HOLLYWOOD SONG

HOLLYWOOD SONG

THE COMPLETE FILM & MUSICAL COMPANION

Volume One: Films A–L

KEN BLOOM

FactsOnFile®

AN INFOBASE HOLDINGS COMPANY

HOLLYWOOD SONG: THE COMPLETE FILM MUSICAL COMPANION

Facts On File, Inc.
460 Park Avenue South
New York NY 10016

Library of Congress Cataloging-in-Publication Data

Bloom, Ken.
Hollywood song : the complete film musical companion / Ken Bloom.
        p. cm.
        Vol. 1: Films A–L
ISBN 0-8160-2002-7 (set). — ISBN 0-8160-2668-8 (v. 1). — ISBN 0-8160-2667-X (v. 2). — ISBN 0-8160-3231-9 (v. 3).
    1. Motion picture music—Bibliography. 2. Songs, English—United States—Indexes. I. Title.
                        ML128.M7B6 1995
        016.7821′4′0973—dc20   90-22261

Facts On File books are available at special discounts when purchased in bulk quantities for businesses, associations, institutions or sales promotions. Please call our Special Sales Department in New York at
                212/682-2244 or 800/322-8755.

Text design by Catherine Rincon Hyman
Jacket design by Soloway/Mitchell
Printed in the United States of America

VB COM 10 9 8 7 6 5 4 3 2 1

This book is printed on acid-free paper.

To

Russell Metheny and

Carl Weaver,

both of whom taught me

a lot and cared a lot

CONTENTS

ACKNOWLEDGMENTS

The compilation and research of this book was a huge undertaking. It couldn't have been completed without the help of many dedicated people. Although I take the responsibility for any errors in *Hollywood Song*, I would like to share any success with many friends and coworkers who helped me.

First and foremost I would like to thank the many dedicated professionals at the various studios where I researched this project. I'm proud to report that no studio turned down my requests, and only one limited my access to their records. While researching the thousands of pieces of paper and cue sheets I grew to appreciate the tremendous work these music and legal departments undertake.

The first studio that allowed me access to their records was Paramount. I want to especially thank Ridge Walker for his enthusiasm and continued support. He and his staff taught me a lot about the music end of motion picture production and helped me get a foothold in the mountain of documents in the Paramount archives. Ridge and his excellent staff, Marc Miller, David Robles, and Charlee Hutton have my utmost respect and gratitude.

Special thanks also to Danny Gould at Warner Brothers and Susan de Christofaro of Twentieth Century-Fox who generously went out of their way to accommodate my requests. Thanks also to Carol Besso at Disney; Julian Bratolyubov, Mark Porter, and Terry Wolff at Universal; Andrew Velcoff and Cathy Manolis at Turner; Jill Coplan at Republic; Monica Ciafardini at Columbia; Steve Pena and Laurence Zwisohn at Twentieth Century-Fox. They were all helpful and kind.

My admiration and thanks to the professionals at the Academy of Motion Picture Arts and Sciences Margaret Herrick Library whose staff is too numerous to mention but who all are experts in both the history of the motion picture industry and in human interaction. They create a uniquely gracious atmosphere for the researcher and movie buff. Thanks too for special understanding to Ruth Spencer of the American Film Institute library.

Thanks to my parents, George and Florence Bloom, whom I can never repay for their love and support.

Thanks to Barry Kleinbart for helping me in California and for being such a close friend.

Thanks to my friends Harry Bagdasian, Kenny Bennett, Bari Biern Sedar, David Bishop, Adrian Bryan-Brown, Hap Erstein, Paul Ford, Sheila Formoy, Kit Grover, Karen Hopkins, Pat Jacobs, Ken Kantor, Paul Newman, Ezio Petersen, Guy Riddick, David Rose, Bill Rudman, Berthe Schuchat, Scott Sedar, Mike Shuster, David Simone, Robert Sixsmith, Bijou Spialek, Joseph Weiss, Max Woodward, Helene Blue, Denis Peshkov, Arthur Siegel, John Thornton, Doug Schulkind, Deborah Brody and Ellen Zeisler who saw me through the good times and bad and listened to me grouse. Thanks to old and new friends in L.A.: Denny Martin Flinn, Barbara Flinn, Ken Olfson, and Michael Shoop.

I'm blessed with a terrific agent, Heide Lange of Greenburger Associates, who deserves a paragraph of her own, and here it is. Thanks Heide for your encouragement, good advice, and friendship.

I'm sure I have forgotten to thank many individuals who helped me compile the enormous amount of material that has gone into making this book. If I have forgotten to thank you please accept my apologies and send your name to me care of Facts On File.

Ken Bloom
New York City

INTRODUCTION

This second volume of the *American Song* series (the first was on musical theater) includes data on songs from almost 7,000 American and foreign films. I attempted to track down all American made films and foreign films distributed in major release by American companies, unproduced films for which songs or scores were written, films in which instrumental pieces were later given lyrics, and silent films which had songs written for them.

Volumes 1 and 2 list all movies alphabetically. Volume 3 contains a chronological listing of titles and complete indexes to personnel and songs.

Most books on Hollywood musicals exclude rock musicals and cowboy pictures. Usually, short subjects are ignored, as are documentaries. I decided that to exclude any picture of any type would be presumptuous. After all, great songs have been written for rock pictures and for cowboy films. I decided to include all films except concert films, which usually do not have music written especially for them. Some concert films do have original songs—for example, *Woodstock*—and those are included. Cartoons are usually included under a generic heading (for example, "Popeye films"), since I couldn't always ascertain which songs were written for which cartoons. Warner Brothers, Disney, and MGM cartoon cue sheets, however, do exist on a film by film basis, and their songs are listed under the film's title.

No films are included if they were produced for video or went straight to video without a release. Films are also omitted if they contained a vocal but the song was not written for the film. For example, films containing only a vocal of a popular tune or public domain standard are excluded.

No information has been included unless it has been verified by programs, sheet music, censorship forms, reviews, scripts, publicity materials, production company records, demo discs, recording and dubbing schedules, publishers' files, ASCAP or BMI lists, or by the composers or lyricists themselves.

Since viewing all the films made by American studios is impossible, and since many prints are incomplete, I used the motion picture companies' cue sheets as my primary source. Songs may have been deleted from prints after the initial road-

show engagements or excised from television prints. But the cue sheets list the songs as they appeared in the films' initial release. For many early films, cue sheets do not exist or are incomplete. In the early thirties cue sheets were pretty much standardized and their quality and reliability were improved.

I didn't make a list of possible films and then look for those cue sheets. Instead in all but one instance (Columbia), I went through every available cue sheet. I also researched all available complementary records. I estimate that I examined over 15,000 cue sheets.

Cue sheets divide music cues into four categories: Background Vocals, Visual Vocals, Background Instrumentals, and Visual.

Here is how the categories work.

TITLE: The title of the film at its initial release is used. Previous titles, alternate titles, and foreign titles are included in the Notes section. If a date in parentheses follows a film's title, it means another film shared the same title. It does not mean the second film had original songs.

STUDIO: For the most part films are credited to releasing companies, not production companies. Thus Goldwyn pictures may be credited under United Artists or MGM.

YEAR: Year of initial release is used. However, dates differ according to various sources. I tried to be as exact as possible, but sometimes a film might open on a limited basis in December for the holiday market and receive broad distribution the next year. Some films are released simply to accommodate contractual obligations and then withdrawn till a later date.

MUSIC SCORE: This category includes the composers of the background instrumental scores.

COMPOSER, LYRICIST: When the majority of a score's songs are written by the same people, I have listed them under these headings instead of repeating their names beside their song titles. Any variations appear after the song in question.

CHOREOGRAPHER: This credit does not often appear on films that obviously have dancing. I tried to include as many as I could find.

PRODUCER: In the early thirties, usually the head of production or head of the studio was listed as Producer. I ignored this credit and usually credited the Associate Producer as the Producer. Later Producers received credit under that title. Some studio heads like Darryl Zanuck did directly oversee a few releases, and they are credited as Producers.

SCREENWRITER, DIRECTOR: These are the official credits according to what appears on the screen. Naturally many uncredited writers and even directors work on films but they are not included unless they did major work. For example, although many writers worked on *The Wizard of Oz*, only those with screen credit are listed. If a writer was credited with Additional Dialogue, in credits, I included him or her under the screenplay credits. If more than one director worked on a film, the Notes section indicates this.

SOURCE: These categories include the original source material upon which the film is based. These are the official sources, not including uncredited or ill disguised stealing of plots. I did not usually list if a film was a remake or a musicalization under these headings. That information appears under notes. If I list Musical under Source that means stage musical.

CAST: All stars are listed, as well as selected character actors and supporting players. If singing voices are dubbed, the dubbers are credited in the Notes section.

SONGS: This category includes all songs written expressly for the film. Songs that are interpolated and operatic arias are listed in the Notes section. Exceptions include interpolations with additional music or lyrics written expressly for the production.

NOTES: This heading includes miscellaneous information, such as other films in which a song appears, alternate titles, a song written but not used for a film, etc.

Ken Bloom
New York City

PART ONE:

FILMS A–L

A

1 ✦ AARON SLICK FROM PUNKIN CRICK
Paramount, 1952

Musical Score Dolan, Robert Emmett
Composer(s) Livingston, Jay; Evans, Ray
Lyricist(s) Livingston, Jay; Evans, Ray
Choreographer(s) O'Curran, Charles

Producer(s) Seaton, George; Perlberg, William
Director(s) Binyon, Claude
Screenwriter(s) Binyon, Claude
Source(s) *Aaron Slick from Punkin Crick* (play) Hare, Walter Benjamin

Cast Shore, Dinah; Merrill, Robert; Young, Alan; Jergens, Adele; Urecal, Minerva; Stewart, Martha

Song(s) Saturday Night in Punkin Crick; Chores; Purt' Nigh, but not Plumb; My Beloved; Still Water; Marshmallow Moon; Why Should I Believe in Love?; I'd Like to Baby You; Life Is a Beautiful Thing; Step Right Up; Soda Shop; The Spider and the Fly [1]; (At) The General Store [1]; Will You Be at Home in Heaven? [1]

Notes The film was released as MARSHMALLOW MOON outside the United States. [1] Not used in final print.

2 ✦ ABBOTT & COSTELLO & DICK POWELL IN THE NAVY
Universal, 1941

Musical Score Skinner, Frank
Composer(s) de Paul, Gene
Lyricist(s) Raye, Don
Choreographer(s) Castle, Nick

Producer(s) Gottlieb, Alex
Director(s) Lubin, Arthur
Screenwriter(s) Horman, Arthur T.; Grant, John

Cast Abbott, Bud; Costello, Lou; Powell, Dick; Dodd, Claire; Foran, Dick; The Andrews Sisters; Howard, Shemp; The Condos Brothers

Song(s) You're a Lucky Fellow, Mr. Smith [2] (C: Burke, Sonny; Prince, Hughie); Starlight, Starbright; Off to See the World; Gimme Some Skin; A Sailor's Life for Me; We're in the Navy [1]; Hula Ba Luau

Notes Also titled IN THE NAVY. [1] Also in HI, BUDDY! [2] Also in BUCK PRIVATES (1941); HI 'YA CHUM and YOU'RE A LUCKY FELLOW, MR. SMITH.

3 ✦ ABBOTT AND COSTELLO IN HOLLYWOOD
Metro–Goldwyn–Mayer, 1945

Composer(s) Blane, Ralph; Martin, Hugh
Lyricist(s) Blane, Ralph; Martin, Hugh
Choreographer(s) Walters, Charles

Producer(s) Simon, S. Sylvan
Director(s) Gosch, Martin A.
Screenwriter(s) Perrin, Nat; Breslow, Lou

Cast Abbott, Bud; Costello, Lou; Rafferty, Frances; Stanton, Robert; Porter, Jean; Anderson, Warner; Mazurki, Mike; Ragland, Rags

Song(s) As I Remember You; I Hope the Band Keeps Playing; Fun on the Wonderful Midway (Loveland); I Like Love [1]; Shake Your Salt on the Bluebird's Tail [1]

Notes [1] Not used.

4 ✦ ABBOTT AND COSTELLO IN JACK AND THE BEANSTALK

See JACK AND THE BEANSTALK.

5 ✦ ABBOTT AND COSTELLO MEET CAPTAIN KIDD
Warner Brothers, 1952

Musical Score Kraushaar, Raoul
Composer(s) Lee, Lester
Lyricist(s) Russell, Bob

Producer(s) Gottlieb, Alex
Director(s) Lamont, Charles
Screenwriter(s) Dimsdale, Howard; Grant, John

Cast Abbott, Bud; Costello, Lou; Laughton, Charles; Brooke, Hillary; Warren, Fran; Shirley, Bill

Song(s) Meet Captain Kidd; A Bachelor's Life; We Sail Tonight; Speak to Me of the Tall Pine; Aye Aye Aye Aye O; North of Nowhere

6 ◆ ABBOTT AND COSTELLO MEET DR. JEKYLL AND MR. HYDE
Universal, 1953

Composer(s) Hughes, Arnold
Lyricist(s) Herbert, Frederick
Choreographer(s) Williams, Kenny

Producer(s) Christie, Howard
Director(s) Lamont, Charles
Screenwriter(s) Loeb, Lee; Grant, John

Cast Abbott, Bud; Costello, Lou; Karloff, Boris; Denny, Reginald; Stevens, Craig; Westcott, Helen

Song(s) Equal Rights; 'E Tipped 'Is 'At

7 ◆ ABBOTT AND COSTELLO MEET THE INVISIBLE MAN
Universal, 1951

Producer(s) Christie, Howard
Director(s) Lamont, Charles
Screenwriter(s) Lees, Robert; Rinaldo, Frederic I.; Grant, John

Cast Abbott, Bud; Costello, Lou; Guild, Nancy; Jergens, Adele; Leonard, Sheldon; Frawley, William; Muir, Gavin

Song(s) Good Old D-D-T (C/L: Herbert, Frederick; Gershenson, Joseph; Rosen, Milton)

8 ◆ ABBOTT AND COSTELLO MEET THE MUMMY
Universal, 1955

Musical Score Mancini, Henry

Producer(s) Christie, Howard
Director(s) Lamont, Charles
Screenwriter(s) Grant, John

Cast Abbott, Bud; Costello, Lou; Windsor, Marie; Deacon, Richard; Ansara, Michael; Seymour, Dan; King, Peggy

Song(s) Dull Dance (C/L: Mancini, Henry); You've Come a Long Way from St. Louis [1] (C: Brooks, John B.; L: Russell, Bob); Faggot Dance (C/L: Mancini, Henry)

Notes It is not known if the Mancini songs actually have lyrics or not. [1] Not written for this picture.

9 ◆ THE ABDICATION
Warner Brothers, 1974

Musical Score Rota, Nino
Composer(s) Rota, Nino

Producer(s) Fryer, Robert; Cresson, James
Director(s) Harvey, Anthony
Screenwriter(s) Wolff, Ruth
Source(s) *The Abdication* (play) Wolff, Ruth

Cast Ullmann, Liv; Finch, Peter; Cusack, Cyril; Rogers, Paul; Dunn, Michael

Song(s) She Swears She'll Never Marry (L: Wilkinson, Marc); Christina's Song (L: Wolff, Ruth)

10 ◆ ABDUL THE BULBUL AMEER
Metro–Goldwyn–Mayer, 1941

Song(s) Abdul the Bulbul Ameer (C: Crumit, Frank; L: Traditional)

Notes Cartoon short.

11 ◆ ABIE'S IRISH ROSE
Paramount, 1929

Composer(s) Zamecnik, J.S.
Lyricist(s) Nichols, Anne

Producer(s) Schulberg, B.P.
Director(s) Fleming, Victor
Screenwriter(s) Nichols, Anne; Mankiewicz, Herman J.; Johnson, Julian
Source(s) *Abie's Irish Rose* (play) Nichols, Anne

Cast Rogers, Charles "Buddy"; Carroll, Nancy; Hersholt, Jean; MacDonald, J. Farrell; Gorcey, Bernard; Kramer, Ida

Song(s) Rosemary; Little Irish Rose

Notes No cue sheet available.

12 ◆ ABOUT FACE
Warner Brothers, 1952

Musical Score Buttolph, David; Heindorf, Ray
Composer(s) De Rose, Peter
Lyricist(s) Tobias, Charles
Choreographer(s) Prinz, LeRoy

Producer(s) Jacobs, William
Director(s) Del Ruth, Roy
Screenwriter(s) Milne, Peter
Source(s) *Brother Rat* (play) Monks Jr., John; Finklehoffe, Fred F.

Cast Grey, Joel; MacRae, Gordon; Wesson, Dick; Bracken, Eddie; Gibson, Virginia; Kirk, Phyllis; Stanley Jr., Aileen; Keating, Larry

Song(s) Reveille; S.M.I. March; Tar Heels; If Someone had Told Me; Wooden Indian; Spring Has Sprung; They Haven't Lost a Father Yet; I'm Nobody (C: Heindorf, Ray; L: Smith, Paul J.; Grey, Joel); Piano, Bass and Drums; No Other Girl for Me (No Other Boy for You)

13 ◆ ABOUT LAST NIGHT
Tri-Star, 1986

Musical Score Goodman, Miles

Producer(s) Brett, Jason; Oxen, Stuart
Director(s) Zwick, Edward
Screenwriter(s) Kazurinsky, Tim; DeClue, Denise

Source(s) *Sexual Perversity in Chicago* (play) Mamet, David

Cast Lowe, Rob; Moore, Demi; Belushi, James; Perkins, Elizabeth; Dicenzo, George; Alldredge, Michael; Thomas, Robin; Kazurinsky, Tim

Song(s) (She's the) Shape of Things to Come (C/L: Oates, John); So Far, So Good (C/L: Snow, Tom; Weil, Cynthia); Natural Love (C/L: Snow, Tom; Weil, Cynthia); Step By Step (C/L: Souther, J.D.; Bonoff, Karla); If We Get Through the Night (C/L: Walsh, Brock); Trials of the Heart (C/L: Bishop, Thom; Day, Michael; Maffit, Rocky); 'Til You Love Somebody (C/L: Marlett, Bob; Shifrin, Sue); If Anybody Had a Heart (C/L: Sother, J.D.; Kortchmar, Danny); Triple Star (C/L: Walsh, Brock); True Love (C/L: Kempner, Scott); Words into Action (C/L: Lesson, Mike; Vale, Peter)

Notes No cue sheet available.

14 ✦ ABOUT MRS. LESLIE
Paramount, 1954

Musical Score Young, Victor

Producer(s) Wallis, Hal B.
Director(s) Mann, Daniel
Screenwriter(s) Frings, Ketti; Kanter, Hal
Source(s) "About Mrs. Leslie" (story) Delmar, Vina

Cast Booth, Shirley; Ryan, Robert; Morgan, Henry

Song(s) I Love You So [1] (C: Young, Victor; L: Lee, Peggy)

Notes There are also vocals of "Kiss the Boys Goodbye" by Victor Schertzinger and Frank Loesser and "I'm in the Mood for Love" by Jimmy McHugh and Dorothy Fields. "I'm in the Mood for Love" also appears in EVERY NIGHT AT EIGHT; PEOPLE ARE FUNNY and THAT'S MY BOY. [1] Lyric written for exploitation only but not accepted by Paramount.

15 ✦ ABOVE THE CLOUDS
Columbia, 1933

Director(s) Neill, Roy William
Screenwriter(s) Coleman, C.C.

Cast Armstrong, Robert; Cromwell, Richard; Wilson, Dorothy; Breese, Edmund; Alberni, Luis

Song(s) Are You Mine [1] (C/L: Rosoff, Charles)

Notes [1] Used instrumentally only. Also used instrumentally in BEYOND THE LAW (1934) and sung in the Republic picture WATERFRONT LADY.

16 ✦ THE ABSENT-MINDED PROFESSOR
Disney, 1961

Musical Score Bruns, George
Composer(s) Sherman, Richard M.; Sherman, Robert B.
Lyricist(s) Sherman, Richard M.; Sherman, Robert B.

Producer(s) Walsh, Bill
Director(s) Stevenson, Robert
Screenwriter(s) Walsh, Bill

Cast MacMurray, Fred; Olson, Nancy; Wynn, Keenan; Kirk, Tommy; Ames, Leon; Reid, Elliott; Andrews, Edward; Lewis, David; Mullaney, Jack; Montrose, Belle; Wynn, Ed

Song(s) The Medfield Fight Song; Flubber Song [1]; Serendipity [2]

Notes [1] Written for exploitation only. [2] Sheet music only.

17 ✦ ABSOLUTE BEGINNERS
Orion, 1986

Producer(s) Woolley, Stephen; Brown, Chris
Director(s) Temple, Julien
Screenwriter(s) Burridge, Richard; Wicking, Christopher; MacPherson, Don
Source(s) *Absolute Beginners* (novel) MacInnes, Colin

Cast O'Connell, Eddie; Kensit, Patsy; Bowie, David; Fox, James; Rice-Davies, Mandy; Ferret, Eve; Hippolyte, Tony; Berkoff, Steven; Adu, Sade; Morris, Anita; Firth, Julian; Blair, Lionel; Coltrane, Robbie; Gaillard, Slim; Syms, Sylvia

Song(s) Absolute Beginners (C/L: Bowie, David)

Notes No cue sheet available.

18 ✦ THE ACCIDENTAL TOURIST
Warner Brothers, 1988

Musical Score Williams, John

Producer(s) Kasdan, Lawrence; Okun, Charles; Grillo, Michael
Director(s) Kasdan, Lawrence
Screenwriter(s) Galati, Frank; Kasdan, Lawrence
Source(s) *The Accidental Tourist* (novel) Tyler, Anne

Cast Hurt, William; Turner, Kathleen; Davis, Geena; Wright, Amy; Stiers, David Ogden; Begley Jr., Ed; Pullman, Bill; Gorman, Robert

Song(s) I'm Gonna Lasso Santa Claus [1] (C/L: Adams, Frankie; Jones, Wilbur)

Notes [1] Not written for film.

19 ✦ ACCUSED (1937)
United Artists, 1937

Musical Score Young, Victor

Producer(s) Hellman, Marcel
Director(s) Freeland, Thornton
Screenwriter(s) Akins, Zoe; Barraud, George

Cast Del Rio, Dolores; Fairbanks Jr., Douglas; Desmond, Florence; Sydney, Basil; Stewart, Athole; Withers, Googie; Culver, Roland

Song(s)   Latin Rhythm [1] (C: Young, Victor)

Notes   No cue sheet available. [1] It is not known if this has lyrics or is an instrumental.

20 ✦ THE ACCUSED (1988)
Paramount, 1988

Musical Score   Fiedel, Brad

Producer(s)   Jaffe, Stanley R.; Lansing, Sherry
Director(s)   Kaplan, Jonathan
Screenwriter(s)   Topor, Tom

Cast   McGillis, Kelly; Foster, Jodie; Colson, Bernie; Rossi, Leo; Hearn, Ann

Song(s)   I'm Talking Love (C: Fiedel, Brad; L: Levinson, Ross)

Notes   No cue sheet available.

21 ✦ ACCUSED OF MURDER
Republic, 1956

Producer(s)   Kane, Joseph
Director(s)   Kane, Joseph
Screenwriter(s)   Williams, Bob; Burnett, W.R.
Source(s)   *Accused of Murder* (novel) Burnett, W.R.

Cast   Brian, David; Ralston, Vera Hruba; Blackmer, Sidney; Grey, Virginia; Stevens, Warren; Van Cleef, Lee; Cook Jr., Elisha

Song(s)   You're in Love (C: Bregman, Buddy; L: Newman, Herb); There's a Song in the Heart of Paree (C: De Lory, Al; L: Gladstone, Jerry)

22 ✦ ACE ELI AND RODGER OF THE SKIES
Twentieth Century–Fox, 1973

Musical Score   Goldsmith, Jerry

Producer(s)   Wilson, Boris
Director(s)   Sampson, Bill
Screenwriter(s)   Rosen, Chips

Cast   Robertson, Cliff; Franklin, Pamela; Shea, Eric; Murphy, Rosemary; Peters, Bernadette; Ghostley, Alice

Song(s)   Who's for Complainin' (C/L: Grady, Jim)

Notes   Based on a story by Steven Spielberg.

23 ✦ ACE IN THE HOLE

See THE BIG CARNIVAL.

24 ✦ ACROSS 110TH STREET
United Artists, 1972

Musical Score   Johnson, J.J.
Composer(s)   Womack, Bobby
Lyricist(s)   Womack, Bobby

Producer(s)   Serpe, Ralph; Said, Fouad
Director(s)   Shear, Barry
Screenwriter(s)   Davis, Luther
Source(s)   (novel) Ferris, Wally

Cast   Quinn, Anthony; Kotto, Yaphet; Franciosa, Anthony; Donaldson, Norma; Fargas, Antonio

Song(s)   Across 110th Street (C: Johnson, J.J.); Quicksand; If You Don't Want My Love (C/L: Womack, Bobby; DeWitty, Gordon); Hang On In There; Do It Right

25 ✦ ACROSS THE BADLANDS
Columbia, 1950

Musical Score   Morton, Arthur
Composer(s)   Burnette, Smiley
Lyricist(s)   Burnette, Smiley

Producer(s)   Clark, Colbert
Director(s)   Sears, Fred F.
Screenwriter(s)   Shipman, Barry

Cast   Starrett, Charles; Mowery, Helen; Elliott, Dick; Andrews, Stanley; Wilke, Robert J.; Burnette, Smiley; Harmonica Bill

Song(s)   Harmonica Bill; I'm Telling Myself I'm Not Afraid

26 ✦ ACROSS THE GREAT DIVIDE
Pacific International, 1978

Musical Score   Kauer, Gene; Lackey, Douglas

Producer(s)   Dubs, Arthur R.
Director(s)   Raffill, Stewart
Screenwriter(s)   Raffill, Stewart

Cast   Logan, Robert; Flower, George Buck; Rattray, Heather; Hall, Mark Edward

Song(s)   Across the Great Divide (C: Kauer, Gene; Lackey, Douglas; L: Badale, Andy; Young, Lucky)

Notes   No cue sheet available.

27 ✦ ACROSS THE SIERRAS
Columbia, 1941

Composer(s)   Drake, Milton
Lyricist(s)   Drake, Milton

Producer(s)   Barsha, Leon
Director(s)   Lederman, D. Ross
Screenwriter(s)   Franklin, Paul

Cast   Elliott, Bill; Fiske, Richard; Walters, Luana; Curtis, Dick; Knowles, Carl; Mason, LeRoy; Robinson, Ruth

Song(s)   Star Spangled Prairie; I Gotta Make Music; Honeymoon Ranch [1]

Notes   [1] Also in SINGING SPURS.

28 ◆ ACROSS THE WIDE MISSOURI
Metro–Goldwyn–Mayer, 1951

Composer(s) Colombo, Alberto
Lyricist(s) Colombo, Alberto

Producer(s) Sisk, Robert
Director(s) Wellman, William A.
Screenwriter(s) Jennings, Talbot

Cast Gable, Clark; Menjou, Adolphe; Montalban, Ricardo; Hodiak, John; Marques, Maria Elena; Naish, J. Carrol; Holt, Jack; Napier, Alan

Song(s) Indian Lament; Indian Lullaby; Across the Wide Missouri [1] (C: Raksin, David; L: Sendrey, Al)

Notes [1] Sheet music credits Ervin Drake and Jimmy Shirl.

29 ◆ ACTION JACKSON
Lorimar, 1988

Musical Score Hancock, Herbie; Kamen, Michael

Producer(s) Silver, Joel
Director(s) Baxley, Craig R.
Screenwriter(s) Reneau, Robert

Cast Weathers, Carl; Nelson, Craig T.; Vanity; Stone, Sharon; Wilson, Thomas F.; Davi, Robert; Thibeau, Jack

Song(s) Action Jackson (C/L: Cooper, Bernadette); He Turned Me Out (C/L: Humes, Lemel; Kurtes, Mary Lee)

Notes No cue sheet available.

30 ◆ ACTION OF THE TIGER
Metro–Goldwyn–Mayer, 1958

Musical Score Searle, Humphrey

Producer(s) Harper, Kenneth
Director(s) Young, Terence
Screenwriter(s) Carson, Robert
Source(s) *Action of the Tiger* (novel) Wellard, James

Cast Johnson, Van; Carol, Martine; Lom, Herbert; Rocco, Gustavo; Nieto, Jose; Connery, Sean

Song(s) Tino, Tino (C/L: Parker, Ross; Kay, Parker)

31 ◆ ACT OF THE HEART
Universal, 1970

Musical Score Freedman, Harry

Producer(s) Almond, Paul
Director(s) Almond, Paul
Screenwriter(s) Almond, Paul

Cast Bujold, Genevieve; Sutherland, Donald; Mitchell, Bill

Song(s) Cantata—The Flame Within [1] (C: Freedman, Harry; L: Almond, Paul); Deux Chansons (C/L: Vigneault, Gilles)

Notes [1] Lyrics adapted from the Bible.

32 ◆ ADA
Metro–Goldwyn–Mayer, 1961

Musical Score Kaper, Bronislau

Producer(s) Weingarten, Lawrence
Director(s) Mann, Daniel
Screenwriter(s) Sheekman, Arthur; Driskill, William
Source(s) *Ada Dallas* (novel) Williams, Wirt

Cast Hayward, Susan; Martin, Dean; Hyde-White, Wilfrid; Meeker, Ralph; Balsam, Martin; Maxwell, Frank; Rainey, Ford

Song(s) May the Lord Bless You Real Good (C/L: Roberts, Warren; Fowler, Wally); Ada [1] (C: Kapes, Bronislau; L: David, Mack)

Notes [1] Written for exploitation only.

33 ◆ ADAM'S RIB
Metro–Goldwyn–Mayer, 1949

Musical Score Rozsa, Miklos

Producer(s) Weingarten, Lawrence
Director(s) Cukor, George
Screenwriter(s) Gordon, Ruth; Kanin, Garson

Cast Tracy, Spencer; Hepburn, Katharine; Holliday, Judy; Ewell, Tom; Wayne, David; Hagen, Jean; Emerson, Hope; Kolb, Clarence; Moran, Polly

Song(s) Farewell, Amanda (C/L: Porter, Cole)

34 ◆ ADAM'S WOMAN
Warner Brothers, 1970

Musical Score Young, Bob
Composer(s) Young, Bob
Lyricist(s) Denton, Kit

Producer(s) Edelman, Louis F.
Director(s) Leacock, Philip
Screenwriter(s) Fieder, Richard

Cast Bridges, Beau; Merrow, Jane; Mills, John; Kier, Andrew; Reed, Tracy

Song(s) Adam's Woman; Home in Old England; Ride with Me to the Bushland; Small Beer; Listen to the Land

Notes All songs are background vocals. This is an Australian film that was briefly released in 1970. Originally titled RETURN OF THE BOOMERANG.

35 ◆ THE ADDING MACHINE
Universal, 1969

Musical Score Williamson, Bill; Leander, Mike

Producer(s) Epstein, Jerome
Director(s) Epstein, Jerome
Screenwriter(s) Epstein, Jerome
Source(s) *The Adding Machine* (play) Rice, Elmer

Cast O'Shea, Milo; Diller, Phyllis; Whitelaw, Billie; Chaplin, Sydney; Glover, Julian; Huntley, Raymond

Song(s) How Small We Are How Little We Know (C/L: Wilson Jr., Earl)

36 ◆ ADIOS ARGENTINA (1935)
Fox, 1935 unproduced

Composer(s) Porter, Cole
Lyricist(s) Porter, Cole

Producer(s) Brock, Lou

Cast Guizar, Tito; Veloz and Yolanda

Song(s) Don't Fence Me In [1]; Adios Argentina; The Chiripah; If You Could Love Me; Side Car; Singing in the Saddle

Notes [1] Later in HOLLYWOOD CANTEEN (Warner Brothers) and DON'T FENCE ME IN (Republic).

37 ◆ ADORABLE
Fox, 1933

Composer(s) Whiting, Richard A.
Lyricist(s) Marion Jr., George
Choreographer(s) Lee, Sammy

Director(s) Dieterle, William
Screenwriter(s) Marion Jr., George; Storm, Jane
Source(s) *Ihre Hoheit Befiehlt (Her Highness Commands)* (film) Frank, Paul; Wilder, Billy

Cast Gaynor, Janet; Garat, Henry; Smith, C. Aubrey; Mundin, Herbert

Song(s) Trara! Jetzt Kommt die Marschmusik [2] (C: Heymann, Werner; L: Gilbert, Robert); Adorable; Bibchen Dies und Bibchen Das [1] (C: Heymann, Werner; L: Marion Jr., George; Neubach, Ernst); My First Love to Last [3]; My Heart's Desire; Frag' Nicht Wie, Frag' Nicht Wo [2] (C: Heymann, Werner; L: Neubach, Ernst); Fanfare [2] (Inst.) (C: Heymann, Werner)

Notes For your information the other number in the original film is "Du Hast Mir Heimlich die Liebe in Hause Gebracht" and has lyrics by Richard Gilbert. [1] Written for the source film. Marion contributed the English lyrics under the title "Soup Song." [2] Used instrumentally only, from the source film. [3] Also used in I LOVED YOU WEDNESDAY.

38 ◆ ADVANCE TO THE REAR

See COMPANY OF COWARDS.

39 ◆ THE ADVENTURERS
Paramount, 1970

Musical Score Jobim, Antonio Carlos

Producer(s) Gilbert, Lewis
Director(s) Gilbert, Lewis
Screenwriter(s) Gilbert, Lewis; Hastings, Michael
Source(s) *The Adventurers* (novel) Robbins, Harold

Cast Fehmiu, Bekim; de Havilland, Olivia; Bergen, Candice; Borgnine, Ernest; Aznavour, Charles; Brazzi, Rossano; Badel, Alan; Taylor-Young, Leigh; Ireland, John; Moffo, Anna; Rey, Fernando

Song(s) Adventure [1] (C: Jobim, Antonio Carlos; L: Gimbel, Norman)

Notes [1] Lyric written for exploitation only.

40 ◆ ADVENTURE'S END
Universal, 1937

Producer(s) Carr, Trem
Director(s) Lubin, Arthur
Screenwriter(s) Kohn, Ben Grauman; Darling, W. Scott; Sutherland, Sidney

Cast Wayne, John; Gibson, Diana; Olsen, Moroni; Love, Montagu

Song(s) Singapore Sadie (C/L: Henderson, Charles); Paradise Isle [1] (C/L: Koki, Sam)

Notes [1] Not written for this picture.

41 ◆ ADVENTURES IN BABYSITTING
Disney, 1987

Musical Score Kamen, Michael

Producer(s) Hill, Debra; Obst, Lynda
Director(s) Columbus, Chris
Screenwriter(s) Simkins, David

Cast Shue, Elisabeth; Brewton, Maia; Coogan, Keith; Rapp, Anthony; Levels, Calvin; D'Onofrio, Vincent; Miller, Penelope Ann; Noonan, John Ford; Canada, Ron

Song(s) Babysitting Blues (C/L: Kraft, Robert; Mueller, Mark); Albert's Smokin' Ice (C/L: Kraft, Robert); Future in Your Eyes (C/L: Lyon, John; Batteaux, Robin); Just Can't Stop (C/L: Goldberg, Barry; Gruska, Jay)

Notes Only songs written for production listed.

42 ◆ ADVENTURES IN DIAMONDS
Paramount, 1940

Producer(s) Fitzmaurice, George
Director(s) Fitzmaurice, George
Screenwriter(s) Lee, Leonard; Schulz, Franz

Cast   Brent, George; Miranda, Isa; Loder, John; Bruce, Nigel; Patterson, Elizabeth; Evans, Rex; Kellaway, Cecil; Truex, Ernest; Forbes, Ralph; Clive, Rex

Song(s)   A Flea Flew in My Flute (C: Boutelje, Phil; L: Loesser, Frank); The Whistler's Ditties (inst.) (C: Loesser, Frank)

Notes   The film was previously titled DIAMONDS ARE DANGEROUS. The film was later titled PORTRAIT IN DIAMONDS.

43 ✦ ADVENTURES OF A ROOKIE
RKO, 1943

Musical Score   Webb, Roy

Producer(s)   Gilroy, Bert
Director(s)   Goodwins, Leslie
Screenwriter(s)   James, Edward

Cast   Brown, Wally; Carney, Alan; Martin, Richard; Gage, Erford; Corday, Rita

Song(s)   Give, Give, Give (C/L: Brown, Wally)

44 ✦ ADVENTURES OF BARON MUNCHAUSEN
Columbia, 1989

Musical Score   Kamen, Michael
Composer(s)   Kamen, Michael
Lyricist(s)   Idle, Eric

Producer(s)   Shuhly, Thomas
Director(s)   Gilliam, Terry
Screenwriter(s)   McKeown, Charles; Gilliam, Terry

Cast   Neville, John; Idle, Eric; Polley, Sarah; Reed, Oliver; McKeown, Charles; Cortese, Valentina; Pryce, Jonathan; Paterson, Bill; Thurman, Uma; Steadman, Alison; Williams, Robin

Song(s)   What Will Become of the Baron? (L: McKeown, Charles; Gilliam, Terry); The Torturer's Apprentice; A Eunuch's Life Is Hard; Play Up and Win the Game; Sea Chanty (L: McKeown, Charles; Gilliam, Terry)

45 ✦ THE ADVENTURES OF BULLWHIP GRIFFIN
Disney, 1967

Musical Score   Bruns, George
Composer(s)   Sherman, Richard M.; Sherman, Robert B.
Lyricist(s)   Sherman, Richard M.; Sherman, Robert B.

Producer(s)   Anderson, Bill
Director(s)   Neilson, James
Screenwriter(s)   Hawley, Lowell S.
Source(s)   *By the Great Horn Spoon* (novel) Fleischman, Sid

Cast   McDowall, Roddy; Pleshette, Suzanne; Malden, Karl; Guardino, Harry; Haydn, Richard; Baddeley, Hermione; Russell, Bryan; Redmond, Liam; Kellaway, Cecil; Baker, Joby; Mazurki, Mike; Hunnicutt, Arthur

Song(s)   Bullwhip Griffin (C: Bruns, George; L: Leven, Mel); Cal-I-For-Nee Gold; The Girls of San Francisco; Whoever You Are

Notes   This was originally serialized on TV.

46 ✦ THE ADVENTURES OF FRONTIER FREMONT
Sunn Classics, 1977

Musical Score   Summers, Bob
Composer(s)   Summers, Bob

Producer(s)   Sellier Jr., Charles
Director(s)   Friedenberg, Richard
Screenwriter(s)   O'Malley, David

Cast   Haggerty, Dan; Pyle, Denver; Miratti, Tony; Goodman, Norman

Song(s)   Jacob's Theme (L: Askey, Penny; Summers, Bob); Carry Me Away (L: Summers, Bob; O'Malley, David); Gon' Up Country (L: O'Malley, David; Friedenberg, Richard)

Notes   No cue sheet available.

47 ✦ ADVENTURES OF HAJJI BABA
Twentieth Century–Fox, 1954

Musical Score   Tiomkin, Dimitri

Producer(s)   Wanger, Walter
Director(s)   Weis, Don
Screenwriter(s)   Collins, Richard

Cast   Derek, John; Stewart, Elaine; Bowe, Rosemarie; Gomez, Thomas; Picerni, Paul; Randolph, Donald; Blake, Amanda; Danson, Linda

Song(s)   Hajji Baba (C: Tiomkin, Dimitri; L: Washington, Ned)

48 ✦ THE ADVENTURES OF HUCKLEBERRY FINN (1939)
Metro–Goldwyn–Mayer, 1939

Musical Score   Waxman, Franz

Producer(s)   Mankiewicz, Joseph L.
Director(s)   Thorpe, Richard
Screenwriter(s)   Butler, Hugo
Source(s)   *The Adventures of Huckleberry Finn* (novel) Twain, Mark

Cast   Rooney, Mickey; Connolly, Walter; Frawley, William; Ingram, Rex; Carver, Lynne; Sayers, Jo Ann

Song(s)   Jim's Song (C/L: Waxman, Franz)

49 ✦ THE ADVENTURES OF ICHABOD AND MR. TOAD

See THE LEGEND OF SLEEPY HOLLOW and THE WIND IN THE WILLOWS.

50 ✦ THE ADVENTURES OF MARK TWAIN
Atlantic, 1986

Musical Score   Scream, Billy

Producer(s)   Vinton, Will
Director(s)   Vinton, Will
Screenwriter(s)   Sadburne, Susan

Cast   Whitmore, James; Ritchie, Chris; Krug, Gary; Mariana, Michele; Morrison, John; Edelman, Carol; McKennon, Dallas; Stone, Marley; Scream, Billy

Song(s)   Heroes (C: Scream, Billy; L: Shadburne, Susan)

Notes   No cue sheet available. Animated feature (Claymation).

51 ✦ ADVENTURES OF SADIE
Twentieth Century–Fox, 1955

Musical Score   Binge, Ronald

Producer(s)   Minter, George
Director(s)   Langley, Noel
Screenwriter(s)   Langley, Noel

Cast   Collins, Joan; Cole, George; More, Kenneth; Hare, Robertson; Fitzgerald, Walter; Jacques, Hattie; Felton, Felix; Gingold, Hermione

Song(s)   Puentecito (C/L: Monreal, M.)

Notes   Originally titled OUR GAL FRIDAY.

52 ✦ THE ADVENTURES OF SCARAMOUCHE
Embassy, 1964

Producer(s)   Levine, Joseph E.
Director(s)   Isasmendi, Antonio Isasi
Screenwriter(s)   Rigel, Arturo; Isasmendi, Antonio Isasi; Mann, Colin

Cast   Barray, Gerard; Canale, Gianna Maria; Giradon, Michele

Song(s)   The Comedians (C/L: Aznavour, Charles)

Notes   No cue sheet available.

53 ✦ THE ADVENTURES OF SHERLOCK HOLMES' SMARTER BROTHER
Twentieth Century–Fox, 1975

Musical Score   Morris, John

Producer(s)   Roth, Richard A.
Director(s)   Wilder, Gene
Screenwriter(s)   Wilder, Gene

Cast   Wilder, Gene; Kahn, Madeline; Feldman, Marty; DeLuise, Dom; McKern, Leo; Kinnear, Roy; Le Mesurier, John; Wilmer, Douglas; Walters, Thorley

Song(s)   You Can't Love As I Do (C: Rubens, Paul; L: Wright, Hugh); Away Away [1] (C/L: Morris, John)

Notes   There are also vocal renditions of "Kangaroo Hop" by Godfrey and "I'm Simply Crazy Over You" by Jean Schwartz. [1] Ten seconds of screen time.

54 ✦ THE ADVENTURES OF SKIPALONG ROSENBLOOM

See SKIPALONG ROSENBLOOM.

55 ✦ ADVENTURES OF THE FLYING CADETS
Universal, 1944

Musical Score   Skinner, Frank

Director(s)   Taylor, Ray; Collins, Lewis D.
Source(s)   (serial)

Cast   Downs, Johnny; Jordan, Bobby; Wood, Ward; Benedict, Billy; Ciannelli, Eduardo; Toomey, Regis; Armstrong, Robert; Jackson, Selmer; Holt, Jennifer

Song(s)   Here Come the Air Cadets (C: Rosen, Milton; L: Carter, Everett)

Notes   This is a serial. The song was the theme of the series.

56 ✦ ADVISE AND CONSENT
Columbia, 1962

Musical Score   Fielding, Jerry

Producer(s)   Preminger, Otto
Director(s)   Preminger, Otto
Screenwriter(s)   Mayes, Wendell
Source(s)   *Advise and Consent* (novel) Drury, Allen

Cast   Fonda, Henry; Laughton, Charles; Murray, Don; Pidgeon, Walter; Lawford, Peter; Tierney, Gene; Tone, Franchot; Ayres, Lew; Meredith, Burgess; Hodges, Eddie; Ford, Paul; Grizzard, George; Swenson, Inga; Andrews, Edward; McGrath, Paul; Geer, Will; White, Betty

Song(s)   Heart of Mine (song from Advise and Consent) (C: Fielding, Jerry; L: Washington, Ned)

Notes   No cue sheet available. The song may have been written for exploitation only.

57 ✦ AFFAIR IN TRINIDAD
Columbia, 1951

Musical Score   Duning, George
Composer(s)   Lee, Lester
Choreographer(s)   Bettis, Valerie

Producer(s) Sherman, Vincent
Director(s) Sherman, Vincent
Screenwriter(s) Gunn, James; Saul, Oscar

Cast Ford, Glenn; Hayworth, Rita [1]; Thatcher, Torin; Buloff, Joseph; Scourby, Alexander; Voskovec, George; Bettis, Valerie

Song(s) Trinidad Lady (L: Russell, Bob; Karger, Fred); I've Been Kissed Before [2] (L: Russell, Bob)

Notes [1] Dubbed by Jo Ann Greer. [2] Also in THREE FOR THE SHOW.

58 ◆ THE AFFAIRS OF DOBIE GILLIS
Metro–Goldwyn–Mayer, 1953

Musical Score Alexander, Van
Choreographer(s) Romero, Alex

Producer(s) Loew Jr., Arthur M.
Director(s) Weis, Don
Screenwriter(s) Shulman, Max

Cast Reynolds, Debbie; Van, Bobby; Ruick, Barbara; Fosse, Bob; Stafford, Hanley; Tuttle, Lurene; Conried, Hans; Freeman, Kathleen

Song(s) You Can't Do Wrong Doin' Right [1] (C/L: Rinker, Al; Huddleston, Floyd); I'm Through with Love [2] (C: Malneck, Matty; Livingston, Fud; L: Kahn, Gus)

Notes There are also vocals of "All I Do Is Dream of You" by Arthur Freed and Nacio Herb Brown and "Believe Me If All Those Endearing Young Charms." Kathleen Freeman leads a band called Happy Stella Kowalski and Her Schottische Five. [1] Also in DUCHESS OF IDAHO and THE SELLOUT. [2] Written in 1931.

59 ◆ AFFAIRS OF GERALDINE
Republic, 1946

Producer(s) Schaefer, Armand
Director(s) Blair, George
Screenwriter(s) Butler, John K.

Cast Withers, Jane; Lydon, Jimmy [1]; Walburn, Raymond; Meek, Donald; Quigley, Charles; Withers, Grant

Song(s) Rip Van Winkle (C/L: Levinson; Handy; Leeds); In the Middle of May (C: Ahlert, Fred E.; L: Stillman, Al)

Notes [1] Billed as James Lydon.

60 ◆ THE AFFAIRS OF SUSAN
Paramount, 1945

Musical Score Hollander, Frederick

Producer(s) Wallis, Hal B.
Director(s) Seiter, William A.

Screenwriter(s) Monroe, Thomas; Gorog, Laszlo; Flournoy, Richard

Cast Fontaine, Joan; Brent, George; O'Keefe, Dennis; Abel, Walter; DeFore, Don; Johnson, Rita

Song(s) Something in My Heart [1] (C: Waxman, Franz; Harburg, E.Y.)

Notes [1] This song does not appear on cue sheets.

61 ◆ AN AFFAIR TO REMEMBER
Twentieth Century–Fox, 1957

Musical Score Friedhofer, Hugo
Composer(s) Warren, Harry
Lyricist(s) Adamson, Harold; McCarey, Leo

Producer(s) Wald, Jerry
Director(s) McCarey, Leo
Screenwriter(s) Daves, Delmer; McCarey, Leo

Cast Grant, Cary; Kerr, Deborah [4]; Denning, Richard; Patterson, Neva; Nesbitt, Cathleen; Lewis, Robert Q.; Bonanova, Fortunio; Moore, Matt

Song(s) An Affair to Remember [2]; You Make It Easy to Be True; Continue [1]; Benton's Commercial No. 1 [3] (C: Gaynor, Jessie L.; L: Darby, Ken); Benton's Commercial No. 2 [3] (C: Gaynor, Jessie L.; L: Darby, Ken); Tomorrow Land; The Tiny Scout

Notes A remake of LOVE AFFAIR (1939). [1] Used instrumentally only though prerecorded. [2] French lyrics by Tanis Chandler. [3] Based on "The Slumber Boat" by Jessie L. Gaynor and Alice Riley. [4] Dubbed by Marni Nixon.

62 ◆ AFFAIR WITH A STRANGER
RKO, 1952

Musical Score Webb, Roy

Producer(s) Sparks, Robert
Director(s) Rowland, Roy
Screenwriter(s) Flournoy, Richard

Cast Lewis, Monica; Simmons, Jean; Mature, Victor; Tarola, Mary Jo; Darwell, Jane; Greer, Dabbs; Joy, Nicholas; Carey, Olive

Song(s) Affair with a Stranger (C/L: Coslow, Sam)

Notes Formerly titled KISS AND RUN and BREAKOUT.

63 ◆ AFRICA—TEXAS STYLE!
Paramount, 1967

Musical Score Arnold, Malcolm

Producer(s) Marton, Andrew
Director(s) Marton, Andrew
Screenwriter(s) White, Andy

Cast O'Brian, Hugh; Mills, John; Green, Nigel

Song(s) Harambee [2] (C/L: Worrod, Charles; Kabaka, Daudi); Swahili Serenade [1] (C: Arnold, Malcolm; L: David, Mack)

Notes [1] Does not appear in film. [2] Not written for film.

64 ✦ AFTER MIDNIGHT

See CAPTAIN CAREY U.S.A.

65 ✦ AFTER THE DANCE
Columbia, 1935

Choreographer(s) Rasch, Albertina

Director(s) Bulgakov, Leo
Screenwriter(s) Shumate, Harold; Manning, Bruce

Cast Carroll, Nancy; Murphy, George; Todd, Thelma; LaRue, Jack; Killian, Victor

Song(s) I Heard a Blind Man Singing (in the Street) [1] (C/L: Muse, Clarence); Without You I'm Just Drifting (C/L: Akst, Harry); Tomorrow Night (C/L: Akst, Harry)

Notes [1] Also in O'SHAUGHNESSY'S BOY (MGM).

66 ✦ AFTER THE FOX
United Artists, 1966

Musical Score Bacharach, Burt
Composer(s) Bacharach, Burt
Lyricist(s) David, Hal

Producer(s) Bryan, John
Director(s) De Sica, Vittorio
Screenwriter(s) Simon, Neil

Cast Sellers, Peter; Mature, Victor; Ekland, Britt; Balsam, Martin; Tamiroff, Akim; Buzzanca, Lando

Song(s) After the Fox; Make a Movie in Sevalio [1]; The Fox in Sevalio [1]; Visiting Day [1]; World of Make Believe [1]

Notes [1] Not used.

67 ✦ AFTER THE THIN MAN
Metro–Goldwyn–Mayer, 1936

Musical Score Stothart, Herbert; Ward, Edward
Choreographer(s) Felix, Seymour

Producer(s) Stromberg, Hunt
Director(s) Van Dyke, W.S.
Screenwriter(s) Goodrich, Frances; Hackett, Albert

Cast Asta; Powell, William; Loy, Myrna; Stewart, James; Calleia, Joseph; Marshal, Alan; Levene, Sam; Landi, Elissa; Ralph, Jessie; Hart, Teddy; McNulty, Dorothy; Mrs. Asta

Song(s) Sing, Sing, Sing (C/L: Prima, Louis); Asta's Love Song (C/L: Wright, Robert; Forrest, George); Blow That Horn (C: Donaldson, Walter; L: Wright, Robert; Forrest, George); Smoke Dreams (C: Brown, Nacio Herb; L: Freed, Arthur)

68 ✦ AFTER TOMORROW
Fox, 1932

Director(s) Borzage, Frank
Screenwriter(s) Levien, Sonya
Source(s) (play) Golden, John; Strange, Hugh

Cast Farrell, Charles; Nixon, Marian; Gombell, Minna; Collier Sr., William

Song(s) All the World Will Smile Again (After Tomorrow) (C/L: Hanley, James F.)

69 ✦ AGAINST A CROOKED SKY
Doty–Dayton, 1976

Musical Score De Azevedo, Alexis K.

Producer(s) Dayton, Lyman D.
Director(s) Bellamy, Earl
Screenwriter(s) Stewart, Douglas C.; Lamb, Eleanor

Cast Boone, Richard; Petersen, Stewart; Land, Geoffrey; Wilcoxon, Henry

Song(s) Against a Crooked Sky (C: De Azevado, Alexis K.; L: David, Mack)

Notes No cue sheet available.

70 ✦ AGAINST ALL ODDS
Columbia, 1984

Musical Score Colombier, Michel; Carlton, Larry

Producer(s) Hackford, Taylor; Gilmore, William S.
Director(s) Hackford, Taylor
Screenwriter(s) Hughes, Eric
Source(s) *Out of the Past* (film) Mainwaring, Daniel

Cast Ward, Richard; Bridges, Jeff; Woods, James; Karras, Alex; Greer, Jane; Widmark, Richard; Harewood, Dorian; Kurtz, Swoosie

Song(s) For Love Alone (C/L: Carlton, Larry); My Male Curiosity (C/L: Darnell, August); Making a Big Mistake (C/L: Rutherford, Michael); Walk Through the Fire (C/L: Gabriel, Peter); Against All Odds (Take a Look at Me Now) (C/L: Collins, Phil); Balcony [1] (C/L: Adamson, Stuart); Violet and Blue [1] (C/L: Nicks, Stephanie)

Notes All of these were written for the picture. [1] Sheet music only.

71 ✦ AIN'T MISBEHAVIN'
Universal, 1955

Musical Score Mancini, Henry
Choreographer(s) Scott, Lee; Williams, Kenny

Producer(s) Marx, Samuel
Director(s) Buzzell, Edward
Screenwriter(s) Rapp, Philip; Freeman, Devery; Buzzell, Edward

Cast Calhoun, Rory; Laurie, Piper; Carson, Jack; Van Doren, Mamie; Gardiner, Reginald; Britton, Barbara; Gaye, Lisa

Song(s) The Dixie Mambo (C: Burke, Sonny; L: Henderson, Charles); A Little Love Can Go a Long, Long Way (C: Fain, Sammy; L: Webster, Paul Francis); I Love That Rickey Tickey Tickey (C: Scott, Johnnie; L: Cahn, Sammy)

Notes "Ain't Misbehavin'" by Andy Razaf, Thomas "Fats" Waller and Harry Brooks is also used vocally.

72 ✦ AIRPORT '77
Universal, 1977

Musical Score Cacavas, John

Producer(s) Frye, William
Director(s) Jameson, Jerry
Screenwriter(s) Scheff, Michael; Spector, David

Cast Lemmon, Jack; Grant, Lee; Vaccaro, Brenda; Cotten, Joseph; de Havilland, Olivia; McGavin, Darren; Lee, Christopher; Foxworth, Robert; Hooks, Robert; Markham, Monte; Quinlan, Kathleen; Gerard, Gil; Lewis, Monica; Golonka, Arlene; Walsh, M. Emmet; Furth, George; Robinson, Dar; Lemmon, Chris; Stewart, James; Kennedy, George

Song(s) Beauty Is in the Eyes of the Beholder (C/L: Sullivan, Tom)

Notes No cue sheet available.

73 ✦ AIR STRIKE
Lippert, 1955

Musical Score Brummer, Andre

Producer(s) Roth, Cy
Director(s) Roth, Cy
Screenwriter(s) Roth, Cy

Cast Denning, Richard; Jean, Gloria; Haggerty, Don; Hudson, Bill; Kirby, John

Song(s) Each Time You Leave Me (C: Brummer, Andre; L: Ostrow, Sylvia)

74 ✦ THE ALAMO
United Artists, 1960

Musical Score Tiomkin, Dimitri
Composer(s) Tiomkin, Dimitri
Lyricist(s) Webster, Paul Francis

Producer(s) Wayne, John
Director(s) Wayne, John
Screenwriter(s) Grant, James Edward

Cast Wayne, John; Widmark, Richard; Harvey, Laurence; Avalon, Frankie; Wayne, Patrick; Cristal, Linda; Wills, Chill; O'Brien, Joan; Calleia, Joseph; Boone, Richard

Song(s) Here's to the Ladies; Green Leaves of Summer; Tennessee Babe; Ballad of the Alamo [1]

Notes [1] Exploitation only.

75 ✦ ALASKAN SLED DOG
Disney, 1956

Musical Score Wallace, Oliver

Producer(s) Sharpsteen, Ben
Director(s) Machetanz, Sara; Machetanz, Fred
Screenwriter(s) Hauser, Dwight

Cast Ewing, Bill

Song(s) Balto [1] (C: Smith, Paul J.; L: Shows, Charlie; Johnson, Bob)

Notes This is a semi-documentary. [1] Not used.

76 ✦ ALASKA PASSAGE
Twentieth Century–Fox, 1959

Musical Score Alexander, Alex

Producer(s) Glasser, Bernard
Director(s) Bernds, Edward
Screenwriter(s) Bernds, Edward

Cast Williams, Bill; Hayden, Nora; Thomas, Lyn; Bradley, Leslie; Dennis, Nick; Kirkpatrick, Jess

Song(s) Tina's Song [1] (C: Alexander, Alex; L: Starr, June)

Notes [1] Used instrumentally only.

77 ✦ ALASKA SEAS
Paramount, 1954

Musical Score Talbot, Irvin

Producer(s) Epstein, Mel
Director(s) Hopper, Jerry
Screenwriter(s) Homes, Geoffrey; Doniger, Walter
Source(s) (story) Willoughby, Barrett

Cast Ryan, Robert; Sterling, Jan; Keith, Brian; Barry, Gene

Song(s) I Wish I Was the Willow [1] (C: Lane, Burton; L: Loesser, Frank)

Notes Also appearing in the cast are Ross Bagdasarian, later remembered as the originator of The Chipmunks, and Aaron Spelling as the Knifer. Mr. Spelling is best known as the producer of the television series DYNASTY. [1] Also in SPAWN OF THE NORTH.

78 ✦ ALEXANDER'S RAGTIME BAND
Twentieth Century–Fox, 1938

Composer(s) Berlin, Irving
Lyricist(s) Berlin, Irving
Choreographer(s) Felix, Seymour

Producer(s) Zanuck, Darryl F.
Director(s) King, Henry
Screenwriter(s) Scola, Kathryn; Trotti, Lamar

Cast Power, Tyrone; Faye, Alice; Ameche, Don; Merman, Ethel; Haley, Jack; Hersholt, Jean; Westley, Helen; Carradine, John; Vernon, Wally; Crehan, Joseph; Dunbar, Dixie; Andrews, Stanley

Song(s) Now It Can Be Told; This Is the Life; For Your Country and My Country [2]; Comedy Song I'm Marching Along with Time [1]

Notes There are also vocals of the following Berlin songs: "Alexander's Ragtime Band," "Ragtime Violin" (also in EASTER PARADE), "The International Rag" (also in CALL ME MADAM), "Everybody's Doin' It," "When the Midnight Choo Choo Leaves for Alabam'" (also in THERE'S NO BUSINESS LIKE SHOW BUSINESS and EASTER PARADE), "I Can Always Find a Little Sunshine in the Y.M.C.A.," "Oh How I Hate to Get Up in the Morning," "We're on Our Way to France" (also in movie THIS IS THE ARMY), "Say It With Music," "A Pretty Girl Is Like a Melody" (also in BLUE SKIES and THERE'S NO BUSINESS LIKE SHOW BUSINESS), "Blue Skies" (also in BLUE SKIES, GLORIFYING THE AMERICAN GIRL and THE JAZZ SINGER), "Pack Up Your Sins and Go to the Devil," "What'll I Do," "My Walking Stick," "Remember" (also in THERE'S NO BUSINESS LIKE SHOW BUSINESS), "Everybody Step" (also in BLUE SKIES), "All Alone," "Easter Parade" (also in EASTER PARADE and HOLIDAY INN) and "Heat Wave" (From stage musical AS THOUSANDS CHEER. Also in films BLUE SKIES and THERE'S NO BUSINESS LIKE SHOW BUSINESS), and instrumentals of "In My Harem," "Cheek to Cheek" (also in TOP HAT) and "Marie." [1] Instrumental use only. [2] Also in THIS IS THE ARMY.

79 ✦ ALEX IN WONDERLAND
Metro–Goldwyn–Mayer, 1971

Musical Score O'Horgan, Tom

Producer(s) Tucker, Larry
Director(s) Mazursky, Paul
Screenwriter(s) Mazursky, Paul; Tucker, Larry

Cast Sutherland, Donald; Burstyn, Ellen; Mazursky, Meg; Sergent, Glenna; Spolin, Viola; Lerner, Michael; Philippe, Andre; Mazursky, Paul; Fellini, Federico; Moreau, Jeanne

Song(s) A Time for This-A Time for That (C: Garon, Timothy; L: Mazursky, Paul; Tucker, Larry); La Reve Est La (C: Delerue, Georges; L: Moreau, Jeanne); Time on Your Side (C/L: Smith, Howlett); Ja-Le-Man-Si (C/L: Broughton, John; Brown, Stanley); O-Me-Ya-Wa-Do (C/L: Broughton, John; Brown, Stanley); Le Vrai Scandale (C: Duhamel, Antoine; L: Moreau, Jeanne)

Notes There are also vocals of "Over the Rainbow" by Harold Arlen and E.Y. Harburg and "Hooray for Hollywood" by Richard A. Whiting and Johnny Mercer.

80 ✦ ALFIE
Paramount, 1966

Musical Score Rollins, Sonny

Producer(s) Gilbert, Lewis
Director(s) Gilbert, Lewis
Screenwriter(s) Naughton, Bill
Source(s) *Alfie* (play) Naughton, Bill

Cast Caine, Michael; Winters, Shelley; Martin, Millicent; Foster, Julia; Asher, Jane; Field, Shirley Anne; Merchant, Vivien; Bron, Eleanor; Elliott, Denholm; Bass, Alfie; Stark, Graham

Song(s) Alfie (C: Bacharach, Burt; L: David, Hal)

81 ✦ ALIAS JESSE JAMES
United Artists, 1959

Musical Score Lilley, Joseph J.

Producer(s) Hope, Jack
Director(s) McLeod, Norman Z.
Screenwriter(s) Bowers, William; Beauchamp, D.D. [1]

Cast Hope, Bob; Corey, Wendell; Fleming, Rhonda; Arness, James; Garner, James; O'Brian, Hugh; Autry, Gene; Davis, Jim; Finn, Mickey; Wright, Will; Mazurki, Mike; Talbott, Gloria; Young, Mary

Song(s) Alias Jesse James (C: Hooven, Marilyn; Hooven, Joe; L: Dunham, "By"); Ain't a Hankerin' (C/L: Burton, Bud; Altman, Arthur); Protection [2] (C/L: Burton, Bud; Altman, Arthur)

Notes This production was made at Paramount but released by United Artists. [1] Billed as Daniel D. Beauchamp. [2] Not on cue sheet.

82 ✦ ALIAS JIMMY VALENTINE
Metro–Goldwyn–Mayer, 1928

Musical Score Axt, William

Director(s) Conway, Jack
Screenwriter(s) Farnham, Joe; Mason, Sarah Y.
Source(s) *Alias Jimmy Valentine* (play) Armstrong, Paul

Cast Haines, William; Barrymore, Lionel; Dane, Karl; Hyams, Leila; Marshall, Tully; Hickman, Howard

Song(s) Love Dreams (C: Axt, William; L: Mendoza, David)

Notes AFI lists additional songwriter credits as Mort Harris and Raymond Klages.

83 ✦ ALIAS THE CHAMP
Republic, 1949

Producer(s) Auer, Stephen
Director(s) Blair, George
Screenwriter(s) De Mond, Albert

Cast Rockwell, Robert; Fuller, Barbara; Long, Audrey; Nolan, Jim; Harmon, John; Menacker, Sammy; Crehan, Joseph

Song(s) C'est Vous [1] (C/L: Newman, Albert; Cherwin, Richard; Washington, Ned)

Notes [1] Also in INSURANCE INVESTIGATOR.

84 ✦ ALI BABA AND THE FORTY THIEVES
Universal, 1943

Musical Score Ward, Edward

Producer(s) Malvern, Paul
Director(s) Lubin, Arthur
Screenwriter(s) Hartmann, Edmund L.

Cast Hall, Jon; Montez, Maria; Puglia, Frank; Katch, Kurt; Bey, Turhan; Devine, Andy; Bonanova, Fortunio; Olsen, Moroni; Beckett, Scotty

Song(s) Forty and One for All (C: Ward, Edward; L: Brennan, J. Keirn)

85 ✦ ALI BABA GOES TO TOWN
Twentieth Century–Fox, 1937

Composer(s) Revel, Harry
Lyricist(s) Gordon, Mack

Producer(s) Zanuck, Darryl F.
Director(s) Butler, David
Screenwriter(s) Tugend, Harry; Yellen, Jack

Cast Cantor, Eddie; Martin, Tony; Young, Roland; Lang, June; Hovick, Louise [2]; Carradine, John; Field, Virginia; Dinehart, Alan; Dumbrille, Douglass; The Raymond Scott Quintet; The Peters Sisters

Song(s) Swing Is Here to Sway; I've Got My Heart Set on You; Vote for Honest Abe [1]; Laugh Your Way Through Life [1]; Twilight in Turkey (Inst.) (C: Scott, Raymond); Arabian Dance (Inst.) (C: Scott, Raymond); Dance of the Seven Veils (Inst.) (C: Scott, Raymond); Arabiana [3]

Notes [1] Same melody. [2] Gypsy Rose Lee. [3] Not used.

86 ✦ ALICE ADAMS
RKO, 1935

Musical Score Webb, Roy

Producer(s) Berman, Pandro S.
Director(s) Stevens, George
Screenwriter(s) Yost, Dorothy; Offner, Mortimer
Source(s) *Alice Adams* (novel) Tarkington, Booth

Cast Hepburn, Katharine; MacMurray, Fred; Stone, Fred; Venable, Evelyn; Albertson, Frank; Shoemaker, Ann; Grapewin, Charley; Sutton, Grady; Hopper, Hedda; Hale, Jonathan; McDaniel, Hattie

Song(s) I Can't Waltz Alone (C: Steiner, Max; L: Fields, Dorothy)

Notes No cue sheet available. The song might have been written for exploitation only.

87 ✦ ALICE IN WONDERLAND (1933)
Paramount, 1933

Composer(s) Tiomkin, Dimitri; Finston, Nat
Lyricist(s) Carroll, Lewis

Producer(s) Lighton, Louis D.
Director(s) McLeod, Norman Z.
Screenwriter(s) Mankiewicz, Joseph L.; Menzies, William Cameron
Source(s) *Alice's Adventures in Wonderland* (novel) Carroll, Lewis

Cast Fields, W.C.; Cooper, Gary; Oakie, Jack; Oliver, Edna May; Grant, Cary; Arlen, Richard; Fazenda, Louise; Ruggles, Charles; Robson, May; Horton, Edward Everett; Skipworth, Alison; Gallagher, Skeets; LeRoy, Baby; Moran, Polly; Henry, Charlotte; Errol, Leon; Sparks, Ned; Hatton, Raymond

Song(s) Twinkle, Twinkle Little Bat; Beautiful Soup [1]; Tweedle Dum; Jabberwocky; Red Queen (C: Traditional); Father William; Drinking Song; Duchess Lullaby; The Walrus and the Carpenter; Lobster Quadrille; Alice in Wonderland (L: Robin, Leo); Walk a Little Faster [2] (C: Franklin, Dave); At the Banquet [2]

Notes [1] Also in YOUNG AND WILLING. [2] Sheet music only.

88 ✦ ALICE IN WONDERLAND (1951)
Disney, 1951

Musical Score Wallace, Oliver
Composer(s) Fain, Sammy
Lyricist(s) Hilliard, Bob

Producer(s) Sharpsteen, Ben
Director(s) Geronimi, Clyde; Luske, Hamilton; Jaxon, Wilfred
Screenwriter(s) Hibler, Winston; Peet, Bill; Rinaldi, Joe; Cottrell, William; Grant, Joe; Connell, Del;

Walbridge, John; Oreb, Tom; Huemer, Dick; Kelsey, Dick; Banta, Milt; Penner, Erdman; Sears, Ted
Source(s) *Alice's Adventures in Wonderland; Through the Looking Glass* (novels) Carroll, Lewis
Voices Beaumont, Kathryn; Angel, Heather; Thompson, Bill; O'Malley, Pat; Felton, Verna; Colonna, Jerry; Holloway, Sterling; Haydn, Richard; Wynn, Ed

Directing Animator(s) Kahl, Milt; Kimball, Ward; Thomas, Franklin; Larson, Eric; Lounsbery, John; Johnston, Ollie; Reitherman, Wolfgang; Davis, Marc; Clark, Les; Ferguson, Norm

Song(s) Alice in Wonderland (1); Alice in Wonderland (2) [1] (C/L: Churchill, Frank E.); In a World of My Own; I'm Late; The Caucus Race; How Do You Do, and Shake Hands [4] (C: Wallace, Oliver; L: Carroll, Lewis); The Walrus and the Carpenter (L: Hilliard, Bob; Carroll, Lewis); Old Father William (C: Wallace, Oliver; L: Carroll, Lewis); We'll Smoke the Blighter Out (C: Wallace, Oliver; L: Sears, Ted; Hibler, Winston); All in the Golden Afternoon; A-E-I-O-U (Caterpillar Song) (C/L: Wallace, Oliver); T'was Brillig (C: de Paul, Gene; L: Raye, Don; Carroll, Lewis); Very Good Advice; Painting the Roses Red; The Unbirthday Song (C/L: David, Mack; Livingston, Jerry; Hoffman, Al); Alice and Bottle [1] (C: Churchill, Frank E.; L: Osborne, Ted); Beautiful Soup [1] (C: de Paul, Gene; L: Raye, Don); Beware the Jabberwock [1] (C: de Paul, Gene; L: Raye, Don); Beyond the Laughing Sky [1] [2]; Curiosity [1] (C/L: David, Mack; Livingston, Jerry; Hoffman, Al); Dream Caravan [1]; Everything Has a Useness [1] [3] (C/L: David, Mack; Livingston, Jerry; Hoffman, Al); Garden Snips [1] (C/L: Churchill, Frank E.); If You'll Believe in Me [1] (C/L: David, Mack; Livingston, Jerry; Hoffman, Al); I'm Odd [1]; It's Crazy to Be Sane [1] (C: Churchill, Frank E.; L: Osborne, Ted); Lobster Quadrille [1] (C: Churchill, Frank E.; L: Carroll, Lewis); Mock Turtle Soup Song [1] (C: Churchill, Frank E.; L: Carroll, Lewis); Pepper Lullaby [1] (C: Churchill, Frank E.; L: Carroll, Lewis)

89 ✦ ALICE IN WONDERLAND (1976)
General National, 1976

Musical Score Searles, Bucky

Producer(s) Osco, William
Director(s) Townsend, Bud
Screenwriter(s) Fredricks, B. Anthony
Source(s) *Alice's Adventures in Wonderland* (novel) Carroll, Lewis

Cast De Bell, Kristine; Gelman, Larry; Novak, Allan; Tsengoles, Tony; Tsengoles, Sue

Song(s) Whole New World (C: Matz, Peter; L: Searles, Bucky); Guess I Was Too Busy Growing Up (C: Matz, Peter; L: Searles, Bucky)

Notes No cue sheet available.

90 ✦ ALICE'S ADVENTURES IN WONDERLAND (1972)
American National, 1972

Composer(s) Barry, John
Lyricist(s) Black, Don

Producer(s) Horne, Derek
Director(s) Sterling, William
Screenwriter(s) Sterling, William
Source(s) *Alice's Adventures in Wonderland; Through the Looking Glass* (novels) Carroll, Lewis

Cast Crawford, Michael; Kaye, Davy; Helpmann, Robert; Sellers, Peter; Moore, Dudley; Richardson, Ralph; Bull, Peter; Robson, Flora; Hordern, Michael; Milligan, Spike; Jayston, Michael; Fullerton, Fiona

Song(s) Curiouser and Curiouser; You've Gotta Know When to Stop; The Last Word Is Mine; Dum and Dee Dance; Nursery Rhyme (L: Carroll, Lewis); The Pun Song; I've Never Been This Far Before; Off with Their Heads; The Moral Song; Will You Walk a Little Faster? (L: Carroll, Lewis); They Told Me You Had Been to Her (L: Carroll, Lewis); The Me I Never Knew

Notes No cue sheet available.

91 ✦ ALICE SIT-BY-THE-FIRE
Paramount, 1946 unproduced

Source(s) *Alice Sit-By-the-Fire* (play) Barrie, James M.

Song(s) Flutter Bye Butterfly (C: Spielman, Fred; L: Goell, Kermit)

Notes Leo Robin was also hired to write two numbers but the production was called off before he could do so.

92 ✦ ALICE'S RESTAURANT
United Artists, 1969

Producer(s) Elkins, Hillard; Manduke, Joe
Director(s) Penn, Arthur
Screenwriter(s) Herndon, Vennable; Penn, Arthur

Cast Guthrie, Arlo; Quinn, Pat; Broderick, James; Seeger, Pete; Hayes, Lee; McClanathan, Michael; Obanhein, William

Song(s) Alice's Restaurant Massacre [1] (C/L: Guthrie, Arlo)

Notes [1] Used instrumentally only according to cue sheet.

93 ✦ THE ALL-AMERICAN
Universal, 1953

Musical Score Lava, William

Producer(s) Rosenberg, Aaron
Director(s) Hibbs, Jesse
Screenwriter(s) Beauchamp, D.D.

Cast   Curtis, Tony; Nelson, Lori; Long, Richard; Van Doren, Mamie; Whitman, Stuart

Song(s)   Have a Beer (C: Hughes, Arnold; L: Herbert, Frederick)

94 ✦ ALL-AMERICAN CO-ED
United Artists, 1941

Musical Score   Ward, Edward
Composer(s)   Samuels, Walter G.
Lyricist(s)   Newman, Charles

Producer(s)   Roach, Hal; Prinz, LeRoy
Director(s)   Prinz, LeRoy
Screenwriter(s)   Fitzsimmons, Cortland; Higgins, Kenneth C.

Cast   Langford, Frances; Downs, Johnny; Woodworth, Marjorie; The Tanner Sisters; Beery Jr., Noah; Dale, Esther; Langdon, Harry; Lane, Allan; Rogers, Kent

Song(s)   I'm a Chap with a Chip on My Shoulder; Up at the Crack of Dawn; The Farmer's Daughter; Out of the Silence (C/L: Norlin, Lloyd R.)

Notes   No cue sheet available.

95 ✦ ALL AMERICAN SWEETHEART
Columbia, 1937

Composer(s)   Oakland, Ben
Lyricist(s)   Drake, Milton

Director(s)   Hillyer, Lambert
Screenwriter(s)   Neville, Grace; Niblo Jr., Fred; Simmons, Michael L.

Cast   Farr, Patricia; Colton, Scott; Morgan, Gene; Eagles, Jimmy; Twerp, Ida

Song(s)   Pop Goes the Bottle; Lazy Rhythm [1] (L: J.P.); The Fight Song (C: Mertz, Paul); Old School (C: Mertz, Paul); Turn on the Tap; My Kid Sister [1]

Notes   [1] Used instrumentally only.

96 ✦ ALL ASHORE
Columbia, 1953

Composer(s)   Wells, Robert; Karger, Fred
Lyricist(s)   Wells, Robert; Karger, Fred
Choreographer(s)   Ivan, Erze; Scott, Lee

Producer(s)   Taps, Jonie
Director(s)   Quine, Richard
Screenwriter(s)   Edwards, Blake; Quine, Richard

Cast   Rooney, Mickey; Haymes, Dick; Ryan, Peggy; McDonald, Ray; Bates, Barbara; Bates, Jody

Song(s)   Boy Meets Girl; Heave Ho; My Hearties; I Love No One but You; All Ashore; Buddy Boy; Catalina; If You Were an Eskimo; I'm So Unlucky; Sir Francis the Dragon; Who Are We to Say

Notes   No cue sheet available. Lee Scott is also credited with songs in some sources.

97 ✦ ALL AT SEA
Metro–Goldwyn–Mayer, 1958

Musical Score   Addison, John

Producer(s)   Van Thal, Dennis
Director(s)   Frend, Charles
Screenwriter(s)   Clarke, T.E.B.

Cast   Guinness, Alec; Browne, Irene; Denham, Maurice; Cuthbertson, Allan; Jeffries, Lionel; Rose, George; Collins, Jackie; Maddern, Victor; Wattis, Richard

Song(s)   Gotta One Way Ticket (C/L: New, Derek)

Notes   Also known as BARNACLE BILL.

98 ✦ ALL BY MYSELF
Universal, 1943

Producer(s)   Burton, Bernard W.
Director(s)   Feist, Felix E.
Screenwriter(s)   Wedlock Jr., Hugh; Snyder, Howard

Cast   Hamilton, Neil; Ankers, Evelyn; Lane, Rosemary; Knowles, Patric

Song(s)   You're Priceless [1] (C/L: Amsterdam, Morey; Romano, Tony); I Don't Believe in Rumors (C/L: Glick, Harry; Lambert, Jimmy); All to Myself (C/L: Pepper, Buddy; James, Inez); Let It Ride [1] (C/L: Morgan, Loumell)

Notes   [1] Not written for picture.

99 ✦ ALLERGIC TO LOVE
Universal, 1944

Producer(s)   Wilson, Warren
Director(s)   Lilley, Edward
Screenwriter(s)   Wilson, Warren

Cast   Beery Jr., Noah; O'Driscoll, Martha; Bruce, David; Pangborn, Franklin; Rosenbloom, Maxie; Knight, Fuzzy; Windheim, Marek; Chandler, George; Howland, Olin; Hamilton, John; Armetta, Henry; The Guadalajara Trio

Song(s)   Carmencita (C/L: Carter, Everett; Rosen, Milton); Rhumba Matumba [1] (C/L: Collazo, Bobby); Farruca (C/L: Matos, Manuel); Teperdi (C/L: Santos, Mario); Music Maestro (C/L: Roberti, Roberto & Marques Jr.)

Notes   No cue sheet available. [1] Also in PAN-AMERICANA.

100   ✦   ALL FOR MARY
United Artists, 1955

Musical Score   Farnon, Robert

Producer(s)   Rank, J. Arthur
Director(s)   Toye, Wendy
Screenwriter(s)   Blackmore, Peter; Soskin, Paul

Cast   Patrick, Nigel; Harrison, Kathleen; Tomlinson, David; Day, Jill; McKern, Leo

Song(s)   All for Mary (C: Farnon, Robert; L: Newell, Norman); Far Away from Everybody (C: Delugg, Milton; L: Hilliard, Bob)

Notes   A Rank Organisation film.

101   ✦   ALL HANDS ON DECK
Twentieth Century–Fox, 1961

Composer(s)   Livingston, Jay; Evans, Ray
Lyricist(s)   Livingston, Jay; Evans, Ray
Choreographer(s)   Belfer, Hal

Producer(s)   Brodney, Oscar
Director(s)   Taurog, Norman
Screenwriter(s)   Sommers, Jay
Source(s)   *Warm Bodies* (novel) Morris, Donald R.

Cast   Boone, Pat; Hackett, Buddy; O'Keefe, Dennis; Eden, Barbara

Song(s)   All Hands on Deck; Somewhere There's a Home; There's No One Like You; I Got It Made; You're Someone Special [1]; Little Friend (Lullaby to a Turkey) [1]

Notes   [1] Not used.

102   ✦   AN ALLIGATOR NAMED DAISY
United Artists, 1955

Musical Score   Black, Stanley
Composer(s)   Coslow, Sam
Lyricist(s)   Coslow, Sam

Producer(s)   Rank, J. Arthur
Director(s)   Thompson, J. Lee
Screenwriter(s)   Davies, Jack
Source(s)   *An Alligator Named Daisy* (book) Terret, Charles

Cast   Sinden, Donald; Dors, Diana; Justice, James Robertson; Carson, Jean; Holloway, Stanley; Culver, Roland; Rutherford, Margaret; Lawson, Wilfred

Song(s)   I'm in Love for the Very First Time (C/L: Roberts, Paddy); Crocodile Crawl; Midnight Madness; First Love

Notes   A British film.

103   ✦   ALL IN A NIGHT'S WORK
Paramount, 1961

Musical Score   Previn, Andre

Producer(s)   Wallis, Hal B.
Director(s)   Anthony, Joseph
Screenwriter(s)   Sheldon, Sidney; Beloin, Edmund; Richlin, Maurice

Cast   MacLaine, Shirley; Martin, Dean; Robertson, Cliff; Ruggles, Charles; Crane, Norma; Gordon, Gale; Cowan, Jerome; Weston, Jack

Song(s)   All in a Night's Work [1] (C/L: Roberts, Ruth; L: Katz, William)

Notes   [1] Written for exploitation only.

104   ✦   ALL IN A NUTSHELL
Disney, 1948

Musical Score   Wallace, Oliver

Director(s)   Hannah, Jack
Screenwriter(s)   Berg, Bill; George, Mick

Song(s)   Main Title (C/L: Wallace, Oliver)

Notes   Short subject.

105   ✦   ALL MEN ARE APES
Adelphia Pictures, 1965

Musical Score   Dweir, Irv

Producer(s)   Sackett, Bernard L.
Director(s)   Mawra, J.P.
Screenwriter(s)   Mazin, Charles E.; Sackett, Barnard L.

Cast   De Passe, Stephanie; Ryan, Mark; Lynn, Grace; Woods, Steve

Song(s)   Voodoo (C/L: Mazin, Charles E.); All Men Are Apes (C/L: Mazin, Charles E.)

Notes   No cue sheet available.

106   ✦   ALL MEN ARE ENEMIES
Fox, 1934

Producer(s)   Rockett, Al
Director(s)   Fitzmaurice, George
Screenwriter(s)   Coffee, Lenore; Hoffenstein, Samuel
Source(s)   *All Men Are Enemies* (novel) Aldington, Richard

Cast   Twelvetrees, Helen; Barrie, Mona; Williams, Hugh

Song(s)   Hear My Heart [1] (C: De Francesco, Louis E.; L: Hoffenstein, Samuel)

Notes   [1] William Kernell is listed in some sources although Hoffenstein (spelled Hoefenstein) is indicated as lyricist on cue sheets.

107 ✦ THE ALLNIGHTER
Universal, 1987

Musical Score Bernstein, Charles
Composer(s) Gutierrez, Louis; Gurley, M. Clark
Lyricist(s) Gutierrez, Louis; Gurley, M. Clark

Producer(s) Hoffs, Tamar Simon
Director(s) Hoffs, Tamar Simon
Screenwriter(s) Kessler, M.L.; Hoffs, Tamar Simon

Cast Hoffs, Susanna; Pfeiffer, Dedee; Cusack, Joan; Shanta, James Anthony; Terlesky, John; Ontkean, Michael; Grier, Pam; Taylor, Meshach

Song(s) Take a Mile; Slow Song; True Love (C/L: Bernstein, Charles)

Notes There are other songs that were not written for the picture.

108 ✦ ALL NIGHT LONG
Universal, 1981

Musical Score Newborn, Ira; Hazard, Richard
Lyricist(s) Richter, W.D.

Producer(s) Goldberg, Leonard; Weintraub, Jerry
Director(s) Tramont, Jean-Claude
Screenwriter(s) Richter, W.D.

Cast Hackman, Gene; Streisand, Barbra; Ladd, Diane; Quaid, Dennis; Dobson, Kevin; Daniels, William

Song(s) Carelessly Tossed (C: Lindgren, Alan); Cheryl's Theme (C: Grusin, Dave)

Notes No cue sheet available.

109 ✦ ALL OVER TOWN
Republic, 1937

Producer(s) Fields, Leonard
Director(s) Horne, James W.
Screenwriter(s) Chodorov, Jerome; Townley, Jack

Cast Olsen, Ole; Johnson, Chic; Howard, Mary; Stockwell, Harry; Pangborn, Franklin; Finlayson, James; Kane, Eddie; Fields, Stanley; Corrigan, D'Arcy

Song(s) MacDougal's Mackeral (C/L: Olsen, Ole; Johnson, Chic)

110 ✦ ALL STAR BOND RALLY
Twentieth Century–Fox, 1945

Musical Score Mockridge, Cyril J.

Producer(s) Fanchon
Director(s) Audley, Michael
Screenwriter(s) Quinn, Don

Cast Crosby, Bing; Hope, Bob; Fibber McGee and Molly; Marx, Harpo; Harry James and His Band; Sinatra, Frank; Grable, Betty

Song(s) Buy a Bond (C: McHugh, Jimmy; L: Adamson, Harold); Elma (Inst.) (C: Marx, Harpo)

Notes Short subject. Vocals of "I'll Be Marching to a Love Song" and "Thanks for the Memory" by Ralph Rainger and Leo Robin; "Saturday Night (Is the Loneliest Night of the Week)" by Jule Styne and Sammy Cahn are also performed. Canadian prints also have the Harry James Band playing "Two O'Clock Jump" by Harry James, Count Basie and Benny Goodman.

111 ✦ ALL-STAR MUSICAL REVUE
Warner Brothers, 1945

Song(s) Once to Every Heart (C: Lane, Burton; L: Koehler, Ted)

Notes Short subject.

112 ✦ ALL STAR VAUDEVILLE
Warner Brothers, 1935

Cast Rooney, Pat; Rooney Jr., Pat; Seeley, Blossom; Fields, Benny

Song(s) Why Don't You Practice What You Preach (C/L: Goodhart, Al); If I Could Be As Clever As My Dad (C/L: Rooney)

Notes Short subject. The film also includes "Between the Devil and the Deep Blue Sea" by Harold Arlen and Ted Koehler.

113 ✦ ALL THAT HEAVEN ALLOWS
Universal, 1955

Musical Score Skinner, Frank

Producer(s) Hunter, Ross
Director(s) Sirk, Douglas
Screenwriter(s) Fenwick, Peg

Cast Wyman, Jane; Hudson, Rock; Talbott, Gloria; Reynolds, William; Moorehead, Agnes; Nagel, Conrad; Grey, Virginia

Song(s) Rovey Eye (C/L: Herbert, Frederick; Hughes, Arnold)

114 ✦ ALL THAT JAZZ
Columbia/Twentieth Century–Fox, 1979

Producer(s) Aurthur, Robert Alan
Director(s) Fosse, Bob
Screenwriter(s) Aurthur, Robert Alan; Fosse, Bob

Cast Scheider, Roy; Lange, Jessica; Reinking, Ann; Palmer, Leland; Gorman, Cliff; Vereen, Ben; Foldi, Erzsebet; Tolan, Michael; Smith, Sammy; Wright, Max; Le Massena, William; Chase, Chris; Holland, Anthony; Margulies, David; Gordon, Keith; Lithgow, John; Drum, Leonard; Troobnick, Eugene; Fisher, Jules; Masters, Ben; Merlin, Joanna; Haynes, Tiger; Townsend, K.C.;

Bayer, Gary; Elmore, Steve; Fosse, Nicole; Mann, P.J.; Hobson, I.M.; McCarty, Mary; Merritt, Theresa; Shawn, Wallace; Shelton, Sloane; Bergman, Sandahl; Schwantes, Leland

Song(s) Take Off with Us (C/L: Tobias, Fred; Lebowsky, Stanley)

Notes There are also vocals of "On Broadway" by Barry Mann, Cynthia Weil, Jerry Leiber and Mike Stoller; "A Perfect Day" by Harry Nilsson; "Everything Old Is New Again" by Peter Allen and Carole Bayer Sager; "After You've Gone" by Henry Creamer and Turner Layton; "There'll Be Some Changes Made" by W.B. Overstreet, B. Higgins, and H. Edwards; "Who's Sorry Now" by Ted Snyder, Bert Kalmar and Harry Ruby; "Some of These Days" by Shelton Brooks; "Bye, Bye, Love" by Boudleaux Bryant and Felice Bryant and "There's No Business Like Show Business" by Irving Berlin.

115 ✦ ALL THE CATS JOIN IN
Disney, 1946

Song(s) All the Cats Join In (C: Sauter, Eddie; L: Wilder, Alec; Gilbert, Ray)

Notes This is part of MAKE MINE MUSIC. It was arranged by Charles Wolcott and Benny Goodman.

116 ✦ ALL THE FINE YOUNG CANNIBALS
Metro–Goldwyn–Mayer, 1960

Musical Score Alexander, Jeff

Producer(s) Berman, Pandro S.
Director(s) Anderson, Michael
Screenwriter(s) Thom, Robert
Source(s) *The Bixby Girls* (novel) Marshall, Rosamond

Cast Wagner, Robert; Wood, Natalie; Kohner, Susan; Hamilton, George; Bailey, Pearl; Seymour, Anne; Albertson, Mabel; Beavers, Louise; Stevens, Onslow; Gregg, Virginia

Song(s) The Doggonedest Feeling (C/L: Coles, Charles L. "Honi"; Payne, Benny); Deep Song (C/L: Cory, George; Cross, Douglas)

Notes Formerly entitled EVER FOR EACH OTHER. There are also vocals of "Happiness Is a Thing Called Joe" by Harold Arlen and E.Y. Harburg; and "God Bless the Child" by Billie Holiday and Arthur Herzog Jr.

117 ✦ ALL THE KING'S HORSES
Paramount, 1935

Composer(s) Coslow, Sam
Lyricist(s) Coslow, Sam
Choreographer(s) Prinz, LeRoy

Producer(s) LeBaron, William
Director(s) Tuttle, Frank

Screenwriter(s) Tuttle, Frank; Stephani, Frederick
Source(s) *All the King's Horses* (musical) Horan, Edward A.; Herendeen, Frederick

Cast Brisson, Carl; Ellis, Mary; Horton, Edward Everett; de Mille, Katherine; Pallette, Eugene; Korff, Arnold

Song(s) Be Careful Young Lady; Dancing the Viennese; A Little White Gardenia [4]; Gypsy Madness; When My Prince Charming Comes Along [5]; King Can Do No Wrong [1]; I Want to Dance a Little, Romance a Little [1]; Our First Rendezvous; If You Were I and I Were You; Goodbye Forever (C: Tosti); Sleep Baby Sleep (C: Unknown; L: Coslow, Sam); Carlo's Song [2]; My Unfinished Symphony of Love [2]; With the Whole World Listening In [2]; You Me and Company [2]; Cabinet Number [2]; Keep Your Fingers Crossed [2] [3]

Notes [1] Same music. [2] Unused. [3] Also not used in TWO FOR TONIGHT. Used with Richard Whiting music for CORONADO. [4] Also in TOO MANY PARENTS. [5] In score of unproduced BUDDY ROGERS MUSICAL.

118 ✦ ALL THE RIGHT MOVES
Twentieth Century–Fox, 1983

Musical Score Campbell, David

Producer(s) Deutsch, Stephen
Director(s) Chapman, Michael
Screenwriter(s) Kane, Michael
Source(s) "Football High" (article) Jordan, Pat

Cast Cruise, Tom; Nelson, Craig T.; Thompson, Lea; Cioffi, Charles; Faison, Sandy; Carafotes, Paul

Song(s) All the Right Moves (C: Snow, Tom; L: Alfonso, Barry); Unison (C/L: Roberts, Bruce; Goldmark, Andy); This Could Be Our Last Chance (C/L: Golde, Franne; Pomerantz, Susan; Shifrin, Sue); The Last Stand (C/L: Kahan, Doug); Easy Street (C/L: Moman, Chips; Emmons, Bobby); Have I Done Anything At All (To Make You Love Me Today) (C/L: Emmons, Bobby); I Don't Wanna Go Down (C/L: O'Neal, Brian); Mr. Popularity (C/L: McMahon, Gerard); Hold Me Close to You (C: St. Louis, Louis; L: Alhanti, Janet); Blue Skies Forever (C: Kerr, Richard; L: Jennings, Will)

Notes It is not known which of these were written for the picture. All are background vocals.

119 ✦ ALL THE WAY HOME
Paramount, 1963

Musical Score Green, Bernard

Producer(s) Susskind, David
Director(s) Segal, Alex
Screenwriter(s) Reisman Jr., Philip

Source(s) *All the Way Home* (play) Mosel, Tad; *A Death in the Family* (novel) Agee, James

Cast Simmons, Jean; Preston, Robert; Hingle, Pat; MacMahon, Aline; Chalmers, Thomas; Cullum, John; Kearney, Michael

Song(s) All the Way Home (C: Styne, Jule; L: Styne, Stanley)

120   ◆   ALL THE YOUNG MEN
Columbia, 1960

Musical Score Duning, George

Producer(s) Bartlett, Hall
Director(s) Bartlett, Hall
Screenwriter(s) Bartlett, Hall

Cast Ladd, Alan; Poitier, Sidney; Johansson, Ingemar; Darren, James; Corbett, Glenn; Sahl, Mort; St. Clair, Ana

Song(s) All the Young Men (C: Duning, George; L: Styne, Stanley)

Notes No cue sheet available.

121   ◆   ALL THIS AND HEAVEN TOO
Warner Brothers, 1940

Musical Score Steiner, Max
Composer(s) Jerome, M.K.
Lyricist(s) Scholl, Jack

Producer(s) Wallis, Hal B.; Warner, Jack L.
Director(s) Litvak, Anatole
Screenwriter(s) Robinson, Casey
Source(s) *All This and Heaven Too* (novel) Field, Rachel

Cast Davis, Bette; Boyer, Charles; Weidler, Virginia; Westley, Helen; Hampden, Walter; Daniell, Henry; Coulouris, George; Lockhart, June; Todd, Ann

Song(s) The War of the Roses; Lullaby; Loti's Song [1]; All This and Heaven Too [2]

Notes All these songs are less than a minute's duration. [1] Sometime listed in sources as "Lotus Song" but not on cue sheets. [2] Not listed on cue sheets.

122   ◆   ALL THIS AND MONEY TOO

See LOVE IS A BALL.

123   ◆   ALL THIS AND WORLD WAR II
Twentieth Century–Fox, 1976

Producer(s) Lieberson, Sandy; Machat, Martin J.
Director(s) Winslow, Susan

Cast Ambrosia; Gabriel, Peter; Reddy, Helen; Wood, Boyd; Sayer, Leo; The Bee Gees; Gross, Henry; Turner, Tina; Laine, Frankie; Ferry, Bryan; Essex, David; John, Elton; Status Quo; The Brothers Johnson

Notes There are no original songs written for this production. The following Lennon/McCartney songs are used on the soundtrack: "Magical Mystery Tour," "Day in the Life," "Strawberry Fields," "Fool on the Hill," "Polyethene Pam," "Long and Winding Road," "Golden Slumbers," "Come Together," "Menace," "Sun King," "I Am the Walrus," "Maxwell's Silver Hammer," "She's Leaving Home," "Let It Be," "Yesterday," "Lucy in the Sky," "It's Getting Better," "Hey Jude," "When I'm Sixty-Four," "With a Little Help from My Friends," "We Can Work It Out," "Nowhere Man," "Because," "Get Back," "Michelle," "Boy You've Got to Carry that Weight," "You Never Give Me Your Money," "One Sweet Dream," "(And In) The End" and "Give Peace a Chance."

124   ◆   ALL THROUGH THE NIGHT
Warner Brothers, 1942

Musical Score Deutsch, Adolph
Composer(s) Schwartz, Arthur
Lyricist(s) Mercer, Johnny

Producer(s) Wallis, Hal B.
Director(s) Sherman, Vincent
Screenwriter(s) Spigelgass, Leonard; Gilbert, Edwin

Cast Bogart, Humphrey; MacLane, Barton; Veidt, Conrad; Darwell, Jane; Verne, Kaaren; McHugh, Frank; Lorre, Peter; Anderson, Judith; Silvers, Phil; Ford, Wallace

Song(s) Cherie I Love You (C/L: Goodman, Lillian Rosedale); All Through the Night

125   ◆   ALL WOMEN HAVE SECRETS
Paramount, 1940

Musical Score Leipold, John; Young, Victor; Bradshaw, Charles W.

Producer(s) LeBaron, William
Director(s) Neumann, Kurt
Screenwriter(s) Johnston, Agnes Christine

Cast Dale, Virginia; Allen Jr., Joseph; Cagney, James

Song(s) Rock-A-Bye Baby [1] (C: Burdette, Robert; Canning, Effie I.; L: Loesser, Frank; Cascales, Johnny); I Live Again (Because I'm In Love Again) (C: Young, Victor; L: Washington, Ned)

Notes Originally titled CAMPUS WIVES. [1] Arranged and with new lyrics by Frank Loesser and Johnny Cascales.

126   ◆   ALMOST ANGELS
Disney, 1962

Choreographer(s) Thomson, Norman

Director(s) Perrin, Steve
Screenwriter(s) Harris, Vernon

Cast The Vienna Boys Choir; Weck, Peter; Holt, Hans; Eckhardt, Fritz; Lobel, Bruni; Phillipp, Gunther; Gilmore, Denis

Notes No original songs. No cue sheet available.

127 ✦ ALMOST MARRIED
Universal, 1942

Musical Score Skinner, Frank
Composer(s) Press, Jacques
Lyricist(s) Cherkose, Eddie

Producer(s) Goldsmith, Ken
Director(s) Lamont, Charles
Screenwriter(s) Wedlock Jr., Hugh; Snyder, Howard

Cast Paige, Robert; Frazee, Jane; Pallette, Eugene; Eburne, Maude

Song(s) After All These Years; Take Your Place in the Sun; Bingee, Bingee, Skootie (C/L: Gaillard, Slim; Squires, Harry D.); The Rhumba; I Won't Take No for an Answer; Just to Be Near You [1] (C: dePaul, Gene; L: Unknown)

Notes [1] Not on cue sheet.

128 ✦ ALMOST SUMMER
Universal, 1978

Producer(s) Clark, Anthony R.
Director(s) Davidson, Martin
Screenwriter(s) Berg, Judith; Berg, Sandra; Reid, Marc; Davidson, Rubel; Davidson, Martin

Cast Kirby, Bruno; Purcell, Lee; Friedrich, John; Conn, Didi; Matheson, Tim

Song(s) Almost Summer (C: Wilson, Brian; Love, Mike; Jardine, Al); Sad, Sad Summer (C/L: Love, Mike); Cruisin' (C/L: Love, Mike); Lookin' Good (C/L: Altbach, Ron); Island Girl/Chief Joseph (C/L: Lloyd, Charles)

Notes There are other licensed songs on the soundtrack.

129 ✦ ALMOST YOU
Twentieth Century–Fox, 1985

Musical Score Elias, Jonathan

Producer(s) Lipson, Mark
Director(s) Brooks, Adam
Screenwriter(s) Horowitz, Mark

Cast Adams, Brooke; Dunne, Griffin; Young, Karen; Watt, Marty; Estabrook, Christine; Mostel, Josh; Dean, Laura; Pinero, Miguel; Gray, Spalding; Metcalf, Mark

Song(s) Almost You (C: Elias, Jonathan; L: Watt, Marty)

Notes No cue sheet available.

130 ✦ ALOMA OF THE SOUTH SEAS
Paramount, 1941

Composer(s) Hollander, Frederick
Lyricist(s) Loesser, Frank
Choreographer(s) Prinz, LeRoy

Producer(s) Bell, Monta
Director(s) Santell, Alfred
Screenwriter(s) Owen, Seena; Butler, Frank; Hayward, Lillie
Source(s) *Aloma of the South Seas* (play) Clemens, Leroy; Hymer, John B.

Cast Lamour, Dorothy; Hall, Jon; Reed, Philip; de Mille, Katherine; Overman, Lynne; Beckett, Scotty; Shaw, Reta

Song(s) The White Blossoms of Tah-Ni [2]; Vana Vana (C/L: Goupil, Augie); Oaoa (C/L: Goupil, Augie); Tearii (C/L: Goupil, Augie); Manue (C/L: Goupil, Augie); Tiare Tahiti (C/L: Goupil, Augie); Paoa (C/L: Goupil, Augie); E Maururu a Vau (C/L: King Pomare V); Aloma of the South Seas [1]; The Faraway Islands [1]

Notes Little of the Tahitian music was written for the film. Much of it was based on traditional sources. [1] Not used. [2] Also in ISLE OF TABU.

131 ✦ ALONE WITH YOU
Fox, 1930

Composer(s) Greer, Jesse
Lyricist(s) Klages, Raymond

Song(s) The Shindig; I'm the Scamp of the Campus; Where Can You Be? [1]; When You Look in My Eyes

Notes No other information available. [1] Also in CHEER UP AND SMILE.

132 ✦ ALONG CAME JONES
RKO, 1945

Musical Score Friedhofer, Hugo

Director(s) Heisler, Stuart
Screenwriter(s) Johnson, Nunnally
Source(s) *Useless Cowboy* (novel) LeMay, Alan

Cast Cooper, Gary; Young, Loretta; Demarest, William; Duryea, Dan; Sully, Frank; Simpson, Russell; Loft, Arthur; Robertson, Willard

Song(s) 'Round and Around (C/L: Lange, Arthur; Stewart, Al)

133 ✦ ALONG CAME LOVE
Paramount, 1936

Producer(s) Rowland, Richard A.
Director(s) Lytell, Bert
Screenwriter(s) Strong, Austin

Cast Starrett, Charles; Hervey, Irene; Kenyon, Doris; Judels, Charles; Warner, H.B.; Franklin, Irene

Song(s) I'm the Gal the Lonesome Cowboy Left Behind (C: Morton, Arthur; L: Franklin, Irene); A Rendezvous with a Dream [1] (C: Rainger, Ralph; L: Robin, Leo)

Notes Originally titled LOVE AND LAUGHTER. There are also sequences of the Irene Franklin character singing a little of Franklin's song "Red Head," and she was heard but not seen singing "Some Day We'll Meet Again" by Con Conrad and Herb Magidson. [1] Also in POPPY and not used in STICK TO YOUR GUNS.

134 ✦ ALONG CAME RUTH
Warner Brothers, 1932

Cast Etting, Ruth

Song(s) Shine on Harvest Moon [1] (C/L: Bayes, Nora; Norworth, Jack); It Cost Me Just a Nickel (C: Fain, Sammy; L: Kahal, Irving); Moonlight on the River (C/L: Green, Bud); My Heart's at Ease (C/L: Waller; Young)

Notes No cue sheet available. No reference to this film is available. It might be a short subject. The date is questionable. Used is the copyright date of the Bud Green song. [1] Not written for film. Whether the other songs were, I don't know. It is also used in I'LL SEE YOU IN MY DREAMS; SHINE ON HARVEST MOON (1938) (Republic) and SHINE ON HARVEST MOON.

135 ✦ ALONG CAME YOUTH
Paramount, 1931

Composer(s) Rainger, Ralph
Lyricist(s) Marion Jr., George

Director(s) Corrigan, Lloyd; McLeod, Norman Z.
Screenwriter(s) Marion Jr., George

Cast Rogers, Charles "Buddy"; Dee, Frances; Erwin, Stuart

Song(s) Sugar Beat [1]; Fate Is Late Again [1]; I Look at You and a Song Is Born

Notes [1] Not used.

136 ✦ ALONG THE NAVAJO TRAIL
Republic, 1945

Composer(s) Elliott, Jack
Lyricist(s) Elliott, Jack
Choreographer(s) Ceballos, Larry

Producer(s) White, Eddy
Director(s) MacDonald, Frank
Screenwriter(s) Geraghty, Gerald
Source(s) (novel) MacDonald, William Colt

Cast Rogers, Roy; Trigger; Hayes, George "Gabby"; Evans, Dale; Rodriguez, Estelita; Fowley, Douglas; Paiva, Nestor; Flint, Sam; Bob Nolan and the Sons of the Pioneers

Song(s) Free As the Wind; It's the Gypsy in Me; Saskatoon; Savin' for a Rainy Day; Cool Water [2] (C/L: Nolan, Bob); Along the Navajo Trail [1] (C/L: Markes, Larry; Charles, Dick; DeLange, Eddie); How're Ya Doin' in the Heart Department (C/L: Newman, Charles; Altman, Arthur); Twenty-One Years Is a Mighty Long Time (C/L: Forster, Gordon)

Notes [1] Also in Columbia's THE BLAZING SUN and in Republic's DON'T FENCE ME IN. The song was originally titled "Prairie Parade" in 1942 as written by Markes and Charles. That song was featured in LAUGH YOUR BLUES AWAY. [2] Also in HANDS ACROSS THE BORDER and DING DONG WILLIAMS (RKO).

137 ✦ ALONG THE OREGON TRAIL
Republic, 1946

Composer(s) Willing, Foy
Lyricist(s) Willing, Foy

Producer(s) Tucker, Melville
Director(s) Springsteen, R.G.
Screenwriter(s) Snell, Earle; Cole, Royal K.

Cast Hale, Monte; Booth, Adrian; Moore, Clayton; Barcroft, Roy; Terhune, Max; Wright, Will; Crosby, Wade; Mason, LeRoy; Foy Willing and the Riders of the Purple Sage; Taylor, Forrest

Song(s) Along the Wagon Trail; Pretty Little Pink (C: Traditional); Oregon

138 ✦ ALONG THE RIO GRANDE
RKO, 1941

Musical Score Sawtell, Paul
Composer(s) Whitley, Ray; Rose, Fred
Lyricist(s) Whitley, Ray; Rose, Fred

Producer(s) Gilroy, Bert
Director(s) Killy, Edward
Screenwriter(s) Jones, Arthur V.; Grant, Morton

Cast Holt, Tim; Whitley, Ray; Rhodes, Betty Jane; Lynn, Emmett

Song(s) Old Monterey Moon; Along the Rio Grande; My Grandpap

139 ✦ THE ALPHABET MURDERS
Metro–Goldwyn–Mayer, 1966

Musical Score Goodwin, Ron

Producer(s) Bachmann, Lawrence P.
Director(s) Tashlin, Frank
Screenwriter(s) Pursall, David; Seddon, Jack
Source(s) *The A.B.C. Murders* (novel) Christie, Agatha

Cast Randall, Tony; Ekberg, Anita; Morley, Robert; Denham, Maurice; Rolfe, Guy; Allen, Sheila; Glover, Julian

Song(s) Amanda (C: Fahey, Brian; L: Newell, Norman)

140 ✦ ALVAREZ KELLY
Columbia, 1966

Musical Score Green, Johnny

Producer(s) Siegel, Sol C.
Director(s) Dmytryk, Edward
Screenwriter(s) Coen, Franklin

Cast Holden, William; Widmark, Richard; Rule, Janice; O'Neal, Patrick; Shaw, Victoria; Franz, Arthur; Carey Jr., Harry

Song(s) The Ballad of Alvarez Kelly (C: Green, Johnny; L: Mercer, Johnny); I Never Like to Kiss [1] (L: Coen, Franklin)

Notes [1] Music based on "The Farmer in the Dell."

141 ✦ ALWAYS A BRIDESMAID
Universal, 1943

Producer(s) Goldsmith, Ken
Director(s) Kenton, Erle C.
Screenwriter(s) Ronson, Mel

Cast Knowles, Patric; McDonald, Grace; Butterworth, Charles; Gilbert, Billy

Song(s) That's My Affair (C: Weiser, Irving; L: Zaret, Hy); As Long As I Have You (C/L: Hanbrich, Earl; Lewis, Al; Simon, Howard); Thanks for the Buggy Ride (C/L: Buffano, Jules); Ride On (C/L: Tolbert, "Skeets"); Yoo-Hoo [1] (C/L: Schoen, Vic; Wilfort, John; Jacobs, Ray)

Notes [1] Sheet music lists music by John Wilfahrt and lyrics by Roy Jordan.

142 ✦ ALWAYS GOODBYE
Fox, 1931

Director(s) MacKenna, Kenneth; Menzies, William Cameron
Screenwriter(s) McLaurin, Kate

Cast Landi, Elissa; Stone, Lewis; Cavanaugh, Paul; Garrick, John

Song(s) Always Goodbye (Toujours Adieu) (C: Hanley, James F.; L: Jerville, Jou)

143 ✦ ALWAYS IN MY HEART
Warner Brothers, 1942

Musical Score Roemheld, Heinz

Producer(s) MacEwen, Walter; Jacobs, William
Director(s) Graham, Jo

Screenwriter(s) Comandini, Adele
Source(s) *Fly Away Home* (play) Bennett, Dorothy; White, Irving

Cast Warren, Gloria; Huston, Walter; Francis, Kay; Minnevitch, Borrah; Hale, Patti; O'Connor, Una; Armida

Song(s) Always in My Heart (C: Lecuona, Ernesto; L: Gannon, Kim)

Notes Rossini's "Una Voce Poca Fa" was also used vocally.

144 ✦ ALWAYS LEAVE THEM LAUGHING
Warner Brothers, 1949

Composer(s) Cahn, Sammy
Lyricist(s) Cahn, Sammy

Producer(s) Wald, Jerry
Director(s) Del Ruth, Roy
Screenwriter(s) Rose, Jack; Shavelson, Melville
Source(s) "The Thief of Broadway" (story) Shulman, Max; Mealand, Richard

Cast Berle, Milton; Lahr, Bert; Roman, Ruth; Mayo, Virginia; Hale, Alan; Hayes, Grace; Cowan, Jerome; Gough, Lloyd; Showalter, Max

Song(s) Always Leave Them Laughing (C: Berle, Milton); This Is Not Goodbye; Give Me a Tam Tam Tambourine (C: Heindorf, Ray); Say Farewell (C: Heindorf, Ray); Clink Your Glasses; The Wonder of It All; You're Too Intense (C: Berle, Milton)

Notes There are also snatches of other popular songs.

145 ✦ AMATEUR DADDY
Fox, 1932

Director(s) Blystone, John
Screenwriter(s) Conselman, William
Source(s) *Scotch Valley* (novel) Cram, Mildred

Cast Baxter, Warner; Nixon, Marian; La Roy, Rita; Powers, Lucille; Pawley, William; Darro, Frankie

Song(s) Now I Lay Me Down to Sleep (C/L: Hanley, James F.)

146 ✦ AMAZING GRACE
United Artists, 1974

Musical Score Perkinson, Coleridge-Taylor
Composer(s) Perkinson, Coleridge-Taylor
Lyricist(s) Robinson, Matt

Producer(s) Robinson, Matt
Director(s) Lathan, Stan
Screenwriter(s) Robinson, Matt

Cast Mabley, Moms; McQueen, Butterfly; Fetchit, Stepin; Sweet, Dolph; Gunn, Moses; Cash, Rosalind; White, Slappy; Karen, James

Song(s) Amazing Grace (How Sweet She Be); Look Out, Baltimore!; Hey Big Dancin' (C: Robinson, Matt); Creola, Where You Goin' and What You Gonna Do to Baltimore When You Get There?; I'm So Glad (Waters Gonna Be the Mayor) (C: Robinson, Matt)

147 ◆ AMAZING GRACE AND CHUCK
Tri-Star, 1987

Musical Score Bernstein, Elmer

Producer(s) Field, David
Director(s) Newell, Mike
Screenwriter(s) Field, David

Cast Curtis, Jamie Lee; Peck, Gregory; Petersen, William L.; Zuehlke, Joshua; English, Alex; Richardson, Lee; Auerbach, Red

Song(s) Chuck's Lament (A Child's Dream) (C/L: Crosby, David; Stills, Stephen; Nash, Graham; Vitale, Joe)

Notes No cue sheet available.

148 ◆ THE AMAZING MRS. HOLLIDAY
Universal, 1943

Producer(s) Riskin, Everett
Director(s) Manning, Bruce
Screenwriter(s) Ryan, Frank; Jacoby, John

Cast Durbin, Deanna; O'Brien, Edmond; Fitzgerald, Barry; Treacher, Arthur; Davenport, Harry; Mitchell, Grant; Inescort, Frieda; Hale, Jonathan; Dale, Esther; Schilling, Gus

Song(s) Chinese Eventide (C/L: Chang, H.H.; Chang, Rosalynde); In Old Vienna [1] (C/L: Palmer, King)

Notes There is also a vocal of "The Old Refrain" by Alice Mattullath and Fritz Kreisler. [1] Sheet music only.

149 ◆ AMBITIOUS PEOPLE
Metro–Goldwyn–Mayer, 1951

Song(s) You Will Play the Star Part (C/L: Timberg, Herman)

Notes No other information available. There are also vocals of The "Prisoner's Song" by Guy Massey and "Ain't She Sweet" by Milton Ager and Jack Yellen.

150 ◆ AMERICAN ANTHEM
Columbia, 1986

Musical Score Silvestri, Alan

Producer(s) Schaffel, Robert; Chapin, Doug
Director(s) Magnoli, Albert
Screenwriter(s) Archerd, Evan; Benjamin, Jeff; Williams, Susan

Cast Gaylord, Mitch; Jones, Janet; Phillips, Michelle; Aprea, John

Song(s) Two Hearts (C/L: Parr, John); Sane Direction (C/L: Morriss, Andrew; Hutchence, Michael); Battle of the Dragon (C: Nicholson, Gary; Jarvis, John; L: Nicks, Stevie); Take It Easy (C/L: Taylor, Andy; Jones, Steve); Run to Her (C/L: Page, Richard; George, Steve; Mastellotto, Pat; Farris, Steve); Angel Eyes (C/L: Taylor, Andy; Jones, Steve); Wings to Fly (C: Moroder, Giorgio; L: Whitlock, Tom); Love and Lonliness (C/L: Garvey, Nick; Hann, Gordon); Wings of Love (C/L: Taylor, Andy; Jones, Steve)

Notes No cue sheet available.

151 ◆ AN AMERICAN DREAM
Warner Brothers, 1966

Musical Score Mandel, Johnny

Producer(s) Conrad, William
Director(s) Gist, Robert
Screenwriter(s) Rubin, Mann
Source(s) *An American Dream* (novel) Mailer, Norman

Cast Whitman, Stuart; Parker, Eleanor; Leigh, Janet; Sullivan, Barry; Nolan, Lloyd; Hamilton, Murray

Song(s) A Time for Love (C: Mandel, Johnny; L: Webster, Paul Francis)

Notes Released in Great Britain as SEE YOU IN HELL, DARLING.

152 ◆ AMERICAN DREAMER
Warner Brothers, 1984

Musical Score Furey, Lewis

Producer(s) Chapin, Doug
Director(s) Rosenthal, Rick
Screenwriter(s) Kouf, Jim; Greenwalt, David

Cast Williams, Jobeth; Conti, Tom; Giannini, Giancarlo; Browne, Coral; Staley, James; Fox, Huckleberry

Song(s) Dreamer (C/L: Furey, Lewis)

Notes No cue sheet available.

153 ◆ AN AMERICAN EAGLE
Mastodon, 1929

Cast Flinn, Brook; Flinn, Dylan; Brown, Jeffrey; Brown, Ronald

Song(s) The Pennsylvania Pastiche (C/L: Martin, Scott); The Senatorial Slide (C/L: Zavin, Jonathan); The Egalitarian Urge (Inst.) (C: Hopkins, Matthew)

Notes No other information available.

154 ✦ AMERICAN EMPIRE
United Artists, 1942

Producer(s) Dickson, Dick
Director(s) McGann, William
Screenwriter(s) Bren, J. Robert; Atwater, Gladys; Kohn, Ben Grauman

Cast Dix, Richard; Carrillo, Leo; Foster, Preston; Gifford, Frances; Williams, Guinn "Big Boy"; Barrat, Robert; LaRue, Jack; Edwards, Cliff; Martin, Chris-Pin

Song(s) Little Pal (C: Ruby, Herman; L: Pollack, Lew)

Notes No cue sheet available.

155 ✦ AMERICAN FLYERS
Warner Brothers, 1985

Musical Score Ritenour, Lee; Mathieson, Greg

Producer(s) Wigan, Gareth; Weinstein, Paula
Director(s) Badham, John
Screenwriter(s) Tesich, Steve

Cast Costner, Kevin; Grant, David; Chong, Rae Dawn; Paul, Alexandra; Rule, Janice; Bercovici, Luca; Townsend, Robert; Amos, John; Grey, Jennifer

Song(s) Brand New Day (C/L: Ritenour, Lee; Mathieson, Greg); American Flyers (C/L: Reede, Jon; Tanner, Marc)

Notes These songs are also used as background vocals, as are other previously recorded pop songs.

156 ✦ THE AMERICAN GAME
World Northal, 1979

Musical Score Kaufman, Jeffrey

Producer(s) Jones, Anthony
Director(s) Freund, Jay; Wolf, David
Screenwriter(s) Freund, Jay; Wolf, David M.

Song(s) The American Game (C/L: Kaufman, Jeffrey); Yesterday Is Gone (C/L: Kaufman, Jeffrey)

Notes A documentary. No cue sheet available.

157 ✦ AMERICAN GIGOLO
Paramount, 1980

Musical Score Moroder, Giorgio
Composer(s) Moroder, Giorgio

Producer(s) Fields, Freddie
Director(s) Schrader, Paul
Screenwriter(s) Schrader, Paul

Cast Gere, Richard; van Pallandt, Nina; Hutton, Lauren; Elizondo, Hector

Song(s) Call Me (L: Harry, Deborah); Love and Passion (L: Schrader, Paul); Something in Return (The Seduction) [1] (L: Lloyd, Michael); The Love I Saw In You Was Just a Mirage (C/L: Robinson, William

"Smokey"; Tarplin, M.); Take Off Your Uniform (C/L: Hiatt, John)

Notes These songs are only background vocals. [1] Does not appear in movie as a song.

158 ✦ AMERICAN HOT WAX
Paramount, 1978

Producer(s) Linson, Art
Director(s) Mutrux, Floyd
Screenwriter(s) Kaye, John

Cast Leno, Jay; Weaver, Carl Earl; McIntire, Tim; Berry, Chuck; Lewis, Jerry Lee; Hawkins, Screaming Jay

Notes There are no original songs in this film. Visual vocals lasting more than one minute include "The ABCs of Love" by Morris Levy; "Little Star" by Vito Picone and Arthur Venosa; "Speedo" by Esther Navarro; "Come Go With Me" by C.E. Quick; "That's Why" by Berry Gordy Jr. and Tyran Carlo; "Hello Mary Lou" by Gene Pitney and Cavet Mangiaracina; "Church Bells May Ring" by Morty Craft and The Willows; "I Wonder Why" by Richard Weeks and Melvin Anderson; "Hushabye" by Doc Pomus and Mort Shuman; "Mister Lee" by Heather Dixon, Helen Gathers, Emma Ruth Pought, Laura Webb and Jannie Pought; "Maybe" by R. Barrett; "Why Do Fools Fall in Love" by Frankie Lymon and Morris Levy; "That Is Rock and Roll" by Jerry Leiber and Mike Stoller; "Rock and Roll Is Here to Stay" by David White; "I Put a Spell on You" by Jay Hawkins; "Mister Blue" by DeWayne Blackwell; "Reelin' & Rockin'" by Chuck Berry; "Roll Over Beethoven" by Chuck Berry; and "Great Balls of Fire" by Jack Hammer and Otis Blackwell.

159 ✦ AN AMERICAN IN PARIS
Metro–Goldwyn–Mayer, 1951

Choreographer(s) Kelly, Gene

Producer(s) Freed, Arthur
Director(s) Minnelli, Vincente
Screenwriter(s) Lerner, Alan Jay

Cast Kelly, Gene; Caron, Leslie; Levant, Oscar; Foch, Nina; Guetary, George; Borden, Eugene; Neill, Noel

Notes There are no original songs in this film. Vocals, all written by George and Ira Gershwin, include: "Nice Work If You Can Get It"; "By Strauss"; "I Got Rhythm"; "Love Is Here to Stay"; "Someone to Watch Over Me"; "Tra-La-La"; "I'll Build a Stairway to Paradise" with lyrics by B.G. deSylva and Arthur Francis (Ira Gershwin); "I Don't Think I'll Fall in Love Today"; "'S Wonderful" and excerpts from "American in Paris" and "Concerto in F" by George Gershwin. Songs that were filmed but not used include "I've Got a Crush on You"; "But Not for Me" and "Liza." There was also to be a "Somebody Loves Me" ballet (lyrics by B.G. DeSylva) but it was not filmed.

160 ✦ THE AMERICANIZATION OF EMILY
Metro–Goldwyn–Mayer, 1965

Musical Score Mandel, Johnny

Producer(s) Ransohoff, Martin
Director(s) Hiller, Arthur
Screenwriter(s) Chayefsky, Paddy
Source(s) *The Americanization of Emily* (novel) Huie, William Bradford

Cast Andrews, Julie; Douglas, Melvyn; Coburn, James; Binns, Edward; Fraser, Liz; Wynn, Keenan; Windom, William; Garner, James

Song(s) Emily [1] (C: Mandel, Johnny; L: Mercer, Johnny)

Notes [1] Used instrumentally only.

161 ✦ AMERICAN NINJA 2: THE CONFRONTATION
Cannon, 1987

Musical Score Clinton, George S.

Producer(s) Golan, Menahem; Globus, Yoram
Director(s) Firstenberg, Sam
Screenwriter(s) Conway, Gary; Booth, James

Cast Dudikoff, Michael; James, Steve; Poindexter, Larry; Conway, Gary; Weston, Jeff

Song(s) Tell Me About Mary (C/L: Bishop, Michael); Move to the City (C/L: Stradlin, Izzy; Weber, Chris); Temptation (C/L: Bishop, Michael; Page, Scott)

Notes No cue sheet available.

162 ✦ THE AMERICANO
RKO, 1955

Musical Score Webb, Roy

Producer(s) Stillman, Robert
Director(s) Castle, William
Screenwriter(s) Trosper, Guy
Source(s) "Six Weeks South of Texas" [1] (magazine serial) White, Leslie T.

Cast Ford, Glenn; Lovejoy, Frank; Romero, Cesar; Thiess, Ursula; Lane, Abbe; Powers, Tom

Song(s) The Americano (C: Cugat, Xavier; L: Rosner, George)

Notes [1] The source is also sometimes known as TROUBLE IN PARADISE.

163 ✦ AN AMERICAN ROMANCE
Metro–Goldwyn–Mayer, 1944

Musical Score Gruenberg, Louis

Producer(s) Vidor, King
Director(s) Vidor, King
Screenwriter(s) Dalmas, Herbert; Ludwig, William

Cast Donlevy, Brian; Richards, Ann; Abel, Walter; McNally, Horace; Qualen, John

Song(s) Lord, Please Send Down Your Love (C: Gruenberg, Louis; L: Vidor, King)

164 ✦ AN AMERICAN TAIL
Universal, 1986

Musical Score Horner, James
Composer(s) Horner, James; Mann, Barry
Lyricist(s) Weil, Cynthia

Producer(s) Bluth, Don; Pomeroy, John; Goldman, Gary
Director(s) Bluth, Don
Screenwriter(s) Geiss, Tony; Freudberg, Judy
Voices Blore, Cathianne; DeLuise, Dom; Finnegan, John; Glasser, Phillip; Green, Amy; Kahn, Madeline; Musick, Pat; Persoff, Nehemiah; Plummer, Christopher

Song(s) Never Say Never; There Are No Cats in America; Give Me Your Tired, Your Poor [1] (C: Horner, James; L: Lazarus, Emma); Somewhere Out There; A Duo

Notes This is an animated feature. [1] Based on the poem by Emma Lazarus.

165 ✦ AMERICATHON
United Artists, 1979

Musical Score Scott, Tom

Producer(s) Roth, Joe
Director(s) Israel, Neal
Screenwriter(s) Proctor, Philip; Bergman, Peter
Source(s) *Gothamathon* (play) Proctor, Philip; Bergman, Peter

Cast Riegert, Peter; Korman, Harvey; Willard, Fred; Buzby, Zane; Morgan, Nancy; Ritter, John; Schaal, Richard; LaSorda, Tommy; Meat Loaf; Chief Dan George; Costello, Elvis; Hesseman, Howard; Carlin, George; Opatoshu, David

Song(s) My Life (C/L: Brown Jr., Earl); Gold (C/L: Pomeranz, David); Car Wars (C/L: Scott, Tom); Without Love (C/L: Lowe, Nick); Get a Move On (C/L: Money, Eddie; Collins, Paul; Chiate, Lowell); Don't You Ever Say No (C/L: Pomeranz, David; Cohen, Lisa Catherine); Open Up Your Heart (C/L: Money, Eddie)

Notes No cue sheet available.

166 ✦ THE AMOROUS ADVENTURES OF MOLL FLANDERS
Paramount, 1965

Musical Score Addison, John

Producer(s) Hellman, Marcel
Director(s) Young, Terence

Screenwriter(s) Cannan, Denis; Kibbee, Roland
Source(s) *Moll Flanders* (novel) Defoe, Daniel

Cast Novak, Kim; Sanders, George; Johnson, Richard; Lansbury, Angela; Palmer, Lilli; De Sica, Vittorio; Massey, Daniel; McKern, Leo; Parker, Cecil

Song(s) Black Velvet Band (C: Traditional; L: Long, Lionel); Lovely Is She [1] (C: Addison, John; L: Newell, Norman)

Notes [1] Written to the melody of the instrumental number "Moll's Tune." Lyric added for exploitation only.

167 ◆ AMUKIRIKI
Paramount, 1955

Producer(s) Smardan, Eddie
Director(s) Smardan, Eddie

Song(s) Amukiriki (The Lord Willing) (C: Livingston, Jerry; L: Russell, Bob)

Notes This is a travelogue.

168 ◆ AMY
Disney, 1981

Musical Score Brunner, Robert F.

Producer(s) Courtland, Jerome
Director(s) McEveety, Vincent
Screenwriter(s) Stone, Noreen

Cast Agutter, Jenny; Newman, Barry; Nolan, Kathleen; Robinson, Chris; Fant, Lou; O'Brien, Margaret; Fabray, Nanette; Rechenberg, Otto; Hollander, David; Moody, Wesley; Branton, Alban; Scribner, Ronnie

Song(s) So Many Ways (C: Brunner, Robert F.; L: Belland, Bruce)

169 ◆ ANASTASIA
Twentieth Century–Fox, 1956

Musical Score Newman, Alfred

Producer(s) Adler, Buddy
Director(s) Litvak, Anatole
Screenwriter(s) Laurents, Arthur
Source(s) *Anastasia* (play) Bolton, Guy

Cast Bergman, Ingrid; Brynner, Yul; Hayes, Helen; Tamiroff, Akim; Hunt, Martita; Aylmer, Felix

Song(s) Anastasia [1] (C: Newman, Alfred; L: Webster, Paul Francis)

Notes [1] Lyric added for exploitation only.

170 ◆ ANCHORS AWEIGH
Metro–Goldwyn–Mayer, 1945

Musical Score Stoll, George
Composer(s) Styne, Jule
Lyricist(s) Cahn, Sammy
Choreographer(s) Kelly, Gene; Donohue, Jack

Producer(s) Pasternak, Joe
Director(s) Sidney, George
Screenwriter(s) Lennart, Isobel

Cast Grayson, Kathryn; Sinatra, Frank; Kelly, Gene; Iturbi, Jose; Stockwell, Dean; Britton, Pamela; Ragland, Rags; Gilbert, Billy; Kennedy, Edgar; Sutton, Grady; Ames, Leon; McManus, Sharon

Song(s) We Hate to Leave; I Begged Her; What Makes the Sunset; My Heart Sings (C/L: Jamblan; Herpin; Rome, Harold); The Worry Song (C: Fain, Sammy; L: Freed, Ralph); The Charm of You; I Fall in Love Too Easily; Waltz Serenade (C: Tchaikowsky, Peter; Brent, Earl); If You Knew Susie [1] (C: Meyer, Joseph; L: DeSylva, B.G.; Cahn, Sammy)

Notes There are also vocals of "Anchors Aweigh" by Zimmerman; "Largo al Factotum" by Rossini; "Wiegenlied" and "Lullaby" by Brahms; "Mother" by Theodore Morse; "Cielito Lindo" by Fernandez; "Jalousie" by Jacob Gade and Vera Bloom; and "El Relajo" by Leyva. [1] Cahn wrote additional lyrics.

171 ◆ . . . AND JUSTICE FOR ALL
Columbia, 1979

Musical Score Grusin, Dave

Producer(s) Jewison, Norman; Palmer, Patrick
Director(s) Jewison, Norman
Screenwriter(s) Curtin, Valerie; Levinson, Barry

Cast Pacino, Al; Warden, Jack; Forsythe, John; Strasberg, Lee; Tambor, Jeffrey; Lahti, Christine; Levene, Sam; Christian, Robert; Nelson, Craig T.

Song(s) There's Something Funny Going On (C: Grusin, Dave; L: Bergman, Alan; Bergman, Marilyn)

Notes No cue sheet available.

172 ◆ AND NOW TOMORROW
Paramount, 1944

Musical Score Young, Victor

Producer(s) Kohlmar, Fred
Director(s) Pichel, Irving
Screenwriter(s) Chandler, Raymond; Partos, Frank
Source(s) *And Now Tomorrow* (novel) Field, Rachel

Cast Ladd, Alan; Sullivan, Barry; Young, Loretta; Hayward, Susan; Bondi, Beulah; Mack, Helen; Kellaway, Cecil; Mitchell, Grant; Hickman, Darryl

Song(s) And Now Tomorrow [1] (C: Young, Victor; L: Heyman, Edward)

Notes [1] Lyric written for exploitation only.

173 ◆ AND THE ANGELS SING
Paramount, 1944

Musical Score Young, Victor; Bradshaw, Charles W.
Composer(s) Van Heusen, James

Lyricist(s) Burke, Johnny
Choreographer(s) Dare, Danny

Producer(s) Leshin, E.D.
Director(s) Marshall, George
Screenwriter(s) Panama, Norman; Frank, Melvin

Cast MacMurray, Fred; Lamour, Dorothy; Hutton, Betty; Lynn, Diana

Song(s) Who's Kidding Who? [1] [3]; His Rocking Horse Ran Away; It Could Happen to You; My Heart's Wrapped Up in Gingham; When Stanislaus Got Married; Bluebirds in My Belfry; Knocking on Your Own Front Door; The First Hundred Years [2]; How Does Your Garden Grow?; Jingle Jangle Jingle [4] (C: Lilley, Joseph J.; L: Loesser, Frank); Shake Hands with Your Neighbor [1] [5] (C: Young, Victor; L: Loesser, Frank); And the Angels Sing [6] (C: Elman, Ziggy; L: Mercer, Johnny)

Notes There is also a vocal of the traditional song "A-Hunting We Will Go." The blackout sketches accompanying "How Does Your Garden Grow?" and "Knocking on Your Own Front Door" (Friendly Finance section) were by Lester Lee and Jerry Seelen. The production was first called FOUR ANGELS. [1] Unused. [2] Seelen and Lee wrote one verse for Dorothy Lamour to sing to Fred MacMurray and so were given credit for additional lyrics. [3] Seelen and Lee wrote some additional lyrics for this song, which was not used. [4] Also in JINGLE JANGLE JINGLE and THE FOREST RANGERS. [5] In UNTAMED. [6] Sheet music only; not in film.

174 ◆ ANDY
Universal, 1965

Musical Score Prince, Robert

Producer(s) Serafian, Richard C.
Director(s) Serafian, Richard C.
Screenwriter(s) Serafian, Richard C.

Cast Alden, Norman; Daykarhanova, Tamura; Scooler, Zvee; Vye, Murvyn; Wedgeworth, Ann; Bond, Sudie

Song(s) It Was Love (C/L: Prince, Robert)

175 ◆ ANDY HARDY COMES HOME
Metro–Goldwyn–Mayer, 1958

Musical Score Alexander, Van
Composer(s) Rooney, Mickey [1]; Spina, Harold
Lyricist(s) Rooney, Mickey [1]; Spina, Harold

Producer(s) Doff, Red
Director(s) Koch, Howard W.
Screenwriter(s) Hutshing, Edward Everett; Dowley, Robert Morris
Source(s) characters by Rouverol, Aurania

Cast Rooney, Mickey; Breslin, Patricia; Holden, Fay; Parker, Cecilia; Haden, Sara; Forman, Joey; Colonna, Jerry; Taylor, Vaughn; Rooney, Teddy; Weissmuller Jr., Johnny

Song(s) Lazy Summer Night; Unkw-in-it [2]; Octavians [3] (C: Ward, S.); U-Gotta-Soda [4]

Notes [1] Credited in cue sheet as by Spina alone. [2] Used instrumentally only. [3] Tune based on "America the Beautiful." [4] Used instrumentally only. Credited to Van Alexander on cue sheet.

176 ◆ ANDY HARDY MEETS DEBUTANTE
Metro–Goldwyn–Mayer, 1940

Musical Score Snell, Dave

Director(s) Seitz, George B.
Screenwriter(s) Whitmore, Annalee; Seller, Thomas
Source(s) characters by Rouverol, Aurania

Cast Rooney, Mickey; Parker, Cecilia; Stone, Lewis; Holden, Fay; Garland, Judy; Rutherford, Ann; Lewis, Diana

Song(s) I Woke Up This Morning (C/L: Edens, Roger)

Notes There are vocals of "Alone" by Nacio Herb Brown and Arthur Freed and "I'm Nobody's Baby" by Benny Davis, Milton Ager and Joseph Santley. Prerecorded but not used were "Buds Won't Bud" by Harold Arlen and E.Y. Harburg and "All I Do Is Dream of You" by Arthur Freed and Nacio Herb Brown.

177 ◆ ANDY HARDY'S PRIVATE SECRETARY
Metro–Goldwyn–Mayer, 1940

Director(s) Seitz, George B.
Screenwriter(s) Murfin, Jane; Ruskin, Jane
Source(s) characters by Rouverol, Aurania

Cast Rooney, Mickey; Stone, Lewis; Holden, Fay; Rutherford, Ann; Haden, Sara; Hunter, Ian; Grayson, Kathryn

Notes There are no original songs in this picture. Vocals include "Voci De Primavera" by Johann Stauss; "Ardon G'Incensi" from Donizetti's LUCIA DE LAMMERMOOR and "I've Got My Eyes on You" by Cole Porter (also appears in BROADWAY MELODY OF 1940).

178 ◆ ANGEL
Paramount, 1937

Producer(s) Lubitsch, Ernst
Director(s) Lubitsch, Ernst
Screenwriter(s) Raphaelson, Samson
Source(s) (play) Lengyel, Melchior

Cast Dietrich, Marlene; Marshall, Herbert; Douglas, Melvyn; Horton, Edward Everett; Crews, Laura Hope; Cossart, Ernest

Song(s) Angel [1] (C: Hollander, Frederick; L: Robin, Leo)

Notes [1] The song appears to have been played only instrumentally on the soundtrack.

179 ◆ ANGELA
Twentieth Century–Fox, 1955

Musical Score   Nascimbene, Mario

Producer(s)   Pallos, Steven
Director(s)   O'Keefe, Dennis
Screenwriter(s)   Rix, Jonathan; Anton, Edoardo

Cast   O'Keefe, Dennis; Lane, Mara; Foa, Arldo; Bentik, Galeazzo; Brazzi, Rossano

Song(s)   Angela [1] (C: Nascimbene, Mario; L: Pinchi); Angel Eyes [1] (C: Nascimbene, Mario; L: Lovelock, Bill; Grace, Wylie)

Notes   [1] Lyric added for exploitation only.

180 ◆ ANGEL AND THE BADMAN
Republic, 1946

Musical Score   Hageman, Richard

Producer(s)   Wayne, John
Director(s)   Grant, James Edward
Screenwriter(s)   Grant, James Edward
Source(s)   "Angel and the Outlaw" (story)

Cast   Wayne, John; Russell, Gail; Rich, Irene; Carey, Harry; Cabot, Bruce; Dixon, Lee; Grant, Stephen; Powers, Tom; Hurst, Paul; Howland, Olin; Barton, Joan

Song(s)   A Little Bit Different (C: Kent, Walter; L: Gannon, Kim)

181 ◆ ANGEL, ANGEL DOWN WE GO
American International, 1969

Musical Score   Karger, Fred
Composer(s)   Mann, Barry; Weil, Cynthia
Lyricist(s)   Mann, Barry; Weil, Cynthia
Choreographer(s)   Taylor, Wilda

Producer(s)   Katzman, Jerome F.
Director(s)   Thom, Robert
Screenwriter(s)   Thom, Robert

Cast   Jones, Jennifer; Christopher, Jordan; McDowall, Roddy; Near, Holly; Rawls, Lou

Notes   No cue sheet available.

182 ◆ AN ANGEL COMES TO BROOKLYN
Republic, 1945

Composer(s)   Green, Sanford
Lyricist(s)   Carroll, June

Producer(s)   Sillman, Leonard
Director(s)   Goodwins, Leslie
Screenwriter(s)   Carroll, June; Paley, Stanley

Cast   Dowd, Kaye; Kemper, Charles; Duke, Robert; Street, David; Perry, Barbara; d'Alvarez, Marguerite; Carroll, June; Beaton, Betzi; Scheerer, Bob

Song(s)   Big Wide Wonderful World (C/L: Rox, John); Heaven Scene; Draping Song; Ad Lib # 1 (C/L: Allen, Cliff; Haygood, Billie); Ad Lib # 2 (C/L: Allen, Cliff; Haygood, Billie); Biggest Gyp on the Nile (C/L: Harris, Laurence; Harris, Buddy); You Better Go Now (C/L: Reichner, Bickley; Graham, Robert); Way Back When

183 ◆ ANGELINA
Fox, 1935

Song(s)   Los Dos Galanes (Habanera) (C: Sanders, Troy; L: Poncela, E. Jardiel)

Notes   No other information available. This might be a Spanish language production.

184 ◆ ANGEL IN MY POCKET
Universal, 1969

Musical Score   Murray, Lyn

Producer(s)   Montagne, Edward J.
Director(s)   Rafkin, Alan
Screenwriter(s)   Fritzell, Jim; Greenbaum, Everett

Cast   Griffith, Andy; Meriwether, Lee; Van Dyke, Jerry; Medford, Kay; Buchanan, Edgar; Collins, Gary; Fennelly, Parker

Song(s)   Girls of All Nations (C/L: Keller, Jerry; Blume, Dave)

185 ◆ ANGEL'S HOLIDAY
Twentieth Century–Fox, 1937

Producer(s)   Stone, John
Director(s)   Tinling, James
Screenwriter(s)   Fenton, Frank; Root, Lynn

Cast   Withers, Jane; Kent, Robert; Davis, Joan; Blane, Sally; Huber, Harold; Chaney Jr., Lon

Song(s)   They Blew Themselves Out of Breath [1] (C: Howard, Harold; Telaak, Bill; L: Howard, Harold; Telaak, Bill; Clare, Sidney)

Notes   There are also vocals of "Who's That Knocking at My Heart" by Burton Lane and "Goodnight Sweetheart" by Ray Noble, Jimmy Campbell and Reg Connelly. [1] Lyric revised by Sidney Clare.

186 ◆ ANGELS WITH BROKEN WINGS
Republic, 1941

Composer(s)   Styne, Jule
Lyricist(s)   Cherkose, Eddie

Producer(s)   Cohen, Albert J.
Director(s)   Vorhaus, Bernard
Screenwriter(s)   Ropes, Bradford; Brown, George Carleton

Cast Barnes, Binnie; Roland, Gilbert; Lee, Mary; Gilbert, Billy; Frazee, Jane; Norris, Edward; Alexander, Katherine; Gorcey, Leo; Ranson, Lois; Lynn, Leni; Blackmer, Sidney; Kennedy, Tom

Song(s) Three Little Wishes; In Buenos Aires; Has to Be

187 ◆ ANGELS WITH DIRTY FACES
Warner Brothers, 1938

Musical Score Steiner, Max

Producer(s) Bischoff, Sam
Director(s) Curtiz, Michael
Screenwriter(s) Wexley, John; Duff, Warren

Cast Bogart, Humphrey; Sheridan, Ann; Bancroft, George; Halop, Billy; Jordan, Bobby; Gorcey, Leo; Punsley, Bernard; Dell, Gabriel; Hall, Huntz

Song(s) Angels with Dirty Faces (C: Spitalny, Maurice; L: Fisher, Fred)

Notes No cue sheet available.

188 ◆ ANIMAL CRACKERS
Paramount, 1930

Musical Score Gorney, Jay; Reese, Max
Composer(s) Ruby, Harry
Lyricist(s) Kalmar, Bert

Producer(s) Wanger, Walter
Director(s) Heerman, Victor
Screenwriter(s) Ryskind, Morrie; Collings, Pierre
Source(s) *Animal Crackers* (musical) Ruby, Harry; Kalmar, Bert; Ryskind, Morrie; Kaufman, George S.

Cast Marx, Groucho; Marx, Chico; Marx, Harpo; Marx, Zeppo; Dumont, Margaret; Roth, Lillian; Metcalf, Edward; Reece, Kathryn

Song(s) Butler's Song; Original Piano Ditty [1] (C: Marx, Chico); Why Am I So Romantic?; Hooray for Captain Spaulding [2]; Abie the Fisherman (No music)

Notes [1] This little tune later had lyrics by Sol Violinsky added for use in the movie MONKEY BUSINESS. It was then titled, "I'm Daffy Over You." It was published in 1950 as "Lucky Little Penny" with credit given to Marx, Violinsky and Benny Davis. [2] In Broadway musical.

189 ◆ ANIMAL HOUSE

See NATIONAL LAMPOON'S ANIMAL HOUSE.

190 ◆ ANNABELLE'S AFFAIRS
Fox, 1931

Director(s) Werker, Alfred
Screenwriter(s) Gordon, Leon

Source(s) *Good Gracious Annabelle* (play) Kummer, Clare

Cast McLaglen, Victor; MacDonald, Jeanette; Young, Roland; Hardy, Sam; Collier Sr., William; Warren, Ruth; Compton, Joyce; Blane, Sally; Prouty, Jed

Song(s) If Someone Should Kiss You Tonight (C/L: Hanley, James F.)

Notes There are also vocal renditions of "Kathleen Mavourneen" and "Prairie Flower."

191 ◆ ANNA CHRISTIE
Metro–Goldwyn–Mayer, 1929

Musical Score Axt, William

Director(s) Brown, Clarence
Screenwriter(s) Marion, Frances
Source(s) *Anna Christie* (play) O'Neill, Eugene

Cast Garbo, Greta; Bickford, Charles; Dressler, Marie; Marion, George F. [1]

Song(s) Original Irish Tune (C/L: Axt, William)

Notes This is the film that was advertised: Garbo Talks! [1] Repeating original stage performance.

192 ◆ ANNA KARENINA
Metro–Goldwyn–Mayer, 1935

Musical Score Stothart, Herbert
Choreographer(s) Wallmann, Margarete; Hale, Chester

Producer(s) Selznick, David O.
Director(s) Brown, Clarence
Screenwriter(s) Dane, Clemence; Viertel, Salka
Source(s) *Anna Karenina* (novel) Tolstoy, Leo

Cast Garbo, Greta; Bartholomew, Freddie; O'Sullivan, Maureen; Robson, May; Rathbone, Basil; Owen, Reginald; Denny, Reginald; Foster, Phoebe; March, Fredric

Song(s) Cafe Russe (C/L: Stothart, Herbert)

Notes There are also vocals from Tschaikowsky's EUGENE ONEGIN and something by Stothart titled "Troop Entrainment" which I don't believe has lyrics.

193 ◆ ANNA LUCASTA
United Artists, 1958

Musical Score Bernstein, Elmer

Producer(s) Harmon, Sidney
Director(s) Laven, Arnold
Screenwriter(s) Yordan, Philip

Cast Kitt, Eartha; Davis Jr., Sammy; O'Neal, Frederick; Scott, Henry; Ingram, Rex; Burke, Georgia

Song(s) That's Anna (C: Bernstein, Elmer; L: Cahn, Sammy)

194 ✦ ANNAPOLIS
Pathe, 1928

Producer(s) McGrew, F.
Director(s) Cabanne, Christy
Screenwriter(s) McGrew, F.; Krafft, John

Cast Brown, Johnny Mack; Allan, Hugh; Loff, Jeanette; Ryan, Maurice; Munson, Byron; Bakewell, William

Song(s) My Annapolis and You (C/L: Weinberg, Charles; Bibo, Irving)

Notes No cue sheet available.

195 ✦ ANNAPOLIS FAREWELL
Paramount, 1935

Producer(s) Lighton, Louis D.
Director(s) Hall, Alexander
Screenwriter(s) Van Every, Dale; Craven, Frank
Source(s) "Target" (story) Avery, Stephen

Cast Cromwell, Richard; Brown, Tom; Standing, Sir Guy

Song(s) Annapolis Farewell [1] (C: Kisco, Charley; L: Coslow, Sam)

Notes [1] This song is used in the film only as an instrumental.

196 ✦ ANN CARVER'S PROFESSION
Columbia, 1932

Composer(s) Rosoff, Charles
Lyricist(s) Rosoff, Charles

Director(s) Buzzell, Edward
Screenwriter(s) Riskin, Robert

Cast Wray, Fay; Raymond, Gene

Song(s) There's Life in Music [1] [2]; Why Can't We Love Forever [1] [2]

Notes "Maybe I Love You Too Much" by Irving Berlin; "Love in the Moonlight" by Lewis and Kisco and "Sweet Georgia Brown" by Ben Bernie, Maceo Pinkard and Bernie Casey are used vocally. [1] Used instrumentally only. [2] Also used instrumentally in THE CRIME OF HELEN STANLEY. Sung in WATERFRONT LADY (Mascot).

197 ✦ ANNE OF THE THOUSAND DAYS
Universal, 1969

Musical Score Delerue, Georges

Producer(s) Wallis, Hal B.
Director(s) Jarrott, Charles
Screenwriter(s) Boland, Bridget; Hale, John
Source(s) *Anne of the Thousand Days* (play) Anderson, Maxwell

Cast Bujold, Genevieve; Papas, Irene; Quayle, Anthony; Colicos, John; Hordern, Michael; Blake, Katherine; Squire, William; Quilley, Denis

Song(s) Farewell My Love [1](C: Delerue, Georges; L: Hale, John)

Notes [1] Titled "Farewell, Farewell" on the sheet music.

198 ✦ ANNIE
Columbia, 1982

Musical Score Burns, Ralph
Composer(s) Strouse, Charles
Lyricist(s) Charnin, Martin
Choreographer(s) Phillips, Arlene

Producer(s) Stark, Ray
Director(s) Huston, John
Screenwriter(s) Sobieski, Carol
Source(s) *Annie* (musical) Charnin, Martin; Strouse, Charles; Meehan, Thomas

Cast Finney, Albert; Burnett, Carol; Quinn, Aileen; Reinking, Ann; Peters, Bernadette; Curry, Tim; Holder, Geoffrey; Minami, Roger; Herrmann, Edward; De Banzie, Lois

Song(s) Maybe; Hard Knock Life; Sandy (Dumb Dog) [1] [2]; I Think I'm Gonna Like It Here; Little Girls; Let's Go to the Movies [1]; We Got Annie [1] [2]; Sign [1]; You're Never Fully Dressed Without a Smile; Tomorrow; Easy Street; I Don't Need Anything But You

Notes All selections except [1] from Broadway score. [2] Cut from Broadway musical.

199 ✦ ANNIE GET YOUR GUN
Metro–Goldwyn–Mayer, 1950

Musical Score Deutsch, Adolph
Composer(s) Berlin, Irving
Lyricist(s) Berlin, Irving
Choreographer(s) Alton, Robert

Producer(s) Freed, Arthur
Director(s) Sidney, George
Screenwriter(s) Sheldon, Sidney
Source(s) *Annie Get Your Gun* (musical) Berlin, Irving; Fields, Dorothy; Fields, Irving

Cast Hutton, Betty; Keel, Howard; Calhern, Louis; Naish, J. Carrol; Arnold, Edward; Wynn, Keenan; Venuta, Benay; Sundberg, Clinton

Song(s) Colonel Buffalo Bill; Doin' What Comes Natur'lly; You Can't Get a Man with a Gun; There's No Business Like Show Business [2]; They Say It's Wonderful; My Defenses Are Down; I'm an Indian Too; The Girl That I Marry; I've Got the Sun in the Morning; Anything You Can Do; Let's Go West Again [1]

Notes Judy Garland prerecorded all of her vocals and filmed two scenes under Busby Berkeley's direction, but was replaced by Hutton. Charles Walters took over from Berkeley but he too was replaced. Frank Morgan was also featured in early takes but his death led to reshooting of his scenes with Louis Calhern. [1] Not used though recorded by Hutton. Only song from score not written for original Broadway production. [2] Also in THERE'S NO BUSINESS LIKE SHOW BUSINESS (20th).

200 ◆ ANOTHER MAN, ANOTHER CHANCE
United Artists, 1977

Musical Score Lai, Francis

Producer(s) Mnouchkine, Alexandre; Danciger, Georges
Director(s) Lelouch, Claude
Screenwriter(s) Lelouch, Claude

Cast Caan, James; Bujold, Genevieve; Huster, Francis; Warren, Jennifer; Tyrrell, Susan

Song(s) La Complainte du Nouveau Monde (C: Lai, Francis; L: Barouh, Pierre)

201 ◆ ANOTHER TIME, ANOTHER PLACE
Paramount, 1958

Producer(s) Kaufman, Joseph
Director(s) Allen, Lewis
Screenwriter(s) Manns, Stanley
Source(s) *Another Time, Another Place* (novel) Coffee, Lenore

Cast Turner, Lana; Connery, Sean; Johns, Glynis; Sullivan, Barry; Stephens, Martin; Hare, Doris; Fraser, Bill

Song(s) Another Time, Another Place [1] (C/L: Livingston, Jay; Evans, Ray)

Notes [1] Instrumental use only in picture.

202 ◆ ANTHONY ADVERSE
Warner Brothers, 1936

Musical Score Korngold, Erich Wolfgang

Director(s) LeRoy, Mervyn
Screenwriter(s) Gibney, Sheridan
Source(s) *Anthony Adverse* (novel) Allen, Hervey

Cast March, Fredric; de Havilland, Olivia [1]; Gwenn, Edmund; Rains, Claude; Louise, Anita; Hayward, Louis; Woods, Donald; Sondergaard, Gale; Beckett, Scotty; Alberni, Luis

Song(s) I'll Wait for You My Love (C: Korngold, Erich Wolfgang); Chant of the Natives (C: Korngold, Erich Wolfgang)

Notes [1] Dubbed by Diana Gaylen.

203 ◆ ANYBODY'S WOMAN
Paramount, 1930

Director(s) Arzner, Dorothy
Screenwriter(s) Akins, Zoe; Anderson, Doris
Source(s) The Better Wife Morris, Gouverneur

Cast Chatterton, Ruth; Brook, Clive; Lukas, Paul; Patricola, Tom

Song(s) Got a Man on My Mind (Worryin' Away) [2] (C: Rainger, Ralph; L: Dietz, Howard [1])

Notes [1] Dietz wrote the song under the pseudonym Dick Howard. [2] Also in JUNE MOON.

204 ◆ ANYONE CAN PLAY
Paramount, 1968

Musical Score Trovajoli, Armando

Producer(s) Lucari, Gianni Hecht
Director(s) Zampa, Luigi
Screenwriter(s) Zampa, Luigi

Cast Andress, Ursula; Lisi, Virna; Cassel, Jean-Pierre; Auger, Claudine; Wolff, Frank; Buzzanca, Lando; Adorf, Mario; Mell, Marisa

Song(s) Anyone Can Play (C: Trovajoli, Armando; L: Nohra, Audrey)

205 ◆ ANYTHING CAN HAPPEN
Paramount, 1952

Musical Score Young, Victor
Composer(s) Young, Victor
Lyricist(s) Livingston, Jay; Evans, Ray

Producer(s) Perlberg, William
Director(s) Seaton, George
Screenwriter(s) Seaton, George; Oppenheimer, George
Source(s) *Anything Can Happen* (book) Papashvily, George; Papashvily, Helen

Cast Ferrer, Jose; Hunter, Kim; Kasznar, Kurt; Leontovich, Eugenie

Song(s) Love Laughs at Kings [1]; Turkish Folk Song

Notes [1] Georgian lyrics by Wladimir Babishwili.

206 ◆ ANYTHING GOES (1936)
Paramount, 1936

Composer(s) Porter, Cole
Lyricist(s) Porter, Cole
Choreographer(s) Prinz, LeRoy

Producer(s) Glazer, Benjamin
Director(s) Milestone, Lewis
Screenwriter(s) De Leon, Walter; Salkow, Sidney; Moffitt, John C.; Martin, Francis
Source(s) *Anything Goes* (musical) Porter, Cole; Wodehouse, P.G.; Crouse, Russel; Bolton, Guy; Lindsay, Howard

Cast Crosby, Bing; Merman, Ethel; Ruggles, Charles; Lupino, Ida

Song(s) Anything Goes [1] [3]; I Get a Kick Out of You [1] [3]; You're the Top [1] [3]; There'll Always Be a Lady Fair [1]; Sailor Beware [6] (C: Whiting, Richard A.; L: Robin, Leo); Moonburn (C: Carmichael, Hoagy; L: Heyman, Edward); My Heart and I [4] (C: Hollander, Frederick; L: Robin, Leo); Shanghai De Ho (C: Hollander, Frederick; Whiting, Richard A.; L: Robin, Leo); I Can't Escape From You [2] [6] [7] (C: Whiting, Richard A.; L: Robin, Leo); Hopelessly in Love [2] [6] (C: Hollander, Frederick; L: Robin, Leo); Lotus Lou [2] (C: Hollander, Frederick; L: Robin, Leo); Be Like the Bluebird [1] [2] [5]

Notes Released for television as TOPS IS THE LIMIT. [1] From original production. [2] Not used. [3] Revised lyrics by Brian Hooker. [4] First titled "Am I Awake." Not used in ROSE OF THE RANCHO. [5] Recorded. [6] Written for film SAILOR BEWARE. [7] In RHYTHM ON THE RANGE.

207 ✦ ANYTHING GOES (1956)
Paramount, 1956

Composer(s) Porter, Cole
Lyricist(s) Porter, Cole
Choreographer(s) Castle, Nick; Petit, Roland; Flatt, Ernest

Producer(s) Dolan, Robert Emmett
Director(s) Lewis, Robert
Screenwriter(s) Sheldon, Sidney
Source(s) *Anything Goes* (musical) Porter, Cole; Lindsay, Howard; Crouse, Russel; Wodehouse, P.G.; Bolton, Guy

Cast Crosby, Bing; O'Connor, Donald; Jeanmaire, Zizi; Gaynor, Mitzi; Harris, Phil; Kasznar, Kurt; Erdman, Richard; Flatt, Ernest; Miller, Buzz; Dalio, Marcel; Kulp, Nancy; Rhodes, Betty Jane; Pepper, Jack

Song(s) Ya Gotta Give the People Hoke (C: Van Heusen, James; L: Cahn, Sammy); Anything Goes [1] [4]; I Get a Kick Out of You [1] [4]; You're the Top [1] [4]; It's Delovely [2]; All Through the Night; You Can Bounce Right Back (C: Van Heusen, James; L: Cahn, Sammy); A Second Hand Turban and a Crystal Ball (C: Van Heusen, James; L: Cahn, Sammy); Blow, Gabriel, Blow [1]; Acey Deucey [3] (C: Van Heusen, James; L: Cahn, Sammy)

Notes [1] From original show. [2] From RED, HOT AND BLUE. [3] Not used. [4] Paramount wanted Porter to update his lyrics but Porter could not because of other commitments. Porter himself suggested Ted Fetter. These had revised lyrics by Ted Fetter. [5] Petit staged the "Jeanmaire Ballet" and "I Get a Kick Out of You." Flatt staged the "Anything Goes" dance number.

208 ✦ ANY WEDNESDAY
Warner Brothers, 1966

Musical Score Duning, George

Producer(s) Epstein, Julius J.
Director(s) Miller, Robert Ellis
Screenwriter(s) Epstein, Julius J.
Source(s) *Any Wednesday* (play) Resnik, Muriel

Cast Fonda, Jane; Robards Jr., Jason; Murphy, Rosemary; Jones, Dean

Song(s) Any Wednesday (C: Duning, George; L: Bergman, Marilyn; Bergman, Alan)

Notes Released in Great Britain as BACHELOR GIRL APARTMENT.

209 ✦ ANY WHICH WAY YOU CAN
Warner Brothers, 1980

Musical Score Dorff, Stephen H.; Garrett, Snuff

Producer(s) Manes, Fritz
Director(s) Van Horn, Buddy
Screenwriter(s) Sherman, Stanford

Cast Eastwood, Clint; Locke, Sondra; Lewis, Geoffrey; Smith, William; Guardino, Harry; Gordon, Ruth; Cavanaugh, Michael; Corbin, Barry

Song(s) Beers to You (C/L: Dorff, Stephen H.; Garrett, Snuff; Durrill, John; Pinkard, Sandy); One Too Many Women in Your Life (C/L: Durrill, John; Everly, Phil); Too Loose (C/L: Brown, Milton L.; Dorff, Stephen H.; Garrett, Snuff); You're the Reason God Made Oklahoma (C/L: Collins, Larry; Pinkard, Sandy); Whiskey Heaven (C/L: Crofford, Cliff; Durrill, John; Garrett, Snuff); The Orangutan Hall of Fame (C/L: Crofford, Cliff; Garrett, Snuff); The Good Guys and the Bad Guys (C/L: Garrett, Snuff; Durrill, John); Any Way You Want Me (C/L: Ofman, Lee); Jelly Roll Song (C/L: Gordon, Ruth); Cow Patti (C/L: Stafford, Jim); Any Which Way You Can (C/L: Brown, Milton; Dorff, Stephen H.; Garrett, Snuff); Acapulco [1] (C/L: Collins, Larry; Heath, Mary)

Notes [1] Sheet music only.

210 ✦ APACHE COUNTRY
Columbia, 1952

Producer(s) Schaefer, Armand
Director(s) Archainbaud, George
Screenwriter(s) Hall, Norman S.

Cast Autry, Gene; Buttram, Pat; Cotton, Carolina; Lauter, Harry; Bushman, Francis X.

Song(s) The Covered Wagon Rolled Right Along [1] [2] (C/L: Wood, Britt; Heath, Hy); I Love to Yodel [1] [3] (C/L: Cotton, Carolina); Cold, Cold Heart [1] (C/L: Williams, Hank); Crime Will Never Pay [1] (C/L: Pepper, Jack; Robison, Willard)

Notes [1] No original songs in this picture. [2] Also in SADDLE PALS (Republic) with Ernest Gold also receiving credit. [3] Also in SMOKEY RIVER SERENADE.

211 ◆ APACHE ROSE
Republic, 1946

Composer(s) Elliott, Jack
Lyricist(s) Elliott, Jack

Producer(s) White, Edward J.
Director(s) Witney, William
Screenwriter(s) Geraghty, Gerald

Cast Rogers, Roy; Trigger; Evans, Dale; Howland, Olin; Meeker, George; Laurenz, John; Vincent, Russ; Urecal, Minerva; Mason, LeRoy; Bob Nolan and the Sons of the Pioneers; Terry, Tex

Song(s) Ride Vaqueros; Jose (C/L: Spencer, Tim; Spencer, Glenn); At the Wishing Well; There's Nothing Like Coffee in the Mornin'; Apache Rose

212 ◆ APPLAUSE
Paramount, 1929

Producer(s) Bell, Monta
Director(s) Mamoulian, Rouben
Screenwriter(s) Fort, Garrett
Source(s) (novel) Brown, Beth

Cast Morgan, Helen; Mellish Jr., Fuller; Wadsworth, Henry; Peers, Joan; Cameron, Jack; Cummings, Dorothy

Song(s) What Wouldn't I Do for that Man [1] (C: Gorney, Jay; L: Harburg, E.Y.); Give Your Little Baby Lots of Lovin' (C: Burke, Joe; L: Morse, Dolly [2]); Doin' the New Raccoon [3] (C: Burke, Joe; L: Morse, Dolly [2])

Notes There are also vocals of "Yaka Hula Hicka Dula" by Pete Wendling, E. Ray Goetz and Joe Young; "I've Got a Feelin' I'm Fallin'" by Thomas "Fats" Waller, Harry Link and Billy Rose; "Pretty Baby" by Egbert Van Alstyne, Tony Jackson and Gus Kahn (also in THE EDDIE CANTOR STORY and I'LL SEE YOU IN MY DREAMS); "Turkey Trot" by Robin Hood Bowers and Edgar Smith; "Waiting for the Robert E. Lee" by Lewis F. Muir and L. Wolfe Gilbert; "Smiles" by J. Will Callahan and Lee Roberts; "Sweetheart of All My Dreams" by Bert Lowe, Art Fitch and Kay Fitch and "That's My Weakness Now" by Bud Green and Sam Stept. [1] Also in GLORIFYING THE AMERICAN GIRL. [2] A pseudonym for Theodora Morse. Others were D.A. Estrom and Dorothy Terriss. [3] Not on cue sheets.

213 ◆ THE APPLE
Cannon, 1980

Musical Score Recht, Coby
Composer(s) Recht, Coby
Lyricist(s) Recht, Iris; Clinton, George S.

Producer(s) Golan, Menahem; Globus, Yoram
Director(s) Golan, Menahem
Screenwriter(s) Golan, Menahem

Cast Stewart, Catherine Mary; Gilmour, George; Kennedy, Grace; Love, Allan; Ackland, Joss; Shell, Ray; Margolyes, Miriam

Song(s) Bim; Universal Melody; Coming; I Found Me; The Apple; Cry for Me; Speed; Creation; Where Has Love Gone; Showbizness; Made for Me; How to Be a Master; Child of Love

Notes No cue sheet available.

214 ◆ THE APPLE DUMPLING GANG
Disney, 1975

Musical Score Baker, Buddy

Producer(s) Anderson, Bill
Director(s) Tokar, Norman
Screenwriter(s) Tait, Don
Source(s) (book) Bickham, Jack M.

Cast Bixby, Bill; Clark, Susan; Knotts, Don; Conway, Tim; Wayne, David; Pickens, Slim; Morgan, Harry; McGiver, John; Knight, Don; Adrian, Iris

Song(s) The Apple Dumpling Gang (C/L: Tatum, Shane)

215 ◆ THE APPOINTMENT
Metro–Goldwyn–Mayer, 1969

Musical Score Phillips, Stu

Producer(s) Poll, Martin
Director(s) Lumet, Sidney
Screenwriter(s) Leonviola, Antonio

Cast Sharif, Omar; Aimee, Anouk; Perego, Didi; Tozzi, Fausto; Proietti, Luigi; Barbara, Paolo; Lenya, Lotte

Song(s) The Empty Man (C: Phillips, Stu; Stone, Bob)

Notes There are two cue sheets for this picture. The other has a score by John Barry and no vocals. The script credits the screenplay to Leonviola. Some other sources credit James Salter.

216 ◆ APPOINTMENT IN HONDURAS
RKO, 1953

Musical Score Forbes, Louis

Producer(s) Bogeaus, Benedict
Director(s) Tourneur, Jacques
Screenwriter(s) De Wolf, Karen

Cast Ford, Glenn; Sheridan, Ann; Scott, Zachary

Song(s) Appointment in Honduras [1] (C/L: Forbes, Louis)

Notes [1] Used instrumentally only.

217 ◆ THE APPRENTICESHIP OF DUDDY KRAVITZ
Paramount, 1974

Composer(s) Myers, Stanley
Lyricist(s) Myers, Stanley

Producer(s) Kemeny, John
Director(s) Kotcheff, Ted
Screenwriter(s) Chetwynd, Lionel
Source(s) *The Apprenticeship of Duddy Kravitz* (novel) Richler, Mordecai

Cast Dreyfuss, Richard; Warden, Jack; Wiseman, Joseph

Song(s) Wonder Boy; Bar Mitzvah Is Over

218 ◆ THE APRIL FOOLS
National General, 1969

Musical Score Hamlisch, Marvin

Producer(s) Carroll, Gordon
Director(s) Rosenberg, Stuart
Screenwriter(s) Dresner, Hal

Cast Lemmon, Jack; Deneuve, Catherine; Lawford, Peter; Weston, Jack; Loy, Myrna; Boyer, Charles; Korman, Harvey; Kellerman, Sally; Dillon, Melinda; Mars, Kenneth; Doyle, David

Song(s) The April Fools (C: Bacharach, Burt; L: David, Hal); Sugar Kite (C: Hamlisch, Marvin; L: Hirschhorn, Joel); Wake Up (C: Hamlisch, Marvin; Hirschhorn, Joel)

Notes No cue sheet available.

219 ◆ APRIL FOOL'S DAY
Paramount, 1986

Musical Score Bernstein, Charles

Producer(s) Mancuso Jr., Frank
Director(s) Walton, Fred
Screenwriter(s) Bach, Danilo

Cast Baker, Jay; Barlow, Pat; Berry, Lloyd; Foreman, Deborah; Goodrich, Deborah; Heaton, Tom; O'Neal, Griffin

Song(s) Too Bad You're Crazy (C/L: Bernstein, Charles)

Notes No cue sheet available.

220 ◆ APRIL IN PARIS
Warner Brothers, 1952

Musical Score Heindorf, Ray; Jackson, Howard
Composer(s) Duke, Vernon
Lyricist(s) Cahn, Sammy
Choreographer(s) Prinz, LeRoy

Producer(s) Jacobs, William
Director(s) Butler, David
Screenwriter(s) Rose, Jack; Shavelson, Melville

Source(s) "Girl from Paris" (story) Rose, Jack; Shavelson, Melville

Cast Day, Doris; Bolger, Ray; Dauphin, Claude; Miller, Eve; Givot, George; Harvey, Paul; Farjeon, Herbert

Song(s) April in Paris [1] (L: Harburg, E.Y.); It Must Be Good; Life Is Such a Pleasure; Give Me Your Lips; I'm Gonna Ring the Bell Tonight; I Know a Place [2]; That's What Makes Paris Paree; I Ask You

Notes [1] Not written for this production. Originally in Broadway revue WALK A LITTLE FASTER. [2] Sometimes listed in sources as "The Place You Hold in My Heart."

221 ◆ APRIL LOVE
Twentieth Century–Fox, 1957

Musical Score Newman, Alfred
Composer(s) Fain, Sammy
Lyricist(s) Webster, Paul Francis
Choreographer(s) Foster, Bill

Producer(s) Weisbart, David
Director(s) Levin, Henry
Screenwriter(s) Miller, Winston
Source(s) *The Phantom Filly* (novel) Chamberlain, George Agnew

Cast Boone, Pat; Jones, Shirley; Michaels, Dolores [3]; O'Connell, Arthur; Crowley, Matt; Nolan, Jeanette; Jackson, Brad [2]

Song(s) April Love; Clover in the Meadow; Give Me a Gentle Girl; The Bentonville Fair; Do It Yourself; Automobiles [1]; High Hopes and Empty Pockets (The Gambler's Lament) [1]

Notes Originally titled HOME IN INDIANA and YOUNG IN LOVE. [1] Not used. [2] Dubbed by Ray Kellogg (who, by the way, is the husband of Eileen Wilson). [3] Dubbed by Eileen Wilson.

222 ◆ APRIL SHOWERS
Warner Brothers, 1948

Producer(s) Jacobs, William
Director(s) Kern, James V.
Screenwriter(s) Milne, Peter
Source(s) "Barbary Host" (story) Laurie Jr., Joe

Cast Carson, Jack; Sothern, Ann; Ellis, Robert; Alda, Robert; Sakall, S.Z.; Rober, Richard

Song(s) Mr. Lovejoy and Mr. Gay (C: Heindorf, Ray; L: Scholl, Jack); The World's Most Beautiful Girl (C: Gannon, Kim; L: Fetter, Ted); Little Trouper (C: Gannon, Kim; L: Kent, Walter)

Notes Vocals also include "Moonlight Bay" by Edward Madden and Percy Wenrich; "April Showers" by Louis Silvers and B.G. DeSylva; "Are You From Dixie" by

George L. Cobb and Jack Yellen; "Put on Your Old Grey Bonnet" by Stanley Murphy and Percy Wenrich; "While Strolling Through the Park One Day" by Ed Haley; "Every Little Movement" by Karl Hoschna and Otto Harbach; "Pretty Baby" by Egbert van Alstyne and Otto Harbach; "Carolina in the Morning" by Walter Donaldson and Gus Kahn and "Mary You're a Little Bit Old-Fashioned" by Henry Marshall and Marion Sunshine.

223 ✦ ARABESQUE
Universal, 1966

Musical Score   Mancini, Henry

Producer(s)   Donen, Stanley
Director(s)   Donen, Stanley
Screenwriter(s)   Mitchell, Julian; Price, Stanley; Marton, Pierre
Source(s)   *The Cipher* (novel) Cottler, Gordon

Cast   Peck, Gregory; Loren, Sophia; Badel, Alan; Moore, Kieron; Merivale, John; Lamont, Duncan; Coulouris, George

Song(s)   Candy (C/L: David, Mack; Whitney, Joan; Kramer, Alex); We've Loved Before [1] (C: Mancini, Henry; L: Livingston, Jay; Evans, Ray)

Notes   [1] Written for exploitation only.

224 ✦ ARE YOU LISTENING?
Metro–Goldwyn–Mayer, 1932

Composer(s)   Axt, William; Snell, Dave
Lyricist(s)   Snell, Dave; Axt, William

Director(s)   Beaumont, Harry
Screenwriter(s)   Taylor, Dwight
Source(s)   (novel) McEvoy, J.P.

Cast   Haines, William; Evans, Madge; Ford, Wallace; Marsh, Joan; Page, Anita; Hamilton, Neil; Hersholt, Jean; Miljan, John; Griffies, Ethel; Morley, Karen

Song(s)   Skating in the Dark; I'm Dreaming of My Indian Sweetheart

Notes   There are also vocals of "Oh, Little Town of Bethlehem" and Romberg and Hammerstein's "Lover Come Back to Me."

225 ✦ ARE YOU THERE
Fox, 1931

Composer(s)   Hamilton, Morris
Lyricist(s)   Henry, Grace

Director(s)   MacFadden, Hamilton
Screenwriter(s)   Thompson, Harlan

Cast   Lillie, Beatrice; Garrick, John; Baclanova, Olga; Sand, Jillian; Hamilton, Lloyd; Von Seyffertitz, Gustav; Grossmith, George

Song(s)   Lady Detectives; Queen of the Hunt Am I; It Must Be the Iron in the Spinach; Bagdad Daddies; Believe in Me [1] (C: Hanley, James F.; L: McCarthy, Joseph)

Notes   [1] Sheet music only.

226 ✦ ARE YOU WITH IT?
Universal, 1948

Musical Score   Scharf, Walter
Composer(s)   Miller, Sidney; James, Inez
Lyricist(s)   Miller, Sidney; James, Inez
Choreographer(s)   Da Pron, Louis

Producer(s)   Arthur, Robert
Director(s)   Hively, Jack
Screenwriter(s)   Brodney, Oscar
Source(s)   *Are You With It?* (musical) Perrin, Sam; Balzer, George

Cast   O'Connor, Donald; San Juan, Olga; Parker, Lew [2]; Stewart, Martha; O'Hanlon, George; Catlett, Walter; Sherman, Ransom; Da Pron, Louis; Gibson, Julie

Song(s)   Are You With It?; Down at Baba's Alley; What Do I Have to Do To Make You Love Me?; Daddy, Surprise Me! [3]; I'm Looking for a Prince of a Fella; (It Only Takes) a Little Imagination; I Gotta Give My Feet a Break [1]

Notes   [1] Instrumental use only. [2] From Broadway musical. [3] Also in HORIZONS WEST.

227 ✦ ARGENTINE NIGHTS
Universal, 1940

Composer(s)   Borne, Hal
Lyricist(s)   Kuller, Sid; Golden, Ray

Producer(s)   Goldsmith, Ken
Director(s)   Rogell, Albert S.
Screenwriter(s)   Horman, Arthur T.; Golden, Ray; Kuller, Sid

Cast   The Andrews Sisters; The Ritz Brothers; Moore, Constance; Reeves, George; Moran, Peggy

Song(s)   Brooklynonga; Rhumboogie (C: Prince, Hughie; L: Raye, Don); The Spirit of 77B; Hit the Road (C/L: Shoen, Vic; Raye, Don; Prince, Hughie); Once Upon a Dream (C: Chaplin, Saul; L: Cahn, Sammy); Amigo, We Go Riding Tonight (C: Chaplin, Saul; L: Cahn, Sammy); The Dowry Song (C: Chaplin, Saul; L: Cahn, Sammy)

228 ✦ ARISE, MY LOVE
Paramount, 1940

Producer(s)   Hornblow Jr., Arthur
Director(s)   Leisen, Mitchell
Screenwriter(s)   Brackett, Charles; Wilder, Billy

Cast   Colbert, Claudette; Milland, Ray; Abel, Walter; O'Keefe, Dennis

Song(s)   Arise My Love [1] (C: Hollander, Frederick; L: Washington, Ned)

Notes   [1] Apparently the song is used only for underscoring.

229 ✦ THE ARISTO-CAT
Warner Brothers, 1943

Director(s)   Jones, Chuck
Screenwriter(s)   Pierce, Ted

Cast   Hubie and Bertie

Song(s)   In an Eighteenth Century Drawing Room (C/L: Scott, Raymond)

Notes   A Merrie Melodie animated cartoon.

230 ✦ THE ARISTOCATS
Disney, 1970

Musical Score   Bruns, George
Composer(s)   Sherman, Richard M.; Sherman, Robert B.
Lyricist(s)   Sherman, Richard M.; Sherman, Robert B.

Producer(s)   Reitherman, Wolfgang; Hibler, Winston
Director(s)   Reitherman, Wolfgang
Screenwriter(s)   Clemmons, Larry; Gerry, Vance; Thomas, Franklin; Svendsen, Julius; Anderson, Ken; Cleworth, Eric; Wright, Ralph
Voices   Harris, Phil; Gabor, Eva; Holloway, Sterling; Crothers, Benjamin "Scatman"; Winchell, Paul; Hudson, Lord Tim; Scotti, Vito; Ravenscroft, Thurl; Kulp, Nancy; Buttram, Pat; Lindsey, George; Evans, Monica; Shelley, Carole; Lane, Charles; Baddeley, Hermione

Directing Animator(s)   Kahl, Milt; Thomas, Franklin; Johnston, Ollie; Lounsbery, John

Song(s)   Thomas O'Malley Cat (C/L: Gilkyson, Terry); Ev'rybody Wants to Be a Cat (C: Rinker, Al; L: Huddleston, Floyd); The Aristocats; Scales and Arpeggios; She Never Felt Alone (Pourquios? And Why); Court Me Slowly [1]; How Much You Mean to Me [1]; Jazz-Razz-Ma-Tazz [1] (C/L: Gilkyson, Terry); Le Jazz Hot [1]; My Way's the Highway [1]; Get In, Get Out of the Rain [1]

Notes   [1] Not used.

231 ✦ THE ARIZONA COWBOY
Republic, 1949

Composer(s)   Allen, Rex
Lyricist(s)   Allen, Rex

Producer(s)   Adreon, Frank
Director(s)   Springsteen, R.G.
Screenwriter(s)   Ropes, Bradford

Cast   Allen, Rex; Loring, Teala; Jones, Gordon; Urecal, Minerva; Cardwell, James; Barcroft, Roy; Andrews, Stanley; Cheshire, Harry V.; Martin, Chris-Pin

Song(s)   Arizona Waltz; Toolie Rollum [1]; Old Chisholm Trail (C: Traditional)

Notes   [1] Also in RODEO KING AND THE SENORITA; SHADOWS OF TOMBSTONE, UTAH WAGON TRAIN and SILVER CITY BONANZA.

232 ✦ ARIZONA CYCLONE
Universal, 1942

Composer(s)   Rosen, Milton
Lyricist(s)   Carter, Everett

Producer(s)   Cowan, Will
Director(s)   Lewis, Joseph H.
Screenwriter(s)   Lowe, Sherman

Cast   Brown, Johnny Mack; Knight, Fuzzy; O'Day, Nell; Adams, Kathryn; Rawlinson, Herbert; Strange, Glenn

Song(s)   On the Trail of Tomorrow [3]; Let's Go [2]; Cross Eyed Kate [1]

Notes   [1] Used instrumentally only. [2] Also in ARIZONA TRAIL and WEST OF CARSON CITY. [3] Also in WEST OF CARSON CITY and TRAIL TO VENGEANCE.

233 ✦ THE ARIZONA KID
Republic, 1939

Producer(s)   Kane, Joseph
Director(s)   Kane, Joseph
Screenwriter(s)   Geraghty, Gerald; Ward, Luci

Cast   Rogers, Roy; Hayes, George "Gabby"; March, Sally; Hamblen, Stuart; Sebastian, Dorothy; Dwire, Earl; Kerwin, David

Song(s)   It's Home Sweet Home to Me (C/L: Samuels, Walter G.); Lazy Old Moon (C/L: Samuels, Walter G.)

234 ✦ ARIZONA LEGION
RKO, 1939

Musical Score   Webb, Roy

Producer(s)   Gilroy, Bert
Director(s)   Howard, David
Screenwriter(s)   Drake, Oliver

Cast   O'Brien, George; Johnson, Laraine; Moore, Carlyle; Wills, Chill

Song(s)   I'd Rather Be Footloose than Free [1] (C/L: Drake, Oliver)

Notes   [1] The Universal film RAIDERS OF SAN JOAQUIN has an Oliver Drake song titled "I'd Rather Be Footloose and Fancy Free." It might be the same song.

235 ✦ ARIZONA MAHONEY
Paramount, 1937

Producer(s) Botsford, A.M.
Director(s) Hogan, James
Screenwriter(s) Yost, Robert; Anthony, Stuart
Source(s) "Stairs of Sand" (story) Grey, Zane

Cast Cummings, Robert; Martel, June; Crabbe, Buster; Cook, Joe; Gateson, Marjorie; Chasen, Dave; Carle, Richard

Song(s) Ida Dunn (C/L: Dempsey, J.E.)

236 ✦ ARIZONA SKETCHES
Paramount, 1941

Musical Score Young, Victor

Song(s) Prairieland Lullaby (C: Young, Victor; L: Loesser, Frank)

Notes Short subject. No cue sheet available. Sheet music only.

237 ✦ ARIZONA STAGE COACH
Monogram

Musical Score Sanucci, Frank

Song(s) Where the Grass Grows High in the Mountains (C/L: Sooter, Rudy)

Notes No other information available.

238 ✦ ARIZONA TO BROADWAY
Fox, 1933

Director(s) Tinling, James
Screenwriter(s) Conselman, William; Johnson, Henry

Cast Dunn, James; Bennett, Joan; Mundin, Herbert; Cohen, Sammy

Song(s) Ain't It Gonna Ring No More (C/L: Burton, Val; Jason, Will); Bono the Steel Skulled Boy (C/L: Dunn, James)

239 ✦ ARIZONA TRAIL
Universal, 1943

Producer(s) Drake, Oliver
Director(s) Keays, Vernon
Screenwriter(s) Lively, William

Cast Ritter, Tex; Knight, Fuzzy; Shaw, Janet

Song(s) Let's Go [1] (C: Rosen, Milton; L: Carter, Everett); Stars of the Midnight Range (C/L: Bond, Johnny); Ridin' Down to Santa Fe (C/L: Bond, Johnny); Stay Away from My Heart [2] (C/L: Marvin, Johnny); The Devil's Gonna Laugh (C: Rosen, Milton; L: Carter, Everett)

Notes [1] Also in ARIZONA CYCLONE (1942) and WEST OF CARSON CITY. [2] Also in I'M FORM ARKANSAS (PRC).

240 ✦ ARIZONA WILDCAT
Twentieth Century–Fox, 1938

Choreographer(s) Castle, Nick; Sawyer, Geneva

Producer(s) Stone, John
Director(s) Leeds, Herbert I.
Screenwriter(s) Trivers, Barry; Cady, Jerry

Cast Carrillo, Leo; Withers, Jane; Moore, Pauline; Henry, William; Wilcoxon, Henry; Harlan, Rosita

Song(s) Tavern Song [1] (C/L: Sanders, Troy)

Notes [1] Also in JESSE JAMES.

241 ✦ THE ARIZONIAN
RKO, 1935

Musical Score Webb, Roy

Producer(s) Reid, Cliff
Director(s) Vidor, Charles
Screenwriter(s) Nichols, Dudley

Cast Dix, Richard; Grahame, Margot; Foster, Preston; Calhern, Louis; Bush, James; Best, Willie

Song(s) Roll Along, Covered Wagon (C/L: Kennedy, Jimmy)

242 ✦ ARKANSAS JUDGE
Republic, 1941

Producer(s) Schaefer, Armand
Director(s) McDonald, Frank
Screenwriter(s) McGowan, Dorrell; McGowan, Stuart
Source(s) *False Witness* (novel) Stone, Irving

Cast Weaver Brothers; Elviry; Rogers, Roy; Byington, Spring; Moore, Pauline; Thomas, Frank M.; Borg, Veda Ann; Weaver, Loretta

Song(s) Naomi Wise (C/L: Robison, Carson J.); Peaceful Valley (C/L: Robison, Willard); Keep on the Sunny Side (C/L: Carter, A.P.)

Notes It is not known if any of these were written for this film. There is also a vocal of the traditional tune, "Happy Little Home in Arkansas."

243 ✦ THE ARKANSAS SWING
Columbia, 1948

Producer(s) Clark, Colbert
Director(s) Nazarro, Ray
Screenwriter(s) Shipman, Barry

Cast Porter, Dorothy; Henry, Gloria; Donahue, Mary Eleanor; Hart, Stuart; Vincent, June; Fowley, Douglas; Ward, Gabe; Taylor, Gil; The Hoosier Hotshots

Song(s) Bread and Butter Woman [2] (C: Lee, Lester; L: Roberts, Allan); Sweetheart of the Blues (C: Lee, Lester; L: Roberts, Allan); Texas Sandman [3] (C: Fisher, Doris; L: Roberts, Allan); It Ain't Nobody's Business What I Do [1] (C/L: Stampsel, S.G.; Markowitz, Morris; Browne, J.A.); Happy Birthday Polka [1] (C/L: Segal, Jack; Bergman, Dewey); Whoopee Hat Brigade [1] (C/L: Siegel, Monty; Jaffe, Moe); Not Today [1] (C/L: Bilder, Robert); What a Lucky Feeling [4] (C: Bilder, Robert; L: Clark, Frances)

Notes Originally titled TEXAS SANDMAN. The Texas Rangers singing group is also heard on the soundtrack. [1] Not written for film. [2] Also in SLIGHTLY FRENCH and PURPLE HEART DIARY. [3] Also in THE STRAWBERRY ROAN. [4] Titled "That Lucky Feeling" in sheet music.

244 ✦ ARMED AND DANGEROUS
Columbia, 1986

Musical Score Meyers, Bill
Composer(s) Meyers, Bill

Producer(s) Grazer, Brian; Keach, James
Director(s) Lester, Mark L.
Screenwriter(s) Ramis, Harold; Torokvei, Peter

Cast Candy, John; Levy, Eugene; Loggia, Robert; McMillan, Kenneth; Ryan, Meg; James, Brion; Stroud, Don; Railsback, Steve

Song(s) Candy's Theme (L: White, Maurice); Armed and Dangerous (C/L: White, Maurice; Page, Martin; Glenn, Garry); Respect, Respect, Respect (C/L: Serafini, Dan); Some Kind of Day (L: Burtnick, Glen); That's the Way It Is (C/L: Henderson, Michael); Steppin' Into the Night (C/L: Glenn, Garry; Quander, Dianne)

Notes These were all written for this picture. Some are background vocals.

245 ✦ ARMY SHOW
Warner Brothers, 1943

Song(s) The Bombardier Song (C: Rodgers, Richard; L: Hart, Lorenz); Hello Mom (C: Dunstedter, Eddie; L: Jones, Arthur; Loesser, Frank); Glide Glider Glide (C/L: Porter, Cole)

Notes Short subject.

246 ✦ AROUND THE WORLD
RKO, 1943

Composer(s) McHugh, Jimmy
Lyricist(s) Adamson, Harold
Choreographer(s) Castle, Nick

Producer(s) Dwan, Allan
Director(s) Dwan, Allan
Screenwriter(s) Spence, Ralph

Cast Kay Kyser and His Band; Auer, Mischa; Davis, Joan; McGuire, Marcy; Brown, Wally; Carney, Alan; Carroll, Georgia; Babbitt, Harry; Kabibble, Ish; Mason, Sully; Conway, Julie; Kay Kyser's Band; Jack & Max; Little Fred's Football Dogs; Armstrong, Robert

Song(s) Don't Believe Everything You Dream [1]; Great News Is in the Making; The Moke from Shamokin; Roodle-Ee-Doo; He's Got a Secret Weapon; Candlelight and Wine; They Just Chopped Down the Old Apple Tree; A Seasick Sailor

Notes No cue sheet available. [1] Also in RADIO STARS ON PARADE.

247 ✦ AROUND THE WORLD IN 80 DAYS
United Artists, 1956

Musical Score Young, Victor

Producer(s) Todd, Michael
Director(s) Anderson, Michael
Screenwriter(s) Perelman, S.J.; Poe, James; Farrow, John
Source(s) *Around the World in 80 Days* (novel) Verne, Jules

Cast Niven, David; Cantinflas; MacLaine, Shirley; Newton, Robert; Boyer, Charles; Brown, Joe E.; Carol, Martine; Carradine, John; Coburn, Charles; Colman, Ronald; Coward, Noel; Devine, Andy; Dietrich, Marlene; Fernandel; Gielgud, John; Gingold, Hermione; Greco, Jose; Hardwicke, Sir Cedric; Howard, Trevor; Johns, Glynis; Keaton, Buster; Lillie, Beatrice; Lorre, Peter; Mills, John; Morley, Robert; Oakie, Jack; Raft, George; Roland, Gilbert; Romero, Cesar; Sinatra, Frank; Skelton, Red

Song(s) Around the World in 80 Days [1] (C: Young, Victor; L: Adamson, Harold); Away Out West [2] (C: Young, Victor; L: Adamson, Harold)

Notes [1] Used instrumentally only. [2] Sheet music only.

248 ✦ ARRIVEDERCI, BABY!
Paramount, 1966

Producer(s) Hughes, Ken
Director(s) Hughes, Ken
Screenwriter(s) Hughes, Ken
Source(s) *The Careful Man* (novel) Deming, Richard

Cast Curtis, Tony; Schiaffino, Rosanna; Kwan, Nancy; Jeffries, Lionel; Gabor, Zsa Zsa

Song(s) Love Me Longer (Francesca's Theme) [1] (C: Farnon, Dennis; L: Shuman, Earl)

Notes Also features the "Kashmiri Song" by A. Woodforde Finden and L. Hope. [1] Not featured in picture.

249 ◆ ART GALLERY
Metro–Goldwyn–Mayer, 1939

Musical Score   Bradley, Scott

Song(s)   Monkey Theme (C: Bradley, Scott; L: Hanna, William)

Notes   This is a cartoon short.

250 ◆ ARTHUR
Orion, 1981

Musical Score   Bacharach, Burt
Composer(s)   Bacharach, Burt
Lyricist(s)   Sager, Carole Bayer

Producer(s)   Greenhut, Robert
Director(s)   Gordon, Steve
Screenwriter(s)   Gordon, Steve

Cast   Moore, Dudley; Minnelli, Liza; Gielgud, John; Fitzgerald, Geraldine; Eikenberry, Jill; Elliott, Stephen; Ross, Ted; Evans, Peter; Lewis, Bobo; Martin, Barney; De Salvo, Anne; Copeland, Maurice; Johnson, Justine

Song(s)   Arthur's Theme [2] (Best That You Can Do) (C/L: Sager, Carole Bayer; Bacharach, Burt; Allen, Peter; Cross, Christopher); Fool Me Again [1]; It's Only Love [3]; Poor Rich Boy [3] (L: Pack, David; Puerta, Joe)

Notes   [1] Instrumental use only. [2] Background vocal use. [3] Sheet music only.

251 ◆ ARTHUR 2: ON THE ROCKS
Warner Brothers, 1988

Musical Score   Bacharach, Burt

Producer(s)   Shapiro, Robert
Director(s)   Yorkin, Bud
Screenwriter(s)   Breckman, Andy

Cast   Moore, Dudley; Minnelli, Liza; Elliott, Stephen; Sikes, Cynthia; Gielgud, John; Benedict, Paul

Song(s)   Love Is My Decision (C: Bacharach, Burt; DeBurgh, Chris; L: Sager, Carole Bayer; DeBurgh, Chris)

252 ◆ ARTISTS AND MODELS (1937)
Paramount, 1937

Composer(s)   Lane, Burton
Lyricist(s)   Koehler, Ted
Choreographer(s)   Prinz, LeRoy

Producer(s)   Gensler, Lewis E.
Director(s)   Walsh, Raoul
Screenwriter(s)   De Leon, Walter; Martin, Francis

Cast   Benny, Jack; Lupino, Ida; Arlen, Richard; Patrick, Gail; Blue, Ben; Canova, Judy; Cunningham, Cecil; Meek, Donald; Hopper, Hedda; Raye, Martha; Andre Kostalanetz and His Orchestra; Russell Patterson's Personettos; Louis Armstrong and His Orchestra; Anne and Zeke; The Yacht Club Boys [2]; Boswell, Connee; Arno, Peter; McClelland, Barclay; Brown, Arthur William; Goldberg, Rube; La Gatta, John; Patterson, Russel

Song(s)   Sasha Pasha Sasha (C/L: The Yacht Club Boys [2]; Koehler, Ted); Pop Goes the Bubble (and Soap Gets in My Eyes); Whispers in the Dark [5] (C: Hollander, Frederick; L: Robin, Leo); Stop! You're Breaking My Heart; Public Melody No. 1 (C: Arlen, Harold); New Love [1] (C: Schwartz, Jean; L: Loman, Jules); Artist and Model [1] (C: Schwartz, Jean; L: Loman, Jules); Mr. Esquire [3] (C: Young, Victor); I Have Eyes [4] (C: Rainger, Ralph; L: Robin, Leo); Laughing Song [1] (C/L: The Yacht Club Boys [2]; Koehler, Ted)

Notes   Arrangements of "Public Melody No. 1," "Stop! You're Breaking My Heart" and "Whispers in the Dark" were by Andre Kostelanetz. [1] Not used. [2] George Kelly, Charles Adler, William B. Mann and James V. Kern. [3] Used instrumentally only but recorded with lyric. [4] Originally written for WAIKIKI WEDDING but not used. Also in PARIS HONEYMOON. Not on cue sheets as being used. [5] Originally written for DESIRE.

253 ◆ ARTISTS AND MODELS (1955)
Paramount, 1955

Composer(s)   Warren, Harry
Lyricist(s)   Brooks, Jack
Choreographer(s)   O'Curran, Charles

Producer(s)   Wallis, Hal B.
Director(s)   Tashlin, Frank
Screenwriter(s)   Tashlin, Frank; Kanter, Hal; Baker, Herbert
Source(s)   *Rock-a-Bye Baby!* (play) Davidson, Michael; Lessing, Norman

Cast   Martin, Dean; Lewis, Jerry; MacLaine, Shirley; Malone, Dorothy; Mayehoff, Eddie; Gabor, Eva; Ekberg, Anita; Winslow, George

Song(s)   Artists and Models; The Bat Lady; Innamorata; The Lucky Song; When You Pretend; You Look So Familiar

254 ◆ ARTISTS AND MODELS ABROAD
Paramount, 1938

Composer(s)   Rainger, Ralph
Lyricist(s)   Robin, Leo
Choreographer(s)   Prinz, LeRoy

Producer(s)   Hornblow Jr., Arthur
Director(s)   Leisen, Mitchell
Screenwriter(s)   Lindsay, Howard; Crouse, Russel; Englund, Ken

Cast   Benny, Jack; Bland, Mary; Woolley, Monty; Grapewin, Charley; Feld, Fritz; Compton, Joyce; Huntley Jr., G.P.; The Yacht Club Boys; Kennedy, Phyllis

Song(s) Do the Buckaroo; You're Broke You Dope (C/L: The Yacht Club Boys [2]); You're Lovely, Madame [4]; What Have You Got That Gets Me; Russian Song [1] (C/L: The Yacht Club Boys [2]); How Would You Feel [3]

Notes Was to be called ARTISTS AND MODELS OF 1938. The film was released as STRANDED IN PARIS in Great Britain. [1] Not used but recorded. [2] George Kelly, Chas. Adler, William B. Mann and James V. Kern. [3] Not used. [4] Also used in NAUGHTY NANETTE.

255 ♦ THE ART OF LOVE
Universal, 1965

Musical Score Coleman, Cy
Composer(s) Coleman, Cy

Producer(s) Hunter, Ross
Director(s) Jewison, Norman
Screenwriter(s) Reiner, Carl

Cast Van Dyke, Dick; Garner, James; Stevens, Naomi; Jacobson, Irving; Carmel, Roger C.; Olaf, Pierre; Merman, Ethel; Sommer, Elke; Dickinson, Angie; Reiner, Carl

Song(s) Monsieur [1] (C: Scharf, Walter; L: Brooks, Jack; Verdie, Paul); The Art of Love [2] (L: Raye, Don); I Wish I Knew Her Name [2] (L: Grand, Murray); Kick Off Your Shoes [2] (L: Grand, Murray); Nikki [2] (L: Lipton, James); So Long Baby [2] (L: Grand, Murray; Coleman, Cy)

Notes [1] Also in BUCCANEER'S GIRL but without Verdie credit. [2] Written for exploitation only.

256 ♦ ASECURE A SU MUMER
Fox, 1934

Song(s) Radiante (C: Piedra, Ernesto; Poncela, E. Jardiel); Sneezing Love (C: Sanders, Troy; Roulien, Raul; L: Roulien, Raul; Poncela, E. Jardiel)

Notes No other information available.

257 ♦ AS GOOD AS MARRIED
Universal, 1937

Producer(s) Asher, E.M.
Director(s) Buzzell, Edward
Screenwriter(s) Herbert, F. Hugh; Starling, Lynn

Cast Boles, John; Nolan, Doris; Mowbray, Alan; Kent, Dorothea

Song(s) Oh, Alec-Oh, Alec (C/L: Lewis, C. Harold); You're in My Heart Again [1] (C: McHugh, Jimmy; L: Adamson, Harold)

Notes [1] Also in BREEZING HOME.

258 ♦ AS HUSBANDS GO
Fox, 1934

Producer(s) Lasky, Jesse L.
Director(s) MacFadden, Hamilton
Screenwriter(s) Levien, Sonya; Behrman, S.N.
Source(s) *As Husbands Go* (play) Crothers, Rachel

Cast Baxter, Warner; Vinson, Helen

Song(s) Parlez-Moi D'Amour (Speak to Me of Love) [1] (C/L: Lenoir, Jean); Ah, Love but a Day [2](C: DeFrancesco, Louis E.; L: Browning, Robert)

Notes [1] Also in THE SAILOR TAKES A WIFE (MGM). [2] From Browning's poem "James Lee's Wife Speaks at the Window."

259 ♦ ASH WEDNESDAY
Paramount, 1973

Musical Score Jarre, Maurice

Producer(s) Dunne, Dominick
Director(s) Peerce, Larry
Screenwriter(s) Tramont, Jean-Claude

Cast Taylor, Elizabeth; Berger, Helmut; Baxter, Keith; Fonda, Henry

Song(s) Summer Green, Autumn Gold [1] (C: Jarre, Maurice; L: Webster, Paul Francis); The Nearness of You [2] (C: Carmichael, Hoagy; L: Washington, Ned)

Notes There is also a vocal of "Ruby" by Heinz Roemheld and Mitchell Parish. [1] Lyric written for exploitation only. [2] Written for unproduced film ROMANCE IN THE ROUGH. Not used in ST. LOUIS BLUES. Recorded but not used in GIRLS! GIRLS! GIRLS!. Finally, this was Paramount's first screen usage!

260 ♦ ASI ES LA VIDA
Sono-Art Productions, 1930

Composer(s) Bohr, Eva; Bohr, Jesse
Lyricist(s) Bohr, Eva; Bohr, Jesse

Producer(s) Goebel, O.E.; Weeks, George W.
Director(s) Crone, George J.
Screenwriter(s) Crespo, Jorge Juan
Source(s) *The Dark Chapter* (novel) Rath, E.J.; *They All Want Something* (play) Savage, Courtenay

Cast Bohr, Jose; Magana, Delia; Vendrill, Lola; Vanoni, Cesar; Acosta, Enrique; Nivon, Marcela; Davidson, Tito

Song(s) Son Cosas de la Vida; Que Tienes en la Mirada; Mi Princessia

Notes No cue sheet available. A Spanish language version of WHAT A MAN.

261 ✦ ASK ANY GIRL
Metro–Goldwyn–Mayer, 1959

Musical Score Alexander, Jeff

Producer(s) Pasternak, Joe
Director(s) Walters, Charles
Screenwriter(s) Wells, George
Source(s) *Ask Any Girl* (novel) Wolfe, Winifred

Cast Niven, David; MacLaine, Shirley; Young, Gig; Taylor, Rod; Backus, Jim; Kelly, Claire; Fraser, Elisabeth

Song(s) Ballad for Beatniks (C: Alexander, Jeff; L: Orenstein, Larry); Blues About Manhattan [1] (C: Alexander, Jeff; L: Orenstein, Larry)

Notes There is also a vocal of "I'm in the Mood for Love" by Dorothy Fields and Jimmy McHugh.

262 ✦ ASKING FOR TROUBLE
Republic, 1942

Musical Score Russell, Kennedy

Producer(s) Orton, Wallace
Director(s) Mitchell, Oswald
Screenwriter(s) Mitchell, Oswald; West, Con

Cast Miller, Max; Lynne, Carol; Hyde-White, Wilfrid; Lester, Mark; Percy, Billy

Song(s) Stars in Your Eyes (C/L: Manny; Shuff); When the Blackbird Says Bye-Bye (C/L: Noel, Art); Come On and Dance (C/L: Miller, Max)

Notes A British National release.

263 ✦ AS LONG AS THEY'RE HAPPY
United Artists, 1955

Musical Score Black, Stanley
Composer(s) Coslow, Sam
Lyricist(s) Coslow, Sam

Producer(s) Rank, J. Arthur; Stross, Raymond
Director(s) Thompson, J. Lee
Screenwriter(s) Melville, Alan
Source(s) *As Long As They're Happy* (play) Sylvaine, Vernon

Cast Buchanan, Jack; Scott, Janette; Carson, Jean; Stephen, Susan; De Banzie, Brenda; Wayne, Jerry; Dors, Diana; McDermott, Hugh

Song(s) You Started Something; Quiet Little Rendezvous; I Hate the Morning (C/L: Gregg, Hubert); (I Don't Know Whether To) Laugh or Cry; Liza's Eyes; My Crazy Little Mixed Up Heart; Be My Guest; Hokey Pokey Polka; Cry (C/L: Kohlman, Churchill); What the Country Needs; Don't Laugh at Me [1] (C: Black, Stanley; L: Wisdom, Norman; Tremayne, June)

Notes [1] Also in UP IN THE WORLD and TROUBLE IN STORE but without Black being credited.

264 ✦ THE ASSASSINATION BUREAU
Paramount, 1969

Musical Score Grainer, Ron
Composer(s) Grainer, Ron
Lyricist(s) Shaper, Hal

Producer(s) Relph, Michael
Director(s) Dearden, Basil
Screenwriter(s) Relph, Michael
Source(s) *The Assassination Bureau Ltd.* (novel) London, Jack; Fish, Robert

Cast Reed, Oliver; Rigg, Diana; Savalas, Telly; Jurgens, Curt; Noiret, Philippe; Mitchell, Warren; Reid, Beryl; Revill, Clive

Song(s) The Student Song; To Know My Love Loves Me; Life Is a Precious Thing

265 ✦ ASSIGNMENT TO KILL
Warner Brothers–Seven Arts, 1969

Musical Score Lava, William
Composer(s) Lava, William
Lyricist(s) Conrad, William

Producer(s) Conrad, William
Director(s) Reynolds, Sheldon
Screenwriter(s) Reynolds, Sheldon
Source(s) "The Assignment" (story) Reynolds, Sheldon

Cast O'Neal, Patrick; Hackett, Joan; Lom, Herbert; Gielgud, John; Portman, Eric; Homolka, Oscar; D'Orsay, Fifi; Van Eyck, Peter

Song(s) Baby, What Makes You So Mean [1]; I'm On the Go [2]; I Should Have Known [2]

Notes [1] Background vocal use only. [2] Background instrumental use only.

266 ✦ AS YOUNG AS WE ARE
Paramount, 1958

Producer(s) Alland, William
Director(s) Girard, Bernard
Screenwriter(s) Dolinsky, Meyer

Cast Harland, Robert; Scott, Pippa; Watkins, Linda

Song(s) As Young As We Are [1] (C/L: Barlow, Harold); Too Young for Love [1] [2] (C/L: Barlow, Harold)

Notes "Stella By Starlight" by Victor Young and Ned Washington is used vocally. [1] These two songs have the same music. [2] The lyric of "Too Young for Love" was rejected and the song was rewritten with a new lyric.

267 ✦ AT GOOD OLD SIWASH
Paramount, 1940

Lyricist(s)   Loesser, Frank

Producer(s)   Reed, Theodore
Director(s)   Reed, Theodore
Screenwriter(s)   Hartman, Don
Source(s)   Siwash Stories (stories) Fitch, George

Cast   Holden, William; Granville, Bonita; Stone, Ezra; Frawley, William; Denning, Richard; Terry, Phillip; Rutherford, Tom; Ladd, Alan

Song(s)   Alpha Ro Song [1] (C: Lambert, Louis); Ode to Joy (Siwash Spring Song) [2] (C: Beethoven, Ludwig von); We're All Here at Siwash (1) [2] (C: Beethoven, Ludwig von); Any Minute Now (C: Loesser, Frank); Siwash Alma Mater [2] (C: Beethoven, Ludwig von); We're All Here at Siwash (2) [3] (C: Brahms, Johannes)

Notes   Released also as THOSE WERE THE DAYS. [1] To the tune of "When Johnny Comes Marching Home." [2] To the music of Beethoven's "Ninth Symphony." [3] Not in final print.

268 ✦ ATHENA
Metro–Goldwyn–Mayer, 1954

Musical Score   Stoll, George; Van Eps, Robert
Composer(s)   Martin, Hugh; Blane, Ralph
Lyricist(s)   Martin, Hugh; Blane, Ralph
Choreographer(s)   Bettis, Valerie

Producer(s)   Pasternak, Joe
Director(s)   Thorpe, Richard
Screenwriter(s)   Ludwig, William; Spigelgass, Leonard

Cast   Powell, Jane; Purdom, Edmund; Reynolds, Debbie; Damone, Vic; Calhern, Louis; Christian, Linda; Varden, Evelyn; Collins, Ray; Reid, Carl Benton; Wendell, Howard; Gibson, Virginia; Nakamura, Henry

Song(s)   Athena [4]; The Girl Next Door [1]; Vocalize [2]; Imagine; Harmonize [2]; Webson's Meat Jingle (C/L: Alexander, Jeff; Stoll, George); Love Can Change the Stars; I Never Felt Better; Venezia; Faster Than Sound [3]

Notes   There is also a vocal of "Chacun le Sait" from DAUGHTER OF THE REGIMENT by Donizetti. [1] Originally in MEET ME IN ST. LOUIS as "The Boy Next Door." [2] Same music. [3] Recorded but not used. [4] Some sheet music credits Bert Pollock with lyrics.

269 ✦ ATLANTIC CITY (1944)
Republic, 1944

Choreographer(s)   Gould, Dave; Felix, Seymour

Producer(s)   Cohen, Albert J.
Director(s)   McCarey, Ray
Screenwriter(s)   Gill, Frank; Gilbert, Doris; Brown, George Carleton

Cast   Moore, Constance; Taylor, Brad; Grapewin, Charley; Colonna, Jerry; Whiteman, Paul; Castaine, Robert; Baker, Belle; Shean, Al; Kenney, Jack; Van, Gus; Marsh, Charles; Armstrong, Louis; Buck and Bubbles [1]; Frisco, Joe

Song(s)   Harlem on Parade (C: Scharf, Walter; L: Duplessie, R.); Rhythm for Sale (C/L: Sublett, John [1]; Washington, Ford [1])

Notes   Vocals include "The Bird on Nellie's Hat" by Arthur J. Lamb and Alfred Sloman; "After You've Gone" by Henry Creamer and Turner Layton; "By the Sea" by Harry Carroll and Harold Atteridge; "On a Sunday Afternoon" by Harry Von Tilzer and Andrew B. Sterling; "That's How You Can Tell They're Irish" by Clarence Gaskill and Grey; "I Ain't Got Nobody" by Roger Graham and Spencer Williams; "Ain't Misbehavin'" by Andy Razaf and Thomas "Fats" Waller; "Mr. Gallagher and Mr. Shean" by Ed Gallagher and Al Shean; "Nobody's Sweetheart" by Gus Kahn, Ernie Erdman and Billy Meyers; "Merrily We Roll Along" by E.P. Christie and Ferd V. D. Garretson; "Rock-A-Bye Baby" by Effie I. Canning; "The Mulberry Bush;" "The Farmer in the Dell" and "London Bridge Is Falling Down." [1] Sublett and Washington are better known as Buck and Bubbles.

270 ✦ ATLANTIC CITY (1981)
Paramount, 1981

Musical Score   Legrand, Michel

Producer(s)   Heroux, Denis
Director(s)   Malle, Louis
Screenwriter(s)   Guare, John

Cast   Lancaster, Burt; Sarandon, Susan; Reid, Kate; Piccoli, Michel; McLaren, Hollis; Joy, Robert; Waxman, Al; Goulet, Robert; Znaimer, Moses

Song(s)   Atlantic City, My Old Friend (C/L: Anka, Paul)

Notes   No cue sheet available.

271 ✦ AT LONG LAST LOVE
Twentieth Century–Fox, 1975

Producer(s)   Bogdanovich, Peter
Director(s)   Bogdanovich, Peter
Screenwriter(s)   Bogdanovich, Peter

Cast   Reynolds, Burt; Shepherd, Cybill; Kahn, Madeline; Brennan, Eileen; Hillerman, John; Natwick, Mildred; Walsh, M. Emmet

Song(s)   Poor Young Millionaire [1] (C: Butler, Artie; Bogdanovich, Peter; L: Porter, Cole)

Notes   The following Cole Porter songs are included as vocals: "Down in the Depths," "Tomorrow," "Which," "You're the Top," "Find Me a Primitive Man," "Friendship," "But in the Morning, No," "Well, Did You Evah" (From stage musical DUBARRY WAS A

LADY and the film HIGH SOCIETY), "From Alpha to Omega," "Let's Misbehave," "It's Delovely," "Just One of Those Things" (also in PANAMA HATTIE and CAN-CAN), "I Get a Kick Out of You," "Most Gentlemen Don't Like Love," "I Loved Him" and "A Picture of You Without Me." [1] Porter's lyrics were not written for this picture.

272 ✦ A TOUT PRENDRE

See TAKE IT ALL.

273 ✦ AT THE CIRCUS
Metro–Goldwyn–Mayer, 1939

Composer(s) Arlen, Harold
Lyricist(s) Harburg, E.Y.
Choreographer(s) Connolly, Bobby

Producer(s) LeRoy, Mervyn
Director(s) Buzzell, Edward
Screenwriter(s) Brecher, Irving

Cast Marx, Groucho; Marx, Chico; Marx, Harpo; Baker, Kenny; Rice, Florence; Arden, Eve; Dumont, Margaret; Pendleton, Nat; Feld, Fritz

Song(s) Step Up and Take a Bow; Two Blind Loves; Lydia the Tattooed Lady; Swingali

Notes There are also vocals of "Blue Moon" by Richard Rodgers and Lorenz Hart and "Oh Susannah" by Stephen Foster.

274 ✦ AT WAR WITH THE ARMY
Paramount, 1950

Composer(s) Livingston, Jerry
Lyricist(s) David, Mack

Producer(s) Finklehoffe, Fred F.
Director(s) Walker, Hal
Screenwriter(s) Finklehoffe, Fred F.
Source(s) *At War with the Army* (play) Allardice, James B.

Cast Martin, Dean; Lewis, Jerry; Kellin, Mike; Bergen, Polly; Ruth, Jean

Song(s) You and Your Beautiful Eyes; Tonda Wanda Hoy; The Navy Gets the Gravy but the Army Gets the Beans; Too Ra Loo Ra Loo Ral [1] (C/L: Shannon, J.R.)

Notes [1] Not written for film.

275 ✦ AUDREY ROSE
United Artists, 1977

Musical Score Small, Michael

Producer(s) Wizan, Joe; De Felitta, Frank
Director(s) Wise, Robert
Screenwriter(s) De Felitta, Frank
Source(s) *Audrey Rose* (novel) De Felitta, Frank

Cast Mason, Marsha; Beck, John; Hopkins, Anthony; Swift, Susan; Walden, Robert; Hillerman, John

Song(s) Winter Winter Go Away (C/L: De Felitta, Frank; Moulton, Leslie)

276 ✦ AUNTIE MAME
Warner Brothers, 1958

Musical Score Kaper, Bronislau
Lyricist(s) Lawrence, Jerome; Lee, Robert E.

Director(s) DaCosta, Morton
Screenwriter(s) Comden, Betty; Green, Adolph
Source(s) *Auntie Mame* (play) Lee, Robert E.; Lawrence, Jerome

Cast Russell, Rosalind; Tucker, Forrest; Browne, Coral; Clark, Fred; Handzlick, Jan; Cass, Peggy; Smith, Roger; Knowles, Patric; Scott, Pippa; Patrick, Lee; Waterman, Willard; Shimoda, Yuki

Song(s) Chu Chin Girl (C: Lawrence, Jerome; Lee, Robert E.); O Rumsun U [1] (C: Schechtman, Saul); Tooralay [1] (C: Schechtman, Saul); Drifting [2] (L: Unknown)

Notes The play is based on the novel of the same name by Patrick Dennis. [1] Background vocal only. [2] Music based on main theme. Lyrics added later.

277 ✦ AUTHOR! AUTHOR!
Twentieth Century–Fox, 1982

Musical Score Grusin, Dave

Producer(s) Winkler, Irwin
Director(s) Hiller, Arthur
Screenwriter(s) Horovitz, Israel

Cast Pacino, Al; Cannon, Dyan; Weld, Tuesday; King, Alan; Dishy, Bob; Elliott, Bob; Goulding, Ray

Song(s) Comin' Home to You (C: Grusin, Dave; L: Bergman, Marilyn; Bergman, Alan)

278 ✦ AUTUMN LEAVES
Columbia, 1956

Musical Score Salter, Hans J.

Producer(s) Goetz, William
Director(s) Aldrich, Robert
Screenwriter(s) Jevne, Jack; Meltzer, Lewis; Blees, Robert

Cast Crawford, Joan; Robertson, Cliff; Miles, Vera; Greene, Lorne; Donnelly, Ruth; Strudwick, Shepperd

Song(s) Autumn Leaves [1] (C: Kosma, Joseph; L: Prevert, Jacques [2])

Notes [1] Not written for film. [2] English lyrics by Johnny Mercer.

279 ✦ AVALANCHE EXPRESS
Twentieth Century–Fox, 1979

Musical Score Ferguson, Allyn

Producer(s) Robson, Mark
Director(s) Robson, Mark
Screenwriter(s) Polonsky, Abraham
Source(s) *Avalanche Express* (novel) Forbes, Colin

Cast Marvin, Lee; Shaw, Robert; Evans, Linda; Schell, Maximilian; Namath, Joe; Buchholz, Horst; Connors, Michael; Cassinelli, Claudia

Song(s) St. Petersburg Song (C/L: Shaw, Robert)

280 ✦ AVANTI!
United Artists, 1972

Producer(s) Wilder, Billy
Director(s) Wilder, Billy
Screenwriter(s) Diamond, I.A.L.; Wilder, Billy
Source(s) *Avanti* (play) Taylor, Samuel

Cast Lemmon, Jack; Mills, Juliet; Revill, Clive; Andrews, Edward; Barra, Gianfranco

Song(s) Core Ngrato [1] (C: Cardillo, S.; L: Cordiferro, R.); Senza Fine [2] (C/L: Paoli, Gino); Un'ora Sola Ti Vorrei (C/L: Bertini; Marchetti, F.D.); Blackmail (C/L: Rustichelli, Carlo); Palocoscenico (C/L: Bonagura, Enzo; Giannini, A.; Chianese, G.)

Notes "Blackmail" may be the only song written for this picture. [1] Also in A MAN ABOUT THE HOUSE (20th). [2] Also in THE FLIGHT OF THE PHOENIX (20th).

281 ✦ THE AVENGING RIDER
RKO, 1942

Musical Score Sawtell, Paul; Dreyer, Dave

Producer(s) Gilroy, Bert
Director(s) Nelson, Sam

Screenwriter(s) Hoyt, Harry O.; Grant, Morton
Source(s) "The Five of Spades" (story) Hoyt, Harry O.

Cast Holt, Tim; Edwards, Cliff; Summers, Ann; Clark, Davison; Willis, Norman; Hackett, Karl; Hodgins, Earle

Song(s) Minnie My Mountain Moocher (C/L: Edwards, Cliff)

282 ✦ THE AWAKENING
United Artists, 1928

Musical Score Riesenfeld, Hugo

Producer(s) Goldwyn, Samuel
Director(s) Fleming, Victor
Screenwriter(s) Wilson, Carey; Hilliker, Katherine; Caldwell, H.H.

Cast Banky, Vilma; Byron, Walter; Wolheim, Louis; Davis, George; Orlamond, William

Song(s) Marie (C/L: Berlin, Irving)

Notes No cue sheet available.

283 ✦ THE AWFUL TRUTH
Columbia, 1937

Composer(s) Oakland, Ben
Lyricist(s) Drake, Milton

Producer(s) McCarey, Leo
Director(s) McCarey, Leo
Screenwriter(s) Delmar, Vina
Source(s) (play) Richman, Arthur

Cast Dunne, Irene; Grant, Cary; Bellamy, Ralph; D'Arcy, Alexander; Cunningham, Cecil; Lamont, Molly; Dale, Esther

Song(s) My Dreams Have Gone with the Wind; I Don't Like Music [1]

Notes Originally called I'LL TAKE ROMANCE. [1] Not on cue sheet.

B

284 ✦ BABES IN ARMS
Metro–Goldwyn–Mayer, 1939

Composer(s) Rodgers, Richard
Lyricist(s) Hart, Lorenz
Choreographer(s) Berkeley, Busby

Producer(s) Freed, Arthur
Director(s) Berkeley, Busby
Screenwriter(s) McGowan, Jack; Van Riper, Kay
Source(s) *Babes in Arms* (musical) Rodgers, Richard; Hart, Lorenz

Cast Rooney, Mickey; Garland, Judy; Winninger, Charles; Kibbee, Guy; Preisser, June; Hayes, Grace; Jaynes, Betty; McPhail, Douglas; Lynn, Leni; Sheffield, John; Shoemaker, Ann; Hamilton, Margaret; Crehan, Joseph

Song(s) Opera Vs. Jazza (C/L: Edens, Roger); Babes in Arms [1]; Indignation March (C/L: Edens, Roger); Nursery March (C/L: Edens, Roger); Where or When [1]; Minstrel Show (Daddy Was a Minstrel Man) (C/L: Edens, Roger); Good Morning [2] (C: Brown, Nacio Herb; L: Freed, Arthur)

Notes There are also vocals of "Broadway Rhythm" (also in BROADWAY MELODY OF 1936, BROADWAY MELODY OF 1938, SINGIN' IN THE RAIN and PRESENTING LILY MARS) and "You Are My Lucky Star" (also in SINGIN' IN THE RAIN, BORN TO SING, and BROADWAY MELODY OF 1936) by Arthur Freed and Nacio Herb Brown; "God's Country" from the Broadway musical HOORAY FOR WHAT! by Harold Arlen and E.Y. Harburg; "I Cried for You" by Arthur Freed, Gus Arnheim and Abe Lyman (also in SOMEBODY LOVES ME and LADY SINGS THE BLUES) and brief snippets of other popular songs. Eddie Larkin assisted on the choreography. [1] From original Broadway show. [2] Also in SINGIN' IN THE RAIN.

285 ✦ BABES IN TOYLAND (1934)
Metro–Goldwyn–Mayer, 1934

Composer(s) Herbert, Victor
Lyricist(s) McDonough, Glen

Producer(s) Roach, Hal
Director(s) Meins, Gus; Rogers, Charles
Screenwriter(s) Butler, Frank; Grinde, Nick
Source(s) *Babes in Toyland* (musical) McDonough, Glen; Herbert, Victor

Cast Laurel, Stan; Hardy, Oliver; Karns, Virginia; Henry, Charlotte; Knight, Felix; Roberts, Florence; Kleinbach, Henry

Song(s) Toyland; Never Mind Bo Peep; Castle in Spain; Go to Sleep

Notes No cue sheet available. All songs from Broadway original. Released to television as MARCH OF THE WOODEN SOLDIERS

286 ✦ BABES IN TOYLAND (1961)
Disney, 1961

Musical Score Bruns, George
Composer(s) Bruns, George
Lyricist(s) Leven, Mel
Choreographer(s) Mahoney, Tom

Director(s) Donohue, Jack
Screenwriter(s) Kimball, Ward; Rinaldi, Joe; Hawley, Lowell S.
Source(s) *Babes in Toyland* (musical) Herbert, Victor; McDonough, Glen

Cast Bolger, Ray; Sands, Tommy; Funicello, Annette [2]; Wynn, Ed; Kirk, Tommy; Corcoran, Kevin; Calvin, Henry; Sheldon, Gene; McCarty, Mary; Jillian, Ann; Corcoran, Brian

Song(s) Castle in Spain [1]; Floretta [1]; Forest of No Return [1]; Go to Sleep [1]; Gypsies [1]; I Can't Do the Sum [1]; Just a Toy [1]; Just a Whisper Away [1]; Lemonade [1]; The Mother Goose Village Square [1]; Never Mind Bo Peep [1]; Tom and Mary [1]; Toyland March [1]; We Won't Be Happy Til We Get It [1]; Work Shop Song [1]; Mary, Mary Quite Contrary (L: Traditional); Slowly, He Sank to the Bottom of the Sea; Jack Be Nimble (L: Traditional); Simple Simon (L: Traditional)

Notes [1] George Bruns adapted the music from Victor Herbert melodies. [2] Billed simply as Annette.

287 ✦ BABES ON BROADWAY
Metro–Goldwyn–Mayer, 1941

Musical Score Stoll, George; Arnaud, Leo; Bassman, George
Composer(s) Lane, Burton
Lyricist(s) Freed, Ralph

Producer(s) Freed, Arthur
Director(s) Berkeley, Busby
Screenwriter(s) Finklehoffe, Fred F.; Ryan, Elaine

Cast Rooney, Mickey; Garland, Judy; Bainter, Fay; McDonald, Ray; Meek, Donald; Weidler, Virginia; Quine, Richard; Woollcott, Alexander

Song(s) Babes on Broadway; Anything Can Happen in New York (L: Harburg, E.Y.); How About You; Hoe Down (C: Edens, Roger); Chin Up! Cheerio! Carry On! (L: Harburg, E.Y.); Bombshell from Brazil (C/L: Edens, Roger); Mama Yo Quiero (C/L: Paiva, Vincente; Paiva, Jararaca); Minstrel Show (C/L: Edens, Roger); Blackout Over Broadway; FDR Jones (C/L: Rome, Harold); Ballad for Americans [1] (C: Robinson, Earl; L: Latouche, John); Tap It Out [2]

Notes There are also vocals of "Yankee Doodle Boy" and "Mary's a Grand Old Name" by George M. Cohan; "I've Got Rings on My Fingers" by Maurice Scott, R.P. Weston and F.J. Barnes; "She Is Ma Daisy" by Harry Lauder and J.D. Harper; "By the Light of the Silvery Moon" by Gus Edwards and Edward Madden and "Waiting for the Robert E. Lee" by Lewis F. Muir and L. Wolfe Gilbert. [1] This number was filmed but deleted. It later turned up complete in BORN TO SING (1943). [2] Not used.

288 ✦ BABES ON SWING STREET
Universal, 1944

Composer(s) Miller, Sidney; James, Inez
Lyricist(s) Miller, Sidney; James, Inez
Choreographer(s) Da Pron, Louis

Producer(s) Burton, Bernard W.
Director(s) Lilley, Edward
Screenwriter(s) Dimsdale, Howard; Conrad, Eugene

Cast Blyth, Ann; Ryan, Peggy; Errol, Leon; Kruger, Alma; Devine, Andy; Gwynne, Anne; Preisser, June; Grant, Kirby; Dunn, Billy; Freddie Slack and His Orchestra; The Rubenettes

Song(s) Take It Easy [1] (C/L: deBru, Albert; Taylor, Irving; Mizzy, Vic); Musical Chairs; Youth Is on the March (C: Rosen, Milton; L: Carter, Everett); I've Got a Way with the Boys; Wrong Thing at the Right Time; Hotcha Sonya; Music and You

Notes There is also a rendition of "Peg O' My Heart" by Alfred Bryan and Fred Fischer. [1] Also in MEET MISS BOBBY SOCKS (Columbia) and YELLOW ROSE OF TEXAS (Republic).

289 ✦ BABY BOOM
United Artists, 1987

Musical Score Conti, Bill

Producer(s) Meyers, Nancy
Director(s) Shyer, Charles
Screenwriter(s) Meyers, Nancy; Shyer, Charles

Cast Keaton, Diane; Ramis, Harold; Shepard, Sam; Wanamaker, Sam; Spader, James; Hingle, Pat; Leach, Britt; Kennedy, Kristina; Ellerbee, Linda; Golden, Annie; Jackson, Victoria; Whitehead, Paxton

Song(s) Everchanging Times (C/L: Bacharach, Burt; Sager, Carole Bayer; Conti, Bill)

Notes No cue sheet available.

290 ✦ BABY DOLL
Warner Brothers, 1956

Musical Score Hopkins, Kenyon

Producer(s) Kazan, Elia
Director(s) Kazan, Elia
Screenwriter(s) Williams, Tennessee

Cast Baker, Carroll; Malden, Karl; Wallach, Eli; Dunnock, Mildred; Chapman, Lonny

Song(s) Shame, Shame, Shame! (C: Hopkins, Kenyon; L: Fisher, Ruby); Baby Doll [1] (C: Hopkins, Kenyon; L: Hanighen, Bernie)

Notes [1] Written for exploitation only.

291 ✦ BABY FACE HARRINGTON
Metro–Goldwyn–Mayer, 1935

Musical Score Johnston, Arthur

Producer(s) Selwyn, Edgar
Director(s) Walsh, Raoul
Screenwriter(s) Johnson, Nunnally; Knopf, Edwin H.; Lederer, Charles
Source(s) *Something to Brag About* (play) Selwyn, Edgar; LeBaron, William

Cast Butterworth, Charles; Merkel, Una; Stephens, Harvey; Pallette, Eugene; Pendleton, Nat; Carle, Richard

Song(s) Hiking (C: Lane, Burton; L: Adamson, Harold)

292 ✦ BABY FACE NELSON
United Artists, 1957

Musical Score Alexander, Van

Producer(s) Zimbalist, Al
Director(s) Siegel, Don
Screenwriter(s) Shulman, Irving; Mainwaring, Daniel

Cast Rooney, Mickey; Jones, Carolyn; Hardwicke, Sir Cedric; Gordon, Leo; De Corsia, Ted; Caruso, Anthony; Elam, Jack

Song(s) I'm So in Love with You (C/L: Spina, Harold; Rooney, Mickey)

Notes It is not known if the song is used vocally or not.

293 ✦ BABY FOLLIES
Metro–Goldwyn–Mayer, 1930

Composer(s) Edwards, Gus
Lyricist(s) Waggner, George

Director(s) Edwards, Gus
Screenwriter(s) Hopkins, Robert E.

Song(s) Booperaboop [1]; As You Come In; Three Little Maids; Scotch Song; On the Beach at Waikiki (C: Kailimai, Henry; L: Stover, G.H.); Rarin' to Go; Baby Follies [2] (L: Johnson, Howard); Opening [2] (L: Johnson, Howard)

Notes Short subject. [1] Also in the short KIDDIE REVUE though credited to Edwards, Waggner and Will D. Cobb. [2] Not on cue sheets.

294 ✦ BABY TAKE A BOW
Fox, 1934

Producer(s) Stone, John
Director(s) Lachman, Harry
Screenwriter(s) Klein, Philip; Paramore Jr., Edward E.

Cast Temple, Shirley; Dunn, James; Trevor, Claire

Song(s) On Account-a I Love You (C: Stept, Sam H.; L: Green, Bud); I've Got You on the Top of My List [1] (C: Gorney, Jay; L: Clare, Sidney)

Notes [1] Also in WILD GOLD.

295 ✦ BABY THE RAIN MUST FALL
Columbia, 1964

Musical Score Bernstein, Elmer
Composer(s) Bernstein, Elmer
Lyricist(s) Sheldon, Ernie

Producer(s) Pakula, Alan J.
Director(s) Mulligan, Robert
Screenwriter(s) Foote, Horton
Source(s) *The Traveling Lady* (play) Foote, Horton

Cast Remick, Lee; McQueen, Steve; Murray, Don; Fix, Paul; Hutchinson, Josephine; White, Ruth; Watts, Charles

Song(s) Baby the Rain Must Fall; Treat Me Right; Shine for Me

296 ✦ BACHELOR IN PARADISE
Metro–Goldwyn–Mayer, 1962

Musical Score Mancini, Henry

Producer(s) Richmond, Ted
Director(s) Arnold, Jack
Screenwriter(s) Davies, Valentine; Kanter, Hal

Cast Hope, Bob; Turner, Lana; Paige, Janis; Hutton, Jim; Prentiss, Paula; Grey, Virginia; Porter, Don; Moorehead, Agnes; Sundstrom, Florence; McGiver, John; Sundberg, Clinton; Hewitt, Alan; Shaw, Reta

Song(s) Bachelor in Paradise (C: Mancini, Henry; L: David, Mack)

297 ✦ BACHELOR MOTHER
RKO, 1939

Producer(s) DeSylva, B.G.
Director(s) Kanin, Garson
Screenwriter(s) Krasna, Norman

Cast Rogers, Ginger; Niven, David; Coburn, Charles; Albertson, Frank; Clive, E.E.; Truex, Ernest

Song(s) Timbalero [1] (C/L: Gonzales, Aaron)

Notes No cue sheet available. [1] Also in THE GIRL AND THE GAMBLER.

298 ✦ BACHELOR OF ARTS
Fox, 1934

Composer(s) Whiting, Richard A.
Lyricist(s) Clare, Sidney

Producer(s) Stone, John
Director(s) King, Louis
Screenwriter(s) Trotti, Lamar
Source(s) (novel) Erskine, John

Cast Brown, Tom; Louise, Anita; Judge, Arline

Song(s) Phi-Phi-Phi; When the Last Year Rolls Around

299 ✦ BACHELOR PARTY
Twentieth Century–Fox, 1984

Musical Score Folk, Robert

Producer(s) Moler, Ron; Israel, Neal
Director(s) Israel, Neal
Screenwriter(s) Israel, Neal; Proft, Pat

Cast Hanks, Tom; Kitaen, Tawny; Zmed, Adrian; Grizzard, George; Sperber, Wendie Jo

Song(s) American Beat (C/L: Zaremba, Peter); Head Over Heels (C/L: Caffey, Charlotte; Valentine, Kathy); Alley Oop (C/L: Frazier, Dallas); Dream of the West (C/L: Evans, Carl); Why Do Good Girls Like Bad Boys (C/L: Cutler, Miriam); Little Demon (C/L: Dunbar, Tommy; Carlin, Alex; Seabury, John); Nature Took Over (C/L: Cutler, Miriam); Gotta Give a Little Love (C/L: Thomas, Timmy); Hall of Fame (C/L: Zaremba, Peter; Streng, Keith); Wind Out (C/L: Berry, Bill; Buck, Peter; Mills, Mike; Stipe, Michael); What Kind of Hell (C/L: McDonald, Eddie; Peters, Mike); Prepare to Energize (C/L: Orbit, William; Mayer, Laurie); Who Do You Want to Be Today (C/L: Elfman, Danny); Something Isn't Right (C/L: Elfman, Danny)

300 ✦ BACK AT THE FRONT

See WILLIE AND JOE IN BACK AT THE FRONT.

301 ✦ BACK IN THE SADDLE
Republic, 1941

Producer(s) Grey, Harry
Director(s) Landers, Lew
Screenwriter(s) Murphy, Richard; Lasky Jr., Jesse

Cast Autry, Gene; Burnette, Smiley; Lee, Mary; Norris, Edward; Wells, Jacqueline [1]; Richards, Addison

Song(s) Swingin' Sam the Cowboy Man (C: Styne, Jule; L: Meyer, Sol); Where the River Meets the Range [3] (C: Styne, Jule; L: Meyer, Sol); Ninety-Nine Bullfrogs (C/L: Burnette, Smiley); There's Nothing Like a Hoedown (C/L: Styne, Jule); Back in the Saddle Again [2] (C/L: Whitley, Ray); When the Cactus Is in Bloom (C/L: Rodgers, Jimmie)

Notes No cue sheet available. There may also be vocals of "You Are My Sunshine" by Jimmie Davis and Charles Mitchell and "After the Ball" by Charles K. Harris. [1] Also known as Julie Bishop. [2] Also in MELODY RANCH, ROVIN' TUMBLEWEEDS and BORDER G-MEN (RKO). Autry is listed as coauthor of the song but he actually didn't write any of it. He had a songwriting agreement with Ray Whitley where he would pay $25 per title as a work for hire and then include his name on the credits. [3] Also in RIDIN' ON A RAINBOW.

302 ✦ BACK ROADS
Warner Brothers, 1981

Musical Score Mancini, Henry

Producer(s) Shedlo, Ronald
Director(s) Ritt, Martin
Screenwriter(s) Devore, Gary

Cast Field, Sally; Jones, Tommy Lee; Keith, David; Colon, Miriam; Gazzo, Michael Vincente; Shor, Dan; Walsh, M. Emmet; Babcock, Barbara; Carter, Nell

Song(s) Ask Me No Questions (I'll Tell You No Lies) (C: Mancini, Henry; L: Bergman, Marilyn; Bergman, Alan)

303 ✦ BACK TO GOD'S COUNTRY
Universal, 1953

Musical Score Skinner, Frank

Producer(s) Christie, Howard
Director(s) Pevney, Joseph
Screenwriter(s) Reed, Tom

Cast Hudson, Rock; Henderson, Marcia; Cochran, Steve; O'Brian, Hugh; Johnson, Chubby; Owen, Tudor; Space, Arthur

Song(s) Beyond the Horizon (C: Herbert, Frederick; L: Hughes, Arnold)

Notes It is not known if this song was written for this film.

304 ✦ BACK TO NATURE
Twentieth Century–Fox, 1936

Producer(s) Golden, Max H.
Director(s) Tinling, James
Screenwriter(s) Ellis, Robert; Logan, Helen

Cast Prouty, Jed; Deane, Shirley; Dunbar, Dixie; Martin, Tony; Byington, Spring; Howell, Kenneth; Ernest, George; Carlson, June

Song(s) The Moon Is Shining (C: Tinling, James; L: Martin, Tony)

305 ✦ BACK TO SCHOOL
Orion, 1986

Musical Score Elfman, Danny

Producer(s) Russell, Chuck
Director(s) Metter, Alan
Screenwriter(s) Kampmann, Steven; Porter, Will; Torokvei, Peter; Ramis, Harold

Cast Dangerfield, Rodney; Kellerman, Sally; Young, Burt; Gordon, Keith; Downey Jr., Robert; Whitehead, Paxton; Zabka, William; Barbeau, Adrienne; Walsh, M. Emmet; Beatty, Ned; Darden, Severn; Kinison, Sam; Vonnegut Jr., Kurt; McClurg, Edie

Song(s) Back to School (C/L: Leonard, Mark); Educated Girl (C/L: Caldwell, Bobby; Goodrum, Randy); I'll Never Forget Your Face (C: Wolf, Richard; L: Wolf, Richard; Perkins, Wayne)

Notes No cue sheet available.

306 ✦ BACK TO THE BEACH
Paramount, 1987

Musical Score Dorff, Stephen H.

Producer(s) Mancuso Jr., Frank
Director(s) Hobbs, Lyndall
Screenwriter(s) Krikes, Peter; Meerson, Steve; Thompson, Christopher

Cast Avalon, Frankie; Funicello, Annette; Loughlin, Lori; Hinkley, Tommy; Stevens, Connie; Holland, Joe; Calvin, John; Adams, Don; Billingsley, Barbara; Denver, Bob; Dow, Tony; Hale, Alan; Mathers, Jerry; Reubens, Paul

Song(s) Catch a Ride (C/L: Kahne, David); Sun, Sun, Sun, Sun, Sun (C/L: Kahne, David); Some Things Live Forever (C/L: Sembello, Michael; Bettis, John)

Notes No cue sheet available.

307 ✦ BACK TO THE FUTURE
Universal, 1985

Musical Score Silvestri, Alan

Producer(s) Gale, Bob; Canton, Neil
Director(s) Zemeckis, Robert
Screenwriter(s) Zemeckis, Robert; Gale, Bob

Cast Fox, Michael J.; Lloyd, Christopher; Thompson, Lea; Glover, Crispin; Wilson, Thomas F.; Wells, Claudia; McClure, Marc; Tolkan, James; Siemaszko, Casey

Song(s) Windows (C/L: Van Halen, Edward; Landee, Donn); Pledging My Love (C/L: Robey, Don D.; Washington, Fats); Back in Time (C/L: Lewis, Huey; Hayes, Chris; Colla, Johnny; Hopper, Sean); The Power of Love (C/L: Lewis, Huey; Hayes, Chris; Colla, Johnny)

308 ✦ BAD BASCOMB
Metro–Goldwyn–Mayer, 1946

Musical Score Snell, Dave
Composer(s) Brent, Earl
Lyricist(s) Brent, Earl

Producer(s) Dull, Orville O.
Director(s) Simon, S. Sylvan
Screenwriter(s) Lipman, William R.; Garrett, Grant

Cast Beery, Wallace; O'Brien, Margaret; Main, Marjorie; Naish, J. Carrol; Rafferty, Frances; Thompson, Marshall

Song(s) Climb Up the Ladder; Wait, Wait, Brother

309 ✦ BAD BOY
Twentieth Century–Fox, 1935

Producer(s) Butcher, Edward
Director(s) Blystone, John
Screenwriter(s) Rivkin, Allen

Cast Dunn, James; Wilson, Dorothy; Fazenda, Louise; Killian, Victor; Wray, John; Alberni, Luis; Bondi, Beulah; Vincent, Allen

Song(s) As I Live and Breathe (I Live and Breathe for You) (C: Pollack, Lew; L: Webster, Paul Francis)

310 ✦ BAD COMPANY
Paramount, 1972

Musical Score Schmidt, Harvey
Composer(s) Schmidt, Harvey

Producer(s) Jaffe, Stanley R.
Director(s) Benton, Robert
Screenwriter(s) Newman, David; Benton, Robert

Cast Bridges, Jeff; Brown, Barry; Davis, Jim; Huddleston, David

Song(s) Theme from Bad Company (Wandering Child) (inst.)

311 ✦ THE BADGE OF MARSHALL BRENNAN
Allied Artists, 1957

Musical Score Idriss, Ramez

Producer(s) Gannaway, Albert C.
Director(s) Gannaway, Albert C.
Screenwriter(s) Hubbard, Thomas G.

Cast Davis, Jim; Whelan, Arleen; Van Cleef, Lee; Heydt, Louis Jean

Song(s) Man on the Run (C: Idriss, Ramez; Gannaway, Albert C. L: Levy, Hal)

312 ✦ BAD GIRL
Fox, 1931

Director(s) Borzage, Frank
Screenwriter(s) Burke, Edwin
Source(s) *Bad Girl* (novel) Delmar, Vina

Cast Eilers, Sally; Dunn, James; Gombell, Minna

Song(s) Come On Baby and Beg for It (C/L: Hanley, James F.)

Notes The novel was turned into a play of the same name.

313 ✦ BADLANDS OF DAKOTA
Universal, 1941

Producer(s) Waggner, George
Director(s) Green, Alfred E.
Screenwriter(s) Geraghty, Gerald

Cast Stack, Robert; Rutherford, Ann; Crawford, Broderick; Herbert, Hugh; Devine, Andy; Knight, Fuzzy; Chaney Jr., Lon; Page, Bradley; Farmer, Frances; Richards, Addison; Dix, Richard

Song(s) Goin' to Have a Big Time Tonight [1] (C/L: Robison, Carson J.)

Notes [1] Also in NATIONAL BARN DANCE (Paramount).

314 ✦ BADLANDS OF MONTANA
Twentieth Century–Fox, 1957

Musical Score Gertz, Irving

Producer(s) Ullman, Daniel B.
Director(s) Ullman, Daniel B.
Screenwriter(s) Ullman, Daniel B.

Cast Reason, Rex; Dean, Maria; Garland, Beverly; Larsen, Keith; Cunningham, Robert; Meyer, Emile

Song(s) The Gallant Gun (C: Gertz, Irving; L: Levy, Hal)

315 ✦ BAD MAN FROM RED BUTTE
Universal, 1940

Composer(s) Rosen, Milton
Lyricist(s) Carter, Everett

Director(s) Taylor, Ray
Screenwriter(s) Robins, Sam

Cast Brown, Johnny Mack; Knight, Fuzzy; Baker, Bob; Gwynne, Anne

Song(s) Gabby the Lawyer; Where the Prairie Meets the Sky [1]; We Want Hornsby

Notes [1] Also in ESCAPE FROM HONG KONG, FRONTIER LAW, I'LL TELL THE WORLD and TWILIGHT ON THE PRAIRIE.

316 ✦ BAD MAN OF BRIMSTONE
Metro–Goldwyn–Mayer, 1937

Musical Score Axt, William

Producer(s) Rapf, Harry
Director(s) Ruben, J. Walter
Screenwriter(s) Hume, Cyril; Maibaum, Richard

Cast Beery, Wallace; Bruce, Virginia; O'Keefe, Dennis; Calleia, Joseph; Stone, Lewis; Kibbee, Guy; Cabot, Bruce; Hatton, Raymond; Beery, Noah; Beckett, Scotty; Williams, Guinn "Big Boy"

Song(s) Save That Last Grave for Me (C: Freed, Arthur; L: Wright, Robert; Forrest, Chet)

Notes No cue sheet available. Script available.

317 ✦ BADMAN'S COUNTRY
Warner Brothers, 1958

Musical Score Gertz, Irving

Producer(s) Kent, Robert E.
Director(s) Sears, Fred F.
Screenwriter(s) Hampton, Orville H.

Cast Montgomery, George; Crabbe, Buster; Atterbury, Malcolm; Brand, Neville; Booth, Karin

Song(s) Badman's Country (C/L: Kent, Robert E.)

318 ✦ BAD MEDICINE
Twentieth Century–Fox, 1985

Musical Score Schifrin, Lalo

Producer(s) Winitsky, Alex; Sellers, Arlene
Director(s) Miller, Harvey
Screenwriter(s) Miller, Harvey
Source(s) *Calling Dr. Horowitz* (novel) Horowitz, Steven; Offen, Neil

Cast Guttenberg, Steve; Arkin, Alan; Hagerty, Julie; Macy, Bill; Armstrong, Curtis; Kavner, Julie; Grifasi, Joe; Gottfried, Gilbert

Song(s) Madera, Madera (C/L: Miller, Harvey); La Bonita Noche (C/L: Miller, Harvey)

Notes No cue sheet available.

319 ✦ BAD MEN OF DEADWOOD
Republic, 1941

Producer(s) Kane, Joseph
Director(s) Kane, Joseph
Screenwriter(s) Webb, James R.

Cast Rogers, Roy; Hayes, George "Gabby"; Adams, Carol; Brandon, Henry; Rawlinson, Herbert; Payne, Sally; Taliaferro, Hal; Novello, Jay; Blue, Monte; Kirk, Jack; Murphy, Horace

Song(s) Call of the Dusty Trail (C/L: Rose, Fred; Whitley, Ray); Joe O'Grady (C: Styne, Jule; L: Meyer, Sol); Sundown on the Rangeland [1] (C/L: Rogers, Roy; Rose, Fred)

Notes [1] Also used in IN OLD CALIENTE.

320 ✦ BAD MEN OF THE BORDER
Universal, 1945

Composer(s) Rosen, Milton
Lyricist(s) Carter, Everett

Producer(s) Fox, Wallace W.
Director(s) Fox, Wallace W.
Screenwriter(s) Huffington, Adele

Cast Grant, Kirby; Knight, Fuzzy; Armida

Song(s) And then I Got Married [2]; Carmencita [3]; Forget Your Boots and Saddle [1]

Notes [1] Used instrumentally only. [2] Also in SON OF ROARING DAN. [3] Also in THE MASKED RIDER.

321 ✦ BAD MEN OF THE HILLS
Columbia, 1942

Producer(s) Fier, Jack
Director(s) Berke, William
Screenwriter(s) Ward, Luci

Cast Starrett, Charles; Hayden, Russell; Edwards, Cliff; Walters, Luana

Song(s) Cherokee Joe (C/L: Unknown); Ladybug (C/L: Unknown); Where Oh Where Is My Blue Eyes? (C/L: Unknown)

Notes No cue sheet available.

322 ✦ BAD NEWS BEARS GO TO JAPAN
Paramount, 1978

Musical Score Chihara, Paul
Composer(s) Chihara, Paul
Lyricist(s) Chihara, Paul

Producer(s) Ritchie, Michael
Director(s) Berry, John
Screenwriter(s) Lancaster, Bill

Cast Curtis, Tony; Haley, Jackie Earle; Wakayama, Tomisaburo; Inoki, Antonio; Chapman, Lonny; Button, Dick; Philbin, Regis

Song(s) Mean Bones; Bird Man [1]; Take Good Care of Her (C: Kent, Arthur; L: Warren, Ed)

Notes Also featured are "Take Me Out to the Ball Game" by Jack Norworth and Albert von Tilzer; the Japanese folk song "Kurodabushi;" "Moon River" by Johnny Mercer and Henry Mancini; "Happy Days" by Charles Fox and Norman Gimbel and "Tangerine" by Johnny Mercer and Victor Schertzinger. [1] Instrumental use only.

323 ✦ BAD NEWS BEARS IN BREAKING TRAINING
Paramount, 1977

Producer(s) Goldberg, Leonard
Director(s) Pressman, Michael
Screenwriter(s) Brickman, Paul

Cast Devane, William; James, Clifton; Haley, Jackie Earle; Baio, Jimmy; Sweet, Dolph; Barnes, Chris; Lutter, Alfred

Song(s) Lookin' Good (C: Safan, Craig; L: Gimbel, Norman); It Just Takes Love [1] (C: Safan, Craig; L: Safan, Craig; Archerd, Evan)

Notes [1] Not used in film. Music based on Tchaikovsky's "1812 Overture."

324 ✦ BAGDAD
Universal, 1949

Musical Score Skinner, Frank
Composer(s) Skinner, Frank
Lyricist(s) Brooks, Jack
Choreographer(s) Horton, Lester

Producer(s) Arthur, Robert
Director(s) Lamont, Charles
Screenwriter(s) Andrews, Robert Hardy

Cast O'Hara, Maureen; Christian, Paul; Sutton, John; Price, Vincent; Corey, Jeff; Puglia, Frank; Leiber, Fritz; Pearce, Ann

Song(s) Bagdad; Love Is Strange [1]; Song of the Desert [2]

Notes [1] Music based on Khachaturian Suite—Gayne Ballet: "Awakening" and "Dance of Myscha." [2] Part of cue titled "Seylaba Dance."

325 ✦ BAGDAD CAFE
Island, 1988

Musical Score Telson, Bob

Producer(s) Adlon, Percy; Adlon, Eleonore
Director(s) Adlon, Percy
Screenwriter(s) Doherty, Christopher

Cast Sagebrecht, Marianne; Pounder, C.C.H.; Palance, Jack; Kaufmann, Christine

Song(s) Calling You (C/L: Telson, Bob); Brenda, Brenda (C: Telson, Bob; L: Breuer, Lee)

Notes No cue sheet available.

326 ✦ BAHAMA PASSAGE
Paramount, 1941

Producer(s) Griffith, Edward H.
Director(s) Griffith, Edward H.
Screenwriter(s) Van Upp, Virginia
Source(s) *Dildo Cay* (novel) Hayes, Nelson

Cast Carroll, Madeleine; Robson, Flora; Kellaway, Cecil; Carroll, Leo G.; Dandridge, Dorothy; Whipper, Leigh; Anderson, Mary; Hayden, Sterling

Song(s) Dominii Dambelli (C/L: Whipper, Leigh)

327 ✦ BALALAIKA
Metro–Goldwyn–Mayer, 1939

Musical Score Stothart, Herbert
Composer(s) Stothart, Herbert
Lyricist(s) Wright, Bob; Forrest, Chet
Choreographer(s) Matray, Ernst

Producer(s) Weingarten, Lawrence
Director(s) Schunzel, Reinhold
Screenwriter(s) Gordon, Leon; Bennett, Charles; Deval, Jacques
Source(s) *Balalaika* (musical) Maschwitz, Eric; Posford, George; Grun, Bernard

Cast Eddy, Nelson; Massey, Ilona; Ruggles, Charles; Morgan, Frank; Atwill, Lionel; Smith, C. Aubrey; Compton, Joyce; Frantz, Dalies

Song(s) Ride Cossack Ride; Tanya; At the Balalaika [1] (C: Posford, George; L: Maschwitz, Eric; Wright, Bob; Forrest, Chet); Flow Flow White Wine [1] (C: Traditional; L: Kahn, Gus); Wishing Episode; Magic of Your Love [1] (C: Lehar, Franz; L: Kahn, Gus; Grey, Clifford); Shadows on the Sand [2]; At Last in Your Arms [3] (C/L: Porter, Cole); My Heart Is a Gypsy [3] (C: Kaper, Bronislau; L: Kahn, Gus)

Notes There are also vocals of "El Ukhnem" by Chaliapine and Koeneman; "Les Tringles des Sistres," "Si Tu M'Aimes," "Votre Toast," and "Je Peux Vous le Rendre" from Bizet's CARMEN; "Scheherezade" by Rimsky-Korsakoff; "Silent Night" by Franz Gruber and "Otchi Tchornyia." [1] Music adapted by Stothart and lyrics added. [2] Sheet music only. [3] Not used.

328 ✦ THE BALLAD OF CABLE HOGUE
Warner Brothers, 1970

Musical Score Goldsmith, Jerry
Composer(s) Gillis, Richard
Lyricist(s) Gillis, Richard

Producer(s) Peckinpah, Sam; Faralla, William
Director(s) Peckinpah, Sam
Screenwriter(s) Crawford, John; Penney, Edmund

Cast Robards Jr., Jason; Warner, David; Stevens, Stella; Martin, Strother; Pickens, Slim; Jones, L.Q.; Whitney, Peter; Freeman, Kathleen

Song(s) Tomorrow Is the Song I Sing (C: Goldsmith, Jerry); Wait for Me, Sunrise; Hogan's Saloon Song; Butterfly Mornin's

329 ✦ BALLAD OF JOSIE
Universal, 1968

Musical Score De Vol, Frank

Producer(s) MacDonnell, Norman
Director(s) McLaglen, Andrew V.
Screenwriter(s) Swanton, Harold

Cast Day, Doris; Graves, Peter; Kennedy, George; Devine, Andy; Talman, William; Hartman, David; Raymond, Guy; Quinn, Teddy; Christie, Audrey; Scott, Timothy; Stroud, Don

Song(s) Ballad of Josie (C: Costa, Don; L: Huddleston, Floyd); Wait Till Tomorrow (C: De Paul, Gene; L: Lloyd, Jack)

330 ✦ BALL OF FIRE
RKO/Goldwyn, 1941

Musical Score Newman, Alfred

Producer(s) Goldwyn, Samuel
Director(s) Hawks, Howard
Screenwriter(s) Wilder, Billy; Brackett, Charles

Cast Cooper, Gary; Stanwyck, Barbara [1]; Andrews, Dana; Jenkins, Allen; Homolka, Oscar; Travers, Henry; Sakall, S.Z.; Marshall, Tully; Kinskey, Leonid; Haydn, Richard; Mather, Aubrey; Duryea, Dan; Lane, Charles; Howard, Kathleen

Song(s) Drumboogie [2] (C/L: Krupa, Gene; Eldridge, Roy)

Notes [1] Dubbed by Irene Daye. [2] Not written for film.

331 ✦ BAL TABARIN
Republic, 1951

Musical Score Butts, Dale
Composer(s) Elliott, Jack
Lyricist(s) Elliott, Jack

Producer(s) Millakowsky, Herman
Director(s) Ford, Philip
Screenwriter(s) Branch, Houston

Cast Lawrence, Muriel; Ching, William; Carleton, Claire; Brodie, Steve; Geray, Steven; Rubini, Jan; Powers, Tom

Song(s) My Heart Says Yes (C: Brahms, Johannes); You've Never Been in Love [1]; Now and Forever More

Notes [1] French lyric by Tom Mack.

332 ✦ BAMBI
Disney, 1942

Musical Score Churchill, Frank E.; Plumb, Ed
Composer(s) Churchill, Frank E.
Lyricist(s) Morey, Larry

Director(s) Hand, David D.
Screenwriter(s) Morey, Larry
Source(s) *Bambi* (novel) Salten, Felix

Supervising Animator(s) Thomas, Franklin; Kahl, Milton; Larson, Eric; Johnston Jr., Oliver M.

Song(s) Love Is a Song; Let's Sing a Gay Little Spring Song; Little April Shower (Rain Drops); Looking for Romance (I Bring You a Song) [2]; I'm Looking for Someone [1]; The Song of the Wind [1]; Thumper's Song [4] (C/L: Bliss, Helen; Sour, Robert; Manners, Henry [3]); Twitterpated [4] (C/L: Bliss, Helen; Sour, Robert; Manners, Henry [3])

Notes [1] Not used. [2] Originally titled "Night Wind." [3] Also known as Harry Katzman. [4] Written for exploitation only.

333 ✦ BAMBOO BLONDE
RKO, 1946

Composer(s) Pollack, Lew
Lyricist(s) Greene, Mort
Choreographer(s) O'Curran, Charles

Producer(s) Schlom, Herman
Director(s) Mann, Anthony
Screenwriter(s) Cooper, Olive; Kimble, Lawrence
Source(s) "Chicago Lulu" (story) Whittaker, Wayne

Cast Langford, Frances; Edwards, Ralph; Wade, Russell; Adrian, Iris; Martin, Richard; Greer, Jane; Vernon, Glenn; Harvey, Paul; Wallace, Regina; Brooks, Jean; Noonan, Tommy [1]; Vaughan, Dorothy

Song(s) Good for Nothing but Love; Dreaming Out Loud [2]; Along About Evening; Moonlight Over the Islands [3]

Notes [1] Billed as Tom Noonan. [2] Also used in FALCON'S ALIBI. [3] Also in THE JUDGE STEPS OUT and MAKE MINE LAUGHS.

334 ✦ BANANAS
United Artists, 1971

Musical Score Hamlisch, Marvin

Producer(s) Grossberg, Jack
Director(s) Allen, Woody
Screenwriter(s) Allen, Woody; Rose, Mickey

Cast Allen, Woody; Lasser, Louise; Montalban, Carlos; Cosell, Howard

Song(s) 'Cause I Believe in Loving You [1] (C: Hamlisch, Marvin; L: Liebling, Howard); Bananas [2] (C/L: Hamlisch, Marvin)

Notes [1] Used instrumentally only. [2] Written for exploitation only.

335 ✦ BANDITI A MILANO

See THE VIOLENT FOUR.

336 ✦ BANDIT RANGER
RKO, 1943

Musical Score Sawtell, Paul; Dreyer, Dave
Composer(s) Rose, Fred; Whitley, Ray
Lyricist(s) Rose, Fred; Whitley, Ray

Producer(s) Gilroy, Bert
Director(s) Selander, Lesley
Screenwriter(s) Cohen, Bennett R.; Grant, Morton

Cast Holt, Tim; Edwards, Cliff; Barclay, Joan; Harlan, Kenneth; Mason, LeRoy; Strange, Glenn

Song(s) Musical Jack; Move Along

337 ✦ BANDITS OF EL DORADO
Columbia, 1949

Composer(s) Burnette, Smiley
Lyricist(s) Burnette, Smiley

Producer(s) Clark, Colbert
Director(s) Nazarro, Ray
Screenwriter(s) Shipman, Barry

Cast Burnette, Smiley; Starrett, Charles; Lewis, George; Sears, Fred F.; Kehner, John; Moore, Clayton; Mahoney, Jock [1]

Song(s) The Rich Get Richer; Tricky Senor; That Last Great Day (C/L: Rice, Frank; Stokes, Ernest L.)

Notes [1] Billed as Jock O'Mahoney.

338 ✦ THE BANDIT TRAIL
RKO, 1941

Musical Score Sawtell, Paul; Webb, Roy

Producer(s) Gilroy, Bert
Director(s) Killy, Edward
Screenwriter(s) Parker, Norton S.

Cast Holt, Tim; Whitley, Ray; White, Lee "Lasses"; Ankrum, Morris

Song(s) On the Outlaw Trail [1] (C/L: Whitley, Ray; Rose, Fred)

Notes Originally titled THE OUTLAW TRAIL. [1] Also in FIGHTING FRONTIER.

339 ✦ BAND OF ANGELS
Warner Brothers–First National, 1957

Musical Score Steiner, Max

Director(s) Walsh, Raoul
Screenwriter(s) Twist, John; Goff, Ivan; Roberts, Ben
Source(s) *Band of Angels* (novel) Warren, Robert Penn

Cast Gable, Clark; De Carlo, Yvonne; Poitier, Sidney; Knowles, Patric; Teal, Ray; Thatcher, Torin; Zimbalist Jr., Efrem

Song(s) Band of Angels (C: Steiner, Max; L: Sigman, Carl)

340 ✦ BAND OF THE HAND
Tri-Star, 1986

Musical Score Rubini, Michael

Producer(s) Rauch, Michael
Director(s) Glaser, Paul Michael
Screenwriter(s) Garen, Leo; Garan, Jack

Cast Lang, Stephen; Carmine, Michael; Holly, Lauren; Mitchell, John Cameron; Quinn, Daniele; Remar, James

Song(s) Band of the Hand (C/L: Dylan, Bob); Carry Me Back Home (C/L: Summers, Andy); Hold On (C/L: Shaffer, Rick); Mission (C/L: Shaffer, Rick); Turn It On (C/L: Shaffer, Rick; Cohen, Bruce)

Notes No cue sheet available.

341 ✦ THE BAND PLAYS ON
Metro–Goldwyn–Mayer, 1934

Producer(s) Marin, Ned
Director(s) Mack, Russell
Screenwriter(s) Schubert, Bernard; Spence, Ralph; Gates, Harvey
Source(s) "Backfield" (story) Morgan, Byron; Bren, J. Robert; "The Gravy Game" (story) Stuhldreher, Harry; Martin, W. Thornton

Cast Young, Robert; Carrillo, Leo; Healy, Ted; Erwin, Stuart; Furness, Betty; Foster, Preston; Hardie, Russell

Song(s) Roll Up the Score (C: Lane, Burton; L: Adamson, Harold); You're So Happy (C: Donaldson, Walter; L: Kahn, Gus)

Notes There is also a vocal of "Jenny Jones."

342 ✦ BANDS ACROSS THE SEA
Warner Brothers, 1945

Song(s) Mama Don't Allow It [2] (C: Davenport, Charles; L: Cahn, Sammy); This Love of Mine (C: Sanicola, Henry; L: Parker, Sol; Sinatra, Frank); That's What the Well-Dressed Man in Harlem Will Wear [1] (C/L: Berlin, Irving)

Notes Short subject. It is not known if any of these were written for the film. [1] From THIS IS THE

ARMY. [2] Also in BARNYARD FOLLIES (Republic); MOUNTAIN MUSIC (Paramount) without Sammy Cahn lyric credit and BOB WILLS AND HIS TEXAS PLAYBOYS with it.

343   ✦   THE BAND WAGON
Metro–Goldwyn–Mayer, 1953

Composer(s)   Schwartz, Arthur
Lyricist(s)   Dietz, Howard
Choreographer(s)   Kidd, Michael

Producer(s)   Freed, Arthur
Director(s)   Minnelli, Vincente
Screenwriter(s)   Comden, Betty; Green, Adolph

Cast   Astaire, Fred; Charisse, Cyd [2]; Levant, Oscar; Fabray, Nanette; Buchanan, Jack; Mitchell, James; Gist, Robert

Song(s)   By Myself [13]; A Shine on Your Shoes [10]; That's Entertainment [1]; Something to Remember You By [6] [14] [15]; High and Low [8]; I Love Louisa [8] [14]; New Sun in the Sky [8]; I Guess I'll Have to Change My Plan [7]; Louisiana Hayride [10]; Triplets [13]; Never Marry a Dancer [3] [11]; Got a Brand New Suit [3] [12]; Alone Together [3] [9] [10]; Two-Faced Woman [3] [5] [10]; Sweet Music [3] [8]; You Have Everything [3] [13]; The Private Eye [4]; The Beggar's Waltz [8] (Inst.); Dancing in the Dark [8] [9]; You and the Night and the Music [9] [11]; Where Can He Be? [1] [16]

Notes   There is also a ballet called "The Girl Hunt" based on themes by Schwartz. [1] Written for this score. [2] Dubbed by India Adams. Pat Michaels was the first dubbing choice but after pre-recording four songs she became ill and was replaced. [3] Deleted from final print. [4] Not used but written for the film. [5] This number's vocal (by India Adams) found it's way into the film TORCH SONG (1953). [6] From THREE'S A CROWD. [7] From THE LITTLE SHOW. [8] Recorded. From THE BAND WAGON. [9] Used instrumentally only. [10] From FLYING COLORS. [11] From REVENGE WITH MUSIC. [12] Recorded. From AT HOME ABROAD. [13] From BETWEEN THE DEVIL. [14] Also in film DANCING IN THE DARK. [15] Also in DANCING IN THE DARK (20th) and HER KIND OF MAN (Warner). [16] Not used.

344   ✦   BANG THE DRUM SLOWLY
Paramount, 1973

Musical Score   Lawrence, Stephen

Producer(s)   Rosenfield, Lois; Rosenfield, Maurice
Director(s)   Hancock, John
Screenwriter(s)   Harris, Mark
Source(s)   *Bang the Drum Slowly* (novel) Harris, Mark

Cast   Ligon, Tom; De Niro, Robert; Moriarty, Michael; Gardenia, Vincent

Song(s)   Look Before You Weep (C/L: Stoeber, Orville); Theme from Bang the Drum Slowly [1] (C: Lawrence, Stephen; L: Hart, Bruce)

Notes   [1] Used instrumentally only.

345   ✦   BANJO ON MY KNEE
Twentieth Century–Fox, 1936

Composer(s)   McHugh, Jimmy
Lyricist(s)   Adamson, Harold

Producer(s)   Johnson, Nunnally
Director(s)   Cromwell, John
Screenwriter(s)   Johnson, Nunnally

Cast   Stanwyck, Barbara; McCrea, Joel; Brennan, Walter; Ebsen, Buddy; Westley, Helen; Catlett, Walter; Martin, Anthony; de Mille, Katherine; Killian, Victor; Gombell, Minna; Charters, Spencer; Humbert, George; Vaughn, Hilda; Weston, Cecil; The Hall Johnson Choir

Song(s)   With a Banjo On My Knee [2]; There's Something in the Air [1]; Where the Lazy River Goes By

Notes   There is also a vocal of "St. Louis Blues" by W.C. Handy which is also in DANCERS IN THE DARK and both films titled ST. LOUIS BLUES. [1] Also in DANCE HALL. [2] Also in YOUTH WILL BE SERVED.

346   ✦   BANJO, THE WOODPILE CAT
United Artists, 1981

Musical Score   Brunner, Robert F.
Composer(s)   Bluth, Don
Lyricist(s)   Bluth, Don

Director(s)   Bluth, Don

Song(s)   He Couldn't Be Good; Off to the City; The Rain Song; Boogie Baby; I'll Stick with You

Notes   An animated cartoon. No other information available.

347   ✦   BANNING
Universal, 1967

Musical Score   Jones, Quincy

Producer(s)   Berg, Dick
Director(s)   Winston, Ron
Screenwriter(s)   Lee, James

Cast   Wagner, Robert; Comer, Anjanette; St. John, Jill; Stockwell, Guy; Farentino, James; Garrison, Sean; Hackman, Gene

Song(s)   The Eyes of Love (C: Jones, Quincy; L: Russell, Bob)

348 ✦ BARBARELLA
Paramount, 1968

Musical Score   Crewe, Bob; Fox, Charles
Composer(s)   Fox, Charles
Lyricist(s)   Crewe, Bob

Producer(s)   De Laurentiis, Dino
Director(s)   Vadim, Roger
Screenwriter(s)   Southern, Terry
Source(s)   *Barbarella* (comic strip) Forest, Jean Claude

Cast   Fonda, Jane; Law, John Phillip; Marceau, Marcel; Hemmings, David; Tognazzi, Ugo

Song(s)   Barbarella; Love Drags Me Down; I Love All the Love in You; An Angel Is Love

349 ✦ THE BARBARIAN
Metro–Goldwyn–Mayer, 1933

Musical Score   Stothart, Herbert

Producer(s)   Hyman, Bernard H.
Director(s)   Wood, Sam
Screenwriter(s)   Loos, Anita; Harris, Elmer
Source(s)   (play) Selwyn, Edgar

Cast   Loy, Myrna; Novarro, Ramon; Denny, Reginald; Hale, Louise Closser; Smith, C. Aubrey; Arnold, Edward; Hopper, Hedda

Song(s)   Love Songs of the Nile (C: Brown, Nacio Herb; L: Freed, Arthur)

Notes   Titled A NIGHT IN CAIRO internationally. A remake of Novarro's 1924 feature, THE ARAB.

350 ✦ BARBARY COAST GENT
Metro–Goldwyn–Mayer, 1944

Musical Score   Snell, Dave

Producer(s)   Dull, Orville O.
Director(s)   Del Ruth, Roy
Screenwriter(s)   Lipman, William R.; Garrett, Grant; Ruskin, Harry

Cast   Beery, Wallace; Barnes, Binnie; Carradine, John; Kellogg, Bruce; Rafferty, Frances; Wills, Chill; Beery, Noah; O'Neill, Henry; Collins, Ray; Beavers, Louise

Song(s)   Star of the Evening (C: Ruthven, Ormond B.; L: Mannheimer, Albert; Brent, Earl)

351 ✦ BARBED WIRE
Columbia, 1952

Producer(s)   Autry, Gene
Director(s)   Archainbaud, George
Screenwriter(s)   Geraghty, Gerald

Cast   Autry, Gene; Champion; Buttram, Pat; Fawcett, William; Frost, Terry; Moore, Clayton; Penn, Leonard; James, Anne

Song(s)   Mexicali Rose [1] (C/L: Tenney, Jack); Old Buckaroo [2] (C/L: Autry, Gene; Allan, Fleming)

Notes   [1] Also in the Republic pictures MEXICALI ROSE and ROOTIN' TOOTIN' RHYTHM both with the additional credit of Helen Stone. [2] Also in PUBLIC COWBOY NUMBER ONE.

352 ✦ THE BAREFOOT EXECUTIVE
Disney, 1970

Musical Score   Brunner, Robert F.

Producer(s)   Anderson, Bill
Director(s)   Butler, Robert
Screenwriter(s)   McEveety, Joseph L.

Cast   Russell, Kurt; Flynn, Joe; Morgan, Harry; Cox, Wally; North, Heather; Hewitt, Alan; Rorke, Hayden; Ritter, John; Raffles

Song(s)   He's Gonna Make It (C: Brunner, Robert F.; L: Belland, Bruce)

353 ✦ BAREFOOT IN THE PARK
Paramount, 1967

Musical Score   Hefti, Neal

Producer(s)   Wallis, Hal B.
Director(s)   Saks, Gene
Screenwriter(s)   Simon, Neil
Source(s)   *Barefoot in the Park* (play) Simon, Neil

Cast   Fonda, Jane; Redford, Robert; Boyer, Charles; Natwick, Mildred

Song(s)   Barefoot in the Park (C: Hefti, Neal; L: Mercer, Johnny); Shama Shama [1] (C: Gould, Danny; L: Balabanoff, Luben)

Notes   [1] The Macedonian words were written by Luben Balabanoff and Neil Simon.

354 ✦ THE BARKLEYS OF BROADWAY
Metro–Goldwyn–Mayer, 1949

Musical Score   Hayton, Lennie
Composer(s)   Warren, Harry
Lyricist(s)   Gershwin, Ira
Choreographer(s)   Alton, Robert [1]

Producer(s)   Freed, Arthur
Director(s)   Walters, Charles
Screenwriter(s)   Comden, Betty; Green, Adolph

Cast   Astaire, Fred; Rogers, Ginger; Burke, Billie; Robbins, Gale; Francois, Jacques; Zucco, George; Levant, Oscar

Song(s) Swing Trot; You'd Be Hard to Replace; Bouncin' the Blues (Inst.); My One and Only Highland Fling; A Weekend in the Country; Shoes with Wings On; Manhattan Downbeat; These Days [2]; There Is No Music [2]; The Poetry of Motion [2]; Call on Us Again [2]; Natchez on the Mississip' [2]; The Courtin' of Elma and Ella [2]; Taking No Chance with You [2]; Second Fiddle to a Harp [2]; Minstrels on Parade [2]

Notes Released in England as THE GAY BARKLEYS. This was originally to have starred Judy Garland. When she left the picture and Ginger Rogers assumed the part many of the songs were then dropped from the score. See [2]. There is also a vocal of "They Can't Take That Away from Me" by George and Ira Gershwin. [1] "Shoes with Wings On" choreographed by Hermes Pan. [2] Not used.

355 ✦ BARNYARD BABIES
Metro–Goldwyn–Mayer, 1935

Song(s) Pig Latin Love (C: Bradley, Scott; L: Hanna, William)

Notes Animated cartoon.

356 ✦ BARNYARD FOLLIES
Republic, 1940

Composer(s) Marvin, Johnny; Rose, Fred
Lyricist(s) Marvin, Johnny; Rose, Fred
Choreographer(s) Earl, Josephine

Producer(s) Schaefer, Armand
Director(s) McDonald, Frank
Screenwriter(s) McGowan, Dorrell; McGowan, Stuart

Cast Lee, Mary; Davis, Rufe; Storey, June; Prouty, Jed; Killian, Victor; Woodbury, Joan; Switzer, Carl "Alfalfa"; Homans, Robert; Harrison, Dorothy [1]

Song(s) Barnyard Holiday; I'd Love to Be a Cowboy (C/L: Macboyle, D.; Gregory, B.; Van Ness, C.); Lollipop Lane [2]; Big Boy Blues; Mama Don't Allow It [3] (C/L: Davenport, Charles); Poppin' the Corn (C: Styne, Jule; L: Meyer, Sol)

Notes [1] The Queen of Dairyland. [2] Also in SILVER CITY BONANZA. [3] Also in MOUNTAIN MUSIC (Paramount) as credited above and the Warner Brothers shorts BANDS ACROSS THE SEA and BOB WILLS AND HIS TEXAS PLAYBOYS with lyrics credited to Sammy Cahn.

357 ✦ BARON MUNCHAUSEN (UNPRODUCED)
Disney

Composer(s) Heath, Hy; Lange, Johnny
Lyricist(s) Heath, Hy; Lange, Johnny

Song(s) The Fabulous Baron

358 ✦ THE BARRETTS OF WIMPOLE STREET
Metro–Goldwyn–Mayer, 1934

Musical Score Stothart, Herbert

Producer(s) Thalberg, Irving G.
Director(s) Franklin, Sidney
Screenwriter(s) Vajda, Ernest; West, Claudine; Stewart, Donald Ogden
Source(s) *The Barretts of Wimpole Street* (play) Besier, Rudolf

Cast Shearer, Norma; March, Fredric; Laughton, Charles; O'Sullivan, Maureen; Alexander, Katherine; Forbes, Ralph; O'Connor, Una; Carroll, Leo G.; Clayton, Marion

Song(s) Wilt Thou Have My Hand (C: Stothart, Herbert; L: Barrett, Elizabeth)

Notes The song was also used in the 1956 remake with a score by Bronislau Kaper.

359 ✦ BARRICADE
Twentieth Century–Fox, 1939

Musical Score Buttolph, David

Producer(s) Zanuck, Darryl F.
Director(s) Ratoff, Gregory
Screenwriter(s) Walker, Granville

Cast Faye, Alice; Baxter, Warner; Winninger, Charles; Treacher, Arthur; Luke, Keye; Fung, Willie

Song(s) There'll Be Other Nights [1] (C: Pollack, Lew; L: Brown, Lew)

Notes No cue sheet available. [1] Cut before release.

360 ✦ THE BARRIER
Paramount, 1937

Musical Score Lawrence, Maurice
Composer(s) Stern, Jack
Lyricist(s) Tobias, Harry

Producer(s) Sherman, Harry
Director(s) Selander, Lesley
Screenwriter(s) Schubert, Bernard; Jacobs, Harrison; Sharp, Mordaunt
Source(s) *The Barrier* (novel) Beach, Rex

Cast Ellison, James; Parker, Jean; Carrillo, Leo; Kruger, Otto

Song(s) Song of the Wild; Moonlit Paradise

Notes There was a search for permission to use the title "Moon Above."

361 ✦ BARS AND STRIPES
Metro–Goldwyn–Mayer, 1937

Musical Score Snell, Dave

Director(s) Sherman, Joseph
Screenwriter(s) Plannette, Jean; Grashin, Mauri

Cast Von, Vyola; Winslow, Dick; Holmes, Maynard

Song(s) Midnight Blue (C: Burke, Joe; L: Leslie, Edgar); In the Sweet Land of Swing (C/L: Wright, Bob; Forrest, Chet)

Notes Short Subject. Originally titled DOING SWING TIME.

362 ✦ BATHING BEAUTY
Metro–Goldwyn–Mayer, 1944

Musical Score Green, Johnny
Choreographer(s) Donohue, Jack; Alton, Robert

Producer(s) Cummings, Jack
Director(s) Sidney, George
Screenwriter(s) Kingsley, Dorothy; Boretz, Allen; Waldman, Frank

Cast Skelton, Red; Williams, Esther; Rathbone, Basil; Goodwin, Bill; Porter, Jean; Ramirez, Carlos; Bryant, Nana; Smith, Ethel; Xavier Cugat and His Orchestra; Romay, Lina; Harry James and His Music Makers; Forrest, Helen; Paige, Janis; Meek, Donald; Dumont, Margaret

Song(s) Bim Bam Bu [1] (C/L: Morales, Noro; Camacho, John A.); Te Quiero Dijiste (C/L: Grever, Maria); I'll Take the High Note (C: Green, Johnny; L: Adamson, Harold); Alma Llanera (C/L: Gutierrez, Pedro Elias); Magic Is the Moonlight [2] (C: Grever, Maria; L: Pasquale, Charles)

Notes There is also a vocal of "I Cried for You" by Arthur Freed, Abe Lyman and Gus Arnheim which was originally filmed but not used in BEST FOOT FORWARD. Ethel Smith played an organ rendition of "Tico Tico No Fuba" by Ervin Drake, Aloysio Oliveira and Zequinha Abreu. "The Water Ballet" was staged by John Murray Anderson. [1] Harold Adamson wrote English lyrics to this song but they aren't used in this picture. He titled the song "Bim Bam Boom." [2] Sheet music only.

363 ✦ BATTLE BEYOND THE STARS

See THE GREEN SLIME.

364 ✦ BATTLE CRY
Warner Brothers, 1955

Musical Score Steiner, Max

Director(s) Walsh, Raoul
Screenwriter(s) Uris, Leon
Source(s) *Battle Cry* (novel) Uris, Leon

Cast Heflin, Van; Ray, Aldo; Hunter, Tab; Whitmore, James; Lupton, John; Lopez, Perry; Parker, Fess; Freeman, Mona; Olson, Nancy; Malone, Dorothy; Francis, Anne

Song(s) Honey-Babe [1] (C: Steiner, Max; L: Webster, Paul Francis)

Notes [1] Also in THE GIRL HE LEFT BEHIND.

365 ✦ BATTLE OF BROADWAY
Twentieth Century–Fox, 1938

Composer(s) Akst, Harry
Lyricist(s) Clare, Sidney

Producer(s) Wurtzel, Sol M.
Director(s) Marshall, George
Screenwriter(s) Patrick, John; Breslow, Lou

Cast McLaglen, Victor; Donlevy, Brian; Hovick, Louise [1]; Walburn, Raymond; Bari, Lynn; Darwell, Jane; Kellard, Robert; Cohen, Sammy; Muir, Esther; Holden, Eddie; McDaniel, Hattie; Tombes, Andrew

Song(s) Top Gallants (Legionaires) [2]; The Daughter of Mademoiselle

Notes [1] Gypsy Rose Lee. She was dubbed by Mary Martin. [2] Also in CRACK UP.

366 ✦ THE BATTLE OF PARIS
Paramount, 1929

Director(s) Florey, Robert
Screenwriter(s) Markey, Gene

Cast Lawrence, Gertrude; Ruggles, Charles; Petrie, Walter; Du Bois, Gladys; Treacher, Arthur; King, Jon

Song(s) (When I Am) Housekeeping for You (C: Gorney, Jay; L: Dietz, Howard [1]); They All Fall in Love (C/L: Porter, Cole); What Makes My Baby Blue [2] [3] (C: Gorney, Jay; L: Dietz, Howard [1]); Here Comes the Bandwagon (C/L: Porter, Cole); Without You [4] (C/L: Porter, Cole)

Notes Paramount memos of the period indicate that Porter wrote four songs, of which only two were used (see [4]). There were also two songs alluded to as having been written by Paramount staff writers. [1] Written under pseudonym Dick Howard. [2] Unused. [3] Published. [4] This song was found in manuscript in the Paramount files. I assume it was written for this picture since Porter didn't write any other Paramount films at the time and the song is filed under 1929.

367 ✦ BATTLE SHOCK

See A WOMAN'S DEVOTION.

368 ✦ BATTLESTAR GALACTICA
Universal, 1978

Musical Score Phillips, Stu

Producer(s) Dykstra, John
Director(s) Colla, Richard A.
Screenwriter(s) Larson, Glen A.

Cast Greene, Lorne; Hatch, Richard; Benedict, Dirk; Jefferson Jr., Herbert; Hyde-White, Wilfrid; Colicos, John; Seymour, Jane; Milland, Ray; Begley Jr., Ed; Springfield, Rick; Oakes, Randi

Song(s) It's Love, Love, Love (C/L: Tartaglia, John Andrew; Collins, Sue; Larson, Glen A.); Galactica Theme (C: Phillips, Stu; L: Larson, Glen A.)

369 ✦ THE BAWDY ADVENTURES OF TOM JONES
Universal, 1976

Musical Score Grainer, Ron
Composer(s) Holden, Paul
Lyricist(s) Holden, Paul

Producer(s) Sadoff, Robert
Director(s) Owen, Cliff
Screenwriter(s) Lloyd, Jeremy
Source(s) *Tom Jones* (novel) Fielding, Henry; *Tom Jones* (musical) MacPherson, Don; Holden, Paul

Cast Henson, Nicky; Howard, Trevor; Terry-Thomas; Lowe, Arthur; Brown, Georgia; McEwan, Geraldine; Collins, Joan; Mervyn, William

Song(s) The Jones Boy (C/L: Matthews, David; Guilgud, Michael); How Do You Explain a Baby; Ingenuity (C/L: Gunning, Christopher; Gunning, Annie); Modus Operandi; I'll Make the Music Play (C/L: Gunning, Christopher; Gunning, Annie); Walkaway; The Real Truth

370 ✦ BAXTER'S BEAUTIES OF 1933

See MOVIE, MOVIE

371 ✦ BAYOU
United Artists, 1957

Musical Score Fried, Gerald
Composer(s) Fessler, E.I.
Lyricist(s) Fessler, E.I.

Producer(s) Riggs, M.A.
Director(s) Daniels, Harold
Screenwriter(s) Fissler, Edward I.

Cast Graves, Peter; Milan, Lita; Fowley, Douglas; Carey, Timothy

Song(s) Bayou Song; Hold Me Close

Notes Also known as POOR WHITE TRASH.

372 ✦ BEACH BALL
Paramount, 1965

Musical Score Wilson, Frank

Producer(s) Patton, Bart
Director(s) Weinrib, Lennie
Screenwriter(s) Malcolm, David

Cast Byrnes, Edward; Diana Ross and the Supremes; Noel, Chris; Logan, Robert; The Four Seasons; The Righteous Brothers; The Hondells; The Walker Brothers

Song(s) Dawn [1] (C/L: Gaudio, Bob; Linzer, Sandy); Surfin' Shindig (C: Wilson, Frank; L: Pipkin, Chester); Baby, What You Want Me to Do [1] (C/L: Reed, J.); We've Got Money (C/L: Capps, Al); My Buddy Seat [1] (C/L: Wilson, Brian; Usher, Gary); Wiggle Like You're Tickled (C: Wilson, Frank; L: Pipkin, Chester); Doin' the Jerk [1] (C/L: Ingel, Scott); Surfer Boy (C/L: Holland, Eddie; Holland, Brian; Dozier, Lamont); Beach Ball (C/L: Holland, Eddie; Holland, Brian; Dozier, Lamont); I Feel So Good (C: Wilson, Frank; L: Pipkin, Chester)

Notes [1] Not written for movie.

373 ✦ BEACH BLANKET BINGO
American International, 1965

Musical Score Baxter, Les
Composer(s) Hemric, Guy; Styner, Jerry
Lyricist(s) Hemric, Guy; Styner, Jerry

Producer(s) Nicholson, James H.; Arkoff, Samuel Z.
Director(s) Asher, William
Screenwriter(s) Asher, William

Cast Avalon, Frankie; Funicello, Annette; Walley, Deborah; Lembeck, Harvey; Ashley, John; McCrea, Jody; Loren, Donna; The Hondells; Rickles, Don; Lynde, Paul; Keaton, Buster; Wilson, Earl; Shaw, Bobbi

Song(s) A Surfer's Life Is Fun

Notes No cue sheet available.

374 ✦ BEACHES
Touchstone, 1989

Musical Score Delerue, Georges
Choreographer(s) Wood, Dee Dee

Producer(s) Bruckheimer-Martell, Bonnie; Midler, Bette; South, Margaret Jennings
Director(s) Marshall, Garry
Screenwriter(s) Donoghue, Mary Agnes
Source(s) *Beaches* (novel) Dart, Iris Rainer

Cast Midler, Bette; Hershey, Barbara; Heard, John; Gray, Spalding; Read, James; Kazan, Lainie

Song(s) Bunny Boy (C/L: Shaiman, Marc); The Wind Beneath My Wings (C/L: Henley, Larry; Silbar, Jeff)

Notes Only original songs listed.

375 ✦ THE BEAR
Embassy, 1984

Musical Score Conti, Bill

Producer(s) Spangler, Larry G.
Director(s) Sarafian, Richard C.
Screenwriter(s) Kane, Michael

Cast Busey, Gary; Leake, Cynthia; Thomas, Carmen; Stanton, Harry Dean; Hexum, John-Erik; Greenstein, Pat

Song(s) I'll Be Home Again (C: Conti, Bill; L: Lambert, Dennis)

Notes No cue sheet available.

376 ✦ THE BEARS AND I
Disney, 1974

Musical Score Baker, Buddy

Producer(s) Hibler, Winston
Director(s) McEveety, Bernard
Screenwriter(s) Whedon, John
Source(s) (book) Leslie, Robert Franklin

Cast Wayne, Patrick; Chief Dan George; Duggan, Andrew; Ansara, Michael; Pine, Robert; DeVargas, Val; Baylor, Hal

Song(s) Sweet Surrender (C/L: Denver, John)

377 ✦ BEAST OF THE CITY
Metro–Goldwyn–Mayer, 1932

Director(s) Brabin, Charles R.
Screenwriter(s) Mahin, John Lee

Cast Huston, Walter; Harlow, Jean; Hersholt, Jean; Ford, Wallace; Peterson, Dorothy; Miljan, John; Naish, J. Carrol

Song(s) Sweet and Lovely [1] (C/L: Arnheim, Gus; Lemare, Jules; Tobias, Harry)

Notes [1] Also in TWO GIRLS AND A SAILOR.

378 ✦ THE BEAST WITHIN
United Artists, 1982

Musical Score Baxter, Les
Composer(s) Baxter, Les
Lyricist(s) Cox, Ronny

Producer(s) Bernhard, Harvey; Katzka, Gabriel
Director(s) Mora, Philippe
Screenwriter(s) Holland, Tom

Cast Cox, Ronny; Besch, Bibi; Clemens, Paul; Moffat, Kitty

Song(s) Teardrops in Heaven; Country Girl

379 ✦ THE BEAT
Vestron, 1988

Musical Score Burwell, Carter
Composer(s) Flanagan, Harley; Mayhew, Kevin
Lyricist(s) Flanagan, Harley; Mayhew, Kevin

Producer(s) Phillips, Julia; Kilik, Jon; Wechsler, Nick
Director(s) Mones, Paul
Screenwriter(s) Mones, Paul
Source(s) *Voorhas* (play) Mones, Paul

Cast Jacobson, David; McNamara, William; Glover, Kara; Alexander, Stuart; McCarthy, David; Flanagan, Markus; Savage, John

Song(s) It's the Limit; Hard Times

Notes No cue sheet available.

380 ✦ THE BEAT GENERATION
Metro–Goldwyn–Mayer, 1959

Musical Score Glasser, Albert
Composer(s) Glasser, Albert
Lyricist(s) Meltzer, Lewis
Choreographer(s) Petroff, Hamil

Producer(s) Zugsmith, Albert
Director(s) Haas, Charles
Screenwriter(s) Matheson, Richard; Meltzer, Lewis

Cast Cochran, Steve; Van Doren, Mamie; Danton, Ray; Spain, Fay; Louis Armstrong and His All-Stars; Hayes, Margaret; Coogan, Jackie; Mitchum, Jim; Crosby, Cathy; Anthony, Ray; Contino, Dick; McCalla, Irish; Vampira; Daniels, Billy; Rosenbloom, Maxie; Chaplin Jr., Charles

Song(s) The Beat Generation (C: Kent, Walter; L: Walton, Tom); To Whom It May Concern [2] (C/L: Cole, Nat "King"; Hawkins, Charlotte); Love [1] (C/L: Blane, Ralph; Martin, Hugh); Someday You'll Be Sorry (C/L: Armstrong, Louis); I'm Off to the Moon; I've Got the Real Gone Nothing Blues; The Beat Is Ours; Speed, Speed, Speed

Notes [1] Also in HALF A HERO and ZIEGFELD FOLLIES. [2] Also in NIGHT OF THE QUARTER MOON.

381 ✦ BEAT STREET
Orion, 1984

Producer(s) Picker, David V.; Belafonte, Harry
Director(s) Lathan, Stan
Screenwriter(s) Davis, Andy; Gilbert, David; Golding, Paul

Cast Chong, Rae Dawn; Davis, Guy; Chardiet, Jon; Grant, Leon W.; Santiago, Saundra; Alice, Mary

Song(s) Beat Street Breakdown (C/L: Glover, Melvin; Griffin, Reggie); Baptize the Beat (C/L: Murphy, Michael; Frank, David); Strangers in a Strange World (C/L: Holmes, Jake); Beat Street Strut (C: Deodato, Eumir; Palanker, Alan; L: Barnes, Milton G.; Barnes, Katreese); Us Girls (C: Levinson, Ross; L: Levinson, Ross; Hooper, Deborah); This Could Be the Night (C/L: Baker, Arthur; Rogers, Evan; B., Tina; Sturken, Carl; Lord-Alge, Chris); Breakers Revenge (C/L: Baker, Arthur); Tu Carino (Carmen's Theme) (C: Franzetti, Carlos; L: Blades, Ruben); Frantic Situation (C: Baker, Arthur; Evans, Leroi; Serrano, Ray; L: Henderson, William; Williams, Ellis; Bambataa Aasim, Afrika; Fowler, Wilford; Miller, John; Allen, Robert)

Notes No cue sheet available.

382 ◆ BEAT THE BAND
RKO, 1946

Musical Score Harline, Leigh
Composer(s) Harline, Leigh
Lyricist(s) Greene, Mort

Producer(s) Kraike, Michel
Director(s) Auer, John H.
Screenwriter(s) Kimble, Lawrence
Source(s) *Beat the Band* (musical) Abbott, George; Green, Johnny; Marion Jr., George

Cast Langford, Frances; Edwards, Ralph; Terry, Phillip; Clayworth, June; Paige, Mabel; Tombes, Andrew; Sutton, Grady; Gene Krupa and His Band

Song(s) I Couldn't Sleep a Wink Last Night [1] (C: McHugh, Jimmy; L: Adamson, Harold); I've Got My Fingers Crossed; Kissin' Well; Shadow Rhapsody (Inst.) (C: Krupa, Gene); I'm in Love

Notes [1] Also in HIGHER AND HIGHER and RADIO STARS ON PARADE.

383 ◆ BEAU BANDIT
Radio, 1930

Producer(s) LeBaron, William
Director(s) Hillyer, Lambert
Screenwriter(s) Smith, Wallace

Cast La Rocque, Rod; Lewis, Mitchell; Kenyon, Doris; Middleton, Charles; Duryea, George; Donlan, James

Song(s) Just a Little Kiss (C/L: Unknown)

Notes No cue sheet available.

384 ◆ BEAU GESTE
Paramount, 1939

Producer(s) Wellman, William A.
Director(s) Wellman, William A.
Screenwriter(s) Carson, Robert

Cast Cooper, Gary; Preston, Robert; Milland, Ray; Donlevy, Brian; Naish, J. Carrol; Dekker, Albert; Crawford, Broderick; Stephenson, James; Barton, Charles; Huntley Jr., G.P.; Hayward, Susan; Thatcher, Heather

Song(s) The Legionnaire's Song [1] (C: Sanders, Troy; L: Loesser, Frank)

Notes [1] Music is from song "Foreign Legion March" by Sanders.

385 ◆ BEAU JAMES
Paramount, 1957

Choreographer(s) Baker, Jack

Producer(s) Rose, Jack
Director(s) Shavelson, Melville

Screenwriter(s) Rose, Jack; Shavelson, Melville
Source(s) *Beau James* (book) Fowler, Gene

Cast Hope, Bob; Miles, Vera [1]; Douglas, Paul; Smith, Alexis; McGavin, Darren; Jessel, George; Catlett, Walter

Song(s) His Honor the Mayor of New York (C: Lilley, Joseph J. L: Cahn, Sammy); Beau James [2] (C/L: Baker, Herbert)

Notes Only original songs listed. Sammy Cahn wrote the Yiddish version of "Will You Love Me in December" originally by James J. Walker and Ernest R. Ball. "Penthouse Serenade" by Will Jason and Val Burton is also used. It also appeared in ONE HOUR LATE and STRANGE LOVE OF MOLLY LOUVAIN (Warner). The song is sometimes referred to as "When We're Alone." [1] Vera Miles dubbed by Imogene Lynn. [2] Written for exploitation only.

386 ◆ THE BEAUTIFUL BLONDE FROM BASHFUL BEND
Twentieth Century–Fox, 1949

Producer(s) Sturges, Preston
Director(s) Sturges, Preston
Screenwriter(s) Sturges, Preston

Cast Grable, Betty; Romero, Cesar; Vallee, Rudy; San Juan, Olga; Holloway, Sterling; Herbert, Hugh; Brendel, El; Hall, Porter; Hamilton, Margaret; Caine, Georgia

Song(s) The Beautiful Blonde from Bashful Bend (C: Newman, Lionel; L: George, Don)

Notes "Every Time I Meet You" by Josef Myrow and Mack Gordon is also given a vocal performance.

387 ◆ BEAUTIFUL BUT BROKE
Columbia, 1944

Producer(s) Briskin, Irving
Director(s) Barton, Charles
Screenwriter(s) Seff, Manuel

Cast Davis, Joan; Hubbard, John; Frazee, Jane; Clark, Judy; Haymes, Bob [4]

Song(s) Shoo Shoo Baby [3] (C/L: Moore, Phil); Mr. Jive Has Gone to War (C: Oakland, Ben; L: Gilbert, L. Wolfe); Just Another Blues (C/L: Charles, Dick; Markes, Larry; Paul, Jimmy); Take the Door to the Left (C: Chaplin, Saul; L: Samuels, Walter G.); Keeping It Private (Me and Private Joe) (C: Donaldson, Walter; L: Greene, Mort); Mama I Wanna Make Rhythm [1] (C/L: Jerome, Jerome; Byron, Richard; Kent, Walter); Pistol Packin' Mama [2] (C/L: Dexter, Al)

Notes I believe "Mr. Jive Has Gone to War" was written for the picture. I don't think any of the others were. [1] Also in MANHATTAN MERRY-GO-ROUND and TENTH AVENUE KID, both Republic pictures. [2] Also in PISTOL PACKIN'

MAMA (Republic). [3] Also in BIG CITY (1948) (MGM); TROCADERO (Republic); SOUTH OF DIXIE (Universal). [4] Also known as Robert Stanton.

388 ✦ THE BEAUTIFUL CHEAT
Universal, 1945

Producer(s) Barton, Charles
Director(s) Barton, Charles
Screenwriter(s) Ullman, Elwood; Markson, Ben

Cast Granville, Bonita; Beery Jr., Noah; Irving, Margaret; Ryan, Irene

Song(s) Is You Is Or Is You Ain't My Baby [1] (C/L: Jordan, Louis; Austin, Billy); Stop and Make Love (C/L: Brooks, Jack); Ooh! What You Do to Me (C: Fairchild, Edgar; L: Brooks, Jack)

Notes [1] Also in EASY TO LOOK AT.

389 ✦ BEAUTIFUL STRANGER

See TWIST OF FATE.

390 ✦ BEAUTY FOR THE ASKING
RKO, 1939

Musical Score Webb, Roy

Producer(s) Fineman, B.P.
Director(s) Tryon, Glenn
Screenwriter(s) Anderson, Doris; Jarrico, Paul

Cast Ball, Lucille; Knowles, Patric; Inescort, Frieda; Woods, Donald

Song(s) Have You Forgotten So Soon (C/L: Heyman, Edward; Coslow, Sam; Silver, Abner)

391 ✦ BECAUSE OF YOU
Universal, 1952

Musical Score Skinner, Frank

Producer(s) Cohen, Albert J.
Director(s) Pevney, Joseph
Screenwriter(s) Frings, Ketti

Cast Young, Loretta; Nicol, Alex; Chandler, Jeff; Dee, Frances; Scourby, Alexander; Clarke, Mae

Song(s) Here's Your Kiss (C: Rosen, Milton; L: Carter, Everett)

Notes There is also a brief rendition of "Spring Will Be a Little Late this Year" by Frank Loesser.

392 ✦ BECAUSE THEY'RE YOUNG
Columbia, 1960

Musical Score Williams, John

Producer(s) Bresler, Jerry
Director(s) Wendkos, Paul
Screenwriter(s) Gunn, James
Source(s) *Harrison High* (novel) Farris, John

Cast Clark, Dick; Callan, Michael; Weld, Tuesday; Shaw, Victoria; Shore, Roberta; Berlinger, Warren; McClure, Doug; Duane Eddy and the Rebels; Darren, James

Song(s) Because They're Young (C: Costa, Don; L: Schroeder, Aaron; Gold, Wally); Shazam (C: Eddy, Duane; L: Hazlewood, Lee); Swingin' School (C/L: Mann, Kal; Lowe, Bernie)

Notes No cue sheet available.

393 ✦ BECAUSE YOU'RE MINE
Metro–Goldwyn–Mayer, 1952

Musical Score Green, Johnny
Composer(s) Brodszky, Nicholas
Lyricist(s) Cahn, Sammy

Producer(s) Pasternak, Joe
Director(s) Hall, Alexander
Screenwriter(s) Tunberg, Karl; Spigelgass, Leonard

Cast Lanza, Mario; Morrow, Doretta; Whitmore, James; Miller, Dean; Corday, Paula; Donnell, Jeff; Porter, Don; Franz, Eduard; Byington, Spring

Song(s) Because You're Mine; Gummy for Your Tummy (C/L: Alexander, Jeff); Fluffy Foam (C/L: Alexander, Jeff); The Song the Angels Sing (C: Traditional; Aaronson, Irving; L: Webster, Paul Francis); Lee-Ah-Loo (C: Sinatra, Raymond; L: Lehman, Johnny); Be My Love [1]; Garbage Can-Can (C/L: Alexander, Jeff)

Notes There are also vocals of "Casta Diva" from Bellini's NORMA; "You Do Something to Me" by Cole Porter; "The Lord's Prayer" by Albert Hay Malotte; "Miserre" and "Il Balen Del Suo Sorriso" from Verdi's IL TROVATORE; "Addio! Addio!" from Verdi's RIGOLETTO; "O Paradiso" from Meyerbeer's L'AFRICAINE and "Granada" by Augustin Lara. [1] Also in LOOKING FOR LOVE and THE TOAST OF NEW ORLEANS.

394 ✦ BEDAZZLED
Twentieth Century–Fox, 1967

Musical Score Moore, Dudley
Composer(s) Moore, Dudley
Lyricist(s) Moore, Dudley

Producer(s) Donen, Stanley
Director(s) Donen, Stanley
Screenwriter(s) Cook, Peter; Moore, Dudley

Cast Moore, Dudley; Cook, Peter; Bron, Eleanor; Welch, Raquel; Noel, Barry

Song(s) Bedazzled (L: Moore, Dudley; Cook, Peter); Love Me; Trampoline; Choir, Vespers, Etc.; Sweet Mouth [1] (L: Cahn, Sammy)

Notes Originally titled GET THEE BEHIND ME. [1] Written for exploitation only.

395 ✦ BEDEVILLED
Metro–Goldwyn–Mayer, 1955

Musical Score Alwyn, William

Producer(s) Berman, Henry
Director(s) Leisen, Mitchell
Screenwriter(s) Eisinger, Jo

Cast Baxter, Anne; Forrest, Steve; Renant, Simone; Teynac, Maurice; Christopher, Robert; Tomelty, Joseph; Francen, Victor

Song(s) Embrasse - Moi Bien (C: Durand, Paul; L: Contet, Henri; Driscoll, Richard)

Notes Richard Thorpe finished the direction of this picture when illness prevented Leisen from continuing.

396 ✦ BEDEVILLED RABBIT
Warner Brothers, 1957

Musical Score Franklyn, Milton J.

Director(s) McKimson, Robert
Screenwriter(s) Maltese, Michael

Cast Bunny, Bugs; The Tasmanian Devil

Song(s) 'Attsa Matta for You (C/L: Maltese, Michael)

Notes Merrie Melodie cartoon.

397 ✦ BEDKNOBS AND BROOMSTICKS
Disney, 1971

Musical Score Kostal, Irwin
Composer(s) Sherman, Richard M.; Sherman, Robert B.
Lyricist(s) Sherman, Richard M.; Sherman, Robert B.
Choreographer(s) McKayle, Donald

Producer(s) Walsh, Bill
Director(s) Stevenson, Robert
Screenwriter(s) Walsh, Bill; DaGradi, Don
Source(s) (novel) Norton, Mary

Directing Animator(s) Kimball, Ward
Cast Lansbury, Angela; Tomlinson, David; McDowall, Roddy; Jaffe, Sam; Ericson, John; Forsyth, Bruce; O'Callaghan, Cindy; Weighill, Ian; O'Shea, Tessie; Owen, Reginald

Song(s) The Old Home Guard; A Step in the Right Direction [2]; The Age of Not Believing; Eglantine; Portobello Road; Portobello Street Dance; The Beautiful Briny; Substitutiary Locomotion; With a Flair [2]; Nobody's Problems [1]; Solid Citizen [1]; Don't Let Me Down [1]

Notes [1] Not used. [2] These numbers were probably deleted after the film's premiere.

398 ✦ THE BED SITTING ROOM
United Artists, 1969

Musical Score Thorne, Ken

Producer(s) Lewenstein, Oscar; Lester, Richard
Director(s) Lester, Richard
Screenwriter(s) Antrobus, John; Milligan, Spike
Source(s) *The Bed Sitting Room* (play) Antrobus, John; Milligan, Spike

Cast Tushingham, Rita; Richardson, Ralph; Cook, Peter; Moore, Dudley; Milligan, Spike; Secombe, Harry; Nichols, Dudley; Hordern, Michael; Kinnear, Roy; Lowe, Arthur

Song(s) God Save Mrs. Ethyl Shroake (C: Traditional; L: Milligan, Spike; Antrobus, John)

399 ✦ A BEDTIME STORY
Paramount, 1932

Composer(s) Rainger, Ralph
Lyricist(s) Robin, Leo
Choreographer(s) Lang, Charles

Producer(s) Cohen, Emanuel
Director(s) Taurog, Norman
Screenwriter(s) Glazer, Benjamin; Young, Waldemar; Johnson, Nunnally
Source(s) *Bellamy the Magnificent* (novel) Horniman, Roy

Cast Chevalier, Maurice; Twelvetrees, Helen; LeRoy, Baby; Michael, Gertrude; Horton, Edward Everett; Ames, Adrienne

Song(s) In a Park in Paree; Look What I've Got; Monsieur Baby [1]; Home Made Heaven; A Bedtime Story [2] (C/L: Towers, Leo; Leon, Harry; Nicholls, Horatio)

Notes [1] Also in LUCKY STARLETS. [2] Sheet music only.

400 ✦ BEEN DOWN SO LONG IT LOOKS LIKE UP TO ME
Paramount, 1971

Composer(s) Sherman, Garry
Lyricist(s) Pistilli, Gene

Producer(s) Rosenthal, Robert
Director(s) Young, Jeffrey
Screenwriter(s) Schlitt, Robert
Source(s) *Been Down So Long It Looks Like Up to Me* (novel) Farina, Richard

Cast Primus, Barry; DeCoff, Linda; Tyrrell, Susan; Downing, David; Coe, John; Davison, Bruce; Jabara, Paul; Julia, Raul; Norman, Zack; Murray the K

Song(s)   Been Down So Long; Play Something Slow; Roll Daddy Roll; It Was You; God Be with You (L: Hopkins, Linda; Pratcher, Mildred; Lane, Mildred); Lettin' Down an Old Friend

401 ✦ BEER AND PRETZELS
Metro–Goldwyn–Mayer, 1933

Cast   Healy, Ted; Howard - Fine and Howard [1]; Bonny

Song(s)   Steins on the Table (C: Goodhart, Al; L: Kahn, Gus)

Notes   Short subject. [1] Better known as the Three Stooges—Moe Howard, Larry Fine and Curly Howard.

402 ✦ THE BEGGAR'S OPERA
Warner Brothers, 1953

Musical Score   Bliss, Sir Arthur
Lyricist(s)   Fry, Christopher

Producer(s)   Olivier, Laurence; Wilcox, Herbert
Director(s)   Brooks, Peter
Screenwriter(s)   Cannan, Denis; Fry, Christopher
Source(s)   *The Beggar's Opera* (play) Gay, John

Cast   Holloway, Stanley; Devine, George; Clare, Mary; Seyler, Athene; Griffith, Hugh; Tutin, Dorothy; Anderson, Daphne; Olivier, Laurence

Notes   The cast was dubbed by Adele Leigh; Jennifer Vyvyan; Joan Cross; John Cameron and Bruce Boyce. Olivier sang his own songs. No cue sheet available.

403 ✦ THE BEGUILED
Universal, 1971

Musical Score   Schifrin, Lalo

Producer(s)   Siegel, Don
Director(s)   Siegel, Don
Screenwriter(s)   Sherry, John B.; Grice, Grimes
Source(s)   (novel) Cullinan, Thomas

Cast   Eastwood, Clint; Page, Geraldine; Hartman, Elizabeth; Harris, Jo Ann; Carr, Darleen; Mercer, Mae; Ferdin, Pamelyn

Song(s)   All My Troubles (C/L: Mercer, Mae); Joys of Living (C/L: Coster, Irwin)

404 ✦ BEHAVE YOURSELF
RKO, 1951

Musical Score   Harline, Leigh

Producer(s)   Wald, Jerry; Krasna, Norman
Director(s)   Beck, George
Screenwriter(s)   Beck, George

Cast   Granger, Farley; Winters, Shelley; Demarest, William; Sullivan, Francis L.; Gillmore, Margalo; Chaney, Lon; Conried, Hans; Cook Jr., Elisha; Anders, Glenn; Jenkins, Allen; Leonard, Sheldon

Song(s)   Behave Yourself (C/L: Ebsen, Buddy; Spence, Lew)

405 ✦ BEHIND CITY LIGHTS
Republic, 1945

Musical Score   Dubin, Joseph S.
Composer(s)   Styne, Jule

Producer(s)   Bercholz, Joseph
Director(s)   English, John
Screenwriter(s)   Weil, Richard
Source(s)   "Retour a L'Aube" (story) Baum, Vicki

Cast   Roberts, Lynne; Cookson, Peter; Cowan, Jerome; Dale, Esther; Terry, William; Killian, Victor; Olsen, Moroni; Forrest, William; Vogan, Emmett

Song(s)   If You're in Love (L: Loesser, Frank); A Change of Heart [1] (L: Adamson, Harold)

Notes   [1] Also in CHANGE OF HEART and HIT PARADE OF 1943.

406 ✦ BEHIND THE EIGHT BALL
Universal, 1942

Composer(s)   de Paul, Gene
Lyricist(s)   Raye, Don

Producer(s)   Benedict, Howard
Director(s)   Cline, Edward F.
Screenwriter(s)   Roberts, Stanley; Ronson, Mel

Cast   The Ritz Brothers; Bruce, Carol; Foran, Dick; Downs, Johnny; Sonny Dunham and His Orchestra

Song(s)   Riverboat Jamboree; Atlas Did It; We Ought to Dance; Keep 'Em Laughing; Mr. Five by Five [1]; Golden Wedding Day; Wasn't It Wonderful; The Bravest of the Brave

Notes   Titled OFF THE BEATEN TRACK internationally. There is also a vocal of "When My Baby Smiles at Me" by Andrew Sterling, Ted Lewis and Bill Munro. [1] Also in NEVER A DULL MOMENT.

407 ✦ BEHIND THE HEADLINES
RKO, 1937

Musical Score   Steiner, Max

Producer(s)   Reid, Cliff
Director(s)   Rossen, Robert
Screenwriter(s)   Hartmann, Edmund L.; Bren, J. Robert

Cast   Tracy, Lee; Gibson, Diana; Meek, Donald; Guilfoyle, Paul; Huston, Paul; Weaver, Doodles

Song(s) I Wish I Were a Fisherman [1] (C: Steiner, Max; L: Eliscu, Edward)

Notes [1] Also in STINGAREE.

408 ✦ BEHIND THE MAKE-UP
Paramount, 1930

Director(s) Milton, Robert [4]
Screenwriter(s) Watters, George Manker; Estabrook, Howard
Source(s) "The Feeder" (story) Cram, Mildred

Cast Powell, William; Francis, Kay; Lukas, Paul [3]; Skelly, Hal; Worth, Lillian; Wray, Fay

Song(s) My Pals (C: Coslow, Sam; L: Robin, Leo); I Will Remember You Will Forget (C/L: Coslow, Sam); Never Say Die (C: Chase, Newell; L: Robin, Leo); Give Me a Kiss Sweetheart [2] (C: Chase, Newell; L: Coslow, Sam); My Lucky Days Are Past [1] (L: Unknown); Hittin' the Sky [5] (C: Harling, W. Franke; L: Robin, Leo); Just a Kiss in the Moonlight (C: Chase, Newell; L: Robin, Leo; Coslow, Sam)

Notes [1] Arrangement of a traditional Russian song, "Oomerle Schastya Dne" by Paul Grey. [2] Not used. [3] Dubbed by Paul Grey. [4] Directed also by Dorothy Arzner. [5] Used instrumentally only. May not have been written for this film.

409 ✦ BEHIND THE MIKE
Universal, 1937

Musical Score Henderson, Charles

Producer(s) Brock, Lou
Director(s) Salkow, Sidney
Screenwriter(s) Trivers, Barry

Cast Gargan, William; Wilson, Don; Barrett, Judith

Song(s) Once You're in Love [1] (C: McHugh, Jimmy; L: Adamson, Harold)

Notes There is also a vocal of "I'm Nobody's Sweetheart Now" by Cliff Friend. [1] Also in NURSE FROM BROOKLYN.

410 ✦ BELIEVE IN ME
Metro–Goldwyn–Mayer, 1971

Musical Score Karlin, Fred

Producer(s) Chartoff, Robert; Winkler, Irwin
Director(s) Hagmann, Stuart
Screenwriter(s) Horovitz, Israel

Cast Sarrazin, Michael; Bisset, Jacqueline; Cypher, Jon; Garfield, Allen; Conway, Kevin; Fargas, Antonio; Ultra Violet; Kamen, Milt

Song(s) Believe in Me (C: Karlin, Fred; L: Kymry, Tylwyth)

Notes Formerly titled SPEED IS OF THE ESSENCE.

411 ✦ BELLE LE GRAND
Republic, 1951

Musical Score Young, Victor

Producer(s) Dwan, Allan
Director(s) Dwan, Allan
Screenwriter(s) Beauchamp, D.D.

Cast Ralston, Vera Hruba; Carroll, John; Lawrence, Muriel; Ching, William; Emerson, Hope; Withers, Grant; Chase, Stephen; Qualen, John; Morgan, Henry

Song(s) Voices of Spring (C: Strauss, Johann; L: de Prete, Lucia)

412 ✦ THE BELLE OF NEW YORK
Metro–Goldwyn–Mayer, 1951

Composer(s) Warren, Harry
Lyricist(s) Mercer, Johnny
Choreographer(s) Alton, Robert

Producer(s) Freed, Arthur
Director(s) Walters, Charles
Screenwriter(s) O'Brien, Robert; Elinson, Irving; Erskine, Chester
Source(s) *The Belle of New York* (play) Morton, Hugh

Cast Astaire, Fred; Vera-Ellen [2]; Main, Marjorie; Wynn, Keenan; Pearce, Alice; Sundberg, Clinton; Robbins, Gale

Song(s) When I'm Out with the Belle of New York; Let a Little Love Come In (C/L: Edens, Roger); Bachelor Dinner Song; Seeing's Believing; Baby Doll; Oops!; Thank You Mr. Currier, Thank You Mr. Ives (A Bride's Wedding Day Song); Naughty but Nice; I Wanna Be a Dancin' Man; I Love to Beat the Big Bass Drum [1]

Notes [1] Not used. [2] Dubbed by Anita Ellis.

413 ✦ BELLE OF OLD MEXICO
Republic, 1949

Composer(s) Kent, Walter
Lyricist(s) Kent, Walter

Producer(s) White, Edward J.
Director(s) Springsteen, R.G.

Cast Rodriguez, Estelita; Rockwell, Robert; Willock, Dave; Brooke, Hillary; Bates, Florence; Jones, Gordon

Song(s) Lost Now (C/L: Kent, Walter; Farrar, Walton); Oh That Rhythm; Yoyo, Yaya (C/L: Martins, Antonio C.); I'll Forget You; Making with the Conversation (C/L: Kent, Walter; Farrar, Walton)

414 ✦ BELLE OF THE NINETIES
Paramount, 1934

Composer(s) Johnston, Arthur
Lyricist(s) Coslow, Sam

Producer(s) LeBaron, William
Director(s) McCarey, Leo
Screenwriter(s) West, Mae

Cast West, Mae; Duke Ellington and His Orchestra; Pryor, Roger; Brown, Johnny Mack [2]; Donlan, James; Baker, Benny; Gargan, Edward

Song(s) How Can I Resist You [3] (C: Revel, Harry; L: Gordon, Mack); Creole Man [3] (C: Revel, Harry; L: Gordon, Mack); You Don't Know What You're Doin' to Me [5] (C: Revel, Harry; L: Gordon, Mack); Memphis Blues [4] (C: Handy, W.C.; L: Norton, George A.; Coslow, Sam); Hesitation Blues (C: Middleton, Scott; L: Smythe, Billy; Trent, Jo); I Met My Waterloo [3]; My Old Flame; I'm in Love with a Tattooed Man; My American Beauty; When a St. Louis Woman Comes Down to New Orleans (C: Johnston, Arthur; L: Austin, Gene; Coslow, Sam); You Can Have It Baby (L: Johnston, Arthur); Belle of the Nineties; Pom Tiddley Om Pom (C: Douglas, R.H.; L: Passmore, Walter; Coslow, Sam); Troubled Waters [1]; Meet the King (C/L: McCarey, Leo); Marahuana [7] [6]; Sympathizin' with Me [7] [8]; Were Your Ears Burning [7] [9]

Notes The production was first titled IT AIN'T NO SIN. [1] Based on spiritual "Troubled Waters." [2] Billed as John Mack Brown. [3] Considered for FOUR HOURS TO KILL. [4] Also in BIRTH OF THE BLUES but with Frank Loesser revising the lyrics. [5] Not used in FOUR HOURS TO KILL. [6] Used in MURDER AT THE VANITIES. [7] Not used. [8] Also not used in COLLEGE HUMOR. Used instrumentally in YOU'RE TELLING ME. [9] Used in SHOOT THE WORKS. Also not used in SHE LOVES ME NOT.

415 ✦ BELLE OF THE YUKON
RKO, 1944

Musical Score Lange, Arthur
Composer(s) Van Heusen, James
Lyricist(s) Burke, Johnny
Choreographer(s) Loper, Don

Producer(s) Seiter, William A.
Director(s) Seiter, William A.
Screenwriter(s) Grant, James Edward

Cast Scott, Randolph; Lee, Gypsy Rose; Shore, Dinah; Marshall, William; Burns, Bob; Winninger, Charles; Williams, Guinn "Big Boy"; Armstrong, Robert; Bates, Florence; McKay, Wanda; Lilian, Victor

Song(s) Belle of the Yukon; Ev'ry Girl Is Diff'rent; Like Someone in Love; Sleigh Ride in July; Ballad of Millicent Devere [1]

Notes There is also a vocal of "I Can't Tell Why I Love You, But I Do, Do, Do" by Gus Edwards and Will D. Cobb. [1] Sheet music only.

416 ✦ BELLES ON THEIR TOES
Twentieth Century–Fox, 1952

Producer(s) Engel, Samuel G.
Director(s) Levin, Henry
Screenwriter(s) Ephron, Henry; Ephron, Phoebe

Source(s) *Belles on Their Toes* (book) Gilbreth Jr., Frank B.; Carey, Ernestine Gilbreth

Cast Crain, Jeanne; Loy, Myrna; Paget, Debra; Hunter, Jeffrey; Arnold, Edward; Carmichael, Hoagy; Bates, Barbara; Arthur, Robert; Felton, Verna

Song(s) Saginaw (C: Daniel, Eliot; L: Ephron, Phoebe; Ephron, Henry); Beans (C/L: Gordon, Mack); The Farmer in the Dell (C: Traditional; L: Ephron, Phoebe; Ephron, Henry)

Notes There are also brief vocals of popular tunes.

417 ✦ BELLS ARE RINGING
Metro–Goldwyn–Mayer, 1960

Musical Score Previn, Andre
Composer(s) Styne, Jule
Lyricist(s) Comden, Betty; Green, Adolph
Choreographer(s) O'Curran, Charles

Producer(s) Freed, Arthur
Director(s) Minnelli, Vincente
Screenwriter(s) Comden, Betty; Green, Adolph
Source(s) *Bells Are Ringing* (musical) Comden, Betty; Green, Adolph; Styne, Jule

Cast Holliday, Judy [3]; Martin, Dean; Clark, Fred; Foy Jr., Eddie; Stapleton, Jean [3]; Storey, Ruth; Clark, Dort [3]; Gorshin, Frank; Allen, Valerie; Peck, Steven; Roberts, Ralph; West, Bernie [3]; Mulligan, Gerry; Linden, Hal [4]

Song(s) Bells Are Ringing; It's a Perfect Relationship; Do It Yourself [1]; It's a Simple Little System; Better Than a Dream [5]; I Met a Girl; I Love Your Sunny Teeth [2]; Oh How It Hurts [2]; Hot and Cold [2]; The Midas Touch; Mississippi Steamboat [2]; Mu Cha Cha; Just in Time; Drop That Name; I'm Going Back; Don't Thank Me [2]; To Love and to Lose [1] [6]; My Guiding Star [7]; Is It a Crime [8]; Where in the World [1] [6]

Notes [1] Only songs written for this film. [2] These are short (under 20 seconds) songs, which the songwriting dentist writes, and are from the Broadway show. [3] From original cast. [4] From Broadway cast as understudy to and replacement for Sidney Chaplin. [5] Interpolated into Broadway show after opening. [6] Not used. [7] Used instrumentally only. [8] Deleted from final print.

418 ✦ BELLS OF CAPISTRANO
Republic, 1942

Producer(s) Grey, Harry
Director(s) Morgan, William
Screenwriter(s) Kimble, Lawrence

Cast Autry, Gene; Burnette, Smiley; Grey, Virginia; Littlefield, Lucien; Conway, Morgan

Song(s) Forgive Me (C: Ager, Milton; L: Yellen, Jack); At Sundown (C/L: Donaldson, Walter); Fort Worth Jail

(C/L: Rinehart, Richard); In Old Capistrano (C/L: Charleston, Jerry; Stryker, Fred); Don't Bite the Hand That's Feeding You (C/L: Hoier, Thomas; Morgan, James)

Notes   No cue sheet available.

419 ✦ BELLS OF CORONADO
Republic, 1949

Composer(s)   Willing, Foy
Lyricist(s)   Robin, Sid

Producer(s)   White, Edward J.
Director(s)   Witney, William
Screenwriter(s)   Nibley, Sloan

Cast   Rogers, Roy; Trigger; Evans, Dale; Brady, Pat; Withers, Grant; Foy Willing and the Riders of the Purple Sage

Song(s)   Got No Time for the Blues; Bells of Coronado [1]; Save a Smile (for a Rainy Day)

Notes   [1] Spanish lyrics by Aaron Gonzalez.

420 ✦ BELLS OF ROSARITA
Republic, 1945

Choreographer(s)   Ceballos, Larry

Producer(s)   White, Eddy
Director(s)   McDonald, Frank
Screenwriter(s)   Townley, Jack

Cast   Rogers, Roy; Trigger; Hayes, George "Gabby"; Evans, Dale; Mara, Adele; Withers, Grant; Richards, Addison; Barcroft, Roy; Martin, Janet; Boychoir, Robert M.; Bob Nolan and the Sons of the Pioneers; Elliott, Wild Bill; Lane, Allan; Barry, Donald; Carson, Sunset; Livingston, Robert

Song(s)   The Bugler's Lullaby (C: Bert, Betty; L: Mitchell, Robert); Bells of Rosarita (C/L: Elliott, Jack); Under a Blanket of Blue (C/L: Levinson, Jerry; Symes, Marty; Neiburg, Al J.); Swinging Down the Road (C: Scott, Raymond; L: Tobias, Harry); Gonna Build a Fence Around Texas (C: Olsen, George; L: Friend, Cliff; Phillips, Katherine); Michael Finnegan (C: Traditional; L: Mitchell, Robert); When the Circus Came to Town [1] (C/L: Eaton, Jimmy; Shand, Terry); Trail Herding Cowboy (C/L: Nolan, Bob)

Notes   [1] Also in VILLAGE BARN DANCE.

421 ✦ THE BELLS OF ST. MARY'S
RKO, 1945

Musical Score   Dolan, Robert Emmett

Producer(s)   McCarey, Leo
Director(s)   McCarey, Leo
Screenwriter(s)   Nichols, Dudley

Cast   Crosby, Bing; Bergman, Ingrid; Travers, Henry; Carroll, Joan; Sleeper, Martha; Gargan, William; Donnelly, Ruth; Williams, Rhys

Song(s)   Aren't You Glad You're You (C: Van Heusen, James; L: Burke, Johnny); The Bells of St. Mary's (C: Adams, A. Emmett; L: Furber, Douglas); In the Land of the Beginning Again [1] (C: Clarke, Grant; L: Meyer, George W.)

Notes   Sequel to GOING MY WAY. There is also a vocal of the traditional song "Varvinda Friska Leka Och Hviska." [1] Written in 1918.

422 ✦ BELLS OF SAN ANGELO
Republic, 1947

Composer(s)   Elliott, Jack
Lyricist(s)   Elliott, Jack

Producer(s)   White, Edward J.
Director(s)   Witney, William
Screenwriter(s)   Nibley, Sloan

Cast   Rogers, Roy; Evans, Dale; Devine, Andy; McGuire, John; Hytten, Olaf; Sharpe, David; Leiber, Fritz; Patterson, Hank; Bob Nolan and the Sons of the Pioneers; Acuff, Eddie; Toones, Fred S.

Song(s)   Bells of San Angelo [1]; Hot Lead (C/L: Spencer, Tim); Cowboy's Dream of Heaven [2]; I Love the West; Early in the Morning; Lazy Days (C/L: Spencer, Tim)

Notes   [1] Spanish lyrics by Aaron Gonzalez. [2] Also in OLD OVERLAND TRAIL.

423 ✦ BELOVED INFIDEL
Twentieth Century–Fox, 1959

Musical Score   Waxman, Franz

Producer(s)   Wald, Jerry
Director(s)   King, Henry
Screenwriter(s)   Bartlett, Sy
Source(s)   *Beloved Infidel* (book) Graham, Sheila; Frank, Gerold

Cast   Peck, Gregory; Kerr, Deborah; Albert, Eddie; Ober, Philip

Song(s)   Beloved Infidel (C: Waxman, Franz; L: Webster, Paul Francis)

424 ✦ BELOW THE BELT
Atlantic Releasing, 1980

Musical Score   Fielding, Jerry
Composer(s)   Fielding, Jerry
Lyricist(s)   Fielding, Jerry; MacKechnie, David

Producer(s)   Miller, Joseph
Director(s)   Fowler, Robert
Screenwriter(s)   Fowler, Robert; Sonnett, Sherrie
Source(s)   *To Smithereens* (novel) Drexler, Rosalyn

Cast Baff, Regina; Becher, John C.; Burke, Mildred; Gammon, James; McGreevey, Annie; Townsend, K.C.

Song(s) She Is My Lady; To Smithereens; Way Down South; Say I'm Purdy; Don't Remember Wakin' Up that Way; We Ride in Limosines; Birmingalabamaham

Notes No cue sheet available.

425 ◆ BEN AND ME
Disney, 1953

Musical Score Wallace, Oliver

Director(s) Luske, Hamilton
Screenwriter(s) Hibler, Winston; Connell, Del; Sears, Ted
Voices Holloway, Sterling

Song(s) Ben and Me [1] (C/L: Wallace, Oliver)

Notes Cartoon. [1] Used instrumentally only.

426 ◆ BENEATH THE PLANET OF THE APES
Twentieth Century–Fox, 1970

Musical Score Rosenman, Leonard

Producer(s) Jacobs, Arthur P.
Director(s) Post, Ted
Screenwriter(s) Dehn, Paul

Cast Franciscus, James; Hunter, Kim; Evans, Maurice; Harrison, Linda; Richards, Paul; Buono, Victor; Corey, Jeff; Gomez, Thomas

Song(s) Psalm of Mendez (C: Rosenman, Leonard; L: Darby, Ken)

427 ◆ BENEATH THE TWELVE MILE REEF
Twentieth Century–Fox, 1953

Musical Score Herrmann, Bernard

Producer(s) Basker, Robert
Director(s) Webb, Robert D.
Screenwriter(s) Bezzerides, A.I.

Cast Wagner, Robert; Moore, Terry; Roland, Gilbert; Naish, J. Carrol; Boone, Richard; Clarke, Angela; Graves, Peter; Novello, Jay; Carey Jr., Harry

Song(s) Yiata—Yiata (Why—Why) (C/L: Harakas, James; Ladas, Andrew)

428 ◆ BENEATH WESTERN SKIES
Republic, 1944

Producer(s) Gray, Louis
Director(s) Bennett, Spencer Gordon
Screenwriter(s) De Mond, Albert; Williams, Bob

Cast Livingston, Bob; Burnette, Smiley; Laird, Effie; London, Tom; Miller, Charles; Jacquet, Frank; Mason, LeRoy; Strauch Jr., Joe

Song(s) Travelin' Man (C/L: Burnette, Smiley)

429 ◆ BENGAZI
RKO, 1955

Musical Score Webb, Roy

Producer(s) Wiesenthal, Sam; Tevlin, Eugene
Director(s) Brahm, John
Screenwriter(s) Bohem, Endre; Vittes, Louis

Cast Conte, Richard; McLaglen, Victor; Powers, Mala; Carlson, Richard; Erdman, Richard; Gonzales-Gonzales, Pedro; Brooke, Hillary

Song(s) She Was Made Only for Kisses (C/L: Webb, Roy); Bengazi [1] (C/L: Arnold, Murray)

Notes [1] Written for exploitation only.

430 ◆ BENJI THE HUNTED
Disney, 1987

Musical Score Box, Euel; Box, Betty

Producer(s) Vaughn, Ben
Director(s) Camp, Joe
Screenwriter(s) Camp, Joe

Cast Benji; Steagall, Red; Inn, Frank

Song(s) Too Many Yesterdays (C: Box, Euel; Box, Betty; L: Camp, Joe)

431 ◆ THE BENNY GOODMAN STORY
Universal, 1955

Producer(s) Rosenberg, Aaron
Director(s) Davies, Valentine
Screenwriter(s) Davies, Valentine

Cast Allen, Steve [1]; Reed, Donna; Gersten, Berta; James, Harry; Krupa, Gene; Tilton, Martha; Wilson, Teddy; Hampton, Lionel; Elman, Ziggy; Ory, Kid; Anderson, Herbert; Simon, Robert F.; Davis Jr., Sammy; Winslow, Dick; Truex, Barry; Averback, Hy

Notes There are no original songs written for this picture. The only vocal is "And the Angels Sing" by Johnny Mercer and Ziggy Elman. [1] Clarinet dubbed by Benny Goodman.

432 ◆ BERNARDINE
Twentieth Century–Fox, 1957

Composer(s) Mercer, Johnny
Lyricist(s) Mercer, Johnny

Producer(s) Engel, Samuel G.
Director(s) Levin, Henry
Screenwriter(s) Reeves, Theodore
Source(s) *Bernardine* (play) Chase, Mary

Cast Boone, Pat; Moore, Terry; Gaynor, Janet; Jagger, Dean; Sargent, Richard; Drury, James; Burns, Ronnie; Abel, Walter; Schafer, Natalie; Jewell, Isabel; Angold, Edith

Song(s) Bernardine (1); Technique (1); Bernardine (2) [1] (C/L: Rome, Harold); Technique (1) [1] (C/L: Rome, Harold); Bernardine (3) (C/L: Rome, Harold)

Notes There is also a vocal of "Love Letters in the Sand" by J. Fred Coots, Nick Kenny and Charles Kenny. [1] Harold Rome had written two songs titled "Bernardine" and one titled "Technique" for the picture but they were "Deemed unacceptable" and returned to him. Mercer was hired to do the score.

433 ✦ BERRY GORDY'S THE LAST DRAGON

See THE LAST DRAGON.

434 ✦ BERT RIGBY, YOU'RE A FOOL
Warner Brothers, 1989

Producer(s) Shapiro, George
Director(s) Reiner, Carl
Screenwriter(s) Reiner, Carl

Cast Lindsay, Robert; Coltrane, Robbie; Bradshaw, Cathryn; Gayle, Jackie; Kirby, Bruno; Bernsen, Corbin; Bancroft, Anne

Song(s) That's How I Turned Out to Be Mister Elvis P. (C/L: Brown, Earl); Whitegold Beer Commercial (C/L: Brown, Earl); They've Opened the Ritz Tonight (C/L: Brown, Earl)

Notes No cue sheet available. Vocals include "The Continental" by Con Conrad and Herb Magidson; "Isn't It Romantic" by Richard Rodgers and Lorenz Hart; "You Are My Lucky Star," "Good Morning," "You Were Meant for Me," "Broadway Rhythm," "Broadway Melody" and "Singin' in the Rain" by Nacio Herb Brown and Arthur Freed; "Fit As a Fiddle" by Al Goodhart, Arthur Freed and Al Hoffman; "Moses Supposes" by Betty Comden, Adolph Green and Roger Edens; "My Little Ukelele" by Jack Cottrell; "I'll See You Again" by Noel Coward; "All of You" by Cole Porter; "Dream a Little Dream" by Wilbur Schwandt, Fabian Andre and Gus Kahn and "Puttin' on the Ritz" by Irving Berlin.

435 ✦ BEST FOOT FORWARD
Metro–Goldwyn–Mayer, 1943

Musical Score Hayton, Lennie
Composer(s) Blane, Ralph; Martin, Hugh
Lyricist(s) Blane, Ralph; Martin, Hugh
Choreographer(s) Walters, Charles

Producer(s) Freed, Arthur
Director(s) Buzzell, Edward
Screenwriter(s) Brecher, Irving; Finklehoffe, Fred F.
Source(s) *Best Foot Forward* (musical) Martin, Hugh; Blane, Ralph; Holm, John Cecil

Cast Ball, Lucille [2]; Gaxton, William; Weidler, Virginia; Dix, Tommy [1]; Allyson, June [1]; De Haven, Gloria; Walker, Nancy [1]; Bowers, Kenny [1]; Jordan, Jack [1]; Harry James and His Music Makers; Wills, Chill

Song(s) Buckle Down, Winsocki; Wish I May; Three Men on a Date; Ev'ry Time; The Three B's; My First Promise; Alive and Kickin'; You're Lucky; That's How I Love the Blues [3]; What Do You Think I Am [3] [4]; I Cried for You [3] [5] (C/L: Freed, Arthur; Arnheim, Gus; Lyman, Abe)

Notes There are also the instrumentals "Two O'Clock Jump" played by Harry James and Rimsky-Korsakoff's "Flight of the Bumblebee." Martin and Blane actually wrote songs separately, not together. [1] From Broadway cast. [2] Dubbed by Gloria Grafton. [3] Deleted from final print. [4] Prerecording used in BROADWAY RHYTHM. [5] Sequence used in BATHING BEAUTY.

436 ✦ BEST FRIENDS
Warner Brothers, 1982

Musical Score Legrand, Michel
Composer(s) Legrand, Michel
Lyricist(s) Bergman, Alan; Bergman, Marilyn

Producer(s) Jewison, Norman; Palmer, Patrick
Director(s) Jewison, Norman
Screenwriter(s) Curtin, Valerie; Levinson, Barry

Cast Reynolds, Burt; Hawn, Goldie; Tandy, Jessica; Hughes, Barnard; Lindley, Audra; Wynn, Keenan; Silver, Ron; Locatell, Carol; Libertini, Richard

Song(s) How Do You Keep the Music Playing?; Think About Love

437 ✦ THE BEST HOUSE IN LONDON
Metro–Goldwyn–Mayer, 1969

Musical Score Spoliansky, Mischa
Composer(s) Cass, Ronnie; Myers, Peter
Lyricist(s) Cass, Ronnie; Myers, Peter

Producer(s) Breen, Philip; Unger, Kurt
Director(s) Saville, Philip
Screenwriter(s) Norden, Denis

Cast Hemmings, David; Pettet, Joanna; Sanders, George; Robin, Dany; Mitchell, Warren; Fraser, Bill; O'Shea, Tessie; Angers, Avril; Cleese, John; Lloyd Pack, Charles; Friday, Carol; Rogers, Marie

Song(s) Little Pussy; Birds of London Town; Wandering Romanies (C/L: Cass, Ronnie)

438 ✦ THE BEST LITTLE WHOREHOUSE IN TEXAS
Universal–RKO, 1982

Musical Score Williams, Patrick
Composer(s) Hall, Carol
Lyricist(s) Hall, Carol
Choreographer(s) Stevens, Tony

Producer(s) Miller, Thomas L.; Milkis, Edward K.; Boyett, Robert
Director(s) Higgins, Colin

Screenwriter(s) Higgins, Colin; King, Larry; Masterson, Peter
Source(s) *The Best Little Whorehouse in Texas* (musical) Hall, Carol; King, Larry; Masterson, Peter

Cast Reynolds, Burt; Parton, Dolly; Durning, Charles; DeLuise, Dom; Nabors, Jim; Mandan, Robert; Nettleton, Lois; Merritt, Theresa; Beery Jr., Noah

Song(s) Twenty Fans [1]; A Lil' Ole Bitty Pissant Country Place [1]; Sneakin' Around (C/L: Parton, Dolly); Watch Dog Theme [1]; Texas Has a Whorehouse in It [1]; Aggie Song and Dance [1]; Sidestep [1]; Hard Candy Christmas [1]; I Will Always Love You (C/L: Parton, Dolly)

Notes [1] From original Broadway musical.

439 ◆ BEST OF ENEMIES
Fox, 1933

Composer(s) Jason, Will; Burton, Val
Lyricist(s) Jason, Will; Burton, Val

Director(s) James, Rian
Screenwriter(s) Mintz, Sam; James, Rian

Cast Rogers, Charles "Buddy"; Nixon, Marian; Morgan, Frank; Nissen, Greta

Song(s) All American Girls; Hans and Gretchen; We Belong to Alma [1]

Notes There are also vocal renditions of "Gypsy Hearts" by Bryan and Stark and "Oh You Beautiful Doll" by Nat D. Ayer and A. Seymour Brown. [1] Not on cue sheet.

440 ◆ THE BEST OF EVERYTHING
Twentieth Century–Fox, 1959

Musical Score Newman, Alfred

Producer(s) Wald, Jerry
Director(s) Negulesco, Jean
Screenwriter(s) Sommer, Edith; Rubin, Mann
Source(s) *The Best of Everything* (novel) Jaffe, Rona

Cast Crawford, Joan; Lange, Hope; Boyd, Stephen; Parker, Suzy; Jourdan, Louis; Hyer, Martha; Evans, Robert; Aherne, Brian

Song(s) The Best of Everything (C: Newman, Alfred; L: Cahn, Sammy); Lonely Lover [1] (C: Newman, Alfred; L: Cahn, Sammy)

Notes [1] Not used.

441 ◆ THE BEST OF TIMES
Universal, 1986

Musical Score Rubinstein, Arthur B.

Producer(s) Carroll, Gordon
Director(s) Spottiswoode, Roger
Screenwriter(s) Shelton, Ron

Cast Williams, Robin; Russell, Kurt; Reed, Pamela; Palance, Holly; Moffat, Donald; Whitton, Margaret;

Walsh, M. Emmet; Scott, Donovan; Armstrong, R.G.; Taylor, Dub; Ballantine, Carl; Freeman, Kathleen; Cameron, Kirk; Lively, Robyn

Song(s) He's Sure the Boy I Love (C/L: Mann, Barry; Weil, Cynthia); Don't Say Nothin' Bad (About My Baby) [1] (C/L: Goffin, Gerry; King, Carole)

Notes There are also vocals of "Remember Then" by Stan Vincent, Beverly Ross and Tony Powers; "The First Time Ever I Saw Your Face" by Ewan Mac Coll; "Close to You" by Hal David and Burt Bacharach and "Land of Hope and Glory" by Sir Edward Elgar and Arthur Benson. [1] Also in SHAMPOO.

442 ◆ THE BEST THINGS IN LIFE ARE FREE
Twentieth Century–Fox, 1956

Choreographer(s) Alexander, Rod

Producer(s) Ephron, Henry
Director(s) Curtiz, Michael
Screenwriter(s) Bowers, William; Ephron, Phoebe

Cast MacRae, Gordon; Dailey, Dan; Borgnine, Ernest; North, Sheree [1]; Noonan, Tommy; Vye, Murvyn; Avery, Phyllis; Keating, Larry; Galento, Tony; Brooks, Norman; d'Amboise, Jacques; Arlen, Roxanne

Notes There were no songs written for this picture. Songs by Ray Henderson, B.G. DeSylva and Lew Brown to receive vocal treatment in this film are: "The Best Things in Life Are Free," "Just a Memory," 'Here I Am—Broken Hearted," "Button Up Your Overcoat," "This Is the Mrs.," "Lucky Day," "Lucky in Love," "Good News," "It All Depends on You," "Don't Hold Everything," "The Black Bottom," "Red Hot Chicago," "One More Time," "You Try Somebody Else," "The Birth of the Blues," "Sonny Boy," "Together," "If I Had a Talking Picture of You," "Sunny Side Up" and "Without Love." [1] Dubbed by Eileen Wilson.

443 ◆ BETRAYAL
Twentieth Century–Fox, 1983

Musical Score Moran, Mike; Muldowney, Dominic

Producer(s) Spiegel, Sam
Director(s) Jones, David
Screenwriter(s) Pinter, Harold
Source(s) *Betrayal* (play) Pinter, Harold

Cast Irons, Jeremy; Kingsley, Ben; Hodge, Patricia; Elgar, Avril

Song(s) Head Bangers No. 2 (C/L: Moran, Mike)

444 ◆ BETRAYED (1954)
Metro–Goldwyn–Mayer, 1954

Musical Score Goehr, Walter

Director(s) Reinhardt, Gottfried
Screenwriter(s) Millar, Ronald; Froeschel, George

Cast Gable, Clark; Turner, Lana; Mature, Victor; Calhern, Louis; Hasse, O.E.; Hyde-White, Wilfrid; Carmichael, Ian; Culver, Roland

Song(s) Betrayed (C: Goehr, Walter; L: Millar, Ronald); Johnny Come Home (C: Goehr, Walter; L: Millar, Ronald)

Notes No cue sheet available.

445 ✦ BETRAYED (1988)
United Artists, 1988

Musical Score Conti, Bill

Producer(s) Winkler, Irwin
Director(s) Costa-Gavras
Screenwriter(s) Eszterhas, Joe

Cast Winger, Debra; Berenger, Tom; Heard, John; Blair, Betsy; Mahoney, John; Levine, Ted; DeMunn, Jeffrey; Hall, Albert; Clennon, David; Swan, Robert; Libertini, Richard

Song(s) The Devil's Right Hand (C/L: Earle, Steve); The Race Is On (C/L: Rollins, Don)

446 ✦ BETTER OFF DEAD
Warner Brothers, 1985

Composer(s) Hine, Rupert
Lyricist(s) Merdur, Torrence

Producer(s) Jaffe, Michael
Director(s) Holland, "Savage" Steve
Screenwriter(s) Holland, "Savage" Steve

Cast Cusack, John; Stiers, David Ogden; Franklin, Diane; Darby, Kim; Wyss, Amanda; Armstrong, Curtis; Schiavelli, Vincent; Waterbury, Laura; Schneider, Daniel

Song(s) One Way Love (C/L: Goldstein, Steve; Hitchings, Duane; Krampf, Craig; Nelson, Eric); A Little Luck (C/L: Rubin, Angie); I've Been Arrested By You; Dancing in Isolation; Come to Your Rescue

Notes No cue sheet available.

447 ✦ BETTY BOOP CARTOONS
Paramount, 1932

Song(s) Betty Boop (C: Green, Johnny; L: Heyman, Edward)

Notes Animated shorts.

448 ✦ BETTY CO-ED
Columbia, 1946

Producer(s) Katzman, Sam
Director(s) Dreifuss, Arthur
Screenwriter(s) Dreifuss, Arthur; Plympton, George

Cast Porter, Jean; Savitt, Jan; Mills, Shirley; Mason, William; La Planche, Rosemary; Moran, Jackie; Meader, George

Song(s) Zig Me with a Gentle Zag [3] (C/L: Cherkose, Eddie; Press, Jacques); Put the Blame on Mame [1] (C/L: Roberts, Allan; Fisher, Doris); You Gotta Do Whatcha Gotta Do [2] (C/L: Roberts, Allan; Fisher, Doris)

Notes There is also a vocal of "Betty Co-Ed" by Rudy Vallee and J.P. Fogarty. [1] Also in GILDA and SENIOR PROM. [2] Also in TALK ABOUT A LADY. [3] Used instrumentally in SWEETHEART OF THE CAMPUS.

449 ✦ BETWEEN TWO WOMEN
Metro–Goldwyn–Mayer, 1944

Choreographer(s) Bate, Jeannette

Producer(s) Wilson, Carey
Director(s) Goldbeck, Willis
Screenwriter(s) Ruskin, Harry

Cast Johnson, Van; Barrymore, Lionel; De Haven, Gloria; Wynn, Keenan; Maxwell, Marilyn; Kruger, Alma; Luke, Keye; Ames, Leon

Song(s) Look at Me (C/L: Brent, Earl)

450 ✦ BEVERLY HILLS COP
Paramount, 1984

Musical Score Faltermeyer, Harold

Producer(s) Simpson, Don; Bruckheimer, Jerry
Director(s) Brest, Martin
Screenwriter(s) Petrie Jr., Daniel

Cast Murphy, Eddie; Eilbacher, Lisa; Berkoff, Steven; Hill, Gilbert R.; Cox, Ronny; Reiser, Paul; Reinhold, Judge; Ashton, John

Song(s) The Heat Is On [1] (C: Faltermeyer, Harold L: Forsey, Keith); New Attitude [1] (C/L: Robinson, Sharon; Gilutin, Jon; Hull, Bunny); Stir It Up [1] (C/L: Sembello, Danny; L: Willis, Allee)

Notes Only songs written for movie included. [1] None of these songs appear as visual vocals. They are strictly background songs.

451 ✦ BEVERLY HILLS COP II
Paramount, 1987

Musical Score Faltermeyer, Harold

Producer(s) Simpson, Don; Bruckheimer, Jerry
Director(s) Scott, Tony
Screenwriter(s) Ferguson, Larry; Skaaren, Warren

Cast Murphy, Eddie; Reinhold, Judge; Prochnow, Jurgen; Cox, Ronny; Ashton, John; Nielsen, Brigitte; Garfield, Allen; Stockwell, Dean; Gottfried, Gilbert; Reiser, Paul

Song(s) Shakedown [1] (C/L: Faltermeyer, Harold; Forsey, Keith; Seger, Bob); Better Way (C/L: Cymone, Andre); I Can't Stand It (C/L: Jones, David Allen; Payne, Harold); I Want Your Sex (C/L: Michael, George); Love/Hate (C/L: Cymone, Andre; Jackson, Julian); Be There (C/L: Willis, Allee; Golde, Franne); 36 Lovers (C/L: Eaton, John; Riley Jr., Melvin); All Revved Up (C: Moroder, Giorgio; L: Whitlock, Tom); Hold On (C/L: Wirrick, James); In Deep (C/L: Sexton, Charlie; Wilk, Scott)

Notes All background vocal use. [1] From BEVERLY HILLS COP.

452 ✦ BEWARE, MY LOVELY
RKO, 1952

Musical Score Stevens, Leith

Producer(s) Young, Collier
Director(s) Horner, Harry
Screenwriter(s) Dinelli, Mel
Source(s) "The Man" (story/play) Dinelli, Mel

Cast Lupino, Ida; Ryan, Robert; Holmes, Taylor; Whiting, Barbara; Williams, James; Whitehead, O.Z.; Pollack, Dee

Song(s) I Found a Friend (C/L: Bennett, Norman)

453 ✦ BEYOND A REASONABLE DOUBT
RKO, 1956

Musical Score Gilbert, Herschel Burke

Producer(s) Friedlob, Bert
Director(s) Lang, Fritz
Screenwriter(s) Morrow, Douglas

Cast Andrews, Dana; Fontaine, Joan; Blackmer, Sidney; Franz, Arthur; Bourneuf, Philip; Binns, Edward; Strudwick, Shepperd; Raymond, Robin; Nichols, Barbara

Song(s) Beyond a Reasonable Doubt (C: Gilbert, Herschel Burke; L: Perry, Alfred)

454 ✦ BEYOND GLORY
Paramount, 1948

Musical Score Young, Victor

Producer(s) Fellows, Robert
Director(s) Farrow, John
Screenwriter(s) Latimer, Jonathan; Warren, Charles Marquis; Haines, William Wister

Cast Ladd, Alan; Reed, Donna; Coulouris, George; Travers, Henry; Murphy, Audie

Song(s) Beyond Glory [1] (C/L: Livingston, Jay; Evans, Ray)

Notes Originally titled THE LONG GREY LINE. [1] Written for exploitation only.

455 ✦ BEYOND THE BLUE HORIZON
Paramount, 1942

Musical Score Young, Victor
Composer(s) Styne, Jule
Lyricist(s) Loesser, Frank

Producer(s) Bell, Monta
Director(s) Santell, Alfred
Screenwriter(s) Butler, Frank

Cast Lamour, Dorothy; Haley, Jack; Denning, Richard; Abel, Walter; Morison, Patricia; Gifford, Frances; Patterson, Elizabeth; Todd, Ann

Song(s) Malay Love Song [1]; Pagan Lullaby [2]; A Full Moon and an Empty Heart (C: Revel, Harry; L: Greene, Mort)

Notes The film was known as MALAYA, PAGAN LULLABY and HER JUNGLE MATE before release. [1] Unused. [2] Recorded but apparently not used.

456 ✦ BEYOND THE LAW
Columbia, 1934

Producer(s) Briskin, Irving
Director(s) Lederman, D. Ross
Screenwriter(s) Shumate, Harold

Cast McCoy, Tim; Grey, Shirley; Richards, Addison

Song(s) Are You Mine [1] (C/L: Rosoff, Charles)

Notes [1] Used instrumentally only. Also used instrumentally in ABOVE THE CLOUDS and sung in the Republic picture WATERFRONT LADY.

457 ✦ BEYOND THE PECOS
Universal, 1944

Producer(s) Drake, Oliver
Director(s) Hillyer, Lambert
Screenwriter(s) Cohen, Bennett R.

Cast Cameron, Rod; Holt, Jennifer; Dew, Eddie

Song(s) Ridin' High (C/L: Tower, J. Leon; Coleman, Lila M.; LaFranz, Sophia Kroeger); Dusty Trail [2] (C/L: Sheely, Betty; Sheely, C. Whitney; List, Bud); The Call of the Range [1] (C: Rosen, Milton; L: Carter, Everett)

Notes [1] Also in FRONTIER LAW, GUNMAN'S CODE and MAN FROM MONTANA (1941). [2] Also in SHADY LADY.

458 ◆ BEYOND THE PURPLE HILLS
Columbia, 1950

Producer(s) Schaefer, Armand
Director(s) English, John
Screenwriter(s) Hall, Norman S.

Cast Autry, Gene; Buttram, Pat; Dennison, Jo; Beddoe, Don; Champion; O'Malley, Pat

Song(s) Dear Hearts and Gentle People (C: Fain, Sammy; L: Hilliard, Bob); Beyond the Purple Hills (C/L: Unknown); The Girl I Left Behind Me (C/L: Unknown)

Notes No cue sheet available.

459 ◆ BEYOND THE RIO GRANDE (1930)
Biltmore Productions, 1930

Producer(s) Freuler, John R.
Director(s) Webb, Harry
Screenwriter(s) Krusada, Carl

Cast Perrin, Jack; Farnum, Franklyn; Burt, Charline; Tansey, Emma; Bill Jr., Buffalo

Song(s) Beyond the Rio Grande (C/L: Taylor, Harry)

Notes No cue sheet available.

460 ◆ BEYOND THE RIO GRANDE (1945)

See MEXICANA.

461 ◆ BEYOND THE SACRAMENTO
Columbia, 1940

Composer(s) Drake, Milton
Lyricist(s) Drake, Milton

Director(s) Hillyer, Lambert
Screenwriter(s) Ward, Luci

Cast Elliott, Bill; Keyes, Evelyn; Taylor, Dub; Beddoe, Don

Song(s) When You're Ridin' for the Law; The West Gets Under My Skin

462 ◆ BEYOND THE VALLEY OF THE DOLLS
Twentieth Century–Fox, 1970

Musical Score Phillips, Stu; Loose, Bill
Composer(s) Phillips, Stu
Lyricist(s) Stone, Bob

Producer(s) Meyer, Russ
Director(s) Meyer, Russ
Screenwriter(s) Ebert, Roger

Cast Read, Dolly; Myers, Cynthia; McBroom, Marcia; LaZar, John; Blodgett, Michael; Gurian, David; Williams, Edy

Song(s) Come with the Gentle People; Find It (C: Carey, Lynn); Incense and Peppermint (C: Carter, John; L: Gilbert, Tim); Beyond This Valley [1]; Girl from the City (C/L: Marshall, Paul); I'm Comin' Home (C/L: Marshall, Paul); Sweet Talking Candy Man; In the Long Run; Look Up at the Bottom; Beyond the Valley of the Dolls; Where Do I Fit [1] (C: Loose, Bill; Phillips, Stu); Once I Had Love [1] (L: Carey, Lynn); Ampersand [2] (L: Phillips, Stu)

Notes [1] Used instrumentally only.

463 ◆ BEYOND TOMORROW
RKO, 1940

Musical Score Tours, Frank

Producer(s) Garmes, Lee
Director(s) Sutherland, Edward
Screenwriter(s) Comandini, Adele

Cast Carlson, Richard; Parker, Jean; Vinson, Helen; Winninger, Charles; Carey, Harry; Smith, C. Aubrey

Song(s) It's Raining Dreams (C/L: Spina, Harold; Newman, Charles); Louisiana Lady (C/L: Tours, Frank)

464 ◆ BE YOURSELF!
United Artists, 1930

Producer(s) Schenck, Joseph M.
Director(s) Freeland, Thornton
Screenwriter(s) Freeland, Thornton; Marcin, Max
Source(s) *The Champ* (book) Jackson, Joseph

Cast Brice, Fanny; Armstrong, Robert; Astor, Gertrude; Green, Harry; Collins, G. Pat

Song(s) When a Woman Loves a Man (C: Rainger, Ralph; L: Rose, Billy); Cooking Breakfast for the One I Love (C: Greer, Jesse; L: Rose, Billy; Tobias, Henry); Kicking a Hole in the Sky (C: Greer, Jesse; L: Rose, Billy; Macdonald, Ballard); Sasha the Passion of the Pascha (C: Greer Jesse; L: Rose, Billy; Macdonald, Ballard; Greer, Jesse); Baby Be Yourself [1] (C: Duke, Vernon; L: Harburg, E.Y.)

Notes No cue sheet available. [1] Not used.

465 ◆ BIG
Twentieth Century–Fox, 1988

Musical Score Shore, Howard

Producer(s) Brooks, James L.; Greenhut, Robert
Director(s) Marshall, Penny
Screenwriter(s) Ross, Gary; Spielberg, Anne

Cast Hanks, Tom; Perkins, Elizabeth; Loggia, Robert; Heard, John; Rushton, Jared; Moscow, David; Lovitz, Jon; Ruehl, Mercedes; Clark, Josh

Song(s) We Go Together (C/L: Frankel, Joel); Workin' for a Livin' (C/L: Cipollina, Mario; Colla, Johnny); Forget Me Nots (C/L: Rushen, Patrice;

Washington, Freddie); It's In Everyone of Us (C/L: Pomeranz, David)

Notes Only songs of more than a minute duration listed. All are background vocals. It is not known if any were written for the film.

466 ✦ THE BIGAMIST
Filmakers, 1953

Musical Score Stevens, Leith

Producer(s) Young, Collier
Director(s) Lupino, Ida
Screenwriter(s) Young, Collier

Cast O'Brien, Edmond; Fontaine, Joan; Lupino, Ida; Gwenn, Edmund; Darwell, Jane; Tobey, Kenneth

Song(s) It Wasn't the Stars (C: Dennis, Matt; L: Gillam, Dave)

467 ✦ THE BIG BEAT
Universal, 1958

Producer(s) Cowan, Will
Director(s) Cowan, Will
Screenwriter(s) Harmon, David P.

Cast The Del Vikings; The Diamonds; Domino, Antoine "Fats"; The Four Aces; James, Harry; The Lancers; Martin, Freddy; Morgan, Russ; The Mills Brothers; The Shearing Quintet; The Thompson Singers; The Cal Tjader Quartet; Martin, Andra; Grant, Gogi; Stone, Jeffrey; Rose Marie; Conried, Hans; Miller, Howard

Song(s) The Big Beat (C/L: Bartholomew, Dave; Domino, Antoine "Fats"); As I Love You (C/L: Livingston, Jay; Evans, Ray); You're Being Followed (C: Altman, Arthur; L: Tobias, Charles); Can't Wait (C/L: Saxon, Grace; Mirkin, Barry); You've Never Been in Love (C/L: Lloyd, Jack; Copeland, Alan); It's Great When You're Doing a Show (C: Pola, Eddie; L: Pola, Eddie; Lloyd, Jack; Copeland, Alan); Where Mary Go (C/L: Lampert, Diane; Gluck Jr., John); Little Darlin' (C/L: Williams, Maurice); Lazy Love (C: Fields, Irving; L: Gasso, Bernard); I Waited So Long (C/L: Livingston, Jay; Evans, Ray); Take My Heart (C/L: Alberts, Al; Mahoney, Dave); Call Me (C: Fields, Irving; L: Gasso, Bernard; Fields, Irving)

468 ✦ THE BIG BONANZA
Republic, 1944

Producer(s) Schaefer, Armand
Director(s) White, Eddy
Screenwriter(s) McGowan, Dorrell; McGowan, Stuart; Gangelin, Paul

Cast Arlen, Richard; Livingston, Robert; Frazee, Jane; Hayes, George "Gabby"; Roberts, Lynne; Driscoll,

Bobby; Kerrigan, J.M.; Simpson, Russell; Reicher, Frank; Hickman, Cordell; Hale, Monte; King Jr., Charles

Song(s) When the Right Man Comes Along (C/L: Elliott, Jack)

469 ✦ THE BIG BOUNCE
Warner Brothers–Seven Arts, 1969

Musical Score Curb, Mike [1]; Hemric, Guy
Composer(s) Curb, Mike [1]; Hemric, Guy
Lyricist(s) Curb, Mike [1]; Hermric, Guy

Producer(s) Dozier, Robert
Director(s) March, Alex
Screenwriter(s) Dozier, Robert
Source(s) *The Big Bounce* (novel) Leonard, Elmore

Cast O'Neal, Ryan; Taylor-Young, Leigh; Daly, James; Heflin, Van; Grant, Lee

Song(s) When Somebody Cares For You; His Name (C/L: Curb, Mike [1]); The Big Bounce; Nancy's Theme; Once in a Lifetime (C/L: Curb, Mike [1]; Hemric, Guy; Styner, Jerry)

Notes All songs are background vocal use. [1] Billed as Michael Curb.

470 ✦ BIG BOY
Warner Brothers, 1930

Director(s) Crosland, Alan
Screenwriter(s) Wells, William K.; Vekroff, Perry
Source(s) *Big Boy* (musical) Atteridge, Harold; DeSylva, B.G.; Hanley, James F.; Meyer, Joseph

Cast Jolson, Al; Hale, Louise Closser; Hughes, Lloyd; Phillips, Eddie; Beery, Noah

Song(s) What Will I Do Without You? [2] (C: Burke, Joe; Dubin, Al); Tomorrow Is Another Day (C: Stept, Sam H.; Green, Bud); Liza Lee (C: Stept, Sam H.; L: Green, Bud); Down South [1] (C/L: Spaeth, Sigmund; Myddleton, George); The Handicap March (C: Rosey, George; L: Reed Jr., Dave); Hooray for Baby and Me (C/L: Mitchell, Sidney D.; Gottler, Archie; Meyer, George W.); Little Sunshine (C/L: Mitchell, Sidney D.; Gottler, Archie; Meyer, George W.)

Notes No cue sheet available. [1] Also in SHOW BOAT (1929) (Universal). [2] Also in THE GOLD DIGGERS OF BROADWAY and SALLY.

471 ✦ THE BIG BROADCAST (1932)
Paramount, 1932

Composer(s) Rainger, Ralph
Lyricist(s) Robin, Leo

Director(s) Tuttle, Frank
Screenwriter(s) Marion Jr., George
Source(s) *Wild Waves* (play) Manley, William Ford

Cast Erwin, Stuart; Crosby, Bing; Smith, Kate; Hyams, Leila; Lynn, Sharon; Barbier, George; Robertson, Ralph; Melish, Alex; Robinson, Dewey; Burns and Allen; The Boswell Sisters; Tracy, Arthur; Novis, Donald; Vincent Lopez and His Orchestra; Cab Calloway and His Orchestra

Song(s) Moon Mad [2]; Here Lies Love [1]; Soliloquy; Please [3]; The Boswell Weeps; Suicide Song; Sob Song; Auditions; Calloway Calling (inst.); Fanfare and Underscoring (inst.)

Notes Only original songs listed. There are also vocals of "Crazy People" by Edgar Leslie and James V. Monaco; "Kickin' the Gong Around" by Harold Arlen and Ted Koehler; "Tiger Rag" by the Original Dixieland Jazz Band and Harry DeCosta (also used instrumentally in IS EVERYBODY HAPPY, BIRTH OF THE BLUES, HAS ANYBODY SEEN MY GAL and NIGHT CLUB GIRL); "Where the Blue of the Night Meets the Gold of the Day" by Bing Crosby, Roy Turk and Fred E. Ahlert and "When the Moon Comes Over the Mountain" by Harry Woods and Howard Johnson (also in DINNER AT EIGHT and HELLO, EVERYBODY). Title clearance for "Living in a Fool's Paradise" was requested and disapproved since L. Wolfe Gilbert had written a song under the same name. The following numbers were filmed for the movie but not used: "Bugle Call Rag," "Piano Echoes," "Blue Rhythm" (played by the Vincent Lopez Orchestra), "Santa Lucia" and "O Sole Mio" (sung by Arthur Tracy) Cab Calloway singing "Reefer Man" (subsequently used in INTERNATIONAL HOUSE); The Boswell Sisters theme based on "Shout Sister Shout" and "Heebie Jeebie Blues" and the Mills Brothers singing "Old Man of the Mountain." [1] Also used in INTERNATIONAL HOUSE and TORCH SINGER. [2] Considered for FOUR HOURS TO KILL but not used. [3] Also in COLLEGE HUMOR.

472 ✦ THE BIG BROADCAST OF 1936
Paramount, 1935

Composer(s) Rainger, Ralph; Whiting, Richard A.
Lyricist(s) Robin, Leo
Choreographer(s) Prinz, LeRoy

Producer(s) Glazer, Benjamin
Director(s) Taurog, Norman
Screenwriter(s) De Leon, Walter; Martin, Francis; Spence, Ralph

Cast Oakie, Jack; Roberti, Lyda; Burns, George; Allen, Gracie; Barrie, Wendy; Tamiroff, Akim; Wadsworth, Henry; Gordon, C. Henry; Baker, Benny; Crosby, Bing; Merman, Ethel; Robinson, Bill; The Nicholas Brothers; Amos 'n' Andy; Boland, Mary; Ruggles, Charles; Tauber, Richard; The Vienna Boys Choir; Ray Noble and His Band; Ina Rae Hutton and Her Band

Song(s) Amargura (Cheating Muchachita) [2] [11] (C: Gardel, Carlos; L: Harper, Marjorie; Lepera, Alfred); Listen in On My Heart [1] [8] (C/L: Ronell, Ann); Beep-Beep-Beep [1] [8] (C/L: Ronell, Ann); Crooner's Lullaby [8] [13] (C: Johnston, Arthur; L: Coslow, Sam); Is Love a Moon Flower? (C: Rainger, Ralph); Through the Doorway of Dreams (I Saw You) (C: Whiting, Richard A.); A Man, A Maid, A Moon (C: Rainger, Ralph); On the Wings of a Waltz (C: Rainger, Ralph; L: Robin, Leo; Shauer, Mel); Chanson de Vovier [2] (Ox-Cart Song) (C: Gardel, Carlos; L: Lepera, Alfred); Delantero Buey [8] (C: Gardel, Carlos; L: Lepera, Alfred); Double Trouble; Miss Brown to You; Why Dream; I Don't Want to Make History (I Just Want to Make Love) [14]; It's the Animal in Me [10] (C: Revel, Harry; L: Gordon, Mack); I Wished on the Moon [4] (C: Rainger, Ralph; L: Parker, Dorothy); No Can Do; New Pan-Ameri-Can-Can [5]; Blossoms on Broadway [3]; Pardon My Dust; My Kingdom for a Kiss [6]; Laughin' at the Weather Man [13]; I'll Be there with Bells On [7]; You'll Never be Sorry [8]; While the Night is Young [9]; Why Stars Come Out at Night [12] [8] (C/L: Noble, Ray)

Notes The film was to be called THE BIG BROADCAST OF 1935. Jessica Dragonette had a specialty in the film; however, preview audiences were lukewarm so the spot was cut. Lubitsch (Paramount's head of production at the time) wrote "We fought until the very last regarding keeping Dragonette in picture but preview audiences unquestionably told us insertion of Dragonette specialty definitely injured the picture." [1] These songs were written by Ronell prior to her employment at Paramount so they were disqualified for inclusion in the film. [2] These numbers only were used in foreign prints. [3] Unused. Also not used in COLLEGE SWING. "Blossoms on Broadway" later used as title tune for a 1937 Paramount picture. [4] Originally intended for movie SAILOR BEWARE. [5] The songwriters originally wanted to call this song "The Panamerican-Can." However Paramount was leery because of the success of the Victor Herbert instrumental hit "Panamericana." The songwriters changed the title but the Hays Office refused the new title because of the word "Can-Can." [6] Darryl Zanuck of 20th Century Fox had reserved the title as the title for a future film but agreed to let the song writers use it. [7] This was previously the title of a George M. Cohan song. [8] Not used. [9] Also not used in GOIN' TO TOWN. [10] This segment was filmed as part of WE'RE NOT DRESSING but not used in that film. It was interpolated into this film. [11] Harper wrote the English lyrics. [12] Though not used, it was published. [13] Used in MILLIONS IN THE AIR. [14] Also in PALM SPRINGS. [15] Sheet music only.

473 ✦ BIG BROADCAST OF 1937
Paramount, 1936

Composer(s) Rainger, Ralph
Lyricist(s) Robin, Leo
Choreographer(s) Prinz, LeRoy

Producer(s) Gensler, Lewis E.
Director(s) Leisen, Mitchell
Screenwriter(s) De Leon, Walter; Martin, Francis; Atteberry, Duke; Perrin, Sam; Phillips, Arthur

Cast Benny, Jack; Raye, Martha; Burns, Bob; Burns, George; Allen, Gracie; Ross, Shirley; Milland, Ray; Stokowski, Leopold; Forrest, Frank; Adler, Larry; Benny Goodman and His Orchestra; Whitney, Eleanore; Fields, Benny

Song(s) You Came to My Rescue; Here's Love in Your Eye; Heigh-ho the Radio; La Bomba; Vote for Mr. Rhythm (L: Siegel, Al; Robin, Leo); Your Minstrel Man; Talking Through My Heart; Jazzing the Wedding March (inst.) (C: Wagner, Richard); Night in Manhattan [5]; The High Hat Hop [1]; Come and See Me Tomorrow [1] (L: de Leon, Martin); New York [1]; Voom Voom [1] [2] (C/L: Coslow, Sam); It Don't Make Sense [1] [4]; The Swing Tap [1] [3]; Casanova [1]

Notes Larry Adler played the Andy Razaf and Leon Berry tune "Christopher Columbus;" Benny Goodman played Elmer Schoebel's "Bugle Call Rag" and Stowkowski conducted Bach's "Impregnable Fortress" (not listed in final print) and "Little Fugue in G Minor." Title searches were undertaken for the following names: "Swing Fever" (not allowed); "Don't Look Now" (Robin rescinded the request). [1] Not used. [2] From an idea by Al Siegel. Also not used in DOUBLE OR NOTHING. Later used in THIS WAY PLEASE. [3] Eventually used instrumentally in THREE CHEERS FOR LOVE. [4] Also not used in GIVE ME A SAILOR. [5] On cue sheet but some sources say it was cut prior to release.

474 ✦ THE BIG BROADCAST OF 1938
Paramount, 1938

Composer(s) Rainger, Ralph
Lyricist(s) Robin, Leo
Choreographer(s) Prinz, LeRoy

Producer(s) Thompson, Harlan
Director(s) Leisen, Mitchell
Screenwriter(s) Englund, Ken; De Leon, Walter; Martin, Francis

Cast Overman, Lynne; Ross, Shirley; Fields, W.C.; Raye, Martha; Hope, Bob; Lamour, Dorothy; Guizar, Tito; Blue, Ben; Erickson, Leif; Bradley, Grace; Flagstad, Kirsten

Song(s) This Little Ripple Had Rhythm (Mr. Ripple's Animation); Don't Tell a Secret to a Rose; You Took the Words Right Out of My Heart; Love in Bloom [7]; Thanks for the Memory [6]; Mama, that Moon Is Here Again; The Waltz Lives On [8]; Heel and Toe Polka; Zuni Zuni (C/L: Guizar, Tito; Hoffman, William); Love with a Capital "You" [1] [2]; Sawing a Woman in Half [1] [5] (C/L: "Jock" [4]); Noche de Ronda [3] (C/L: Lara, Maria Teresa); Virgencita [1] (C/L: Guizar, Tito); What Goes On Here (In My Heart) [1] [9]

Notes Flagstad sings an aria from Act II Scene I of DIE WALKURE and W.C. Fields vocalizes. Someone identified as Honey Child sings "Dixie" by Dan Emmett. The following titles were requested for clearance: "They're Going Hollywood in Harlem," "I've Got Manhattan in My Soul," "And," "Sittin' Out a Dance," "Hallelujah Jones," "The Pan American Can" (see THE BIG BROADCAST OF 1936 answer was the same this time and "Down with the Devil." No lyrics were submitted to the censor for these titles and songs of the same name don't appear in other movies, so I believe the songs were not written. [1] Not used. [2] Also not used in COLLEGE SWING and MAN ABOUT TOWN. Used in $1,000 A TOUCHDOWN. [3] Released in Latin America only. Also in SOMBRERO (MGM); MASQUERADE IN MEXICO (Paramount); HAVANA ROSE (Republic) and RIDE CLEAR OF DIABLO (Universal). [4] A pseudonym for Jack Rock. [5] Jock had written a previous song of the same title with Kay Swift and Al Silverman. [6] Oscar winner. Also in THANKS FOR THE MEMORY. [7] Also in NEW YORK TOWN; $1,000 A TOUCHDOWN; and SHE LOVES ME NOT and not used in KISS AND MAKE UP. [8] Also in STAR BRIGHT. [9] Not used in COLLEGE SWING. Used in GIVE ME A SAILOR.

475 ✦ THE BIG BUS
Paramount, 1976

Producer(s) Freeman, Fred; Cohen, Lawrence J.
Director(s) Frawley, James
Screenwriter(s) Freeman, Fred; Cohen, Lawrence J.

Cast Gould, Harold; Channing, Stockard; Bologna, Joseph; Beck, John; Auberjonois, Rene; Dishy, Bob; Redgrave, Lynn; Kellerman, Sally; Mulligan, Richard; Ferrer, Jose; Hagman, Larry; Beatty, Ned

Song(s) Six Months to Live (C: Dunne, Murphy; L: Dunne, Murphy; Cohen, Larry; Freeman, Fred); Doggie Doctor (C/L: Dunne, Murphy)

476 ✦ BIG BUSINESS
Gaumont-British

Composer(s) Green, Johnny
Lyricist(s) Dyrenforth, James C.

Cast Lawrence, Gertrude

Song(s) Not Bad; An Hour Ago This Minute; What Now?

Notes No cue sheet available. No other information available.

477 ✦ BIG BUSINESS GIRL
Warner Brothers–First National, 1931

Director(s) Seiter, William A.
Screenwriter(s) Lord, Robert

Cast   Young, Loretta; Cortez, Ricardo; Albertson, Jack; Blondell, Joan; Jordan, Bobby

Song(s)   Constantly (C/L: Unknown)

Notes   No cue sheet available.

478 ✦ THE BIG CARNIVAL
Paramount, 1951

Producer(s)   Wilder, Billy
Director(s)   Wilder, Billy
Screenwriter(s)   Wilder, Billy; Samuels, Lesser; Newman, Walter

Cast   Douglas, Kirk; Arthur, Robert; Benedict, Richard; Sterling, Jan; Hall, Porter

Song(s)   We're Coming, Leo (C/L: Livingston, Jay; Evans, Ray)

Notes   Movie also released as ACE IN THE HOLE. "The Hut Sut Song" by Leo V. Killion, Ted McMichael and Jack Owens is also used in the movie for less then a minute—slightly shorter than the time devoted to the Livingston/Evans tune.

479 ✦ BIG CITY
Metro–Goldwyn–Mayer, 1948

Musical Score   Perl, Lothar
Choreographer(s)   Donen, Stanley

Producer(s)   Pasternak, Joe
Director(s)   Taurog, Norman
Screenwriter(s)   Cook, Whitfield; Chapin, Anne Morrison; Kandel, Aben

Cast   O'Brien, Margaret; Preston, Robert; Thomas, Danny; Murphy, George; Booth, Karin; Arnold, Edward; Jenkins, Jackie "Butch"; Garrett, Betty; Lehmann, Lotte

Song(s)   I'm Gonna See a Lot of You (C: Spielman, Al; L: Torre, Janice); Shoo Shoo Baby [1] (C/L: Moore, Phil); Ok'l Baby Dok'l (C: James, Inez; L: Miller, Sidney); Yippee-O, Yippee-Ay (C/L: Popp; Seelen, Jerry)

Notes   The first film for Betty Garrett and Lotte Lehmann and the last for Butch Jenkins. There are also vocals of "Kol Nidre" and "Traumerei" by Schumann; "Kerry Dance" by Molloy; "God Bless America" and "What'll I Do" by Irving Berlin and "Don't Blame Me" by Jimmy McHugh and Dorothy Fields. [1] Also in BEAUTIFUL BUT BROKE (Columbia); TROCADERO (Republic) and SOUTH OF DIXIE (Universal).

480 ✦ BIG CITY BLUES
Warner Brothers, 1932

Producer(s)   Wallis, Hal B.
Director(s)   LeRoy, Mervyn
Screenwriter(s)   Morehouse, Ward; Hayward, Lillie
Source(s)   (play) Morehouse, Ward

Cast   Linden, Eric; Catlett, Walter; Blondell, Joan; Courtney, Inez; Knapp, Evalyn; Bogart, Humphrey; Howland, Jobyna; Sparks, Ned; Kibbee, Guy

Song(s)   Every Day Can't Be a Sunday (C/L: Jolson, Al); Whistle and Blow Your Blues Away (C: Lombardo, Carmen; L: Young, Joseph)

481 ✦ THE BIG CLOCK
Paramount, 1948

Producer(s)   Maibaum, Richard
Director(s)   Farrow, John
Screenwriter(s)   Latimer, Jonathan

Cast   Laughton, Charles; Milland, Ray; O'Sullivan, Maureen; Lanchester, Elsa; Macready, George; Johnson, Rita; Morgan, Henry

Song(s)   The Big Clock [1] (C/L: Livingston, Jay; Evans, Ray)

Notes   [1] Written for exploitation only.

482 ✦ THE BIG CUBE
Warner Brothers, 1969

Musical Score   Johns, Valgean

Producer(s)   Parsons, Lindsley
Director(s)   Davison, Tito
Screenwriter(s)   Lansford, William Douglas

Cast   Turner, Lana; Mossberg, Karin; Chakiris, George; O'Herlihy, Dan; Egan, Richard; The Finks

Song(s)   Lean on Me (C: Johns, Valgean; L: Finkelstein, Howard)

483 ✦ THE BIG EASY
Columbia, 1987

Musical Score   Fiedel, Brad

Producer(s)   Friedman, Stephen
Director(s)   McBride, Jim
Screenwriter(s)   Petrie Jr., Daniel

Cast   Quaid, Dennis; Barkin, Ellen; Beatty, Ned; Goodman, John; Persky, Lisa Jane; Smith, Ebbe Roe; O'Brien, Tom; Ludlam, Charles; Zabriskie, Grace; Lawrence, Marc; Simien, Terrance

Song(s)   Closer to You (C: Quaid, Dennis; Simien, Terrance; L: Quaid, Dennis); Oh, Yeh, Ya! (C/L: Simien, Terrance); For Your Love I Would Pay Any Price (C/L: Simien, Terrance)

Notes   No cue sheet available.

484 ✦ THE BIG FIX
Universal, 1978

Musical Score   Conti, Bill

Producer(s)   Borack, Carl; Dreyfuss, Richard
Director(s)   Kagan, Jeremy Paul

Screenwriter(s) Simon, Roger L.
Source(s) *The Big Fix* (novel) Simon, Roger L.

Cast Dreyfuss, Richard; Anspach, Susan; Bedelia, Bonnie; Lithgow, John; Medina, Ofelia; Coster, Nicolas; Abraham, F. Murray; Weaver, Fritz; Rifkin, Ron

Song(s) Seduced (C/L: Tigerman, Gary)

Notes No cue sheet available.

485 ✦ THE BIG GAME
RKO, 1936

Producer(s) Berman, Pandro S.
Director(s) Nichols Jr., George
Screenwriter(s) Shaw, Irwin

Cast Huston, Philip; Gleason, James; Travis, June; Cabot, Bruce; Devine, Andy; Williams, Guinn "Big Boy"; Arledge, John; Gordon, C. Henry; Berwanger, Jay; Shakespeare, William; Wilson, Robert; Moscrip, James "Monk"; Klein, Irwin "King Kong"; Jones, Gomer; Hamilton, Robert "Bones"; Alustiza, Frank

Song(s) For Old Atlantic (C: Shilkret, Nathaniel; L: Ormont, David)

486 ✦ THE BIGGEST BUNDLE OF THEM ALL
Metro–Goldwyn–Mayer, 1967

Musical Score Ortolani, Riz

Producer(s) Shaftel, Josef
Director(s) Annakin, Ken
Screenwriter(s) Salkowitz, Sy

Cast Welch, Raquel; Wagner, Robert; Cambridge, Godfrey; Spinetti, Victor; De Sica, Vittorio; Robinson, Edward G.

Song(s) Most Of All There's You (C: Ortolani, Riz; L: Newell, Norman); The Biggest Bundle of Them All (C/L: Cordell, Ritchie; Trimachi, Sal); Along About Now [1] (C: Ortolani, Riz; L: Sigman, Carl)

Notes [1] Sheet music only.

487 ✦ THE BIG LAND
Warner Brothers, 1957

Musical Score Buttolph, David

Producer(s) Bertholon, George
Director(s) Douglas, Gordon M.
Screenwriter(s) Dortort, David; Rackin, Martin
Source(s) *Buffalo Grass* (novel) Gruber, Frank

Cast Ladd, Alan; Mayo, Virginia; Caruso, Anthony; O'Brien, Edmond

Song(s) I Leaned on a Man (C: Rosenman, Leonard; L: Shanklin, Wayne)

488 ✦ THE BIG LIFT
Twentieth Century–Fox, 1950

Producer(s) Perlberg, William
Director(s) Seaton, George
Screenwriter(s) Seaton, George

Cast Clift, Montgomery; Douglas, Paul; Borchers, Cornell; Loebel, Burni; Hasse, O.E.; Davenport, Danny

Song(s) Vielleicht Sollst Du Mein Gluck Sein (C/L: Neumann, Gunther)

Notes There are also vocals of "Mariandl" by Hans Lang and Kurt Nachmann; "Chattanooga Choo Choo" by Harry Warren and Mack Gordon with German lyrics by Carl Ulrich Blecher and "In Einem Kleinen Cafe in Hernals" by Hermann Leopoldi and Peter Herz.

489 ✦ THE BIG MONEY
United Artists, 1958

Musical Score Phillips, Van

Producer(s) Rank, J. Arthur
Director(s) Mack, Russell
Screenwriter(s) De Leon, Walter; Mack, Russell

Cast Carmichael, Ian; Lee, Belinda; Harrison, Kathleen; Helpmann, Robert; Ireland, Jill

Song(s) Kiss Me (C/L: Phillips, Van)

490 ✦ THE BIG NIGHT
Paramount, 1960

Musical Score Sparks, Randy

Producer(s) Alves, Vern
Director(s) Salkow, Sidney
Screenwriter(s) Hardman, Ric

Cast Sparks, Randy; Stevenson, Venetia; Foran, Dick; White, Jesse; Contino, Dick

Song(s) The Big Night (C/L: Sparks, Randy)

491 ✦ THE BIG PARTY
Fox, 1930

Composer(s) Kernell, William
Lyricist(s) Kernell, William

Director(s) Blystone, John
Screenwriter(s) Robbins, J. Edwin

Cast Carol, Sue; Lee, Dixie; Catlett, Walter; Albertson, Frank; Keene, Richard; Judell, Walter; Smith, Jack

Song(s) Day Dreams [1] (C/L: Kernell, William); Good for Nothing but Love [5]; Bluer Than Blue Over You [4] (L: Thompson, Harlan); Nobody Knows But Rosie (C: Hanley, James F.; L: McCarthy, Joseph); I'm Climbing Up a Rainbow [3] (C: Nelson, Edward G.; L: Pease, Harry); Riding on a Moonbeam [2] (C: Burke, Johnny; L: Little, George A.)

492 ✦ THE BIG POND

Notes [1] Not used. [2] Used instrumentally only (may not have been used at all; the early Fox cue sheets can be very confusing). [3] Written for but not used in LET'S GO PLACES. [4] Also in ON YOUR BACK. [5] Also in ON THE LEVEL and SONG OF KENTUCKY.

492 ✦ THE BIG POND
Paramount, 1930

Composer(s) Fain, Sammy; Norman, Pierre
Lyricist(s) Kahal, Irving

Producer(s) Bell, Monta
Director(s) Henley, Hobart
Screenwriter(s) Fort, Garrett; Presnell, Robert; Sturges, Preston
Source(s) (play) Middleton, George; Thomas, E.A.

Cast Chevalier, Maurice; Colbert, Claudette; Barbier, George; Ballou, Marion; Corday, Andree; Pendleton, Nat; Koch, Elaine

Song(s) You Brought a New Kind of Love to Me [3]; Mia Cara; Je N'Peux Pas Vivre Sans Amour [1] (C/L: Pearly, Fred; Gabaroche, G.); Frere Jacques [1] (C/L: Traditional); Livin' in the Sunlight, Lovin' in the Moonlight (C: Sherman, Al; L: Lewis, Al); Lucky Days [2] (C/L: Henderson, Ray); Do Something [4] (C: Stept, Sam H.; L: Green, Bud)

Notes [1] In French release only. [2] Originally in GEORGE WHITE'S SCANDALS OF 1926. [3] Later used as the title song in the movie A NEW KIND OF LOVE. [4] Also used in NOTHING BUT THE TRUTH.

493 ✦ BIG RED
Disney, 1962

Musical Score Wallace, Oliver
Composer(s) Sherman, Richard M.; Sherman, Robert B.
Lyricist(s) Sherman, Richard M.; Sherman, Robert B.

Producer(s) Hibler, Winston
Director(s) Tokar, Norman
Screenwriter(s) Pelletier, Louis
Source(s) *Big Red* (novel) Kjelgaard, Jim

Cast Pidgeon, Walter; Payant, Gilles; Genest, Emile; Bertrand, Janette; Bouvier, Georges

Song(s) Theme from Big Red; Mon Amour Perdu (My Lost Love)

494 ✦ THE BIG SHOW
Republic, 1936

Composer(s) Stept, Sam H.

Producer(s) Schaefer, Armand
Director(s) Wright, Mack V.
Screenwriter(s) McGowan, Dorrell; McGowan, Stuart

Cast Autry, Gene; Burnette, Smiley; Hughes, Kay; Payne, Sally; Terhune, Max; Judels, Charles; The Sons of the Pioneers; Jones Boys; Beverly Hill Billies; The Light Crust Doughboys

Song(s) Lady Known as Lulu (L: Washington, Ned); Happy Go Lucky Vagabonds (C/L: Light Crust Doughboys); I'm Mad About You [1] (L: Koehler, Ted); Ride, Ranger, Ride [3] (C/L: Spencer, Tim); Wild and Wooly West (L: Koehler, Ted); Nobody's Darling (C/L: Davis, Jimmie); Roll Wagon Roll (C/L: Spencer, Tim); Old Faithful (C/L: Kennedy, C.); The Martins and the Coys [2] (C/L: Weems, Ted; Camaron, Al)

Notes [1] Also in DANGEROUS HOLIDAY. [2] Also in MAN FROM OKLAHOMA. [3] Also in GANGSTERS OF THE FRONTIER (PRC), KING OF THE COWBOYS, RIDE, RANGER, RIDE and TEXANS NEVER CRY (Columbia).

495 ✦ THE BIG SHOW-OFF
Republic, 1945

Producer(s) Williams, Sydney M.
Director(s) Bretherton, Howard
Screenwriter(s) Vadnay, Laslo [1]; Weil, Richard

Cast Lake, Arthur; Evans, Dale; Stander, Lionel; Meeker, George; Hurst, Paul; Anson Weeks and His Orchestra

Song(s) Whoops My Dear (C/L: Oppenheim, Dave); There's Only One You (C/L: Evans, Dale); Cleo from Rio [2] (C/L: Oppenheim, Dave; Ingraham, Roy)

Notes [1] Billed as Leslie Vadnay. [2] Sheet music only.

496 ✦ BIG SISTER BLUES
Paramount, 1948

Cast Maxey, Virginia; The Lyttle Sisters; Slaughter, Anna Mae; Patrick, Lee

Song(s) The Secretary Song [1] (C: Fain, Sammy; L: Barnett, Jackie); I Hain't, Tain't, Ain't (C/L: Livingston, Jay; Evans, Ray); Them There Eyes [1] (C/L: Pinkard, Maceo; Tracey, William; Tauber, Doris); I'm My Own Grandmaw [2] (C/L: Latham, Dwight; Jaffe, Moe)

Notes Short subject. [1] Not written for this short. [2] Not used.

497 ✦ THE BIG SKY
RKO, 1952

Musical Score Tiomkin, Dimitri
Composer(s) Tiomkin, Dimitri
Lyricist(s) Clarke, Gordon

Producer(s) Hawks, Howard
Director(s) Hawks, Howard
Screenwriter(s) Nichols, Dudley
Source(s) *The Big Sky* (novel) Guthrie Jr., A.B.

VOLUME 1 ✦ HOLLYWOOD SONG:

Cast Douglas, Kirk; Martin, Dewey; Threatt, Elizabeth; Hunnicutt, Arthur; Baer, Buddy; Geray, Steven

Song(s) Quand Je Reve (When I Dream) [2] ; Charlotte; The Big Sky [1] (L: Jones, Stan)

Notes There is also a vocal of "Brandy Leave Me Alone" by Josef Marais. [1] Lyric written for exploitation only. [2] English lyrics written by Gordon Clarke and Paul Logan but not used in film.

---

498 ✦ THE BIG SLEEP (1946)
Warner Brothers–First National, 1946

Musical Score Steiner, Max

Producer(s) Hawks, Howard
Director(s) Hawks, Howard
Screenwriter(s) Faulkner, William; Brackett, Leigh; Furthman, Jules
Source(s) *The Big Sleep* (novel) Chandler, Raymond

Cast Bogart, Humphrey; Bacall, Lauren; Ridgely, John; Vickers, Martha; Malone, Dorothy; Knudsen, Peggy; Toomey, Regis; Cook Jr., Elisha

Song(s) And Her Tears Flowed Like Wine [1] (C/L: Kenton, Stan; Lawrence, Charles; Greene, Joe)

Notes [1] Not written for film. Also in TWO GUYS FROM MILWAUKEE.

---

499 ✦ THE BIG SLEEP (1978)
United Artists, 1978

Musical Score Fielding, Jerry

Producer(s) Kastner, Elliott; Winner, Michael
Director(s) Winner, Michael
Screenwriter(s) Winner, Michael
Source(s) *The Big Sleep* (novel) Chandler, Raymond

Cast Mitchum, Robert; Miles, Sarah; Boone, Richard; Clark, Candy; Collins, Joan; Fox, Edward; Mills, John; Stewart, James; Reed, Oliver; Andrews, Harry; Blakely, Colin; Todd, Richard

Song(s) Won't Somebody Dance with Me (C/L: de Paul, Linsey)

Notes No cue sheet available.

---

500 ✦ THE BIG SOMBRERO
Columbia, 1949

Producer(s) Schaefer, Armand
Director(s) McDonald, Frank
Screenwriter(s) Cooper, Olive

Cast Autry, Gene; Verdugo, Elena; Dunne, Stephen; Lewis, George; Champion

Song(s) Solamente Una Vez (You Belong to My Heart) [4] (C: Lara, Augustin; L: Gilbert, Ray); Rancho Pillow [2] (C/L: Newman, Charles; Wrubel, Allie); My Adobe Hacienda [1] (C/L: Massey, Louise; Penny, Lee); Good-by Old Mexico (C/L: Butcher, Dwight); The Trail to Mexico [3] (C/L: Traditional); I'm Thankful for Small Favors (C: dePaul, Gene; L: Raye, Don)

Notes No cue sheet available. There are also vocals of "La Golondrina" and "Oh, My Darling Clementine," whether they had additional music or lyrics is unknown. [1] Also in ON THE OLD SPANISH TRAIL (Republic) and BOB WILLS AND THE TEXAS PLAYBOYS (Warner). [2] Also in HEART Of THE RIO GRANDE (Republic). [3] This may be the traditional song which is also in THE FURIES (Paramount). [4] Also in THE THREE CABALLEROS (Disney), MR. IMPERIUM (MGM) and THE GAY RANCHERO (Republic).

---

501 ✦ THE BIG SONG AND DANCE
Paramount, 1952 unproduced

Composer(s) Schwartz, Arthur
Lyricist(s) Fields, Dorothy

Song(s) The Profezzor; Now Is Wonderful; I Did It and I'm Glad; Goin' with the Birds; Where Do I Go From You [1]; Dance Me Around; I'm Proud of You; Boys Are Better than Girls

Notes This musical was not produced. There were title searches for the following numbers although no music is in the Paramount files: "The Love Department," "Fun Is for People," "Tuscaloosa" (cut from Broadway musical A TREE GROWS IN BROOKLYN), "It's Not Where You Start (It's Where You Finish)" (title later used for a song in the Broadway musical SEESAW), "X Marks the Spot," "Oysters in July," "Have You Got a Sister? ('Cause I Don't Like You)," "April Fooled Me" (the title of a later Fields song written to music left by Jerome Kern after his death) and "The Lone Pilot in the Sky." [1] A song with the same title was cut from the MGM musical EXCUSE MY DUST.

---

502 ✦ THE BIG STORE
Metro–Goldwyn–Mayer, 1941

Choreographer(s) Appell, Arthur

Producer(s) Sidney, Louis K.
Director(s) Riesner, Charles F.
Screenwriter(s) Kuller, Sid; Fimberg, Hal; Golden, Ray

Cast Marx, Groucho; Marx, Chico; Marx, Harpo; Martin, Tony; Grey, Virginia; Dumont, Margaret; Dumbrille, Douglass

Song(s) If It's You (C/L: Oakland, Ben; Shaw, Artie; Drake, Milton); Sing While You Sell (C: Borne, Hal; L: Fimberg, Hal; Kuller, Sid); Tenement Symphony in Four Flats (C: Borne, Hal; L: Kuller, Sid; Golden, Ray)

503 ◆ BIG STREET
RKO, 1942

Musical Score Webb, Roy
Composer(s) Revel, Harry
Lyricist(s) Greene, Mort
Choreographer(s) Hale, Chester

Producer(s) Runyon, Damon
Director(s) Reis, Irving
Screenwriter(s) Spigelgass, Leonard
Source(s) "Little Pinks" (story) Runyon, Damon

Cast Fonda, Henry; Ball, Lucille [2]; MacLane, Barton; Pallette, Eugene; Moorehead, Agnes; Levene, Sam; Collins, Ray; Martin, Marion; Orr, William T.; Cleveland, George; Gordon, Vera; Ozzie Nelson and His Orchestra

Song(s) Who Knows; Your Face Looks Familiar [1]

Notes [1] Used instrumentally only. [2] Dubbed by Martha Mears.

504 ◆ BIG TIME (1929)
Fox, 1929

Producer(s) Sprague, Chandler
Director(s) Hawks, Kenneth
Screenwriter(s) Lanfield, Sidney; Wells, William K.
Source(s) "Little Ledna" (story) Smith, William Wallace

Cast Tracy, Lee; Clarke, Mae; Pollard, Daphne; Fetchit, Stepin; Ford, John

Song(s) Nobody Knows You Like I Do (C/L: Lanfield, Sidney)

505 ◆ BIG TIME (1978)
Motown, 1978

Musical Score Robinson, William "Smokey"
Composer(s) Robinson, William "Smokey"
Lyricist(s) Robinson, William "Smokey"

Producer(s) Joy, Christopher; Isaac, Leon; Georgias, Andrew; Gross, Lou
Director(s) Georgias, Andrew
Screenwriter(s) Diether, Anton; Isaac, Leon; Joy, Christopher; Robinson, William "Smokey"

Cast Joy, Christopher; Mayo, Tobar; Kennedy, Jayne; Mosley, Roger E.; Evans, Art

Song(s) Big Time; Hip Trip (C: Bradford, James; L: Bradford, James; Robinson, William "Smokey"); So Nice to Be with You (L: Jones, Rosella; Robinson, William "Smokey"); If We're Gonna Act Like Lovers (C/L: Robinson, William "Smokey"; Jones, Kennis); He Is the Light of the World; Agony & Ecstacy; JJ's Theme; Shana's Theme

Notes No cue sheet available.

506 ◆ BIG TIME (1988)
Island Visual Arts, 1988

Musical Score Waits, Tom

Producer(s) Roeg, Luc
Director(s) Blum, Chris

Cast Waits, Tom; Blair, Michael; Carney, Ralph; Cohen, Greg; Ribot, Marc; Schwarz, Willie

Song(s) Straight to the Top (C/L: Waits, Tom; Cohen, Greg); Strange Weather (C/L: Waits, Tom; Brennan, Kathleen)

Notes No cue sheet available.

507 ◆ BIG TIME REVUE
Warner Brothers, 1946

Song(s) Broken Hearted Troubadour, A (C: Green, Sanford; L: David, Mack); Clementine (From New Orleans) (C: Warren, Harry; L: Creamer, Henry)

Notes Short subject.

508 ◆ BIG TOP PEEWEE
Paramount, 1988

Musical Score Elfman, Danny

Producer(s) Reubens, Paul; Hill, Debra
Director(s) Kleiser, Randal
Screenwriter(s) Reubens, Paul; McGrath, George

Cast Reubens, Paul; Miller, Penelope Ann; Kristofferson, Kris; Golino, Valeria; Tyrrell, Susan; White, Wayne; Henderson, Albert; Mann, Terrence; Hall, Kevin Peter

Song(s) Big Top Finale (C: Elfman, Danny; L: Kleiser, Randal; McGrath, George; Reubens, Paul); The Girl on the Flying Trapeze [1] (C: Elfman, Danny; L: Reubens, Paul; McGrath, George)

Notes [1] Not on cue sheet.

509 ◆ THE BIG TOWN
Columbia, 1987

Musical Score Melvoin, Michael

Producer(s) Ransohoff, Martin
Director(s) Bolt, Ben
Screenwriter(s) Pool, Robert Roy
Source(s) *The Arm* (novel) Howard, Clark

Cast Dillon, Matt; Lane, Diane; Jones, Tommy Lee; Dern, Bruce; Grant, Lee; Skerritt, Tom; Amis, Suzy; Grant, David Marshall; Francks, Don; Close, Del

Song(s) Big Town (C/L: Self, Ronnie)

Notes No cue sheet available.

510 ✦ BIG TOWN GIRL
Twentieth Century–Fox, 1937

Composer(s) Akst, Harry
Lyricist(s) Clare, Sidney

Producer(s) Feld, Milton
Director(s) Strayer, Frank R.
Screenwriter(s) Breslow, Lou; Patrick, John; Ellis, Robert; Logan, Helen

Cast Trevor, Claire; Woods, Donald; Dinehart, Alan; Baxter, Alan; Alper, Murray; Charters, Spencer; Cass, Maurice; Bacon, Irving; Chandler, George; Hale, Jonathan

Song(s) I'll Settle for Love; Argentine Swing; Don't Throw Kisses

511 ✦ THE BIG TREES
Warner Brothers–First National, 1952

Musical Score Roemheld, Heinz

Producer(s) Edelman, Louis F.
Director(s) Feist, Felix E.
Screenwriter(s) Twist, John; Webb, James R.

Cast Douglas, Kirk; Miller, Eve; Wymore, Patrice; Buchanan, Edgar; Archer, John; Hale Jr., Alan; Roberts, Roy

Song(s) The Soubrette on the Police Gazette [1] (C: Jerome, M.K.; L: Scholl, Jack)

Notes [1] Also in MOVIELAND MAGIC.

512 ✦ BIG TROUBLE IN LITTLE CHINA
Twentieth Century–Fox, 1986

Musical Score Carpenter, John; Howarth, Alan

Producer(s) Franco, Larry J.
Director(s) Carpenter, John
Screenwriter(s) Goldman, Gary; Weinstein, David Z.

Cast Russell, Kurt; Cattrall, Kim; Dun, Dennis; Hong, James; Wong, Victor; Burton, Kate; Li, Donald; Wong, Carter

Song(s) Big Trouble in Little China (C/L: Carpenter, John)

Notes No cue sheet available.

513 ✦ THE BIG WASH
Disney, 1947

Musical Score Wallace, Oliver

Director(s) Geronimi, Clyde
Screenwriter(s) Berg, Bill; Banta, Milt

Song(s) Glorious Dolorious (C/L: Wallace, Oliver)

Notes Short subject.

514 ✦ THE BIG WAVE
Allied Artists, 1962

Musical Score Mayuzumi, Toshiro

Producer(s) Danielewski, Tad
Director(s) Danielewski, Tad
Screenwriter(s) Buck, Pearl S.; Danielewski, Tad
Source(s) Buck, Pearl S.

Cast Hayakawa, Sessue; Itami, Ichizo; Curtis, Mickey; Shitara, Koji

Song(s) Be Ready at Dawn (C: Mayuzumi, Toshiro; L: Danielewski, Tad)

Notes No cue sheet available.

515 ✦ BIG WEDNESDAY
Warner Brothers, 1978

Musical Score Poledouris, Basil

Producer(s) Feitshans, Buzz
Director(s) Milius, John
Screenwriter(s) Milius, John; Aaberg, Dennis

Cast Vincent, Jan-Michael; Katt, William; Busey, Gary; D'Arbanville, Patti; Purcell, Lee; Melville, Sam; Fetty, Darrell; Kanaly, Steve; Hale, Barbara; Englund, Robert

Song(s) Three Friends Theme (C: Poledouris, Basil; L: Beamer, Keola; Beamer, Kapono)

Notes No cue sheet available.

516 ✦ THE BIG WHEEL
United Artists, 1949

Musical Score Finston, Nat

Producer(s) Popkin, Harry M.; Stiefel, Samuel H.; Briskin, Mort
Director(s) Ludwig, Edward
Screenwriter(s) Smith, Robert

Cast Rooney, Mickey; Mitchell, Thomas; O'Shea, Michael; Byington, Spring; Hatcher, Mary; McDaniel, Hattie; Brodie, Steve; Romay, Lina; Jenkins, Allen

Song(s) Que Bueno (C/L: Spielman, Fred; Goell, Kermit)

517 ✦ BIKINI BEACH
American International, 1964

Musical Score Baxter, Les
Composer(s) Hemric, Guy; Styner, Jerry
Lyricist(s) Hemric, Guy; Styner, Jerry

Producer(s) Nicholson, James H.; Arkoff, Samuel Z.
Director(s) Asher, William
Screenwriter(s) Asher, William; Townsend, Leo; Dillon, Robert

Cast Avalon, Frankie; Funicello, Annette; Hyer, Martha; Lembeck, Harvey; Rickles, Don; Ashley, John; McCrea, Jody; MacRae, Meredith; Wonder, Little Stevie; The Pyramids; Wynn, Keenan

Song(s) Bikini Beach; Love's a Secret Weapon; Gimme Your Love; Yeah, Yeah, Yeah; How About That (C/L: Usher, Gary; Christian, Roger); Because You're You (C/L: Usher, Gary; Christian, Roger); This Time It's Love (C/L: Usher, Gary; Christian, Roger); Happy Feelin' Dance and Shout (C/L: Usher, Gary; Christian, Roger); Bikini Drag (C/L: Usher, Gary; Christian, Roger); Record Run (C/L: Usher, Gary; Christian, Roger); Gotcha Where I Wantcha (C/L: Merrill, Jack; Gilson, Red)

Notes No cue sheet available.

518 ✦ BILL AND COO
Republic, 1947

Composer(s) Buttolph, David; Newman, Lionel
Lyricist(s) Foster, Royal

Producer(s) Murray, Ken
Director(s) Riesner, Dean
Screenwriter(s) Foster, Royal; Riesner, Dean

Cast George Burton's Love Birds; Curley Twiford's Jimmy the Crow; Burton, George; Walters, Elizabeth

Song(s) Tweet Tweet [1] (C: Henderson, Ray; L: DeSylva, B.G.; Brown, Lew); Hum a Little Tune; Off to the Circus

Notes [1] Written for show GEORGE WHITE'S SCANDALS OF 1925.

519 ✦ BILL CRACKS DOWN
Republic, 1937

Composer(s) Stept, Sam H.
Lyricist(s) Washington, Ned

Producer(s) Berke, William
Director(s) Nigh, William
Screenwriter(s) McGowan, Dorrell; McGowan, Stuart

Cast Withers, Grant; Roberts, Beatrice; Weeks, Ranny; Allen, Judith; Caine, Georgia

Song(s) On a Certain Saturday Night; You Grow Sweeter Every Day

520 ✦ BILLIE
United Artists, 1965

Musical Score Frontiere, Dominic
Composer(s) Ross, Bernice; Crane, Lor; Gold, Jack
Lyricist(s) Ross, Bernice; Crane, Lor; Gold, Jack
Choreographer(s) Winters, David

Producer(s) Weis, Don
Director(s) Weis, Don

Screenwriter(s) Alexander, Ronald
Source(s) *Time Out for Ginger* (play) Alexander, Ronald

Cast Duke, Patty; Backus, Jim; Greer, Jane; Berlinger, Warren; De Wolfe, Billy; Lane, Charles; Sargent, Dick; Deacon, Richard; Seaforth, Susan

Song(s) Billie (C: Frontiere, Dominic; L: Lampert, Diane); Lonely Little in Between; Funny Little Butterflies; The Girl Is a Girl Is a Girl

521 ✦ BILLION DOLLAR HOBO
International Picture Show Company, 1978

Musical Score Leonard, Michael

Producer(s) Elliott, Lang; McGowan, Stuart
Director(s) McGowan, Stuart
Screenwriter(s) McGowan, Stuart; Conway, Tim; Beatty, Roger

Cast Conway, Tim; Geer, Will; Weston, Eric; Myhers, John; Silvera, Frank; Weber, Sharon; Tessler, Sheela

Song(s) Half Sung Song (C/L: Leonard, Michael)

Notes No cue sheet available.

522 ✦ BILLION DOLLAR SCANDAL
Paramount, 1933

Producer(s) Rogers, Charles R.
Director(s) Brown, Harry Joe
Screenwriter(s) Mack, Willard; Banyard, Beatrice

Cast Armstrong, Robert; Cummings, Constance; Morgan, Frank; Baclanova, Olga; Gleason, James; Albertson, Frank; Toler, Sidney

Song(s) South Dakota (C/L: Knight, Fuzzy)

Notes "California Here I Come" by Al Jolson, B.G. DeSylva and Joseph Meyer is also used in the film.

523 ✦ BILLY JACK
Warner Brothers, 1971

Musical Score Lowe, Mundell

Producer(s) Solti, Mary Rose
Director(s) Frank, T.C. [2]
Screenwriter(s) Christina, Frank [2]; Christina, Teresa [1]

Cast Laughlin, Tom; Taylor, Delores; Howat, Clark; Freed, Bert; Webb, Julie; Tobey, Kenneth; Izay, Victor

Song(s) One Tin Soldier (C/L: Lambert, Dennis; Potter, Brian); The Old and the New (C/L: Lowe, Mundell); Johnnie (C/L: Kelly, Teresa); When Will Billy Love Me (C/L: Baker, Lynn); Freedom Over Men (C/L: Smith, Gwen); A Rainbow Made of Children (C/L: Baker, Lynn); The Ring Song (C/L: Moffat, Katy); Look, Look to the Mountain (C/L: Kelly,

Teresa); Mary and the Jesus Babe (C/L: Etelson, Robbyn)

Notes [1] Delores Taylor. [2] Tom Laughlin.

524 ✦ BILLY ROSE'S DIAMOND HORSESHOE

See DIAMOND HORSESHOE.

525 ✦ BILLY ROSE'S JUMBO
Metro–Goldwyn–Mayer, 1963

Musical Score Edens, Roger
Composer(s) Rodgers, Richard
Lyricist(s) Hart, Lorenz

Producer(s) Pasternak, Joe; Melcher, Martin
Director(s) Walters, Charles
Screenwriter(s) Sheldon, Sidney
Source(s) *Jumbo* (musical) Hecht, Ben; MacArthur, Charles; Rodgers, Richard; Hart, Lorenz

Cast Day, Doris; Boyd, Stephen [7]; Durante, Jimmy; Raye, Martha; Jagger, Dean; Waring, Joseph; Wood, Lynn; Watts, Charles; Chandler, James; Sutton, Grady; Christiani, Corky

Song(s) My Romance [1]; The Circus Is on Parade [1]; Over and Over Again [1] [6]; Why Can't I [3]; Romeo and Juliet [2] (C/L: Edens, Roger); This Can't Be Love [4]; The Most Beautiful Girl in the World [1]; Little Girl Blue [1]; Sawdust and Spangles and Dreams [5] (C: Rodgers, Richard; Edens, Roger; L: Edens, Roger); Working Chant [5] (C: Rodgers, Richard; Edens, Roger; L: Edens, Roger); We Got Clowns [5] (C: Rodgers, Richard; Edens, Roger; L: Edens, Roger)

Notes The second unit director was Busby Berkeley. [1] From original production. [2] An interlude to "Why Can't I." [3] From Broadway musical SPRING IS HERE. [4] From the Broadway musical THE BOYS FROM SYRACUSE. Also used in the Universal film version of that show. [5] Rodgers gets credit on these numbers because Edens used some of Rodgers' music. For example "We Got Clowns" is part of the production number surrounding "The Circus Is on Parade." [6] Music originally used for "The Party Waltz" in film HOLLYWOOD PARTY (1934). [7] Dubbed by James Joyce.

526 ✦ BILLY THE KID (1930)
Metro–Goldwyn–Mayer, 1930

Director(s) Vidor, King
Screenwriter(s) Stallings, Laurence; Tuchock, Wanda; MacArthur, Charles
Source(s) *Saga of Billy the Kid* (book) Burns, Walter Noble

Cast Brown, Johnny Mack; Johnson, Kay; Dane, Karl; Beery, Wallace

Song(s) Heigh-Ho (C/L: Montgomery, Reggie)

Notes This film was shot in both 70 mm and 35 mm, and was exhibited in 70 millimetre in major cities.

527 ✦ BILLY THE KID (1941)
Metro–Goldwyn–Mayer, 1941

Producer(s) Asher, Irving
Director(s) Miller, David
Screenwriter(s) Fowler, Gene
Source(s) *The Saga of Billy the Kid* (book) Burns, Walter Noble

Cast Taylor, Robert; Donlevy, Brian; Hunter, Ian; Lockhart, Gene; Howard, Mary; Chaney Jr., Lon; Wills, Chill; Withers, Grant

Song(s) Viva La Vida (C/L: Ruthven, Ormond B.; Mannheimer, Albert); Lazy Acres (C/L: Ruthven, Ormond B.)

528 ✦ BILLY THE KID RETURNS
Republic, 1938

Composer(s) Cherkose, Eddie
Lyricist(s) Cherkose, Eddie

Producer(s) Ford, Charles E.
Director(s) Kane, Joseph
Screenwriter(s) Natteford, Jack

Cast Rogers, Roy; Burnette, Smiley; Hart, Mary; Wallace, Morgan; Kohler, Fred; Boteler, Wade; Stanley, Edwin; Crehan, Joseph; Keane, Robert Emmett

Song(s) Born to the Saddle [1]; Trail Blazin'; Sing a Little Song About Anything (C/L: Cherkose, Eddie; Burnette, Smiley); When the Sun Is Setting on the Prairie (C: Colombo, Alberto); Parade Song (C/L: Cherkose, Eddie; Burnette, Smiley); Dixie Instrumental Song (C/L: Cherkose, Eddie; Burnette, Smiley); When I Camped Under the Stars (C: Spencer, Tim)

Notes [1] Also in PHANTOM STALLION and UNDER MEXICALI STARS.

529 ✦ BIMBO THE GREAT
Warner Brothers, 1961

Musical Score Mackeben, Theo; Orgermann, Klaus
Composer(s) Mizzy, Vic
Lyricist(s) Parish, Mitchell

Producer(s) Gruter, Alexander
Director(s) Philipp, Harold
Screenwriter(s) Raspotnik, Hans

Cast Holm, Claus; Damar, Germaine; Karlowa, Elma; Orschel, Marina; Schmidt, Helmut

Song(s)   Angel Baby; The Torch Burns at Midnight

Notes   No cue sheet available.

530 ✦ THE BINGO LONG TRAVELING ALL-STARS AND MOTOR KINGS
Universal, 1976

Musical Score   Goldstein, William

Producer(s)   Cohen, Rob
Director(s)   Badham, John
Screenwriter(s)   Barwood, Hal; Robbins, Matthew
Source(s)   (novel) Brashler, William

Cast   Williams, Billy Dee; Jones, James Earl; Pryor, Richard; Dawson, Rico; Brison, Sam "Birmingham"; Brown, Jophery; King, Mabel; Ross, Ted; Childress, Alvin

Song(s)   Steal On Home (C/L: Miller, Ron; Gordy Jr., Berry); Razzle Dazzle (C: Goldstein, William; L: Miller, Ron)

531 ✦ BIRD
Warner Brothers, 1988

Musical Score   Niehaus, Lennie

Producer(s)   Eastwood, Clint
Director(s)   Eastwood, Clint
Screenwriter(s)   Oliansky, Joel

Cast   Whitaker, Forest; Venora, Diane; Zelniker, Michael; Wright, Samuel E.; David, Keith; McGuire, Michael

Song(s)   Albino Red Blues (C: Niehaus, Lennie; L: Oliansky, Joel)

532 ✦ BIRD OF PARADISE (1932)
RKO, 1932

Musical Score   Steiner, Max
Choreographer(s)   Berkeley, Busby

Producer(s)   Selznick, David O.
Director(s)   Vidor, King
Screenwriter(s)   Root, Wells; Tuchock, Wanda; Praskins, Leonard
Source(s)   Bird of Paradise (play) Tully, William Watson

Cast   McCrea, Joel; Del Rio, Dolores; Halliday, John; Gallagher, Skeets [3]; Roach, Bert; Chaney, Creighton [2]; Boteler, Wade

Song(s)   Out of the Blue [1] (C: Steiner, Max; L: Eliscu, Edward)

Notes   [1] The cue sheet doesn't indicate if this is used vocally or not. Also used in RED MORNING, probably instrumentally only. [2] Lon Chaney Jr. [3] Billed as Richard "Skeets" Gallagher.

533 ✦ BIRD OF PARADISE (1951)
Twentieth Century–Fox, 1951

Musical Score   Amfitheatrof, Daniele

Producer(s)   Daves, Delmer
Director(s)   Daves, Delmer
Screenwriter(s)   Daves, Delmer

Cast   Jourdan, Louis; Paget, Debra; Chandler, Jeff; Sloane, Everett; Schwartz, Maurice; Elam, Jack

Song(s)   Chant to the Name of Tenga (C/L: Bray Sr., David); Kona Kai Opua (Ka Laau—Stick Dance) (C/L: Messer, Helen); Song of Kalua (Offering Song B) (C/L: Darby, Ken); Love Chant of Lokalia (Kuu Aloha E Kua Aloha) (C/L: Montgomery, Lokalia); Chant for the Purification by Fire (Mai Kahi Ki Mai Ka Wahl O Pele) (C/L: Bray Sr., David); Imi Au Oe Ia (King's Serenade) (C/L: King, Charles E.); Pata'uta'u A Pere (A Chant to Pele) (C: Ceran, George Marcel Archer; L: Garnier, Gerald); Ku'u Lei Awapohi (C/L: Taylor, Emily K.); Chant for the Soul of Kalua (Ke Po Mai Lapuna Po Hilo) (C/L: Bray Sr., David); Bird of Paradise [1] (C: De Rose, Peter; L: Rosa, Malia)

Notes   [1] Written for exploitation only.

534 ✦ THE BIRDS
Universal, 1963

Producer(s)   Hitchcock, Alfred
Director(s)   Hitchcock, Alfred
Screenwriter(s)   Hunter, Evan
Source(s)   The Birds (novel) du Maurier, Daphne

Cast   Hedren, Tippi; Taylor, Rod; Tandy, Jessica; Pleshette, Suzanne; Cartwright, Veronica; Griffies, Ethel; McGraw, Charles

Song(s)   Risselty Rosselty (C: Traditional; L: Hunter, Evan)

535 ✦ BIRDS AND THE BEES (1947)

See THREE DARING DAUGHTERS.

536 ✦ THE BIRDS AND THE BEES (1956)
Paramount, 1956

Musical Score   Scharf, Walter
Composer(s)   Warren, Harry
Lyricist(s)   David, Mack
Choreographer(s)   Castle, Nick

Producer(s)   Jones, Paul
Director(s)   Taurog, Norman
Screenwriter(s)   Sheldon, Sidney; Sturges, Preston

Cast   Gobel, George; Gaynor, Mitzi; Niven, David; Gardiner, Reginald; Clark, Fred

Song(s) (The Same Thing Happens with) The Birds and the Bees; La Parisienne; The Songs I Sing [1] (C: Scharf, Walter; L: Hartman, Don); Each Time I Dream (1) [1] (C: Scharf, Walter; L: Hartman, Don); Each Time I Dream (2) [2]; Little Miss Tippy-Toes [2] (L: Adamson, Harold)

Notes A remake of THE LADY EVE. [1] These two songs have the same music but neither were used. The music was based on a theme in the film. [2] Not used.

537 ✦ BIRDS DO IT
Columbia, 1966

Musical Score Matlovsky, Samuel

Producer(s) Colbert, Stanley
Director(s) Marton, Andrew
Screenwriter(s) Kogen, Arnie; Arthur, Art

Cast Sales, Soupy; Hunter, Tab; O'Connell, Arthur; Andrews, Edward

Song(s) Birds Do It (C/L: Greenfield, Howard; Keller, Jack)

Notes No cue sheet available.

538 ✦ BIRTH OF A NOTION
Warner Brothers, 1947

Musical Score Stalling, Carl

Director(s) McKimson, Robert
Screenwriter(s) Foster, Warren

Cast Duck, Daffy; Lorre, Peter

Song(s) When My Dreamboat Comes Home (C/L: Friend, Cliff; Franklin, Dave)

539 ✦ BIRTH OF THE BLUES
Paramount, 1941

Producer(s) Bell, Monta
Director(s) Schertzinger, Victor
Screenwriter(s) De Leon, Walter; Tugend, Harry

Cast Crosby, Bing; Donlevy, Brian; Teagarden, Jack; Martin, Mary; Anderson, Eddie "Rochester"; Naish, J. Carrol; Kellaway, Cecil; Hymer, Warren; MacMahon, Horace; Barris, Harry; Elzy, Ruby; Lee, Carolyn

Song(s) Memphis Blues [1] (C: Handy, W.C.; L: Norton, George A.; Loesser, Frank); The Waiter and the Porter and the Upstairs Maid (C/L: Mercer, Johnny); Gotta Go to the Jailhouse (C: Dolan, Robert Emmett; L: Tugend, Harry)

Notes Other songs that are interpolated into the score are: "Birth of the Blues" by B.G. DeSylva, Lew Brown and Ray Henderson; "By the Light of the Silvery Moon" by Edward Madden and Gus Edwards; "Waiting at the Church" by Fred W. Leigh and Henry E. Pether; "Cuddle Up a Little Closer" by Karl Hoschna and Otto Harbach; "Wait Til the Sun Shines Nellie" by Andrew B. Sterling and Harry Von Tilzer; "Melancholy Baby" by George A. Norton and Ernie Burnett and "St. Louis Blues" by W.C. Handy. Although B.G. DeSylva is credited as producer, it is more accurate to list the associate producer when the producer of note was head of production and therefore not responsible for the everyday producing chores. [1] Also in BELLE OF THE NINETIES but with Sam Coslow revising the lyrics.

540 ✦ THE BISCUIT EATER
Disney, 1971

Musical Score Brunner, Robert F.

Producer(s) Anderson, Bill
Director(s) McEveety, Vincent
Screenwriter(s) Watkin, Lawrence Edward

Cast Holliman, Earl; Crowley, Pat; Ayres, Lew; Cambridge, Godfrey; Richards, Beah; James, Clifton; Whitaker, Johnny; Moreland, Mantan

Song(s) Moreover and Me (C/L: Tatum, Shane)

541 ✦ THE BISHOP'S WIFE
RKO, 1947

Musical Score Friedhofer, Hugo

Producer(s) Goldwyn, Samuel
Director(s) Koster, Henry
Screenwriter(s) Sherwood, Robert E.; Bercovici, Leonardo
Source(s) *In Barley Fields* (novel) Nathan, Robert

Cast Grant, Cary; Niven, David; Young, Loretta; Woolley, Monty; Gleason, James; Cooper, Gladys; Lanchester, Elsa; Haden, Sara; The Mitchell Boys' Choir

Song(s) O Sing to God—Noel (C: Gounod, Charles; L: Webb, Roy); Lost April (C/L: DeLange, Eddie; Newman, Emil; Spencer, Herbert)

Notes [1] Used instrumentally only.

542 ✦ BITTER SWEET (1933)
United Artists, 1933

Composer(s) Coward, Noel
Lyricist(s) Coward, Noel

Producer(s) Wilcox, Herbert
Director(s) Wilcox, Herbert
Screenwriter(s) Wilcox, Herbert; Hayward, Lydia; Hoffe, Monckton
Source(s) *Bitter Sweet* (operetta) Coward, Noel

Cast   Neagle, Anna; Gravet, Fernand [1]; Percy, Esme; Heatherly, Clifford; St. Helier, Ivy; Mander, Miles; Hammond, Kay

Song(s)   I'll See You Again

Notes   No cue sheet available. [1] Later to spell his last name Gravet. The name was really spelled Gravey.

543 ◆ BITTER SWEET (1940)
Metro–Goldwyn–Mayer, 1940

Composer(s)   Coward, Noel
Lyricist(s)   Coward, Noel
Choreographer(s)   Matray, Ernst

Producer(s)   Saville, Victor
Director(s)   Van Dyke II, W.S.
Screenwriter(s)   Samuels, Lesser
Source(s)   *Bitter Sweet* (operetta) Coward, Noel

Cast   MacDonald, Jeanette; Eddy, Nelson; Sanders, George; Bressart, Felix; Carver, Lynne; Hunter, Ian; Ashley, Edward; Lewis, Diana; Rumann, Sig; Judels, Charles; Beecher, Janet

Song(s)   I'll See You Again; What Is Love?; Tokay; Love in Any Language (L: Kahn, Gus); Dear Little Cafe (L: Kahn, Gus); Kiss Me; Ladies of the Town (L: Kahn, Gus); Zeigeuner; If You Could Only Come to Me; The Call of Life [1]; If Love Were All [1]

Notes   Previous film version produced in Great Britain in 1933. Some of the Kahn lyrics are based on Coward's originals, some are not. However, there is no indication as to which were originally Kahn's. No cue sheet available. [1] Recorded but not used.

544 ◆ BITTERSWEET BLUES
Publix, 1928

Song(s)   Bitter Sweet Blues (C/L: Dietrich, James; Lewis, Bobby)

Notes   No cue sheet available. Sheet music only.

545 ◆ BLACK ANGEL
Universal, 1946

Musical Score   Skinner, Frank
Composer(s)   Fairchild, Edgar; Brooks, Jack
Lyricist(s)   Brooks, Jack; Fairchild, Edgar

Producer(s)   Neill, Roy William; McKnight, Tom
Director(s)   Neill, Roy William
Screenwriter(s)   Chanslor, Roy
Source(s)   *Black Angel* (novel) Woolrich, Cornell

Cast   Duryea, Dan; Dowling, Constance; Bennett, Joan; Vincent, June; Lorre, Peter; Crawford, Broderick; Ford, Wallace; Cavanaugh, Hobart

Song(s)   Heartbreak; I Want to Be Talked About; Time Will Tell

546 ◆ THE BLACK BANDIT
Universal, 1938

Musical Score   Sanucci, Frank
Composer(s)   Allan, Fleming
Lyricist(s)   Allan, Fleming

Producer(s)   Carr, Trem
Director(s)   Waggner, George
Screenwriter(s)   West, Joseph

Cast   Baker, Bob; Reynolds, Marjorie; Taylor, Forrest

Song(s)   Starlight on the Prairie; Cowboy Song for Sale; My Old Paint Pony and Me; Dry and Dusty

547 ◆ BLACK BEAUTY
Paramount, 1971

Producer(s)   Andrews, Peter; Hayworth, Malcolm
Director(s)   Hill, James
Screenwriter(s)   Mankowitz, Wolf
Source(s)   *Black Beauty* (novel) Sewell, Anna

Cast   Lester, Mark; Slezak, Walter; Mower, Patrick; Lawrence, Peter Lee

Song(s)   Black Beauty Theme (inst.) (C: Bart, Lionel)

548 ◆ THE BLACKBOARD JUNGLE
Metro–Goldwyn–Mayer, 1955

Musical Score   Wolcott, Charles

Producer(s)   Berman, Pandro S.
Director(s)   Brooks, Richard
Screenwriter(s)   Brooks, Richard
Source(s)   *The Blackboard Jungle* (novel) Hunter, Evan

Cast   Ford, Glenn; Francis, Anne; Calhern, Louis; Hayes, Margaret; Hoyt, John; Kiley, Richard; Meyer, Emile; Ruysdael, Basil; Anderson, Warner; Poitier, Sidney; Morrow, Vic; Terranova, Dan; Campos, Rafael; Mazursky, Paul

Song(s)   Lover, Lover (Why Must We Part?) (C/L: Wolcott, Charles)

Notes   There is also a vocal of "Rock Around the Clock" by Max C. Freedman and Jimmy De Knight (also in ROCK AROUND THE CLOCK).

549 ◆ THE BLACK CAMEL
Fox, 1931

Director(s)   MacFadden, Hamilton
Screenwriter(s)   Connors, Barry; Klein, Philip
Source(s)   *Black Camel* (novel) Biggers, Earl Derr

Cast   Oland, Warner; Eilers, Sally; Lugosi, Bela; Revier, Dorothy

Song(s) Uhuehuene [1] (C/L: King); I Have a Thought in My Heart for You [2] (C/L: Hoopii Jr., Sol)

Notes [1] Not written for the film. [2] Also in THE MAN WHO CAME BACK (1931).

550 ✦ THE BLACK CAULDRON
Disney, 1985

Musical Score Bernstein, Elmer

Producer(s) Hale, Joe
Director(s) Berman, Ted; Rich, Richard J.
Screenwriter(s) Jonas, David; Gerry, Vance; Berman, Ted; Rich, Richard J.; Hale, Joe; Wilson, Al; Morita, Roy; Young, Pete; Stevens, Art; Disney, Roy Edward; Sisson, Rosemary Anne
Source(s) Chronicles of Prydain series (novels) Alexander, Lloyd
Voices Huston, John; Bardsley, Grant; Sheridan, Susan; Jones, Freddie; Hawthorne, Nigel; Byner, John; Malet, Arthur; Fonacaro, Phil; Hurt, John

Song(s) Fflewddur's Song (C: Bowden, Richard; L: Rich, Richard J.)

Notes Animated cartoon.

551 ✦ BLACK EYE
Warner Brothers, 1974

Musical Score Garson, Mort

Producer(s) Rooney, Pat
Director(s) Arnold, Jack
Screenwriter(s) Haggard, Mark; Martin, Jim
Source(s) *Murder on the Wild Side* (novel) Jack, Jeff

Cast Williamson, Fred; Forsyth, Rosemary; Graves, Teresa; Morrison, Bret; Anderson, Richard

Song(s) I Know Where We've Been (C: Garson, Mort; L: Wilson, Jacques)

552 ✦ BLACK GOLD
Warner Brothers, 1963

Musical Score Jackson, Howard

Producer(s) Barnett, Jim
Director(s) Martinson, Leslie H.
Screenwriter(s) Duncan, Bob; Duncan, Wanda
Source(s) "Wyoming Wildcatter" (story) Whittington, Harry

Cast Carey, Philip; McBain, Diane; Cody, Iron Eyes; Best, James; Akins, Claude; Spain, Fay

Song(s) Nobody Lied (When They Said That I Cried Over You) (C: Weber, Edwin J.; L: Berry, Hyatt; Norman, Karyl)

Notes It is not known if this was written for the picture.

553 ✦ BLACK HILLS
Eagle Lion, 1948

Musical Score Greene, Walter

Producer(s) Thomas, Jerry
Director(s) Taylor, Ray
Screenwriter(s) Poland, Joseph

Cast Dean, Eddie; Ates, Roscoe; Patterson, Shirley; Frost, Terry

Song(s) Black Hills [1] (C/L: Dean, Eddie; Blair, Hal); Punchinello (C/L: Gates, Pete); Let's Go Sparkin' (C/L: Dean, Eddie; Blair, Hal)

Notes [1] Also in HAWK OF POWDER RIVER.

554 ✦ THE BLACK KLANSMAN
SGS Prods., 1966

Musical Score Mendoza-Nava, Jaime

Producer(s) Mikels, Ted V.
Director(s) Nikels, Ted V.
Screenwriter(s) Wilson, John T.; Names, Arthur A.

Cast Gilden, Richard; Kutner, Rima; Lovejoy, Harry

Song(s) The Black Klansman (C/L: Harris, Tony)

Notes No cue sheet available.

555 ✦ BLACK OAK CONSPIRACY
New World, 1977

Musical Score Peake, Don

Producer(s) Vint, Jesse; Clark, Tom
Director(s) Kelljan, Bob
Screenwriter(s) Vint, Jesse; Smith, Hugh

Cast Vint, Jesse; Carlson, Karen; Salmi, Albert; Cassel, Seymour

Song(s) Jingo's Song (C/L: Peake, Don; Everly, Phil)

Notes No cue sheet available.

556 ✦ THE BLACK ORCHID
Paramount, 1958

Musical Score Cicognini, Alessandro

Producer(s) Ponti, Carlo; Girosi, Marcello
Director(s) Ritt, Martin
Screenwriter(s) Stefano, Joseph

Cast Loren, Sophia; Quinn, Anthony; Richman, Mark; Vincent, Virginia; Bissell, Whit; Balin, Ina

Song(s) The Hurdy-Gurdy Song (The Black Orchid Street Melody) [1] (C: Cicognini, Alessandro; L: David, Mack)

Notes [1] Used instrumentally only.

557 ✦ **BLACK SAMSON**
Warner Brothers, 1974

Musical Score Toussaint, Allen

Producer(s) Cady, Daniel B.
Director(s) Bail, Chuck [1]
Screenwriter(s) Hamilton Jr., Warren

Cast Tarkington, Rockne; Smith, William; Strickland, Connie; Speed, Carol; Payne, Michael

Song(s) Black Samson (C/L: Toussaint, Allen)

Notes Billed as Charles Bail.

558 ✦ **BLACK SHEEP**
Twentieth Century–Fox, 1935

Producer(s) Wurtzel, Sol M.
Director(s) Dwan, Allan
Screenwriter(s) Rivkin, Allen

Cast Lowe, Edmund; Trevor, Claire; Brown, Tom; Pallette, Eugene; Ames, Adrienne; Mundin, Herbert; Sterling, Ford; Prouty, Jed; Bevan, Billy; Torrence, David

Song(s) In Other Words I'm in Love (C: Levant, Oscar; L: Clare, Sidney)

Notes From a letter from Sam Fox: "We are confronted with many problmes respecting the exploitation of film songs. First, we must have good songs and while the songs may be fine production material, very often they are not favorably accepted by the important radio artists, orchestras, sponsors, program directors, etc. It has been our experience that we cannot make a hit of any song unless we land the important plugs and these do not use or ask for our printed orchestrations inasmuch as they use their own special arrangements. We have found that usually after the important plugs have used a particular number with their own special arrangement, there is a demand for printed orchestrations and thereupon we publish such printed orchestrations. It is costly to get out orchestrations and find there is no demand for same."

559 ✦ **BLACK SPURS**
Paramount, 1965

Producer(s) Lyles, A.C.
Director(s) Springsteen, R.G.
Screenwriter(s) Fisher, Steve

Cast Calhoun, Rory; Moore, Terry; Arlen, Richard; Brady, Scott; Darnell, Linda; Cabot, Bruce; Chaney Jr., Lon

Song(s) Black Spurs (C: Haskell, Jimmie; L: Dunham, "By" [1])

Notes [1] Pseudonym for William D. Dunham.

560 ✦ **BLACK STARLET**
Omni Pictures, 1978

Musical Score Hinton, Joe; Ervin, Dee
Composer(s) Hinton, Joe; Ervin, Dee
Lyricist(s) Hinton, Joe; Ervin, Dee

Producer(s) Cady, Daniel B.
Director(s) Munger, Chris
Screenwriter(s) Ostroff, Howard

Cast Brown, Juanita; Mason, Eric; King, Damu; Tarkington, Rockne; Holden, Diane; Keen, Noah

Song(s) Up Is Down; Hollywood Faces; Fire Sign; Go On and Find Your Star

Notes No cue sheet available.

561 ✦ **THE BLACK SWAN**
Twentieth Century–Fox, 1942

Producer(s) Bassler, Robert
Director(s) King, Henry
Screenwriter(s) Hecht, Ben; Miller, Seton I.
Source(s) *The Black Swan* (novel) Sabatini, Rafael

Cast Power, Tyrone; O'Hara, Maureen; Cregar, Laird; Mitchell, Thomas; Sanders, George; Quinn, Anthony; Zucco, George; Bonanova, Fortunio

Song(s) Heave Ho (C: Newman, Alfred; L: Henderson, Charles)

562 ✦ **BLACK TUESDAY**
United Artists, 1954

Musical Score Dunlap, Paul

Producer(s) Goldstein, Robert
Director(s) Fregonese, Hugo
Screenwriter(s) Boehm, Sydney

Cast Robinson, Edward G.; Graves, Peter; Stone, Milburn; Parker, Jean; Stevens, Warren; Kelly, Jack

Song(s) Black Tuesday Blues (C/L: Parrish, Bob)

563 ✦ **THE BLACK WATCH**
Twentieth Century–Fox, 1929

Director(s) Ford, John; Hare, Lumsden
Screenwriter(s) McGuinness, James Kevin
Source(s) *King of the Khyber Rifles* (novel) Mundy, Talbot

Cast McLaglen, Victor; Loy, Myrna; King, Claude; Rollins, David; Hare, Lumsden; D'Arcy, Roy; Lewis, Mitchell

Song(s) Flowers of Delight (C: Kernell, William; L: Thompson, Harlan)

564 ✦ BLACK WIDOW
Twentieth Century–Fox, 1987

Musical Score   Small, Michael

Producer(s)   Schneider, Harold
Director(s)   Rafelson, Bob
Screenwriter(s)   Bass, Ronald

Cast   Winger, Debra; Russell, Theresa; Frey, Sami; Hopper, Dennis; Williamson, Nicol; O'Quinn, Terry; Hong, James; Moffett, D.W.; Woronov, Mary

Song(s)   Magic Island (C/L: Rafelson, Peter); Night Hearts [1] (C/L: Rafelson, Peter)

Notes   [1] Not on cue sheet. Only in *Academy Index*.

565 ✦ THE BLACK WINDMILL
Universal, 1974

Musical Score   Budd, Roy

Producer(s)   Siegel, Don
Director(s)   Siegel, Don
Screenwriter(s)   Vance, Leigh
Source(s)   *Seven Days to a Killing* (novel) Egleton, Clive

Cast   Caine, Michael; Pleasence, Donald; Vernon, John; Seyrig, Delphine

Song(s)   Mother Nature (C: Budd, Roy; L: Fishman, Jack)

Notes   "Chestnut Tree" by Jimmy and Hamilton Kennedy and Tommy Connor is also used vocally.

566 ✦ BLAME IT ON RIO
Twentieth Century–Fox, 1984

Composer(s)   Wannberg, Ken
Lyricist(s)   Spiegel, Dennis

Producer(s)   Donen, Stanley
Director(s)   Donen, Stanley
Screenwriter(s)   Peters, Charlie; Gelbart, Larry

Cast   Caine, Michael; Bologna, Joseph; Harper, Valerie; Moore, Demi

Song(s)   Blame It on Rio (C: Coleman, Cy; L: Harnick, Sheldon); I Must Be Doing Something Right (C: Coleman, Cy; L: Harnick, Sheldon); Nothing to Say; PB #1 (C: Castro-Neves, Oscar; L: Blanc, Aldir); PB #7 (C: Castro-Neves, Oscar; L: Blanc, Aldir); Afterthought; Alone with Me; Misunderstood; Time Out [1]; Chasing at Images; Strong Is the Urge

Notes   [1] Instrumental use only.

567 ✦ BLAME IT ON THE NIGHT
Tri-Star, 1984

Composer(s)   Neeley, Ted; Scott, Tom
Lyricist(s)   Neeley, Ted

Producer(s)   Taft, Gene
Director(s)   Taft, Gene
Screenwriter(s)   Jenkin, Len

Cast   Mancuso, Nick; Thames, Byron; Ackerman, Leslie; Bakalyan, Richard [1]; Granger, Leeyan; Ludwick, Rex; Wilding, Michael

Song(s)   Lost in the Light (C: Neeley, Ted); Ol' Grinnin' Moon (C: Neeley, Ted); Blame It on the Night; Another One Night Stand; Takin' Care of Each Other; One By One (C: Neeley, Ted; L: Neeley, Ted; Myers-Mark, Judith); Stone Me (L: Neeley, Ted; Taft, Gene); A Man without a Woman (L: Neeley, Ted; Taft, Gene)

Notes   No cue sheet available. [1] Billed as Dick Bakalyan.

568 ✦ BLAME IT ON THE SAMBA
Disney, 1948

Song(s)   Blame It on the Samba [1] (C: Nazareth, Ernesto; L: Nazareth, Ernesto; Gilbert, Ray); Apanhei-Te-Cavaquinho [1] (C: Nazareth, Ernesto; L: Gilbert, Ray)

Notes   Short subject. No credit sheet available. [1] Gilbert provided the English lyrics.

569 ✦ THE BLAZE OF NOON
Paramount, 1947

Producer(s)   Fellows, Robert
Director(s)   Farrow, John
Screenwriter(s)   Sheekman, Arthur; Wead, Frank
Source(s)   (novel) Gann, Ernest K.

Cast   Holden, William; Hayden, Sterling; Baxter, Anne; Bendix, William; Tufts, Sonny; Da Silva, Howard; Wallace, Jean; Corrigan, Lloyd; Sands, Johnny; Wright, Will

Song(s)   The Blaze of Noon [1] (C: Deutsch, Adolph; L: Henderson, Charles)

Notes   [1] Written for exploitation only.

570 ✦ BLAZE O' GLORY
Sono-Art, 1930

Composer(s)   Hanley, James F.
Lyricist(s)   Dowling, Eddie; Macdonald, Ballard; McCarthy, Joseph; Brockman, James

Director(s)   Hoffman, Renaud; Cronenaud, George J.
Screenwriter(s)   McCarty, Henry
Source(s)   "The Long Shot" (story) Boyd, Thomas Alexander

Cast   Dowling, Eddie; Compson, Betty; Schuman-Heinck, Ferdinand; Darro, Frankie; Walthall, Henry B.; The Rounders

Song(s) The Doughboy's Lullaby (L: Dowling, Eddie; Brockman, James); Put a Little Salt on the Bluebird's Tail (L: Dowling, Eddie; Brockman, James); Wrapped in a Red Red Rose (L: Dowling, Eddie; McCarthy, Joseph); Welcome Home (L: Macdonald, Ballard)

Notes No cue sheet available. After the New York premiere the film was cut down and several of the songs were shortened. There is also a Spanish version: SOMBRAS DE GLORIA.

571 ✦ BLAZING SADDLES
Warner Brothers, 1974

Musical Score Morris, John
Composer(s) Brooks, Mel
Lyricist(s) Brooks, Mel

Producer(s) Hertzberg, Michael
Director(s) Brooks, Mel
Screenwriter(s) Brooks, Mel; Steinberg, Norman; Bergman, Andrew; Pryor, Richard; Uger, Alan

Cast Little, Cleavon; Wilder, Gene; Korman, Harvey; Karras, Alex; Kahn, Madeline; Brooks, Mel

Song(s) Blazing Saddles [1] (C: Morris, John; Brooks, Mel); Ballad of Rock Ridge; I'm Tired; French Mistake

Notes [1] Background vocal use only.

572 ✦ BLAZING SIXES
Warner Brothers, 1937

Composer(s) Jerome, M.K.
Lyricist(s) Scholl, Jack

Producer(s) Foy, Bryan
Director(s) Smith, Noel
Screenwriter(s) Neville, John Thomas
Source(s) "Miracle Mountain" (story) Coldeway, Anthony

Cast Foran, Dick; Valkis, Helen; Hart, Gordon; Foran, Tom; Strange, Glenn

Song(s) In a Little Country Town; Ridin' on to Monterey

Notes No cue sheet available.

573 ✦ THE BLAZING SUN
Columbia, 1950

Producer(s) Autry, Gene
Director(s) English, John
Screenwriter(s) Townley, Jack

Cast Autry, Gene; Champion; Duncan, Kenne; Barton, Gregg; Norris, Edward; London, Tom; Buttram, Pat; Hale Jr., Alan; Marvin, Frankie

Song(s) Along the Navajo Trail [1] [2] (C/L: Markes, Larry; Charles, Dick; De Lange, Eddie); Brush Those Tears From Your Eyes [2] (C/L: Haldeman, Oakley; Trave, Al; Lee, Jimmy)

Notes [1] Originally titled "Prairie Parade," with words and music by Larry Markes and Dick Charles in 1942. It was performed in the film LAUGH YOUR BLUES AWAY. As "Along the Navajo Trail" it was used in the Republic Picture of the same name and in DON'T FENCE ME IN. [2] Not written for this picture.

574 ✦ BLESSED EVENT
Warner Brothers, 1932

Producer(s) Griffith, Ray
Director(s) Del Ruth, Roy
Screenwriter(s) Green, Howard J.
Source(s) *Blessed Event* (play) Seff, Manuel; Wilson, Forrest

Cast Tracy, Lee; Brian, Mary; Jenkins, Allen; Donnelly, Ruth; Sparks, Ned; Powell, Dick

Song(s) How Can You Say No When All the World Is Saying Yes? (C: Burke, Joe; L: Kahal, Irving; Dubin, Al); I'm Making Hay in the Moonlight (C: Greer, Jesse; L: Seymour, Tot)

Notes No cue sheet available.

575 ✦ BLESS THE BEASTS AND CHILDREN
Columbia, 1971

Musical Score Botkin Jr., Perry; De Vorzon, Barry

Producer(s) Kramer, Stanley
Director(s) Kramer, Stanley
Screenwriter(s) Benoff, Mac
Source(s) *Bless the Beasts & the Children* (novel) Swarthout, Glendon

Cast Mumy, Billy [1]; Robins, Barry; Chapin, Miles; Claser, Darel; Swofford, Ken

Song(s) Bless the Beasts and Children (C/L: Botkin Jr., Perry; De Vorzon, Barry)

Notes [1] Billed as Bill Mumy.

576 ✦ BLIND DATE
Tri-Star, 1987

Musical Score Mancini, Henry

Producer(s) Adams, Tony
Director(s) Edwards, Blake
Screenwriter(s) Launer, Dale

Cast Basinger, Kim; Willis, Bruce; Larroquette, John; Daniels, William; Coe, George; Blum, Mark; Hartman, Phil; Van Patten, Joyce; Shimono, Sab

Song(s) Simply Meant to Be (C/L: Mancini, Henry; Merrill, George; Rubicam, Shannon); Anybody Seen Her (C/L: Brown, L. Russell; Vera, Billy); Treasures (C/L: Jordan, Stanley)

Notes No cue sheet available.

577 ✦ THE BLISS OF MRS. BLOSSOM
Paramount, 1968

Musical Score Ortolani, Riz
Composer(s) Ortolani, Riz
Lyricist(s) Newell, Norman

Producer(s) Shaftel, Josef
Director(s) McGrath, Joseph
Screenwriter(s) Coppel, Alec; Norden, Denis
Source(s) *The Bliss of Mrs. Blossom* (play) Coppel, Alec; (story) Shaftel, Josef

Cast MacLaine, Shirley; Attenborough, Richard; Booth, James

Song(s) The Way That I Live; Let's Live for Love; Paree - Paree - Paree; I Think I'm Beginning to Fall in Love (C/L: Stephens, Geoffrey)

578 ✦ BLITZ WOLF
Metro–Goldwyn–Mayer, 1942

Song(s) Blitz Wolf (C/L: Bradley, Scott)

Notes Animated cartoon.

579 ✦ THE BLOB
Paramount, 1958

Musical Score Carmichael, Ralph

Producer(s) Harris, Jack H.
Director(s) Yeaworth Jr., Irvin
Screenwriter(s) Simonson, Theodore; Phillips, Kate

Cast McQueen, Steve; Benson, John; Corseaut, Aneta; Rowe, Earl; Howland, Olin

Song(s) The Blob (C: Bacharach, Burt; L: David, Mack)

580 ✦ THE BLONDE CHEAT
RKO, 1938

Producer(s) Sistrom, William
Director(s) Santley, Joseph
Screenwriter(s) Kaufman, Charles; Yawitz, Paul; Shore, Viola Brothers; Segall, Harry

Cast Fontaine, Joan; de Marney, Derrick; Kellaway, Cecil; Cunningham, Cecil; Coote, Robert

Song(s) It Must Be Love (C/L: Dreyer, Dave; Ruby, Herman)

581 ✦ BLONDE CRAZY
Warner Brothers, 1931

Director(s) Del Ruth, Roy
Screenwriter(s) Glasmon, Kubec; Bright, John

Cast Cagney, James; Blondell, Joan; Calhern, Louis; Francis, Noel; Milland, Ray

Song(s) When Your Lover Has Gone (C/L: Swan, E.A.); I Can't Write the Words (C: Marks, Gerald; L: Fields, Buddy); Ain't That the Way It Goes [1] (C: Ahlert, Fred E.; L: Turk, Roy)

Notes Released in Great Britain as LARCENY LANE. [1] Instrumental use only indicated in cue sheet.

582 ✦ BLONDE FROM BROOKLYN
Columbia, 1945

Producer(s) Richmond, Ted
Director(s) Lord, Del
Screenwriter(s) Lazarus, Erna

Cast Stanton, Robert; Merrick, Lynn; Hall, Thurston; Treen, Mary

Song(s) Lost (A Wonderful Girl) (C: Hanley, James F.; L: Davis, Benny); Save Him for Me (C/L: Scherman, Robert); Comin' Around the Corner (C/L: Davis, Mac; Wilson, Robert); Just a Prayer Away (C: Kapp, David; L: Tobias, Charles); Yip Yip Dehootie (My Baby Said Yes) (C/L: Robin, Sid; Walters, Teddy); Alabamy Bound (C: Henderson, Ray; L: DeSylva, B.G.; Green, Bud)

583 ✦ BLONDE RANSOM
Universal, 1945

Musical Score Skinner, Frank
Choreographer(s) Da Pron, Louis

Producer(s) Lewis, Gene
Director(s) Beaudine, William
Screenwriter(s) Webster, M. Coates

Cast Cook, Donald; Grey, Virginia; Lee, Pinky; Lyons, Collette

Song(s) Hinky Dinky Pinky (C/L: Sherman, Al); The Life of the Party (C/L: Brooks, Jack); Got a Million Dollar Worth of Dreams (C/L: Brooks, Jack; Berens, Norman); Musical Wedding (C: Mendelssohn, Felix; Wagner, Richard; L: Brooks, Jack)

584 ✦ BLONDE TROUBLE
Paramount, 1937

Producer(s) Jones, Paul
Director(s) Archainbaud, George
Screenwriter(s) Hayward, Lillie
Source(s) *June Moon* (play) Kaufman, George S.; Lardner, Ring

Cast Downs, Johnny [4]; Brendel, El; Davis, Eddie; Whitney, Eleanore; Overman, Lynne

Song(s) Montana Moon [1] (C/L: Kaufman, George S.; Lardner, Ring); As a Rose in June [2] (C/L: Kaufman, George S.; Lardner, Ring); Life is a Game [2] (C/L: Kaufman, George S.; Lardner, Ring); She Came Rollin' Down the Mountain [5] (C: Sherwin, Manning; L: Lippman, Arthur; Richman, Harry); Hello Tokio [3] (C/L: Kaufman, George S.; Lardner, Ring); It Was All in Fun (C: Lane, Burton; L: Freed, Ralph)

Notes The picture was originally titled GOOD NIGHT LADIES and ADVENTURE WITH MUSIC before release. See JUNE MOON. [1] Originally in the stage show JUNE MOON. [2] Same music. [3] This was an earlier song not written for the film. It appeared in JUNE MOON (the movie). [4] Buddy Clark recorded "It's All in Fun" for the soundtrack including the end title. He probably dubbed the vocals for Johnny Downs. [5] Also in SHIP CAFE, though used only instrumentally.

585 ✦ BLONDE VENUS
Paramount, 1932

Musical Score Poteker, Oscar

Director(s) von Sternberg, Josef
Screenwriter(s) Lauren, S.K.; Furthman, Jules

Cast Dietrich, Marlene; Marshall, Herbert; Grant, Cary; Moore, Dickie; Toler, Sidney

Song(s) Hot Voo-Doo [1] (C: Rainger, Ralph; L: Robin, Leo; Coslow, Sam); I Couldn't Be Annoyed (C: Whiting, Richard A.; L: Robin, Leo); You Little So-and-So [3] (C: Coslow, Sam; L: Robin, Leo); I'm Getting What I Want [4] [5] (C: Whiting, Richard A.; L: Robin, Leo); You Threw Me Overboard [5] (C/L: Coslow, Sam); Cher Ami [2] (inst.) (C: Coslow, Sam)

Notes Dietrich also sings "Leise Ziert Durch Mein Gemut" by Mendelssohn and "Ein Mannlein Steht Im Walde" by Humperdinck and Wette. Robin was hired to punch up the lyrics for songs already written. [1] Robin retained only four lines and the title while adding an extra chorus and the verse. [2] Not listed in final rundown of songs. [3] Robin retained Coslow's title and first verse as written. The other two verses and second chorus were written by Robin. [4] The title was by J.C. Lewis. Robin retained six lines of Lewis' lyrics in the first chorus and added an additional chorus and verse. Whiting had originally written the song with Lewis but when Robin was brought in he rewrote the lyric. [5] Unused.

586 ✦ BLONDIE GOES LATIN
Columbia, 1941

Composer(s) Forrest, Chet; Wright, Bob
Lyricist(s) Forrest, Chet; Wright, Bob
Choreographer(s) Kay, Marie

Producer(s) Sparks, Robert
Director(s) Strayer, Frank R.
Screenwriter(s) Flournoy, Richard; De Wolf, Karen
Source(s) *Blondie* (comic strip) Young, Chic

Cast Singleton, Penny; Lake, Arthur; Simms, Larry; Daisy; Mummert, Danny; Guizar, Tito; Hale, Jonathan; Bacon, Irving; Terry, Ruth; Grant, Kirby; Acuff, Eddie

Song(s) Solteiro e Melhor [1] (C/L: Soares, Rubens; Silva, Felisberto); You Don't Play a Drum You Beat It; I Hate Music Lessons; Querida [2]; You Can't Cry on My Shoulder

Notes Titled CONGA SWING in Great Britain. [1] English lyrics by Bill Morgan. Not written for this picture. [2] Spanish lyrics written by M. de Zarraga.

587 ✦ BLONDIE GOES TO COLLEGE
Columbia, 1942

Composer(s) Chaplin, Saul
Lyricist(s) Cahn, Sammy

Producer(s) Sparks, Robert
Director(s) Strayer, Frank R.
Screenwriter(s) Breslow, Lou
Source(s) *Blondie* (comic strip) Young, Chic

Cast Parks, Larry; Singleton, Penny; Lake, Arthur; Simms, Larry; Daisy; Blair, Janet; Mummert, Danny; Mara, Adele; Bridges, Lloyd; Melton, Sid; Tombes, Andrew; Hale, Jonathan

Song(s) Loyal Sons of Leighton; Do I Need You [1]

Notes Released as THE BOSS SAID "NO" in Great Britain. [1] Not used.

588 ✦ BLONDIE MEETS THE BOSS
Columbia, 1940

Musical Score Harline, Leigh
Choreographer(s) Larkin, Eddie

Producer(s) Sparks, Robert
Director(s) Strayer, Frank R.
Screenwriter(s) Flournoy, Richard
Source(s) *Blondie* (comic strip) Young, Chic

Cast Singleton, Penny; Lake, Arthur; Simms, Larry; Daisy; Skinnay Ennis and His Band; Moore, Dorothy; Hale, Jonathan

Song(s) Y' Had It Comin' to You (C: Oakland, Ben; L: Lerner, Sam)

589 ✦ BLONDIE OF THE FOLLIES
Metro–Goldwyn–Mayer, 1932

Musical Score Axt, William

Director(s) Goulding, Edmund
Screenwriter(s) Loos, Anita

Cast Davies, Marion; Montgomery, Robert; Dove, Billie; Durante, Jimmy; Gleason, James; Pitts, ZaSu; Toler, Sidney; Dumbrille, Douglass

Song(s) Why Don't You Take Me (C/L: Goulding, Edmund); Don't Take Your Girl to the Grand Hotel (C/L: Snell, Dave); One Night, One Spring [1] (C/L: Goulding, Edmund)

Notes Other songs used instrumentally are "Goodnight, My Love" by Harry Tobias, Gus Arnheim and Jules Lemare; "Tell Me While We're Dancing" by Harry Link and Nick Kenney; "Three on a Match" by Raymond B. Egan and Ted Fiorito; "Goin' Fishin'" by Walter G. Samuels and Leonard Whitcup and "It Was So

Beautiful" by Arthur Freed and Harry Barris. [1] Used instrumentally only.

590 ✦ BLONDIE'S BLESSED EVENT
Columbia, 1941

Producer(s) Sparks, Robert
Director(s) Strayer, Frank R.
Screenwriter(s) Flournoy, Richard; Lee, Connie; De Wolf, Karen
Source(s) *Blondie* (comic strip) Young, Chic

Cast Singleton, Penny; Lake, Arthur; Simms, Larry; Mummert, Danny; Brown, Stanley; Daisy; Hale, Jonathan; Conried, Hans; Wickes, Mary; Harvey, Paul

Song(s) Ah Loo Loo (C: Chaplin, Saul; L: Cahn, Sammy)

591 ✦ BLOOD ALLEY
Warner Brothers, 1955

Musical Score Webb, Roy

Director(s) Wellman, William A.
Screenwriter(s) Fleischman, A.S.
Source(s) *Blood Alley* (novel) Fleischman, A.S.

Cast Wayne, John; Bacall, Lauren; Fix, Paul; Mazurki, Mike; Ekberg, Anita

Song(s) Blood Alley Song (C: Webb, Roy; L: Hsueh, W.F.)

592 ✦ BLOOD AND SAND
Twentieth Century–Fox, 1941

Musical Score Gomez, Vincente
Composer(s) Gomez, Vincente
Lyricist(s) Gomez, Vincente

Producer(s) Zanuck, Darryl F.
Director(s) Mamoulian, Rouben
Screenwriter(s) Swerling, Jo
Source(s) *Blood and Sand* (novel) Ibanez, Vincente Blasco

Cast Power, Tyrone; Darnell, Linda; Hayworth, Rita; Nazimova; Quinn, Anthony; Naish, J. Carrol; Carradine, John; Cregar, Laird; Bari, Lynn; Gomez, Vincente; Montague, William [1]; Reeves, George; Bonanova, Fortunio; Killian, Victor; de Cordoba, Pedro

Song(s) Tu No Te Llamas (C/L: Bonanova, Fortunio); Chi-Qui-Chi (L: Tuvim, Abe); Saeta; Verde Luna

Notes [1] Monty Banks.

593 ✦ BLOOD HOOK
Troma, 1987

Musical Score Naunas, Thomas A.

Producer(s) Herbert, David
Director(s) Mallon, James
Screenwriter(s) Edgerton, Larry; Galligan, John

Cast Jacobs, Mark; Danz, Patrick; Drake, Paul; Hauser, Sara; Todd, Lisa; Winters, Don

Song(s) Fishing for Your Love (C/L: Harper, Victor); Things Aren't What They Seem (C/L: Naunas, Thomas A.)

Notes No cue sheet available.

594 ✦ BLOODHOUNDS ON BROADWAY
Twentieth Century–Fox, 1952

Choreographer(s) Sidney, Robert

Producer(s) Jessel, George
Director(s) Jones, Harmon
Screenwriter(s) Gomberg, Sy
Source(s) "Bloodhounds on Broadway" (story) Runyon, Damon

Cast Gaynor, Mitzi; Brady, Scott; Green, Mitzi; Chapman, Marguerite; O'Shea, Michael; Vernon, Wally; Slate, Henry

Song(s) Bye Low (C/L: Daniel, Eliot); Jack of Diamonds (C: Oakland, Ben; L: Webster, Paul Francis); Do the New York [1] (C/L: Murray, J.P.; Trivers, Barry; Oakland, Ben)

Notes There are many other vocals of past Fox songs. [1] Not used.

595 ✦ BLOODSPORT
Cannon, 1988

Musical Score Hertzog, Paul

Producer(s) DiSalle, Mark
Director(s) Arnold, Newt
Screenwriter(s) Lettich, Sheldon; Cosby, Christopher; Friedman, Mel

Cast Van Damme, Jean Claude; Gibb, Donald; Ayres, Leah; Burton, Norman; Whitaker, Forrest

Song(s) Fight to Survive (C/L: Shandi; Hertzog, Paul); On My Own—Alone (C/L: Shandi; Hertzog, Paul)

Notes No cue sheet available.

596 ✦ BLOSSOMS
Publix, 1928

Song(s) Blossoms That Bloom in the Moonlight (C/L: Dietrich, James; Black, Ben)

Notes No cue sheet available. Sheet music only.

597 ✦ BLOSSOMS IN THE DUST
Metro–Goldwyn–Mayer, 1941

Musical Score Stothart, Herbert

Producer(s) Asher, Irving
Director(s) LeRoy, Mervyn
Screenwriter(s) Loos, Anita

Cast Pidgeon, Walter; Garson, Greer; Bressart, Felix; Hunt, Marsha; Holden, Fay; Hinds, Samuel S.

Song(s) Blossoms in the Dust (C: Stothart, Herbert; L: Brent, Earl)

598 ✦ BLOSSOMS ON BROADWAY
Paramount, 1937

Composer(s) Sherwin, Manning
Lyricist(s) Loesser, Frank

Producer(s) Schulberg, B.P.
Director(s) Wallace, Richard
Screenwriter(s) Reeves, Theodore

Cast Ross, Shirley; Davis, Rufe; Arnold, Edward; Frawley, William; Trent, John

Song(s) Blossoms on Broadway [1] (C: Rainger, Ralph; L: Robin, Leo); No Ring on Her Finger [5]; You Can't Tell a Man by His Hat; Police Line Up (Grand Finale in Police Station); Operatum (Greek Opera Sequence) [3] (L: Freed, Ralph); The Rhythm of the Moon [2] (C: Rainger, Ralph; L: Robin, Leo); Snug as a Bug in a Rug [4] (C: Malneck, Matty)

Notes The picture was originally titled PARK AVENUE FOLLIES. [1] Originally written for COLLEGE SWING but not used. Also not used in THE BIG BROADCAST OF 1936. [2] Written for WE'RE NOT DRESSING but not used. This was also not used for BLOSSOMS ON BROADWAY. [3] The music was compiled by Phil Boutelje. [4] Unused. Finally filmed in THE GRACIE ALLEN MURDER CASE. [5] Also in FLAMING FEATHER and THE PARSON OF PANIMINT.

599 ✦ BLOWING WILD
Warner Brothers, 1953

Musical Score Tiomkin, Dimitri

Producer(s) Sperling, Milton
Director(s) Fregonese, Hugo
Screenwriter(s) Yordan, Philip

Cast Cooper, Gary; Stanwyck, Barbara; Quinn, Anthony; Roman, Ruth; Bond, Ward

Song(s) Blowing Wild (C: Tiomkin, Dimitri; L: Webster, Paul Francis)

600 ✦ BLOW-UP
Metro–Goldwyn–Mayer, 1968

Musical Score Hancock, Herbie

Producer(s) Ponti, Carlo
Director(s) Antonioni, Michelangelo
Screenwriter(s) Antonioni, Michelangelo; Guerra, Tonino; Bond, Edward

Cast Redgrave, Vanessa; Miles, Sarah; Hemmings, David; Castle, John; Hills, Gillian; Verushka; Chagrin, Claude; Birkin, Jane; Bowles, Peter; Chagrin, Julian

Song(s) Did You Ever Make Up Your Mind? (C/L: Sebastian, John); Stroll On (C/L: Yardbirds, The)

601 ✦ THE BLUE ANGEL (1930)
Paramount, 1930

Composer(s) Hollander, Frederick
Lyricist(s) Hollander, Frederick

Producer(s) Pommer, Erich
Director(s) von Sternberg, Josef
Screenwriter(s) Liebman, Robert [2]
Source(s) *Professor Unrath* (book) Mann, Heinrich

Cast Jannings, Emil; Dietrich, Marlene

Song(s) Falling in Love Again; Beware of Blonde Women; Gotta Get a Man; Just a Man; Throw Away the Key; Spring Has Come

Notes [2] Von Sternberg claimed to have written the screenplay.

602 ✦ THE BLUE ANGEL (1959)
Twentieth Century–Fox, 1959

Musical Score Friedhofer, Hugo

Producer(s) Cummings, Jack
Director(s) Dymtryk, Edward
Screenwriter(s) Balchin, Nigel

Cast Jurgens, Curt; Britt, May; Bikel, Theodore; Banner, John; Mioni, Fabrizio; Stossel, Ludwig

Song(s) Lola—Lola (C/L: Livingston, Jay; Evans, Ray)

Notes A remake of THE BLUE ANGEL with a screenplay by Karl Zuckmayer, Karl Vollmoeller and Robert Liebman which was based on the novel by Heinrich Mann. There is also a vocal of "Falling in Love Again" by Frederick Hollander and also "I, Yi, Yi, Yi, Yi (I Like You Very Much)" by Harry Warren and Mack Gordon.

603 ✦ BLUE BAYOU
Disney, 1946

Song(s) Blue Bayou (C: Worth, Bobby; L: Gilbert, Ray)

Notes This cartoon is part of MAKE MINE MUSIC.

604 ✦ BLUEBEARD'S TEN HONEYMOONS
Allied Artists, 1960

Musical Score Elms, Albert

Producer(s) Parkinson, Roy
Director(s) Wilder, W. Lee
Screenwriter(s) Wilder, Myles

Cast Sanders, George; Calvet, Corinne; Kent, Jean; Roc, Patricia; Audley, Maxine; Gynt, Greta; Coulouris, George; Lawrence, Sheldon; Fleming, Ian

Song(s) Challenge of Love (C: Elms, Albert; L: Caryll, Joseph)

Notes No cue sheet available. Note Ian Fleming's inclusion in the cast list.

605 ✦ THE BLUEBIRD (1940)
Twentieth Century–Fox, 1940

Musical Score Newman, Alfred
Composer(s) Newman, Alfred
Lyricist(s) Bullock, Walter
Choreographer(s) Castle, Nick

Producer(s) Zanuck, Darryl F.
Director(s) Lang, Walter
Screenwriter(s) Pascal, Ernest
Source(s) *The Bluebird* (play) Maeterlinck, Maurice

Cast Temple, Shirley; Byington, Spring; Bruce, Nigel; Sondergaard, Gale; Collins, Eddie; Jason, Sybil; Ralph, Jessie; Ericson, Helen; Hicks, Russell; Crews, Laura Hope; Loftus, Cecilia; Shean, Al; Reynolds, Gene

Song(s) Lay-De-O; Kingdom of the Future; Someday You'll Find Your Bluebird [1] (L: Gordon, Mack)

Notes A traditional German Christmas carol titled "Ihr Kinderlein Kommet" is also used and titled "Oh, Come Little Children." [1] Lyric written for exploitation only.

606 ✦ THE BLUE BIRD (1976)
Twentieth Century–Fox, 1976

Musical Score Petrov, Andre; Kostal, Irwin
Composer(s) Petrov, Andre
Lyricist(s) Harrison, Tony

Producer(s) Maslansky, Paul
Director(s) Cukor, George
Screenwriter(s) Whitemore, Hugh; Hayes, Alfred
Source(s) *The Bluebird* (play) Maeterlinck, Maurice

Cast Taylor, Elizabeth; Fonda, Jane; Gardner, Ava; Tyson, Cicely; Morley, Robert; Andrews, Harry; Kensit, Patsy; Geer, Will; Washbourne, Mona; Cole, George

Song(s) Grandparent's Song; Blue Halloo; You're in the Hands of Fate (C: Kostal, Irwin); Once I Held a Bluebird; Wings in the Sky [1]; Clock Song [1] (C/L: Kostal, Irwin); Maternal Love [1]

Notes [1] Instrumental use only.

607 ✦ BLUE CANADIAN ROCKIES
Columbia, 1952

Producer(s) Schaefer, Armand
Director(s) Archainbaud, George
Screenwriter(s) Geraghty, Gerald

Cast Autry, Gene; Buttram, Pat; Davis, Gail; Cotton, Carolina; Champion; The Cass County Boys

Song(s) Mama Don't Like Music (C/L: Unknown); The Blue Canadian Rockies [1] (C/L: Unknown); Anytime (C/L: Unknown); Yodel, Yodel, Yodel (C/L: Unknown)

Notes No cue sheet available. There are also vocals of "Old Chisholm Trail" and "Froggy Went A-Courtin'." [1] Also in GENE AUTRY AND THE MOUNTIES.

608 ✦ BLUE CITY
Paramount, 1986

Musical Score Cooder, Ry

Producer(s) Hayward, William; Hill, Walter
Director(s) Manning, Michelle
Screenwriter(s) Heller, Lukas; Hill, Walter
Source(s) *Blue City* (novel) MacDonald, Ross

Cast Nelson, Judd; Sheedy, Ally; Caruso, David; Winfield, Paul; Wilson, Scott; Morris, Anita

Song(s) Blue City Down (C/L: Cooder, Ry; Dickinson, Jim); Tell Me Somthing Slick and Make It Quick (C/L: Cooder, Ry; Dickinson, Jim)

Notes No cue sheet available.

609 ✦ BLUE COLLAR
Universal, 1978

Musical Score Nitzsche, Jack

Producer(s) Guest, Ron
Director(s) Schrader, Paul
Screenwriter(s) Schrader, Paul; Schrader, Leonard
Source(s) material by Glass, Sydney A.

Cast Pryor, Richard; Keitel, Harvey; Kotto, Yaphet; Begley Jr., Ed; Bellaver, Harry; Memmoli, George; Saroyan, Lucy; Smith, Lane

Song(s) Hard Workin' Man (C: Nitzsche, Jack; L: Schrader, Paul; Nitzsche, Jack)

Notes Only original song listed.

610 ✦ THE BLUE DAHLIA
Paramount, 1946

Composer(s) Wayne, Bernie
Lyricist(s) Raleigh, Ben

Producer(s) Houseman, John
Director(s) Marshall, George
Screenwriter(s) Chandler, Raymond

Cast Ladd, Alan; Lake, Veronica; Bendix, William; Da Silva, Howard; Dowling, Doris; Powers, Tom; Wright, Will; Beaumont, Hugh; Faylen, Frank

Song(s) The Blue Dahlia [1]; That Ain't Right [1]

Notes Vocals of "Accentuate the Positive" by Harold Arlen and Johnny Mercer and "It's Easy to Remember" by Richard Rodgers and Lorenz Hart are also included. [1] Used instrumentally only.

611 ✦ BLUE DENIM
Twentieth Century–Fox, 1959

Musical Score Herrmann, Bernard

Producer(s) Brackett, Charles
Director(s) Dunne, Philip
Screenwriter(s) Sommer, Edith; Dunne, Philip
Source(s) *Blue Denim* (play) Herlihy, James Leo; Noble, William

Cast Lynley, Carol; de Wilde, Brandon; Carey, Macdonald; Hunt, Marsha; Berlinger, Warren; Class, Buck

Song(s) Who Baby [1] (C/L: Carroll, Jeanne; Olofson, Bill)

Notes [1] Also in SING BOY SING.

612 ✦ THE BLUE GARDENIA
Warner Brothers, 1953

Musical Score Kraushaar, Raoul

Producer(s) Gottlieb, Alex
Director(s) Lang, Fritz
Screenwriter(s) Hoffman, Charles
Source(s) "The Gardenia" (story) Caspary, Vera

Cast Baxter, Anne; Conte, Richard; Sothern, Ann; Burr, Raymond; Donnell, Jeff; Erdman, Richard; Reeves, George

Song(s) Blue Gardenia (C: Lee, Lester; L: Russell, Bob)

613 ✦ BLUE HAWAII
Paramount, 1961

Choreographer(s) O'Curran, Charles

Producer(s) Wallis, Hal B.
Director(s) Taurog, Norman
Screenwriter(s) Kanter, Hal
Source(s) "Beach Boy" (story) Weiss, Allan

Cast Presley, Elvis; Lansbury, Angela; Blackman, Joan; Winters, Roland; Walters, Nancy; Adrian, Iris

Song(s) Blue Hawaii [1] (C: Rainger, Ralph; L: Robin, Leo); Almost Always True [2] (C: Traditional; L: Wise, Fred; Weisman, Ben); Aloha Oe [1] (C/L: Liliuokalani, Queen); No More [3] (C: Yradier, Sebastian; L: Robertson, Don); Can't Help Falling in Love [4] (C/L: Weiss, George David; Peretti, Hugo; Creatore, Luigi); Hawaiian Sunset (C/L: Tepper, Sid; Bennett, Roy C.); Rockahula Baby (C: Weisman, Ben; L: Fuller, Dolores; Wise, Fred); Moonlight Swim (C: Weisman, Ben; L: Dee, Sylvia); Hawaiian Sweetheart (Ku-U-I-Po) (C/L: Weiss, George David; Peretti, Hugo; Creatore, Luigi);

Ito Eats (C/L: Tepper, Sid; Bennett, Roy C.); Slicin' Sand (C/L: Tepper, Sid; Bennett, Roy C.); You're Stepping Out of Line (C: Weisman, Ben; L: Wise, Fred; Fuller, Dolores); Beach Boy Blues (C/L: Tepper, Sid; Bennett, Roy C.); Island of Love (Kauai) (C/L: Tepper, Sid; Bennett, Roy C.); Hawaiian Wedding Song (C: King, Charles E.; L: Hoffman, Al; Manning, Dick); Hawaiian Shave and a Haircut (C/L: Brooks, Dudley; O'Curran, Charles); Mele Kalikimaka [5] (C/L: Anderson, R. Alex)

Notes [1] Not written for film. Originally in WAIKIKI WEDDING. [2] Based on French song "Alouette." [3] Based on "La Paloma." Robertson and Hal Blair credited on sheet music. [4] Adapted from "Plaisir D'Amour" by G. Martini and Jean Florian. [5] Not used.

614 ✦ THE BLUE IGUANA
Paramount, 1988

Musical Score James, Ethan

Producer(s) Sighvatsson, Sigurjon; Golin, Steven
Director(s) Lafia, John
Screenwriter(s) Lafia, John

Cast McDermott, Dylan; Harper, Jessica; Russo, James; Feldshuh, Tovah; Stockwell, Dean

Song(s) Blue Iguana (C/L: Blow, Kurtis; Green, Michael); Cruel and Unusual World (C: James, Ethan; Shayne, Stephanie); Gee, What a Guy (C: McCoy, Van; L: Warwick, Dionne)

615 ✦ THE BLUE MAX
Twentieth Century–Fox, 1966

Musical Score Goldsmith, Jerry

Producer(s) Ferry, Christian
Director(s) Guillermin, John
Screenwriter(s) Hanley, Gerald; Pursall, David; Seddon, Jack
Source(s) *The Blue Max* (novel) Hunter, Jack D.

Cast Peppard, George; Mason, James; Andress, Ursula; Kemp, Jeremy; Vogler, Karl Michael; Schell, Carl

Song(s) May Wine [1] (C: Goldsmith, Jerry; L: Sheldon, Ernie)

Notes [1] Used instrumentally only.

616 ✦ BLUE MONTANA SKIES
Republic, 1939

Composer(s) Marvin, Johnny; Rose, Fred

Producer(s) Grey, Harry
Director(s) Eason, B. Reeves
Screenwriter(s) Geraghty, Gerald
Source(s) Marvin, Johnny; Rose, Fred

Cast   Autry, Gene; Burnette, Smiley; Storey, June; Woods, Harry; Marshall, Tully; Bridge, Al; Shrum, Walt; Colorado The Hillbillies

Song(s)   Rockin' in the Saddle; Old Geezer; 'Neath the Blue Montana Sky; I Just Want You; Famous Men of the West (C/L: Marvin, Johnny; Rose, Fred; Cherkose, Eddie); Colorado Swing (C/L: Cooley, Spade); Away Out Yonder [1]

Notes   [1] Also in ROVIN' TUMBLEWEEDS.

617 ✦ BLUES BUSTERS
Monogram, 1950

Composer(s)   Wayne, Bernie; Raleigh, Ben
Lyricist(s)   Wayne, Bernie; Raleigh, Ben

Producer(s)   Grippo, Jan
Director(s)   Beaudine, William
Screenwriter(s)   Marion, Charles R.; Lawrence, Bert

Cast   Hall, Huntz; Gorcey, Leo; Gorcey, Bernard; Jergens, Adele; Stevens, Craig; Dell, Gabriel; Coates, Phyllis; Benedict, William; Gorcey, David; King, Marty

Song(s)   Wasn't It You?; You Walk By; Bluebirds Keep Singin' in the Rain (C/L: Lange, Johnny; Daniel, Eliot)

Notes   No cue sheet available. A Bowery Boys picture.

618 ✦ BLUES FOR LOVERS
Twentieth Century–Fox, 1966

Musical Score   Black, Stanley
Composer(s)   Charles, Ray
Lyricist(s)   Charles, Ray

Producer(s)   Blaser, Herman
Director(s)   Henreid, Paul
Screenwriter(s)   Wohl, Burton

Cast   Charles, Ray; Bell, Tom; Peach, Mary; Addams, Dawn; Bishop, Piers; McDowell, Betty; The Ray Charles Orchestra

Song(s)   Let the Good Times Roll (C/L: Lee, Leonard); Hit the Road Jack (C/L: Unknown); Lucky Old Sun (C/L: Smith, Beasley); Hallelujah I Love Her So; Talking About You; Don't Tell Me Your Troubles (C/L: Gibson, Don); I Gotta Woman; Careless Love (C/L: Handy, W.C.); Busted (C/L: Howard, Harlan); What'd I Say [1]; Unchain My Heart (C/L: Jones, Agnes; James, Freddy)

Notes   It is not known which of these songs, if any, were written for the film. [1] Also in VIVA LAS VEGAS and SWINGIN' ALONG.

619 ✦ BLUES IN THE NIGHT
Warner Brothers, 1941

Composer(s)   Arlen, Harold
Lyricist(s)   Mercer, Johnny

Producer(s)   Blanke, Henry
Director(s)   Litvak, Anatole
Screenwriter(s)   Rossen, Robert
Source(s)   *Hot Nocturne* (play) Gilbert, Edwin

Cast   Lane, Priscilla; Field, Betty; Nolan, Lloyd; Carson, Jack; Whorf, Richard; Ford, Wallace; Halop, Billy; Kazan, Elia; Jimmy Lunceford and His Band; Will Osborne and His Band

Song(s)   Blues in the Night; Hang on to Your Lids Kids; This Time the Dream's on Me; Wait Till It Happens to You; Says Who? Says You, Says I

620 ✦ BLUE SKIES
Paramount, 1946

Composer(s)   Berlin, Irving
Lyricist(s)   Berlin, Irving
Choreographer(s)   Pan, Hermes

Producer(s)   Siegel, Sol C.
Director(s)   Heisler, Stuart
Screenwriter(s)   Sheekman, Arthur

Cast   Caulfield, Joan [2]; Astaire, Fred; Crosby, Bing; De Wolfe, Billy; San Juan, Olga

Song(s)   A Couple of Song and Dance Men; Getting Nowhere; Have You Ever Tried Drinking Water? [1]; I'll Dance Rings Around You [1]; It's a Lovely Day for a Walk [1]; Serenade to an Old-Fashioned Girl; Wilhelmina [1]; You Keep Coming Back Like a Song; The Race Horse and the Flea [3]; I Want You to Meet My Girl [3]; My Old Pal [3]; Rhythmic Boogie Woogie [4] (inst.) (C: Astaire, Fred)

Notes   There are also vocals of "Puttin' on the Ritz," "Heat Wave" (from stage musical AS THOUSANDS CHEER and the films ALEXANDER'S RAGTIME BAND and THERE'S NO BUSINESS LIKE SHOW BUSINESS), "How Deep Is the Ocean," "A Pretty Girl Is Like a Melody" (Sung by tenor soloist James O'Brien) (also used in ALEXANDER'S RAGTIME BAND and THERE'S NO BUSINESS LIKE SHOW BUSINESS, both 20th Century-Fox pictures), "I'll See You in C-U-B-A," "I've Got My Captain Working for Me Now," "You'd Be Surprised" (also in THERE'S NO BUSINESS LIKE SHOW BUSINESS), "All By Myself," "Blue Skies" (also in GLORIFYING THE AMERICAN GIRL, ALEXANDER'S RAGTIME BAND and THE JAZZ SINGER) and "Everybody Step" (also in ALEXANDER'S RAGTIME BAND). The Berlin songs "Any Bonds Today," "This Is the Army Mr. Jones," "White Christmas," "Always," "The Little Things in Life," "Not for All the Rice in China" and "Russian Lullaby" are sung in montage sequences. A Radio Montage sung by Bing Crosby and Betty Finch and incorporating the songs "I'm Putting All My Eggs in One Basket," "Cheek to Cheek," "Blues Skies" and "You Keep Coming Back Like a Song" were recorded but not used. [1] Unused. Copies of the music are in

Paramount's files. [2] Dubbed by Betty Finch for "Serenade to an Old Fashioned Girl." And dubbed by Betty Russell in "All By Myself." [3] Unused. No copy at Paramount. [4] Used for Astaire's dance solo in "Heat Wave."

Paramount had begun filming the movie with Paul Draper opposite Crosby but wasn't happy with the results. Draper was replaced with Fred Astaire on a loan-out even though MGM had Astaire under a multiple picture deal and had a picture in pre-production. After Astaire finished Blue Skies his doctor advised him to give up pictures and the dancer retired. This threw MGM into a tizzy and it wasn't until Easter Parade two years later that Astaire returned to the screen.

621 ✦ BLUE SUNSHINE
Cinema Shares, 1979

Musical Score   Gross, Charles

Producer(s)   Manasse, George
Director(s)   Lieberman, Jeff
Screenwriter(s)   Lieberman, Jeff

Cast   King, Zalman; Winters, Deborah; Goddard, Mark; Walden, Robert; Siebert, Charles; Cooper, Ann; Ghostley, Alice; Gierasch, Stefan; King, Meegan

Song(s)   Blue Sunshine (C/L: Jackson, Billy; Ferguson, Jay; Griffin, Paul); Disco Blue (C/L: Jackson, Billy; Ferguson, Jay; Griffin, Paul); The Music of Love (C: Leslie, Diane; L: Leigh, Carolyn)

Notes   No cue sheet available.

622 ✦ BLUE VELVET
De Laurentiis Entertainment, 1986

Musical Score   Badalamenti, Angelo

Producer(s)   Caruso, Fred
Director(s)   Lynch, David
Screenwriter(s)   Lynch, David

Cast   MacLachlan, Kyle; Rossellini, Isabella; Hopper, Dennis; Dern, Laura; Lange, Hope; Stockwell, Dean; Dickerson, George; Pointer, Priscilla; Bay, Frances; Dourif, Brad

Song(s)   Mysteries of Love (C: Badalamenti, Angelo; L: Lynch, David)

Notes   No cue sheet available.

623 ✦ BLUME IN LOVE
Warner Brothers, 1973

Producer(s)   Mazursky, Paul
Director(s)   Mazursky, Paul
Screenwriter(s)   Mazursky, Paul

Cast   Segal, George; Anspach, Susan; Kristofferson, Kris; Mason, Marsha; Winters, Shelley; Mazursky, Paul

Song(s)   I'm in Love with You (C/L: Crume, Dillard; Crume, Rufus E.); Settle Down and Get Along (C/L: Kristofferson, Kris); Chester the Goat (C/L: Kristofferson, Kris)

Notes   There is also an rendition of "You've Got a Friend" by Carole King. It is not known if the other songs were written for the picture.

624 ✦ THE BOATNIKS
Disney, 1970

Musical Score   Brunner, Robert F.
Composer(s)   Brunner, Robert F.

Producer(s)   Miller, Ron
Director(s)   Tokar, Norman
Screenwriter(s)   Julian, Arthur

Cast   Morse, Robert; Powers, Stefanie; Silvers, Phil; Fell, Norman; Shaughnessy, Mickey; Cox, Wally; Ameche, Don; Forman, Joey; Ross, Joe E.; Lewis, Al; Lamb, Gil

Song(s)   Boatniks (L: Belland, Bruce); Lotus Baby (L: Jackman, Bob)

625 ✦ BOBBIKINS
Twentieth Century–Fox, 1959

Musical Score   Green, Philip
Composer(s)   Bygraves, Max
Lyricist(s)   Bygraves, Max

Producer(s)   Brodney, Oscar
Director(s)   Day, Robert
Screenwriter(s)   Brodney, Oscar

Cast   Jones, Shirley; Bygraves, Max; Stocker, Steven; Whitelaw, Billie; Shelley, Barbara; Gordon, Dolin; Tingwell, Charles; Jeffries, Lionel; Carson, Charles; Davies, Rupert

Song(s)   Funny Little Clown; World of Dreams (C/L: Stone, Wilson); Bobbikins' Lullaby; Last Night I Dreamed

626 ✦ THE BOBO
Warner Brothers–Seven Arts, 1967

Musical Score   Lai, Francis
Composer(s)   Lai, Francis
Lyricist(s)   Cahn, Sammy

Producer(s)   Gershwin, Jerry; Kastner, Elliott
Director(s)   Parrish, Robert
Screenwriter(s)   Schwartz, David R.
Source(s)   The Bobo (play) Schwartz, David R.

Cast   Sellers, Peter; Ekland, Britt; Brazzi, Rossano; Celi, Adolfo; Jacques, Hattie; Griffith, Kenneth

Song(s)   The Bulls of Salamanca (C/L: Martin, George; Kretzmer, Herbert); Imagine [1]; Girl from Barcelona (C/L: Martin, George; Kretzmer, Herbert); The Blue Matador [1]; The Bobo [2]

Notes   The play is based on the novel *Olympia* by Burt Cole. [1] Background vocal only. [2] Not used.

627 ✦ BOB WILLS AND HIS TEXAS PLAYBOYS
Warner Brothers, Unknown

Cast   Bob Wills and His Texas Playboys

Song(s)   Ride On (My Prairie Pinto) (C/L: Blackmore, Alice; Cortez, Carmen); My Adobe Hacienda [2] (C/L: Massey, Louise; Penny, Lee); Mama Don't Allow It [1] (C: Davenport, Charles; L: Cahn, Sammy); San Antonio Rose [3] (C/L: Wills, Bob)

Notes   It is not known if any of these were written for this short subject. [1] Also in BARNYARD FOLLIES (Republic) and MOUNTAIN MUSIC (Paramount) without Sammy Cahn credit; and with it in BANDS ACROSS THE SEA. [2] Also in THE BIG SOMBRERO (Columbia) and ON THE OLD SPANISH TRAIL (Republic). [3] Also in RHYTHM ROUND-UP (Columbia), UNDER COLORADO SKIES (Republic), SAN ANTONIO ROSE (Universal) and HONKYTONK MAN.

628 ✦ THE BODY SNATCHER
RKO, 1945

Musical Score   Webb, Roy

Producer(s)   Lewton, Val
Director(s)   Wise, Robert
Screenwriter(s)   MacDonald, Philip; Keith, Carlos [1]
Source(s)   "The Body Snatcher" (story) Stevenson, Robert Louis

Cast   Karloff, Boris; Lugosi, Bela; Daniell, Henry; Corday, Rita; Wade, Russell; Atwater, Edith

Song(s)   Spit Song (C: Lewton, Val; L: Bennett, Norman)

Notes   The song lasts only 30 seconds. [1] Pseudonym for Val Lewton.

629 ✦ THE BOHEMIAN GIRL
Metro–Goldwyn–Mayer, 1936

Producer(s)   Roach, Hal
Director(s)   Horne, James W.; Rogers, Charles
Source(s)   *The Bohemian Girl* (operetta) Balfe, Michael W.; Bunn, Alfred

Cast   Laurel, Stan; Hardy, Oliver; Hood, Darla; Wells, Jacqueline; Hodges, Jon; Finlayson, James; Busch, Mae; Moreno, Antonio; Bowers, Harry; Todd, Thelma

Song(s)   Heart of a Gypsy (C: Shilkret, Nathaniel; L: Shayon, Robert)

Notes   No cue sheet available. Songs from the original operetta given vocal treatment include "I Dreamt That I Dwelt in Marble Halls," "Then You'll Remember Me," "The Heart Bowed Down," "But Memory Is the Only Friend That Grief Can Call Its Own."

630 ✦ THE BOLD AND THE BRAVE
RKO, 1955

Producer(s)   Chester, Hal E.
Director(s)   Foster, Lewis R.
Screenwriter(s)   Lewin, Robert

Cast   Corey, Wendell; Taylor, Don; Rooney, Mickey; Maurey, Nicole

Song(s)   The Bold and the Brave (C/L: Rooney, Mickey; Bagdasarian, Ross)

631 ✦ BOLERO
Paramount, 1934

Producer(s)   Glazer, Benjamin
Director(s)   Ruggles, Wesley
Screenwriter(s)   Wilson, Carey; Glasmon, Kubec; Jackson, Horace

Cast   Raft, George; Lombard, Carole; Michael, Gertrude; Frawley, William; Drake, Frances; Rand, Sally; Milland, Ray

Song(s)   Raftero (Inst.) (C: Rainger, Ralph)

632 ✦ BOMBALERA
Paramount

Choreographer(s)   Earl, Josephine

Song(s)   Los Hijos de Buda (C/L: Hernandez, Rafael); Tonight Is Our Night [2] (C: Pafumy, Jose; L: Salinas, A.; Valerinia, C.; Drake, Ervin); Tico Tico No Fuba [1] [2] (C: Abreu, Zequinha; L: Oliveira, Aloysio; Drake, Ervin); Babalu (C: Lecuona, Margarita; L: Russell, S.K.)

Notes   Short subject. No cue sheet available. [1] Also in BATHING BEAUTY (MGM), COPACABANA (UA) and the Columbia pictures GAY SENORITA and KANSAS CITY KITTY. [2] Drake provided the English lyrics.

633 ✦ BOMBARDIER
RKO, 1943

Musical Score   Webb, Roy

Producer(s)   Fellows, Robert
Director(s)   Wallace, Richard
Screenwriter(s)   Twist, John

Cast O'Brien, Pat; Scott, Randolph; Shirley, Anne; Albert, Eddie; Reed, Walter; Ryan, Robert; MacLane, Barton; Strong, Leonard

Song(s) Song of the Bombardiers (C: Jerome, M.K.; L: Scholl, Jack)

634 ✦ BONDAGE
Fox, 1933

Composer(s) Jason, Will; Burton, Val
Lyricist(s) Jason, Will; Burton, Val

Director(s) Santell, Alfred
Screenwriter(s) Kober, Arthur; Malloy, Doris
Source(s) (novel) Leake, Grace S.

Cast Jordan, Dorothy; Kirkland, Alexander; Jewell, Isabel; Darwell, Jane

Song(s) Penthouse Lament [1]; Command to Love

Notes [1] This is a sequel to "Penthouse Serenade (When We're Alone)."

635 ✦ BONGO
Disney, 1947

Musical Score Wallace, Oliver; Baker, Buddy; Daniel, Eliot
Composer(s) Daniel, Eliot
Lyricist(s) Kaye, Buddy

Director(s) Kinney, Jack
Screenwriter(s) Nolley, Lance; Oreb, Tom
Source(s) (story) Lewis, Sinclair

Cast Shore, Dinah

Song(s) I'm a Happy-Go-Lucky Fellow [2] (C: Harline, Leigh; L: Washington, Ned); Too Good to Be True; Lazy Countryside (C/L: Worth, Bobby); The Air Grew Still; Say It with a Slap; Slap! Slap! Slap! (That's Love) [1] (C/L: Worth, Bobby); Did I Do Somethin' I Shouldn't? [1] (C/L: Worth, Bobby)

Notes This cartoon is part of FUN AND FANCY FREE. [1] Not used. [2] This is a prerecorded song cut from PINOCCHIO. Cliff Edwards (who played Jiminy Cricket in PINOCCHIO) sings it on the soundtrack.

636 ✦ BONJOUR TRISTESSE
Columbia, 1958

Musical Score Auric, Georges

Producer(s) Preminger, Otto
Director(s) Preminger, Otto
Screenwriter(s) Laurents, Arthur
Source(s) *Bonjour Tristesse* (novel) Sagan, Francoise

Cast Kerr, Deborah; Niven, David; Seberg, Jean; Demongeot, Mylene; Chiari, Walter; Horne, Geoffrey; Hunt, Martita; Culver, Roland; Greco, Juliette

Song(s) Bonjour Tristesse (C: Auric, Georges; L: Laurents, Arthur)

637 ✦ BONNIE AND CLYDE
Warner Brothers, 1967

Musical Score Strouse, Charles
Composer(s) Strouse, Charles

Producer(s) Beatty, Warren
Director(s) Penn, Arthur
Screenwriter(s) Newman, David; Benton, Robert

Cast Beatty, Warren; Dunaway, Faye; Pollard, Michael J.; Hackman, Gene; Parsons, Estelle; Pyle, Denver; Wilder, Gene

Song(s) Bonnie and Clyde [1] (L: Strouse, Charles); We Will Find a Way [1] (L: Adams, Lee)

Notes No original songs. [1] Lyrics written for exploitation only.

638 ✦ BONNIE SCOTLAND
Metro–Goldwyn–Mayer, 1935

Musical Score Shields, LeRoy

Producer(s) Roach, Hal
Director(s) Horne, James W.
Screenwriter(s) Butler, Frank; Noffitt, Jeff

Cast Laurel, Stan; Hardy, Oliver; Lang, June; Janney, William; Grey, Anne; Steel, Vernon; Finlayson, James; Pollard, Daphne; Belmore, Lionel

Song(s) Dixie (C/L: Hardy, Oliver)

639 ✦ BON VOYAGE
Disney, 1962

Musical Score Smith, Paul J.; Marks, Franklyn
Composer(s) Smith, Paul J.
Lyricist(s) George, Gil

Producer(s) Walsh, Bill; Miller, Ron
Director(s) Neilson, James
Screenwriter(s) Walsh, Bill
Source(s) *Bon Voyage* (novel) Hayes, Joseph; Hayes, Marijane

Cast MacMurray, Fred; Wyman, Jane; Callan, Michael; Walley, Deborah; Landis, Jessie Royce; Kirk, Tommy; Anys, Georgette; Corcoran, Kevin; Desny, Ivan

Song(s) Bon Voyage (C/L: Sherman, Richard M.; L: Sherman, Robert B.); Words to My Music; The First Time; Hey Tiger (C: Marks, Franklyn; L: Jackman, Bob); Old Familiar Places (C/L: Marks, Franklyn); Transcontinental (C/L: Marks, Franklyn); The Whistling Polka (C: Marks, Franklyn; L: Jackman, Bob); Demimonde; Streets of Paris; Parisian Cha Cha (C: Marks, Franklyn; L: Jackman, Bob)

640 ✦ BON VOYAGE, CHARLIE BROWN (AND DON'T COME BACK)
Paramount, 1980

Producer(s)   Mendelson, Lee; Melendez, Bill
Director(s)   Melendez, Bill
Screenwriter(s)   Schulz, Charles M.
Source(s)   *Peanuts* (comic strip) Schulz, Charles M.
Voices   Anderson, Daniel; Carlson, Casey; Patts, Patricia; Skelley, Arrin; Bortolin, Annalisa; Beach, Scott

Song(s)   I Want to Remember This (C/L: Bogas, Ed; Munsen, Judy)

Notes   No cue sheet available. An animated feature.

641 ✦ THE BOOB TUBE
Independent–International, 1976

Producer(s)   Adler, Jerry; Burton, Al
Screenwriter(s)   Odin, Christopher

Cast   Alderman, John; Kelly, Sharon; Torena, Lyllah

Song(s)   Soap (C/L: Kaye, Billy; Kaye, Richard)

Notes   No cue sheet available.

642 ✦ BOOGIE WOOGIE
Paramount, 1945

Composer(s)   Wayne, Bernie
Lyricist(s)   Raleigh, Ben
Choreographer(s)   Earl, Josephine

Producer(s)   Harris, Lou
Director(s)   Madison, Noel

Cast   Mathews, Barbara; Benchley, Robert

Song(s)   Please Don't Ration the Boogie Woogie [2]; My Heart Should Know [1]

Notes   Short subject. [1] This song was previously titled "When My Man Comes Home," written for, but not used in, OUT OF THIS WORLD. [2] Not used for OUT OF THIS WORLD.

643 ✦ BOOLOO
Paramount, 1938

Composer(s)   Hollander, Frederick
Lyricist(s)   Coslow, Sam

Producer(s)   Elliott, Clyde
Director(s)   Elliott, Clyde
Screenwriter(s)   Welsh, Robert E.

Cast   Tapley, Colin; Regan, Jayne

Song(s)   Beside a Moonlit Stream; Booloo [1]

Notes   [1] Not used but recorded and published. "Beside a Moonlit Stream" was also published.

644 ✦ BOOM
Universal, 1968

Musical Score   Barry, John

Producer(s)   Heyman, John
Director(s)   Losey, Joseph
Screenwriter(s)   Williams, Tennessee
Source(s)   *The Milk Train Doesn't Stop Here Anymore* (play) Williams, Tennessee

Cast   Taylor, Elizabeth; Coward, Noel; Burton, Richard; Shimkus, Joanna; Dunn, Michael

Song(s)   Hideaway (C: Dankworth, John; L: Black, Don)

645 ✦ BOOTS AND SADDLES
Republic, 1937

Producer(s)   Siegel, Sol C.
Director(s)   Kane, Joseph
Screenwriter(s)   Natteford, Jack; Drake, Oliver

Cast   Autry, Gene; Burnette, Smiley; Allen, Judith; Elliott, Gordon

Song(s)   Salvo Vaquero (C/L: Gonzales, Aaron); Ridin' the Range [1] (C/L: Allan, Fleming; Autry, Gene; Shawn, Nelson); Dusty Roads (C/L: Burnette, Smiley); Si Quires (C/L: Gonzales, Aaron); Take Me Back to My Boots and Saddle [2] (C/L: Powell, Teddy; Whitcup, Leonard; Samuels, Walter G. G.); The One Rose (C/L: McIntyre, Lani; Lyon, Del)

Notes   No cue sheet available. [1] Also in SIERRA SUE with additional credit to Jule Styne. [2] Also in CALL OF THE CANYON and PEPPER (20th) as "Take Me Back to My Boots and Saddle."

646 ✦ BOP GIRL GOES CALYPSO
United Artists, 1957

Musical Score   Baxter, Les
Composer(s)   Baxter, Les
Lyricist(s)   Adelson, Lenny

Producer(s)   Schenck, Aubrey
Director(s)   Koch, Howard W.
Screenwriter(s)   Belgard, Arnold

Cast   Tyler, Judy; Troup, Bobby; Woode, Margo; Littlefield, Lucien; O'Hanlon, George

Song(s)   Rhythm and Blues (C/L: Carter, Cecil); So Hard to Laugh, So Easy to Cry (C/L: Askin, Rich; Carter, Cecil); Calypso Rock (C/L: Kaye, Norman); Rovin' Gal (L: Baxter, Jim); Be Bop (C/L: Lord Flea); Hard Rock Candy Baby; Calypso Boogie (L: Baxter, Jim); Wow (C/L: Winley, Paul; Clowney, David; Kornegay, Bob); I'm Gonna Rock and Roll Till I Die (C/L: Towne, Fred; Morris, Heywood; Greefield,

Mannie); Way Back in San Francisco; Calypso Jamboree (C/L: Lord Flea); Oo-Ba-Lo; De Rain

Notes Also released as BOP GOES CALYPSO.

647 ✦ BOP GOES CALYPSO

See BOP GIRL GOES CALYPSO.

648 ✦ THE BORDER
Universal–RKO, 1982

Musical Score Cooder, Ry
Composer(s) Cooder, Ry
Lyricist(s) Hiatt, John; Dickinson, J.

Producer(s) Bronfman Jr., Edgar
Director(s) Richardson, Tony
Screenwriter(s) Washburn, Deric; Green, Walon; Freeman, David

Cast Nicholson, Jack; Perrine, Valerie; Keitel, Harvey; Oates, Warren; Carillo, Elpidia; Wilcox, Shannon

Song(s) Across the Borderline; Too Late; No Quiero (C/L: Samudio, Domingo); El Americanado (C/L: Ontiveros, Ernesto); Texas Bop (C/L: Dickinson, J.); Building Fires (C/L: Dickinson, J.; Penn, D.; Christopher, J.); Cat Walks Away (C/L: Cooder, Ry); Skin Game

649 ✦ BORDER FLIGHT
Paramount, 1936

Producer(s) Botsford, A.M.
Director(s) Lovering, Otho
Screenwriter(s) Anthony, Stuart; Beckhard, Arthur

Cast Cummings, Robert; Farmer, Frances; Howard, John

Song(s) I Feel Like a Feather in the Breeze [1] (C: Revel, Harry; L: Gordon, Mack)

Notes [1] Also in COLLEGIATE.

650 ✦ BORDER G-MAN
RKO, 1938

Producer(s) Gilroy, Bert
Director(s) Howard, David
Screenwriter(s) Drake, Oliver

Cast Johnson, Laraine; Whitley, Ray; O'Brien, George

Song(s) To Watch the Setting Sun (C/L: Whitley, Ray); Wagon Train (C/L: Phelps, Norman); Back in the Saddle Again [1] (C/L: Whitley, Ray)

Notes [1] Later when the song was appropriated as his theme song, Gene Autry was given coauthor credit though he did not contribute to it. Also in Autry films: BACK IN THE SADDLE, MELODY RANCH and ROVIN' TUMBLEWEEDS.

651 ✦ THE BORDER LEGION
Republic, 1940

Producer(s) Kane, Joseph
Screenwriter(s) Stevens, Louis; Cooper, Olive

Cast Rogers, Roy; Hayes, George "Gabby"; Hughes, Carol; Sawyer, Joe; Eburne, Maude; Taliaferro, Hal; Novello, Jay

Song(s) With My Guitar and You [1] (C: Snyder, Ted; L: Harris, Mort; Heyman, Edward)

Notes [1] Also in SWING HIGH (Pathe).

652 ✦ BORDERLINE
Universal, 1950

Musical Score Salter, Hans J.

Producer(s) Bren, Milton; Seiter, William A.
Director(s) Seiter, William A.
Screenwriter(s) Freeman, Devery

Cast Trevor, Claire; MacMurray, Fred; Burr, Raymond; Roberts, Roy; Torvay, Jose; Ankrum, Morris; Baron, Lita

Song(s) Carlotta (C/L: Cahn, Sammy)

653 ✦ BORDER ROMANCE
Tiffany Productions, 1930

Composer(s) Jason, Will; Burton, Val
Lyricist(s) Jason, Will; Burton, Val

Producer(s) Scott, Lester F.
Director(s) Thorpe, Richard
Screenwriter(s) Natteford, Jack

Cast Armida; Terry, Don; Kane, Marjorie "Babe"; Potel, Victor; Barry, Wesley; Martan, Nita; Glendon, Frank

Song(s) Song of the Rurales; The Girl from Topolobombo; Yo Te Adoro; My Desert Rose

Notes No cue sheet available.

654 ✦ BORDER SADDLEMATES
Republic, 1952

Producer(s) White, Edward J.
Director(s) Witney, William
Screenwriter(s) De Mond, Albert

Cast Allen, Rex; Kay, Mary Ellen; Pickens, Slim; Barcroft, Roy; Taylor, Forrest

Song(s) Wait for the Wagon (C/L: Buckley, R.); Roll On Border Moon [1] (C/L: Elliott, Jack)

Notes [1] Same song as "Roll on Texas Moon."

655 ✦ BORDER WOLVES
Universal, 1938

Composer(s)   Taconis; Gayne
Lyricist(s)   Taconis; Gayne

Director(s)   Waggner, George
Screenwriter(s)   Parker, Norton S.

Cast   Baker, Bob; Moore, Constance; Knight, Fuzzy; Jones, Dickie; Fung, Willie; Strange, Glenn; O'Shea, Oscar

Song(s)   Ridin' the Hoot Owl Trail; Blaze Away Cowboy; Bowlegged; Wyoming Moon

656 ✦ BORN AGAIN
Avco Embassy, 1978

Musical Score   Baxter, Les

Producer(s)   Capra Jr., Frank
Director(s)   Rapper, Irving
Screenwriter(s)   Bloch, Walter
Source(s)   *Born Again* (book) Colson, Charles

Cast   Jones, Dean; Francis, Anne; Robinson, Jay; Andrews, Dana; St. Jacques, Raymond; Brent, George

Song(s)   Born Again (C: Baxter, Les; L: Johnson, Craig)

Notes   No cue sheet available.

657 ✦ BORN FREE
Columbia, 1966

Musical Score   Barry, John

Producer(s)   Jaffe, Sam; Radin, Paul
Director(s)   Hill, James
Screenwriter(s)   Copley, Gerald L.C.
Source(s)   *Born Free* (book) Adamson, Joy

Cast   McKenna, Virginia; Travers, Bill; Keen, Geoffrey; Lukoye, Peter; Chambati, Omar

Song(s)   Born Free (C: Barry, John; L: Black, Don)

Notes   No cue sheet available.

658 ✦ BORN IN EAST L.A.
Universal, 1987

Musical Score   Holdridge, Lee

Producer(s)   MacGregor-Scott, Peter
Director(s)   Marin, Richard "Cheech"
Screenwriter(s)   Marin, Richard "Cheech"
Source(s)   "Born in East L.A." (song) Springsteen, Bruce; Marin, Richard "Cheech"

Cast   Marin, Richard "Cheech"; Rodriguez, Paul; Stern, Daniel; Vincent, Jan-Michael; Lopez, Kamala

Song(s)   Born in East L.A. [1] (C: Springsteen, Bruce; L: Marin, Richard "Cheech")

Notes   There are also vocals of "Sukiyaki" by El Rohusuke and Hachidai Nakamura; "Summertime

Blues" by Eddie Cochran and Jerry Capeheart; "Twist and Shout" by Bert Russell and Phil Medley; "Purple Haze" by Jimi Hendrix; "America" by Neil Diamond and "Sabor a Mi" by Mel Mitchell and Alvaro Carrillo. [1] Based on Springsteen's "Born in the U.S.A."

659 ✦ BORN ON THE FOURTH OF JULY
Universal, 1990

Musical Score   Williams, John

Producer(s)   Stone, Oliver; Ho, A. Kitman
Director(s)   Stone, Oliver
Screenwriter(s)   Stone, Oliver; Kovic, Ron
Source(s)   (book) Kovic, Ron

Cast   Cruise, Tom; Larkin, Bryan; Barry, Raymond J.; Kva, Caroline; Getz, John; Warshofsky, David; Dafoe, Willem; Hoffman, Abbie; Gedrick, Jason

Song(s)   We Don't Need Arms (C/L: Palmer, James L.); Hace Un Ano (C/L: Leal, F. Valdes)

Notes   Only original songs listed.

660 ✦ BORN RECKLESS
Warner Brothers, 1959

Musical Score   Bregman, Buddy
Composer(s)   Bregman, Buddy
Lyricist(s)   Styne, Stanley

Producer(s)   Schenck, Aubrey
Director(s)   Koch, Howard W.
Screenwriter(s)   Landau, Richard

Cast   Van Doren, Mamie; Richards, Jeff; Hunnicutt, Arthur; Ohmart, Carol; Dugan, Tom; Williams, Tex

Song(s)   Born Reckless; Home Type Girl; Song of the Rodeo; Something to Dream About (C/L: Singleton, Charles; Coleman, Larry); A Little Longer; Separate the Men from the Boys; You Lovable You (C/L: Ram, Buck)

661 ✦ BORN TO BE KISSED

See THE GIRL FROM MISSOURI.

662 ✦ BORN TO BE LOVED
Universal, 1959

Musical Score   Steininger, Franz
Composer(s)   Steininger, Franz

Producer(s)   Haas, Hugo
Director(s)   Haas, Hugo
Screenwriter(s)   Haas, Hugo

Cast   Morris, Carol; Vague, Vera; Haas, Hugo; Kallman, Dick; Fontaine, Jacqueline; Bird, Billie

Song(s)   Born to Be Loved (L: Bullock, Walter); One Good Kiss Deserves Another (L: Pola, Eddie)

663 ✦ BORN TO BE WILD
Republic, 1938

Producer(s)   Shumate, Harold
Director(s)   Kane, Joseph
Screenwriter(s)   West, Nathanael

Cast   Byrd, Ralph; Weston, Doris; Bond, Ward; Keane, Robert Emmett

Song(s)   Danger Ahead (C: Tinturin, Peter; L: Lawrence, Jack); Camioneros (C/L: Durant, Eddie); A Story as Old as the Hills (C/L: Tinturin, Peter; L: Lawrence, Jack)

664 ✦ BORN TO DANCE
Metro–Goldwyn–Mayer, 1936

Composer(s)   Porter, Cole
Lyricist(s)   Porter, Cole
Choreographer(s)   Gould, Dave

Producer(s)   Cummings, Jack
Director(s)   Del Ruth, Roy
Screenwriter(s)   McGowan, Jack; Silvers, Sid

Cast   Powell, Eleanor; Stewart, James; Bruce, Virginia; Merkel, Una; Silvers, Sid; Langford, Frances; Walburn, Raymond; Dinehart, Alan; Ebsen, Buddy; Georges and Jalna

Song(s)   Rolling Home; Rap Tap on Wood; Hey Babe Hey; Entrance Lucy James; Love Me, Love My Pekinese; Easy to Love [1]; I've Got You Under My Skin; Swingin' the Jinx Away [2]

Notes   [1] Also used in the MGM film EASY TO LOVE. [2] Also in I DOOD IT.

665 ✦ BORN TO KILL
RKO, 1946

Musical Score   Sawtell, Paul; Webb, Roy

Producer(s)   Schlom, Herman
Director(s)   Wise, Robert
Screenwriter(s)   Greene, Eve; Macaulay, Richard
Source(s)   *Deadlier Than the Male* (novel) Gunn, James

Cast   Tierney, Lawrence; Trevor, Claire; Slezak, Walter; Terry, Phillip; Long, Audrey; Cook Jr., Elisha; Jewell, Isabel; Howard, Esther

Song(s)   Jive Bomb (C/L: Webb, Roy; Rose, Gene); Jumpin' Jack [1] (C/L: Rose, Gene; Webb, Roy)

Notes   [1] Used instrumentally only.

666 ✦ BORN TO SING
Metro–Goldwyn–Mayer, 1942

Composer(s)   Brent, Earl
Lyricist(s)   Brent, Earl
Choreographer(s)   Lee, Sammy

Producer(s)   Stephani, Frederick
Director(s)   Ludwig, Edward
Screenwriter(s)   Clork, Harry; Spencer, Franz G.

Cast   Weidler, Virginia; McDonald, Ray; Gorcey, Leo; McPhail, Douglas; O'Neill, Henry; Ragland, Rags; Leonard, Sheldon; Nunn, Larry; Dumont, Margaret; Hood, Darla

Song(s)   I'll Love Ya (C/L: Hayton, Lennie; Brent, Earl); I Hate the Conga (C/L: Brent, Earl); Here I Am, Eight Years Old; Two A.M.; Ballad for Americans [1] (C: Robinson, Earl; L: Latouche, John)

Notes   There are also some brief vocals of several popular songs including "You Are My Lucky Star" (also appeared in SINGIN' IN THE RAIN BROADWAY MELODY OF 1936 and BABES IN ARMS) and "Alone" (also in A NIGHT AT THE OPERA), both by Arthur Freed and Nacio Herb Brown. [1] Busby Berkeley directed the finale: "Ballad for Americans" which was an outtake from the movie BABES ON BROADWAY (1942).

667 ✦ BORN TO THE SADDLE
Universal, 1939

Lyricist(s)   Cherkose, Eddie

Song(s)   Sing a Little Song About Anything; Parade Song; Dixie Instrumental Suite

Notes   No cue sheet available.

668 ✦ BORSALINO
Paramount, 1970

Musical Score   Bolling, Claude

Producer(s)   Delon, Alain
Director(s)   Deray, Jacques
Screenwriter(s)   Carriere, Jean-Claude; Sautet, Claude; Deray, Jacques
Source(s)   *Bandits at Marseilles* (novel) Saccomano, Eugene

Cast   Belmondo, Jean-Paul; Delon, Alain; Rouvel, Catherine; Adani, Laura; Guiomar, Julien

Song(s)   Prends-Moi Matelot (C: Bolling, Claude; L: Deray, Jacques); Theme from Borsalino [1] (C: Bolling, Claude; L: Delange, Pierre)

Notes   [1] Not in picture.

669 ✦ BOSKO'S EASTER EGGS
Metro–Goldwyn–Mayer, 1937

Musical Score   Bradley, Scott

Song(s)   Easter Eggs (C/L: Bradley, Scott)

Notes   Animated cartoon.

670 ✦ BOSS OF BOOMTOWN
Universal, 1944

Musical Score Rosen, Milton
Composer(s) Marvin, Johnny
Lyricist(s) Marvin, Johnny

Producer(s) Drake, Oliver
Director(s) Taylor, Ray
Screenwriter(s) Lively, William

Cast Cameron, Rod; Tyler, Tom

Song(s) Texas; My Proud Beauty; Ninety-Nine Days

671 ✦ BOSS OF BULLION CITY
Universal, 1940

Musical Score Skinner, Frank

Director(s) Taylor, Ray
Screenwriter(s) St. Claire, Arthur; McLeod, Victor

Cast Brown, Johnny Mack; Knight, Fuzzy; O'Day, Nell; Brown, Harry

Song(s) Mi Morena (My Brunette) (C/L: Castillon, Jesus)

672 ✦ BOSS OF HANGTOWN MESA
Universal, 1942

Producer(s) Drake, Oliver
Director(s) Lewis, Joseph H.
Screenwriter(s) Drake, Oliver

Cast Brown, Johnny Mack; Knight, Fuzzy; Farnum, William; Lease, Rex

Song(s) Ain't Got Nothin' and Nothin' Worries Me (C: Rosen, Milton; L: Drake, Oliver); Trail Dreamin' [2] (C: Rosen, Milton; L: Wakely, Jimmy; Drake, Oliver); Pappy Was a Gunman (C/L: Drake, Oliver); Song of the Prairie [1] (C: Rosen, Milton; L: Carter, Everett)

Notes [1] Also in RIDERS OF PASCO BASIN. [2] Also in THE LONE STAR TRAIL and TRIGGER TRAIL.

673 ✦ THE BOSS' SON
Lagoon, 1980

Musical Score Markowitz, Richard
Composer(s) Markowitz, Richard
Lyricist(s) Dunham, K. Lawrence

Producer(s) White, Jeffrey
Director(s) Roth, Bobby
Screenwriter(s) Roth, Bobby

Cast Brauner, Asher; Solari, Rudy; Moreno, Rita; Sanders, Henry G.; Darren, James; Havens, Richie; Verdugo, Elena

Song(s) From Day One; Why Don't You Walk Away

Notes No cue sheet available.

674 ✦ BOTANY BAY
Paramount, 1953

Producer(s) Sistrom, Joseph
Director(s) Farrow, John
Screenwriter(s) Latimer, Jonathan

Cast Ladd, Alan; Mason, James; Medina, Patricia; Hardwicke, Sir Cedric; Bolster, Anita

Song(s) Botany Bay [1] (L: Livingston, Jay; Evans, Ray)

Notes [1] The songwriters also did music revisions on what is a traditional melody. The number was not used in the picture.

675 ✦ BOTH ENDS OF THE CANDLE

See THE HELEN MORGAN STORY.

676 ✦ BOTTLES
Metro–Goldwyn–Mayer, 1936

Song(s) Cry Baby Song (C: Bradley, Scott; L: Hanna, William); Spirits of Ammonia (C: Bradley, Scott; L: Hanna, William)

Notes Animated Cartoon. There are also vocals of "Rocked in the Cradle of the Deep" by Mrs. Willard and Joseph Philip Knight; "Little Brown Jug" and "When Yuba Plays the Rumba on the Tuba" by Herman Hupfeld.

677 ✦ BOTTOMS UP
Fox, 1934

Composer(s) Lane, Burton
Lyricist(s) Adamson, Harold

Producer(s) DeSylva, B.G.
Director(s) Butler, David
Screenwriter(s) DeSylva, B.G.; Butler, David; Silvers, Sid

Cast Tracy, Spencer; Boles, John; Patterson, Pat; Todd, Thelma

Song(s) Turn on the Moon; I'm Throwing My Love Away; Sidioso (C: Silvers); Little Did I Dream; Waiting at the Gate for Katy (C: Whiting, Richard A.; L: Kahn, Gus); Bottoms Up [1]

Notes There are also renditions of "Who's Afraid of the Big Bad Wolf" by Frank Churchill and "Is I in Love, I Is" by J. Russel Robinson. [1] Used instrumentally only.

678 ✦ BOULDER DAM
Warner Brothers, 1936

Musical Score Roemheld, Heinz
Composer(s) Wrubel, Allie
Lyricist(s) Dixon, Mort

Producer(s) Bischoff, Sam
Director(s) McDonald, Frank
Screenwriter(s) Bartlett, Cy; Block, Ralph

Cast Alexander, Ross; Ellis, Patricia; Talbot, Lyle; Acuff, Eddie; O'Neill, Henry; Brecher, Egon; Howland, Olin

Song(s) My Long Gone Baby Came Home; Toddlin' Along with You [1]

Notes [1] May also be in BRIGHT LIGHTS (1935).

679 ✦ BOULEVARD NIGHTS
Warner Brothers, 1981

Musical Score Schifrin, Lalo
Composer(s) Schifrin, Lalo
Lyricist(s) Prestopino, Gregory; Locatell, Carol

Producer(s) Benenson, Bill
Director(s) Pressman, Michael
Screenwriter(s) Nakano, Desmond

Cast Yniquez, Richard; De La Paz, Danny; Du Bois, Marta; Victor, James; Carvalho, Betty

Song(s) On the Boulevard; Street Tattoo (L: Garnett, Gale); Shotgun (C/L: Dewalt, Autry); Restless Lovin'

Notes All are background vocals. Some are very short.

680 ✦ BOUND FOR GLORY
United Artists, 1977

Musical Score Rosenman, Leonard

Producer(s) Blumofe, Robert F.; Leventhal, Harold
Director(s) Ashby, Hal
Screenwriter(s) Getchell, Robert

Cast Carradine, Robert; Cox, Ronny; Dillon, Melinda; Strickland, Gail

Song(s) Woody & Memphis Sue (C/L: Thomas, Guthrie; Getchell, Robert)

Notes This is a biopic of Woody Guthrie. Vocals, all by Guthrie unless otherwise indicated, include "California Water Tastes Like Cherry Wine," "Curly Headed Baby," "Nine Hundred Miles" (Traditional), "Jesus Christ," "Talking Dust Bowl Blues," "Pie in the Sky" (Traditional), "Columbus Stockade," "Takin' It Easy" (written with Paul Campbell), "Down in the Valley" (Traditional), "So Long It's Been Good to Know You (Dusty Old Dust)," "This Train Is Bound for Glory," "Oklahoma Hills" (written with Jack Guthrie), "Hobo's Lullaby" (written by Goebel Reeves), "I Ain't Got No Home," "Hard Travelin'," "Deportee," "Do Re Mi;" "Howdido;" "Union Maid," "Lonesome Valley," "Pastures of Plenty," "This Land Is Your Land," "Better World," "Gypsy Davy," "I'm in the Mood for Love" (by Dorothy Fields and Jimmy McHugh), "Tom Joad,"

"Sinking of the Reuben James;" "Going Down the Road (I Ain't Going to Be Treated This Way)" (written with Lee Hays), "Hard Travelin'," and "Roll on Columbia" written by Guthrie and music based on "Goodnight Irene" by Huddie Ledbetter and John Lomax.

681 ✦ BOWERY CHAMPS
Monogram, 1944

Musical Score Kay, Edward J.

Producer(s) Katzman, Sam; Dietz, Jack
Director(s) Beaudine, William
Screenwriter(s) Snell, Earle

Cast Gorcey, Leo; Hall, Huntz; Benedict, Billy; Jordan, Bobby; Dell, Gabriel; Ford, Francis; Cherkose, Eddie; Brent, Evelyn

Song(s) Hotcha Chornia Brown [1] (C: Stept, Sam H.; L: Green, Bud)

Notes [1] Written in 1934.

682 ✦ BOWERY TO BROADWAY
Universal, 1944

Composer(s) Ward, Edward
Lyricist(s) Carter, Everett
Choreographer(s) Da Pron, Louis; Romero, Carlos; Boyle, Johnny

Producer(s) Grant, John
Director(s) Lamont, Charles
Screenwriter(s) Joseph, Edmund; Lytton, Bart; Horman, Arthur T.

Cast Oakie, Jack; Cook, Donald; Montez, Maria; Foster, Susanna; Blyth, Ann; Albritton, Louise; McHugh, Frank; De Camp, Rosemary; Carrillo, Leo; Devine, Andy; O'Connor, Donald; Ryan, Peggy; Carter, Ben; Moreland, Mantan; Bey, Turhan [1]

Song(s) Here You Are (C/L: Gannon, Kim; Kent, Walter); There'll Always Be A Moon; Lullaby of the Bells (L: Waggner, George); My Song of Romance (C: George, Don; L: Franklin, Dave); Montevideo (C/L: Gannon, Kim; Kent, Walter); The Love Waltz; He Took Her for a Sleighride (C/L: Greene, Mort; Curtis, Mann; Gottler, Archie; Jerome, William); Sing What's In Your Heart; Coney Island Moon (C/L: Gannon, Kim; Kent, Walter)

Notes Only original songs listed. Other vocals included: "Wait 'Till the Sun Shines, Nellie" by Andrew B. Sterling and Harry Von Tilzer; "Just Because She Made Dem Goo-Goo Eyes" by John Queen and Hughie Cannon; "Little Annie Rooney" by Michael Nolan; "Under the Bamboo Tree" by Bob Cole and J. Rosamond Johnson; "Daisy Bell" by Sylvester Krause and Harry Dacre and "Yip-I-Addy-I-Ay" by Will D. Cobb and J.H. Flynn. [1] Dubbed by Lee Sweetland.

683 ✦ BOY, DID I GET A WRONG NUMBER!
United Artists, 1966

Musical Score LaSalle, Richard
Composer(s) LaSalle, Richard
Lyricist(s) Dunham, "By"

Producer(s) Small, Edward
Director(s) Marshall, George
Screenwriter(s) Styler, Burt; Lewin, Albert; Kennett, George

Cast Hope, Bob; Sommer, Elke; Diller, Phyllis; Danova, Cesare; Lord, Marjorie; Thorsdon, Kelly; Baker, Benny; Von Zell, Harry

Song(s) Commercial-Hurdle Girdle; Murder Me

684 ✦ BOY FRIEND (1939)
Twentieth Century–Fox, 1939

Producer(s) Stone, John
Director(s) Tinling, James
Screenwriter(s) Hoffman, Joseph; Trivers, Barry

Cast Withers, Jane; Whelan, Arleen; Bond, Richard; Fowley, Douglas; Hymer, Warren; Shaw, Robert; Watson, Minor

Song(s) Doin' the Socialite (C: Akst, Harry; L: Clare, Sidney)

685 ✦ THE BOY FRIEND (1972)
Metro–Goldwyn–Mayer/EMI, 1972

Composer(s) Wilson, Sandy
Lyricist(s) Wilson, Sandy
Choreographer(s) Gable, Christopher; Gregory, Gillian; Gilbert, Terry; Members of the Cast

Producer(s) Russell, Ken
Director(s) Russell, Ken
Screenwriter(s) Russell, Ken
Source(s) *The Boy Friend* (musical) Wilson, Sandy

Cast Twiggy; Gable, Christopher; Adrian, Max; Pringle, Bryan; Hale, Georgina; Melvin, Murray; Fraser, Moyra; Sheybal, Vladek; Bryant, Sally; Tune, Tommy; Murphy, Brian; Armitage, Graham; Ellis, Antonia; Little, Caryl; Jameson, Ann; Willmer, Catherine; La'Bassiere, Robert; Windsor, Barbara; Jackson, Glenda

Song(s) I Could Be Happy with You; Perfect Young Ladies; The Boy Friend; Won't You Charleston with Me?; Fancy Forgetting; Sur La Plage; A Room in Bloomsbury [1]; Safety in Numbers; Poor Little Pierrette; The Riviera; It's Never too Late to Fall in Love; The You-Don't-Want-to-Play-with- Me Blues; It's Nicer in Nice

Notes All songs are from the stage show. The American version had songs deleted. The British version contained more musical numbers. This list contains all the filmed musical numbers (as far as we know). There

are also vocals of "All I Do Is Dream of You" and "You Are My Lucky Star" by Arthur Freed and Nacio Herb Brown. [1] Part of this number was cut after initial release.

686 ✦ BOY MEETS GIRL
Warner Brothers, 1938

Musical Score Jackson, Howard

Producer(s) Wallis, Hal B.
Director(s) Bacon, Lloyd
Screenwriter(s) Spewack, Bella; Spewack, Sam
Source(s) *Boy Meets Girl* (play) Spewack, Bella; Spewack, Sam

Cast Cagney, James; Foran, Dick; Bellamy, Ralph; McHugh, Frank; Reagan, Ronald; Singleton, Penny

Song(s) With a Pain in My Heart (C: Jerome, M.K.; L: Scholl, Jack)

687 ✦ BOY ON A DOLPHIN
Twentieth Century–Fox, 1957

Musical Score Friedhofer, Hugo

Producer(s) Engel, Samuel G.
Director(s) Negulesco, Jean
Screenwriter(s) Moffat, Ivan; Taylor, Dwight
Source(s) *The Boy on a Dolphin* (novel) Divine, David

Cast Ladd, Alan; Webb, Clifton; Loren, Sophia; Minotis, Alexis; Naismith, Laurence

Song(s) Boy on a Dolphin [1] (C: Friedhofer, Hugo; L: Webster, Paul Francis); Tinafto (C: Morakis, Takis; L: Fermanoglou, John)

Notes [1] Based on "Tinafto." The music was adapted by Friedhofer.

688 ✦ BOYS FROM BRAZIL
Twentieth Century–Fox, 1978

Musical Score Goldsmith, Jerry

Producer(s) Richards, Martin; O'Toole, Stanley
Director(s) Schaffner, Franklin J.
Screenwriter(s) Gould, Heywood
Source(s) *Boys from Brazil* (novel) Levin, Ira

Cast Peck, Gregory; Olivier, Laurence; Mason, James; Palmer, Lilli; Hagen, Uta; Guttenberg, Steve; Elliott, Denholm; Harris, Rosemary; Dehner, John; Rubeinstein, John; Meara, Anne; Black, Jeremy

Song(s) We're Home Again (C: Goldsmith, Jerry; L: Shaper, Hal)

689 ✦ THE BOYS FROM SYRACUSE
Universal, 1940

Musical Score Skinner, Frank
Composer(s) Rodgers, Richard

Lyricist(s) Hart, Lorenz
Choreographer(s) Gould, Dave

Producer(s) Levey, Jules
Director(s) Sutherland, Edward
Screenwriter(s) Spigelgass, Leonard; Grayson, Charles
Source(s) *The Boys from Syracuse* (musical) Abbott, George; Hart, Lorenz; Rodgers, Richard

Cast Jones, Allan; Penner, Joe; Raye, Martha; Lane, Rosemary; Butterworth, Charles; Hervey, Irene; Mowbray, Alan; Blore, Eric; Hinds, Samuel S.

Song(s) The Greeks Have No Word for It; Who Are You; Sing for Your Supper [1]; He and She [1]; Falling in Love with Love [1]; This Can't Be Love [1] [2]

Notes [1] From original Broadway production. [2] Also in BILLY ROSE'S JUMBO.

690 ✦ BOYS IN COMPANY "C"
Columbia, 1977

Musical Score Mendoza-Nava, Jaime

Producer(s) Morgan, Andre
Director(s) Furie, Sidney J.
Screenwriter(s) Natkin, Rick; Furie, Sidney J.

Cast Shaw, Stan; Sevens, Andrew; Canning, James; Lembeck, Michael; Wasson, Craig; Hylands, Scott; Whitmore Jr., James

Song(s) Here I Am (C/L: Wasson, Craig)

691 ✦ BOYS' NIGHT OUT
Metro–Goldwyn–Mayer, 1963

Musical Score De Vol, Frank
Composer(s) Van Heusen, James
Lyricist(s) Cahn, Sammy

Producer(s) Ransohoff, Martin
Director(s) Gordon, Michael
Screenwriter(s) Wallach, Ira

Cast Novak, Kim; Garner, James; Randall, Tony; Blair, Janet; Page, Patti; Landis, Jessie Royce; Homolka, Oscar; Morris, Howard; Jeffreys, Anne; Duff, Howard; Gabor, Zsa Zsa; Backus, Jim; Keating, Larry; Bendix, William; Clark, Fred; McDevitt, Ruth

Song(s) Boys' Night Out; Cathy

692 ✦ THE BOYS OF PAUL STREET
Twentieth Century–Fox, 1969

Musical Score Petrovics, Emil

Producer(s) Bohem, Endre
Director(s) Fabri, Zoltan
Screenwriter(s) Fabri, Zoltan
Source(s) (novel) Molnar, Ferenc

Cast Kemp, Anthony; Burleigh, William; Moulder-Brown, John; Holdaway, Julien; Toroscik, Mri; Pecsi, Sandor

Song(s) Golden Dust (C: Petrovics, Emil; L: Bohem, Endre)

693 ✦ BOYS' RANCH
Metro–Goldwyn–Mayer, 1946

Musical Score Shilkret, Nathaniel

Producer(s) Sisk, Robert
Director(s) Rowland, Roy
Screenwriter(s) Ludwig, William

Cast Jenkins, Jackie "Butch"; Craig, James; Homeier, Skip [1]; Patrick, Dorothy; Collins, Ray; Hickman, Darryl

Song(s) Blood on the Saddle [2] (C/L: Johnston, Gene; Cheatman, E.)

Notes [1] Billed as Skippy Homeier. [2] Also in HORSE PLAY (Universal).

694 ✦ BOYS TOWN
Metro–Goldwyn–Mayer, 1938

Musical Score Ward, Edward

Producer(s) Considine Jr., John W.
Director(s) Taurog, Norman
Screenwriter(s) Meehan, John; Schary, Dore

Cast Tracy, Spencer; Rooney, Mickey; Hull, Henry; Fenton, Leslie; Reynolds, Gene

Song(s) Boys Town on Parade (C: Ward, Edward; L: Wright, Bob; Forrest, Chet)

Notes There is also a vocal of "Ave Maria."

695 ✦ THE BOYS WILL NEVER BELIEVE IT
Metro–Goldwyn–Mayer, 1972

Musical Score Heiman, Nachum; Krivoshei, David
Composer(s) Heiman, Nachum; Krivoshei, David

Producer(s) Deshe, A.
Director(s) Zohar, Uri
Screenwriter(s) Clement, Dick; Hefer, Haim

Cast Topol; Topol, Galia; Levy, Ori

Song(s) The Boys Will Never Believe It (L: Newell, Norman); All the Words [1] (L: Mallows, Michael)

Notes Also known as THE ROOSTER. [1] Used instrumentally only.

696 ✦ A BOY TEN FEET TALL
Paramount, 1965

Producer(s) Mason, Hal
Director(s) Mackendrick, Alexander
Screenwriter(s) Cannan, Denis
Source(s) *Sammy Going South* (novel) Canaway, W.H.

Cast   McClelland, Fergus; Robinson, Edward G.; Cummings, Constance; Walker, Zena

Song(s)   A Boy Ten Feet Tall [1] (C: Baxter, Les; L: Washington, Ned)

Notes   Released as SAMMY GOING SOUTH in Great Britain. Also titled SAMMY GO SOUTH. [1] Not used in picture.

697 ✦ THE BOY WHO COULD FLY
Twentieth Century–Fox, 1986

Musical Score   Broughton, Bruce

Producer(s)   Adelson, Gary
Director(s)   Castle, Nick
Screenwriter(s)   Castle, Nick

Cast   Deakins, Lucy; Underwood, Jay D.; Bedelia, Bonnie; Savage, Fred; Dewhurst, Colleen; Gwynne, Fred; Cohn, Mindy

Song(s)   Back of the Bus (C: Broughton, Bruce; L: Castle, Nick)

698 ✦ BOY WITH GREEN HAIR
RKO, 1949

Musical Score   Harline, Leigh

Producer(s)   Ames, Stephen
Director(s)   Losey, Joseph
Screenwriter(s)   Barzman, Ben; Levitt, Alfred Lewis

Cast   O'Brien, Pat; Ryan, Robert; Hale, Barbara; Stockwell, Dean; Lyon, Richard; Catlett, Walter; Hinds, Samuel S.; Toomey, Regis; Hickman, Dwayne

Song(s)   Nature Boy (C/L: Ahbez, Eden)

699 ✦ BRADDOCK: MISSING IN ACTION III
Cannon, 1988

Musical Score   Chattaway, Jay

Producer(s)   Golan, Menahem; Globus, Yoram
Director(s)   Norris, Aaron
Screenwriter(s)   Bruner, James; Norris, Chuck

Cast   Norris, Chuck; Aleong, Aki; Harrah, Roland; Kim, Miki

Song(s)   Freedom Again (C/L: Bloom, Ron); In Your Eyes (C/L: Bloom, Ron)

Notes   No cue sheet available.

700 ✦ THE BRAIN
Paramount, 1969

Producer(s)   Poire, Alain
Director(s)   Oury, Gerard
Screenwriter(s)   Oury, Gerard

Cast   Niven, David; Belmondo, Jean-Paul; Bourvil; Wallach, Eli

Song(s)   The Brain (C: Delerue, Georges; L: Kusik, Larry; Snyder, Eddie); Cento Giorni (C/L: Soffici, Pierre; Mogol)

701 ✦ THE BRAVE ONE
RKO, 1956

Musical Score   Young, Victor

Producer(s)   King, Maurice; King, Frank
Director(s)   Rapper, Irving
Screenwriter(s)   Franklin, Harry; White, Merrill G.

Cast   Ray, Michael; Hoyos, Rodolfo; Cardenas, Elsa; Navarro, Carlos; Lansing, Joi

Song(s)   El Jocalito (C/L: Esperon, Manuel)

702 ✦ BRAZIL (1944)
Republic, 1944

Musical Score   Barroso, Ary
Composer(s)   Barroso, Ary
Lyricist(s)   Barroso, Ary
Choreographer(s)   Daniels, Billy

Producer(s)   North, Robert
Director(s)   Santley, Joseph
Screenwriter(s)   Kerr, Laura; Gill, Frank, Jr.

Cast   Guizar, Tito; Bruce, Virginia; Horton, Edward Everett; Livingston, Robert; Lane, Richard; Puglia, Frank; Bonanova, Fortunio; Veloz, Frank; Veloz and Yolanda; deSilva, Henry; Seymour, Dan

Song(s)   Brazil (L: Russell, Bob); Upa Upa; Vaquero Song (C/L: Barroso, Ary; Oliveira, Aloysio); Tonight You're Mine [3] (C/L: Barroso, Ary; Oliveira, Aloysio); Ki Ki Ki Ri (C/L: Barroso, Ary; de Carbalho, J.); Hands Across the Border [1] (C: Carmichael, Hoagy; L: Washington, Ned); Rio De Janeiro (C: Barroso, Ary; L: Washington, Ned); A Batucada Comecou [2]; Blim Blem Blao [2]; Quando Eu Penso Na Bahia [2]

Notes   [1] Also in HANDS ACROSS THE BORDER. [2] Sheet music only. [3] English lyrics by Ned Washington.

703 ✦ BRAZIL (1985)
Twentieth Century–Fox, 1985

Musical Score   Kamen, Michael

Producer(s)   Milchan, Arnon
Director(s)   Gilliam, Terry
Screenwriter(s)   Gilliam, Terry; Stoppard, Tom; McKeown, Charles

Cast   Pryce, Jonathan; De Niro, Robert; Helmond, Katherine; Holm, Ian; Hoskins, Bob; Palin, Michael; Richardson, Ian; Vaughan, Peter; Jones, Simon

Song(s)   Singing Messenger (C/L: Gilliam, Terry)

704 ✦ BREAD AND CHOCOLATE
World Northal, 1978

Musical Score Patucchi, Daniele

Producer(s) Lodi-Fe, Maurizo
Director(s) Brusati, Franco
Screenwriter(s) Brusati, Franco; Fiastri, Iaia; Manfredi, Nino

Cast Manfredi, Nino; Turco, Paolo; D'Alessio, Ugo; Barbra, Gianfranco

Song(s) L'Uomo non E'di Legno (C: Calise, Ugo; L: Fiastri, Iaia

Notes No cue sheet available.

705 ✦ BREAKER! BREAKER!
American International, 1977

Musical Score Hulette, Don
Composer(s) Hulette, Don

Producer(s) Hulette, Don
Director(s) Hulette, Don
Screenwriter(s) Chambers, Terry

Cast Norris, Chuck; Murdock, George; DiFusco, John; O'Connor, Terry; Gentry, Don

Song(s) Breaker! Breaker! (L: DiFusco, John; Hulette, Don); I've Heard These Words (L: Chambers, Terry); We Never Said Hello (L: Thomas, Thomas G.); You Woke Up This Morning (L: Hulette, Don)

Notes No cue sheet available.

706 ✦ BREAKFAST AT TIFFANY'S
Paramount, 1961

Musical Score Mancini, Henry

Producer(s) Shepherd, Richard; Jurow, Martin
Director(s) Edwards, Blake
Screenwriter(s) Axelrod, George
Source(s) "Breakfast at Tiffany's" (novella) Capote, Truman

Cast Hepburn, Audrey; Neal, Patricia; Peppard, George; Rooney, Mickey; Ebsen, Buddy; Balsam, Martin; McGiver, John

Song(s) Moon River [1] (C: Mancini, Henry; L: Mercer, Johnny); Lovers in the Park [2] (C: Mancini, Henry; L: Livingston, Jay; Evans, Ray)

Notes [1] Oscar winner. [2] Lyric written for exploitation only.

707 ✦ THE BREAKFAST CLUB
Universal, 1985

Musical Score Forsey, Keith; Chang, Gary

Producer(s) Tanen, Ned; Hughes, John
Director(s) Hughes, John
Screenwriter(s) Hughes, John

Cast Estevez, Emilio; Gleason, Paul; Hall, Anthony Michael; Kapelos, John; Nelson, Judd; Ringwald, Molly; Sheedy, Ally; Crawford, Perry

Song(s) Don't You (Forget About Me) (C/L: Forsey, Keith; Schiff, Steve); Fire in the Twilight (C: Forsey, Keith; Schiff, Steve; L: Schiff, Steve; Forsey, Keith; Hues, Jack); We Are Not Alone (C/L: De Vito, Karla; Benson, Robby; Goldstein, Steve); Heart Too Hot to Hold (C: Forsey, Keith; Forsey, Laurie; L: Forsey, Keith; Forsey, Laurie; Johnson, Jesse; Frondelli, Michael)

708 ✦ BREAKIN'
MGM/UA–Cannon, 1984

Musical Score Remel, Gary; Boyd, Michael

Producer(s) DeBevoise, Allen; Zito, David
Director(s) Silberg, Joel
Screenwriter(s) Parker, Charles; DeBevoise, Allen; Scaife, Gerald

Cast Dickey, Lucinda; Quinones, Adolfo "Shabba-Doo"; Chambers, Michael "Boogaloo Shrimp"; Newborn III, Phineas; McDonald, Christopher; Lokey, Ben; Solomon, Timothy; Sanchez, Ana; Morrow, Tracey "Ice-T"; Bromilow, Peter

Song(s) Tibetan Jam (C: Storrs, David; L: Morrow, Tracey "Ice-T"); Heart of the Beat (C/L: Hart, Don; Midnight, Charlie); Reckless [1] (C: Storrs, David; L: Morrow, Tracey "Ice-T"); Breakin' There's No Stopping Us (C/L: Brown, Ollie E.; Knight, Jerry); Showdown (C/L: Brown, Ollie E.; Curiale, John); 99 1/2 (C/L: Footman, Joe; Anderson, Maxi); Street People (C/L: Brown, Ollie E.; Knight, Jerry); Ain't Nobody (C/L: Wolinski, David); Body Work (C/L: Hudson, Curtis); Cut It (C/L: Fishman, Paul); Freakshow on the Dance Floor (C/L: Alexander, James; Beard, Michael)

Notes No cue sheet available. [1] Chris Taylor credited with lyrics on sheet music.

709 ✦ BREAKIN' 2 ELECTRIC BOOGALOO
Tri-Star, 1984

Composer(s) Brown, Ollie E.; Giles, Attala Z.; Regan, Russ
Lyricist(s) Brown, Ollie E.; Giles, Attala Z.; Regan, Russ

Producer(s) Golan, Menahem; Globus, Yoram
Director(s) Firstenberg, Sam
Screenwriter(s) Ventura, Jan; Reichert, Julia

Cast Dickey, Lucinda; Quinones, Adolfo "Shabba-Doo"; Chambers, Michael "Boogaloo Shrimp"; Bono, Susie; Caesar, Harry; de Winter, Jo; Ewing, John Christy; Notario, Steve "Sugarfoot"; Leonard, Lu; Olfson, Ken

Song(s) Electric Boogaloo; Radiotron; Action; Go Off (C: Storrs, David; L: Morrow, Tracey "Ice-T"; Storrs,

David); When I.C.U. (C/L: Brown, Ollie E.; Knight, Jerry; Giles, Attala Z.)

Notes   No cue sheet available.

710 ◆ BREAKING AWAY
Twentieth Century–Fox, 1979

Composer(s)   Williams, Patrick
Lyricist(s)   Williams, Patrick

Producer(s)   Yates, Peter
Director(s)   Yates, Peter
Screenwriter(s)   Tesich, Steve

Cast   Christopher, Dennis; Quaid, Dennis; Stern, Daniel; Haley, Jackie Earle; Barrie, Barbara; Dooley, Paul; Bochner, Hart; Wright, Amy

Song(s)   You Don't Even Try; Loosen It Up; The La La Song

Notes   All background vocal uses.

711 ◆ BREAKING THE ICE
RKO, 1938

Composer(s)   Churchill, Frank E.
Lyricist(s)   Webster, Paul Francis

Producer(s)   Lesser, Sol
Director(s)   Cline, Edward F.
Screenwriter(s)   McCall Jr., Mary C.; Seff, Manuel; Schubert, Bernard

Cast   Breen, Bobby; Dare, Irene; Ruggles, Charles; Costello, Dolores; Barrat, Robert; Peterson, Dorothy; King, John; Gilbert, Billy; Hamilton, Margaret

Song(s)   Happy As a Lark; Put Your Heart Into a Song; The Sunny Side of Things; Telling My Troubles to a Mule (C: Young, Victor); Goodbye, My Dreams, Goodbye [1] (C: Young, Victor)

Notes   No cue sheet available. [1] Music based on Schubert's "Serenade."

712 ◆ BREAK OF HEARTS
RKO, 1935

Musical Score   Steiner, Max

Producer(s)   Berman, Pandro S.
Director(s)   Moeller, Philip
Screenwriter(s)   Mason, Sarah Y.; Heerman, Victor; Veiller, Anthony

Cast   Hepburn, Katharine; Boyer, Charles; Beal, John; Hersholt, Jean

Song(s)   Happy-Go-Lucky (C: Steiner, Max; L: Scholl, Jack)

713 ◆ BREAK THE NEWS
Monogram, 1941

Composer(s)   Porter, Cole
Lyricist(s)   Porter, Cole

Director(s)   Clair, Rene
Screenwriter(s)   Kerr, Geoffrey

Cast   Chevalier, Maurice; Buchanan, Jack; Knight, June

Song(s)   It All Belongs to You; Don't Let It Get You Down [1]

Notes   Produced in England in 1937. [1] Not used. Later put in score of stage musical YOU NEVER KNOW.

714 ◆ BREATH OF SCANDAL
Paramount, 1960

Musical Score   Cicognini, Alessandro

Producer(s)   Ponti, Carlo; Girosi, Marcello
Director(s)   Curtiz, Michael
Screenwriter(s)   Howard, Sidney [2]; Bernstein, Walter
Source(s)   *Olympia* (play) Molnar, Ferenc

Cast   Loren, Sophia; Gavin, John; Chevalier, Maurice; Lansbury, Angela; Jeans, Isabel

Song(s)   A Breath of Scandal (C: Stolz, Robert; L: Stillman, Al); A Smile in Vienna [1] (C: Fellner, Sepp; L: Michael, Patrick; Schneider, Karl)

Notes   The film was also known as OLYMPIA. A remake of HIS GLORIOUS NIGHT (MGM). [1] Used instrumentally only. [2] The Sidney Howard script (he died in 1939) was written in 1938. Ponti bought it from MGM and hired Bernstein.

715 ◆ BREEZING HOME
Universal, 1937

Composer(s)   McHugh, Jimmy
Lyricist(s)   Adamson, Harold

Producer(s)   Grainger, Edmund
Director(s)   Carruth, Milton
Screenwriter(s)   Grayson, Charles

Cast   Barrie, Wendy; Gargan, William; Barnes, Binnie; Baxter, Alan; Walburn, Raymond; Kruger, Alma; Loring, Michael; Cook Jr., Elisha; Best, Willie

Song(s)   I'm Hittin' the Hot Spots [1]; You're in My Heart Again [2]

Notes   [1] Also in WHEN LOVE IS YOUNG and MISSISSIPPI GAMBLER (1942). [2] Also in AS GOOD AS MARRIED.

716 ◆ BREEZY
Universal, 1973

Musical Score   Legrand, Michel

Producer(s)   Daley, Robert
Director(s)   Eastwood, Clint
Screenwriter(s)   Heims, Jo

Cast   Holden, William; Lenz, Kay; Hotchkis, Joan; Dusay, Marj; Morrison, Shelley; Jackson, Jamie Smith

Song(s) Breezy's Song (C: Legrand, Michel; L: Bergman, Alan; Bergman, Marilyn)

717 ✦ BREWSTER MCCLOUD
Metro–Goldwyn–Mayer, 1971

Musical Score Page, Gene
Composer(s) Phillips, John
Lyricist(s) Phillips, John

Producer(s) Adler, Lou
Director(s) Altman, Robert
Screenwriter(s) Cannon, Doran William

Cast Cort, Bud; Kellerman, Sally; Murphy, Michael; Windom, William; Schuck, John; Hamilton, Margaret; Salt, Jennifer; Fischer, Corey; Remsen, Bert; Wood, G.; Duvall, Shelley; Auberjonois, Rene; Keach, Stacy

Song(s) First and Last Thing You Do; White Feather Wings; Last of the Unnatural Acts; Promise Not to Tell

Notes This film has a credit reading: Title Song: Francis Scott Key.

718 ✦ BREWSTER'S MILLIONS (1935)
United Artists, 1935

Composer(s) Noble, Ray
Lyricist(s) Furber, Douglas

Producer(s) Wilcox, Herbert
Director(s) Wilcox, Herbert
Screenwriter(s) Wimperis, Arthur; Wilhelm, W.; Joseph, Michael; Grey, Clifford; Pedelty, Donovan
Source(s) *Brewster's Millions* (play) Smith, Winchell; Ongley, Byron; *Brewster's Millions* (novel) McCutcheon, George Barr

Cast Buchanan, Jack; Damita, Lily; O'Neil, Nance; Fairbrother, Sidney; McLean, Ian; Emmy, Fred; Aynsworth, Allan; Shaw, Sebastian; Hoey, Dennis

Song(s) La Caranga; I Think I Can; One Good Tune Deserves Another; Pull Down the Blinds

Notes No cue sheet available. Versions of this story were filmed in 1914, 1921, 1945 and 1984 and again in Britain in 1961 as THREE ON A SPREE.

719 ✦ BREWSTER'S MILLIONS (1985)
Universal, 1985

Musical Score Cooder, Ry

Producer(s) Gordon, Lawrence; Silver, Joel
Director(s) Hill, Walter
Screenwriter(s) Weingrod, Herschel; Harris, Timothy
Source(s) *Brewster's Millions* (novel) McCutcheon, George Barr; *Brewster's Millions* (play) Smith, Winchell; Ongley, Byron

Cast Pryor, Richard; Candy, John; McKee, Lonette; Collins, Stephen; Orbach, Jerry; Hingle, Pat; Feldshuh,

Tovah; Cronyn, Hume; Grifasi, Joe; Dempsey, Jerome; Smirnoff, Yakov; Moranis, Rick; Janis, Conrad; Le Noire, Rosetta; Santoni, Reni

Song(s) Living in Materialisticality (C/L: Cooder, Ry; King, Bobby); Baby You're My Everything For Now (C/L: Cooder, Ry); Meet Me at No Special Place (L: Robinson, J. Russel; L: Pyle, Harry; Terker, Arthur); In the Nick of Time (C/L: Lewis, Huey; Cooder, Ry)

720 ✦ THE BRIBE
Metro–Goldwyn–Mayer, 1949

Musical Score Rozsa, Miklos
Lyricist(s) Katz, William

Producer(s) Berman, Pandro S.
Director(s) Leonard, Robert Z.
Screenwriter(s) Roberts, Marguerite
Source(s) (story) Nebel, Frederick

Cast Taylor, Robert; Gardner, Ava [1]; Laughton, Charles; Price, Vincent; Hodiak, John; Hinds, Samuel S.; Hoyt, John; Rinaldo, Tito

Song(s) Situation Wanted (C: Brown, Nacio Herb); La Perica (C: Rozsa, Miklos); Fiesta (C: Rozsa, Miklos)

Notes [1] Dubbed by Eileen Wilson.

721 ✦ BRIDAL SUITE
MGM, 1939

Producer(s) Selwyn, Edgar
Director(s) Thiele, William
Screenwriter(s) Hoffenstein, Samuel

Cast Annabella; Young, Robert; Connolly, Walter; Owen, Reginald; Lockhart, Gene; Treacher, Arthur; Burke, Billie; Field, Virginia; Bressart, Felix

Song(s) When I Gave My Smile to You [1] (C: Buddie, Bill; L: Kahn, Gus); When I Called You My Sweetheart (C/L: Buddie, Bill; Orban, Jeff); One Little Drink to You (C: Gutmann, Arthur; L: Kahn, Gus)

Notes No cue sheet available. [1] Jeff Orban also credited by ASCAP though not sheet music.

722 ✦ THE BRIDE
Bryanston, 1976

Musical Score Berinstein, Peter

Producer(s) Grissmer, John
Director(s) Pelissie, Jean-Marie
Screenwriter(s) Grissmer, John; Pelissie, Jean-Marie

Cast Strasser, Robin; Roberts, Arthur; Beal, John

Song(s) Can't Help Loving You (C: Berinstein, Peter; L: Ross, Susan)

Notes No cue sheet available.

723 ✦ BRIDE OF THE REGIMENT
Warner Brothers–First National, 1930

Composer(s)   Ward, Edward
Lyricist(s)   Bryan, Alfred; Dubin, Al
Choreographer(s)   Haskell, Jack

Director(s)   Dillon, John Francis
Screenwriter(s)   Harris, Ray; Pearson, Humphrey
Source(s)   *Lady in Ermine* (musical) Schanzer, Rudolph; Wellisch, Ernst

Cast   Segal, Vivienne; Prior, Allan; Pidgeon, Walter; Fazenda, Louise; Sterling, Ford; Lane, Lupino; Loy, Myrna

Song(s)   Broken-Hearted Lover (L: Bryan, Alfred); Dream Away (L: Bryan, Alfred); Heart of Heaven; I'd Like to Be a Happy Bride; One Kiss, Sweetheart, Then Goodbye; Cook's Song; Through the Miracle of Love; One Life One Love (L: Bryan, Alfred); You Still Retain Your Girlish Figure

Notes   No cue sheet available. Titled LADY OF THE ROSE in Great Britain. The German title of the source is DIE FRAU IM HERMELIN. It is not known whether Bryan and Dubin collaborated.

724 ✦ BRIDE OF VENGEANCE
Paramount, 1949

Musical Score   Friedhofer, Hugo
Composer(s)   Sanders, Troy
Lyricist(s)   Livingston, Jay; Evans, Ray

Producer(s)   Maibaum, Richard
Director(s)   Leisen, Mitchell
Screenwriter(s)   Hogan, Michael; Hume, Cyril; Dane, Clemence

Cast   Lund, John; Carey, Macdonald; Goddard, Paulette; Gilbert, Billy; Burr, Raymond; Dekker, Albert

Song(s)   The Nightingale and the Rose (C: Young, Victor L: Dane, Clemence); Give Thy Love; The Wine of Old Giuseppe

Notes   The production was first titled A MASK FOR LUCRETIA.

725 ✦ THE BRIDE WALKS OUT
RKO, 1936

Producer(s)   Small, Edward
Director(s)   Jason, Leigh
Screenwriter(s)   Wolfson, P.J.; Epstein, Philip G.

Cast   Raymond, Gene; Stanwyck, Barbara; Young, Robert; Sparks, Ned; Broderick, Helen; Best, Willie; Warwick, Robert; Gilbert, Billy; Boteler, Wade; McDaniel, Hattie

Song(s)   It Happened When Your Eyes Met Mine (C: Akst, Harry; L: Turk, Roy)

Notes   Formerly titled MARRY THE GIRL.

726 ✦ THE BRIDE WORE CRUTCHES
Twentieth Century–Fox, 1941

Producer(s)   Hubbard, Lucien
Director(s)   Traube, Shepard
Screenwriter(s)   Verdier, Edward

Cast   Roberts, Lynne; North, Ted; Kennedy, Edgar; Armstrong, Robert; Stander, Lionel; Mitchell, Grant; MacMahon, Horace

Song(s)   Dearest One (C: Newman, Emil; L: Holden, Cally)

727 ✦ THE BRIDE WORE RED
Metro–Goldwyn–Mayer, 1937

Musical Score   Waxman, Franz
Choreographer(s)   Raset, Val

Producer(s)   Mankiewicz, Joseph L.
Director(s)   Arzner, Dorothy
Screenwriter(s)   Slesinger, Tess; Foote, Bradbury
Source(s)   *The Girl from Trieste* (play) Molnar, Ferenc

Cast   Crawford, Joan; Tone, Franchot; Burke, Billie; Young, Robert; Owen, Reginald; Moore, Dickie; Zucco, George

Song(s)   Who Wants Love? (C: Waxman, Franz; L: Kahn, Gus); Canzone-Scherzo (C/L: Waxman, Franz)

728 ✦ THE BRIDGE OF SAN LUIS REY
United Artists, 1944

Musical Score   Tiomkin, Dimitri
Composer(s)   Tiomkin, Dimitri
Lyricist(s)   Stahlberg, Herbert

Producer(s)   Bogeaus, Benedict
Director(s)   Lee, Rowland V.
Screenwriter(s)   Estabrook, Howard
Source(s)   *The Bridge of San Luis Rey* (novel) Wilder, Thornton

Cast   Bari, Lynn; Tamiroff, Akim; Lederer, Francis; Nazimova; Calhern, Louis; Yurka, Blanche; Woods, Donald; Dunn, Emma; Urecal, Minerva

Song(s)   Poor Poor Mama; The Devil Will Get You

729 ✦ BRIEF MOMENT
Columbia, 1933

Director(s)   Burton, David
Screenwriter(s)   Marlow, Brian; Fitzgerald, Edith
Source(s)   *Brief Moment* (play) Behrman, S.N.

Cast   Lombard, Carole; Raymond, Gene; Owsley, Monroe; Cook, Donald; Hohl, Arthur

Song(s)   Say What You Mean, and Mean What You're Saying to Me (C: Marks, Gerald; L: Young, Joe); Since You Have Chosen Me (C: Rosoff, Charles; L: Young, Joe)

Notes   No cue sheet available.

730 ◆ BRIGADOON
Metro–Goldwyn–Mayer, 1954

Composer(s) Loewe, Frederick
Lyricist(s) Lerner, Alan Jay
Choreographer(s) Kelly, Gene

Producer(s) Freed, Arthur
Director(s) Minnelli, Vincente
Screenwriter(s) Lerner, Alan Jay
Source(s) *Brigadoon* (musical) Lerner, Alan Jay;
Loewe, Frederick

Cast Johnson, Van; Kelly, Gene; Charisse, Cyd [2];
Stewart, Elaine; Jones, Barry; Laing, Hugh; Sharpe,
Albert; Bosler, Virginia; Thompson, Jimmy [1]; Heath,
Dody; Chakiris, George; Quillan, Eddie

Song(s) Brigadoon; Down on Mac Connachy Square;
Waitin' for My Dearie; I'll Go Home with Bonnie Jean;
The Heather on the Hill; Almost Like Being in Love;
The Chase; There But for You Go I [3]; Come to Me,
Bend to Me [4]

Notes All songs from the Broadway musical although
the cue titles may not match. [1] Dubbed by John
Gustafson. [2] Dubbed by Carole Richards. [3] Deleted
from final print. [4] Prerecorded but not used.

731 ◆ BRIGHT EYES
Fox, 1934

Producer(s) Wurtzel, Sol M.
Director(s) Butler, David
Screenwriter(s) Conselman, William

Cast Temple, Shirley; Withers, Jane; Dunn, James;
Allen, Judith

Song(s) (On the) Good Ship Lollipop (C: Whiting,
Richard A.; L: Clare, Sidney)

732 ◆ BRIGHT LIGHTS (1930)
Warner Brothers–First National, 1930

Lyricist(s) Washington, Ned; Magidson, Herb
Choreographer(s) Ceballos, Larry

Producer(s) North, Robert
Director(s) Curtiz, Michael
Screenwriter(s) Pearson, Humphrey

Cast Mackaill, Dorothy; Beery, Noah; Fay, Frank;
Courtney, Inez; Nugent, Eddie; Breese, Edmund;
Pollard, Daphne; McHugh, Frank

Song(s) Nobody Cares If I'm Blue (C: Akst, Harry; L:
Clarke, Grant); I'm Crazy for Cannibal Love (C: Ward,
Edward; L: Bryan, Alfred); Song of the Congo (C:
Perkins, Ray); Every Little Girl He Sees (C: Akst, Harry;
L: Clarke, Grant); A Man About Town (C: Cleary,
Michael); Rubberneckin' Around (C: Akst, Harry;
Perkins, Ray)

Notes No cue sheet available. There is also a vocal of
"Chinatown" by Jean Schwartz and William Jerome.

733 ◆ BRIGHT LIGHTS (1935)
Warner Brothers (First National), 1935

Composer(s) Wrubel, Allie
Lyricist(s) Dixon, Mort

Producer(s) Brown, Harry Joe
Director(s) Berkeley, Busby
Screenwriter(s) Kalmar, Bert; Ruby, Harry

Cast Brown, Joe E.; Dvorak, Ann; Ellis, Patricia;
Gargan, William; Cawthorn, Joseph; O'Neill, Henry;
Treacher, Arthur; Westcott, Gordon; Demarest, William

Song(s) She Was an Acrobat's Daughter (C: Ruby,
Harry; L: Kalmar, Bert); Powder My Back [1]; You're an
Eyeful of Heaven; Toddlin' Along with You [2]; Bright
Lights [3]

Notes Released in Great Britain as FUNNY FACE.
Originally titled: BROADWAY JOE. [1] Also in CITY
FOR CONQUEST. [2] Also in BOULDER DAM. [3]
Not on cue sheets.

734 ◆ BRIGHT LIGHTS, BIG CITY
United Artists, 1988

Musical Score Fagen, Donald

Producer(s) Rosenberg, Mark; Pollack, Sydney
Director(s) Bridges, James
Screenwriter(s) McInerney, Jay
Source(s) *Bright Lights, Big City* (novel) McInerney, Jay

Cast Fox, Michael J.; Sutherland, Kiefer; Cates,
Phoebe; Kurtz, Swoosie; Sternhagen, Frances; Pollan,
Tracy; Houseman, John; Schlatter, Charlie; Robards Jr.,
Jason; Warrilow, David; Wiest, Dianne; Hickey, William;
Robards, Sam

Song(s) Love Attack (C/L: Dawson, Shannon; Jay, G.
"Love"); Pump Up the Volume (C/L: Young, Martyn;
Young, Steve); Bright Lights, Big City (C/L: Reed,
Jimmy); Good Love (C/L: Prince); Kiss and Tell (C/L:
Leonard, Patrick; Kamen, Chester; Ferry, Bryan); True
Faith (C/L: New Order; Hague, Stephen); Ice Cream
Days (C/L: Hall, Jennifer; Tarney, Alan); Pleasure, Little
Treasure (C/L: Gore, M.L.); Obsessed (C/L: Leiber,
Oliver); Divine Emotions (C/L: Walden, Narada
Michael; Cohen, Jeffrey); Century's End (C: Fagen,
Donald; L: Meher, Timothy)

Notes It is not known if any of the above were written
for this film. There is also a vocal of "Let's Have Another
Cup of Coffee" by Irving Berlin.

735 ◆ BRIGHT ROAD
Metro–Goldwyn–Mayer, 1953

Musical Score Rose, David

Producer(s) Fielding, Sol Baer
Director(s) Mayer, Gerald
Screenwriter(s) Lavery, Emmet

Source(s) "See How They Run" (story) Vroman, Mary Elizabeth

Cast Dandridge, Dorothy; Hepburn, Philip; Belafonte, Harry; Sanders, Barbara Ann; Horton, Robert; Norman, Maidie

Song(s) Suzanne (Ev'ry Night when the Sun Goes Down) (C/L: Belafonte, Harry; Thomas, Millard)

---

736 ✦ BRING ME THE HEAD OF ALFREDO GARCIA
United Artists, 1974

Musical Score Fielding, Jerry

Producer(s) Baum, Martin
Director(s) Peckinpah, Sam
Screenwriter(s) Peckinpah, Sam; Dawson, Gordon

Cast Oates, Warren; Vega, Isela; Da Silva, Nico; Dantine, Helmut; Levy, Don; Sahl, Mort; Scott, Bill; Kristofferson, Kris

Song(s) Bennie's Tune (C/L: Vega, Isela); Bad Blood Baby (C/L: Peckinpah, Sam)

Notes There are also several public domain tunes given brief vocal treatments.

---

737 ✦ BRING ON THE GIRLS
Paramount, 1945

Musical Score Young, Victor; Dolan, Robert Emmett
Composer(s) McHugh, Jimmy
Lyricist(s) Adamson, Harold
Choreographer(s) Dare, Danny

Producer(s) Kohlmar, Fred
Director(s) Lanfield, Sidney
Screenwriter(s) Ware, Darrell; Tunberg, Karl

Cast Reynolds, Marjorie [5]; Bracken, Eddie; Tufts, Sonny; Lake, Veronica; Mitchell, Grant; Mowbray, Alan; Hall, Porter; Spike Jones and His Orchestra; Faylen, Frank; Hall, Huntz; Hall, Thurston; Arno, Sig; Coy, Johnny; Daniels, Billy

Song(s) You Moved Right In; Uncle Sammy Hit Miami; If It Could Happen [1] [2]; Bring on the Girls; How Would You Like to Take My Picture; I'm Gonna Hate Myself in the Morning; True to the Navy; Egyptian-Ella [3] (C: Doyle, Walter; L: Doyle, Walter; Tufts, Sonny); The Gold Diggers Are Back Again [1]: At the Yankee Doodle Ball [1]; Preacher and the Bear [4] (C/L: Arizona, Joe)

Notes Spike Jones presents his versions of "Chloe" by Gus Kahn and Neil Moret. He recorded Rossini's "William Tell Overture" but the number was not used in the final print. The recording call for "You Moved Right In" and "How Would You Like to Take My Picture" called for the following talent: Martha Mears, Marjorie Reynolds, Billy Daniels, and Danny Dare. [1] Unused. [2] The song was originally titled "It Could Happen to Me" but because of the similarity to the Burke and Van Heusen song "It Could Happen to You" the title was changed. Finally the number was taken out of production although Eddie Bracken did record the number for use in the film. (One reviewer claims the song was a highlight of the movie, perhaps he was talking of another number.) To add insult to injury 51 seconds of the Burke and Van Heusen number was instrumentally added to the soundtrack. [3] The original lyrics for the song were denied by the Hays office because "of its basically vulgar and suggestive flavor . . . we feel should not be included in your production if this picture is to meet the requirements of the Production Code." Sonny Tufts then rewrote the lyrics. [4] This number was recorded by the Golden Gate Quartette but not included in the release print. [5] Dubbed by Martha Mears.

---

738 ✦ BRING YOUR SMILE ALONG
Columbia, 1955

Composer(s) Lee, Lester; Roberts, Allan
Lyricist(s) Lee, Lester; Roberts, Allan

Producer(s) Taps, Jonie
Director(s) Edwards, Blake
Screenwriter(s) Edwards, Blake

Cast Laine, Frankie; Brasselle, Keefe; Towers, Constance; Marlow, Lucy; Leslie, William; Albertson, Jack; Clark, Bobby; Warren, Ruth; Siletti, Mario

Song(s) If Spring Never Comes (C: Carey, Bill; L: Fischer, Carl); Gandy Dancers Ball (C: Weston, Paul; L: Howard, Paul Mason); When a Girl Is Beautiful (C: Lee, Lester; L: Roberts, Allan); Every Baby Needs a Da-Da-Daddy (C: Lee, Lester; L: Roberts, Allan); Mama Mia (Italian Mother Song) (C: Lee, Lester; L: Washington, Ned); Bring Your Smile Along (C/L: Fischer, Carl; Davis, Benny)

Notes No cue sheet available. There is also a vocal of "Don't Blame Me" by Dorothy Fields and Jimmy McHugh and one of "Side By Side" by Harry Woods.

---

739 ✦ BROADWAY
Universal, 1929

Musical Score Jackson, Howard
Composer(s) Conrad, Con; Gottler, Archie
Lyricist(s) Mitchell, Sidney D.; Conrad, Con
Choreographer(s) Kusell, Maurice L. [2]

Producer(s) Laemmle Jr., Carl
Director(s) Fejos, Paul
Screenwriter(s) Lowe Jr., Edward T.; Furthman, Charles; Dunning, Philip; Abbott, George
Source(s) *Broadway* (play) Dunning, Philip; Abbott, George

Cast Tryon, Glenn; Jackson, Thomas E. [1]; Porcasi, Paul [1]; Brent, Evelyn; Kennedy, Merna; Ellie, Robert;

Harlan, Otis; Lord, Marion; Feld, Fritz; Gus Arnheim and the Cocoanut Grove Orchestra

Song(s) Broadway; The Chicken or the Egg; Hot Footin' It; Hittin' the Ceiling; Sing a Little Love Song; Bounce a Little Ball at Your Baby [3]

Notes No cue sheet available. [1] From original Broadway production. The film is comprised solely of the stage dialogue. What the other screenwriters contributed is a question. According to *Variety*, Dunning was the sole author of the play, with Abbott receiving credit for "some construction work on it." [2] *Film Daily Yearbook* credits John Mattison with choreography. [3] Not used.

740 ◆ BROADWAY AHEAD

See SWEETHEART OF THE CAMPUS.

741 ◆ BROADWAY BABIES
Warner Brothers–First National, 1929

Musical Score Forbstein, Leo
Composer(s) Meyer, George W.
Lyricist(s) Bryan, Alfred

Director(s) LeRoy, Mervyn
Screenwriter(s) Katterjohn, Monte; Pearson, Humphrey
Source(s) "Broadway Musketeers" (story) Gelzer, Jay

Cast White, Alice; Delaney, Charles; Kohler, Fred; Dugan, Tom; Eilers, Sally; Byron, Marion

Song(s) Wishing and Waiting for Love [1] (C: Akst, Harry; L: Clarke, Grant); Jig Jig Jigaloo; The Broadway Baby Dolls

Notes No cue sheet available. [1] Also in DANCING SWEETIES.

742 ◆ BROADWAY BAD
Fox, 1933

Director(s) Lanfield, Sidney
Screenwriter(s) Kober, Arthur; Fulton, Maude

Cast Blondell, Joan; Cortez, Ricardo; Rogers, Ginger; Ames, Adrienne

Song(s) Forget the Past (C: Akst, Harry; L: Mitchell, Sidney D.)

743 ◆ BROADWAY GONDOLIER
Warner Brothers, 1935

Composer(s) Warren, Harry
Lyricist(s) Dubin, Al

Producer(s) Bischoff, Sam
Director(s) Bacon, Lloyd
Screenwriter(s) Duff, Warren; Herzig, Sig

Cast Powell, Dick; Blondell, Joan; Fazenda, Louise; Menjou, Adolphe; The Mills Brothers; The Canova Family; Ted Fiorito and His Band

Song(s) Flagenheim's Odorless Cheese; Outside of You; The Pig and the Cow, and the Dog and the Cat [2]; Lonely Gondolier; The Rose in Her Hair; Lulu's Back in Town; You Can Be Kissed; Sweet and Slow [1]

Notes [1] This is given 46 seconds of instrumental use. It is not known if it was written for this picture but it is also used in BROADWAY HOSTESS and also briefly in STARS OVER BROADWAY. [2] Also in I FOUND STELLA PARRISH.

744 ◆ THE BROADWAY HOOFER
Columbia, 1929

Producer(s) Cohn, Harry
Director(s) Archainbaud, George
Screenwriter(s) Lehman, Gladys

Cast Saxon, Marie; Egan, Jack; Fazenda, Louise; Hickman, Howard

Song(s) Mediterranean Moon (C/L: Valentine; King; Fiorito, Ted); Hawaiian Love Song (C: Franklin, Dave; L: Macdonald, Ballard); Wanting You [1] (C/L: Sizemore, Arthur; Grossman, Bernie; Abrahams, Maurice); I Live to Love Only You (C: Rich, Max; L: Gordon, Mack)

Notes There are also vocal renditions of "Moonlight Bay" by Percy Wenrich; "By the Light of the Silvery Moon" by Gus Edwards and Edward Madden; "Dear Old Moonlight" by an unknown composer and "Shine on Harvest Moon" by Jack Norworth and Nora Bayes. [1] Instrumental use only.

745 ◆ BROADWAY HOSTESS
Warner Brothers–First National, 1935

Composer(s) Wrubel, Allie
Lyricist(s) Dixon, Mort
Choreographer(s) Connolly, Bobby

Producer(s) Foy, Bryan
Director(s) McDonald, Frank
Screenwriter(s) Bricker, George

Cast Shaw, Winifred; Tobin, Genevieve; Talbot, Lyle; Jenkins, Allen; Regan, Phil; Wilson, Marie; Byington, Spring

Song(s) Sweet and Slow [1] (C: Warren, Harry; L: Dubin, Al); Dancing with Tears in My Eyes [2] (C: Burke, Joe; L: Dubin, Al); Weary; He Was Her Man; Who But You; Let It Be Me; Playboy of Paree; The Lady in Red [4]; Only the Girl [3] (C: Jerome, M.K.; L: Ruby, Herman); Help Yourself To My Love [5] (C: Jerome, M.K.; L: Ruby, Herman)

Notes [1] Used for 20 seconds. Used instrumentally in BROADWAY GONDOLIER and, for an even briefer period, in STARS OVER BROADWAY. [2] Used for 33 seconds. Cut from print of DANCING SWEETIES. [3] Listed in some sources but not on cue sheets. Also in THE PAINTED ANGEL. [4] Also in IN CALIENTE. [5] Sheet music only.

746 ♦ BROADWAY MELODY
Metro–Goldwyn–Mayer, 1928

Composer(s) Brown, Nacio Herb
Lyricist(s) Freed, Arthur

Director(s) Beaumont, Harry
Screenwriter(s) Houston, Norman; Gleason, James

Cast King, Charles; Page, Anita; Love, Bessie; Prouty, Jed; Thomson, Kenneth; Doran, Mary

Song(s) Broadway Melody [2]; Love Boat; You Were Meant for Me [1]; Wedding of the Painted Doll [3]; Boy Friend; Truthful Parson Brown (C/L: Robertson, W.); Lovely Lady [4]

Notes Theaters advertised "All Talking! All Singing! All Dancing!" for this, the first all-talking production by MGM. This is also the first film for which the cast lip-synched to an already produced soundtrack. This was made necessary since the "Wedding of the Painted Doll" number was reshot after a disappointing preview. [1] Also in DOUGHBOYS, THE SHOW OF SHOWS, SINGIN' IN THE RAIN and HOLLYWOOD REVUE OF 1929. [2] Also in SINGIN' IN THE RAIN, BROADWAY MELODY OF 1936 and BROADWAY MELODY OF 1938. [3] Also in SINGIN' IN THE RAIN. [4] Not used.

747 ♦ BROADWAY MELODY OF 1936
Metro–Goldwyn–Mayer, 1936

Composer(s) Brown, Nacio Herb
Lyricist(s) Freed, Arthur
Choreographer(s) Gould, Dave; Rasch, Albertina

Producer(s) Considine Jr., John W.
Director(s) Del Ruth, Roy
Screenwriter(s) McGowan, Jack; Silvers, Sid; Conn, Harry W.

Cast Benny, Jack; Powell, Eleanor; Taylor, Robert; Merkel, Una; Silvers, Sid; Knight, June; Stockwell, Harry; Langford, Frances; Ebsen, Buddy; Ebsen, Vilma; Long Jr., Nick

Song(s) Broadway Melody [1] [2] [5] [10]; You Are My Lucky Star [1] [5] [6] [7]; I've Got a Feelin' You're Foolin' [4] [5]; Sing Before Breakfast [2]; All I Do Is Dream of You [5]; On a Sunday Afternoon [3]; Broadway Rhythm [2] [5] [7] [8]; Something's Gotta Happen Soon [9]

Notes [1] From BROADWAY MELODY. [2] Also in BROADWAY MELODY OF 1938. [3] Also in MAN-PROOF. [4] Also in SINGIN' IN THE RAIN

and WITH A SONG IN MY HEART. [5] Also in SINGIN' IN THE RAIN. [6] Also in BABES IN ARMS. [7] Also in BORN TO DANCE. [8] Also in PRESENTING LILY MARS. [9] Not used. [10] Roger Edens can be clearly seen seated at a piano rolled onto the dance floor to accompany Eleanor Powell's solo in this number. He also appears as a rehearsal pianist during Powell's audition as a "French" star.

748 ♦ BROADWAY MELODY OF 1938
Metro–Goldwyn–Mayer, 1937

Composer(s) Brown, Nacio Herb
Lyricist(s) Freed, Arthur
Choreographer(s) Gould, Dave

Producer(s) Cummings, Jack
Director(s) Del Ruth, Roy
Screenwriter(s) McGowan, Jack

Cast Taylor, Robert; Powell, Eleanor [3]; Murphy, George; Ebsen, Buddy; Garland, Judy; Walburn, Raymond; Howard, Willie; Barnes, Binnie; Tucker, Sophie; Cogin, Charles Igor; Benchley, Robert; Grapewin, Charley; Wildhack, Robert; Gorin, Igor

Song(s) Broadway Melody [1] [2] [6]; Yours and Mine [8]; Follow in My Footsteps; Everybody Sing; Sing Before Breakfast [2]; I'm Feelin' Like a Million; Your Broadway and My Broadway; Broadway Rhythm [2] [5] [6] [7]; Got a Pair of New Shoes [4]; Dear Mr. Gable (C/L: Edens, Roger); Sun Showers [9]; Broadway [9]

Notes There are also vocals from CARMEN by Bizet ("Toreador Song"); "Some of These Days" by Shelton Brooks; "Largo Al Factotum" from Rossini's THE BARBER OF SEVILLE; "You Made Me Love You" by James V. Monaco and Joseph McCarthy and several popular songs of around 15 seconds each. [1] Also in BROADWAY MELODY. [2] Also in BROADWAY MELODY OF 1936. [3] Dubbed by Marjorie Lane. [4] Deleted from final print. Heard briefly in "Finale." In THOROUGHBREDS DON'T CRY with additional lyrics by Roger Edens. [5] Also in PRESENTING LILY MARS. [6] Also in SINGIN' IN THE RAIN. [7] Also in BABES IN ARMS. [8] Also in TEST PILOT. [9] Sheet music only.

749 ♦ BROADWAY MELODY OF 1940
Metro–Goldwyn–Mayer, 1940

Composer(s) Porter, Cole
Lyricist(s) Porter, Cole
Choreographer(s) Connolly, Bobby

Producer(s) Cummings, Jack
Director(s) Taurog, Norman
Screenwriter(s) Gordon, Leon; Oppenheimer, George

Cast Astaire, Fred; Powell, Eleanor; Murphy, George; Morgan, Frank; Hunter, Ian; Rice, Florence; Carver, Lynne

Song(s) Please Don't Monkey with Broadway; All Ashore (C/L: Edens, Roger); Between You and Me; I've Got My Eyes on You [2] [4]; I Concentrate on You; Begin the Beguine [1]; I Happen to Be in Love [3]; I'm So in Love with You [3] [4]

Notes There is also a vocal of "Il Bacio" by Arditi. [1] From the Broadway show JUBILEE. This song was included because of the popularity of Artie Shaw's Bluebird recording. [2] Also in ANDY HARDY'S PRIVATE SECRETARY. [3] Not used. [4] Same music.

750 ✦ BROADWAY MUSKETEERS
Warner Brothers–First National, 1938

Musical Score Roemheld, Heinz
Composer(s) Jerome, M.K.
Lyricist(s) Scholl, Jack

Producer(s) Foy, Bryan
Director(s) Farrow, John
Screenwriter(s) Ryan, Don; Gamet, Kenneth
Source(s) "Three Girls on Broadway" (story) Ryan, Don; Gamet, Kenneth

Cast Lindsay, Margaret; Sheridan, Ann; Wilson, Marie

Song(s) Has It Ever Occurred to You; Who Said That This Isn't Love; As Sure As You're in Love [1]

Notes [1] Used as a background instrumental only. Also used instrumentally in THE PERFECT SPECIMEN.

751 ✦ BROADWAY RHYTHM
Metro–Goldwyn–Mayer, 1944

Musical Score Green, Johnny
Composer(s) de Paul, Gene
Lyricist(s) Raye, Don
Choreographer(s) Walters, Charles; Donohue, Jack; Alton, Robert; Loper, Don

Producer(s) Cummings, Jack
Director(s) Del Ruth, Roy
Screenwriter(s) Kingsley, Dorothy; Clork, Harry
Source(s) *Very Warm for May* (musical) Kern, Jerome; Hammerstein II, Oscar

Cast Murphy, George; Simms, Ginny; Winninger, Charles; De Haven, Gloria; Walker, Nancy; Blue, Ben; Horne, Lena; Anderson, Eddie "Rochester"; Tommy Dorsey and His Orchestra; Scott, Hazel; Bowers, Kenny; The Ross Sisters; Murphy, Dean

Song(s) Good Girl [2] (C: Kern, Jerome; L: Hammerstein II, Oscar); Contrary Mary [2] (C: Kern, Jerome; L: Hammerstein II, Oscar); Irresistible You; What Do You Think I Am [3] (C/L: Blane, Ralph; Martin, Hugh); Amor [1] (C: Ruiz, Gabriel; L: Skylar, Sunny; Mendez, Ricardo Lopez); Brazilian Boogie (C/L: Blane, Ralph; Martin, Hugh); Solid Potato Salad [5] (C: de Paul, Gene; Prince, Hughie; L: Raye, Don); I Love Corny Music; Milkman Keep Those Bottles Quiet;

Who's Who; That Lucky Fellow (C: Kern, Jerome; L: Hammerstein II, Oscar); In Other Words Seventeen (C: Kern, Jerome; L: Hammerstein II, Oscar); All in Fun (C: Kern, Jerome; L: Hammerstein II, Oscar); All the Things You Are (C: Kern, Jerome; L: Hammerstein II, Oscar); My Moonlight Madonna [4] (C: Fibich, Zdenko; Scotti, William; L: Webster, Paul Francis)

Notes This is also a vocal of "Pretty Baby" by Tony Jackson, Egbert Van Alstyne and Gus Kahn and "Somebody Loves Me" by George Gershwin, B.G. DeSylva and Ballard Macdonald; and brief (15 second) snippets of other popular songs. The Kern/Hammerstein songs are from VERY WARM FOR MAY and are all given brief renditions except "All the Things You Are." [1] English lyrics by Skylar. [2] Written for the proposed film version of VERY WARM FOR MAY when it was to be produced by Arthur Freed. [3] Used in this film, prerecorded for BEST FOOT FORWARD. [4] Sheet music only. [5] Prince not credited on cue sheets.

752 ✦ BROADWAY SCANDALS
Columbia, 1929

Choreographer(s) LeMaire, Rufus

Producer(s) Cohn, Harry
Director(s) Archainbaud, George
Screenwriter(s) Lehman, Gladys; Houston, Norman

Cast Egan, Jack; O'Neil, Sally; Myers, Carmel; Adair, Alice; La Marr, Laura; Raft, George; Marseilles, Maurine; The Cheer Leader Quartette

Song(s) Can You Read In My Eyes (C/L: Coslow, Sam); What Is Life Without Love [1] (C/L: Franklin, Dave; Thompson, Fred; Stone, Jack); Does An Elephant Love Peanuts [2] (C/L: Hanley, James F.); Rhythm of the Tambourine (C/L: Franklin, Dave); Love's the Cause of All My Blues (C/L: Trent, Jo; Daniels, Charles); Spell of the Blues (C/L: Dreyer, Dave; Ruby, Herman; Johnston, Arthur); Kickin' the Blues Away [2] (C/L: Hanley, James F.; Franklin, Dave); I'd Love To Love You (C/L: Dreyer, Dave; Clare, Sidney)

Notes [1] Originally written by Fred Thompson, Jack Stone and Jack Stern. It was rewritten for the picture. [2] These were the only two songs specifically written for the picture.

753 ✦ BROADWAY SERENADE
Metro–Goldwyn–Mayer, 1939

Musical Score Stothart, Herbert; Ward, Edward
Choreographer(s) Felix, Seymour; Berkeley, Busby

Producer(s) Leonard, Robert Z.
Director(s) Leonard, Robert Z.
Screenwriter(s) Lederer, Charles

Cast MacDonald, Jeanette; Ayres, Lew; Hunter, Ian; Morgan, Frank; Vernon, Wally; Johnson, Rita; Gargan, William; Shean, Al; Pangborn, Franklin; Stevens, Kenneth

Song(s) For Every Lonely Heart [1] (C: Stothart, Herbert; L: Kahn, Gus); High Flyin' (C: Ward, Edward; L: Wright, Bob; Forrest, Chet); One Look at You (C: Ward, Edward; L: Wright, Bob; Forrest, Chet); No Time to Argue (C: Romberg, Sigmund; L: Kahn, Gus); Time Changes Everything but Love (C: Donaldson, Walter; L: Kahn, Gus); Broadway Serenade (C: Stothart, Herbert; L: Kahn, Gus)

Notes Titled SERENADE internationally. There are also vocals of "Yip I Addy I Ay!" by John H. Flynn and Will D. Cobb; "Un Bel Di Vedremo" from Puccini's MADAME BUTTERFLY; "What You Going to Do When the Rent Comes Round" by Von Tilzer and Sterling; "Hearts Win You Lose" by Andrew Sterling; and "Love's Old Sweet Song" by James Lyman Molloy and G. Clifton Bingham. [1] Based on music by Tchaikovsky.

754 ✦ BROADWAY THRU A KEYHOLE
United Artists, 1933

Composer(s) Revel, Harry
Lyricist(s) Gordon, Mack

Producer(s) Goetz, William; Griffith, Raymond
Director(s) Sherman, Lowell
Screenwriter(s) Towne, Gene

Cast Guinan, Texas; Cummings, Constance; Columbo, Russ; Kelly, Paul; Ratoff, Gregory; Williams, Frances; Foy Jr., Eddie; Cavanaugh, Hobart; Gilbert, Billy; Seeley, Blossom

Song(s) Doin' the Uptown Lowdown; I Love You Pizzicato; You're My Past, Present and Future; When You Were the Girl on the Scooter and I Was the Boy on the Bike

Notes No cue sheet available.

755 ✦ BROADWAY TO HOLLYWOOD
Metro–Goldwyn–Mayer, 1933

Choreographer(s) Rasch, Albertina; Lee, Sammy

Producer(s) Rapf, Harry
Director(s) Mack, Willard
Screenwriter(s) Mack, Willard; Woolf, Edgar Allan

Cast Brady, Alice; Morgan, Frank; Cooper, Jackie; Hardie, Russell; Evans, Madge; Rooney, Mickey; Quillan, Eddie; Durante, Jimmy; Templeton, Fay; Robson, May; Albertina Rasch Ballet; Eddy, Nelson

Song(s) We Are the Two Hackets (C/L: Goodhart, Al); The March of Time (C: Alter, Louis; L: Unknown); When Old New York Was Young (C: Edwards, Gus; L: Johnson, Howard)

Notes Also released as MARCH OF TIME, the title by which it was originally filmed. It was to be a revue but a plot was added and the film retitled. Released as RINGING UP THE CURTAIN internationally. This was Nelson Eddy's film debut and Mickey Rooney's first

MGM picture. There are also vocals of "Ma Blushin' Rosie" by Edgar Smith and John Stromberg; "Come Down Ma Evenin' Star" by Robert B. Smith and John Stromberg; "Hiawatha" by James O'Dea and Neil Moret; "Bedelia" by William Jerome and Jean Schwartz; "(There'll Be a) Hot Time in the Old Town (Tonight)" by Joseph Hayden and Theodore M. Metz and "In the Garden of My Heart" by Caro Roma and Ernest R. Ball.

756 ✦ BROKEN STAR
United Artists, 1955

Musical Score Dunlap, Paul

Producer(s) Koch, Howard W.
Director(s) Selander, Lesley
Screenwriter(s) Higgins, John C.

Cast Duff, Howard; Turich, Felipe; Baron, Lita; Williams, Bill; Dominquez, Joe; Richards, Addison

Song(s) I Hate You (C: Dunlap, Paul; L: Higgins, John C.)

757 ✦ THE BROKEN WING
Paramount, 1932

Director(s) Corrigan, Lloyd
Screenwriter(s) McNutt, William Slavens; Jones, Grover
Source(s) (play) Dickey, Paul; Goddard, Charles W.

Cast Velez, Lupe; Carrillo, Leo; Douglas, Melvyn; Barbier, George

Song(s) Maybe in a Dream [1] (C/L: Rainger, Ralph); Te Traigo Flores (C: Rainger, Ralph; Pasternacki, Stephen; Coslow, Sam; L: Grever, Maria)

Notes [1] This is based on a Spanish song "O Es Una Ilusion" with lyrics by Maria Grever.

758 ✦ BRONCO BILLY
Warner Brothers, 1980

Musical Score Dorff, Stephen H.; Garrett, Snuff

Producer(s) Hackin, Dennis; Dobrofsky, Neal
Director(s) Eastwood, Clint
Screenwriter(s) Hackin, Dennis

Cast Eastwood, Clint; Locke, Sondra; Lewis, Geoffrey; Crothers, Benjamin "Scatman"; McKinney, Bill; Bottoms, Sam

Song(s) Cowboys and Clowns (C/L: Dorff, Stephen H.; Garrett, Snuff; Harju, Gary; Herbstritt, Larry); Bayou Lullaby (C: Crofford, Cliff; Garrett, Snuff); Barroom Buddies (C/L: Brown, Milton; Crofford, Cliff; Dorff, Stephen H.; Garrett, Snuff); Misery and Gin (C/L: Durrill, John; Garrett, Snuff); Bronco Billy (C/L: Brown, Milton; Dorff, Stephen H.; Garrett, Snuff); Misery Loves Company [1] (C/L: Reed, Jerry)

Notes [1] Sheet music only.

759 ✦ BROOKLYN GOES TO NEW ORLEANS
Universal, 1958

Song(s)   Bourbon Street (C/L: Pichon, Walter "Fats")

Notes   Short subject.

760 ✦ THE BROTHER FROM ANOTHER PLANET
Cinecom International, 1984

Musical Score   Daring, Mason
Composer(s)   Daring, Mason
Lyricist(s)   Daring, Mason

Producer(s)   Rajski, Peggy; Renzi, Maggie
Director(s)   Sayles, John
Screenwriter(s)   Sayles, John

Cast   Morton, Joe; Carter, Rosanna; Ramirez, Ray; Rene, Yves; Jackson, Leonard; Woods, Ren; Sayles, John; Strathairn, David; Le Noire, Rosetta; Stevens, Fisher; Bridgewater, Dee Dee; Mostel, Josh

Song(s)   Burning My Heart Out; Boss of the Block; Getaway; You Can't Get to Heaven from Here; Homeboy (L: Sayles, John); Dinero [1] (C: London, Frank; Daring, Mason; L: Salgado, Efrain); El Calle (C/L: London, Frank); Promised Land (L: Sayles, John)

Notes   No cue sheet available. [1] Also in KEY EXCHANGE.

761 ✦ THE BROTHERHOOD
Paramount, 1968

Musical Score   Schifrin, Lalo

Producer(s)   Douglas, Kirk
Director(s)   Ritt, Martin
Screenwriter(s)   Carlino, Lewis John

Cast   Douglas, Kirk; Cord, Alex; Papas, Irene; Adler, Luther

Song(s)   The Brotherhood Dance (The Dance We Didn't Dance) [1] [2] (C: Traditional; L: Gimbel, Norman); The Taste of Love [2] (C: Schifrin, Lalo; L: Gimbel, Norman)

Notes   [1] Music based on Sicilian folk song titled "Vitti 'Na Crozza." [2] Lyric written for exploitation only.

762 ✦ BROTHERLY LOVE
Metro–Goldwyn–Mayer, 1970

Musical Score   Addison, John
Choreographer(s)   Watson, Bobby

Producer(s)   Ginna, Robert Emmett
Director(s)   Thompson, J. Lee
Screenwriter(s)   Kennaway, James

Cast   O'Toole, Peter; Craig, Michael; Andrews, Harry; Cusack, Cyril; Blessed, Brian; Malicz, Mark; Milne, Lennox

Song(s)   My Romance [1] (C: Young, Victor; L: Washington, Ned)

Notes   Released as COUNTRY DANCE in the United Kingdom. [1] Written in 1932.

763 ✦ BROTHER ORCHID
Warner Brothers, 1940

Musical Score   Roemheld, Heinz

Producer(s)   Warner, Jack L.; Wallis, Hal B.
Director(s)   Bacon, Lloyd
Screenwriter(s)   Baldwin, Earl

Cast   Robinson, Edward G.; Sothern, Ann; Bellamy, Ralph; Bogart, Humphrey; Crisp, Donald; Jenkins, Allen; Brown, Charles; Kellaway, Cecil

Song(s)   My Little Buckaroo [1] (C: Jerome, M.K.; L: Scholl, Jack)

Notes   [1] Also in THE CHEROKEE STRIP, SONGS OF THE RANGE, WEST OF THE ROCKIES and DON'T FENCE ME IN (Republic).

764 ✦ BROTHERS (1929)
Imperial Photoplays, 1929

Director(s)   Pembroke, Scott
Screenwriter(s)   Hoerl, Arthur

Cast   Keefe, Cornelius; Rankin, Arthur; Bedford, Barbara; Carle, Richard; Chesebro, George; O'Flynn, Paddy; Cain, James; Anderson, Edward

Song(s)   I'm Dreaming (C/L: Dougherty, Dan)

Notes   No cue sheet available.

765 ✦ BROTHERS (1930)
Columbia, 1930

Director(s)   Lang, Walter
Screenwriter(s)   Neville, John Thomas; Condon, Charles
Source(s)   (play) Ashton Jr., Herbert

Cast   Lytell, Bert; Sebastian, Dorothy; Morris, William; Tucker, Richard; Black, Maurice; McCormack, Frank; McDowell, Claire

Song(s)   I'm Dreaming [1] (C/L: Dougherty, Dan)

Notes   [1] Listed instrumentally only on cue sheets.

766 ✦ BROTHERS (1977)
Warner Brothers, 1977

Musical Score   Taj Mahal
Composer(s)   Taj Mahal
Lyricist(s)   Taj Mahal

Producer(s) Lewis, Edward; Lewis, Mildred
Director(s) Barron, Arthur
Screenwriter(s) Lewis, Edward; Lewis, Mildred

Cast Casey, Bernie; McGee, Vonetta; O'Neal, Ron; Roker, Renny; Gilliam, Stu; Lehne, John; Pace, Owen

Song(s) Night Rider; Brothers Doin' Time; Love Theme No. 1; Free the Brothers; Love Theme in the Key of D

Notes All background vocal use.

767 ✦ BROTHER SUN, SISTER MOON
Paramount, 1973

Composer(s) Donovan
Lyricist(s) Donovan

Producer(s) Perugia, Luciano
Director(s) Zeffirelli, Franco
Screenwriter(s) D'Amico, Suso Cecchi; Ross, Kenneth; Wertmuller, Lina; Zeffirelli, Franco

Cast Faulkner, Graham; Bowker, Judi; Guinness, Alec

Song(s) Crusaders Song; Lullaby; Lovely Day; God Bless the Master; Brother Sun, Sister Moon; Little Church; Rain Song; Lord Make Me an Instrument; There's a Shape in the Sky

768 ✦ BRUBAKER
Twentieth Century–Fox, 1980

Musical Score Schifrin, Lalo
Composer(s) Schifrin, Lalo

Producer(s) Silverman, Ron
Director(s) Rosenberg, Stuart
Screenwriter(s) Richter, W.D.

Cast Redford, Robert; Kotto, Yaphet; Alexander, Jane; Hamilton, Murray; Keith, David; Freeman, Morgan; Clark, Matt; McIntyre, Tim; Ward, Richard

Song(s) All for the Love of Sunshine (L: Curb, Mike; Hatcher, Harley); Rolling Down (L: Nelson, Steve; Chay, Elfrieda); So Far from Love (L: Nelson, Steve)

769 ✦ THE BRUTE MAN
PRC, 1946

Producer(s) Pivar, Ben
Director(s) Yarbrough, Jean
Screenwriter(s) Bricker, George; Webster, M. Coates

Cast Hatton, Rondo; Adams, Jane; Neal, Tom; Wiley, Jan

Song(s) Mr. Bach and Mr. Boogie # 2 (C: Pine, Lester; L: Brooks, Jack); Once Upon a Dream (C: Salter, Hans J.; L: Brooks, Jack)

Notes This is a Universal film that was turned over to PRC for distribution when Universal forswore B pictures. Cue sheet does not differentiate between vocals and instrumentals.

770 ✦ B.S. I LOVE YOU
Twentieth Century–Fox, 1971

Musical Score Shekter, Mark
Composer(s) Shekter, Mark
Lyricist(s) Shekter, Mark

Producer(s) Broidy, Arthur M.
Director(s) Stern, Steven Hillard
Screenwriter(s) Stern, Steven Hillard

Cast Kastner, Peter; Cameron, JoAnna; Sorel, Louise; Burghoff, Gary; Shull, Richard B.; Barnes, Joanna; Gerstad, John

Song(s) Ordinary Man; Life Going Down; Gold Star Promotion (C/L: Dale, Jimmy; Black, Terry; Kennedy, Steve); Is There a Place; You Better Find It; Diana By the Sea; Going to Take a Ride (C/L: Shekter, Mark; Dale, Jimmy; Black, Terry; Kennedy, Steve); Valhalla, East Side (C/L: Dale, Jimmy); 'Cause I Don't Have You; We're Almost There

771 ✦ BUBBLES
Publix, 1928

Song(s) Bubbles (Beautiful Bubbles of Love) (C: Lucas, Gene; L: Black, Ben)

Notes No cue sheet available. Sheet music only.

772 ✦ THE BUCCANEER
Paramount, 1958

Musical Score Bernstein, Elmer
Composer(s) Bernstein, Elmer

Producer(s) Wilcoxon, Henry
Director(s) Quinn, Anthony
Screenwriter(s) Lasky Jr., Jesse; Mosk, Berenice

Cast Brynner, Yul; Heston, Charlton; Boyer, Charles; Bloom, Claire; Stevens, Inger; Hull, Henry; Greene, Lorne; Marshall, E.G.; Dumbrille, Douglass; Adrian, Iris

Song(s) Mawbee Chant (L: Lasky Jr., Jesse); Street Cry (L: Lasky Jr., Jesse); Lover's Gold (Love Song from The Buccaneer) [1] [2] (L: David, Mack); Bowlin' Chant [1] (L: Bernstein, Elmer); My Lady Fair [1] (L: Bernstein, Elmer)

Notes Produced under the personal supervision of Cecil B. DeMille. A remake of a screenplay by Harold Lamb, Edwin Justus Mayer and C. Gardner Sullivan based on Jeanie Macpherson's adaptation of "Lafitte the Pirate" by Lyle Saxon. [1] Not used. [2] From a theme in the film.

773 ✦ BUCCANEER'S GIRL
Universal, 1950

Musical Score Scharf, Walter
Composer(s) Scharf, Walter
Lyricist(s) Brooks, Jack

Producer(s) Arthur, Robert
Director(s) de Cordova, Frederick
Screenwriter(s) Shumate, Harold; Hoffman, Joseph

Cast De Carlo, Yvonne; Friend, Philip; Douglas, Robert; Lanchester, Elsa; Lloyd, Norman; King, Andrea; Flippen, Jay C.; Daniell, Henry; Dumbrille, Douglasss; Felton, Verna

Song(s) Here's to the Ladies; Pralines (L: Brodney, Oscar); Monsieur [1]; Because You're in Love; A Sailor Sails the Seven Seas

Notes [1] Also in THE ART OF LOVE but with additional credit to Paul Verdie. Maybe he wrote a French lyric.

774 ✦ BUCK BENNY RIDES AGAIN
Paramount, 1940

Musical Score Young, Victor
Composer(s) McHugh, Jimmy
Lyricist(s) Loesser, Frank
Choreographer(s) Prinz, LeRoy

Producer(s) Sandrich, Mark
Director(s) Sandrich, Mark
Screenwriter(s) Beloin, Edmund; Morrow, William

Cast Day, Dennis; Benny, Jack; Harris, Phil; Drew, Ellen [2] [3]; Dale, Virginia [2] [3]; Cornell, Lillian; Devine, Andy; Bond, Ward; Lane, Charles; Harris, Theresa

Song(s) My! My!; Say It (Over and Over Again) [2]; My Kind of Country; Drums in the Night [3]; Music from Paradise [1] [4]; That Friendly Feeling [1]; Roses 'Round My Room [1]

Notes [1] Unused. [2] This is sung in the radio audition scene by Lillian Cornell, Tilton and Virginia Dale. [3] Sung by Lillian Cornell, Noyes and Van Brunt. [4] The lyrics were originally written to a tune by Manning Sherwin. McHugh's tune was later used in the motion picture RIDING HIGH (1943).

775 ✦ BUCK PRIVATES
Universal, 1941

Composer(s) Prince, Hughie
Lyricist(s) Raye, Don

Producer(s) Gottlieb, Alex
Director(s) Lubin, Arthur
Screenwriter(s) Horman, Arthur T.

Cast Abbott, Bud; Costello, Lou; Bowman, Lee; Curtis, Alan; The Andrews Sisters; Pendleton, Nat; Frazee, Jane; Hinds, Samuel S.; Howard, Shemp

Song(s) You're a Lucky Fellow, Mr. Smith [3] (C: Burke, Sonny; Prince, Hughie); I Wish You Were Here (C: Prince, Hughie; Schoen, Vic); When Private Brown Becomes a Captain; Boogie Woogie Bugle Boy [1]; Bounce Me Brother with a Solid Four [2]

Notes There is also a vocal of "I'll Be with You in Apple Blossom Time" by Neville Fleeson and Albert Von Tilzer. [1] Also in SWINGTIME JOHNNY. [2] Also in WILLIE AND JOE IN BACK AT THE FRONT and ONE EXCITING WEEK (Republic). [3] Also in ABBOTT & COSTELLO & DICK POWELL IN THE NAVY, HI 'YA CHUM and YOU'RE A LUCKY FELLOW, MR. SMITH.

776 ✦ BUCK PRIVATES COME HOME
Universal, 1947

Musical Score Schumann, Walter

Producer(s) Arthur, Robert
Director(s) Barton, Charles
Screenwriter(s) Grant, John; Rinaldo, Frederic I.; Lees, Robert

Cast Abbott, Bud; Costello, Lou; Simmons, Beverly; Pendleton, Nat; Brown, Tom; Fulton, Joan; Beddoe, Don; Porter, Don; MacBride, Donald

Song(s) We're Goin' Home (C: Schumann, Walter; L: Brooks, Jack)

777 ✦ BUCK ROGERS—IN THE 25TH CENTURY
Universal, 1979

Musical Score Phillips, Stu

Producer(s) Caffey, Richard
Director(s) Haller, Daniel
Screenwriter(s) Larson, Glen A.; Stevens, Leslie
Source(s) *Buck Rogers* (comic strip) Nowlan, Philip Francis

Cast Gerard, Gil; Hensley, Pamela; Gray, Erin; Silva, Henry

Song(s) Theme from Buck Rogers (Suspension) (C/L: Larson, Glen A.)

778 ✦ BUDDY BUDDY
Metro–Goldwyn–Mayer, 1981

Musical Score Schifrin, Lalo

Producer(s) Weston, Jay
Director(s) Wilder, Billy
Screenwriter(s) Wilder, Billy; Diamond, I.A.L.
Source(s) (play/story) Veber, Francis

Cast Lemmon, Jack; Matthau, Walter; Prentiss, Paula; Kinski, Klaus; Elcar, Dana; Chapin, Miles; Begley Jr., Ed; Ensign, Michael

Song(s) CuCuRuCuCu Paloma (C/L: Mendez, Tomas)

Notes There is also a vocal of "Cecelia" by Dave Dreyer and Herman Ruby.

779 ✦ BUDDY ROGERS MUSICAL
Paramount, 1930 unproduced

Composer(s) Akst, Harry
Lyricist(s) Clarke, Grant

Song(s) Here You Are ; Poor Blind Men; She's the Reason; Crystal Waters; The Sound of the Gourd [2]; Play It Slow and Easy—I'll Dance All Night [1]; When My Prince Charming Comes Along; Too Late; Red Roses and Pale White Moonlight; It's Paradise

Notes [1] A song of the same title is also listed under MONTE CARLO (1930) but with different songwriter credits. [2] Also in the unproduced THE LOVE MOON.

780 ✦ THE BUDDY SYSTEM
Twentieth Century–Fox, 1984

Musical Score Williams, Patrick

Producer(s) Chammas, Alain
Director(s) Jordan, Glenn
Screenwriter(s) Donoghue, Mary Agnes

Cast Dreyfuss, Richard; Sarandon, Susan; Allen, Nancy; Stapleton, Jean; Wheaton, Wil

Song(s) Some History (C/L: Williams, Patrick); Here's That Sunny Day (C: Williams, Patrick; L: Jennings, Will)

781 ✦ BUGSY MALONE
Paramount, 1976

Musical Score Williams, Paul
Composer(s) Williams, Paul
Lyricist(s) Williams, Paul
Choreographer(s) Gregory, Gillian

Producer(s) Marshal, Alan
Director(s) Parker, Alan
Screenwriter(s) Parker, Alan

Cast Baio, Scott; Dugger, Florrie; Foster, Jodie; Casssisi, John; Lev, Martin; Murphy, Paul; Jenkins, Albin

Song(s) Bugsy Malone; Fat Sam's Grand Slam; Tomorrow; Bad Guys; I'm Feeling Fine; My Name Is Tallulah; So You Wanna Be a Boxer; Ordinary Fool; Down and Out; You Give a Little Love; Show Business (C: Arthur, Ernest; L: Gregory, Gillian)

782 ✦ BULLDOG DRUMMOND
United Artists, 1929

Producer(s) Goldwyn, Samuel
Director(s) Jones, F. Richard
Screenwriter(s) Smith, Wallace; Howard, Sidney
Source(s) *Bulldog Drummond* (play) du Maurier, Gerald

Cast Colman, Ronald; Bennett, Joan; Tashman, Lilyan; Love, Montagu; Grant, Lawrence; Benge, Wilson; Allister, Claud; Milar, Adolph

Song(s) (I Says to Myself Says I) There's the One for Me (C: Akst, Harry; L: Yellen, Jack)

Notes No cue sheet available.

783 ✦ BULLET CODE
RKO, 1940

Musical Score Dreyer, Dave; Sawtell, Paul

Producer(s) Gilroy, Bert
Director(s) Howard, David
Screenwriter(s) Schroeder, Doris

Cast O'Brien, George; Vale, Virginia; Whitaker, Slim; Hickman, Howard

Song(s) Wagon Train [1] (C/L: Whitley, Ray)

Notes [1] In WAGON TRAIN but with credit to Fred Rose also.

784 ✦ BULLFIGHTER AND THE LADY
Republic, 1951

Musical Score Young, Victor

Producer(s) Boetticher, Budd
Director(s) Boetticher, Budd
Screenwriter(s) Boetticher, Budd; Nazarro, Ray

Cast Stack, Robert; Page, Joy; Roland, Gilbert; Grey, Virginia; Hubbard, John; Jurado, Katy

Song(s) Esta Noche (Tonight) [1] (C: Young, Victor; L: Elliott, Jack); How Strange [2] (C: Young, Victor; L: Lee, Peggy)

Notes There is also a vocal of "Luto En El Alma" by Claudio Estrada. [1] Sung in Spanish only. Spanish lyric by Aaron Gonzalez. [2] Lyric written for exploitation only.

785 ✦ THE BULLFIGHTERS
Twentieth Century–Fox, 1945

Musical Score Buttolph, David

Producer(s) Girard, William
Director(s) St. Clair, Malcolm
Screenwriter(s) Darling, W. Scott

Cast Costello, Diosa; Laurel, Stan; Hardy, Oliver; Woode, Margo; Lane, Richard; Andrews, Carol; Novello, Jay

Song(s) Bim Bam Boom [1] (C/L: Morales, Noro)

Notes [1] Not written for this picture.

786 ✦ BULLIES
Universal, 1986

Musical Score Zaza, Paul
Composer(s) Zaza, Paul; Fargo, Stew
Lyricist(s) Fargo, Stew; Zaza, Paul

Producer(s) Simpson, Peter
Director(s) Lynch, Paul
Screenwriter(s) Sheppard, John; McCann, Bryan

Cast Crombie, Jonathan; Green, Janet Laine; Hunter, Stephen B.; Berti, Dehl

Song(s) Vern's Garage (C/L: Zaza, Paul); Just a Guitar Man [1] (C: Zaza, Paul; L: Cuff, Bill); An Easy Love; Right Now (C/L: Zaza, Paul); Slow Down (C/L: Baird, Don; Whitlock, Paula); Country Gigolo (C/L: Fargo, Stew); Got Some Livin' to Do; Out of the Fire (C/L: Zaza, Paul; Simpson, Peter)

Notes [1] Also used in MY BLOODY VALENTINE (Paramount) but without Bill Cuff credit.

787 ✦ BULLWHIP
Allied Artists, 1958

Musical Score Stevens, Leith

Producer(s) Ainsworth, Helen
Director(s) Jones, Harmon
Screenwriter(s) Buffington, Adele

Cast Madison, Guy; Fleming, Rhonda; Griffith, James; Beddoe, Don; Adams, Peter; Sheridan, Don

Song(s) Bullwhip (C/L: Hopper, Hal; Griffith, James)

788 ✦ BUNDLE OF JOY
RKO, 1956

Composer(s) Myrow, Josef
Lyricist(s) Gordon, Mack
Choreographer(s) Castle, Nick

Producer(s) Grainger, Edmund
Director(s) Taurog, Norman
Screenwriter(s) Krasna, Norman; Carson, Robert; Sheekman, Arthur

Cast Fisher, Eddie; Reynolds, Debbie; Menjou, Adolphe; Noonan, Tommy; Talbot, Nita; Merkel, Una; Cooper, Melville; Treen, Mary

Song(s) Worry About Tomorrow, Tomorrow; Polly's Entrance; All About Love; Someday Soon; Lullaby in Blue; I Never Felt This Way Before; Bundle of Joy; Tempo Fugit [1]; What's So Good About Good Morning [1]

Notes [1] Not used.

789 ✦ BUNNY AND CLAUDE
Warner Brothers, 1968

Musical Score Lava, William

Director(s) McKimson, Robert

Cast Bunny and Claude

Song(s) The Ballad of Bunny and Claude (C: Lava, William; L: Hendricks, William L.)

Notes Looney Tune.

790 ✦ BUONA SERA MRS. CAMPBELL
United Artists, 1968

Musical Score Ortolani, Riz

Producer(s) Frank, Melvin
Director(s) Frank, Melvin
Screenwriter(s) Keller, Sheldon; Norden, Denis; Frank, Melvin

Cast Lollobrigida, Gina; Winters, Shelley; Silvers, Phil; Lawford, Peter; Savalas, Telly; Grant, Lee; Margolin, Janet

Song(s) Buona Sera Mrs. Campbell (C: Ortolani, Riz; L: Frank, Melvin)

791 ✦ THE BURBS
Universal, 1989

Musical Score Goldsmith, Jerry

Producer(s) Brezner, Larry; Finnell, Michael
Director(s) Dante, Joe
Screenwriter(s) Olsen, Dana

Cast Dern, Bruce; Fisher, Carrie; Ducommun, Rick; Feldman, Corey; Hanks, Tom; Brother Theodore; Schaal, Wendy; Gibson, Henry; Gordon, Gale

Song(s) Machine (C/L: Mitchell, Alex; Sunshine, Gary; Mahler, Ricky Beck); Bloodstone (C/L: Finn, Mickey; Radice, Mark; Rod, Fernie; Rowe, Billy); Locked in a Cage (C/L: Finn, Mickey; Rowe, Billy; Rod, Fernie; Yaffa, Sam); Make Some Noise (C/L: Finn, Mickey; Rowe, Billy; Rod, Fernie; Yaffa, Sam; Tostenson, Rod)

792 ✦ BURGLAR
Warner Brothers, 1987

Musical Score Levay, Sylvester

Producer(s) McCormick, Kevin; Hirsh, Michael
Director(s) Wilson, Hugh
Screenwriter(s) Loeb III, Joseph; Weisman, Matthew; Wilson, Hugh
Source(s) (novels) Block, Lawrence

Cast Goldberg, Whoopi; Goldthwait, Bobcat [1]; Bailey, G.W.; Warren, Lesley Ann; Handy, James; De Salvo, Anne

Song(s) I'm the Burglar (C/L: Edwards, Bernard; Bova, Jeff; Martinez, Eddie; Thompson, Tony; Hart, Robert; Kelly, Tom; Steinberg, Billy); Check In, Check Out (C/L: Jackson, Jackie; Jackson, Randy; Edwards, Bernard; Oland, Pamela Phillips; Bova, Jeff; Martinez, Eddie; Thompson, Tony; Hart, Robert); Dancing in the City (C/L: Kelly, Tom; Steinberg, Billy); New Way of Living (C/L: Edwards, Bernard; Bova, Jeff; Martinez, Eddie; Thompson, Tony; Hart, Robert); Tough Guys (C/L: Edwards, Bernard; Bova, Jeff; Martinez, Eddie; Thompson, Tony; Hart, Robert; Pasquale, Joe); Time Out for the Burglar (C/L: Jackson, Jackie; Jackson,

Randy; Edwards, Bernard; Oland, Pamela Phillips; Bova, Jeff; Martinez, Eddie; Thompson, Tony; Hart, Robert)

Notes   [1] Billed as Bob Goldthwait.

793 ✦ BURIED LOOT
Metro–Goldwyn–Mayer, 1935

Musical Score   Axt, William

Director(s)   Seitz, George B.
Screenwriter(s)   Seitz, George B.

Cast   Taylor, Robert

Song(s)   Lazy River Love Song (C/L: Axt, William)

Notes   Short subject. Number one in the "Crime Does Not Pay" series.

794 ✦ BURKE & WILLS
Hemdale, 1987

Musical Score   Sculthorpe, Peter

Producer(s)   Clifford, Graeme; Sexton, John
Director(s)   Clifford, Graeme
Screenwriter(s)   Thomas, Michael

Cast   Thompson, Jack; Havers, Nigel; Scacchi, Greta; Fargher, Matthew; Forsythe, Drew

Song(s)   O Mistress Mine (C: Sculthorpe, Peter; L: Shakespeare, William)

Notes   No cue sheet available.

795 ✦ BURMA CONVOY
Universal, 1941

Producer(s)   Grant, Marshall
Director(s)   Smith, Noel
Screenwriter(s)   Rubin, Stanley; Chanslor, Roy

Cast   Bickford, Charles; Ankers, Evelyn; Albertson, Frank; Kellaway, Cecil; Fung, Willie; Bey, Turhan; Bradley, Truman

Song(s)   You've Got That Look (C: Hollander, Frederick; L: Loesser, Frank); I'm in Glory (C: McHugh, Jimmy; L: Adamson, Harold)

796 ✦ BURY ME NOT ON THE LONE PRAIRIE
Universal, 1941

Director(s)   Taylor, Ray
Screenwriter(s)   Lowe, Sherman; McLeod, Victor

Cast   Brown, Johnny Mack; Knight, Fuzzy; O'Day, Nell

Song(s)   I'm a Happy Cowboy (C/L: Wakely, Jimmy); Bears Give Me the Bird [1] (C: Rosen, Milton; L: Carter, Everett)

Notes   [1] Sheet music only.

797 ✦ THE BUSHBABY
Metro–Goldwyn–Mayer, 1969

Musical Score   Reed, Les

Producer(s)   Maxwell, Robert; Trent, John
Director(s)   Trent, John
Screenwriter(s)   Stevenson, William H.; Maxwell, Robert
Source(s)   *The Bushbaby* (novel) Stevenson, William H.

Cast   Brooks, Margaret; Gossett, Lou; Houston, Donald; Naismith, Laurence; Maitland, Marne; Gwillim, Jack

Song(s)   Kwaheri (C: Reed, Les; L: Maxwell, Robert; Magwaza, Roger [1])

Notes   [1] Swahili lyric.

798 ✦ BUSINESS AND PLEASURE
Fox, 1932

Director(s)   Butler, David
Screenwriter(s)   Conselman, William; Towne, Gene
Source(s)   *The Plutocrat* (novel) Tarkington, Booth

Cast   Rogers, Will; Goudal, Jetta; McCrea, Joel; Peterson, Dorothy

Song(s)   Old Aunt Mariah (C/L: Hanley, James F.)

799 ✦ BUSINESS AS USUAL
Cannon, 1988

Musical Score   Scott, Andrew; Weller, Paul

Producer(s)   Geater, Sara
Director(s)   Barrett, Lezli-An
Screenwriter(s)   Barrett, Lezli-An

Cast   Jackson, Glenda; Thaw, John; Tyson, Cathy; McGann, Mark; Boland, Eamon; Hazeldine, James

Song(s)   Cost of Loving (C/L: Weller, Paul)

Notes   No cue sheet available.

800 ✦ BUS STOP
Twentieth Century–Fox, 1956

Musical Score   Newman, Alfred; Mockridge, Cyril J.

Producer(s)   Adler, Buddy
Director(s)   Logan, Joshua
Screenwriter(s)   Axelrod, George
Source(s)   *Bus Stop* (play) Inge, William

Cast   Monroe, Marilyn; Murray, Don; O'Connell, Arthur; Field, Betty; Heckart, Eileen; Bray, Robert; Lange, Hope; Conried, Hans

Song(s)   A Paper of Pins (The Bus Stop Song) (C/L: Darby, Ken); The Right Kind [1] (C: Newman, Lionel; Henderson, Charles; L: George, Don)

Notes "That Old Black Magic" by Johnny Mercer and Harold Arlen and the traditional songs "Kiss Me Quick and Go" and "Rye Whiskey" are used vocally. [1] BMI list only.

801 ◆ BUSTER
Hemdale, 1988

Musical Score Dudley, Anne
Composer(s) Dozier, Lamont
Lyricist(s) Collins, Phil

Producer(s) Heyman, Norma
Director(s) Green, David
Screenwriter(s) Shindler, Colin

Cast Collins, Phil; Walters, Julie; Lamb, Larry; Lawrence, Stephanie; Beaven, Ellie; Attwell, Michael; Brown, Ralph; Hancock, Sheila; Quayle, Anthony

Song(s) Two Hearts (One Mind); Goin' Loco Down in Acapulco; Big Noise; Groovy Kind of Love (C: Wine, Toni; L: Sager, Carole Bayer); I Got You Babe (C/L: Bono, Sonny); I Just Don't Know What to Do With Myself (C: Bacharach, Burt; L: David, Hal); Keep on Running (C/L: Edwards, Jackie); Loco in Acapulco (L: Collins, Phil); Sweets for My Sweet (C: Shuman, Mort; L: Pomus, Doc)

Notes No cue sheet available. Not all songs written for this film.

802 ◆ BUSTER AND BILLIE
Columbia, 1973

Musical Score De Lory, Al
Composer(s) Axton, Hoyt
Lyricist(s) Axton, Hoyt

Producer(s) Silverman, Ron
Director(s) Petrie, Daniel
Screenwriter(s) Turbeville, Ron

Cast Vincent, Jan-Michael; Goodfellow, Joan; Martin, Pamela Sue; James, Clifton

Song(s) Billie's Theme; Lightnin' Bar Blues; Long Lonesome Road (C/L: Casey, Claude); Anytime (C/L: Lawson, Herbert "Happy"); Hillbilly Gal (C/L: Casey, Claude; Martin, Troy L.)

803 ◆ THE BUSTER KEATON STORY
Paramount, 1957

Producer(s) Sheldon, Sidney; Smith, Robert
Director(s) Sheldon, Sidney
Screenwriter(s) Sheldon, Sidney; Smith, Robert

Cast O'Connor, Donald; Blyth, Ann; Fleming, Rhonda; Lorre, Peter; Coogan, Jackie

Song(s) Buster [1] (C: Young, Victor; L: Stone, Wilson)

Notes [1] Used instrumentally only.

804 ◆ BUSTIN' LOOSE
Universal, 1981

Musical Score Davis, Mark

Producer(s) Pryor, Richard; Glick, Michael S.
Director(s) Scott, Oz
Screenwriter(s) Simon, Roger L.

Cast Pryor, Richard; Tyson, Cicely; Ramirez, Angel; Hughes, Jimmy; De Leon, Edwin

Song(s) Lovin' You (Is Such An Easy Thang to Do) (C/L: Miller, Marcus); Hittin' Me Where It Hurts (C/L: Smith, William; Wakefield, Kathy); Just When I Needed You (C/L: Flack, Roberta; Mercury, Eric); Children's Song (C/L: Flack, Roberta; Miles, Barry; Watkins, Dwight); Love (Always Commands) (C/L: Flack, Roberta; Mercury, Eric)

805 ◆ BUTCH CASSIDY AND THE SUNDANCE KID
Twentieth Century–Fox, 1969

Musical Score Bacharach, Burt
Composer(s) Bacharach, Burt
Lyricist(s) David, Hal

Producer(s) Foreman, John
Director(s) Hill, George Roy
Screenwriter(s) Goldman, William

Cast Newman, Paul; Redford, Robert; Ross, Katharine; Martin, Strother; Jones, Henry; Corey, Jeff; Furth, George; Leachman, Cloris; Cassidy, Ted; Mars, Kenneth

Song(s) Raindrops Keep Fallin' on My Head; Blue Seas [1]; Where There's a Heartache There Must Be a Heart [2]

Notes [1] Lyric written for exploitation only. [2] Not used.

806 ◆ BUTCH MINDS THE BABY
Universal, 1942

Musical Score Skinner, Frank
Composer(s) de Paul, Gene
Lyricist(s) Raye, Don

Director(s) Rogell, Albert S.
Screenwriter(s) Spigelgass, Leonard
Source(s) "Butch Minds the Baby" (story) Runyon, Damon

Cast Crawford, Broderick; Barnitz, Michael; Bruce, Virginia; Foran, Dick; Howard, Shemp; Hall, Porter; Withers, Grant; Knight, Fuzzy; Six Hits and a Miss

Song(s) You Don't Know What Love Is [2]; The Boy with the Wistful Eyes [1]; People Like You [3]

Notes [1] Also in KEEP 'EM FLYING. [2] Also in TWO TICKETS TO LONDON. [3] Not used.

807 ✦ BUTTERFLIES ARE FREE
Columbia, 1972

Musical Score Alcivar, Robert

Producer(s) Frankovich, M.J.
Director(s) Katselas, Milton
Screenwriter(s) Gershe, Leonard
Source(s) *Butterflies Are Free* (play) Gershe, Leonard

Cast Hawn, Goldie; Albert, Edward; Heckart, Eileen; Glaser, Michael; Warren, Mike

Song(s) Carry Me (C: Alcivar, Robert; L: McNeill, Randy); Butterflies Are Free [1] (C/L: Schwartz, Stephen)

Notes [1] Written for the Broadway production.

808 ✦ BUTTERFLY
Analysis, 1982

Musical Score Morricone, Ennio

Producer(s) Cimber, Matt
Director(s) Cimber, Matt
Screenwriter(s) Goff, John; Cimber, Matt

Cast Keach, Stacy; Zadora, Pia; Welles, Orson; Nettleton, Lois; Albert, Edward; Franciscus, James; Whitman, Stuart; Lockhart, June; McMahon, Ed

Song(s) Butterfly (C: Morricone, Ennio; L: Connors, Carol)

Notes No cue sheet available.

809 ✦ BYE BYE BARBARA
Paramount, 1970

Producer(s) Bodard, Mag
Director(s) Deville, Michel
Screenwriter(s) Companez, Nina; Deville, Michel

Cast Swann, Ewa; Avron, Philippe; Cremer, Bruno; Stewart, Alexandra; Duchaussoy, Michel

Song(s) Bye Bye Barbara (C: Companez, Nina; L: Bodard, Mag)

810 ✦ BYE BYE BIRDIE
Columbia, 1963

Composer(s) Strouse, Charles
Lyricist(s) Adams, Lee
Choreographer(s) White, Onna

Producer(s) Kohlmar, Fred
Director(s) Sidney, George
Screenwriter(s) Brecher, Irving
Source(s) *Bye Bye Birdie* (musical) Stewart, Michael; Strouse, Charles; Adams, Lee

Cast Leigh, Janet; Van Dyke, Dick [2]; Ann-Margaret; Stapleton, Maureen; Rydell, Bobby; Pearson, Jesse; Sullivan, Ed; Lynde, Paul [2]; LaRoche, Mary; Evans,

Michael; Paige, Robert; Albertson, Frank; Sully, Frank; Lamb, Gil

Song(s) Bye Bye Birdie; Kids; Honestly Sincere; Put on a Happy Face; Telephone Hour; A Lot of Livin' to Do; Rosie; One Last Kiss; One Boy; Hymn for a Sunday Evening; How Lovely to Be a Woman; The Shriner Ballet [1]

Notes Diana Lee dubbed one of the teenagers, who were all dubbed. She is the daughter of dubber Bill Lee. All songs but [1] were in the original Broadway musical. [2] From original cast.

811 ✦ BYE BYE BRAVERMAN
Warner Brothers, 1968

Musical Score Matz, Peter

Producer(s) Lumet, Sidney
Director(s) Lumet, Sidney
Screenwriter(s) Sargent, Herbert
Source(s) "To An Early Grave" (story) Markfield, Wallace

Cast Segal, George; Warden, Jack; Wiseman, Joseph; Booke, Sorrell; Walter, Jessica; Newman, Phyllis; Lampert, Zohra; Cambridge, Godfrey; King, Alan; Holland, Anthony

Song(s) Braverman's Waltz (C: Matz, Peter; L: Sargent, Herbert); Down in the Valley (Parody) (C: Traditional; L: Traditional; Sargent, Herbert)

812 ✦ BYE BYE BRAZIL
Unifilm, 1981

Musical Score Buarque, Chico; Menescal, Roberto; Dominguinhos

Producer(s) Barreto, Luiz Carlos; Barreto, Lucy
Director(s) Diegues, Carlos
Screenwriter(s) Diegues, Carlos

Cast Faria, Betty; Wilker, Jose; Junior, Fabio; Zambelli, Zaira; Nabor, Principe

Song(s) Bye Bye Brazil (C/L: Buarque, Chico)

Notes No cue sheet available.

813 ✦ BY HOOK OR BY CROOK

See I DOOD IT.

814 ✦ BY LOVE POSSESSED
United Artists, 1961

Musical Score Bernstein, Elmer

Producer(s) Mirisch, Walter
Director(s) Sturges, John
Screenwriter(s) Dennis, John

Cast Bel Geddes, Barbara; Mitchell, Thomas; Kohner, Susan; O'Connor, Carroll; Turner, Lana; Zimbalist Jr., Efrem; Robards Jr., Jason; Hamilton, George

Song(s) By Love Possessed (C: Bernstein, Elmer; L: Cahn, Sammy)

Notes No cue sheet available.

815 ✦ BY THE LIGHT OF THE SILVERY MOON
Warner Brothers, 1953

Choreographer(s) Saddler, Donald

Producer(s) Jacobs, William
Director(s) Butler, David
Screenwriter(s) O'Brien, Robert; Elinson, Irving
Source(s) *Penrod*; *Penrod and Sam* (novels) Tarkington, Booth

Cast Day, Doris; MacRae, Gordon; De Camp, Rosemary; Wickes, Mary; Gray, Billy

Notes There are no original songs in this musical. Vocals include "By the Light of the Silvery Moon" By Gus Edwards and Edward Madden; "My Home Town Is a One-Horse Town but It's Big Enough for Me" by Abner Silver and Alexander Gerber; "Your Eyes Have Told Me So" by Walter Blaufuss, Egbert Van Alstyne and Gus Kahn; "Be My Little Baby Bumble Bee" by Henry Marshall and Stanley Murphy; "Ain't We Got Fun" by Richard A. Whiting, Gus Kahn and Raymond B. Egan; "If You Were the Only Girl in the World" by Nat D. Ayer and Clifford Grey; "Moonlight Bay" by Percy Wenrich and Edward Madden; "Just One Girl" by Lyn Udall and Karl Kennett; "King Chanticleer" by A. Seymour Brown and Nat D. Ayer and "I'll Forget You" by Ernest R. Ball and Annelu Burns.

C

816 ✦ CABARET
Allied Artists/ABC, 1972

Composer(s)   Kander, John
Lyricist(s)   Ebb, Fred

Producer(s)   Feuer, Cy
Director(s)   Fosse, Bob
Screenwriter(s)   Allen, Jay Presson
Source(s)   *Cabaret* (musical) Kander, John; Ebb, Fred; Masteroff, Joe

Cast   Minnelli, Liza; York, Michael; Griem, Helmut; Grey, Joel; Wepper, Fritz; Berenson, Marisa; Neumann-Viertel, Elisabeth; Vita, Helen; Vespermann, Gerd

Song(s)   Money [1]; Mein Herr [1]; Willkommen; Maybe This Time [3]; Two Ladies; Tomorrow Belongs to Me; If You Could See Her; Cabaret; Married [2]

Notes   Mark Lambert dubbed the song "Tomorrow Belongs to Me." [1] Written for this film. [2] Sung in German as "Heiraten" by Greta Keller. [3] An older Kander and Ebb song interpolated into this score.

817 ✦ CABIN IN THE SKY
Metro–Goldwyn–Mayer, 1943

Musical Score   Edens, Roger
Composer(s)   Arlen, Harold
Lyricist(s)   Harburg, E.Y.

Producer(s)   Freed, Arthur
Director(s)   Minnelli, Vincente
Screenwriter(s)   Schrank, Joseph
Source(s)   *Cabin in the Sky* (musical) Duke, Vernon; Latouche, John; Root, Lynn

Cast   Waters, Ethel [2]; Anderson, Eddie "Rochester"; Horne, Lena; Armstrong, Louis; Ingram, Rex [2]; Duke Ellington and His Orchestra; The Hall Johnson Choir; Spencer, Kenneth; Polk, Oscar; Moreland, Mantan; Best, Willie; Buck and Bubbles [3] [4]; McQueen, Butterfly; Dandridge, Ruby; Nicodemus; Whitman, Ernest

Song(s)   Li'l Black Sheep [1]; Happiness Is a Thing Called Joe; Cabin in the Sky [2] (C: Duke, Vernon; L: Latouche, John); Taking a Chance on Love [2] (C: Duke, Vernon; L: Latouche, John; Fetter, Ted); Life's Full of Consequence; Honey in the Honeycomb [2] (C: Duke, Vernon; L: Latouche, John); Going Up (Inst.)

(C: Ellington, Duke); Ain't It de Truth [5] [7]; I Got a Song [5] [6]; Things Ain't What They Used to Be [8] (C: Ellington, Mercer; L: Parsons, Ted); Jezebel Jones [9]

Notes   There are also vocals of spirtuals and "S-H-I-N-E" by Cecil Mack, Lew Brown and Ford Dabney. [1] Harmonized by Hall Johnson who also revised the lyrics. [2] From the Broadway production. [3] John Bubbles' real name was John W. Sublett. [4] Buck's real name was Ford L. Washington. [5] Deleted from final print. [6] The song later turned up in the Broadway musical BLOOMER GIRL. [7] The song later turned up in the Broadway musical JAMAICA. The footage was later used in an MGM short subject. [8] Sheet music only. [9] Not used.

818 ✦ CABIN KIDS
Educational, 1935

Song(s)   Little Bit of Rhythm (in the Best of Us) (C/L: Herman, Pincus; Chaplin, Saul; Cahn, Sammy)

Notes   No other information available. Short subject.

819 ✦ CACTUS FLOWER
Columbia, 1969

Musical Score   Jones, Quincy
Composer(s)   Jones, Quincy

Producer(s)   Frankovich, M.J.
Director(s)   Saks, Gene
Screenwriter(s)   Diamond, I.A.L.
Source(s)   *Cactus Flower* (play) Barillet and Gredy [1]

Cast   Matthau, Walter; Bergman, Ingrid; Hawn, Goldie; Weston, Jack; Lenz, Rick; Scotti, Vito

Song(s)   A Time for Love Is Anytime (L: Weil, Cynthia); I Needs to Be Bee'd With (L: Shelby, Ernie)

Notes   [1] English version by Abe Burrows.

820 ✦ THE CADDY
Paramount, 1953

Composer(s)   Warren, Harry
Lyricist(s)   Brooks, Jack
Choreographer(s)   Baker, Jack

Producer(s)   Jones, Paul
Director(s)   Taurog, Norman
Screenwriter(s)   Hartmann, Edmund L.; Arnold, Danny; Englund, Ken

Cast   Martin, Dean; Lewis, Jerry; Bates, Barbara; Reed, Donna; Clark, Fred

Song(s)   What Wouldcha Do Without Me; That's Amore; You're the Right One; It's a Whistle-in' Kinda Mornin'; A Gay Continental Am I; (It Takes A Lot of Little Likes to Make) One Big Love; Easy, Brother, Easy [1]; Mine to Love [2] (C: Young, Victor; L: Blake, Bebe)

Notes   [1] Not used. [2] Sheet music only.

821 ✦ CADDYSHACK
Orion, 1980

Musical Score   Mandel, Johnny
Composer(s)   Loggins, Kenny
Lyricist(s)   Loggins, Kenny

Producer(s)   Kenney, Douglas
Director(s)   Ramis, Harold
Screenwriter(s)   Doyle-Murray, Brian; Ramis, Harold; Kenney, Douglas

Cast   Chase, Chevy; Knight, Ted; Dangerfield, Rodney; O'Keefe, Michael; Murray, Bill; Holcomb, Sarah; Colomby, Scott; Doyle-Murray, Brian; McConnachie, Brian

Song(s)   I'm Alright; Lead the Way; Mr. Night

Notes   No cue sheet available.

822 ✦ CADDYSHACK II
Warner Brothers, 1988

Musical Score   Newborn, Ira

Producer(s)   Canton, Neil
Director(s)   Arkush, Allan
Screenwriter(s)   Ramis, Harold; Torokvei, Peter

Cast   Mason, Jackie; Chase, Chevy; Aykroyd, Dan; Cannon, Dyan; Stack, Robert; Merrill, Dina; Silverman, Jonathan; Phillips, Chynna

Song(s)   Heart of Glass (C/L: Champlin, Tamara; Champlin, Bill; Gaitsch, Bruce); Nobody's Fool (C/L: Loggins, Kenny; Towers, Michael)

Notes   I only listed the song that seemed to be written for the movie. The others are all from records.

823 ✦ CADET GIRL
Twentieth Century–Fox, 1941

Composer(s)   Rainger, Ralph
Lyricist(s)   Robin, Leo

Producer(s)   Wurtzel, Sol M.
Director(s)   McCarey, Ray
Screenwriter(s)   Rauh, Stanley; Hanemann, H.W.

Cast   Landis, Carole; Montgomery, George; Shepperd, John; Tracy, William; Carter, Janis; Lowery, Robert; Chandler, Chick; Bacon, Irving; Jones, Edna Mae

Song(s)   She's a Good Neighbor; My Old Man Was an Army Man; It Happened, It's Over, Let's Forget It; I'll Settle for You; I'm Making a Play for You [1]; It Won't Be Fun (But It's Gotta Be Done); You Started Something [2]; Uncle Sam Gets Around

Notes   [1] Not used. Later in RISE AND SHINE. [2] Also in MOON OVER MIAMI.

824 ✦ CAFE METROPOLE
Twentieth Century–Fox, 1937

Producer(s)   Johnson, Nunnally
Director(s)   Griffith, Edward H.
Screenwriter(s)   Deval, Jacques

Cast   Young, Loretta; Power, Tyrone; Menjou, Adolphe; Ratoff, Gregory; Winninger, Charles; Westley, Helen; Gottschalk, Ferdinand; Kinskey, Leonid; Kaliz, Armand; Porcasi, Paul

Song(s)   Fond of You (C: Revel, Harry; L: Gordon, Mack)

Notes   No cue sheet available.

825 ✦ CAFE SOCIETY
Paramount, 1939

Choreographer(s)   Prinz, LeRoy

Producer(s)   Lazarus, Jeff
Director(s)   Griffith, Edward H.
Screenwriter(s)   Van Upp, Virginia

Cast   MacMurray, Fred; Carroll, Madeleine; Ross, Shirley; Joslyn, Allyn; Ralph, Jessie; Gillingwater, Claude

Song(s)   Park Avenue Gimp (C: Shuken, Leo; L: Loesser, Frank); Kiss Me With Your Eyes [3] (C: Lane, Burton; L: Loesser, Frank); Bluebirds in the Moonlight [1] [2] (C: Rainger, Ralph; L: Robin, Leo)

Notes   [1] Unused. [2] Later used in GULLIVER'S TRAVELS. Also not used for MAN ABOUT TOWN and PARIS HONEYMOON. [3] This is the same music as a song "Do You Ever Dream," also with lyrics by Frank Loesser.

826 ✦ CAHILL: UNITED STATES MARSHALL
Warner Brothers, 1973

Musical Score   Bernstein, Elmer

Producer(s)   Wayne, Michael
Director(s)   McLaglen, Andrew V.
Screenwriter(s)   Fink, Harry Julian; Fink, Rita M.

Cast   Wayne, John; Grimes, Gary; O'Brien, Clay; Kennedy, George; Brand, Neville; Windsor, Marie

Song(s) Man Gets to Thinkin', A (C: Bernstein, Elmer; L: Black, Don)

Notes Released in Great Britain as CAHILL. Only second page of cue sheet available.

827 ✦ CAIN AND MABEL
Warner Brothers, 1936

Musical Score Warren, Harry
Composer(s) Warren, Harry
Lyricist(s) Dubin, Al
Choreographer(s) Connolly, Bobby

Producer(s) Bischoff, Sam
Director(s) Bacon, Lloyd
Screenwriter(s) Doyle, Laird

Cast Gable, Clark; Davies, Marion; Karns, Roscoe; Jenkins, Allen; Catlett, Walter; Carlyle, David; Cavanaugh, Hobart; Donnelly, Ruth; Kelton, Pert; Clive, E.E.

Song(s) Coney Island [1]; (I'll Sing You A) Thousand Love Songs; (Here Comes) Chiquita

Notes Vocal performances of Warren and Dubin's "The Shadow Waltz" and "The Rose in Her Hair" are also included briefly as part of the "I'll Sing You A Thousand Love Songs" sequence along with "L'Amour Toujours L'Amour" by Rudolf Friml; "Who" by Jerome Kern, Oscar Hammerstein II and Otto Harbach and Wagner's "Bridal Chorus." [1] Performed instrumentally only. [1] Also in STARS OVER BROADWAY.

828 ✦ CAIRO
Metro–Goldwyn–Mayer, 1942

Musical Score Stothart, Herbert
Composer(s) Schwartz, Arthur
Lyricist(s) Harburg, E.Y.
Choreographer(s) Lee, Sammy

Director(s) Van Dyke II, W.S.
Screenwriter(s) McClain, John

Cast MacDonald, Jeanette; Young, Robert; Waters, Ethel; Owen, Reginald; Mitchell, Grant; Atwill, Lionel; Ciannelli, Eduardo; Wilson, Dooley

Song(s) The Waltz Is Over; Steamboat (C/L: Stothart, Herbert); Keep the Light Burning Bright in the Harbor (L: Dietz, Howard; Harburg, E.Y.); Cairo; Buds Won't Bud (C: Arlen, Harold); A Man Without a Woman [1]

Notes There are also vocals of "Les Filles De Cadix" by Delibes; "A Heart That's Free" by Alfred George Robyn and Railey; "We Did It Before" by Cliff Friend and Charles Tobias; "From the Land of The Sky Blue Water" by Charles Wakefield Cadman and Nelle Richmond Eberhart; "Beautiful Ohio" by Mary Earl (Robert A. King) and Ballard Macdonald; "Waiting for the Robert E. Lee" by Lewis F. Muir and L. Wolfe Gilbert; "Avalon" by Al Jolson, B.G. DeSylva and Vincent Rose

and a few other short (under 30 seconds) renditions of popular songs and classical pieces. [1] Not used but recorded. The Harburg estate titles this song "A Woman without a Man."

829 ✦ CALAMITY JANE
Warner Brothers, 1953

Musical Score Heindorf, Ray; Buttolph, David; Jackson, Howard
Composer(s) Fain, Sammy
Lyricist(s) Webster, Paul Francis
Choreographer(s) Donohue, Jack

Producer(s) Jacobs, William
Director(s) Butler, David
Screenwriter(s) O'Hanlon, James

Cast Day, Doris; Keel, Howard; McLerie, Allyn Ann; Carey, Philip; Wesson, Dick; Harvey, Paul; Robbins, Gale

Song(s) The Deadwood Stage (Whip-Crack-Away!); Hive Full of Honey; I Can Do Without You; 'Tis Harry I'm Plannin' to Marry; Just Blew in from the Windy City; Keep It Under Your Hat; Higher than a Hawk (Deeper than a Well); A Woman's Touch; The Black Hills of Dakota; Secret Love

830 ✦ CALCUTTA
Paramount, 1947

Choreographer(s) Jonsy, Roberta

Producer(s) Miller, Seton I.
Director(s) Farrow, John
Screenwriter(s) Miller, Seton I.

Cast Duprez, June; Ladd, Alan; Bendix, William; Russell, Gail

Song(s) This Is Madness (C: Wayne, Bernie; L: Raleigh, Ben)

831 ✦ CALENDAR GIRL
Republic, 1946

Composer(s) McHugh, Jimmy
Lyricist(s) Adamson, Harold

Producer(s) Dwan, Allan
Director(s) Dwan, Allan
Screenwriter(s) Loos, Mary; Sale, Richard; Loeb, Lee

Cast Frazee, Jane; Marshall, William [1]; Patrick, Gail; Baker, Kenny; McLaglen, Victor; Rich, Irene; Ellison, James; Pangborn, Franklin; Schilling, Gus; Arnt, Charles; Martin, Janet

Song(s) Calendar Girl; A Bluebird Is Singing to Me; Lovely Night to Go Dancing; At the Fireman's Ball; New York Is a Nice Place to Visit; (Have I Told You Lately) I'm Telling You Now; Let's Have Some Pretzels and Beer

Notes [1] Dubbed.

832 ✦ CALIFORNIA
Paramount, 1946

Musical Score Young, Victor
Composer(s) Robinson, Earl
Lyricist(s) Harburg, E.Y.

Producer(s) Miller, Seton I.
Director(s) Farrow, John
Screenwriter(s) Butler, Frank; Strauss, Theodore

Cast Stanwyck, Barbara; Milland, Ray; Coulouris, George; Fitzgerald, Barry; Faylen, Frank; Quinn, Anthony; Ciannelli, Eduardo

Song(s) Lily-I-Lay-De-O; California or Bust; Said I to My Heart, Said I; California; The Gold Rush (Gold Discovery Montage); I Should'a Stood in Pennsylvania

833 ✦ CALIFORNIA DREAMING
American International, 1979

Musical Score Karlin, Fred
Composer(s) Karlin, Fred
Lyricist(s) Karlin, Fred

Producer(s) Whittaker, Christian
Director(s) Hancock, John
Screenwriter(s) Wynn, Ned

Cast O'Connor, Glynnis; Cassel, Seymour; Tristan, Dorothy; Christopher, Dennis; Playten, Alice; Roberts, Tanya; Susman, Todd; Calvin, John; Wynn, Ned

Song(s) Everybody's Dancin'; Forever; Among the Yesterdays (L: Royer, Robb); Pass You By (L: Royer, Robb); Keep It In the Family (C/L: Cummings, Burton); Come on and Get Ready (C/L: Albano, Vincent); I'm in Love Again; See It My Way

Notes No cue sheet available.

834 ✦ CALIFORNIA FIREBRAND
Republic, 1948

Composer(s) Willing, Foy
Lyricist(s) Robin, Sid

Producer(s) Tucker, Melville
Director(s) Ford, Philip
Screenwriter(s) Cheyney, J. Benton; Butler, John K.; Cole, Royal K.

Cast Hale, Monte; Booth, Adrian; Hurst, Paul; Tyrrell, Alice; Coffin, Tristram; Mason, LeRoy; Evans, Douglas; Foy Willing and the Riders of the Purple Sage; York, Duke

Song(s) Trail to California; Gonna Have a Big Time Tonight; Cindy (C: Traditional; L: Willing, Foy)

Notes There are also vocals of the traditional songs: "When the Work's All Done This Fall," "Cowboy Jack," "All Day on the Prairie" and "Streets of Laredo."

835 ✦ CALIFORNIA HOLIDAY

See SPINOUT.

836 ✦ THE CALIFORNIA MAIL
Warner Brothers, 1936

Composer(s) Jerome, M.K.
Lyricist(s) Scholl, Jack

Producer(s) Foy, Bryan
Director(s) Smith, Noel
Screenwriter(s) Buckley, Harold; Chanslor, Roy
Source(s) "The Pony Express Rider" (story) Buckley, Harold; Chanslor, Roy

Cast Foran, Dick; Perry, Linda; Farley, James

Song(s) Ridin' the Mail [1]; Love Begins at Evening [1]

Notes [1] Also used in PONY EXPRESS RIDER.

837 ✦ CALIFORNIA PASSAGE
Republic, 1950

Musical Score Scott, Nathan
Composer(s) Spina, Harold
Lyricist(s) Elliott, Jack

Producer(s) Kane, Joseph
Director(s) Kane, Joseph
Screenwriter(s) Grant, James Edward

Cast Tucker, Forrest; Mara, Adele; Rodriguez, Estelita; Davis, Jim; Miles, Peter; Kemper, Charles; Williams, Bill; Williams, Rhys; Fix, Paul

Song(s) I'm Goin' 'Round in Circles; Second Hand Romance

838 ✦ CALLAWAY WENT THATAWAY
Metro–Goldwyn–Mayer, 1951

Musical Score Skiles, Marlin

Producer(s) Panama, Norman; Frank, Melvin
Director(s) Panama, Norman; Frank, Melvin
Screenwriter(s) Panama, Norman; Frank, Melvin

Cast MacMurray, Fred; McGuire, Dorothy; Keel, Howard; White, Jesse; Roope, Fay; Schafer, Natalie; Kennedy, Douglas; Taylor, Elizabeth; Gable, Clark; Williams, Esther

Song(s) I'll Be Waitin' for You Where the Tumbleweed Is Blue [1] (C/L: Wolcott, Charles)

Notes [1] Also in SLANDER.

839 ✦ CALL HER SAVAGE
Fox, 1932

Director(s) Dillon, John Francis
Screenwriter(s) Burke, Edwin
Source(s) *Call Her Savage* (novel) Thayer, Tiffany

Cast   Bow, Clara; Owsley, Monroe; Roland, Gilbert;
Todd, Thelma; Taylor, Estelle

Song(s)   I Want to Be a Chambermaid (C/L: Sullivan,
William)

840   ◆   CALLING ALL KIDS
Metro–Goldwyn–Mayer, 1943

Musical Score   Terr, Max; Shilkret, Nathaniel
Composer(s)   Bernard, Felix
Lyricist(s)   Baerwitz, Sam
Choreographer(s)   Granger, Steven

Director(s)   Baerwitz, Sam
Screenwriter(s)   Baerwitz, Sam

Cast   Our Gang [1]

Song(s)   Salute to the Army, the Navy and the Marines;
Manual of Arms; Our Favorite Stars

Notes   There is also a vocal of "I Yi, Yi, Yi, Yi (I Like
You Very Much)" by Harry Warren and Mack Gordon in
this Our Gang Comedy Short. [1] Including Buckwheat,
Froggy and Mickey.

841   ◆   CALL IT LUCK
Fox, 1934

Producer(s)   Stone, John
Director(s)   Tinling, James
Screenwriter(s)   Nichols, Dudley; Trotti, Lamar;
Cunningham, Joseph; McCoy, Harry

Cast   Patterson, Pat; Starrett, Charles

Song(s)   I'll Bet on You (C: Whiting, Richard A.; L:
Clare, Sidney); A Merry-O Cheerio Drinking Song
(C/L: Clare, Sidney)

842   ◆   CALL ME
Vestron, 1988

Musical Score   Frank, David

Producer(s)   Martel, Kenneth; Quill, John E.
Director(s)   Mitchell, Sollace
Screenwriter(s)   Kay, Karyn

Cast   Charbonneau, Patricia; McHattie, Stephen; Gaines,
Boyd; Freed, Sam; Buscemi, Steve; D'Arbanville, Patti

Song(s)   To Tylko Slowa (C: Urbaniak, Michael; L:
Ostrowska, Malgorzata)

Notes   No cue sheet available.

843   ◆   CALL ME BWANA
United Artists, 1963

Musical Score   Norman, Monty; Mathieson, Muir

Producer(s)   Broccoli, Albert R.
Director(s)   Douglas, Gordon M.
Screenwriter(s)   Monaster, Nate; Harwood, Johanna

Cast   Hope, Bob; Ekberg, Anita; Adams, Edie; Jeffries,
Lionel; Palmer, Arnold

Song(s)   (They) Call Me Bwana (C/L: Norman, Monty)

844   ◆   CALL ME MADAM
Twentieth Century–Fox, 1953

Composer(s)   Berlin, Irving
Lyricist(s)   Berlin, Irving
Choreographer(s)   Alton, Robert

Producer(s)   Siegel, Sol C.
Director(s)   Lang, Walter
Screenwriter(s)   Sheekman, Arthur
Source(s)   *Call Me Madam* (musical) Berlin, Irving;
Crouse, Russel; Lindsay, Howard

Cast   Merman, Ethel; O'Connor, Donald; Vera-Ellen
[2]; Sanders, George; De Wolfe, Billy; Dantine, Helmut;
Slezak, Walter; Skala, Lilia

Song(s)   The Hostess with the Mostes' on the Ball [1];
Washington Square Dance [1]; Lichtenburg [1]; Can
You Use Any Money Today [1]; Marrying for Love [1];
It's a Lovely Day Today [1]; The International Rag [3];
You're Just in Love [1]; (Dance to the Music of) The
Ocarina [1]; Something to Dance About [1]; Mrs. Sally
Adams [1]; The Best Things for You [1]; What Chance
Have I With Love [4]

Notes   [1] From Broadway production. [2] Dubbed by
Carole Richards. [3] Also in ALEXANDER'S
RAGTIME BAND. [4] Written for stage musical
LOUISIANA PURCHASE. Recorded but not used for
the film version.

845   ◆   CALL ME MISTER
Twentieth Century–Fox, 1951

Musical Score   Harline, Leigh
Composer(s)   Rome, Harold
Lyricist(s)   Rome, Harold
Choreographer(s)   Berkeley, Busby

Producer(s)   Kohlmar, Fred
Director(s)   Bacon, Lloyd
Screenwriter(s)   Lewin, Albert; Styler, Burt
Source(s)   *Call Me Mister* (musical revue) Rome,
Harold; Auerbach, Arnold M.; Horwitt, Arnold B.

Cast   Grable, Betty; Dailey, Dan; Thomas, Danny;
Robertson, Dale; Venuta, Benay; Boone, Richard;
Hunter, Jeffrey; Fontaine, Frank; Von Zell, Harry;
Willock, Dave; Ellis, Robert; Paris, Jerry; Spencer, Lou;
Stanley, Art

Song(s)   Jodie Chant [1] (L: Alexander, Jeff); Call Me
Mister; Japanese Girl Like 'Merican Boy (Too
Much—Too Much) (C: Fain, Sammy; L: Gordon,
Mack); I'm Gonna Love That Guy (Like He's Never
Been Loved Before) (C/L: Ash, Frances); Lament to the
Pots and Pans (C: Brent, Earl; L: Seelen, Jerry); Going

Home Train; I Just Can't Do Enough for You—Baby (C: Fain, Sammy; L: Gordon, Mack); Military Life (The Jerk Song) (L: Seelen, Jerry); Love Is Back in Business (C: Fain, Sammy; L: Gordon, Mack); It's a Man's World [2] (C: Myrow, Josef; L: Gordon, Mack); Whistle and Walk Away [1] (C: Fain, Sammy; L: Gordon, Mack); Happy Little Verse and Chorus [3] [5] (C: Arlen, Harold; L: Blane, Ralph); Kiss and Make Up Feeling [3] [4] (C/L: Unknown)

Notes   "South America, Take It Away," from the original musical revue, is heard as background music. "Red Ball Express" was set to be in the production, budgeted and put on the schedule but it was replaced. [1] Recorded but not used. [2] Shot but not used. [3] Not used. [4] This might have been an early title for "I'm Gonna Love That Guy." [5] Used in MY BLUE HEAVEN.

846   ✦   CALL NORTHSIDE 777
Twentieth Century–Fox, 1948

Musical Score   Newman, Alfred

Producer(s)   Lang, Otto
Director(s)   Hathaway, Henry
Screenwriter(s)   Cady, Jerry; Dratler, Jay
Source(s)   articles by McGuire, James P.

Cast   Stewart, James; Conte, Richard; Cobb, Lee J.; Walker, Helen; Garde, Betty; Orzazewski, Kasia; de Bergh, Joanne; Smith, Howard; Marshall, E.G.

Song(s)   Drinking Song (C: Newman, Alfred; L: Dzierzgowka, Irene)

847   ✦   CALL OF THE CANYON
Republic, 1942

Producer(s)   Grey, Harry
Director(s)   Santley, Joseph
Screenwriter(s)   Cooper, Olive

Cast   Autry, Gene; Burnette, Smiley; The Sons of the Pioneers; Terry, Ruth; Hall, Thurston; Strauch Jr., Joe; Nazarro, Cliff; Kent, Dorothea; MacDonald, Edmund; Lawrence, Marc

Song(s)   Coronation March (C: Meyerbeer, Giacomo; L: Meyer, Sol); Somebody Else is Taking My Place [1] (C/L: Howard, Dick; Ellsworth, Bob; Morgan, Russ); Take Me Back to My Boots and Saddle [2] (C/L: Powell, Teddy; Samuels, Walter G. G.; Whitcup, Leonard); Montana Plains (C/L: Montana, Patsy); When It's Chilly Down in Chile (C: Styne, Jule; L: Meyer, Sol); Call of the Canyon (C/L: Hill, Billy)

Notes   [1] Also in STRICTLY IN THE GROOVE (Universal). [2] Also in BOOTS AND SADDLES (as "Take Me Back to My Boots and Saddles") and PEPPER.

848   ✦   CALL OF THE CIRCUS
Pickwick, 1930

Musical Score   Nase, Ralph J.

Director(s)   O'Connor, Frank
Screenwriter(s)   Alton, Maxine
Source(s)   *Call of the Circus* (play) Alton, Maxine

Cast   Bushman, Francis X.; Clayton, Ethel; Wyndham, Joan; Kirby, William C.; Gay, Dorothy; Wilson, Sunburnt Jim

Song(s)   Life Is Just a Circus (C: Stauffer, Aubrey; L: Alton, Maxine)

Notes   No cue sheet available.

849   ✦   CALL OF THE FLESH
Metro–Goldwyn–Mayer, 1930

Composer(s)   Stothart, Herbert
Lyricist(s)   Grey, Clifford

Director(s)   Brabin, Charles R.
Screenwriter(s)   Colton, John

Cast   Novarro, Ramon; Jordan, Dorothy; Adoree, Renee; O'Neil, Nance; Torrence, Ernest

Song(s)   Today; Not Quite Good Enough for Me; Lonely (L: Novarro, Ramon)

Notes   Also known as THE SINGER OF SEVILLE. Renee Adoree's last film. There are also some excerpts from operas.

850   ✦   CALL OF THE PRAIRIE
Paramount, 1936

Producer(s)   Sherman, Harry
Director(s)   Bretherton, Howard
Screenwriter(s)   Schroeder, Doris; Smith, Vernon

Cast   Boyd, William; Ellison, James; Hayes, George "Gabby"; Evans, Muriel; Conklin, Chester; Mann, Hank

Song(s)   Call of the Prairie [1] (C: Lawnhurst, Vee; L: Seymour, Tot)

Notes   [1] The song was originally intended for RHYTHM ON THE RANGE.

851   ✦   CALL OF THE ROCKIES
Republic, 1944

Producer(s)   Gray, Louis
Director(s)   Selander, Lesley
Screenwriter(s)   Williams, Bob

Cast   Burnette, Smiley; Carson, Sunset [1]; Hall, Ellen; Alyn, Kirk; Woods, Harry; Jaquet, Frank; Kirk, Jack

Song(s)   Tain't Worth It (C/L: Burnette, Smiley)

Notes   [1] Billed as Sonny "Sunset" Carson.

852 ✦ CALL OF THE SOUTH SEAS
Republic, 1944

Musical Score   Knudson, Thurston
Composer(s)   Knudson, Thurston
Lyricist(s)   Knudson, Thurston

Producer(s)   Goetz, Walter
Director(s)   English, John
Screenwriter(s)   De Mond, Albert

Cast   Martin, Janet; Lane, Allan; Barcroft, Roy; Henry, William; Mara, Adele; Jacquet, Frank; Renaldo, Duncan; Vernon, Wally

Song(s)   Vahine Hinemoa; Te Hura Virviri; Upaupa Arue; War Chant; Aue Tau Tane; Blue Island (C: Newman, Evan; L: Washington, Ned)

853 ✦ CALL OUT THE MARINES
RKO, 1942

Composer(s)   Revel, Harry
Lyricist(s)   Greene, Mort

Producer(s)   Benedict, Howard
Director(s)   Ryan, Frank; Hamilton, William
Screenwriter(s)   Ryan, Frank; Hamilton, William

Cast   McLaglen, Victor; Lowe, Edmund; Barnes, Binnie; Kelly, Paul; Smith, Robert; Lovett, Dorothy; Pangborn, Franklin; The King's Men; Six Hits and a Miss

Song(s)   Call Out the Marines; Beware [1]; Zana Zoranda; The Light of My Life; Hands Across the Border

Notes   [1] Also in FALLEN SPARROW.

854 ✦ CALM YOURSELF
Metro–Goldwyn–Mayer, 1935

Musical Score   Maxwell, Charles

Producer(s)   Hubbard, Lucien
Director(s)   Seitz, George B.
Screenwriter(s)   Kober, Arthur
Source(s)   *Calm Yourself* (novel) Hope, Edward

Cast   Young, Robert; Furness, Betty; Pendleton, Nat; Gillingwater, Claude; Hatton, Raymond; Evans, Madge; Morgan, Ralph; Albright, Hardie; Ross, Shirley; Bing, Herman

Song(s)   The Tattooed Lady [1] (C/L: O'Keefe, Walter)

Notes   There is also a vocal of "Schnitzelbank." [1] Also in O'SHAUGHNESSY'S BOY and ELMER AND ELSIE (Paramount).

855 ✦ CALYPSO HEAT WAVE
Columbia, 1957

Musical Score   Mertz, Paul; DiMaggio, Ross
Choreographer(s)   Earl, Josephine

Producer(s)   Katzman, Sam
Director(s)   Sears, Fred F.
Screenwriter(s)   Chandler, David

Cast   Desmond, Johnny; Anders, Merry; Myles, Meg; Landon, Paul; Grey, Joel; The Tarriers [2]; The Hi-Lo's; Angelou, Maya; Hood, Darla; Whittinghill, Dick; Lyden, Pierce; Perkins, Gil; Mac Niles and the Calypsonians

Song(s)   Calypso Heat Wave [1] (C: Karger, Fred; L: Styne, Stanley); Calypso Joe (C/L: O'Neale, Marge; Darian, Fred); My Sugar Is So Refined (C: Lippman, Sidney; L: Dee, Sylvia); Consideration (C/L: Desmond, Johnny; Keddington, Ruth); Jody (C/L: Johnson, Scott; Darnell, Rayon); Rock Joe (C/L: Gilbeaux, Gene; Trenier, Claude; Trenier, Cliff); Treat Me Like a Lady (C/L: Reed, Don; Thorne, George); Trinidad Hubbub (C/L: Mertz, Paul); The Market Place (C/L: Angelou, Maya); Tastes Like Strawberries (C/L: Orentlick, Paul; Schlenger, Betty); Banana Boat Song (C/L: Darling, Erik; Carey, Bob; Arkin, Alan); Run Joe (C/L: Willoughby, Joe; Merrick, Walt; Jordan, Louis); Chaucoun (C/L: Darling, Erik; Carey, Bob; Arkin, Alan); Day Old Bread and Canned Beans (C/L: Trenier, Claude; Hill, Don; Jo, Damita); Stewed Pig Knuckles (C/L: Mac Niles, C.)

Notes   [1] Only song written for the picture. [2] Including Alan Arkin.

856 ✦ CAMELOT
Warner Brothers, 1967

Musical Score   Newman, Alfred
Composer(s)   Loewe, Frederick
Lyricist(s)   Lerner, Alan Jay
Choreographer(s)   Schwab, Buddy

Producer(s)   Warner, Jack L.
Director(s)   Logan, Joshua
Screenwriter(s)   Lerner, Alan Jay
Source(s)   *Camelot* (musical) Lerner, Alan Jay; Loewe, Frederick

Cast   Redgrave, Vanessa; Harris, Richard; Nero, Franco [1]; Hemmings, David; Jeffries, Lionel; Naismith, Laurence; Olaf, Pierre; Winwood, Estelle; Marshall, Garry

Song(s)   Guenevere; How to Handle a Woman; I Wonder What the King Is Doing Tonight; Follow Me; The Simple Joys of Maidenhood; St. Genevieve; Camelot; C'est Moi; The Lusty Month of May; Take Me to the Fair; What Do the Simple Folk Do; If Ever I Would Leave You; I Loved You Once in Silence

Notes   All songs were in the Broadway musical. [1] Dubbed by Gene Merlino.

857 ✦ CAMEO KIRBY
Twentieth Century–Fox, 1930

Composer(s)   Donaldson, Walter
Lyricist(s)   Leslie, Edgar

Director(s) Cummings, Irving
Screenwriter(s) Orth, Marion
Source(s) *Cameo Kirby* (play) Tarkington, Booth; Wilson, Harry Leon

Cast Murray, J. Harold; Terris, Norma; Gilmore, Douglas; Edeson, Robert; Morton, Charles; Fetchit, Stepin; Hyams, John; Loy, Myrna

Song(s) Tankard and Bowl (C/L: Brady, Edward; Strauss, Fred); I'm a Peaceful Man (C/L: Brady, Edward; Strauss, Fred); Sweet Romance; Home Is Heaven, Heaven Is Home; After a Million Dreams; Long Day [1]; Burgundy and Wine [1]; Behind an Old Spanish Fan [1] (C: Jensen, John D.; L: Hyde, Helen M.)

Notes [1] Not used.

858 ✦ CAMPUS HONEYMOON
Republic, 1947

Composer(s) Sale, Richard
Lyricist(s) Sale, Richard

Producer(s) Fanchon
Director(s) Sale, Richard
Screenwriter(s) Sale, Richard; Gruskin, Jerry

Cast Wilde, Lyn; Wilde, Lee; Mara, Adele; Crane, Richard; Hackett, Hal; Bachelor, Stephanie; Wood, Wilson; Smith, Charles

Song(s) Who's Got a Tent for Rent; Are You Happening to Me; It's Nice to Have a Man Around the House; The Opalocka Song (C: Scott, Nathan); How Does It Feel to Fall in Love

859 ✦ CAMPUS MAN
Paramount/RKO, 1987

Musical Score Newton-Howard, James

Producer(s) Fowler, Peggy; Landau, Jon
Director(s) Casden, Ron
Screenwriter(s) Dorff, Matt; Horvat, Alex; Baere, Geoffrey

Cast Dye, John; Lyon, Steve; Delaney, Kim; Wilhoite, Kathleen; O'Keefe, Miles; Fairchild, Morgan; Welsh, John

Song(s) Lookin' Up (C/L: Sembello, Michael; Rublcava, Alfred; Rudolph, Dick); Money Makes the Heart Grow Fonder (C/L: Sembello, Michael; Sembello, Danny; Rudolph, Dick); Rock Until You Drop (C/L: Sembello, Michael; Sembello, Danny; Rudolph, Dick)

Notes No cue sheet available.

860 ✦ CAMPUS RHYTHM
Monogram, 1943

Composer(s) Kay, Edward J.
Lyricist(s) Cherkose, Eddie

Producer(s) Parsons, Lindsley
Director(s) Dreifuss, Arthur
Screenwriter(s) Marion, Charles R.

Cast Downs, Johnny; Storm, Gale; Lowery, Robert; Candido, Candy; Pearson, Ge-Ge; Leavitt, Douglas

Song(s) Walking the Chalk Line (C: Herscher, Louis; L: Loman, Jules); Swing Your Way Through College (C: Herscher, Louis; L: Long, Andy Iona); It's Great to Be a College Girl (C/L: Herscher, Louis); College Sweetheart (C/L: Herscher, Louis); But Not You; You Character; It's a Mutiny

Notes No cue sheet available.

861 ✦ CAMPUS SLEUTH
Monogram, 1948

Composer(s) Robin, Sid
Lyricist(s) Jason, Will

Producer(s) Jason, Will
Director(s) Jason, Will
Screenwriter(s) Collins, Hal

Cast Stewart, Freddie; Preisser, June; Mills, Warren; Neill, Noel; MacBride, Donald; Collins, Monte; Ross, Stan; Bobby Sherwood and His Orchestra; Gallian, Gerri

Song(s) Baby, You Can Count on Me; What Happened?; Neither Could I; Jungle Rhumba; Sherwood's Forest

Notes No cue sheet available. Tilted SMART POLITICS internationally.

862 ✦ THE CANARY COMES ACROSS
Metro–Goldwyn–Mayer, 1938

Musical Score Snell, Dave
Composer(s) Jason, Will; Burton, Val
Lyricist(s) Jason, Will; Burton, Val

Director(s) Jason, Will
Screenwriter(s) Goldstone, Richard; Rauh, Stanley

Cast Rhodes, Erik; Black, Maurice; Grey, Virginia; O'Shea, Oscar

Song(s) Lawburn Alma Mater; Goodnight Angela; I'm His Moll; Doin' the Atlanta; The Busy Bee (C/L: Snell, Dave; Burton, Val; Jason, Will)

Notes This is a short subject.

863 ✦ CAN-CAN
Twentieth Century–Fox, 1960

Composer(s) Porter, Cole
Lyricist(s) Porter, Cole
Choreographer(s) Pan, Hermes

Producer(s) Cummings, Jack
Director(s) Lang, Walter
Screenwriter(s) Kingsley, Dorothy; Lederer, Charles
Source(s) *Can-Can* (musical) Burrows, Abe; Porter, Cole

Cast Sinatra, Frank; MacLaine, Shirley; Chevalier, Maurice; Jourdan, Louis; Prowse, Juliet; Dalio, Marcel; Belasco, Leon; Paiva, Nestor; Chase, Barrie

Song(s) You Do Something to Me; Let's Do It (Let's Fall in Love); Just One of Those Things [4]; I Love Paris [1]; Montmart' [1]; Maidens Typical of France [1]; C'est Magnifique [1] [3]; Live and Let Live [1]; It's All Right with Me [1]; Come Along with Me [1]; Quadrille [1] (Inst.); Can-Can [2]; Allez-Vous-En, Go Away [2]; Never, Never Be an Artist [2]; Every Man Is a Stupid Man [2]; Never Give Anything Away [2]

Notes Early memos indicate Sammy Davis Jr. was to sing "Blow Gabriel Blow" in the film. Appearing in the chorus are Marni Nixon and Norma Zimmer. [1] From original production. [2] From original production but used instrumentally only. [3] Lyrics to the verse were written by Saul Chaplin. [4] Also in PANAMA HATTIE and AT LONG LAST LOVE.

864 ✦ CANCEL MY RESERVATION
Warner Brothers, 1972

Musical Score Frontiere, Dominic

Producer(s) Oliver, Gordon
Director(s) Bogart, Paul
Screenwriter(s) Marx, Arthur; Fisher, Robert
Source(s) "The Broken Gun" (story) L'Amour, Louis

Cast Hope, Bob; Saint, Eva Marie; Bellamy, Ralph; Tucker, Forrest; Archer, Anne; Wynn, Keenan; Vigran, Herb

Song(s) Cancel My Reservation (C: Frontiere, Dominic; L: Hart, Bobby)

865 ✦ THE CANDIDATE
Warner Brothers, 1972

Musical Score Rubinstein, John
Composer(s) Rubinstein, John
Lyricist(s) Colloff, David

Producer(s) Coblenz, Walter
Director(s) Ritchie, Michael
Screenwriter(s) Larner, Jeremy

Cast Redford, Robert; Carlson, Karen; Boyle, Peter; Douglas, Melvyn; Porter, Don; Redeker, Quinn; Upton, Morgan

Song(s) Better Way; Just a Friend

866 ✦ CANDLELIGHT IN ALGERIA
Twentieth Century–Fox, 1943

Producer(s) Stafford, John
Director(s) King, George
Screenwriter(s) Williams, Brock; Strueby, Katherine

Cast Mason, James; Lehmann, Carla; Lovell, Raymond; Stamp-Taylor, Enid

Song(s) Flamme d'Amour (C/L: May, Hans); It's Love (C: Watson, Muriel L: Denby, Jack); Algerian Serenade (C/L: Turner, James; Douglas, Roy)

867 ✦ CANDLES AT NINE
Anglo-American, 1944

Director(s) Harlow, John
Screenwriter(s) Mason, Basil; Harlow, John
Source(s) *The Mouse Who Couldn't Play Ball* (novel) Gilbert, Anthony

Cast Matthews, Jessie; Stuart, John; Lehmann, Beatrix

Song(s) Marry Another (C/L: Butcher, Ernest); I'd Like to Share (C: Davis, H.P.; L: Purcell, Harold); Coconuts (C: Purdell, R.; Williams, C.; L: Purdell, R.)

Notes A British National picture.

868 ✦ CANDY AND NANCY (UNPRODUCED)
Disney

Composer(s) Keyes, Baron
Lyricist(s) Keyes, Baron

Song(s) Have You Ever Seen a Peanut Butterfly; Mickey Mouse Where Have You Been

Notes Unproduced. "Have You Ever Seen a Peanut Butterfly" is much in the spirit of "When I See an Elephant Fly" from DUMBO.

869 ✦ CAN HEIRONYMUS MERKIN EVER FORGET MERCY HUMPPE AND FIND TRUE HAPPINESS?
Universal, 1969

Musical Score Newley, Anthony
Composer(s) Newley, Anthony
Lyricist(s) Kretzmer, Herbert

Producer(s) Newley, Anthony
Director(s) Newley, Anthony
Screenwriter(s) Raucher, Herman; Newley, Anthony

Cast Newley, Anthony; Collins, Joan; Berle, Milton; Jessel, George; Kreski, Connie; Forsyth, Bruce; Kaye, Stubby; Hayes, Patricia

Song(s) When You Gotta Go; Piccadilly Lily; On the Boards; If All the World's a Stage; Sweet Love Child; Chalk and Cheese; Lullaby; Black Mass (Oh, What a Son of a Bitch I Am) (L: Newley, Anthony); I'm All I Need; Once Upon a Time

870 ♦ CANNONBALL
New World, 1976

Musical Score   Axelrod, David A.

Producer(s)   Gelfman, Samuel W.
Director(s)   Bartel, Paul
Screenwriter(s)   Bartel, Paul; Simpson, Donald

Cast   McKinney, Bill; Carradine, David; Hamel, Veronica; Graham, Gerrit; Carradine, Robert; Canova, Judy; Keach, James; Woronov, Mary; Bartel, Paul

Song(s)   He's Just a Man (C: Axelrod, David A.; L: Bramlett, Delaney)

Notes   No cue sheet available.

871 ♦ CANNONBALL RUN
Twentieth Century–Fox, 1981

Producer(s)   Ruddy, Albert S.
Director(s)   Needham, Hal
Screenwriter(s)   Yates, Brock

Cast   Reynolds, Burt; Moore, Roger; Fawcett, Farrah; DeLuise, Dom; Martin, Dean; Davis Jr., Sammy; Elam, Jack; Barbeau, Adrienne; Chan, Jackie; Convy, Bert; Fonda, Peter; Furth, George; Jagger, Bianca

Song(s)   Cannonball (C/L: Stevens, Ray); If and When (C/L: Peters, Ben); Just for the Hell of It (C/L: Stevens, Ray); Gotta Have a Dream (C/L: Capps, Al; Garrett, Snuff; Molinary, Phyllis)

Notes   It is not known which of these was written for the film.

872 ♦ CANNONBALL RUN II
Warner Brothers, 1984

Musical Score   Capps, Al

Producer(s)   Ruddy, Albert S.
Director(s)   Needham, Hal
Screenwriter(s)   Needham, Hal; Ruddy, Albert S.; Miller, Harvey

Cast   Reynolds, Burt; DeLuise, Dom; Martin, Dean; Davis Jr., Sammy; Farr, Jamie; Henner, Marilu; Savalas, Telly; MacLaine, Shirley; Anton, Susan; Bach, Catherine; Brooks, Foster; Caesar, Sid; Chan, Jackie; Conway, Tim; Danza, Tony; Elam, Jack; Kiel, Richard; Knotts, Don; Montalban, Ricardo; Nabors, Jim; Nye, Louis; Picon, Molly; Reilly, Charles Nelson; Rocco, Alex; Sinatra, Frank; Theismann, Joe; Tillis, Mel; Vigoda, Abe; Dreyer, Fred; Johnson, Arte; Lemmon, Chris; Lindsey, George; McClure, Doug; Rizzo, Jilly; Taylor, Dub

Song(s)   Like a Cannonball (C/L: Brown, Milton; Dorff, Stephen H.; Garrett, Snuff)

Notes   No cue sheet available.

873 ♦ CANTACLARO
Fox, 1946

Musical Score   Esperon, Manuel
Composer(s)   Esperon, Manuel
Lyricist(s)   Esperon, Manuel

Director(s)   Bracho, Julio

Song(s)   La Tierra de Mi Querer (C/L: Bonnet, Carlos; Esperon, Manuel); Alma Llanera (C: Gutierrez, Pedro Elias); La Madrugada; Copias Mata Ahorcado

Notes   No other information available.

874 ♦ CAN'T BUY ME LOVE
Disney, 1987

Musical Score   Folk, Robert
Choreographer(s)   Abdul, Paula

Producer(s)   Mount, Thom
Director(s)   Rash, Steve
Screenwriter(s)   Swerdlick, Michael

Cast   Dempsey, Patrick; Peterson, Amanda; Gains, Courtney; Caspary, Tina; Green, Seth; Farrell, Sharon; Dugan, Dennis

Song(s)   Love Thing (C/L: Folk, Robert)

875 ♦ CAN'T HELP SINGING
Universal, 1945

Composer(s)   Kern, Jerome
Lyricist(s)   Harburg, E.Y.

Producer(s)   Jackson, Felix
Director(s)   Ryan, Frank
Screenwriter(s)   Foster, Lewis R.; Ryan, Frank
Source(s)   "Girl of the Overland Trail" (story) Warshawsky, Curtis B.; Warshawsky, Samuel J.

Cast   Durbin, Deanna; Collins, Ray; Tamiroff, Akim; Kinskey, Leonid; Blandick, Clara; Bruce, David; Howland, Olin; Vincent, June; Gomez, Thomas; Tombes, Andrew; Cleveland, George

Song(s)   Elbow Room; Can't Help Singing; March (Inst.); Honky-Tonk (Inst.); Any Moment Now; Swing Your Sweetheart; More and More; Californ-i-ay; I'll Follow Your Smile [1]; There'll Come a Day [1]; Once in a Million Moons [1]

Notes   Originally titled CAROLINE. [1] Not used.

876 ♦ CAN THIS BE DIXIE
Twentieth Century–Fox, 1936

Composer(s)   Akst, Harry
Lyricist(s)   Clare, Sidney

Producer(s) Wurtzel, Sol M.
Director(s) Marshall, George
Screenwriter(s) Trotti, Lamar

Cast Withers, Jane; Summerville, Slim; Wood, Helen; Beck, Thomas; Haden, Sara; Gillingwater, Claude; Cook, Donald; Burke, James; Prouty, Jed; McDaniel, Hattie; Brown, Troy; Harlan, Otis

Song(s) Pick Pick Pickaninny; Does You Wanna Go to Hebben; Uncle Tom's Cabin Is a Cabaret; It's Julep Time in Dixie Land; Ancestors [1]

Notes [1] Not used.

---

877 ✦ CAN'T STOP THE MUSIC
Allan Carr, 1980

Composer(s) Morali, Jacques
Lyricist(s) Hurtt, Phil; Whitehead, Burris

Producer(s) Carr, Allan; Morali, Jacques; Belolo, Henri
Director(s) Walker, Nancy
Screenwriter(s) Carr, Allan; Woodard, Bronte

Cast Simpson, Ray [1]; Hodo, David [1]; Rose, Felipe [1]; Jones, Randy [1]; Hughes, Glenn [1]; Briley, Alix [1]; Perrine, Valerie; Jenner, Bruce; Guttenberg, Steve; Sand, Paul; Grimes, Tammy; Rush, Barbara; Havoc, June; Davis, Altovise; Sokol, Marilyn; Nype, Russell; Weston, Jack; Taylor-Young, Leigh; Patterson, Dick; Lewis, Bobo; Trueman, Paula; Nelson, Portia; Smith-Lee, Jacqui; Draher, Dodie

Song(s) Can't Stop the Music; Liberation; I Love You to Death; YMCA (L: Belolo, Henri; Willis, Victor); Give Me a Break (L: Belolo, Henri; Brown, Vera; Draher, Dodie; Smith-Lee, Jacqui); Go West (L: Belolo, Henri; Willis, Victor); Manhattan Woman (L: Belolo, Henri; Willis, Victor); Magic Night (L: Willis, Victor); Milk Shake (L: Willis, Victor); Samantha (L: Belolo, Henri; Hurtt, Phil); Sophistication (L: Belolo, Henri; Hurtt, Phil; Brown, Vera; Draher, Dodie; Smith-Lee, Jacqui); Sound of the City (L: Belolo, Henri; Hurtt, Phil)

Notes No cue sheet available. [1] Members of The Village People.

---

878 ✦ CANYON PASSAGE
Universal, 1946

Musical Score Skinner, Frank
Composer(s) Carmichael, Hoagy
Lyricist(s) Carmichael, Hoagy

Producer(s) Wanger, Walter
Director(s) Tourneur, Jacques
Screenwriter(s) Pascal, Ernest
Source(s) "Canyon Passage" (story) Haycox, Ernest

Cast Andrews, Dana; Donlevy, Brian; Bond, Ward; Hayward, Susan; Roc, Patricia; Carmichael, Hoagy;

Devine, Andy; Devine, Ted; Devine, Dennis; Hobart, Rose; Hobbes, Halliwell; Bridges, Lloyd; Ridges, Stanley; Holden, Fay

Song(s) Rogue River Valley; Silver Saddle; I'm Gettin' Married in the Morning; Ole Buttermilk Sky (L: Brooks, Jack)

---

879 ✦ CANYONS OF THE SUN
Twentieth Century–Fox, 1945

Song(s) Riding on the Trails of Colorado [1] (C: Von Tilzer, Albert; L: Mahoney, Jock)

Notes This is a Movietone Adventure short subject. [1] Based on the song "Drifting" by Albert Von Tilzer and R.C. MacPherson.

---

880 ✦ CAP'N JERICHO

See HELL AND HIGH WATER.

---

881 ✦ CAPRICE
Twentieth Century–Fox, 1967

Musical Score Marks, Larry

Producer(s) Rosenberg, Aaron; Melcher, Martin
Director(s) Tashlin, Frank
Screenwriter(s) Jayson, Jay; Tashlin, Frank

Cast Day, Doris; Harris, Richard; Walston, Ray; Kruschen, Jack; Mulhare, Edward; Skala, Lilia; Tsu, Irene; Pollard, Michael J.; Romanoff, Michael

Song(s) Caprice (C/L: Marks, Larry)

---

882 ✦ CAPTAIN CAREY, U.S.A.
Paramount, 1950

Musical Score Friedhofer, Hugo

Producer(s) Maibaum, Richard
Director(s) Leisen, Mitchell
Screenwriter(s) Thoeren, Robert
Source(s) *After Midnight* (book) Albrand, Martha

Cast Ladd, Alan; Hendrix, Wanda; Winters, Roland

Song(s) Mona Lisa [2] (C/L: Livingston, Jay; Evans, Ray); After Midnight [1] (C/L: Livingston, Jay; Evans, Ray)

Notes The production was originally titled AFTER MIDNIGHT. [1] Not used. This song has the same tune as "Mona Lisa" but when the film's title was changed the lyrics were changed also. [2] English lyrics not used in film. Troy Sanders of Paramount wrote on the composition sheet "'Mona Lisa'" is unusual and good, and it is hoped that it will be exploited with the picture." Oscar winner.

883 ✦ CAPTAIN CAUTION
United Artists, 1940

Musical Score Ohman, Phil
Composer(s) Ohman, Phil
Lyricist(s) Carling, Foster

Producer(s) Roach, Hal; Wallace, Richard
Director(s) Wallace, Richard
Screenwriter(s) Jones, Grover
Source(s) *Captain Caution* (novel) Roberts, Kenneth

Cast Mature, Victor; Platt, Louise; Carrillo, Leo; Cabot, Bruce; Osborne, Vivienne; Barrat, Robert; Mander, Miles; Brendel, El; Ates, Roscoe; O'Malley, Pat; Tombes, Andrew; Mather, Aubrey; Ladd, Alan; Corrigan, Lloyd; Osborn, Ted; Watkins, Pierre; Jamison, Bud

Song(s) Apple Song; Hilda; On a Little Island by a Sunlit Sea; Only One; Que Voulez-Vous?

Notes No cue sheet available.

884 ✦ CAPTAIN CHINA
Paramount, 1949

Musical Score Cailliet, Lucien

Producer(s) Pine, William; Thomas, William
Director(s) Foster, Lewis R.
Screenwriter(s) Foster, Lewis R.; Bagni, Gwen

Cast Payne, John; Russell, Gail; Lynn, Jeffrey; Chaney, Lon; Bergen, Edgar; O'Shea, Michael; Corby, Ellen; Armstrong, Robert

Song(s) Oh Brandy Leave Me Alone [1] (C/L: Marais, Joseph)

Notes [1] This song wasn't written for this film. Later used in HATARI!

885 ✦ CAPTAIN EO
Disney, 1987

Musical Score Horner, James; Carlin, Tom; Truman, Tim
Composer(s) Jackson, Michael
Lyricist(s) Jackson, Michael
Choreographer(s) Hornaday, Jeffrey

Producer(s) Lemorande, Rusty
Director(s) Coppola, Francis Ford

Cast Jackson, Michael; Huston, Anjelica; Shawn, Dick

Song(s) We Are Here to Change the World; Another Part of Me

Notes This is an attraction at Disneyland and Disneyworld. Filmed in 3-D.

886 ✦ CAPTAIN JANUARY
Twentieth Century–Fox, 1936

Composer(s) Pollack, Lew
Lyricist(s) Mitchell, Sidney D.
Choreographer(s) Donohue, Jack

Producer(s) Zanuck, Darryl F.
Director(s) Butler, David
Screenwriter(s) Hellman, Sam; Lehman, Gladys; Tugend, Harry

Cast Temple, Shirley; Kibbee, Guy; Summerville, Slim; Ebsen, Buddy; Haden, Sara; Darwell, Jane; Lang, June; Carradine, John

Song(s) Early Bird; At the Codfish Ball; Right Somebody to Love (L: Yellen, Jack)

887 ✦ CAPTAIN NEWMAN, M.D.
Universal, 1963

Musical Score Skinner, Frank

Producer(s) Arthur, Robert
Director(s) Miller, David
Screenwriter(s) Breen, Richard L.; Ephron, Phoebe; Ephron, Henry
Source(s) *Captain Newman M.D.* (novel) Rosten, Leo

Cast Peck, Gregory; Darin, Bobby; Albert, Eddie; Duvall, Robert; Dickinson, Angie; Curtis, Tony; Withers, Jane; Storch, Larry; Sargent, Dick; Simon, Robert F.

Song(s) Yankee Doodle (C: Traditional; L: Herbert, Frederick; Breen, Richard L.)

888 ✦ CAPTAIN OF THE GUARD
Universal, 1930

Composer(s) Roemheld, Heinz
Lyricist(s) Dugan, William Francis

Director(s) Robertson, John; Fejos, Paul
Screenwriter(s) Branch, Houston; Watters, George Manker

Cast Boles, John; La Plante, Laura; De Grasse, Sam; Marcus, James; Harlan, Otis

Song(s) Song of the Guard; For You; Maids on Parade; You, You Alone; Can It Be; It's a Sword

Notes No cue sheet available. There is also a vocal of "La Marseillaise."

889 ✦ CAPTAINS COURAGEOUS
Metro–Goldwyn–Mayer, 1937

Musical Score Waxman, Franz
Composer(s) Waxman, Franz
Lyricist(s) Kahn, Gus

Producer(s) Lighton, Louis D.
Director(s) Fleming, Victor
Screenwriter(s) Mahin, John Lee; Connelly, Marc; Van Every, Dale
Source(s) "Captains Courageous" (story) Kipling, Rudyard

Cast Bartholomew, Freddie; Tracy, Spencer; Barrymore, Lionel; Douglas, Melvyn

Song(s) Don't Cry Little Fish; Ooh!, What a Terrible Man; A Vida Do Pescador (L: Yaconelli, Z.)

890 ✦ THE CAPTAIN'S KID
Warner Brothers–First National, 1936

Musical Score Jackson, Howard
Composer(s) Jerome, M.K.
Lyricist(s) Scholl, Jack

Producer(s) Foy, Bryan
Director(s) Grinde, Nick
Screenwriter(s) Reed, Tom
Source(s) "Way for a Pirate" (story) Felton, Earl

Cast Kibbee, Guy; Jason, Sybil; Robson, May; Purcell, Dick; Treen, Mary

Song(s) Drifting Along; (I'm the) Captain's Kid

891 ✦ CAPTAINS OF THE CLOUDS
Warner Brothers, 1942

Musical Score Steiner, Max

Producer(s) Wallis, Hal B.
Director(s) Curtiz, Michael
Screenwriter(s) Horman, Arthur T.; Macaulay, Richard; Raine, Norman Reilly
Source(s) "Bush Pilots" (story) Horman, Arthur T.; Gillette, Roland

Cast Cagney, James; Morgan, Dennis; Marshall, Brenda; Hale, Alan; Tobias, George; Cavanagh, Paul; Gardiner, Reginald; Denny, Reginald

Song(s) Captains of the Clouds (C: Arlen, Harold; L: Mercer, Johnny)

Notes "Bless 'Em All" by Jimmy Hughes, Frank Lake and Al Stillman is also used though not written for the picture. It is also used in CHAIN LIGHTNING and many, many other Warner Brothers pictures.

892 ✦ THE CAPTAIN'S PUP
Metro–Goldwyn–Mayer, 1938

Song(s) The Captain's Pup (C/L: Lewis, Elbert C.)

Notes Animated cartoon.

893 ✦ CAPTAIN SWAGGER
Pathe, 1928

Director(s) Griffith, Edward H.
Screenwriter(s) Perez, Paul; Heilbron, Adelaide

Cast La Rocque, Rod; Carol, Sue; Tucker, Richard; Potel, Victor; Haupt, Ullrich

Song(s) Captain Swagger, All the Girls Adore You (C/L: Weinberg, Charles; Bibo, Irving)

Notes No cue sheet available.

894 ✦ CAPTAIN TUGBOAT ANNIE
Republic, 1945

Producer(s) Burkett, James S.
Director(s) Rosen, Phil
Screenwriter(s) Callahan, George
Source(s) characters by Raine, Norman Reilly

Cast Darwell, Jane; Kennedy, Edgar; Gordon, Charles; Moreland, Mantan; Blake, Pamela; Albright, Hardie; Warner, H.B.; Norton, Jack; Feld, Fritz; Crehan, Joseph

Song(s) Tugboat Annie (C/L: Bibo, Irving)

895 ✦ CARAMBOLAGES
Metro–Goldwyn–Mayer, 1966

Musical Score Calvi, Gerard

Producer(s) Bluwal, Marcel
Director(s) Bluwal, Marcel
Screenwriter(s) Tchernia, Pierre; Audiard, Michel; Kasak, Fred
Source(s) (novel) Kassak, Fred

Cast Brialy, Jean-Claude; de Funes, Louis; Serrault, Michel; Daumier, Sophie; Adam, Alfred

Song(s) Jours d'Ennui (C: Calvi, Gerard; L: Hardy, Francoise)

Notes Also known as A KILLING SUCCESS.

896 ✦ CARAVAN
Fox, 1934

Composer(s) Heymann, Werner
Lyricist(s) Kahn, Gus

Producer(s) Kane, Robert T.
Director(s) Charell, Erik
Screenwriter(s) Raphaelson, Samson

Cast Boyer, Charles; Young, Loretta; Parker, Jean

Song(s) Gypsy Song; Happy I Am Happy; Ha Cha Cha; Wine Song

897 ✦ CARAVANS
Universal, 1978

Musical Score Batt, Michael

Producer(s) Williams, Elmo
Director(s) Fargo, James
Screenwriter(s) Crawford, Nancy Voyles; McMahon, Thomas A.; Williams, Lorraine
Source(s) *Caravans* (novel) Michener, James A.

Cast Quinn, Anthony; O'Neill, Jennifer; Sarrazin, Michael; Vosoughi, Behrooz; Lee, Christopher; Sullivan, Barry

Song(s) Caravan Song (C/L: Batt, Michael)

898 ✦ THE CARAVAN TRAIL
PRC, 1946

Musical Score Hajos, Karl

Director(s) Emmett, Robert
Screenwriter(s) Kavanaugh, Frances

Cast Dean, Eddie; Lynn, Emmett; LaRue, Al "Lash"; Carlin, Jean; Malcolm, Robert; King, Charles; Taylor, Forrest; Chesebro, George

Song(s) Wagon Wheels [1] (C/L: De Rose, Peter; Hill, Billy); Crazy Cowboy Song (C/L: Dean, Eddie; Bond, Johnny); You're Too Pretty to Be Lonesome (C/L: Dean, Eddie; Herscher, Louis; Porter, Lew)

Notes [1] From ZIEGFELD FOLLIES OF 1934. Also in WAGON WHEELS (Paramount).

899 ✦ THE CARDINAL
Columbia, 1963

Musical Score Moross, Jerome
Composer(s) Moross, Jerome
Lyricist(s) Leigh, Carolyn
Choreographer(s) Schwab, Buddy

Producer(s) Preminger, Otto
Director(s) Preminger, Otto
Screenwriter(s) Dozier, Robert
Source(s) *The Cardinal* (novel) Robinson, Henry Morton

Cast Tryon, Tom; Lynley, Carol; Gish, Dorothy; McNamara, Maggie; Hayes, Bill; Prud'homme, Cameron; Kellaway, Cecil; Smith, Loring; Saxon, John; Huston, John; Duval, Jose; Morse, Robert; Meredith, Burgess; Haworth, Jill; Vallone, Raf; Carminati, Tullio; Davis, Ossie; Wills, Chill; Merande, Doro; O'Neal, Patrick; Hamilton, Murray; Schneider, Romy; Hunnicutt, Arthur

Song(s) They Haven't Got All the Girls (L: Stillman, Al); The Cardinal [1]; Stay with Me [1]; Fallen Woman [1]; Tango [1]

Notes [1] Lyric added for exploitation only.

900 ✦ THE CARE BEARS ADVENTURE IN WONDERLAND
Cineplex Odeon, 1987

Musical Score Cullen, Patricia
Composer(s) Sebastian, John
Lyricist(s) Sebastian, John

Producer(s) Hirsh, Michael; Loubert, Patrick; Smith, Clive A.
Director(s) Jafelice, Raymond
Screenwriter(s) Snooks, Susan; De Klein, John
Voices Dermer, Bob; Almos, Eva; Hennessey, Dan; Henshaw, Jim; Lukofsky, Maria; Goy, Luba

Song(s) Rise & Shine (C/L: Solomon, Maribeth); Have You Seen this Girl; Mad About Hats; Wonderland; King of Wonderland

Notes No cue sheet available. Animated feature.

901 ✦ CARE BEARS MOVIE II: A NEW GENERATION
Columbia, 1986

Musical Score Cullen, Trish
Composer(s) Parks, Dean; Parks, Carol
Lyricist(s) Parks, Dean; Parks, Carol

Producer(s) Nelvana Limited
Director(s) Schott, Dale
Screenwriter(s) Sauder, Peter
Voices Kay, Hadley; Wiggins, Chris; Francks, Cree Summer; Court, Alyson; Fantini, Michael

Song(s) Our Beginning; Flying My Colors; I Care for You; Growing Up; The Fight Song; Forever Young

Notes Animated feature.

902 ✦ CAREER
Paramount, 1959

Musical Score Waxman, Franz

Producer(s) Wallis, Hal B.
Director(s) Anthony, Joseph
Screenwriter(s) Lee, James
Source(s) *Career* (play) Lee, James

Cast Martin, Dean; Franciosa, Anthony; MacLaine, Shirley; Jones, Carolyn; Blackman, Joan; Middleton, Robert

Song(s) (Love Is A) Career! (C: Van Heusen, James; L: Cahn, Sammy)

903 ✦ CAREER GIRL
PRC, 1943

Producer(s) Schwarz, Jack
Director(s) Fox, Wallace W.
Screenwriter(s) Neuman, Sam

Cast Langford, Frances; Norris, Edward; Adrian, Iris; Wood, Craig; Brent, Linda; Judels, Charles

Notes No cue sheet available. The song credits above are from Hirschhorn's *The Hollywood Musical*. The *Film Daily Yearbook* completely reverses the credits of the two songwriting teams.

904 ✦ CAREERS
Warner Brothers–First National, 1929

Producer(s) Marin, Ned
Director(s) Dillon, John Francis
Screenwriter(s) Halsey, Forrest

Source(s) *Karriere* (play) Schirokauer, Alfred; Rosenhayn, Paul

Cast Dove, Billie; Moreno, Antonio; Beery, Noah; Herbert, Holmes; Myers, Carmel; Todd, Thelma; Faust, Marte

Song(s) I Love You, I Hate You [1] (C: Meyer, George W.; L: Bryan, Alfred); My Sweet Helene (C: Myer, George W.; L: Bryan, Alfred)

Notes No cue sheet available. [1] Also in DANCING SWEETIES.

905 ✦ CAREFREE
RKO, 1938

Musical Score Bennett, Russell
Composer(s) Berlin, Irving
Lyricist(s) Berlin, Irving
Choreographer(s) Pan, Hermes

Producer(s) Berman, Pandro S.
Director(s) Sandrich, Mark
Screenwriter(s) Scott, Allan; Pagano, Ernest

Cast Astaire, Fred; Rogers, Ginger; Bellamy, Ralph; Gear, Luella; Carson, Jack; Kolb, Clarence; Pangborn, Franklin

Song(s) I Used to Be Color Blind; The Yam; Change Partners; Since They Turned Loch Lomand Into Swing [1]; The Night Is Filled with Music [2]

Notes [1] Used instrumentally only. [2] Sheet music only.

906 ✦ THE CARELESS AGE
Warner Brothers–First National, 1929

Director(s) Wray, John Griffith
Screenwriter(s) Shumate, Harold
Source(s) *Diversion* (play) van Druten, John

Cast Fairbanks Jr., Douglas; Myers, Carmel; Young, Loretta; Herbert, Holmes; Thomson, Kenneth; Noy, Wilfred; Chase, Ilka

Song(s) Melody Divine (C: Ruby, Herman; L: Spencer, Norman); Say It with a Solitaire (C: Perkins, Ray; L: Ruby, Herman)

Notes No cue sheet available.

907 ✦ CARELESS LADY
Fox, 1932

Composer(s) Hanley, James F.

Director(s) MacKenna, Kenneth
Screenwriter(s) Bolton, Guy

Cast Bennett, Joan; Boles, John; Gombell, Minna; Heyburn, Weldon; Lane, Nora; Bonanova, Fortunio; Hull, Josephine; Pawley, William; Kirkwood, James

Song(s) Souvenir of Love (L: Hanley, James F.); When You Hear this Song Remember Me (L: Freed, Ralph)

908 ✦ THE CARELESS YEARS
United Artists, 1957

Musical Score Stevens, Leith

Producer(s) Lewis, Edward
Director(s) Hill, Arthur
Screenwriter(s) Lewis, Edward

Cast Stockwell, Dean; Trundy, Natalie; Larch, John; Billingsley, Barbara; Stephenson, John; Hyatt, Bobby

Song(s) The Careless Years (C/L: Dubin, Joseph S.)

909 ✦ CARGO OF INNOCENTS

See STAND BY FOR ACTION.

910 ✦ THE CARHOPS
NMD Film, 1977

Musical Score Frangipane, Ronald

Producer(s) Buckley, Jim
Director(s) Locke, Peter
Screenwriter(s) Ross, Paul; Blank, Michael

Cast Carl, Kitty; Farringer, Lisa; de Witt, Fay; Miller, Pamela

Song(s) Kitty's Theme (C/L: Kaplan, Artie); San Francisco Affair (C/L: Kaplan, Artie); The Carhops (C: Singer, Roy; L: Ellis, Tom)

Notes No cue sheet available.

911 ✦ CARIBBEAN HOLIDAY

See ONE NIGHT IN THE TROPICS.

912 ✦ CARIBBEAN ROMANCE
Paramount, 1945

Cast San Juan, Olga; Lydon, Jimmy; Blore, Eric

Song(s) Tonight Will Live (Oracion Caribe) [1] (C: Lara, Augustin; L: Washington, Ned; Lara, Augustin); Alo Alo [2] (C/L: Filho, Andre); Paran-Pan-Pan [2] (C/L: Pozo, Luciano); Bim Bam Bum [2] (C/L: Hernandez, Rafael)

Notes Short subject. [1] Washington wrote the English lyrics. Also in TROPICAL MASQUERADE and TROPIC HOLIDAY. [2] Not written for film.

913 ✦ CARMEN JONES
Twentieth Century–Fox, 1954

Composer(s) Bizet, Georges
Lyricist(s) Hammerstein II, Oscar
Choreographer(s) Ross, Herbert

Producer(s)   Preminger, Otto
Director(s)   Preminger, Otto
Screenwriter(s)   Kleiner, Harry
Source(s)   *Carmen Jones* (musical) Hammerstein II, Oscar

Cast   Dandridge, Dorothy [8]; Belafonte, Harry [9]; James, Olga; Bailey, Pearl; Carroll, Diahann [10]; Glenn, Roy [11]; Stewart, Nick [12]; Adams, Joe [13]; Peters, Brock; Lewis, Sandy; Lynn, Mauri; Covan, DeForest; de Lavallade, Carmen; Savage, Archie

Song(s)   Send Along Anudder Load; Lift 'Em Up an' Put 'Em Down; Dat's Love (Habanera); You Talk 'Jus Like My Man; You Go for Me; Carmen Jones is Goin' to Jail; Dere's a Cafe on de Corner; Dis Flower [1]; Beat Out Dat Rhythm on a Drum [2]; Stan' Up an' Fight; Whizzen' Away Along de Track [3]; Blow on 'em Sugar [4]; String Me High on a Tree; Final Duet [5]; Toreador Song; My Joe [6]; Card Song [7]

Notes   All songs from Broadway production. All music based on themes from CARMEN. [1] Based on the "Flower Song." [2] Based on "Gypsy Song." [3] Based on "Quintet." [4] Based on "Habanera." [5] Based on "Duet & Final Chorus." [6] Based on "Aria" from Act 3. [7] Based on "Card Song" from Act 3. [8] Dubbed by Marilyn Horne. [9] Dubbed by Le Vern Hutcherson. [10] Dubbed by Bernice Peterson. [11] Dubbed by Brock Peters. [12] Dubbed by Joe Crawford. [13] Dubbed by Marvin Hayes.

914 ✦ THE CARNATION KID
Paramount, 1929

Producer(s)   Christie, Al
Director(s)   Hopper, E. Mason; Pearce, A. Leslie
Screenwriter(s)   Huffsmith, Arthur; Cohn, Alfred A.

Cast   MacLean, Douglas; Lee, Frances; Davidson, William B.; Eddy, Lorraine; Mailes, Charles Hill; McDonald, Francis

Song(s)   Carnations Remind Me Of You (C/L: Sherwin, Sterling)

Notes   No cue sheet available.

915 ✦ CARNEGIE HALL
United Artists, 1947

Producer(s)   Morros, Boris; LeBaron, William
Director(s)   Ulmer, Edgar G.
Screenwriter(s)   Kamb, Karl

Cast   Rubinstein, Arthur; Heifitz, Jascha; Walter, Bruno; Stokowski, Leopold; Pons, Lily; Stevens, Rise; Pinza, Ezio; Peerce, Jan; Harry James and His Band; Monroe, Vaughn; Hunt, Marsha; Prince, William; McHugh, Frank; Yaray, Hans; Buloff, Joseph; Boreo, Emile; D'Artega, Alfonso

Song(s)   Beware My Heart (C/L: Coslow, Sam); Sometime We Will Meet Again (C/L: LeBaron, William; Morros, Boris; Stone, Gregory); The Brown Danube (C/L: Borne, Hal); All the World Is Mine (C: Portnoff, Mischa; Portnoff, Wesley; L: Dick, Dorothy); Pleasure's All Mine (C/L: Ryerson, Frank; Moore, Wilton); Romance in Carnegie Hall (C/L: D'Artega, Alfonso; Kaye, Buddy)

Notes   No cue sheet available. There are also several classical music numbers.

916 ✦ CARNIVAL BOAT
RKO, 1932

Musical Score   Steiner, Max

Producer(s)   Rogell, Charles R.
Director(s)   Rogell, Albert S.
Screenwriter(s)   Seymour, James

Cast   Boyd, William [1]; Rogers, Ginger; Kohler, Fred; Bosworth, Hobart; Prevost, Marie; Kennedy, Edgar; Sweet, Harry

Song(s)   How I Could Go for You (C/L: Grossman, Bernie; Lewis, Harold; Sizemore)

Notes   Originally titled BAD TIMBER. [1] Billed as Bill Boyd.

917 ✦ CARNIVAL IN COSTA RICA
Twentieth Century–Fox, 1947

Musical Score   Lecuona, Ernesto
Composer(s)   Lecuona, Ernesto
Lyricist(s)   Lecuona, Ernesto
Choreographer(s)   Massine, Leonide

Producer(s)   Bacher, William A.
Director(s)   Ratoff, Gregory
Screenwriter(s)   Larkin, John; Hoffenstein, Samuel; Reinhardt, Elizabeth

Cast   Haymes, Dick; Vera-Ellen [5]; Romero, Cesar; Holm, Celeste; Revere, Anne; Naish, J. Carrol; The Lecuona Cuban Boys; de Cordoba, Pedro; Whiting, Barbara; Paiva, Nestor; Feld, Fritz; Ivo, Tommy; Aguglia, Mimi

Song(s)   Costa Rica [1] (L: Ruby, Harry; Skylar, Sunny; Stillman, Al; Lecuona, Ernesto); I'll Know It's Love [1] (L: Ruby, Harry; Lecuona, Ernesto); Gui-Pi-Pia (1) [2]; Gui-Pi-Pia (2) [2]; Blue Caribbean Sea [4] (L: Harper, Marjorie) (C: Ruby, Harry; L: Skylar, Sunny; Ruby, Harry; Stillman, Al); Mi Vida [1] [3] (L: Ruby, Harry; Lecuona, Ernesto); Another Night Like This (L: Ruby, Harry); Why Do Men Bring Out the Mother in Me (C/L: Ruby, Harry); Maracas [1] (L: Lecuona, Ernesto; Ruby, Harry); Rumba Bomba [1] (L: Lecuona, Ernesto; Ruby, Harry); Fiesta (1); Punto Guanacasteco; Las Carretas; Harvest Song; Wedding Music (Inst.); Fiesta

(2) [4] (L: Skylar, Sunny; Stillman, Al); An Orchid for Remembrance [4] (L: Skylar, Sunny; Stillman, Al); Song of the Carreterro [4] (L: Skylar, Sunny; Stillman, Al); Gloomy on the Sunny Side of Twenty [4] (L: Skylar, Sunny; Stillman, Al); Cucca Chilena (Inst.); Pasillo Guanacasteco

Notes Originally titled CITY OF FLOWERS. Stillman and Skylar wrote lyrics for the Lecuona melodies. These lyrics were rejected and rewritten by Harry Ruby who kept, in "Gui-Pi Pia," three rhymes and in "Costa Rica" four lines of the Stillman and Skyler contributions. Therefore, they all receive credit although the work is mainly Ruby's. [1] Lecuona contributed the Spanish lyrics. The song is performed with both sets of lyrics. [2] This song has two distinct melodies, one with Spanish lyrics and one in English. [3] Stillman and Skylar wrote a set of lyrics that were rejected. Ruby's lyrics did not retain any of the previous work, therefore no credit was given. [4] Not used. [5] Dubbed.

918 ✦ CARNIVAL IN PARIS
Metro–Goldwyn–Mayer, 1937

Musical Score Snell, Dave
Composer(s) Burton, Val; Jason, Will
Lyricist(s) Burton, Val; Jason, Will

Director(s) Thiele, William
Screenwriter(s) Goldstone, Richard

Cast Brandon, Henry; Rutherford, Ann; Burns, Harry; Gottschalk, Ferdinand

Song(s) Mon Paree; Chi.i Boum Boum; Falling Star

Notes Short subject.

919 ✦ CARNIVAL STORY

See TEXAS CARNIVAL.

920 ✦ CAROLINA
Fox, 1934

Producer(s) Sheehan, Winfield
Director(s) Sheehan, Winfield
Screenwriter(s) Berkeley, Reginald
Source(s) (play) Green, Paul

Cast Gaynor, Janet; Young, Robert; Barrymore, Lionel

Song(s) Carolina (C: Gorney, Jay; L: Brown, Lew); Moaning (C/L: DeFrancesco, Louis E.); Bright New Mo'nin' [1] (C: Hollander, Frederick; L: Brown, Forman); Put on Yo' Workin' Shoes [2] (C: DeFrancesco, Louis E.; L: Kernell, William); The Sun Shines Brighter (When You Go Singing Along) [2] (C: DeFrancesco, Louis E.; L: Kernell, William)

Notes [1] Not used. [2] Sheet music only.

921 ✦ CAROLINA BLUES
Columbia, 1944

Composer(s) Styne, Jule
Lyricist(s) Cahn, Sammy
Choreographer(s) Lee, Sammy

Producer(s) Bischoff, Sam
Director(s) Jason, Leigh
Screenwriter(s) Hoffman, Joseph; Martin, Al; Henley, Jack

Cast Kay Kyser and His Band; Miller, Ann; Moore, Victor; Donnell, Jeff; Freeman, Howard; Carroll, Georgia; Kabibble, Ish; Babbitt, Harry; Mason, Sully; Nicholas, Harold; The Cristianis; The Layson Brothers; The Four Step Brothers

Song(s) Mr. Beebe (L: Cahn, Sammy; Brooks, Dudley); Thinkin' About the Wabash (L: Cahn, Sammy; Bullock, Walter); Thanks A Lot; Poor Little Rhode Island; You Make Me Dream Too Much; There Goes that Song Again

Notes Originally titled BATTLESHIP BLUES. Also might have once been known as THANKS A LOT.

922 ✦ CAROLINA CANNONBALL
Republic, 1954

Composer(s) Kahn, Donald; Elliott, Jack
Lyricist(s) Kahn, Donald; Elliott, Jack

Producer(s) Picker, Sidney
Director(s) Lamont, Charles
Screenwriter(s) Shipman, Barry

Cast Canova, Judy; Clyde, Andy; Elliott, Ross; Rumann, Sig; Askin, Leon; Kruschen, Jack; Wilcox, Frank

Song(s) Carolina Cannonball; Wishin' and Waitin'; Busy As a Beaver

923 ✦ CAROLINA MOON
Republic, 1940

Producer(s) Berke, William
Director(s) McDonald, Frank
Screenwriter(s) Miller, Winston

Cast Autry, Gene; Burnette, Smiley; Storey, June; Lee, Mary; Waller, Eddy; Albright, Hardie; Niebert, Terry; Dale, Frank; Jimmy Lewis and His Texas Cowboys; Ritter, Fred

Song(s) At the Rodeo (C/L: Autry, Gene; Tobias, Harry); Carolina Moon (C: Burke, Joe; L: Davis, Benny); Me and My Echo (C/L: Lee, Connie); Dreams That Won't Come True (C: Autry, Gene; Marvin, Johnny; Tobias, Harry); Say Si Si [1] (C/L: Lecuona, Ernesto; Stillman, Al; Luban, Francia)

Notes [1] Also in SAMBAMANIA (Paramount). Stillman wrote the English lyrics.

924 ✦ CAROUSEL
Twentieth Century–Fox, 1956

Musical Score Newman, Alfred
Composer(s) Rodgers, Richard
Lyricist(s) Hammerstein II, Oscar
Choreographer(s) Alexander, Rod; de Mille, Agnes [2]

Producer(s) Ephron, Henry
Director(s) King, Henry
Screenwriter(s) Ephron, Phoebe; Ephron, Henry
Source(s) *Carousel* (musical) Hammerstein II, Oscar; Rodgers, Richard

Cast MacRae, Gordon; Jones, Shirley [1]; Mitchell, Cameron; Ruick, Barbara; Turner, Claramae; Rounsville, Robert; Lockhart, Gene; Christie, Audrey; Luckey, Susan [4]; Le Massena, William; Dehner, John; d'Amboise, Jacques

Song(s) Carousel Waltz (Inst.); Mister Snow; If I Loved You; June Is Bustin' Out All Over; Soliloquy; When the Children Are Asleep; A Real Nice Clambake; What's the Use of Wond'rin'; You'll Never Walk Alone; You're a Queer One, Julie Jordan [3]; Blow High, Blow Low [3]; There's Nothin' So Bad for a Woman (Stonecutters)

Notes All songs are from the Broadway musical. There is also a cue labeled "I'm a Tomboy." Frank Sinatra was the original choice to play Billy Bigelow and did do some filming and recording. He recorded "If I Loved You" on August 16 and 17, and according to a memo of September 13, 1955, "Sinatra was not in voice, due to having recorded the night before at Capitol and being unable to sleep." "Blow High Blow Low" was also recorded with Sinatra in duet with Cameron Mitchell and a male chorus. Luckily they also recorded the number without Sinatra at the same time. [1] According to a playback list of October 6, 1955, Marni Nixon dubbed "If I Loved You" on August 30, 1955. She has no recollection of having dubbed it. [2] Louise's ballet based on the original by de Mille. [3] "You're a Queer One, Julie Jordan" and "Blow High, Blow Low" did not appear on the cue sheets. [4] Dubbed by Marie Greene.

925 ✦ THE CARPETBAGGERS
Paramount, 1964

Producer(s) Levine, Joseph E.
Director(s) Dmytryk, Edward
Screenwriter(s) Hayes, John Michael
Source(s) *The Carpetbaggers* (novel) Robbins, Harold

Cast Peppard, George; Baker, Carroll; Ladd, Alan; Cummings, Robert; Hyer, Martha; Ayres, Lew; Balsam, Martin; Erickson, Leif; Totter, Audrey; Ashley, Elizabeth

Song(s) Monica (Love Theme from the Carpetbaggers) [1] (C: Bernstein, Elmer; L: Shuman, Earl)

Notes [1] Lyrics for exploitation only.

926 ✦ CARSON CITY KID
Republic, 1940

Composer(s) Tinturin, Peter
Lyricist(s) Tinturin, Peter

Producer(s) Kane, Joseph
Director(s) Kane, Joseph
Screenwriter(s) Geraghty, Gerald; Yost, Robert

Cast Rogers, Roy; Hayes, George "Gabby"; Beery Jr., Noah; Steele, Bob; Moore, Pauline; Loft, Arthur; MacDonald, Francis; Rosner, George; Taliaferro, Hal

Song(s) The Gold Digger Song; Are You the One; Sonora Moon

927 ✦ THE CARTER CASE
Republic, 1942

Producer(s) Fields, Leonard
Director(s) Vorhaus, Bernard
Screenwriter(s) Sheldon, Sidney; Robert, Ben
Source(s) "Mr. District Attorney" (radio program) Lord, Phillips H.

Cast Ellison, James; Gilmore, Virginia; Pangborn, Franklin; Harvey, Paul; Charters, Spencer; Acuff, Eddie

Song(s) William Tell Routine (C: Styne, Jule; L: Meyer, Sol)

928 ✦ CAR WASH
Universal, 1976

Musical Score Whitfield, Norman
Composer(s) Whitfield, Norman
Lyricist(s) Whitfield, Norman

Producer(s) Linson, Art; Stromberg, Gary
Director(s) Schultz, Michael
Screenwriter(s) Schumacher, Joel

Cast Pryor, Richard; The Pointer Sisters; Ajaye, Franklyn; Carlin, George; Corey, Irwin; Morris, Garrett; Serna, Pepe; King, Henry; Pinkey, Leon; Gary, Lorraine; Fargas, Antonio; Bryant, Sully

Song(s) Car Wash; Zig Zag (C/L: Royce, Rose); Daddy Rich; You Gotta Believe; I Want to Get Next to You; Born to Love You (C/L: Whitfield, Norman; Royce, Rose); I'm Going Down; Put Your Money Where Your Mouth Is; You're on My Mind (C/L: Jobe, L.; Garner Jr., Henry; Whitfield, Norman)

929 ✦ CASABLANCA
Warner Brothers, 1943

Musical Score Steiner, Max
Composer(s) Scholl, Jack; Jerome, M.K.
Lyricist(s) Scholl, Jack; Jerome, M.K.

Producer(s) Wallis, Hal B.
Director(s) Curtiz, Michael

Screenwriter(s) Epstein, Julius J.; Epstein, Philip G.; Koch, Howard W.
Source(s) *Everybody Goes to Rick's* (play) Burnett, Murray; Alison, Joan

Cast Wilson, Dooley [2]; Bogart, Humphrey; Henreid, Paul; Bergman, Ingrid; Rains, Claude; Sakall, S.Z.; Greenstreet, Sydney; Veidt, Conrad; Lorre, Peter

Song(s) As Time Goes By [1] (C/L: Hupfeld, Herman); Knock on Wood [3]; Thats What Noah Done [3]; Muse's Call [3]

Notes There is also a visual vocal of "Tango Delle Rose" by F. Schreirer, A. Bottero and Carol Raven. [1] Not written for picture. Originally featured in Broadway revue EVERYBODY'S WELCOME. [2] Dooley Wilson's piano playing was dubbed by Elliot J. Carpenter. [3] Not on cue sheet.

930 ✦ CASA MANANA
Monogram, 1951

Producer(s) Parsons, Lindsley
Director(s) Yarbrough, Jean
Screenwriter(s) Raynor, Bill

Cast Clarke, Robert; Welles, Virginia; Karnes, Robert; Roux, Tony; Brewster, Carol; Maxey, Paul; Richey, Jean; The Rio Brothers; Eddie LeBaron and His Orchestra; Cooley, Spade; Jiminez, Yadira; Zaro and D'Lores; The Mercer Brothers; Armando and Lits; Betty and Beverly; Perez, Olga; Davis and Johnson

Notes No cue sheet available.

931 ✦ CASANOVA IN BURLESQUE
Republic, 1944

Composer(s) Kent, Walter
Lyricist(s) Gannon, Kim

Producer(s) Cohen, Albert J.
Director(s) Goodwins, Leslie
Screenwriter(s) Gill, Frank, Jr.

Cast Brown, Joe E.; Evans, Dale; Havoc, June; Gateson, Marjorie; Imhoff, Roger; Tombes, Andrew; Tyler, Harry; Knox, Patricia

Song(s) Casanova Joe; Five a Day Fatima; Mess Me Up [1]; Who Took Me Home Last Night [2] (C: Styne, Jule; L: Adamson, Harold); Willie the Shake; Taming of the Shrew Finale

Notes This might be an incomplete cue sheet. [1] Also in MURDER IN THE MUSIC HALL. [2] Also in CHANGE OF HEART, HIT PARADE OF 1943, THE PHANTOM SPEAKS and THUMBS UP.

932 ✦ CASANOVA'S BIG NIGHT
Paramount, 1954

Musical Score Murray, Lyn
Choreographer(s) Earl, Josephine

Producer(s) Jones, Paul
Director(s) McLeod, Norman Z.
Screenwriter(s) Kanter, Hal; Hartmann, Edmund L.

Cast Hope, Bob; Fontaine, Joan; Dalton, Audrey; Rathbone, Basil; Marlowe, Hugh; Carradine, John; Emerson, Hope; Burr, Raymond; Chaney, Lon

Song(s) Pretty Mandolin (Tic-A-Tic-A-Tic) (C/L: Livingston, Jay; Evans, Ray); The Gondolier's Serenade [1] (C: Lilley, Joseph J.; L: David, Mack; Blake, Bebe)

Notes [1] Used instrumentally only.

933 ✦ CASBAH
Universal, 1948

Musical Score Scharf, Walter
Composer(s) Arlen, Harold
Lyricist(s) Robin, Leo
Choreographer(s) Pearce, Bernard

Producer(s) Goldstone, Nat G.
Director(s) Berry, John
Screenwriter(s) Bus-Fekete, Ladislaus; Manoff, Arnold
Source(s) *Pepe Le Moko* (novel) Ashelbe, Detective

Cast Martin, Tony; Toren, Marta; Haas, Hugo; Lorre, Peter; De Carlo, Yvonne; Gomez, Thomas; Dick, Douglas; Rudley, Herbert; Dunham, Katherine

Song(s) For Every Man There's a Woman; Hooray for Love; Odette's Cafe (Inst.); Heart Thief (Inst.); It Was Written in the Stars; What's Good About Goodbye; The Monkey Sat in the Cocoanut Tree [1]

Notes [1] Not used.

934 ✦ THE CASE OF THE CURIOUS BRIDE
Warner Brothers, 1935

Producer(s) Brown, Harry Joe
Director(s) Curtiz, Michael
Screenwriter(s) Reed, Tom; Holmes, Brown
Source(s) *The Case of the Curious Bride* (novel) Gardner, Erle Stanley

Cast William, Warren; Flynn, Errol; Woods, Donald; Dodd, Claire; Jenkins, Allen; MacLane, Barton; Shaw, Winifred; Hymer, Warren

Song(s) It Was a Dark and Stormy Night (C: Fain, Sammy; L: Kahal, Irving)

935 ✦ CASEY AT THE BAT
Disney, 1946

Director(s) Geronimi, Clyde
Screenwriter(s) Brightman, Homer; Gurney, Eric
Source(s) "Casey at the Bat" (poem) Thayer, Ernest

Song(s) Casey (The Pride of Them All) (C: Darby, Ken; Daniel, Eliot; L: Gilbert, Ray)

Notes This cartoon is part of MAKE MINE MUSIC.

936 ✦ CASEY'S SHADOW
Columbia, 1978

Musical Score Bernstein, Elmer
Composer(s) Tempchin, Jack
Lyricist(s) Tempchin, Jack

Producer(s) Stark, Ray
Director(s) Ritt, Martin
Screenwriter(s) Sobieski, Carol
Source(s) "Ruidoso" (story) McPhee, John

Cast Matthau, Walter; Smith, Alexis; Webber, Robert; Hamilton, Murray; Rubin, Andrew A.; Burns, Stephen; Myers, Susan; Bissell, Whit

Song(s) Coonass [1] (C/L: Rebennack, Mac); Let Me Go Til I'm Gone [1] (C: Williams, Patrick; Jennings, Wilbur); It Takes Love; I Wanna Win; Dream Angel

Notes The cue sheet credited the score to Patrick Williams. The academy's *Annual Index to Motion Picture Credits* is what I used above. [1] Songs on cue sheet (as opposed to those in *Academy Guide*).

937 ✦ CASH MCCALL
Warner Brothers, 1959

Musical Score Steiner, Max

Producer(s) Blanke, Henry
Director(s) Pevney, Joseph
Screenwriter(s) Coffee, Lenore; Hargrove, Marion
Source(s) *Cash McCall* (novel) Hawley, Cameron

Cast Garner, James; Wood, Natalie; Foch, Nina; Jagger, Dean; Jones, Henry; Marshall, E.G.; Kruger, Otto

Song(s) Skipping Rope (C: Steiner, Max; L: Hargrove, Marion)

Notes This number lasted 25 seconds on the screen.

938 ✦ CASH ON DELIVERY
RKO, 1956

Musical Score Williamson, Lambert

Producer(s) Schrift, Ben; Rogers, Peter
Director(s) Box, Muriel
Screenwriter(s) McDougall, Roger
Source(s) *To Dorothy, a Son* (play) McDougall, Roger

Cast Winters, Shelley; Gregson, John; Cummins, Peggy; Hyde-White, Wilfrid; Washbourne, Mona; Power, Hartley; Miller, Martin; Mather, Aubrey; Bass, Alfie

Song(s) Give Me a Man (C/L: Roberts, Paddy); You're the Only One (C/L: Abram, Jacques)

Notes Released as TO DOROTHY, A SON in Great Britain. Some sources also list the "Juke-Box Ballet" by Fred G. Morritt and George Thorne as being from this film.

939 ✦ CASINO DE PAREE

See GO INTO YOUR DANCE.

940 ✦ THE CASINO MURDER CASE
Metro–Goldwyn–Mayer, 1935

Musical Score Tiomkin, Dimitri

Producer(s) Hubbard, Lucien
Director(s) Marin, Edwin L.
Screenwriter(s) Ryerson, Florence; Woolf, Edgar Allan
Source(s) *The Casino Murder Case* (novel) Van Dine, S.S.

Cast Lukas, Paul; Cook, Donald; Byron, Arthur; Blore, Eric; Fazenda, Louise; Jewell, Isabel; Healy, Ted; Russell, Rosalind; Skipworth, Alison

Song(s) I've Got a Feeling I'm Going Spanish Now [1] (C/L: Snell, Dave)

Notes [1] Also in CAUGHT SHORT.

941 ✦ CASINO ROYALE
Columbia, 1967

Musical Score Bacharach, Burt
Composer(s) Bacharach, Burt
Lyricist(s) David, Hal

Producer(s) Feldman, Charles K.; Bresler, Jerry
Director(s) Huston, John; Hughes, Ken; Guest, Val; Parrish, Robert; McGrath, Joseph
Screenwriter(s) Mankowitz, Wolf; Law, John; Sayers, Michael
Source(s) *Casino Royale* (novel) Fleming, Ian

Cast Sellers, Peter; Andress, Ursula; Niven, David; Welles, Orson; Pettet, Joanna; Lavi, Daliah; Allen, Woody; Kerr, Deborah; Holden, William; Boyer, Charles; Huston, John; Kasznar, Kurt; Raft, George; Belmondo, Jean-Paul; Cooper, Terence; Bisset, Jacqueline [1]

Song(s) The Look of Love; Casino Royale

Notes [1] Billed as Jacky Bisset.

942 ✦ CASPER CARTOONS
Paramount

Song(s) Casper the Friendly Ghost (C: Livingston, Jerry; L: David, Mack); Casper Casper (C: Krondes, Jimmy; L: Jacobson, Sid)

Notes Animated cartoons. First produced in 1950.

943 ✦ CAST A GIANT SHADOW
United Artists, 1966

Musical Score Bernstein, Elmer
Composer(s) Bernstein, Elmer

Producer(s)   Shavelson, Melville
Director(s)   Shavelson, Melville
Screenwriter(s)   Shavelson, Melville
Source(s)   *Cast a Giant Shadow* (book) Berkman, Ted

Cast   Douglas, Kirk; Berger, Senta; Dickinson, Angie; Topol [1]; Wayne, John; Sinatra, Frank; Brynner, Yul; Adler, Luther; Merrill, Gary

Song(s)   Love Me True (L: Sheldon, Ernie); Lila Lel (L: Almagor, Dan); Next Year in Jerusalem (C: Traditional; L: Seltzer, Dov); Cast a Giant Shadow [2] (L: Sheldon, Ernie)

Notes   There are other public domain vocals. [1] Billed as Haym Topol. [2] Lyric written for exploitation only.

944 ♦ CASTAWAY
Cannon, 1987

Musical Score   Myers, Stanley

Producer(s)   McCallum, Rick
Director(s)   Roeg, Nicolas
Screenwriter(s)   Scott, Allan
Source(s)   (book) Irvine, Lucy

Cast   Reed, Oliver; Donohoe, Amanda; Hale, Georgina; Barber, Frances

Song(s)   Be Kind to My Mistakes (C/L: Bush, Kate)

Notes   No cue sheet available.

945 ♦ THE CASTILIAN
Warner Brothers, 1963

Musical Score   Buenagu, Jose
Composer(s)   Faith, Robert
Lyricist(s)   Marcucci, Robert

Producer(s)   Pink, Sidney W.
Director(s)   Seto, Javier
Screenwriter(s)   Pink, Sidney W.
Source(s)   *Valley of the Swords* (screenplay) Diaz, Paulino R.; Seto, Javier; de Los Arcos, Luis

Cast   Santony, Spartaco; Velasquez, Teresa; Avalon, Frankie; Romero, Cesar; Rey, Fernando; Crawford, Broderick

Song(s)   Ballad of Ferman (C: Buenagu, Jose); Ferman's Love Song; Valley of the Swords

946 ♦ CASUAL SEX?
Universal, 1988

Musical Score   Parks, Van Dyke

Producer(s)   Herzberg, Ilona; Kahn, Sheldon
Director(s)   Robert, Genevieve
Screenwriter(s)   Toll, Judy; Goldman, Wendy
Source(s)   *Casual Sex?* (play) Toll, Judy; Goldman, Wendy

Cast   Thompson, Lea; Jackson, Victoria; Shellen, Stephen; Levine, Jerry; Clay, Andrew Dice; Gross, Mary; Breiman, Valeri

Song(s)   (No More) Casual Sex (C/L: Darnell, August; Browder Jr., Stoney); Hot Hot Hot [1] (C/L: Cassell, Alphonsus)

Notes   [1] Sheet music only.

947 ♦ CATALINA
Paramount, 1946 unproduced

Composer(s)   Livingston, Jay; Evans, Ray
Lyricist(s)   Livingston, Jay; Evans, Ray

Song(s)   Catalina [1]; King Cocoa; Who? Where? When?; I Love You Truly; Avalon

Notes   [1] Later used in the short CATALINA INTERLUDE.

948 ♦ CATALINA INTERLUDE
Paramount, 1948

Producer(s)   Grey, Harry
Director(s)   Ganzer, Alvin

Cast   Maxey, Virginia; Webb, Richard; Jimmy Dorsey and His Orchestra

Song(s)   Catalina (C/L: Livingston, Jay; Evans, Ray)

Notes   Short subject. There are also vocals of "My Ideal" by Leo Robin, Richard Whiting and Newell Chase and "Hit the Road to Dreamland" by Harold Arlen and Johnny Mercer.

949 ♦ THE CAT AND THE FIDDLE
Metro–Goldwyn–Mayer, 1933

Composer(s)   Kern, Jerome
Lyricist(s)   Harbach, Otto

Director(s)   Howard, William K.
Screenwriter(s)   Spewack, Bella; Spewack, Sam
Source(s)   *The Cat and the Fiddle* (musical) Harbach, Otto; Kern, Jerome

Cast   Novarro, Ramon; MacDonald, Jeanette; Morgan, Frank; Hersholt, Jean; Butterworth, Charles; Segal, Vivienne

Song(s)   The Night Was Made for Love; One Moment Alone; Poor Pierrot; She Didn't Say Yes; Don't Ask Me Not to Sing; I Watch the Love Parade; A New Love Is Old

Notes   All music from the Broadway original.

950 ♦ CAT BALLOU
Columbia, 1965

Musical Score   De Vol, Frank
Composer(s)   Livingston, Jerry
Lyricist(s)   David, Mack

Producer(s) Hecht, Harold
Director(s) Silverstein, Elliott
Screenwriter(s) Newman, Walter; Pierson, Frank R.
Source(s) *The Ballad of Cat Ballou* (novel) Chanslor, Roy

Cast Fonda, Jane; Marvin, Lee; Callan, Michael; Hickman, Dwayne; Cole, Nat "King"; Kaye, Stubby; Denny, Reginald; Flippen, Jay C.; Hunnicutt, Arthur; Cabot, Bruce

Song(s) The Prologue; Ballad of Cat Ballou; They Can't Make Her Cry; Pray Jezabel; Wolf City; Roodle Doodle; Kid Shelleen; Trip to the Hole in the Wall; Running Patter; Tarnished Virtue

951 ✦ CATCH MY SOUL
Cinerama Releasing, 1974

Composer(s) White, Tony Joe
Lyricist(s) Good, Jack

Producer(s) Good, Jack; Rosenbloom, Richard
Director(s) McGoohan, Patrick
Screenwriter(s) Good, Jack
Source(s) *Othello* (play) Shakespeare, William

Cast Havens, Richie; LeGault, Lance; Hubley, Season; White, Tony Joe; Tyrrell, Susan

Song(s) Othello (C/L: White, Tony Joe); Working on a Building (C/L: White, Tony Joe); Wash Us Clear; Eat the Bread, Drink the Wine; Book of Prophecy; Catch My Soul; That's What God Said (C/L: Bramlett, Delaney); Chug a Lug (C/L: Bramlett, Delaney); I Found Jesus (C/L: Bramlett, Delaney); Looking Back (C/L: White, Tony Joe; Bramlett, Delaney); Open Our Eyes (C/L: Lumkins, Leon); Last of the Blood (C: Pohlman, Ray); Put Out the Light (C: Pohlman, Ray); Tickle His Fancy (C: Zoughby, Emil Dean)

Notes No cue sheet available. There is also a vocal of the traditional song "Run Shaker Life."

952 ✦ CAT ON A HOT TIN ROOF
Metro–Goldwyn–Mayer, 1958

Musical Score Previn, Andre

Producer(s) Weingarten, Lawrence
Director(s) Brooks, Richard
Screenwriter(s) Brooks, Richard; Poe, James
Source(s) *Cat on a Hot Tin Roof* (play) Williams, Tennessee

Cast Taylor, Elizabeth; Newman, Paul; Ives, Burl; Carson, Jack; Anderson, Judith; Sherwood, Madeleine; Gates, Larry; Taylor, Vaughn

Song(s) Lost in a Summer Night [1] (C: Previn, Andre; L: Raskin, Milton)

Notes [1] Used instrumentally only.

953 ✦ CAT PEOPLE
RKO–Universal, 1982

Musical Score Moroder, Giorgio

Producer(s) Fries, Charles
Director(s) Schrader, Paul
Screenwriter(s) Ormsby, Alan

Cast Kinski, Nastassia; McDowell, Malcolm; O'Toole, Annette; Dee, Ruby; Begley Jr., Ed; Faison, Frankie; Paulin, Scott; Laroquette, John

Song(s) Theme from Cat People (C: Moroder, Giorgio; L: Bowie, David)

Notes No cue sheet available.

954 ✦ CATTLE ANNIE AND LITTLE BRITCHES
Universal, 1983

Musical Score Greene, Richard

Producer(s) Hitzig, Rupert; King, Alan
Director(s) Johnson, Lamont
Screenwriter(s) Eyre, David; Ward, Robert
Source(s) *Cattle Annie and Little Britches* (novel) Ward, Robert

Cast Glenn, Scott; Gleeson, Redmond; Russ, William; Call, Ken; Savage, John; Taylor, Buck; Plummer, Amanda; Lancaster, Burt; Conrad, Michael; Lang, Perry; Steiger, Rod; Ford, Steven

Song(s) Cattle Annie (C/L: Slocum, Tom; Berti, Sanh; Berti, Dehl Franke); Oh Death (C/L: Slocum, Tom; Berti, Sanh)

955 ✦ CATTLE DRIVE
Universal, 1951

Producer(s) Rosenberg, Aaron
Director(s) Neumann, Kurt
Screenwriter(s) Natteford, Jack; Hayward, Lillie

Cast Stockwell, Dean; McCrea, Joel; Ames, Leon; Wills, Chill; Brandon, Henry; Petrie, Howard; Steele, Bob

Song(s) Ten Thousand Cattle Gone Astray (C: Traditional L: Herbert, Frederick)

956 ✦ CATTLE TOWN
Warner Brothers, 1952

Musical Score Lava, William

Producer(s) Foy, Bryan
Director(s) Smith, Noel
Screenwriter(s) Blackburn, Tom

Cast Morgan, Dennis; Blake, Amanda; Moreno, Rita; Teal, Ray

Song(s) West Virginia [2] (C/L: Blane, Ralph); Underneath a Western Sky [1] (C: Jerome, M.K.; Fiorito, Ted; L: Scholl, Jack)

Notes [1] Also used in COWBOY QUARTERBACK and RETURN OF THE FRONTIERSMAN. This is the only film which uses this song which credits Fiorito. Scholl and Jerome wrote another song with the title "Underneath the Western Skies." It might be the same song or only similar to it. [2] Also in ONE SUNDAY AFTERNOON.

957 ✦ CAUGHT IN THE DRAFT
Paramount, 1941

Musical Score Young, Victor

Producer(s) DeSylva, B.G.
Director(s) Butler, David
Screenwriter(s) Tugend, Harry

Cast Hope, Bob; Lamour, Dorothy; Overman, Lynne; Bracken, Eddie; Kolb, Clarence

Song(s) Love Me As I Am [1] (C: Alter, Louis; L: Loesser, Frank)

Notes [1] Featured instrumentally only although recorded vocally.

958 ✦ CAUGHT PLASTERED
RKO, 1931

Producer(s) LeBaron, William
Director(s) Seiter, William A.
Screenwriter(s) Spence, Ralph; Welch, Eddie

Cast Wheeler, Bert; Woolsey, Robert; Lee, Dorothy; Beaumont, Lucy; Robards, Jason; Middleton, Charles

Song(s) I'm That Way About You (C/L: Schertzinger, Victor)

959 ✦ CAUGHT SHORT
Metro–Goldwyn–Mayer, 1930

Director(s) Riesner, Charles F.
Screenwriter(s) Mack, Willard; Hopkins, Robert E.
Source(s) *Caught Short* (joke book) Cantor, Eddie

Cast Dressler, Marie; Moran, Polly; Page, Anita; Morton, Charles

Song(s) I've Got a Feeling I'm Going Spanish Now [1] (C: Snell, Dave; L: Egan, Raymond B.); Somebody (C: Ahlert, Fred E.; L: Turk, Roy)

Notes [1] Also in THE CASINO MURDER CASE.

960 ✦ CAVALCADE
Fox, 1933

Composer(s) Coward, Noel
Lyricist(s) Coward, Noel

Producer(s) Sheehan, Winfield
Director(s) Lloyd, Frank
Screenwriter(s) Berkeley, Reginald
Source(s) *Cavalcade* (play) Coward, Noel

Cast Lindsay, Margaret; Brook, Clive; Granville, Bonita; Warburton, John; Mundin, Herbert; O'Connor, Una; Jeans, Ursula; Mercer, Beryl; Bevan, Billy

Song(s) Girls of the C.I.V. [1]; Finale (Musical Comedy Sequence); Lover of My Dreams (Mirabelle Waltz); Twentieth Century Blues; You Are My Day Dream (C/L: DeFrancesco, Louis E.; Berkeley, Reginald); Cavalcade [2] (C: DeFrancesco, Louis E.; L: Berkeley, Reginald)

Notes There are also many World War I (and earlier) period songs given vocals. These include "Soldiers of the Queen" by Leslie Stuart (Thomas Barrett); "When Johnny Comes Marching Home" by Louis Lambert (Patrick Sarsfield Gilmore); "Shall We Gather at the River" by Reverend R. Lowry; "Rule Britannia" by Thomas Arne; "I'll Make a Man of You" (from THE PASSING SHOW) by Herman Finck and Arthur Wimperis; "Your King and Country Want You" by Paul Rubens; "Military Mary Ann" by Louis A. Hirsch and Edward Madden; "It's a Long Way to Tipperary" by Jack Judge and Harry Williams; "Pack Up Your Troubles in Your Old Kit Bag and Smile Smile Smile" by Felix Powell and George Asaf; "Keep the Home Fires Burning" by Ivor Novello and Lena G. Ford; "Oh You Beautiful Doll" by Nat D. Ayer and A. Seymour Brown; "Annie Laurie;" "Auld Lang Syne" by Robert Burns; "God Save the King" by Henry Carey. [1] This may be Coward's arrangement of a Boer War song. [2] Used instrumentally only.

961 ✦ THE CAVALIER
Tiffany–Stahl, 1928

Director(s) Willat, Irvin
Screenwriter(s) Anthony, Walter
Source(s) *The Black Rider* (novel) Brand, Max

Cast Talmadge, Richard; Bedford, Barbara; Cecil, Nora; Torrence, David; Mir, David

Song(s) My Cavalier (C: Riesenfeld, Hugo; L: Willson, Meredith)

Notes No cue sheet available.

962 ✦ CAVEMAN
United Artists, 1981

Musical Score Schifrin, Lalo

Producer(s) Turman, Lawrence; Foster, David
Director(s) Gottlieb, Carl
Screenwriter(s) De Luca, Rudy; Gottlieb, Carl

Cast Starr, Ringo; Quaid, Dennis; Bach, Barbara; Matuszak, John; Long, Shelley

Song(s) The Caveman Song (C/L: Schifrin, Lalo)

963 ◆ THE CAVERN
Twentieth Century–Fox, 1965

Musical Score Rustichelli, Carlo

Producer(s) Ulmer, Edgar G.
Director(s) Ulmer, Edgar G.
Screenwriter(s) Pertwee, Michael; Davis, Jack

Cast Saxon, John; Schiaffino, Rosanna; Hagman, Larry; Marshall, Peter L.; Aherne, Brian; Castelnuovo, Nino; von Borody, Hans

Song(s) The Cavern (C/L: Coates, Carroll); Anna's Song (C: Rustichelli, Carlo; L: Unknown)

964 ◆ CEASE FIRE (1953)
Paramount, 1953

Musical Score Tiomkin, Dimitri

Producer(s) Wallis, Hal B.
Director(s) Crump, Owen
Screenwriter(s) Doniger, Walter

Song(s) (We Are) Brothers in Arms (C: Tiomkin, Dimitri; L: Washington, Ned)

Notes This is a documentary featuring infantry soldiers in Korea. There is also a vocal of "Battle Hymn of the Republic" with new lyrics by Owen Crump.

965 ◆ CEASE FIRE (1985)
CineWorld, 1985

Musical Score Fry, Gary

Producer(s) Grefe, William
Director(s) Nutter, David
Screenwriter(s) Fernandez, George
Source(s) *Vietnam Trilogy* (play) Fernandez, George

Cast Johnson, Don; Blount, Lisa; Lyons, Robert F.; Chaves, Richard; Richards, Rick; Gil, Jorge

Song(s) We've Got Each Other (C/L: Fry, Gary)

Notes No cue sheet available.

966 ◆ CENTENNIAL SUMMER
Twentieth Century–Fox, 1946

Composer(s) Kern, Jerome
Lyricist(s) Robin, Leo
Choreographer(s) Fox, Dorothy

Producer(s) Preminger, Otto
Director(s) Preminger, Otto
Screenwriter(s) Kanin, Michael
Source(s) *Centennial Summer* (novel) Idell, Albert E.

Cast Crain, Jeanne [4]; Wilde, Cornel; Darnell, Linda [5]; Eythe, William; Brennan, Walter; Bennett, Constance; Gish, Dorothy; Whiting, Barbara; Stevens, Larry; Howard, Kathleen; Swan, Buddy; Dingle, Charles; Long, Avon; Gordon, Gavin; Dunn, Eddie; Austin, Lois

Song(s) Centennial; Long Live Our Free America; All Through the Day (L: Hammerstein II, Oscar); Railroad Song; The Right Romance; Up with the Lark; In Love in Vain; Two Dachshunds (Inst.); Square Dance (Inst.); Cinderella Sue (L: Harburg, E.Y.); Happy Anniversary [1] [6]; The Clock (Inst.); Two Hearts Are Better Than One (Duettino) [1] [3] (L: Mercer, Johnny); Pepper Pot [1]; Opening of Exposition [1] [2] (Inst.); Waltzing Around the Maypole [1] [2] (Inst.); Cradle of Democracy [1] [2] (Inst.); The Things That Most Appeal to Me [1] [2] (Inst.); A Little Quaker [1] [2] (Inst.); Drifting Along the Delaware [1] [2] (Inst.); German Town [1] [2] (Inst.); Dom Pedro of Brazil [1] [2] (Inst.); Drowsy Lullaby [1] [2] (Inst.); Strolling and Patrolling [1] [2] (Inst.)

Notes [1] Not used. [2] The instrumental titles in this group were what Twentieth Century–Fox originally purchased from Kern. They did not have lyrics at the time. Perhaps these were Kern's titles and they were made into songs by Robin et al. Anyway, I thought I'd list them for your information. [3] This number was listed on a memo of 1/30/46, coming between "In Love in Vain" and "Cinderella Sue." Louanne Hogan made a commercial recording of this song. [4] Dubbed by Louanne Hogan. [5] Dubbed. [6] Originally part of "Centennial" and "Long Live Our Free America."

967 ◆ CENTRAL PARK
Warner Brothers–First National, 1932

Composer(s) Hess, Cliff
Lyricist(s) Hess, Cliff

Producer(s) Griffith, Ray
Director(s) Adolfi, John
Screenwriter(s) Morehouse, Ward; Baldwin, Earl

Cast Blondell, Joan; Kibbee, Guy; Ford, Wallace; Ellis, Patricia; Walthall, Henry B.

Song(s) Young Love [1]; Central Park [1]

Notes [1] No songs indicated on cue sheets.

968 ◆ A CERTAIN SMILE
Twentieth Century–Fox, 1958

Musical Score Newman, Alfred

Producer(s) Ephron, Henry
Director(s) Negulesco, Jean
Screenwriter(s) Goodrich, Frances; Hackett, Albert
Source(s) *A Certain Smile* (novel) Sagan, Francoise

Cast Brazzi, Rossano; Fontaine, Joan; Dillman, Bradford; Carere, Christine; Franz, Eduard

Song(s) A Certain Smile (C: Fain, Sammy; L: Webster, Paul Francis)

969 ✦ CHA-CHA-CHA BOOM!
Columbia, 1956

Choreographer(s) Barton, Earl

Producer(s) Katzman, Sam
Director(s) Sears, Fred F.
Screenwriter(s) Gordon, James B.

Cast Prado, Perez; The Mary Kaye Trio; Grayco, Helen; Arcaraz, Luis; Lopez, Manny; Dunne, Stephen; Talton, Alix; Gonzales, Jose Gonzales; Lewis, Sylvia; Hal Mooney Orchestra

Notes No cue sheet available. There were no songs written for this picture. Vocals include: "Get Happy" by Harold Arlen and Ted Koehler; "Lonesome Road," "Save Your Sorrow," "Lilly's Lament," "Year Round Love" and the instrumentals "Cuban Rock and Roll," "Voodoo Suite," "Crazy Crazy" and "Mambo No. 8."

970 ✦ THE CHAIRMAN
Twentieth Century–Fox, 1969

Musical Score Goldsmith, Jerry

Producer(s) Abrahams, Mort
Director(s) Thompson, J. Lee
Screenwriter(s) Maddow, Ben
Source(s) (novel) Kennedy, Jay Richard

Cast Peck, Gregory; Heywood, Anne; Hill, Arthur; Dobie, Alan; Luke, Keye

Song(s) The World That Only Lovers See [1] (C: Goldsmith, Jerry; L: Shaper, Hal)

Notes [1] Lyric written for exploitation only.

971 ✦ A CHALLENGE FOR ROBIN HOOD
Twentieth Century–Fox, 1968

Musical Score Hughes, Gary

Producer(s) Parkes, Clifford
Director(s) Pennington-Richards, C.M.
Screenwriter(s) Bryan, Peter

Cast Ingham, Barrie; Hayter, James; Greene, Leon; Blythe, Peter; Hamilton, Guy; Bass, Alfie

Song(s) Robin Hood Theme (C/L: Cox, Tony; Brown, Macrae)

Notes A Hammer film.

972 ✦ THE CHAMP
Metro–Goldwyn–Mayer, 1931

Director(s) Vidor, King
Screenwriter(s) Praskins, Leonard; Tuchock, Wanda

Cast Beery, Wallace; Cooper, Jackie; Rich, Irene; Ates, Roscoe; Brophy, Edward S.; Hamilton, Hale; Jones, Marcia Mae; Scott, Jesse

Song(s) Don't Tell Her What Happened to Me (C/L: DeSylva, B.G.)

973 ✦ CHAMPAGNE AND ORCHIDS
Metro–Goldwyn–Mayer, 1935 unproduced

Composer(s) Kern, Jerome
Lyricist(s) Hammerstein II, Oscar

Song(s) When I've Got the Moon (Banjo Song); Champagne and Orchids; Dance Like a Fool; Out on the Broad Prairie (Broad Western Prairie); Singing a Song in Your Arms; Prelude to Champagne and Orchids (inst.)

974 ✦ CHAMPAGNE FOR TWO
Paramount, 1947

Producer(s) Grey, Harry
Director(s) Epstein, Mel

Cast Isabelita

Song(s) The Lamp on the Corner (Farolito) [1] (C: Lara, Augustin; L: Lara, Augustin; Washington, Ned); Chiu, Chiu [2] [3] (C/L: Molinare, Nicanor); Mi Caballo [2] (C/L: Santos, Mario; Morales, Isi); Ho Ho Jose (C/L: Livingston, Jay; Evans, Ray)

Notes Short subject. [1] Washington wrote the English lyrics. Also in LAS VEGAS NIGHTS and TROPIC HOLIDAY. [2] Not written for this film. [3] Also in YOU WERE NEVER LOVELIER.

975 ✦ CHAMPAGNE WALTZ
Paramount, 1937

Composer(s) Ronell, Ann
Lyricist(s) Ronell, Ann

Producer(s) Thompson, Harlan
Director(s) Sutherland, Edward
Screenwriter(s) Hartman, Don; Butler, Frank

Cast MacMurray, Fred; Oakie, Jack; Leiber, Fritz; Swarthout, Gladys; Baker, Benny; Veloz and Yolanda

Song(s) Paradise in Waltz Time (C: Hollander, Frederick; L: Coslow, Sam); When Is a Kiss not a Kiss (C: Lane, Burton; L: Freed, Ralph); The Lorelei; Merry Go Round [4]; Could I Be In Love (C: Daly, William; L: Robin, Leo); Welcome Song [1] (C: Mucke, Franz; L: Boutelje, Phil); Twilight, Twilight [2] [3]; Music of My Heart [3]; Singin'-with-the-Band [3]; Rhythmania [3] (C/L: Coslow, Sam); You're the You [3]; Some Fun, Hey Kid [3]; Say It with Handies [3]; Blue Danube Waltz (C: Strauss, Johann; L: Robin, Leo); The Champagne Waltz [5] (C/L: Conrad, Con; Oakland, Ben; Drake, Milton)

Notes   This movie was first titled MOON OVER VIENNA. The movie also features a short version of "The Lorelei," a German folk song by Frederich Silcher. There is also a few bars of Swarthout and Frank Forrest singing "My Heart At Thy Sweet Voice" by Saint-Saens. [1] This was an old classic with new lyrics. Apparently another "Welcome Song" with music by Wagner and lyrics by Coslow was recorded but not used. [2] This was based on "The Elegy" by Massenet. It was not used in the film. [3] Unused. [4] This is sung in the film by Joaquin Garay. The song was a trunk tune that had received two unauthorized performances in two Radio City Music Hall extravaganzas—CALLIOPE of July 25, 1935 and SEASIDE PARK of August 23, 1934. It also appeared in THE PARSON OF PANAMINT. [5] Not in film. Published for exploitation only.

976 ✦ CHAMPION
United Artists, 1949

Musical Score   Tiomkin, Dimitri

Producer(s)   Kramer, Stanley
Director(s)   Robson, Mark
Screenwriter(s)   Foreman, Carl

Cast   Douglas, Kirk; Maxwell, Marilyn; Kennedy, Arthur; Stewart, Paul; Roman, Ruth; Albright, Luis

Song(s)   Never Be It Said (C: Tiomkin, Dimitri; L: Goldmark, Golde)

977 ✦ CHANCE MEETING
Paramount, 1959

Producer(s)   Deutsch, David
Director(s)   Losey, Joseph
Screenwriter(s)   Barzman, Ben; Lampell, Millard

Cast   Kruger, Hardy; Baker, Stanley; Presle, Micheline

Song(s)   Chance Meeting [1] (C/L: Roberts, Ruth; L: Katz, William)

Notes   [1] Written for exploitation only.

978 ✦ CHANEL SOLITAIRE
United Film Distribution, 1981

Musical Score   Musy, Jean

Producer(s)   Spangler, Larry G.
Director(s)   Kaczender, George
Screenwriter(s)   More, Julian
Source(s)   *Chanel Solitaire* (book) Delay, Claude

Cast   Pisier, Marie-France; Dalton, Timothy; Hauer, Rutger; Black, Karen; Fossey, Brigitte; Frechet, Lella

Song(s)   One and Only (C: Musy, Jean; L: Allen, Peter)

Notes   No cue sheet available.

979 ✦ CHANGE OF HABIT
Universal, 1969

Musical Score   Goldenberg, Billy [1]
Composer(s)   Weisman, Ben
Lyricist(s)   Kaye, Buddy

Producer(s)   Connelly, Joe
Director(s)   Graham, William
Screenwriter(s)   Lee, James; Schweitzer, S.S.; Bercovici, Eric

Cast   Presley, Elvis; Moore, Mary Tyler; McNair, Barbara; Elliott, Jane; Kirk, Lorena; Asner, Edward; Emhardt, Robert; Toomey, Regis; Vincent, Virginia

Song(s)   Change of Habit; Chi Ki, Chi Ki (C/L: Goldenberg, Billy [1]); Have a Happy (C/L: Kaye, Buddy; Weisman, Ben; Fuller, Darryl); Let Us Pray; Rubberneckin' (C: Warren, Bunny; L: Jones, Dory)

Notes   [1] Billed as William Goldenberg.

980 ✦ CHANGE OF HEART (1934)
Fox, 1934

Producer(s)   Sheehan, Winfield
Director(s)   Tinling, James
Screenwriter(s)   Hyland, Frances; Ray, Albert

Cast   Gaynor, Janet; Farrell, Charles

Song(s)   College Stunts (C: Zamecnik, J.S.; L: O'Keefe); So What (C/L: Akst, Harry)

Notes   "My Time Is Your Time" by Leo Dance is also used vocally.

981 ✦ CHANGE OF HEART (1943)

See HIT PARADE OF 1943.

982 ✦ CHANGE OF HEART (1949)
Republic, 1949

Composer(s)   Styne, Jule
Lyricist(s)   Adamson, Harold

Producer(s)   Cohen, Albert J.
Director(s)   Rogell, Albert S.
Screenwriter(s)   Hyland, Frances; Gill, Frank, Jr.

Cast   Carroll, John; Hayward, Susan; Patrick, Gail; Catlett, Walter; Arden, Eve; Freddy Martin and His Orchestra; Count Basie and His Orchestra; Ray McKinley and His Orchestra; The Golden Gate Quartette; Pops and Louis; The Three Cheers; The Music Maids

Song(s)   Limpwitz Little Liver Pills (C/L: Newman, Albert; Gill, F.); Tahm Boom Bah; That's How to Write a Song; Who Took Me Home Last Night [2]; Harlem Sandman; Do These Old Eyes Deceive Me; A Change of Heart [1]; Yankee Doodle Tan (C: Johnson, J.C.; L: Razaf, Andy)

Notes   This is a revised version of HIT PARADE OF 1943. I have not cross referenced songs in both. [1] Also in BEHIND CITY LIGHTS. [2] Also in CASANOVA IN BURLESQUE; THE PHANTOM SPEAKS and THUMBS UP.

983 ◆ A CHANGE OF SEASONS
Twentieth Century–Fox, 1980

Musical Score   Mancini, Henry

Producer(s)   Ransohoff, Martin
Director(s)   Lang, Richard
Screenwriter(s)   Segal, Erich; Kern, Ronni; Segal, Fred

Cast   MacLaine, Shirley; Hopkins, Anthony; Derek, Bo; Brandon, Michael; Hurt, Mary Beth; Winter, Ed

Song(s)   Where Do You Catch the Bus for Tomorrow (C: Mancini, Henry; L: Bergman, Marilyn; Bergman, Alan)

984 ◆ CHAPTER TWO
Columbia, 1979

Musical Score   Hamlisch, Marvin

Producer(s)   Stark, Ray
Director(s)   Moore, Robert
Screenwriter(s)   Simon, Neil
Source(s)   *Chapter Two* (play) Simon, Neil

Cast   Caan, James; Mason, Marsha; Bologna, Joseph; Harper, Valerie; Fudge, Alan

Song(s)   I'm on Your Side (C: Hamlisch, Marvin; L: Sager, Carole Bayer)

Notes   No cue sheet available.

985 ◆ CHARADE
Universal, 1964

Musical Score   Mancini, Henry

Producer(s)   Donen, Stanley
Director(s)   Donen, Stanley
Screenwriter(s)   Stone, Peter

Cast   Hepburn, Audrey; Grant, Cary; Matthau, Walter; Kennedy, George; Coburn, James; Glass, Ned; Marin, Jacques; Bonifas, Paul; Minot, Dominique

Song(s)   Charade (C: Mancini, Henry; L: Mercer, Johnny)

986 ◆ CHARLEY AND THE ANGEL
Disney, 1973

Musical Score   Baker, Buddy

Producer(s)   Anderson, Bill
Director(s)   McEveety, Vincent
Screenwriter(s)   Rogers, Roswell

Source(s)   *The Golden Evenings of Summer* (novel) Stanton, Will

Cast   MacMurray, Fred; Leachman, Cloris; Morgan, Harry; Russell, Kurt; Cody, Kathleen; Van Patten, Vincent; Kolden, Scott; Lindsey, George; Andrews, Edward; Bakalyan, Richard; Nichols, Barbara; Tolsky, Susan

Song(s)   Livin' One Day at a Time [1] (C/L: Tatum, Shane)

Notes   [1] Ed Scott is also given writing credit on credit sheet but not on cue sheet.

987 ◆ CHARLEY-ONE-EYE
Paramount, 1973

Musical Score   Cameron, John

Producer(s)   Swann, James
Director(s)   Chaffey, Don
Screenwriter(s)   Leonard, Keith

Cast   Roundtree, Richard; Thinnes, Roy; Davenport, Nigel

Song(s)   Don't You Wish That It Might Rain (C/L: Cameron, John)

988 ◆ CHARLEY VARRICK
Universal, 1973

Musical Score   Schifrin, Lalo

Producer(s)   Siegel, Don
Director(s)   Siegel, Don
Screenwriter(s)   Rodman, Howard; Riesner, Dean
Source(s)   *The Looters* (novel) Reese, John

Cast   Matthau, Walter; Robinson, Andy; Baker, Joe Don; Farr, Felicia; Vernon, John; North, Sheree; Fell, Norman; Fong, Benson; Schallert, William; Scott, Jacqueline

Song(s)   I Painted Her [1] (C: Mooney, Hal; L: Riesner, Dean); You Can Make a Memory Out of Me (C/L: Schifrin, Lalo; Vance, Paul)

Notes   [1] Also in ROOSTER COGBURN.

989 ◆ CHARLIE CHAN AT THE OPERA
Twentieth Century–Fox, 1936

Composer(s)   Levant, Oscar
Lyricist(s)   Kernell, William

Producer(s)   Stone, John
Director(s)   Humberstone, H. Bruce
Screenwriter(s)   Darling, W. Scott; Belden, Charles
Source(s)   Charlie Chan series (novels) Biggers, Earl Derr

Cast   Oland, Warner; Karloff, Boris; Luke, Keye; Henry, Charlotte; Harrigan, Nedda; Demarest, William

Song(s) Carnival Then Farewell; Carnival—Ah Romantic Love Dream; Carnival—King and Country Call

990 ✦ CHARLIE CHAN AT TREASURE ISLAND
Twentieth Century–Fox, 1939

Producer(s) Wurtzel, Sol M.
Director(s) Foster, Norman
Screenwriter(s) Larkin, John
Source(s) Charlie Chan series (novels) Biggers, Earl Derr

Cast Toler, Sidney; Romero, Cesar; Moore, Pauline; Yung, Sen; Dumbrille, Douglass; Blane, Sally; Heydt, Louis Jean

Song(s) Laau (Hawaiaan Dance) (C/L: Hoopii Jr., Sol); Pakalana (C/L: Hoopii Jr., Sol)

991 ✦ CHARLIE CHAN IN PANAMA
Twentieth Century–Fox, 1940

Producer(s) Wurtzel, Sol M.
Director(s) Foster, Norman
Screenwriter(s) Larkin, John; Ziffren, Lester
Source(s) Charlie Chan series (novels) Biggers, Earl Derr

Cast Toler, Sidney; Rogers, Jean; Atwill, Lionel; Nash, Mary; Yung, Sen; Richmond, Kane; LaRue, Jack; Richards, Addison

Song(s) Negra Mia (C/L: Ruffino, Carlos); Vereda Tropical (C/L: Curiel, Gonzalo)

Notes It is not known if either of these were written for this film.

992 ✦ CHARLIE CHAN IN RIO
Twentieth Century–Fox, 1941

Composer(s) Warren, Harry
Lyricist(s) Gordon, Mack

Producer(s) Wurtzel, Sol M.
Director(s) Lachman, Harry
Screenwriter(s) Engel, Samuel G.; Ziffren, Lester
Source(s) Charlie Chan series (novels) Biggers, Earl Derr

Cast Dahli, Jacqueline [1]; Toler, Sidney; Hughes, Mary Beth; Wright Jr., Cobina; North, Ted; Jory, Victor; Yung, Sen; Derr, Richard

Song(s) They Met in Rio (A Midnight Serenade) [2]; I Yi, Yi, Yi, Yi (I Like You Very Much) [2]

Notes [1] Dubbed by Andrea Marsh. [2] Also in THAT NIGHT IN RIO.

993 ✦ CHARLIE CHAN IN SHANGHAI
Twentieth Century–Fox, 1935

Producer(s) Stone, John
Director(s) Tinling, James
Screenwriter(s) Lowe, Edward T.; Fairlie, Gerard
Source(s) Charlie Chan series (novels) Biggers, Earl Derr

Cast Oland, Warner; Hervey, Irene; Locher, Charles [1]; Hicks, Russell; Luke, Keye; Hobbes, Halliwell

Song(s) The Prince and Ming Lo Fu (C/L: Sanders, Troy)

Notes [1] Changed name to Jon Hall.

994 ✦ CHARLIE CHAN'S COURAGE
Fox, 1934

Producer(s) Stone, John
Director(s) Hadden, George
Screenwriter(s) Miller, Seton I.
Source(s) Charlie Chan series (novels) Biggers, Earl Derr

Cast Oland, Warner; Leyton, Drue; Woods, Donald

Song(s) Holly's Song (C/L: Jenks, Si)

995 ✦ CHARLIE MCCARTHY, DETECTIVE
Universal, 1939

Producer(s) Tuttle, Frank
Director(s) Tuttle, Frank
Screenwriter(s) Eliscu, Edward

Cast McCarthy, Charlie; Bergen, Edgar; Cummings, Robert; Moore, Constance; Sutton, John; Calhern, Louis; Kennedy, Edgar; Hymer, Warren; Hinds, Samuel S.

Song(s) Almost (C: Oakland, Ben; L: Lerner, Sam); Charlie McCarthy, Detective (C/L: Block, Hal; Press, Jacques; Cherkose, Eddie); How Was I to Know [1] (C: Press, Jacques; L: Cherkose, Eddie)

Notes [1] Used instrumentally only.

996 ✦ CHARLIE, THE LONESOME COUGAR
Disney, 1967

Musical Score Marks, Franklyn

Producer(s) Hibler, Winston
Screenwriter(s) Speirs, Jack

Cast Charlie the Lonesome Cougar; Brown, Ron; Wilson, Jim; Sample, Lewis; Russell, Bryan [2]; Wallace, Linda; Peterson, Clifford; Moller, Edward C.; Allen, Rex

Song(s) About Charlie [1] (C: Marks, Franklyn; L: Speirs, Jack; Hibler, Winston)

Notes [1] Hibler is listed on the cue sheet but not the credits. [2] Spelled Brian Russell on the credits sheet.

997 ✦ CHARLOTTE'S WEB
Paramount, 1973

Composer(s) Sherman, Richard M.; Sherman, Robert B.
Lyricist(s) Sherman, Richard M.; Sherman, Robert B.

Producer(s) Barbera, Joseph; Hanna, William
Director(s) Nichols, Charles; Takamoto, Iwao
Screenwriter(s) Hammer, Earl, Jr.
Source(s) *Charlotte's Web* (novel) White, E.B.
Voices Reynolds, Debbie; Lynde, Paul; Gibson, Henry; Allen, Rex; Madden, Dave; Moorehead, Agnes; White, William B.

Song(s) There Must Be Something More; I Can Talk; Chin Up; We've Got Lots in Common; Deep in the Dark; Charlotte's Web; Mother Earth and Father Time; A Veritable Smorgasboard; Zuckerman's Famous Pig

Notes Animated feature.

998 ✦ THE CHARM SCHOOL

See COLLEGIATE.

999 ✦ CHARRO!
National General, 1969

Musical Score Montenegro, Hugo
Composer(s) Montenegro, Hugo
Lyricist(s) Bergman, Alan; Bergman, Marilyn

Producer(s) Warren, Charles Marquis
Director(s) Warren, Charles Marquis
Screenwriter(s) Warren, Charles Marquis

Cast Presley, Elvis; Balin, Ina; French, Victor; Sikking, James B.; Werle, Barbara; Sturges, Solomon

Song(s) Charro! (C: Montenegro, Hugo; L: Bergman, Alan; Bergman, Marilyn); Charro (C/L: Strange, Billy; Davis, Scott)

Notes No cue sheet available.

1000 ✦ CHARTROOSE CABOOSE
Universal, 1960

Musical Score Calker, Darrell

Producer(s) Dougherty, Stanley W.
Director(s) Peterson, Rod
Screenwriter(s) Reynolds, William "Red"

Cast McGreevey, Michael; Bee, Molly; Cooper, Ben; Buchanan, Edgar; Whitehead, O.Z.; Pickens, Slim

Song(s) Chartroose Caboose (C/L: Atkerson, Paul; Peterson, Rod); Night, Night (C/L: Liebert, William; Atkerson, Paul; Peterson, Rod)

1001 ✦ CHASING RAINBOWS
Metro–Goldwyn–Mayer, 1930

Composer(s) Ager, Milton
Lyricist(s) Yellen, Jack

Director(s) Riesner, Charles F.
Screenwriter(s) Root, Wells; Riesner, Charles F.; Hopkins, Robert E.; Nicholson, Kenyon; Boasberg, Al

Cast Love, Bessie; King, Charles; Benny, Jack; Arthur, George K.; Moran, Polly; Lee, Gwen; Martan, Nita; Phillips, Eddie; Dressler, Marie; Troubetzkoy, Youcca

Song(s) The Woman in the Shoe [1] (C: Brown, Nacio Herb; L: Freed, Arthur); Happy Days Are Here Again [2]; Lucky Me, and Loveable You; Do I Know What I'm Doing; Everybody Tap; Poor but Honest (C: Edwards, Gus; L: Murray, John T.); Love Ain't Nothing but the Blues (C: Alter, Louis; L: Goodwin, Joe); Dynamic Personality (C/L: Fisher, Fred; Montgomery, Reggie; Ward, Edward)

Notes [1] In foreign prints only. Some of the other songs are not in the foreign version. [2] Also in RAIN OR SHINE (Columbia).

1002 ✦ CHATTERBOX (1943)
Republic, 1943

Composer(s) Akst, Harry
Lyricist(s) Meyer, Sol

Producer(s) Cohen, Albert J.
Director(s) Santley, Joseph
Screenwriter(s) Brown, George Carleton; Gill, Frank, Jr.

Cast Brown, Joe E.; Canova, Judy; Lane, Rosemary; Hubbard, John; Clute, Chester; Vogan, Emmett; Schilling, Gus; Jeffreys, Anne; Byron, George

Song(s) Welcome to Victory Ranch; Mad About Him, Sad Without Him, How Can I Be Glad Without Him Blues [1] (C/L: Markes, Larry; Charles, Dick); Sweet Lucy Brown (C/L: Rene, Lou; Rene, Otis); Why Can't I Sing a Love Song [2]; Guy From Albuquerque [3]

Notes [1] Also in FOLLOW THE BOYS (Universal). [2] Also in ROSIE THE RIVETER. [3] Sheet music only.

1003 ✦ CHATTERBOX (1977)
American International, 1977

Musical Score Karger, Fred

Producer(s) Curtis, Bruce Cohn
Director(s) DeSimone, Tom
Screenwriter(s) Rosin, Mark; Yonemoto, Norman

Cast Rialson, Candice; Gelman, Larry; Kean, Jane; Bullington, Perry

Song(s) Sad Eyes (C/L: Sedaka, Neil; Cody, Phil)

Notes No cue sheet available.

1004 ✦ CHE!
Twentieth Century–Fox, 1969

Musical Score Schifrin, Lalo

Producer(s) Bartlett, Sy
Director(s) Fleischer, Richard
Screenwriter(s) Wilson, Michael; Bartlett, Sy

Cast Sharif, Omar; Palance, Jack; Danova, Cesare; Loggia, Robert; Strode, Woody; Luna, Barbara; Silvera, Frank; Troupe, Tom

Song(s) Tiempo Pasado (C/L: Schifrin, Lalo)

1005 ✦ CHECK AND DOUBLE CHECK
RKO, 1930

Producer(s) LeBaron, William
Director(s) Brown, Melville
Screenwriter(s) Kalmar, Bert; Ruby, Harry

Cast Godsen, Freeman F.; Correll, Charles J.; Carol, Sue; Rich, Irene; Harolde, Ralf; Martindel, Edward; Duke Ellington and His Cotton Club Orchestra; Morton, Charles [1]

Song(s) Three Little Words (C: Ruby, Harry; L: Kalmar, Bert); Old Man Blues (C: Ellington, Duke; L: Mills, Irving); Ring Dem Bells (C: Ellington, Duke; L: Mills, Irving); Nobody Knows But de Lawd (C: Ruby, Harry; L: Kalmar, Bert)

Notes The cue sheet does not differentiate between vocals and instrumentals. It titles the Ellington song "Awn-Awn" ("Awa Blues" in the script) and "Ring Dem Bells" does not appear. [1] Dubbed by Bing Crosby.

1006 ✦ CHECKERED FLAG OR CRASH
Universal, 1977

Musical Score Mandel, Mel; Sachs, Norman

Producer(s) Weintraub, Fred; Heller, Paul
Director(s) Gibson, Alan
Screenwriter(s) Allin, Michael

Cast Baker, Joe Don; Sarandon, Susan; Hagman, Larry; Vint, Alan; Jones, Parnelli

Song(s) Checkered Flag or Crash (C: Sachs, Norman; L: Mandel, Mel)

1007 ✦ CHECK YOUR GUNS
Eagle Lion, 1947

Musical Score Greene, Walter

Producer(s) Thomas, Jerry
Director(s) Taylor, Ray
Screenwriter(s) O'Donnell, Joseph

Cast Dean, Eddie; Ates, Roscoe; Gates, Nancy; Cambro, George

Song(s) Miserable Ornery Ole Coyote (C/L: Dean, Eddie; Blair, Hal); God's Little Lanterns (C/L: Gates, Pete); Moseyin' Along (C/L: Gates, Pete)

1008 ✦ CHEECH AND CHONG'S NEXT MOVIE
Universal, 1980

Producer(s) Brown, C. and C.
Director(s) Chong, Thomas
Screenwriter(s) Marin, Richard "Cheech"; Chong, Thomas

Cast Marin, Richard "Cheech"; Chong, Thomas; Guerrero, Evelyn; Kennedy, Betty; Kramer, Sy

Song(s) Hell on Wheels (C: Davis, Mark; L: Runnells, Rochelle); My Scrotum (C/L: Marin, Richard "Cheech"); Mexican American (C/L: Marin, Richard "Cheech"); Beaners (C/L: Chong, Thomas); Aztec Chant (C/L: Davis, Mark)

1009 ✦ CHEECH AND CHONG'S UP IN SMOKE

See UP IN SMOKE.

1010 ✦ CHEER UP AND SMILE
Twentieth Century–Fox, 1930

Composer(s) Klages, Raymond
Lyricist(s) Greer, Jesse

Director(s) Lanfield, Sidney
Screenwriter(s) Green, Howard J.

Cast Lee, Dixie; Lake, Arthur; Baclanova, Olga; Judels, Charles; Smith, Jack

Song(s) The Scamp of the Campus; Where Can You Be? [1]; You May Not Like It But It's a Great Idea; Shindig; When You Look in My Eyes

Notes No cue sheet available. [1] Also in ALONE WITH YOU.

1011 ✦ THE CHEROKEE STRIP
Warner Brothers–First National, 1937

Musical Score Jackson, Howard
Composer(s) Jerome, M.K.
Lyricist(s) Scholl, Jack

Producer(s) Foy, Bryan
Director(s) Smith, Noel
Screenwriter(s) Watson, Joseph K.; Ward, Luci
Source(s) "Cherokee Strip Stampeders" (story) Repp, Ed Earl

Cast Foran, Dick; Bryan, Jane; Bupp, Tommy; Cobb, Edmund; Crehan, Joseph

Song(s) My Little Buckaroo [1]; Along the Old Frontier; Down the Cottonwood Trail

Notes Released in Great Britain as STRANGE LAWS. [1] Also in DON'T FENCE ME IN (Republic), BROTHER ORCHID, SONGS OF THE RANGE and WEST OF THE ROCKIES.

1012 ✦ CHEYENNE
Warner Brothers, 1947

Musical Score Steiner, Max
Lyricist(s) Koehler, Ted
Choreographer(s) Prinz, LeRoy

Producer(s) Buckner, Robert
Director(s) Walsh, Raoul
Screenwriter(s) LeMay, Alan; Williamson, Thames

Cast Morgan, Dennis; Wyman, Jane; Paige, Janis; Bennett, Bruce; Kennedy, Arthur; Hale, Alan; MacLane, Barton

Song(s) Going Back to Old Cheyenne (C: Steiner, Max); I'm So in Love (I Don't Know What I'm Doin') (C: Jerome, M.K.)

1013 ✦ CHICAGO BEN
Twentieth Century–Fox, 1938

Producer(s) Black, Edward
Director(s) Varnel, Marcel
Screenwriter(s) Edgar, Marion; Guest, Val; Orton, J.O.C.

Cast Hay, Will; Kennedy, Edgar; Bupp, Tommy; Burns, David; Duprez, Fred; Pola, Eddie; McDowall, Roddy

Song(s) Happy and Free (C: Williams)

Notes A Gainsborough picture distributed in the U.S. by Twentieth Century–Fox. Titled HEY HEY U.S.A. in Great Britain. Edgar Kennedy and David Burns are not to be confused with the American actors of the same name.

1014 ✦ CHICAGO SYNDICATE
Columbia, 1955

Director(s) Sears, Fred F.
Screenwriter(s) Hoffman, Joseph

Cast O'Keefe, Dennis; Lane, Abbe; Stewart, Paul; Cugat, Xavier; Hayes, Allison; Cutting, Richard

Song(s) Cuban Mambo (C: Cugat, Xavier; L: Argulo, Rafael); Cumparsita Mambo (C/L: Rodrigues; Matos, G.H.; Du Fault, Rudy); One at a Time (C/L: Raleigh, Ben; Wayne, Bernie); Greek Bolero (C/L: Spartacos, John)

Notes No cue sheet available.

1015 ✦ CHICKEN WAGON FAMILY
Twentieth Century–Fox, 1939

Producer(s) Wurtzel, Sol M.
Director(s) Leeds, Herbert I.
Screenwriter(s) Shore, Viola Brothers
Source(s) *Chicken-Wagon Family* (novel) Benefield, Barry

Cast Withers, Jane; Carrillo, Leo; Weaver, Marjorie; Byington, Spring; Richmond, Kane; Cavanaugh, Hobart; MacFadden, Hamilton; Palange, Inez

Song(s) The Daughter of Mademoiselle (C: Akst, Harry; L: Clare, Sidney)

1016 ✦ A CHILD IS WAITING
United Artists, 1962

Musical Score Gold, Ernest

Producer(s) Langner, Philip
Director(s) Cassavetes, John
Screenwriter(s) Mann, Abby
Source(s) (teleplay) Mann, Abby

Cast Lancaster, Burt; Garland, Judy; Rowlands, Gena; Ritchey, Bruce; Tierney, Lawrence; Hill, Steven; Wilson, Elizabeth

Song(s) Snowflake (C/L: Kurtz, Marjorie)

1017 ✦ CHILD OF MANHATTAN
Columbia, 1933

Director(s) Buzzell, Edward
Screenwriter(s) Purcell, Gertrude
Source(s) *Child of Manhattan* (play) Sturges, Preston

Cast Carroll, Nancy; Boles, John; Jones, Buck; Ralph, Jessie; Darwell, Jane

Song(s) Take Everything But You [1] (C/L: Abrahams, Maurice; Colby, Elmer [2])

Notes [1] Used instrumentally only. It was not written for this picture. [2] Pseudonym of B.G. DeSylva, Lew Brown and Ray Henderson.

1018 ✦ CHILDREN OF DREAMS
Warner Brothers, 1931

Composer(s) Romberg, Sigmund
Lyricist(s) Hammerstein II, Oscar

Director(s) Crosland, Alan
Screenwriter(s) Hammerstein II, Oscar

Cast Gregory, Paul; Schilling, Margaret; Patricola, Tom; Winninger, Charles; Winston, Bruce; Byron, Marion; Skipworth, Alison; Alberni, Luis; Litel, John; Boley, May; Porcasi, Paul

Song(s) Fruit Pickers' Song; Oh, Couldn't I Love that Girl; Children of Dreams; Sleeping Beauty; If I Had a

Girl Like You; That Rare Romance; Yes, Sir; Tango D'Amour

Notes No cue sheet available. Hirshhorn in *The Hollywood Musical* also lists songs "Her Professor" and "Seek Love."

1019 ✦ CHILDREN OF PLEASURE
Metro–Goldwyn–Mayer, 1930

Composer(s) Fisher, Fred
Lyricist(s) Rice, Andy
Choreographer(s) Lee, Sammy

Director(s) Beaumont, Harry
Screenwriter(s) Wilbur, Crane
Source(s) (play) Wilbur, Crane

Cast Gray, Lawrence; Rubin, Benny; Johnson, Helen; Gibson, Wynne

Song(s) A Couple of Birds (C: Montgomery, Reggie; L: Johnson, Howard; Ward, George); Dust; Girl Trouble (L: Fisher, Fred); Better Things of Life; Leave It That Way; The Whole Darned Thing's For You (C: Ahlert, Fred E.; L: Turk, Roy); Dynamic Personality [1] (C/L: Fisher, Fred; Ward, George; Montgomery, Reggie)

Notes [1] Not used.

1020 ✦ THE CHILDREN OF SANCHEZ
Lone Star Pictures, 1978

Musical Score Mangione, Chuck

Producer(s) Bartlett, Hall
Director(s) Bartlett, Hall
Screenwriter(s) Zavattini, Cesare; Bartlett, Hall
Source(s) (book) Lewis, Oscar

Cast Quinn, Anthony; Frerer, Lupita; Giallelis, Stathis; Mendez, Lucia; Quinn, Duncan; Del Rio, Dolores; Jurado, Katy; Tarso, Ignacio Lopez; Montejo, Carmen

Song(s) The Children of Sanchez (C/L: Mangione, Chuck); Lullaby (C/L: Mangione, Chuck)

Notes No cue sheet available.

1021 ✦ CHILDREN OF THE RITZ
Warner Brothers–First National, 1929

Director(s) Dillon, John Francis
Screenwriter(s) Heilbron, Adelaide
Source(s) "Children of the Ritz" (story) Woolrich, Cornell

Cast Mackaill, Dorothy; Mulhall, Jack; Ford, James; Carlyle, Richard; Hall, Evelyn; McGuire, Kathryn; Crayne, Frank

Song(s) Some Sweet Day (C: Shilkret, Nathaniel; L: Pollack, Lew)

Notes No cue sheet available.

1022 ✦ CHILD'S PLAY
United Artists, 1988

Musical Score Renzetti, Joe

Producer(s) Kirschner, David
Director(s) Holland, Tom
Screenwriter(s) Mancini, Don; Lafia, John; Holland, Tom

Cast Hicks, Catherine; Sarandon, Chris; Vincent, Alex; Dourif, Brad; Manoff, Dinah

Song(s) Second Sight (C/L: Kitah, D.; Darling, Denver); I'm Hanging (C/L: Boyle, B.); Is It Really Love (C/L: Bell, R.; Lanning, M.)

1023 ✦ CHINA GATE
Twentieth Century–Fox, 1957

Producer(s) Fuller, Samuel
Director(s) Fuller, Samuel
Screenwriter(s) Fuller, Samuel

Cast Barry, Gene; Dickinson, Angie; Cole, Nat "King"; Dubov, Paul; Van Cleef, Lee; Givot, George; Milton, Gerald

Song(s) China Gate (C: Young, Victor; L: Adamson, Harold)

1024 ✦ CHINA GIRL
Vestron, 1987

Musical Score Delia, Joe

Producer(s) Nizik, Michael
Director(s) Ferrara, Abel
Screenwriter(s) St. John, Nicholas

Cast Russo, James; Panebianco, Richard; Chang, Sari; Caruso, David; Wong, Russell; Chin, Joe; Malina, Judith; Hong, James; Miano, Robert; Hipp, Paul; Chan, Doreen

Song(s) Compulsion (C/L: Cioe, Crispin; Delia, Joe; Marshall, Sherryl); Hot and Bothered (C/L: Delia, Joe; Ferrara, Abel; Hipp, Paul); Chinatown Tonight (C/L: Delia, Joe; Ferrara, Abel); Midnight for You (C/L: Hipp, Paul)

Notes No cue sheet available.

1025 ✦ CHINA PASSAGE
RKO, 1937

Musical Score Steiner, Max

Producer(s) Reid, Cliff
Director(s) Killy, Edward
Screenwriter(s) Hartmann, Edmund L.; Bren, J. Robert

Cast Worth, Constance; Haworth, Vinton; Fenton, Leslie; Jones, Gordon; Craig, Alec; Elliott, Dick; Thomas, Frank M.; Irving, George; Gilbert, Billy; Compton, Joyce; Ahn, Philip

Song(s)   I Never Saw a Better Night [1] (C: Gensler, Lewis E.; L: Mercer, Johnny)

Notes   [1] Also in OLD MAN RHYTHM.

1026 ✦ CHINA SEAS
Metro–Goldwyn–Mayer, 1935

Musical Score   Stothart, Herbert

Producer(s)   Lewin, Albert
Director(s)   Garnett, Tay
Screenwriter(s)   Furthman, Jules; McGuinness, James Kevin
Source(s)   *China Seas* (novel) Garstin, Crosbie

Cast   Gable, Clark; Harlow, Jean; Beery, Wallace; Russell, Rosalind; Stone, Lewis; Smith, C. Aubrey; Digges, Dudley; Benchley, Robert

Song(s)   China Seas [1] (C: Brown, Nacio Herb; L: Freed, Arthur)

Notes   No cue sheet available. Song may have been written for exploitation. [1] Same music as "By the Taj Mahal" in STUDENT TOUR.

1027 ✦ THE CHINA SYNDROME
Columbia, 1979

Producer(s)   Douglas, Michael
Director(s)   Bridges, James
Screenwriter(s)   Gray, Mike; Cook, T.S.; Bridges, James

Cast   Fonda, Jane; Lemmon, Jack; Douglas, Michael; Brady, Scott; Hampton, James; Donat, Peter; Brimley, Wilford; Herd, Richard

Song(s)   Somewhere in Between (C/L: Bishop, Stephen)

Notes   No cue sheet available.

1028 ✦ CHIP AND DALE CARTOONS
Disney

Song(s)   Chip and Dale (C: Wallace, Oliver; L: George, Gil)

Notes   Cartoons.

1029 ✦ CHIP OFF THE OLD BLOCK
Universal, 1944

Composer(s)   Shannon, Grace
Lyricist(s)   Crago, Bill
Choreographer(s)   Da Pron, Louis

Producer(s)   Burton, Bernard W.
Director(s)   Lamont, Charles
Screenwriter(s)   Townsend, Leo; Conrad, Eugene

Cast   O'Connor, Donald; Ryan, Peggy; Blyth, Ann; Kupperman, Joel; Vinson, Helen; Broderick, Helen; Treacher, Arthur; Knowles, Patric; Bromberg, J. Edward; Truex, Ernest; Gombell, Minna

Song(s)   The Sperling Prep Song; Sailor Song (C/L: Conrad, Eugene; James, Inez; Miller, Sidney); It's Mighty Nice to Have Met You; My Song [2] (C: Henderson, Ray; L: Brown, Lew); Love Is Like Music (C/L: James, Inez; Miller, Sidney; Schwarzwald, Milton); Make Way for a Smile (C/L: James, Inez; Miller, Sidney); I Gotta Give My Feet a Break (C/L: James, Inez; Miller, Sidney); The Captain's Kids (C/L: James, Inez; Miller, Sidney); I'll Make Love to You with a Song; Is It Good or Is It Bad (C/L: Tobias, Charles); You Look Good to Me [1] (C/L: Pepper, Buddy; James, Inez; Miller, Sidney)

Notes   [1] Used instrumentally only. [2] Written in 1931.

1030 ✦ CHIP OF THE FLYING U
Universal, 1940

Composer(s)   Rosen, Milton
Lyricist(s)   Carter, Everett

Director(s)   Staub, Ralph
Screenwriter(s)   Rhine, Larry; Bennison, Andrew

Cast   Brown, Johnny Mack; Baker, Bob; Knight, Fuzzy; Weston, Doris; Taylor, Forrest; The Texas Rangers

Song(s)   Mr. Moon; Ride On; Git Along

Notes   No cue sheet available.

1031 ✦ CHISUM
Warner Brothers, 1970

Musical Score   Frontiere, Dominic
Composer(s)   Frontiere, Dominic

Producer(s)   Fenady, Andrew J.
Director(s)   McLaglen, Andrew V.
Screenwriter(s)   Fenady, Andrew J.
Source(s)   "Chisum & the Lincoln County Cattle War" (story) Fenady, Andrew J.

Cast   Wayne, John; Tucker, Forrest; Knowles, Patric; Deuel, Geoffrey; McMyler, Pamela; Johnson, Ben; Corbett, Glenn; George, Christopher

Song(s)   Chisum (L: Fenady, Andrew J.); Turn Me Around (L: Gimbel, Norman)

1032 ✦ CHITTY CHITTY BANG BANG
United Artists, 1968

Musical Score   Sherman, Robert B.; Sherman, Richard M.
Composer(s)   Sherman, Robert B.; Sherman, Richard M.
Lyricist(s)   Sherman, Robert B.; Sherman, Richard M.
Choreographer(s)   Breaux, Marc; Wood, Dee Dee

Producer(s)   Broccoli, Albert R.
Director(s)   Hughes, Ken
Screenwriter(s)   Dahl, Roald; Hughes, Ken
Source(s)   *Chitty Chitty Bang Bang* (novel) Fleming, Ian

Cast Van Dyke, Dick; Hall, Adrian; Ripley, Heather; Howes, Sally Ann; Justice, James Robertson; Frobe, Gert; Jeffries, Lionel; Hill, Benny; Quayle, Anna; Helpmann, Robert

Song(s) You Two; Toot Sweets; Hushabye Mountain; Me Ol' Bamboo; Chitty Chitty Bang Bang; Truly Scrumptious; This Lovely Lonely Man; Posh; Roses of Success; Hushabye Mountain; Chuchi Face; Doll on a Music Box; Funfair [1]; Vulgarian March [1]

Notes [1] Sheet music only.

1033 ✦ THE CHOCOLATE SOLDIER
Metro–Goldwyn–Mayer, 1941

Composer(s) Straus, Oscar
Lyricist(s) Stange, Stanislaus
Choreographer(s) Matray, Ernst

Producer(s) Saville, Victor
Director(s) Del Ruth, Roy
Screenwriter(s) Lee, Leonard; Winter, Keith
Source(s) *The Guardsman* (play) Molnar, Ferenc

Cast Eddy, Nelson; Stevens, Rise; Bruce, Nigel; Bates, Florence

Song(s) My Hero [1]; Alexius the Heroic; Evening Star [4] (C: Wagner, Richard; L: Kahn, Gus); Sympathy [2]; Seek the Spy [1]; While My Lady Sleeps (C: Kaper, Bronislau; L: Kahn, Gus); Finale Act I [1]; The Letter Song [3] (L: Freed, Ralph); The Chocolate Soldier [1]; Finale (C: Stothart, Herbert; Kaper, Bronislau; L: Kahn, Gus); Tiralala [5]; The Trout [6] (C: Salabert, Franz; L: Freed, Ralph)

Notes The Straus/Stange songs are from the operetta THE CHOCOLATE SOLDIER. There are also vocals of "Mon Coeur S'Ouvre a Ta Voix" by Saint-Saens; "Song of the Flea" by Moussorgsky; "La Ci Darem La Mano" from Mozart's DON GIOVANNI. [1] Music adapted by Herbert Stothart and Bronislau Kaper. Lyric adapted by Gus Kahn. [2] Music adapted by Bronislau Kaper and lyrics by Gus Kahn. [3] Music adapted by Herbert Stothart and Bronislau Kaper. [4] Same music used for song of same name with lyrics by Jack Brooks in Universal's THAT'S THE SPIRIT. [5] Sheet music only. [6] Not used.

1034 ✦ CHOOSE ME
Island Alive, 1984

Producer(s) Pfeiffer, Carolyn; Blocker, David
Director(s) Rudolph, Alan
Screenwriter(s) Rudolph, Alan

Cast Carradine, Keith; Warren, Lesley Ann; Bujold, Genevieve; Bauchau, Patrick; Chong, Rae Dawn; Larroquette, John

Song(s) Choose Me (C/L: Vandross, Luther; Miller, Marcus; Masser, Michael; Weil, Cynthia)

Notes No cue sheet available.

1035 ✦ CHOOSE YOUR PARTNERS

See TWO GIRLS ON BROADWAY.

1036 ✦ CHORUS CALL
Entertainment Ventures, 1978

Musical Score Shepherd, Antonio

Producer(s) Williams, Allen; Freeman, Davis
Director(s) Shepherd, Antonio
Screenwriter(s) Shepherd, Antonio

Cast Parker, Kay; Rains, Darby Lloyd; London, Susan; Anne, Beth; Pepe

Song(s) Chorus Call (C/L: Shepherd, Antonio); Six Tits in a Row (C/L: Shepherd, Antonio)

Notes No cue sheet available.

1037 ✦ A CHORUS LINE
Columbia, 1985

Composer(s) Hamlisch, Marvin
Lyricist(s) Kleban, Edward
Choreographer(s) Hornaday, Jeffrey

Producer(s) Feuer, Cy; Martin, Ernest H.
Director(s) Attenborough, Richard
Screenwriter(s) Schulman, Arnold
Source(s) *A Chorus Line* (musical) Hamlisch, Marvin; Kirkwood, James; Dante, Nicholas; Kleban, Edward

Cast Blevins, Michael; Borges, Yamil; Boyd, Jan Gan; Brown, Sharon; Burge, Gregg; Douglas, Michael; English, Cameron; Fields, Tony; Fosse, Nicole; Frederick, Vicki; Jones, Janet; Johnston, Michelle; Landers, Audrey; Klinger, Pam; Mann, Terrence; McGowan, Charles; Reed, Alyson; Ross, Justin; Savage, Blane; Wiest, Matt

Song(s) Surprise, Surprise [1]; Let Me Dance for You [1]; I Hope I Get It; Who Am I Anyway?; I Can Do That; At the Ballet; Nothing; Dance: Ten, Looks: Three; What I Did for Love; One

Notes [1] Written for film version. All other songs from Broadway show.

1038 ✦ CHRISTINA
Fox, 1929

Director(s) Howard, William K.
Screenwriter(s) Lauren, S.K.

Cast Gaynor, Janet; Morton, Charles; Dorraine, Lucy; Schildkraut, Joseph; Cording, Harry

Song(s) Christina (C/L: Conrad, Con; Gottler, Archie; Mitchell, Sidney D.)

1039 ◆ CHRISTMAS HOLIDAY
Universal, 1944

Producer(s) Jackson, Felix
Director(s) Siodmak, Robert
Screenwriter(s) Mankiewicz, Herman J.
Source(s) *Christmas Holiday* (novel) Maugham, W. Somerset

Cast Durbin, Deanna; Kelly, Gene; Whorf, Richard; Harens, Dean; George, Gladys; Sondergaard, Gale; Bruce, David

Song(s) Spring Will Be a Little Late This Year (C/L: Loesser, Frank); Always [1] (C/L: Berlin, Irving)

Notes [1] Not written for this film.

1040 ◆ CHRISTMAS IN CONNECTICUT
Warner Brothers, 1945

Musical Score Hollander, Frederick

Producer(s) Jacobs, William
Director(s) Godfrey, Peter
Screenwriter(s) Houser, Lionel; Comandini, Adele

Cast Stanwyck, Barbara; Greenstreet, Sydney; Morgan, Dennis; Gardiner, Reginald; Sakall, S.Z.; O'Connor, Una

Song(s) The Wish That I Wish Tonight (C: Jerome, M.K.; L: Scholl, Jack)

1041 ◆ CHUBASCO
Warner Brothers, 1968

Musical Score Lava, William
Composer(s) Lava, William
Lyricist(s) Conrad, William

Producer(s) Conrad, William
Director(s) Milner, Allen H.
Screenwriter(s) Milner, Allen H.

Cast Jones, Christopher; Strasberg, Susan; Sothern, Ann; Totter, Audrey; Foster, Preston; Egan, Richard

Song(s) Chubasco Queridinho (C/L: Beelby, Malcolm; Serrano, Louis Duprat); If It's Love; To Love You

1042 ◆ CHU CHU AND THE PHILLY FLASH
Twentieth Century–Fox, 1981

Musical Score Rugolo, Pete

Producer(s) Weston, Jay
Director(s) Rich, David Lowell
Screenwriter(s) Dana, Barbara

Cast Arkin, Alan; Burnett, Carol; Warden, Jack; Aiello, Danny; Arkin, Adam; Glover, Danny; Buzzi, Ruth; Scotti, Vito; Jacobi, Lou

Song(s) Oh Baby (C/L: Arkin, Alan)

1043 ◆ CIGARETTE GIRL
Columbia, 1947

Composer(s) Fisher, Doris; Roberts, Allan
Lyricist(s) Fisher, Doris; Roberts, Allan

Producer(s) Bloom, William
Director(s) Fritsch, Gunther V.
Screenwriter(s) Mortiz, Henry K.

Cast Brooks, Leslie; Lloyd, Jimmy; Donath, Ludwig; Russ Morgan and His Orchestra

Song(s) It's All in the Mind; How Can You Tell [2]; They Won't Let Me Sing; Honeymoon on a Dime; The More We Get Together [1]

Notes [1] Based on "Ach Du Lieber Augustin." [2] Also in I SURRENDER DEAR.

1044 ◆ CIMARRON
Metro–Goldwyn–Mayer, 1961

Musical Score Waxman, Franz

Producer(s) Grainger, Edmund
Director(s) Mann, Anthony
Screenwriter(s) Schulman, Arnold
Source(s) *Cimarron* (novel) Ferber, Edna

Cast Ford, Glenn; Schell, Maria; Baxter, Anne; O'Connell, Arthur; Tamblyn, Russ; McCambridge, Mercedes; Morrow, Vic; Keith, Robert; McGraw, Charles; Morgan, Henry (Harry); Opatoshu, David; MacMahon, Aline; Darvas, Lili; Buchanan, Edgar; Wickes, Mary; Dano, Royal

Song(s) Cimarron (C: Waxman, Franz; L: Webster, Paul Francis)

1045 ◆ THE CINCINNATI KID
Metro–Goldwyn–Mayer, 1966

Musical Score Schifrin, Lalo

Producer(s) Ransohoff, Martin
Director(s) Jewison, Norman
Screenwriter(s) Lardner Jr., Ring; Southern, Terry
Source(s) *The Cincinnati Kid* (novel) Jessup, Richard

Cast McQueen, Steve; Robinson, Edward G.; Ann-Margaret; Malden, Karl; Weld, Tuesday; Blondell, Joan; Torn, Rip; Weston, Jack; Calloway, Cab; Corey, Jeff

Song(s) Nobody Knows the Way I Feel This Mornin' (C/L: Delaney, Tom; Delaney, Pearl); The Cincinnati Kid (C: Schifrin, Lalo; L: Cochran, Dorcas)

1046 ✦ CINDERELLA
Disney, 1950

Musical Score Wallace, Oliver; Smith, Paul J.
Composer(s) David, Mack; Livingston, Jerry; Hoffman, Al
Lyricist(s) David, Mack; Livingston, Jerry; Hoffman, Al

Producer(s) Sharpsteen, Ben
Director(s) Jackson, Wilfred; Luske, Hamilton; Geronimi, Clyde
Screenwriter(s) Peed, William; Sears, Ted; Brightman, Homer; Anderson, Ken; Penner, Erdman; Hibler, Winston; Reeves, Harry; Rinaldi, Joe
Source(s) "Cinderella" (story) Perrault, Charles
Voices Woods, Ilene; Audley, Eleanor; Felton, Verna; DuBrey, Claire; Williams, Rhoda; MacDonald, James; Stanley, Helene; Van Rooten, Luis; Barclay, Don; Douglas, Mike; Phipps, William

Directing Animator(s) Larson, Eric; Kahl, Milt; Thomas, Franklin; Lounsbery, John; Reitherman, Wolfgang; Kimball, Ward; Johnston, Ollie; Davis, Marc; Clark, Les; Ferguson, Norm

Song(s) Cinderella; A Dream Is a Wish Your Heart Makes; Oh Sing Sweet Nightingale; The Work Song; Bibbidi-Bobbidi-Boo (The Magic Song); So This Is Love; Cinderella Work Song [1]; Dancing on a Cloud [1] (C: Wolcott, Charles; L: Morey, Larry); The Dress That My Mother Wore [1] (C: Wolcott, Charles; L: Morey, Larry); The Face That I See in the Night [1] (C: Wolcott, Charles; L: Morey, Larry); Horse-Sense [1]; I Lost My Heart At the Ball [1] (C: Wolcott, Charles; L: Morey, Larry); I'm in the Middle of a Muddle [1]; Mouse Song [1] (C: Wolcott, Charles; L: Morey, Larry); Pretending [1] (C: Wolcott, Charles; L: Morey, Larry); Raga-Daga-Day [1]; Sing a Little, Dream a Little [1] [2] (C: Wolcott, Charles; L: Morey, Larry); Sleepy Time [1] [2] (C: Wolcott, Charles; L: Dodd, Jimmy); Tee Hee Hee, You Can't Scare Me [1]

Notes Animated cartoon. [1] Not used. [2] Same music.

1047 ✦ CINDERELLA JONES
Warner Brothers, 1946

Musical Score Hollander, Frederick
Composer(s) Styne, Jule
Lyricist(s) Cahn, Sammy

Producer(s) Gottlieb, Alex
Director(s) Berkeley, Busby
Screenwriter(s) Hoffman, Charles
Source(s) "Judy Adjudicates" (story) Wylie, Philip

Cast Alda, Robert; Leslie, Joan; Bishop, Julie; Prince, William; Sakall, S.Z.; Horton, Edward Everett; Cook Jr., Elisha; Donnelly, Ruth; Cavanaugh, Hobart

Song(s) If You're Waiting I'm Waiting Too; Cinderella Jones; You Never Know Where You're Going Till You

Get There; When the One You Love Simply Won't Love Back; Our Theme [1]

Notes [1] Background instrumental use only.

1048 ✦ CINDERELLA LIBERTY
Twentieth Century–Fox, 1973

Musical Score Williams, John
Composer(s) Williams, John
Lyricist(s) Williams, Paul

Producer(s) Rydell, Mark
Director(s) Rydell, Mark
Screenwriter(s) Ponicsan, Darryl
Source(s) (novel) Ponicsan, Darryl

Cast Caan, James; Mason, Marsha; Calloway, Kirk; Wallach, Eli; Young, Burt; Coleman, Dabney; McLerie, Allyn Ann

Song(s) Wednesday Special; Nice to Be Around [1]

Notes [1] Used instrumentally only.

1049 ✦ CINDERELLA SWINGS IT
RKO, 1943

Producer(s) Brandt, Jerrold T.
Director(s) Cabanne, Christy
Screenwriter(s) Simmons, Michael L.

Cast Warren, Gloria; Kibbee, Guy; Parrish, Helen; Hogan, Dick; Kinskey, Leonid; Best, Willie; Watkin, Pierre

Song(s) The Flag's Still There Mr. Key [1] (C: Oakland, Ben; L: Jessel, George); I Heard You Cried Last Night (C: Grouya, Ted; L: Kruger, Jerrie)

Notes No cue sheet available. [1] This was originally titled SCATTERGOOD SWINGS IT.

1050 ✦ CINDERFELLA
Paramount, 1960

Musical Score Scharf, Walter
Composer(s) Warren, Harry
Lyricist(s) Brooks, Jack
Choreographer(s) Castle, Nick

Producer(s) Lewis, Jerry
Director(s) Tashlin, Frank
Screenwriter(s) Tashlin, Frank

Cast Lewis, Jerry; Wynn, Ed; Anderson, Judith; Silva, Henry; Hutton, Robert; Basie, Count; Williams, Joe; Alberghetti, Anna Maria

Song(s) Somebody; Let Me Be a People (Plain Old Me); The Princess Waltz (Once Upon a Time) [2] (C: Warren, Harry; Scharf, Walter); The Other Fella; Turn It On [1]; The Cricket Song [3] (C: Scharf, Walter); I'm Going to the Ball [3]; I'm Part of a Family [3] (C/L: Scharf, Walter; Brooks, Jack); Tick-Dee [3] (C/L:

Scharf, Walter; Brooks, Jack); We're Going to the Ball [3] (C/L: Scharf, Walter; Brooks, Jack); Work Some More [3] (C/L: Scharf, Walter)

Notes   [1] Not used but recorded. [2] Lyric added for exploitation. [3] Not used.

1051 ✦ CIRCUS OF HORRORS
American International, 1960

Musical Score   Reizenstein, Franz; Mathieson, Muir

Producer(s)   Priggen, Norman
Director(s)   Hayers, Sidney
Screenwriter(s)   Baxt, George

Cast   Diffring, Anton; Remberg, Erika; Monlaur, Yvonne; Pleasence, Donald; Griffith, Kenneth; Gwillim, Jack; Merivale, John

Song(s)   Look for a Star (C/L: Anthony, Mark)

Notes   No cue sheet available.

1052 ✦ CIRCUS WORLD
Paramount, 1964

Producer(s)   Bronston, Samuel
Director(s)   Hathaway, Henry
Screenwriter(s)   Hecht, Ben; Grant, James Edward; Halevy, Julian

Cast   Wayne, John; Hayworth, Rita; Cardinale, Claudia; Nolan, Lloyd; Conte, Richard

Song(s)   Circus World (C: Tiomkin, Dimitri; L: Washington, Ned)

Notes   Titled THE MAGNIFICENT SHOWMAN in Great Britain.

1053 ✦ THE CISCO KID
Fox, 1931

Director(s)   Cummings, Irving
Screenwriter(s)   Cohn, Alfred A.
Source(s)   (story) Henry, O.

Cast   Baxter, Warner; Lowe, Edmund; Montenegro, Conchita; Lane, Nora

Song(s)   Song of the Cisco Kid [1] (C/L: Baxter, Warner); Song of the Fisher Maidens [2] (C/L: Kernell, William)

Notes   [1] The song is used again in THE RETURN OF THE CISCO KID in 1939. [2] Sheet music only.

1054 ✦ CISCO PIKE
Columbia, 1971

Composer(s)   Kristofferson, Kris
Lyricist(s)   Kristofferson, Kris

Producer(s)   Ayres, Gerald
Director(s)   Norton, Bill L.
Screenwriter(s)   Norton, Bill L.

Cast   Kristofferson, Kris; Black, Karen; Hackman, Gene; Bang, Joy; Viva; Browne, Roscoe Lee; Stanton, Harry Dean

Song(s)   Loving Her Was Easier (Than Anything I'll Ever Do Again) [1]; I'd Rather Be Sorry; The Pilgrim: Chapter 33; Michoacan (C: Allen, Atwood; L: Fowley, Kim); Breakdown; Funky Lady (C/L: Montgomery, Herman L. (Lee))

Notes   [1] Also in HONEYSUCKLE ROSE (Warner Brothers).

1055 ✦ CITADEL OF CRIME
Republic, 1941

Musical Score   Glickman, Mort

Producer(s)   Sherman, George
Director(s)   Sherman, George
Screenwriter(s)   Ryan, Don

Cast   Armstrong, Robert; Albertson, Frank; Hayes, Linda; Simpson, Russell; Gallagher, Skeets; Haade, William; Novello, Jay; Fix, Paul

Song(s)   Stars Over the Prairie [1] (C/L: Tinturin, Peter)

Notes   [1] Also in NEVADA CITY.

1056 ✦ CITIZEN KANE
RKO, 1941

Musical Score   Herrmann, Bernard

Producer(s)   Welles, Orson
Director(s)   Welles, Orson
Screenwriter(s)   Welles, Orson; Mankiewicz, Herman J.

Cast   Cotten, Joseph; Comingore, Dorothy; Moorehead, Agnes; Warrick, Ruth; Collins, Ray; Sanford, Erskine; Sloane, Everett; Alland, William; Welles, Orson; Stewart, Paul; Coulouris, George

Song(s)   A Poco No [1] (C: Guizar, Pepe; L: Ruby, Herman)

Notes   There is also a vocal of "Una Voce Poco Fa" by Rossini. [1] Ruby added new lyrics.

1057 ✦ CITIZEN'S BAND
Paramount, 1977

Producer(s)   Fields, Freddie
Director(s)   Demme, Jonathan
Screenwriter(s)   Brickman, Paul

Cast   Le Mat, Paul; McGill, Bruce; Clark, Candy; Rodd, Marcia; Wedgeworth, Ann; Napier, Charles

Song(s)   I'm Not in Love [1] (C/L: Stewart, Eric; Gouldman, Graham); You Are So Beautiful [1] (C/L: Preston, Billy; Fisher, Bruce); You Heard the Song [1] (C: Conti, Bill; L: Gimbel, Norman)

Notes   This film was re-released as HANDLE WITH CARE. [1] These songs are all background vocals.

1058 ✦ CITY BENEATH THE SEA
Universal, 1952

Composer(s)   Hughes, Arnold
Lyricist(s)   Herbert, Frederick

Producer(s)   Cohen, Albert J.
Director(s)   Boetticher, Budd
Screenwriter(s)   Harvey, Jack; Romero, Ramon
Source(s)   *Port Royal—Ghost City Beneath the Sea* (novel) Reisberg, Harry E.

Cast   Stepanek, Karel; Ryan, Robert; Quinn, Anthony; Mathews, George; Rios, Lalo; Hattie, Hilo; Strode, Woody

Song(s)   Damballa (C/L: Antoine, Le Roi); Sippa-A-Sip; Handle with Care; Time for Love [1]

Notes   [1] Sheet music only.

1059 ✦ CITY FOR CONQUEST
Warner Brothers, 1940

Musical Score   Steiner, Max
Choreographer(s)   Vreeland, Robert

Producer(s)   Litvak, Anatole
Director(s)   Litvak, Anatole
Screenwriter(s)   Wexley, John
Source(s)   *City for Conquest* (novel) Kandel, Aben

Cast   Cagney, James; Sheridan, Ann; Kennedy, Arthur; Craven, Frank; Crisp, Donald; McHugh, Frank; Tobias, George; Cowan, Jerome; Quinn, Anthony; Patrick, Lee; Yurka, Blanche; Kazan, Elia

Song(s)   Powder My Back [1] (C: Wrubel, Allie; L: Dixon, Mort); Where Were You When the Moon Came Out (C/L: Redmond, John; Altman, Arthur; Cavanaugh, Jimmy)

Notes   It is not known if the songs were written for the film. [1] Also in BRIGHT LIGHTS (1935).

1060 ✦ CITY GIRL
Fox, 1930

Musical Score   Kay, Arthur

Director(s)   Murnau, F.W.; Van Buren, A.H.; Erickson, A.F.
Screenwriter(s)   Lester, Elliott
Source(s)   *The Mad Turtle* (play) Lester, Elliott

Cast   Farrell, Charles; Duncan, Mary; Torrence, David; Yorke, Edith; O'Day, Dawn; Maguire, Tom; Alexander, Dick; Rooney, Pat; Ates, Roscoe

Song(s)   Chicago Song [2] (C: Traditional; L: MacFarlane, George); In the Valley of My Dreams [1] (C: Hanley, James F.; L: Norman, Pierre)

Notes   Originally titled OUR DAILY BREAD. [1] Unclear if used instrumentally or vocally. [2] Based on "The Irish Washerwoman."

1061 ✦ CITY HEAT
Warner Brothers, 1987

Musical Score   Niehaus, Lennie

Producer(s)   Manes, Fritz
Director(s)   Benjamin, Richard
Screenwriter(s)   Brown, Sam O. [1]; Stinson, Joseph C.

Cast   Eastwood, Clint; Reynolds, Burt; Alexander, Jane; Kahn, Madeline; Torn, Rip; Cara, Irene; Roundtree, Richard; LoBianco, Tony; Sanderson, William

Song(s)   City Heat Blues (C: Niehaus, Lennie; L: Cara, Irene; Roberts, Bruce)

Notes   The rendition of "Let's Do It" on the soundtrack is an unreleased master furnished by Rudy Vallee. [1] Pseudonym for Blake Edwards.

1062 ✦ CITY OF BAD MEN
Twentieth Century–Fox, 1953

Producer(s)   Goldstein, Leonard
Director(s)   Jones, Harmon
Screenwriter(s)   George, George W.; Slavin, George F.

Cast   Crain, Jeanne; Robertson, Dale; Boone, Richard; Bridges, Lloyd; Mathews, Carole; Betz, Carl; Acosta, Rodolfo

Song(s)   Love Me, Love Me, Love Me (C: Newman, Lionel; L: Daniel, Eliot)

1063 ✦ CITY ON A HUNT
United Artists, 1953

Musical Score   Shefter, Bert
Composer(s)   Shefter, Bert
Lyricist(s)   Bennett, Charles

Producer(s)   Mackenzie, Hugh; Freed, Matt
Director(s)   Bennett, Charles
Screenwriter(s)   Bennett, Charles

Cast   Steele, Marjorie; Tufts, Sonny; Martin, Lewis; Ayres, Lew; Griffith, James

Song(s)   Grossett Jingle; Sally Doyle Jingle; Pinker Jingle; No Escape

Notes   Orignally titled NO ESCAPE.

1064 ✦ CLAMBAKE
United Artists, 1967

Musical Score   Alexander, Jeff
Choreographer(s)   Romero, Alex

Producer(s)   Levy, Jules V.; Gardner, Arthur; Laven, Arnold

Director(s)   Nadel, Arthur
Screenwriter(s)   Browne Jr., Arthur

Cast   Hutchins, Will [1]; Presley, Elvis; Fabares, Shelley; Bixby, Bill; Gregory, James; Harley, Amanda; Merrill, Gary

Song(s)   Clambake [2] (C: Wiesman, Ben; Alexander, Jeff) (L: Wayne, Sid); Who Needs Money [2] (C: Alexander, Jeff; L: Starr, Roy); Confidence (C/L: Tepper, Sid; Bennett, Roy C.); A House That Has Everything (C/L: Tepper, Sid; Bennett, Roy C.); The Girl I Never Loved (C/L: Starr, Randy); Hey! Hey! Hey! (C/L: Byers, Joy); You Don't Know Me (C/L: Walker, C.; Arnold, E.)

Notes   [1] Dubbed. [2] Alexander not credited on sheet music.

1065 ✦ CLASH BY NIGHT
RKO, 1952

Musical Score   Webb, Roy

Producer(s)   Parsons, Harriet
Director(s)   Lang, Fritz
Screenwriter(s)   Hayes, Alfred
Source(s)   *Clash By Night* (play) Odets, Clifford

Cast   Stanwyck, Barbara; Douglas, Paul; Ryan, Robert; Monroe, Marilyn; Naish, J. Carrol; Minciotti, Silvio; Andes, Keith

Song(s)   Theatre Sequence (C/L: Fragos, George; Baker, Jack; Gasparre, Dick) (C: Webb, Roy; L: Bennett, Norman); I Hear a Rhapsody; Don't Cry [1] (C/L: Skylar, Sunny); Don't Get Married Till You Fall in Love [1] (C: Carpenter, Imogene; L: Webber, Billie)

Notes   [1] Sheet music only.

1066 ✦ THE CLASS OF MISS MACMICHAEL
Brut Pictures, 1979

Musical Score   Myers, Stanley

Producer(s)   Bernard, Judd
Director(s)   Narizzano, Silvio
Screenwriter(s)   Bernard, Judd
Source(s)   *Eff Off* (novel) Hutson, Sandy

Cast   Jackson, Glenda; Reed, Oliver; Murphy, Michael; Cash, Rosalind; Standing, John; Adabusi, Riba

Song(s)   Mayfair Magic (C/L: Myers, Stanley); Playing in School (C/L: Renoir)

Notes   No cue sheet available.

1067 ✦ CLASS OF 1984
American Films, 1982

Musical Score   Schifrin, Lalo

Producer(s)   Kent, Arthur
Director(s)   Lester, Mark

Screenwriter(s)   Lester, Mark; Saxton, John; Holland, Tom

Cast   King, Perry; Ross, Merrie Lynn; Van Patten, Timothy; McDowall, Roddy; Arngrim, Stefan; Fox, Michael J.

Song(s)   I Am the Future (C: Schifrin, Lalo; L: Osborne, Gary); You Better Not Step Out of Line (C: Schifrin, Lalo; Baxter, Jeff "Skunk"; L: Osborne, Gary); Suburbanite (C/L: Schifrin, Lalo)

Notes   No cue sheet available.

1068 ✦ CLAUDIA
Twentieth Century–Fox, 1943

Musical Score   Newman, Alfred

Producer(s)   Perlberg, William
Director(s)   Goulding, Edmund
Screenwriter(s)   Ryskind, Morrie
Source(s)   *Claudia* (play) Franken, Rose

Cast   McGuire, Dorothy; Young, Robert; Claire, Ina; Gardiner, Reginald; Baclanova, Olga; Howard, Jean; Tweddell, Frank; Fenton, Frank

Song(s)   From Yesterday Till Tomorrow (C: Newman, Alfred; L: Henderson, Charles); Cow Call (C: Goulding, Edmund; L: Baclanova, Olga)

1069 ✦ CLAUDINE
Twentieth Century–Fox, 1974

Musical Score   Mayfield, Curtis
Composer(s)   Mayfield, Curtis
Lyricist(s)   Mayfield, Curtis

Producer(s)   Weinstein, Hannah
Director(s)   Berry, John
Screenwriter(s)   Pine, Tina; Pine, Lester

Cast   Carroll, Diahann; Jones, James Earl; Hilton-Jacobs, Lawrence; Tamu; Kruger, David; Curtis, Yvette; Wade, Adam

Song(s)   On and On; The Makings of You; Mr. Welfare; Hold On; To Be Invisible; Make Yours a Happy Home

1070 ✦ CLEOPATRA JONES AND THE CASINO OF GOLD
Warner Brothers, 1975

Musical Score   Frontiere, Dominic

Producer(s)   Tennant, William; Shaw, Run Run
Director(s)   Bail, Chuck
Screenwriter(s)   Tennant, William

Cast   Dobson, Tamara; Stevens, Stella; Fell, Norman; Popwell, Albert

Song(s) You're Playing with Fire (C: Frontiere, Dominic; L: Kerner, Kenny; Wise, Richie)

Notes Background vocal use only.

1071 ✦ THE CLIMAX
Universal, 1944

Musical Score Ward, Edward
Composer(s) Ward, Edward
Lyricist(s) Waggner, George

Producer(s) Waggner, George
Director(s) Waggner, George
Screenwriter(s) Siodmak, Curt
Source(s) (play) Locke, Edward

Cast Karloff, Boris; Foster, Susanna; Bey, Turhan; Sondergaard, Gale; Gomez, Thomas; Vincent, June; Dolenz, George

Song(s) Now at Last [1]; Some Day I Know

Notes Operatic sequences staged by Lester Horton. [1] Music based on themes by Chopin and F. Schubert. The name of the supposed opera is THE MAGIC VOICE.

1072 ✦ CLIMBING THE GOLDEN STAIRS
Metro–Goldwyn–Mayer, 1929

Composer(s) Edwards, Gus
Lyricist(s) Brockman, James

Cast King, Charles; The Pearl Twins; Bo Ling and Bo Ching (The Chinese Twins); The Aber Twins; The Clute Twins; Jarvis, Sidney

Song(s) Heart of Broadway; Climbing Those Golden Stairs; Cop Number (L: Unknown); Hello Melody, Goodbye Jazz (L: Hilliam, J.C.)

Notes Short subject. There are also a few bars of "Side By Side" by Harry Woods and "St. Louis Blues" by W.C. Handy.

1073 ✦ THE CLOCK
Metro–Goldwyn–Mayer, 1945

Musical Score Bassman, George

Producer(s) Freed, Arthur
Director(s) Minnelli, Vincente
Screenwriter(s) Nathan, Robert; Schrank, Joseph
Source(s) "The Clock" (story) Gallico, Paul; Gallico, Pauline

Cast Garland, Judy; Walker, Robert; Gleason, James; Wynn, Keenan; Thompson, Marshall

Song(s) Song of the City (C/L: Bassman, George)

Notes There is also a vocal of "Whispering" by Malvin Schoenberger, Richard Coburn and John Schoenberger and one of "That's How I Need You" by Al Piantadosi, Joseph McCarthy and Joe Goodwin.

1074 ✦ THE CLOCK SHOP
Metro–Goldwyn–Mayer, 1930

Musical Score Alter, Louis
Composer(s) Alter, Louis
Lyricist(s) Johnson, Howard

Director(s) Brooks, Marty

Cast Edwards, Cliff; Heller, Jackie; MacMahon, Doris; Betty and Ramon

Song(s) Rolland from Holland (C/L: Johnson, Howard); Ghost of Grandfather's Clock; Cuckoo Clock; Gotta Feelin' for You (L: Trent, Jo); Big Ben Family

Notes Short subject.

1075 ✦ THE CLOCK STRIKES 8

See COLLEGE SCANDAL.

1076 ✦ THE CLOCK WATCHER
Disney, 1945

Musical Score Wallace, Oliver

Song(s) Royal Work Song (C: Wallace, Oliver; L: Wallace, Oliver; Cox, Rex)

Notes Short subject. No credit sheet available.

1077 ✦ CLOSE HARMONY
Paramount, 1929

Composer(s) Whiting, Richard A.
Lyricist(s) Robin, Leo

Director(s) Cromwell, John; Sutherland, Edward
Screenwriter(s) Heath, Percy; Weaver, John V.A.

Cast Carroll, Nancy; Rogers, Charles "Buddy"; Oakie, Jack; Gallagher, Skeets; Green, Harry

Song(s) America I Love You (C/L: Gottler, Archie); I Wanna Go Places and Do Things; Wild Party Girl (inst.); I'm All A-Twitter (and All A-Twirl) [2]; She's So I Don't Know; Strutters' Ball (C/L: Brooks, Shelton); Margie (C: Conrad, Con; Robinson, J. Russel; L: Davis, Benny); Twelfth Street Rag (C: Bowman, Uday; L: Summer, James S.); Here Comes My Ball and Chain [1]; I Still Belong to You [1]; Doin' the Raccoon [1]

Notes [1] These songs are listed on a Paramount (New York) Theater program but not on the cue sheets. [2] Also in WOMAN TRAP.

1078 ✦ THE CLOWN
Metro–Goldwyn–Mayer, 1953

Musical Score Rose, David

Producer(s) Wright, William H.
Director(s) Leonard, Robert Z.
Screenwriter(s) Rackin, Martin

Cast   Skelton, Red; Considine, Tim; Greer, Jane; Smith, Loring; Ober, Philip

Song(s)   I Never Knew [1] (C/L: Pitts, Tom; Egan, Raymond B.; Marsh, Roy)

Notes   [1] Also used in THREE FACES OF EVE (20th) and the Universal pictures THE CRIMSON CANARY and STRICTLY IN THE GROOVE. Written in 1920 for show THE MIDNIGHT ROUNDERS.

1079 ✦ CLUB LIFE
CineWorld, 1986

Musical Score   Conrad, Jack

Producer(s)   Vane, Norman Thaddeus
Director(s)   Vane, Norman Thaddeus
Screenwriter(s)   Vane, Norman Thaddeus

Cast   Parsekian, Tom; Parks, Michael; Barrett, Jamie; Curtis, Tony; Stone, Dee Wallace

Song(s)   Club Life (C/L: Musker, Frank; Lamers, Elizabeth; Lawrence, Trevor)

Notes   No cue sheet available.

1080 ✦ CLUB PARADISE
Warner Brothers, 1986

Musical Score   Mansfield, David; Parks, Van Dyke
Composer(s)   Cliff, Jimmy
Lyricist(s)   Cliff, Jimmy

Producer(s)   Shamberg, Michael
Director(s)   Ramis, Harold
Screenwriter(s)   Ramis, Harold; Doyle-Murray, Brian

Cast   Williams, Robin; O'Toole, Peter; Moranis, Rick; Cliff, Jimmy; Twiggy; Caesar, Adolph; Levy, Eugene; Cassidy, Joanna; Martin, Andrea; Doyle-Murray, Brian; Flaherty, Joe; Gross, Mary

Song(s)   Seven Day Weekend (C/L: Cliff, Jimmy; Costello, Elvis); The Lion Awakes; Shining Star; American Plan; Club Paradise; Free I Soul (C/L: Mansfield, David; Carlin, Daniel A.; Parks, Van Dyke); Third World People; You Can't Keep a Good Man Down

Notes   There are other songs which are from albums. Most of these songs above were background vocals.

1081 ✦ CLUNY BROWN
Twentieth Century–Fox, 1946

Producer(s)   Lubitsch, Ernst
Director(s)   Lubitsch, Ernst
Screenwriter(s)   Hoffenstein, Samuel; Reinhardt, Elizabeth
Source(s)   *Cluny Brown* (novel) Sharp, Margery

Cast   Boyer, Charles; Jones, Jennifer; Lawford, Peter; Walker, Helen; Owen, Reginald; Gardiner, Reginald; Smith, C. Aubrey; Haydn, Richard; Allgood, Sara; Cossart, Ernest; O'Connor, Una; Leonard, Queenie

Song(s)   Stinker (C/L: Evans, Rex)

1082 ✦ C'MON LET'S LIVE A LITTLE
Paramount, 1966

Composer(s)   Crawford, Don
Lyricist(s)   Crawford, Don

Producer(s)   Starr, June; Hertelandy, John
Director(s)   Butler, David
Screenwriter(s)   Starr, June

Cast   Kelly, Patsy; Smith, Ethel; Vee, Bobby; Ireland Jr., John; Evans, Mark; De Shannon, Jackie; Hodges, Eddie

Song(s)   C'mon Let's Live a Little; What Fools These Mortals Be; Instant Girl; Baker Man; Way Back Home; Over and Over; For Granted; Let's Go-Go [1] (C/L: Brown, Melvin; Pinkard, James); Back Talk; Tonight's the Night

Notes   [1] Not written for film.

1083 ✦ COAL MINER'S DAUGHTER
Universal, 1980

Producer(s)   Schwartz, Bernard
Director(s)   Apted, Michael
Screenwriter(s)   Rickman, Tom
Source(s)   (book) Lynn, Loretta; Vescey, George

Cast   Spacek, Sissy; Jones, Tommy Lee; D'Angelo, Beverly; Boyens, Phyllis; Helm, Levon; Sanderson, William; Elkins, Robert; Hannah, Bob

Notes   There are no original songs in this movie. Vocals include "Walking the Floor Over You" by Ernest Tubb; "Blue Moon of Kentucky" by Bill Monroe; "Coal Miner's Daughter" by Loretta Lynn; "It Wasn't God Who Made Honky Tonk Angels" by J.D. Miller; "The Titanic" by Maybell Sara and A.P. Carter; "Have I Told You Lately That I Love You" by Scott Wiseman; "There He Goes" by Eddie Miller, Durwood Haddock and W.S. Stevenson; "I'm a Honky Tonk Girl" by Loretta Lynn; "Amazing Grace" and "Walking After Midnight" by Don Hecht and Alan Block; "Satisfied Mind" by Jack Rhodes and Red Hayes; "I Fall to Pieces" by Hank Cochran and Harlan Howard; "Sweet Dreams" by Don Gibson; "Back in Baby's Arms" by Bob Montgomery; "You Ain't Woman Enough to Take My Man" by Loretta Lynn; "You're Lookin' at Country" by Loretta Lynn; "Fist City" by Loretta Lynn and "One's on the Way" by Shel Silverstein.

1084 ✦ COAST TO COAST
Paramount, 1980

Musical Score Bernstein, Charles

Producer(s) Tisch, Steve; Avnet, Jon
Director(s) Sargent, Joseph
Screenwriter(s) Weiser, Stanley

Cast Cannon, Dyan; Blake, Robert; Redeker, Quinn; Lerner, Michael; Stuart, Maxine

Song(s) Coast to Coast (C/L: Wilson, Johnny; Bomar, Woody); Pickin' Up Strangers (C/L: Hill, Byron); Fool That I Am (C/L: Sager, Carole Bayer; Roberts, Bruce)

Notes No cue sheet available.

1085 ✦ COBRA
Warner Brothers, 1986

Musical Score Levay, Sylvester

Producer(s) Golan, Menahem; Globus, Yoram
Director(s) Cosmatos, George P.
Screenwriter(s) Stallone, Sylvester
Source(s) *Fair Game* (novel) Gosling, Paula

Cast Stallone, Sylvester; Nielsen, Brigitte; Santoni, Reni; Robinson, Andrew; La Fleur, Art; Avery, Val; Williams, Bert; Thompson, Brian; Garlington, Lee

Song(s) Suave (C/L: Estefan, Gloria; Garcia, Enrique); Angel in the City (C/L: Tepper, Robert); Voice of America's Sons (C/L: Cafferty, John)

1086 ✦ THE COCA-COLA KID
Cinecom, 1985

Musical Score Notzing, William
Composer(s) Finn, Tom
Lyricist(s) Finn, Tom

Producer(s) Roe, David
Director(s) Makevejev, Dusan
Screenwriter(s) Moorhouse, Frank
Source(s) "The Americans"; "Baby"; "The Electrical Experience" (stories) Moorhouse, Frank

Cast Roberts, Eric; Scacchi, Greta; Kerr, Bill; Haywood, Chris; McQuade, Kris; Gilles, Max; Barry, Tony

Song(s) Home for My Heart; Coca-Cola Jingle; Straight Night

Notes No cue sheet available.

1087 ✦ COCKEYED CAVALIERS
RKO, 1934

Musical Score Webb, Roy
Composer(s) Burton, Val; Jason, Will
Lyricist(s) Burton, Val; Jason, Will

Producer(s) Brock, Lou
Director(s) Sandrich, Mark
Screenwriter(s) Kaufman, Edward; Holmes, Ben; Garrett, Grant; Spence, Ralph

Cast Wheeler, Bert; Woolsey, Robert; Todd, Thelma; Lee, Dorothy; Beery, Noah; Greig, Robert; Sedley, Henry

Song(s) Opening Chorus; And the Big Bad Wolf Is Dead; Dilly Dally

1088 ✦ THE COCKEYED WORLD
Fox, 1929

Composer(s) Conrad, Con; Gottler, Archie
Lyricist(s) Conrad, Con; Mitchell, Sidney D.

Director(s) Walsh, Raoul
Screenwriter(s) Wells, William K.
Source(s) *Tropical Twins* (play) Stallings, Laurence; Anderson, Maxwell

Cast McLaglen, Victor; Lowe, Edmund; Damita, Lily; Brendel, El; Erwin, Stuart; Burns, Bob; Brown, Joe

Song(s) So Dear to Me; So Long; Elenita

Notes A sequel to WHAT PRICE GLORY. There are also vocals of "K-K-K-Katy" by Geoffrey O'Hara; "Over There" by George M. Cohan; "Rose of No Man's Land" by James Caddigan and James Brennan; "Hinky Dinky Parley Voo" by Al Dubin, Irving Mills and Jimmy McHugh; "You're the Cream in My Coffee" by Lew Brown, B.G. DeSylva and Ray Henderson; and "Glorianna" by Sidney Clare and Lew Pollack.

1089 ✦ COCK O' THE WALK
Sono-Art, 1930

Producer(s) Cruze, James
Director(s) Neill, Roy William
Screenwriter(s) Bell, Ralph; Marlow, Brian
Source(s) Un Seguro Sobre la Dicha Mom, Arturo S.

Cast Schildkraut, Joseph; Loy, Myrna; Sleeman, Philip; Peil, Edward; Beck, John; Tell, Olive; Lucas, Wilfred; Jonasson, Frank

Song(s) Play Me a Tango Tune (C/L: Titsworth, Paul; Cowan, Lynn)

Notes No cue sheet available.

1090 ✦ COCKTAIL
Touchstone, 1988

Musical Score Robinson, J. Peter

Producer(s) Field, Ted; Cort, Robert W.
Director(s) Donaldson, Roger
Screenwriter(s) Gould, Heywood
Source(s) (book) Gould, Heywood

Cast Cruise, Tom; Brown, Bryan; Shue, Elisabeth; Banes, Lisa; Lynch, Kelly; Luckinbill, Laurence

Song(s) Powerful Stuff (C/L: Wilson, Wally; Henderson, Michael; Field, Robert S.); Wild Again (C/L: Bettis, John; Clark, Michael)

Notes Only original songs listed.

1091 ✦ COCKTAIL HOUR
Columbia, 1933

Director(s) Schertzinger, Victor
Screenwriter(s) Purcell, Gertrude; Schayer, Richard

Cast Daniels, Bebe; Scott, Randolph; Ralph, Jessie; Kirkland, Muriel; Blackmer, Sidney; Norton, Barry; Gateson, Marjorie

Song(s) Listen Heart of Mine (C/L: Schertzinger, Victor)

1092 ✦ COCOANUT GROVE
Paramount, 1938

Producer(s) Arthur, George M.
Director(s) Santell, Alfred
Screenwriter(s) Bartlett, Sy; Cooper, Olive

Cast MacMurray, Fred; Hilliard, Harriet; Arden, Eve; Blue, Ben; Davis, Rufe; Harry Owens and His Orchestra; The Yacht Club Boys

Song(s) Dreamy Hawaiian Moon (C/L: Owens, Harry); The Four of Us Went to Sea (C/L: The Yacht Club Boys [1]); Says My Heart [4] (C: Lane, Burton; L: Loesser, Frank); You Leave Me Breathless (C: Hollander, Frederick; L: Freed, Ralph); Swami Song (Use Swami Salts) (C: Lane, Burton; L: Santell, Alfred); Ten Easy Lessons [6] (C: "Jock" [2]; Lane, Burton; L: "Jock" [2]; Loesser, Frank); The Musketeers' Song (We're Four of the Three Musketeers) [5] (C: Ruby, Harry; L: The Yacht Club Boys [1]; Kalmar, Bert); Two Bits a Pair [3] (C/L: "Jock" [2]); (In a) Cocoanut Grove [8] (C/L: Owens, Harry); You're a Blessing to Me [3] (C: Rainger, Ralph; L: Robin, Leo); Trailer Song [7] (C/L: The Yacht Club Boys [1])

Notes [1] The Yacht Club Boys were George Kelly, Charles Adler, William B. Mann and James V. Kern. [2] "Jock" is a pseudonym for Jack Rock. [3] Not used. [4] Originally written for COLLEGE SWING with music by Manning Sherwin. Lane wrote new music for inclusion in COCOANUT GROVE. [5] This number is based on the Kalmar and Ruby song "We're Four of the Three Musketeers," which appeared in the Marx Brothers' Broadway musical ANIMAL CRACKERS. [6] This song was from a "Suggestion by 'Jock'." [7] This song was written to accompany the trailers or previews in theatres that would be showing the movie. Whether or not it was used is not known. [8] This song, also known as "There's a Cocoanut Grove," and published as "Cocoanut Grove," was used instrumentally only.

1093 ✦ THE COCOANUTS
Paramount, 1929

Composer(s) Berlin, Irving
Lyricist(s) Berlin, Irving

Producer(s) Bell, Monta
Director(s) Florey, Robert; Santley, Joseph
Screenwriter(s) Kaufman, George S.
Source(s) *The Cocoanuts* (musical) Kaufman, George S.

Cast Marx, Groucho; Marx, Harpo; Marx, Chico; Marx, Zeppo; Eaton, Mary; Shaw, Oscar; Francis, Kay; Ruysdael, Basil; Dumont, Margaret

Song(s) When My Dreams Come True [3]; I Lost My Shirt [1] [2]; Florida by the Sea [2]; Monkey-Doodle-Doo [2]; The Bell-Hops; Ballet Music [4] (inst.) (C: Tours, Frank)

Notes [1] Melody based on "Toreador Song" from Bizet's CARMEN. Cut from final print. [2] In original show. [4] From MUSIC BOX REVUE. The number comes right after "Monkey Doodle-Doo." [3] Berlin's first song written for a sound film.

1094 ✦ COCOON
Twentieth Century–Fox, 1985

Musical Score Horner, James

Producer(s) Zanuck, Richard D.; Brown, David; Zanuck, Lili Fini
Director(s) Howard, Ron
Screenwriter(s) Benedek, Tom

Cast Ameche, Don; Brimley, Wilford; Cronyn, Hume; Dennehy, Brian; Gilford, Jack; Guttenberg, Steve; Stapleton, Maureen; Tandy, Jessica; Verdon, Gwen; Ware, Herta; Welch, Tahnee; Oliver, Barret; Harrison, Linda; Power Jr., Tyrone; Howard, Clint; Gil, Jorge

Song(s) That's What We Call Dancing (C/L: Newman, Lionel); Gravity [1] (C/L: Sembello, Cruz)

1095 ✦ CODE OF THE LAWLESS
Universal, 1945

Producer(s) Fox, Wallace W.
Director(s) Fox, Wallace W.
Screenwriter(s) Harper, Patricia

Cast Grant, Kirby; Knight, Fuzzy; Adams, Poni

Song(s) The Jackass Song (C/L: Bricker, George)

1096 ✦ CODE OF THE OUTLAW
Republic, 1942

Producer(s) Gray, Louis
Director(s) English, John
Screenwriter(s) Shipman, Barry
Source(s) characters by MacDonald, William Colt

Cast Steele, Bob; Tyler, Tom; Davis, Rufe; Heyburn, Weldon; Bartlett, Bennie; Leighton, Melinda; Curtis, Donald

Song(s) Rootin' Shootin' Terror of the West (C/L: Heath, Hy)

1097 ✦ CODE OF THE PRAIRIE
Republic, 1944

Producer(s) Gray, Louis
Director(s) Bennett, Spencer Gordon
Screenwriter(s) De Mond, Albert; Coldeway, Anthony

Cast Burnette, Smiley; Carson, Sunset; Stewart, Peggy; Chatterton, Tom; Barcroft, Roy; Heyburn, Weldon; Geary, Bud; London, Tom; Kirk, Jack

Song(s) They Won't Pay Me (C/L: Burnette, Smiley)

1098 ✦ CODE OF THE WEST
RKO, 1947

Musical Score Sawtell, Paul; Webb, Roy

Producer(s) Schlom, Herman
Director(s) Berke, William
Screenwriter(s) Houston, Norman
Source(s) *Code of the West* (novel) Grey, Zane

Cast Warren, James; Alden, Debra; Laurenz, John; Brodie, Steve; Lynn, Rita; Burr, Raymond

Song(s) Rainbow Valley [2] (C: Harris, Harry; L: Pollack, Lew); Ooh! La! La! [1] (C: Shilkret, Nathaniel; L: Wrubel, Allie)

Notes [1] Also in TOAST OF NEW YORK. [2] Also in GIRL RUSH (1944).

1099 ✦ COLD TURKEY (1951)
Disney, 1951

Musical Score Smith, Paul J.

Director(s) Nichols, Charles
Screenwriter(s) Salkin, Leo; Bertino, Al

Song(s) Lucky Turkey (C/L: Smith, Paul J.)

Notes Short subject.

1100 ✦ COLD TURKEY (1971)
United Artists, 1971

Musical Score Newman, Randy

Producer(s) Lear, Norman
Director(s) Lear, Norman
Screenwriter(s) Lear, Norman

Cast Newhart, Bob; Horton, Edward Everett; Van Dyke, Dick; Gardenia, Vincent; Bond, Sudie; Scott, Pippa; Bob and Ray [1]; Poston, Tom

Song(s) He Gives Us All His Love (C/L: Newman, Randy)

Notes [1] Bob Elliott and Ray Goulding.

1101 ✦ COLLEEN
Warner Brothers, 1936

Composer(s) Warren, Harry
Lyricist(s) Dubin, Al
Choreographer(s) Connolly, Bobby

Producer(s) Lord, Robert
Director(s) Green, Alfred E.
Screenwriter(s) Milne, Peter; Herbert, F. Hugh; Herzig, Sig

Cast Powell, Dick; Keeler, Ruby; Herbert, Hugh; Blondell, Joan; Oakie, Jack; Fazenda, Louise; Draper, Paul; Wilson, Marie; Alberni, Luis; Cavanaugh, Hobart

Song(s) You Gotta Know How to Dance; I Don't Have to Dream Again; A Boulevardier from the Bronx; An Evening with You; Summer Night [1]

Notes The last Dick Powell/Ruby Keeler musical. [1] Used instrumentally with humming only. Used in SING ME A LOVE SONG.

1102 ✦ COLLEGE COACH
Warner Brothers, 1933

Composer(s) Fain, Sammy
Lyricist(s) Kahal, Irving

Producer(s) Lord, Robert
Director(s) Wellman, William A.
Screenwriter(s) Seff, Manuel; Busch, Niven

Cast O'Brien, Pat; Byron, Arthur; Dvorak, Ann; Talbot, Lyle; Herbert, Hugh; Pendleton, Nat; Meek, Donald; Powell, Dick

Song(s) Men of Calvert (Football Song); Lonely Lane; Meet Me in the Gloaming [2] (C: Goodhart, Al; Hoffman, Al); L: Freed, Arthur); What Will I Do Without You? [3] (C: Gottlieb, Hilda; L: Mercer, Johnny); Fit As a Fiddle [4] (C: Goodhart, Al; Hoffman, Al; L: Freed, Arthur)

Notes Released in Great Britain as FOOTBALL COACH. There is five seconds of "Just One More Chance" by Arthur Johnston and Sam Coslow. [2] Instrumental, according to cue sheet. Freed not credited on cue sheet. [3] Instrumental according to cue sheet. Gottlieb and Mercer not mentioned on cue sheet. Lewis

E. Gensler credited. [4] Not used. Later in SINGIN' IN THE RAIN.

1103 ✦ COLLEGE CONFIDENTIAL
Universal, 1960

Musical Score   Elliott, Dean
Composer(s)   Sparks, Randy
Lyricist(s)   Sparks, Randy

Producer(s)   Zugsmith, Albert
Director(s)   Zugsmith, Albert
Screenwriter(s)   Shulman, Irving

Cast   Allen, Steve; Wilson, Earl; Graham, Sheila; Winchell, Walter; Sobol, Louis; Meadows, Jayne; Van Doren, Mamie; Crosby, Cathy; Marshall, Herbert; Bryant, Theona; Twitty, Conway; Sparks, Randy; Marciano, Rocky; Mason, Pamela; Cook Jr., Elisha; Montgomery Jr., Robert; Wellman Jr., William

Song(s)   College Confidential; College Confidential Ball (C/L: Twitty, Conway); Playmates; So Be It! [1] (C/L: Allen, Steve)

Notes   [1] Sheet music only.

1104 ✦ COLLEGE HOLIDAY
Paramount, 1936

Composer(s)   Rainger, Ralph
Lyricist(s)   Robin, Leo
Choreographer(s)   Prinz, LeRoy

Producer(s)   Thompson, Harlan
Director(s)   Tuttle, Frank
Screenwriter(s)   McEvoy, J.P.; Ware, Harlan; Gorney, Jay; Myers, Henry

Cast   Raye, Martha; Burns, George; Allen, Gracie; Blue, Ben; Downs, Johnny; Whitney, Eleanore; Benny Goodman and His Orchestra; Boland, Mary; Hunt, Marsha; Erickson, Leif

Song(s)   Sweetheart Waltz (C: Lane, Burton; L: Freed, Ralph); A Rhyme for Love; So What [3]; I Adore You [2]; Minstrel Show Opening (C: Lane, Burton; L: Freed, Ralph); Who's That Knockin' at My Heart (C: Lane, Burton; L: Freed, Ralph); What a Pleasure to Work with You [1] (C: Lane, Burton; L: Robin, Leo); Grecian Ballet (inst); My Heart Sings [1]; Honey Chile [1]; The Prom Waltz [1] [4]; Wo! Ho! That's Love! [1]; Fifty Million Sweethearts [1]

Notes   Benny Goodman sings "The Volga Boatman" and there are also vocals of the "Stein Song" and "Far Above Cayuga's Waters." [1] Not used. [2] Originally titled "Enchanted." [3] Originally titled "Don't Let It Get You Down," but that was not cleared since Wright and Forrest had previously registered the lyric. The Gershwins were happy to approve the title "So What,"

which they had used previously. [4] Used in TEMPO OF TOMORROW.

1105 ✦ COLLEGE HUMOR
Paramount, 1933

Composer(s)   Johnston, Arthur
Lyricist(s)   Coslow, Sam

Producer(s)   LeBaron, William
Director(s)   Ruggles, Wesley
Screenwriter(s)   Binyon, Claude; Butler, Frank

Cast   Crosby, Bing; Carlisle, Mary; Arlen, Richard; Oakie, Jack; Burns, George; Allen, Gracie

Song(s)   Play Ball [1]; Down the Old Ox Road; Moonstruck; Learn to Croon [4]; Please [5] (C: Rainger, Ralph; L: Robin, Leo); Colleen O'Killarney (L: Robin, Leo); Irish Jig (inst.); Sympathizin' with Me [2]; I'm a Bachelor of the Art of Ha Cha Cha [3]

Notes   There are also vocals of "Just an Echo in the Valley" by James Campbell, Harry Woods and Reg Connelly and "I Surrender Dear" by Gordon Clifford and Harry Barris (also in the Columbia picture I SURRENDER DEAR). [1] Part of this number was titled "Alma Mater." [2] Not used. Used later instrumentally only in "You're Telling Me." Also not used in BELLE OF THE NINETIES. [3] Used instrumentally only. [4] Also in HELL AND HIGH WATER and TOO MUCH HARMONY. [5] Also in THE BIG BROADCAST.

1106 ✦ COLLEGE LOVERS
Warner Brothers–First National, 1930

Director(s)   Adolfi, John
Screenwriter(s)   Doty, Douglas

Cast   Hopton, Russell; Whiting, Jack; McHugh, Frank; Williams, Guinn "Big Boy"; Nixon, Marian; Boteler, Wade; Crane, Phyllis; Tucker, Richard

Song(s)   Up an' at 'Em (C: Cleary, Michael; L: Magidson, Herb; Washington, Ned); One Minute of Heaven [2] (C: Cleary, Michael; L: Magidson, Herb; Washington, Ned); Kiss Waltz [1] (C/L: Burke, Joe; Dubin, Al); Spending An Evening with You (C: Mencher, Murray; L: Tobias, Charles)

Notes   Only "Up an' at 'Em" is positively identified as a vocal on the cue sheet. However, the cue sheet lists the others as "duped." [1] Also in FOOTSTEPS IN THE DARK and DANCING SWEETIES. [2] Also in THE FORWARD PASS.

1107 ✦ COLLEGE QUEEN
Paramount, 1946

Producer(s)   Templeton, George
Director(s)   Templeton, George

Cast Forbes, Ralph; Neill, Noel; Tilton, Elizabeth; Young, Audrey

Song(s) I'm Learning A Lot in College (C: Wayne, Bernie; L: Raleigh, Ben)

Notes Short subject. There are also two medleys of popular songs of the day.

1108 ◆ COLLEGE RHYTHM
Paramount, 1934

Composer(s) Revel, Harry
Lyricist(s) Gordon, Mack
Choreographer(s) Prinz, LeRoy

Producer(s) Lighton, Louis D.
Director(s) Taurog, Norman
Screenwriter(s) De Leon, Walter; McDermott, John; Martin, Francis

Cast Oakie, Jack; Roberti, Lyda; Penner, Joe; Ross, Lanny; Mack, Helen

Song(s) We're Here to State; Love and Kisses Finnegan; Stay As Sweet As You Are [6]; Stacey Cheer; College Rhythm; Haberdashers Department [3]; Stacey Closets; Housewear Department [3]; Let's Give Three Cheers for Love; Goo Goo; Take a Number from One to Ten; You Hit a New High [1]; You Went Over with a Bang [1]; You Say that to All the Girls [1]; Let's Double Up [1]; Love and Let Love [1]; My Heart Is an Open Book [1] [4]; Sit Down and Tell Me Where I Stand [1] [2]; Doin' the Dumb-Bell [1]; Powder, Lipstick and Rouge [1] [5]

Notes [1] Not used. [2] This song was originally intended for SITTING PRETTY but didn't make it in there either. The title was somewhat different: "Sit Down and Tell Me How I Stand." [3] There are additional short jingles like "Toy Department," "Furniture Department," "Shower Department," "Music Department," etc. [4] Used in LOVE IN BLOOM. [5] Used in THE DOLLY SISTERS (20th). [6] Also used in COLLEGIATE, RUMBA and STOLEN HARMONY.

1109 ◆ COLLEGE SCANDAL
Paramount, 1935

Producer(s) Lewis, Albert
Director(s) Nugent, Elliott
Screenwriter(s) Partos, Frank; Brackett, Charles; Roberts, Marguerite

Cast Downs, Johnny; Barrie, Wendy; Taylor, Kent; Judge, Arline; Frawley, William; Baker, Benny; Nugent, Edward

Song(s) In the Middle of a Kiss [1] (C/L: Coslow, Sam); Varsity Dance (inst.) (C: Coslow, Sam)

Notes Titled THE CLOCK STRIKES 8 in Great Britain. [1] Not used in SHOOT THE WORKS.

1110 ◆ COLLEGE SWING
Paramount, 1938

Lyricist(s) Loesser, Frank
Choreographer(s) Prinz, LeRoy

Producer(s) Gensler, Lewis E.
Director(s) Walsh, Raoul
Screenwriter(s) De Leon, Walter; Martin, Francis; Sturges, Preston

Cast Grable, Betty; Ennis, Skinnay; The Four Playboys; Coogan, Jackie; The Slate Brothers; Raye, Martha; George, Florence; Allen, Gracie; Burns, George; Payne, John; Hope, Bob; Colonna, Jerry

Song(s) College Swing (C: Carmichael, Hoagy); What Did Romeo Say to Juliet (C: Lane, Burton); You're a Natural (C: Sherwin, Manning); Says My Heart [1] [16] (C: Sherwin, Manning); Love with a Capital "You" [1] [2] [18] (C: Rainger, Ralph; L: Robin, Leo); I Fell Up to Heaven [1] [11] (C: Rainger, Ralph; L: Robin, Leo); What Goes on Here (In My Heart) [1] (C: Rainger, Ralph; L: Robin, Leo); The Old School Bell (C: Sherwin, Manning); Mary, Mary, Quite Contrary [1] [3] (C: Lane, Burton); Junior [1] [9] (C: Lane, Burton); What a Rumba Does to Romance (C: Sherwin, Manning); I Fall in Love with You Every Day [19] (C: Sherwin, Manning; Altman, Arthur); A Penny for Your Dreams [1] [15] (C: Hollander, Frederick; L: Freed, Ralph); How'dja Like to Love Me [12] (C: Lane, Burton); Beans [1] (C: Sherwin, Manning); I'm Tired (of Carrying Trays Around) [8] (C/L: Slate Brothers); Moments Like This [14] (C: Lane, Burton); There's a Building Boom [1] (C: Rainger, Ralph; L: Robin, Leo); Tonight We Love [1] [17] (C: Rainger, Ralph; L: Robin, Leo); That's for Me [1] (C: Rainger, Ralph; L: Robin, Leo); Prom Waltz [1] (C: Rainger, Ralph; L: Robin, Leo); Blossoms on Broadway [1] [4] (C: Rainger, Ralph; L: Robin, Leo); All Right for You [1] (C: Rainger, Ralph; L: Robin, Leo); April in My Heart Again [1] [5] (C: Carmichael, Hoagy; L: Meinardi, Helen); Sweeter Than Ever [1] (C: Hollander, Frederick; L: Freed, Ralph); No Stoop No Squat No Squint [1] [6] (C/L: "Jock" [13]); The Engine Went Puff Puff Puff [1] [7] (C/L: Siegel, Al); Those Eyes You're Wearing [1] (C: Lane, Burton); Sweet Dreams [1] [9] (C: Lane, Burton; L: Freed, Ralph); The Gay Desperado [1] [10] (C: Lane, Burton; L: Freed, Ralph)

Notes Titled SWING, TEACHER, SWING in Great Britain. There is also a satire of the Robins and Rainger song "Please" sung by Jerry Colonna. [1] Not used. [2] Used in MAN ABOUT TOWN, and $1,000 A TOUCHDOWN. [3] This number was used in LAS VEGAS NIGHTS and cut from DANCING ON A DIME. [4] This number was also not used in THE BIG BROADCAST OF 1936 and finally appeared in BLOSSOMS ON BROADWAY. [5] Originally written for DOUBLE OR NOTHING but not used. [6] This title was the slogan for Philco advertising. There was another song of the same title by Clarence Gaskill. [7] The censors at the Hays Office objected to the lyric "I've Got a Tender Behind." The song wasn't used. [8] This song's title originally was "I'm Tired of all the Songs About the South." [9] Same music. "Junior" was written later and finally appeared in ST. LOUIS BLUES (1938). [10] Same music as "The Song in My Heart Is a Rhumba" which was cut from ST. LOUIS BLUES (1938). [11] Later in A SONG IS BORN. [12] Also in ST. LOUIS BLUES (1939). [13] Pseudonym for Jack Rock. [14] Also in LAS VEGAS NIGHTS; MONEY FROM HOME; and recorded but not used in TRUE TO LIFE. [15] Used in ROMANCE IN THE ROUGH. [16] Burton Lane wrote new music and the song was used in COCOANUT GROVE. [17] In ROMANCE IN THE DARK. [18] Not used in BIG BROADCAST OF 1938. Used in GIVE ME A SAILOR. [19] Altman not credited on sheet music.

1111 ✦ COLLEGIATE
Paramount, 1936

Composer(s) Revel, Harry
Lyricist(s) Gordon, Mack

Producer(s) Lighton, Louis D.
Director(s) Murphy, Ralph
Screenwriter(s) De Leon, Walter; Martin, Francis
Source(s) "The Charm School" (story) Miller, Alice Duer

Cast Gordon, Mack [4]; Revel, Harry [4]; Grable, Betty; Oakie, Jack; Cooper, Betty Jane; Langford, Frances

Song(s) My Grandfather's Clock in the Hallway; Bevans, Dear Bevans; Who Am I; With My Eyes Wide Open I'm Dreaming [9]; Stay As Sweet As You Are [7]; You Hit the Spot; Introduction to Betty Jane Cooper; Rhythmatic; I Feel Like a Feather in the Breeze [6]; Guess Again [2] [5]; Learn to Be Lovely [1] [2]; Will I Ever Know [2] [8]; Sport a Sport [2] [3]; Fashion Show [2]; A Smile Will Do the Trick [2]

Notes Titled THE CHARM SCHOOL internationally. There is also a brief rendition of "Take a Number from One to Ten" from COLLEGE RHYTHM. The recording of "You Hit the Spot" includes vocals by Jack Oakie, Frances Langford and Mack Gordon and piano accompaniment by Harry Revel. [1] Used only as an instrumental background. [2] Not used. [3] This was recorded by Betty Grable to a piano track. [4] Gordon and Revel had parts leading a singing class. [5] Not used but published. In THE OLD FASHIONED WAY and READY FOR LOVE. [6] Also in BORDER FLIGHT. [7] Also in COLLEGE RHYTHM, RUMBA and STOLEN HARMONY. [8] Used in PALM SPRINGS. [9] Also used in ONE HOUR LATE, SHOOT THE WORKS and STOLEN HARMONY.

1112 ✦ COLORADO
Republic, 1940

Producer(s) Kane, Joseph
Director(s) Kane, Joseph
Screenwriter(s) Stevens, Louis; Jacobs, Harrison

Cast Rogers, Roy; Hayes, George "Gabby"; Moore, Pauline; Stone, Milburn; Eburne, Maude; Loft, Arthur; Taliaferro, Hal

Song(s) Night on the Prairie [1] (C/L: Hamilton, Albert; Gluck, Nate)

Notes There are also vocals of several Stephen Foster songs, including: "Ring De Banjo," "Oh Susannah," "Polly Wolly Doodle" and "De Camptown Races." [1] Also in THE GOLDEN STALLION.

1113 ✦ COLORADO SERENADE
PRC, 1946

Director(s) Tansey, Robert Emmett
Screenwriter(s) Kavanaugh, Frances

Cast Dean, Eddie; Ates, Roscoe; Sharpe, David; Kenyon, Mary; Taylor, Forrest; King, Charles

Song(s) Ridin' Down to Rawhide (C/L: Armstrong, Sam); Ridin' to the Top of the Mountain (C/L: Dean, Eddie; Hoefle, Carl); Western Lullaby (C/L: Dean, Eddie; Canova, H.L.)

1114 ✦ COLORADO SUNDOWN
Republic, 1951

Musical Score Butts, Dale

Producer(s) White, Edward J.
Director(s) Witney, William
Screenwriter(s) Taylor, Eric; Lively, William

Cast Allen, Rex; Kay, Mary Ellen; Pickens, Slim; Beavers, Louise; Vincent, June; The Republic Rhythm Riders

Song(s) Under California Stars [1] (C/L: Elliott, Jack)

Notes There is also a vocal of "Down by the River." [1] Also in UNDER CALIFORNIA STARS.

1115 ✦ COLORADO SUNSET
Republic, 1939

Producer(s) Berke, William
Director(s) Sherman, George
Screenwriter(s) Burbridge, Betty; Roberts, Stanley

Cast Autry, Gene; Burnette, Smiley; Storey, June; Pepper, Barbara; Crabbe, Buster [1]; Barrat, Robert; Lincoln, Elmo

Song(s) Poor Little Dogies [3] (C/L: Rose, Fred); The Merry Way Back Home (C/L: Samuels, Walter G.); Colorado Sunset [2] (C: Conrad, Con; L: Gilbert, L.

Wolfe); Seven Years (with the Wrong Woman) [4] (C/L: Nolan, Bob); Vote for Autry (C/L: Unknown)

Notes   No cue sheet available. [1] Billed as Larry "Buster" Crabbe. [2] Also in WESTERN JAMBOREE. [3] There is a similarly titled song, "Get Along Little Doggie" by Johnny Marvin and Fred Rose in WESTERN JAMBOREE. [4] Also in WESTERN JAMBOREE.

1116   ✦   THE COLOR OF MONEY
Touchstone, 1986

Musical Score   Robertson, Robbie

Producer(s)   Axelrad, Irving; De Fina, Barbara
Director(s)   Scorsese, Martin
Screenwriter(s)   Price, Richard
Source(s)   (novel) Tevis, Walter

Cast   Newman, Paul; Cruise, Tom; Mastrantonio, Mary Elizabeth; Shaver, Helen; Turturro, John; Cobbs, Bill

Song(s)   My Baby's In Love with Another Guy (C/L: Lucie, Lawrence; Brightman, Herman); Who Owns This Place? (C/L: Henley, Don; Kortchmar, Danny; Sother, J.D.); Let Yourself In for It (C/L: Palmer, Robert); Two Brothers and a Stranger (C/L: Knopfler, Mark); Don't Tell Me Nothin' (C/L: Dixon, Willie); It's in the Way You Use It (C/L: Clapton, Eric; Robertston, Robbie); Standing on the Edge (C/L: Williams, Jerry)

Notes   Only original songs listed.

1117   ✦   THE COLOR PURPLE
Warner Brothers, 1985

Musical Score   Jones, Quincy
Composer(s)   Jones, Quincy

Producer(s)   Kennedy, Kathleen; Marshall, Frank; Spielberg, Steven; Jones, Quincy
Director(s)   Spielberg, Steven
Screenwriter(s)   Meyjes, Menno
Source(s)   *The Color Purple* (novel) Walker, Alice

Cast   Goldberg, Whoopi; Glover, Danny; Caesar, Adolph; Avery, Margaret; Chong, Rae Dawn; Winfrey, Oprah; Busia, Akosua

Song(s)   Makidada (L: Jones, Quincy; Meyjes, Menno; Temperton, Rod); Pa's Wedding Hymn [1] (L: Jones, Quincy; Temperton, Rod; Richie, Lionel); Miss Celie's Blues [1] (L: Jones, Quincy; Temperton, Rod; Richie, Lionel); I Ain't Gonna Sing No Mo' (C/L: Jones, Quincy; Terry, Saunders Sonny); Don't Make Me No Never Mind (Slow Drag) (C/L: Jones, Quincy; Ingram, James); Maybe God Is Tryin' to Tell You Somethin' (C/L: Jones, Quincy; Crouch, Andrae; Maxwell, Bill; Del Sesto, David); Heaven Belongs to You (C/L: Crouch, Andrae; Crouch, Sandra)

Notes   [1] Same song.

1118   ✦   COLORS
Orion, 1988

Musical Score   Hancock, Herbie

Producer(s)   Solo, Robert H.
Director(s)   Hopper, Dennis
Screenwriter(s)   Schiffer, Michael

Cast   Penn, Sean; Duvall, Robert; Alonso, Maria Conchita; Brooks, Randy; Bush, Grand L.; Wayans, Damon

Song(s)   Colors (C: Ice-T; Islam, Afrika; L: Ice-T)

Notes   No cue sheet available.

1119   ✦   COMANCHE
United Artists, 1956

Musical Score   Gilbert, Herschel Burke

Producer(s)   Krueger, Carl
Director(s)   Sherman, George
Screenwriter(s)   Krueger, Carl

Cast   Andrews, Dana; Smith, Kent; Paiva, Nestor; Brandon, Henry; Litel, John; Sherman, Reed; Cristal, Linda

Song(s)   A Man Is As Good As His Word (C: Gilbert, Herschel Burke; L: Perry, Alfred)

1120   ✦   THE COMANCHEROS
Twentieth Century–Fox, 1961

Musical Score   Bernstein, Elmer

Producer(s)   Sherman, George
Director(s)   Curtiz, Michael
Screenwriter(s)   Grant, James Edward; Huffaker, Clair
Source(s)   *The Comancheros* (novel) Wellman, Paul I.

Cast   Wayne, John; Whitman, Stuart; Balin, Ina; Persoff, Nehemiah; Marvin, Lee; Ansara, Michael; Wayne, Patrick; Cabot, Bruce; Buchanan, Edgar; Daniell, Henry; Mobley, Roger

Song(s)   The Comancheros [1] (C/L: Franks, Tillman)

Notes   [1] Written for exploitation only.

1121   ✦   COME BACK CHARLESTON BLUE
Warner Brothers, 1972

Producer(s)   Goldwyn Jr., Samuel
Director(s)   Warren, Mark
Screenwriter(s)   Schweig, Bontche [1]; Elliott, Peggy
Source(s)   *The Heat's On* (novel) Himes, Chester

Cast   Allen, Jonelle; Cambridge, Godfrey; St. Jacques, Raymond

Song(s)   Come Back Charleston Blue (C: Jones, Quincy; Cleveland, Al; L: Hathaway, Donny)

Notes   Other songs seemed to be interpolated and not written for the picture. [1] Ernest Kinoy.

1122   ✦   COME BACK TO ME

See DOLL FACE.

1123   ✦   COME BLOW YOUR HORN
Paramount, 1963

Composer(s)   Van Heusen, James
Lyricist(s)   Cahn, Sammy

Producer(s)   Yorkin, Bud; Lear, Norman
Director(s)   Yorkin, Bud
Screenwriter(s)   Lear, Norman
Source(s)   *Come Blow Your Horn* (play) Simon, Neil

Cast   Sinatra, Frank; Picon, Molly; Cobb, Lee J.; St. John, Jill; Bill, Tony

Song(s)   Come Blow Your Horn; The Look of Love

1124   ✦   THE COMEDIANS
Metro–Goldwyn–Mayer, 1968

Musical Score   Rosenthal, Laurence

Producer(s)   Glenville, Peter
Director(s)   Glenville, Peter
Screenwriter(s)   Greene, Graham
Source(s)   *The Comedians* (novel) Greene, Graham

Cast   Burton, Richard; Taylor, Elizabeth; Guinness, Alec; Ustinov, Peter; Ford, Paul; Gish, Lillian; Browne, Roscoe Lee; Foster, Gloria; Jones, James Earl; Brown, George Stanford; Mokae, Zakes; Seck, Douta; St. Jacques, Raymond; Tyson, Cicely

Song(s)   Requin La (C/L: Laviny, Gerard)

1125   ✦   COME FLY WITH ME
Metro–Goldwyn–Mayer, 1963

Musical Score   Murray, Lyn

Producer(s)   de Grunwald, Anatole
Director(s)   Levin, Henry
Screenwriter(s)   Roberts, William
Source(s)   *Girl on a Wing* (novel) Glemser, Bernard

Cast   Hart, Dolores; O'Brian, Hugh; Boehm, Karl; Tiffin, Pamela; Nettleton, Lois; Addams, Dawn; Malden, Karl; Wattis, Richard; Cruickshank, Andrew; Dobson, James

Song(s)   Come Fly with Me (C: Van Heusen, James; L: Cahn, Sammy)

Notes   There is also a vocal of "La Chansonnette" by M. Phillipe Gerard and Jean Drejac.

1126   ✦   COME NEXT SPRING
Republic, 1955

Musical Score   Steiner, Max

Producer(s)   Yates, Herbert J.
Director(s)   Springsteen, R.G.
Screenwriter(s)   Pittman, Montgomery

Cast   Sheridan, Ann; Cochran, Steve; Brennan, Walter; Buchanan, Edgar; Tufts, Sonny; Shannon, Harry; Fulton, Rad; Clarke, Mae; Ates, Roscoe; Ruby, Wade; Best, James

Song(s)   Come Next Spring (C: Steiner, Max; L: Adelson, Lenny)

Notes   There is also a vocal of "God Moves in a Mysterious Way."

1127   ✦   COME ON DANGER
RKO, 1941

Musical Score   Dreyer, Dave; Sawtell, Paul
Composer(s)   Whitley, Ray; Rose, Fred
Lyricist(s)   Whitley, Ray; Rose, Fred

Producer(s)   Gilroy, Bert
Director(s)   Hill, Robert
Screenwriter(s)   Lewis, David; Ilfeld, Lester

Cast   Keene, Tom; Haydon, Julie; Ates, Roscoe; Ellis, Robert; Scott, William

Song(s)   Come On Danger; On the Trail Again; Old Bowlegged Jones

Notes   Formerly titled THE LAW RIDES.

1128   ✦   COME ON MARINES
Paramount, 1932 unproduced

Composer(s)   Rainger, Ralph
Lyricist(s)   Robin, Leo

Song(s)   Hula Holiday; Oh Baby, Obey [1]

Notes   This production was abandoned. The movie was finally made in 1934 but without the song. [1] Also not used in FOUR HOURS TO KILL and GIVE ME A SAILOR.

1129   ✦   COME ON RANGERS
Republic, 1938

Composer(s)   Kent, Walter
Lyricist(s)   Cherkose, Eddie

Producer(s)   Ford, Charles E.
Director(s)   Kane, Joseph
Screenwriter(s)   Geraghty, Gerald; Natteford, Jack

Cast   Rogers, Roy; Hart, Mary; Hatton, Raymond; McDonald, J. Farrell; Pratt, Purnell; Woods, Harry; MacFarlane, Bruce; Chandler, Lane

Song(s) Song of the West; Let Me Hum a Western Tune; I've Learned a Lot About Women (C/L: Marvin, Johnny)

1130 ✦ COMES A HORSEMAN
United Artists, 1978

Musical Score Small, Michael

Producer(s) Kirkwood, Gene; Paulson, Dan
Director(s) Pakula, Alan J.
Screenwriter(s) Clark, Dennis Lynton

Cast Caan, James; Fonda, Jane; Robards Jr., Jason; Grizzard, George; Farnsworth, Richard; Harmon, Mark

Song(s) Old Paint (C/L: Small, Michael); I Got No Use for the Women (C/L: Small, Michael)

1131 ✦ COME SEPTEMBER
Universal, 1961

Musical Score Salter, Hans J.
Composer(s) Darin, Bobby
Lyricist(s) Darin, Bobby

Producer(s) Arthur, Robert
Director(s) Mulligan, Robert
Screenwriter(s) Shapiro, Stanley; Richlin, Maurice

Cast Hudson, Rock; Slezak, Walter; Lollobrigida, Gina; Dee, Sandra; Darin, Bobby; Grey, Joel; De Banzie, Brenda; Howard, Ron

Song(s) Come September; Multiplication

1132 ✦ COME SPY WITH ME
Twentieth Century–Fox, 1967

Musical Score Bowers, Robert C.

Producer(s) Heller, Paul
Director(s) Stone, Marshall
Screenwriter(s) Berg, Cherney

Cast Donahue, Troy; Dromm, Andrea; Dekker, Albert

Song(s) Come Spy with Me (C/L: Robinson Jr., William); Shark (C: Bowers, Robert C.; L: Butler, J.)

1133 ✦ COME TO THE STABLE
Twentieth Century–Fox, 1949

Musical Score Mockridge, Cyril J.

Producer(s) Engel, Samuel G.
Director(s) Koster, Henry
Screenwriter(s) Millard, Oscar; Benson, Sally

Cast Young, Loretta; Holm, Celeste; Marlowe, Hugh [1]; Lanchester, Elsa; Gomez, Thomas; Patrick, Dorothy [2]; Ruysdael, Basil; Wilson, Dooley; Toomey, Regis; Mazurki, Mike

Song(s) Through a Long and Sleepless Night (C: Newman, Alfred; L: Gordon, Mack); Canticle (C: Newman, Alfred; L: Wagner, Roger); My Bolero [3] (C/L: Kennedy, James; Simon, Nat)

Notes [1] Dubbed by Ken Darby. [2] Dubbed by Eileen Wilson. [3] Not on cue sheets though in some sources.

1134 ✦ COME UP SMILING

See SING ME A LOVE SONG.

1135 ✦ COMFORT AND JOY
Universal, 1984

Musical Score Knopfler, Mark
Composer(s) Park, Andy
Lyricist(s) Park, Andy

Producer(s) Belling, Davina; Parsons, Clive
Director(s) Forsyth, Bill
Screenwriter(s) Forsyth, Bill

Cast Paterson, Bill; David, Eleanor; Grogan, C.P.; Norton, Alex; Bernardi, Patrick

Song(s) Love Over Gold (C/L: Knopfler, Mark); 6 O'Clock Jingle; News ID; News Jingle; Time to Get Up Jingle; Dicky Bird Jingle; Lookalike Jingle; Traffic Jingle; Station ID; Time Alone (C/L: Anderson; Clark); Rufus Jingle; Keep Fit Programme; Recipe Jingle

1136 ✦ COMING HOME
United Artists, 1978

Composer(s) Carradine, Robert; Jones, Robert C.
Lyricist(s) Carradine, Robert; Jones, Robert C.

Producer(s) Hellman, Jerome
Director(s) Ashby, Hal
Screenwriter(s) Salt, Waldo; Jones, Robert C.

Cast Voight, Jon; Fonda, Jane; Dern, Bruce; Ginty, Robert; Milford, Penelope; Carradine, Robert; Cyphers, Charles

Song(s) What Is Tomorrow; Follow (C/L: Merrick, Jerry); Too Many Days

Notes Only what I believe are original songs listed.

1137 ✦ COMING OUT PARTY
Fox, 1934

Producer(s) Lasky, Jesse L.
Director(s) Blystone, John
Screenwriter(s) Unger, Gladys; Lasky Jr., Jesse

Cast Dee, Frances; Raymond, Gene

Song(s) I Think You're Wonderful (C: Lane, Burton; L: Adamson, Harold)

1138 ◆ COMING TO AMERICA
Paramount, 1988

Musical Score Rodgers, Nile

Producer(s) Wachs, Robert D.; Folsey Jr., George
Director(s) Landis, John
Screenwriter(s) Sheffield, David; Blaustein, Barry

Cast Murphy, Eddie; Hall, Arsenio; Jones, James Earl; Amos, John; Sinclair, Madge; Headley, Shari

Song(s) She's Your Queen to Be (C/L: Blaustein, Barry; Sheffield, David); I Got It (C/L: Rodgers, Nile); All Dressed Up (Ready to Hit the Town) (C/L: Moffett, Jonathan Phillip); Vocal Rap Pattern (C/L: Blaustein, Barry; Sheffield, David); Better Late Than Never (C/L: Scott, Alan Roy; Washington, Freddie); Come Into My Life (C/L: Chiten, Paul; Phillips-Oland, Pamela); Transparent (C/L: Willis, Allee; Sembello, Danny); I Like It Like That [2] (C/L: Rodgers, Michael; Tolbert, Lloyd); Addicted to You (C/L: Levert, Gerald; Levert, Eddie; Gordon, Marc); Livin' the Good Life (C: Rodgers, Nile; L: Cole, Gardner); Coming to America (C: Rodgers, Nile; L: Huang, Nancy); Comin' Correct [1]; (C/L: Dre, Dr.); That's The Way It Is [1] (C/L: Waterman, Stock)

Notes [1] Sheet music only. [2] Titled "I Like It That Way" on sheet music.

1139 ◆ COMIN' ROUND THE MOUNTAIN (1936)
Republic, 1936

Composer(s) Stept, Sam H.
Lyricist(s) Drake, Oliver

Producer(s) Schaefer, Armand
Director(s) Wright, Mack V.
Screenwriter(s) Drake, Oliver; McGowan, Dorrell; McGowan, Stuart

Cast Autry, Gene; Rutherford, Ann; Burnette, Smiley; Mason, Roy; Cooper, Ken; Lane, Tracy

Song(s) Chiquita; When the Campfire Is Low on the Prairie [1] (L: Stept, Sam H.); Don Juan of Seville

Notes No cue sheet available. [1] Also in THE RANGER AND THE LADY. [2] Also in INDIAN TERRITORY (Columbia) and GUNSMOKE RANCH (with Sidney Mitchell credited for lyrics).

1140 ◆ COMIN' ROUND THE MOUNTAIN (1951)
Universal, 1951

Musical Score Skinner, Frank
Composer(s) Wood, Britt
Lyricist(s) Beatty, George
Choreographer(s) Belfer, Hal

Producer(s) Christie, Howard
Director(s) Lamont, Charles
Screenwriter(s) Lees, Robert; Rinaldo, Frederic I.

Cast Abbott, Bud; Costello, Lou; Shay, Dorothy; Grant, Kirby; Sawyer, Joe; Wilkerson, Guy; Strange, Glenn; Moore, Ida; Cogan, Shaye

Song(s) Agnes Clung (C/L: Smith, Hessie; Shay, Dorothy); Why Don't Someone Marry Mary Anne; Sagebrush Sadie; You Broke Your Promise (C/L: Taylor, Irving; Wyle, George; Pola, Eddie); Another Notch on Father's Shotgun (C/L: Wrubel, Allie; Ray, Joey; Wrubel, Robert)

1141 ◆ COMMANDO
Twentieth Century–Fox, 1985

Musical Score Horner, James

Producer(s) Silver, Joel
Director(s) Lester, Mark L.
Screenwriter(s) de Souza, Steven E.

Cast Schwarzenegger, Arnold; Chong, Rae Dawn; Hedaya, Dan; Wells, Vernon; Olson, James; Kelly, David Patrick; Milano, Alyssa

Song(s) We Fight for Love (C: Horner, James; L: Des Barres, Michael)

Notes No cue sheet available.

1142 ◆ COMMANDOS STRIKE AT DAWN
Columbia, 1942

Musical Score Gruenberg, Louis

Producer(s) Cowan, Lester
Director(s) Farrow, John
Screenwriter(s) Shaw, Irwin
Source(s) "The Commandos" (story) Forester, C.S.

Cast Muni, Paul; Lee, Anna; Gish, Lillian; Hardwicke, Sir Cedric; Coote, Robert; Collins, Ray; De Camp, Rosemary; Derr, Richard; Knox, Alexander; Cameron, Rod; Heydt, Louis Jean; Bridges, Lloyd; Van Zandt, Philip

Song(s) Commandos March (C: Ronell, Ann; Gruenberg, Louis L: Ronell, Ann); Out to Pick the Berries (C/L: Ronell, Ann)

1143 ◆ COMMON CLAY
Fox, 1930

Director(s) Fleming, Victor
Screenwriter(s) Furthman, Jules
Source(s) *Common Clay* (novel) Kincaid, Cleves

Cast Bennett, Constance; Ayres, Lew; Marshall, Tully; Kemp, Matty; Pratt, Purnell; Mercer, Beryl

Song(s)   I Feel That Certain Feeling Coming On (C: Monaco, James V.; L: Friend, Cliff)

Notes   No cue sheet available.

1144 ✦ THE COMMON TOUCH
Republic, 1941

Musical Score   Russell, Kennedy
Composer(s)   Russell, Kennedy
Lyricist(s)   O'Connor, Desmond

Producer(s)   Baxter, John
Director(s)   Baxter, John
Screenwriter(s)   Emary, Barbara K.; Orme, Geoffrey

Cast   Gynt, Greta; Hibbert, Geoffrey; Howard, Joyce; Welchman, Harry; Miles, Bernard; Gibbons, Carroll

Song(s)   Harmonize; Round the Back of the Arches; The Cubanoca

Notes   A British National picture.

1145 ✦ COMPANY OF COWARDS
Metro–Goldwyn–Mayer, 1966

Musical Score   Sparks, Randy
Composer(s)   Sparks, Randy
Lyricist(s)   Sparks, Randy

Producer(s)   Richmond, Ted
Director(s)   Marshall, George
Screenwriter(s)   Peeples, Samuel A.; Bowers, William
Source(s)   *The Company of Cowards* (novel) Chamberlain, William

Cast   Ford, Glenn; Stevens, Stella; Douglas, Melvyn; Backus, Jim; Blondell, Joan; Prine, Andrew; Pearson, Jesse; Hale, Alan; Bissell, Whit

Song(s)   Company of Cowards; This Ol' Riverboat; Ladies; Today; Abe

Notes   Titled ADVANCE TO THE REAR internationally.

1146 ✦ THE COMPETITION
Columbia, 1980

Musical Score   Schifrin, Lalo

Producer(s)   Sackheim, William
Director(s)   Oliansky, Joel
Screenwriter(s)   Oliansky, Joel

Cast   Stern, Adam; Henderson, Ty; Kriegler, Vickie; Remick, Lee; Irving, Amy; Dreyfuss, Richard; Sikking, James B.

Song(s)   People Alone (C: Schifrin, Lalo; L: Jennings, Wilbur)

Notes   No cue sheet available.

1147 ✦ COMPULSION
Twentieth Century–Fox, 1959

Musical Score   Newman, Lionel

Producer(s)   Zanuck, Richard D.
Director(s)   Fleischer, Richard
Screenwriter(s)   Murphy, Richard
Source(s)   *Compulsion* (novel) Levin, Meyer

Cast   Welles, Orson; Varsi, Diane; Stockwell, Dean; Dillman, Bradford; Marshall, E.G.; Milner, Martin; Anderson, Richard; Binns, Edward; MacLeod, Gavin

Song(s)   Evil's in Me [1] (C: Myrow, Fred; L: Surmagne, Jacques)

Notes   [1] Written for exploitation only.

1148 ✦ COMPUTER KILLERS

See HORROR HOSPITAL.

1149 ✦ THE COMPUTER WORE TENNIS SHOES
Disney, 1969

Musical Score   Brunner, Robert F.

Producer(s)   Anderson, Bill
Director(s)   Butler, Robert
Screenwriter(s)   McEveety, Joseph L.

Cast   Russell, Kurt; Romero, Cesar; Flynn, Joe; Schallert, William; Hewitt, Alan; Bakalyan, Richard; Provost, Jon; Harrington Jr., Pat; Feld, Fritz

Song(s)   The Computer Wore Tennis Shoes (C: Brunner, Robert F.; L: Belland, Bruce)

1150 ✦ COMRADE X
Metro–Goldwyn–Mayer, 1940

Musical Score   Kaper, Bronislau

Producer(s)   Reinhardt, Gottfried
Director(s)   Vidor, King
Screenwriter(s)   Hecht, Ben; Lederer, Charles

Cast   Gable, Clark; Lamarr, Hedy; Homolka, Oscar; Arden, Eve; Bressart, Felix

Song(s)   The Little Man Who Wasn't There (C: Hanighen, Bernie; L: Adamson, Harold); Burial Chant (C: Kaper, Bronislau; L: Tolstoi, Andrei); We Are Free (C: Kaper, Bronislau; L: Tolstoi, Andrei)

1151 ✦ THE CONCORDE—AIRPORT '79
Universal, 1979

Musical Score   Schifrin, Lalo

Producer(s)   Lang, Jennings
Director(s)   Rich, David Lowell

Screenwriter(s)   Roth, Eric
Source(s)   *Airport* (novel) Hailey, Arthur

Cast   Wagner, Robert; Blakely, Susan; Delon, Alain; Kristel, Sylvia; Albert, Eddie; Andersson, Bibi; Charo; Davidson, John; Raye, Martha; Tyson, Cicely; Warner, David; McCambridge, Mercedes; Begley Jr., Ed

Song(s)   You're a Miracle [1] (C: Schifrin, Lalo; L: Garnett, Gale)

Notes   [1] Used instrumentally only in later version of the movie (1981) when just titled CONCORDE not THE CONCORDE—AIRPORT '79.

1152 ✦ CONDEMNED
United Artists, 1929

Producer(s)   Goldwyn, Samuel
Director(s)   Ruggles, Wesley; Digges, Dudley
Screenwriter(s)   Howard, Sidney
Source(s)   *Condemned to Devil's Island* (novel) Niles, Blair

Cast   Colman, Ronald; Harding, Ann; Digges, Dudley; Wolheim, Louis; Elmer, William; Kingsley, Albert

Song(s)   Song of the Condemned (C: Wendling, Pete; L: Meskill, Jack)

Notes   No cue sheet available.

1153 ✦ CONEY ISLAND
Twentieth Century–Fox, 1943

Composer(s)   Rainger, Ralph
Lyricist(s)   Robin, Leo
Choreographer(s)   Pan, Hermes

Producer(s)   Perlberg, William
Director(s)   Lang, Walter
Screenwriter(s)   Seaton, George

Cast   Grable, Betty; Montgomery, George; Romero, Cesar; Winninger, Charles; Silvers, Phil; Briggs, Matt; Hurst, Paul; Orth, Frank; Tombes, Andrew; Seymour, Harry

Song(s)   Beautiful Coney Island; There's Danger in a Dance; Take It From There; Miss Lulu from Louisville; Get the Money; Old Demon Rum [1]

Notes   "Put Your Arms Around Me, Honey" by Albert Von Tilzer and Junie McCree; "Who Threw the Overalls in Mistress Murphy's Chowder?" by George L Giefer; "In My Harem" by Irving Berlin; "When Irish Eyes Are Smiling" by Ernest R. Ball, Chauncey Olcott and George Graff; "Cuddle Up a Little Closer, Lovey Mine" by Karl Hoschna and Otto Harbach; "Pretty Baby" by Tony Jackson and Egbert Van Alstyne and "I'm Looking for a Sweetheart" by Raymond A. Browne are also used vocally. [1] Not used.

1154 ✦ CONFESSION
Warner Brothers–First National, 1937

Musical Score   Kreuder, Peter

Producer(s)   Wallis, Hal B.
Director(s)   May, Joe; Logan, Stanley
Screenwriter(s)   Epstein, Julius J.; Levino, Margaret
Source(s)   "Mazurka" (story) Rameau, Hans

Cast   Francis, Kay; Rathbone, Basil; Hunter, Ian; Crisp, Donald; Bryan, Jane; Crews, Laura Hope; Borg, Veda Ann

Song(s)   One Hour of Romance (C: Kreuder, Peter; L: Scholl, Jack)

1155 ✦ CONFESSIONS OF A CO-ED
Paramount, 1931

Director(s)   Burton, David; Murphy, Dudley

Cast   Sidney, Sylvia; Holmes, Phillips; Foster, Norman

Song(s)   Out of Nowhere [1] (C: Green, Johnny; L: Heyman, Edward); Ya Got Love (C: Goodhart, Al; Hoffman, Al; L: Nelson, Ed G.)

Notes   Released as HER DILEMMA in Great Britain. [1] Also in THE FIVE PENNIES.

1156 ✦ CONFESSIONS OF A POP PERFORMER
Columbia, 1975

Musical Score   Welch, Ed
Composer(s)   Bugatti, Dominic; Musker, Frank
Lyricist(s)   Bugatti, Dominic; Musker, Frank

Producer(s)   Smith, Greg
Director(s)   Cohen, Norman
Screenwriter(s)   Wood, Christopher
Source(s)   Confession series (novels) Lea, Timothy

Cast   Askwith, Robin; Booth, Anthony; Hare, Doris; White, Sheila; Gascoine, Jill; Lenska, Rula; Maynard, Bill

Song(s)   Confessions of Timmy Lee; Kipper; I Need You

Notes   There was one more song on the cue sheet that could not be identified: "The—pham."

1157 ✦ CONFIRM OR DENY
Twentieth Century–Fox, 1941

Producer(s)   Hammond, Len
Director(s)   Mayo, Archie
Screenwriter(s)   Swerling, Jo

Cast   Ameche, Don; Bennett, Joan; McDowall, Roddy; Loder, John; Walburn, Raymond; Shields, Arthur; Blore, Eric; Reynolds, Helene; Leonard, Queenie; Bevan, Billy

Song(s)   Bless 'Em All [1] (C/L: Hughes, Jimmy; Lake, Frank; Stillman, Al)

Notes   [1] Not written for this production.

1158 ✦ CONGORILLA
Twentieth Century–Fox, 1932

Producer(s) Johnson, Martin; Johnson, Osa
Director(s) Johnson, Martin; Johnson, Osa

Song(s) Congorilla (C: DeFrancesco, Louis E.; L: Bryan, Alfred)

Notes This is a documentary.

1159 ✦ CONGO SWING

See BLONDIE GOES LATIN.

1160 ✦ CONGRESS DANCES
United Artists, 1932

Composer(s) Heymann, Werner
Lyricist(s) Gilbert, Roland

Producer(s) Pommer, Erich
Director(s) Charell, Erik
Screenwriter(s) Falk, Norbert; Nachmann, Kurt

Cast Harvey, Lilian; Garat, Henry; Veidt, Conrad; Dagover, Lil; McLaughlin, Gibb; Purdell, Reginald

Song(s) Only Happens Once (Das Gibts Nur Einmal) (L: Phillips, Felicia; Harold, Peter); The Music Was So Gay (Es Muss Doch Was Gaeschehn); Vienna In May (Das Muss Ein Stueck vom Himmel Sein); Live, Laugh and Love [1] (L: Leigh, Rowland); Just Once for All Time [1] (L: Leigh, Rowland); When the Music Plays [1] (L: Leigh, Rowland)

Notes This is a UFA studio German picture (originally titled DIE KONGRESS TANZT) released by United Artists. It was later also released by Republic. English lyrics by Phillips and Harold used only. [1] Sheet music only.

1161 ✦ A CONNECTICUT YANKEE
Fox, 1931

Composer(s) Kernell, William
Lyricist(s) Kernell, William

Director(s) Butler, David
Screenwriter(s) Conselman, William
Source(s) *A Connecticut Yankee in King Arthur's Court* (novel) Twain, Mark

Cast Rogers, Will; O'Sullivan, Maureen; Loy, Myrna; Albertson, Frank

Song(s) Goodnight; Springtime

1162 ✦ A CONNECTICUT YANKEE IN KING ARTHUR'S COURT
Paramount, 1949

Musical Score Young, Victor
Composer(s) Van Heusen, James
Lyricist(s) Burke, Johnny

Producer(s) Fellows, Robert
Director(s) Garnett, Tay
Screenwriter(s) Beloin, Edmund
Source(s) *A Connecticut Yankee in King Arthur's Court* (novel) Twain, Mark

Cast Fleming, Rhonda; Crosby, Bing; Bendix, William; Hardwicke, Sir Cedric

Song(s) If You Stub Your Toe on the Moon; 'Twixt Myself and Me [1]; When Is Sometime?; Once and for Always; Busy Doing Nothing

Notes Rodgers and Hammerstein were approached to write additional numbers for the film. The first consideration was that the team required that the music be published by Williamson (Rodgers and Hammerstein's publishing company) but Harms (the original publisher of the Rodgers and Hart score) had the rights to all new songs by Rodgers and Hammerstein. The songwriters were busy putting ALLEGRO together and Hammerstein felt he would be tied up during the time when the new songs would have to be written. Rodgers indicated in a memo that he would be willing to work with another lyricist. A copy of that memo was sent to Frank Loesser. Before anyone had time to react to that suggestion (including Crosby who had veto power), Rodgers and Hammerstein decided they would have time after all. At this point the Rodgers and Hart songs "Thou Swell" and "My Heart Stood Still" were slated to be in the production. Crosby was amenable to whoever would write the songs and suggested Deanna Durbin as his costar. Paramount was leery since her last few pictures had not done well. Crosby decided to go see OKLAHOMA! in New York and check up on Mary Hatcher who was appearing therein. Paramount was also interested in Jo Stafford who was beginning to attain some renown. But she was deemed too tall for Crosby. Beryl David was also considered and rejected, although Paramount felt "she will probably achieve popularity comparable to Dinah Shore's."

Rodgers then decided that if he were to do it he would have to collaborate with Hammerstein. Money was discussed but still the spectre of the work left on Allegro loomed. Finally on June 5, 1947, it was mutually agreed that the team would not write new songs. On June 13, 1947, Burke and Van Heusen, already under contract to Paramount, were assigned the picture.

Warners originally had the rights to the novel by Mark Twain from the author's estate and rights to the musical comedy. Warners had an agreement with Harms that any new songs would be published by Harms. When Paramount bought the rights from Warners they also signed the contract containing the clause giving publishing rights to Paramount. Paramount then decided to base its screenplay entirely on the novel and not use any Rodgers and Hart songs, thereby avoiding having to have any songs published by Harms and instead having its own publishing house, Famous Music, own the songs. Rodgers and Hammerstein contacted Paramount to offer their services after January 1, 1948 to write an original motion picture score. MGM had begun production on WORDS AND MUSIC based on the lives of Rodgers and Hart. Unfortunately for MGM, Paramount had the rights to the songs from A CONNECTICUT YANKEE as well as the Rodgers and Hart songs from early Paramount pictures. Paramount sold rights to the early numbers and insisted that as far as "Thou Swell" was concerned, since it was already filmed, MGM could use it but had to delete all references to the number originally being in A CONNECTICUT YANKEE. Paramount further stated that if MGM wanted to also use "My Heart Stood Still" they could not release their picture until two years had passed—February 22, 1950. After much more legal wrangling and reminders of favors of past times (see BLUE SKIES), Paramount agreed to let MGM use "My Heart Stood Still" for one chorus as sung by an unseen chorus. [1] Not used.

1163 ✦ THE CONQUEROR
RKO, 1956

Musical Score Young, Victor
Choreographer(s) Sidney, Robert

Producer(s) Powell, Dick
Director(s) Powell, Dick
Screenwriter(s) Millard, Oscar

Cast Wayne, John; Hayward, Susan; Armendariz, Pedro; Moorehead, Agnes; Gomez, Thomas; Hoyt, John; Conrad, William; De Corsia, Ted

Song(s) Oriental Lament [1] (C/L: Bakaleinikoff, Constantin); The Conqueror (C: Young, Victor; L: Heyman, Edward)

Notes [1] Lyric written for exploitation only.

1164 ✦ CONSPIRACY
RKO, 1939

Musical Score Tours, Frank

Producer(s) LeBaron, William
Director(s) Cabanne, Christy
Screenwriter(s) Dix, Beulah Marie

Cast Love, Bessie; Sparks, Ned; Trevor, Hugh

Song(s) Take the World Off Your Shoulders [1] (C: Fain, Sammy; L: Brown, Lew)

Notes [1] Also in MEXICAN SPITFIRE AT SEA.

1165 ✦ THE CONSTANT NYMPH
Warner Brothers–First National, 1943

Musical Score Korngold, Erich Wolfgang [1]

Producer(s) Blanke, Henry
Director(s) Goulding, Edmund
Screenwriter(s) Scola, Kathryn

Source(s) *The Constant Nymph* (play) Kennedy, Margaret; Dean, Basil

Cast Boyer, Charles [1]; Fontaine, Joan; Smith, Alexis; Coburn, Charles; Whitty, Dame May; Lorre, Peter; Reynolds, Joyce

Song(s) Tomorrow (C: Korngold, Erich Wolfgang; L: Kennedy, Margaret)

Notes [1] Korngold's piano playing is heard on the soundtrack dubbing for Charles Boyer.

1166 ✦ CONTINENTAL DIVIDE
Universal, 1981

Musical Score Small, Michael

Producer(s) Larson, Bob
Director(s) Apted, Michael
Screenwriter(s) Kasdan, Lawrence

Cast Belushi, John; Brown, Blair; Goorwitz, Allen; Glynn, Carlin; Ganios, Tony; Avery, Val

Song(s) Never Say Goodbye (C: Small, Michael; L: Sager, Carole Bayer)

Notes No cue sheet available.

1167 ✦ CONVOY
United Artists, 1979

Musical Score Davis, Chip

Producer(s) Sherman, Robert M.
Director(s) Peckinpah, Sam
Screenwriter(s) Norton, B.W.L.
Source(s) (song) McCall, C.W.

Cast Kristofferson, Kris; MacGraw, Ali; Borgnine, Ernest; Young, Burt; Sinclair, Madge; Ajaye, Franklyn; Davies, Brian; Cassel, Seymour; Yates, Cassie

Song(s) Convoy (C: Davis, Chip; L: Fries, Bill); Charge of the Semi-Light Brigade (C: Davis, Chip; L: Fries, Bill)

Notes Only original songs listed.

1168 ✦ COOGAN'S BLUFF
Universal, 1968

Musical Score Schifrin, Lalo
Composer(s) Schifrin, Lalo
Lyricist(s) Holmes, Wally

Producer(s) Siegel, Don
Director(s) Siegel, Don
Screenwriter(s) Miller, Herman; Riesner, Dean; Rodman, Howard

Cast Eastwood, Clint; Stroud, Don; Cobb, Lee J.; Clark, Susan; Sterling, Tisha; Field, Betty

Song(s) Pigeon-Toed Orange Peel; Everybody

1169 ✦ COOL BREEZE
Metro–Goldwyn–Mayer, 1972

Musical Score Burke Sr., Solomon V.
Composer(s) Burke Sr., Solomon V.
Lyricist(s) Burke Jr., Solomon

Producer(s) Corman, Gene
Director(s) Pollack, Barry
Screenwriter(s) Pollack, Barry
Source(s) *The Asphalt Jungle* (novel) Burnett, W.R.

Cast Rasulala, Thalmus; Pace, Judy; Watkins, Jim; Kelly, Paula; Kilpatrick, Lincoln; Grier, Pam; St. Jacques, Raymond

Song(s) Cool Breeze; Everlasting Life (C/L: Frazier, Thurston); We're Almost Home; Get Up and Do Something for Yourself; Love Affair [1]; It Must Be Love [1]; The Bus [1]; Fight Back [1]

Notes A remake of THE ASPHALT JUNGLE. [1] Used instrumentally only.

1170 ✦ COOL HAND LUKE
Warner Brothers, 1967

Musical Score Schifrin, Lalo

Producer(s) Carroll, Gordon
Director(s) Rosenberg, Stuart
Screenwriter(s) Pearce, Donn; Pierson, Stuart

Cast Newman, Paul; Kennedy, George; Cannon, J.D.; Antonio, Lou; Drivas, Robert; Martin, Strother; Van Fleet, Jo

Song(s) Plastic Jesus (C/L: Cromarty, George; Rush, Ed); Down Here on the Ground [1] (C: Schifrin, Lalo; L: Garnett, Gale)

Notes It is not known if this was written for the film. [1] Lyric written for exploitation only.

1171 ✦ THE COOL ONES
Warner Brothers, 1967

Musical Score Freeman, Ernie
Composer(s) Hazlewood, Lee
Lyricist(s) Hazlewood, Lee

Producer(s) Conrad, William
Director(s) Nelson, Gene
Screenwriter(s) Geller, Joyce
Source(s) "The Swingers" (story) Geller, Joyce

Cast McDowall, Roddy; Watson, Debbie; Peterson, Gil; Harris, Phil; Coote, Robert; Talbot, Nita; Furth, George; Miller, Mrs.; Campbell, Glen; The Bantams; The Leaves; T.J. and the Fourmations

Song(s) The Cool One's Prologue; The Cool Ones (C/L: Hazlewood, Lee; Strange, Billy); Doctor Stone (C/L: Pons, Jim; Beck, John); This Town; High (C/L: Hazlewood, Lee; Strange, Billy); Panorama Pa-Cliff-Ic (C/L: Strange, Billy); Hey Hey Ronnie (C/L: Senter, Bruce); The Tantrum; It's Your World; Olivera Street Kids Running (C/L: Strange, Billy); Hands; Where Did I Go Wrong (C/L: Lloyd, Jack; Strange, Billy); Baby, Baby, Your Love Is All I Need; A Bad Woman's Love

Notes Some of these songs last less than one minute. There are also renditions of "It's Magic" by Sammy Cahn and Jule Styne; "The Birth of the Blues" by B.G. DeSylva, Lew Brown and Ray Henderson; "Just One of Those Things" by Cole Porter; "Secret Love" by Sammy Fain and Paul Francis Webster and "What Is This Thing Called Love" by Cole Porter.

1172 ✦ CO-OPTIMISTS
New Era, 1930

Director(s) Greenwood, Edwin
Source(s) *Co-Optimists* (musical revue) Gideon, Melville; Burnby, Davy; de Bear, Archibald

Cast Burnaby, Dave; Monkman, Phyllis; Cliff, Laddie; Chester, Betty; Pepper, Harry; MacFarlane, Elsa; Childs, Gilbert; Gideon, Melville

Notes No cue sheet available. This is basically a filmed version of the British musical comedy revue.

1173 ✦ COPACABANA
United Artists, 1947

Musical Score Ward, Edward
Composer(s) Coslow, Sam
Lyricist(s) Coslow, Sam

Producer(s) Coslow, Sam
Director(s) Green, Alfred E.
Screenwriter(s) Vadnay, Laslo; Boretz, Allen; Harris, Howard

Cast Marx, Groucho; Miranda, Carmen; Cochran, Steve; Jean, Gloria; Russell, Andy; Sanford, Ralph; Tombes, Andrew; Sobol, Louis; Wilson, Earl; Green, Abel

Song(s) Je Vous Aime [2]; If You Want to Make a Hit with Fifi; Stranger Things Have Happened [2]; Go West Young Man [2] (C: Ruby, Harry; L: Kalmar, Bert); My Heart Was Doing a Bolero; Let's Do the Copacabana [2]; I Haven't Got a Thing to Sell; We've Come to the Copa [2]; Tico Tico No Fuba [1] (C: Abreu, Zequinha; L: Oliveira, Aloysio; Drake, Ervin)

Notes [1] Also used in BOMBALERA (Paramount), the Columbia pictures GAY SENORITA and KANSAS CITY KITTY, IT'S A PLEASURE (RKO) and BATHING BEAUTY (MGM). [2] Edward Ward is also credited with music on cue sheet, probably for incidental music during the songs or for small contributions.

1174 ✦ COP-OUT
Cinerama Releasing, 1968

Musical Score   Scott, Patrick John

Producer(s)   de Grunwald, Dimitri
Director(s)   Rouve, Pierre
Screenwriter(s)   Rouve, Pierre
Source(s)   *Strangers in the House* (novel) Simenon, Georges

Cast   Darin, Bobby; Mason, James; Chaplin, Geraldine; Bertoya, Paul; Ogilvy, Ian

Song(s)   Ain't That So (C: Scott, Patrick John; L: Briggs, Vic)

Notes   No cue sheet available.

1175 ✦ COPPER CANYON
Paramount, 1950

Musical Score   Amfitheatrof, Daniele
Choreographer(s)   Earl, Josephine

Producer(s)   Epstein, Mel
Director(s)   Farrow, John
Screenwriter(s)   Latimer, Jonathan

Cast   Faylen, Frank; Emerson, Hope; Milland, Ray; Lamarr, Hedy; Carey, Macdonald; Freeman, Mona; Carey Jr., Harry

Song(s)   Copper Canyon (C/L: Livingston, Jay; Evans, Ray); Square Dance Calls (C/L: Boutelje, Phil; Gotcher, Les)

1176 ✦ COPPER SKY
Twentieth Century–Fox, 1957

Musical Score   Kraushaar, Raoul

Producer(s)   Stabler, Robert W.
Director(s)   Warren, Charles Marquis
Screenwriter(s)   Norden, Eric

Cast   Morrow, Jeff; Gray, Coleen; Martin, Strother; Brinegar, Paul; Lomas, Jack

Song(s)   Copper Sky (C: Krashaar, Raoul; L: Hooven, Marilyn; Hooven, Joe)

1177 ✦ COQUETTE
United Artists, 1929

Director(s)   Taylor, Sam
Screenwriter(s)   Taylor, Sam
Source(s)   *Coquette* (play) Abbott, George; Bridgers, Anne P.

Cast   Pickford, Mary; Brown, Johnny Mack; Moore, Matt; Sainpolis, John; Janney, William; Beavers, Louise

Song(s)   Coquette (C/L: Berlin, Irving)

Notes   No cue sheet available.

1178 ✦ CORKY
Metro–Goldwyn–Mayer, 1971

Musical Score   Parker, John Carl

Producer(s)   Geller, Bruce
Director(s)   Horn, Leonard
Screenwriter(s)   Price, Eugene

Cast   Blake, Robert; Rampling, Charlotte; O'Neal, Patrick; Connelly, Christopher; Payton-Wright, Pamela; Johnson, Ben; Luckinbill, Laurence; Stevens, Pamela; Allison, Bobby; Allison, Donnie; Baker, Buddy; Petty, Richard; Yarborough, Cale

Song(s)   Boy Would I Be Lookin' Good (C/L: Murray, Larry); Lookin' Good (C/L: Barry, Jeff); Softly and Tenderly (C/L: Hendricks, James)

1179 ✦ CORONADO
Paramount, 1935

Composer(s)   Whiting, Richard A.
Lyricist(s)   Coslow, Sam
Choreographer(s)   Prinz, LeRoy

Producer(s)   LeBaron, William
Director(s)   McLeod, Norman Z.
Screenwriter(s)   Hartman, Don; Butler, Frank

Cast   Eddy Duchin and His Orchestra; Burgess, Betty; Downs, Johnny; The Nicholas Brothers; Haley, Jack; Errol, Leon; Wells, Jacqueline

Song(s)   You Took My Breath Away; The Beautiful Isle of Oomph [5]; All's Well (In Coronado By the Sea); How Do I Rate with You; Midsummer Madness [1]; Mashed Potatoes [1] [2]; Keep Your Fingers Crossed [4]; I've Got Some New Shoes (L: Bullock, Walter; Coslow, Sam); Pampas Moon [3] (L: Marion, George)

Notes   Duchin plays instrumental versions of the Whiting and Rainger song "Why Dream," the Sam Coslow tune "The Middle of a Kiss" and the Rainger and Dorothy Parker tune "I Wished on the Moon." [1] Not used. [2] Recorded for the soundtrack. [3] Instrumental only. [4] Originally written for ALL THE KING'S HORSES, with music by Coslow, and considered for TWO FOR TONIGHT. [5] Published as "Down on the Isle of Oomph."

1180 ✦ THE CORPSE CAME C.O.D.
Columbia, 1947

Producer(s)   Bischoff, Sam
Director(s)   Levin, Henry
Screenwriter(s)   Bricker, George; Babcock, Dwight
Source(s)   (novel) Starr, Jimmy

Cast   Brent, George; Blondell, Joan; Jergens, Adele; Bannon, Jim; Brooks, Leslie; Berkes, John; Sears, Fred F.; O'Connor, Una

Song(s) (He's Got a) Warm Kiss (C/L: Fisher, Doris; Roberts, Allan)

1181 ✦ THE CORRUPT ONES
Warner Brothers, 1967

Musical Score Garvarentz, Georges

Producer(s) Brauner, Arthur
Director(s) Hill, James
Screenwriter(s) Clemens, Brian

Cast Stack, Robert; Sommer, Elke; Kwan, Nancy; Peters, Werner; Marquand, Christian

Song(s) The Corrupt Ones (C: Garvarentz, Georges; L: Kaye, Buddy)

Notes Released in Great Britain as THE PEKING MEDALLION.

1182 ✦ CORVETTE SUMMER
Metro–Goldwyn–Mayer, 1978

Musical Score Safan, Craig
Composer(s) Safan, Craig
Lyricist(s) Safan, Craig

Producer(s) Barwood, Hal
Director(s) Robbins, Matthew
Screenwriter(s) Barwood, Hal; Robbins, Matthew

Cast Hamill, Mark; Potts, Annie; Roche, Eugene

Song(s) Give Me the Night; When We Get Lovin'

Notes Formerly titled STINGRAY. Titled THE HOT ONE internationally.

1183 ✦ THE COTTON CLUB
Orion, 1984

Musical Score Barry, John

Producer(s) Evans, Robert
Director(s) Coppola, Francis Ford
Screenwriter(s) Kennedy, William; Coppola, Francis Ford

Cast Gere, Richard; Hines, Gregory; Lane, Diane; McKee, Lonette; Remar, James; Cage, Nicolas; Garfield, Allen; Gwynne, Fred; Verdon, Gwen; Persky, Lisa Jane; Hines, Maurice; Beck, Julian; Nelson, Novella; Waits, Tom; Grey, Jennifer; Smith, Wynonna; Carpenter, Thelma; Coles, Charles "Honi"; Marshall, Larry; Dallesandro, Joe; Venora, Diane; Strode, Woody; Graham, Bill; Allen, Dayton; Hoskins, Bob; Leake, Damien; Jones, Robert Earl

Notes No cue sheet available. There are no original songs in this film.

1184 ✦ COTTON COMES TO HARLEM
United Artists, 1970

Musical Score MacDermot, Galt
Composer(s) MacDermot, Galt
Lyricist(s) Lewis, Joe

Producer(s) Goldwyn Jr., Samuel
Director(s) Davis, Ossie
Screenwriter(s) Davis, Ossie; Perl, Arnold
Source(s) *Cotton Comes to Harlem* (novel) Himes, Chester

Cast Cambridge, Godfrey; St. Jacques, Raymond; Lockhart, Calvin; Foxx, Redd; Pace, Judy

Song(s) Black Enough (L: Davis, Ossie); Going Home; Cotton Comes to Harlem; Down in My Soul (L: Dumaresq, William); My Salvation (L: Dunbar, Paul Lawrence)

1185 ✦ COUNTDOWN
Warner Brothers, 1968

Musical Score Rosenman, Leonard

Producer(s) Conrad, William
Director(s) Altman, Robert
Screenwriter(s) Mandel, Loring
Source(s) *Pilgrim Project* (novel) Searls, Hank

Cast Caan, James; Duvall, Robert; Moore, Joanna; Baxley, Barbara; Aidman, Charles; Ihnat, Steve

Song(s) John Henry Astronaut (C/L: Ridgley, Robert)

Notes "April in Paris" by E.Y. Harburg and Vernon Duke is also used.

1186 ✦ COUNTERBLAST
Republic, 1948

Musical Score May, Hans
Composer(s) May, Hans
Lyricist(s) Stranks, Alan

Producer(s) Jackson, Louis H.
Director(s) Stein, Paul
Screenwriter(s) Whitingham, Jack

Cast Beatty, Robert; Johns, Mervyn; Pilbeam, Nova; Scott, Margaretta; Wheatley, Alan

Song(s) Love Again [1]; Faithful; Somewhere in This Great Big World

Notes This is a British National picture. There is also a vocal of "Oh, Oh, Antonio" by C.W. Murphy and Dan Lipton. [1] Also in SPRING SONG.

1187 ✦ THE COUNTERFEIT TRAITOR
Paramount, 1961

Producer(s) Perlberg, William
Director(s) Seaton, George

Screenwriter(s)   Seaton, George
Source(s)   *Double Dealers* (book) Klein, Alexander

Cast   Holden, William; Palmer, Lilli; Griffith, Hugh; Kinski, Klaus; Schnabel, Stefan

Song(s)   Marianna [1] (C: Newman, Alfred; L: Webster, Paul Francis)

Notes   [1] Lyrics added for exploitation.

1188 ✦ COUNTERPLOT
United Artists, 1958

Musical Score   Sawtell, Paul; Shefter, Bert

Producer(s)   Neumann, Kurt
Director(s)   Neumann, Kurt
Screenwriter(s)   Blake, Richard

Cast   Tucker, Forrest; Hayes, Allison; Milton, Gerald

Song(s)   Say Au Revoir (C/L: Neumann, Kurt)

1189 ✦ THE COUNTESS OF MONTE CRISTO
Universal, 1948

Musical Score   Scharf, Walter
Composer(s)   Chaplin, Saul
Lyricist(s)   Brooks, Jack
Choreographer(s)   Da Pron, Louis

Producer(s)   Beck, John
Director(s)   de Cordova, Frederick
Screenwriter(s)   Bowers, William

Cast   Henie, Sonja; San Juan, Olga; Hart, Dorothy; Kirby, Michael; Treacher, Arthur; French, Hugh; Trenkler, Freddie

Song(s)   Friendly Polka; Count Your Blessings; Who Believes in Santa Claus?

1190 ✦ THE COUNT OF MONTE CRISTO
United Artists, 1934

Musical Score   Newman, Alfred

Producer(s)   Small, Edward
Director(s)   Lee, Rowland V.
Screenwriter(s)   Dunne, Philip; Totheroh, Dan; Lee, Rowland V.
Source(s)   *The Count of Monte Cristo* (novel) Dumas, Alexandre

Cast   Donat, Robert; Landi, Elissa; Calhern, Louis; Blackmer, Sidney; Walburn, Raymond; Heggie, O.P.; Farnum, William; Caine, Georgia; Alberni, Luis; Hervey, Irene; Compton, Juliette; Muse, Clarence; Ames, Leon [1]

Song(s)   The World Is Mine (C: Green, Johnny; L: Harburg, E.Y.); Love Is in Command (C: Pollack, Lew; L: Young, Joe)

Notes   No cue sheet available. [1] Billed as Leon Waycoff.

1191 ✦ A COUNTRY COYOTE GOES HOLLYWOOD
Disney, 1967

Musical Score   Bruns, George

Producer(s)   Hibler, Winston
Screenwriter(s)   Speirs, Jack

Cast   Allen, Rex

Song(s)   When the Neon Is in Bloom (C: Bruns, George; L: Speirs, Jack)

1192 ✦ COUNTRY DANCE

See BROTHERLY LOVE (1970).

1193 ✦ COUNTRY FAIR
Republic, 1941

Producer(s)   Schaefer, Armand
Director(s)   McDonald, Frank
Screenwriter(s)   McGowan, Dorrell; McGowan, Stuart

Cast   Foy Jr., Eddie; Lulu Belle and Scotty; Clyde, June; Williams, Guinn "Big Boy"; Demarest, William; Harold Huber and Radio Entertainers; Peary, Harold; Ford, White; The Vass Family; The Simp Phonies

Song(s)   Chewing Chawing Gum (C/L: Wiseman, Scott); You Can't Never Sometimes Most Always Tell (C/L: Burnette, Smiley); Sierra Sue [1] (C/L: Carey, Joseph B.); Morning on the Farm (C/L: Elliott, Jack)

Notes   There is also a vocal of "Mademoiselle from Armentiere" with a special lyric. [1] Also in SIERRA SUE.

1194 ✦ THE COUNTRY GIRL
Paramount, 1954

Musical Score   Young, Victor
Composer(s)   Arlen, Harold
Lyricist(s)   Gershwin, Ira
Choreographer(s)   Alton, Robert

Producer(s)   Perlberg, William
Director(s)   Seaton, George
Screenwriter(s)   Seaton, George
Source(s)   *The Country Girl* (play) Odets, Clifford

Cast   Crosby, Bing; Kelly, Grace; Holden, William; Ross, Anthony; Reynolds, Gene; Fontaine, Jacqueline; Ryder, Eddie; Kent, Robert; Reynolds, John W.

Song(s)   It's Mine It's Yours (The Pitchman); The Search Is Through; The Land Around Us; Dissertation on the State of Bliss (Love and Learn); Beer Commercial

1195 ✦ COUNTRY MUSIC HOLIDAY
Paramount, 1958

Producer(s)   Serpe, Ralph; Kreitsek, Howard B.
Director(s)   Ganzer, Alvin
Screenwriter(s)   Cross, H.B.

Cast   Husky, Ferlin; Gabor, Zsa Zsa; Duke, Patty; White, Jesse; Carter, June; Norton, Cliff; Parker, Lew; Fisher, Al; Graziano, Rocky; Young, Faron; The Jordanaires; Miller, Drifting Johnny; Lonzo & Oscar; Nee, Bernie

Song(s)   My Home Town (C/L: Burnette, Smiley); The Face of Love (C/L: Lebowsky, Stanley; Lehman, Johnny); Terrific Together (C/L: Williams, Jimmy; Hill, Dave); Ninety-Nine Percent [1] (C/L: Benton, Brook; Otis, Clyde); Somewhere There's Sunshine (C/L: Ballard, Pat); Wang Dang Doo (C/L: Adams, J.T.; Norris, Jean; Beasley, William); Just One More Chance [2] (C: Johnston, Arthur; L: Coslow, Sam); Little Miss Ruby (C/L: Matthews, Neal); Goodbye My Darlin' (C/L: Otis, Clyde; Benton, Brook; Colacrai, Cirino); Wide Wide World (C/L: Owens, Cliff; Dreyer, Dave); When It Rains It Pours (C/L: Slavin, Slick); Don't Walk Away from Me [1] (C/L: Benton, Brook; Otis, Clyde); Country Music Holiday [1] (C: Bacharach, Burt; L: David, Hal); Albuquerque [3] (C/L: Miller, J.)

Notes   [1] Background vocal only. [2] Also in LEMON DROP KID (1934), THE MAGNIFICENT LIE and THIS RECKLESS AGE. [3] BMI list only.

1196 ✦ COUNT THE WAYS
New Yorker, 1977

Musical Score   Samuels, Danny

Producer(s)   Perry, Ann
Director(s)   Perry, Ann
Screenwriter(s)   Perry, Ann

Cast   Green, Yvonne; Wells, Jason; Gale, Tome

Song(s)   Thoughts of You (C/L: Samuels, Danny); Cake Walk (C/L: Samuels, Danny)

Notes   No cue sheet available.

1197 ✦ COURAGE OF BLACK BEAUTY
Twentieth Century–Fox, 1957

Musical Score   Alperson Jr., Edward L.; Herrick, Paul

Producer(s)   Alperson, Edward L.
Director(s)   Schuster, Harold
Screenwriter(s)   Fisher, Steve

Cast   Crawford, Johnny; Gibson, Mimi; Bryant, John; Brewster, Diane; O'Malley, J. Pat

Song(s)   Donkey Game Theme (C: Alperson Jr., Edward L.; L: Stapley, Richard; Hughes, Dick); Black Beauty (C: Alperson Jr., Edward L.; L: Herrick, Paul)

1198 ✦ COURAGE OF THE WEST
Universal, 1938

Composer(s)   Allan, Fleming
Lyricist(s)   Allan, Fleming

Director(s)   Lewis, Joseph H.
Screenwriter(s)   Baker, Jay Norton

Cast   Baker, Bob; MacDonald, J. Farrell; Cox, Buddy

Song(s)   Restin' Beside the Trail; Free Ranger's Song; Snag Tooth Sal (C/L: Knight, Fuzzy); Song of the Trail

1199 ✦ THE COURT JESTER
Paramount, 1956

Musical Score   Schoen, Vic
Composer(s)   Fine, Sylvia
Lyricist(s)   Fine, Sylvia; Cahn, Sammy
Choreographer(s)   Starbuck, James

Producer(s)   Panama, Norman; Frank, Melvin
Director(s)   Panama, Norman; Frank, Melvin
Screenwriter(s)   Panama, Norman; Frank, Melvin

Cast   Kaye, Danny; Johns, Glynis; Rathbone, Basil; Lansbury, Angela; Parker, Cecil; Natwick, Mildred; Middleton, Robert; Carradine, John; Hermine's Midgets

Song(s)   Baby, Let Me Take You Dreaming [1]; The Maladjusted Jester (Nobody's Fool) (L: Fine, Sylvia); Life Could Not Better Be; My Heart Knows a Lovely Song; Outfox the Fox; Where Walks My True Love [2]; Pass the Basket [3]; Ritual of Knighthood [4]

Notes   [1] Originally titled "Loo, Loo, Loo, I'll Take You Dreaming." [2] Used instrumentally only. [3] Not used but recorded. [4] Not used.

1200 ✦ THE COURTSHIP OF EDDIE'S FATHER
Metro–Goldwyn–Mayer, 1963

Musical Score   Stoll, George

Producer(s)   Pasternak, Joe
Director(s)   Minnelli, Vincente
Screenwriter(s)   Gay, John

Cast   Ford, Glenn; Jones, Shirley; Stevens, Stella; Merrill, Dina; Sherwood, Roberta; Howard, Ron; Van Dyke, Jerry

Song(s)   The Rose and the Butterfly (C: Young, Victor; L: Unger, Stella); Whistle Bait [1] (C: Stoll, George; Van Eps, Bob; L: Pasternak, Joe; Winn, Jerry)

Notes   No cue sheet available. [1] Sheet music only.

1201 ✦ COUSINS
Paramount, 1989

Musical Score   Badalamenti, Angelo

Producer(s)   Allyn, William
Director(s)   Schumacher, Joel
Screenwriter(s)   Metcalfe, Stephen

Cast Danson, Ted; Rossellini, Isabella; Young, Sean; Petersen, William L.; Bridges, Lloyd; Coogan, Keith; Coe, George; Aleandro, Norma

Song(s) I Love You For Today (C: Badalamenti, Angelo; L: Badalamenti, Angelo; Schumacher, Joel); Time to Dance the Bamba (C: Traditional; L: Valentino, Luis); Speak Softly Love (C: Rota, Nino; L: Kusik, Larry); A Time for Us (C: Rota, Nino; L: Kusik, Larry; Snyder, Eddie); With or Without You (C/L: U2 [1])

Notes A remake of the French film COUSIN, COUSINE by Jean-Charles Tacchella. [1] Consists of Paul David Hewson, David Evans, Adam Clayton and Larry Mullen Jr.

1202 ◆ COVER GIRL
Columbia, 1944

Composer(s) Kern, Jerome
Lyricist(s) Gershwin, Ira
Choreographer(s) Kelly, Gene; Donen, Stanley; Raset, Val; Felix, Seymour

Producer(s) Schwartz, Arthur
Director(s) Vidor, Charles
Screenwriter(s) Van Upp, Virginia

Cast Kelly, Gene; Bowman, Lee; Hayworth, Rita [2]; Silvers, Phil; Barker, Jess; Brooks, Leslie; Falkenburg, Jinx; Arden, Eve; Colby, Anita; Kruger, Otto; Hall, Thurston; Winters, Shelley

Song(s) The Show Must Go On; Who's Complaining; Sure Thing; Make Way for Tomorrow (L: Gershwin, Ira; Harburg, E.Y.); Long Ago and Far Away; Cover Girl (That Girl on the Cover); Put Me to the Test [3]; I've Turned the Corner [1]; What I Love to Hear [4]; Tropical Night [4]; Time: The Present [4]; That's the Best of All [4]; Midnight Music [4] [5]

Notes "Poor John" by Fred W. Leigh and Henry E. Pether is also used vocally. [1] Instrumental use only. [2] Dubbed by Martha Mears. [3] Lyric Similar to "Put Me to the Test" in DAMSEL IN DISTRESS (RKO) with Gershwin music. However, the song is used instrumentally only in that picture. [4] Not used. [5] Same music.

1203 ◆ COVER ME BABE
Twentieth Century–Fox, 1970

Musical Score Karlin, Fred
Composer(s) Karlin, Fred
Lyricist(s) Posey, Art; Session, Honey

Producer(s) Linsk, Lester
Director(s) Black, Noel
Screenwriter(s) Wells, George

Cast Forster, Robert; Locke, Sondra; Benton, Susanne; Kercheval, Ken; Waterston, Sam; Toomey, Regis

Song(s) So You Say (L: Royer, Robb; Griffin, James A.); Just Take Your Time; Cover Me Babe (L: Newman, Randy); I Don't Hear Them Anymore (C/L: Reich, George); What Will I Do After That (C/L: Reich, George)

1204 ◆ THE COWBOY AND THE INDIANS
Columbia, 1949

Producer(s) Schaefer, Armand
Director(s) English, John
Screenwriter(s) Cummings, Dwight; Yost, Dorothy

Cast Autry, Gene; Ryan, Sheila; Richards, Frank; Patterson, Hank; Silverheels, Jay; Champion

Song(s) Here Comes Santa Claus (C/L: Unknown); One Little Indian Boy (C/L: Unknown)

Notes No cue sheet available. There are also vocals of "Silent Night" and "America."

1205 ◆ COWBOY AND THE SENORITA
Republic, 1944

Composer(s) Ohman, Phil
Lyricist(s) Washington, Ned

Producer(s) Grey, Harry
Director(s) Kane, Joseph
Screenwriter(s) Kahn, Gordon

Cast Rogers, Roy; Lee, Mary; Evans, Dale; Hubbard, John; Williams, Guinn "Big Boy"; Knight, Fuzzy; Christy, Dorothy; Taliaferro, Hal; Kirk, Jack; Sons of the Pioneers

Song(s) The Cowboy and the Senorita; The Bunkhouse Bugle Boy (C/L: Nolan, Bob; Spencer, Tim); What'll I Use for Money; 'Round Her Neck She Wears a Yeller Ribbon (C/L: Norton, George A.); The Enchilada Man

1206 ◆ COWBOY CANTEEN
Columbia, 1943

Composer(s) Chaplin, Saul
Lyricist(s) Samuels, Walter G.

Producer(s) Fier, Jack
Director(s) Landers, Lew
Screenwriter(s) Gangelin, Paul; Adler, Felix

Cast Starrett, Charles; Frazee, Jane; Vague, Vera; Ritter, Tex; Williams, Guinn "Big Boy"; Terhune, Max; Taylor, Dub; The Mills Brothers; Jimmy Wakely and His Saddle Pals; Chickie and Buck; Roy Acuff and His Smoky Mountain Boys and Girls; The Tailor Maids; Hughes, Bill

Song(s) Boogie Woogie Special; Spot in Arizona; You Man You; Come On and Whistle (C/L: Piantadosi, Al; Bibo, Irving)

Notes Originally titled BARNYARD CANTEEN. There are also vocals of "Ridin' Herd on a Cloud" by Perry Botkin, Bernie Schwartz and Jon Bushallow Jr.;

"Goin' to Lasso a Rainbow for You" by Elmer Sioux Scarberry, and Connie Glore; "Wait for the Light to Shine" by Fred Rose; "Walking Down the Lane with You" by Jimmy Wakeley; "Lazy River" by Hoagy Carmichael and Sidney Arodin; "Night Train to Memphis" by Beasley Smith, Marvin Hughes and Owen Bradley (also in NIGHT TRAIN TO MEMPHIS); and "Paper Doll" by Johnny Black.

1207 ✦ COWBOY FROM BROOKLYN
Warner Brothers, 1938

Musical Score Deutsch, Adolph
Composer(s) Whiting, Richard A.
Lyricist(s) Mercer, Johnny

Producer(s) Wallis, Hal B.
Director(s) Bacon, Lloyd
Screenwriter(s) Baldwin, Earl
Source(s) *Howdy Stranger* (play) Peletier, Louis; Sloane, Robert

Cast Powell, Dick; O'Brien, Pat; Lane, Priscilla; Foran, Dick; Sheridan, Ann

Song(s) I've Got a Heart Full of Music; Ride Tenderfoot, Ride; I'll Dream Tonight; Howdy Stranger; Cowboy from Brooklyn [1] (C: Warren, Harry)

Notes [1] Only used for 3 seconds of vocal. The remainder of the use is background instrumental.

1208 ✦ COWBOY IN MANHATTAN
Universal, 1943

Musical Score Skinner, Frank
Composer(s) Rosen, Milton
Lyricist(s) Carter, Everett

Producer(s) Malvern, Paul
Director(s) Woodruff, Frank
Screenwriter(s) Wilson, Warren

Cast Paige, Robert; Langford, Frances; Errol, Leon; Catlett, Walter

Song(s) Whistle Your Blues to a Bluebird [2]; Need I Say More? [4]; Private Cowboy Jones; Mister Moon [4]; A Cowboy Is Happy [3]; Got Love [1]

Notes [1] Used instrumentally only. [2] Also in the short IN THE GROOVE and in TOO MANY BLONDES. [3] Also in GUN TOWN and RAWHIDE RANGERS. [4] Also in SIX LESSONS FROM MADAM LA ZONGA. [4] Also used in TWILIGHT ON THE PRAIRIE.

1209 ✦ COWBOY IN THE CLOUDS
Columbia, 1943

Producer(s) Fier, Jack
Director(s) Kline, Benjamin
Screenwriter(s) Beecher, Elizabeth

Cast Starrett, Charles; Taylor, Dub; Duncan, Julie; The Jesters; Jimmy Wakely and His Saddle Pals

Song(s) She Lived Next Door to a Firehouse (C/L: Klein, Lou; Phillips, Fred); There's a Rainbow on the Rio Colorado [1] (C/L: Autry, Gene; Rose, Fred); There's a Tavern in the Town (C/L: Hills, William; Vallee, Rudy); Cowboy in the Clouds (C/L: Cavanaugh, James; Redmond, John; Weldon, Frank)

Notes There are no original songs in this film. [1] Also in SONS OF NEW MEXICO.

1210 ✦ A COWBOY NEEDS A HORSE
Disney, 1956

Musical Score Bruns, George

Director(s) Justice, Bill
Screenwriter(s) Kinney, Dick; Williams, Roy

Song(s) A Cowboy Needs a Horse (C/L: Mills, Billy; Howard, Paul Mason)

Notes Short subject.

1211 ✦ COWBOY QUARTERBACK
Warner Brothers, 1939

Musical Score Jackson, Howard

Producer(s) Foy, Bryan
Director(s) Smith, Noel
Screenwriter(s) Niblo Jr., Fred
Source(s) "Hurry Kane" (story) Lardner, Ring; *Elmer the Great* (1933) (play) Cohan, George M.

Cast Wheeler, Bert; Dickson, Gloria; Wilson, Marie; Hopper, DeWolf; Demarest, William; Foy Jr., Eddie; Gould, William

Song(s) Underneath a Western Sky [1] (C: Jerome, M.K.; L: Scholl, Jack)

Notes [1] Only 27 seconds of vocals used. Also in CATTLE TOWN (with Ted Fiorito credit also) and RETURN OF THE FRONTIERSMAN. Scholl and Jerome also wrote a song titled "Underneath the Western Skies" which is used in SONG OF THE SADDLE. It might be the same song or only similar to it.

1212 ✦ COWBOY SERENADE
Republic, 1942

Producer(s) Grey, Harry
Director(s) Morgan, William
Screenwriter(s) Cooper, Olive

Cast Autry, Gene; Burnette, Smiley; McKenzie, Fay; Cunningham, Cecil; Richards, Addison; Brooks, Rand; Coffin, Tristram; Andrews, Lloyd "Slim"; Leighton, Melinda; Berke, Johnnie

Song(s) Sweethearts or Strangers [2] (C/L: Davis, Jimmie); Tahiti Honey (C: Styne, Jule; L: Brown, George; Meyer, Sol); Nobody Knows (C: Styne, Jule; L: Meyer, Sol); Cowboy Serenade (C: Hall, Rich; L: Meyer, Sol); There's Nothing Like a Gold Ole Fashioned Hoedown [1] (C/L: Autry, Gene); You Are My Sunshine [1] (C/L: Davis, Jimmie; Mitchell, Charles)

Notes [1] May have been used instrumentally; records unclear. Also in I'M FROM ARKANSAS (PRC); RIDIN' ON A RAINBOW and STRICTLY IN THE GROOVE (Universal). [2] Also in STRICTLY IN THE GROOVE (Universal).

1213 ✦ COW TOWN
Columbia, 1950

Producer(s) Schaefer, Armand
Director(s) English, John
Screenwriter(s) Geraghty, Gerald

Cast Autry, Gene; Davis, Gail; Shannon, Harry; Mahoney, Jock; Burroughs, Clark; Champion; O'Malley, Pat

Song(s) Powder Your Face with Sunshine (C: Lombardo, Carmen; L: Rochinski, Stanley)

Notes No cue sheet available. There are also vocals of "Down in the Valley," "Buffalo Gal" and "The Dying Cowboy."

1214 ✦ THE COYOTE'S LAMENT
Disney, 1968

Musical Score Bruns, George; Smith, Paul J.; Wallace, Oliver

Song(s) Coyote's Lament (C: Bruns, George; L: Nichols, Charles)

Notes No credit sheet available.

1215 ✦ CRACKERJACK

See MAN WITH A 100 FACES.

1216 ✦ CRACKERS
Universal, 1984

Musical Score Chihara, Paul
Composer(s) Summers, Bob; Roberts, S.; Escovedo, P.
Lyricist(s) Summers, Bob; Roberts, S.; Escovedo, P.

Producer(s) Lewis, Edward; Cortes, Robert
Director(s) Malle, Louis
Screenwriter(s) Fiskin, Jeffrey Alan

Cast Sutherland, Donald; Warden, Jack; Penn, Sean; Shawn, Wallace; Riley, Larry; Baranski, Christine; Woodard, Charlaine; Horsford, Anna Maria

Song(s) We Got More Than We Need (C/L: McDonald, Michael; Sanford, Ed); City Boy Lover; Suzi Plastic [2]; Berro E Sombaro (C/L: Brown, Charles; Tillary, Donald; Buchanan, John; Johnson, Curtis; Fleming, Leroy; Wilder, Jerry; Gerran, Gregory; Wellman, Ricardo); London Town (C/L: Summers, Bob; Roberts, S.; Ham, L.); Que Pequena [1] (C/L: Ciani, Suzanne)

Notes A remake of BIG DEAL ON MADONNA STREET (1958). [1] Also in THE INCREDIBLE SHRINKING WOMAN. [2] Also in SMOKEY AND THE BANDIT—PART 3.

1217 ✦ CRACK IN THE MIRROR
Twentieth Century–Fox, 1960

Musical Score Jarre, Maurice

Producer(s) Zanuck, Darryl F.
Director(s) Fleischer, Richard
Screenwriter(s) Canfield, Mark
Source(s) *Drama in the Mirror* (novel) Haedrich, Marcel

Cast Welles, Orson; Greco, Juliette; Dillman, Bradford; Knox, Alexander; Lacey, Catherine; Matalon, Vivian

Song(s) Song Eponine (C: Patterson, Henri; L: Canfield, Mark)

1218 ✦ CRACK IN THE WORLD
Paramount, 1965

Musical Score Douglas, Johnny

Producer(s) Glasser, Bernard; Sansom, Lester A.
Director(s) Marton, Andrew
Screenwriter(s) White, Jon Manchip; Halevy, Julian

Cast Andrews, Dana; Scott, Janette; Moore, Kieron; Knox, Alexander

Song(s) Time [1] (C: Douglas, Johnny; L: Davies, John)

Notes [1] Lyric written for exploitation only. Based on cue titled "Admiration."

1219 ✦ CRACK UP
Twentieth Century–Fox, 1936

Producer(s) Engel, Samuel G.
Director(s) St. Clair, Malcolm
Screenwriter(s) Kenyon, Charles; Mintz, Sam

Cast Lorre, Peter; Donlevy, Brian; Wood, Helen; Morgan, Ralph; Beck, Thomas; Linaker, Kay; Matthews, Lester; Foxe, Earle; Naish, J. Carrol; Roy, Gloria; Apfel, Oscar

Song(s) Top Gallants (Legionaires) [1] (C: Akst, Harry; L: Clare, Sidney)

Notes Also in BATTLE OF BROADWAY.

1220 ✦ CRADLE SONG
Paramount, 1933

Director(s) Leisen, Mitchell
Screenwriter(s) Sparks, Robert; Partos, Frank
Source(s) *Cradle Song* (play) Connelly, Marc

Cast Wieck, Dorothea; Venable, Evelyn; Dresser, Louise; Taylor, Kent; Standing, Sir Guy

Song(s) Lonely Little Senorita [2] (C: Hajos, Karl; Rainger, Ralph; L: Robin, Leo); Children of Mary (C: Harling, W. Franke; L: White, Jerome); Lullaby (Cantilena to the Infant Jesus) (C/L: Harling, W. Franke); Cradle Song [1] (C: Rainger, Ralph; L: Robin, Leo); Flowers of the Verdant Spring (Concordia Loelitia) (C: Traditional L: White, Jerome); Beautiful Mary (Omnis Expertem) (C: Traditional L: White, Jerome)

Notes [1] Not used but published. [2] Also in SWING HIGH, SWING LOW but without the Rainger credit.

1221 ✦ CRASHING THRU
Monogram, 1938

Composer(s) Loman, Jules
Lyricist(s) Brooks, Jack

Producer(s) Krasne, Philip N.
Director(s) Clifton, Elmer
Screenwriter(s) Lowe, Sherman
Source(s) *Renfrew Rides the Range* (novel) Erskine, Laurie York

Cast Newill, James; Hull, Warren; Carmen, Jean; Stone, Milburn; Byron, Walter; Blystone, Stanley

Song(s) Mounted Men [1] (C/L: Lively, Robert; Laidlaw, Betty); Center of Attraction; Crimson Sunset

Notes Also in DANGER AHEAD, FIGHTIN' MAN, MURDER ON THE YUKON, RENFREW AND THE GREAT WHITE TRAIL, SKY BANDITS and YUKON FLIGHT.

1222 ✦ CRASHIN' THROUGH DANGER
Excelsior, 1938

Producer(s) Neufeld, Sigmund; Simmonds, Leslie
Director(s) Newfield, Sam
Screenwriter(s) Houston, Norman

Cast Blane, Sally; Walker, Ray; Williams, Guinn "Big Boy"; Bush, James; Usher, Guy

Song(s) I Fell Off the Flying Trapeze (C/L: Hume; Stross; Zahler, Lee; Wood, John Hickory)

1223 ✦ CRAWL SPACE
Empire Releasing, 1986

Musical Score Donaggio, Pino

Producer(s) Bessi, Roberto
Director(s) Schmoeller, David
Screenwriter(s) Schmoeller, David

Cast Kinski, Klaus; Balsam, Talia; Whinnery, Barbara; Francis, Carol

Song(s) Lovers Tonight (C: Donaggio, Pino; L: Schmoeller, David); If I Had Enough Money, I'd Buy Me a Man (C: Donaggio, Pino; L: Schmoeller, David)

Notes No cue sheet available.

1224 ✦ CRAZY HOUSE (1930)
Metro–Goldwyn–Mayer, 1930

Cast Rubin, Benny; Dent, Vernon; Moran, Polly; Dane, Karl; Shy, Gus; Edwards, Cliff; Snake Hips; Albertina Rasch Ballet

Song(s) Goodbye (C/L: Montgomery, Reggie); Mars Ballet (Inst.) (C: Tiomkin, Dimitri)

Notes Short subject.

1225 ✦ CRAZY HOUSE (1943)
Universal, 1943

Choreographer(s) Hale, George

Producer(s) Kenton, Erle C.
Director(s) Cline, Edward F.
Screenwriter(s) Lees, Robert; Rinaldo, Frederic I.

Cast Olsen, Ole; Johnson, Chic; Knowles, Patric; O'Driscoll, Martha; Daley, Cass; Kilbride, Percy; Noble, Leighton; Gomez, Thomas; Kennedy, Edgar; Pangborn, Franklin; Curtis, Alan; Jones, Allan; Gilbert, Billy; Conried, Hans; Howard, Shemp; Chaney Jr., Lon; Devine, Andy; Paige, Robert; The Glenn Miller Singers; Hutton, Marion; Count Basie and His Band; De Marco, Tony; De Marco, Sally; Chandra; The Kaly Dancers; The Laison Brothers; The Five Hertzogs; The Delta Rhythm Boys; The Bobby Brooks Quartet; Tombes, Andrew; Rathbone, Basil; Bruce, Nigel

Song(s) Lament of a Laundry Girl (C/L: Shapiro, Ted; Seelen, Jerry; Lee, Lester); Jealous [2] (C: Little, Little Jack; L: Malie, Tommie; Finch, Dick); There Goes That Song Again (C/L: Wrubel, Allie); Moonlight Serenade (C: Miller, Glenn; L: Parish, Mitchell); Baby, Won't You Please Come Home (C/L: Warfield, Charles; Williams, Clarence); I'll See You in My Dreams [3] (C: Jones, Isham; L: Kahn, Gus); My Rainbow Song (C/L: Signorelli, Frank; Malneck, Matty; Parish, Mitchell); I Ought to Dance (C: Chaplin, Saul; L: Cahn, Sammy); Tropicana (C: de Paul, Gene; L: Raye, Don); Crazy House (C: Rosen, Milton; L: Cherkose, Eddie); Someday Maybe I'll Dream Again [4] (C/L: Piantadosi, Al; Bibo, Irving); Donkey Serenade [1] (C: Friml, Rudolf; Stothart, Herbert; L: Forrest, Chet; Wright, Bob); Get On Board, Little Children (C: de Paul, Gene; L: Raye, Don); Pocket Full o' Pennies (C: Steininger, Franz; L: Cherkose, Eddie)

Notes Some of these were not written for this film. [1] Also in THE FIREFLY. [2] Also in THE FEMININE TOUCH (MGM). [3] Also in I'LL SEE YOU IN MY

DREAMS. [4] Stanley Joseloff is co-credited as lyricist on sheet music.

1226 ✦ CRAZYLEGS, ALL-AMERICAN
Republic, 1953

Musical Score Stevens, Leith

Producer(s) Bartlett, Hall
Director(s) Lyon, Francis D.
Screenwriter(s) Bartlett, Hall

Cast Hirsch, Elroy "Crazylegs"; Nolan, Lloyd; Vohs, Joan; Millican, James; Waterfield, Bob; Kelley, Bob; Brown, James; Field, Norman; Lorimer, Louise; Crehan, Joseph; Brundige, Bill; Hirsch, Win; Arnold, Melvyn; Brink, Larry; Dahms, Tom; Daugherty, Dick; Dwyer, Jack; Fears, Tom; Gambold, Bob; Hecker, Norbert; Lane, Dick; Lewis, Woodley; McLaughlin, Leon; Paul, Don; Putnam, Duane; Quinlan, Volney; Towler, Dan; Van Brocklin, Norman; Waterfield, Bob; West, Stan; Winkler, Jim; Younger, Paul

Song(s) The Rams' Fight Song (C: Stevens, Leith; L: Bartlett, Hall)

Notes Many of the players were on the Los Angeles Rams football team.

1227 ✦ CRAZY OVER DAISY
Disney, 1949

Musical Score Wallace, Oliver

Director(s) Hannah, Jack
Screenwriter(s) Williams, Roy; Banta, Milt

Song(s) Daisy Mae (C/L: Wallace, Oliver)

Notes Cartoon.

1228 ✦ CRAZY THAT WAY
Fox, 1930

Producer(s) Middleton, George
Director(s) MacFadden, Hamilton
Screenwriter(s) MacFadden, Hamilton; Orth, Marion
Source(s) *In Love with Love* (play) Lawrence, Vincent

Cast Bennett, Joan; MacKenna, Kenneth; Toomey, Regis; Robards, Jason; Hare, Lumsden

Song(s) Let's Do (C: Nelson, Edward G.; L: Pease, Harry)

Notes Originally titled IN LOVE WITH LOVE.

1229 ✦ CRAZY WORLD OF JULIUS VROODER
Twentieth Century–Fox, 1974

Producer(s) Rissien, Edward; Hiller, Arthur
Director(s) Hiller, Arthur
Screenwriter(s) Henry, Daryl

Cast Bottoms, Timothy; Seagull, Barbara; Pressman, Lawrence; Salmi, Albert; Marshall, George; Dysart, Richard; Dietrich, Dena; Scott, Debralee; Frizzell, Lou

Song(s) We'll Come to Be There (C: Alcivar, Robert; L: Caldwell, Gayle)

Notes Originally titled VROODER'S HOOCH.

1230 ✦ CRIA!
Jason Allen, 1977

Musical Score Perales, J.L.

Producer(s) Querejeta, Elias
Director(s) Saura, Carlos
Screenwriter(s) Saura, Carlos

Cast Chaplin, Geraldine; Torrent, Ana; Perez, Conchita

Song(s) Porque te Vas (C/L: Pereles, J.L.); Palabras Promesas (C/L: Pereles, J.L.)

Notes No cue sheet available.

1231 ✦ CRIME BY NIGHT
Warner Brothers, 1944

Musical Score Lava, William

Producer(s) Jacobs, William
Director(s) Clemens, William
Screenwriter(s) Weil, Richard; Malone, Joel
Source(s) "Forty Whacks" (story) Homes, Geoffrey

Cast Cowan, Jerome; Wyman, Jane; Emerson, Faye; Lang, Charles; Parker, Eleanor; Crawford, Stuart

Song(s) Two Tables Apart (C: Altman, Arthur; L: Gannon, Kim)

1232 ✦ CRIME INC.
PRC, 1945

Musical Score Greene, Walter

Producer(s) Fromkess, Leon
Director(s) Landers, Lew
Screenwriter(s) Schrock, Raymond
Source(s) (book) Mooney, Martin

Cast Carrillo, Leo; Neal, Tom

Song(s) I'm Guilty (C/L: Livingston, Jay; Evans, Ray); That's It (C: Brown Jr., Nacio Herb; L: Shelton, Marla); What a Fool I Was (C: Brown Jr., Nacio Herb; L: Shelton, Marla); Dream After Dream (C/L: Worth, Bobby; Cowan, Stanley)

1233 ✦ THE CRIME OF DOCTOR FORBES
Twentieth Century–Fox, 1936

Producer(s) Wurtzel, Sol M.
Director(s) Marshall, George
Screenwriter(s) Hyland, Frances; Elkins, Saul

Cast Stuart, Gloria; Kent, Robert; Armetta, Henry; Bromberg, J. Edward; Haden, Sara; Dinehart, Alan; Lane, Charles; McVey, Paul

Song(s) Doctor Song (C: Rose, Gene; L: Clare, Sidney)

1234 ◆ THE CRIME OF HELEN STANLEY
Columbia, 1934

Director(s) Lederman, D. Ross
Screenwriter(s) Shumate, Harold

Cast Bellamy, Ralph; Grey, Shirley; Patrick, Gail

Song(s) There's Life in Music [1] (C/L: Rosoff, Charles)

Notes [1] Used instrumentally only. Also used instrumentally in ANN CARVER'S PROFESSION. Sung in WATERFRONT LADY (Mascot).

1235 ◆ CRIMES OF PASSION
New World, 1984

Musical Score Wakeman, Rick

Producer(s) Sandler, Barry
Director(s) Russell, Ken
Screenwriter(s) Sandler, Barry

Cast Turner, Kathleen; Perkins, Anthony; Laughlin, John; Potts, Annie; Davison, Bruce

Song(s) It's a Lovely Life (C: Wakeman, Rick; L: Gimbel, Norman)

Notes No cue sheet available.

1236 ◆ CRIMINAL LAWYER
RKO, 1936

Musical Score Steiner, Max

Producer(s) Reid, Cliff
Director(s) Cabanne, Christy
Screenwriter(s) Atwater, C.V.; Lennon, Thomas

Cast Tracy, Lee; Grahame, Margot; Ciannelli, Eduardo; Rhodes, Erik; Lawford, Betty

Song(s) Tonight Lover Tonight [1] (C: Stern, Jack; L: Tobias, Harry)

Notes [1] Also in PACIFIC LINER.

1237 ◆ THE CRIMSON CANARY
Universal, 1945

Musical Score Fairchild, Edgar

Producer(s) Blankfort, Henry
Director(s) Hoffman, John
Screenwriter(s) Blankfort, Henry; Phillips, Peggy

Cast Beery Jr., Noah; Collier, Lois; Litel, John; Geray, Steven

Song(s) I Never Knew [1] (C/L: Pitts, Tom; Egan, Raymond B.; Marsh, Roy); One Meat Ball (C/L: Zaret, Hy; Singer, Lou)

Notes [1] Also in STRICTLY IN THE GROOVE, THE THREE FACES OF EVE (20th) and THE CLOWN (MGM).

1238 ◆ CRITTERS
New Line, 1986

Musical Score Newman, David

Producer(s) Harvey, Rupert
Director(s) Herek, Stephen
Screenwriter(s) Muri, Domanic; Herek, Stephen

Cast Stone, Dee Wallace; Walsh, M. Emmet; Bush, Billy "Green"; Grimes, Scott; Van Der Velde, Nadine; Zane, Billy; Mann, Terrence

Song(s) Power of the Night (C/L: Mann, Terrence; Vetter, Richie; Pettit, Dodie); Leather (C/L: Vetter, Richie); Still You Turn Me On (C/L: Ducks, Brian)

Notes No cue sheet available.

1239 ◆ CROCODILE DUNDEE
Paramount, 1986

Musical Score Best, Peter

Producer(s) Cornell, John
Director(s) Faiman, Peter
Screenwriter(s) Hogan, Paul; Shakie, Ken; Cornell, John

Cast Hogan, Paul; Kozlowski, Linda; Blum, Mark; Gulpilil, David; Lombard, Michael; Meillon, John

Song(s) Only One Like You (C/L: Prestwich, Stephen); Mad, Bad and Dangerous (C/L: Best, Peter); I Give My Heart to You (C/L: Crane, Jimmie; Jacobs, Al; Brewster, Jimmy); Live It Up (C/L: Smith, Greedy); Different World (C/L: Farriss, Andrew; Hutchence, Michael); Coroboree (C/L: Best, Peter)

1240 ◆ CROONER
Warner Brothers, 1932

Producer(s) Hubbard, Lucien
Director(s) Bacon, Lloyd
Screenwriter(s) Kenyon, Charles

Cast Manners, David [1]; Murray, Ken; Dvorak, Ann; Nugent, Eddie; Naish, J. Carrol; Kibbee, Guy

Song(s) I Send My Love with the Roses (C: Burke, Joe; L: Dubin, Al); Three's a Crowd (C: Warren, Harry; L: Dubin, Al; Kahal, Irving); Sweethearts Forever (C: Friend, Cliff; L: Caesar, Irving); Now You've Got Me Worrying for You (C: Fain, Sammy; L: Young, Joe);

Banking on the Weather (C: Fain, Sammy; L: Young, Joe)

Notes No cue sheet available. [1] Dubbed by Brick Holton.

1241 ✦ CROSSING DELANCEY
Warner Brothers, 1988

Musical Score Chihara, Paul

Producer(s) Nozik, Michael
Director(s) Silver, Joan Micklin
Screenwriter(s) Sandler, Susan
Source(s) (play) Sandler, Susan

Cast Irving, Amy; Riegert, Peter; Bozyk, Feizl; Krabbe, Jeroen; Miles, Sylvia; Martin, George

Song(s) Come Softly to Me (C/L: Christopher, Gretchen; Ellis, Barbara; Troxel, Gary); Pounding (C/L: Roche, Terre; Roche, Suzzy); Nocturne (C/L: Roche, Margaret A.); Get Your Hands Off Her (C/L: Oleszko, Pat); Lucky (C/L: Roche, Terre; Roche, David)

1242 ✦ CROSS MY HEART (1946)
Paramount, 1946

Musical Score Dolan, Robert Emmett
Composer(s) Van Heusen, James
Lyricist(s) Burke, Johnny

Producer(s) Tugend, Harry
Director(s) Berry, John
Screenwriter(s) Binyon, Claude; Tugend, Harry; Schnee, Charles
Source(s) *True Confession* (play) Verneuil, Louis; Berr, Georges

Cast Hutton, Betty; Les Brown and His Orchestra; Donnelly, Ruth; Tufts, Sonny; Adrian, Iris; Williams, Rhys; Bridge, Alan; Chekhov, Michael

Song(s) It Hasn't Been Chilly in Chile (Since Lilly O'Reilly's Around); Does Baby Feel All Right?; How Do You Do It?; That Little Dream Got Nowhere; Love Is the Darndest Thing; Cross My Heart [1] (C: Dolan, Robert Emmett; L: Neill, Larry)

Notes Movie originally titled TOO GOOD TO BE TRUE. [1] This number was used only for the exploitation of the picture.

1243 ✦ CROSS MY HEART (1987)
Universal, 1987

Musical Score Broughton, Bruce

Producer(s) Kasdan, Lawrence
Director(s) Bernstein, Armyan
Screenwriter(s) Bernstein, Armyan; Parent, Gail

Cast Short, Martin; O'Toole, Annette; Reiser, Paul; Kerns, Joanna; Puscas, Jessica; Arenberg, Lee

Song(s) One Heartbeat (C/L: Legassick, Steve; Ray, Brian); Hot in the Flames of Love (C/L: Walden, Narada Michael; Cohen, Jeffrey; Glass, Preston); Perfect World (C/L: Byrne, David; Frantz, Chris); Holding Back the Years (C/L: Hucknall, Mick; Moss, Neil); So Much in Love (C/L: Jackson, William; Williams, George; Straigis, Roy)

Notes It is not known which if any of these were written for this film.

1244 ✦ CROSSROADS (1942)
Metro–Goldwyn–Mayer, 1942

Musical Score Kaper, Bronislau

Producer(s) Knopf, Edwin H.
Director(s) Conway, Jack
Screenwriter(s) Trosper, Guy

Cast Powell, William; Lamarr, Hedy; Trevor, Claire; Rathbone, Basil; Wycherly, Margaret; Bressart, Felix; Warner, H.B.; Rumann, Sig; Merivale, Philip

Song(s) 'Til You Return (C: Schwartz, Arthur; L: Dietz, Howard)

1245 ✦ CROSSROADS (1986)
Columbia, 1986

Musical Score Cooder, Ry

Producer(s) Carliner, Mark
Director(s) Hill, Walter
Screenwriter(s) Fusco, John

Cast Macchio, Ralph; Seneca, Joe; Gertz, Jami; Morton, Joe; Judd, Robert; Vai, Steve

Song(s) Crossroads (C/L: Johnson, Robert); Nitty Gritty Mississippi (C/L: Burch, Fred; Hill, Donald); Made a Woman Out of Me (C/L: Burch, Fred; Hill, Donald); She's More to Be Pitied (C/L: Rakes, Ruby); If I Lose (C/L: Stanley, Ralph); Cotton Needs Pickin' (C/L: Price, John; Frost, Frank; Holmes, Richard; Taylor, Otis); Maintenance Man (C/L: Price, John; Frost, Frank); Willie Brown Blues (C: Cooder, Ry; L: Seneca, Joe)

1246 ✦ CROSS-UP
United Artists, 1958

Musical Score Black, Stanley

Producer(s) Berman, Monty; Baker, Robert S.
Director(s) Gilling, John
Screenwriter(s) Gilling, John; Goldbeck, Willis
Source(s) *I'll Never Come Back* (novel) Mair, John

Cast Parks, Larry; Smith, Constance; Daniely, Lisa

Song(s) I Know Love (C: Black, Stanley; L: Collins, Syd)

Notes A British production titled TIGER BY THE TAIL in England.

1247 ✦ CROSSWINDS
Paramount, 1951

Producer(s) Thomas, William; Pine, William
Director(s) Foster, Lewis R.
Screenwriter(s) Burtis, Thomson
Source(s) *New Guinea Gold* (novel) Burtis, Thomson

Cast Payne, John; Fleming, Rhonda; Tucker, Forrest

Song(s) Crosswinds (C/L: Livingston, Jay; Evans, Ray)

1248 ✦ CRUISIN' DOWN THE RIVER
Columbia, 1953

Choreographer(s) Scott, Lee

Producer(s) Taps, Jonie
Director(s) Quine, Richard
Screenwriter(s) Edwards, Blake; Quine, Richard

Cast Haymes, Dick; Totter, Audrey; Daniels, Billy; Kellaway, Cecil; Russell, Connie; Fowley, Douglas; Blake, Larry; Downs, Johnny; Payne, Benny; The Bell Sisters; Crockett, Dick; Foulger, Byron; Ivan, Erze

Song(s) Cruisin' Down the River (C/L: Beadell, Eily; Tollerton, Nell)

Notes No cue sheet available. Songs include "Sing You Sinners" by Sam Coslow and W. Franke Harling; "I Never Knew" and "Pennies from Heaven" by Johnny Burke and Arthur Johnston; "There Goes that Song Again" by Jule Styne and Sammy Cahn; "Swing Low Sweet Chariot," "My Honey Man," "Has Your Mother Any More Like You" and "Father, Dear Father" by Emmet G. Coleman; "More to Be Pitied Than Censured."

1249 ✦ CRUISING
Lorimar/United Artists, 1980

Musical Score Nitzsche, Jack

Producer(s) Weintraub, Jerry
Director(s) Friedkin, William
Screenwriter(s) Friedkin, William
Source(s) (novel) Walker, Gerald

Cast Pacino, Al; Sorvino, Paul; Allen, Karen; Cox, Richard; Scardino, Don; Spinell, Joe; Remar, James; Burmeister, Leo; Boothe, Powers

Song(s) Heart of the Moment (C/L: DeVille, Willy); Loneliness (C/L: O'Brien, Shawn; Lusson, Robert; Baer, John); Spy Boy (C/L: Hiatt, John); When I Close My Eyes I See Blood (C/L: Lee, Phil); Shakedown (C: Staples, Kevin; L: Pope, Carol); Pullin' My String (C/L: DeVille, Willy); Lions Share (C/L: Darby, Crash & Pat);

Hypnotize (C/L: Lusson, Robert; O'Brien, Shawn); It's So Easy (C/L: DeVille, Willy)

Notes No cue sheet available.

1250 ✦ THE CRUSADES
Paramount, 1935

Composer(s) Kopp, Rudolph
Lyricist(s) Lamb, Harold

Producer(s) De Mille, Cecil B.
Director(s) De Mille, Cecil B.
Screenwriter(s) Lamb, Harold; Young, Waldemar; Nichols, Dudley

Cast Wilcoxon, Henry; Young, Loretta; Keith, Ian; de Mille, Katherine; Smith, C. Aubrey; Schildkraut, Joseph; Hale, Alan; Farnum, William; Love, Montagu; Auer, Mischa

Song(s) Richard Ruled in England [1] (C: Traditional); Hymn of Joy; The Man in the Moon; Blondel's Love Song; Song of the Crusades (C: Whiting, Richard A.; Kopp, Rudolph; L: MacPherson, Jeanie [2]; Robin, Leo); Soldier's Song

Notes [1] Written to tune of "Son of a Gambolier." [2] MacPherson was credited with the choral lyric.

1251 ✦ CRY BABY
Universal, 1990

Musical Score Williams, Patrick
Choreographer(s) Eastside, Lori

Producer(s) Talalay, Rachel
Director(s) Waters, John
Screenwriter(s) Waters, John

Cast Depp, Johnny [1]; Locane, Amy [2]; Tyrrell, Susan; Pop, Iggy; Lake, Ricki; Lords, Traci; Bergen, Polly; McGuire, Kim; Donahue, Troy; Mink Stole; Dallesandro, Joe; Heatherton, Joey; Nelson, David; Hearst, Patricia; Dafoe, Willem; Mailer, Stephen [3]

Song(s) King Cry Baby (C/L: Pomus, Doc; Alvin, Dave); Doin' Time for Bein' Young (C/L: Sother, J.D.; Wachtel, Waddy); High School Hellcats (C/L: Alvin, Dave); Cry Baby (C/L: Robinson, Morgan C.; Robinson, Lawrence); Fingertips (C/L: Prysock, Red)

Notes No cue sheet available. Lyric adaptations by Dave Alvin, Al Kooper and Rachel Sweet. It is not known if all the above songs were written for this film. There are also vocals of "Sh Boom" by James Keyes, Claude Feaster, Carl Feaster, Floyd F. McRae and James Edwards; "A Teenage Prayer" by Bix Reichner and Bernie Lowe; "Teardrops Are Falling" by The Five Wings; "Bunny Hop" by Ray Anthony and Leonard Auletti; "Mister Sandman" by Pat Ballard and "Please, Mister Jailer" by Winona Carr. There are other fifties songs performed on the soundtrack. [1] Dubbed by James Intveld. [2] Dubbed by Rachel Sweet. [3] Dubbed by Gerry Beckley.

1252 ✦ THE CRY BABY KILLER
Allied Artists, 1958

Musical Score   Fried, Gerald

Producer(s)   Corman, Roger
Director(s)   Addiss, Jus
Screenwriter(s)   Gordon, Leo

Cast   Lauter, Harry; Nicholson, Jack; Mitchell, Carolyn; Halsey, Brett; Cartwright, Lynn; Nelson, Ed; McCall, Mitzi

Song(s)   The Cry Baby Killer (C/L: Kallman, Dick)

Notes   No cue sheet available.

1253 ✦ CRY FREEDOM
Universal, 1987

Musical Score   Fenton, George; Gwangwa, Jonas
Composer(s)   Troyte, Arthur
Lyricist(s)   Angless, Edwin; Mpange, Swai

Producer(s)   Attenborough, Richard
Director(s)   Attenborough, Richard
Screenwriter(s)   Briley, John
Source(s)   *Biko*; *Asking for Trouble* (books) Woods, Donald James

Cast   Kline, Kevin; Wilton, Penelope; Washington, Denzel; Hargreaves, John; McCowen, Alec; McNally, Kevin; Mokae, Zakes; Richardson, Ian; Simon, Josette; West, Timothy; Glover, Julian

Song(s)   Senzeni Na [1]; Nongoongoo (To Those We Love) (C/L: Makeba, Miriam); Nkosi Sikelel I—Afrika (C/L: Sontonga, Enoch Mankayi)

Notes   [1] Music in public domain. Lyric credit is for adaptation and arrangement.

1254 ✦ THE CRY OF LAUGHING OWLS
Universal, 1965

Musical Score   Green, Johnny

Song(s)   The World of the Heart (C: Green, Johnny; L: Mercer, Johnny)

Notes   No other information available.

1255 ✦ CUANDO EL AMOR RIE

See THE LOVE GAMBLER (1931).

1256 ✦ CUBAN FIREBALL
Republic, 1951

Composer(s)   Elliott, Jack
Lyricist(s)   Elliott, Jack

Producer(s)   Picker, Sidney
Director(s)   Beaudine, William
Screenwriter(s)   Roberts, Charles E.; Townley, Jack

Cast   Rodriguez, Estelita; Douglas, Warren; Aguglia, Mimi; Belasco, Leon

Song(s)   Un Poquito de Tu Amor [1] (C/L: Gutierrez, Julio); A Slave [2]; Lost and Found; Tobacco

Notes   [1] English lyrics by Ernest Rosecrans. [2] Spanish lyrics by Aaron Gonzalez.

1257 ✦ CUBAN LOVE SONG
Metro–Goldwyn–Mayer, 1931

Musical Score   Stothart, Herbert
Lyricist(s)   Fields, Dorothy

Director(s)   Van Dyke, W.S.
Screenwriter(s)   Sullivan, C. Gardner; Meredyth, Bess; Colton, John; Emery, Gilbert; Hopkins, Robert E.; Fox, Paul Harvey

Cast   Tibbett, Lawrence; Velez, Lupe; Morley, Karen; Torrence, Ernest; Durante, Jimmy; Fazenda, Louise; Ernesto Lecuona and the Palau Brothers' Cuban Orchestra

Song(s)   Tramps at Sea (C: Stothart, Herbert; McHugh, Jimmy); Cuban Love Song [1] (C: Stothart, Herbert)

Notes   There are also vocals of "The Peanut Vendor" by Marion Sunshine, L. Wolfe Gilbert and Moises Simons and "Buche Y Pluma" by Hernandez. [1] Sheet music and ASCAP credit Stothart and McHugh.

1258 ✦ CUBAN PETE
Universal, 1946

Producer(s)   Cowan, Will
Director(s)   Yarbrough, Jean
Screenwriter(s)   Presnell, Robert; Webster, M. Coates

Cast   Arnaz, Desi; Porter, Don; de Wit, Jacqueline; Fulton, Joan; Simmons, Beverly; Smith, Ethel; de Cordoba, Pedro; The King Sisters

Song(s)   El Cumbanchero (C/L: Hernandez, Rafael); Rhumba Matumba [1] (C/L: Collazo, Bobby); Cuban (C/L: Golden, Jack); Cuban Pete (C/L: Norman, Jose); After Tonight (C/L: Brooks, Jack; Arnaz, Desi; Schwarzwald, Milton)

Notes   Titled DOWN CUBA WAY in Great Britain. There is also a vocal of "Cielito Lindo" by C. Fernandez and an instrumental of "The Breeze and I" by Ernesto Lecuona and Al Stillman. It is not known if any of the above were written for this film. [1] Also in HOLLYWOOD BOND CARAVAN (Paramount) and MY GAL LOVES MUSIC.

1259 ✦ THE CUCKOO PATROL
Twentieth Century–Fox, 1965

Composer(s)   Garrity, Freddie
Lyricist(s)   Garrity, Freddie

Producer(s)   Wilson, Maurice J.
Director(s)   Wood, Duncan
Screenwriter(s)   Schwartz, Lew

Cast   Freddie and the Dreamers; Connor, Kenneth; Maddern, Victor; Le Mesurier, John; Mullard, Arthur

Song(s)   The Cuckoo Patrol; It Wasn't Me; It Seems Like Things Are Turning Out Fine Again

1260 ✦ THE CUCKOOS
Radio, 1930

Composer(s)   Ruby, Harry
Lyricist(s)   Kalmar, Bert
Choreographer(s)   Eaton, Pearl

Producer(s)   LeBaron, William
Director(s)   Sloane, Paul
Screenwriter(s)   Wood, Cyrus
Source(s)   *The Ramblers* (musical) Bolton, Guy; Ruby, Harry; Kalmar, Bert

Cast   Wheeler, Bert; Woolsey, Robert; Clyde, June; Trevor, Hugh; Lee, Dorothy; Lebedeff, Ivan; Padula, Marguerita; Lewis, Mitchell; Howland, Jobyna

Song(s)   I'm a Gypsy; Wherever You Are [2]; I Love You So Much; Cabelleros Number; Oh How We Love Our Alma Mater; All Alone Monday; California Skies; Sleep Baby Sleep [1]; Goodbye; Laugh Today and Cry Tomorrow; Dancing the Devil Away; If I Were a Travelling Salesman [3] (C: Burke, Joe; L: Dubin, Al)

Notes   Cue sheets do not differentiate between vocals and instrumentals. These songs are from comparing the cue sheet and script. [1] Only a few seconds long. [2] Credited in some sources as by Charles Tobias and Cliff Friend. [3] Sheet music only.

1261 ✦ CURLY TOP
Fox, 1935

Composer(s)   Henderson, Ray
Lyricist(s)   Koehler, Ted
Choreographer(s)   Donohue, Jack

Producer(s)   Sheehan, Winfield
Director(s)   Cummings, Irving
Screenwriter(s)   McNutt, Patterson; Beckhard, Arthur

Cast   Temple, Shirley; Boles, John; Hudson, Rochelle

Song(s)   Animal Crackers in My Soup (C: Caesar, Irving; Koehler, Ted); It's All So New to Me (L: Heyman, Edward); Simple Things in Life; When I Grow Up (L: Heyman, Edward); Curly Top; Busy! Keepin' Happy [1]; How Can There Be So Many Moons? [1] (L: Caesar, Irving; Koehler, Ted); One Way Street [1] (L: Caesar, Irving; Koehler, Ted); Spreading Love Around [1] (L: Heyman, Edward)

Notes   [1] Not used.

1262 ✦ CURSE OF THE CAT PEOPLE
RKO, 1944

Musical Score   Webb, Roy

Producer(s)   Lewton, Val
Director(s)   Fritsch, Gunther V.; Wise, Robert
Screenwriter(s)   Bodeen, DeWitt

Cast   Simon, Simone; Smith, Kent; Randolph, Jane; Carter, Ann; Sir Lancelot; March, Eve; Dean, Julia

Song(s)   September (C/L: Ambrose, Paul; Jackson, Helen Hunt)

1263 ✦ CUSTER OF THE WEST
Cinerama Releasing, 1968

Musical Score   Segall, Bernard
Composer(s)   Segall, Bernard
Lyricist(s)   Holt, Will

Producer(s)   Lerner, Irving
Director(s)   Siodmak, Robert
Screenwriter(s)   Gordon, Bernard

Cast   Shaw, Robert; Ure, Mary; Hunter, Jeffrey; Hardin, Ty; Ryan, Robert

Song(s)   Marching Song; Maxwell House; Heroes Die

Notes   No cue sheet available.

1264 ✦ CUTTER & BONE
United Artists, 1981

Musical Score   Nitzsche, Jack

Producer(s)   Gurian, Paul R.
Director(s)   Passer, Ivan
Screenwriter(s)   Fiskin, Jeffrey Alan
Source(s)   *Cutter & Bone* (novel) Thornburg, Newton

Cast   Bridges, Jeff; Heard, John; Eichorn, Lisa; Dusenberry, Ann; Elliott, Stephen; Rosenberg, Arthur; van Pallandt, Nina

Song(s)   We're Old Enough to Know (C: Nitzsche, Jack; L: Byrum, John)

Notes   There were also some licensed songs in Spanish. Also known as CUTTER'S WAY.

1265 ✦ CUTTER'S WAY

See CUTTER & BONE.

1266 ✦ CYCLONE ON HORSEBACK
RKO, 1941

Musical Score   Dreyer, Dave; Sawtell, Paul
Composer(s)   Whitley, Ray; Rose, Fred
Lyricist(s)   Whitley, Ray; Rose, Fred

Producer(s)   Gilroy, Bert
Director(s)   Killy, Edward
Screenwriter(s)   Parker, Norton S.

Cast Holt, Tim; Reynolds, Marjorie; Whitley, Ray; White, Lee "Lasses"; Worth, Harry; Whitaker, Slim

Song(s) Bangtail; Tumbleweed Cowboy; Blue Nightfall

1267 ✦ CYNTHIA
Metro–Goldwyn–Mayer, 1947

Musical Score Kaper, Bronislau

Producer(s) Knopf, Edwin H.
Director(s) Leonard, Robert Z.
Screenwriter(s) Buchman, Harold; Kaufman, Charles
Source(s) *The Rich and Full Life* (play) Delmar, Vina

Cast Taylor, Elizabeth; Murphy, George; Sakall, S.Z.; Astor, Mary; Lockhart, Gene; Byington, Spring; Lydon, Jimmy [2]; Beckett, Scotty

Song(s) Melody of Spring [1] (C: Green, Johnny; L: Freed, Ralph)

Notes Originally titled THE RICH FULL LIFE. There is also a vocal of "Buckle Down Winsocki" by Hugh Martin and Ralph Blane. [1] From music by Johann Strauss. [2] Billed as James Lydon.

1268 ✦ CZAR OF BROADWAY
Universal, 1930

Producer(s) Sullivan, C. Gardner
Director(s) Craft, William James
Screenwriter(s) Towne, Gene

Cast Wray, John; Compson, Betty; Harron, John; Allister, Claud; Mack, Wilbur; Baggot, King; Breese, Edmund

Song(s) That Homestead Steady of Mine (C: Handman, Lou; L: Ryan, Ben)

Notes No cue sheet available. No other information available.

D

Disney, 1970

Musical Score   Bruns, George

Producer(s)   Kimball, Ward
Director(s)   Kimball, Ward
Screenwriter(s)   Berman, Ted

Cast   Russell, Kurt; Thompson, Chris; Quinn, Spencer; White, Jesse; Renoudet, Pete

Song(s)   Wheels (C/L: Lindley, David)

1270 ✦ DADDY LONG LEGS (1931)
Fox, 1931

Director(s)   Santell, Alfred
Source(s)   *Daddy Long Legs* (novel) Webster, Jean

Cast   Gaynor, Janet; Farrell, Charles; Brendel, El; O'Sullivan, Lawrence

Song(s)   Mush (C/L: Hanley, James F.)

1271 ✦ DADDY LONG LEGS (1952)
Twentieth Century–Fox, 1952 unproduced

Composer(s)   Wilder, Alec
Lyricist(s)   Engvick, William

Song(s)   Daddy Long Legs; Oh, What a Lovely Time; Alma Mater (Moon and Alma Mater); Judy; The Moon Just Winked at Me; Great Fortunes I've Earned; Who Are You?; Forty-Eight Reasons; The Family Is Home; The Trouble with Children; The Skating Song; Corn Meal Mush; All I Want to Do Is Dance; Carol

Notes   This version was unproduced. A subsequent score was written by Johnny Mercer. Engvick's lyrics still exist at Fox.

1272 ✦ DADDY LONG LEGS (1955)
Twentieth Century–Fox, 1955

Musical Score   North, Alex
Composer(s)   Mercer, Johnny
Lyricist(s)   Mercer, Johnny
Choreographer(s)   Astaire, Fred; Robel, David; Petit, Roland [4]

Producer(s)   Engel, Samuel G.
Director(s)   Negulesco, Jean
Screenwriter(s)   Ephron, Henry; Ephron, Phoebe
Source(s)   *Daddy Long Legs* (novel) Webster, Jean

Cast   Astaire, Fred; Caron, Leslie; Moore, Terry; Ritter, Thelma; Clark, Fred; Austin, Charlotte; Keating, Larry; Ray Anthony and His Orchestra

Song(s)   The History of the Beat [1]; Guardian Angel [2]; Tango (Inst.); C-A-T Spells Cat; Daddy Long Legs; Welcome Egg-Head; Texas Romp and Square Dance; Dream [3]; Sluefoot; Something's Gotta Give; Mambo (Inst.); Dancing Through Life [2]; Blues Theme (Inst.); First Auto Theme [5]; Second Auto Theme [5]; First Chinese Theme [5]; Hare Pieces [5]; Julie's Dream (Ballet) [5]; Minor Nursery [5]; Montage Theme [5]; Third Day Rag [5]; Texas Waltz [5]; Texas March [5]

Notes   In 1952 Alec Wilder and William Engvick wrote a complete score for DADDY LONG LEGS, but it wasn't used. See DADDY LONG LEGS (1952). The music of the Paris, Hong Kong and Rio ballets was written by Alex North. [1] Formerly titled "That'll Get It." [2] Used instrumentally only. [3] Not written for this film. [4] Petit choreographed the ballets. [5] Not used.

1273 ✦ DADDY'S GONE A-HUNTING
National General, 1969

Musical Score   Williams, John

Producer(s)   Robson, Mark
Director(s)   Robson, Mark
Screenwriter(s)   Cohen, Larry; Semple Jr., Lorenzo

Cast   White, Carol; Hylands, Scott; Burke, Paul; Powers, Mala; Sikking, James B.

Song(s)   Daddy's Gone A-Hunting (C: William, John; L: Previn, Dory)

Notes   No cue sheet available.

1274 ✦ THE DAKOTA KID
Republic, 1951

Producer(s)   Ralston, Rudy
Director(s)   Ford, Philip
Screenwriter(s)   Lively, William

Cast Chapin, Michael; Janssen, Eilene; Bell, James; Morton, Dean; Field, Margaret; Barcroft, Roy

Song(s) What Are Cowboys Made Of [1] (C: Styne, Jule; L: Cherkose, Eddie)

Notes [1] Also in MELODY RANCH.

1275 ◆ DAKOTA LIL
Twentieth Century–Fox, 1949

Musical Score Tiomkin, Dimitri

Producer(s) Alperson, Edward L.
Director(s) Selander, Lesley
Screenwriter(s) Geraghty, Maurice

Cast Montgomery, George; Cameron, Rod; Windsor, Marie; Emery, John; Ford, Wallace

Song(s) Matamoros (C: Tiomkin, Dimitri; L: Geraghty, Maurice); Ecstasy [1] (C: Kraushaar, Raoul; Coster, Irwin; L: Geraghty, Maurice; Jungmeyer Jr., Jack); Rose of Cimarron [2] (C/L: Geraghty, Maurice)

Notes [1] Based on the old Scotch song "Charlie Is My Darling." [2] Sheet music only.

1276 ◆ THE DALTON GIRLS
United Artists, 1957

Musical Score Baxter, Les

Producer(s) Koch, Howard W.
Director(s) LeBorg, Reginald
Screenwriter(s) Tombragel, Maurice

Cast Anders, Merry; Davis, Lisa; Edwards, Penny; George, Sue; Russell, John; Hinton, Ed

Song(s) A Gun Is My True Love (C: Baxter, Les; L: Unknown)

1277 ◆ DAMAGED LOVE
Sono-Art, 1930

Director(s) Willat, Irvin
Screenwriter(s) Broadhurst, Thomas William
Source(s) *Our Pleasant Sins* (play) Broadhurst, Thomas William

Cast Collyer, June; Starrett, Charles; Taylor, Eloise; Garde, Betty; Trowbridge, Charles

Song(s) In Each Other's Arms (C: Pascal, Milton; L: Pearson, M. Homer)

Notes No cue sheet available.

1278 ◆ THE DAM BUSTERS
Warner Brothers, 1955

Musical Score Coates, Eric; Lucas, Leighton

Director(s) Anderson, Michael
Screenwriter(s) Sherriff, R.C.

Source(s) *The Dam Busters* (book) Brickhill, Paul; *Enemy Coast Ahead* (book) Gibson, Wing Commander

Cast Todd, Richard; Redgrave, Michael; Jeans, Ursula; Sydney, Basil; Barr, Patrick; Clark, Ernest

Song(s) Sing Everybody Sing [1] (C/L: Long, J.P.)

Notes [1] Also in HI, BEAUTIFUL (Universal) with additions by Al Stillman.

1279 ◆ DAMES
Warner Brothers, 1934

Composer(s) Warren, Harry
Lyricist(s) Dubin, Al
Choreographer(s) Berkeley, Busby

Producer(s) Lord, Robert
Director(s) Enright, Ray
Screenwriter(s) Daves, Delmer

Cast Powell, Dick; Keeler, Ruby; Herbert, Hugh; Blondell, Joan; Kibbee, Guy; Pitts, ZaSu; Vinton, Arthur; Fain, Sammy

Song(s) When You Were a Smile on Your Mother's Lips (And a Twinkle in Your Daddy's Eye) [2] (C: Fain, Sammy; L: Kahal, Irving); I Only Have Eyes for You [1]; Try to See It My Way Baby (C: Wrubel, Allie; L: Dixon, Mort); Girl at the Ironing Board; Dames

Notes [1] Later in MONEY FROM HOME (Paramount). [2] Also in SWEETHEART SERENADE.

1280 ◆ DAMNATION ALLEY
Twentieth Century–Fox, 1977

Musical Score Goldsmith, Jerry

Producer(s) Zeitman, Jerome M.; Maslansky, Paul
Director(s) Smight, Jack
Screenwriter(s) Sharp, Alan; Heller, Lukas
Source(s) *Damnation Alley* (novel) Zelazny, Roger

Cast Vincent, Jan-Michael; Peppard, George; Sanda, Dominique; Winfield, Paul; Haley, Jackie Earle; Niven, Kip

Song(s) Again (C: Newman, Lionel; L: Cochran, Dorcas)

1281 ◆ DAMN YANKEES
Warner Brothers, 1958

Composer(s) Adler, Richard; Ross, Jerry
Lyricist(s) Adler, Richard; Ross, Jerry
Choreographer(s) Fosse, Bob; Ferrier, Pat

Producer(s) Abbott, George; Donen, Stanley
Director(s) Abbott, George; Donen, Stanley
Screenwriter(s) Abbott, George
Source(s) *Damn Yankees* (musical) Abbott, George; Adler, Richard; Ross, Jerry

Cast Hunter, Tab; Walston, Ray; Verdon, Gwen; Bolin, Shannon

Song(s) Six Months Out of Every Year; Heart; Goodbye, Old Girl; Shoeless Joe from Hannibal, Mo.; There's Something About an Empty Chair [1] (C/L: Adler, Richard); A Little Brains, A Little Talent; Whatever Lola Wants (Lola Gets); Those Were the Good Old Days; Who's Got the Pain; Two Lost Souls

Notes Released as WHAT LOLA WANTS in Great Britain. The Broadway musical is based on *The Year the Yankees Lost the Pennant*, a novel by Douglas Wallop. [1] Only song written for picture.

1282 ◆ A DAMSEL IN DISTRESS
RKO, 1937

Musical Score Bennett, Russell
Composer(s) Gershwin, George
Lyricist(s) Gershwin, Ira
Choreographer(s) Pan, Hermes

Producer(s) Berman, Pandro S.
Director(s) Stevens, George
Screenwriter(s) Wodehouse, P.G.; Pagano, Ernest; Lauren, S.K.
Source(s) *A Damsel in Distress* (novel) Wodehouse, P.G.

Cast Astaire, Fred; Burns, George; Allen, Gracie; Fontaine, Joan; Gardiner, Reginald [1]; Noble, Ray; Collier, Constance; Love, Montagu; Watson, Harry

Song(s) I Can't Be Bothered Now; Jolly Tar and the Milk-Maid; Things Are Looking Up; Stiff Upper Lip; Sing of Spring; Foggy Day; Nice Work If You Can Get It; Put Me to the Test [2]; Pay Some Attention to Me [3]

Notes There is also a vocal of "Heaven Above Forgive Thee" from MARTHA by Von Flotow. [1] Dubbed by Mario Berini. [2] Used instrumentally only. Lyric similar to "Put Me to the Test" in COVER GIRL where it was set to Jerome Kern music. [3] Not used.

1283 ◆ DANCE, CHARLIE, DANCE
Warner Brothers–First National, 1937

Composer(s) Jerome, M.K.
Lyricist(s) Scholl, Jack

Producer(s) Foy, Bryan
Director(s) McDonald, Frank
Screenwriter(s) Wilbur, Crane; Jacobs, William
Source(s) *The Butter and Egg Man* (play) Kaufman, George S.

Cast Erwin, Stuart; Muir, Jean; Farrell, Glenda; Jenkins, Allen; Richards, Addison; Foy, Charles; Clute, Chester

Song(s) Ballet de Bunk [1]; Dance, Charlie, Dance

Notes [1] Instrumental use only.

1284 ◆ DANCE, FOOLS, DANCE!
Metro–Goldwyn–Mayer, 1931

Director(s) Beaumont, Harry
Screenwriter(s) Rouverol, Aurania; Schayer, Richard

Cast Crawford, Joan; Vail, Lester; Edwards, Cliff; Bakewell, William; Holden, William; Gable, Clark; Hamilton, Hale

Song(s) A Gay Caballero (C: Crumit, Frank; L: Klein, Lou)

1285 ◆ DANCE, GIRL, DANCE
RKO, 1940

Musical Score Ward, Edward
Composer(s) Ward, Edward
Lyricist(s) Wright, Robert; Forrest, Chet
Choreographer(s) Matray, Ernst

Producer(s) Pommer, Erich
Director(s) Arzner, Dorothy
Screenwriter(s) Slesinger, Tess; David, Frank

Cast O'Hara, Maureen; Hayward, Louis; Ball, Lucille; Field, Virginia; Bellamy, Ralph; Carlisle, Mary; Alexander, Katherine; Brophy, Edward S.; Abel, Walter; Huber, Harold; Ouspenskaya, Maria

Song(s) The Beer Barrel Polka (C: Vejvoda, Jaromir; L: Brown, Lew); Morning Star; Mother What Do I Do Now? (C: Wright, Robert; Forrest, Chet); Jitterbug Bite

1286 ◆ DANCE GYPSY
Studio Unknown, 1940

Lyricist(s) Drake, Milton

Song(s) Vodka; Guitar Serenade; Volga Olga; Ortchi Tchornya

Notes No other information available.

1287 ◆ DANCE HALL (1930)
RKO, 1930

Producer(s) LeBaron, William
Director(s) Brown, Melville
Screenwriter(s) Murfin, Jane; Ruben, J. Walter

Cast Lake, Arthur; Borden, Olive; Cawthorn, Joseph; Seddon, Margaret; Emerson, Ralph

Song(s) Someone [1] (C: Levant, Oscar; L: Clare, Sidney)

Notes [1] Also in JAZZ HEAVEN.

1288 ◆ DANCE HALL (1941)
Twentieth Century–Fox, 1941

Producer(s) Wurtzel, Sol M.
Director(s) Pichel, Irving
Screenwriter(s) Rauh, Stanley; Hill, Ethel
Source(s) *Giant Swing* (novel) Burnett, W.R.

Cast Landis, Carole; Romero, Cesar; Henry, William; Storey, June; Bromberg, J. Edward

Song(s) There's Something in the Air [1] (C: McHugh, Jimmy; L: Adamson, Harold); There's a Lull in My Life [2] (C: Revel, Harry; L: Gordon, Mack)

Notes [1] Also in BANJO ON MY KNEE. [2] Also in WAKE UP AND LIVE.

1289 ✦ THE DANCE OF LIFE
Paramount, 1929

Composer(s) Whiting, Richard A.
Lyricist(s) Robin, Leo; Coslow, Sam
Choreographer(s) Lindsay, Earl

Producer(s) Selznick, David O.
Director(s) Sutherland, Edward; Cromwell, John
Screenwriter(s) Watters, George Manker; Glazer, Benjamin
Source(s) *Burlesque* (play) Hopkins, Arthur; Watters, George Manker

Cast Skelly, Hal; Carroll, Nancy; Boley, May; Levant, Oscar; Revier, Dorothy; Theodore, Ralph; Brown, Charles D.; Sutherland, Edward [2]; Cromwell, John [3]

Song(s) True Blue Lou; King of Jazzmania; (I Want to Cuddle Some) Cuddlesome Baby; Ladies of the Dance; The Flippity Flop; Horses Horses (L: Gay, Byron); Mightiest Matador

Notes AFI also lists the songs "Sam, the Accordian Man" and "In the Gloaming." There are also vocals of "Yes Sir, That's My Baby" by Walter Donaldson and Gus Kahn (also in THE EDDIE CANTOR STORY and I'LL SEE YOU IN MY DREAMS); "I'll Get By" by Fred Ahlert and Roy Turk; "(She's the) Daughter of Rosie O'Grady" by Walter Donaldson and Monty C. Brice; and "Sweeping the Cobwebs off the Moon" by Oscar Levant, Sam Lewis and Joe Young. [1] Not written for the film. [2] Sutherland appears as a theater attendant. [3] Cromwell appears as the doorkeeper.

1290 ✦ THE DANCERS
Fox, 1930

Director(s) Sprague, Chandler
Screenwriter(s) Burke, Edwin

Cast Holmes, Phillips; Moran, Lois; Clarke, Mae; Byron, Walter; Campbell, Mrs. Patrick; Davis, Tyrrell

Song(s) Doing the Boom Boom [1] (C/L: Conrad, Con; Gottler, Archie; Mitchell, Sidney D.); Love Has Passed Me By [2] (C: Monaco, James V.; L: Friend, Cliff)

Notes A remake of the 1925 silent version by Fox which was based on Hubert Parsons' THE DANCERS (1923). [1] Originally used in WHY LEAVE HOME? [2] Copyright registration lists this as originally written for a Fox film titled PLAY CALLED LIFE. I could find no reference to this title.

1291 ✦ DANCERS IN THE DARK
Paramount, 1932

Director(s) Burton, David
Screenwriter(s) Mankiewicz, Herman J.

Cast Oakie, Jack; Hopkins, Miriam; Collier Jr., William; Raft, George; Roberti, Lyda; Pallette, Eugene

Song(s) It's the Darndest Thing (C: McHugh, Jimmy; L: Fields, Dorothy); All I Want Is Just One (C: Whiting, Richard A.; L: Robin, Leo); I'm In Love with a Tune (C/L: Rainger, Ralph); Live and Love Tonight [2] [1] (C: Johnston, Arthur; L: Coslow, Sam); You Didn't Know the Music [2] (C/L: Coslow, Sam); My Hour Has Come [2] [3] (C/L: Rainger, Ralph)

Notes Formerly titled DANCE PALACE. There are also vocals of "Lady of Spain" by Tolchard Evans and Erell Reaves and "St. Louis Blues" by W.C. Handy (also in the two films titled ST. LOUIS BLUES and in BANJO ON MY KNEE). [1] Also not used in WE'RE NOT DRESSING, but used in MURDER AT THE VANITIES. [2] Not used. [3] Not used in TWO KINDS OF WOMAN.

1292 ✦ DANCE WITH ME HENRY
United Artists, 1957

Musical Score Dunlap, Paul

Producer(s) Goldstein, Bob
Director(s) Barton, Charles
Screenwriter(s) Freeman, Devery

Cast Costello, Lou; Abbott, Bud; Perreau, Gigi; Hamer, Rusty; Wickes, Mary; De Corsia, Ted; Hargrave, Ron; Alberoni, Sherry; Reeves, Richard

Song(s) Oogly-Boogly (C/L: Hargrave, Ron); Scooby Dooby (C/L: Hargrave, Ron)

Notes Abbott and Costello's last movie as a team.

1293 ✦ DANCING CO-ED
Metro–Goldwyn–Mayer, 1939

Musical Score Ward, Edward; Snell, Dave
Composer(s) Shaw, Artie
Choreographer(s) King, George

Producer(s) Selwyn, Edgar
Director(s) Simon, S. Sylvan
Screenwriter(s) Mannheimer, Albert

Cast Turner, Lana; Carlson, Richard; Artie Shaw and His Band; Rutherford, Ann; Bowman, Lee; Hall, Thurston; Errol, Leon; Karns, Roscoe; Woolley, Monty; Preisser, June; Kingsford, Walter

Song(s) Nightmare (Inst.); Non-Stop Flight (Inst.); The Blues—An Improvisation (Inst.); Double Mellow (Inst.); Gang Busters (Inst.); Everything Is Jumpin' [1] (C: Shaw, Artie); Jungle Drums [1] (C: Lecuona, Ernesto; L: Lombardo, Carmen; O'Flynn, Charles);

One Foot in the Groove [1] (C/L: Shaw, Artie; Davry, Wen); Traffic Jam (inst.) [1] (C: Shaw, Artie; McRae, Teddy)

Notes Titled EVERY OTHER INCH A LADY internationally. There is a vocal of "I've Got a Feelin' You're Foolin'" by Nacio Herb Brown and Arthur Freed. Some of the instrumentals were not written specifically for this film. [1] Sheet music only.

1294 ✦ DANCING FEET
Republic, 1936

Musical Score Stept, Sam H.
Composer(s) Stept, Sam H.
Lyricist(s) Mitchell, Sidney D.

Producer(s) Clark, Colbert
Director(s) Santley, Joseph
Screenwriter(s) Chodorov, Jerome; Cooper, Olive; Totman, Wellyn
Source(s) (novel) Eden, Bob

Cast Lyon, Ben; Marsh, Joan; Nugent, Eddie; Jewell, Isabel; Burke, James; Pratt, Purnell; Barnett, Vince; Condos, Nick; Rawlinson, Herbert; J.C. Edwards and His Band

Song(s) Every Time I Look at You; Here Comes Love (L: Stept, Sam H.); Dancing Feet; And Then [1]; Get in Step [1]

Notes [1] Not used.

1295 ✦ THE DANCING FOOL

See HAROLD TEEN.

1296 ✦ DANCING IN MANHATTAN
Columbia, 1945

Producer(s) MacDonald, Wallace
Director(s) Levin, Henry
Screenwriter(s) Lazarus, Erna

Cast Brady, Fred; Donnell, Jeff; Wright, William; Savage, Ann

Notes No cue sheet available.

1297 ✦ DANCING IN THE DARK
Twentieth Century–Fox, 1949

Choreographer(s) Felix, Seymour

Producer(s) Jessel, George
Director(s) Reis, Irving
Screenwriter(s) McCall Jr., Mary C.

Cast Powell, William; Stevens, Mark; Drake, Betsy [1]; Menjou, Adolphe; Stuart, Randy; Corrigan, Lloyd; Emerson, Hope; Catlett, Walter; Beddoe, Don; Hersholt, Jean; Grauman, Sid; Wescott, Helen; Ferguson, Frank

Notes No original songs in this film. Vocals include the Arthur Schwartz and Howard Dietz songs "Dancing in the Dark;" "Something to Remember You By" (also in THE BAND WAGON and HER KIND OF MAN); "New Sun in the Sky" (also in THE BAND WAGON) and "I Love Louisa" (also in THE BAND WAGON). [1] Dubbed by Bonnie Lou Williams.

1298 ✦ DANCING LADY
Metro–Goldwyn–Mayer, 1933

Composer(s) Lane, Burton
Lyricist(s) Adamson, Harold
Choreographer(s) Lee, Sammy; Prinz, Eddie

Producer(s) Selznick, David O.
Director(s) Leonard, Robert Z.
Screenwriter(s) Rivkin, Allen; Wolfson, P.J.
Source(s) (novel) Bellah, James Warner

Cast Crawford, Joan; Tone, Franchot; Gable, Clark; Lightner, Winnie; Astaire, Fred; Robson, May; Benchley, Robert; Ted Healy and His Stooges [1]; Eddy, Nelson; Holloway, Sterling

Song(s) Hey Young Fella; Hold Your Man [3] (C: Brown, Nacio Herb; L: Freed, Arthur); Everything I Have Is Yours; My Dancing Lady (C: McHugh, Jimmy; L: Fields, Dorothy); (That's the) Rhythm of the Day (C: Rodgers, Richard; L: Hart, Lorenz); Heigh Ho the Gang's All Here [4]; Let's Go Bavarian; Dancing Lady (1) [2] (C: Rodgers, Richard; L: Hart, Lorenz); Dancing Lady (2) [2] (C: Rodgers, Richard; L: Hart, Lorenz); Life Is a Merry-Go-Round [2] (C: Brown, Nacio Herb; L: Freed, Arthur)

Notes Fred Astaire's film debut. [1] Moe Howard, Jerry Howard and Larry Fine. [2] Not used. [3] Also in HOLD YOUR MAN. [4] Written for stage show EARL CARROLL'S VANITIES OF 1931.

1299 ✦ DANCING ON A DIME
Paramount, 1941

Musical Score Young, Victor
Composer(s) Lane, Burton
Lyricist(s) Loesser, Frank
Choreographer(s) Prinz, LeRoy

Producer(s) Botsford, A.M.
Director(s) Santley, Joseph
Screenwriter(s) Rapf, Maurice; Chapin, Anne Morrison; Rivkin, Allen

Cast Paige, Robert; MacDonald, Grace; Dale, Virginia; Frawley, William; Hayes, Peter; Cornell, Lillian; Quillan, Eddie; Jenks, Frank

Song(s) I Hear Music [2]; Loveable Sort of Person (C: Young, Victor); Manana; Debutante Number One (C: Young, Victor); Dancing on a Dime; Mary, Mary, Quite Contrary [1]; Operatic Prelude to Show (C: Styne, Jule)

Notes [1] Not used. Appeared in LAS VEGAS NIGHTS and was also not used in COLLEGE SWING. [2] Jule Styne (vocal arranger on the picture) wrote some special lyrics for this song with Loesser which were titled "Recording Version."

1300 ✦ DANCING ON THE CEILING
Metro–Goldwyn–Mayer, 1937

Composer(s) Lane, Burton
Lyricist(s) Adamson, Harold

Director(s) Roth, Murray

Song(s) Locker Room Sequence; See Your Dentist Once a Day; In the Office (C/L: Vaughan, C.); Walking on the Ceiling

Notes Short subject.

1301 ✦ DANCING ON THE MOON
Paramount, 1935

Producer(s) Fleischer, Max

Song(s) Dancing on the Moon (C: Mencher, Murray; L: Tobias, Charles)

Notes This is an animated cartoon.

1302 ✦ DANCING PIRATE
RKO, 1936

Musical Score Newman, Alfred; Penso, Raphael
Composer(s) Rodgers, Richard
Lyricist(s) Hart, Lorenz
Choreographer(s) Lewis, Russell

Producer(s) Sparks, John
Director(s) Corrigan, Lloyd
Screenwriter(s) Harris, Ray; Faragoh, Francis Edwards
Source(s) "Glorious Buccaneer" (story) Lindsey-Squier, Emma

Cast Duna, Steffi; Collins, Charles; Morgan, Frank; Alberni, Luis; Varconi, Victor; LaRue, Jack; Real, Alma; Mong, William V.; The Dancing Cansinos [1]

Song(s) Are You My Love; When You're Dancing the Waltz

Notes [1] Including the future Rita Hayworth.

1303 ✦ DANCING SWEETIES
Warner Brothers, 1930

Director(s) Enright, Ray
Screenwriter(s) Rigby, Gordon; Jackson, Joseph
Source(s) Three Flights Up Fried, Harry

Cast Withers, Grant; Carol, Sue; Murphy, Edna; Marshall, Tully; Phillips, Eddie; Price, Kate; Vaughn, Ada Mae; Clayton, Eddie; Barnett and Clark

Song(s) Wishing and Waiting for Love [4] (C: Akst, Harry; L: Clarke, Grant); Hullabaloo (C: Dolan, Robert Emmett; L: O'Keefe, Walter); Kiss Waltz [3] (C: Burke, Joe; L: Dubin, Al); I Love You, I Hate You [2] (C: Meyer, Joseph; L: Bryan, Alfred); Dancing with Tears in My Eyes [1] (C: Burke, Joe; L: Dubin, Al)

Notes No cue sheet available. [1] Cut from final print. Used for less than a minute in BROADWAY HOSTESS. [2] Also in CAREERS. [3] Also in COLLEGE LOVERS and FOOTSTEPS IN THE DARK. [4] Also in BROADWAY BABIES.

1304 ✦ A DANDY IN ASPIC
Columbia, 1968

Musical Score Jones, Quincy

Producer(s) Gilliatt, Leslie
Director(s) Mann, Anthony
Screenwriter(s) Marlowe, Derek

Cast Harvey, Laurence; Courtenay, Tom; Farrow, Mia; Stander, Lionel; Andrews, Harry; Cook, Peter

Song(s) If You Want Love (C: Jones, Quincy; L: Sheldon, Ernie); The Spell You Spin, the Web You Weave (C: Grusin, Dave; Jones, Quincy; L: Russell, Bob)

Notes No cue sheet available.

1305 ✦ DANGER AHEAD
Monogram, 1940

Composer(s) Lange, Johnny
Lyricist(s) Porter, Lew

Director(s) Staub, Ralph
Screenwriter(s) Halperin, Edward
Source(s) "Renfrew of the Royal Mounted" (stories) Erskine, Laurie York

Cast Newill, James; Kent, Dorothea; Usher, Guy; O'Brien, Dave; Allen, Maude; Shaw, Al

Song(s) Spare the Rod and Spoil the Child; That's the Kind of Girl for Me; Mounted Men [1] (C/L: Laidlow, Betty; Lively, Robert)

Notes [1] Also in CRASHING THRU, FIGHTING MAN, MURDER ON THE YUKON, RENFREW AND THE GREAT WHITE TRAIL, SKY BANDITS and YUKON FLIGHT.

1306 ✦ DANGER: DIABOLIK!
Paramount, 1968

Producer(s) De Laurentiis, Dino
Director(s) Bava, Mario
Screenwriter(s) Bava, Mario; Baracco, Adriano; Maiuri, Dino

Cast Law, John Phillip; Mell, Marisa

Song(s) Deep Down (C: Morricone, Ennio; L: Nohra, Audrey)

1307 ✦ DANGER—LOVE AT WORK
Twentieth Century–Fox, 1937

Producer(s) Wilson, Harold
Director(s) Preminger, Otto
Screenwriter(s) Grant, James Edward; Markson, Ben

Cast Sothern, Ann; Haley, Jack; Boland, Mary; Horton, Edward Everett; Carradine, John; Catlett, Walter; Bartlett, Bennie; Cass, Maurice; Dinehart, Alan; Girardot, Etienne; Clive, E.E.

Song(s) Danger—Love at Work [1] (C: Revel, Harry; L: Gordon, Mack)

Notes [1] Also in YOU CAN'T HAVE EVERYTHING.

1308 ✦ DANGER ON THE AIR
Universal, 1938

Producer(s) Starr, Irving
Director(s) Garrett, Otis
Screenwriter(s) Lively, Robert
Source(s) *Death Catches Up with Mr. Cluck* (novel) Xantippe

Cast Woods, Donald; Grey, Nan; Prouty, Jed; Churchill, Berton; Lundigan, William; Gallagher, Skeets; Van Sloan, Edward; Meeker, George; Cobb, Lee J.

Song(s) Where Are You? [1] (C: McHugh, Jimmy; L: Adamson, Harold)

Notes There are also vocals of "Una Voce Poca Fa" from Rossini's BARBER OF SEVILLE; "When the Blue of the Night" by Henderson and "My Time Is Your Time" by Eric Little and Leo Dance. [1] Also in TOP OF THE TOWN.

1309 ✦ A DANGEROUS BRUNETTE
Warner Brothers, 1932

Cast Merkel, Una

Song(s) I'm Dancing with Tears in My Eyes [1] (C: Burke, Joe; L: Dubin, Al)

Notes Although there is a cue sheet at Warner Brothers, I can't find any other reference to this film under this name. [1] Used in KID NIGHTINGALE.

1310 ✦ THE DANGEROUS DAYS OF KIOWA JONES
Metro–Goldwyn–Mayer, 1966

Musical Score Matlovsky, Samuel

Producer(s) Youngstein, Max E.; Karr, David
Director(s) March, Alex
Screenwriter(s) Fenton, Frank; Thompson, Robert E.

Cast Horton, Robert; Baker, Diane; Mineo, Sal; Persoff, Nehemiah; Harris, Robert H.; Chapman, Lonny; Merrill, Gary; Dano, Royal

Song(s) Kiowa Jones (C: Karliski, Steve; L: Kolber, Larry)

1311 ✦ DANGEROUS HOLIDAY
Republic, 1937

Composer(s) Stept, Sam H.
Lyricist(s) Washington, Ned

Producer(s) Berke, William
Director(s) Barrows, Nicholas T.
Screenwriter(s) Barrows, Nicholas T.

Cast Hould, Ray; Hopper, Hedda; Williams, Guinn "Big Boy"; LaRue, Jack; Prouty, Jed; Roberts, Lynne; Newell, William; Pangborn, Franklin; Sutton, Grady; Boteler, Wade; Young, Carleton; Sale, Virginia

Song(s) I'm Mad About You [1] (L: Koehler, Ted); Happy Go Lucky [2]; Let's Finish the Dream [2]

Notes [1] Also in THE BIG SHOW. [2] Not used.

1312 ✦ THE DANGEROUS NAN MCGREW
Paramount, 1930

Director(s) St. Clair, Malcolm
Screenwriter(s) Smith, Paul Gerard; Collings, Pierre

Cast Kane, Helen; Moore, Victor; Erwin, Stuart; Morgan, Frank; Hale, Louise Closser; Hall, James

Song(s) Aw! C'mon, Whatta Ya Got to Lose? (C: Whiting, Richard A.; L: Robin, Leo); Prisoner's Song [2] (C/L: Massey, Guy); Dangerous Nan McGrew (C: Goodhart, Al; L: Hartman, Don); I Owe You (C: Goodhart, Al; L: Hartman, Don); Once a Gypsy Told Me (You Were Mine) [1] (C: Fain, Sammy; Norman, Pierre; L: Kahal, Irving)

Notes [1] Instrumental use only. [2] Also in HONEY.

1313 ✦ DANGEROUS PARADISE
Paramount, 1930

Director(s) Wellman, William A.
Screenwriter(s) Jones, Grover; McNutt, William Slavens
Source(s) *Victory* (novel) Conrad, Joseph

Cast Arlen, Richard; Carroll, Nancy; Von Seyffertitz, Gustav; Oland, Warner; McDonald, Francis

Song(s) Smiling Skies (C: Whiting, Richard A.; L: Robin, Leo); Moonlight Love (C/L: Spencer, James Ponia); Surabaya Love Song [1] (C/L: Spencer, James Ponia)

Notes This movie was titled VICTORY and FLESH OF EVE before production. "My Honolulu Tomboy" by Sonny Cunha is also sung in the film though not written for it. [1] This is presented instrumentally only.

1314 ✦ DANGEROUS PARTNERS
Metro–Goldwyn–Mayer, 1945

Musical Score Snell, Dave

Producer(s) Field, Arthur L.
Director(s) Cahn, Edward L.
Screenwriter(s) Parsonnet, Marion

Cast   Craig, James; Hasso, Signe; Gwenn, Edmund; Totter, Audrey; Paige, Mabel; Warburton, John; Withers, Grant; O'Neill, Henry; Bressart, Felix; Anderson, Warner

Song(s)   His (C/L: Brent, Earl)

1315 ✦ DANGEROUS WHEN WET
Metro–Goldwyn–Mayer, 1953

Composer(s)   Schwartz, Arthur
Lyricist(s)   Mercer, Johnny
Choreographer(s)   Daniels, Billy; Walters, Charles

Producer(s)   Wells, George
Director(s)   Walters, Charles
Screenwriter(s)   Kingsley, Dorothy

Cast   Williams, Esther; Lamas, Fernando; Carson, Jack; Greenwood, Charlotte; Darcel, Denise; Demarest, William; Corcoran, Donna; Whiting, Barbara; Tom and Jerry

Song(s)   I Got Out of Bed on the Right Side; I Like Men; Fifi; In My Wildest Dreams; Ain't Nature Grand; C'est La Guerre [1]

Notes   [1] Not used.

1316 ✦ DANGEROUS YOUTH
Warner Brothers, 1958

Musical Score   Black, Stanley
Composer(s)   Moreton, Peter; Waller, Bert
Lyricist(s)   Moreton, Peter; Waller, Bert

Producer(s)   Neagle, Anna
Director(s)   Wilcox, Herbert
Screenwriter(s)   Story, Jack Trevor
Source(s)   "These Dangerous Years" (story) Story, Jack Trevor

Cast   Vaughan, Frankie; Lesley, Carole; Baker, George; Kath, Katherine; Byrnes, Edward; Lane, Jackie

Song(s)   These Dangerous Years; Cold Cold Shower; Isn't This a Lovely Evening

Notes   No cue sheet available. Released in Great Britain as THESE DANGEROUS YEARS. The *The 50th Anniversary* book lists Richard Mullen as a co-song writer.

1317 ✦ DANGER ROUTE
United Artists, 1968

Musical Score   Mayer, John

Producer(s)   Rosenberg, Max J.; Subotsky, Milton
Director(s)   Holt, Seth
Screenwriter(s)   Roberts, Meade
Source(s)   *The Eliminator* (novel) York, Andrew

Cast   Johnson, Richard; Lynley, Carol; Bouchet, Barbara; Syms, Sylvia; Dors, Diana; Andrews, Harry; Wanamaker, Sam

Song(s)   Danger Route (C/L: Bart, Lionel)

Notes   No cue sheet available.

1318 ✦ DANIEL BOONE
RKO, 1936

Producer(s)   Hirliman, George A.
Director(s)   Howard, David
Screenwriter(s)   Jarrett, Daniel

Cast   Carradine, John; O'Brien, George; Angel, Heather; Regas, George; Forbes, Ralph; Muse, Clarence; Jones, Dickie

Song(s)   Roll on Wheel (C/L: Muse, Clarence); Make Way (C: Stern, Jack; Tobias, Harry; Hamilton, Grace); In My Garden (C: Stern, Jack; L: Hamilton, Grace)

Notes   [1] Sheet music only.

1319 ✦ DANIEL BOONE, TRAIL BLAZER
Republic, 1957

Musical Score   Lavista, Raul
Composer(s)   Gannaway, Albert C.
Lyricist(s)   Levy, Hal

Producer(s)   Gannaway, Albert C.
Director(s)   Gannaway, Albert C.; Rodriguez, Ismael
Screenwriter(s)   Hubbard, Tom; Patrick, Jack

Cast   Bennett, Bruce; Chaney, Lon; Young, Faron; Kibbs, Kem; Evans, Jacqueline; Kohler Jr., Fred

Song(s)   Long Green Valley; Stand Firm in the Faith; Dan'l Boone [1]; Yankee Fiddle-de-dee [2]

Notes   [1] Used instrumentally only. [2] Not used.

1320 ✦ DARBY O'GILL AND THE LITTLE PEOPLE
Disney, 1959

Musical Score   Wallace, Oliver
Composer(s)   Wallace, Oliver
Lyricist(s)   Watkin, Lawrence Edward

Director(s)   Stevenson, Robert
Screenwriter(s)   Watkin, Lawrence Edward
Source(s)   Darby O'Gill stories (stories) Kavanagh, H.T.

Cast   Sharpe, Albert; Munro, Janet; Connery, Sean; O'Dea, Jimmy; Moore, Kieron; Winwood, Estelle; Fitzgerald, Walter

Song(s)   Wishing Song; Pretty Irish Girl; Dance of the Leprechauns (Inst.)

1321 ✦ DARBY'S RANGERS
Warner Brothers, 1958

Musical Score   Steiner, Max

Producer(s)   Rackin, Martin
Director(s)   Wellman, William A.

Screenwriter(s) Trosper, Guy
Source(s) (book) Altieri, Major James

Cast Garner, James; Warden, Jack; Byrnes, Edward; Thatcher, Torin; Brown, Peter; Hamilton, Murray; King, Andrea

Song(s) Ranger Chant (C/L: Altieri, James J.)

1322 ✦ DARK CITY
Paramount, 1950

Musical Score Waxman, Franz

Producer(s) Wallis, Hal B.
Director(s) Dieterle, William
Screenwriter(s) Bercovici, Leonardo; Lucas, John Meredyth

Cast Heston, Charlton; Scott, Lizabeth; Lindfors, Viveca; Jagger, Dean; DeFore, Don; Webb, Jack; Morgan, Henry

Song(s) (What Would I Do) If I Didn't Have You (C: Spina, Harold; L: Elliott, Jack)

Notes Only original song listed. "A Letter from a Lady in Love" by Maurice Ellenhorn and Judy Bennett and "I Don't Want to Walk Without You" are also used vocally.

1323 ✦ THE DARK HORSE
Universal, 1946

Producer(s) Welsch, Howard
Director(s) Jason, Will
Screenwriter(s) Marion, Charles R.; Solomon, Leo

Cast Terry, Phillip; MacBride, Donald; Savage, Ann; Jenkins, Allen; Darwell, Jane; Gargan, Edward; Lee, Ruth; Gordon, Mary; The Merry Macs

Song(s) George Washington Kelly (C/L: Jason, Will)

1324 ✦ DARK PURPOSE
Universal, 1964

Musical Score Lavagnino, Angelo Francesco

Producer(s) Barclay, Steve
Director(s) Marshall, George
Screenwriter(s) Harmon, David P.

Cast Jones, Shirley; Brazzi, Rossano; Sanders, George; Moll, George

Song(s) Ravello (C/L: Baron, Paul)

Notes No cue sheet available.

1325 ✦ DARK SKIES
Biltmore Productions, 1929

Director(s) Webb, Harry
Screenwriter(s) Natteford, Jack

Cast Mason, Shirley; MacDonald, Wallace; Mong, William V.; O'Brien, Tom; Swickard, Josef; Moore, Juanita [1]; Brent, Evelyn [1]

Song(s) Juanita (C/L: Sheridan, Walter; Zahler, Lee)

Notes Some sources refer to this film as DARKENED SKIES. [1] Sources differ on who was the female lead.

1326 ✦ DARK VICTORY
Warner Brothers, 1939

Musical Score Steiner, Max

Director(s) Goulding, Edmund
Screenwriter(s) Robinson, Casey
Source(s) *Dark Victory* (play) Brewer Jr., George; Bloch, Bertram

Cast Davis, Bette; Fitzgerald, Geraldine; Reagan, Ronald; Bogart, Humphrey; Travers, Henry; Witherspoon, Cora; Brissac, Virginia; Brent, George

Song(s) Oh Give Me Time for Tenderness (C: Goulding, Edmund; L: Janis, Elsie)

1327 ✦ DARLING, HOW COULD YOU!
Paramount, 1951

Musical Score Van Cleave, Nathan; Sanders, Troy; Hollander, Frederick

Producer(s) Tugend, Harry
Director(s) Leisen, Mitchell
Screenwriter(s) Smith, Dodie; Samuels, Lesser
Source(s) *Alice-Sit-By-the-Fire* (play) Barrie, James M.

Cast Fontaine, Joan; Freeman, Mona; Lund, John

Song(s) Twilight Song [1] (C: Brahms, Johannes; L: Livingston, Jay; Evans, Ray); Rendezvous [2] (C/L: Livingston, Jay; Evans, Ray); Darling, How Could You [2] (C: Livingston, Jerry; L: David, Mack)

Notes The film was first titled RENDEZVOUS. [1] Music based on "Waltz in A Major." [2] Not used. [2] Written for exploitation only. Not used in picture.

1328 ✦ DARLING LILI
Paramount, 1970

Composer(s) Mancini, Henry
Lyricist(s) Mercer, Johnny
Choreographer(s) Pan, Hermes

Producer(s) Edwards, Blake
Director(s) Edwards, Blake
Screenwriter(s) Edwards, Blake; Blatty, William Peter

Cast Andrews, Julie; Hudson, Rock

Song(s) Darling Lili; Smile Away Each Rainy Day; I'll Give You Three Guesses; Whistling Away the Dark; The Girl in No Man's Land; Skal (Let's Have Another on Me); Les P'tits Oiseaux (The Little Birds); Your

Good-Will Ambassador; Piccadilly Circus [1]; Steal Two Eggs [1]

Notes A vocal rendition of the Jack Judge and Harry Williams tune "It's a Long, Long Way to Tipperary" is used as is "Pack Up Your Troubles in Your Old Kit Bag" by George Asaf and Felix Powell and "La Marseillaise" by Rouget de Lisle. [1] Not used.

1329 ✦ D.A.R.Y.L.
Paramount, 1985

Musical Score Hamlisch, Marvin

Producer(s) Heyman, John
Director(s) Wincer, Simon
Screenwriter(s) Ambrose, David; Scott, Allan; Ellis, Jeffrey

Cast Hurt, Mary Beth; McKean, Michael; Walker, Kathryn; Camp, Colleen; Sommer, Josef; Oliver, Barret

Song(s) Somewhere I Belong (C: Hamlisch, Marvin; L: Pitchford, Dean); Back to the City [1] (C/L: Keel, Ron; Chaisson, Kenny)

Notes [1] Not used.

1330 ✦ DATE WITH DUKE
Paramount, 1947

Composer(s) Ellington, Duke

Producer(s) Pal, George
Director(s) Pal, George

Song(s) Sonata (inst.) [1] (C: Strayhorn, Billy); Strange Feeling (inst.) (C: Strayhorn, Billy; Ellington, Duke); Dancers in Love (inst.)

Notes This is a George Pal Puppetoon short subject. [1] Also titled "Balcony Serenade."

1331 ✦ A DATE WITH JUDY
Metro–Goldwyn–Mayer, 1948

Choreographer(s) Donen, Stanley

Producer(s) Pasternak, Joe
Director(s) Thorpe, Richard
Screenwriter(s) Cooper, Dorothy; Kingsley, Dorothy
Source(s) A Date with Judy (radio characters) Leslie, Aleen

Cast Beery, Wallace; Powell, Jane; Taylor, Elizabeth [1]; Miranda, Carmen; Stack, Robert; Beckett, Scotty; Xavier Cugat and His Orchestra; Ames, Leon; Royle, Selena; Sundberg, Clinton; Cleveland, George; Corrigan, Lloyd

Song(s) It's a Most Unusual Day (C: McHugh, Jimmy; L: Adamson, Harold); Through the Years (C: Youmans, Vincent; L: Heyman, Edward); Love Is Where You Find It [2] (C: Brown, Nacio Herb; L: Brent, Earl); I'm Strictly on the Corny Side (C: Templeton, Alec; L:

Unger, Stella); Judaline (C: de Paul, Gene; L: Raye, Don); Cuanto Le Gusta (C: Ruiz, Gabriel; L: Gilbert, Ray); Cookin' with Gas (C: Oliveira, Louis; L: Gilbert, Ray)

Notes [1] Dubbed. [2] Also in THE KISSING BANDIT.

1332 ✦ THE DAUGHTER OF ROSIE O'GRADY
Warner Brothers, 1950

Composer(s) Jerome, M.K.
Lyricist(s) Scholl, Jack
Choreographer(s) Prinz, LeRoy

Producer(s) Jacobs, William
Director(s) Butler, David
Screenwriter(s) Rose, Jack; Shavelson, Melville; Milne, Peter

Cast Haver, June; MacRae, Gordon; Barton, James; Sakall, S.Z.; Nelson, Gene; Darwell, Jane; Reynolds, Debbie

Song(s) Farm Off Old Broadway; My Own True Love and I; What Am I Gonna Tell Them at the Yacht Club; As We Are Today (C: Lecuona, Ernesto; L: Tobias, Charles); Winter Comes; Winter Serenade

Notes Some old songs interpolated into the score include "The Daughter of Rosie O'Grady" by Walter Donaldson and Monty Brice; "Rose of Tralee" by Glover; "The Picture That Hung Toward the Wall" by Charles Graham; "Ma' Blushin' Rosie, Ma Posie Sweet" by John Stromberg and Edgar Smith and "Winter" by Alfred Bryan and Albert Gumble.

1333 ✦ DAUGHTERS COURAGEOUS
Warner Brothers, 1939

Musical Score Steiner, Max

Producer(s) Wallis, Hal B.
Director(s) Curtiz, Michael
Screenwriter(s) Epstein, Julius J.; Epstein, Philip G.
Source(s) Fly Away Home (play) Bennett, Dorothy; White, Irving

Cast Rains, Claude; Bainter, Fay; Crisp, Donald; Lane, Priscilla; Garfield, John; Robson, May

Song(s) They Say [1] (C: Mann, Paul; Weiss, Stephan; L: Heyman, Edward)

Notes Previously titled A FAMILY AFFAIR. [1] Also in JOHNNY APOLLO (20th).

1334 ✦ DAVID AND BATHSHEBA
Twentieth Century–Fox, 1951

Musical Score Newman, Alfred
Choreographer(s) Cole, Jack

Producer(s) Zanuck, Darryl F.
Director(s) King, Henry
Screenwriter(s) Dunne, Philip

Cast Peck, Gregory; Hayward, Susan; Massey, Raymond; Moore, Kieron; Justice, James Robertson; Meadows, Jayne; Bushman, Francis X.

Song(s) Rapture of Love—Twenty-Third Psalm (C: Newman, Alfred; L: King James Version); David and Bathsheba [1] (C/L: Jenkins, Gordon; Roberts, Allan; Allen, Robert)

Notes [1] Sheet music only

1335 ◆ DAVY
Metro–Goldwyn–Mayer, 1960

Musical Score Rogers, Eric

Producer(s) Dearden, Basil
Director(s) Relph, Michael
Screenwriter(s) Rose, William

Cast Secombe, Harry; Randell, Ron; Knox, Alexander; Dean, Isabel

Song(s) My World Is Your World (C: Evans, Tolchard; L: Grafton, Jimmy)

Notes Made in England in 1957 by Ealing. Released in the United States in 1960. There is also a vocal of "The Mastersingers" by R. Wagner.

1336 ◆ DAVY CROCKETT AND THE RIVER PIRATES
Disney, 1956

Musical Score Bruns, George
Composer(s) Bruns, George
Lyricist(s) Blackburn, Tom

Producer(s) Walsh, Bill
Director(s) Foster, Norman
Screenwriter(s) Blackburn, Tom; Foster, Norman

Cast Parker, Fess; Ebsen, Buddy; York, Jeff; Tobey, Kenneth; Crockett, Dick; Catlett, Walter; Bevans, Clem

Song(s) Ballad of Davy Crockett; King of the River; Yaller, Yaller Gold

1337 ◆ DAVY CROCKETT, KING OF THE WILD FRONTIER
Disney, 1955

Musical Score Bruns, George
Composer(s) Bruns, George

Producer(s) Walsh, Bill
Director(s) Foster, Norman
Screenwriter(s) Blackburn, Tom

Cast Parker, Fess; Ebsen, Buddy; Ruysdael, Basil; Conried, Hans; Tobey, Kenneth; Mazurki, Mike

Song(s) Ballad of Davy Crockett (L: Blackburn, Tom); Farewell (L: Traditional); Old Betsy (L: George, Gil); Be Sure You're Right [1] (C/L: Parker, Fess; Ebsen, Buddy)

Notes [1] Written for exploitation only.

1338 ◆ A DAY AT THE BEACH
Paramount, 1970

Musical Score Shuman, Mort

Producer(s) Gutowski, Gene
Director(s) Hesera, Simon
Screenwriter(s) Polanski, Roman
Source(s) *Een Dagje Naar Het Strand* (novel) Heeresma, Heere

Cast Burns, Mark; Edney, Beatrice; Sellers, Peter

Song(s) Where Are We Going? (C: Shuman, Mort; L: Lynch, Kenny)

1339 ◆ A DAY AT THE RACES
Metro–Goldwyn–Mayer, 1937

Musical Score Kaper, Bronislau; Jurmann, Walter
Composer(s) Kaper, Bronislau; Jurmann, Walter
Lyricist(s) Kahn, Gus
Choreographer(s) Gould, Dave; Connolly, Bobby

Director(s) Wood, Sam
Screenwriter(s) Pirosh, Robert; Seaton, George; Oppenheimer, George

Cast Anderson, Ivie; The Crinoline Choir; Marx, Groucho; Marx, Chico; Marx, Harpo; Jones, Allan; O'Sullivan, Maureen; Dumont, Margaret; Ceeley, Leonard; Dumbrille, Douglass; Muir, Esther; Rumann, Sig; Middlemass, Robert; Fay, Vivien

Song(s) Blue Venetian Waters; Tomorrow Is Another Day; Barn Episode (C/L: Edens, Roger); All God's Chillun Got Rhythm; A Message from the Man in the Moon; Cosi Cosa (Inst.) [1]; Doctor Hackenbush [2] (C: Ruby, Harry; L: Kalmar, Bert)

Notes 1] Also in EVERYBODY SING and A NIGHT AT THE OPERA. [2] Sheet music only.

1340 ◆ THE DAY BEFORE SPRING
Metro–Goldwyn–Mayer, 1946 unproduced

Composer(s) Green, Johnny
Lyricist(s) Loesser, Frank

Producer(s) Cummings, Jack
Screenwriter(s) Oppenheimer, George; Diamond, I.A.L.
Source(s) *The Day Before Spring* (musical) Loewe, Frederick; Lerner, Alan Jay

Song(s) The Statue Song; Opening; My Sentimental Nature; Bing, Bang; Who Could Forget You; It's Time for the Love Scene; Ibbedy Bibbedy Sibbedy Sab; You're So Reliable

1341 ✦ THE DAYDREAMER
Embassy, 1960

Musical Score Laws, Maury
Composer(s) Laws, Maury
Lyricist(s) Bass, Jules

Producer(s) Roemer, Larry
Director(s) Bass, Jules
Screenwriter(s) Rankin Jr., Arthur
Source(s) Stories and characters by Andersen, Hans Christian
Voices Bankhead, Tallulah; Ives, Burl; Borge, Victor; Hayakawa, Sessue; Karloff, Boris; Ritchard, Cyril; Wynn, Ed; Duke, Patty; Mills, Hayley; Terry-Thomas; Goulet, Robert

Cast Gilford, Jack; Bolger, Ray; O'Keefe, Paul; Hamilton, Margaret; Harter, Robert

Song(s) The Daydreamer; Wishes and Teardrops; Luck to Sell; Happy Guy; Who Can Tell; Simply Wonderful; Isn't It Cozy Here?; Tivoli Bells; Voyage of the Walnut Shell; Waltz for a Mermaid

Notes No cue sheet available.

1342 ✦ A DAY OF FURY
Universal, 1956

Producer(s) Arthur, Robert
Director(s) Jones, Harmon
Screenwriter(s) Edmiston, James; Brodney, Oscar

Cast Robertson, Dale; Mahoney, Jock; Corday, Mara; Reid, Carl Benton; Merlin, Jan; Dehner, John; Carroll, Dee; Bromley, Sheila

Song(s) Take Me to Town [1] (C/L: Shapiro, Dan; Lee, Lester)

Notes [1] Also in TAKE ME TO TOWN and WYOMING MAIL.

1343 ✦ DAY OF THE ANIMALS
Warner Brothers, 1976

Musical Score Schifrin, Lalo

Producer(s) Montoro, Edward L.
Director(s) Girdler, William
Screenwriter(s) Norton, William; Norton, Eleanor

Cast George, Christopher; Nielsen, Leslie; George, Lynda Day; Jaeckel, Richard; Ansara, Michael; Roman, Ruth

Song(s) Bob's Tune (C/L: Girdler, Bill)

1344 ✦ THE DAY OF THE LOCUST
Paramount, 1975

Producer(s) Hellman, Jerome
Director(s) Schlesinger, John
Screenwriter(s) Salt, Waldo
Source(s) *The Day of the Locust* (novel) West, Nathanael

Cast Atherton, William; Black, Karen; Meredith, Burgess; Page, Geraldine; Dysart, Richard; Hopkins, Bo; Goldoni, Lelia; Barty, Billy; Kennedy, Madge; Schafer, Natalie; Stewart, Paul

Song(s) Miss Lonely Hearts [1] (C: Barry, John; L: Williams, Paul)

Notes [1] Not used in film.

1345 ✦ DAYS OF JESSE JAMES
Republic, 1939

Composer(s) Tinturin, Peter
Lyricist(s) Tinturin, Peter

Producer(s) Kane, Joseph
Director(s) Kane, Joseph
Screenwriter(s) Snell, Earle

Cast Rogers, Roy; Hayes, George "Gabby"; Barry, Donald; Moore, Pauline; Woods, Harry; Loft, Arthur; Boteler, Wade; Wales, Ethel; Beckett, Scotty

Song(s) Echo Mountain; I'm a Son of a Cowboy; Saddle Your Dreams

1346 ✦ DAYS OF WINE AND ROSES
Warner Brothers, 1963

Musical Score Mancini, Henry

Producer(s) Manulis, Martin
Director(s) Edwards, Blake
Screenwriter(s) Miller, J.P.
Source(s) "Days of Wine and Roses" (television play) Miller, J.P.

Cast Lemmon, Jack; Remick, Lee; Megowan, Debbie; Bickford, Charles; Klugman, Jack; Hewitt, Alan; Palmer, Tom

Song(s) Days of Wine and Roses (C: Mancini, Henry; L: Mercer, Johnny)

1347 ✦ DAYTON'S DEVILS
Commonwealth United, 1968

Musical Score Skiles, Marlin

Producer(s) Stabler, Robert W.
Director(s) Shea, Jack
Screenwriter(s) De Gorter, Fred

Cast Calhoun, Rory; Nielsen, Leslie; Kazan, Lainie [1]; Gudegast, Hans; Sadler, Barry

Song(s) Sunny (C/L: Hebb, Bobby)

Notes [1] Lainie Kazan's film debut.

1348 ✦ D.C. CAB
Universal, 1983

Composer(s) Moroder, Giorgio

Producer(s) Carew, Topper
Director(s) Schumacher, Joel
Screenwriter(s) Schumacher, Joel

Cast Gail, Max; Baldwin, Adam; Mr. T; Barnet, Charlie; Gifford, Gloria; Busey, Gary; Warfield, Marsha; Maher, Bill; Rodriguez, Paul; Barbarian, Peter; Mayo, Whitman; Barbarian, David; Cara, Irene; Diehl, John; De Salvo, Anne; Guilford-Grey, Ann; Canada, Ron

Song(s) D.C. Cab (C/L: Feldman, Richard; Kelly, Rick; McNally, Larry John); D.C. Cha-Cha (C/L: Donovan, Lisa Ann; Garfield, Harry Asher); One More Time Around the Block (C/L: Galdston, Phil; Thom, Peter); World Champion (C/L: Finch, Ron; Ross, Daryl); Party Me Tonight (L: Bellotte, Pete); Single Heart (L: Bellotte, Pete); The Dream (L: Cara, Irene; Bellotte, Pete)

1349 ✦ DEAD CERT
United Artists, 1974

Musical Score Addison, John

Producer(s) Hartley, Neil
Director(s) Richardson, Tony
Screenwriter(s) Richardson, Tony; Oaksey, John
Source(s) *Dead Cert* (novel) Francis, Dick

Cast Antony, Scott; Dench, Judi; Williams, Michael; Hogg, Ian; Thomas, Nina; Dignam, Mark; Glover, Julian

Song(s) Brand New Car (C/L: Knapp, John); Universe (C/L: Pizier, Robin)

Notes Incomplete cue sheet.

1350 ✦ DEAD END DRIVE-IN
New World, 1986

Producer(s) Williams, Andrew
Director(s) Trenchard-Smith, Brian
Screenwriter(s) Smalley, Peter
Source(s) "Crabs" (story) Carey, Peter

Cast Manning, Ned; McCurry, Natalie; Whitford, Peter; Wilde, Wilbur; Gibson, Dave; Lillingston, Sandie

Song(s) Playing with Fire [1] (L: Dembowski, Eve)

1351 ✦ DEAD END STREET
Cannon, 1985

Composer(s) Springsteen, Bruce
Lyricist(s) Springsteen, Bruce

Producer(s) Shapira, David; Kol, Itzhak
Director(s) Yosha, Yaky
Screenwriter(s) Tavor, Eli; Yosha, Yaky

Cast Gaon, Yehoram; Atzmon, Anat; Almagor, Gila; Dayan, Tiky

Song(s) Point Blank; Hungry Heart; Jungle Land

Notes No cue sheet available. It is not known if the Springsteen songs were written for this film.

1352 ✦ DEADFALL
Twentieth Century–Fox, 1968

Musical Score Barry, John

Producer(s) Monash, Paul
Director(s) Forbes, Bryan
Screenwriter(s) Forbes, Bryan
Source(s) (novel) Cory, Desmond

Cast Caine, Michael; Ralli, Giovanna; Portman, Eric; Newman, Nanette; Buck, David; Pierre, Carlos; Rossiter, Leonard

Song(s) My Love Has Two Faces (C: Barry, John; L: Lawrence, Jack)

Notes There is also a guitar concerto, titled "Romance for Guitar and Orchestra," written by Barry for the picture.

1353 ✦ DEAD HEAT
New World, 1988

Musical Score Troost, Ernest

Producer(s) Meltzer, Michael; Helpern, David
Director(s) Goldblatt, Mark
Screenwriter(s) Black, Terry

Cast Williams, Treat; Piscopo, Joe; Frost, Lindsay; McGavin, Darren; Price, Vincent; Kirkconnell, Clare; Luke, Keye; Lewis, Monica

Song(s) Dead Heat (C/L: Huckert, John W.; Johnson, Patrick Read; Settle, Phillip)

Notes No cue sheet available.

1354 ✦ DEADLIER THAN THE MALE
Universal, 1967

Musical Score Lockyer, Malcolm

Producer(s) Box, Betty E.; Box, Sydney; Newbery, Bruce
Director(s) Thomas, Ralph
Screenwriter(s) Sangster, Jimmy; Osborn, David; Charles-Williams, Liz
Source(s) Bulldog Drummond series (stories) Sapper

Cast Johnson, Richard; Sommer, Elke; Koscina, Sylva; Green, Nigel; Naismith, Laurence; Rossiter, Leonard

Song(s) Deadlier Than the Male (C/L: Franz, John; Engel, Scott)

1355 ✦ THE DEADLY BEES
Paramount, 1967

Musical Score Josephs, Wilfred

Producer(s) Rosenberg, Max J.
Director(s) Francis, Freddie
Screenwriter(s) Bloch, Robert; Marriott, Anthony
Source(s) *A Taste of Honey* (novel) Heard, H.F.

Cast Leigh, Suzanna; Finlay, Frank; Doleman, Guy; Cossins, James; Gwynn, Michael

Song(s) It's Not What I Need You For [1] (C/L: Wood, Ronald); Stop the Music [1] (C/L: Westlake, Clive; L: Subotsky, Milton); Baby Let Me Love You [1] (C: Westlake, Clive; L: Lynch, Kenny)

Notes [1] All uses are background vocal.

1356 ✦ THE DEADLY COMPANIONS
Pathe-America, 1961

Musical Score Kraushaar, Raoul

Producer(s) FitzSimons, Charles B.
Director(s) Peckinpah, Sam
Screenwriter(s) Fleischman, A.S.

Cast O'Hara, Maureen; Keith, Brian; Cochran, Steve; Wills, Chill; Martin, Strother; Wright, Will; O'Hara, Jim

Song(s) A Dream of Love (C/L: Skiles, Marlin; FitzSimons, Charles B.)

Notes No cue sheet available.

1357 ✦ DEADLY ILLUSION
CineTel, 1988

Musical Score Gleeson, Patrick

Producer(s) Meyer, Irwin
Director(s) Tannen, William; Cohen, Larry
Screenwriter(s) Cohen, Larry

Cast Williams, Billy Dee; Vanity; Fairchild, Morgan; Beck, John; Cortese, Joe; Wilding Jr., Michael

Song(s) Illusions Are Real (C: Gleeson, Patrick; L: Connors, Carol)

Notes No cue sheet available.

1358 ✦ DEAD OR ALIVE
PRC, 1944

Musical Score Zahler, Lee; Grigor, Nico

Producer(s) Alexander, Arthur
Director(s) Clifton, Elmer
Screenwriter(s) Fraser, Harry

Cast Ritter, Tex; O'Brien, Dave; Clements, Marjorie; Wilkerson, Guy; King, Charles; Randall, Rebel

Song(s) I'm Gonna Leave You Like I Found You (C/L: Ritter, Tex; Harford, Frank); I Don't Care Since You Told Me Good Bye (C/L: Ritter, Tex; Dodd, Barney)

1359 ✦ DEAD POETS SOCIETY
Touchstone, 1989

Musical Score Jarre, Maurice

Producer(s) Haft, Steven; Witt, Paul Junger; Thomas, Tony
Director(s) Weir, Peter
Screenwriter(s) Schulman, Tom

Cast Williams, Robin; Leonard, Robert Sean; Hawke, Ethan; Charles, Josh; Hansen, Gale; Kussman, Dylan; Ruggiero, Allelon; Waterston, James; Powers, Alexandra; Lloyd, Norman; Smith, Kurtwood; Martin, George

Song(s) Welton School Song (C/L: Faulkner, Jack); Ridgeway High School Fight Song—Cadence One (C/L: Rehbert, Jerry); Snack Food (C/L: Walker, Larry); Le Reve De Jeannine (Jeannine's Dream) (C/L: Marron, Jeannine)

1360 ✦ DEAD RECKONING
Columbia, 1947

Producer(s) Biddell, Sidney
Director(s) Cromwell, John
Screenwriter(s) Garrett, Oliver H.P.; Fisher, Steve

Cast Bogart, Humphrey; Scott, Lizabeth; Cromwell, John; Chandler, George; Ford, Wallace; Carnovsky, Morris; Dandridge, Ruby; Miller, Marvin

Song(s) Either It's Love or It Isn't (C/L: Fisher, Doris; Roberts, Allan)

1361 ✦ DEALING: OR THE BERKELEY-TO-BOSTON FORTY-BRICK LOST-BAG BLUES
Warner Brothers, 1972

Musical Score Small, Michael

Producer(s) Pressman, Edward R.
Director(s) Williams, Paul
Screenwriter(s) Odell, David; Williams, Paul

Cast Lyons, Robert F.; Lithgow, Robert; Hershey, Barbara; Durning, Charles

Song(s) I Can't Turn You Loose (C/L: Redding, Otis); I'm Stepping Out with a Memory Tonight (C/L: Wrubel, Allie; Magidson, Herb); Bluebird (C/L: Stills, Stephen); You Got What It Takes (C/L: Gordy Jr., Berry; Carlo, Tyran; Gordy, Gwen)

Notes It is not known if any of these were written for the film.

1362 ✦ DEAL OF THE CENTURY
Warner Brothers, 1983

Musical Score   Rubinstein, Arthur B.

Producer(s)   Yorkin, Bud
Director(s)   Friedkin, William
Screenwriter(s)   Brickman, Paul

Cast   Chase, Chevy; Weaver, Sigourney; Hines, Gregory; Edwards, Vince; Marquez, William; Shawn, Wallace

Song(s)   Shine (C: Rubinstein, Arthur B.; L: Morrow, Cynthia)

Notes   Vocal renditions of "Someone to Watch Over Me" by George and Ira Gershwin and "Santa Claus Is Coming to Town" by Haven Gillespie and J. Fred Coots are heard on the soundtrack.

1363 ✦ DEAR HEART
Warner Brothers, 1965

Musical Score   Mancini, Henry

Producer(s)   Manulis, Martin
Director(s)   Mann, Delbert
Screenwriter(s)   Mosel, Tad
Source(s)   "The Out-of-Towners" (story) Mosel, Tad

Cast   Page, Geraldine; Ford, Glenn; Lansbury, Angela; Anderson Jr., Michael; Nichols, Barbara; Barry, Patricia; Drake, Charles; Pearce, Alice

Song(s)   Dear Heart (C: Mancini, Henry; L: Livingston, Jay; Evans, Ray); I Wish We Were Playing Post Office (C/L: Mosel, Tad)

1364 ✦ DEAR RUTH
Paramount, 1947

Musical Score   Dolan, Robert Emmett

Producer(s)   Jones, Paul
Director(s)   Russell, William D.
Screenwriter(s)   Sheekman, Arthur
Source(s)   *Dear Ruth* (play) Krasna, Norman

Cast   Caulfield, Joan; Holden, William; Freeman, Mona; Arnold, Edward; De Wolfe, Billy; Philips, Mary; Welles, Virginia

Song(s)   Fine Thing! [1] (C: Dolan, Robert Emmett; L: Mercer, Johnny)

Notes   [1] Used instrumentally only.

1365 ✦ DEAR WIFE
Paramount, 1949

Producer(s)   Maibaum, Richard
Director(s)   Haydn, Richard
Screenwriter(s)   Sheekman, Arthur; Nash, Richard

Cast   Holden, William; Caulfield, Joan; De Wolfe, Billy; Freeman, Mona; Arnold, Edward; Von Zell, Harry

Song(s)   Dear Wife [1] (C/L: Livingston, Jay; Evans, Ray)

Notes   This is a sequel to DEAR RUTH. The original movie is based on a play by Norman Krasna. [1] Did not appear in film.

1366 ✦ DEATH OF A GUNFIGHTER
Universal, 1969

Musical Score   Nelson, Oliver

Producer(s)   Lyons, Richard E.
Director(s)   Smithee, Allen
Screenwriter(s)   Calvelli, Joseph
Source(s)   (novel) Patten, Lewis B.

Cast   Widmark, Richard; O'Connor, Carroll; Horne, Lena; Saxon, John; Smith, Kent; Gates, Larry; Woodward, Morgan; Lydon, Jimmy [1]

Song(s)   Sweet Apple Wine (C: Nelson, Oliver; L: Hall, Carol)

Notes   [1] Billed as James Lydon.

1367 ✦ DEATH ON THE DOWNBEAT
Studio Unknown, 1947

Composer(s)   Jason, Will; Robin, Sid
Lyricist(s)   Jason, Will; Robin, Sid

Song(s)   Baby, You Can Count on Me; Neither Could I; What Happened?

Notes   No other information available.

1368 ✦ DEATH WISH 4: THE CRACKDOWN
Cannon, 1987

Musical Score   McCallum, Paul; McCallum, Valentine; Bisharat, John

Producer(s)   Kohner, Pancho
Director(s)   Thompson, J. Lee
Screenwriter(s)   Hickman, Gail Morgan

Cast   Bronson, Charles; Lenz, Kay; Ryan, John P.; Lopez, Perry; Dickerson, George; Oh, Soon-Teck

Song(s)   In Some Brazil (C/L: Bishop, Michael); The Hunger (C/L: Bishop, Michael)

Notes   No cue sheet available.

1369 ✦ DECEPTION
Warner Brothers–First National, 1946

Musical Score   Korngold, Erich Wolfgang
Choreographer(s)   Prinz, LeRoy

Producer(s)   Blanke, Henry
Director(s)   Rapper, Irving

Screenwriter(s)   Collier, John; Than, Joseph
Source(s)   *Jealousy (Monsieur Lamberthier)* (play)
Verneuil, Louis

Cast   Davis, Bette; Rains, Claude; Henreid, Paul;
Abbott, John; Fong, Benson; Crandall, Suzi

Song(s)   Radio Commercial (C: Jerome, M.K.; L:
Scholl, Jack); Too Marvelous for Words [1] (C: Whiting,
Richard A.; L: Mercer, Johnny)

Notes   [1] Also in READY, WILLING AND ABLE and
YOUNG MAN WITH A HORN.

1370 ✦ DECISION BEFORE DAWN
Twentieth Century–Fox, 1951

Musical Score   Waxman, Franz

Producer(s)   Litvak, Anatole
Director(s)   Litvak, Anatole
Screenwriter(s)   Viertel, Peter
Source(s)   *Call It Treason* (novel) Howe, George

Cast   Basehart, Richard; Merrill, Gary; Werner, Oskar;
Neff, Hildegarde; Blanchar, Dominique; Seyferth,
Wilfried

Song(s)   Erika (C/L: Niel, Hans); Du Bist Die Rose
Vom Wortherse (C: Lang, Hans; L: Meder, Erich); Paris
(Paris Ich Liebe Dich) (C: Mackeben, Theo; L:
Beckmann, Hans Fritz)

1371 ✦ THE DEEP
Columbia, 1977

Musical Score   Barry, John

Producer(s)   Guber, Peter
Director(s)   Yates, Peter
Screenwriter(s)   Benchley, Peter; Wynn, Tracy
Keenan
Source(s)   *The Deep* (novel) Benchley, Peter

Cast   Shaw, Robert; Bisset, Jacqueline; Nolte, Nick;
Gossett, Lou; Wallach, Eli

Song(s)   Down Deep Inside (C: Barry, John; L: Barry,
John; Summer, Donna)

1372 ✦ DEEP ADVENTURE
Warner Brothers, 1957

Musical Score   Jackson, Howard

Producer(s)   Francis, Cedric
Director(s)   Welborn, Charles
Screenwriter(s)   Crump, Owen

Cast   Allen, Ross; Phillips, Dottie Lee; Fuller, William

Song(s)   Velvet Moon (C/L: DeLange, Eddie; Myrow,
Josef); You Must Have Been a Beautiful Baby [1] (C:
Warren, Harry; L: Mercer, Johnny)

Notes   [1] Also used in THE EDDIE CANTOR
STORY, HARD TO GET (1938), THE HARD WAY,
MILDRED PIERCE and MY DREAM IS YOURS.

1373 ✦ DEEP BLUE SEA
Twentieth Century–Fox, 1955

Musical Score   Arnold, Malcolm

Producer(s)   Brackett, Charles
Director(s)   Fleischer, Richard
Screenwriter(s)   Reisch, Walter; Brackett, Charles

Cast   Milland, Ray; Collins, Joan; Granger, Farley;
Adler, Luther; Skinner, Cornelia Otis; Farrell, Glenda;
Robbins, Gale

Song(s)   The Deep Blue Sea [1] (C: Chagrin, Francis;
L: Bradford, Roy)

Notes   [1] Roy Hamilton credited with lyrics on cue
sheet.

1374 ✦ DEEP END
Paramount, 1971

Producer(s)   Jedele, Helmut
Director(s)   Skolimowski, Jerzy
Screenwriter(s)   Gruza, J.; Sulik, B.; Skolimowski, Jerzy

Cast   Moulder-Brown, John; Asher, Jane; Sandford,
Christopher; Dors, Diana

Song(s)   But I Might Die Tonight (C/L: Stevens, Cat);
Mother Sky (C/L: Can, The)

1375 ✦ DEEP IN MY HEART
Metro–Goldwyn–Mayer, 1954

Composer(s)   Romberg, Sigmund
Choreographer(s)   Loring, Eugene

Producer(s)   Edens, Roger
Director(s)   Donen, Stanley
Screenwriter(s)   Spigelgass, Leonard
Source(s)   *Deep in My Heart* (book) Arnold, Elliott

Cast   Ferrer, Jose; Oberon, Merle; Traubel, Helen;
Avedon, Doe; Pidgeon, Walter; Henreid, Paul;
Toumanova, Tamara; Stewart, Paul; Elsom, Isobel;
Burns, David; Backus, Jim; Clooney, Rosemary; Kelly,
Gene; Kelly, Fred; Powell, Jane; Damone, Vic; Miller,
Ann; Olvis, William; Charisse, Cyd; Mitchell, James;
Keel, Howard; Martin, Tony; Weldon, Joan

Song(s)   Leg of Mutton (L: Edens, Roger);
Jazzadadadoo (L: Edens, Roger; Atteridge, Harold)

Notes   There were no songs written for this film
although Edens did write lyrics to some previously
composed instrumental pieces. All All music is by
Sigmund Romberg. Songs include "Deep In My Heart,
Dear," "Your Land and My Land," "Girls, Good Bye!,"
and "Serenade" with lyrics by Dorothy Donnelly; "Will
You Remember Vienna," "Lover Come Back to Me,"

"Stouthearted Men" and "Softly As in a Morning Sunrise" with lyrics by Oscar Hammerstein II; "I Love to Say Hello to the Girls" with lyrics by Alex Gerber; "Mr. and Mrs." with lyrics by J. Hickory Wood; "I Love to Go Swimmin' with Wimmen" and "Fat, Fat, Fatima" with lyrics by Ballard Macdonald; "The Road to Paradise" and "Will You Remember?" with lyrics by Rida Johnson Young; "The Very Next Girl I See" with lyrics by Harold Atteridge; "It" and "One Alone" with lyrics by Oscar Hammerstein II and Otto Harbach and "Auf Wiedersehen" with lyrics by Herbert Reynolds. "One Kiss" and "Dance My Darlings," both with lyrics by Oscar Hammerstein II, were recorded but not used.

1376 ✦ DEEP IN THE HEART OF TEXAS
Universal, 1942

Producer(s) Drake, Oliver
Director(s) Clifton, Elmer
Screenwriter(s) Drake, Oliver

Cast Brown, Johnny Mack; Ritter, Tex; Knight, Fuzzy; Holt, Jennifer

Song(s) Deep in the Heart of Texas [1] (C: Swander, Don; L: Hershey, June); Song of the Sage (C/L: Bond, Johnny)

Notes [1] Also in the Republic pictures HEART OF THE RIO GRANDE, HI, NEIGHBOR and KING OF THE COWBOYS and the Fox picture I'LL GET BY.

1377 ✦ DELICIOUS
Fox, 1931

Composer(s) Gershwin, George
Lyricist(s) Gershwin, Ira

Director(s) Butler, David
Screenwriter(s) Levien, Sonya; Bolton, Guy

Cast Gaynor, Janet; Farrell, Charles; Brendel, El; O'Sullivan, Lawrence

Song(s) Delishious; Dream Sequence; Somebody from Somewhere; Katinkitshka; Blah Blah Blah; You Started It (Inst.); Rhapsody in Rivets (Inst.)

1378 ✦ DELIGHTFULLY DANGEROUS
United Artists, 1945

Composer(s) Gould, Morton
Lyricist(s) Heyman, Edward
Choreographer(s) Matray, Ernst

Producer(s) Rogers, Charles R.
Director(s) Lubin, Arthur
Screenwriter(s) De Leon, Walter; Phillips, Arthur

Cast Powell, Jane; Moore, Constance; Bellamy, Ralph; Treacher, Arthur; Beavers, Louise; Tobey, Ruth; Robinson, Ruth; Charlot, Andre; Hunter, Shirley; Morton Gould and His Orchestra; Williams, Hunter

Song(s) I'm Only Teasin'; In a Shower of Stars; Mynah Bird; Through Your Eyes to Your Heart; Once Upon a Song; Mr. Strauss Goes to Town (C: Strauss, Johann)

Notes No cue sheet available. Hirschhorn credits ONCE UPON A SONG to John Jacob Loeb and Redd Evans—sheet music does not.

1379 ✦ THE DELIGHTFUL ROGUE
RKO, 1929

Producer(s) LeBaron, William
Director(s) Pearce, A. Leslie; Shores, Lynn
Screenwriter(s) Smith, Wallace
Source(s) "A Woman Decides" (story) Smith, Wallace

Cast La Rocque, Rod; La Roy, Rita; Boyer, Charles; Moorehouse, Bert; Brady, Ed; Semels, Harry; Blum, Samuel

Song(s) Gay Love [1] (C: Levant, Oscar; L: Clare, Sidney)

Notes [1] Also in LOVE COMES ALONG.

1380 ✦ DEPORTED
Universal, 1950

Musical Score Scharf, Walter

Producer(s) Buckner, Robert
Director(s) Siodmak, Robert
Screenwriter(s) Buckner, Robert

Cast Toren, Marta; Chandler, Jeff; Dauphin, Claude; Berti, Marina

Song(s) Street Song (C/L: Scharf, Walter; Romito, Vittorio; Cibelli, Amalia E.)

1381 ✦ DERELICT
Paramount, 1930

Director(s) Lee, Rowland V.
Screenwriter(s) McNutt, William Slavens; Jones, Grover; Marcin, Max

Cast Bancroft, George; Landis, Jessie Royce; Boyd, William; Durkin, James; Stuart, Donald

Song(s) Over the Sea of Dreams (C: King, Jack; L: Robin, Leo)

1382 ✦ THE DESERT HORSEMAN
Columbia, 1945

Composer(s) Burnette, Smiley
Lyricist(s) Burnette, Smiley

Producer(s) Clark, Colbert
Director(s) Nazarro, Ray
Screenwriter(s) Lowe, Sherman

Cast Starrett, Charles; Roberts, Adelle; Walt Shrum and His Colorado Hillbillies; Burnette, Smiley

Song(s) He Was an Amateur Once; Ring the Bell; There's a Tear in Your Eye [1] (C/L: Shrum, Walt; Hoag, Robert; Washburn, Charles)

Notes Originally titled PHANTOM OF THE DESERT. [1] Not written for the picture.

1383 ✦ THE DESERT RAVEN
Allied Artists, 1965

Musical Score LaSalle, Richard

Producer(s) Dunn, Cal
Director(s) Lee, Alan S.
Screenwriter(s) Romen, Rachel; Lee, Alan S.

Cast Romen, Rachel; Roberts, Rosalind; Terry, Robert N.

Song(s) The Desert Raven (C/L: Steele, John)

Notes No cue sheet available.

1384 ✦ DESERT SANDS
United Artists, 1955

Musical Score Dunlap, Paul

Producer(s) Koch, Howard W.
Director(s) Selander, Lesley
Screenwriter(s) George, George W.; Slavin, George F.; Arnold, Danny
Source(s) *Primitive Action* (novel) Robb, John

Cast Meeker, Ralph; Naish, J. Carrol; Larsen, Keith; Carradine, John; English, Marla

Song(s) Desert Sands (C: Dunlap, Paul; L: Heyman, Edward)

1385 ✦ THE DESERT SONG (1929)
Warner Brothers, 1929

Composer(s) Romberg, Sigmund
Lyricist(s) Hammerstein II, Oscar

Director(s) Del Ruth, Roy
Screenwriter(s) Gates, Harvey
Source(s) *The Desert Song* (musical) Harbach, Otto; Schwab, Laurence; Mandel, Frank; Hammerstein II, Oscar; Romberg, Sigmund

Cast Boles, John; King, Carlotta; Fazenda, Louise; Miljan, John; Arthur, Johnny; Martindel, Edward; Pratt, Jack; Hoffman, Otto; Loy, Myrna

Song(s) Ho! (The Riff Song); It; French Military Marching Song; Then You Will Know; The Desert Song; Song of the Brass Key; One Flower Grows Alone in Your Garden; The Sabre Song; Romance; One Alone; Farewell; My Little Castagnette

Notes No cue sheet available. All songs from Broadway original. This list of songs is a compilation of those listed in *The Rodgers and Hammerstein Fact Book* (which excludes "Song of the Brass Key" and "My Little

Castagnette") and Clive Hirschhorn's *The Hollywood Musical* (which excludes "Farewell" and "It"). The *AFI Catalog* lists "Love's Dear Yearning," a number that was cut before the Broadway opening.

1386 ✦ THE DESERT SONG (1943)
Warner Brothers, 1943

Musical Score Roemheld, Heinz
Composer(s) Romberg, Sigmund
Lyricist(s) Hammerstein II, Oscar; Harbach, Otto
Choreographer(s) Prinz, LeRoy

Producer(s) Buckner, Robert
Director(s) Florey, Robert
Screenwriter(s) Buckner, Robert
Source(s) *The Desert Song* (musical) Schwab, Laurence; Harbach, Otto; Mandel, Frank; Romberg, Sigmund; Hammerstein II, Oscar

Cast Morgan, Dennis; Manning, Irene; Cabot, Bruce; Lockhart, Gene; Overman, Lynne; Emerson, Faye; Francen, Victor; Bois, Curt; LaRue, Jack; Dalio, Marcel

Song(s) Mal El Sham (C/L: Bonnesar, Dave); Ho! (The Riff Song) [1]; Asmar El Loon (C/L: Bonnesar, Dave); Fifi's Song (L: Scholl, Jack); Gay Parisienne (C: Walter, Serge; L: Scholl, Jack); Romance [1]; Howid Men Hina (C/L: Bonnesar, Dave); One Alone [1]; The Desert Song [1]; Long Live the Night (L: Silva, Mario; Scholl, Jack); French Military Marching Song [1]; One Flower Grows Alone in Your Garden [1] [2]

Notes There are brief instrumental backgrounds of other songs from the original production including "It," "Dance of Triumph," "Prelude" and "Margot and I Want a Kiss." [1] From Broadway original. [2] Not on cue sheet.

1387 ✦ THE DESERT SONG (1953)
Warner Brothers, 1953

Musical Score Steiner, Max
Composer(s) Romberg, Sigmund
Lyricist(s) Hammerstein II, Oscar; Harbach, Otto
Choreographer(s) Prinz, LeRoy

Producer(s) Fehr, Rudi
Director(s) Humberstone, H. Bruce
Screenwriter(s) Kibbee, Roland
Source(s) *The Desert Song* (musical) Schwab, Laurence; Harbach, Otto; Mandel, Frank; Romberg, Sigmund; Hammerstein II, Oscar

Cast MacRae, Gordon; Grayson, Kathryn; Massey, Raymond; Cochran, Steve; Collins, Ray; McLerie, Allyn Ann; Wesson, Dick; Picerni, Paul; Conrad, William

Song(s) Ho! (The Riff Song); Romance; The Desert Song; Gay Parisienne (C: Walter, Serge; L: Scholl, Jack); Azuri's Dance [1]; One Flower Grows Alone in Your Garden; One Alone; Long Live the Night (L: Silva, Mario; Scholl, Jack)

Notes Only those songs by Romberg, Hammerstein II and Harbach were in the original production. The others were written for the 1943 film version of the musical. [1] Hummed.

1388 ✦ DESERT WONDERLAND
Twentieth Century–Fox, 1942

Song(s) Desert Wonderland [1] (C: Hulbert, Lee; Stock, Larry; L: Stillman, Al

Notes This is a Lowell Thomas Magic Carpet of Movietone travelogue. [1] Based on "A Lone Wolf on the Indian Trail."

1389 ✦ DESIGN FOR LIVING
Paramount, 1933

Producer(s) Lubitsch, Ernst
Director(s) Lubitsch, Ernst
Screenwriter(s) Hecht, Ben
Source(s) *Design for Living* (play) Coward, Noel

Cast Cooper, Gary; March, Fredric; Hopkins, Miriam; Horton, Edward Everett; Pangborn, Franklin; Jewell, Isabel; Darwell, Jane

Song(s) My Design for Living [1] (C: Revel, Harry; L: Gordon, Mack)

Notes [1] Not used in film.

1390 ✦ DESIGNING WOMAN
Metro–Goldwyn–Mayer, 1957

Musical Score Previn, Andre
Choreographer(s) Cole, Jack

Producer(s) Schary, Dore
Director(s) Minnelli, Vincente
Screenwriter(s) Wells, George

Cast Peck, Gregory; Bacall, Lauren; Gray, Dolores; Levene, Sam; Shaughnessy, Mickey; Helmore, Tom; White, Jesse; Connors, Chuck; Platt, Edward; Moore, Alvy; Cole, Jack; Veazie, Carol

Song(s) Designing Woman (C: Previn, Andre; L: Brooks, Jack); Music Is Better Than Words [1] (C: Previn, Andre; L: Comden, Betty; Green, Adolph)

Notes There is also a vocal of "There'll Be Some Changes Made" by W. Benton Overstreet and Billy Higgins. [1] Also in IT'S ALWAYS FAIR WEATHER with additional lyric credit for Roger Edens.

1391 ✦ DESIRE
Paramount, 1936

Composer(s) Hollander, Frederick
Lyricist(s) Robin, Leo

Producer(s) Lubitsch, Ernst
Director(s) Borzage, Frank

Screenwriter(s) Hoffenstein, Samuel; Young, Waldemar; Mayer, Edwin Justus
Source(s) (play) Szekely, Hans; Stemmle, R.A.

Cast Dietrich, Marlene; Cooper, Gary; Halliday, John; Frawley, William; Cossart, Ernest; Tamiroff, Akim; Mowbray, Alan; Tilbury, Zeffie; Lawrence, Marc

Song(s) Awake in a Dream; Cielito Lindo (C: Traditional); I Love to Be in Love [1]; I Wonder [1]; Whispers in the Dark [1]; Desire [1]

Notes The movie was originally titled THE PEARL NECKLACE. [1] Not used.

1392 ✦ DÉSIRÉE
Twentieth Century–Fox, 1954

Producer(s) Blaustein, Julian
Director(s) Koster, Henry
Screenwriter(s) Taradash, Daniel
Source(s) *Desiree* (novel) Selinko, Annemarie

Cast Brando, Marlon; Simmons, Jean; Oberon, Merle; Rennie, Michael; Mitchell, Cameron; Sellars, Elizabeth; Nesbitt, Cathleen; Napier, Alan; Jones, Carolyn

Song(s) We Meet Again (Desiree Waltz) [1] (C: Newman, Alfred; L: Darby, Ken)

Notes [1] Lyric written for exploitation only.

1393 ✦ A DESPERATE ADVENTURE
Republic, 1938

Producer(s) Auer, John H.
Director(s) Auer, John H.
Screenwriter(s) Trivers, Barry

Cast Novarro, Ramon; Marsh, Marian; Blore, Eric; Tallichet, Margaret; Tombes, Andrew; Rutherford, Tom; Nazarro, Cliff; Sedan, Rolfe; Collier, Lois

Song(s) We Live for Art (C: Colombo, Alberto; L: Cherkose, Eddie)

1394 ✦ THE DESPERATE HOURS
Paramount, 1955

Producer(s) Wyler, William
Director(s) Wyler, William
Screenwriter(s) Hayes, Joseph
Source(s) *The Desperate Hours* (novel, play) Hayes, Joseph

Cast Bogart, Humphrey; Martin, Dewey; Middleton, Robert; March, Fredric; Scott, Martha; Eyer, Richard; Murphy, Mary; Young, Gig; Collins, Ray

Song(s) Desperate Hours [1] (C: Bacharach, Burt; L: Stone, Wilson)

Notes [1] Written for exploitation only.

1395 ✦ DESPERATE TRAILS
Universal, 1939

Producer(s) Ray, Albert
Director(s) Ray, Albert
Screenwriter(s) Bennison, Andrew

Cast Brown, Johnny Mack; Knight, Fuzzy

Song(s) Ridin' Home [1] (C: McHugh, Jimmy; L: Adamson, Harold)

Notes [1] Also in ROAD AGENT, THE ROAD TO RENO, STRICTLY IN THE GROOVE and TENTING TONIGHT ON THE OLD CAMP GROUND.

1396 ✦ DESTINATION GOBI
Twentieth Century–Fox, 1953

Musical Score Kaplan, Sol

Producer(s) Rubin, Stanley
Director(s) Wise, Robert
Screenwriter(s) Freeman, Everett

Cast Widmark, Richard; Taylor, Don; Adams, Casey; Vye, Murvyn; Hickman, Darryl; Milner, Martin; Bagdasarian, Ross; Acosta, Rodolfo; Collins, Russell

Song(s) Mongolian Funeral Chant (C/L: Kaplan, Sol); Buddhist Temple (C/L: Kaplan, Sol)

1397 ✦ DESTINATION MURDER
RKO, 1952

Musical Score Gertz, Irving

Producer(s) Cahn, Edward L.; Suess, Maurie M.
Director(s) Cahn, Edward L.
Screenwriter(s) Martin, Don

Cast Steve Gibson's Redcaps; MacKenzie, Joyce; Clements, Stanley; Hatfield, Hurd; Dekker, Albert; Dell, Myrna

Song(s) Palace of Stone (C/L: Springs, James)

1398 ✦ DESTINY
Universal, 1945

Musical Score Skinner, Frank

Producer(s) Neill, Roy William
Director(s) Duvivier, Julien; LeBorg, Reginald
Screenwriter(s) Chanslor, Roy; Pascal, Ernest

Cast Curtis, Alan; Jean, Gloria; Craven, Frank; McDonald, Grace; Fenton, Frank; Gombell, Minna

Song(s) Who Knows Why April Dances (C: Tansman, Alexandre; L: Webster, Paul Francis)

Notes There is also a vocal of "I'll See You in My Dreams" by Gus Kahn and Isham Jones. This was originally to be the fourth chapter of FLESH AND FANTASY, but instead LeBorg was brought in to film an additional 30 minutes and make it a programmer on its own.

1399 ✦ DESTRY
Universal, 1954

Composer(s) Hughes, Arnold
Lyricist(s) Herbert, Frederick

Producer(s) Rubin, Stanley
Director(s) Marshall, George
Screenwriter(s) Beauchamp, D.D.; North, Edmund
Source(s) *Destry Rides Again* (novel) Brand, Max

Cast Murphy, Audie; Blanchard, Mari; Bettger, Lyle; Buchanan, Edgar; Wickes, Mary; Mitchell, Thomas; Nelson, Lori; Ford, Wallace; Hale Jr., Alan; Wallace, George

Song(s) The Bang Song (Bang! Bang!); If You Can Can-Can; Empty Arms [1]

Notes [1] Also in IMITATION OF LIFE.

1400 ✦ DESTRY RIDES AGAIN
Universal, 1939

Composer(s) Hollander, Frederick
Lyricist(s) Loesser, Frank

Producer(s) Pasternak, Joe
Director(s) Marshall, George
Screenwriter(s) Jackson, Felix; Purcell, Gertrude; Myers, Henry
Source(s) *Destry Rides Again* (novel) Brand, Max

Cast Dietrich, Marlene; Merkel, Una; Auer, Mischa; Stewart, James; Donlevy, Brian; Winninger, Charles; Hinds, Samuel S.; Hervey, Irene; Jenkins, Allen; Hymer, Warren; Gilbert, Billy; Fadden, Tom; Carson, Jack; Jones, Dickie; Todd, Ann

Song(s) Little Joe, the Wrangler [1]; You've Got that Look; The Boys in the Backroom

Notes This is a remake of the 1932 Tom Mix movie of the same name. It was remade in 1950 as FRENCHIE and in 1954 as DESTRY. [1] Also in LITTLE JOE, THE WRANGLER, MAN FROM MONTANA and THE OLD TEXAS TRAIL.

1401 ✦ THE DEVIL AND MAX DEVLIN
Disney, 1980

Musical Score Baker, Buddy
Composer(s) Hamlisch, Marvin

Producer(s) Courtland, Jerome
Director(s) Stern, Steven Hillard
Screenwriter(s) Rodgers, Mary

Cast Cosby, Bill; Anspach, Susan; Rich, Adam; Budd, Julie

Song(s)   Any Fool Could See (L: Willis, Allee); Roses and Rainbows (L: Sager, Carole Bayer)

1402 ◆ THE DEVIL IN LOVE
Warner Brothers, 1968

Musical Score   Trovajoli, Armando

Producer(s)   Gori, Mario Cecchi
Director(s)   Scola, Ettore
Screenwriter(s)   Scola, Ettore; Maccari, Ruggero

Cast   Gassman, Vittorio; Rooney, Mickey; Auger, Claudine; Manni, Ettore

Song(s)   Allelujah Per Due (C: Trovajoli, Armando; L: Calabrese, Giorgio)

1403 ◆ THE DEVIL IS A SISSY
Metro–Goldwyn–Mayer, 1936

Musical Score   Stothart, Herbert

Producer(s)   Davis, Frank
Director(s)   Van Dyke, W.S.
Screenwriter(s)   Mahin, John Lee; Schayer, Richard

Cast   Bartholomew, Freddie; Cooper, Jackie; Rooney, Mickey; Hunter, Ian; Conklin, Peggy; Alexander, Katherine; Lockhart, Gene; Lockhart, Kathleen

Song(s)   Say Ah! (C: Brown, Nacio Herb; L: Freed, Arthur)

Notes   Released as THE DEVIL TAKES THE COUNT in Great Britain.

1404 ◆ THE DEVIL IS A WOMAN
Paramount, 1935

Musical Score   Rainger, Ralph; Setaro, Andrea
Composer(s)   Rainger, Ralph
Lyricist(s)   Robin, Leo

Director(s)   von Sternberg, Josef
Screenwriter(s)   Dos Passos, John
Source(s)   "Woman and the Puppet" (story) Louys, Pierre

Cast   Dietrich, Marlene; Romero, Cesar; Atwill, Lionel; Skipworth, Alison; Horton, Edward Everett

Song(s)   Three Sweethearts Have I; Then It Isn't Love [1]

Notes   The film was originally titled CAPRICE ESPAGNOLE. [1] Not used but recorded for soundtrack by Dietrich and published.

1405 ◆ THE DEVIL MAKES THREE
Metro–Goldwyn–Mayer, 1952

Musical Score   Kaper, Bronislau

Producer(s)   Goldstone, Richard
Director(s)   Marton, Andrew
Screenwriter(s)   Davis, Jerry

Cast   Kelly, Gene; Angeli, Pier; Rober, Richard; Egan, Richard; Clausen, Claus; Seyferth, Wilfried

Song(s)   Can Love Come Back Again? [1] (C: Kaper, Bronislau; L: Brooks, Jack; Hollander, Frederick); Oh Christmas Tree (C: Kaper, Bronislau; L: Brooks, Jack); Wer Soll Das Bezahlen? [2] (C: Schmitz, Juff; L: Stein, Walter; Goldstone, Richard)

Notes   There is also a vocal of "On the Atchison, Topeka and the Santa Fe" by Harry Warren and Johnny Mercer. [1] German lyrics by Frederick Hollander. [2] English lyrics by Goldstone.

1406 ◆ DEVIL-MAY-CARE
Metro–Goldwyn–Mayer, 1929

Composer(s)   Stothart, Herbert
Lyricist(s)   Grey, Clifford
Choreographer(s)   Rasch, Albertina

Director(s)   Franklin, Sidney; Brooke, J. Clifford
Screenwriter(s)   Sears, Zelda
Source(s)   La Bataille Des Dames (play) Scribe, Eugene; Legouve, Ernest

Cast   Novarro, Ramon; Jordan, Dorothy; Harris, Marion; Miljan, John

Song(s)   March of the Old Guard; The Gang Song; Why Waste Your Charms?; Madam Pompadour; Charming; If He Cared; Shepherd's Serenade

Notes   The beginning of Herbert Stothart's long MGM tenure. Dimitri Tiomkin contributed the ballet music.

1407 ◆ THE DEVIL'S HAIRPIN
Paramount, 1957

Musical Score   Van Cleave, Nathan

Producer(s)   Wilde, Cornel
Director(s)   Wilde, Cornel
Screenwriter(s)   Wilde, Cornel; Edmiston, James

Cast   Wilde, Cornel; Wallace, Jean; Astor, Mary; Franz, Arthur; Bagdasarian, Ross

Song(s)   The Touch of Love (C/L: Bagdasarian, Ross); Swing It Just a Little More (C: Bagdasarian, Ross; L: Wilde, Cornel)

1408 ◆ DEVIL'S HOLIDAY
Paramount, 1930

Musical Score   Goulding, Edmund

Director(s)   Goulding, Edmund
Screenwriter(s)   Goulding, Edmund

Cast   Carroll, Nancy; Holmes, Phillips; Kirkwood, James; Bosworth, Hobart; Sparks, Ned; Farley, Morgan; Prouty, Jed; Pitts, ZaSu; Downey, Morton; Pringle, Jessie

Song(s)   You Are a Song (C: Goulding, Edmund; Terr, Max; L: Robin, Leo)

1409 ✦ THE DEVIL'S IN LOVE
Fox, 1933

Director(s) Dieterle, William
Screenwriter(s) Estabrook, Howard

Cast Young, Loretta; Jory, Victor; Manners, David; Osborne, Vivienne; Naish, J. Carrol

Song(s) Mon Papa (C/L: Jason, Will; Burton, Val)

1410 ✦ DEVIL'S ISLAND
Warner Brothers, 1940

Musical Score Jackson, Howard

Producer(s) Foy, Bryan
Director(s) Clemens, William
Screenwriter(s) Gamet, Kenneth; Ryan, Don
Source(s) (story) Coldeway, Anthony; Schrock, Raymond

Cast Karloff, Boris; Stephenson, James; Harrigan, Nedda; Kuznetzoff, Adia

Song(s) Song of the Doomed (C: Jerome, M.K.; L: Scholl, Jack)

Notes *50th Anniversary* lists the screenwriters as Anthony Coldeway and Manley P. Hall.

1411 ✦ THE DEVIL'S LOTTERY
Fox, 1932

Director(s) Taylor, Sam
Screenwriter(s) Bolton, Guy
Source(s) (novel) Bartley, Nalbro

Cast Landi, Elissa; McLaglen, Victor; Kirkland, Alexander; Morgan, Ralph

Song(s) Hangin' at the End of a Rope (C/L: Hanley, James F.)

1412 ✦ THE DEVIL'S PARTY
Universal, 1936

Producer(s) Grainger, Edmund
Director(s) McCarey, Ray
Screenwriter(s) Chanslor, Roy
Source(s) *Hell's Kitchen Has a Party* (novel) Chase, Borden

Cast Renschler, Mickey; Beckett, Scotty; Bupp, Tommy; Jones, Dickie; Quigley, Juanita; McLaglen, Victor; Gargan, William; Kelly, Paul; Roberts, Beatrice; Hinds, Samuel S.; Gargan, Edward; Gallaudet, John

Song(s) Things Are Coming My Way (C: McHugh, Jimmy; L: Adamson, Harold)

1413 ✦ DEVIL'S SADDLE LEGION
Warner Brothers, 1937

Musical Score Jackson, Howard
Composer(s) Jerome, M.K.
Lyricist(s) Scholl, Jack

Producer(s) Hollingshead, Gordon
Director(s) Connolly, Bobby
Screenwriter(s) Repp, Ed Earl
Source(s) "Hell's Saddle Legion" (story) Repp, Ed Earl

Cast Foran, Dick; Nagel, Anne; Hart, Gordon

Song(s) My Texas Home [1]; When Moonlight Is Riding the Range; God's Country

Notes [1] Also in SONGS OF THE RANGE and WEST OF THE ROCKIES.

1414 ✦ A DEVIL WITH WOMEN
Fox, 1930

Producer(s) Middleton, George
Director(s) Cummings, Irving
Screenwriter(s) Nichols, Dudley; Johnson, Henry
Source(s) "Dust and Sun" (story) Ripley, Clements

Cast McLaglen, Victor; Maris, Mona; Bogart, Humphrey; Alcaniz, Luana

Song(s) Amor Mio (C: Monaco, James V.; L: Friend, Cliff)

Notes Originally titled ON THE MAKE.

1415 ✦ THE D.I.
Warner Brothers, 1957

Musical Score Heindorf, Ray; Buttolph, David

Producer(s) Webb, Jack
Director(s) Webb, Jack
Screenwriter(s) Barrett, James Lee
Source(s) "Murder of a Sandflea" (teleplay) Barrett, James Lee

Cast Webb, Jack; Dubbins, Don; Loughery, Jackie; Lewis, Monica; Gregg, Virginia

Song(s) (If You Don't) Somebody Else Will (C: Conniff, Ray; Weismantel, Fred)

1416 ✦ DIAMOND HORSESHOE
Twentieth Century–Fox, 1945

Composer(s) Warren, Harry
Lyricist(s) Gordon, Mack
Choreographer(s) Pan, Hermes

Producer(s) Perlberg, William
Director(s) Seaton, George
Screenwriter(s) Seaton, George
Source(s) (play) Nicholson, Kenyon

Cast Grable, Betty; Haymes, Dick; Silvers, Phil; Gaxton, William; Kay, Beatrice; Cavallaro, Carmen; Solar, Willie; Dumont, Margaret; Benson, Roy; Acuff, Eddie; Gargan, Edward

Song(s) Welcome to the Diamond Horseshoe; Cooking Up a Show; In Acapulco; The More I See You; I Wish I Knew; The Old and the New Prelude; Play Me an Old Fashioned Melody; A Nickel's Worth of Jive; Dessert

Finale; China Boy (C/L: Boutelje, Phil; Winfree, Dick); Mink Lament [1]; Moody [1]

Notes Also known as BILLY ROSE'S DIAMOND HORSESHOE. "My Melancholy Baby" by Ernie Burnett and George A. Norton; "Carrie (Carrie Marry Harry)" by Albert Von Tilzer and Junie McCree; "Let Me Call You Sweetheart" by Leo Friedman and Beth Slater Whitson; "(I'd Climb the Highest Mountain) If I Knew I'd Find You" by Lew Brown and Sidney Clare; "The Aba-Daba Honeymoon" by Arthur Fields and Walter Donovan and "On the Gay White Way" by Ralph Rainger and Leo Robin are all also used vocally. [1] Listed in Tony Thomas' biography of Warren but not on cue sheets. [2] Not used.

1417 ◆ THE DIAMOND QUEEN
Warner Brothers, 1953

Musical Score Sawtell, Paul

Producer(s) Melford, Frank
Director(s) Brahm, John
Screenwriter(s) Englander, Otto

Cast Lamas, Fernando; Roland, Gilbert; Dahl, Arlene; Leonard, Sheldon

Song(s) The Lucky Sailor (C/L: Sawtell, Paul); The Bugle Played (C/L: Sawtell, Paul)

1418 ◆ DIAMONDS ARE FOREVER
United Artists, 1971

Musical Score Barry, John

Producer(s) Saltzman, Harry; Broccoli, Albert R.
Director(s) Hamilton, Guy
Screenwriter(s) Maibaum, Richard
Source(s) *Diamonds Are Forever* (novel) Fleming, Ian

Cast Connery, Sean; St. John, Jill; Gray, Charles; Smith, Putter; Glover, Bruce; Wood, Lana; Dean, Jimmy; Cabot, Bruce; Lee, Bernard; Llewelyn, Desmond; Maxwell, Lois

Song(s) Diamonds Are Forever (C: Barry, John; L: Black, Don)

1419 ◆ DIAMONDS FOR BREAKFAST
Paramount, 1969

Musical Score Kaye, Norman

Producer(s) Ponti, Carlo; Rouve, Pierre
Director(s) Morahan, Christopher
Screenwriter(s) Simpson, N.F.; Rouve, Pierre; Harwood, Ronald

Cast Mastroianni, Marcello; Tushingham, Rita; Taylor, Elaine; Blye, Maggie; Mitchell, Warren; Rossiter, Leonard; Fraser, Bill

Song(s) Diamonds for Breakfast (C: Kaye, Norman; L: Shaper, Hal)

Notes The film never opened in the United States. ABC Pictures owned the American rights.

1420 ◆ DIE LAUGHING
Orion, 1980

Musical Score Safan, Craig
Composer(s) Benson, Robby
Lyricist(s) Segal, Jerry

Producer(s) Canton, Mark; Benson, Robby
Director(s) Werner, Jeff
Screenwriter(s) Segal, Jerry; Benson, Robby; Parker, Scott

Cast Benson, Robby; Grovenor, Linda; Durning, Charles; Lanchester, Elsa; Cort, Bud; Taggart, Rita; Zagon, Marty

Song(s) Mr. Weinstein; All I Want Is Love; Far Side of a Dream

Notes No cue sheet available.

1421 ◆ A DIFFERENT STORY
Avco Embassy, 1978

Musical Score Frank, David

Producer(s) Belkin, Alan
Director(s) Aaron, Paul
Screenwriter(s) Olek, Henry

Cast King, Perry; Foster, Meg; Curtin, Valerie; Donat, Peter; Bull, Richard; Collenitine; Barbara; Barry, Guerin

Song(s) Let Tomorrow Be (C/L: Wahler, Robert)

Notes No cue sheet available.

1422 ◆ DIMPLES
Twentieth Century–Fox, 1936

Composer(s) McHugh, Jimmy
Lyricist(s) Koehler, Ted

Producer(s) Zanuck, Darryl F.
Director(s) Seiter, William A.
Screenwriter(s) Sheekman, Arthur; Perrin, Nat

Cast Temple, Shirley; Morgan, Frank; Westley, Helen; Kent, Robert; Fetchit, Stepin; Allwyn, Astrid; Byron, Delmer; The Hall Johnson Choir; Carradine, John

Song(s) Hey What Did the Blue Jay Say; He Was a Dandy; Shirley and the Two Black Dots (Inst.); Picture Me Without You; Dixie Anna; Oh Mister Man Up in the Moon [1]; Wings of the Morning [2]

Notes Originally titled BOWERY PRINCESS. [1] Sheet music only. [2] Not used.

1423 ✦ DINER
Metro–Goldwyn–Mayer, 1982

Producer(s) Weintraub, Jerry
Director(s) Levinson, Barry
Screenwriter(s) Levinson, Barry

Cast Guttenberg, Steve; Stern, Daniel; Rourke, Mickey; Bacon, Kevin; Daly, Timothy; Barkin, Ellen; Reiser, Paul; James, Jessica

Song(s) You're My Heaven (C/L: Brody, Bruce; Kral, Ivan)

Notes Only original song listed.

1424 ✦ DINGAKA
Paramount, 1965

Composer(s) Egnos, Bertha
Lyricist(s) Egnos, Bertha
Choreographer(s) Wartski, Sheila

Producer(s) Uys, Jamie
Director(s) Uys, Jamie
Screenwriter(s) Uys, Jamie

Cast Baker, Stanley; Prowse, Juliet; Gampu, Ken; Mynhardt, Siegfried

Song(s) Python Dance (L: Gray, Basil); Tula Baba; Tribal Prayer (L: Gray, Basil; Domingo, Eddie); When the Roll Is Called Up Yonder (C/L: Black, James); Body and Bones (L: Domingo, Eddie); Song of the Convicts; Placating the Gods (L: Gray, Basil)

1425 ✦ DING DONG WILLIAMS
RKO, 1945

Musical Score Harline, Leigh
Composer(s) McHugh, Jimmy
Lyricist(s) Adamson, Harold

Producer(s) Schlom, Herman
Director(s) Berke, William
Screenwriter(s) Weisberg, Brenda; Webster, M. Coates
Source(s) "Strictly Ding Dong" (stories) English, Richard

Cast Vernon, Glenn; McGuire, Marcy; Bressart, Felix; Jeffreys, Anne; Warren, James; Davidson, William b.; Noonan, Tommy [1]; Nazarro, Cliff; Robards, Jason; Bob Nolan and the Sons of the Pioneers

Song(s) Cool Water [3] (C/L: Nolan, Bob); Candlelight and Wine [2]; I Saw You First [4]

Notes [1] Billed as Tom Noonan. [2] Also in FALCON'S ADVENTURE. [3] Also in the Republic pictures ALONG THE NAVAJO TRAIL and HANDS ACROSS THE BORDER. [4] Also in HIGHER AND HIGHER and RACE STREET.

1426 ✦ DINNER AT EIGHT
Metro–Goldwyn–Mayer, 1933

Producer(s) Selznick, David O.
Director(s) Cukor, George
Screenwriter(s) Marion, Frances; Mankiewicz, Herman J.; Stewart, Donald Ogden
Source(s) *Dinner at Eight* (play) Kaufman, George S.; Ferber, Edna

Cast Dressler, Marie; Barrymore, John; Beery, Wallace; Harlow, Jean; Barrymore, Lionel; Tracy, Lee; Lowe, Edmund; Burke, Billie; Evans, Madge; Hersholt, Jean; Morley, Karen; Holmes, Phillips; Robson, May; Hale, Louise Closser; Mitchell, Grant; Patterson, Elizabeth

Song(s) When the Moon Comes Over the Mountain [1] (C: Woods, Harry; L: Johnson, Howard); Dinner at Eight [2] (C: McHugh, Jimmy; L: Fields, Dorothy)

Notes [1] Also in the Paramount films THE BIG BROADCAST and HELLO, EVERYBODY (1933). [2] Sheet music only.

1427 ✦ DIPLOMANIACS
RKO, 1933

Composer(s) Akst, Harry
Lyricist(s) Eliscu, Edward
Choreographer(s) Ceballos, Larry

Producer(s) Jaffe, Sam
Director(s) Seiter, William A.
Screenwriter(s) Mankiewicz, Joseph L.; Meyers, Henry

Cast Wheeler, Bert; Woolsey, Robert; White, Marjorie; Calhern, Louis; Barry, Phyllis; Herbert, Hugh; Kennedy, Edgar; Carle, Richard

Song(s) Sing to Me [1]; In the Red; Paris; No No War

Notes [1] Also in ROMANCE IN MANHATTAN.

1428 ✦ DIRT
American Cinema, 1979

Musical Score Halligan, Richard
Composer(s) Oldfield, Alan
Lyricist(s) Talon, Johnny

Producer(s) Bodoh, Allan F.; Graham, John Patrick
Director(s) Carson, Eric; Naylor, Cal
Screenwriter(s) Schweitzer, S.S.; Friedgen, Bud; Madigan, Tom; Young, R.R.

Cast Gordon, Clarke; Credel, Curtis; Griswold, Kenny; Gunn, Debbie

Song(s) Swamp Buggy; Snow, Climb; Jeep Bridge Runners

Notes No cue sheet available.

1429 ✦ DIRTY DANCING
Vestron, 1987

Musical Score Morris, John

Producer(s) Gottlieb, Linda
Director(s) Ardolino, Emile
Screenwriter(s) Bergstein, Eleanor

Cast Swayze, Patrick; Grey, Jennifer; Orbach, Jerry; Rhodes, Cynthia; Weston, Jack; Bishop, Kelly; Price, Lonny; Coles, Charles "Honi"; Morrow, "Cousin Brucie"; Trueman, Paula

Song(s) Where Are You Tonight (C/L: Scola, Mark); Hungry Eyes (C/L: Previte, Franke; DeNicola, John); Overload (C/L: Zappacosta, Alfie; Luciani, Marko); Yes (C/L: Fryer, Terry; Cavanaugh, Neal; Graf, Tom); She's Like the Wind (C/L: Swayze, Patrick; Widelitz, Stacy); I've Had the Time of My Life (C/L: Previte, Franke; Markowitz, Donald; DeNicola, John); Do You Love Me (C/L: Gordy Jr., Berry); Hey Baby! (C/L: Cobb, Margaret; Channel, Bruce); Love Man (C/L: Redding, Otis)

Notes No cue sheet available. Not all songs written for this film.

1430 ✦ DIRTY DINGUS MAGEE
Metro–Goldwyn–Mayer, 1970

Musical Score Strange, Billy; Alexander, Jeff

Producer(s) Kennedy, Burt
Director(s) Kennedy, Burt
Screenwriter(s) Waldman, Tom; Waldman, Frank; Heller, Joseph
Source(s) *The Ballad of Dingus Magee* (novel) Markson, David

Cast Sinatra, Frank; Kennedy, George; Jackson, Anne; Nettleton, Lois; Elam, Jack; Carey, Michele; Carey Jr., Harry

Song(s) Dirty Dingus Magee [1] (C/L: Alexander, Jeff; Curb, Mike; David, Mack)

Notes [1] Mike Curb credited on cue sheet only. Jeff Alexander not credited on sheet music.

1431 ✦ THE DIRTY DOZEN
Metro–Goldwyn–Mayer, 1967

Musical Score De Vol, Frank
Composer(s) De Vol, Frank

Producer(s) Hyman, Kenneth
Director(s) Aldrich, Robert
Screenwriter(s) Johnson, Nunnally; Heller, Lukas
Source(s) *The Dirty Dozen* (novel) Nathanson, E.M.

Cast Marvin, Lee; Borgnine, Ernest; Bronson, Charles; Brown, Jim; Cassavetes, John; Jaeckel, Richard; Kennedy, George; Lopez, Trini; Meeker, Ralph; Ryan, Robert; Savalas, Telly; Sutherland, Donald; Walker, Clint; Webber, Robert

Song(s) Einsam (L: Siegfried, Sybille); Bramble Bush (L: David, Mack)

1432 ✦ DIRTY MARY—CRAZY LARRY
Twentieth Century–Fox, 1974

Musical Score Haskell, Jimmie

Producer(s) Herman, Norman H.
Director(s) Hough, John
Screenwriter(s) Chapman, Leigh; Santean, Antonio
Source(s) *The Chase* (novel) Unekis, Richard

Cast Fonda, Peter; George, Susan; Roarke, Adam; Morrow, Vic; McDowall, Roddy

Song(s) Time (Is Such a Funny Thing) (C: Janssen, Danny; L: Hart, Bobby); Dirty Mary Crazy Larry [1] (C/L: Kanew, Jeff)

Notes [1] Sheet music only.

1433 ✦ DISC JOCKEY
Allied Artists, 1951

Producer(s) Duke, Maurice
Director(s) Jason, Will
Screenwriter(s) Reynolds, Clarke

Cast Simms, Ginny; O'Shea, Michael; Drake, Tom; Nigh, Jane; Morgan, Russ; Kent, Lenny; Dorsey, Tommy; Shearing, George; Lucas, Nick; Jeffries, Herb; Vaughan, Sarah; The Weavers; Cowan, Jerome; Foy Willing and the Riders of the Purple Sage; Norvo, Red; Pollack, Ben; Venuti, Joe; Fina, Jack

Song(s) Let's Meander Through the Meadow (C/L: Steuben, S.; Gordon, Roz); Show Me Your Love Me (C/L: Steuben, S.; Gordon, Roz); Nobody Wants Me (C/L: Gordon, Roz); After Hours (C/L: Gordon, Roz); Disc Jockey (C/L: Jeffries, Herb; Hazard, Dick); In My Heart (C/L: Jeffries, Herb; Hazard, Dick); Peaceful Country (C/L: Willing, Foy); Riders of the Purple Sage (C/L: Willing, Foy); Brain Wave (inst.) (C: Shearing, George); Oh Look at Me Now (C: Bushkin, Joe; L: De Vries, John); The Roving Kind (C/L: Cavanaugh, Jessie; Stanton, Arnold)

Notes No cue sheet available. Not all songs written for this picture.

1434 ✦ DISGRACED
Paramount, 1933

Producer(s) Veiller, Bayard
Director(s) Kenton, Erle C.
Screenwriter(s) Miller, Alice Duer; Martin, Francis

Cast Twelvetrees, Helen; Cabot, Bruce; Ames, Adrienne; Murray, Ken

Song(s) Any Place Is Paradise (As Long As You Are There) (C: Pasternacki, Stephen; L: Coslow, Sam)

Notes Sam Coslow sang the song for the scene where the stars are listening to the Victrola. The writers originally envisioned using the Dietz and Schwartz song "Alone Together."

1435 ✦ DISK-O-TEK HOLIDAY
Allied Artists, 1966

Producer(s) Slay Jr., Frank; de Lane Lea, Jacques
Director(s) Scarza, Vince; Hickox, Douglas

Cast Peter and Gordon; The Bachelors; The Chiffons; Freddie and the Dreamers; Cannon, Freddy; A Band of Angels; Roy, Caroline; The Vagrants; Paxton, Casey; Great, Johnny B.; Cordet, Louise; The Applejacks; Jackie and the Raindrops; The Merseybeats; The Rockin' Ramrods; The Orchids; Small, Millie

Notes No cue sheet available. It is not known if there are any original songs in this film.

1436 ✦ THE DISORDERLY ORDERLY
Paramount, 1964

Producer(s) Jones, Paul
Director(s) Tashlin, Frank
Screenwriter(s) Tashlin, Frank

Cast Lewis, Jerry; Oliver, Susan; Farrell, Glenda; Sloane, Everett; Sharpe, Karen; Freeman, Kathleen

Song(s) The Disorderly Orderly (C: Carr, Leon; L: Shuman, Earl)

1437 ✦ DISORGANIZED CRIME
Disney, 1989

Musical Score Newman, David

Producer(s) Bigelow, Lynn
Director(s) Kouf, Jim
Screenwriter(s) Kouf, Jim

Cast Axton, Hoyt; Bernsen, Corbin; Blades, Ruben; Gwynne, Fred; O'Neill, Ed; Phillips, Lou Diamond; Roebuck, Daniel; Russ, William

Song(s) Short Cut (C/L: Fleischer, Charles); Take Mine (C/L: Stowell, Jim); Too Fine a Lady (C/L: Stowell, Jim); Mind's Eye (C/L: Fleischer, Charles); Red Eyes, White Whiskey, Blue Heart (C/L: Stowell, Jim)

Notes Originally titled BANK JOB.

1438 ✦ DISTANT THUNDER
Paramount, 1988

Musical Score Jarre, Maurice

Producer(s) Schaffel, Robert
Director(s) Rosenthal, Rick
Screenwriter(s) Stitzel, Robert

Cast Macchio, Ralph; Lithgow, John; Keane, Kerrie; Brown, Reb; Margolin, Janet

Song(s) Distant Thunder (C/L: Thumm, Bill; Fairbairn, R.D.)

Notes No cue sheet available. There is also a vocal of "Wake the Town and Tell the People" by Jerry Livingston and Sammy Gallop.

1439 ✦ DIVE BOMBER
Warner Brothers, 1941

Musical Score Steiner, Max

Producer(s) Wallis, Hal B.
Director(s) Curtiz, Michael
Screenwriter(s) Wead, Frank; Buckner, Robert
Source(s) "Beyond the Blue Sky" (story) Wead, Frank

Cast Flynn, Errol; Smith, Alexis; MacMurray, Fred; Bellamy, Ralph

Song(s) What's New [1] (C: Haggart, Bob; L: Burke, Johnny); We Watch the Sky-ways [2] (C: Steiner, Max; L: Kahn, Gus)

Notes It is not known if this was written for the picture. [2] Lyric written for exploitation only.

1440 ✦ THE DIVINE LADY
Warner Brothers–First National, 1929

Director(s) Lloyd, Frank
Screenwriter(s) Johnston, Agnes Christine; Halsey, Forrest
Source(s) *The Divine Lady: a Romance of Nelson and Emma Hamilton* (novel) Barrington, E.

Cast Griffith, Corinne [1]; Varconi, Victor; Dressler, Marie; Warner, H.B.; Keith, Ian; Love, Montagu; Hall, Evelyn

Song(s) Lady Divine (C: Kountz, Richard; L: Pasternack, Joseph)

Notes No cue sheet available. [1] Singing and piano playing both dubbed.

1441 ✦ THE DIVINE OBSESSION
Melody Picatures, 1976

Producer(s) Kaufman, Lloyd; Wynn, David
Director(s) Kaufman, Lloyd
Screenwriter(s) Kalen, Robert

Cast Franklin, Julia; Anthony, Bree; National Velvet; Dexter, Tony

Song(s) The Divine Obsession Theme Song (C/L: Hobler, Randolph)

Notes No cue sheet available.

1442 ✦ DIVORCE MADE EASY
Paramount, 1929

Producer(s) Christie, Al
Director(s) Graham, Walter
Screenwriter(s) Collison, Wilson

Cast MacLean, Douglas; Prevost, Marie

Song(s) So Sweet (C/L: Sherwin, Sterling)

Notes No cue sheet available. Sheet music only.

1443 ✦ DIXIANA
RKO, 1930

Musical Score Tierney, Harry
Composer(s) Tierney, Harry
Lyricist(s) Caldwell, Anne
Choreographer(s) Eaton, Pearl

Producer(s) LeBaron, William
Director(s) Reed, Luther
Screenwriter(s) Reed, Luther; Caldwell, Anne

Cast Daniels, Bebe; Marshall, Everett; Wheeler, Bert; Woolsey, Robert; Cawthorn, Joseph; Howland, Jobyna; Lee, Dorothy; Harolde, Ralf; Robinson, Bill [1]

Song(s) Mr. & Mrs. Sippi; Clown's March; I Am Your Baby Now; Here's to the Old Days [4]; A Tear, a Kiss, a Smile; Creole Number; My One Ambition Is You; Dixiana (L: Davis, Benny); Each Life Is a Card Game; A Lady Loved a Soldier [2]; Guiding Star [3]

Notes The cue sheet does not differentiate between vocals and instrumentals. [1] Apparently Robinson's numbers were shown only in those theaters part of the R-K-O circuit. [2] Titled "The Lady and the Soldier" in script. [3] Titled "Silver Star" in script. [4] Titled "Good Old Pals" in script.

1444 ✦ DIXIE
Paramount, 1943

Musical Score Dolan, Robert Emmett
Composer(s) Van Heusen, James
Lyricist(s) Burke, Johnny
Choreographer(s) Felix, Seymour

Producer(s) Jones, Paul
Director(s) Sutherland, Edward
Screenwriter(s) Tunberg, Karl; Ware, Darrell

Cast Foy Jr., Eddie; Crosby, Bing; De Wolfe, Billy; Overman, Lynne; Warwick, Robert; Reynolds, Marjorie; Lamour, Dorothy; Walburn, Raymond; Mitchell, Grant; Conlin, Jimmy

Song(s) Sunday, Monday or Always [6]; Laughing Tony; Opening—4 Show (C: Lilley, Joseph J.; L: Bradshaw, Charles W.); She's From Missouri; Opening—2nd Minstrel Show; A Horse that Knows the Way Back Home; If You Please [1] [4]; Kinda Peculiar

Brown [1] [3]; The Opening of the 40 Man Minstrel Show [1] [2]; Miss Jemima Walks By [1] [5]

Notes Bing and a chorus also sing "Swing Low Sweet Chariot" and "The Last Rose of Summer." There is also a vocal of "Dixie" by Dan Emmett. [1] Used instrumentally only. [2] This was based on the song titled "Miss Jemima Walks By" and was recorded. [3] Recorded and published. [4] Published though not used. [5] Later used in THE GIRL RUSH (1955). [6] Also used in ROAD TO UTOPIA and TAKE IT BIG.

1445 ✦ DIXIE JAMBOREE
PRC, 1944

Composer(s) Breen, Michael
Lyricist(s) Neuman, Sam

Producer(s) Schwarz, Jack
Director(s) Cabanne, Christy
Screenwriter(s) Neuman, Sam

Cast Langford, Frances; Kibbee, Guy; Talbot, Lyle; The Ben Carter Negro Choir; D'Orsay, Fifi; Quillan, Eddie

Song(s) Dixie Show Boat; (You Ain't Right with the Lord) Repent Brother Repent; If It's a Dream; No, No, No!

Notes Hirschhorn also lists the song "Big Stuff," though it's not on the cue sheet.

1446 ✦ DIXIELAND JAMBOREE
Warner Brothers, 1945

Song(s) I Don't Know Why You Feel This Way (C/L: Reed, Leonard); To Have You To Hold You (C: Revel, Harry; L: Gordon, Mack)

Notes Short subject.

1447 ✦ DIZZY DAMES
Liberty, 1935

Producer(s) Hoffman, M.H.
Director(s) Nigh, William
Screenwriter(s) Waggner, George
Source(s) (story) Wodehouse, P.G.

Cast Rambeau, Marjorie; Miles, Lillian; McKinney, Florine; Gray, Lawrence; Courtney, Inez; Warburton, John; Churchill, Berton; Knight, Fuzzy; Kelly, Kitty

Song(s) Martinique (C: Alter, Louis; L: Swanstrom, Arthur; Waggner, George); Love Is the Thing (C: Moret, Neil; L: Tobias, Harry); I Was Taken By Storm (C: Alter, Louis; L: Heyman, Edward); Let's Be Frivolous (C: Jackson, Howard; L: Waggner, George)

Notes No cue sheet available.

1448 ✦ D.O.A.
Disney, 1988

Musical Score Janek, Chaz

Producer(s) Sander, Ian; Ziskin, Laura
Director(s) Morton, Rocky; Jankel, Annabel
Screenwriter(s) Pogue, Charles Edward

Cast Quaid, Dennis; Ryan, Meg; Rampling, Charlotte; Stern, Daniel; Kaczmarek, Jane; Neame, Christopher; Knepper, Rob

Song(s) Too Much Sex, Not Enough Affection (C/L: MacDonald, Pat)

Notes No cue sheet available. A remake of D.O.A.

1449 ✦ DOC SAVAGE: OR THE MAN OF BRONZE
Warner Brothers, 1975

Musical Score De Vol, Frank

Producer(s) Pal, George
Director(s) Anderson, Michael
Screenwriter(s) Morhaim, Joseph; Pal, George
Source(s) *Doc Savage* (novel) Robeson, Kenneth

Cast Ely, Ron; Hensley, Pamela; Wexler, Paul G.; Zwerling, Darrell; Miller, Michael

Song(s) Doc Savage March [1] (C: Sousa, John Philip; De Vol, Frank; L: Black, Don)

Notes [1] Music based on Sousa's march "The Thunderer."

1450 ✦ THE DOCTOR AND THE DEVILS
Twentieth Century–Fox, 1985

Musical Score Morris, John

Producer(s) Sanger, Jonathan
Director(s) Francis, Freddie
Screenwriter(s) Harwood, Ronald

Cast Dalton, Timothy; Pryce, Jonathan; Twiggy; Sands, Julian; Rea, Stephen; Logan, Phyllis; McKenna, T.P.; Phillips, Sian

Song(s) Whisper and I Shall Hear (C: Morris, John; L: Newcombe, C. Hubi)

Notes This is based on an original screenplay by Dylan Thomas.

1451 ✦ DOCTOR AT SEA
Republic, 1955

Musical Score Montgomery, Bruce

Producer(s) Box, Betty E.
Director(s) Thomas, Ralph
Screenwriter(s) Phipps, Nicholas; Davies, Jack

Cast Bogarde, Dirk; Bardot, Brigitte; De Banzie, Brenda; Justice, James Robertson; Denham, Maurice; Purcell, Noel

Song(s) Je Ne Sais Pas (C/L: Gregg, Hubert)

1452 ✦ DR. BROADWAY
Paramount, 1942

Producer(s) Siegel, Sol C.
Director(s) Mann, Anthony
Screenwriter(s) Arthur, Art

Cast Carey, Macdonald; Phillips, Jean; Naish, J. Carrol

Song(s) Dolores [1] (C: Alter, Louis; L: Loesser, Frank)

Notes [1] Also in LAS VEGAS NIGHTS and SAIGON.

1453 ✦ DR. DETROIT
Universal, 1983

Musical Score Schifrin, Lalo

Producer(s) Weiss, Robert K.
Director(s) Pressman, Michael
Screenwriter(s) Gottlieb, Carl; Boris, Robert; Friedman, Bruce Jay

Cast Aykroyd, Dan; Hesseman, Howard; Dixon, Donna; Lei, Lydia; Carter, T.K.; Drescher, Fran; Headly, Glenne; Furth, George; Martin, Nan; Duggan, Andrew

Song(s) Theme from Dr. Detroit (C/L: Mothersbaugh, Mark; Casale, Gerald V.); Superfreak (C/L: James, Rick; Miller, A.); Luv-Luv (C/L: Mothersbaugh, M.; Casale, Gerald V.); Hold Him (C/L: Brooks, Pattie; Newborn, Ira); The Best Time of My Life (C/L: Schifrin, Lalo); You Are the One (C: Schifrin, Lalo; L: Ballard, Glen); Bustin' Loose (C/L: Brown, C.); Get Up Offa That Thing (C/L: Brown, James); King of Soul (C/L: Newborn, Ira); Get It On and Have a Party (C/L: Brooks, Pattie; Newborn, Ira)

1454 ✦ DOCTOR DOLITTLE
Twentieth Century–Fox, 1967

Musical Score Bricusse, Leslie
Composer(s) Bricusse, Leslie
Lyricist(s) Bricusse, Leslie
Choreographer(s) Ross, Herbert

Producer(s) Jacobs, Arthur P.
Director(s) Fleischer, Richard
Screenwriter(s) Bricusse, Leslie
Source(s) Doctor Dolittle series (novels) Lofting, Hugh

Cast Harrison, Rex; Eggar, Samantha [2]; Newley, Anthony; Attenborough, Richard; Bull, Peter; Holder, Geoffrey; Nelson, Portia; Varden, Norma

Song(s) My Friend the Doctor; The Vegetarian; Talk to the Animals; At the Crossroads; I've Never Seen Anything Like It; Beautiful Things; When I Look In

Your Eyes; Like Animals; After Today; Fabulous Places; I Think I Like You; Doctor Dolittle; Something In Your Smile [1]; Where Are the Words [1]; A Man Can Do Anything [3]; Children Want to Know Why [3]; If I Could Be Anyone at All [3]; I Don't Want to Be King [3]; A World Full of Miracles [3]; Animalitarians [3] (C/L: Flanders, Michael; Swann, Donald); I Won't Be a King [3] (C/L: Flanders, Michael; Swann, Donald); A Total Vegetarian [3] (C/L: Flanders, Michael; Swann, Donald); Goodbye to Sophie! [3] (C/L: Flanders, Michael; Swann, Donald); How Would You Like It [3]; Maybe I Was Wrong [3]; I'll Fight a Lion [3]; The Punga Leaf [3]; Better Than You Know Yourself [3]

Notes Sidney Poitier was originally to be in the film and Gilbert Price was hired to dub his singing. [1] Filmed but not used. [2] Dubbed by Diana Lee. Eggar's lead-in dialogue (to the songs) was used on the sound track of the film. However, Lee re-recorded that dialogue so that Eggar does not appear at all on the soundtrack album. [3] Not used.

1455 ✦ DR. GOLDFOOT AND THE BIKINI MACHINE
American International, 1965

Musical Score Baxter, Les

Producer(s) Nicholson, James H.; Arkoff, Samuel Z.
Director(s) Taurog, Norman
Screenwriter(s) Ullman, Elwood

Cast Price, Vincent; Avalon, Frankie; Hickman, Dwayne; Hart, Susan; Mullaney, Jack; Clark, Fred

Song(s) Dr. Goldfoot and the Bikini Machine (C/L: Hemric, Guy; Styner, Jerry)

Notes No cue sheet available.

1456 ✦ DR. GOLDFOOT AND THE GIRL BOMBS
American International, 1966

Musical Score Baxter, Les

Producer(s) Lucisano, Fulvio
Director(s) Bava, Mario
Screenwriter(s) Heyward, Louis M.; Kaufman, Robert

Cast Price, Vincent; Fabian; Franco and Ciccio; Antonelli, Laura

Song(s) Dr. Goldfoot and the Girl Bombs (C/L: Hemric, Guy; Styner, Jerry)

Notes No cue sheet available.

1457 ✦ DR. JEKYLL AND MR. HYDE
Paramount, 1932

Director(s) Mamoulian, Rouben
Screenwriter(s) Hoffenstein, Samuel; Heath, Percy

Source(s) *Dr. Jekyll and Mr. Hyde* (novel) Stevenson, Robert Louis

Cast Hopkins, Miriam; March, Fredric; Hobart, Rose; Herbert, Holmes; Hobbes, Halliwell

Song(s) Champagne Charley Was His Name [1] (C: Lee, Alfred; L: Whymark, H.J.)

Notes [1] Character sings lyric "Champagne Ivy" but song is the same.

1458 ✦ DOCTOR RHYTHM
Paramount, 1938

Composer(s) Monaco, James V.
Lyricist(s) Burke, Johnny
Choreographer(s) Crosby, Jack

Producer(s) Cohen, Emanuel
Director(s) Tuttle, Frank
Screenwriter(s) Swerling, Jo [3]; Connell, Richard; Titheridge, Dion
Source(s) "The Badge of Policeman O'Roon" (short story) Henry, O.

Cast Crosby, Bing; Lillie, Beatrice; Holloway, Sterling; Carlisle; Mary; Devine, Andy; Armstrong, Louis; Crews, Laura Hope; Keating, Fred; Pangborn, Franklin; Davis, Rufe

Song(s) P.S. Forty-Three; My Heart Is Taking Lessons; Rhythm [1] (C: Rodgers, Richard; L: Hart, Lorenz); On the Sentimental Side; Only a Gypsy Knows; The Trumpet Player's Lament [2]; This Is My Night to Dream [2]; Doctor Rhythm [2]; Zing, Zing Go the Tambourines [2]

Notes The picture was originally called THE BADGE OF POLICEMAN O'ROON. [1] Also known as "There's Rhythm in That Heart of Mine" and in the Broadway show THE SHOW IS ON. [2] Not used. [3] Titheridge wrote additional comedy scenes.

Comments from a telegram re: title of movie. "Agree title Swing Along Ladies probably inadvisable...Feel title At Your Service too colorless and flat. Suggest what I think exceptionally good title for this picture from every angle, namely Doctor Rhythm. Reams of publicity printed about Crosby being made Doctor of Music by Gonzaga University, Crosby's last night's radio program from Gonzaga devoted almost entirely to Bing's Doctor Degree and thousands of future references in print over radio, etc. that will undoubtedly be made to Bing as doctor, combined with fact he plays role of doctor in O'Roon makes this title in my opinion a natural. I like Doctor Rhythm better than any variations of same idea such as Doctor of Rhythm, Doctor of Music, etc. because first named title is shorter, snappier, gayer, less heavy and indicates more clearly musical comedy than others. I would grab this title quick, use it for picture and for song in picture. You can imagine Doctor Crosby singing song called Doctor Rhythm in which he prescribes a dash of swing for a heartache, a soothing waltz for the blues and warns that a big apple a day won't keep this doctor away."

A later letter to New York: "Complication on Doctor Rhythm title arises in fact that president of Gonzaga University has protested to Crosby against use of title, evidently due to repercussion against giving degree and fact that event was received as humorous and not serious, was especially heard at Town Hall program which caricatured whole event including the president. Crosby not disposed to combat the University in their feeling concerning title. Therefore, not safe set it for this picture. Everybody here believes Come Along Lady best substitute since it can carry advertising pictorially with Crosby as cop expostulating with either Lillie or Mary Carlisle."

1459 ✦ DOCTORS DON'T TELL
Republic, 1941

Producer(s) Cohen, Albert J.
Director(s) Tourneur, Jacques
Screenwriter(s) Reeves, Theodore; Dawn, Isabel

Cast Beal, John; Rice, Florence; Norris, Edward; Sutton, Grady; Shirley, Bill; Fowley, Douglas; Bond, Ward

Song(s) Lilly and Billy (C: Styne, Jule; L: Meyer, Sol); Take My Heart (C: Styne, Jule; L: Cherkose, Eddie)

1460 ✦ DOCTORS' WIVES
Fox, 1931

Director(s) Borzage, Frank
Screenwriter(s) Watkins, Maurine

Cast Baxter, Warner; Bennett, Joan; Loftus, Cecilia; Warren, Ruth

Song(s) Tiddly-Umpty-Aye (C/L: Loftus, Cecilia)

1461 ✦ DR. TERROR'S HOUSE OF HORRORS
Paramount, 1965

Musical Score Lynch, Kenny

Producer(s) Subotsky, Milton; Rosenberg, Max J.
Director(s) Francis, Freddie
Screenwriter(s) Subotsky, Milton

Cast Cushing, Peter; Lee, Christopher; Sutherland, Donald; Howells, Ursula; Lee, Bernard; Adrian, Max

Song(s) Everybody's Got Love (C/L: Lynch, Kenny); Give Me Love (C/L: Lynch, Kenny)

1462 ✦ DOCTOR, YOU'VE GOT TO BE KIDDING!
Metro–Goldwyn–Mayer, 1966

Musical Score Hopkins, Kenyon
Composer(s) Vance, Paul

Lyricist(s) Pockriss, Lee
Choreographer(s) Barton, Earl

Producer(s) Laurence, Douglas
Director(s) Tewksbury, Peter
Screenwriter(s) Shuken, Phillip
Source(s) *Three for a Wedding* (novel) Mahan, Pette Wheat

Cast Dee, Sandra [1]; Hamilton, George; Holm, Celeste; Bixby, Bill; Kallman, Dick; Sahl, Mort; Jenkins, Allen; Hickman, Dwayne

Song(s) Walk Tall Like a Man; I Haven't Got Anything Better to Do; Little Girl (C/L: Birmingham, Rodney Lee); Talkin' Law [2] (C: Hopkins, Kenyon; L: Wasserman, Dale)

Notes Previously titled THREE FOR A WEDDING and THIS WAY OUT PLEASE. There are also vocals of "Be My Love" by Nicholas Brodszky and Sammy Cahn; "All I Do Is Dream of You" by Arthur Freed and Nacio Herb Brown; "Everything I Have Is Yours" by Burton Lane and Harold Adamson and "The Trolley Song" by Ralph Blane and Hugh Martin. [1] Dubbed by Marie Greene. [2] Also in MISTER BUDDWING.

1463 ✦ DR. ZHIVAGO
Metro–Goldwyn–Mayer, 1966

Musical Score Jarre, Maurice

Producer(s) Ponti, Carlo
Director(s) Lean, David
Screenwriter(s) Bolt, Robert
Source(s) *Dr. Zhivago* (novel) Pasternak, Boris

Cast Chaplin, Geraldine; Christie, Julie; Courtenay, Tom; Guinness, Alec; McKenna, Siobhan; Richardson, Ralph; Sharif, Omar; Steiger, Rod; Tushingham, Rita; Kinski, Klaus

Song(s) Somewhere My Love [1] (C: Jarre, Maurice; L: Webster, Paul Francis)

Notes [1] Lyric added for exploitation only. Titled "Lara's Theme," as an instrumental.

1464 ✦ DODGE CITY TRAIL
Columbia, 1937

Composer(s) Stept, Sam H.
Lyricist(s) Washington, Ned

Director(s) Coleman Jr., C.C.
Screenwriter(s) Shumate, Harold

Cast Starrett, Charles; Grayson, Donald; Weldon, Marion; Hicks, Russell

Song(s) Lonesome River; Out in the Cow Country; Pancho's Widow; Strike While the Iron Is Hot

1465 ✦ **DOG GONE SOUTH**
Warner Brothers, 1950

Musical Score Stalling, Carl

Director(s) Jones, Chuck

Cast Dog, Charlie

Song(s) Southern Discomfort (C/L: Maltese, Michael)

Notes Merrie Melodie cartoon.

1466 ✦ **DOGPOUND SHUFFLE**
Paramount, 1975

Musical Score White, David
Composer(s) White, David
Lyricist(s) Bloom, Jeffrey

Producer(s) Bloom, Jeffrey
Director(s) Bloom, Jeffrey
Screenwriter(s) Bloom, Jeffrey

Cast Moody, Ron; Soul, David; McMyler, Pamela; Stricklyn, Ray; Sutton, Raymond; Scruffy

Song(s) If I'm Going to See You Tomorrow [1]; Instant Cleanser [2]

Notes Also called SPOT. The film was held in the can then tried out in Buffalo under the name SPOT in 1975. As late as 1976 Peter Hammond, writing to the *Hollywood Reporter*, bemoaned the fact that the film had still not been released. [1] Sung on soundtrack by Lynne Marta. [2] Sung on soundtrack by David White.

1467 ✦ **DOGS IN SPACE**
Skouras, 1987

Producer(s) Rowe, Glenys
Director(s) Lowenstein, Richard
Screenwriter(s) Lowenstein, Richard

Cast Hutchence, Michael; Post, Saskia; Needles, Nique; Bond, Deanna

Song(s) Rooms for the Memory (C/L: Olsen, Ollie); Dogs in Space (C/L: Sejavka, Sam; Lewis, Mike); Winlose (C/L: Olsen, Ollie)

Notes No cue sheet available.

1468 ✦ **DOIN' THEIR BIT**
Metro–Goldwyn–Mayer, 1942

Musical Score Hayton, Lennie
Choreographer(s) Murray, Bud

Director(s) Glazer, Herbert

Cast Our Gang [1]

Song(s) The Flag of Freedom (C: Hayton, Lennie; L: Freed, Ralph)

Notes Short subject. There is also a vocal of "I Love a Man in Uniform" by James V. Monaco, Billy Rose and Ballard Macdonald. [1] Including Spanky and Froggy.

1469 ✦ **DOIN' TIME**
Warner Brothers, 1985

Musical Score Fox, Charles

Director(s) Mendeluk, George

Cast Altman, Jeff; Young, Dey; Mulligan, Richard; Vernon, John; Landers, Judy

Song(s) That's the Way It's Done (C/L: Lover, Sam; Innis, Dave); All Fucked Up (C/L: Zwang, Ron; Wilcox, Pete); Breakin' Out (C/L: Carl, Max; Kastner, Andrew); Shoot for the Top [1] (C/L: Howell, Kurt; Maslin, Harry); Big House (C/L: Zwang, Ron; Wilcox, Pete)

Notes [1] Also in POLICE ACADEMY IV: CITIZENS ON PATROL.

1470 ✦ **$**
Columbia, 1971

Musical Score Jones, Quincy
Composer(s) Jones, Quincy
Lyricist(s) Jones, Quincy

Producer(s) Frankovich, M.J.
Director(s) Brooks, Richard
Screenwriter(s) Brooks, Richard

Cast Beatty, Warren; Hawn, Goldie; Frobe, Gert; Webber, Robert; Brady, Scott

Song(s) Money Is; Do It—To It

1471 ✦ **DOLL FACE**
Twentieth Century–Fox, 1945

Composer(s) McHugh, Jimmy
Lyricist(s) Adamson, Harold
Choreographer(s) Williams, Kenny

Producer(s) Foy, Bryan
Director(s) Seiler, Lewis
Screenwriter(s) Praskins, Leonard
Source(s) (play) Hovick, Louise [3]

Cast Blaine, Vivian; O'Keefe, Dennis; Como, Perry; Miranda, Carmen; Stewart, Martha; Dunn, Michael; Hadley, Reed; Prager, Stanley

Song(s) Somebody's Walkin' in My Dreams; Red, Hot and Beautiful; 'Bout Eighty Miles Outside of Atlanta [2]; The Parisian Trot [1] (C: Newman, Lionel); Here Comes Heaven Again; Dig You Later (A-Hubba-Hubba-Hubba); Chico Chico (From Porto Rico); Always True to the Navy [4]; Wouldn't It Be Nice? [5]

Notes Titled COME BACK TO ME in Great Britain. [1] Previously used in THE LODGER. [2] Written for

SOMETHING FOR THE BOYS. Special lyrics by Nick Castle and Charles Henderson. [3] Gypsy Rose Lee. [4] Cut from final print. [5] Sheet music only.

1472 ✦ THE DOLL SHOP
Metro–Goldwyn–Mayer, 1929

Composer(s) Edwards, Gus
Lyricist(s) Bryan, Vincent; Snell, Dave [1]

Director(s) Lee, Sammy

Cast Belmore, Lionel; Dees, Buster; Kahn, Cy; Murray, Joyce

Song(s) Wake Up; Broken Hearted Dolly (L: Bryan, Vincent); Hot Chocolate (C: Alter, Louis; L: Trent, Jo); Tin Soldiers on Parade

Notes Short subject. [1] The lyric credits are not certain. Snell usually wrote music. However, Edwards is credited with music on cue sheets and Byran and Snell are listed also under "Songs By" on the credits. Therefore, I assumed they wrote the lyrics to Edwards' melodies.

1473 ✦ THE DOLLY SISTERS
Twentieth Century–Fox, 1945

Composer(s) Monaco, James V.
Lyricist(s) Gordon, Mack
Choreographer(s) Felix, Seymour

Producer(s) Jessel, George
Director(s) Cummings, Irving
Screenwriter(s) Larkin, John; Spitzer, Marian

Cast Grable, Betty; Payne, John; Haver, June; Sakall, S.Z.; Gardiner, Reginald; Latimore, Frank; Marshall, Trudy; Sheldon, Gene; Rumann, Sig; Thomas, Evan

Song(s) I Can't Begin to Tell You; We Have Been Around (C: Henderson, Charles); Don't Be Too Old Fashioned (Old Fashioned Girl) (C: Henderson, Charles); Powder, Lipstick and Rouge [1] (C: Revel, Harry)

Notes Other vocals include: "The Vamp" by Byron Gay; "Give Me the Moonlight, Give Me the Girl" by Alfred Von Tilzer and Lew Brown; "Carolina in the Morning" by Walter Donaldson and Gus Kahn; "I'm Always Chasing Rainbows" by Harry Carroll and Joseph McCarthy; "The Darktown Strutter's Ball" by Shelton Brooks; "Arrah Go On, I'm Gonna Go Back to Oregon" by Bert Grant, Sam M. Lewis and Joe Young; "Smiles" by Lee S. Roberts and J. Will Callahan; "Mademoiselle from Armentieres (Hinky- Dinky Parlex-vous);" "Oh! Frenchy" by Con Conrad and Sam Erlich; "Pack Up Your Troubles in Your Old Kit Bag and Smile, Smile, Smile" by Felix Powell and George Asaf; "On the Mississippi" by Harry Carroll and Buddy Fields and "The Sidewalks of New York" by Charles B. Lawlor and

James W. Blake. [1] Not used in COLLEGE RHYTHM (Paramount).

1474 ✦ THE DOMINO PRINCIPLE
Avco Embassy, 1977

Musical Score Goldenberg, Billy

Producer(s) Kramer, Stanley
Director(s) Kramer, Stanley
Screenwriter(s) Kennedy, Adam
Source(s) (novel) Kennedy, Adam

Cast Hackman, Gene; Bergen, Candice; Wallach, Eli; Widmark, Richard; Rooney, Mickey; Albert, Edward; Swofford, Ken; Patterson, Neva; Novello, Jay

Song(s) Some Day Soon (C: Goldenberg, Billy; L: Shannon, Harry)

Notes No cue sheet available.

1475 ✦ DONALD AND THE WHEEL
Disney, 1961

Musical Score Baker, Buddy
Composer(s) Leven, Mel
Lyricist(s) Leven, Mel

Director(s) Luske, Hamilton
Screenwriter(s) Berg, Bill

Cast Duck, Donald

Song(s) Principle of the Thing; The Wheel; Wheels of Progress; A Small Canoe [1] (C: Baker, Buddy; L: Jackman, Bob)

Notes Cartoon short. [1] Used instrumentally only.

1476 ✦ DONALD DUCK CARTOONS
Disney, 1947 - present

Cast Duck, Donald

Song(s) Donald Duck Song (C/L: Wallace, Oliver); Happy Happy Birthday to You (C/L: Silversher, Michael; Silversher, Patty); Der Fuehrer's Face [1] (C/L: Wallace, Oliver)

Notes Cartoon shorts. [1] From the Short DER FUHRER'S FACE (1942), also known as DONALD DUCK IN NUTZI LAND.

1477 ✦ DONALD GETS DRAFTED
Disney, 1941

Musical Score Smith, Paul J.

Cast Duck, Donald

Song(s) The Army's Not the Army Anymore [1] (C: Harline, Leigh; L: Quenzer, Arthur)

Notes Cartoon short. No credit sheet available. [1] Also used in THE VANISHING PRIVATE.

1478 ◆ DONALD IN MATHMAGIC LAND
Disney, 1959

Musical Score Baker, Buddy

Screenwriter(s) Banta, Milt; Berg, Bill; Haber, Dr. Heinz

Cast Duck, Donald

Song(s) Wish I May, Wish I Might (C: Baker, Buddy; L: Jackman, Bob); College March (Inst.) (C: Baker, Buddy)

Notes Animated cartoon.

1479 ◆ DONALD'S DIARY
Disney, 1953

Musical Score Plumb, Ed

Director(s) Kinney, Jack
Screenwriter(s) Mack, Brick; Kinney, Dick

Cast Duck, Donald

Song(s) Dreamboat (C: Plumb, Ed; L: Unknown)

Notes Cartoon short.

1480 ◆ DONALD'S LUCKY DAY
Disney, 1939

Musical Score Wallace, Oliver

Cast Duck, Donald

Song(s) Ducky's Lucky Day (C/L: Wallace, Oliver)

Notes Cartoon short. No credit sheet available.

1481 ◆ THE DON IS DEAD
Universal, 1973

Musical Score Goldsmith, Jerry

Producer(s) Wallis, Hal B.
Director(s) Fleischer, Richard
Screenwriter(s) Albert, Marvin H.
Source(s) (novel) Quarry, Nick

Cast Forrest, Frederic; Forster, Robert; Quinn, Anthony; Cioffi, Charles; Meredith, Jo Anne; Zorich, Louis

Song(s) Our Last Night (C: Goldsmith, Jerry; L: Goldsmith, Carol)

1482 ◆ DO NOT DISTURB
Twentieth Century–Fox, 1965

Producer(s) Rosenberg, Aaron; Melcher, Martin
Director(s) Levy, Ralph
Screenwriter(s) Rosen, Milton; Breen, Richard L.

Cast Day, Doris; Taylor, Rod; Baddeley, Hermione; Fantoni, Sergio; Gardiner, Reginald; Romanoff, Michael; McGiveney, Maura; Askin, Leon

Song(s) Do Not Disturb (C: Raleigh, Ben; L: Barkan, Mark); Au-Revoir Is Goodbye with a Smile [1] (C: Garson, Mort; L: Hilliard, Bob)

Notes [1] Mort Greene is credited on cue sheets.

1483 ◆ DONOVAN'S REEF
Paramount, 1963

Producer(s) Ford, John
Director(s) Ford, John
Screenwriter(s) Nugent, Frank; Grant, Edward

Cast Wayne, John; Marvin, Lee; Mazurki, Mike; Warden, Jack; Allan, Elizabeth; Lamour, Dorothy; Romero, Cesar

Song(s) The First Night of the Full Moon [1] (C: Perry, Alfred Kealoha; L: David, Hal)

Notes [1] Not used in film.

1484 ◆ DON'T BOTHER TO KNOCK
Twentieth Century–Fox, 1952

Producer(s) Blaustein, Julian
Director(s) Baker, Roy
Screenwriter(s) Taradash, Daniel
Source(s) *Mischief* (novel) Armstrong, Charlotte

Cast Widmark, Richard; Monroe, Marilyn; Bancroft, Anne; Corcoran, Donna; Cagney, Jeanne; Tuttle, Lurene; Cook Jr., Elisha; Backus, Jim; Felton, Verna; Beddoe, Don

Song(s) A Rollin' Stone (C: Newman, Lionel; L: Darby, Ken; Russell, Bob)

Notes "How About You" by Burton Lane and Ralph Freed; "Manhattan" by Richard Rodgers and Lorenz Hart; "There's a Lull in My Life" by Harry Revel and Mack Gordon (also in WAKE UP AND LIVE); "How Blue the Night" by Jimmy McHugh and Harold Adamson (also in FOUR JILLS IN A JEEP) and "Chattanooga Choo Choo" by Harry Warren and Mack Gordon (also in SUN VALLEY SERENADE) are also given vocal performances.

1485 ◆ DON'T CRY IT'S ONLY THUNDER
Sanrio, 1982

Musical Score Jarre, Maurice

Producer(s) deFaria, Walt
Director(s) Werner, Peter
Screenwriter(s) Hensler, Paul

Cast Christopher, Dennis; Saint James, Susan; Brown, Roger Aaron; Englund, Robert; Whitmore Jr., James

Song(s) Questions and Answers (C: Jarre, Maurice; L: Gimbel, Norman)

Notes No cue sheet available.

1486 ✦ DON'T FENCE ME IN
Republic, 1945

Choreographer(s) Ceballos, Larry

Producer(s) Brown, Donald H.
Director(s) English, John
Screenwriter(s) Butler, John K.; McGowan, Dorrell; McGowan, Stuart

Cast Rogers, Roy; Trigger; Hayes, George "Gabby"; Evans, Dale; Livingston, Robert; Olsen, Moroni; Lawrence, Marc; Gleason, Lucille; Tombes, Andrew; Harvey, Paul

Song(s) Don't Fence Me In [2] (C/L: Porter, Cole); A Kiss Goodnight (C/L: Victor, Floyd; Herman, R.N.; Slack, Freddie); Choo Choo Polka (C/L: Manners, Zeke; Shore, Mike); My Little Buckaroo [4] (C: Jerome, M.K.; L: Scholl, Jack); The Last Round-Up [3] (C/L: Hill, Billy); Along the Navajo Trail [1] (C/L: Markes, Larry; Charles, Dick; Delange, Eddie); Tumbling Tumbleweeds [4] (C/L: Nolan, Bob)

Notes [1] Also in Columbia's THE BLAZING SUN and Republic's ALONG THE NAVAJO TRAIL. It was originally titled "Prairie Parade" in 1942 when written by Markes and Charles. That song was featured in LAUGH YOUR BLUES AWAY. [2] Also in HOLLYWOOD CANTEEN (Warner Brothers) and written for ADIOS ARGENTINA (Fox). [3] Also in ONE HOUR LATE (Paramount), SINGING HILL, STAND UP AND CHEER (Fox) and THE LAST ROUNDUP (Columbia). [4] Also in BROTHER ORCHID, THE CHEROKEE STRIP, SONGS OF THE RANGE and WEST OF THE ROCKIES, all Warner films. [4] Also in RHYTHM ROUND-UP (Columbia); IN OLD MONTEREY; SILVER SPURS; TUMBLING TUMBLEWEEDS and HOLLYWOOD CANTEEN (Warner).

1487 ✦ DON'T GET PERSONAL
Universal, 1942

Musical Score Skinner, Frank
Composer(s) Berens, Norman
Lyricist(s) Brooks, Jack

Producer(s) Goldsmith, Ken
Director(s) Lamont, Charles
Screenwriter(s) Waggner, George

Cast Herbert, Hugh; Auer, Mischa; Frazee, Jane; Gwynne, Anne; Paige, Robert; Holloway, Sterling

Song(s) It Doesn't Make Sense; Every Time a Moment Goes By; Now What Do We Do?

1488 ✦ DON'T GO IN THE HOUSE
Film Ventures, 1980

Producer(s) Hammill, Ellen
Director(s) Ellison, Joseph

Screenwriter(s) Ellison, Joseph; Hammill, Ellen; Masefield, Joseph R.

Cast Grimaldi, Dan; Bonet, Charlie; Ricci, Bill; Osth, Robert

Song(s) Dancin' Close to You (C/L: Daryll, Ted); Straight Ahead (C/L: Daryll, Ted); Late Night Surrender (C/L: Heller, Bill); Boogie Lightning (C/L: Heller, Bill)

Notes No cue sheet available.

1489 ✦ DON'T GO NEAR THE WATER
Metro–Goldwyn–Mayer, 1957

Musical Score Kaper, Bronislau

Producer(s) Weingarten, Lawrence
Director(s) Walters, Charles
Screenwriter(s) Kingsley, Dorothy; Wells, George
Source(s) Don't Go Near the Water (novel) Brinkley, William

Cast Ford, Glenn; Scala, Gia; Holliman, Earl; Francis, Anne; Wynn, Keenan; Clark, Fred; Gabor, Eva; Tamblyn, Russ; Richards, Jeff; Smith, Howard; Shaughnessy, Mickey; Brent, Romney; Wickes, Mary; Nichols, Robert

Song(s) Don't Go Near the Water (C: Kaper, Bronislau; L: Cahn, Sammy); Melora [1] (C: Kaper, Bronislau; L: Webster, Paul Francis)

Notes [1] Sheet music only.

1490 ✦ DON'T JUST STAND THERE
Universal, 1972

Musical Score Perito, Nick

Producer(s) Margulies, Stan
Director(s) Winston, Ron
Screenwriter(s) Williams, Charles
Source(s) The Wrong Venus (novel) Williams, Charles

Cast Wagner, Robert; Johns, Glynis; Rhoades, Barbara; Korman, Harvey; Beck, Vincent

Song(s) Don't Just Stand There (C: Perito, Nick; L: Charles, Ray)

1491 ✦ DON'T KNOCK THE ROCK
Columbia, 1956

Choreographer(s) Barton, Earl

Producer(s) Katzman, Sam
Director(s) Sears, Fred F.
Screenwriter(s) Kent, Robert E.; Gordon, James B.; Kline, Benjamin

Cast Haley, Bill; Dale, Alan; Freed, Alan; The Treniers; Little Richard; Dave Appell and His Applejacks; Hardy, Patricia

Song(s)   Apple Jack (C/L: Appell, Dave; Appell, Ed; Joyce, Norman); Country Dance (C/L: Jones, Ollie); Don't Knock the Rock (C: Karger, Fred; L: Kent, Robert E.); Hook, Line and Sinker (C/L: Haley, Bill; Khoury, Ed; Bonner, Ronnie); Out of the Bushes (C/L: Haley, Bill; Khoury, Ed; Bonner, Ronnie); Your Love Is My Love (C/L: Edwards, Francis); You're Just Right (C/L: Attili, G.D.; de Jesus, G.); Goofin' Around (C/L: Beecher, F.; Grande, J.); Rip It Up (C/L: Blackwell, Robert; Marascalco, John); Rockin' on Sunday Night (C/L: Holtzman, M.; Ellis, R.); Gonna Run Not Walk That Aisle (C/L: Attili, G.D.; de Jesus, G.); Long Tall Sally (C/L: de Jesus, G.; Johnson, E.); Tutti Frutti [1] (C/L: Penniman, Richard; La Bostrie, Dorothy; Lubin, Joe)

Notes   No cue sheet available. No songs written for this film. Vocals include: "Rock Around the Clock;" "Hook, Line & Sinker;" "Tutti Frutti;" "Long Tall Sally."

1492 ◆ DON'T LOOK NOW
Paramount, 1973

Producer(s)   Katz, Peter
Director(s)   Roeg, Nicolas
Screenwriter(s)   Scott, Allan; Bryant, Chris
Source(s)   "Don't Look Now" (story) du Maurier, Daphne

Cast   Sutherland, Donald; Christie, Julie; Serato, Massimo; Mason, Hilary; Matania, Cielia

Song(s)   Salvatore (C/L: Giannantonio, Leo Di); Lu Primo Amore (C/L: Gaber, Giorgio; Simonetta, Umberto); Per Amore (C/L: Donaggio, Pino)

1493 ◆ DON'T MAKE WAVES
Metro–Goldwyn–Mayer, 1967

Musical Score   Mizzy, Vic

Producer(s)   Calley, John; Ransohoff, Martin
Director(s)   Mackendrick, Alexander
Screenwriter(s)   Wallach, Ira; Kirgo, George
Source(s)   *Muscle Beach* (novel) Wallach, Ira

Cast   Curtis, Tony; Cardinale, Claudia; Tate, Sharon; Webber, Robert; Barnes, Joanna; Draper, David; London, Marc; Bergen, Edgar; Sahl, Mort

Song(s)   Don't Make Waves (C/L: McGuinn, Jim; Hillman, Chris)

1494 ◆ DON'T RAISE THE BRIDGE, LOWER THE RIVER
Columbia, 1968

Musical Score   Whitaker, David

Producer(s)   Shenson, Walter
Director(s)   Paris, Jerry
Screenwriter(s)   Wilk, Max

Cast   Lewis, Jerry; Pearce, Jacqueline; Cribbins, Barnard; Routledge, Patricia; Parsons, Nicholas; Terry-Thomas

Song(s)   Don't Raise the Bridge, Lower the River (C: Whitaker, David; L: Shaper, Hal)

Notes   No cue sheet available.

1495 ◆ DON WINSLOW OF THE COAST GUARD
Universal, 1943

Musical Score   Skinner, Frank; Rosen, Milton

Director(s)   Taylor, Ray; Beebe, Ford
Source(s)   (comic strip) Martinek, Frank V.

Cast   Terry, Don; Sande, Walter; Boteler, Wade; Scott, Paul; Litel, John; Leeds, Peter; Nagel, Anne; Dodd, Claire; Lackteen, Frank

Song(s)   Full Speed with Guns Up (C: Rosen, Milton; L: Carter, Everett)

Notes   This is a serial.

1496 ◆ DO THE RIGHT THING
Universal, 1989

Musical Score   Lee, Bill

Producer(s)   Lee, Spike
Director(s)   Lee, Spike
Screenwriter(s)   Lee, Spike

Cast   Aiello, Danny; Davis, Ossie; Dee, Ruby; Edson, Richard; Esposito, Giancarlo; Lee, Spike; Nunn, Bill; Turturro, John; Savage, John; Harris, Robin; Benjamin, Paul; Faison, Frankie; Perez, Rosie

Song(s)   Fight the Power (C/L: Ridenhour, Carlton; Shocklee, Hank; Sadler, Eric; Shocklee, Keith); Don't Shoot Me (C/L: Lee, Spike; Warren, Mervyn; McKnight III, Claude V.; Thomas, David); Prove to Me (C/L: Jones, Raymond; McKinney, Sami); Can't Stand the Heat (C/L: Hinds, David R.); Party Hearty (C/L: House, William "Ju Ju"; Wood, Kent); My Fantasy [1] (C/L: Riley, Teddy; Griffin, Gene); We Love (C/L: Warren, Mervyn; Kibble, Mark); Hard to Say I Love You (C/L: Jones, Raymond); Feels So Good (C/L: McKinney, Sami; Perry, Lori; O'Hara, Michael); Why Don't We Try (C/L: DeCarmine, Larry; Jones, Raymond; Morris, Vince); Never Explain Love (C/L: Block, Cathy; Jones, Raymond)

Notes   It is not known which of these were written for this film. [1] Sheet music credits Griffin and William Aquart.

1497 ◆ DOUBLE CROSSBONES
Universal, 1951

Musical Score   Skinner, Frank
Composer(s)   Shapiro, Dan; Lee, Lester

Lyricist(s) Shapiro, Dan; Lee, Lester
Choreographer(s) Belfer, Hal

Producer(s) Goldstein, Leonard
Director(s) Barton, Charles T.
Screenwriter(s) Brodney, Oscar; Grant, John

Cast O'Connor, Donald; Napier, Alan; Barrat, Robert; Bacigalupi, Louis; Emerson, Hope; Carter, Helena; Geer, Will; Emery, John; Givney, Kathryn

Song(s) Percy Had a Heart; Song of Adventure

1498 ✦ DOUBLE CROSS ROADS
Fox, 1930

Director(s) Werker, Alfred; Middleton, George
Screenwriter(s) Estabrook, Howard
Source(s) *Yonder Grow the Daisies* (novel) Lipman, William R.

Cast Lee, Lila; Love, Montagu; Ames, Robert; Sparks, Ned; Chapman, Edythe; MacFarlane, George

Song(s) Too Wonderful for Words [3] (C: Stamper, Dave; Kernell, William; L: Joseph, Edmund; Smith, Paul Gerard); Look What You've Done to Me [1] (C/L: Conrad, Con; Gottler, Archie; Mitchell, Sidney D.); (Song of) My Lonely Heart (C: Cadman, Charles Wakefield; L: Kernell, William); Show Me the Way (C/L: Kernell, William); Daisies [2] (C: Nelson, Edward G.; L: Pease, Harry); Do You Believe in Love at First Sight [4] (C: Fiorito, Ted; L: Kahn, Gus)

Notes [1] Also in WHY LEAVE HOME? and FOX MOVIETONE FOLLIES OF 1929. [2] Used as incidental music in THE BIG PARTY. Ascribed to DOUBLE CROSS ROADS, though I can find no record in files. [3] Also in WORDS AND MUSIC (1929). [4] Sheet music only.

1499 ✦ DOUBLE DEAL
International Roadshow, 1939

Composer(s) Brooks, Shelton
Lyricist(s) Brooks, Shelton

Producer(s) Merwin, Dixon R.
Director(s) Dreifuss, Arthur
Screenwriter(s) Hoerl, Arthur

Cast Hawley, Monte; LeGon, Jeni; Thompson, Eddie; O'Brien, Florence; Jackson, Freddie; Woods, Buck; Sheffield, Maceo; Miller, F.E.; Brooks, Shelton

Notes No other information available. There are songs by Peter Tinturin, Harry Tobias and Floyd Tillman.

1500 ✦ DOUBLE DYNAMITE
RKO, 1952

Musical Score Harline, Leigh
Composer(s) Styne, Jule
Lyricist(s) Cahn, Sammy

Producer(s) Cummings Jr., Irving
Director(s) Cummings, Irving
Screenwriter(s) Shavelson, Melville; Crane, Harry

Cast Russell, Jane; Marx, Groucho; Sinatra, Frank; McGuire, Don; Freeman, Howard; Paiva, Nestor

Song(s) It's Only Money; Stone Walls (C/L: Lovelace, Richard); Kisses and Tears

1501 ✦ DOUBLE OR NOTHING
Paramount, 1937

Musical Score Young, Victor
Choreographer(s) Prinz, LeRoy

Producer(s) Glazer, Benjamin
Director(s) Reed, Theodore
Screenwriter(s) Lederer, Charles; Gelsey, Erwin; Atteberry, Duke; Moffitt, John C.

Cast Raye, Martha; Crosby, Bing; Carlisle, Mary; Frawley, William; Hinds, Samuel S.; Faye, Frances; Devine, Andy; Baker, Benny

Song(s) Double or Nothing (C: Young, Victor; L: Burke, Johnny); (You Know It All) Smarty (C: Lane, Burton; L: Freed, Ralph); All You Want to Do Is Dance (C: Johnston, Arthur; L: Burke, Johnny); It's the Natural Thing to Do (C: Johnston, Arthur; L: Burke, Johnny); It's On, It's Off [3] (C: Siegel, Al; L: Coslow, Sam); The Moon Got In My Eyes (C: Johnston, Arthur; L: Burke, Johnny); Listen My Children and You Shall Hear (C: Lane, Burton; L: Freed, Ralph); After You (C: Siegel, Al; L: Coslow, Sam); I'd Like to Do Things for You [1] (C/L: Coslow, Sam); She's a Girl Scout at Heart (Park Number) [1] (C/L: Coslow, Sam); Heaven Help a Sailor on a Night Like This [1] (C: Siegel, Al; L: Coslow, Sam); Voom Voom [1] [2] (C/L: Coslow, Sam); There's April in My Heart [1] (C: Carmichael, Hoagy; L: Adams, Stanley); To the Hum of My Heart [1] (C: Carmichael, Hoagy; L: Adams, Stanley); Two of You [1] (C: Carmichael, Hoagy; L: Adams, Stanley); Between a Kiss and a Sigh [1] (C: Johnston, Arthur; L: Burke, Johnny)

Notes [1] Not used. [2] Also not used in THE BIG BROADCAST. Used in THIS WAY PLEASE. [3] Originally titled "Let's Call the Whole Thing Off."

1502 ✦ DOUBLE RHYTHM
Paramount, 1946

Composer(s) Livingston, Jay; Evans, Ray
Lyricist(s) Livingston, Jay; Evans, Ray

Producer(s) Templeton, George
Director(s) Templeton, George
Screenwriter(s) Rosenwald, Franz; Tashlin, Frank

Cast Boyce, Helen; Dixon, Lee; Higson, Jimmy; The Nilsson Twins

Song(s) The Wife of the Life of the Party (C: Livingston, Jay; Evans, Ray; Lilley, Joseph J.); Jig Time in Texas (C/L: Dixon, Lee); Have the Last Kiss on Me; Numb, Dumb and Glum; Long Long Ago [1] (C: Bayly, T.H.; L: Livingston, Jay; Evans, Ray; Bayly, T.H.)

Notes Short subject. [1] Not written for this production. Livingston and Evans added lyrics.

1503 ✦ DOUBLE TROUBLE
Metro–Goldwyn–Mayer, 1967

Musical Score Alexander, Jeff
Choreographer(s) Romero, Alex

Producer(s) Bernard, Judd; Winkler, Irwin
Director(s) Taurog, Norman
Screenwriter(s) Heims, Jo

Cast Presley, Elvis; Williams, John; Romain, Yvonne; Day, Annette; The Wiere Brothers; Rafferty, Chips

Song(s) Double Trouble (C: Pomus, Doc; L: Shuman, Mort); Baby If You'll Give Me All Your Love (C/L: Byers, Joy); Could I Fall in Love (C/L: Starr, Randy); The Long Legged Girl with the Short Dress On (C/L: McFarland, Leslie; Scott, Winfield); City by Night (C/L: Giant, Bill; Kaye, Florence; Baum, Bernie); Old MacDonald (C/L: Starr, Randy); I Love Only One Girl (C/L: Tepper, Sid; Bennett, Roy C.); There Is So Much World to See (C/L: Weisman, Ben; Wayne, Sid)

1504 ✦ DOUGHBOYS
Metro–Goldwyn–Mayer, 1930

Choreographer(s) Lee, Sammy

Director(s) Sedgwick, Edward
Screenwriter(s) Boasberg, Al; Schayer, Richard

Cast Edwards, Cliff; Eilers, Sally; Keaton, Buster; Brophy, Edward S.; Potel, Victor

Song(s) Mister Military Man (C/L: Sedgwick, Edward); Are We Going Out Tonight (C/L: Edwards, Cliff); You Never Did That Before (C: Ahlert, Fred E.; L: Turk, Roy); You Were Meant for Me [1] (C: Brown, Nacio Herb; L: Freed, Arthur); Sing (C/L: Meyer, Joseph; Johnson, Howard)

Notes Original title: THE BIG SHOT. Released internationally as FORWARD MARCH. There are also vocals of "In the Good Old Summertime" by George Evans and Ren Shields; and "Sweet Adeline" by Richard H. Gerard and Henry W. Armstrong. [1] Also in BROADWAY MELODY, SINGIN' IN THE RAIN, THE SHOW OF SHOWS, HOLLYWOOD REVUE OF 1929.

1505 ✦ DOUGHBOYS IN IRELAND
Columbia, 1943

Producer(s) Fier, Jack
Director(s) Landers, Lew
Screenwriter(s) Green, Howard J.; Brice, Monte

Cast Baker, Kenny; Donnell, Jeff; Merrick, Lynn; Bonham, Guy; Latham, Red; Carlson, Wamp; Mitchum, Robert [1]

Notes No cue sheet available. It is not known if there are any original songs in this film. Vocals include: "Mother Machree" by Rida Johnson Young, Chauncey Olcott and Ernest R. Ball; "When Irish Eyes Are Smiling" by Ball," Olcott and George Graff Jr.; "My Wild Irish Rose" by Olcott; "All or Nothing at All" by Jack Lawrence and Arthur Altman; "I Have Faith," "I Knew" and "Little American Boy;" by Yetta Cohen; "McNamara's Band" by Shamus O'Conner and John J. Stamford and "There Must Be an Easier Way to Make a Living." [1] Billed as Bob Mitchum.

1506 ✦ THE DOVE
Paramount, 1975

Musical Score Barry, John

Producer(s) Peck, Gregory
Director(s) Jarrott, Charles
Screenwriter(s) Beagle, Peter S.; Kennedy, Adam
Source(s) *Dove* (book) Graham, Robin Lee; Gill, Derek

Cast Bottoms, Joseph; Raffin, Deborah; McLiam, John; Coleman, Dabney

Song(s) Sail the Summer Winds (C: Barry, John; L: Black, Don)

1507 ✦ DOWN AMONG THE SHELTERING PALMS
Twentieth Century–Fox, 1952

Musical Score Harline, Leigh
Composer(s) Arlen, Harold
Lyricist(s) Blane, Ralph; Arlen, Harold
Choreographer(s) Felix, Seymour

Producer(s) Kohlmar, Fred
Director(s) Goulding, Edmund
Screenwriter(s) Binyon, Claude; Lewin, Albert; Styler, Burt

Cast Lundigan, William [3]; Greer, Jane; Gaynor, Mitzi; Wayne, David; De Haven, Gloria; Lockhart, Gene; Paar, Jack; Greenman, Alvin; Gilbert, Billy; Kulky, Henry

Song(s) I'm a Ruler of a South Sea Island; The Friendly Islands [4] (L: Blane, Ralph); Who Will It Be When the Time Comes?; 27 Elm Street; The Drum Dance (C/L: Darby, Ken); The Drum Chant (C/L: Darby, Ken); What Make De Diff'rence; Back Where I Come From [1]; The Opposite Sex [2]; When You're in Love [2]

Notes   Originally titled FRIENDLY ISLAND. There are also vocals of "Down Among the Sheltering Palms" by Abe Olman and James Brockman; "Pata' U Ta' U A Pere" by George Marcel Archer Ceran and Gerald Garnier and "All of Me" by Seymour Simons and Gerald Marks. [1] Not used. [2] Recorded but not used. [3] Dubbed by Bill Lee. [4] The introduction is titled "From Island to Island." The song is also in MY BLUE HEAVEN.

1508 ✦ DOWN AND OUT IN BEVERLY HILLS
Disney, 1986

Musical Score   Summers, Andy

Producer(s)   Mazursky, Paul
Director(s)   Mazursky, Paul
Screenwriter(s)   Mazursky, Paul; Capetanos, Leon

Cast   Nolte, Nick; Midler, Bette; Dreyfuss, Richard; Little Richard; Nelson, Tracy; Pena, Elizabeth; Richard, Evan; Mazursky, Paul; Curtin, Valerie; Primus, Barry; Tsu, Irene

Song(s)   Great Gosh a Might (It's a Matter of Time) (C/L: Little Richard; Preston, Billy)

Notes   No cue sheet available.

1509 ✦ DOWN ARGENTINE WAY
Twentieth Century–Fox, 1940

Composer(s)   Warren, Harry
Lyricist(s)   Gordon, Mack
Choreographer(s)   Castle, Nick; Sawyer, Geneva

Producer(s)   Zanuck, Darryl F.
Director(s)   Cummings, Irving
Screenwriter(s)   Ware, Darrell; Tunberg, Karl

Cast   Ameche, Don; Grable, Betty; Miranda, Carmen; Greenwood, Charlotte; Naish, J. Carrol; Stephenson, Henry; Aldridge, Katharine; Kinskey, Leonid; Martin, Chris-Pin; Conway, Robert; Gaye, Gregory; Stone, Bobby; Judels, Charles; The Nicholas Brothers

Song(s)   Down Argentina Way; South American Way (C: McHugh, Jimmy; L: Albert, Carlos); Nenita; Two Dreams Met; Mamae Eu Quero (C: Paiva, Vincente; Paiva, Jararaca; L: Paiva, Vincente; Paiva, Jararaca; Stillman, Al [3]); Bambu (C/L: Almirante [1]); Sing to Your Senorita; Clavel del Aire [2] (C: Filiberto, Juan de Dios; L: Valdes, Fernan Silva)

Notes   [1] Pseudonym for Henri Que Foreis. [2] Used in South American prints. [3] Stillman's lyrics not used in film. His song titled "I Want My Mama."

1510 ✦ DOWN CUBA WAY

See CUBAN PETE.

1511 ✦ DOWN DAKOTA WAY
Republic, 1949

Producer(s)   White, Edward J.
Director(s)   Witney, William
Screenwriter(s)   Butler, John K.; Nibley, Sloan

Cast   Rogers, Roy; Trigger; Evans, Dale; Brady, Pat; Montana, Monte; Foy Willing and the Riders of the Purple Sage

Song(s)   Down Dakota Way (C: Butts, Dale; L: Nibley, Sloan); Candy Kisses [1] (C/L: Morgan, George); The ABC Song (Xylophone) (C: Willing, Foy; L: Robin, Sid)

Notes   [1] Considered for but not used in LOVING YOU (Paramount).

1512 ✦ DOWNHILL RACER
Paramount, 1969

Musical Score   Hopkins, Kenyon

Producer(s)   Gregson, Richard
Director(s)   Ritchie, Michael
Screenwriter(s)   Salter, James
Source(s)   *The Downhill Racers* (novel) Hall, Oakley

Cast   Redford, Robert; Hackman, Gene; Sparv, Camilla; Vogler, Karl Michael; Coleman, Dabney

Song(s)   You Got Me Climbing Up the Wall (C/L: Hopkins, Kenyon); It Was a Long Happy Day [1] (C/L: Hopkins, Kenyon); Open Up and Let Me In [1] (C/L: Hopkins, Kenyon; Fridkin, Dennis)

Notes   Formerly titled THE POUNDING MOMENT, DOWNHILL, and THE DOWNHILL RACERS. [1] Not used.

1513 ✦ DOWN IN ARKANSAW
Republic, 1938

Producer(s)   Schaefer, Armand
Director(s)   Grinde, Nick
Screenwriter(s)   McGowan, Dorrell; McGowan, Stuart

Cast   Byrd, Ralph; Weaver, Leon; Weaver, Frank; Elviry; Storey, June; Tomlin, Pinky; Churchill, Berton; Williams, Guinn "Big Boy"; Miller, Walter; Green, Gertrude; Jackson, Selmer

Song(s)   The Farmer's Not in the Dell (C: Kent, Walter; L: Cherkose, Eddie); Lula Wall (C/L: Carter, June); The Heart of the City that Has No Heart (C/L: Allen, Thomas S.; Daly, Joseph M.)

1514 ✦ DOWN LIBERTY ROAD
Warner Brothers, 1956

Musical Score   Koff, Charles

Song(s)   Legend of the Alamo (C/L: Bowers, Jane)

Notes   This might be a short. There are no existing references.

1515 ✦ DOWN MEXICO WAY
Republic, 1941

Producer(s)   Grey, Harry
Director(s)   Santley, Joseph
Screenwriter(s)   Cooper, Olive; Duffy, Albert

Cast   Autry, Gene; Burnette, Smiley; McKenzie, Fay; Huber, Harold; Blackmer, Sidney; Tombes, Andrew; Herrara Sisters; Renaldo, Duncan

Song(s)   Down Mexico Way [2] (C: Styne, Jule; L: Cherkose, Eddie; Meyer, Sol); Beer Barrel Polka (Roll Out the Barrel) (C/L: Styne, Jule); Las Altenitas (C: Espinosa, J.J.; L: Tuvim, Abe; Luban, Francia); Maria Elena [4] (C: Barcelata, Lorenzo; L: Barcelata, Lorenzo; Russell, S.K.); South of the Border [3] (C/L: Kennedy, Jimmy; Carr, Michael); Cowboy and the Lady [1] (C/L: Quenzer, Arthur; Newman, L.)

Notes   No cue sheet available. There are also vocals of "La Cachita" and "Guadalajara." [1] May also be in EL RANCHO GRANDE. [2] Also in THE GOLDEN STALLION, HOME IN WYOMING and YELLOW ROSE OF TEXAS. [3] Also in SOUTH OF THE BORDER. [1] Russell wrote the English lyrics.

1516 ✦ DOWN MISSOURI WAY
PRC, 1946

Musical Score   Hajos, Karl
Composer(s)   Kent, Walter
Lyricist(s)   Gannon, Kim

Director(s)   Berne, Joseph
Screenwriter(s)   Neuman, Sam

Cast   O'Driscoll, Martha; Wright, William

Song(s)   There's a Rose that Grows in the Ozarks; Just Can't Get that Guy; Never Knew that I Could Sing [2]; Monkey Business; The Big Town Gal; If Somethin' Don't Happen Soon; I'm So in Love with You; Jane Loves Mike [1] (L: Kent, Walter); Old Missouri Hayride

Notes   [1] The cue sheet doesn't differentiate between vocals and instrumentals. This might be background scoring. [2] Also in HEARTACHES.

1517 ✦ DOWN THE WYOMING TRAIL
Monogram, 1939

Musical Score   Sanucci, Frank

Producer(s)   Finney, Edward
Director(s)   Herman, Al
Screenwriter(s)   Dixon, Peter

Cast   Ritter, Tex; Murphy, Horace; Brodel, Mary; Lawson, Bobby; King, Charles; Terry, Bob; Ingram, Jack; LaRue, Frank

Song(s)   In Elk Valley (C: Lange, Johnny; L: Porter, Lew); Goin' Back to Texas (C/L: Robison, Carson J.); It Makes No Difference Now (C/L: Davis, Jimmie)

Notes   No cue sheet available. There is also a vocal of "Little Town of Bethlehem" by I.H. Redner.

1518 ✦ DOWN TO EARTH
Columbia, 1947

Composer(s)   Fisher, Doris
Lyricist(s)   Roberts, Allan
Choreographer(s)   Cole, Jack

Producer(s)   Hartman, Don
Director(s)   Hall, Alexander
Screenwriter(s)   Blum, Edwin; Hartman, Don

Cast   Hayworth, Rita [1]; Parks, Larry [2]; Platt, Marc; Jergens, Adele [3]; Macready, George; Culver, Roland; Gleason, James; Horton, Edward Everett; Frawley, William; Littlefield, Lucien; Haney, Carol

Song(s)   Swinging the Muses; Let's Stay Young Forever; They Can't Convince Me; This Can't Be Legal; People Have More Fun Than Anyone

Notes   [1] Dubbed by Anita Ellis. [2] Dubbed by Hal Derwin. [3] Dubbed by Kay Starr.

1519 ✦ DOWN TO THEIR LAST YACHT
RKO, 1934

Producer(s)   Brock, Lou
Director(s)   Sloane, Lou
Screenwriter(s)   Dix, Marion; Starling, Lynn

Cast   Boland, Mary; Moran, Polly; Sparks, Ned; Fox, Sidney; Blackmer, Sidney; Holloway, Sterling; Gateson, Marjorie; Franklin, Irene; Coleman, Charles

Song(s)   Funny Little World [1] (C/L: Ronell, Ann); Tiny Little Finger on Your Hand (C/L: Burton, Val; Jason, Will); There's Nothing Else to Do in Malakamokalu (C/L: Mitchell, Sidney D.; Friend, Cliff); South Sea Bolero (C/L: Ronell, Ann; Steiner, Max); Beach Boy (C/L: Ronell, Ann)

Notes   Titled HAWAIIAN NIGHTS internationally. [1] Max Steiner also credited on sheet music.

1520 ✦ DOWN TO THE SEA
Republic, 1936

Producer(s)   Schaefer, Armand
Director(s)   Collins, Lewis D.
Screenwriter(s)   Totman, Wellyn; Johnson, Robert Lee

Cast   Hardie, Russell; Lyon, Ben; Rutherford, Ann; Pichel, Irving; Leiber, Fritz; Barnett, Vince

Song(s) Beneath the Sea (C/L: Grey, Harry)

Notes There are also several traditional Greek songs.

1521 ◆ DOWN TO THE SEA IN SHIPS
Twentieth Century–Fox, 1949

Producer(s) Lighton, Louis D.
Director(s) Hathaway, Henry
Screenwriter(s) Mahin, John Lee

Cast Widmark, Richard; Barrymore, Lionel; Stockwell, Dean; Kellaway, Cecil; Lockhart, Gene; Kroeger, Berry; McIntire, John; Morgan, Henry; Davenport, Harry; Flippen, Jay C.; Knight, Fuzzy

Song(s) Ol' Briny (C: Newman, Alfred; L: Darby, Ken)

1522 ◆ DOWNTWISTED
Cannon, 1987

Musical Score Berlin Game
Composer(s) Berlin Game
Lyricist(s) Berlin Game

Producer(s) Golan, Menahem; Globus, Yoram
Director(s) Pyun, Albert F.
Screenwriter(s) O'Neill, Gene; Tobin, Noreen

Cast Lowell, Carey; Rocket, Charles; Dochtermann, Trudi; Mathews, Thom; Cox, Courteney

Song(s) De Repente; I'm Closer Now; The Candle of My Life Went Out Tonight

Notes No cue sheet available.

1523 ◆ DO YOU LOVE ME?
Twentieth Century–Fox, 1946

Composer(s) McHugh, Jimmy
Lyricist(s) Adamson, Harold
Choreographer(s) Felix, Seymour

Producer(s) Jessel, George
Director(s) Ratoff, Gregory
Screenwriter(s) Ellis, Robert; Logan, Helen

Cast O'Hara, Maureen; Haymes, Dick; James, Harry; Gardiner, Reginald; Gaines, Richard; Prager, Stanley; Harry James and His Music Makers; Pully, B.S.; Chandler, Chick; Kruger, Alma; Sessions, Almira; Briggs, Harlan

Song(s) (I'm Sorry) I Didn't Mean a Word I Said; The Flower Song [1]; Do You Love Me (C/L: Ruby, Harry); As If I Didn't Have Enough on My Mind (C: James, Harry; Newman, Lionel; L: Henderson, Charles); Moonlight Propaganda (C: Malneck, Matty; L: Magidson, Herb)

Notes Originally titled KITTEN ON THE KEYS. There is also a vocal of "The More I See You" by Harry Warren and Mack Gordon from BILLY ROSE'S DIAMOND HORSESHOE. Instrumentals include the

"Back Beat Boogie" by Harry James; "St. Louis Blues" by W.C. Handy and the "Symphony No. 4 Finale" by Peter Tchaikovsky. [1] Only lasts 12 seconds.

1524 ◆ DRACULA A.D. 1972
Warner Brothers, 1972

Musical Score Vickers, Mike

Producer(s) Douglas, Josephine
Director(s) Gibson, Alan
Screenwriter(s) Houghton, Don

Cast Lee, Christopher; Cushing, Peter; Beacham, Stephanie; Munro, Caroline

Song(s) You Better Come Through (C/L: Barnes, Tim); Alligator Man (C/L: Valentino, Sal)

1525 ◆ DRAG
Warner Brothers–First National, 1929

Composer(s) Meyer, George W.
Lyricist(s) Bryan, Alfred

Director(s) Lloyd, Frank
Screenwriter(s) King, Bradley
Source(s) Drag Pelley, William Dudley

Cast Barthelmess, Richard; Day, Alice; Littlefield, Lucien; Ward, Katherine; Parker, Charlie; Dugan, Tom; Lee, Lila

Song(s) My Song of the Nile; I'm Too Young to Be Careful (And Too Sweet to Be Good)

Notes No cue sheet available.

1526 ◆ DRAGNET (1954)
Warner Brothers, 1954

Musical Score Schumann, Walter

Producer(s) Meyer, Stanley
Director(s) Webb, Jack
Screenwriter(s) Breen, Richard L.

Cast Webb, Jack; Alexander, Ben; Boone, Richard; Robinson, Ann; Harris, Stacy; Gregg, Virginia; Arquette, Cliff

Song(s) Foggy Night in San Francisco (C: Saunders, Herman; L: Miller, Sidney)

Notes No cue sheet available. A movie version of the famous TV Series.

1527 ◆ DRAGNET (1987)
Universal, 1987

Musical Score Newborn, Ira
Composer(s) Jam, Jimmy; Lewis, Terry
Lyricist(s) Jam, Jimmy; Lewis, Terry

Producer(s) Permut, David; Weiss, Robert K.
Director(s) Mankiewicz, Tom

Screenwriter(s) Aykroyd, Dan; Zweibel, Alan; Mankiewicz, Tom

Cast Aykroyd, Dan; Hanks, Tom; Plummer, Christopher; Morgan, Harry; Paul, Alexandra; O'Halloran, Jack; Ashley, Elizabeth; Coleman, Dabney; Freeman, Kathleen

Song(s) Just the Facts; Helplessly in Love with You; City of Crime (C/L: Aykroyd, Peter; Aykroyd, Dan; Thrall, Pat)

1528 ✦ DRAGONWYCK
Twentieth Century–Fox, 1946

Musical Score Newman, Alfred

Producer(s) Zanuck, Darryl F.
Director(s) Mankiewicz, Joseph L.
Screenwriter(s) Mankiewicz, Joseph L.
Source(s) *Dragonwyck* (novel) Seton, Anya

Cast Tierney, Gene; Huston, Walter; Price, Vincent; Langan, Glenn; Revere, Anne; Byington, Spring; Marshall, Connie; Morgan, Henry; Tandy, Jessica; Ford, Ruth

Song(s) Creole Lullaby (C: Newman, Alfred; L: Henderson, Charles)

1529 ✦ DREAMBOAT
Twentieth Century–Fox, 1952

Musical Score Mockridge, Cyril J.

Producer(s) Siegel, Sol C.
Director(s) Binyon, Claude
Screenwriter(s) Binyon, Claude

Cast Webb, Clifton; Rogers, Ginger; Francis, Anne; Hunter, Jeffrey; Lanchester, Elsa; Clark, Fred; Harvey, Paul; Collins, Ray; Stanley, Helene

Song(s) Prunectar Prune Juice (C/L: Darby, Ken)

Notes "You'll Never Know" by Mack Gordon and Harry Warren also receives a featured vocal in this picture.

1530 ✦ DREAMER
Twentieth Century–Fox, 1979

Musical Score Conti, Bill

Producer(s) Lobell, Michael
Director(s) Nosseck, Noel
Screenwriter(s) Proctor, James; Bischof, Larry

Cast Matheson, Tim; Blakely, Susan; Warden, Jack; Shull, Richard B.; Clark, Matt

Song(s) Reach for the Top (C/L: Conti, Bill; Lerios, Cory; Jenkins, David)

Notes No cue sheet available.

1531 ✦ DREAM GIRL
Paramount, 1948

Musical Score Young, Victor
Choreographer(s) Daniels, Billy

Producer(s) Wolfson, P.J.
Director(s) Leisen, Mitchell
Screenwriter(s) Sheekman, Arthur
Source(s) *Dream Girl* (play) Rice, Elmer

Cast Hutton, Betty [2]; Carey, Macdonald; Knowles, Patric; Field, Virginia; Wood, Peggy; Abel, Walter

Song(s) Drunk with Love (C/L: Livingston, Jay; Evans, Ray); Dream Girl [1] (C/L: Livingston, Jay; Evans, Ray)

Notes [1] Used only instrumentally. [2] Dubbed by Nadine Connor for operatic sequences.

1532 ✦ DREAMING OUT LOUD
RKO, 1940

Musical Score Moraweck, Lucien

Producer(s) Votion, Jack
Director(s) Young, Harold
Screenwriter(s) Green, Howard J.; Trivers, Barry; Andrews, Robert

Cast Lum & Abner [1]; Langford, Frances; Craven, Frank; Watson, Bobs; Bacon, Irving; Blandick, Clara; Wilcox, Robert; Briggs, Donald

Song(s) Dreaming Out Loud (C/L: Coslow, Sam)

Notes No cue sheet available. [1] Chester Lauck and Norris Goff.

1533 ✦ DREAMS OF GLASS
Universal, 1968

Musical Score Freebairn-Smith, Ian

Producer(s) Clouse, Robert
Director(s) Clouse, Robert
Screenwriter(s) Clouse, Robert

Cast Denoa, Robert; Barrett, Caroline; Lo Presti, Joe

Song(s) Dreams of Glass (C: Freebairn-Smith, Ian; L: Brown, W. Earl)

1534 ✦ THE DREAM TEAM
Universal, 1989

Musical Score McHugh, David

Producer(s) Knight, Christopher W.
Director(s) Zieff, Howard
Screenwriter(s) Connolly, Jon; Loucka, David

Cast Keaton, Michael; Lloyd, Christopher; Boyle, Peter; Furst, Stephen; Boutsikaris, Dennis; Bracco,

Lorraine; O'Shea, Milo; Bosco, Philip; Remar, James; Dixon, MacIntyre

Song(s) Walk the Dinosaur (C/L: Was, Dave; Was, Don; Jacobs, Randy); Further On Up the Road (C/L: Veasey, Joe Medwich; Robey, Don D.)

Notes Only songs written for this film are listed.

1535 ✦ DREAM WIFE
Metro–Goldwyn–Mayer, 1953

Musical Score Salinger, Conrad

Producer(s) Schary, Dore
Director(s) Sheldon, Sidney
Screenwriter(s) Sheldon, Sidney; Baker, Herbert; Levitt, Alfred Lewis

Cast Grant, Cary; Kerr, Deborah; Pidgeon, Walter; St. John, Betta; Franz, Eduard; Tremayne, Les

Song(s) Tarji's Song (C/L: Wolcott, Charles; Shebani, Jamshid); Ghi-Li, Ghi-Li, Ghi-Li (C/L: Wolcott, Charles; Shebani, Jamshid)

1536 ✦ DRESSED TO KILL (1941)
Twentieth Century–Fox, 1941

Producer(s) Wurtzel, Sol M.
Director(s) Forde, Eugene
Screenwriter(s) Rauh, Stanley; O'Connor, Manning
Source(s) *The Dead Take No Bows* (novel) Burke, Richard

Cast Nolan, Lloyd; Hughes, Mary Beth; Ryan, Sheila; Demarest, William; Carter, Ben; Brissac, Virginia; Kalser, Erwin

Song(s) I've Got You All to Myself [1] (C: Rainger, Ralph; L: Robin, Leo)

Notes [1] Also in MOON OVER MIAMI.

1537 ✦ DRESSED TO KILL (1946)
Universal, 1946

Composer(s) Brooks, Jack
Lyricist(s) Brooks, Jack

Producer(s) Neill, Roy William
Director(s) Neill, Roy William
Screenwriter(s) Lee, Leonard

Cast Rathbone, Basil; Morison, Patricia; Breon, Edmond; Worlock, Frederick; Bruce, Nigel; Glyn, Anita

Song(s) Ya Never Know Just 'Oo Yer Gonna Meet; The Swag Man [1]

Notes This is the last in the Universal Sherlock Holmes series. [1] Used instrumentally only.

1538 ✦ DRESSED TO THRILL
Fox, 1935

Composer(s) Pollack, Lew
Lyricist(s) Webster, Paul Francis

Producer(s) Kane, Robert T.
Director(s) Lachman, Harry
Screenwriter(s) Raphaelson, Samson
Source(s) *La Couturiere de Luneville* (play) Savior, Alfred

Cast Rolf, Tutta; Brook, Clive; Westman, Nydia

Song(s) My One Big Moment; My Heart Is a Violin; Be Still My Sorrow [1] (C: Traditional; L: Pollack, Lew; Webster, Paul Francis)

Notes "Dark Eyes" and "Mademoiselle from Armentieres" are also sung. [1] Based on the traditional song "Still, Be Still My Sorrow."

1539 ✦ DRIFTIN' RIVER
PRC, 1946

Musical Score Hajos, Karl

Director(s) Tansey, Robert Emmett
Screenwriter(s) Kavanaugh, Frances

Cast Dean, Eddie; Patterson, Shirley

Song(s) Driftin' River (C/L: Porter, Lew; Tansy, Robert); I'm a Lonesome Cowboy (C/L: Dean, Eddie; Bond, Johnny)

1540 ✦ DRIP-ALONG DAFFY
Warner Brothers, 1951

Musical Score Stalling, Carl

Director(s) Jones, Chuck
Screenwriter(s) Maltese, Michael

Cast Duck, Daffy; Pig, Porky; Canasta, Nasty

Song(s) The Flower of Gower Gulch (C/L: Maltese, Michael)

Notes Merrie Melodie cartoon.

1541 ✦ DRUM BEAT
Warner Brothers, 1954

Musical Score Young, Victor

Producer(s) Ladd, Alan
Director(s) Daves, Delmer
Screenwriter(s) Daves, Delmer

Cast Ladd, Alan; Rorke, Hayden; Bronson, Charles; Dalton, Audrey; Pavan, Marisa

Song(s) Drum Beat (C: Young, Victor; L: Washington, Ned)

1542 ◆ DRUMS OF AFRICA
Metro–Goldwyn–Mayer, 1963

Musical Score   Mandel, Johnny

Producer(s)   Zimbalist, Al; Krasne, Philip N.
Director(s)   Clark, James B.
Screenwriter(s)   Estridge, Robin; Hoerl, Arthur

Cast   Bochner, Lloyd; Hartley, Mariette; Avalon, Frankie; Thatcher, Torin; Pate, Michael

Song(s)   The River Love (C/L: Faith, Russell; Marcucci, Robert)

1543 ◆ DRUMS OF THE CONGO
Universal, 1942

Composer(s)   Rosen, Milton
Lyricist(s)   Carter, Everett

Producer(s)   McRae, Henry
Director(s)   Cabanne, Christy
Screenwriter(s)   Chanslor, Roy

Cast   Terry, Don; Moran, Peggy; Lane, Richard; Munson, Ona; Bledsoe, Jules; Erwin, Stuart; Bey, Turhan; Dandridge, Dorothy; Whitman, Ernest

Song(s)   River Man; 'Round the Bend; Hear the Drums Beat Out [1]

Notes   [1] Sheet music only.

1544 ◆ DUBARRY WAS A LADY
Metro–Goldwyn–Mayer, 1943

Choreographer(s)   Walters, Charles

Producer(s)   Freed, Arthur
Director(s)   Del Ruth, Roy
Screenwriter(s)   Brecher, Irving; Mahoney, Wilkie
Source(s)   *DuBarry Was a Lady* (musical) DeSylva, B.G.; Fields, Herbert; Porter, Cole

Cast   Skelton, Red; Kelly, Gene; Ball, Lucille [2]; O'Brien, Virginia; Ragland, Rags; Mostel, Zero; Tommy Dorsey and His Orchestra; Beavers, Louise; Dumbrille, Douglass; Meek, Donald; Givot, George

Song(s)   DuBarry Was a Lady (C: Lane, Burton; L: Freed, Ralph); Do I Love You [1] (C/L: Porter, Cole); Salome [4] (C: Edens, Roger; L: Harburg, E.Y.); I Love an Esquire Girl (C: Edens, Roger; L: Freed, Ralph; Brown, Lew); Ladies of the Bath (C/L: Edens, Roger); Katie Went to Haiti [1] (C/L: Porter, Cole); Madame, I Love Your Crepes Suzettes (C: Lane, Burton; L: Freed, Ralph; Brown, Lew); Song of Rebellion (C/L: Edens, Roger); Friendship [1] (C/L: Porter, Cole); A Pretty Girl Is Like a Melody [3] (C/L: Martin, Hugh; Blane, Ralph)

Notes   This was Mostel's film debut. Charles Walters appeared in the Broadway original. There are also vocals of "Thinking of You" by Walter Donaldson and Paul

Ash; "A Cigarette, Sweet Music and You" by Roy Ringwald; "Do You Ever Think of Me" by Harry D. Kerr and Earl Burtnett; "Sleepy Lagoon" by Jack Lawrence and Eric Coates and "You Are My Sunshine" by Jimmie Davis and Charles Mitchell. [1] From original Broadway musical. [2] Dubbed by Martha Mears. [3] Deleted from final print. [4] Recording from PANAMA HATTIE but not used there.

1545 ◆ DUCHESS AND THE DIRTWATER FOX
Twentieth Century–Fox, 1976

Musical Score   Fox, Charles
Composer(s)   Fox, Charles
Lyricist(s)   Cahn, Sammy; Frank, Melvin

Producer(s)   Frank, Melvin
Director(s)   Frank, Melvin
Screenwriter(s)   Frank, Melvin; Sandler, Barry; Rose, Jack

Cast   Segal, George; Hawn, Goldie; Janis, Conrad; David, Thayer; Lee, Jennifer

Song(s)   Please Don't Touch My Plums; Fools Gold; Blimey; The Touch of Love; Lemon Drops, Lollipops & Sunbeams

1546 ◆ DUCHESS OF IDAHO
Metro–Goldwyn–Mayer, 1950

Musical Score   Stoll, George; Sendrey, Al
Composer(s)   Rinker, Al; Huddleston, Floyd
Lyricist(s)   Rinker, Al; Huddleston, Floyd
Choreographer(s)   Donohue, Jack

Producer(s)   Pasternak, Joe
Director(s)   Leonard, Robert Z.
Screenwriter(s)   Cooper, Dorothy; Davis, Jerry

Cast   Williams, Esther; Johnson, Van; Lund, John; Raymond, Paula; Sundberg, Clinton; Haines, Connie; Torme, Mel; Blake, Amanda; Farrell, Tommy; Arno, Sig; Horne, Lena; Powell, Eleanor

Song(s)   Let's Choo Choo Choo to Idaho; Baby, Come Out of the Clouds (C/L: Nemo, Henry; Pearl, Lee); Of All Things; You Can't Do Wrong Doin' Right [2]; Warm Hands Beguine [1]

Notes   [1] Used instrumentally only. [2] Also in THE AFFAIRS OF DOBIE GILLIS and THE SELLOUT.

1547 ◆ DUCK SOUP
Paramount, 1933

Composer(s)   Ruby, Harry
Lyricist(s)   Kalmar, Bert

Director(s)   McCarey, Leo
Screenwriter(s)   Kalmar, Bert; Ruby, Harry; Perrin, Nat; Sheekman, Arthur

Cast   Marx, Groucho; Marx, Harpo; Marx, Chico; Marx, Zeppo; Dumont, Margaret; Torres, Raquel; Calhern, Louis

Song(s)   His Excellency Is Due; Freedonia Hymn; Part Two Opening; Peanut Vendor (C: Simons, Moises; L: Gilbert, L. Wolfe; Sunshine, Marion); The Country's Going to War; Sylvanian Hymn (inst.); Doin' What You're Doin' [1]; The King Can Do No Wrong [1]

Notes   [1] Not used.

1548 ✦ DUDE COWBOY
RKO, 1943

Composer(s)   Rose, Fred; Whitley, Ray
Lyricist(s)   Rose, Fred; Whitley, Ray

Producer(s)   Gilroy, Bert
Director(s)   Howard, David
Screenwriter(s)   Grant, Morton

Cast   Holt, Tim; Reynolds, Marjorie; Whitley, Ray; White, Lee "Lasses"; Currie, Louise

Song(s)   Dude Cowboy; End of the Canyon Trail; Silver River; Wildweed

1549 ✦ DUEL IN THE JUNGLE
Warner Brothers, 1954

Producer(s)   Hellman, Marcel; Owen, Tony
Director(s)   Marshall, George
Screenwriter(s)   Marx, Sam; Morrison, T.J.

Cast   Andrews, Dana; Crain, Jeanne; Farrar, David; Barr, Patrick; Coulouris, George; Hyde-White, Wilfrid

Song(s)   The Night Belongs to Me (C: Spoliansky, Mischa L: Newell, Norman)

Notes   No cue sheet available.

1550 ✦ DUEL IN THE SUN
Selznick, 1946

Musical Score   Tiomkin, Dimitri
Choreographer(s)   Losch, Tilly; Shaw, Lloyd [1]

Producer(s)   Selznick, David O.
Director(s)   Vidor, King
Screenwriter(s)   Selznick, David O.; Garrett, Oliver H.P.
Source(s)   *Duel in the Sun* (novel) Busch, Niven

Cast   Jones, Jennifer; Cotten, Joseph; Peck, Gregory; Barrymore, Lionel; Gish, Lillian; Huston, Walter; Marshall, Herbert; Bickford, Charles; Carey, Harry; Kruger, Otto; Blackmer, Sidney; Losch, Tilly; McQueen, Butterfly; Killian, Victor

Song(s)   Gotta Get Me Somebody to Love (C/L: Wrubel, Allie); Duel in the Sun (C: Tiomkin, Dimitri; L: Adams, Stanley; Judell, Maxson); Gotta Get Me

Somebody to Love (C/L: Wrubel, Allie); Headin' Home (C: Tiomkin, Dimitri; L: Herbert, Frederick)

Notes   No cue sheet available. [1] Choreographed group dances.

1551 ✦ DUFFY
Columbia, 1968

Musical Score   Freeman, Ernie

Producer(s)   Manulis, Martin
Director(s)   Parrish, Robert
Screenwriter(s)   Cammell, Donald; Brown Jr., Harry Joe

Cast   Coburn, James; Mason, James; Fox, James; York, Susannah; Alderton, John

Song(s)   I'm Satisfied (C/L: Weil, Cynthia; Mann, Barry; Freeman, Ernie)

Notes   No cue sheet available.

1552 ✦ DUFFY'S TAVERN
Paramount, 1945

Musical Score   Dolan, Robert Emmett
Choreographer(s)   Daniels, Billy

Producer(s)   Dare, Danny
Director(s)   Walker, Hal
Screenwriter(s)   Panama, Norman; Frank, Melvin
Source(s)   "Duffy's Tavern" (radio series) Gardner, Ed

Sketchwriter(s)   White, George; Davis, Eddie; Brooks, Matt; Burrows, Abe [2]; Dean, Barney; Panama, Norman; Frank, Melvin
Cast   Gardner, Ed; Moore, Victor; Reynolds, Marjorie; Sullivan, Barry; Crosby, Bing; Crosby, Gary; Crosby, Dennis; Crosby, Lin; Crosby, Phillip; Hutton, Betty; Goddard, Paulette; Ladd, Alan; Lamour, Dorothy; Bracken, Eddie; Donlevy, Brian; Tufts, Sonny; Lake, Veronica; de Cordova, Arturo; Fitzgerald, Barry; Daley, Cass; Lynn, Diana; Benchley, Robert; Demarest, William; Da Silva, Howard; De Wolfe, Billy; Abel, Walter; Coy, Johnny; San Juan, Olga; Watson, Bobby

Song(s)   The Hard Way (C: Van Heusen, James; L: Burke, Johnny); Now We're Getting Somewhere [1] (C: Van Heusen, James; L: Burke, Johnny); You Can't Blame a Gal for Tryin' (C: Wayne, Bernie; L: Raleigh, Ben)

Notes   The movie consists of snatches of tunes associated with the careers of Betty Hutton and Bing Crosby. Most of these are only a few seconds in length. I have listed only those songs original to this picture. "Swingin' on a Star" by Burke and Van Heusen is given a long version with a rewritten lyric by Johnny Burke. [1] This song is only given an instrumental treatment; the finale in particular is based on the tune's melody. [2] Billed as Abram S. Burrows.

1553 ✦ THE DUKE STEPS OUT
Metro–Goldwyn–Mayer, 1929

Director(s) Cruze, James
Screenwriter(s) Schrock, Raymond; Van Every, Dale

Cast Crawford, Joan; Dane, Karl; Haines, William; Daves, Delmer; Nugent, Edward; Holtz, Tenen

Song(s) Just You (C: Axt, William; Mendoza, David; L: Klages, Raymond)

1554 ✦ DUMBO
Disney, 1941

Musical Score Wallace, Oliver
Composer(s) Churchill, Frank E.
Lyricist(s) Washington, Ned

Director(s) Sharpsteen, Ben
Screenwriter(s) Grant, Joe; Huemer, Dick
Source(s) (story) Aberson, Helen; Pearl, Harold
Voices Brophy, Edward S.; Holloway, Sterling; Bing, Herman; Edwards, Cliff; Felton, Verna

Directing Animator(s) Tytla, Vladimir; Moore, Fred; Kimball, Ward; Lounsbery, John; Babbitt, Art; Reitherman, Woolie

Song(s) Look Out for Mr. Stork; Casey Junior (1); Baby Mine; Pink Elephants on Parade (C: Wallace, Oliver); When I See an Elephant Fly (C: Wallace, Oliver); Song of the Roustabouts; It's Circus Day Again [1]; Casey Junior (2) [2] (L: Huemer, Dick; Grant, Joe); Clown Song [2] (C: Wallace, Oliver; L: Quenzer, Arthur); It's Spring Again [2]; Pink Elephant Polka [2] (L: Huemer, Dick; Grant, Joe); Sing a Song of Cheese [2] (L: Huemer, Dick; Grant, Joe); Spread Your Wings [1]

Notes Feature cartoon. [1] Used instrumentally only. [2] Not used.

1555 ✦ DUSTY AND SWEETS MCGEE
Warner Brothers, 1971

Producer(s) Laughlin, Michael S.
Director(s) Mutrux, Floyd

Song(s) Woo-Woo Arnie Ginsberg's Theme Song (C/L: Ginsberg, Arnie); Don't Leave Me (C/L: Nilsson, Harry); Into the Mystic (C/L: Morrison, Van); Book of Love (C/L: Davis, Warren; Malone, George; Patrick, Charles); Runaway (C/L: Shannon, Del; Crook, Max); So Close (C/L: Holmes, Jake)

Notes It is not known if any of these were written for this production. The movie consists of actual drug addicts plopped in front of the cameras.

1556 ✦ DYNAMITE
Metro–Goldwyn–Mayer, 1929

Producer(s) De Mille, Cecil B.
Director(s) De Mille, Cecil B.
Screenwriter(s) MacPherson, Jeanie; Lawson, John Howard; Unger, Gladys

Cast Nagel, Conrad; Johnson, Kay; Bickford, Charles; McCrea, Joel; Faye, Julia; Edeson, Robert; Holden, William; Columbo, Russ [1]

Song(s) How Am I To Know [2] (C: King, Jack; L: Parker, Dorothy)

Notes [1] Played a Mexican prisoner. [2] Also in THE HOODLUM SAINT and HE'S MY GUY (Universal).

E

1557 ✦ EADIE WAS A LADY
Columbia, 1945

Choreographer(s) Cole, Jack

Producer(s) Kraike, Michel
Director(s) Dreifuss, Arthur
Screenwriter(s) Brice, Monte

Cast Miller, Ann; Besser, Joe; Wright, William; Donnell, Jeff; Little, Jimmy; Howard, Kathleen; Hal McIntyre and His Orchestra; Dugan, Tom

Song(s) She's a Gypsy from Brooklyn (C: Oakland, Ben; L: Gilbert, L. Wolfe); You Came Along (Out of Nowhere) (C: Chaplin, Saul; L: Cahn, Sammy); I'm Gonna See My Baby [1] (C/L: Moore, Phil); Tabby the Cat [1] (C/L: Dickinson, Harold; Gibeling, Howard); Eadie Was a Lady [1] [2] (C: Whiting, Richard A.; Brown, Nacio Herb; L: DeSylva, B.G.)

Notes [1] Not written for this picture. [2] Also in TAKE A CHANCE.

1558 ✦ THE EAGLE'S BROOD
Paramount, 1935

Producer(s) Sherman, Harry
Director(s) Bretherton, Howard
Screenwriter(s) Schroeder, Doris; Jacobs, Harrison
Source(s) *Hopalong Cassidy and the Eagle's Brood* (novel) Mulford, Clarence E.

Cast Boyd, William; Ellison, James; Hayes, George "Gabby"; Woodbury, Joan; Farnum, William

Song(s) Free with Love (C: Stept, Sam H.; L: Mitchell, Sidney D.); Following the Stars (C: Stept, Sam H.; L: Franklin, Dave)

1559 ✦ EAGLE SQUADRON
Universal, 1942

Musical Score Skinner, Frank
Choreographer(s) Lavelle, Doris; Pierre, M.

Producer(s) Wanger, Walter
Director(s) Lubin, Arthur
Screenwriter(s) Raine, Norman Reilly
Source(s) (story) Forester, C.S.

Cast Stack, Robert; Loder, John; Albert, Eddie; Erickson, Leif; Barrier, Edgar; Hall, Jon; Barrymore, Diana; Bruce, Nigel; Ankers, Evelyn; Elsom, Isobel; Cooper, Gladys; Hale Jr., Alan; Porter, Don

Song(s) The Sign of the "V" (C: de Paul, Gene; L: Raye, Don)

1560 ✦ EARL CARROLL SKETCHBOOK
Republic, 1946

Composer(s) Styne, Jule
Lyricist(s) Cahn, Sammy

Producer(s) North, Robert
Director(s) Rogell, Albert S.
Screenwriter(s) Levy, Parke; Gill, Frank, Jr.

Cast Moore, Constance; Marshall, William; Goodwin, Bill; Coy, Johnny; Vague, Vera; Horton, Edward Everett; Brooke, Hillary; Babb, Dorothy; Homans, Robert

Song(s) Vivo; I've Never Forgotten; Mother Hubbard's Bunion Pads (C/L: Newman, Albert); The Lady with the Mop; I Was Silly, I Was Headstrong and Impetuous; What Makes You Beautiful, Beautiful; Oh Henry; You're So Good to Me [2]; I've Got a Right to Sing the Blues (C: Arlen, Harold; L: Koehler, Ted); Hittin' the Bottle (C: Arlen, Harold; L: Koehler, Ted); Salvo [1]

Notes Titled HATS OFF TO RHYTHM. [1] Not used. [2] Also in TELL IT TO A STAR and YOUTH ON PARADE.

1561 ✦ EARL CARROLL VANITIES
Republic, 1945

Composer(s) Kent, Walter
Lyricist(s) Gannon, Kim
Choreographer(s) Lee, Sammy

Producer(s) Cohen, Albert J.
Director(s) Santley, Joseph
Screenwriter(s) Gill, Frank, Jr.

Cast O'Keefe, Dennis; Moore, Constance; Arden, Eve; Kruger, Otto; Mowbray, Alan; Bachelor, Stephanie; Lee, Pinky; Forbes, Mary; Parkyakarkus; Belasco, Leon; Dugan, Tom; Clute, Chester; Alexander, Jimmy; Woody Herman and His Orchestra; Liliane and Mario

Song(s) Riverside Jive (C/L: Newman, Albert); I've Been So Good for So Long; Rock-A-Bye Boogie; Endlessly; The Last Man in Town; Who Dat Up Der (L: Russell, Bob); You Beautiful Thing You

1562 ✦ EARL OF PUDDLESTONE
Republic, 1940

Musical Score Lava, Bill

Producer(s) Meins, Gus
Director(s) Meins, Gus
Screenwriter(s) Burton, Val; Adamson, Ewart

Cast Gleason, James; Gleason, Russell; Davenport, Harry; Ranson, Lois; Ryan, Tommy; Blore, Eric; Blythe, Betty; Harvey, Forrester

Song(s) Here Comes Romance (C: Kraushaar, Raoul; L: Tinturin, Peter); Jumpin' Jehosophat (C/L: Cowan, Stanley; Worth, Bobby)

1563 ✦ THE EARLY BIRD AND THE WORM
Metro–Goldwyn–Mayer, 1936

Musical Score Bradley, Scott

Song(s) The Early Bird (C: Bradley, Scott; L: Ising, Rudolf)

Notes Animated cartoon.

1564 ✦ THE EARTHLING
Filmways, 1981

Musical Score De Benedictis, Dick
Composer(s) Kasha, Al; Hirschhorn, Joel; Lloyd, Michael
Lyricist(s) Kasha, Al; Hirschhorn, Joel; Lloyd, Michael

Producer(s) Schick, Elliot; Strong, John
Director(s) Collinson, Peter
Screenwriter(s) Cotler, Lanny

Cast Holden, William; Schroder, Ricky; Thompson, Jack; Hamnett, Olivia; Nielson, Harry

Song(s) Halfway Home (C/L: Shire, David; Connors, Carol); Fast Women and Slow Dancin'; He'll Never Fill My Shoes; Blind Faith (C/L: Lloyd, Michael); Stay with Me (C/L: Lloyd, Michael); Run to Me (C/L: Lloyd, Michael; D'Andrea, John)

Notes No cue sheet available.

1565 ✦ THE EASIEST WAY
Metro–Goldwyn–Mayer, 1931

Director(s) Conway, Jack
Screenwriter(s) Ellis, Edith
Source(s) *The Easiest Way* (play) Walter, Eugene

Cast Bennett, Constance; Menjou, Adolphe; Montgomery, Robert; Rambeau, Marjorie; Gable, Clark; Blandick, Clara

Song(s) Blame It on the Moonlight (C: Ager, Milton; L: Yellen, Jack)

Notes First filmed in 1917.

1566 ✦ EASTER PARADE
Metro–Goldwyn–Mayer, 1948

Composer(s) Berlin, Irving
Lyricist(s) Berlin, Irving
Choreographer(s) Alton, Robert

Producer(s) Freed, Arthur
Director(s) Walters, Charles
Screenwriter(s) Sheldon, Sidney; Goodrich, Frances; Hackett, Albert

Cast Garland, Judy; Astaire, Fred; Lawford, Peter; Miller, Ann; Munshin, Jules; Sundberg, Clinton; Beavers, Richard

Song(s) Happy Easter; Drum Crazy; It Only Happens When I Dance with You; A Fella with an Umbrella; It Only Happens When I Dance with You; Steppin' Out with My Baby; A Couple of Swells; Better Luck Next Time; Mister Monotony [1] [4]; I Love You—You Love Him [1]; Let's Take an Old Fashioned Walk [1] [2]; A Pretty Girl Is Like a Melody [1] [3]

Notes There are also vocals of the following Berlin songs: "Easter Parade" (also in HOLIDAY INN and ALEXANDER'S RAGTIME BAND), "I Want to Go Back to Michigan (Down on the Farm)," "I Love a Piano," "Snookey Ookums," "Ragtime Violin" (also in ALEXANDER'S RAGTIME BAND), "When the Midnight Choo-Choo Leaves for Alabam'" (also in ALEXANDER'S RAGTIME BAND and THERE'S NO BUSINESS LIKE SHOW BUSINESS), "Shaking the Blues Away" and "The Girl on the Magazine Cover." Astaire replaced Gene Kelly just prior to production. [1] Deleted from final print. [2] Put into stage musical MISS LIBERTY. [3] From ZIEGFELD FOLLIES. [4] Later put into and deleted from Broadway musicals MISS LIBERTY and CALL ME MADAM. It finally opened on Broadway in JEROME ROBBINS ON BROADWAY.

1567 ✦ EAST SIDE OF HEAVEN
Universal, 1939

Composer(s) Monaco, James V.
Lyricist(s) Burke, Johnny
Choreographer(s) Raset, Val

Director(s) Butler, David
Screenwriter(s) Conselman, William

Cast Crosby, Bing; Baby Sandy; Blondell, Joan; Auer, Mischa; Jones, Jane; The Music Maids; Smith, C. Aubrey; Cowan, Jerome; Travers, Mary

Song(s) Golden Wedding Song; Song of the Newlyweds; Sing a Song of Sunbeams; Hang Your Heart on a Hickory Limb; That Sly Old Gentleman from

Featherbed Lane; East Side of Heaven; I'm in Love with a Jitterbug [1]

Notes [1] Not used.

1568 ✦ EASY COME, EASY GO (1947)
Paramount, 1947

Musical Score Webb, Roy

Producer(s) Macgowan, Kenneth
Director(s) Farrow, John
Screenwriter(s) Faragoh, Francis Edwards; McNulty, John; Froelick, Anne
Source(s) sketches by McNulty, John

Cast Fitzgerald, Barry; Lynn, Diana; Tufts, Sonny; Foran, Dick; McHugh, Frank; Jenkins, Allen; Litel, John; Shields, Arthur; Faylen, Frank; Burke, James; Cleveland, George

Song(s) Easy Come, Easy Go [1] (C/L: Livingston, Jay; Evans, Ray); New York! Oh What a Charming City [2] (C/L: Gairdner, I.A.)

Notes [1] Not used but published. [2] Not written for film.

1569 ✦ EASY COME—EASY GO (1965)
Paramount, 1965 unproduced

Song(s) Surf City (C/L: Wilson, Brian; Berry, Jan); I Found a Girl (C/L: Sloan, Phil; Barri, Steve); The Little Old Lady from Pasadena (C/L: Altfeld, Don; Christian, Roger); Drag City (C/L: Christian, Roger; Berry, Jan; Wilson, Brian)

1570 ✦ EASY COME, EASY GO (1967)
Paramount, 1967

Musical Score Lilley, Joseph J.
Choreographer(s) Winters, David

Producer(s) Wallis, Hal B.
Director(s) Rich, John
Screenwriter(s) Weiss, Allan; Lawrence, Anthony

Cast Presley, Elvis; Marshall, Dodie; Priest, Pat; Harrington Jr., Pat; Ward, Skip; McHugh, Frank; Lanchester, Elsa; Carey, Gil

Song(s) Easy Come, Easy Go (C: Weisman, Ben; L: Wayne, Sid); I'll Take Love (C/L: Fuller, Dee; Larkan, Mark); Sing You Children, Sing (C/L: Nelson, Gerald; Burch, Fred); The Love Machine (C/L: Nelson, Gerald; Burch, Fred; Taylor, Chuck); Yoga Is As Yoga Does (C/L: Nelson, Gerald; Burch, Fred); You Gotta Stop (C/L: Giant, Bill; Baum, Bernie; Kaye, Florence); Go Go Jo [1] (C/L: LeGault, Lance); Freak Out [1] (C/L: LeGault, Lance)

Notes Previously named EASY DOES IT. [1] Not written for film.

1571 ✦ EASY LIVING (1937)
Paramount, 1937

Producer(s) Hornblow Jr., Arthur
Director(s) Leisen, Mitchell
Screenwriter(s) Sturges, Preston

Cast Arthur, Jean; Arnold, Edward; Dale, Esther; Alberni, Luis; Milland, Ray; Nash, Mary; Pangborn, Franklin; Demarest, William

Song(s) Easy Living [1] (C: Rainger, Ralph; L: Robin, Leo)

Notes [1] The number is only used instrumentally. It is later used vocally in the RKO film EASY LIVING.

1572 ✦ EASY LIVING (1949)
RKO, 1949

Musical Score Webb, Roy

Producer(s) Sparks, Robert
Director(s) Tourneur, Jacques
Screenwriter(s) Schnee, Charles
Source(s) "The Education of the Heart" (story) Shaw, Irwin

Cast Mature, Victor; Ball, Lucille; Scott, Lizabeth; Tufts, Sonny; Nolan, Lloyd; Stewart, Paul; Paar, Jack; Donnell, Jeff; Baker, Art; Lang, Charles; The Los Angeles Rams

Song(s) Easy Living [1] (C: Rainger, Ralph; L: Robin, Leo)

Notes [1] Previously used instrumentally in the Paramount film EASY LIVING.

1573 ✦ EASY MONEY
Orion, 1983

Musical Score Rosenthal, Laurence

Producer(s) Nicolella, John
Director(s) Signorelli, James
Screenwriter(s) Dangerfield, Rodney; Endler, Michael; O'Rourke, P.J.; Blair, Dennis

Cast Dangerfield, Rodney; Pesci, Joe; Fitzgerald, Geraldine; Axxara, Candy; Avery, Val; Noonan, Tommy [1]; Jones, Jeffrey; Ewell, Tom; Leigh, Jennifer Jason

Song(s) Easy Money (C/L: Joel, Billy)

Notes No cue sheet available. [1] Not the same as Tommy Noonan (he died in 1968).

1574 ✦ EASY RIDER
Columbia, 1969

Producer(s) Fonda, Peter
Director(s) Hopper, Dennis
Screenwriter(s) Fonda, Peter; Hopper, Dennis; Sothern, Terry

Cast Fonda, Peter; Hopper, Dennis; Anders, Luana; Askew, Luke; Black, Karen; Walker, Robert; Nicholson, Jack

Song(s) The Pusher (C/L: Axton, Hoyt); Born to Be Wild (C/L: Bonfire, Mars); I Wasn't Born to Follow (C/L: Goffin, Gerry; King, Carole); The Weight (C/L: Robertston, Robbie); If You Want to Be a Bird (C/L: Duren, Antonio); Don't Bogart Me (C/L: Ingber, Elliott; Wagner, Larry); If Six Was Nine (C/L: Hendrix, Jimi); Let's Turky Trot (C/L: Goffin, Gerry; Keller, Jack); Kyrie Eleison (C/L: Axelrod, David A.); Flash, Bam, Pow (C/L: Bloomfield, Mike); It's Alright Ma (I'm Only Bleeding) (C/L: McGuinn, Roger; Dylan, Bob); Ballad of Easy Rider [1] (C/L: Dylan, Bob; McGuinn, Roger)

Notes No cue sheet available. [1] Dylan not credited on sheet music.

1575 ✦ EASY TO LOOK AT
Universal, 1945

Musical Score Skinner, Frank
Composer(s) Newman, Charles; Altman, Arthur
Lyricist(s) Newman, Charles; Altman, Arthur

Producer(s) Blankfort, Henry
Director(s) Beebe, Ford
Screenwriter(s) Blankfort, Henry

Cast Jean, Gloria; Grant, Kirby; Bromberg, J. Edward; Dolenz, George; Blore, Eric; Belasco, Leon; French, Dick; The Delta Rhythm Boys

Song(s) Come Along My Heart; Is You Is Or Is You Ain't My Baby [1] (C/L: Jordan, Louis; Austin, Billy); That Does It!; Umbrella with a Silver Lining; Just for the Devil of It; Swing Low Sweet Lariat

Notes [1] Also in THE BEAUTIFUL CHEAT.

1576 ✦ EASY TO LOVE (1934)
Warner Brothers, 1934

Producer(s) Blanke, Henry
Director(s) Keighley, William
Screenwriter(s) Erickson, Carl; Seff, Manuel
Source(s) *As Good As New* (play) Buchanan, Thompson

Cast Menjou, Adolphe; Tobin, Genevieve; Astor, Mary; Horton, Edward Everett; Ellis, Patricia; Herbert, Hugh; Cavanaugh, Hobart; Kibbee, Guy

Song(s) Easy to Love (C: Fain, Sammy; L: Kahal, Irving)

Notes No cue sheet available.

1577 ✦ EASY TO LOVE (1953)
Metro–Goldwyn–Mayer, 1953

Composer(s) Mizzy, Vic
Lyricist(s) Curtis, Mann
Choreographer(s) Berkeley, Busby

Producer(s) Pasternak, Joe
Director(s) Walters, Charles
Screenwriter(s) Vadnay, Laslo; Roberts, William

Cast Williams, Esther [1]; Johnson, Van; Martin, Tony; Bromfield, John; Skinner, Edna; Donovan, King; Bryar, Paul; Baker, Carroll

Song(s) Didja' Ever!; Look Out! I'm Romantic; Coquette [2] (C: Lombardo, Carmen; Green, Johnny; L: Kahn, Gus); Easy to Love [3] (C/L: Porter, Cole); That's What a Rainy Day Is For

Notes Carroll Baker's first film. [1] Dubbed by Betty Wand. [2] Also used in the MGM film BORN TO DANCE. [3] Written in 1928.

1578 ✦ EASY TO WED
Metro–Goldwyn–Mayer, 1946

Composer(s) Green, Johnny
Lyricist(s) Blane, Ralph
Choreographer(s) Donohue, Jack

Producer(s) Cummings, Jack
Director(s) Buzzell, Edward
Screenwriter(s) Kingsley, Dorothy

Cast Williams, Esther; Johnson, Van; Ball, Lucille [2]; Wynn, Keenan; Kellaway, Cecil; Ramirez, Carlos; Blue, Ben; Smith, Ethel

Song(s) The Continental Polka; Viva Mexico [4] (C: Galindo, Pedro; L: Galindo, Pedro; Stewart, Al); Acercate Mas (Come Closer to Me) (C: Farres, Osvaldo; L: Stewart, Al); Boneca De Pixe (C/L: Barroso, Ary); Gonna Fall in Love with You [1]; Toca Tu Samba (C/L: Soler, Raoul); Easy To Wed [3] (L: Duncan, Ted); It Shouldn't Happen to a Duck [3] (L: Franklin, Robert); Someone Shoulda Told Me [5] (C: Barroso, Ary; L: Kipp, L.T.); Let's Get This War Over With [6]; Tell Ya What I'm Gonna Do [6]

Notes A remake of LIBELED LADY. [1] Used instrumentally only. [2] Dubbed by Virginia Rees. [3] In some sources but not on cue sheet. [4] Stewart's English lyrics not used in film [5] Sheet music only. [6] Not used.

1579 ✦ EATING RAOUL
Twentieth Century–Fox, 1982

Musical Score Ober, Arlon
Composer(s) Ober, Arlon
Lyricist(s) Ober, Arlon

Producer(s) Kimmel, Anne
Director(s) Bartel, Paul
Screenwriter(s) Blackburn, Richard; Bartel, Paul

Cast Bartel, Paul; Woronov, Mary; Beltran, Robert; Saiger, Susan; Hobart, Lynn; Paul, Richard

Song(s) Gimme the Cash Jack; Doggie King Commercial (L: Bartel, Paul); El Amante Triste [1] (L:

Beltran, Robert); Devil with the Blue Dress On [1] (C/L: Stevenson, William; Long, Frederick)

Notes [1] Not on cue sheet.

1580 ◆ EATIN' ON THE CUFF
Warner Brothers, 1942

Musical Score Stalling, Carl

Director(s) Clampett, Bob
Screenwriter(s) Foster, Warren

Song(s) The Moth and the Flame (C/L: Ford, Mickey)

Notes Looney Tune. It is not known if the song was written for this cartoon.

1581 ◆ EBB TIDE
Paramount, 1937

Musical Score Young, Victor

Producer(s) Hubbard, Lucien
Director(s) Hogan, James
Screenwriter(s) Millhauser, Bertram
Source(s) *Ebb Tide* (novel) Stevenson, Robert Louis; Osborne, Lloyd

Cast Nolan, Lloyd; Farmer, Frances; Basquette, Lina; Judels, Charles; Homolka, Oscar; Fitzgerald, Barry

Song(s) Ebb Tide (C: Rainger, Ralph; L: Robin, Leo); Hula Baloo (C: Rainger, Ralph; L: Robin, Leo); I Know What Aloha Means (C: Rainger, Ralph; L: Robin, Leo)

1582 ◆ ECHOES
Entertainment Professionals, 1983

Musical Score Schwartz, Stephen
Composer(s) Schwartz, Stephen
Lyricist(s) Schwartz, Stephen

Producer(s) Nice, George R.; Belsky, Valerie Y.
Director(s) Seidelman, Arthur Allen
Screenwriter(s) Anthony, Richard J.

Cast Alfieri, Richard; Nell, Nathalie; Roman, Ruth; Sondergaard, Gale; McCambridge, Mercedes; Kellin, Mike; Crofoot, Leonard

Song(s) Time Out of Mind; Tailspin; A Night on the Town

Notes No cue sheet available.

1583 ◆ ECHOES OF A SUMMER
United Artists, 1976

Musical Score James, Terry

Producer(s) Joseph, Robert L.
Director(s) Taylor, Don
Screenwriter(s) Joseph, Robert L.

Cast Harris, Richard; Nettleton, Lois; Fitzgerald, Geraldine; Windom, William; Savage, Brad; Foster, Jodie

Song(s) The Last Castle [1] (C/L: Harris, Richard)

Notes Originally titled THE LAST CASTLE. [1] It is not known if this is a song with lyrics or just vocalizing.

1584 ◆ ECHO MOUNTAIN
Warner Brothers, 1936

Musical Score Jackson, Howard
Composer(s) Jerome, M.K.
Lyricist(s) Scholl, Jack

Song(s) Echo Mountain [1]; Swiss Chalet

Notes Short subject. [1] Also in EXPENSIVE HUSBANDS.

1585 ◆ EDDIE AND THE CRUISERS
Embassy, 1983

Musical Score Cafferty, John; Vance, Kenny
Composer(s) Cafferty, John
Lyricist(s) Cafferty, John

Producer(s) Brooks, Joseph; Lifton, Robert K.
Director(s) Davidson, Martin
Screenwriter(s) Davidson, Martin; Davidson, Arlene
Source(s) *Eddie and the Cruisers* (novel) Kluge, P.F.

Cast Berenger, Tom; Pare, Michael; Pantoliano, Joe; Laurance, Matthew; Schneider, Helen; Barkin, Ellen; Vance, Kenny

Song(s) On the Dark Side; Tender Years; Down on My Knees; Season in Hell, Fire Suite; Wild Summer Nights; Boardwalk Angel

Notes No cue sheet available.

1586 ◆ THE EDDIE CANTOR STORY
Warner Brothers, 1953

Choreographer(s) Prinz, LeRoy

Producer(s) Skolsky, Sidney
Director(s) Green, Alfred E.
Screenwriter(s) Weidman, Jerome; Sherdeman, Ted; Skolsky, Sidney

Cast Brasselle, Keefe [1]; Erskine, Marilyn; MacMahon, Aline; Forrest, William; Doran, Ann; March, Hal; Rogers Jr., Will; Windsor, Marie

Notes There are vocals of "Meet Me Tonight in Dreamland" by Beth Slater Whitson and Leo Friedman; "Bedelia" by William Jerome and Jean Schwartz; "Will You Love Me in December (As You Do in May?)" by Ernest R. Ball and James J. Walker; "Be My Little Baby Bumble Bee" by Stanley Murphy and Henry Marshall; "If I Was a Millionaire" by Will D. Cobb and Gus Edwards; "Love Me and the World Is Mine" by Ernest R. Ball and Dave Reed Jr.; "Row Row Row" by William Jerome and James V. Monaco; "How Ya Gonna Keep

'Em Down on the Farm, After They've Seen Paree" by Walter Donaldson and Joe Young; "Oh You Beautiful Doll" by A. Seymour Brown and Nat D. Ayer; "If You Knew Susie (Like I Know Susie)" by Joseph Meyer and B.G. DeSylva; "Bye Bye Blackbird" by Ray Henderson and Mort Dixon; "Pretty Baby" by Tony Jackson, Egbert Van Alstyne and Gus Kahn (also in APPLAUSE and I'LL BE SEEING YOU); "Yes Sir, That's My Baby" by Walter Donaldson and Gus Kahn (also in THE DANCE OF LIFE and I'LL SEE YOU IN MY DREAMS); "Josephine Please No Lean on Da Bell" by Harry Pease and Duke Leonard; "Yes, We Have No Bananas" by Frank Silver and Irving Conn; "Ida (Sweet As Apple Cider)" by Eddie Leonard and Eddie Munson; "Makin' Whoopee" by Walter Donaldson and Gus Kahn; "(Potatoes Are Cheaper, Tomatoes Are Cheaper) Now's the Time to Fall in Love" and "When I'm the President" by Al Sherman and Al Lewis; "One Hour with You" by Richard A. Whiting and Leo Robin; "You Must Have Been a Beautiful Baby" by Harry Warren and Johnny Mercer (also in DEEP ADVENTURE; HARD TO GET; THE HARD WAY; MILDRED PIERCE and MY DREAM IS YOURS); "Margie" by Benny Davis, Con Conrad and J.R. Robinson and "Ma (He's Makin' Eyes at Me)" by Sidney Clare and Con Conrad. Some of these songs are included in medleys. None of these songs were written for this picture. [1] Dubbed by Eddie Cantor.

1587 ◆ EDDIE MACON'S RUN
Universal, 1983

Musical Score Buffalo, Norton
Lyricist(s) Buffalo, Norton

Producer(s) Stroller, Louis A.
Director(s) Kanew, Jeff
Screenwriter(s) Kanew, Jeff
Source(s) *Eddie Macon's Run* (novel) McLendon, James

Cast Douglas, Kirk; Schneider, John; Purcell, Lee; Dunsheath, Lisa; Noonan, Tommy [1]; Quinn, J.C.; Rogers, Gil; Sanders, Jay O.

Song(s) It's Gonna Be Alright (C: Buffalo, Norton); Havin' You Back (C: Buffalo, Norton; Hinton, Mike); Forevermore (C: Buffalo, Norton; Hinton, Mike); Potts Mexicano (C/L: Kanew, Jeff; Buffalo, Norton; Bogas, Ed)

Notes [1] Not the same as Tommy Noonan.

1588 ◆ EDDIE MURPHY: RAW
Paramount, 1987

Producer(s) Wachs, Robert D.; Wayans, Keenan Ivory
Director(s) Townsend, Robert
Screenwriter(s) Murphy, Eddie; Wayans, Keenan Ivory

Cast Allen, Billie; Jackson, Samuel L.; Jackson, Leonard; Murphy, Eddie; Wayans, Damon

Song(s) Raw (C/L: Murphy, Eddie; Jones, David Allen; Antoon, Rod); Kick the Kan (C/L: Jones, David Allen)

Notes No cue sheet available.

1589 ◆ EDDY DUCHIN STORY
Columbia, 1956

Musical Score Duning, George

Producer(s) Wald, Jerry
Director(s) Sidney, George
Screenwriter(s) Taylor, Samuel

Cast Power, Tyrone; Novak, Kim; Shaw, Victoria; Whitmore, James; Thompson, Rex; Maga, Mickey; Strudwick, Shepperd; Inescort, Frieda; Holden, Gloria; Keating, Larry; Albertson, Jack

Notes There are no original songs in this picture. Vocals include "You're My Everything" by Mort Dixon, Harry Warren and Joe Young and "Brazil" by Ary Barroso and S.K. (Bob) Russell. The piano recordings are by Carmen Cavallaro.

1590 ◆ THE EDUCATION OF SONNY CARSON
Paramount, 1974

Musical Score Perkinson, Coleridge-Taylor; Diggs, Benny; New York Community Choir, The
Composer(s) Perkinson, Coleridge-Taylor
Lyricist(s) Kessler, Bob

Producer(s) Yablans, Irwin
Director(s) Campus, Michael
Screenwriter(s) Hudson, Fred
Source(s) (book) Carson, Sonny

Cast Clanton, Rony; Gordon, Don; Walker, Joyce; Benjamin, Paul; Alice, Mary; Hopkins, Linda

Song(s) Girl, Girl, Girl; Where Do I Go (From Here?); Let's Go Higher (C/L: Wright, Timothy)

1591 ◆ EGGS DON'T BOUNCE
Paramount, 1943

Song(s) Now Ya Done It (C: Timberg, Sammy; L: Kaye, Buddy; Wise, Fred)

Notes A Little Lulu cartoon. No cue sheet available. Sheet music only.

1592 ◆ THE EGYPTIAN
Twentieth Century–Fox, 1954

Musical Score Newman, Alfred; Herrmann, Bernard

Producer(s) Zanuck, Darryl F.
Director(s) Curtiz, Michael
Screenwriter(s) Dunne, Philip; Robinson, Casey
Source(s) *Sinuhe the Egyptian* (novel) Waltari, Mika

Cast Simmons, Jean; Mature, Victor; Tierney, Gene; Wilding, Michael; Darvi, Bella; Ustinov, Peter; Purdom, Edmund; Evelyn, Judith; Daniell, Henry; Carradine, John; Rettig, Tommy; de Lavallade, Carmen

Song(s) Hymn to Aton [1] (C: Newman, Alfred; L: Steindorff, George; Seele, Keith C.)

Notes [1] Lyrics from the book *When Egypt Ruled the East.*

1593 ✦ EIGHT BALL BUNNY
Warner Brothers, 1950

Musical Score Stalling, Carl

Director(s) Jones, Chuck
Screenwriter(s) Maltese, Michael

Cast Bunny, Bugs

Song(s) Calypso Bunny (C/L: Maltese, Michael)

Notes Looney Tune cartoon.

1594 ✦ EIGHT GIRLS IN A BOAT
Paramount, 1934

Lyricist(s) Coslow, Sam

Producer(s) Rogers, Charles R.
Director(s) Wallace, Richard
Screenwriter(s) Robinson, Casey; Rebner, Arthur
Source(s) (story) Brandis, Helmut

Cast Montgomery, Douglass; Wilson, Dorothy; Johnson, Kay; Connolly, Walter

Song(s) A Day without You (C: Rebner, Arthur); This Little Piggy Went to Market [2] (C: Lewis, Harold); Eight Girls in a Boat [1] (C: Lewis, Harold)

Notes *Variety* lists the lyricist as Gilbert Warrenton. [1] Not used. [2] Also used in SHE MADE HER BED.

1595 ✦ EIGHT MEN OUT
Orion, 1988

Musical Score Daring, Mason

Producer(s) Pillsbury, Sarah; Sanford, Midge
Director(s) Sayles, John
Screenwriter(s) Sayles, John
Source(s) (book) Asinof, Eliot

Cast Cusack, John; Strathairn, David; Sweeney, D.B.; Mahoney, John; Clapp, Gordon; Rooker, Michael; Sheen, Charlie; Harvey, Don; Lerner, Michael; James, Clifton; Lloyd, Christopher; Sayles, John; Lang, Perry; Terkel, Studs; Mantell, Michael

Song(s) I Be Blue (C: Daring, Mason; L: Sayles, John; Daring, Mason)

Notes No cue sheet available.

1596 ✦ 80 STEPS TO JONAH
Warner Brothers, 1969

Musical Score Vincent, Don; Shearing, George
Composer(s) Vincent, Don
Lyricist(s) Newton, Wayne

Producer(s) Oswald, Gerd
Director(s) Oswald, Gerd
Screenwriter(s) Fox, Frederic Louis

Cast Newton, Wayne; Rooney, Mickey; Van Fleet, Jo; Ewing, Diana; Mineo, Sal; Pickens, Slim; Wynn, Keenan; Armstrong, R.G.

Song(s) My World; Tender Lovin' Care; If I Could Be to You; It's Such a Lonely Time of Year (C/L: Gorgoni, Al; Taylor, Chip)

1597 ✦ EL DORADO
Paramount, 1967

Musical Score Riddle, Nelson

Producer(s) Hawks, Howard
Director(s) Hawks, Howard
Screenwriter(s) Brackett, Leigh
Source(s) *The Stars in Their Courses* (novel) Brown, Harry

Cast Wayne, John; Mitchum, Robert; Caan, James; George, Christopher; Carey, Michael; Asner, Edward; Hunnicutt, Arthur; Holt, Charlene

Song(s) El Dorado (C: Riddle, Nelson; L: Gabriel, John)

1598 ✦ ELECTRA GLIDE IN BLUE
United Artists, 1973

Composer(s) Guercio, James William

Producer(s) Guercio, James William
Director(s) Guercio, James William
Screenwriter(s) Boris, Robert; Butler, Michael

Cast Blake, Robert; Bush, Billy "Green"; Ryan, Mitchell; Riley, Jeannine; Cook Jr., Elisha; Dano, Royal

Song(s) Meadow Mountain Top (C/L: Spoelstra, Mark); Song of Sad Bottles (C/L: Spoelstra, Mark); Tell Me (C/L: Guercio, James William); Free from the Devil Suite (Excerpt) (C/L: De Carlo, Alan; Wolinski, David; Salomone, Ross)

Notes There is also a background vocal of "Most of All" by Alan Freed and Harvey Fuqua.

1599 ✦ ELECTRIC DREAMS
MGM/UA, 1984

Musical Score Moroder, Giorgio

Producer(s) Lemorande, Rusty; De Waay, Larry
Director(s) Barron, Steve
Screenwriter(s) Lemorande, Rusty

Cast Von Dohlen, Lenny; Madsen, Virginia; Caulfield, Maxwell; Cort, Bud; Fellows, Don; Polonsky, Alan; Margolyes, Miriam

Song(s) Electric Dreams (C/L: O'Dowd, George; Pickett, Phil); Now You're Mine (C: Moroder, Giorgio; L: St. John, Helen; Lemorande, Rusty); Video (C/L: Lynne, Jeff); Let It Run (C/L: Lynne, Jeff); Love Is Love (C/L: Culture Club); The Dream (C/L: Culture Club); Together in Electric Dreams (C: Moroder, Giorgio; L: Oakey, Phil); Chaserunner (C/L: Marsh, Ian Craig; Ware, Martyn; Gregory, Glen)

Notes No cue sheet available.

1600 ✦ THE ELECTRIC HORSEMAN
Universal–Columbia, 1979

Musical Score Grusin, Dave

Producer(s) Stark, Ray
Director(s) Pollack, Sydney
Screenwriter(s) Garland, Robert

Cast Redford, Robert; Fonda, Jane; Perrine, Valerie; Nelson, Willie; Saxon, John; Coster, Nicolas; Arbus, Allan; Brimley, Wilford; Sikking, James B.

Song(s) Disco Magic (C/L: Grusin, Dave; Austin, Patti)

Notes There are also vocals of the following songs (It is not known if they were written for this film): "My Heroes Have Always Been Cowboys" by Sharon Vaughn; "Mammas Don't Let Your Babies Grow Up to Be Cowboys" by Ed Bruce and Patsy Bruce; "Midnight Rider" by Gregory Allman and "Hands on the Wheel" by Bill Callery.

1601 ✦ ELEPHANT GUN
United Artists, 1959

Musical Score Bernard, James

Producer(s) Stafford, John
Director(s) Annakin, Ken
Screenwriter(s) Elmes, Guy

Cast Lee, Belinda; Craig, Michael; McGoohan, Patrick; Gaylor, Anna

Song(s) Nor the Moon By Night (C: Bernard, James; L: Fishman, Jack)

Notes This is a British production titled NOR THE MOON BY NIGHT.

1602 ✦ ELEPHANT WALK
Paramount, 1954

Musical Score Waxman, Franz
Choreographer(s) Gopal, Ram

Producer(s) Asher, Irving
Director(s) Dieterle, William

Screenwriter(s) Mahin, John Lee
Source(s) *Elephant Walk* (novel) Standish, Robert

Cast Taylor, Elizabeth; Finch, Peter; Andrews, Dana; Sofaer, Abraham

Song(s) Many Dreams Ago [1] (C: Waxman, Franz; L: David, Mack)

Notes [1] Used instrumentally only.

1603 ✦ 11 HARROWHOUSE
Twentieth Century–Fox, 1974

Musical Score Lewis, Michael J.
Composer(s) Lewis, Michael J.
Lyricist(s) Shaper, Hal

Producer(s) Kastner, Elliott
Director(s) Avakian, Aram
Screenwriter(s) Bloom, Jeffrey
Source(s) *Eleven Harrowhouse* (novel) Browne, Gerald A.

Cast Grodin, Charles; Bergen, Candice; Gielgud, John; Howard, Trevor; Mason, James; Cherry, Helen

Song(s) Day After Day; Long Live Love

1604 ✦ ELLE COURT, ELLE COURT, LA BANLIEUE
United Artists, 1973

Musical Score Welch, Ed

Producer(s) Braunberger, Pierre
Director(s) Pires, Gerard
Screenwriter(s) De Buron, Nicole
Source(s) (novel) Gros, Brigitte

Cast Keller, Martha; Higelin, Jacques; Cordy, Annie; Lanoux, Victor; Courval, Nathalie

Song(s) Paradise in Suburb Land (C/L: Welch, Ed); Marlene (C/L: Higelin, Jacques; Bloch-Laine, O.); They Never Told Us (C/L: Welch, Ed); Surprise Party (C/L: Higelin, Jacques; Bloch-Laine, O.); I Couldn't Wait to Tell You (C: Welch, Ed; L: Paxton, Tom)

1605 ✦ ELMER AND ELSIE
Paramount, 1934

Director(s) Pratt, Gilbert
Screenwriter(s) Pearson, Humphrey
Source(s) *To the Ladies* (play) Kaufman, George S.; Connelly, Marc

Cast Bancroft, George; Fuller, Frances; Karns, Roscoe; Barbier, George

Song(s) The Tattooed Lady [1] (C/L: O'Keefe, Walter)

Notes [1] Also in the MGM films CALM YOURSELF and O'SHAUGHNESSY'S BOY.

1606 ✦ EL MILAGRO DE LA CALLE MAYOR
Twentieth Century–Fox, 1939

Musical Score Salter, Hans J.; Jurmann, Walter
Composer(s) Salter, Hans J.; Jurmann, Walter
Lyricist(s) Salter, Hans J.; Jurmann, Walter

Song(s) Canto de Las Posadas (C/L: Unknown);
Canzonetta; Lullaby; City of Angels

Notes No other information available.

1607 ✦ EL OTRO SOY YO

See THE PRODIGAL RETURNS.

1608 ✦ EL PASO
Paramount, 1949

Musical Score Calker, Darrell
Composer(s) Calker, Darrell
Lyricist(s) Bilder, Robert

Producer(s) Pine, William; Thomas, William
Director(s) Foster, Lewis R.
Screenwriter(s) Foster, Lewis R.

Cast Payne, John; Russell, Gail; Hayden, Sterling;
Hayes, George "Gabby"; Foran, Dick; Hull, Henry;
Warner, H.B.

Song(s) My Love [1]; El Paso [1]

Notes [1] These songs are only used instrumentally as
background themes.

1609 ✦ EL PRINCIPE GONDOLERO
Paramount, 1931

Composer(s) Harling, W. Franke
Lyricist(s) Coslow, Sam

Director(s) Venturini, Edward

Song(s) You'll Fall in Love with Venice [1] [4];
Dantarini (Italian Comedy Song) (C/L: Grever, Maria);
Un Sueno (C/L: Grever, Maria; Coslow, Sam); I
Understand Tonight [1] [2]; I'm Afraid to Waltz with
You [1] [2] [3]

Notes This is a Spanish remake of HONEYMOON
HATE, a 1927 film. The Harling and Coslow songs
were written for a proposed English musical remake of
the silent film but it wasn't produced. See
HONEYMOON HATE for complete list of songs
proposed for that movie. [1] Spanish lyrics by Maria
Grever. [2] Not used. [3] Also not used in FOUR
HOURS TO KILL. Not used in TROUBLE IN
PARADISE. [4] Not used in TROUBLE IN
PARADISE.

1610 ✦ EL RANCHO GRANDE
Republic, 1940

Composer(s) Rose, Fred; Marvin, Johnny; Autry, Gene
Lyricist(s) Rose, Fred; Autry, Gene; Marvin, Johnny

Producer(s) Berke, William
Director(s) McDonald, Frank
Screenwriter(s) Burbridge, Betty; Ropes, Bradford

Cast Autry, Gene; Burnette, Smiley; Storey, June; Lee,
Mary; Hogan, Dick; Lowe, Ellen E.; Taylor, Ferris;
Barcroft, Roy

Song(s) Whistle; Dude Ranch Cowhands [4]; The
Swing of the Range (C: Marvin, Johnny; L: Tobias,
Harry); There'll Never Be Another Pal Like You (C:
Marvin, Johnny; L: Autry, Gene); You Can Take the Boy
Out of the Country (C/L: Burnette, Smiley); I Don't
Belong in Your World; Autry's Your Man [1] [2] (C/L:
Samuels, Walter G.); A Cowboy's Gal [1] (C: Fain,
Sammy; L: Brown, Lew); Joggin' Down the Trail [1]
(C/L: Marvin, Johnny); The Cowboy and the Lady [1]
[3] (C/L: Quenzer, Arthur; Newman, L.); Belles of the
Bunkhouse [1] (C/L: Samuels, Walter G.)

Notes There is also a vocal of "Alla en el Rancho
Grande" by Silvano Ramos and J.D. Del Moral, with
English lyrics by Bartley Costello. [1] These songs are in
manuscript form at the Republic collection at Brigham
Young but do not appear on cue sheets. [2] In
WESTERN JAMBOREE. [3] Also in DOWN MEXICO
WAY. [4] Also in GOLD MINE IN THE SKY.

1611 ✦ EL REY DE LOS GITANOS
Fox, 1933

Composer(s) Vecsei, Armand
Lyricist(s) Gilbert, L. Wolfe

Director(s) Strayer, Frank R.

Cast Mojica, Jose; Moreno, Rosita; Villareal, Julio

Song(s) Song of the Romany Band; Without Love in a
Palace of Dreams; Fortune Telling Song; Serenade; Love
Calls; Carnival Song [1]

Notes No other information available. [1] Also in
NADA MAS QUE UNA MUJER and also in RASCALS
with lyrics credited to Harry Akst and Sidney Clare.

1612 ✦ EL TROVADOR DE LA RADIO
Paramount, 1938

Composer(s) Guizar, Tito
Lyricist(s) Noriega, Nenette

Producer(s) Faralla, Dario
Director(s) Harlan, Richard [5]
Screenwriter(s) Jones, Arthur V. [4]

Cast Guizar, Tito; Duarte, Robina [2]; Tana; Ellis,
Paul; Moreno, Paco

Song(s) Sueno De Amor (C: Guizar, Tito; Gama, Rafael); Presumida; Cantor del Pueblo; Trovador (C: Guizar, Tito; Gama, Rafael); Mujeres Latinas; Caprice Gitane [1] [3] (L: Tana); Matarili-ri-li-ron [1]; Tal Vez [1] [6]; Vagabundo [1] [6]; El Dia Que Yo Pueda [1]; Luna de Castilla [1] (C/L: Longas, Frederico; Rose, Ed; Schips, Tito)

Notes [1] Not used. [2] Formerly known as Jeanne Kelly. [3] In THE PRODIGAL RETURNS. [4] Spanish screenplay by Gabriel Navarro. [5] Dialogue director Gabriel Navarro. [6] Used in THE PRODIGAL RETURNS.

1613 ◆ EL ULTIMO VARON SOBRE LA TIERRA

See IT'S GREAT TO BE ALIVE.

1614 ◆ ELVIRA, MISTRESS OF THE DARK
New World, 1988

Musical Score Campbell, James

Producer(s) Gardner, Eric; Pierson, Mark
Director(s) Signorelli, James
Screenwriter(s) Egan, Sam; Paragon, John; Peterson, Cassandra

Cast Peterson, Cassandra; Greene, Daniel; Kellermann, Susan; Conaway, Jeff; McClurg, Edie; Rubenstein, Phil; Freeman, Damita Jo

Song(s) Here I Am (C: Poirot, Gary; L: Paragon, John)

Notes No cue sheet available.

1615 ◆ EMIL AND THE DETECTIVES
Disney, 1965

Musical Score Schreiter, Heinz

Director(s) Tewksbury, Peter
Screenwriter(s) Carothers, A.J.
Source(s) *Emil and the Detectives* (novel) Kastner, Erich

Cast Slezak, Walter; Russell, Bryan; Mobley, Roger; Schubert, Heinz

Song(s) My Pretty Baby Loves Me So (C: Schreiter, Heinz; L: Schaertel, Alan); Don't You Cry My Little Barbi-Jane [1] (C/L: Schaertel, Alan)

Notes [1] Not used.

1616 ◆ EMMANUELLE—THE JOYS OF A WOMAN
Paramount, 1976

Producer(s) Rousset-Rouard, Yves
Director(s) Giacobetti, Francis
Screenwriter(s) Giacobetti, Francis; Elia, Bob
Source(s) (book) Arsan, Emmanuelle

Cast Kristel, Sylvia; Orsini, Umberto; Laurence, Caroline; Lagache, Frederic; Rivet, Catherine

Song(s) Emmanuelle—The Joys of a Woman (C: Lai, Francis; L: Kusik, Larry)

1617 ◆ EMPEROR OF THE NORTH POLE
Twentieth Century–Fox, 1973

Musical Score De Vol, Frank

Producer(s) Hough, Stan
Director(s) Aldrich, Robert
Screenwriter(s) Knopf, Christopher

Cast Marvin, Lee; Borgnine, Ernest; Carradine, Keith; Tyner, Charles; Oakland, Simon

Song(s) A Man and a Train (C: De Vol, Frank; L: David, Hal)

1618 ◆ THE EMPEROR WALTZ
Paramount, 1948

Musical Score Young, Victor
Choreographer(s) Daniels, Billy

Producer(s) Brackett, Charles
Director(s) Wilder, Billy
Screenwriter(s) Wilder, Billy; Brackett, Charles

Cast Crosby, Bing; Haydn, Richard; Fontaine, Joan; Culver, Roland; Watson, Lucile; Rumann, Sig

Song(s) Friendly Mountains [1] (C: Lilley, Joseph J.; L: Burke, Johnny); The Kiss in Your Eyes [2] (C: Heuberger, Richard); L: Burke, Johnny); I Kiss Your Hand Madame [3] (C: Erwin, Ralph; L: Lewis, Sam M.; Young, Joe); Get Yourself a Phonograph [4] (C: Van Heusen, Jimmy; L: Burke, Johnny); Emperor Waltz [5] (C: Strauss, Johann; L: Burke, Johnny)

Notes The tune "The Whistler and His Dog" by Arthur Pryor is also used extensively in this film. [1] Music based on "Chambre Separee" by Richard Heuberger. [2] Music based on the Austrian folk songs entitled "Tyroler Sind Lustig" and "Erzherzog Johann." [3] Not written for picture. [4] Not used but apparently recorded. [5] Music based on Johann Strauss' "Emperor Waltz."

1619 ◆ EMPTY HOLSTERS
Warner Brothers–First National, 1937

Musical Score Jackson, Howard
Composer(s) Jerome, M.K.
Lyricist(s) Scholl, Jack

Producer(s) Foy, Bryan
Director(s) Eason, B. Reeves
Screenwriter(s) Neville, John Thomas

Cast Foran, Dick; Walthall, Pat; Vogan, Emmett

Song(s) I Gotta Get Back to My Gal [1]; By the Old Corral; The Prairie Is My Home [2]

Notes [1] Also in GOLD IS WHERE YOU FIND IT, SONGS OF THE RANGE and WEST OF THE ROCKIES. [2] Also in THE LAND BEYOND THE LAW, PRAIRIE THUNDER and GUNS OF THE PECOS.

1620 ◆ THE END
United Artists, 1978

Musical Score Williams, Paul; Freebairn-Smith, Ian

Producer(s) Gordon, Lawrence
Director(s) Reynolds, Burt
Screenwriter(s) Belson, Jerry

Cast Reynolds, Burt; DeLuise, Dom; Field, Sally; Martin, Strother; Steinberg, David; Woodward, Joanne; Fell, Norman; McNichol, Kristy; Loy, Myrna; Benson, Robby; Reiner, Carl

Song(s) What a Fine Mess (Here's Another Mess) (C/L: Williams, Paul)

1621 ◆ ENDANGERED SPECIES
Metro–Goldwyn–Mayer, 1982

Musical Score Wright, Gary

Producer(s) Pfeiffer, Carolyn
Director(s) Rudolph, Alan
Screenwriter(s) Rudolph, Alan; Binder, John

Cast Urich, Robert; Williams, Jobeth; Dooley, Paul; Axton, Hoyt; Coyote, Peter; Kanter, Marin; Carey Jr., Harry

Song(s) Beautiful Brown Eyes (C/L: Delmore, Alton; Smith, Arthur; Capehart, Jerry); Boozers Are Losers (C/L: Axton, Hoyt); Cold Places (C/L: Wright, Gary); Mac's Theme (C/L: Wright, Gary)

1622 ◆ ENDLESS LOVE
Universal, 1981

Musical Score Tunick, Jonathan

Producer(s) Barish, Keith; Lovell, Dyson
Director(s) Zeffirelli, Franco
Screenwriter(s) Rascoe, Judith
Source(s) *Endless Love* (novel) Spencer, Scott

Cast Hewitt, Martin; Shields, Brooke; Murray, Don; Knight, Shirley; Kiley, Richard; Straight, Beatrice; Spader, James; Milford, Penelope

Song(s) Endless Love (C/L: Richie, Lionel); Dreaming of You (C/L: Richie, Lionel; McClary, Thomas)

Notes Only original songs listed.

1623 ◆ ENEMY OF THE LAW
PRC, 1945

Musical Score Zahler, Lee; Grigor, Nico

Producer(s) Alexander, Arthur
Director(s) Fraser, Harry
Screenwriter(s) Fraser, Harry

Cast Ritter, Tex; O'Brien, Dave; Wilkerson, Guy; Hughes, Kay; Ingram, Jack; King, Charles; Maynard, Kermit

Song(s) Teach Me to Forget (C/L: Ritter, Tex; Harford, Frank); You Will Have to Pay (C/L: Ritter, Tex; Todd, Bonnie; Cooper, Sarah Jane)

1624 ◆ ENTER LAUGHING
Columbia, 1967

Musical Score Jones, Quincy

Producer(s) Stein, Joseph; Reiner, Carl
Director(s) Reiner, Carl
Screenwriter(s) Reiner, Carl
Source(s) *Enter Laughing* (play) Stein, Joseph

Cast Ferrer, Jose; Winters, Shelley; Carter, Mel; May, Elaine; Santoni, Reni; Opatoshu, David; Rickles, Don; Kovack, Nancy; Reiner, Rob; Gilford, Jack; Pollard, Michael J.; Deacon, Richard; Stein, Danny; Faye, Herbie; Moreland, Mantan

Song(s) Enter Laughing (C: Jones, Quincy; L: David, Mack)

1625 ◆ ERASERHEAD
David K. Lynch Productions; American Film Institute, 1976

Musical Score Ivers, Peter; Waller, Thomas "Fats"

Producer(s) Lynch, David
Director(s) Lynch, David
Screenwriter(s) Lynch, David

Cast Nance, John; Stewart, Charlotte; Bates, Jeanne; Joseph, Allen; Near, Laurel

Song(s) In Heaven (Everything Is Fine) (C: Ivers, Peter; L: Lynch, David)

Notes No cue sheet available.

1626 ◆ ERNEST GOES TO CAMP
Disney, 1987

Musical Score Keister, Shane
Composer(s) Keister, Shane; Keister, Alice
Lyricist(s) Keister, Alice

Producer(s) Williams, Stacy
Director(s) Cherry, John
Screenwriter(s) Cherry, John; Sams, Coke

Cast Varney, Jim; Racimo, Victoria; Alzado, Lyle; Sartain, Gailard; Butler, Daniel; Cody, Iron Eyes; Vernon, John

Song(s) Gee, I'm Glad It's Rainin'; Brave Hearts; Quando Condo (C/L: Patten, Jay; Vitello, Ralph)

1627 ✦ ERNEST HEMINGWAY'S THE KILLERS

See THE KILLERS (1964).

1628 ✦ ERNEST SAVES CHRISTMAS
Disney, 1988

Musical Score Snow, Mark

Producer(s) Williams, Stacy; Claybourne, Doug
Director(s) Cherry, John
Screenwriter(s) Kline, Benjamin; Turner, Ed

Cast Varney, Jim; Clarke, Oliver; Parker, Noelle; Sartain, Gailard; Bird, Billie; Byrge, Bill; Seale, Douglas

Song(s) Uncle Joey's Treehouse (C/L: Rowland, Joanie Diener)

1629 ✦ THE ERRAND BOY
Paramount, 1962

Musical Score Scharf, Walter

Producer(s) Glucksman, Ernest D.
Director(s) Lewis, Jerry
Screenwriter(s) Lewis, Jerry; Richmond, Bill

Cast Lewis, Jerry; Donlevy, Brian; Rumann, Sig; Adrian, Iris; McNear, Howard; Taylor, Renee; Adams, Stanley; Freeman, Kathleen; Weaver, Doodles; Feld, Fritz; Ritts, Paul; Ritts, Mary

Song(s) That's My Way (C: Brown, Louis Yule; L: Lewis, Jerry; Richmond, Bill)

1630 ✦ ESCAPADE
Metro–Goldwyn–Mayer, 1935

Musical Score Kaper, Bronislau; Jurmann, Walter

Producer(s) Hyman, Bernard H.
Director(s) Leonard, Robert Z.
Screenwriter(s) Mankiewicz, Herman J.
Source(s) *Maskerade* (movie) Reisch, Walter

Cast Powell, William; Rainer, Luise; Morgan, Frank; Christians, Mady; Owen, Reginald; Bruce, Virginia; Crews, Laura Hope

Song(s) You're All I Need [1] (C: Kaper, Bronislau; Jurmann, Walter; L: Kahn, Gus; Adamson, Harold)

Notes [1] Adamson only credited on cue sheet. Sheet music and ASCAP do not credit him.

1631 ✦ ESCAPADE IN JAPAN
RKO, 1957

Musical Score Steiner, Max

Producer(s) Lubin, Arthur
Director(s) Lubin, Arthur
Screenwriter(s) Miller, Winston

Cast Wright, Teresa; Mitchell, Cameron; Ober, Philip; Provost, Jon; Nakgawa, Roger; Miyake, Kuniko; Fujita, Susumu; Haida, Katsuhiko; Saito, Tatsuo

Song(s) The Lonely Song (C: Steiner, Max; L: Bennett, Norman)

Notes The Japanese lyrics are by Tak Shindo. There are also vocals of "Autumn Dance" and "Kutsuganaru" by Ryutaro Hirota and Katsura Shimizu; "Yaryuken" by Goken Maeda and "Rice Ear Dance."

1632 ✦ ESCAPE FROM ALCATRAZ
Paramount, 1979

Producer(s) Siegel, Don
Director(s) Siegel, Don
Screenwriter(s) Tuggle, Richard
Source(s) *Escape from Alcatraz* (novel) Bruce, J. Campbell

Cast Eastwood, Clint; Ward, Fred; Thibeau, Jack; McGoohan, Patrick; Fischer, Bruce

Song(s) "D" Block Blues (C/L: Thomas Jr., Gilbert)

1633 ✦ ESCAPE FROM FORT BRAVO
Metro–Goldwyn–Mayer, 1953

Musical Score Alexander, Jeff

Producer(s) Nayfack, Nicholas
Director(s) Sturges, John
Screenwriter(s) Fenton, Frank

Cast Holden, William; Parker, Eleanor; Forsythe, John; Demarest, William; Campbell, William; Bergen, Polly

Song(s) Yellow Stripes [1] (C/L: Jones, Stan); Soothe My Lonely Heart (C/L: Alexander, Jeff); Mescalero Death Chant (C/L: Alexander, Jeff)

Notes [1] Also in RIO GRANDE (Republic).

1634 ✦ ESCAPE FROM HONG KONG
Universal, 1942

Producer(s) Grant, Marshall
Director(s) Nigh, William
Screenwriter(s) Chanslor, Roy

Cast Terry, Don; Carrillo, Leo; Devine, Andy; Lord, Marjorie; Emery, Gilbert

Song(s) Where the Prairie Meets the Sky [1] (C: Rosen, Milton; L: Carter, Everett)

Notes [1] Also in BAD MAN FROM RED BUTTE, FRONTIER LAW, I'LL TELL THE WORLD and TWILIGHT ON THE PRAIRIE.

1635 ✦ ESCAPE ME IF YOU CAN

See ST. BENNY THE DIP.

1636 ✦ ESCAPE ME NEVER
Warner Brothers, 1947

Musical Score Korngold, Erich Wolfgang
Composer(s) Korngold, Erich Wolfgang
Choreographer(s) Prinz, LeRoy

Producer(s) Blanke, Henry
Director(s) Godfrey, Peter
Screenwriter(s) Williamson, Thomas
Source(s) *Escape Me Never* (play) Kennedy, Margaret; *Fool of the Family* (novel) Kennedy, Margaret

Cast Flynn, Errol; Lupino, Ida [1]; Parker, Eleanor; Young, Gig

Song(s) O Nene (L: Franchetti, Aldo); Love for Love (L: Koehler, Ted)

Notes [1] Dubbed by Peg LaCentra.

1637 ✦ ESCAPE TO ATHENA
ITC Entertainment, 1979

Musical Score Blue, Barry; Temperton, Rod

Producer(s) Niven Jr., David; Wiener, Jack
Director(s) Cosmatos, George P.
Screenwriter(s) Anhalt, Edward; Lochte, Richard S.

Cast Moore, Roger; Savalas, Telly; Gould, Elliott; Niven, David; Powers, Stefanie; Cardinale, Claudia; Roundtree, Richard; Bono, Sonny

Song(s) Keep Tomorrow for Me (C/L: Blue, Barry; Temperton, Rod)

Notes No cue sheet available.

1638 ✦ ESCAPE TO HAPPINESS

See INTERMEZZO.

1639 ✦ ESCORT WEST
United Artists, 1958

Musical Score Vars, Henry

Producer(s) Morrison, Robert E.; Edwards, Nate H.
Director(s) Lyon, Francis D.
Screenwriter(s) Gordon, Leo; Hartsook, Fred

Cast Mature, Victor; Stewart, Elaine; Domergue, Faith; Waters, Reba; Ching, William; Beery Jr., Noah; Pickens, Slim; Carey Jr., Harry

Song(s) Come with Me [1] (C/L: Dunham, "By")

Notes [1] "By" Dunham is a pseudonym for William Dunham.

1640 ✦ ETERNALLY YOURS
United Artists, 1939

Producer(s) Wanger, Walter
Director(s) Garnett, Tay
Screenwriter(s) Towne, Gene; Baker, Graham

Cast Young, Loretta; Niven, David; Herbert, Hugh; Smith, C. Aubrey; Burke, Billie; Crawford, Broderick; Walburn, Raymond; Pitts, ZaSu; Field, Virginia; Graves, Ralph; Arden, Eve; Pape, Lionel

Song(s) Eternally Yours (C: Janssen, Werner; L: Gilbert, L. Wolfe)

Notes No cue sheet available.

1641 ✦ EVA
Times Film, 1965

Musical Score Legrand, Michel

Producer(s) Hakim, Robert; Hakim, Raymond
Director(s) Losey, Joseph
Screenwriter(s) Butler, Hugo; Jones, Evan

Cast Moreau, Jeanne; Baker, Stanley; Lisi, Virna; Medici, Nona

Song(s) Adam and Eve (C: Legrand, Michel; L: Losey, Joseph; Jones, Evan)

Notes No cue sheet available.

1642 ✦ EVE KNEW HER APPLES
Columbia, 1945

Producer(s) McDonald, Wallace
Director(s) Jason, Will
Screenwriter(s) Moran, E. Edwin

Cast Miller, Ann; Wright, William; Williams, Robert; Walker, Ray; Brown, Charles D.; Eldredge, John; Bruce, Eddie

Song(s) Someone to Love (C/L: Warren, Bob); I'll Remember April (C/L: de Paul, Gene; Raye, Don; Johnston, Pat)

Notes No cue sheet available. There are two other songs in this film.

1643 ✦ EVE OF ST. MARK
Twentieth Century–Fox, 1944

Producer(s) Perlberg, William
Director(s) Stahl, John M.
Screenwriter(s) Seaton, George
Source(s) *The Eve of St. Mark* (play) Anderson, Maxwell

Cast   Baxter, Anne; Eythe, William; O'Shea, Michael; Price, Vincent; Nelson, Ruth; Collins, Ray; Prager, Stanley; Morgan, Henry; Bailey, Robert

Song(s)   Beer Barrel Polka (Roll Out the Barrel) [1] (C/L: Brown, Lew; Voda, Vej)

Notes   [1] Not written for this film.

1644 ◆ EVERGREEN
Gaumont–British, 1935

Composer(s)   Woods, Harry
Lyricist(s)   Woods, Harry
Choreographer(s)   Bradley, Buddy

Producer(s)   Balcon, Michael
Director(s)   Saville, Victor
Screenwriter(s)   Gaffney, Marjorie; Williams, Emlyn
Source(s)   *Ever Green* (musical) Rodgers, Richard; Hart, Lorenz; Levy, Benn W.

Cast   Matthews, Jessie [1]; Hale, Sonnie [1]; Balfour, Betty; MacKay, Barry; MacLaren, Ivor; Power, Hartley

Song(s)   If I Give in to You [1] (C: Rodgers, Richard; L: Hart, Lorenz); Dear, Dear [1] (C: Rodgers, Richard; L: Hart, Lorenz); Dancing on the Ceiling [1] (C: Rodgers, Richard; L: Hart, Lorenz); When You've Got a Little Springtime in Your Heart; Tinkle, Tinkle, Tinkle; Just By Your Example; Over My Shoulder

Notes   No cue sheet available. There are also vocals of "Daddy Wouldn't Buy Me a Bow-Wow" by Joseph Tabrar and "I Wouldn't Leave My Little Wooden Hut for You" by Tom Mellor and Charles Collins. [1] From original London production.

1645 ◆ THE EVERGREEN EMPIRE
Twentieth Century–Fox, 1939

Song(s)   Out Where the Trail Winds Into the Sky [1] (C: Tandler, H.J.; L: Lehr, Lew)

Notes   This is a Lowell Thomas Magic Carpet of Movietone travelogue. [1] Based on "When Twilight Comes" by Tandler.

1646 ◆ EVER SINCE EVE (1934)
Fox, 1934

Producer(s)   Wurtzel, Sol M.
Director(s)   Marshall, George
Screenwriter(s)   Johnson, Henry; Anthony, Stuart
Source(s)   *Heir to the Horrah* (play) Armstrong, Paul

Cast   O'Brien, George; Brian, Mary; Blythe, Peggy

Song(s)   Horsey (C: Holden, Cally; L: Marshall, George)

1647 ◆ EVER SINCE EVE (1937)
Warner Brothers–First National, 1937

Producer(s)   Wallis, Hal B.
Director(s)   Bacon, Lloyd

Screenwriter(s)   Riley, Lawrence; Baldwin, Earl; Hayward, Lillie

Cast   Davies, Marion; Montgomery, Robert; McHugh, Frank; Ralston, Marcia; Fazenda, Louise; MacLane, Barton

Song(s)   Wreath of Flowers (C/L: Kaaia; Hoopii Jr., Sol); Ever Since Eve (C: Jerome, M.K.; L: Scholl, Jack)

1648 ◆ EVER SINCE VENUS
Columbia, 1943

Composer(s)   Lee, Lester; Harris, Harry
Lyricist(s)   Lee, Lester; Harris, Harry
Choreographer(s)   Boyle, Jack

Director(s)   Dreifuss, Arthur
Screenwriter(s)   Dreifuss, Arthur; Moore, McElbert; McLeod, Victor; Lee, Connie

Cast   Herbert, Hugh; Ina Rae Hutton and Her Orchestra; Hunter, Ross; Savage, Ann; Gilbert, Billy; Feld, Fritz; Gateson, Marjorie; Mowbray, Alan; Farrell, Glenda; Hall, Thurston

Song(s)   Wedding of the Boogie and the Samba (C/L: Wayne, Bernie; Raleigh, Ben); Glamour for Sale; Rosebud I Love You; Do I Need You [1] (C: Chaplin, Saul; L: Cahn, Sammy)

Notes   [1] Written for BLONDIE GOES TO COLLEGE.

1649 ◆ EVERYBODY'S ALL AMERICAN
Warner Brothers, 1988

Musical Score   Howard, James Newton

Producer(s)   Hackford, Taylor; Ziskin, Laura; Sander, Ian
Director(s)   Hackford, Taylor
Screenwriter(s)   Rickman, Tom
Source(s)   (novel) Deford, Frank

Cast   Quaid, Dennis; Lange, Jessica; Hutton, Timothy; Goodman, John; Baker, Raymond; Lumbly, Carl

Song(s)   Until Forever (C/L: Howard, James Newton; Ballard, Glen; Walden, Narada Michael)

1650 ◆ EVERYBODY'S CHEERING

See TAKE ME OUT TO THE BALL GAME (1949).

1651 ◆ EVERYBODY'S DOIN' IT
RKO, 1937

Musical Score   Webb, Roy; Shilkret, Nathaniel

Producer(s)   Sistrom, William
Director(s)   Cabanne, Christy
Screenwriter(s)   Bren, J. Robert; Joseph, Edmund; Segall, Harry

Cast Foster, Preston; Eilers, Sally; Kellaway, Cecil; Krueger, Lorraine; Williams, Guinn "Big Boy"; Lake, Arthur; Ward, Solly

Song(s) Put Your Heart Into Your Feet and Dance (C: Borne, Hal; L: Greene, Mort)

1652 ◆ EVERYBODY SING
Metro–Goldwyn–Mayer, 1938

Musical Score Kaper, Bronislau; Jurmann, Walter
Composer(s) Kaper, Bronislau; Jurmann, Walter
Lyricist(s) Kahn, Gus
Choreographer(s) Gould, Dave; Felix, Seymour [2]

Producer(s) Rapf, Harry
Director(s) Marin, Edwin L.
Screenwriter(s) Ryerson, Florence; Woolf, Edgar Allan; Gruen, James

Cast Jones, Allan; Brice, Fanny; Garland, Judy; Burke, Billie; Owen, Reginald; Carver, Lynne; Gardiner, Reginald; Armetta, Henry

Song(s) Swing Mister Mendelssohn; The One I Love; Early Morning Sequence; Cosi Cosa [3] (L: Washington, Ned); Melody Farm; I'm Gonna Pack My Bag (C/L: Edens, Roger); Bus Sequence [1] (C: Verdi, Giuseppe; L: Kahn, Gus); Sweet Chariot (C/L: Edens, Roger); Quainty, Dainty Me (C: Ruby, Harry; L: Kalmar, Bert); The Show Must Go On (L: Edens, Roger; Kahn, Gus); Why? Because! (C: Ruby, Harry; L: Kalmar, Bert); Ever Since the World Began (C/L: Edens, Roger); Shall I Sing a Melody? (C/L: Edens, Roger)

Notes [1] Based on "Quartet" from RIGOLETTO. [2] Felix only staged "Quainty, Dainty Me." [3] Also in A DAY AT THE RACES (instrumentally) and A NIGHT AT THE OPERA.

1653 ◆ EVERYBODY'S OLD MAN
Twentieth Century–Fox, 1936

Producer(s) Rogers, Bogart
Director(s) Flood, James
Screenwriter(s) McNutt, Patterson; Thomas, A.E.

Cast Cobb, Irvin S.; Hudson, Rochelle; Downs, Johnny; Foster, Norman; Dinehart, Alan; Haden, Sara; Meek, Donald; Hymer, Warren

Song(s) Franklin's Foods (C: Pollack, Lew; L: Yellen, Jack)

1654 ◆ EVERY DAY'S A HOLIDAY (1936)
Paramount, 1936 unproduced

Song(s) Our Little Home on Wheels (Rolling Along) [1] (C/L: Coslow, Sam); Along the Broadway Trail [1] (C: Coslow, Sam; L: Coslow, Sam; Trivers, Barry)

Notes This film was also called IT'S ALL FREE. See also EVERY DAY'S A HOLIDAY (1937). [1] Also not

used in the produced version of EVERY DAY'S A HOLIDAY. [2] Also not used in THRILL OF A LIFETIME.

1655 ◆ EVERY DAY'S A HOLIDAY (1937)
Paramount, 1937

Choreographer(s) Prinz, LeRoy

Producer(s) Cohen, Emanuel
Director(s) Sutherland, Edward
Screenwriter(s) West, Mae

Cast West, Mae; Lowe, Edmund; Nolan, Lloyd; Butterworth, Charles; Winninger, Charles; Catlett, Walter; Conklin, Chester; Armstrong, Louis

Song(s) Flutter By Little Butterfly (C/L: Coslow, Sam); Every Day's a Holiday [6] (C: Coslow, Sam; L: Trivers, Barry; Coslow, Sam); Fifi (C/L: Coslow, Sam); Jubilee (C: Carmichael, Hoagy; L: Adams, Stanley); I Love You Like My Old Felt Hat [1] (C/L: Unknown); April in My Heart [1] [4] (C: Carmichael, Hoagy; L: Meinardi, Helen [2]); Our Little Home on Wheels (Rolling Along) [1] [7] [8] (C/L: Coslow, Sam); That Gal Salome [1] (C/L: Coslow, Sam); I've Got Manhattan on My Mind [1] [3] (C/L: Coslow, Sam); Our Little Home on the Highway [1] [8] (C/L: Coslow, Sam); Along the Broadway Trail [1] [5] (C: Coslow, Sam; L: Trivers, Barry; Coslow, Sam); Opening for Fifi Number [1] (C/L: Coslow, Sam); Riding on a Rainbow [1] (C: Carmichael, Hoagy)

Notes Some of these songs were intended for a cancelled film, also titled EVERY DAY'S A HOLIDAY. They may not all have been considered for this film, but the files indicate they were. This picture was originally titled SAPPHIRE SAL. Charles Winninger also performs "L'Estudiantina." The number "Vote for McCarey" is part of the number "Jubilee." [1] Not used. [2] She was Carmichael's sister-in-law. [3] Also called "I've Got Manhattan in My Soul." [4] Originally intended for COLLEGE SWING. Used in SAY IT IN FRENCH. [5] Written for the 1936 unproduced film EVERY DAY'S A HOLIDAY. Also not used in THRILL OF A LIFETIME. [6] Written for unproduced film SHADOW OF GLORY but without Trivers credit. [7] Written for the 1936 unproduced film EVERY DAY'S A HOLIDAY. [8] These sound like they might be the same song.

1656 ◆ EVERY LITTLE CROOK AND NANNY
Metro–Goldwyn–Mayer, 1972

Musical Score Karlin, Fred

Producer(s) Ackerman, Leonard J.
Director(s) Howard, Cy
Screenwriter(s) Howard, Cy; Axelrod, Jonathan; Klane, Robert
Source(s) *Every Little Crook and Nanny* (novel) Hunter, Evan

Cast Redgrave, Lynn; Mature, Victor; Sand, Paul; Blye, Maggie; Pendleton, Austin; Astin, John; DeLuise, Dom; Sorel, Louise; Morita, Pat; Harrington Jr., Pat; Darden, Severn

Song(s) Big Ben (C: Karlin, Fred; L: Kymry, Tylwyth)

1657 ◆ EVERY NIGHT AT EIGHT
Paramount, 1935

Composer(s) McHugh, Jimmy
Lyricist(s) Fields, Dorothy

Producer(s) Wanger, Walter
Director(s) Walsh, Raoul
Screenwriter(s) Towne, Gene; Baker, Graham; Hanlon, Bert
Source(s) "Three on a Mike" (story) Garvey, Stanley

Cast Raft, George; Faye, Alice; Langford, Frances; Kelly, Patsy; Catlett, Walter; Bing, Herman; Barris, Harry; The Radio Rogues; Miller, James [3]

Song(s) Take It Easy; I Feel a Song Coming On [4] (L: Oppenheimer, George; Fields, Dorothy); Speaking Confidentially; Every Night at Eight; I'm in the Mood for Love [1]; It's Great to Be in Love Again [2]; That's the Hollywood Low-Down [2]

Notes There are also vocals of "Don't Say Goodnight" by Harry Warren and Al Dubin (Also in the Warner Brothers film WONDER BAR) and "Then You've Never Been Blue" by Ted Fiorito, Joe Young and Frances Langford (Sam Lewis, not Frances Langford, is credited on the sheet music.) [1] Also used in ABOUT MRS. LESLIE; PEOPLE ARE FUNNY and THAT'S MY BOY. [2] Not used. [3] Singer of "I Feel a Song Coming On" during the Raft broadcast. [4] Oppenheimer contributed the title only.

1658 ◆ EVERY OTHER INCH A LADY

See DANCING CO-ED.

1659 ◆ EVERY SATURDAY NIGHT
Twentieth Century–Fox, 1936

Producer(s) Golden, Max H.
Director(s) Tinling, James
Screenwriter(s) Eliscu, Edward

Cast Lang, June; Beck, Thomas; Prouty, Jed; Byington, Spring; Roberts, Florence; Howell, Kenneth; Ernest, George; Carlson, June; The Paxton Sisters; Fraser, Phyllis

Song(s) I Sing of Spring (C: Sanders, Troy; L: Clare, Sidney); Breathes There a Man (C: Lane, Burton; L: Magidson, Herb)

1660 ◆ EVERY SUNDAY
Metro–Goldwyn–Mayer, 1936

Director(s) Feist, Felix E.
Screenwriter(s) Grashin, Mauri

Cast Garland, Judy; Durbin, Deanna

Song(s) Americana (C/L: Conrad, Con); Waltz with a Swing (C/L: Edens, Roger)

Notes Short subject.

1661 ◆ EVERYTHING HAPPENS TO US

See HI 'YA CHUM.

1662 ◆ EVERYTHING I HAVE IS YOURS
Metro–Goldwyn–Mayer, 1952

Musical Score Rose, David
Choreographer(s) Castle, Nick; Champion, Gower

Producer(s) Wells, George
Director(s) Leonard, Robert Z.
Screenwriter(s) Wells, George

Cast Champion, Marge; Champion, Gower; O'Keefe, Dennis; Lewis, Monica; Miller, Dean; Franz, Eduard

Song(s) My Heart Skips a Beat (C: Donaldson, Walter; L: Wright, Bob; Forrest, Chet); Like Monday Follows Sunday (C/L: Green, Johnny; Grey, Clifford; Newman, Gretrex; Furber, Douglas); Seventeen Thousand Telephone Poles (C/L: Chaplin, Saul); Derry Down Dilly (C: Green, Johnny; L: Mercer, Johnny); General Hiram Johnson Jefferson Brown [1] (C: Donaldson, Walter; L: Kahn, Gus)

Notes There is also a vocal of "Everything I Have Is Yours" by Burton Lane and Harold Adamson. [1] Written in 1934.

1663 ◆ EVERYTHING'S DUCKY
Columbia, 1961

Musical Score Green, Bernard
Composer(s) Spina, Harold
Lyricist(s) Spina, Harold

Producer(s) Doff, Red
Director(s) Taylor, Don
Screenwriter(s) Murray, John Fenton; Freedman, Benedict

Cast Rooney, Mickey; Hackett, Buddy; Cooper, Jackie; Sommers, Joanie; Winters, Roland; Moore, Alvy; Winslow, Dick; Kennedy, Harold J.

Song(s) Everything's Ducky; Moonlight Music; Scuttlebutt Walk

Notes No cue sheet available.

1664 ✦ EVERYTHING'S ON ICE
RKO, 1939

Producer(s) Lesser, Sol
Director(s) Kenton, Erle C.
Screenwriter(s) Landis, Adrian; Lowe, Sherman

Cast Dare, Irene; Karns, Roscoe; Kennedy, Edgar; Meeker, George; Hart, Mary; Watson, Bobby; Winchell, Paul

Song(s) Everything's on Ice (C: Stryker, Fred; L: Drake, Milton); Birth of a Snowbird (C: Young, Victor; L: Webster, Paul Francis); Georgie Porgie [1] (C: Stryker, Fred; L: Drake, Milton)

Notes [1] Not on cue sheets.

1665 ✦ EVERY WHICH WAY BUT LOOSE
Warner Brothers, 1978

Musical Score Dorff, Stephen H.; Garrett, Snuff

Producer(s) Daley, Robert
Director(s) Fargo, James
Screenwriter(s) Kronsberg, Jeremy Joe

Cast Eastwood, Clint; Locke, Sondra; D'Angelo, Beverly; Clyde; Gordon, Ruth; Chandler, George

Song(s) Every Which Way but Loose (C/L: Dorff, Stephen H.; Garrett, Snuff; Brown, Milton); Send Me Down to Tucson (C/L: Garrett, Snuff; Crofford, Cliff); I Seek the Night (C/L: Diamond, Neil); Coca Cola Cowboy (C/L: Pinkard, James; Dain, Irving; Dorff, Stephen H.; Atchely, Sam); Monkey See, Monkey Do (C/L: Crofford, Cliff; Garrett, Snuff); I Can't Say No to a Truck Drivin' Man (C/L: Crofford, Cliff); Ain't Love Good Tonight (C/L: Sklerov, Gloria; Cate, Randy; Howe, George); Red Eye Special (C/L: Collins, Larry; Pinkard, James; Garrett, Snuff); A Six Pack to Go (C/L: Thompson, Hank; Howe, James; Hart, D.); Biker's Theme (C/L: Brown, Milton; Dorff, Stephen H.; Garrett, Snuff); Don't Say You Don't Love Me No More (C/L: Everly, Phil; Page, Joey); I'll Wake You up When I Get Home (C/L: Dorff, Stephen H.; Brown, Milton L.); Behind Closed Doors (C/L: O'Dell, Kenny)

Notes Some of these are background vocal uses. It is not known which were written for the picture.

1666 ✦ EVERYWOMAN'S MAN

See THE PRIZE FIGHTER AND THE LADY.

1667 ✦ EVIDENCE
Warner Brothers, 1929

Director(s) Adolfi, John
Screenwriter(s) Alexander, J. Grubb
Source(s) *Evidence* (play) MacPherson, J. Du Rocher

Cast Frederick, Pauline; Tearle, Conway; Sherman, Lowell; Francis, Alec B.; Loy, Myrna

Song(s) Little Cavalier (C: Jerome, M.K.; L: Dubin, Al)

Notes No cue sheet available.

1668 ✦ EXCUSE MY DUST
Metro–Goldwyn–Mayer, 1951

Composer(s) Schwartz, Arthur
Lyricist(s) Fields, Dorothy
Choreographer(s) Pan, Hermes

Producer(s) Cummings, Jack
Director(s) Rowland, Roy
Screenwriter(s) Wells, George

Cast Skelton, Red; Forrest, Sally [1]; Carey, Macdonald; Demarest, William; Lewis, Monica; Walburn, Raymond

Song(s) I'd Like to Take You Out Dreaming; Lorelei Brown; Goin' Steady; Spring Has Sprung; Get a Horse; That's for Children; Where Can I Run from You [2]; It Couldn't Happen to Two Nicer People [2]

Notes [1] Dubbed by Gloria Grey. [2] Not used.

1669 ✦ EXPENSIVE HUSBANDS
Warner Brothers, 1937

Musical Score Roemheld, Heinz
Composer(s) Jerome, M.K.
Lyricist(s) Scholl, Jack

Producer(s) Foy, Bryan
Director(s) Connolly, Bobby
Screenwriter(s) Negulesco, Jean; Hayward, Lillie; Brennan, Jay
Source(s) "She Hired a Husband" (story) de Shishmareff, Kyrill

Cast Roberts, Beverly; Knowles, Patric; Joslyn, Allyn; Oliver, Gordon; Feld, Fritz

Song(s) Four Little Maids; Echo Mountain [1]; Shall We Dream Again

Notes [1] Also in ECHO MOUNTAIN (short).

1670 ✦ THE EXPERTS
Paramount, 1989

Musical Score Hamlisch, Marvin

Producer(s) Keach, James
Director(s) Thomas, Dave
Screenwriter(s) Thiel, Nick; Greene, Steven; Alter, Eric

Cast Travolta, John; Smith, Charles Martin; Ducommun, Rick; Murray, Bryan Doyle; Keach, James; Foreman, Deborah; Gross, Arye; Preston, Kelly

Song(s) Take the Heat (C/L: Kraus, Andrew; Deaton, Jerry); Get On Up (C/L: Soto, Francisco; Herrera, Lawrence; Pro, John); Hometown U.S.A. (C/L: Payne, Harold; Luboff, Pete; Luboff, Pat); Read My Mind (C/L: Previn, Anne); Party Time (C/L: Malloy, Anthony; Goddard, Henley; Aaron, Linden; Thomas, Herbert); Hard to Get (C/L: Santis, Jimmy; Kofsky, Don Peter; Forbes, Alexandra)

1671 ✦ THE EXPLOSIVE GENERATION
United Artists, 1961

Musical Score Borne, Hal

Producer(s) Colbert, Stanley
Director(s) Kulik, Buzz
Screenwriter(s) Landon, Joseph

Cast Shatner, William; McCormack, Patty; Kinsolving, Lee; Field, Virginia

Song(s) Wait for Me (C/L: Borne, Hal)

1672 ✦ EXPRESSO BONGO
Continental Dist., 1960

Composer(s) Norman, Monty; ; Heneker, David
Lyricist(s) Norman, Monty; Heneker, David; More, Julian
Choreographer(s) MacMillan, Kenneth

Producer(s) Guest, Val
Director(s) Guest, Val
Screenwriter(s) Mankowitz, Wolf
Source(s) *Expresso Bongo* (London musical) Mankowitz, Wolf; More, Julian; Norman, Monty; Heneker, David

Cast Harvey, Laurence; Syms, Sylvia; Donlan, Yolande; Richard, Cliff; Tzelnicker, Meier; Philpotts, Ambrosine; Baddeley, Hermione; Bunnage, Avis; Hampshire, Susan

Song(s) Nausea [1]; Shrine on the Second Floor [1]; I've Never Had It So Good [1]; Voice in the Wilderness (C: Paramor, Norrie; L: Lewis, Bunny)

Notes No cue sheet available. There are other songs by Robert Farnon, Val Guest and Paddy Roberts. [1] From London stage version.

1673 ✦ THE EXTERMINATOR
Avco Embassy, 1980

Musical Score Renzetti, Joe

Producer(s) Buntzman, Mark
Director(s) Glickenhaus, James
Screenwriter(s) Glickenhaus, James

Cast George, Christopher; Eggar, Samantha; Ginty, Robert; James, Steve

Song(s) Heal It (C/L: Hill, Byron; Reid, Mike); Theme for an American Hero (C/L: Taylor, Chip)

Notes No cue sheet available.

1674 ✦ EXTERMINATOR 2
Cannon, 1984

Musical Score Spear, David

Producer(s) Buntzman, Mark; Sachs, William
Director(s) Buntzman, Mark
Screenwriter(s) Buntzman, Mark; Sachs, William

Cast Ginty, Robert; Van Peebles, Mario; Geffner, Deborah; Faison, Frankie

Song(s) Return to Cinder (C/L: Bernstein, Peter); Shake It to Bake It (C/L: Covell, Jim); Under Fire (C/L: Harrison, Benny); Rally 'Round the Moon (C/L: Webster, David)

Notes No cue sheet available.

1675 ✦ EXTREMITIES
Atlantic, 1986

Musical Score Redford, J.A.C.

Producer(s) Sugarman, Burt
Director(s) Young, Robert M.
Screenwriter(s) Mastrosimone, William
Source(s) *Extremities* (play) Mastrosimone, William

Cast Fawcett, Farrah; Russo, James; Woodard, Alfre; Scarwid, Diana; Martin, Sandy; Velez, Eddie

Song(s) Stand Up to the Night (C: Redford, J.A.C.; Kerr, Richard; L: Jennings, Will)

Notes No cue sheet available.

1676 ✦ AN EYE FOR WEATHER
Disney, 1959

Musical Score Bruns, George

Producer(s) Kimball, Ward
Director(s) Kimball, Ward
Screenwriter(s) Dunn, John; Bosche, William; Kimball, Ward

Cast Frees, Paul

Song(s) Weather Song (C: Bruns, George; L: Adair, Tom)

Notes Short. Also known as EYES IN OUTER SPACE.

1677 ✦ EYES OF LAURA MARS
Columbia, 1978

Musical Score Kane, Artie

Producer(s) Peters, Jon
Director(s) Kershner, Irvin
Screenwriter(s) Carpenter, John; Goodman, David Zelag

Cast Dunaway, Faye; Jones, Tommy Lee; Dourif, Brad; Auberjonois, Rene; Julia, Raul; Adonis, Frank; Fluegel, Darlanne

Song(s) Prisoner (C/L: Lawrence, Karen; Desautels, John); Burn (C/L: Michalski, George; Oosterveen,

Niki); Let's All Chant (C/L: Fields, Alvin; Zager, Michael); Native New Yorker (C/L: Randell, Denny; Linzer, Sandy); Shake Your Booty (C/L: Finch, Richard; Casey, Harry)

Notes No cue sheet available.

1678 ✦ EYES OF TEXAS
Republic, 1948

Composer(s) Spencer, Tim
Lyricist(s) Spencer, Tim

Producer(s) White, Edward J.
Director(s) Witney, William
Screenwriter(s) Nibley, Sloan

Cast Rogers, Roy; Trigger; Roberts, Lynne; Devine, Andy; Bryant, Nana; Barcroft, Roy; Morton, Danny; Ford, Francis; Bob Nolan and the Sons of the Pioneers

Song(s) Texas Trails; Padre of Old San Antone [1]; Graveyard Filler of the West

Notes [1] Spanish lyrics by Aaron Gonzalez.

1679 ✦ THE FABULOUS DORSEYS
United Artists, 1947

Producer(s)   Rogers, Charles R.
Director(s)   Green, Alfred E.
Screenwriter(s)   English, Richard; Arthur, Art; Kenyon, Curtis

Cast   Dorsey, Tommy; Dorsey, Jimmy; Allgood, Sara; Fields, Arthur; Eberly, Bob; Barnet, Charlie; Elman, Ziggy; Tatum, Art; Whiteman, Paul; O'Connell, Helen; Blair, Janet; Lundigan, William; Flavin, James; Bakewell, William; Ward, Bobby; Buckley, Buz

Song(s)   Dorsey Concerto (Inst.) (C: Shuken, Leo)

Notes   There are no original songs written for this film. Vocals include "Marie" by Irving Berlin; "Green Eyes" ("Aquellos Ojos Verdes") by Nilo Menendez, E. Rivera, E. Woods and Adolph Utera; "To Me" by Allie Wrubel and Don George and "The Object of My Affection" by Pinky Tomlin, Coy Poe and Jimmy Grier. There are featured instrumentals of "At Sundown" by Walter Donaldson;" "Runnin' Wild" by A.H. Gibbs, Joe Grey and Leo Wood; "Southern Roses" by Johann Strauss; "Der Blumen Lied" by Gustav Lange; "When You and I Were Young Maggie" by J.A. Butterfield; "Everybody's Doing It Now" by Irving Berlin; "Original" by Art Tatum; "The Blues" arranged by the Dorseys and "Molle Roone."

1680 ✦ THE FABULOUS SENORITA
Republic, 1952

Producer(s)   Picker, Sidney
Director(s)   Springsteen, R.G.
Screenwriter(s)   Roberts, Charles E.; Townley, Jack

Cast   Rodriguez, Estelita; Clarke, Robert; Paiva, Nestor; Kaplan, Marvin; Moreno, Rita; Belasco, Leon; Renaldo, Tito; Del Ray, Nita

Song(s)   A Carida le da el Santo (C/L: Silva, Rodriguez); You've Changed (C: Young, Victor; Martin, Tony; L: Heyman, Edward); La Virgen de la Macarena (C/L: Monterde, B.B.; Calero, A.O.)

Notes   Originally titled AN OLD SPANISH CUSTOM.

1681 ✦ A FACE IN THE CROWD
Warner Brothers, 1957

Musical Score   Glazer, Tom
Composer(s)   Glazer, Tom
Lyricist(s)   Schulberg, Budd

Producer(s)   Kazan, Elia
Director(s)   Kazan, Elia
Screenwriter(s)   Schulberg, Budd

Cast   Griffith, Andy; Neal, Patricia; Franciosa, Anthony; Matthau, Walter; Remick, Lee; Waram, Percy; Medford, Kay

Song(s)   Jail Song; Free Man in the Morning; Vitajex Jingle; Just Pain Folks; Old Fashioned Marriage; Mama Guitar; A Face in the Crowd [1]

Notes   [1] Sheet music only.

1682 ✦ FACE IN THE SKY
Fox, 1933

Director(s)   Lachman, Harry; Collier Sr., William
Screenwriter(s)   Pearson, Humphrey

Cast   Tracy, Spencer; Nixon, Marian; Erwin, Stuart; Hardy, Sam; Lee, Lila

Song(s)   Parade of the "Ads" (C: Burton, Val; Jason, Will; Lange, Arthur; L: Burton, Val; Jason, Will)

Notes   From correspondence in the files. "To James O'Keefe of Fox. January 31, 1933. . . . The movement that is afoot on the Coast among writers of motion picture music is justified and I certainly would welcome concerted action on the part of these writers in respect to getting better recognition in the American Society (ASCAP). The 'powers that be' in the Society look upon strictly motion picture music as a lot of junk. They term this music 'agitato and hurry music' and do not consider it requires any real genius to write this class of music. Everything you say about the Broadwayites is true and the 'hams' who can grind out a few popular ditties are given more credit than real musicians who contribute hundreds of beautiful compositions that play an important part in the production of motion pictures. Signed Sam Fox."

O'Keefe replied, "There is considerable agitation here on the coast among picture music writers who are members of the Song Writers Protective Association and/or the American Society and writers not members of either organization. They have discussed among them the advisability of paying the expenses of a delegation to New York to approach the Amerian Society to honor those writers who write background music in picture scoring and who have no standing whatsoever in the eyes of the Society. They realize that a certain musical Broadway yokelry can approach the American Society after having a few misfit compositions published and obtain membership and share in the melons which the Society divides annually, whereas this group are capable musicians who write reams of beautiful music and still gaze upon the crushed publishers wondering if business will ever come back. However, if I know these song writers, and their crusades, as well as I think I do I feel that they will generally botch anything that they attempt to do, so matters may not come to a head." [1] Sheet music only.

1683 ✦ FACES IN THE FOG
Republic, 1944

Producer(s) Millakowsky, Herman
Director(s) English, John
Screenwriter(s) Heilbron, Adelaide; Townley, Jack

Cast Withers, Jane; Kelly, Paul; Patrick, Lee; Litel, John

Song(s) So Little Time (So Much to Do) (C/L: Hill, Billy; De Rose, Peter)

1684 ✦ FACE TO FACE
Paramount, 1976

Composer(s) Skifs, Bjorn; Palmers, Bengt
Lyricist(s) Skifs, Bjorn; Palmers, Bengt

Producer(s) Bergman, Ingmar
Director(s) Bergman, Ingmar
Screenwriter(s) Bergman, Ingmar

Cast Ullmann, Liv; Josephson, Erland; Bjornstrand, Gunnar; Taube-Henrikson, Aino

Song(s) Out of the Blue; Why Don't You Go Your Way; You've Got to Tell It Like It Is; The Devil Made Me Do It (C/L: Palmers, Bengt)

1685 ✦ FACE WITHOUT A NAME

See MR. BUDDWING.

1686 ✦ THE FACTS OF LIFE
United Artists, 1960

Musical Score Harline, Leigh

Producer(s) Panama, Norman
Director(s) Frank, Melvin
Screenwriter(s) Panama, Norman; Frank, Melvin

Cast Hope, Bob; Ball, Lucille; Hussey, Ruth; DeFore, Don; Nye, Louis; Ober, Philip; Stewart, Marianne; Leeds, Peter; Irving, Hollis; Beavers, Louise; Mazurki, Mike

Song(s) The Facts of Life (C/L: Mercer, Johnny)

1687 ✦ FADE IN
Paramount, 1973

Musical Score Lauber, Ken
Composer(s) Hadjidakis, Manos
Lyricist(s) Landron, Jack

Producer(s) Bernard, Judd; Narizzano, Silvio
Director(s) Taylor, Jud
Screenwriter(s) Ludwig, Jerry; Crowley, Matt

Cast Reynolds, Burt; Loden, Barbara

Song(s) Why Ask Why? [1] (C: Lauber, Ken; L: Gimbel, Norman); Visions [2]; Can't Work [2]; The Myth of Love [2]; I Kinda Think She Goes for Me [2]; Love Is a Moment; Crazy People [2]

Notes The film was made in 1968. [1] Lyric added for exploitation. [2] Not used. Manos Hadjidakis wrote a score that was rejected.

1688 ✦ FADE TO BLACK
American Cinema, 1980

Musical Score Safan, Craig

Producer(s) Braunstein, George; Hamady, Ron
Director(s) Zimmerman, Vernon
Screenwriter(s) Zimmerman, Vernon

Cast Christopher, Dennis; Kerridge, Linda; Barkin, Marcey; Thomerson, Tim; Gilford, Gwynne; Luisi, James; Rourke, Mickey

Song(s) Fade to Black (C/L: Connors, Carol)

Notes No cue sheet available.

1689 ✦ FAIR WIND TO JAVA
Republic, 1953

Musical Score Young, Victor

Producer(s) Kane, Joseph
Director(s) Kane, Joseph
Screenwriter(s) Tregaskis, Richard

Cast MacMurray, Fred; Ralston, Vera Hruba; Douglas, Robert; McLaglen, Victor; Russell, John; Baer, Buddy; Jarman Jr., Claude; Withers, Grant; Ahn, Philip

Song(s) Bound for the Open Sea [1] (C: Traditional; L: Roberts, Gerald)

Notes [1] Based on the song "Rio Grande."

1690 ♦ FAITHFUL IN MY FASHION
Metro–Goldwyn–Mayer, 1946

Musical Score Shilkret, Nathaniel

Producer(s) Houser, Lionel
Director(s) Salkow, Sidney
Screenwriter(s) Houser, Lionel

Cast Reed, Donna; Drake, Tom; Horton, Edward Everett; Byington, Spring; Rumann, Sig; Phillips, Wm. "Bill"; Davenport, Harry; Hamilton, Margaret

Song(s) I Don't Know Why [1] (C: Ahlert, Fred E.; L: Turk, Roy)

Notes There is also a vocal of "L'Amour Toujours L'Amour" by Rudolf Friml. [1] Written in 1931.

1691 ♦ FALCON AND THE COEDS
RKO, 1943

Musical Score Webb, Roy

Producer(s) Geraghty, Gerald
Director(s) Clemens, William
Screenwriter(s) Wray, Ardel; Geraghty, Gerald
Source(s) characters by Arlen, Michael

Cast Conway, Tom; Brooks, Jean; Corday, Rita; Ward, Amelita; Jewell, Isabel; Givot, George; Clark, Cliff; Gargan, Edward; Howland, Olin

Song(s) Bluecliff Alma Mater (C: Webb, Roy; L: Bennett, Norman)

1692 ♦ THE FALCON AND THE SNOWMAN
Orion, 1985

Musical Score Metheny, Pat; Mays, Lyle

Producer(s) Katzka, Gabriel; Schlesinger, John
Director(s) Schlesinger, John
Screenwriter(s) Zallian, Steven
Source(s) *The Falcon and the Snowman* (book) Lindsey, Robert

Cast Hutton, Timothy; Penn, Sean; Hingle, Pat; Dysart, Richard; Singer, Lori; Suchet, David; Harewood, Dorian; Pointer, Priscilla; Pryor, Nicholas; Van Patten, Joyce

Song(s) This Is Not America (C/L: Bowie, David; Metheny, Pat; Mays, Lyle)

Notes No cue sheet available.

1693 ♦ FALCON IN MEXICO
RKO, 1944

Musical Score Webb, Roy

Producer(s) Geraghty, Maurice
Director(s) Berke, William
Screenwriter(s) Yates, George Worthing; Geraghty, Gerald
Source(s) characters by Arlen, Michael

Cast Conway, Tom; Maris, Mona; MacVicar, Martha [1]; Paiva, Nestor; Currier, Mary; Callejo, Cecilia; Parnell, Emory; Vitale, Joseph; de Cordoba, Pedro; Alvarado, Fernando; Washburn, Bryant

Song(s) Negrita No Me Dejes [2] (C/L: Gonzales, Aaron)

Notes [1] Martha Vickers. [2] Also in MEXICAN SPITFIRE and WITHOUT RESERVATION.

1694 ♦ FALCON OUT WEST
RKO, 1944

Musical Score Webb, Roy

Producer(s) Geraghty, Maurice
Director(s) Clemens, William
Screenwriter(s) Jones, Billy; Grant, Morton
Source(s) characters by Arlen, Michael

Cast Conway, Tom; Gallagher, Carole; Hale, Barbara; Barclay, Joan; Clark, Cliff; Gargan, Edward; Watson, Minor; Talbot, Lyle

Song(s) Texas Spurs (C/L: Webb, Roy; Jones, Billy; Bennett, Norman); Valley of the Sun (C/L: Sawtell, Paul; Webb, Roy)

1695 ♦ FALCON'S ADVENTURE
RKO, 1946

Musical Score Sawtell, Paul; Webb, Roy

Producer(s) Schlom, Herman
Director(s) Berke, William
Screenwriter(s) Wisberg, Aubrey; Kent, Robert E.
Source(s) characters by Arlen, Michael

Cast Conway, Tom; Meredith, Madge; Brophy, Edward S.; Warwick, Robert; Dell, Myrna; Brodie, Steve; Wolfe, Ian; Robards, Jason

Song(s) Candlelight and Wine [1] (C: McHugh, Jimmy; L: Adamson, Harold)

Notes [1] Also in DING DONG WILLIAMS.

1696 ♦ FALCON'S ALIBI
RKO, 1945

Musical Score Webb, Roy

Producer(s) Berke, William
Director(s) McCarey, Ray
Screenwriter(s) Yawitz, Paul
Source(s) characters by Arlen, Michael

Cast Conway, Tom; Corday, Rita; Barnett, Vince; Greer, Jane; Cook Jr., Elisha; Parnell, Emory; Bridge, Al; Howard, Esther

Song(s) It Just Happens to Happen [2] (C: Revel, Harry; L: Greene, Mort); Come Out, Come Out Wherever You Are [3] (C: Styne, Jule; L: Cahn, Sammy); Dreaming Out Loud [1] (C: Pollack, Lew; L: Greene, Mort)

Notes [1] Also used in BAMBOO BLONDE. [2] Also used in SING YOUR WORRIES AWAY. [3] Used in STEP LIVELY (1944).

1697 ✦ THE FALCON TAKES OVER
RKO, 1942

Musical Score Webb, Roy

Producer(s) Benedict, Howard
Director(s) Reis, Irving
Screenwriter(s) Root, Lynn; Fenton, Frank
Source(s) (characters) Arlen, Michael; *Farewell, My Lovely* (novel) Chandler, Raymond

Cast Sanders, George; Bari, Lynn; Gleason, James; Jenkins, Allen; Gilbert, Helen

Song(s) The First Time I Saw You [1] (C: Shilkret, Nathaniel; L: Wrubel, Allie)

Notes [1] Also in LAW OF THE UNDERWORLD, OUT OF THE PAST and TOAST OF NEW YORK.

1698 ✦ FALLEN ANGEL
Twentieth Century–Fox, 1945

Musical Score Raksin, David

Producer(s) Preminger, Otto
Director(s) Preminger, Otto
Screenwriter(s) Kleiner, Harry
Source(s) *Fallen Angel* (novel) Holland, Matty

Cast Faye, Alice; Andrews, Dana; Darnell, Linda; Bickford, Charles; Revere, Anne; Cabot, Bruce; Carradine, John; Kilbride, Percy; Conlin, Jimmy

Song(s) Slowly [1] (C: Raksin, David; L: Goell, Kermit)

Notes [1] Performed on juke box by Dick Haymes.

1699 ✦ FALLEN SPARROW
RKO, 1943

Musical Score Webb, Roy
Composer(s) Revel, Harry
Lyricist(s) Greene, Mort

Producer(s) Fellows, Robert
Director(s) Wallace, Richard
Screenwriter(s) Duff, Warren
Source(s) *The Fallen Sparrow* (novel) Hughes, Dorothy B.

Cast Garfield, John; O'Hara, Maureen; Slezak, Walter; Morison, Patricia; O'Driscoll, Martha; Edwards, Bruce; Banner, John; Miljan, John

Song(s) Beware [1]; You're Bad for Me [2]

Notes [1] Also in CALL OUT THE MARINES. [2] Also in THE MAYOR OF 44TH STREET.

1700 ✦ FALL GUY
Monogram, 1946

Producer(s) Mirisch, Walter
Director(s) LeBorg, Reginald
Screenwriter(s) O'Dea, John; Warner, Jerry
Source(s) "Cocaine" (story) Woolrich, Cornell

Cast Penn, Clifford; Loring, Teala; Armstrong, Robert; Dale, Virginia; Cook Jr., Elisha; Fowley, Douglas; Adrian, Iris; Carleton, Bob

Song(s) Tootin' My Own Horn (C/L: Kay, Edward J.; Cherkose, Eddie)

Notes No cue sheet available.

1701 ✦ FALLING IN LOVE AGAIN
International Picture Show Company, 1980

Musical Score Legrand, Michel
Composer(s) Legrand, Michel

Producer(s) Paul, Steven
Director(s) Paul, Steven
Screenwriter(s) Paul, Steven; Allan, Ted; York, Susannah

Cast Gould, Elliott; York, Susannah; Paul, Stuart; Pfeiffer, Michelle; Ballard, Kaye; Paul, Steven; Paul, Bonnie

Song(s) Yesterday's Dreams (L: Connors, Carol); The First Time (L: Lambert, Dennis); You Had to Be There (L: Lambert, Dennis); Being Good for My Baby (L: Cahn, Sammy)

Notes No cue sheet available.

1702 ✦ FALSE FACES
Republic, 1943

Musical Score Glickman, Mort

Producer(s) Sherman, George
Director(s) Sherman, George
Screenwriter(s) Siodmak, Curt

Cast Ridges, Stanley; Henry, William; Williams, Rex; Shaw, Janet; Whitney, Claire; Borg, Veda Ann; Nicodemus; Crehan, Joseph

Song(s) A Trifle on the Triflin' Side (C: Scharf, Walter; L: Darby, Ken)

1703 ✦ FALSE WITNESS

See ZIG ZAG.

1704 ✦ FAME
Metro–Goldwyn–Mayer, 1980

Musical Score Gore, Michael
Composer(s) Gore, Michael
Lyricist(s) Pitchford, Dean
Choreographer(s) Falco, Louis

Producer(s)   De Silva, David; Marshal, Alan
Director(s)   Parker, Alan
Screenwriter(s)   Gore, Christopher

Cast   Allen, Debbie; Belzer, Richard; Bongiorno, Frank; Vitolo, Frank X.; Ramirez, Ray; Massenburg, Carol; Fischbarg, Victor; Bunin, Nicholas; Canuelas, Cindy; Barth, Eddie; Cara, Irene; Curreri, Lee; Dean, Laura; Franceschi, Antonia; Gaines, Boyd; Hague, Albert; Hughes, Tresa; Inwood, Steven; McCrane, Paul; Meara, Anne; Merlin, Joanna; Miller, Barry; Moody, Jim; Ray, Gene Anthony; Teefy, Maureen

Song(s)   Red Light; Dogs in the Yard (C/L: Bugatti, Dominic; Musker, Frank); Hot Lunch Jam (C/L: Gore, Michael; Gore, Lesley; Colesberry, Robert F.); Fame; Never Alone (C/L: Evans, Anthony); Out Here On My Own (C/L: Gore, Michael; Gore, Lesley); Is It Okay If I Call You Mine? (C/L: McCrane, Paul); Time Warp (C/L: O'Brien, Richard); Miss E. Flat (C/L: Oteri, Frank); I Sing the Body Electric

Notes   There is also a vocal of "The Way We Were" by Marvin Hamlisch and Alan and Marilyn Bergman.

1705 ✦ FAMILY HONEYMOON
Universal, 1949

Musical Score   Skinner, Frank

Producer(s)   Beck, John; Griffin, Z. Wayne
Director(s)   Binyon, Claude
Screenwriter(s)   Lussier, Dane
Source(s)   *Family Honeymoon* (novel) Croy, Homer

Cast   Colbert, Claudette; MacMurray, Fred; Hunt, Jimmy; Miles, Peter; Perreau, Gigi; Johnson, Rita; Daniell, Henry; Wills, Chill; McDaniel, Hattie

Song(s)   Happy Homecoming to You (C: Schwarzwald, Milton; L: Lussier, Dane)

1706 ✦ THE FAMILY JEWELS
Paramount, 1965

Musical Score   King, Pete

Producer(s)   Lewis, Jerry
Director(s)   Lewis, Jerry
Screenwriter(s)   Lewis, Jerry; Richmond, Bill

Cast   Lewis, Jerry; Butterworth, Donna; Cabot, Sebastian; Baylos, Gene; Faye, Herbie; Corby, Ellen; Hamilton, Neil; Strauss, Robert; Gary Lewis and the Playboys

Song(s)   This Diamond Ring [1] (C/L: Kooper, Al; Brass, Bob; Levine, Irwin); Little Miss Go-Go [1] (C/L: Brown, Louis Yule; Russell, Leon; Lesslie, Thomas); So Warm, My Love [2] (C: King, Pete; L: Webster, Paul Francis)

Notes   [1] Not written for picture. [2] Lyric written for exploitation only.

1707 ✦ THE FAMILY WAY
Warner Brothers, 1967

Musical Score   McCartney, Paul
Composer(s)   Head, Murray
Lyricist(s)   Head, Murray

Producer(s)   Boulting, John; Boulting, Roy
Director(s)   Boulting, John; Boulting, Roy
Screenwriter(s)   Naughton, Bill
Source(s)   *All in Good Time* (play) Naughton, Bill

Cast   Mills, Hayley; Comer, John; Bennett, Hywell; Mills, John; Rhodes, Marjorie; Head, Murray; Foster, Barry; Angers, Avril; Pickles, Wilfred; Frazer, Liz

Song(s)   Time You Went; Roses (C: Adams, Stephen; L: Weatherly, F.E.); Someday Soon; How Long, How Long Blues

1708 ✦ THE FAN
Paramount, 1981

Composer(s)   Hamlisch, Marvin
Lyricist(s)   Rice, Tim

Producer(s)   Stigwood, Robert
Director(s)   Bianchi, Edward
Screenwriter(s)   Chapman, Priscilla; Hartwell, John
Source(s)   *The Fan* (novel) Randall, Bob

Cast   Bacall, Lauren; Garner, James; Stapleton, Maureen; Elizondo, Hector; Johnson, Kurt; Biehn, Michael

Song(s)   A Remarkable Woman; Hearts, Not Diamonds; In Paris (C/L: St. Louis, Louis); Hot Love Baby Tonight (C/L: St. Louis, Louis; Fernandez, Roberto)

Notes   Only original songs listed. Others are all background vocal.

1709 ✦ FANCY PANTS
Paramount, 1950

Musical Score   Van Cleave, Nathan
Composer(s)   Livingston, Jay; Evans, Ray
Lyricist(s)   Livingston, Jay; Evans, Ray

Producer(s)   Welch, Robert L.
Director(s)   Marshall, George
Screenwriter(s)   Hartmann, Edmund L.; O'Brien, Robert
Source(s)   "Ruggles of Red Gap" (story) Wilson, Harry Leon

Cast   Hope, Bob; Ball, Lucille [2]; Cabot, Bruce; Kirkwood, Jack; Blore, Eric; Penman, Lea; Vitale, Joseph; French, Hugh

Song(s)   Yes M'Lord [1]; Fancy Pants [1]; Home Cookin'

Notes   Originally titled WHERE MEN ARE MEN and LARIAT LOOP. [1] Similar music. [2] Dubbed.

1710 ◆ FANNY
Warner Brothers, 1961

Musical Score Rome, Harold

Producer(s) Logan, Joshua
Director(s) Logan, Joshua
Screenwriter(s) Epstein, Julius J.
Source(s) *Fanny* (musical) Behrman, S.N.; Logan, Joshua; Rome, Harold

Cast Caron, Leslie; Chevalier, Maurice; Boyer, Charles; Buchholz, Horst; Baccaloni, Salvatore; Jeffries, Lionel

Song(s) Oysters, Cockles and Mussels (C/L: Rome, Harold)

Notes The musical's fine score was used as background music. The songs were identified on the cue sheet as "Panisse and Son," "Fanny," "Never Too Late for Love," "Restless Heart," "Octopus Song," "Be Kind to Your Parents," "Hakim's Cellar," "Nautch Dance," "I Like You Very Much," "I Have to Tell You," "Waltz" and "Love Is a Very Light Thing."

1711 ◆ THE FAR COUNTRY
Universal, 1955

Musical Score Skinner, Frank

Producer(s) Rosenberg, Aaron
Director(s) Mann, Anthony
Screenwriter(s) Chase, Borden

Cast Stewart, James; Brennan, Walter; McIntire, John; Roman, Ruth; Calvet, Corinne; Flippen, Jay C.; Morgan, Henry; Brodie, Steve; Gilchrist, Connie

Song(s) Pretty Little Primrose (C: Rosen, Milton; L: Herbert, Frederick)

1712 ◆ FAREWELL ILLUSIONS
International Home Cinema, 1986

Musical Score Gundersen, Svein

Producer(s) Wam, Svend; Vennerod, Petter
Director(s) Wam, Svend; Vennerod, Petter
Screenwriter(s) Wam, Svend; Vennerod, Petter

Cast Hungnes, Svein Sturla; Husebo, Knut; Kjellsby, Jorunn; Foss, Wenche

Song(s) Brave Man (C: Gundersen, Svein; L: Hamo, Asbjorn); Man's World (C: Gundersen, Svein; L: Hamo, Asbjorn)

Notes No cue sheet available.

1713 ◆ A FAREWELL TO ARMS
Twentieth Century–Fox, 1957

Musical Score Nascimbene, Mario

Producer(s) Selznick, David O.
Director(s) Vidor, Charles

Screenwriter(s) Hecht, Ben
Source(s) *A Farewell to Arms* (novel) Hemingway, Ernest

Cast Hudson, Rock; Jones, Jennifer; De Sica, Vittorio; Sordi, Alberto; Homolka, Oscar; McCambridge, Mercedes; Stritch, Elaine; Kasznar, Kurt; Francen, Victor

Song(s) A Farewell to Arms [1] (C: Nascimbene, Mario; L: Webster, Paul Francis)

Notes [1] Lyric added for exploitation only.

1714 ◆ FAREWELL TO FAME

See LET'S GO COLLEGIATE.

1715 ◆ FAR FROM THE MADDING CROWD
Metro–Goldwyn–Mayer, 1967

Musical Score Bennett, Richard Rodney

Producer(s) Janni, Joseph
Director(s) Schlesinger, John
Screenwriter(s) Raphael, Frederic
Source(s) *Far from the Madding Crowd* (novel) Hardy, Thomas

Cast Christie, Julie; Stamp, Terence; Finch, Peter; Bates, Alan

Song(s) Far from the Madding Crowd [1] (C: Ornadel, Cyril; L: Shaper, Hal); Far from the Madding Crowd [1] [2] (C: Bennett, Richard R.; L: Webster, Paul Francis)

Notes [1] Written for exploitation only.

1716 ◆ THE FAR FRONTIER
Republic, 1948

Producer(s) White, Edward J.
Director(s) Witney, William
Screenwriter(s) Nibley, Sloan

Cast Rogers, Roy; Trigger; Davis, Gail; Devine, Andy; Foy Willing and the Riders of the Purple Sage

Song(s) The Far Frontier (C/L: Elliott, Jack); I Still Love the West (C/L: Willing, Foy); The Casual Cowboy Song (C/L: Elliott, Jack)

1717 ◆ THE FARGO KID
RKO, 1940

Musical Score Leipold, John
Composer(s) Whitley, Ray; Rose, Fred
Lyricist(s) Whitley, Ray; Rose, Fred

Producer(s) Gilroy, Bert
Director(s) Killy, Edward
Screenwriter(s) Grant, Morton; Jones, Arthur V.

Cast Holt, Tim; Whitley, Ray; Lynn, Emmett; Drummond, Jane; Kendall, Cyrus W.

Song(s) Crazy Ole Trails Ahead [1]; Twilight on the Prairie [2]

Notes [1] May be same song as "Crazy Old Trails" in SAGEBRUSH LAW. [2] Also in RED RIVER ROBIN HOOD and, without the Rose credit, in TRIGGER TRAIL (Universal).

1718 ✦ THE FARMER
Columbia, 1977

Musical Score Montenegro, Hugo

Producer(s) Conway, Gary
Director(s) Berlatsky, David
Screenwriter(s) Fargo, George; Regan, Patrick; Colson-Dodge, Janice; Carmody, John

Cast Conway, Gary; Tompkins, Angel; Dante, Michael

Song(s) There's Only Me and You (C/L: Segal, Jack; Irwin, Ivy)

Notes No cue sheet available.

1719 ✦ THE FARMER'S DAUGHTER
Paramount, 1940

Producer(s) Thomas, William
Director(s) Hogan, James
Screenwriter(s) Foster, Lewis R.

Cast Raye, Martha; Ruggles, Charles; Michael, Gertrude; Denning, Richard

Song(s) Jungle Jingle (C: Hollander, Frederick; L: Loesser, Frank)

Notes Martha Raye also sings "Jeanie with the Light Brown Hair" by Stephen Foster.

1720 ✦ THE FARMER TAKES A WIFE
Twentieth Century–Fox, 1953

Musical Score Mockridge, Cyril J.
Composer(s) Arlen, Harold
Lyricist(s) Fields, Dorothy
Choreographer(s) Cole, Jack

Producer(s) Rosenberg, Frank P.
Director(s) Levin, Henry
Screenwriter(s) Bullock, Walter; Benson, Sally; Fields, Joseph
Source(s) *The Farmer Takes a Wife* (play) Elser, Frank B.; Connelly, Marc; *Rome Haul* (novel) Edmonds, Walter D.

Cast Robertson, Dale; Grable, Betty; Ritter, Thelma; Carroll, John; Foy Jr., Eddie; Austin, Charlotte; Crowley, Kathleen; Anders, Merry; Hickey, Donna Lee

Song(s) Today, I Love Ev'rybody; The Erie Canal; Can You Spell Schenectady?; We're Doin' It for the Natives in Jamaica; Somethin' Real Special; With the Sun Warm Upon Me; We're in Business; I Could Cook [3]; We're Native Women [1] (C: Schaefer, Hal; L: Cole, Jack);

Opening; When I Close My Door [4]; Look Who's Been Dreaming [2]; I Was Wearing Horseshoes [2]; The Evils of Drink! [2]; Why Am I Happy? [3]; Yes [3]; Happy the Bride the Sun Shines Upon [1]

Notes All lyrics including cut songs are at Fox. [1] Not used. [2] Recorded but not used. [3] Patter and toasts written by Charles Henderson. [4] Used instrumentally although vocals were recorded.

1721 ✦ FASHIONS IN LOVE
Paramount, 1929

Composer(s) Schertzinger, Victor
Lyricist(s) Robin, Leo

Director(s) Schertzinger, Victor
Screenwriter(s) Long, Louise; Baker, Melville
Source(s) *The Concert* (play) Bahr, Hermann

Cast Menjou, Adolphe; Compton, Fay; Miljan, John; Seegar, Miriam

Song(s) I Still Believe in You; Delphine

Notes A remake of THE CONCERT (1921). Evelyn Winters of Paramount's music department sent a telegram to Washington lawyer Fulton Brylawski asking him to research the song title "I Still Believe in You." The telegram read: "Please Search Number Quote I Still Believe in You." Brylawski wrote back to Evelyn Winters at Paramount: "The telegraph company tried to deliver this wire to me on Sunday afternoon while I was engaged in the arduous task of chasing a golf ball around the golf links.

"My wife asked the operator to give her the wire, but this was refused on the operator's statement that it appeared to be 'quite personal' and she naturally was very curious to know why I was getting personal telegrams from ladies in California.

"However, I am hopeful that no really serious results will follow."

Evelyn Winters wrote back: "'I STILL BELIEVE IN YOU' but I would not be so foolish as to wire this to you. I tried to put it over by implication.

"I laughed when I read your letter. Some gal in the telegraph office must be romantic. Mr. Schertzinger, who wrote the song, would be delighted to hear that there are gals throughout the country who can be impressed with all this sentiment. I, too, am hopeful that you will have no serious results because of this declaration of mine."

1722 ✦ FASHIONS OF 1934
Warner Brothers–First National, 1934

Composer(s) Fain, Sammy
Choreographer(s) Berkeley, Busby

Director(s) Dieterle, William; Logan, Stanley
Screenwriter(s) Herbert, F. Hugh; Brickson, Carl

Cast Powell, William; Davis, Bette; McHugh, Frank; Teasdale, Verree; Owen, Reginald; Herbert, F. Hugh; O'Neill, Henry; Reed, Philip; Westcott, Gordon

Song(s) Spin a Little Web of Dreams (L: Kahal, Irving); Enough of You (Inst.); Pardon the Expression (Inst.); We Shouldn't Have Done It (Inst.); Broken Melody [1] (L: Kahal, Irving)

Notes The instrumental numbers above were background music. It is not known if they were ever intended as songs but I listed them anyway. [1] Listed in Burton but not on cue sheets.

1723 ◆ FAST BREAK
Columbia, 1979

Musical Score Shire, David; DiPasquale, James
Composer(s) Shire, David
Lyricist(s) Connors, Carol

Producer(s) Friedman, Stephen
Director(s) Smight, Jack
Screenwriter(s) Stern, Sandor

Cast Kaplan, Gabriel; Sylvester, Harold; Warren, Michael; King, Bernard; Brown, Reb; Washington, Mavis

Song(s) Go For It; He Didn't Stay Long Enough to Say Goodbye (C: DiPasquale, James; Connors, Carol; L: Connors, Carol); With You I'm Born Again

Notes No cue sheet available.

1724 ◆ FAST CHARLIE ... THE MOONBEAM RIDER
Universal, 1978

Musical Score Phillips, Stu

Producer(s) Corman, Roger; Krugman, Saul
Director(s) Carver, Steve
Screenwriter(s) Gleason, Michael

Cast Carradine, David; Vaccaro, Brenda; Clay, Whit; Kiser, Terry

Song(s) Prison Blues (C/L: Phillips, Stu)

1725 ◆ FAST COMPANY (1929)
Paramount, 1929

Director(s) Sutherland, Edward
Screenwriter(s) Ryerson, Florence; Kearney, Patrick; Butterfield, Walton
Source(s) *Elmer the Great* (play) Lardner, Ring; Cohan, George M.

Cast Brent, Evelyn; Oakie, Jack; Gallagher, Skeets; Hardy, Sam; Housman, Arthur; Conklin, Chester; Besserer, Eugenie

Song(s) You Want Lovin', I Want Love (C/L: Coslow, Sam)

Notes There are also cameos from the following baseball players: Irish Meusel, Arnold "Jigger" Statz, Truck Hannah, Gus Sanberg, Ivan Olson, Wally Rehg, Jack Adams, George Boehler, Howard Burkett, Red

Rollings, Frank Greene and Lez Smith. [1] Billed as Richard "Skeets" Gallagher.

1726 ◆ FAST COMPANY (1953)
Metro–Goldwyn–Mayer, 1953

Producer(s) Berman, Henry
Director(s) Sturges, John
Screenwriter(s) Roberts, William

Cast Keel, Howard; Bergen, Polly; Main, Marjorie; Foch, Nina; Burton, Robert; Nugent, Carol; Arno, Sig; MacMahon, Horace

Song(s) Pepito [1] (C/L: Wolcott, Charles)

Notes There is also a vocal of "Adelita." [1] Also in GYPSY COLT.

1727 ◆ THE FASTEST GUITAR ALIVE
Metro–Goldwyn–Mayer, 1967

Musical Score Karger, Fred
Composer(s) Orbison, Roy
Lyricist(s) Dees, Bill
Choreographer(s) Taylor, Wilda

Producer(s) Katzman, Sam
Director(s) Moore, Michael
Screenwriter(s) Kent, Robert E.

Cast Orbison, Roy; Jackson, Sammy; Pierce, Maggie; Freeman, Joan; Bettger, Lyle; Lessy, Ben

Song(s) The Fastest Guitar Alive; Snuggle Huggle (C: Karger, Fred; L: Kent, Robert E.); Pistolero; Good Time Party; River; Whirlwind; Medicine Man; Rollin' On

1728 ◆ FAST FORWARD
Columbia, 1985

Musical Score Hayes, Jack
Choreographer(s) Attwell, Rick

Producer(s) Veitch, John Patrick
Director(s) Poitier, Sidney
Screenwriter(s) Wesley, Richard

Cast Clough, John Scott; Franklin, Don; Mark, Tamara; Silver, Tracy; Worth, Irene; McGee, Cindy

Song(s) Goin' to the Warehouse (C/L: Bahler, Tom; Van Tongeren, John; Hull, Bunny); Breakin' Out (C/L: Vieha, Mark; Ingram, James; Brown, Ollie E.; Walsh, Brock); Survive (C/L: Bahler, Tom; Walsh, Brock); Long As We Believe (C/L: Glass, Preston; Walden, Narada Michael; Afanasieff, Walter; Bahler, Tom; Garrett, Siedah); How Do You Do (C/L: Walsh, Brock; Vieha, Mark); Showdown (C/L: Jellybean; Bray, Stephen; C., Toni); Curves (C/L: Glass, Preston; Walden, Narada Michael); Do You Want It Right Now (C/L: Burton, China; Straker, Nick); Taste (C/L: Swanson, David; Garrett, Siedah); Zoo #2 (C/L: Pershing, D'Vaughn); Mystery (C/L: Anderson, Rusty);

Pretty Girl (C/L: Scott, Jef); Fast Forward (C/L: Walsh, Brock; Bahler, Tom; Van Tongeren, John; Hull, Bunny)

1729 ♦ FAST LIFE
Warner Brothers–First National, 1929

Composer(s) Perkins, Ray
Lyricist(s) Ruby, Herman

Director(s) Dillon, John Francis
Screenwriter(s) Goodrich, John
Source(s) *Fast Life* (play) Shipman, Samuel; Hymer, John B.

Cast Fairbanks Jr., Douglas; Young, Loretta; Morris, Chester; Holden, William [1]; Hallor, Ray

Song(s) Since I Found You; A Fast Life and a Hot One

Notes No cue sheet available. [1] Not the same person as the later star.

1730 ♦ FAST WORKERS
Metro–Goldwyn–Mayer, 1933

Director(s) Browning, Tod
Screenwriter(s) Stallings, Laurence
Source(s) *Rivets* (play) McDermott, John W.

Cast Gilbert, John; Armstrong, Robert; Clarke, Mae; Kirkland, Muriel; Barnett, Vince; Cherrill, Virginia; Holloway, Sterling

Song(s) Louisian' (C/L: Snell, Dave)

1731 ♦ FATAL BEAUTY
MGM/UA, 1987

Musical Score Faltermeyer, Harold

Producer(s) Kroll, Leonard
Director(s) Holland, Tom
Screenwriter(s) Henkin, Hilary; Riesner, Dean

Cast Goldberg, Whoopi; Elliott, Sam; Blades, Ruben; Yulin, Harris; Ryan, John P.; Warren, Jennifer; Dourif, Brad

Song(s) Sin City (C/L: Faltermeyer, Harold; Wilk, Scott; Never, Linda); Make It My Night (C/L: Sembello, Danny; Haynes, Tony); Just That Type of Girl (C/L: Cooper, Bernadette; Mimms, Cornelius; Bokowski, John); On the Edge of Love (C/L: Weil, Cynthia; Cutler, Scott); Didn't I Blow Your Mind (C/L: Murphy, Mic; Frank, David); Criminal (C/L: Levay, Sylvester; Whitlock, Tom); Casanova [1] (C/L: Calloway, Reggie)

Notes I don't know which of these were written for this film. [1] Also in THE PICK-UP ARTIST (Fox).

1732 ♦ FATAL LADY
Paramount, 1936

Composer(s) Young, Victor
Lyricist(s) Coslow, Sam

Producer(s) Wanger, Walter
Director(s) Ludwig, Edward
Screenwriter(s) Ornitz, Samuel; Thayer, Tiffany

Cast Ellis, Mary; Pidgeon, Walter; Foster, Norman; Halliday, John; Donnelly, Ruth; Mowbray, Alan; Kennedy, Edgar

Song(s) Bal Masque [3]; William Tell Overture (C: Rossini, Giacomo; L: Robin, Leo); Isabelle [2] (C: Carbonara, Gerard; L: Ormont, David); Death Scene (C: Carbonara, Gerard; L: Ormont, David); Je Vous Adore; Brazilian Love Song [1]

Notes This picture was originally titled BRAZEN. [1] Only used instrumentally. [2] This was a grand opera in French. The story of the opera was by Leo Robin and Max Terr. [3] Later in THE LOST WEEKEND.

1733 ♦ THE FATAL WEDDING

See GOOD INTENTIONS.

1734 ♦ FATHER AND SON
Columbia, 1929

Musical Score Bakaleinikoff, Constantin

Director(s) Kenton, Erle C.
Screenwriter(s) Hatton, Frederic; Hatton, Fanny; Townley, Jack

Cast Holt, Jack; McBan, Mickey; Revier, Dorothy

Song(s) Dear Little Boy (C/L: Unknown)

1735 ♦ FATHER GOOSE
Universal, 1965

Musical Score Coleman, Cy

Producer(s) Arthur, Robert
Director(s) Nelson, Ralph
Screenwriter(s) Tarloff, Frank; Stone, Peter
Source(s) *A Place of Dragons* (novel) Barnett, S.H.

Cast Grant, Cary; Caron, Leslie; Howard, Trevor; Good, Jack; Sparke, Pip

Song(s) Pass Me By (C: Coleman, Cy; L: Leigh, Carolyn); Little Girl Don't Cry [1] (C/L: Coleman, Cy)

Notes [1] Used instrumentally only.

1736 ♦ FATHER TAKES A WIFE
RKO, 1941

Musical Score Webb, Roy; Gonzales, Aaron

Producer(s) Marcus, Lee
Director(s) Hively, Jack
Screenwriter(s) Fields, Dorothy; Fields, Herbert

Cast Menjou, Adolphe; Swanson, Gloria; Howard, John; Arnaz, Desi; Broderick, Helen; Rice, Florence

Song(s) Perfidia [1] (C/L: Dominguez, Alberto); Mi Amor (C/L: Webb, Roy; Gonzales, Aaron)

Notes [1] Also in STARDUST ON THE SAGE (Republic) with additional English lyrics and in MASQUERADE IN MEXICO (Paramount).

1737 ◆ FAZIL
Fox, 1928

Composer(s) Kernell, William
Lyricist(s) Mojica, Jose

Director(s) Hawks, Howard
Screenwriter(s) Miller, Seton I.
Source(s) *L'Insoumise* (play) Frondaie, Pierre

Cast Farrell, Charles; Nissen, Greta; Busch, Mae; Uraneff, Vadim; Brooke, Tyler; Sturgis, Eddie; Boles, John; Murray, John T.

Song(s) Allah Hear Our Call; My Serenata; Narrative (C: Sanders, Troy; Mojica, Jose); Nocturne Arabe; Call to Arms; Neopolitan Nights [1] (C: Zamecnik, J.S.; L: Kerr, Harry D.)

Notes Originally titled LA LEY DEL HARUN. The cue sheet is dated 1932. [1] Sheet music only.

1738 ◆ FEARLESS FAGAN
Metro–Goldwyn–Mayer, 1952

Producer(s) Knopf, Edwin H.
Director(s) Donen, Stanley
Screenwriter(s) Brennan, Frederick Hazlitt

Cast Leigh, Janet; Carpenter, Carleton; Wynn, Keenan; Anderson, Richard; Corby, Ellen

Song(s) Loveliest Night of the Year [1] (C: Traditional; L: Webster, Paul Francis)

Notes There is also a vocal of "What Do You Think I Am" by Hugh Martin and Ralph Blane. [1] Also in CIMARRON (1961).

1739 ◆ FEAR NO EVIL
Avco Embassy, 1981

Musical Score LaLoggia, Frank; Spear, David

Producer(s) LaLoggia, Frank; LaLoggia, Charles M.
Director(s) LaLoggia, Frank
Screenwriter(s) LaLoggia, Frank

Cast Arngrim, Stefan; Hoffman, Elizabeth; Rowe, Kathleen

Song(s) Fear No Evil (C/L: Paly, Andy)

Notes No cue sheet available.

1740 ◆ FEDERAL AGENT AT LARGE
Republic, 1950

Producer(s) Auer, Stephen
Director(s) Blair, George
Screenwriter(s) De Mond, Albert

Cast Patrick, Dorothy; Rockwell, Robert; Taylor, Kent; Rodriguez, Estelita

Song(s) Miguelito [1] (C/L: Elliott, Jack); Corazon a Corazon [2] (C: Ruiz, Gabriel; L: Washington, Ned)

Notes [1] Spanish lyric by Aaron Gonzales. Also in HOME IN OKLAHOMA. [2] Also in MEXICANA.

1741 ◆ FEDS
Warner Brothers, 1988

Musical Score Edelman, Randy

Producer(s) Blum, Len; Herzberg, Ilona
Director(s) Goldberg, Dan
Screenwriter(s) Blum, Len; Goldberg, Dan

Cast de Mornay, Rebecca; Gross, Mary; Marshall, Ken; Cedar, Larry; Luisi, James; Singer, Raymond; Thompson, Fred Dalton

Song(s) Special Kind of Lovin' (C/L: Goldberg, Barry)

1742 ◆ FEET FIRST
Paramount, 1930

Producer(s) Lloyd, Harold
Director(s) Bruckman, Clyde
Screenwriter(s) Adler, Felix; Neal, Lex; Smith, Paul Gerard

Cast Lloyd, Harold; Kent, Barbara; McWade, Robert; Leighton, Lillian; Best, Willie

Song(s) Hawaiian Memories [1] (C/L: Cowan, Lynn; Titsworth, Paul); The Whole World Knows I Love You [1] (C/L: Cowan, Lynn; Titsworth, Paul)

Notes [1] Neither of these songs made the final cut.

1743 ◆ FELIX THE CAT CARTOONS
Paramount/Pathe

Song(s) Felix the Wonderful Cat (C/L: Sharples, Winston); Felix the Cat (C: Wendling, Pete; Kortlander, Max; L: Bryan, Alfred); Felix Kept on Walking (C: David, Hubert; L: Bryant, Ed)

Notes Animated shorts.

1744 ◆ FELLINI'S CASANOVA
Universal, 1976

Musical Score Rota, Nino [1]
Composer(s) Rota, Nino [1]

Producer(s) Grimaldi, Alberto
Director(s) Fellini, Federico
Screenwriter(s) Fellini, Federico; Zapponi, Bernardino

Cast Sutherland, Donald; Aumont, Tina; Browne, Cicely; Scarpitta, Carmen; Algranti, Clara; Gatti, Daniela; Clementi, Margaret

Song(s) Canto Della Buranella (L: Zanzotto, A.); L'Intermezzo Della Mantide Religiosa (L: Amurri,

Antonio); L'Uccello Magico a Dresda (L: Wolken, K.A.); Il Duca Di Wurttenberg (L: Wolken, K.A.)

Notes [1] Billed as Giovanni Rota.

1745 ✦ THE FEMININE TOUCH
Metro–Goldwyn–Mayer, 1941

Musical Score Waxman, Franz

Producer(s) Mankiewicz, Joseph L.
Director(s) Van Dyke II, W.S.
Screenwriter(s) Oppenheimer, George; Hartmann, Edmund L.; Nash, Ogden

Cast Russell, Rosalind; Ameche, Don; Francis, Kay; Heflin, Van; Meek, Donald

Song(s) Jealous [1] (C: Little, Little Jack; L: Malie, Tommie; Finch, Dick)

Notes [1] Also in CRAZY HOUSE (Universal).

1746 ✦ FERRIS BUELLER'S DAY OFF
Paramount, 1986

Musical Score Newborn, Ira; Baker, Arthur; Robie, John
Choreographer(s) Ortega, Kenny

Producer(s) Hughes, John; Jacobson, Tom
Director(s) Hughes, John
Screenwriter(s) Hughes, John

Cast Broderick, Matthew; Ruck, Alan; Sara, Mia; Jones, Jeffrey; Grey, Jennifer; Pickett, Cindy; McClurg, Edie; Sheen, Charlie; Close, Del; Capers, Virginia

Song(s) Beat City (C/L: Watkins, Ben; Peters, Adam); I'm Afraid (C/L: Joyner, David; Mansfield, David)

1747 ✦ FERRY CROSS THE MERSEY
United Artists, 1965

Musical Score Martin, George
Composer(s) Marsden, Gerry
Lyricist(s) Marsden, Gerry

Producer(s) Holden, Michael
Director(s) Summers, Jeremy
Screenwriter(s) Uncredited

Cast Marsden, Gerry; Marsden, Fred; Chadwick, Lee; Maguire, Les; Samuel, Julie; Barker, Eric; McKenna, T.P.; Black, Cilla; Seville, Jimmy

Song(s) It's Gonna Be Alright; Slow Down (C/L: Williams, Larry); Why Oh Why?; Ferry Cross the Mersey; Fall in Love; This Thing Called Love; Think About Love; Only Girl for Me; I'll Wait for You; Baby You're So Good to Me; I Love You Too (C/L: Jacques; Ryan); Shake Your Tailfeather (C/L: Hayes, Otha M.; Williams, Andree; Rice, Verlie); Why Don't You Love Me (C/L: McDermott; Trimmell; Little; Gornall); I've Got a Woman (C/L: Griffiths, Lenny); Is It Love? (C/L: Willis, Bobby)

Notes The Marsdens, Chadwick and Maguire were members of Gerry and the Pacemakers.

1748 ✦ FERRY TO HONG KONG
J. Arthur Rank, 1959

Musical Score Jones, Kenneth V.

Producer(s) Maynard, George
Director(s) Gilbert, Lewis
Screenwriter(s) Gilbert, Lewis; Harris, Vernon; Mortimer, John
Source(s) *Ferry to Hong Kong* (novel) Catto, Max

Cast Jurgens, Curt; Welles, Orson; Syms, Sylvia; Spenser, Jeremy; Purcell, Noel

Song(s) Ferry to Hong Kong (C/L: Sharples, Bob; Roberts, Paddy)

Notes A Rank picture distributed by Twentieth Century–Fox.

1749 ✦ FEUDIN', FUSSIN', AND A-FIGHTIN'
Universal, 1948

Musical Score Stevens, Leith
Choreographer(s) Da Pron, Louis

Producer(s) Goldstein, Leonard
Director(s) Sherman, George
Screenwriter(s) Beauchamp, D.D.
Source(s) "The Wonderful Race at Rimrock" (story) Beauchamp, D.D.

Cast O'Connor, Donald; Main, Marjorie; Kilbride, Percy; Edwards, Penny; Besser, Joe; Shannon, Harry; Kohler Jr., Fred

Notes "Feudin' & Fightin'" by Burton Lane, Al Dubin and Frank Loesser (uncredited); "Me and My Shadow" by Al Dubin, Billy Rose and Dave Dryer; "S'Posin'" by Andy Razaf and Paul Denniker were given vocal treatments. There are no original songs in this film.

1750 ✦ FEVER HEAT
Paramount, 1968

Producer(s) Doughten Jr., Russell
Director(s) Doughten Jr., Russell
Screenwriter(s) Felsen, Henry Gregor
Source(s) *Fever Heat* (novel) Vicker, Angus [1]

Cast Adams, Nick; Riley, Jeannine; Alden, Norman

Song(s) Fever Heat (C: Mendoza-Nava, Jaime; L: Allman, Lee)

Notes [1] Pseudonym for Henry Gregor Felsen.

1751 ✦ FIDDLER ON THE ROOF
United Artists, 1971

Musical Score Williams, John
Composer(s) Bock, Jerry

Lyricist(s) Harnick, Sheldon
Choreographer(s) Robbins, Jerome [2]

Producer(s) Jewison, Norman
Director(s) Jewison, Norman
Screenwriter(s) Stein, Joseph
Source(s) *Fiddler on the Roof* (musical) Stein, Joseph; Bock, Jerry; Harnick, Sheldon

Cast Topol [1]; Crane, Norma; Harris, Rosalind; Frey, Leonard; Marsh, Michele; Picon, Molly; Mann, Paul; Small, Neva; Glaser, Michael; Collier, Patience; Lemkow, Tutte [3]

Song(s) Tradition; Matchmaker; If I Were a Rich Man; Sabbath Prayer; To Life; Tevye's Monologue; Miracle of Miracles; Tevye's Dream; Sunrise, Sunset; Tevye's Rebuttal; Do You Love Me; Far From the Home I Love; Chava Ballet; Anatevka

Notes All songs from Broadway musical. [1] Billed as Chaim Topol. [2] Robbins' original Broadway choreography adapted by Tom Abbott and Sammy Bayes. [3] Played the enponymous Fiddler. His fiddling was dubbed by Isaac Stern.

1752 ✦ THE FIENDISH PLOT OF DR. FU MANCHU
Orion, 1980

Musical Score Wilkinson, Marc

Producer(s) Braun, Zev; Nolan, Leland
Director(s) Haggard, Piers
Screenwriter(s) Moloney, Jim; Dochtermann, Rudy
Source(s) *Fu Manchu* series of novels by Rohmer, Sax

Cast Sellers, Peter; Mirren, Helen; Tomlinson, David; Caesar, Sid; Williams, Simon; Johns, Stratford

Song(s) Rock a Fu (C: Wilkinson, Marc; L: Haggard, Piers; Nolan, Leland)

Notes No cue sheet available.

1753 ✦ FIESTA (1941)
United Artists, 1941

Musical Score Ward, Edward
Composer(s) Ward, Edward
Lyricist(s) Wright, Robert; Forrest, Chet
Choreographer(s) Prinz, LeRoy

Producer(s) Prinz, LeRoy
Director(s) Prinz, LeRoy
Screenwriter(s) Fitzsimmons, Cortland

Cast Ayars, Ann; Negrete, George; Armida; Givot, George; Moreno, Antonio; Moro, Nico

Song(s) Quien Sabe; Never Trust a Jumping Bean; I'll Never Forget Fiesta (C: Menendez, Nilo); Fiesta (C: Wright, Robert; Forrest, Chet); El Relajo (C/L: Leyva, Lamberto; Castillon, Jesus; Felix, Oscar)

Notes No cue sheet available.

1754 ✦ FIESTA (1947)
Metro–Goldwyn–Mayer, 1947

Musical Score Green, Johnny
Choreographer(s) Loring, Eugene

Producer(s) Cummings, Jack
Director(s) Thorpe, Richard
Screenwriter(s) Bruce, George; Cole, Lester

Cast Williams, Esther; Tamiroff, Akim; Astor, Mary; Bonanova, Fortunio; Haas, Hugo; Charisse, Cyd; Carroll, John; Montalban, Ricardo

Song(s) La Luna Enamorada (C: de Villajos, Angel Ortiz; L: Recio, Miriano Bolanos; Durango, Leocadio Martinez); Romeria Vasca (C/L: Los Bocheros); Las Mananitas (C/L: Ponce, Manuel)

Notes There are also vocals of "La Bamba" by Luis Martinez Serrano and "La Barca de Oro." Aaron Copland and Johnny Green wrote the instrumental piece "Fantasia Mexicana."

1755 ✦ FIFTH AVENUE GIRL
RKO, 1939

Musical Score Bennett, Russell

Producer(s) La Cava, Gregory
Director(s) La Cava, Gregory
Screenwriter(s) Scott, Allan

Cast Rogers, Ginger; Connolly, Walter; Ellison, James; Adams, Kathryn; Teasdale, Verree; Holt, Tim; Pangborn, Franklin

Song(s) Tropicana (C/L: Gonzales, Aaron)

1756 ✦ 55 DAYS AT PEKING
Allied Artists, 1963

Musical Score Tiomkin, Dimitri
Composer(s) Tiomkin, Dimitri
Lyricist(s) Webster, Paul Francis

Producer(s) Bronston, Samuel
Director(s) Ray, Nicholas
Screenwriter(s) Yordan, Philip; Gordon, Bernard
Narrator(s) Welles, Orson

Cast Heston, Charlton; Gardner, Ava; Niven, David; Robson, Flora; Ireland, John; Andrews, Harry; Genn, Leo; Helpmann, Robert; Itami, Ichizo; Kasznar, Kurt; Lukas, Paul

Song(s) So Little Time; Fifty Five Days at Peking; Natasha

Notes No cue sheet available.

1757 ✦ FIFTY ROADS TO TOWN
Twentieth Century–Fox, 1937

Producer(s) Griffith, Raymond
Director(s) Taurog, Norman

Screenwriter(s)   Marion Jr., George; Conselman, William

Cast   Ameche, Don; Sothern, Ann; Summerville, Slim; Darwell, Jane; Qualen, John; Fowley, Douglas; Lane, Allan; Dinehart, Alan; Fetchit, Stepin; Hurst, Paul; Apfel, Oscar; Hicks, Russell

Song(s)   Never in a Million Years [1] (C: Revel, Harry; L: Gordon, Mack)

Notes   [1] From WAKE UP AND LIVE.

1758 ✦ 52ND STREET
United Artists, 1937

Composer(s)   Spina, Harold
Lyricist(s)   Bullock, Walter

Producer(s)   Wanger, Walter
Director(s)   Young, Harold
Screenwriter(s)   Jones, Grover

Cast   Hunter, Ian; Patterson, Pat [1]; Carrillo, Leo; Baker, Kenny; Pitts, ZaSu; Peterson, Dorothy; Silvers, Sid; White, Jack; Shean, Al; Shelton, Marla; Burrud, Bill; Lyons, Collette

Song(s)   I Still Love to Kiss You Good Night; Nothing Can Stop Me Now; I'd Like to See Some Mo' of Samoa; Don't Save Your Love for a Rainy Day; Fifty-Second Street; 23-Skidoo; Let Down Your Hair and Sing; We Love the South

Notes   No cue sheet available. [1] Dubbed by Virginia Verrill.

1759 ✦ 52 MILES TO TERROR

See HOT RODS TO HELL.

1760 ✦ FIGARO AND CLEO
Disney, 1953

Musical Score   Smith, Paul J.

Cast   Figaro; Cleo

Song(s)   Sweepin' (C: Smith, Paul J.; L: Quenzer, Arthur); Figaro and Cleo [1] (C: Harline, Leigh; Smith, Paul J.; L: Washington, Ned)

Notes   Cartoon short. No credit sheet available. [1] Used instrumentally only.

1761 ✦ FIGARO AND FRANKIE
Disney, 1946

Musical Score   Wallace, Oliver

Director(s)   Nichols, Charles
Screenwriter(s)   Gurney, Eric; De La Torre, Bill

Cast   Figaro; Frankie

Song(s)   Figaro (C: Harline, Leigh; L: Washington, Ned)

Notes   Cartoon short.

1762 ✦ FIGHTER ATTACK
Allied Artists, 1953

Musical Score   Skiles, Marlin

Producer(s)   Calihan Jr., William
Director(s)   Selander, Lesley
Screenwriter(s)   Wincelberg, Simon

Cast   Hayden, Sterling; Naish, J. Carrol; Page, Joy; Tobey, Kenneth; Caruso, Anthony

Song(s)   Oh Susanna (C: Foster, Stephen; L: Wincelberg, Simon); Nina (C: Skiles, Marlin; L: Meyer, Sol)

1763 ✦ FIGHTER SQUADRON
Warner Brothers, 1948

Musical Score   Steiner, Max

Producer(s)   Miller, Seton I.
Director(s)   Walsh, Raoul
Screenwriter(s)   Miller, Seton I.; Rackin, Martin

Cast   O'Brien, Edmond; Stack, Robert; Rodney, John; D'Andrea, Tom; Hull, Henry; Strudwick, Shepperd; Larson, Jack; Hudson, Rock

Song(s)   We Watch the Skyways [1] (C: Steiner, Max; Kahn, Gus)

Notes   [1] Used as a background instrumental only.

1764 ✦ FIGHT FOR YOUR LADY
RKO, 1938

Producer(s)   Lewis, Albert
Director(s)   Stoloff, Benjamin
Screenwriter(s)   Pagano, Ernest; Segall, Harry; Kussell, Harold

Cast   Boles, John; Oakie, Jack; Lupino, Ida; Grahame, Margot; Rhodes, Erik; Gilbert, Billy; Judels, Charles

Song(s)   Blame It on the Danube (C: Akst, Harry; L: Loesser, Frank)

1765 ✦ FIGHTING BILL FARGO
Universal, 1941

Composer(s)   Rosen, Milton
Lyricist(s)   Carter, Everett

Producer(s)   Cowan, Will
Director(s)   Taylor, Ray
Screenwriter(s)   Franklin, Paul; Jones, Arthur V.; Cochran, Dorcas

Cast   Brown, Johnny Mack; Knight, Fuzzy; Kelly, Jeanne

Song(s) Welcome Home [2]; Happiness Corral; Geraldine [1]

Notes [1] Also in FRONTIER LAW. [2] Also in THE LONE STAR TRAIL.

1766 ✦ THE FIGHTING ENGINEERS
Warner Brothers, 1943

Musical Score Jackson, Howard

Song(s) The Fighting Engineers (C: Carleton, Bob; Dixon, Cliff; Kearney, Major R.E.)

Notes Short subject.

1767 ✦ FIGHTING FRONTIER
RKO, 1943

Composer(s) Whitley, Ray; Rose, Fred
Lyricist(s) Whitley, Ray; Rose, Fred

Producer(s) Gilroy, Bert
Director(s) Hillyer, Lambert
Screenwriter(s) Cheney, J. Benton; Parker, Norton S.

Cast Holt, Tim; Edwards, Cliff; Summers, Ann; Dew, Eddie; Gould, William; Clark, Davison; Whitaker, Slim

Song(s) On the Outlaw Trail [1]; The Edwards and the Drews

Notes [1] Also in THE BANDIT TRAIL.

1768 ✦ THE FIGHTING GRINGO
RKO, 1939

Producer(s) Gilroy, Bert
Director(s) Howard, David
Screenwriter(s) Drake, Oliver

Cast O'Brien, George; Tovar, Lupita; Villegas, Lucio; Royle, William; Strange, Glenn; Whitaker, Slim; Mason, LeRoy

Song(s) Tumble on Tumble Weed [1] (C: Dreyer, Dave; L: Scholl, Jack)

Notes [1] Also in GUN LAW and SILLY BILLIES.

1769 ✦ FIGHTING MAD
Twentieth Century–Fox, 1976

Musical Score Langhorne, Bruce

Producer(s) Corman, Roger
Director(s) Demme, Jonathan
Screenwriter(s) Demme, Jonathan

Cast Fonda, Peter; Lowry, Lynn; Doucette, John; Carey, Philip; Northup, Harry

Song(s) The Bleeding Heart Inn (C/L: Zorro and the Blue Footballs)

1770 ✦ FIGHTING MAN
Monogram, 1940

Composer(s) Loman, Jules
Lyricist(s) Brooks, Jack

Producer(s) Krasne, Philip N.
Source(s) "Renfrew of the Royal Mounted" (stories) Erskine, Laurie York

Cast Newill, James

Song(s) Trail's End; The Lady's in Distress; Mounted Men [1] (C/L: Lively, Robert; Laidlow, Betty)

Notes [1] Also in CRASHING THRU, DANGER AHEAD, RENFREW AND THE GREAT WHITE TRAIL, SKY BANDITS and YUKON FLIGHT.

1771 ✦ THE FIGHTING O'FLYNN
Universal, 1948

Musical Score Skinner, Frank

Producer(s) Fairbanks Jr., Douglas
Director(s) Pierson, Arthur
Screenwriter(s) Fairbanks Jr., Douglas; Thoeren, Robert
Source(s) (novel) McCarthy, Justin Huntly

Cast Fairbanks Jr., Douglas; Carter, Helena; Hare, Lumsden; Greene, Richard; Medina, Patricia; Shields, Arthur; Kerrigan, J.M.; Donath, Ludwig

Song(s) Irish Recruiting Song (C: Skinner, Frank; L: Brooks, Jack)

1772 ✦ THE FIGHTING SEABEES
Republic, 1944

Producer(s) Cohen, Albert J.
Director(s) Ludwig, Edward; Kane, Joseph
Screenwriter(s) Van Every, Dale; Hill, Ethel; MacKenzie, Aeneas; Chase, Borden

Cast Wayne, John; O'Keefe, Dennis; Hayward, Susan; Frawley, William; Richards, Addison; Fix, Paul; Withers, Grant

Song(s) Song of the Seabees (C: De Rose, Peter; L: Lewis, Sam M.): Where Do Ya Worka John [2] (C/L: Weinberg, Mortimer; Marks, Charley; Warren, Harry); (Adios Mi Amor) Wake Up Your Heart [1] (C: Vargas, Don; L: Lewis, Sam M.; Wendling, Pete)

Notes There is also a vocal of "Ireland Must Be Heaven" by Fred Fisher, Joseph McCarthy and Howard Johnson. [1] Not used. [2] Written in 1923.

1773 ✦ FINDERS KEEPERS
United Artists, 1967

Musical Score Paramor, Norrie
Composer(s) Shadows, The
Lyricist(s) Shadows, The

Producer(s) Brown, George H.
Director(s) Hayers, Sidney
Screenwriter(s) Pertwee, Michael

Cast Richard, Cliff [1]; Welch, Bruce [1]; Marvin, Hank B. [1]; Bennett, Brian [1]; Morley, Robert; Venture, Viviane; Stark, Graham; Le Mesurier, John; Mount, Peggy

Song(s) Time Drags By; Washer Woman; La La La; My Way; Oh Senorita; Paella; Finders Keepers

Notes [1] Members of The Shadows.

1774 ✦ FINE AND DANDY

See THE WEST POINT STORY.

1775 ✦ A FINE MESS
Columbia, 1986

Musical Score Mancini, Henry

Producer(s) Adams, Tony
Director(s) Edwards, Blake
Screenwriter(s) Edwards, Blake

Cast Danson, Ted; Mandel, Howie; Mulligan, Richard; Margolin, Stuart; Alonso, Maria Conchita; Edwards, Jennifer; Sorvino, Paul

Song(s) A Fine Mess (C: Mancini, Henry; L: Lambert, Dennis)

1776 ✦ FINIAN'S RAINBOW (1954)
Distributors Corporation of America, 1954
unproduced

Composer(s) Lane, Burton
Lyricist(s) Harburg, E.Y.

Producer(s) Hubley, John
Director(s) Hubley, John
Source(s) *Finian's Rainbow* (musical) Harburg, E.Y.; Saidy, Fred

Cast Sinatra, Frank; Logan, Ella; Fitzgerald, Barry; Fitzgerald, Ella; Armstrong, Louis; Backus, Jim

Notes This proposed animated film was never completed though scoring and recording were completed.

1777 ✦ FINIAN'S RAINBOW (1968)
Warner Brothers, 1968

Composer(s) Lane, Burton
Lyricist(s) Harburg, E.Y.
Choreographer(s) Pan, Hermes

Producer(s) Landon, Joseph
Director(s) Coppola, Francis Ford
Screenwriter(s) Harburg, E.Y.; Saidy, Fred
Source(s) *Finian's Rainbow* (musical) Harburg, E.Y.; Saidy, Fred; Lane, Burton

Cast Astaire, Fred; Clark, Petula; Francks, Don; Wynn, Keenan; Freeman Jr., Al; Hancock, Barbara; Steele, Tommy; Colby, Ronald; Sweet, Dolph

Song(s) Look to the Rainbow; This Time of the Year; How Are Things in Glocca Morra?; Old Devil Moon; Something Sort of Grandish; That Great Come-And-Get-It-Day; When the Idle Poor Become the Idle Rich; Oh Dem Golden Slippers [1] (C: Traditional; L: Traditional; Harburg, E.Y.); The Begat; When I'm Not Near the Girl I Love; If This Isn't Love; Necessity [1]

Notes All songs from Broadway musical. [1] Recorded but not used.

1778 ✦ FIREBALL 500
American International, 1966

Musical Score Baxter, Les
Composer(s) Hemric, Guy; Styner, Jerry
Lyricist(s) Hemric, Guy; Styner, Jerry

Producer(s) Nicholson, James H.; Arkoff, Samuel Z.
Director(s) Asher, William
Screenwriter(s) Asher, William

Cast Avalon, Frankie; Funicello, Annette; Fabian; Wills, Chill; Lembeck, Harvey; Parrish, Julie; Garner, Ed; Scully, Vince; The Don Randi Trio Plus One; The Carole Lombard Singers

Song(s) Fireball 500; Step Right Up; A Chance Like That; Country Carnival; My Way; Turn Around

Notes No cue sheet available.

1779 ✦ FIRE DOWN BELOW
Columbia, 1957

Choreographer(s) Foster, Bill

Producer(s) Allen, Irving; Broccoli, Albert R.
Director(s) Parrish, Robert
Screenwriter(s) Shaw, Irwin
Source(s) *Five Down Below* (novel) Catto, Max

Cast Hayworth, Rita; Lemmon, Jack; Mitchum, Robert; Lom, Herbert; Lee, Bernard; Newley, Anthony; Colleano, Bonar; Connor, Edric

Song(s) Fire Down Below [1] (C: Lee, Lester; L: Washington, Ned); Harmonica Theme from Fire Down Below (inst.) (C: Lemmon, Jack); Limbo [2] (C: Lee, Lester; L: Washington, Ned)

Notes [1] Originally titled "Woman Intended for Love" in 1956. [2] Sheet music only.

1780 ✦ THE FIREFLY
Metro–Goldwyn–Mayer, 1937

Musical Score Stothart, Herbert
Composer(s) Friml, Rudolf
Lyricist(s) Wright, Bob; Forrest, Chet
Choreographer(s) Rasch, Albertina

Producer(s)   Stromberg, Hunt
Director(s)   Leonard, Robert Z.
Screenwriter(s)   Goodrich, Frances; Hackett, Albert
Source(s)   *The Firefly* (musical) Harbach, Otto; Friml, Rudolf; Stothart, Herbert

Cast   MacDonald, Jeanette; Jones, Allan; William, Warren; Gilbert, Billy; Dumbrille, Douglass

Song(s)   English March; Happy Subjects (C: Stothart, Herbert); Festival (C: Stothart, Herbert); Love Is Like a Firefly (L: Harbach, Otto; Wright, Bob; Forrest, Chet); Spanish Folk Song (C: Stothart, Herbert); A Woman's Kiss [2]; The Donkey Serenade [1] (C: Friml, Rudolf; Stothart, Herbert); No Me Digas No (C/L: Maciste); Para La Salud (C/L: Stothart, Herbert); Ojos Rojos (C/L: Maciste); Giannina Mia (L: Harbach, Otto); He Who Loves and Runs Away (L: Kahn, Gus); Sympathy (L: Harbach, Otto; Kahn, Gus); When a Maid Comes Knocking At Your Heart (L: Harbach, Otto; Wright, Bob; Forrest, Chet)

Notes   [1] Also in CRAZY HOUSE (Universal). [2] Probably based on Friml's instrumental piece "A Woman's Smile."

1781 ✦ FIRE WITH FIRE
Paramount, 1986

Musical Score   Shore, Howard

Producer(s)   Nardino, Gary
Director(s)   Gibbins, Duncan
Screenwriter(s)   Phillips, Bill; Skaaren, Warren; Boorstin, Paul; Boorstin, Sharon

Cast   Madsen, Virginia; Sheffer, Craig; Cohen, Jeffrey Jay; Reid, Kate; Polito, Jon; Sweeney, D.B.

Song(s)   I'm In It for Love (C/L: Goldmark, Andy; Henderson, Patrick); Fire with Fire (C/L: Sanford, Charles); If Anybody Had a Heart (C/L: Kortchmar, Danny; Sother, J.D.)

1782 ✦ FIRST A GIRL
Gaumont-British, 1935

Composer(s)   Sigler, Maurice; Goodhart, Al; Hoffman, Al
Lyricist(s)   Sigler, Maurice; Goodhart, Al; Hoffman, Al

Director(s)   Saville, Victor
Screenwriter(s)   Gaffney, Marjorie
Source(s)   *Viktor und Viktoria* (movie) Schunzel, Reinhold

Cast   Matthews, Jessie; Hale, Sonnie; Lee, Anna; Jones, Griffith; Drayton, Alfred; Hunt, Martita

Song(s)   Everything's in Rhythm with My Heart; The Little Silkworm; Say the Word and It's Yours; I Can Wiggle My Ears

Notes   No cue sheet available. This is a British picture. Sheet music only. The American film VICTOR/VICTORIA is based on the same source.

1783 ✦ THE FIRST BABY
Twentieth Century–Fox, 1936

Director(s)   Seiler, Lewis

Cast   Downs, Johnny; Dean, Shirley; Darwell, Jane; Dunbar, Dixie; McDaniel, Hattie

Song(s)   Joan of Arkansaw [1] (C: Green, Johnny; L: Heyman, Edward); Phi-Phi-Phi (C: Whiting, Richard A.; L: Clare, Sidney); Spreadin' Rhythm Around (C: McHugh, Jimmy; L: Koehler, Ted); She and I (C/L: Mockridge, Cyril J.; L: Robinson, Bill)

Notes   No cue sheet available. [1] Originally in PROFESSIONAL SOLDIER.

1784 ✦ FIRST BLOOD
Orion, 1982

Musical Score   Goldsmith, Jerry

Producer(s)   Feitshans, Buzz
Director(s)   Kotcheff, Ted
Screenwriter(s)   Kozoll, Michael; Sackheim, William; Stallone, Sylvester
Source(s)   *Young Blood* (novel) Morrell, David

Cast   Stallone, Sylvester; Crenna, Richard; Dennehy, Brian; Caruso, David

Song(s)   It's a Long Road (C: Goldsmith, Jerry; L: Shaper, Hal)

Notes   No cue sheet available.

1785 ✦ THE FIRST HUNDRED YEARS
Metro–Goldwyn–Mayer, 1938

Musical Score   Axt, William

Producer(s)   Krasna, Norman
Director(s)   Thorpe, Richard
Screenwriter(s)   Baker, Melville

Cast   Montgomery, Robert; Bruce, Virginia; William, Warren; Barnes, Binnie; Dinehart, Alan

Song(s)   Misunderstood (C/L: Wright, Bob; Forrest, Chet)

1786 ✦ THE FIRST KISS
Paramount, 1928

Composer(s)   Robinson, J. Russel
Lyricist(s)   Dubin, Al

Director(s)   Lee, Rowland V.
Source(s)   *Four Brothers* (novel) Tupper, Tristam

Cast   Wray, Fay; Cooper, Gary; Chandler, Lane; Fenton, Leslie

Song(s)   The First Kiss; Anne Lee

Notes   No cue sheet available.

1787 ✦ FIRST LOVE (1939)
Universal, 1939

Producer(s)   Pasternak, Joe
Director(s)   Koster, Henry
Screenwriter(s)   Manning, Bruce; Houser, Lionel

Cast   Durbin, Deanna; Stack, Robert; Parrish, Helen; Pallette, Eugene; Joy, Leatrice; Howard, Lewis

Song(s)   Drink It Down to Old McKinley (C/L: Previn, Charles); Spring in My Heart (C: Strauss, Johann; L: Freed, Ralph)

Notes   There is also a vocal of "Amapola" by Jos. M. LaCalle and Albert Gamse and "One Fine Day" from Puccini's MADAME BUTTERFLY.

1788 ✦ FIRST LOVE (1977)
Paramount, 1977

Producer(s)   Turman, Lawrence
Director(s)   Darling, Joan
Screenwriter(s)   Hitchcock, Jane Stanton; Freeman, David
Source(s)   "Sentimental Education" (story) Brodkey, Harold

Cast   Katt, William; Dey, Susan; Heard, John; D'Angelo, Beverly; Loggia, Robert

Song(s)   Child for a Day (C/L: Gordon, David; Travis, Paul); That's Enough for Me (C/L: Williams, Paul)

1789 ✦ THE FIRST NUDIE MUSICAL
Paramount, 1976

Composer(s)   Kimmel, Bruce
Lyricist(s)   Kimmel, Bruce

Producer(s)   Reeves, Jack
Director(s)   Haggard, Mark; Kimmel, Bruce
Screenwriter(s)   Kimmel, Bruce

Cast   Nathan, Stephen; Williams, Cindy; Kimmel, Bruce

Song(s)   The First Nudie Musical; I Wanna; The Lights and the Smiles; Pain Us; Come Come Now; I'm Not Deformed; Orgasm; Lesbian Butch Dyke; Dancing Dildos; Perversion; Where Is a Man; Honey, What Ya Doin' Tonight?; Let 'Em Eat Cake; But Touch Me, I'm You; I Don't Have to Hide Anymore

1790 ✦ THE FIRST TIME
United Artists, 1969

Musical Score   Hopkins, Kenyon

Producer(s)   Smith, Roger; Carr, Allan
Director(s)   Neilson, James
Screenwriter(s)   Heims, Jo

Cast   Bisset, Jacqueline; Stern, Wes; Kelman, Rick; Roberts, Wink; Parkes, Gerard; Acker, Sharon; Lee, Cosette

Song(s)   Sweet Love in the Beginning (C: Hopkins, Kenyon; L: Clough, Michael; Crowley, Michael); Walkin' in the Night (C/L: Hopkins, Kenyon)

Notes   International title: YOU DON'T NEED PYJAMAS AT ROSIE'S.

1791 ✦ THE FIRST TRAVELING SALESLADY
RKO, 1956

Musical Score   Gertz, Irving
Composer(s)   Gertz, Irving
Lyricist(s)   Levy, Hal

Producer(s)   Lubin, Arthur
Director(s)   Lubin, Arthur
Screenwriter(s)   Freeman, Devery; Longstreet, Stephen

Cast   Rogers, Ginger; Nelson, Barry; Channing, Carol; Brian, David; Arness, James; Eastwood, Clint; Simon, Robert F.; Wilcox, Frank

Song(s)   First Traveling Saleslady; A Corset Can Do a Lot for a Lady

1792 ✦ FISHERMAN'S WHARF
RKO, 1939

Composer(s)   Young, Victor

Producer(s)   Lesser, Sol
Director(s)   Vorhaus, Bernard
Screenwriter(s)   Schubert, Bernard; Hunter, Ian McLellan; Lewis, Herbert Clyde

Cast   Breen, Bobby; Carrillo, Leo; Armetta, Henry; Patrick, Lee; Bupp, Tommy; Belasco, Leon

Song(s)   Fisherman's Chanty (L: Howe, William; Myers, Harlan); Sell Your Cares for a Song (L: Newman, Charles); Blue Italian Waters (C: Churchill, Frank E.; L: Webster, Paul Francis); Song of Italy (C: Churchill, Frank E.; L: Webster, Paul Francis)

Notes   No cue sheet available.

1793 ✦ THE FISH THAT SAVED PITTSBURGH
United Artists, 1979

Musical Score   Bell, Thom
Composer(s)   Bell, Thom; Bell, Leroy M.; James, Casey
Lyricist(s)   Bell, Leroy M.; James, Casey

Producer(s)   Stromberg, Gary; Dashey, David
Director(s)   Moses, Gilbert
Screenwriter(s)   Starkes, Jaison; Stevens, Edmond

Cast   Erving, Julius; Winters, Jonathan; Lemon, Meadowlark; Kehoe, Jack; Avery, Margaret; Bond III, James; Channing, Stockard

Song(s) Ragtime (C: Bell, Thom; L: Robinson, Jack); Moses's Theme; Follow Every Dream; Magic Mona (L: Robinson, Jack); Chance of a Lifetime (C: Bell, Thom); Jesus, Won't You Walk with Me (C: Traditional; L: Bell, Leroy M.; James, Casey; Bell, Thom); The Fish That Saved Pittsburgh (C: Bell, Thom); Tyrone's Theme (C: Bell, Thom; L: Bell, Leroy M.); Is It Love (Must Be Love) (C: Bell, Thom; L: Bell, Leroy M.); Do It, Do It (No One Does It Better) (C: Bell, Thom); Mighty, Mighty Pisces (C: Bell, Thom)

1794 ✦ F.I.S.T.
United Artists, 1978

Musical Score Conti, Bill

Producer(s) Jewison, Norman
Director(s) Jewison, Norman
Screenwriter(s) Eszterhas, Joe; Stallone, Sylvester

Cast Stallone, Sylvester; Steiger, Rod; Dillon, Melinda; Conway, Kevin; LoBianco, Tony; Yates, Cassie

Song(s) Union Song (C/L: Setaro, John)

1795 ✦ A FISTFUL OF DOLLARS
United Artists, 1964

Musical Score Morricone, Ennio

Producer(s) Colombo, Arrigo; Papi, George
Director(s) Leone, Sergio
Screenwriter(s) Leone, Sergio; Tessari, Duccio

Cast Eastwood, Clint; Koch, Marianne; Calvo, Pepe; Volonte, Gian Maria; Lukschy, Wolfgang; Rupp, Sieghardt; Lozano, Margherita; Martin, Daniel

Song(s) Quantos Amores (C: Morricone, Ennio; L: Orlandi)

Notes This was released in the United States in 1967. At that time most of the Italian names in the credits and cast were Americanized. I list the real names. The movie was a remake of YOJIMBO (1961).

1796 ✦ FITZWILLY
United Artists, 1967

Musical Score Williams, John

Producer(s) Mirisch, Walter
Director(s) Mann, Delbert
Screenwriter(s) Lennart, Isobel
Source(s) *A Garden of Cucumbers* (novel) Tyler, Poyntz

Cast Van Dyke, Dick; Feldon, Barbara; McGiver, John; Townes, Harry; Kleeb, Helen; Seymour, Anne; Evans, Edith; Waterston, Sam; Fiedler, John; Fell, Norman; Kellaway, Cecil

Song(s) Make Me Rainbows (C: Williams, John; L: Bergman, Marilyn; Bergman, Alan)

1797 ✦ FIVE BRANDED WOMEN
Paramount, 1960

Musical Score Lavagnino, Angelo Francesco

Producer(s) De Laurentiis, Dino
Director(s) Ritt, Martin
Screenwriter(s) Perilli, Ivo
Source(s) (novel) Pirro, Ugo

Cast Heflin, Van; Mangano, Silvana; Miles, Vera; Moreau, Jeanne; Bel Geddes, Barbara

Song(s) Jovanka (C: Lavagnino, Angelo Francesco; L: Mattone, Ugo); Military Song (C: Lavagnino, Angelo Francesco; L: Simoni, Sylvana; Fange, Angelo)

Notes Formerly titled JOVANKA AND THE OTHERS.

1798 ✦ 5 CARD STUD
Paramount, 1968

Musical Score Jarre, Maurice

Producer(s) Wallis, Hal B.
Director(s) Hathaway, Henry
Screenwriter(s) Roberts, Marguerite
Source(s) (novel) Gaulden, Ray

Cast Martin, Dean; Mitchum, Robert; Stevens, Inger; McDowall, Roddy; Anderson, John; Bissell, Whit; Kotto, Yaphet

Song(s) Five Card Stud (C: Jarre, Maurice; L: Washington, Ned)

1799 ✦ FIVE DAYS FROM HOME
Universal, 1979

Musical Score Conti, Bill

Producer(s) Peppard, George
Director(s) Peppard, George
Screenwriter(s) Moore, William

Cast Peppard, George; Brand, Neville; Boucher, Sherry; Campos, Victor; Donner, Robert

Song(s) Love Theme (C: Conti, Bill; L: Gimbel, Norman)

Notes No cue sheet available.

1800 ✦ FIVE FINGERS
Twentieth Century–Fox, 1952

Musical Score Herrmann, Bernard

Producer(s) Lang, Otto
Director(s) Mankiewicz, Joseph L.
Screenwriter(s) Wilson, Michael
Source(s) *Operation Cicero* (book) Moyzisch, L.C.

Cast Mason, James; Darrieux, Danielle; Rennie, Michael; Hampden, Walter; Berghof, Herbert

Song(s) J'Ai Peur De T'Aimer (C: Newman, Alfred; L: Chandler, Tanis)

Notes "Monsieur Lenoble" by Michel Emer and "Adieu mon Coeur" by Marguerite Monnot and Henri Contet are also sung as are several operatic arias.

1801 ✦ FIVE OF A KIND
Twentieth Century–Fox, 1938

Producer(s) Wurtzel, Sol M.
Director(s) Leeds, Herbert I.
Screenwriter(s) Breslow, Lou; Patrick, John

Cast Dionne Quintuplets; Hersholt, Jean; Trevor, Claire; Romero, Cesar; Summerville, Slim; Wilcoxon, Henry; Courtney, Inez; Darwell, Jane; Tombes, Andrew

Song(s) All Mixed Up (C: Pokrass, Sam; L: Clare, Sidney)

1802 ✦ FIVE ON THE BLACK HAND SIDE
United Artists, 1973

Musical Score Barnum, H.B.
Composer(s) Barnum, H.B.

Producer(s) Peters, Brock; Tolan, Michael
Director(s) Williams, Oscar
Screenwriter(s) Russell, Charlie L.

Cast Taylor, Clarice; Jackson, Leonard; Turman, Glynn; Martin, D'Urville; Dubois, Ja'net; Banfield, Bonnie; Capers, Virginia; Franklin, Carl Mikal

Song(s) Five on the Black Hand Side (L: Barnum, H.B.; Cobbin, James D.; Murray, Ronald L.; Wilson, Jerome L.); Freedom (L: Barnum, H.B.); Tell Me You Love Me (L: Barnum, H.B.; Cobbin, James D.); They Keep Comin' (L: Barnum, H.B.; Marlow, Mexi); I'll Give You Love (L: Barnum, H.B.; Cobbin, James D.; Murray, Ronald L.; Wilson, Jerome L.)

1803 ✦ THE FIVE PENNIES
Paramount, 1959

Musical Score Stevens, Leith
Composer(s) Fine, Sylvia
Lyricist(s) Fine, Sylvia
Choreographer(s) Barton, Earl

Producer(s) Rose, Jack
Director(s) Shavelson, Melville
Screenwriter(s) Shavelson, Melville; Rose, Jack

Cast Kaye, Danny [2]; Armstrong, Louis; Manne, Shelly; Troup, Bobby; Daley, Ray; Crosby, Bob; Guardino, Harry; Weld, Tuesday; Bel Geddes, Barbara [1]

Song(s) Follow the Leader; Red's Rabbit; Lullaby in Ragtime; Goodnight—Sleep Tight; The Five Pennies

Notes This is a film biography of Red Nichols. Other proposed titles were INTERMISSION and THE RED

NICHOLS STORY. Only original songs listed. Sylvia Fine also wrote special lyrics to "When the Saints Go Marching In" and "Indiana." [1] Dubbed by Eileen Wilson. [2] Trumpet playing by Red Nichols.

1804 ✦ THE 5,000 FINGERS OF DR. T
Columbia, 1953

Musical Score Hollander, Frederick
Composer(s) Hollander, Frederick
Lyricist(s) Seuss, Dr.
Choreographer(s) Loring, Eugene

Producer(s) Kramer, Stanley
Director(s) Rowland, Roy
Screenwriter(s) Geisel, Theodore [2]; Scott, Allan

Cast Hayes, Peter Lind; Healy, Mary; Conried, Hans; Rettig, Tommy; Heasley, John; Heasley, Robert; Cravat, Noel; Kulky, Henry

Song(s) Ten Happy Fingers; Dream Stuff; Hypnotic Duel; Get-Together Weather; Kid's Song; Victory Procession; Dungeon Elevator; Dr. T's Dressing Song; The Grindstone [1]; Hypnotic Chant [1]; Many Questions Have No Answers [1]; Money [1]; You Opened My Eyes [1] (L: Brooks, Jack); Because We're Kids [3]

Notes [1] Instrumental only. [2] Dr. Seuss. [3] Sheet music only.

1805 ✦ FIVE WEEKS IN A BALLOON
Twentieth Century–Fox, 1962

Musical Score Sawtell, Paul

Producer(s) Allen, Irwin
Director(s) Allen, Irwin
Screenwriter(s) Bennett, Charles; Allen, Irwin; Gail, Albert
Source(s) *Five Weeks in a Balloon* (novel) Verne, Jules

Cast Buttons, Red; Fabian; Eden, Barbara; Hardwicke, Sir Cedric; Lorre, Peter; Haydn, Richard; Luna, Barbara; Gilbert, Billy; Marshall, Herbert; Owen, Reginald; Daniell, Henry; Mazurki, Mike

Song(s) Five Weeks in a Balloon [1] (C: Thielman, Urban; L: Desmond, Jodi)

Notes [1] Music based on an Italian folk song.

1806 ✦ THE FIXER
Metro–Goldwyn–Mayer, 1968

Musical Score Jarre, Maurice

Producer(s) Lewis, Edward
Director(s) Frankenheimer, John
Screenwriter(s) Trumbo, Dalton
Source(s) *The Fixer* (novel) Malamud, Bernard

Cast   Bates, Alan; Bogarde, Dirk; Brown, Georgia; Griffith, Hugh; Hartman, Elizabeth; Holm, Ian; Opatoshu, David; Warner, David; White, Carol

Song(s)   Wedding Dance (C: Jarre, Maurice; L: Traditional)

1807 ◆ FLAME AND THE FLESH
Metro–Goldwyn–Mayer, 1954

Composer(s)   Brodszky, Nicholas
Lyricist(s)   Lawrence, Jack

Producer(s)   Pasternak, Joe
Director(s)   Brooks, Richard
Screenwriter(s)   Deutsch, Helen
Source(s)   *Naples, Au Baiser De Feu* (novel) Bailly, Auguste

Cast   Turner, Lana; Angeli, Pier; Thompson, Carlos; Colleano, Bonar

Song(s)   Peddler Man (Then I Loved); By Candlelight; No One but You [1]; Languida

Notes   There is also a vocal of "Serenade of the Roses" by Di Capua. [1] Also in TEN THOUSAND BEDROOMS.

1808 ◆ THE FLAME OF NEW ORLEANS
Universal, 1941

Composer(s)   Previn, Charles
Lyricist(s)   Lerner, Sam

Producer(s)   Pasternak, Joe
Director(s)   Clair, Rene
Screenwriter(s)   Krasna, Norman

Cast   Dietrich, Marlene; Young, Roland; Cabot, Bruce; Auer, Mischa; Devine, Andy; Jenks, Frank; Quillan, Eddie; Crews, Laura Hope; Pangborn, Franklin; Muse, Clarence; Cooper, Melville; Revere, Anne

Song(s)   Salt o' the Sea; Sweet Is the Blush of May; Oh, Joyful Day

1809 ◆ FLAME OF THE BARBARY COAST
Republic, 1944

Choreographer(s)   Ceballos, Larry

Producer(s)   Kane, Joseph
Director(s)   Kane, Joseph
Screenwriter(s)   Chase, Borden
Source(s)   "King of the Barbary Coast" (story) Chaplin, Prescott

Cast   Wayne, John; Dvorak, Ann; Schildkraut, Joseph; Grey, Virginia; Hicks, Russell; Frawley, William; Fix, Paul; Ullrich, Jan; McQueen, Butterfly; Taliaferro, Hal

Song(s)   That Man (Is Always on My Mind) (C: Grossman, Bernie; L: Lewis, Harold); Baby Blue Eyes (C/L: Elliott, Jack); Have a Heart (C/L: Elliott, Jack)

Notes   There are also vocals of "Cubanola Glide" by Harry Von Tilzer and Vincent Bryan; "Lover, Here Is My Heart" by Leo Silesu and Adrian Ross; "In the Sweet Bye and Bye" by Webster and Bennett (the famous song of the same name was written by Vincent P. Bryan and Harry Von Tilzer, but this may be a mistake on the cue sheet), "Dear Old Girl" by Theodore Morse and Richard Henry Buck; "Carrie" by Junie McCree and Albert Von Tilzer; "By the Light of the Silvery Moon" by Edward Madden and Gus Edwards and "There'll Be a Hot Time in the Old Town Tonight" by Joe Hayden and Theodore M. Metz.

1810 ◆ FLAME OF THE ISLANDS
Republic, 1955

Musical Score   Riddle, Nelson
Composer(s)   Burke, Sonny
Lyricist(s)   Elliott, Jack

Producer(s)   Ludwig, Edward
Director(s)   Ludwig, Edward
Screenwriter(s)   Manning, Bruce
Source(s)   *Rebel Island* (novel) Comandini, Adele; Horwin, Jerry

Cast   De Carlo, Yvonne; Duff, Howard; Scott, Zachary; Kasznar, Kurt; O'Neil, Barbara; Arness, James; Inescort, Frieda; Matthews, Lester

Song(s)   Bahama Mama; Take It or Leave It

Notes   There is also a vocal of "Matilda Hold the Light."

1811 ◆ FLAMING BULLETS
PRC, 1945

Musical Score   Zahler, Lee; Grigor, Nico

Producer(s)   Alexander, Arthur
Director(s)   Fraser, Harry
Screenwriter(s)   Fraser, Harry

Cast   Ritter, Tex; O'Brien, Dave; Wilkerson, Guy; King, Charles; Knox, Patricia; Maynard, Kermit

Song(s)   Be Honest with Me [1] (C/L: Rose, Fred; Autry, Gene)

Notes   [1] Also in SIERRA SUE (Republic) and STRICTLY IN THE GROOVE (Universal).

1812 ◆ FLAMING FEATHER
Paramount, 1951

Musical Score   Sawtell, Paul

Producer(s)   Holt, Nat
Director(s)   Enright, Ray
Screenwriter(s)   Adams, Gerald Drayson; Gruber, Frank

Cast   Hayden, Sterling; Whelan, Arleen; Jory, Victor; Arlen, Richard; Rush, Barbara; Tucker, Forrest;

Buchanan, Edgar; Thurston, Carol; McDonald, Ian; Cleveland, George

Song(s) No Ring on Her Finger [2] (C: Sherwin, Manning; L: Loesser, Frank); He Met Her on the Prairie [3] (C: Rainger, Ralph; L: Robin, Leo); You Can't Blame Polly [1] (C: Lee, Lester; L: Seelen, Jerry)

Notes There is also a vocal of "Adios Mariquita Linda" by Marcos A. Jimenez. [1] Not used. Used in A WOMAN OF THE TOWN (UA). [2] Also in BLOSSOMS ON BROADWAY and THE PARSON OF PANAMINT. [3] Also in ROSE OF THE RANCHO.

1813 ✦ THE FLAMINGO KID
Twentieth Century–Fox, 1984

Musical Score Sobel, Curt

Producer(s) Phillips, Michael
Director(s) Marshall, Garry
Screenwriter(s) Marshall, Neal; Marshall, Garry

Cast Dillon, Matt; Elizondo, Hector; McCarthy, Molly; Gehman, Martha; Crenna, Richard; Walter, Jessica; Davis, Carole R.; Jones, Janet; Stevens, Fisher; Pinchot, Bronson; Stahl, Richard; Grifasi, Joe; Allen, Mel; Barbarian Brothers; Chadman, Christopher

Song(s) Breakaway (C: Salvay, Bennett; Walden, Snuffy; L: Matza, Arlene)

Notes No cue sheet available.

1814 ✦ FLAMING STAR
Twentieth Century–Fox, 1960

Musical Score Mockridge, Cyril J.

Producer(s) Weisbart, David
Director(s) Siegel, Don
Screenwriter(s) Huffaker, Clair; Johnson, Nunnally
Source(s) *Flaming Lance* (novel) Huffaker, Clair

Cast Presley, Elvis; Forrest, Steve; Eden, Barbara; Del Rio, Dolores; McIntire, John; Acosta, Rodolfo; Swenson, Karl; Rainey, Ford; Jaeckel, Richard

Song(s) Flaming Star (C: Edwards, Sherman; L: Wayne, Sid); A Cane and a High Starch Collar (C/L: Tepper, Sid; Bennett, Roy C.)

1815 ✦ FLAP
Warner Brothers, 1970

Musical Score Hamlisch, Marvin
Composer(s) Hamlisch, Marvin

Producer(s) Adler, Jerry
Director(s) Reed, Carol
Screenwriter(s) Huffaker, Clair
Source(s) "Nobody Loves a Drunken Indian" (story) Huffaker, Clair

Cast Quinn, Anthony; Akins, Claude; Bill, Tony; Jory, Victor; Collier, Don; Winters, Shelley

Song(s) If Nobody Loves (L: Levitt, Estelle); Joy Palace; Give us Our Land [1] (L: Liebling, Howard)

Notes "L'Amour, Toujours L'Amour" by Rudolf Friml and Catherine Chisholm Cushing was also used as a background vocal. [1] Only visual vocal.

1816 ✦ FLAREUP
Metro–Goldwyn–Mayer, 1970

Musical Score Baxter, Les
Composer(s) Baxter, Les
Lyricist(s) Baxter, Les

Producer(s) Fromkess, Leon
Director(s) Neilson, James
Screenwriter(s) Rodgers, Mark

Cast Welch, Raquel; Stacy, James; Askew, Luke; Chastain, Don; Rifkin, Ron; Byron, Jean; Peters, Kay

Song(s) Raquel; The One I Remember; Flareup (C: Baxter, Les; L: Adelson, Lenny)

1817 ✦ FLASHDANCE
Paramount, 1983

Musical Score Moroder, Giorgio
Choreographer(s) Hornaday, Jeffrey

Producer(s) Guber, Peter; Peters, Jon
Director(s) Lyne, Adrian
Screenwriter(s) Hedley, Tom; Eszterhas, Joe

Cast Beals, Jennifer [1]; Nouri, Michael; Skala, Lilia; Johnson, Sunny; Heffner, Kyle T.

Song(s) Flashdance ... What a Feeling (C: Moroder, Giorgio; L: Forsey, Keith; Cara, Irene); He's a Dream (C/L: Sinnamon, Shandi; Magness, Ronald); Maniac (C/L: Sembello, Michael; Matkosky, Dennis); I Love Rock 'n' Roll (C/L: Hooker, Jake; Merrill, Alan); It's Just Begun (C/L: Castor, Jimmy; Pruitt, John; Thomas, Gerry); Manhunt (C/L: Cotler, Douglas M.; Gilbert, Richard L.); Gloria (C/L: Bigazzi, Giancarlo; Tozzi, Umberto; Veitch, Trevor); Imagination (C/L: Hey, Jerry; Boddicker, Michael; Sembello, Michael; Ramone, Phil); Romeo (C/L: Bellotte, Pete; Levay, Sylvester); Seduce Me Tonight (C: Moroder, Giorgio; L: Forsey, Keith); I'll Be Here Where the Heart Is (C/L: Carnes, Kim; Hitchings, Duane; Krampf, Craig); Lady Lady Lady [2] (C: Moroder, Giorgio; L: Forsey, Keith)

Notes Most of the music is background vocals. [1] Dancing dubbed by Marine Jahan. [2] Sheet music only.

1818 ✦ FLASH GORDON
Universal, 1981

Musical Score Blake, Howard; Queen
Composer(s) Queen
Lyricist(s) Queen

Producer(s)   De Laurentiis, Dino
Director(s)   Hodges, Mike
Screenwriter(s)   Semple Jr., Lorenzo
Source(s)   *Flash Gordon* (comic strip) Raymond, Alex

Cast   Jones, Sam J.; Anderson, Melody; Topol; Von Sydow, Max; Muti, Ornella; Dalton, Timothy; Blessed, Brian; Wyngarde, Peter

Song(s)   Flash Gordon; Kiss; Ajax/Battle Rocket; Vultan and Flash; Wedding Anthem; Ming Spiked; Thanks Flash

1819 ✦ FLASHPOINT
Tri-Star, 1984

Musical Score   Tangerine Dream

Producer(s)   Short, Skip
Director(s)   Tannen, William
Screenwriter(s)   Shryack, Dennis; Butler, Michael
Source(s)   *Flashpoint* (novel) La Fountaine, George

Cast   Kristofferson, Kris; Williams, Treat; Torn, Rip; Conway, Kevin; Smith, Kurtwood; Ferrer, Miguel; Smart, Jean; Harper, Tess

Song(s)   Flashpoint (C/L: Richardson, Scott); Who's that Memory in Your Eyes (C/L: Richardson, Scott)

Notes   No cue sheet available.

1820 ✦ A FLEA IN HER EAR
Twentieth Century–Fox, 1968

Musical Score   Kaper, Bronislau

Producer(s)   Kohlmar, Fred
Director(s)   Charon, Jacques
Screenwriter(s)   Mortimer, John
Source(s)   *A Flea in Her Ear* (play) Feydeau, Georges

Cast   Harrison, Rex; Harris, Rosemary; Jourdan, Louis; Roberts, Rachel; Williams, John; Aslan, Gregoire; Sen Yung, Victor

Song(s)   A Flea in Her Ear (C: Kaper, Bronislau; L: Cahn, Sammy)

1821 ✦ THE FLEET'S IN
Paramount, 1942

Composer(s)   Schertzinger, Victor
Lyricist(s)   Mercer, Johnny
Choreographer(s)   Donohue, Jack

Producer(s)   Jones, Paul
Director(s)   Schertzinger, Victor
Screenwriter(s)   De Leon, Walter; Silvers, Sid; Spence, Ralph
Source(s)   *Sailor Beware* (play) Nicholson, Kenyon; Robinson, Charles

Cast   Lamour, Dorothy; Holden, William; Bracken, Eddie; Hutton, Betty; Rhodes, Betty Jane; Erickson, Leif; Daley, Cass; Lamb, Gil; Britton, Barbara; Jimmy Dorsey and His Orchestra; Eberly, Bob; O'Connell, Helen

Song(s)   The Fleet's In; Tangerine; When You Hear the Time Signal; If You Build a Better Mousetrap; (Somebody Else's Moon —) Not Mine; I Remember You; Arthur Murray Taught Me Dancing in a Hurry; Tomorrow You Belong to Uncle Sammy; I'm Cookin' with Gas [1]; On the Friendly Side [1]

Notes   [1] Not used.

1822 ✦ FLETCH
Universal, 1985

Musical Score   Faltermeyer, Harold

Producer(s)   Greisman, Alan; Douglas, Peter
Director(s)   Ritchie, Michael
Screenwriter(s)   Bergman, Andrew
Source(s)   *Fletch* (novel) McDonald, Gregory

Cast   Chase, Chevy; Baker, Joe Don; Wheeler-Nicholson, Dana; Libertini, Richard; Matheson, Tim; Walsh, M. Emmet; Wendt, George; Mars, Kenneth; Davis, Geena; Henderson, Bill

Song(s)   Bit By Bit (C: Faltermeyer, Harold; L: Golde, Franne); Fletch, Get Outta Town (C/L: Hartman, Don; Midnight, Charlie)

1823 ✦ FLETCH LIVES
Universal, 1989

Musical Score   Faltermeyer, Harold
Composer(s)   Dural, Stanley
Lyricist(s)   Dural, Stanley

Producer(s)   Greisman, Alan; Douglas, Peter
Director(s)   Ritchie, Michael
Screenwriter(s)   Capetanos, Leon

Cast   Chase, Chevy; Holbrook, Hal; Phillips, Julianne; Ermey, R. Lee; Libertini, Richard; Cobb, Randall "Tex"; Little, Cleavon; Vandis, Titos

Song(s)   Ain't No Use Baby; Gospel Song for Mimsi (C/L: Ritchie, Michael); Kings of the Road (C/L: Faltermeyer, Harold); 1234 Zydeco

1824 ✦ FLIGHT AT MIDNIGHT
Republic, 1939

Producer(s)   Schaefer, Armand
Director(s)   Salkow, Sidney
Screenwriter(s)   Gibbons, Eliot

Cast   Parker, Jean; Regan, Phil; Armstrong, Robert; Beery Jr., Noah; Turner, Roscoe; Briggs, Harlan

Song(s)   I Never Thought I'd Fall in Love Again (C: Lane, Burton; L: Freed, Ralph)

1825 ✦ FLIGHT COMMAND
MGM, 1940

Musical Score   Waxman, Franz

Producer(s)   Ruben, J. Walter
Director(s)   Borzage, Frank
Screenwriter(s)   Root, Wells; Haislip, Harvey

Cast   Taylor, Robert; Hussey, Ruth; Pidgeon, Walter; Kelly, Paul; Pendleton, Nat; Strudwick, Shepperd; Skelton, Red; Purcelll, Dick

Song(s)   Eyes of the Fleet (C/L: McElduff, J.V.)

Notes   No cue sheet available.

1826 ✦ FLIGHT NURSE
Republic, 1953

Musical Score   Young, Victor

Producer(s)   Dwan, Allan
Director(s)   Dwan, Allan
Screenwriter(s)   LeMay, Alan

Cast   Leslie, Joan; Tucker, Forrest; Franz, Arthur; Donnell, Jeff; Cooper, Ben; Holden, James; Miller, Kristine

Song(s)   Gimme My Chute [1] (C: Traditional; L: Dwan, Allan)

Notes   [1] To the tune of "Blue Tail Fly."

1827 ✦ THE FLIGHT OF THE PHOENIX
Twentieth Century–Fox, 1965

Musical Score   De Vol, Frank

Producer(s)   Aldrich, Robert
Director(s)   Aldrich, Robert
Screenwriter(s)   Heller, Lukas
Source(s)   *The Flight of the Phoenix* (novel) Trevor, Elleston

Cast   Stewart, James; Attenborough, Richard; Finch, Peter; Kruger, Hardy; Borgnine, Ernest; Bannen, Ian; Fraser, Ronald; Duryea, Dan; Kennedy, George

Song(s)   Senza Fine [1] (C: Paoli, Gino; L: Paoli, Gino; Wilder, Alec)

Notes   [1] Wilder wrote the English lyrics. Also in AVANTI! without Wilder lyrics.

1828 ✦ FLIPPER
Metro–Goldwyn–Mayer, 1963

Musical Score   Vars, Henry

Producer(s)   Tors, Ivan
Director(s)   Clark, James B.
Screenwriter(s)   Weiss, Arthur

Cast   Connors, Chuck; Halpin, Luke; Scott, Connie; Rose, Jane; Higgins, Joe; White, Robertson; Applewhite, George; Maguire, Kathleen; Flipper

Song(s)   Flipper (C: Vars, Henry; L: Dunham, "By")

1829 ✦ FLIPPER'S NEW ADVENTURE
Metro–Goldwyn–Mayer, 1964

Musical Score   Vars, Henry
Composer(s)   Vars, Henry
Lyricist(s)   Dunham, "By"

Producer(s)   Tors, Ivan
Director(s)   Benson, Leon
Screenwriter(s)   Arthur, Art
Source(s)   characters by Browning, Ricou; Cowden, Jack

Cast   Halpin, Luke; Franklin, Pamela; Cherry, Helen; Helmore, Tom; Anis, Francesca; Kelly, Brian; Flipper

Song(s)   Flipper; It's a Cotton Candy World; Imagine

Notes   Titled FLIPPER AND THE PIRATES internationally.

1830 ✦ FLIRTATION WALK
Warner Brothers–First National, 1934

Composer(s)   Wrubel, Allie
Lyricist(s)   Dixon, Mort
Choreographer(s)   Connolly, Bobby

Director(s)   Borzage, Frank
Screenwriter(s)   Daves, Delmer

Cast   Powell, Dick; Keeler, Ruby; O'Brien, Pat; Alexander, Ross

Song(s)   Song of the Islands [5] (C/L: King, Charles E.); The Four Isles, (C/L: King, Charles E.); King's Serenade [4] (C/L: King, Charles E.); Pinch Me Slowly (C/L: King, Charles E.); No Horse, No Wife, No Mustache; Mr. & Mrs. Is the Name; Flirtation Walk; Soft Green Seas [1]; I See Two Lovers [2] [3]; When Do We Eat? [2]; Smoking in the Dark [2]

Notes   [1] Not on cue sheets but found on a list made up by Warner music department head Danny Gould. [2] Not on cue sheets. [3] Also in SWEET MUSIC. [4] Also in MUSICAL MOVIELAND. [5] Also in MELODY LANE (Universal) and SONG OF THE ISLANDS (20th).

1831 ✦ FLIRTING WITH FATE
Metro–Goldwyn–Mayer, 1938

Musical Score   Young, Victor
Composer(s)   Samuels, Walter G.
Lyricist(s)   Newman, Charles

Producer(s)   Loew, David L.
Director(s)   McDonald, Frank
Screenwriter(s)   March, Joseph Moncure; La Blanche, Ethel; Melson, Charles; Clork, Harry

Cast Brown, Joe E.; Carrillo, Leo; Roberts, Beverly; Gibson, Wynne; Duna, Steffi; Kinskey, Leonid; Judels, Charles; Fields, Stanley; Franklin, Irene

Song(s) Ride Bandoleros; Dim Marimba Moon; Mate; Gaucho Gonzales [1]

Notes [1] Used instrumentally only.

1832 ✦ FLORIDA, LAND OF FLOWERS
Twentieth Century–Fox, 1940

Song(s) Moon Dream Shore (C: Lockhart, E.; L: Unknown)

Notes This is a Lowell Thomas Magic Carpet of Movietone travelogue.

1833 ✦ FLORIDA SPECIAL
Paramount, 1936

Producer(s) Wanger, Walter
Director(s) Ludwig, Edward
Screenwriter(s) Boehm, David; Roberts, Marguerite; Perelman, S.J.; Perelman, Laura
Source(s) "Magazine Car" (story) Kelland, Clarence Budington

Cast Heller, Jackie; Oakie, Jack; Eilers, Sally; Taylor, Kent; Drake, Frances

Song(s) It's You I'm Talking About (C: Revel, Harry; L: Gordon, Mack); When Grimble Hits the Cymbal [1] (C: Revel, Harry; L: Gordon, Mack)

Notes "Harrigan" by George M. Cohan is used in the picture. [1] Not used.

1834 ✦ THE FLORODORA GIRL
Metro–Goldwyn–Mayer, 1930

Composer(s) Stothart, Herbert
Lyricist(s) Grey, Clifford; Rice, Andy

Director(s) Beaumont, Harry
Screenwriter(s) Markey, Gene; Spence, Ralph; Boasberg, Al; Hopkins, Robert E.

Cast Davies, Marion; Gray, Lawrence; Catlett, Walter; Chase, Ilka; Prouty, Jed; Oakland, Vivian; Allister, Claud; Hardy, Sam; O'Neil, Nance; Chandler, George; Louise, Anita

Song(s) My Kind of Man; Pass the Beer and Pretzels

Notes Titled THE GAY NINETIES internationally. There are also vocals of "Just One Girl" and "Stay in Your Own Backyard" by Karl Kennett and Lyn Udall; "My Mother Was a Lady" by Edward B. Marks and Joseph W. Stern; "Say 'Au Revoir' but not 'Goodbye'" by Harry Kennedy; "Just Break the News to Mother" by Charles K. Harris; (There'll Be) A Hot Time in the Old Town (Tonight)" by Joseph Hayden and Theodore M. Metz; "Little Annie Rooney" by Michael Nolan; "Swing Me a Little Higher, Obediah" by Rick and Scott; "The

Old Oaken Bucket" and "On the Banks of the Wabash" by Paul Dresser; "Stand Up and Cheer" by Breitenfeld; "Sextette from Florodora" by Leslie Stuart and Owen Hall; and "Won't You Tell Me Dearie" by Bedford and Walton.

1835 ✦ FLOWER DRUM SONG
Universal, 1961

Composer(s) Rodgers, Richard
Lyricist(s) Hammerstein II, Oscar
Choreographer(s) Pan, Hermes

Producer(s) Hunter, Ross; Fields, Joseph
Director(s) Koster, Henry
Screenwriter(s) Fields, Joseph
Source(s) *Flower Drum Song* (musical) Rodgers, Richard; Hammerstein II, Oscar; Fields, Joseph

Cast Umeki, Miyoshi [1]; Soo, Jack [1]; Shigeta, James; Kwan, Nancy [2]; Hall, Juanita [1]; Fong, Benson; Sen Yung, Victor; Sato, Reiko [3]; Tong, Kam [4]; Adiarte, Patrick; Yong, Soo

Song(s) A Hundred Million Miracles; Fan Tan Fanny; The Other Generation; I Enjoy Being a Girl; I Am Going to Like It Here; Chop Suey; Grant Avenue; Gliding Through My Memoree; Love Look Away; You Are Beautiful; Sunday; Don't Marry Me

Notes All songs from the original Broadway show. [1] From Broadway cast. [2] Dubbed by B.J. Baker. [3] Dubbed by Marilyn Horne. [4] Dubbed by John Dodson.

1836 ✦ FLOWER GARDEN
Metro–Goldwyn–Mayer, 1930

Musical Score Alter, Louis
Composer(s) Alter, Louis
Lyricist(s) Johnson, Howard

Director(s) Brooks, Marty

Cast Edwards, Cliff; Howell, Lottice; Locust Sisters; Weaver, Alice; Berkey, Inez; Rutledge & Taylor

Song(s) Planting Flowers of Happiness; Ching, Ching, Ching (C: Fisher, Fred; L: Brooks, Marty); I'm Trailing Arbutus; Dance of the Daffodils; Moonlight, Starlight (C/L: Gilberte, Annie; Gilberte, Hallet)

Notes Short subject.

1837 ✦ FLOWERS FOR MADAME
Warner Brothers, 1935

Composer(s) Wrubel, Allie
Lyricist(s) Dixon, Mort

Song(s) Flowers for Madame; Powder My Back

Notes Short subject. Merrie Melodie. No cue sheet available.

1838 ✦ THE FLY
Twentieth Century–Fox, 1986

Musical Score Shore, Howard

Producer(s) Cornfeld, Stuart
Director(s) Cronenberg, David
Screenwriter(s) Pogue, Charles Edward; Cronenberg, David

Cast Goldblum, Jeff; Davis, Geena; Getz, John; Boushel, Joy; Carlson, Les; Chuvalo, George

Song(s) Help Me (C/L: Rodgers, Nile; Ferry, Bryan)

Notes No cue sheet available.

1839 ✦ FLYING DEVILS
RKO, 1933

Producer(s) Lewis, David
Director(s) Birdwell, Russell J.
Screenwriter(s) Stevens, Louis; Morgan, Byron

Cast Cabot, Bruce; Linden, Eric; Judge, Arline; Bellamy, Ralph; Edwards, Cliff

Song(s) You've Got What Gets Me [1] (C: Gershwin, George; L: Gershwin, Ira)

Notes [1] Also in GIRL CRAZY (1932).

1840 ✦ FLYING DOWN TO RIO
RKO, 1933

Musical Score Steiner, Max
Composer(s) Youmans, Vincent
Lyricist(s) Eliscu, Edward; Kahn, Gus
Choreographer(s) Gould, Dave

Producer(s) Brock, Lou
Director(s) Freeland, Thornton
Screenwriter(s) Hume, Cyril; Hanemann, H.W.; Gelsey, Erwin
Source(s) (play) Caldwell, Anne

Cast Del Rio, Dolores; Raymond, Gene; Roulien, Raul; Rogers, Ginger; Astaire, Fred; Moten, Etta; Walker, Walter; Frederici, Blanche

Song(s) Orchids in the Moonlight; Flying Down to Rio; Waiters' Song [1]; Music Makes Me; Carioca; The Three Greeks [1]; Street Scene (Inst.)

Notes Cue sheet does not list any songs as vocals except a short rendition of "Just a Gigolo" by Leonello Casucci. [1] Used instrumentally only.

1841 ✦ THE FLYING FLEET
Metro–Goldwyn–Mayer, 1928

Director(s) Hill, George
Screenwriter(s) Schayer, Richard

Cast Novarro, Ramon; Graves, Ralph; Page, Anita; Nugent, Eddie; Nye, Carroll

Song(s) You're the Only One for Me (C: Axt, William; Mendoza, David); L: Klages, Raymond

Notes No cue sheet available.

1842 ✦ THE FLYING FOOL
Pathe, 1929

Composer(s) Green, George
Lyricist(s) Waggner, George

Producer(s) Sistrom, William
Director(s) Garnett, Tay
Screenwriter(s) Gleason, James

Cast Boyd, William; Prevost, Marie; Gleason, Russell; O'Brien, Tom

Song(s) If I Had My Way; I'm That Way About Baby

Notes No cue sheet available.

1843 ✦ FLYING HIGH
Metro–Goldwyn–Mayer, 1931

Composer(s) McHugh, Jimmy
Lyricist(s) Fields, Dorothy
Choreographer(s) Berkeley, Busby

Producer(s) White, George
Director(s) Riesner, Charles F.
Screenwriter(s) Younger, A.P.; Hopkins, Robert E.
Source(s) *Flying High* (musical) DeSylva, B.G. [3]; Brown, Lew; Henderson, Ray; McGowan, John

Cast Lahr, Bert [2]; Greenwood, Charlotte; O'Brien, Pat; Crawford, Kathryn; Winninger, Charles; Hopper, Hedda; Kibbee, Guy; Braggiotti, Herbert; Gus Arnheim and His Orchestra

Song(s) I'll Make a Happy Landing [4]; This Will Be the First Time for Me (C: Henderson, Ray; L: DeSylva, B.G.; Brown, Lew); Examination; We'll Dance Until Dawn [5]; Mrs. Krause's Blue Eyed Baby Boy [1] (C: Henderson, Ray; L: DeSylva, B.G.; Brown, Lew); Air Minded [1] (C: Henderson, Ray; L: DeSylva, B.G.; Brown, Lew)

Notes Titled HAPPY LANDING internationally. [1] Used instrumentally only. [2] From Broadway cast. [3] Billed as George G. DeSylva (his real name). [4] Also in PLANE NUTS. [5] Also in RED-HEADED WOMAN and PLANE NUTS.

1844 ✦ FLYING HOSTESS
Universal, 1937

Producer(s) Rogers, Charles R.
Director(s) Roth, Murray
Screenwriter(s) Holmes, Brown; Gates, Harvey; Clork, Harry
Source(s) "Sky Fever" (story) Sayre, George

Cast Barrett, Judith; Logan, Ella; Allwyn, Astrid; Randall, Addison; Gargan, William; Hall, William; Devine, Andy

Song(s) Bang, the Bell Rang (C: Actman, Irving; L: Loesser, Frank)

1845 ✦ THE FLYING MOUSE
Disney, 1934

Musical Score Lewis, Bert
Composer(s) Churchill, Frank E.
Lyricist(s) Morey, Larry

Song(s) If I Were a Bird; You're Nothin' but a Nothin'

Notes Cartoon short. No credit sheet available.

1846 ✦ FLYING WITH MUSIC
United Artists, 1942

Composer(s) Ward, Edward
Lyricist(s) Wright, Bob; Forrest, Chet

Producer(s) Roach, Hal
Director(s) Archainbaud, George
Screenwriter(s) Webster, M. Coates; Kaye, Louis S.

Cast Givot, George; Woodworth, Marjorie; Marshall, William; Gargan, Edward; Bergen, Jerry; Varden, Norma

Song(s) If It's Love; Pennies for Peppino; Carribean Magic; Song of the Lagoon; Rotana

Notes No cue sheet available.

1847 ✦ FM
Universal, 1978

Producer(s) Holston, Rand
Director(s) Alonzo, John A.
Screenwriter(s) Sacks, Ezra

Cast Brandon, Michael; Brennan, Eileen; Little, Cleavon; Yates, Cassie; Karras, Alex; Mull, Martin; Brandt, Janet

Song(s) FM (C/L: Becker, Walter; Fagen, Donald)

Notes Only original song listed. The songwriters are known as Steely Dan.

1848 ✦ FOLIES BERGERE
Twentieth Century–Fox, 1935

Composer(s) Stern, Jack
Lyricist(s) Meskill, Jack
Choreographer(s) Gould, Dave

Producer(s) Zanuck, Darryl F.
Director(s) Del Ruth, Roy
Screenwriter(s) Meredyth, Bess; Long, Hal
Source(s) *The Red Cat* (play) Adler, Hans; Lothar, Rudolph

Cast Chevalier, Maurice; Oberon, Merle; Sothern, Ann; Blore, Eric; Byron, Walter; Hare, Lumsden; Greig, Robert; Hobbes, Halliwell; Dare, Phillip

Song(s) I Was Lucky; Rhythm of the Rain; Singing a Happy Song; Au Revoir L'Amour; You Took the Words Right Out of My Mouth (C: Lane, Burton; L: Adamson, Harold); I Don't Stand a Ghost of a Chance with You [1] (C: Young, Victor; L: Crosby, Bing; Washington, Ned)

Notes No cue sheet available. Remade as THAT NIGHT IN RIO (1941) and again as ON THE RIVIERA (1952). [1] Also in A MILLIONAIRE FOR CHRISTY (20th).

1849 ✦ FOLLIES GIRL
PRC, 1943

Composer(s) Wise, Fred; Kaye, Buddy; Lippman, Sidney
Lyricist(s) Wise, Fred; Kaye, Buddy; Lippman, Sidney

Producer(s) Rowland, William
Director(s) Rowland, William
Screenwriter(s) Klauber, Marcy; Robinson, Charles

Cast Barrie, Wendy; Oliver, Gordon; Nulan, Doris; Long, Johnny; Byrne, Bobby; Heatherton, Ray; Holst, Ernie; Charles Weidman Dance Group; Lazaa and Castellanos; The Song Spinners; The Heat Waves; Thompson, Gil; Claire and Arena

Song(s) Keep the Flag A-Flying (C/L: Schaeffer, Mary); No Man in the House (C: Burke, Sonny; L: Kenny, Nick; Kenny, Charles); Someone to Love (C/L: Warren, Robert); I Told a Lie (C/L: Kenny, Nick; Gannon, Kim; Lane, Ken); Shall We Gather at the Rhythm (C: Burke, Sonny; L: Kenny, Nick; Murphy, John); Fascination; I Knew Your Father's Son; Thoity Poiple Boids

Notes No cue sheet available.

1850 ✦ FOLLOW ME
Cinerama Releasing, 1969

Musical Score Phillips, Stu
Composer(s) Phillips, Stu

Producer(s) McCabe, Gene
Director(s) McCabe, Gene
Screenwriter(s) Ross, Stanley Ralph

Cast Codgen, Claude; McGinnis, Mary Lou; Purvey, Bob; Hill, Bonnie

Song(s) Through Spray Colored Glasses (L: Gates, David); Just Lookin' for Someone (L: Gates, David); Surfers 3 (L: Margules, Mike; Freeman, Jim; MacGillvray); Hello Linda (L: Margules, Mike; Freeman, Jim; MacGillvray)

Notes No cue sheet available.

1851 ✦ FOLLOW ME BOYS!
Disney, 1967

Musical Score Bruns, George

Producer(s) Hibler, Winston
Director(s) Tokar, Norman
Screenwriter(s) Pelletier, Louis
Source(s) *God and My Country* (book) Kantor, MacKinlay

Cast MacMurray, Fred; Miles, Vera; Gish, Lillian; Ruggles, Charles; Reid, Elliott; Russell, Kurt; Patten, Luana; Murray, Ken

Song(s) Follow Me, Boys (C/L: Sherman, Richard M.; L: Sherman, Robert B.)

1852 ✦ FOLLOW THAT BIRD

See SESAME STREET PRESENTS FOLLOW THAT BIRD.

1853 ✦ FOLLOW THAT DREAM
United Artists, 1961

Musical Score Salter, Hans J.

Producer(s) Weisbart, David
Director(s) Douglas, Gordon M.
Screenwriter(s) Lederer, Charles
Source(s) *Pioneer Go Home* (novel) Powell, Richard

Cast Presley, Elvis; O'Connell, Arthur; Helm, Anne; Moore, Joanna; Ogles, Pam; Koon, Gavin; Koon, Robert; Kruschen, Jack; Oakland, Simon

Song(s) What a Wonderful Life (C: Livingston, Jerry; L: Wayne, Sid); Advice (C/L: Giant, Bill; Baum, Bernie; Kaye, Florence); Follow That Dream (C: Weisman, Bernie; L: Wise, Fred) (C/L: Tepper, Sid; Bennett, Roy C.); I'm not the Marrying Kind [1] (C: Edwards, Sherman; L: David, Mack)

Notes [1] Sheet music only.

1854 ✦ FOLLOW THE BAND
Universal, 1943

Composer(s) Rosen, Milton
Lyricist(s) Carter, Everett

Producer(s) Malvern, Paul
Director(s) Yarbrough, Jean
Screenwriter(s) Wilson, Warren; Bennett, Dorothy
Source(s) (story) English, Richard

Cast Langford, Frances; Quillan, Eddie; Hughes, Mary Beth; Rooney, Anne; The King's Men; The King Sisters

Song(s) Swingin' the Blues; Spellbound [1]

Notes There are also vocals of "Juanita;" "What Do You Want to Make Those Eyes At Me For?" by Joseph McCarthy, Howard Johnson and James Monaco; "Killarney" by M.W. Balfe; "Mush, Mush (Don't Tread on the Tail of Me Coat);" "My Melancholy Baby" by George Norton and Maybelle Watson; "Hilo Hattie" by Harold Adamson, Don McDiarmid and Johnny Noble; "My Devotion" by Roc Hillman and Johnny Napton; "Ain't Misbeahvin'" by Andy Razaf, Thomas "Fats" Waller and Harry Brooks; "Rosie the Riveter" by Redd Evans and John J. Loeb and "Army Air Corps Song" by Robert Crawford. [1] Also in GOOD MORNING, JUDGE.

1855 ✦ FOLLOW THE BOYS (1944)
Universal, 1944

Choreographer(s) Hale, George; Schoenfeld, Joe

Producer(s) Feldman, Charles K.
Director(s) Sutherland, Edward
Screenwriter(s) Breslow, Lou; Purcell, Gertrude

Cast Raft, George; Zorina, Vera; The Andrews Sisters; The Delta Rhythm Boys; Shore, Dinah; MacDonald, Jeanette; Fields, W.C.; Rubinstein, Arthur; Welles, Orson; Dietrich, Marlene; O'Connor, Donald; Ryan, Peggy; Tucker, Sophie; Amaya, Carmen; The Bricklayers; Ted Lewis and His Orchestra; Freddie Slack and His Orchestra; Charlie Spivak and His Orchestra; Louis Jordan and His Orchestra; Grapewin, Charley; McDonald, Grace; Butterworth, Charles; Macready, George; Patterson, Elizabeth; Toomey, Regis; Allbritton, Louise; Ankers, Evelyn; Beery Jr., Noah; Bey, Turhan; Beavers, Louise; Bruce, Nigel; Chaney Jr., Lon; Collier, Lois; Devine, Andy; Foster, Susanna; Gomez, Thomas; Hinds, Samuel S.; Jean, Gloria; Montez, Maria; Muse, Clarence; Paige, Robert; O'Driscoll, Martha; Rosenbloom, Maxie; Scott, Randolph; Sondergaard, Gale

Song(s) Tonight (C: Donaldson, Walter; L: Goell, Kermit); The Bigger the Army and Navy (C/L: Yellen, Jack; Dougherty, Dan; Shapiro, Ted); Kittens with their Mittens Laced (C/L: Pepper, Buddy; James, Inez); Mad About Him, Sad Without Him, How Can I Be Glad Without Him Blues [1] (C/L: Markes, Larry; Charles, Dick); Shoo Shoo Baby (C/L: Moore, Phil); A Better Day Is Comin' (C: Styne, Jule; L: Cahn, Sammy); I'll Walk Alone [2] (C: Styne, Jule; L: Cahn, Sammy); Is You Is or Is You Ain't [2] (C/L: Jordan, Louis; Austin, Billy); Where Did You Learn to Love? [2] (C: Styne, Jule; L: Cahn, Sammy)

Notes It is not known if all the above were written for this picture. There are also vocals of "Some of These Days" by Shelton Brooks; "Good Night" by Irving Bibo, Con Conrad and Leo Wood; "I'll See You in My Dreams" by Gus Kahn and Isham Jones with a special lyric by Irving Bibo; "The House I Live In" by Lewis Allan and Earl Robinson; "Beyond the Blue Horizon" by Leo Robin, Richard Whiting and Franke Harling and a medley consisting of "Bei Mir Bist Du Schoen" by Jacob Jacobs, Sholem Secunda, Sammy Cahn and Saul Chaplin; "Well, All Right" by Frances Faye, Don Raye and Dan

Howell; "Hold Tight" by Kent Brandow and Robinson Ware Spotswood; "Beer Barrel Polka" by Lew Brown and Jaromir Vejvoda; "Boogie Woogie Bugle Boy" by Don Raye and Hughie Prince; "I'll Be With You in Apple Blossom Time" by Neville Fleeson and Albert Von Tilzer; "Pennsylvania Polka" by Lester Lee and Zeke Manners; "Strip Polka" by Johnny Mercer and "Victory Polka" by Jule Styne and Sammy Cahn. Arthur Rubinstein plays Chopin's "Polonaise in A Flat Major." [1] Also in CHATTERBOX (Republic). [2] Sheet music only.

1856 ◆ FOLLOW THE BOYS (1965)
Metro–Goldwyn–Mayer, 1965

Musical Score Goodwin, Ron; Courage, Alexander
Composer(s) Murry, Ted
Lyricist(s) Davis, Benny

Producer(s) Bachmann, Lawrence P.
Director(s) Thorpe, Richard
Screenwriter(s) Chantler, David T.; Osborn, David

Cast Francis, Connie; Prentiss, Paula; Robin, Dany; Tamblyn, Russ; Long, Richard; Randell, Ron; Perry, Roger; Paige, Janis; Nichols, Robert

Song(s) Follow the Boys; Italian Lullaby (C/L: Francis, Connie); Waiting for Billy; Tonight's My Night; Intrigue [1]

Notes [1] Used instrumentally only

1857 ◆ FOLLOW THE FLEET
RKO, 1936

Composer(s) Berlin, Irving
Lyricist(s) Berlin, Irving
Choreographer(s) Pan, Hermes

Producer(s) Berman, Pandro S.
Director(s) Sandrich, Mark
Screenwriter(s) Taylor, Dwight; Scott, Allan
Source(s) *Shore Leave* (play) Osborne, Hubert

Cast Astaire, Fred; Rogers, Ginger; Scott, Randolph; Hilliard, Harriet; Allwyn, Astrid; Grable, Betty; Beresford, Harry; Hicks, Russell; Ball, Lucille

Song(s) We Saw the Sea; Let Yourself Go; I'd Rather Lead a Band; Let's Face the Music and Dance; But Where Are You?; I'm Putting All My Eggs in One Basket; Get Thee Behind Me Satan [1]

Notes [1] Not used in TOP HAT.

1858 ◆ FOLLOW THE LEADER (1930)
Paramount, 1930

Director(s) Taurog, Norman; Parker, Albert
Screenwriter(s) Purcell, Gertrude; Silvers, Sid

Source(s) *Manhattan Mary* (musical) Brown, Lew; Henderson, Ray; DeSylva, B.G.; White, George; Wells, William K.

Cast Wynn, Ed; Rogers, Ginger; Smith, Stanley; Holtz, Lou; Kane, Lida; Merman, Ethel; Foster, Preston; Watson, Bobby

Song(s) Broadway, the Heart of the World [1] (C: Henderson, Ray; L: DeSylva, B.G.; Brown, Lew); Satan's Holiday [4] (C: Fain, Sammy; L: Kahal, Irving); Brother, Just Laugh It Off [2] [3] (C: Schwartz, Arthur; Rainger, Ralph; L: Harburg, E.Y.); Laugh It Down [2] (C: Duke, Vernon; L: Harburg, E.Y.); Can't Get Along [2] (C: Green, Johnny; L: Harburg, E.Y.)

Notes "The Marseillaise" is also performed vocally. [1] From MANHATTAN MARY. [2] Instrumental use only. [3] Ralph Rainger is credited in some sources but not on cue sheet, but then neither was Henderson for his song. Some sources indicate this is a vocal. Also in QUEEN HIGH. See note under QUEEN HIGH. [4] Sheet music also credits Pierre Norman and Al Segal.

1859 ◆ FOLLOW THE LEADER (1944)
Monogram, 1944

Musical Score Kay, Edward J.

Producer(s) Katzman, Sam; Dietz, Jack
Director(s) Beaudine, William
Screenwriter(s) Crowley, William X.; Sachs, Beryl

Cast Gorcey, Leo; Hall, Huntz; Dell, Gabriel; Benedict, Billy; Marsh, Joan; LaRue, Jack; Austin, Gene; The Sherrill Sisters

Song(s) Now and Then (C/L: Austin, Gene); All I Wanna Do Is Play the Drum (C/L: Austin, Gene)

1860 ◆ FOLLOW THRU
Paramount, 1930

Composer(s) Henderson, Ray
Lyricist(s) DeSylva, B.G.; Brown, Lew
Choreographer(s) Bennett, David

Producer(s) Schwab, Laurence
Director(s) Schwab, Laurence; Corrigan, Lloyd
Screenwriter(s) Schwab, Laurence; Corrigan, Lloyd
Source(s) *Follow Thru* (musical) Henderson, Ray; DeSylva, B.G.; Brown, Lew; Schwab, Laurence

Cast Rogers, Charles "Buddy"; Carroll, Nancy; Haley, Jack [1]; O'Neal, Zelma [1]; Todd, Thelma; Pallette, Eugene; Dee, Frances; King, Claude; Givney, Kathryn; Lee, Margaret [1]; Tomkins, Don [1]

Song(s) Button Up Your Overcoat [1]; A Peach of a Pair (C: Whiting, Richard A.; L: Marion Jr., George); Then I'll Have Time for You [1]; I Want to Be Bad [1]; It Must Be You (C: Sherwin, Manning; L: Eliscu, Edward); Fire Music (inst.) (C: Duke, Vernon); It Never Happened Before [2] (C: Rodgers, Richard; L: Hart,

Lorenz); I'm Hard to Please (C: Rodgers, Richard; L: Hart, Lorenz); Softer Than a Kitten (That's My Feeling for You) [2] (C: Rodgers, Richard; L: Hart, Lorenz); Because We're Young [2] (C: Rodgers, Richard; L: Hart, Lorenz); You Wouldn't Fool Me Would You [1] [3]

Notes [1] From Broadway production. [2] Not used. [3] Listed in the *Blue Book of Hollywood Musicals* but not in cue sheets.

1861 ✦ FOLLOW YOUR HEART
Republic, 1936

Composer(s) Schertzinger, Victor
Lyricist(s) Bullock, Walter

Producer(s) Fields, Leonard
Director(s) Scotto, Aubrey
Screenwriter(s) Cooper, Olive; Ornitz, Samuel; West, Nathanael; Cole, Lester

Cast Talley, Marion; Bartlett, Michael; Bruce, Nigel; Alberni, Luis; Crosman, Henrietta; Osborne, Vivienne; Catlett, Walter; Blue, Ben; The Hall Johnson Choir

Song(s) Follow Your Heart (L: Mitchell, Sidney D.); Magnolias in the Moonlight [1]; Who Minds 'Bout Me

Notes There are also vocals of "La Miserie" from Verdi's IL TROVATORE; "King's Hunt;" "Oh! Marie" by E. Di Capua; "Cavatine du Page" from Meyerbeer's LES HUGUENOTS; "Sextette" from Donizetti's LUCIA DI LAMMERMOOR; "John Henry;" "It's All Over Me;" and "Work in the Morning." [1] Also in RAGS TO RICHES.

1862 ✦ FOOL FOR LOVE
Cannon, 1985

Musical Score Burt, George
Composer(s) Rogers, Sandy
Lyricist(s) Rogers, Sandy

Producer(s) Golan, Menahem; Globus, Yoram
Director(s) Altman, Robert
Screenwriter(s) Shepard, Sam
Source(s) *Fool for Love* (play) Shepard, Sam

Cast Shepard, Sam; Basinger, Kim; Stanton, Harry Dean; Quaid, Randy; Crawford, Martha

Song(s) Let's Ride; It Comes and Goes; Go Rosa; You Lied Your Way; First and Last Real Cowboy; Call Me Up; Love Shy; Why Wyoming

Notes No cue sheet available.

1863 ✦ FOOLIN' AROUND
Columbia, 1980

Musical Score Bernstein, Charles

Producer(s) Kopelson, Arnold
Director(s) Heffron, Richard T.
Screenwriter(s) Kane, Michael; Swift, David

Cast Busey, Gary; O'Toole, Annette; Calvin, John; Albert, Eddie; Leachman, Cloris; Randall, Tony; Macy, W.H.

Song(s) Foolin' Around (C: Bernstein, Charles; L: Seals, Jim); These Moments Never Live Again (C: Bernstein, Charles; L: Seals, Jim)

Notes No cue sheet available.

1864 ✦ FOOLISH WIVES
Universal, 1922

Musical Score Romberg, Sigmund

Director(s) Von Stroheim, Erich
Screenwriter(s) Von Stroheim, Erich

Cast Von Stroheim, Erich; Christiana, Rudolph; George, Maude; Busch, Mae; Dupont, Miss

Song(s) Foolish Wives (C/L: Stern, Jack; Marks, Clarence; Haymond, Norah)

Notes A silent film with orchestral score by Romberg.

1865 ✦ FOOLS FOR SCANDAL
Warner Brothers, 1938

Musical Score Deutsch, Adolph
Composer(s) Rodgers, Richard
Lyricist(s) Hart, Lorenz
Choreographer(s) Connolly, Bobby

Producer(s) LeRoy, Mervyn
Director(s) LeRoy, Mervyn
Screenwriter(s) Fields, Joseph; Fields, Herbert
Source(s) *Food for Scandal* (play) Hamilton, Nancy; Casey, Rosemary; Shute, James

Cast Lombard, Carole; Gravet, Fernand; Bellamy, Ralph; Jenkins, Allen; Jeans, Isabel; Wilson, Marie; Ralston, Marcia; Les Hite and His Orchestra

Song(s) There's a Boy in Harlem [3]; How Can You Forget; Food for Scandal; Once I Was Young [1]; Love Knows Best [1]; Wedding March [1]; Just a Simple Melody [1] (C: Chaplin, Saul; L: Cahn, Sammy); Let's Sing a Song About Nothing [2]

Notes This might have originally been titled SCRIPT GIRL. [1] Used for background instrumentals only. [2] Not used. [3] Also in THIS WAS PARIS.

1866 ✦ FOOTBALL COACH

See COLLEGE COACH.

1867 ✦ FOOTLIGHT PARADE
Warner Brothers, 1933

Composer(s) Fain, Sammy
Lyricist(s) Kahal, Irving
Choreographer(s) Berkeley, Busby

Producer(s) Lord, Robert
Director(s) Bacon, Lloyd; Keighley, William
Screenwriter(s) Seff, Manuel; Seymour, James

Cast Cagney, James; Kibbee, Guy; Hohl, Arthur; Blondell, Joan; Powell, Dick; Keeler, Ruby; Donnelly, Ruth; Dodd, Claire; Herbert, Hugh; McHugh, Frank

Song(s) Ah The Moon Is Here; Sittin' on a Backyard Fence; By a Waterfall; Honeymoon Hotel (C: Warren, Harry; L: Dubin, Al); Shanghai Lil (C: Warren, Harry; L: Dubin, Al)

Notes There is a note in the Warner's files that refers to the song "One Step Ahead of My Shadow" but I can't find any other reference to it.

1868 ✦ FOOTLIGHT RHYTHM
Paramount, 1948

Composer(s) Livingston, Jay; Evans, Ray
Lyricist(s) Livingston, Jay; Evans, Ray

Director(s) Daniels, Billy

Cast Rawlinson, Sally; Ruiz, Al; Field, Margaret

Song(s) Mississippi Siren; What's Under Your Mask, Madame?; Bamboula

Notes Short subject. "Whispers in the Dark" by Frederick Hollander and Leo Robin is also given a vocal treatment. Betty Russell, Annette Warren and Bill Roberts may have dubbed the cast. The cast names do not appear on recording calls but the others do.

1869 ✦ FOOTLIGHTS AND FOOLS
Warner Brothers, 1929

Composer(s) Meyer, George W.
Lyricist(s) Bryan, Alfred

Director(s) Seiter, William A.
Screenwriter(s) Brush, Katherine; Geraghty, Tom J.; Wilson, Carey

Cast Moore, Colleen; Hackett, Raymond; March, Fredric; Corbin, Virginia Lee; Martindel, Edward; Bennett, Mickey

Song(s) If I Can't Have You; You Can't Believe My Eyes; Ophelia Will Fool You; Pilly Pom Pom Plee

Notes No cue sheet available. The *Variety* review says there were five vocal numbers. The AFI catalog lists only "If I Can't Have You" and "You Can't Believe My Eyes" and credits them to Ray Perkins, Norman Spencer and Herman Ruby.

1870 ✦ FOOTLIGHT SERENADE
Twentieth Century–Fox, 1942

Composer(s) Rainger, Ralph
Lyricist(s) Robin, Leo
Choreographer(s) Pan, Hermes

Producer(s) LeBaron, William
Director(s) Ratoff, Gregory
Screenwriter(s) Ellis, Robert; Logan, Helen; Starling, Lynn

Cast Payne, John; Grable, Betty; Mature, Victor; Wyman, Jane; Gleason, James; Silvers, Phil; Wright Jr., Cobina; Lang, June; Moreland, Mantan; Bacon, Irving

Song(s) Except with You; Are You Kiddin'?; I'm Still Crazy For You; I'll Be Marching to a Love Song [2]; I Heard the Birdies Sing; Land on Your Feet [1]; Living High (On a Western Hill) [1]

Notes [1] Instrumental use only. [2] This number was abridged, and cut-footage appears in a Fox short.

1871 ✦ FOOTLIGHT VARIETIES
RKO, 1951

Producer(s) Bilson, George
Director(s) Yates, Hal
Screenwriter(s) Yates, Hal; Adler, Felix

Cast Errol, Leon; The Sportsmen; Liberace; Jerry Murad's Harmonicats; Frankie Carle and His Orchestra; Buttons, Red; Inesita; West, Buster; Paar, Jack

Song(s) The Show Must Go On (C: Jenkins, Gordon; L: Adair, Tom)

Notes Frankie Carle plays "La Paloma" by Sebastian Yradier. There is a dance to "I Get the Neck of the Chicken." Inesita does a Spanish dance. Liberace plays Liszt's "Hungarian Rhapsody." Jerry Murad's Harmonicats play "Fantasy Impromptu" and Kabelevsky's "The Galloping Comedians." There is a dance to "Love Rhumba" and, finally, Buster West and Melissa Mason dance to "Dixieland Time."

1872 ✦ FOOTLOOSE
Paramount, 1984

Lyricist(s) Pitchford, Dean

Producer(s) Rachmil, Lewis J.; Zaden, Craig
Director(s) Ross, Herbert
Screenwriter(s) Pitchford, Dean

Cast Bacon, Kevin; Lithgow, John; Singer, Lori; Penn, Christopher; Wiest, Dianne; Youngs, Jim

Song(s) Footloose (C: Loggins, Kenny; L: Loggins, Kenny; Pitchford, Dean); The Girl Gets Around (C: Hagar, Sammy); Dancing in the Streets (C: Wolfer, Bill); Somebody's Eyes (C: Snow, Tom); Holding Out for a Hero (C: Steinman, Jim); Never (C: Gore, Michael); Let's Hear It for the Boy (C: Snow, Tom); Almost Paradise (C: Carmen, Eric); I'm Free (Heaven Helps the Man) (C: Loggins, Kenny)

Notes Only original songs listed.

1873 ✦ FOOTSTEPS IN THE DARK
Warner Brothers, 1941

Musical Score Hollander, Frederick

Producer(s) Lord, Robert
Director(s) Bacon, Lloyd
Screenwriter(s) Cole, Lester; Wexley, John
Source(s) *Blondie White* (play) Fodor, Ladislas

Cast Flynn, Errol; Marshall, Brenda; Hale, Alan; Bellamy, Ralph; Patrick, Lee; Jenkins, Allen; Watson, Lucile; Frawley, William; Karns, Roscoe; Mitchell, Grant; LaRue, Jack; Bey, Turhan

Song(s) Love Me (C: Jerome, M.K.; L: Scholl, Jack); Kiss Waltz [1] (C: Burke, Joe; L: Dubin, Al)

Notes [1] Also in COLLEGE LOVERS and DANCING SWEETIES.

1874 ✦ FORBIDDEN (1931)
Columbia, 1931

Composer(s) Bibo, Irving
Lyricist(s) Bibo, Irving

Director(s) Capra, Frank
Screenwriter(s) Swerling, Jo

Cast Stanwyck, Barbara; Menjou, Adolphe; Bellamy, Ralph; Peterson, Dorothy; Fresholtz, Myrna; Hobbes, Halliwell

Song(s) It's a Nice Day Today; Cupid's Holiday (C/L: Fyling)

Notes "My Curly Headed Baby" by Clutsam is interpolated.

1875 ✦ FORBIDDEN (1953)
Universal, 1953

Musical Score Skinner, Frank

Producer(s) Richmond, Ted
Director(s) Mate, Rudolph
Screenwriter(s) Sackheim, William; Doud, Gil

Cast Curtis, Tony; Dru, Joanne; Bettger, Lyle; Miller, Marvin; Sen Yung, Victor; Miller, Marvin

Song(s) You Belong to Me (C/L: King, Pee Wee; Stewart, Redd; Price, Chilton)

1876 ✦ FORBIDDEN VALLEY
Universal, 1938

Producer(s) MacRae, Henry
Director(s) Gittens, Wyndham
Screenwriter(s) Gittens, Wyndham
Source(s) *Mountains Are My Kingdom* (novel) Hardy, Stuart

Cast Beery Jr., Noah; Robinson, Frances; Kohler, Fred; Price, Alonzo; Hinds, Samuel S.; Andrews, Stanley; Charters, Spencer

Song(s) Get Along Little Pony (C/L: Kellogg, Kay)

1877 ✦ FORBIDDEN ZONE
Sutton Marketing, 1980

Musical Score Elfman, Danny

Producer(s) Elfman, Richard
Director(s) Elfman, Richard
Screenwriter(s) Elfman, Richard; Martinson, Nick L.; Bright, Matthew; James, Nick
Source(s) *The Hercules Family* (film) Elfman, Richard

Cast Villechaize, Herve; Tyrrell, Susan; Elfman, Marie-Pascale; Rose, Virginia

Song(s) Forbidden Zone (C/L: Elfman, Danny); Witch's Egg (C/L: Mishalski, George; Tyrrell, Susan)

Notes No cue sheet available.

1878 ✦ A FOREIGN AFFAIR
Paramount, 1948

Musical Score Hollander, Frederick
Composer(s) Hollander, Frederick
Lyricist(s) Hollander, Frederick

Producer(s) Brackett, Charles
Director(s) Wilder, Billy
Screenwriter(s) Brackett, Charles; Wilder, Billy; Breen, Richard L.

Cast Arthur, Jean; Lund, John; Dietrich, Marlene; Mitchell, Millard; Prager, Stanley

Song(s) Illusions; The Ruins of Berlin; Black Market

Notes First titled OPERATION CANDYBAR. "Daisy Bell" (with changed lyrics) and "Shine on Harvest Moon" (whistled only); the Soviet Army song "Meadowlands" by Lev Knipper and Victor Gussev (also appeared in the 1957 film JET PILOT [RKO]; and "Iowa Corn Song" by Edward Riley, George Botsford, Ray W. Lockard and George Hamilton are also sung.

1879 ✦ THE FOREST RANGERS
Paramount, 1942

Musical Score Young, Victor

Producer(s) Sisk, Robert
Director(s) Marshall, George
Screenwriter(s) Shumate, Harold

Cast Goddard, Paulette; Hayward, Susan; MacMurray, Fred; Dekker, Albert; Overman, Lynne; Pallette, Eugene; Toomey, Regis

Song(s) Tall Grows the Timber (C: Hollander, Frederick; L: Loesser, Frank); Jingle Jangle Jingle [1] (C: Lilley, Joseph J.; L: Loesser, Frank)

Notes [1] Also used in AND THE ANGELS SING and JINGLE JANGLE JINGLE.

1880 ✦ FOREVER, DARLING
Metro–Goldwyn–Mayer, 1956

Musical Score Kaper, Bronislau

Producer(s) Arnaz, Desi
Director(s) Hall, Alexander
Screenwriter(s) Deutsch, Helen

Cast Ball, Lucille; Arnaz, Desi; Mason, James; Calhern, Louis; Emery, John; Schafer, Natalie; Hoyt, John; Albertson, Mabel

Song(s) Forever, Darling (C: Kaper, Bronislau; L: Cahn, Sammy)

1881 ✦ FOREVER FEMALE
Paramount, 1953

Musical Score Young, Victor

Producer(s) Duggan, Pat
Director(s) Rapper, Irving
Screenwriter(s) Epstein, Julius J.; Epstein, Philip G.
Source(s) *Rosalind* (play) Barrie, James M.

Cast Rogers, Ginger; Holden, William; Douglas, Paul; Gleason, James; White, Jesse; Rambeau, Marjorie; Reeves, George; Donovan, King; Crowley, Pat

Song(s) Say What You Will [1] (C: Young, Victor; L: Heyman, Edward); Change of Heart [1] (C: Young, Victor; L: Heyman, Edward)

Notes [1] These songs are used only as part of the instrumental background.

1882 ✦ FOREVER MY LOVE
Paramount, 1961

Producer(s) Marischka, Ernst
Director(s) Marischka, Ernst
Screenwriter(s) Marischka, Ernst

Cast Schneider, Romy; Boehm, Karl

Song(s) Forever My Love (C: Bacharach, Burt; L: David, Hal)

1883 ✦ FOREVER YOUNG, FOREVER FREE
Universal, 1977

Musical Score Holdridge, Lee

Producer(s) Pieterse, Andre
Director(s) Lazarus, Ashley
Screenwriter(s) Lazarus, Ashley

Cast Ferrer, Jose; Valentine, Karen; Finney, Bess

Song(s) Forever Young (C: Holdridge, Lee; L: McKuen, Rod)

Notes No cue sheet available.

1884 ✦ FORGED PASSPORT
Republic, 1939

Producer(s) Auer, John H.
Director(s) Auer, John H.
Screenwriter(s) Coen, Franklin; Loeb, Lee

Cast Kelly, Paul; Lang, June; Talbot, Lyle; Gilbert, Billy; Nazarro, Lyle; Murphy, Maurice; Robinson, Dewey; Puglia, Frank

Song(s) Uno Dos Tres (C: Feuer, Cy; L: Cherkose, Eddie); So Far, So Good, So What (C/L: Sackheim, Bill; Cherkose, Eddie)

1885 ✦ FORGOTTEN FACES
Paramount, 1936

Producer(s) Botsford, A.M.
Director(s) Dupont, E.A.
Screenwriter(s) Roberts, Marguerite; Yost, Robert; Marlow, Brian
Source(s) "A Whiff of Heliotrope" (story) Child, Richard Washburn

Cast Cummings, Robert; Rhodes, Betty Jane; Kisco, Charley; Michael, Gertrude; Marshall, Herbert

Song(s) Walking the Floor [1] (C: Rainger, Ralph; L: Robin, Leo)

Notes [1] Written for FOUR HOURS TO KILL but not used.

1886 ✦ FOR KEEPS
Tri-Star, 1988

Musical Score Conti, Bill

Producer(s) Belson, Jerry; Coblenz, Walter
Director(s) Avildsen, John G.
Screenwriter(s) Kazurinsky, Tim; DeClue, Denise

Cast Ringwald, Molly; Batinkoff, Randall; Mars, Kenneth; Flynn, Miriam; Brown, Sharon; Ong, Jack

Song(s) Pow! You Got Me Where I Live (C/L: Dozier, Lamont)

Notes No cue sheet available.

1887 ✦ FOR LOVE OF IVY
Cinerama Releasing, 1968

Musical Score Jones, Quincy
Composer(s) Jones, Quincy

Producer(s)   Scherick, Edgar J.; Weston, Jay
Director(s)   Mann, Daniel
Screenwriter(s)   Aurthur, Robert Alan

Cast   Poitier, Sidney; Lincoln, Abbey; Bridges, Beau; Martin, Nan; Bibb, Leon; Peters, Lauri; O'Connor, Carroll; Hurd, Hugh

Song(s)   For Love of Ivy (L: Russell, Bob); You Put It on Me (L: Angelou, Maya); My Side of the Sky (L: Cashman, Pistill & West)

Notes   No cue sheet available.

1888 ✦ FOR ME AND MY GAL
Metro–Goldwyn–Mayer, 1942

Choreographer(s)   Connolly, Bobby

Producer(s)   Freed, Arthur
Director(s)   Berkeley, Busby
Screenwriter(s)   Sherman, Richard; Finklehoffe, Fred F.; Silvers, Sid

Cast   Garland, Judy; Murphy, George; Kelly, Gene; Blue, Ben; Eggerth, Marta; McNally, Horace [1]; Quine, Richard; Wynn, Keenan; Norman, Lucille

Song(s)   The Doll Shop (C/L: Edens, Roger); Don't Leave Me Daddy (C/L: Verges); When Johnny Comes Marching Home (C/L: Lambert, Louis; Edens, Roger); I Never Knew [2] (C/L: Edens, Roger); Three Cheers for the Yanks [2] (C/L: Martin, Hugh; Blane, Ralph)

Notes   Gene Kelly's debut. There are also vocals of "Oh You Beautiful Doll" by Nat D. Ayer and A. Seymour Brown; "For Me and My Gal" by George W. Meyer, Edgar Leslie and E. Ray Goetz; "When You Wore a Tulip" by Percy Wenrich and Jack Mahoney; "They Go Wild, Simply Wild Over Me" by Fred Fisher and Joseph McCarthy; "Do I Love You?" by Henri Christine and E. Ray Goetz; "After You've Gone" by Henry Creamer and Turner Layton; "Tell Me" by Max Kortlander and Will Callahan; "Till We Meet Again" by Richard A. Whiting and Raymond B. Egan; "We Don't Want the Bacon, What We Want Is a Piece of the Rhine" by Howard Carr, Harry Russell and Jimmie Havens; "Ballin' the Jack" by Chris Smith and James Henry Burris; "What Are You Going to Do to Help the Boys" by Egbert Van Alstyne and Gus Kahn; "How 'Ya Gonna Keep 'Em Down on the Farm" by Walter Donaldson, Sam M. Lewis and Joe Young; "There's a Long Long Trail" by Zo Elliott and Stoddard King; "Where Do We Go From Here" by Howard Johnson and Percy Wenrich and a medley of other popular World War I-era songs. [1] He later changed his name to Stephen McNally. [2] Deleted from final print.

1889 ✦ FOR PETE'S SAKE
Columbia, 1974

Producer(s)   Erlichman, Martin; Shapiro, Stanley
Director(s)   Yates, Peter
Screenwriter(s)   Shapiro, Stanley; Richlin, Maurice

Cast   Streisand, Barbra; Sarrazin, Michael; Parsons, Estelle; Redfield, William; Picon, Molly; Zorich, Louis; Ward, Richard; Bonnell, Vivian; Broun, Heywood Hale

Song(s)   Don't Let Him Down (C: Butler, Artie; L: Lindsay, Mark)

Notes   Originally titled JULY PORKBELLIES.

1890 ✦ FORT ALGIERS
United Artists, 1953

Musical Score   Michelet, Michel

Producer(s)   Ermolieff, Joseph E.
Director(s)   Selander, Lesley
Screenwriter(s)   St. John, Theodore

Cast   De Carlo, Yvonne; Thompson, Carlos; Burr, Raymond; Erickson, Leif; Caruso, Anthony; Dehner, John

Song(s)   I'll Follow You [1] (C: Michelet, Michel; L: Fragey, Margot; De Carlo, Yvonne)

Notes   [1] English lyric by De Carlo.

1891 ✦ FORT APACHE, THE BRONX
Twentieth Century–Fox, 1981

Musical Score   Tunick, Jonathan

Producer(s)   Richards, Martin; Fiorello, Tom
Director(s)   Petrie, Daniel
Screenwriter(s)   Gould, Heywood

Cast   Newman, Paul; Asner, Edward; Wahl, Ken; Aiello, Danny; Ticotin, Rachel; Grier, Pam

Song(s)   Family Tradition (C/L: Williams Jr., Hank); The Blue Side (C/L: Lasley, David; Willis, Allee); It's Time to Party Now (C/L: Parker Jr., Ray); Guajira (C/L: Brown, D.; Reyez, R.; Reyez, C.); Steppin' Out (C/L: Starr, Billy); Bad Girls (C/L: Summer, Donna; Sudano, Bruce); Last Dance (C/L: Jabara, Paul)

Notes   It is not known which, if any, of these were written for the production.

1892 ✦ FOR THE FIRST TIME
Metro–Goldwyn–Mayer, 1960

Musical Score   Stoll, George

Producer(s)   Gruter, Alexander
Director(s)   Mate, Rudolph
Screenwriter(s)   Solt, Andrew

Cast   Lanza, Mario; Von Koczian, Johanna; Kasznar, Kurt; Sonker, Hans; Rosar, Annie; Giglio, Sandro; Rilla, Walter; Gabor, Zsa Zsa

Song(s)   Come Prima (For the First Time) [1] (C: De Paola Panzeri, Taccani; L: Ram, Buck); Capri, Capri (C/L: Stoll, George); Wer Einmal Nur in Munchen War

(Bavarian Beer Song) (C/L: Bette, Karl); Pineapple Picker (C/L: Stoll, George)

Notes Lanza's last film appearance. There are also vocals of "La Donna e Mobile" and "Bella Figlia Del'Amore" from Verdi's RIGOLETTO; "O Sole Mio" by E. diCapua; "Vesti la Giubba" from Leoncavallo's PAGLIACCI; Mozart's "The Laughing Song Trio" from COSI FAN TUTTI; "Ich Liebe Dich" by Grieg; "The Death Scene" from Verdi's OTELLO; "Ave Maria" by Franz Schubert; "Je N'en Connais Pas La Fin" by Monnot and Asso and "Ritorna Vincitor" from Verdi's AIDA. [1] English lyrics by Ram.

1893 ✦ FOR THE LOVE OF BENJI
Mulberry Square, 1977

Musical Score Box, Euel

Producer(s) Vaughn, Ben
Director(s) Camp, Joe
Screenwriter(s) Camp, Joe

Cast Vasil, Art; Fiuzat, Allen; Garrett, Patsy; Smith, Cynthia

Song(s) Sunshine Smiles (C: Box, Euel; L: Box, Betty; Camp, Joe)

Notes No cue sheet available.

1894 ✦ FOR THE LOVE OF MIKE
Twentieth Century–Fox, 1960

Musical Score Lavista, Raul

Producer(s) Sherman, George
Director(s) Sherman, George
Screenwriter(s) Beauchamp, D.D.

Cast Basehart, Richard; Erwin, Stuart; Shields, Arthur; Silvestre, Armando; Allen, Rex; Cardenas, Elsa

Song(s) Charro Bravo (C/L: Allen, Rex)

Notes No cue sheet available.

1895 ✦ FOR THOSE WHO THINK YOUNG
United Artists, 1964

Musical Score Fielding, Jerry
Composer(s) O'Hanlon, James; O'Hanlon, George
Lyricist(s) O'Hanlon, James; O'Hanlon, George

Producer(s) Benson, Hugh
Director(s) Martinson, Leslie H.
Screenwriter(s) O'Hanlon, George; O'Hanlon, James; Beaumont, Dan

Cast Darren, James; Tiffin, Pamela; Woodbury, Woody; Lynde, Paul; Louise, Tina; Sinatra, Nancy; Denver, Bob

Song(s) For Those Who Think Young (C: Livingston, Jerry; L: David, Mack); Back to the Farm; Woody Weedin' Time; Ho-Daddy (C: Fielding, Jerry); I'm Gonna Walk All Over This Land (C: Fielding, Jerry; L: Griffin, Jimmy)

1896 ✦ FORTUNE AND MEN'S EYES
Metro–Goldwyn–Mayer, 1971

Musical Score MacDermot, Galt
Composer(s) MacDermot, Galt

Producer(s) Persky, Lester; Allen, Lewis M.
Director(s) Hart, Harvey
Screenwriter(s) Herbert, John
Source(s) *Fortune and Men's Eyes* (play) Herbert, John

Cast Burton, Wendell; Greer, Michael [1]; Hall, Zooey; Freedman, Danny; Perkins, Larry; Barron, James

Song(s) Fortune and Men's Eyes (L: Shakespeare, William); When Rain Touches Summer (L: Dumaresq, William); It's Free (C/L: Greer, Michael)

Notes [1] From Off-Broadway cast.

1897 ✦ THE FORTUNE COOKIE
United Artists, 1966

Musical Score Previn, Andre

Producer(s) Wilder, Billy
Director(s) Wilder, Billy
Screenwriter(s) Wilder, Billy; Diamond, I.A.L.

Cast Lemmon, Jack; Matthau, Walter; Rich, Ron; Osmond, Cliff; West, Judi; Holcombe, Harry

Song(s) Lindenbaum's Linoleum (C: Previn, Andre; L: Diamond, I.A.L.); The Fortune Cookie [1] (C: Previn, Andre; L: Previn, Dory)

Notes Released internationally as MEET WHIPLASH WILLIE. There is also a vocal of Cole Porter's "You'd Be So Nice to Come Home To." [1] Lyric written for exploitation only.

1898 ✦ 48 HOURS
Paramount, 1982

Producer(s) Gordon, Lawrence
Director(s) Hill, Walter
Screenwriter(s) Hill, Walter; Spottiswoode, Roger; Gross, Larry; de Souza, Steven E.

Cast Nolte, Nick; Murphy, Eddie; O'Toole, Annette; Kelly, David Patrick; Remar, James; Landham, Sonny

Song(s) (The Boys Are) Back in Town (C/L: O'Neal, Brian); New Shoes (C/L: O'Neal, Brian)

1899 ✦ FORTY GUNS
Twentieth Century–Fox, 1957

Musical Score Sukman, Harry
Lyricist(s) Adamson, Harold

Producer(s) Fuller, Samuel
Director(s) Fuller, Samuel
Screenwriter(s) Fuller, Samuel

Cast Stanwyck, Barbara; Sullivan, Barry; Jagger, Dean; Ericson, John; Barry, Gene; Brent, Eve

Song(s) High Ridin' Woman (C: Sukman, Harry); God Has His Arms Around Me (C: Young, Victor)

Notes Originally titled WOMAN WITH A WHIP.

1900 ✦ FORTY LITTLE MOTHERS
Metro–Goldwyn–Mayer, 1940

Producer(s) Rapf, Harry
Director(s) Berkeley, Busby
Screenwriter(s) Yost, Dorothy; Pagano, Ernest

Cast Cantor, Eddie; Anderson, Judith; Morgan, Ralph; Johnson, Rita; Lewis, Diana; Granville, Bonita; Westman, Nydia

Song(s) Banquet Scene (C/L: Edens, Roger); Little Curly Hair in a High Chair (C: Simon, Nat; L: Tobias, Charles)

Notes There is also a vocal of "You Were Meant for Me" by Arthur Freed and Nacio Herb Brown.

1901 ✦ FORTY NAUGHTY GIRLS
RKO, 1937

Composer(s) Dreyer, Dave
Lyricist(s) Ruby, Herman

Producer(s) Sistrom, William
Director(s) Cline, Edward F.
Screenwriter(s) Grey, John

Cast Gleason, James; Pitts, ZaSu; Lord, Marjorie; Shelley, George; Woodbury, Joan; Thomas, Frank M.; Kennedy, Tom

Song(s) Forty Naughty Girls; What a Day; Widow in Lace (C: Spina, Harold; L: Bullock, Walter)

Notes There is also a vocal of "Hooray for Love" by Jimmy McHugh and Dorothy Fields (also in HOORAY FOR LOVE).

1902 ✦ 40 POUNDS OF TROUBLE
Universal, 1962

Musical Score Lindsey, Mort
Composer(s) Lindsey, Mort
Lyricist(s) Shaw, Sydney

Producer(s) Margulies, Stan
Director(s) Jewison, Norman
Screenwriter(s) Hargrove, Marion

Cast Curtis, Tony; Pleshette, Suzanne; Wilcox, Claire; Silvers, Phil; Kaye, Stubby; Storch, Larry; Morris, Howard; McCarthy, Kevin

Song(s) What's the Scene; If You

1903 ✦ 42ND STREET
Warner Brothers, 1933

Composer(s) Warren, Harry
Lyricist(s) Dubin, Al
Choreographer(s) Berkeley, Busby

Producer(s) Wallis, Hal B.
Director(s) Bacon, Lloyd
Screenwriter(s) James, Rian; Seymour, James
Source(s) *42nd Street* (novel) Ropes, Bradford

Cast Baxter, Warner; Daniels, Bebe; Brent, George; Merkel, Una; Keeler, Ruby; Kibbee, Guy; Sparks, Ned; Powell, Dick; Rogers, Ginger; Jenkins, Allen; Walthall, Henry B.; Nugent, Edward J.; Akst, Harry; Nordstrom, Clarence; Stone, George E.

Song(s) It Must Be June; You're Getting to Be a Habit with Me; Forty Second Street; Shuffle Off to Buffalo; Young and Healthy; Pretty Lady [1]; Love Theme (Inst.) [1] [2]

Notes [1] Used for background instrumentals only. [2] Recorded by Peter Mintun for his record DEEP PURPLE (Cue Records #103).

1904 ✦ FORWARD MARCH

See DOUGHBOYS.

1905 ✦ THE FORWARD PASS
Warner Brothers–First National, 1929

Composer(s) Cleary, Michael
Lyricist(s) Magidson, Herb; Washington, Ned

Director(s) Cline, Edward F. [1]
Screenwriter(s) Rogers, Howard Emmett

Cast Fairbanks Jr., Douglas; Young, Loretta; Rome, Bert; Chandler, Lane; Williams, Guinn "Big Boy"; Lane, Allan; Byron, Marion

Song(s) One Minute of Heaven [2]; I Gotta Have You; H'Lo Baby; Huddlin'; Give It!; I Love to Hit Myself on the Head with a Hammer; Nobody but You; Football Song [3]

Notes No cue sheet available. [1] Billed as Eddie Cline. [2] Also in COLLEGE LOVERS. [3] Not used.

1906 ✦ FOR WHOM THE BELL TOLLS
Paramount, 1943

Musical Score Young, Victor

Producer(s) Wood, Sam
Director(s) Wood, Sam
Screenwriter(s) Nichols, Dudley
Source(s) *For Whom the Bell Tolls* (novel) Hemingway, Ernest

Cast Cooper, Gary; Bergman, Ingrid; Tamiroff, Akim; de Cordova, Arturo; Sokoloff, Vladimir

Song(s) A Love Like This [1] (C: Young, Victor; L: Washington, Ned); For Whom the Bell Tolls [2] (C: Kent, Walter; L: Drake, Milton)

Notes [1] Lyric added for exploitation only. [2] Song used for exploitation only.

1907 ◆ FOR WHOM THE BULLS TOIL
Disney, 1952

Musical Score Dubin, Joseph S.

Director(s) Kinney, Jack
Screenwriter(s) Mack, Brick; Kinney, Dick

Song(s) El Torero Chapucero [1] (C: Dubin, Joseph S.; L: Santos, Edmundo)

Notes Animated short. [1] Used instrumentally only.

1908 ◆ FOR YOUR EYES ONLY
United Artists, 1981

Musical Score Conti, Bill

Producer(s) Broccoli, Albert R.
Director(s) Glen, John
Screenwriter(s) Maibaum, Richard; Wilson, Michael G.
Source(s) *For Your Eyes Only* (novel) Fleming, Ian

Cast Moore, Roger; Bouquet, Carole; Glover, Julian; Topol; Harris, Cassandra; Johnson, Lynn-Holly; Llewelyn, Desmond; Maxwell, Lois

Song(s) For Your Eyes Only (C: Conti, Bill; L: Leeson, Mike); Unknown (C: Conti, Bill; L: Conti, Shelby; West, Chris)

1909 ◆ FOUL PLAY
Paramount, 1978

Producer(s) Miller, Thomas L.; Milkis, Edward K.
Director(s) Higgins, Colin
Screenwriter(s) Higgins, Colin

Cast Chase, Chevy; Hawn, Goldie; Meredith, Burgess; Roberts, Rachel; Moore, Dudley; Lawrence, Marc

Song(s) Ready to Take a Chance Again (C: Fox, Charles; L: Gimbel, Norman)

1910 ◆ FOUR DAYS IN NOVEMBER
United Artists, 1964

Musical Score Bernstein, Elmer

Producer(s) Stuart, Mel
Director(s) Stuart, Mel
Screenwriter(s) Strauss, Theodore

Song(s) In the Summer of His Years (C: Lee, David; L: Kretzmer, Herbert)

Notes A documentary about the assasination of President Kennedy.

1911 ◆ FOUR DEVILS
Fox, 1929

Musical Score Rothafel, S.L. [1]

Director(s) Murnau, F.W.; Van Buren, A.H.
Screenwriter(s) Mayer, Carl; Booth, John Hunter
Source(s) *De Fire Djaevle* (novel) Bang, Herman Joachim

Cast MacDonald, J. Farrell; Randolf, Anders; McDowell, Claire; Parker, Jack; O'Day, Dawn; Gaynor, Janet; Morton, Charles; Drexel, Nancy

Song(s) Marion (C: Rapee, Erno; L: Pollack, Lew); Destiny (C: Rapee, Erno; L: Pollack, Lew)

Notes No cue sheet available. [1] S.L. Rothafel is best known as the originator of the motion picture palace. His best known triumph was the theater named after him—the Roxy in New York City.

1912 ◆ FOUR FOR TEXAS
Warner Brothers, 1964

Musical Score Riddle, Nelson

Producer(s) Aldrich, Robert
Director(s) Aldrich, Robert
Screenwriter(s) Sherman, Teddi; Aldrich, Robert

Cast Sinatra, Frank; Martin, Dean; Ekberg, Anita; Andress, Ursula; Bronson, Charles; Buono, Victor; Connor, Edric; Jaeckel, Richard; Mazurki, Mike; Addy, Wesley; Dennis, Nick; Feld, Fritz; Elam, Jack; Sutton, Grady; The Three Stooges; Teddy Buckner and His All Stars

Song(s) Lonesome Polecat (C: Riddle, Nelson; L: Styne, Stanley); Four for Texas [1] (C: Van Heusen, James; L: Cahn, Sammy)

Notes [1] Written for exploitation only.

1913 ◆ FOUR FRIGHTENED PEOPLE
Paramount, 1934

Producer(s) De Mille, Cecil B.
Director(s) De Mille, Cecil B.
Screenwriter(s) Coffee, Lenore; Cormack, Bartlett
Source(s) (novel) Arnot-Robertson, E.

Cast Colbert, Claudette; Marshall, Herbert; Boland, Mary; Gargan, William; Carrillo, Leo; Griffies, Ethel

Song(s) I Wonder What's Become of Yaaka Hickey Doola Lou [1] [3] (C: Donaldson, Walter; L: Kahn, Gus); Four Frightened People [2] (C: Rainger, Ralph; L: Robin, Leo); Just Follow the Sun [2] (C: Donaldson, Walter; L: Kahn, Gus); As Long As There's a Song to Sing [2] [3] (C: Donaldson, Walter; L: Kahn, Gus)

Notes [1] This song was first written for the movie when it was titled CRUISE TO NOWHERE. It was not included when the film was retitled. There was a previous song with the same music, titled "As Long As There's a Song to Sing," that seems to have been written for the earlier film. There is also reference to the song replacing one titled "Just Follow the Sun." [2] Not used. [3] Same music.

1914 ✦ THE FOUR HORSEMEN OF THE APOCALYPSE
Metro–Goldwyn–Mayer, 1962

Musical Score Previn, Andre

Producer(s) Blaustein, Julian
Director(s) Minnelli, Vincente
Screenwriter(s) Ardrey, Robert; Gay, John
Source(s) *Four Horsemen of the Apocalypse* (novel) Ibanez, Vincente Blasco

Cast Ford, Glenn; Thulin, Ingrid [1]; Boyer, Charles; Cobb, Lee J.; Lukas, Paul; Mimieux, Yvette; Boehm, Karl; Henreid, Paul; Dolenz, George; Paiva, Nestor

Song(s) Mine for the Moment (C: Previn, Andre; L: Langdon, Dory)

Notes [1] Speaking voice dubbed by Angela Lansbury.

1915 ✦ FOUR HOURS TO KILL
Paramount, 1935

Composer(s) Rainger, Ralph
Lyricist(s) Robin, Leo

Producer(s) Hornblow Jr., Arthur
Director(s) Leisen, Mitchell
Screenwriter(s) Krasna, Norman
Source(s) *Small Miracle* (play) Krasna, Norman

Cast Barthelmess, Richard; Wilson, Charles; Madison, Noel; Milland, Ray; Mack, Helen; Travers, Henry; Karns, Roscoe

Song(s) Let's Make a Night of It [14]; A Penny in My Pocket [18]; Hate to Talk About Myself [16] (C: Rainger, Ralph; Whiting, Richard A.); Do a Little Rumba with Me [1]; I Lost My Heart [2] [17] (C: Gensler, Lewis E.; L: Robin, Leo); Moon Mad [2] [4]; Oh Baby, Obey [2] [5]; I'm Afraid to Waltz with You [2] [6] (C: Harling, W. Franke; L: Coslow, Sam); It Looks to Me Like Love [2] [7] (C: Gensler, Lewis E.; L: Thompson, Harlan); Remember Cherie [2] (C/L: Coslow, Sam; Norman, Pierre; Grier, Jimmy); I Knew [2] [8] (C: Gensler, Lewis E.; L: Robin, Leo); You're a Blessing to Me [2] [13]; How Can I Resist You [2] [3] (C: Revel, Harry; L: Gordon, Mack); I'm a Seeker of Beauty [2] [9] (C: Johnston, Arthur; L: Coslow, Sam); Creole Man [2] [3] (C: Revel, Harry; L: Gordon, Mack); I'm Gonna Take Possession of You [2] [12] (C/L: Eliscu, Edward; Coslow, Sam); I Ain't Gonna Carry No Torch [2] [10] (C/L: Coslow, Sam); I Met My Waterloo [2] [3] (C: Johnston, Arthur; L: Coslow, Sam); Dance with Me [2] (C: Lombardo, Carmen; L: Coslow, Sam); You Don't Know What You're Doin' to Me [2] [3] (C: Revel, Harry; L: Gordon, Mack); Give Me a Thrill [2] [11] (C/L: Brooks, Harvey; Ellison, Ben; DuBois, Gladys); Walking the Floor [2] [15]

Notes The film was first titled SMALL MIRACLE. [1] Used instrumentally only. [2] Not used. These were all trunk songs written for other pictures that Paramount considered putting into film when titled SMALL MIRACLE. [3] Written for BELLE OF THE NINETIES. [4] Written for THE BIG BROADCAST (1932). [5] Written for COME ON MARINES. Later also not used in GIVE ME A SAILOR. [6] Written for the Spanish version of HONEYMOON HATE titled EL PRINCIPE GONDOLERO and not used there. Also not used in TROUBLE IN PARADISE. [7] Written for FUNNY PAGE. [8] Written for HER MASTER'S VOICE and also not used in HERE IS MY HEART and IT'S A GREAT LIFE. [9] Written for SEARCH FOR BEAUTY. [10] Written for Helen Morgan to sing in YOU BELONG TO ME but not used there. [11] Written for I'M NO ANGEL. [12] Not written for any particular production. [13] Written for HERE IS MY HEART but not used there and also not used in COCOANUT GROVE; GIVE ME A SAILOR and WAIKIKI WEDDING. [14] Written for BEDTIME STORY. [15] Later also not used in FORGOTTEN FACES but published. [16] Written for the unproduced musical SAILOR BEWARE (1936) without the Rainger credit and used for STOLEN HEAVEN. [17] Written for IT'S A GREAT LIFE. [18] Also in MILLIONS IN THE AIR.

1916 ✦ FOUR JACKS AND A JILL
RKO, 1941

Composer(s) Revel, Harry
Lyricist(s) Greene, Mort

Producer(s) Twist, John
Director(s) Hively, Jack
Screenwriter(s) Twist, John

Cast Bolger, Ray; Shirley, Anne [1]; Havoc, June; Arnaz, Desi; Durant, Jack; Foy Jr., Eddie; Feld, Fritz; Daniell, Henry

Song(s) I'm in Good Shape; I Haven't a Thing to Wear [2]; Karinina; Boogie Woogie Conga; Wherever You Are; You Go Your Way

Notes [1] Dubbed by Martha Mears. [2] Also in WHAT A BLONDE.

1917 ✦ FOUR JILLS IN A JEEP
Twentieth Century–Fox, 1944

Composer(s) McHugh, Jimmy
Lyricist(s) Adamson, Harold
Choreographer(s) Loper, Don

Producer(s) Starr, Irving
Director(s) Seiter, William A.
Screenwriter(s) Ellis, Robert; Logan, Helen; Werris, Snag

Cast Faye, Alice; Grable, Betty; Miranda, Carmen; Jessel, George; Haymes, Dick; Harvey, John; Silvers,

Phil; Jimmy Dorsey and His Orchestra; Francis, Kay; Landis, Carole; Raye, Martha; Mayfair, Mitzi

Song(s) How Blue the Night; You Send Me; How Many Times Do I Have to Tell You [2]; Crazy Me; Ohio [1]; It's the Old Army Game [1]; Comin'in on a Wing and a Prayer [2]; S.N.A.F.U.[3]

Notes "Cuddle Up a Little Closer, Lovey Mine" by Karl Hoschna and Otto Harbach is used vocally. The track was originally recorded and used in CONEY ISLAND. "Over There" by George M. Cohan; "You'll Never Know" and "I Yi Yi Yi (I Like You Very Much)" by Harry Warren and Mack Gordon and "(If You Can't Sing It) You'll Have to Swing It," better known as "Mr. Paganini," by Sam Coslow are also used vocally. [1] Instrumental use only. [2] Also used in IN THE MEANTIME DARLING. [2] Cut from final print. [3] Recorded but not used.

1918 ✦ FOUR MOTHERS
Warner Brothers, 1941

Musical Score Roemheld, Heinz

Producer(s) Blanke, Henry
Director(s) Keighley, William
Screenwriter(s) Avery, Stephen Morehouse
Source(s) "Sister Act" (story) Hurst, Fannie

Cast Lane, Priscilla; Lane, Rosemary; Lane, Lola; Page, Gale; Rains, Claude; Lynn, Jeffrey; Albert, Eddie; Robson, May; McHugh, Frank; Foran, Dick; Lewis, Vera

Song(s) Moonlight and Tears (C: Roemheld, Heinz; L: Scholl, Jack)

1919 ✦ FOUR SONS
Fox, 1928

Director(s) Ford, John
Screenwriter(s) Klein, Philip; Hilliker, Katherine; Caldwell, H.H.
Source(s) "Grandmother Bernle Learns Her Letters" (story) Ross, Ida Alexa

Cast Hall, James; Mann, Margaret; Foxe, Earle; Morton, Charles; Bushman Jr., Francis X.; Meeker, George

Song(s) Little Mother (C: Rapee, Erno; L: Pollack, Lew)

Notes No cue sheet available.

1920 ✦ THE FOX
Warner Brothers, 1968

Musical Score Schifrin, Lalo

Producer(s) Stross, Raymond
Director(s) Rydell, Mark
Screenwriter(s) Carlino, Lewis John; Koch, Howard W.
Source(s) The Fox (novel) Lawrence, D.H.

Cast Dennis, Sandy; Dullea, Keir; Heywood, Anne

Song(s) Roll It Over (C/L: Brand, Oscar); That Night [1] (C: Schifrin, Lalo; L: Gimbel, Norman)

Notes [1] Lyric written for exploitation only.

1921 ✦ THE FOX AND THE HOUND
Disney, 1981

Musical Score Baker, Buddy
Composer(s) Stafford, Jim
Lyricist(s) Stafford, Jim

Producer(s) Reitherman, Wolfgang; Stevens, Art
Director(s) Stevens, Art; Berman, Ted; Rich, Richard J.
Screenwriter(s) Clemmons, Larry; Berman, Ted; Young, Pete; Hulett, Steve; Gerry, Vance; Michener, David; Mattinson, Burny; Kress, Earl
Source(s) The Fox and the Hound (novel) Mannix, Daniel P.
Voices Rooney, Mickey; Russell, Kurt; Bailey, Pearl; Albertson, Jack; Duncan, Sandy; Nolan, Jeanette; Buttram, Pat; Fiedler, John; McIntire, John; Bakalyan, Richard [3]

Song(s) Appreciate the Lady; A Huntin' Man [2]; Lack of Education; Best of Friends (C: Johnston, Richard O.; L: Fidel, Stan); Goodbye May Seem Forever (C: Rich, Richard J.; L: Patch, Jeffrey); Farewell My Friend [1] (C: Bellson, Louis; L: Bailey, Pearl); Let Your Body Go [1] (C/L: Connors, Carol)

Notes Animated feature. [1] Not used. [2] Previously titled "Moonshine Night." [3] Billed as Dick Bakalyan.

1922 ✦ FOXES
United Artists, 1980

Musical Score Moroder, Giorgio
Composer(s) Moroder, Giorgio

Producer(s) Puttnam, David; Ayres, Gerald
Director(s) Lyne, Adrian
Screenwriter(s) Ayres, Gerald

Cast Foster, Jodie; Baio, Scott; Kellerman, Sally; Quaid, Randy; Smith, Lois; Faith, Adam

Song(s) Fly Too High (L: Ian, Janis); 20th Century Foxes (C/L: Dimino, Frank; Giuffria, Gregg); Virginia (C/L: Meadows, Punky); Rock & Roll Dancin' (C/L: Beckmeier, F.; Beckmeier, S.); More Than a Feeling (C/L: Scholz, Donald T.); Shake It (C: Esposito, Joseph; Hokenson, Eddie; L: Sudano, Bruce); Bad Love (L: Cher); Greedy Man (C: Moroder, Giorgio; Forsey, Keith; L: Forsey, Keith); Ship of Fools (C/L: Seger, Bob); On the Radio (L: Summer, Donna)

Notes No cue sheet available.

1923 ✦ THE FOXES OF HARROW
Twentieth Century–Fox, 1947

Musical Score Buttolph, David

Producer(s) Bacher, William A.
Director(s) Stahl, John M.

Screenwriter(s) Tuchock, Wanda
Source(s) *The Foxes of Harrow* (novel) Yerby, Frank

Cast Harrison, Rex; O'Hara, Maureen; Haydn, Richard; McLaglen, Victor; Brown, Vanessa; Medina, Patricia; Lockhart, Gene

Song(s) There Was a Woman in Our Town (C: Henderson, Charles; L: Traditional); Drunk Song (C/L: Ricardi, Enrico); Erzilee (Voodoo Chant) (C/L: Hairston, Jester)

Notes These are very brief pieces. There are also vocals of spirituals and other public domain material.

1924 ✦ FOXFIRE
Universal, 1955

Musical Score Mancini, Henry

Producer(s) Rosenberg, Aaron
Director(s) Pevney, Joseph
Screenwriter(s) Frings, Ketti

Cast Russell, Jane; Chandler, Jeff; Duryea, Dan; MacLane, Barton; Lovsky, Celia

Song(s) Foxfire (C: Mancini, Henry; L: Chandler, Jeff)

1925 ✦ FOX MOVIETONE ENTERTAINMENT #2
Fox, 1928

Cast Lawrence, Gertrude; Murray, J. Harold; The Rio Rita Girls [1]

Song(s) I Don't Know (C/L: Unknown); Rangers' Song [1] (C: Tierney, Harry; L: McCarthy, Joseph); Spring Fever [3] (C: Bloom, Rube); Kitten on the Keys [2] (C: Confrey, Zez)

Notes Short subject. Lawrence sings "I Don't Know." Murray sings "The Ranger Song." [1] From RIO RITA. [2] Duo-pianists Constance Mering and Muriel Pollock. [3] May not have been used.

1926 ✦ FOX MOVIETONE ENTERTAINMENT #6
Fox, 1928

Cast Meller, Raquel

Song(s) Flor Del Mal (A Lament of the Girl of the Streets) (C/L: Wolter, F.); La Tarde Del Corpus (C: Reyna, Manuel Bertran; L: Prado, Fiel)

Notes Short subject.

1927 ✦ FOX MOVIETONE ENTERTAINMENT #7
Fox, 1928

Cast Meller, Raquel

Song(s) La Mujer del Torero (The Wife of the Toreador) (C/L: Unknown); El Noi de La Mare (A Song of Motherhood) (C: Martinez, C. Perez; L: Albiesa, Santos)

Notes Short subject.

1928 ✦ FOX MOVIETONE ENTERTAINMENT #8
Fox, 1928

Cast Lightner, Winnie

Song(s) Nagasaki Butterfly (C/L: Unknown); Everybody Loves My Girl (C/L: Unknown)

Notes Short subject.

1929 ✦ FOX MOVIETONE ENTERTAINMENT #9
Fox, 1928

Cast Ben Bernie and His Orchestra

Song(s) A Lane in Spain (C: Lombardo, Carmen; L: Lewis, Al); Are You Going to Be Home (C/L: Dixon, Mort; Stept, Sam H.; Dubin, Al); Scheherazade (C: Rimsky-Korsakov, Nicholas)

Notes Short subject.

1930 ✦ FOX MOVIETONE ENTERTAINMENT #11
Fox, 1928

Cast Kentucky Jubilee Choir; Tarisova, Nina

Song(s) Old Kentucky Home; Swing Low Sweet Chariot; There Were Once Happy Days (C/L: Unknown)

Notes Short subject. Tarisova sings "There Were Once Happy Days." The other two are sung by the choir.

1931 ✦ FOX MOVIETONE ENTERTAINMENT #15
Fox, 1928

Cast Lillie, Beatrice

Song(s) Rambling Along the Highway (C/L: Kernell, William); The Roses Have Made Me Remember (C/L: Coward, Noel)

Notes Short subject.

1932 ✦ FOX MOVIETONE FOLLIES OF 1929
Fox, 1929

Composer(s) Gottler, Archie; Conrad, Con
Lyricist(s) Mitchell, Sidney D.; Conrad, Con
Choreographer(s) Fanchon and Marco; Gottler, Archie

Director(s)   Butler, David; Silver, Marcel
Screenwriter(s)   Wells, William K.

Cast   Breeden, John; Lane, Lola; Jennings, DeWitt; Fetchit, Stepin; Gottler, Archie [1]; Hymer, Warren; Carol, Sue; Lynn, Sharon; Lee, Dixie

Song(s)   Legs; Why Can't I Be Like You; That's You Baby; The Breakaway [3]; Pearl of Old Japan; Walking with Suzie [5]; Big City Blues; Pony Dance (Inst.) (C: Stamper, Dave); Look What You've Done to Me [4]; Bring Back Old Broadway [6] (C: Stamper, Dave; L: Smith, Paul Gerard; Joseph, Edmund); Love Makes the World Go 'Round [6]

Notes   [1] Plays the stage manager. [2] Not on cue sheet. [3] Used in HIGH SOCIETY BLUES. [4] Also in DOUBLE CROSS ROADS and WHY LEAVE HOME? [5] Also in THE MAN WHO DARED. [6] Not used.

1933 ✦ FRAMED
Paramount, 1975

Composer(s)   Stanton, Frank; Kent, Arthur
Lyricist(s)   Stanton, Frank; Kent, Arthur

Producer(s)   Briskin, Mort; Briskin, Joel
Director(s)   Karlson, Phil
Screenwriter(s)   Briskin, Mort
Source(s)   (novel) Powers, Art; Misenheimer, Mike

Cast   Baker, Joe Don; Van Dyke, Conny; Dell, Gabriel; Peters, Brock

Song(s)   Nearer My Love, to You; He's My Lover; I'll Never Make It Easy (C/L: Peters, Ben)

1934 ✦ FRANCIS JOINS THE WACS
Universal, 1954

Musical Score   Gertz, Irving

Producer(s)   Richmond, Ted
Director(s)   Lubin, Arthur
Screenwriter(s)   Freeman, Devery; Allardice, James B.

Cast   O'Connor, Donald; Bari, Lynn; Adams, Julia; Van Doren, Mamie; Pitts, ZaSu; Wills, Chill

Song(s)   Francis Joins the Wacs [1] (C: Wood, Britt; Beatty, George; L: Wood, Britt; Beatty, George; Herbert, Frederick)

Notes   [1] Based on "Old Paint's Complaint" by Wood and Beatty.

1935 ✦ FRANCIS OF ASSISI
Twentieth Century–Fox, 1961

Musical Score   Nascimbene, Mario
Composer(s)   Darby, Ken
Lyricist(s)   Darby, Ken

Producer(s)   Skouras, Plato
Director(s)   Curtiz, Michael
Screenwriter(s)   Vale, Eugene; Forsyth, James; Thomas, Jack
Source(s)   (novel) de Wohl, Louis

Cast   Dillman, Bradford; Hart, Dolores; Whitman, Stuart; Armendariz, Pedro; Kellaway, Cecil; Franz, Eduard; Napier, Russell

Song(s)   The Hills of Assisi [1] (C: Vance, Paul; L: Pockriss, Lee); Tavern Song (C/L: Nascimbene, Mario); I'm Never Alone [1]; I Reach for a Star [1]; Follow the Footsteps of Our Lord [1]

Notes   [1] Not used.

1936 ✦ FRANKENSTEIN MEETS THE WOLF MAN
Universal, 1943

Musical Score   Salter, Hans J.

Producer(s)   Waggner, George
Director(s)   Neill, Roy William
Screenwriter(s)   Siodmak, Curt

Cast   Lugosi, Bela; Chaney Jr., Lon; Ouspenskaya, Maria; Knowles, Patric; Massey, Ilona; Hoey, Dennis; Atwill, Lionel

Song(s)   Faro-La, Faro-Li (C/L: Salter, Hans J.)

1937 ✦ FRANKIE AND JOHNNY
United Artists, 1965

Musical Score   Karger, Fred
Choreographer(s)   Barton, Earl

Producer(s)   Small, Edward
Director(s)   de Cordova, Frederick
Screenwriter(s)   Gottlieb, Alex

Cast   Presley, Elvis; Douglas, Donna [1]; Morgan, Harry; Langdon, Sue Ane; Kovack, Nancy; Christie, Audrey; Strauss, Robert; Eisley, Anthony; Cowen, Jerome

Song(s)   Come Along (C/L: Hoss, David); Petunia, The Gardener's Daughter (C/L: Tepper, Sid; Bennett, Roy C.); Chesay (C/L: Karger, Fred; Weisman, Ben; Wayne, Sid); Look Out Broadway (C/L: Wise, Fred; Starr, Randy); Frankie and Johnny Routine (C/L: Gottlieb, Alex; Karger, Fred; Weisman, Ben); What Every Woman Lives For (C/L: Pomus, Doc; Shuman, Mort); Shout It Out [2] (C/L: Giant, Bill; Baum, Bernie; Kaye, Florence); Hard Luck (C/L: Weisman, Ben; Wayne, Sid); Please Don't Stop Loving Me (C/L: Byers, Joy); Everybody Come Aboard (C/L: Giant, Bill; Baum, Bernie; Kaye, Florence); Down by the Riverside [3] (C/L: Giant, Bill; Baum, Bernie; Kaye, Florence); When the Saints Go Marching In [2] (C/L: Giant, Bill; Baum, Bernie; Kaye, Florence)

Notes   [1] Dubbed by Eileen Wilson. [2] Not used in ROUSTABOUT. [3] Sheet music only.

1938 ✦ FRANTIC
Warner Brothers, 1988

Musical Score   Morricone, Ennio

Producer(s)   Mount, Thom; Hampton, Tim
Director(s)   Polanski, Roman
Screenwriter(s)   Polanski, Roman; Brach, Gerard

Cast   Ford, Harrison; Buckley, Betty; Mahoney, John; Weeks, Jimmie Ray; Voyagis, Yorgo

Song(s)   I'm Gonna Lose You (C/L: Hucknall, Mick)

Notes   No cue sheet available.

1939 ✦ FRATERNITY ROW
Paramount, 1977

Composer(s)   Hutton, John-Phillips
Lyricist(s)   Row, Matthew

Producer(s)   Allison, Charles Gary
Director(s)   Tobin, Thomas J.
Screenwriter(s)   Allison, Charles Gary

Cast   Fox, Peter; Harrison, Gregory; Newman, Scott; Morgan, Nancy; Phillips, Wend

Song(s)   Pinning Call-Out Song; Oh Brotherhood; Hey Gamma Nu; We're Looking Towards a New Life; The Pattern Is Broken (C/L: McLean, Don); If You Can Dream (C/L: McLean, Don)

Notes   No cue sheet available.

1940 ✦ FRAULEIN
Twentieth Century–Fox, 1958

Musical Score   Amfitheatrof, Daniele

Producer(s)   Reisch, Walter
Director(s)   Koster, Henry
Screenwriter(s)   Townsend, Leo
Source(s)   *Fraulein* (novel) McGovern, James

Cast   Ferrer, Mel; Wynter, Dana; Michaels, Dolores; Dantine, Helmut; Bikel, Theodore; Triessault, Ivan; Britt, May; Kruschen, Jack

Song(s)   My Fraulein [1] (C: Amfitheatrof, Daniele; L: Livingston, Jay; Evans, Ray); Nitchevo, Nitchevo, Nitchevo (C/L: Amfitheatrof, Daniele)

Notes   [1] Lyric added for exploitation only.

1941 ✦ FREAKY FRIDAY
Disney, 1977

Musical Score   Mandel, Johnny

Producer(s)   Miller, Ron
Director(s)   Nelson, Gary

Screenwriter(s)   Rodgers, Mary
Source(s)   *Freaky Friday* (novel) Rodgers, Mary

Cast   Harris, Barbara; Foster, Jodie; Astin, John; Kelly, Patsy; Van Patten, Dick; Schreck, Vicki; Booke, Sorrell; Oppenheimer, Alan; Buzzi, Ruth; Ballard, Kaye; Cabot, Ceil

Song(s)   I'd Like to Be You for a Day (C/L: Kasha, Al; Hirschhorn, Joel)

1942 ✦ FREDDIE SLACK AND HIS ORCHESTRA
Universal, 1949

Cast   Freddie Slack and His Orchestra

Song(s)   Goodbye Romance (C/L: James, Inez; Elliott, Jack)

Notes   There are other vocals in this short subject.

1943 ✦ FREDDIE STEPS OUT
Monogram, 1946

Choreographer(s)   Boyle, Jack

Producer(s)   Katzman, Sam
Director(s)   Dreifuss, Arthur
Screenwriter(s)   Collins, Hal

Cast   Stewart, Freddie; Preisser, June; Rooney, Anne; Mills, Warren; Neill, Noel; Moran, Jackie; Darro, Frankie

Song(s)   Patience and Fortitude (C/L: Moore Jr., Billy; Warren, Blackie); Let's Drop the Subject (C/L: Collins, Hal; Sanns, Joe)

Notes   No cue sheet available. There is also a vocal of "Don't Blame Me" by Dorothy Fields and Jimmy McHugh.

1944 ✦ FREE AND EASY
Metro–Goldwyn–Mayer, 1930

Composer(s)   Ahlert, Fred E.
Lyricist(s)   Turk, Roy
Choreographer(s)   Lee, Sammy

Director(s)   Sedgwick, Edward
Screenwriter(s)   Schayer, Richard; Boasberg, Al

Cast   Keaton, Buster; Page, Anita; Friganza, Trixie; Montgomery, Robert; Niblo, Fred; Dearing, Edgar; Miljan, John; Barrymore, Lionel; Haines, William; Sebastian, Dorothy; Dane, Karl; Burton, David; Lee, Gwen

Song(s)   It Must Be You; Land of Mystery; Oh, King Oh, Queen!; The Free and Easy; Cubanita [1] (C/L: Kernell, William); Penitentiary Blues [1] (C/L: Kernell, William); You've Got Me that Way [1] (C/L: Kernell, William)

Notes   [1] Not on cue sheet.

1945 ✦ FREEBIE AND THE BEAN
Warner Brothers, 1974

Musical Score Frontiere, Dominic
Composer(s) Frontiere, Dominic
Lyricist(s) Janssen, Danny; Hart, Bobby

Producer(s) Mutrux, Floyd
Director(s) Rush, Richard
Screenwriter(s) Kaufman, Robert

Cast Arkin, Alan; Caan, James; Harper, Valerie

Song(s) You and Me Babe; When You Need Someone; Hard Core Man

1946 ✦ A FREE PEOPLE
Warner Brothers, 1965

Composer(s) Adlam, Basil
Lyricist(s) Hendricks, William L.

Song(s) Freedom's Flame; This Land Is Your Land (C/L: Guthrie, Woody); Climb Upon a Mountain [1]; Early in the Morning (C/L: Stookey, Paul); Winning of the Land; Wagon Trains West; The Wagoner's Song (C/L: Sparks; Grasso; Posell); Civil War [1]; Don't Cry, Suzanne (C/L: Wadsworth, T.); The Iron Horse [1]; Journey to the Sky; Saddle a Rocket and Ride; The Lighted Lamp

Notes Short subject. All background vocals. It is not known which of these were written for the movie.

1947 ✦ FREEWHEELIN'
Turtle, 1976

Musical Score Freud, Stephen; Cohn, Steve
Composer(s) Freud, Stephen; Cohn, Steve
Lyricist(s) Freud, Stephen; Cohn, Steve

Producer(s) Dittrich, Scott
Director(s) Dittrich, Scott
Screenwriter(s) Van Noy, George

Cast Peralta, Stacy; Darrin, Camille; Howell, Russ; Means, Ken

Song(s) Rollin' with You; Free and Alive; Freewheelin'

Notes No cue sheet available.

1948 ✦ THE FRENCH CONNECTION
Twentieth Century–Fox, 1971

Musical Score Ellis, Don

Producer(s) D'Antoni, Philip
Director(s) Friedkin, William
Screenwriter(s) Tidyman, Ernest
Source(s) (book) Moore, Robin

Cast Hackman, Gene; Rey, Fernando; Scheider, Roy; LoBianco, Tony; Bozzuffi, Marcel; De Pasquale, Frederic

Song(s) Everybody's Goin' to the Moon (C/L: King, Kenneth)

1949 ✦ THE FRENCH LINE
RKO, 1954

Musical Score Scharf, Walter
Composer(s) Myrow, Josef
Lyricist(s) Blane, Ralph; Wells, Robert
Choreographer(s) Daniels, Billy

Producer(s) Grainger, Edmund
Director(s) Bacon, Lloyd
Screenwriter(s) Loos, Mary; Sale, Richard

Cast Russell, Jane; Roland, Gilbert; Hunnicutt, Arthur; McCarty, Mary; MacKenzie, Joyce; Corday, Paula; Elliott, Scott; Stevens, Craig; Geray, Steven

Song(s) Well! I'll Be Switched; With a Kiss; Comment Allez Vous; Wait Till You See Paris; What Is This That I Feel; Poor Andre; Any Gal from Texas; By Madame Firelle; Lookin' for Trouble [2]; The French Line [1]

Notes This is a 3-D movie. There are three different scripts on file: Original Version, New York Version and Code Version. [1] Used instrumentally only. [2] The uncensored version of this song has a spoken interlude but not additional musical material.

1950 ✦ FRENCHMAN'S CREEK
Paramount, 1944

Musical Score Young, Victor

Producer(s) DeSylva, B.G.; Lewis, David
Director(s) Leisen, Mitchell
Screenwriter(s) Jennings, Talbot
Source(s) *Frenchman's Creek* (novel) du Maurier, Daphne

Cast Fontaine, Joan; de Cordova, Arturo; Rathbone, Basil; Forbes, Ralph; Kellaway, Cecil; Bruce, Nigel; Daniels, Billy

Song(s) The Life of Nelly [1] (L: Lee, Lester); Que Drole (C: Bennett, Robert Russell; L: Sanders, Troy)

Notes [1] This has no music.

1951 ✦ A FRENCH MISTRESS
Films Around the World, 1960

Musical Score Addison, John

Producer(s) Boulting, John
Director(s) Boulting, Roy
Screenwriter(s) Boulting, Roy; Dell, Jeffrey

Cast Parker, Cecil; Justice, James Robertson; Bannen, Ian; Laurent, Agnes; Huntley, Raymond; Handl, Irene; Seyler, Athene

Song(s) Madeleine (C: Addison, John; L: Boulting, Roy)

Notes No cue sheet available.

1952 ✦ FRENCH POSTCARDS
Paramount, 1979

Musical Score Holdridge, Lee

Producer(s) Katz, Gloria
Director(s) Huyck, Willard
Screenwriter(s) Huyck, Willard; Katz, Gloria

Cast Chapin, Miles; Baker, Blanche; Grant, David Marshall; Quennessen, Valerie; Winger, Debra; Pisier, Marie-France; Rochefort, Jean

Song(s) The Thing of It Is (C: Kander, John; L: Ebb, Fred)

1953 ✦ FRESH HORSES
Weintraub Entertainment, 1988

Musical Score Foster, David; Williams, Patrick

Producer(s) Berg, Dick
Director(s) Anspaugh, David
Screenwriter(s) Ketron, Larry
Source(s) *Fresh Horses: A Play* (play) Ketron, Larry

Cast Ringwald, Molly; McCarthy, Andrew; D'Arbanville, Patti; Stiller, Ben; Russom, Leon

Song(s) No Tomorrow (C/L: Foster, David; Loggins, Kenny; Matza, Arlene)

Notes No cue sheet available.

1954 ✦ FRESHMAN LOVE
Warner Brothers, 1936

Musical Score Jerome, M.K.
Composer(s) Jerome, M.K.

Producer(s) Foy, Bryan
Director(s) McGann, William
Screenwriter(s) Felton, Earl; Bricker, George

Cast McHugh, Frank; Ellis, Patricia; Hull, Warren; Cawthorn, George E.; Stone, Mary Treen; O'Neill, Henry

Song(s) Collegiana (L: Scholl, Jack); Romance After Dark (L: Jasmyn, Joan); Freshman Love (L: Scholl, Jack); Del Rio Tango (Inst.) (C: Warren, Harry); That's What I Mean [1] (L: Scholl, Jack)

Notes Released in Great Britain as RHYTHM ON THE RIVER. [1] Presented Instrumentally only.

1955 ✦ FRESHMAN YEAR
Universal, 1938

Musical Score Skinner, Frank

Producer(s) Bilson, George
Director(s) MacDonald, Frank
Screenwriter(s) Grayson, Charles

Cast Lundigan, William; Truex, Ernest; The Three Diamond Brothers; The Three Murtha Sisters; The Lucky Seven Choir; Dunbar, Dixie; Moore, Constance; Ladd, Alan

Song(s) Sons of Carlton (C: Previn, Charles; L: Bilson, George; Grayson, Charles); Chasing You Around (C: Actman, Irving; L: Loesser, Frank); Swing That Cheer (C/L: McCarthy, Joseph; Barris, Harry); We're on Relief (C/L: Henderson, Charles); Ain't That Marvelous (C/L: McCarthy, Joseph; Barris, Harry)

1956 ✦ FRIDAY THE 13TH, PART VI: JASON LIVES
Paramount, 1986

Musical Score Manfredini, Harry
Composer(s) Cooper, Alice; Roberts, Kane
Lyricist(s) Cooper, Alice; Roberts, Kane

Producer(s) Behrns, Don
Director(s) McLoughlin, Tom
Screenwriter(s) McLoughlin, Tom

Cast Mathews, Thom; Cooke, Jennifer; Kagen, David; Jones, Renee

Song(s) He's Back (The Man Behind the Mask) (C/L: Cooper, Alice; Roberts, Kane; Kelly, Tom); Teenage Frankenstein; Animal (C/L: Spry, Jeffrey; Spry, C.J.); Hard Rock Summer

1957 ✦ FRIDAY THE 13TH—THE FINAL CHAPTER
Paramount, 1984

Musical Score Manfredini, Harry

Producer(s) Mancuso Jr., Frank
Director(s) Zito, Joseph
Screenwriter(s) Cohen, Barney

Cast Anderson, E. Erich; Aronson, Judie; Barton, Peter; Beck, Kimberly; Feldman, Corey; Glover, Crispin

Song(s) Love Is a Lie (C/L: Swan, Cal)

Notes No cue sheet available.

1958 ✦ FRIDAY THE 13TH . . . THE ORPHAN
World Northal, 1979

Musical Score Macero, Teo

Director(s) Ballard, John
Screenwriter(s) Ballard, John

Cast Feury, Peggy; Miles, Joanna; Whyte, Donn; Owens, Mark; Ajayi, Afolabi; House, Jane

Song(s) I Need to Live Alone Again (C/L: Ian, Janis)

Notes No cue sheet available.

1959 ✦ FRIENDLY NEIGHBORS
Republic, 1940

Producer(s) Schaefer, Armand
Director(s) Grinde, Nick
Screenwriter(s) McGowan, Stuart; McGowan, Dorrell

Cast Weaver, Leon; Weaver, Frank; Weaver, June; Weaver, Loretta; Elviry; Ranson, Lois; Charters, Spencer; Edwards, Cliff; Hartley, John; Shean, Al; Hall, Thurston; Seddon, Margaret; St. John, Al

Song(s) On the Ozark Trail (C/L: Skidmore, William E.; Walker, M.); Weaver Specialty (C: Styne, Jule; L: Brown, George; Meyer, Sol)

Notes There is also a vocal of "Breezin' Along with the Breeze" by Richard A. Whiting, Haven Gillespie and Seymour Simons.

1960 ✦ FRIENDLY PERSUASION
Metro–Goldwyn–Mayer, 1956

Musical Score Tiomkin, Dimitri
Composer(s) Tiomkin, Dimitri
Lyricist(s) Webster, Paul Francis

Producer(s) Wyler, William
Director(s) Wyler, William
Screenwriter(s) Wyler, Robert; West, Jessamyn
Source(s) *The Friendly Persuasion* (novel) West, Jessamyn

Cast Cooper, Gary; McGuire, Dorothy; Perkins, Anthony; Eyer, Richard; Middleton, Robert; Love, Phyllis; Catlett, Walter; Main, Marjorie

Song(s) Friendly Persuasion (Thee I Love); Coax Me a Little (Mocking Bird); Indiana Holiday; Marry Me, Marry Me; Mocking Bird in the Willow Tree [1]

Notes [1] Sheet music only.

1961 ✦ FRIENDS
Paramount, 1971

Composer(s) John, Elton; Taupin, Bernie
Lyricist(s) John, Elton; Taupin, Bernie

Producer(s) Gilbert, Lewis
Director(s) Gilbert, Lewis
Screenwriter(s) Russell, Jack; Harris, Vernon

Cast Bury, Sean; Alvina, Anicee

Song(s) Friends; Honey Roll; Can I Put You On; Michelle's Song; Seasons

1962 ✦ THE FRIGHTENED CITY
Allied Artists, 1962

Musical Score Paramor, Norrie
Composer(s) Paramor, Norrie
Lyricist(s) Lewis, Bunny

Producer(s) Lemont, John; Vance, Leigh
Director(s) Lemont, John
Screenwriter(s) Vance, Leigh

Cast Lom, Herbert; Gregson, John; Connery, Sean; Marks, Alfred; Romain, Yvonne; McFarland, Olive

Song(s) Marvelous Lie; I Laughed at Love

Notes No cue sheet available.

1963 ✦ FRIGHT NIGHT
Columbia, 1985

Musical Score Fiedel, Brad

Producer(s) Jaffe, Herb
Director(s) Holland, Tom
Screenwriter(s) Holland, Tom

Cast Sarandon, Chris; Ragsdale, William; Bearse, Amanda; McDowall, Roddy; Geoffreys, Stephen; Stark, Jonathan

Song(s) Let's Talk (C/L: Mothersbaugh, Mark); Boppin' Tonight (C/L: Goetzman, Gary; Piccirillo, Mike); Rock Myself to Sleep (C/L: Rew, Kimberly; De La Cruz, Vince); Armies of the Night (C/L: Mael, Ron; Mael, Russell); Good Man in a Bad Time (C/L: Tanner, Marc; Reede, Jon; Aniello, Ron); You Can't Hide from the Beast Inside (C/L: Plunkett, Steve); Fright Night (C/L: Lamont, Joe)

1964 ✦ FRISCO SAL
Universal, 1945

Musical Score Ward, Edward
Choreographer(s) Horton, Lester

Producer(s) Waggner, George
Director(s) Waggner, George
Screenwriter(s) Siodmak, Curt; Geraghty, Gerald

Cast Bey, Turhan; Foster, Susanna

Song(s) I Just Got In [2] (C: Berens, Norman; L: Brooks, Jack); Good Little, Bad Little Lady [1] (C/L: Brooks, Jack); Beloved (C: Ward, George; L: Waggner, George); Ace in the Hole (C/L: Dempsey, James; Mitchell, George); Percy (C: Ward, George; L: Waggner, George)

Notes [1] Later in RIDE TO HANGMAN'S TREE. [2] Also in GUN TOWN.

1965 ✦ FROM HELL TO HEAVEN
Paramount, 1933

Director(s) Kenton, Erle C.
Screenwriter(s) Heath, Percy; Buchman, Sidney
Source(s) (play) Hazard, Lawrence

Cast Oakie, Jack; Lombard, Carole; Blackmer, Sidney; Page, Bradley; Grey, Shirley

Song(s) Nova Scotia Moonlight (C: Johnston, Arthur; L: Coslow, Sam)

1966 ✦ FROM HERE TO ETERNITY
Columbia, 1953

Musical Score Duning, George
Composer(s) Karger, Fred
Lyricist(s) Wells, Bob

Producer(s) Adler, Buddy
Director(s) Zinnemann, Fred

Screenwriter(s)   Taradash, Daniel
Source(s)   *From Here to Eternity* (novel) Jones, James

Cast   Lancaster, Burt; Clift, Montgomery; Kerr, Deborah; Reed, Donna; Sinatra, Frank; Ober, Philip; Shaughnessy, Mickey; Bellaver, Harry; Borgnine, Ernest; Warden, Jack; Travis, Merle; Ryan, Tim; Akins, Claude; Reeves, George

Song(s)   Re-Enlistment Blues (L: Jones, James; Wells, Robert); From Here to Eternity [1]; I'll See You in Hawaii [1]

Notes   [1] Sheet music only.

1967 ✦ FROM NOON TILL THREE
United Artists, 1976

Musical Score   Bernstein, Elmer

Producer(s)   Frankovich, M.J.; Self, William
Director(s)   Gilroy, Frank D.
Screenwriter(s)   Gilroy, Frank D.
Source(s)   *From Noon Till Three* (novel) Gilroy, Frank D.

Cast   Bronson, Charles; Ireland, Jill; Fowley, Douglas; Williams, Bert; Lanteau, William

Song(s)   Hello and Goodbye (C: Bernstein, Elmer; L: Bergman, Alan; Bergman, Marilyn)

1968 ✦ FROM RUSSIA WITH LOVE
United Artists, 1964

Musical Score   Barry, John

Producer(s)   Saltzman, Harry; Broccoli, Albert R.
Director(s)   Young, Terence
Screenwriter(s)   Maibaum, Richard
Source(s)   *From Russia with Love* (novel) Fleming, Ian

Cast   Connery, Sean; Bianchi, Daniela; Armendariz, Pedro; Lenya, Lotte; Shaw, Robert; Lee, Bernard; Maxwell, Lois

Song(s)   From Russia with Love (C/L: Bart, Lionel)

1969 ✦ FROM THIS DAY FORWARD
RKO, 1946

Musical Score   Harline, Leigh

Producer(s)   Pereira, William L.
Director(s)   Berry, John
Screenwriter(s)   Butler, Hugo; Sommer, Edith; Schnee, Charles
Source(s)   *All Brides Are Beautiful* (novel) Bell, Thomas

Cast   Stevens, Mark; Fontaine, Joan; De Camp, Rosemary; Morgan, Henry; Brown, Wally; Judge, Arline; McEvoy, Renny; Driscoll, Bobby; Treen, Mary; Smith, Queenie

Song(s)   From This Day Forward (C: Harline, Leigh; L: Greene, Mort)

1970 ✦ THE FRONT
Columbia, 1976

Musical Score   Grusin, Dave

Producer(s)   Ritt, Martin
Director(s)   Ritt, Martin
Screenwriter(s)   Bernstein, Walter

Cast   Allen, Woody; Mostel, Zero; Bernardi, Herschel; Murphy, Michael; Marcovicci, Andrea; Ramsay, Remak; Gough, Lloyd; Rose, Norman; Shelley, Joshua; Sommer, Josef; Aiello, Danny; Kimbrough, Charles; Dixon, MacIntyre; Faye, Joey; Sokol, Marilyn; Flippen, Lucy Lee

Song(s)   Anything for a Laugh (C: Hoffman, Cary; L: Gasman, Ira)

Notes   No cue sheet available.

1971 ✦ FRONTIER FUGITIVES
PRC, 1945

Musical Score   Zahler, Lee; Grigor, Nico

Producer(s)   Alexander, Arthur
Director(s)   Fraser, Harry
Screenwriter(s)   Clifton, Elmer

Cast   O'Brien, Dave; Ritter, Tex; Miller, Lorraine; Wilkerson, Guy; Ingram, Jack; King, Charles

Song(s)   Too Late to Worry, Too Late to Cry (C/L: Dexter, Al); I'll Wait for You (C/L: Dexter, Al)

Notes   Cue sheet doesn't differentiate between vocals and instrumentals.

1972 ✦ FRONTIER GAL
Universal, 1946

Composer(s)   Fairchild, Edgar
Lyricist(s)   Brooks, Jack

Producer(s)   Pagano, Ernest; Fessier, Michael
Director(s)   Lamont, Charles
Screenwriter(s)   Pagano, Ernest; Fessier, Michael

Cast   De Carlo, Yvonne; Cameron, Rod; Simmons, Beverly; Fessier, Michael; Devine, Andy; Knight, Fuzzy; Tombes, Andrew; Leonard, Sheldon; Blandick, Clara

Song(s)   What Is Love?; Johnny's Comin' Home (C: Knight, Fuzzy); Set 'Em Up Joe [1]

Notes   [1] Also in IDEA GIRL and THE WISTFUL WIDOW OF WAGON GAP.

1973 ✦ FRONTIER LAW
Universal, 1944

Composer(s)   Rosen, Milton
Lyricist(s)   Carter, Everett

Producer(s)   Drake, Oliver
Director(s)   Clifton, Elmer
Screenwriter(s)   Clifton, Elmer

Cast Hayden, Russell; Knight, Fuzzy

Song(s) The Bears Give Me the Bird; The Call of the Range [1]; Geraldine [2]; Where the Prairie Meets the Sky [3]

Notes [1] Also in BEYOND THE PECOS, GUNMAN'S CODE and MAN FORM MONTANA (1941). [2] Also in FIGHTING BILL FARGO. [3] Also in BAD MAN FROM RED BUTTE, ESCAPE FROM HONG KONG, I'LL TELL THE WORLD and TWILIGHT ON THE PRAIRIE.

1974 ✦ FRONTIER MARSHALL (1934)
Fox, 1934

Producer(s) Wurtzel, Sol M.
Director(s) Seiler, Lewis
Screenwriter(s) Conselman, William; Anthony, Stuart
Source(s) *Wyatt Earp - Frontier Marshall* (novel) Lake, Stuart N.

Cast O'Brien, George; Bentley, Irene; Stone, George E.

Song(s) Some Day (C: Friedhofer, Hugo; L: Kernell, William)

1975 ✦ FRONTIER MARSHALL (1939)
Twentieth Century–Fox, 1939

Producer(s) Wurtzel, Sol M.
Director(s) Dwan, Allan
Screenwriter(s) Hellman, Sam
Source(s) *Wyatt Earp - Frontier Marshall* (novel) Lake, Stuart N.

Cast Scott, Randolph; Kelly, Nancy; Romero, Cesar; Barnes, Binnie; Carradine, John; Foy Jr., Eddie; Bond, Ward; Chaney Jr., Lon

Song(s) I've Taken a Fancy to You [1] (C: Pollack, Lew; L: Clare, Sidney)

Notes There are also vocals of "Heaven Will Protect the Working Girl" by A. Baldwin Sloane and Edgar Smith (from show TILLIE'S NIGHTMARE) and "Throw Him Down McGinty" (published as "Throw Him Down McClosky") by John W. Kelly. [1] Also in In OLD CHICAGO and WILD GEESE CALLING.

1976 ✦ FRONTIER PONY EXPRESS
Republic, 1939

Producer(s) Kane, Joseph
Director(s) Kane, Joseph
Screenwriter(s) Hall, Norman S.

Cast Rogers, Roy; Hart, Mary; Hatton, Raymond; Keane, Edward; Blue, Monte; Dillaway, Donald; Johnson, Noble; Royle, William

Song(s) The Mail Must Go Through (C/L: Samuels, Walter G. G.); Rusty Spurs (C/L: Wood, W.; Wood, R.)

1977 ✦ FROZEN JUSTICE
Fox, 1929

Director(s) Dwan, Allan; Lester, Elliott
Screenwriter(s) Davis, Owen
Source(s) Norden For Lov Og Ret: en Alaska-Historie Mikkelsen, Ejnar

Cast Ulric, Lenore; Frazer, Robert; Wolheim, Louis; Brendel, El; Patricola, Tom; Judels, Charles; MacFarlane, George

Song(s) Lanak Is Coming (C/L: Kay, Arthur; Spencer, James Ponia); Medicine Man Song (C/L: Spencer, James Ponia); Igloo Song (C: Baer, Abel; L: Gilbert, L. Wolfe); Wicky Wicky (C/L: Spencer, James Ponia); The Right Kind of Man (C: Baer, Abel; L: Gilbert, L. Wolfe); Ai-Ya-Ga-Uk [1] (C/L: Spencer, James Ponia)

Notes [1] Not used.

1978 ✦ THE FUEHRER'S FACE
Disney, 1942

Musical Score Wallace, Oliver

Cast Duck, Donald

Song(s) Der Fuehrer's Face (C/L: Wallace, Oliver)

Notes Cartoon short.

1979 ✦ THE FUGITIVE KIND
United Artists, 1959

Musical Score Hopkins, Kenyon

Producer(s) Jurow, Martin; Shepherd, Richardy
Director(s) Lumet, Sidney
Screenwriter(s) Roberts, Meade
Source(s) *Orpheus Descending* (play) Williams, Tennessee

Cast Brando, Marlon; Magnani, Anna; Woodward, Joanne; Jory, Victor; Armstrong, R.G.; Stapleton, Maureen; Richardson, Emory; Madame Spivy; Gracie, Sally; Benson, Lucille

Song(s) Let Me Out (C/L: Hopkins, Kenyon); Not a Soul (C: Hopkins, Kenyon; L: Williams, Tennessee)

Notes The play was originally titled BATTLE OF ANGELS (1939) before being rewritten.

1980 ✦ FUGITIVE LOVERS
Metro–Goldwyn–Mayer, 1934

Musical Score Axt, William

Producer(s) Hubbard, Lucien
Director(s) Boleslawski, Richard [1]
Screenwriter(s) Hackett, Albert; Goodrich, Frances; Seitz, George B.

Cast Montgomery, Robert; Evans, Madge; Healy, Ted; Pendleton, Nat; Gordon, C. Henry; Selwyn, Ruth; Fine, Larry; Howard, Moe; Howard, Jerry

Song(s) Full of the Devil (C: McHugh, Jimmy; L: Fields, Dorothy); You'll Never Know (C/L: Healy, Ted); Under the Stars (C/L: Snell, Dave)

Notes [1] His name is sometimes spelled Boleslavsky.

1981 ✦ FUGITIVES
Fox, 1929

Producer(s) Hawks, Kenneth
Director(s) Beaudine, William
Screenwriter(s) Stone, John
Source(s) "The Exiles and Other Stories" (stories) Davis, Richard Harding

Cast Bellamy, Madge; Terry, Don; Stone, Arthur; Foxe, Earle; Betz, Matthew; Hare, Lumsden; Yorke, Edith

Song(s) Why Are You Always Breaking My Heart (C/L: Russotto, Leo; Coombes, James P.)

Notes "Cheatin' on You" by Lew Pollack is also used.

1982 ✦ FUGITIVE VALLEY
Monogram, 1941

Musical Score Sanucci, Frank

Producer(s) Weeks, George W.
Director(s) Luby, S. Roy
Screenwriter(s) Drake, Oliver

Cast Corrigan, Ray; King, John; Terhune, Max; Duncan, Julie; Strange, Glenn; Kortman, Bob

Song(s) My Little Prairie Annie (C: George, Jean [1]; L: Tobias, Harry); Ridin' Along [2] (C: George, Jean [1]; L: Tobias, Harry)

Notes [1] Pseudonym for Lucille Nolte. [2] Used instrumentally only.

1983 ✦ FUN AND FANCY FREE
Disney, 1947

Musical Score Daniel, Eliot; Wallace, Oliver; Smith, Paul J.

Cast Bergen, Edgar; Shore, Dinah; Snerd, Mortimer; McCarthy, Charlie

Song(s) Fun and Fancy Free (C/L: Benjamin, Ben; Weiss, George David); Dreamin' Again [1] (C: Daniel, Eliot; L: Gilbert, Ray)

Notes This is a compilation of cartoon shorts. The cartoons include BONGO and MICKEY AND THE BEANSTALK. See the individual cartoons for their songs. [1] Not used.

1984 ✦ FUN IN ACAPULCO
Paramount, 1963

Musical Score Lilley, Joseph J.
Choreographer(s) O'Curran, Charles

Producer(s) Wallis, Hal B.
Director(s) Thorpe, Richard
Screenwriter(s) Weiss, Allan

Cast Presley, Elvis; Andress, Ursula; Lukas, Paul; Rey, Alejandro; Domasin, Larry; Carricart, Robert; Hope, Teri

Song(s) Vino, Dinero Y Amor (C/L: Tepper, Sid; Bennett, Roy C.); I Think I'm Gonna Like It Here (C/L: Robertson, Don; Blair, Hal); Mexico (C: Tepper, Sid; Bennett, Roy C.; L: Tepper, Sid; Bennett, Roy C.; O'Curran, Charles); El Toro (C/L: Giant, Bill; Baum, Bernie; Kaye, Florence); Marguerita (C/L: Robertson, Don); The Bull Fighter Was a Lady (C/L: Tepper, Sid; Bennett, Roy C.); There's No Room to Rhumba in a Sports Car (C/L: Wise, Fred; Manning, Dick); Bossa Nova, Baby (C/L: Leiber, Jerry; Stoller, Mike); You Can't Say No in Acapulco (C/L: Feller, Sid; Fuller, Dee; Morris, Lee); Fun In Acapulco [1] (C: Weisman, Ben; L: Wayne, Sid); Keep It Under Your Hat [1] (C/L: Tepper, Sid; Bennett, Roy C.)

Notes There is also a vocal of "Guadalajara" by Pepe Guizar. It also appeared in WEEKEND AT THE WALDORF (MGM), MEXICANA (Republic) and PAN AMERICANA (RKO). [1] Not used.

1985 ✦ FUNNY FACE
Paramount, 1957

Composer(s) Edens, Roger
Lyricist(s) Gershe, Leonard; Edens, Roger
Choreographer(s) Loring, Eugene; Astaire, Fred

Producer(s) Edens, Roger
Director(s) Donen, Stanley
Screenwriter(s) Gershe, Leonard

Cast Hepburn, Audrey; Astaire, Fred; Auclair, Michael; Thompson, Kay; Flemyng, Robert; Parker, Suzy; Lee, Ruta

Song(s) On How to Be Lovely; How Long Has This Been Going On [1] (C: Gershwin, George; L: Gershwin, Ira); Funny Face [1] (C: Gershwin, George; L: Gershwin, Ira); Think Pink!; Hold It! [2]; Bonjour, Paree!; 'S Wonderful (C: Gershwin, George; L: Gershwin, Ira); He Loves and She Loves [1] (C: Gershwin, George; L: Gershwin, Ira); Clap Yo' Hands [3] (C: Gershwin, George; L: Gershwin, Ira); Let's Kiss and Make Up [1] (C: Gershwin, George; L: Gershwin, Ira)

Notes Paramount bought the project, then titled WEDDING DAY, from MGM; it included the talents of Roger Edens, Fred Astaire and Stanley Donen. [1] Additional lyrics by Leonard Gershe and Roger Edens. [2] Not used. [3] Additional music by Roger Edens.

1986 ✦ FUNNY GIRL
Columbia, 1968

Composer(s) Styne, Jule
Lyricist(s) Merrill, Bob
Choreographer(s) Ross, Herbert

Producer(s) Stark, Ray
Director(s) Wyler, William
Screenwriter(s) Lennart, Isobel
Source(s) *Funny Girl* (musical) Lennart, Isobel; Styne, Jule; Merrill, Bob

Cast Streisand, Barbra; Sharif, Omar; Medford, Kay; Francis, Anne; Pidgeon, Walter; Allen, Lee; Questel, Mae; Mohr, Gerald; Faylen, Frank; Lawrence, Mittie

Song(s) If a Girl Isn't Pretty; I'm the Greatest Star; Roller Skate Rag [1]; Nicky Arnstein; His Love Makes Me Beautiful; People; You Are Woman, I Am Man; Don't Rain on My Parade; Sadie, Sadie; The Swan [1]; Funny Girl [1]; Pink Velvet Jail [1] [2]; Who Taught Her Everything She Knows [2]

Notes The Autumn Bride was dubbed by Betty Wand. There are also vocals of "I'd Rather Be Blue" by Fred Fisher and Billy Rose; "Second Hand Rose" by Grant Clarke and James F. Hanley (also in MY MAN); and "My Man" by Maurice Yvain, A. Willemetz, Jacques Charles and Channing Pollock (also in the Warner film MY MAN). One cue sheet lists "Cornet Man" but the song does not appear in any prints or listed in any other source. [1] Written for film. All other songs are from the original stage musical which also starred Barbra Streisand. [2] Prerecorded but not used. Cue sheet reads "Locked in a Pink Satin Jail." There is also a prerecording of an unused reprise of "Don't Rain on My Parade."

1987 ✦ FUNNY LADY
Columbia, 1975

Musical Score Hamlisch, Marvin
Composer(s) Kander, John
Lyricist(s) Ebb, Fred
Choreographer(s) Ross, Herbert

Producer(s) Stark, Ray
Director(s) Ross, Herbert
Screenwriter(s) Allen, Jay Presson; Schulman, Arnold
Source(s) (musical)

Cast Streisand, Barbra; Caan, James; Sharif, Omar; McDowall, Roddy; Vereen, Ben; Wells, Carole; Gates, Larry; O'Rourke, Heidi

Song(s) Blind Date; Nicky Arnstein [1] (C: Styne, Jule; L: Merrill, Bob); I Like Him; So Long Honey Lamb; How Lucky Can You Get; Isn't This Better; Let's Hear It for Me

Notes [1] Written for FUNNY GIRL Broadway show. There are also vocals of "More Than You Know" by Vincent Youmans, Billy Rose and Edward Eliscu; "It's Only a Paper Moon" by Harold Arlen, Billy Rose and

E.Y. Harburg (from the play THE GREAT MAGOO and also in the Paramount film TAKE A CHANCE); "Beautiful Face, Have a Heart" by Fred Fisher, Billy Rose and James V. Monaco; "I Found a Million Dollar Baby (In a Five and Ten Cent Store)" by Harry Warren, Billy Rose and Mort Dixon (also in the Warner Brothers' MILLION DOLLAR BABY); "Fifty Million Frenchmen Can't Be Wrong" by Fred Fisher, Billy Rose and William Raskin; "Clap Hands Here Comes Charley" by Joseph Meyer, Billy Rose and Ballard Macdonald; "If You Want the Rainbow" by Oscar Levant, Billy Rose and Mort Dixon; "Am I Blue?" by Harry Akst and Grant Clarke; "I Got a Code in My Doze" by Billy Rose, Arthur Fields and Fred Hall; "Great Day" by Vincent Youmans, Billy Rose and Edward Eliscu; "If I Love Again" by Ben Oakland and J.P. Murray and "Me and My Shadow" by Al Jolson, Dave Dreyer and Billy Rose.

1988 ✦ FUNNY PAGE
Paramount, 1933 unproduced

Composer(s) Gensler, Lewis E.
Lyricist(s) Thompson, Harlan

Song(s) Shanty; Song of the Cannibals; Blondie; It Looks to Me Like Love [1]; The Ark That Boob Built

Notes [1] Later considered for FOUR HOURS TO KILL.

1989 ✦ A FUNNY THING HAPPENED ON THE WAY TO THE FORUM
United Artists, 1966

Musical Score Thorne, Ken
Composer(s) Sondheim, Stephen [2]
Lyricist(s) Sondheim, Stephen [2]
Choreographer(s) Martin, George; Martin, Ethel

Producer(s) Frank, Melvin
Director(s) Lester, Richard
Screenwriter(s) Frank, Melvin; Pertwee, Michael
Source(s) *A Funny Thing Happened on the Way to the Forum* (musical) Sondheim, Stephen; Gelbart, Larry; Shevelove, Burt

Cast Mostel, Zero [2]; Gilford, Jack [2]; Crawford, Michael; Andre, Annette; Keaton, Buster [1]; Silvers, Phil; Jessel, Patricia; Hordern, Michael; Greene, Leon

Song(s) Comedy Tonight; Lovely; Everybody Ought to Have a Maid; Bring Me My Bride; Dirge

Notes [1] Keaton's last film. [2] From Broadway original.

1990 ✦ FUN TIME
Paramount, 1944

Producer(s) Harris, Lou
Director(s) Shea, William
Screenwriter(s) Brode, Robert Stephen

Cast Neill, Noel; Foy Jr., Eddie

Song(s) When Birds Want Romance [1] (C/L: Harris, Harry; Lee, Lester)

Notes Short subject. "Did You Ever See a Dream Walking" by Mack Gordon and Harry Revel is also given a vocal treatment. [1] Originally titled "How About You and Me."

1991 ◆ FUN WITH DICK AND JANE
Columbia, 1977

Musical Score Gold, Ernest; Goldenberg, Billy
Composer(s) Dozier, Lamont; Page, Gene
Lyricist(s) Dozier, Lamont; Page, Gene

Producer(s) Bart, Peter; Pavlesky, Max
Director(s) Kotcheff, Ted
Screenwriter(s) Giler, David; Belson, Jerry; Richler, Mordecai

Cast Segal, George; Fonda, Jane; McMahon, Ed; Gautier, Dick; Miller, Allan; Garcia, Hank

Song(s) Ahead of the Game (C/L: Barnes, Peter; Morgan, Michael); Love Ain't Nothing but a Game; While the Cat's Away; Straw Boss

1992 ◆ FUN WITH MR. FUTURE
Disney, 1982

Musical Score McIntosh, Tom

Song(s) There's a Great Big Beautiful Tomorrow [1] (C/L: Sherman, Richard M.; Sherman, Robert B.)

Notes Short subject. No credit sheet available. [1] This song was written for the General Electric exhibit at the 1964-65 New York World's Fair.

1993 ◆ THE FURIES
Paramount, 1950

Musical Score Waxman, Franz

Producer(s) Wallis, Hal B.
Director(s) Mann, Anthony
Screenwriter(s) Schnee, Charles
Source(s) *The Furies* (novel) Busch, Niven

Cast Stanwyck, Barbara; Huston, Walter; Anderson, Judith; Corey, Wendell; Roland, Gilbert; Gomez, Thomas; Bondi, Beulah; Dekker, Albert; Yurka, Blanche

Song(s) T.C. Roundup Time (C/L: Livingston, Jay; Evans, Ray)

Notes There is also a vocal of the traditional song "The Trail to Mexico."

1994 ◆ THE FURY
Twentieth Century–Fox, 1978

Musical Score Williams, John

Producer(s) Yablans, Frank
Director(s) De Palma, Brian
Screenwriter(s) Farris, John
Source(s) *The Fury* (novel) Farris, John

Cast Douglas, Kirk; Cassavetes, John; Snodgress, Carrie; Durning, Charles; Irving, Amy; Lewis, Fiona; Stevens, Andrew

Song(s) I'm Tired (C: Williams, John; L: Williams, Joseph); Hold You [1] (C: Williams, John; L: Williams, Joseph)

Notes [1] Sheet music only.

G

1995 ✦ GABRIELA
Allianz, 1950

Musical Score Jary, Michael
Composer(s) Jary, Michael
Lyricist(s) Schwebach, Kurt; Wyner, Joe

Producer(s) Trebitsch, Gyula
Director(s) von Cziffra, Geza
Screenwriter(s) von Cziffra, Geza

Cast Leander, Zarah; Raddatz, Carl; Molnar, Vera

Song(s) A Woman's a Fool; Floating There Afar; When Will You Ask Me (L: Schwebach, Kurt; von Cziffra, Geza)

Notes A German film released in the U.S.

1996 ✦ GABRIELLA
United Artists, 1982

Musical Score Jobim, Antonio Carlos
Composer(s) Jobim, Antonio Carlos
Lyricist(s) Jobim, Antonio Carlos

Producer(s) Nebenzal, Harold; Moussa, Ibrahim
Director(s) Barreto, Bruno
Screenwriter(s) Serran, Leopoldo; Barreto, Bruno
Source(s) (novel) Armado, Jorge

Cast Braga, Sonia; Mastroianni, Marcello; Cantafora, Antonio; Goulart, Paulo

Song(s) Origins; Fejao na Panela; Caminho da Mata; Lament; Gabriela

1997 ✦ THE GAIETY GIRLS
United Artists, 1938

Composer(s) Spoliansky, Mischa
Lyricist(s) Kernell, William

Director(s) Freeland, Thornton
Screenwriter(s) MacRae, Arthur

Cast Hulbert, Jack; Ellis, Patricia; Riscoe, Arthur; Withers, Googie; Fairbrother, Sydney; Watson, Wylie; Tree, David; Culver, Roland

Song(s) When You Hear Music; It's a Paradise for Two; Kiss Me Good Night

Notes No cue sheet available. Titled PARADISE FOR TWO in England, where it was produced.

1998 ✦ GAILY, GAILY
United Artists, 1969

Musical Score Mancini, Henry
Composer(s) Mancini, Henry
Lyricist(s) Bergman, Marilyn; Bergman, Alan

Producer(s) Jewison, Norman
Director(s) Jewison, Norman
Screenwriter(s) Ginnes, Abram S.
Source(s) *Gaily, Gaily* (book) Hecht, Ben

Cast Bridges, Beau; Mercouri, Melina; Keith, Brian; Kennedy, George; Cronyn, Hume; Kidder, Margot; Hyde-White, Wilfrid

Song(s) Tomorrow Is My Friend; There's Enough to Go Around; Gaily Gaily [1]

Notes [1] Not used.

1999 ✦ GALA DAY AT DISNEYLAND
Disney, 1959

Musical Score Bruns, George

Producer(s) Luske, Hamilton
Screenwriter(s) Clemmons, Larry

Song(s) Climb the Mountain [1] (C: Marks, Franklyn; L: Dunham, "By"); La Gaviota (C: Bruns, George; L: Adair, Tom)

Notes Short subject. [1] Also in THIRD MAN ON THE MOUNTAIN.

2000 ✦ GALLAGHER
Disney, 1964

Musical Score Brunner, Robert F.

Song(s) Gallagher (C/L: Sherman, Richard M.; Sherman, Robert B.)

Notes No other information available.

2001 ✦ THE GALLANT HOURS
United Artists, 1960

Musical Score Wagner, Roger
Composer(s) Wagner, Roger
Lyricist(s) Costello, Ward

Producer(s)   Montgomery, Robert
Director(s)   Montgomery, Robert
Screenwriter(s)   Gilroy, Frank D.; Lay Jr., Beirne

Cast   Cagney, James; Weaver, Dennis; Jaeckel, Richard

Song(s)   The Gallant Hours; Remembrance; I Know a Man

2002 ✦ THE GALLANT LEGION
Republic, 1948

Composer(s)   Elliott, Jack
Lyricist(s)   Elliott, Jack

Producer(s)   Kane, Joseph
Director(s)   Kane, Joseph
Screenwriter(s)   Adams, Gerald Drayson

Cast   Elliott, William; Booth, Adrian; Schildkraut, Joseph; Cabot, Bruce; Devine, Andy; Withers, Grant; Mara, Adele; Rawlinson, Herbert

Song(s)   Lady From Monterey; Kiss or Two; A Gambler's Life

2003 ✦ GALS, INCORPORATED
Universal, 1943

Composer(s)   Rosen, Milton
Lyricist(s)   Carter, Everett
Choreographer(s)   Hilton, Arthur

Producer(s)   Cowan, Will
Director(s)   Goodwins, Leslie
Screenwriter(s)   Dein, Edward

Cast   Errol, Leon; Hilliard, Harriet; McDonald, Grace; Kean, Betty; Glen Gray and His Casa Loma Orchestra; The Pied Pipers

Song(s)   Hep! Hep! Hooray!; All The Time It's You; Take It and Git [1] (C/L: Chapman, William; Chapman, Melvin; Marshall, James T.; Green, Johnny); Here's Your Kiss

Notes   There are also vocals of "Brazil" by S.K. Russell and Ary Barroso; "Can't Get Stuff in Your Cuff" by Sy Oliver and Sammy Cahn and "What Can I Say After I Say I'm Sorry" by Walter Donaldson and Abe Lyman. [1] Also in HOW'S ABOUT IT.

2004 ✦ THE GAL WHO TOOK THE WEST
Universal, 1949

Musical Score   Skinner, Frank

Producer(s)   Arthur, Robert
Director(s)   de Cordova, Frederick
Screenwriter(s)   Bowers, William; Brodney, Oscar

Cast   Todd, James; Brady, Scott; Russell, John; De Carlo, Yvonne; Bevans, Clem; Stevenson, Houseley; Simpson, Russell; Coburn, Charles

Song(s)   Killarney (C: Traditional; L: Brooks, Jack); Frankie and Johnny (C: Traditional; L: Brooks, Jack)

Notes   Brooks wrote special lyrics for this film. There is also a vocal of "Clancy Lowered the Boom" by Johnny Lange and Hy Heath.

2005 ✦ GAMBIT
Universal, 1966

Musical Score   Jarre, Maurice

Producer(s)   Fuchs, Leo L.
Director(s)   Neame, Ronald
Screenwriter(s)   Davies, Jack; Sargent, Alvin
Source(s)   "Who Is Mr. Dean" (story) Carroll, Sidney

Cast   Caine, Michael; MacLaine, Shirley; Lom, Herbert

Song(s)   I'm Gonna Spread My Wings (C: MacKay, Harper; L: Godkin, Paul)

2006 ✦ THE GAMBLER FROM NATCHEZ
Twentieth Century–Fox, 1954

Producer(s)   Goldstein, Leonard
Director(s)   Levin, Henry
Screenwriter(s)   Adams, Gerald Drayson; Wallace, Irving

Cast   Robertson, Dale; Paget, Debra; Gomez, Thomas; Daniels, Lisa; McCarthy, Kevin; Novello, Jay; Strode, Woody

Song(s)   Rami Ramineau (Chimney Sweep) (C/L: Hairston, Jester)

2007 ✦ GAMBLING
Fox, 1934

Producer(s)   Franklin, Harold B.
Director(s)   Lee, Rowland V.
Screenwriter(s)   Graham, Barrett
Source(s)   (play) Cohan, George M.

Cast   Cohan, George M.; Burgess, Dorothy; Gibson, Wynne

Song(s)   Dr. Watson and Mr. Holmes (C: Hannighen, Bernie; L: Mercer, Johnny)

Notes   There is also a vocal of "My Little Girl" by George M. Cohan.

2008 ✦ GAME OF DEATH
Columbia, 1979

Musical Score   Barry, John

Producer(s)   Chow, Raymond
Director(s)   Clouse, Robert
Screenwriter(s)   Spears, Jan

Cast   Lee, Bruce; Young, Gig; Jagger, Dean; O'Brian, Hugh; Camp, Colleen; Wall, Robert; Novak, Mel; Abdul-Jabbar, Kareem; Norris, Chuck

Song(s)   Will This Be the Song I'll Be Singing Tomorrow (C/L: Barry, John)

Notes   No cue sheet available.

2009 ✦ THE GAMES
Twentieth Century–Fox, 1970

Musical Score Lai, Francis
Composer(s) Lai, Francis
Lyricist(s) Shaper, Hal

Producer(s) Linsk, Lester
Director(s) Winner, Michael
Screenwriter(s) Segal, Erich
Source(s) (book) Atkinson, Hugh

Cast Crawford, Michael; Baker, Stanley; O'Neal, Ryan; Aznavour, Charles; Kemp, Jeremy; Smith, Kent

Song(s) From Denver to L.A.; This Lovely Night; Warm Summer Rain; My Love (C/L: Villar, Ray)

2010 ✦ THE GANG'S ALL HERE
Twentieth Century–Fox, 1943

Composer(s) Warren, Harry
Lyricist(s) Robin, Leo
Choreographer(s) Berkeley, Busby

Producer(s) LeBaron, William
Director(s) Berkeley, Busby
Screenwriter(s) Bullock, Walter

Cast Faye, Alice; Miranda, Carmen; Baker, Phil; Benny Goodman and His Orchestra; Pallette, Eugene; Greenwood, Charlotte; Horton, Edward Everett; De Marco, Tony; Ellison, James; Ryan, Sheila; Willock, Dave

Song(s) You Discover You're in New York; Minnie's in the Money [1]; A Journey to a Star; The Lady in the Tutti Frutti Hat; Silent Senorita; No Love, No Nothin' [2]; Paducah; The Polka Dot Polka; Soft Winds (Inst.) [5] (C: Goodman, Benny); The Jitters (Inst.) [4] (C: Rose, Gene); The Polka Dot Ballet (Inst.) (C: Raksin, David); Carnival [6]; Drums and Dreams [7]

Notes Titled THE GIRL HE LEFT BEHIND in Great Britain. Four bars of "I've Got a Gal in Kalamazoo" by Harry Warren and Mack Gordon are also used vocally. There is also a vocal of "Brazil" ("Aquarela Do Brasil") by Ary Barroso. [1] Arrangement by Eddie Sauter. [2] Arrangement by Benny Carter. [3] Robin wrote another song with the same name for RIDING HIGH (1943) but it wasn't used. [4] Mrs. Potter and Beezy dance. [5] Andy and Eadie dance. [6] Not in cue sheet but in Thomas' biography of Warren. [7] Not used.

2011 ✦ GANGS OF SONORA
Republic, 1941

Producer(s) Gray, Louis
Director(s) English, John
Screenwriter(s) De Mond, Albert; Schroeder, Doris
Source(s) characters by MacDonald, William Colt

Cast Livingston, Robert; Steele, Bob; Davis, Rufe; Johnson, June; McTaggart, Ward; MacKellar, Helen; Frazer, Robert

Song(s) Printer's Lament (C: Styne, Jule; L: Meyer, Sol)

2012 ✦ GANGSTER'S BOY
Monogram, 1938

Director(s) Nigh, William
Screenwriter(s) Andrews, Robert; Brown, Karl

Cast Cooper, Jackie; Warwick, Robert; Lorimer, Louise; Jackson, Selmer; Wonder, Tommy; Blythe, Betty

Song(s) Stop Beatin' Round the Mulberry Bush (C/L: Boland, Clay; Reichner, Bickley)

Notes No cue sheet available.

2013 ✦ GANGSTERS OF THE FRONTIER
Producers Releasing Corporation, 1944

Musical Score Zahler, Lee; Grigor, Nico

Producer(s) Alexander, Arthur
Director(s) Clifton, Elmer
Screenwriter(s) Clifton, Elmer

Cast Ritter, Tex; O'Brien, Dave; Wilkerson, Guy; McCarthy, Patti; Miles, Betty; King, Charles

Song(s) Please Remember Me (C/L: Ritter, Tex); He's Gone Up the Trail [1] (C/L: Spencer, Tim); Ride, Ranger, Ride [2] (C/L: Spencer, Tim)

Notes [1] Also in SONS OF THE PIONEERS (Republic). [2] Also in THE BIG SHOW, KING OF THE COWBOYS and RIDE, RANGER, RIDE (all Republic) and TEXANS NEVER CRY (Columbia).

2014 ✦ GANG WAR
FBO Pictures, 1928

Director(s) Glennon, Bert
Screenwriter(s) Woolf, Edgar Allan

Cast Raker, Lorin; Albertson, Mabel; Mc Kee, Jack; Hartman, David; Borden, Olive; Pickford, Jack; Gribbon, Eddie; Long, Walter; Chews, Frank

Song(s) Low Down (C/L: Trent, Jo; De Rose, Peter); I Love Me (C/L: Mahoney, Will); My Suppressed Desire (C: Cohn, Chester; L: Miller, Ned); Ya Comin' Up Tonight - Huh? (C/L: Sherman, Al; Lewis, Al; Lyman, Abe)

Notes No cue sheet available.

2015 ✦ GANGWAY FOR TOMORROW
RKO, 1943

Musical Score Webb, Roy

Producer(s) Auer, John H.
Director(s) Auer, John H.
Screenwriter(s) Oboler, Arch

Cast Margo; Carradine, John; Ryan, Robert; Ward, Amelita; Terry, William; Davenport, Harry; Bell, James; Carney, Alan

Song(s) C'est Mon Couer [1] (C/L: Morgan, Stephen); Je Cherche Un Homme (C/L: Clarke,

Gordon); Humpty Dumpty Heart [2] (C: Van Heusen, James; L: Burke, Johnny)

Notes   [1] Also in JOURNEY INTO FEAR and VARIETY TIME. [2] Also in PLAYMATES.

2016   ✦   THE GARBAGE PAIL KIDS MOVIE
Atlantic, 1987

Musical Score   Lloyd, Michael; D'Andrea, John; Smalley, Jack

Producer(s)   Amateau, Rod
Director(s)   Amateau, Rod
Screenwriter(s)   Palmer, Melinda; Amateau, Rod

Cast   Newley, Anthony; Astin, Mackenzie; Barberi, Katie; MacLachlan, Ron; Amateau, J.P.

Song(s)   The Working Song (C/L: Tyrell, Stephanie; Hall, Ashley); You Can Be a Garbage Pail Kid (C/L: Lloyd, Michael)

Notes   No cue sheet available.

2017   ✦   GARBANCITO DE LA MANCHA
Twentieth Century–Fox, 1945

Composer(s)   Guerrero, Jacinto
Lyricist(s)   Guerrero, Jacinto

Song(s)   Beloj; Cancion de los Gusamos (C/L: Bisbe, J.); Garbancito y Gallinas; Cancion del Labrador; Madre y Garbancito; Cancion Chopos; Isle de las Hades; Lenador y Garbancito; A Tres Ninos Melos Entran Castillo; Garbancito Perdido en el Desierto; Garbancito y Caramanca

Notes   No other information available.

2018   ✦   GARDEN OF EVIL
Twentieth Century–Fox, 1954

Musical Score   Herrmann, Bernard

Producer(s)   Brackett, Charles
Director(s)   Hathaway, Henry
Screenwriter(s)   Fenton, Frank

Cast   Cooper, Gary; Hayward, Susan; Widmark, Richard; Marlowe, Hugh; Mitchell, Cameron; Moreno, Rita

Song(s)   Aqui [1] (C: Newman, Lionel; L: Darby, Ken)

Notes   "La Negra Noche" by Emilio D. Uranga is also used vocally. [1] Based on the traditional Mexican folk song "La Paloma Axul."

2019   ✦   GARDEN OF THE MOON
Warner Brothers–First National, 1938

Composer(s)   Warren, Harry
Lyricist(s)   Mercer, Johnny; Dubin, Al

Producer(s)   Edelman, Louis F.
Director(s)   Berkeley, Busby
Screenwriter(s)   Wald, Jerry; Macaulay, Richard

Cast   O'Brien, Pat; Lindsay, Margaret; Payne, John; Davis, Johnnie; Cooper, Melville; Jeans, Isabel; Todd, Mabel; Singleton, Penny; Purcell, Dick; Bois, Curt; Bates, Granville; Colonna, Jerry; Fidler, Jimmy; Joe Venuti and His Swing Cats; Mayer, Ray

Song(s)   Confidentially; Garden of the Moon; Love Is Where You Find It; The Lady on the Two Cent Stamp; The Girl Friend of the Whirling Dervish

2020   ✦   GAS
Paramount, 1981

Musical Score   Zaza, Paul

Producer(s)   Heroux, Claude
Director(s)   Rose, Les
Screenwriter(s)   Wolf, Richard A.

Cast   Anspach, Susan; Mandel, Howie; Hayden, Sterling; Shaver, Helen; Currie, Sandee; Aykroyd, Peter; Sutherland, Donald

Song(s)   Gas (C: Terry, George; L: Woodson, Kitty)

Notes   No cue sheet available.

2021   ✦   GAS HOUSE KIDS GO WEST
PRC, 1947

Musical Score   Sommer, Hans

Producer(s)   Baerwitz, Sam
Director(s)   Beaudine, William
Screenwriter(s)   Kent, Robert E.

Cast   Switzer, Carl "Alfalfa"; Bartlett, Bennie; Wissler, Rudy; Bond, Tommy; Williams, Chili

Song(s)   West of the Pecos [1] (C/L: Gates, V.W.)

Notes   [1] Also in RANGE BEYOND THE BLUE.

2022   ✦   GAS HOUSE KIDS IN HOLLYWOOD
PRC, 1947

Musical Score   Glasser, Albert

Producer(s)   Baerwitz, Sam
Director(s)   Cahn, Edward L.
Screenwriter(s)   Kent, Robert E.

Cast   Switzer, Carl "Alfalfa"; Wissler, Rudy; Bartlett, Bennie; Bond, Tommy; Burke, James

Song(s)   I'm So in Love (C: Kent, Walter; L: Gannon, Kim)

2023   ✦   GATOR
United Artists, 1976

Musical Score   Bernstein, Charles

Producer(s)   Levy, Jules V.; Gardner, Arthur
Director(s)   Reynolds, Burt
Screenwriter(s)   Norton, William

Cast Reynolds, Burt; Douglas, Mike; Reed, Jerry; Weston, Jack; Hutton, Lauren; Ghostley, Alice

Song(s) The Ballad of Gator McKlusky (Gator) (C/L: Hubbard, Jerry R.); Hey Country Girl (C/L: Richards, Rusty); For a Little While (C/L: Goldsboro, Bobby)

Notes A sequel to WHITE LIGHTNING.

2024 ✦ GATORBAIT
Sebastian Films, 1979

Musical Score Sebastian, Ferd

Producer(s) Sebastian, Ferd; Sebastian, Beverly C.
Director(s) Sebastian, Ferd; Sebastian, Beverly C.
Screenwriter(s) Sebastian, Beverly C.

Cast Jennings, Claudia; Gilman, Sam; Dirkson, Doug; Sebastian, Ben; Sebastian, Tracy

Song(s) Desiree (C: Sebastian, Ferd; L: Sebastian, Beverly C.)

Notes No cue sheet available.

2025 ✦ GAUCHO SERENADE
Republic, 1940

Producer(s) Berke, William
Director(s) McDonald, Frank
Screenwriter(s) Ropes, Bradford; Burbridge, Betty

Cast Autry, Gene; Burnette, Smiley; Storey, June; Lee, Mary; Renaldo, Duncan; Severn Jr., Clifford; Crehan, Joseph

Song(s) Keep Rollin' Lazy Longhorns (C/L: Autry, Gene; Marvin, Johnny); A Song at Sunset (C/L: Autry, Gene; Marvin, Johnny; Tobias, Harry); Headin' for the Wide Open Spaces (C/L: Autry, Gene; Marvin, Johnny; Tobias, Harry); Give Out with a Song (C/L: Lee, Connie); Something About the West (C: Marvin, Johnny; L: Tobias, Harry)

Notes No cue sheet available.

2026 ✦ THE GAY BARKLEYS

See THE BARKLEYS OF BROADWAY.

2027 ✦ THE GAY BRIDE
Metro–Goldwyn–Mayer, 1934

Musical Score Virgil, Jack

Producer(s) Considine Jr., John W.
Director(s) Conway, Jack
Screenwriter(s) Spewack, Bella; Spewack, Sam
Source(s) "Repeal" (story) Coe, Charles Francis

Cast Lombard, Carole; Morris, Chester; Carrillo, Leo; Hardy, Sam; Pitts, ZaSu; Pendleton, Nat

Song(s) Mississippi Honeymoon (C: Donaldson, Walter; L: Kahn, Gus)

2028 ✦ THE GAY DESPERADO
United Artists, 1936

Producer(s) Pickford, Mary; Lasky, Jesse L.
Director(s) Mamoulian, Rouben
Screenwriter(s) Smith, Wallace

Cast Martini, Nino; Carrillo, Leo; Lupino, Ida; Huber, Harold; Auer, Mischa; Blakely, James; Fields, Stanley; Rosely, Adrian

Song(s) The World Is Mine Tonight (C: Posford, George; L: Marvell, Holt); Farewell My Country (C: Sandoval, Miguel; L: Mitchell, Sidney D.); A Gay Ranchero (C: Espinosa, J.J.; L: Luban, Francia; Tuvim, Abe); Gypsy Lament (C/L: Powell, Teddy; Samuels, Walter G. G.; Whitcup, Leonard; Grever, Maria)

Notes No cue sheet available.

2029 ✦ THE GAY DIVORCEE
RKO, 1934

Composer(s) Revel, Harry
Lyricist(s) Gordon, Mack
Choreographer(s) Gould, Dave

Producer(s) Berman, Pandro S.
Director(s) Sandrich, Mark
Screenwriter(s) Marion Jr., George; Yost, Dorothy; Kaufman, Edward
Source(s) *The Gay Divorce* (musical) Taylor, Dwight; Porter, Cole

Cast Astaire, Fred; Rogers, Ginger; Brady, Alice; Horton, Edward Everett; Rhodes, Erik; Blore, Eric; Miles, Lillian; Grable, Betty

Song(s) Don't Let It Bother You [1]; A Needle in a Haystack (C/L: Magidson, Herb; Conrad, Con); Let's Knock Knees; Night and Day [2] (C/L: Porter, Cole); The Continental (C: Conrad, Con; L: Magidson, Herb)

Notes [1] Also in JOAN OF PARIS. [2] Also in ROSALIE (MGM) and NIGHT AND DAY (Warner).

2030 ✦ THE GAY NINETIES

See THE FLORODORA GIRL.

2031 ✦ GAY PURR-EE
Warner Brothers, 1962

Musical Score Lindsey, Mort
Composer(s) Arlen, Harold
Lyricist(s) Harburg, E.Y.

Producer(s) Saperstein, Henry J.
Director(s) Levitow, Abe
Screenwriter(s) Jones, Dorothy; Jones, Chuck
Voices Garland, Judy; Buttons, Red; Goulet, Robert; Gingold, Hermione; Frees, Paul; Amsterdam, Morey; Blanc, Mel; Bennett, Julie; Gardner, Joan

Song(s) Take My Hand Paree; Mewsette; Little Drops of Rain; Paris Is a Lonely Town; Roses Red, Violets Blue; The Money Cat; The Horse Won't Talk; Bubbles

Notes An animated cartoon feature.

2032 ◆ THE GAY RANCHERO
Republic, 1947

Producer(s) White, Edward J.
Director(s) Witney, William
Screenwriter(s) Nibley, Sloan

Cast Rogers, Roy; Trigger; Guizar, Tito; Frazee, Jane; Devine, Andy; Rodriguez, Estelita; Meeker, George; Mason, LeRoy; Moore, Dennis; Richards, Keith; Gagnon, Betty; Rose, Robert; Bob Nolan and the Sons of the Pioneers

Song(s) The Gay Ranchero (Las Altenitas) [1] (C: Espinosa, J.J.; L: Tuvim, Abe; Luban, Francia); Wait'll I Get My Sunshine in the Moonlight (C/L: Glick, Harry; Lambert, Jack; Olson, D.); Cowboy Country (C/L: Spencer, Tim)

Notes There are also vocals of "Granada" by Augustin Lara and "You Belong to My Heart" (also in THE BIG SOMBRERO, THE THREE CABALLEROS and MR. IMPERIUM) by Augustin Lara and Ray Gilbert. [1] English lyrics by Tuvim and Luban. Also in KING OF THE COWBOYS and in THE GAY RANCHERO (1942).

2033 ◆ THE GAY SENORITA
Columbia, 1945

Producer(s) Gorney, Jay
Director(s) Dreifuss, Arthur
Screenwriter(s) Eliscu, Edward

Cast Falkenburg, Jinx; Bannon, Jim; Cochran, Steve; Sylva, Marguerita; Mura, Corinna; Amaral, Nestor; Oliveira, Jose

Song(s) Linda Mujer (You Never Say Yes) [2] (C: Duchesne, Raphael; L: Caesar, Irving); Samba Lele (C/L: Barbosa, Paulo); Llanero Es (Joropo Venezolano) (C/L: Matos, Manuel); Buenas Noches (C/L: Walter, Serge; George, Don); Negra Leono [3] (C/L: Walter, Serge; George, Don); Tico Tico No Fuba [4] (C: Abreu, Zequinha; L: Oliveira, Aloysio; Drake, Ervin; Marcotte, Don); Lincoln and Juarez (C: Gorney, Jay; L: Eliscu, Edward; Myers, Henry); Alla En El Rancho Grande [1] (C: Ramos, Silvano; L: Costello, Bartley); Te Quiero Besar [5] (C/L: Matos, Manuel)

Notes [1] This song was deleted from prints after 1962. The original Spanish lyricist is J. Dal Moral. The song was previously used in TAHITI NIGHTS. [2] The original Spanish lyrics are by Duchesne. The Spanish version was used in THRILL OF BRAZIL. [3] Also used in THE HEAT'S ON, PAN AMERICANA (RKO) and SLIGHTLY SCANDALOUS (Universal) and credited to

Antonio Fernandez. [4] This film is the only one to give credit to Don Marcotte. Also in KANSAS CITY KITTY, COPACABANA (UA), BATHING BEAUTY (MGM), BOMBALERA (Paramount) and IT'S A PLEASURE (RKO). [5] Sheet music only.

2034 ◆ THE GAZEBO
Metro–Goldwyn–Mayer, 1960

Musical Score Alexander, Jeff

Producer(s) Weingarten, Lawrence
Director(s) Marshall, George
Screenwriter(s) Wells, George
Source(s) *The Gazebo* (play) Coppel, Alec

Cast Reynolds, Debbie; Ford, Glenn; Reiner, Carl; McGiver, John; Albertson, Mabel; Merande, Doro; Landau, Martin

Song(s) Something Called Love (C: Kent, Walter; L: Farrar, Walton)

2035 ◆ THE GEISHA BOY
Paramount, 1958

Musical Score Scharf, Walter

Producer(s) Lewis, Jerry
Director(s) Tashlin, Frank
Screenwriter(s) Tashlin, Frank

Cast Lewis, Jerry; Pleshette, Suzanne; McDonald, Marie; Hayakawa, Sessue; MacLane, Barton; McCarthy, Nobu

Song(s) The Geisha Boy [1] (C: Scharf, Walter; L: Brooks, Jack)

Notes [1] Used instrumentally only.

2036 ◆ GENE AUTRY AND THE MOUNTIES
Columbia, 1951

Producer(s) Schaefer, Armand
Director(s) English, John
Screenwriter(s) Hall, Norman S.

Cast Autry, Gene; Buttram, Pat; Verdugo, Elena; Young, Carleton; Rawlinson, Herbert; Champion; Gray, Billy

Song(s) The Blue Canadian Rockies [1] (C/L: Unknown); Onterro (C/L: Unknown)

Notes No cue sheet available. [1] Also in BLUE CANADIAN ROCKIES.

2037 ◆ THE GENE KRUPA STORY
Columbia, 1959

Musical Score Stevens, Leith

Producer(s) Waxman, Philip A.
Director(s) Weis, Don
Screenwriter(s) Jannings, Orin

Cast Mineo, Sal; Nichols, Red; Darren, James; Kohner, Susan; Craig, Yvonne; Troup, Bobby; O'Day, Anita; Lester, Buddy; Manne, Shelly; MacLeod, Gavin

Notes There are no original songs in this picture. Those that receive vocal renditions include "Royal Garden Blues" by Clarence Williams and Spencer Williams; "Way Down Yonder in New Orleans" by Henry Creamer and Turner Layton; "I Love My Baby" by Bud Green and Harry Warren; "Sunny Side of the Street" by Dorothy Fields and Jimmy McHugh; "Indiana" by James F. Hanley and Ballard Macdonald; "Cherokee" by Ray Noble; "Memories of You" by Andy Razaf and Eubie Blake; "I Love You, I Love You" by Art Fitch, Kay Fitch and Bert Lowe; "In the Mood" by Andy Razaf and Joseph Garland; "Song of India" by Rimsky-Korsakoff; "Let There Be Love" by Ian Grand and Lionel Rand and "Exactly Like You" by Dorothy Fields and Jimmy McHugh.

2038 ✦ GENERATION
Avco Embassy, 1969

Producer(s) Brisson, Frederick
Director(s) Schaefer, George
Screenwriter(s) Goodhart, William
Source(s) *Generation* (play) Goodhart, William

Cast Janssen, David; Darby, Kim; Reiner, Carl; Duel, Peter; Prine, Andrew; Coco, James; Waterston, Sam

Song(s) Generation (C/L: Fekaris, Dino; Zesses, Nick; Verdi, Bea)

Notes No cue sheet available.

2039 ✦ GENTE ALEGRE
Paramount, 1935

Song(s) Through the Looking Glass (C/L: Alvarez, Mario); El Tenorio de Broadway (The Tenor of Broadway) (C: Gorney, Jay; L: Ribalto, J. Carner); Igual Que Tu (The Same of You) [1] (C: Gorney, Jay; Harburg, E.Y.); Pasion (C: Hajos, Karl; L: Grever, Maria); No Me Creas (Don't Believe Me) [1] [2] (C: Gorney, Jay; L: Harburg, E.Y.)

Notes [1] Spanish lyrics by Maria Grever. [2] Not used.

2040 ✦ GENTLEMEN ARE BORN
Warner Brothers–First National, 1934

Composer(s) Fain, Sammy
Lyricist(s) Kahal, Irving

Producer(s) Chodorov, Edward
Director(s) Green, Alfred E.
Screenwriter(s) Solow, Eugene; Johnson, Robert Lee

Cast Tone, Franchot; Muir, Jean; Lindsay, Margaret; Dvorak, Ann; Alexander, Ross; Foran, Dick; Gateson, Marjorie

Song(s) When the Roll Is Called Alma Mater [1]

Notes [1] Also in TROUBLE ALONG THE WAY.

2041 ✦ GENTLEMEN MARRY BRUNETTES
United Artists, 1955

Musical Score Farnon, Robert
Choreographer(s) Cole, Jack

Producer(s) Sale, Richard; Waterfield, Robert
Director(s) Sale, Richard
Screenwriter(s) Loos, Mary; Sale, Richard

Cast Russell, Jane; Crain, Jeanne [1]; Young, Alan; Vallee, Rudy; Middleton, Guy; Brady, Scott [2]; Pohlmann, Eric; Mayne, Ferdy; Sachs, Leonard; Lorraine, Guido; Sydney, Derek

Song(s) Gentlemen Marry Brunettes (C/L: Hagen, Earle; Spencer, Herbert; Sale, Richard)

Notes There are also vocals of the following songs: "You're Driving Me Crazy" by Walter Donaldson; "Miss Annabelle Lee" by Sydney Clare and Lew Pollack; "I Wanna Be Loved By You" by Herbert Stothart, Harry Ruby and Bert Kalmar; "Ain't Misbehavin'" by Fats Waller, Harry Brooks and Andy Razaf; "Daddy" by Bobby Troup; and "Have You Met Miss Jones," "My Funny Valentine" and "I've Got Five Dollars" by Rodgers and Hart. [1] Dubbed by Anita Ellis. [2] Dubbed by Robert Farnon.

2042 ✦ GENTLEMEN OF POLISH
Metro–Goldwyn–Mayer, 1934

Director(s) Goulding, Alf

Cast Shaw and Lee

Song(s) Feelin' High (C: Donaldson, Walter; L: Dietz, Howard)

Notes Short subject.

2043 ✦ GENTLEMEN PREFER BLONDES
Twentieth Century–Fox, 1953

Composer(s) Styne, Jule
Lyricist(s) Robin, Leo
Choreographer(s) Cole, Jack

Producer(s) Siegel, Sol C.
Director(s) Hawks, Howard
Screenwriter(s) Lederer, Charles
Source(s) *Gentlemen Prefer Blondes* (musical) Fields, Joseph; Loos, Anita; Styne, Jule; Robin, Leo

Cast Russell, Jane [7]; Monroe, Marilyn [6]; Coburn, Charles; Reid, Elliott; Noonan, Tommy; Winslow, George; Dalio, Marcel; Holmes, Taylor; Varden, Norma; Wendell, Howard; Geray, Steven

Song(s) A Little Girl from Little Rock [1] [3]; Diamonds Are a Girl's Best Friend [1]; Bye Bye Baby

[1]; Ain't There Anyone Here for Love (C: Carmichael, Hoagy; L: Adamson, Harold); When Love Goes Wrong (Nothin' Goes Right) (C: Carmichael, Hoagy; L: Adamson, Harold); Definitely No (C/L: Schaefer, Hal); You're in Love [8] (C: Newman, Lionel; L: Daniel, Eliot); My Conversation [4] (C: Carmichael, Hoagy; L: Adamson, Harold); Make Me Make You Mine [2] (C: Carmichael, Hoagy; L: Adamson, Harold); (When the Wild Wild Women Go in Swimmin' Down in) Bimini Bay [2] (C: Carmichael, Hoagy; L: Adamson, Harold); Down Boy [2] [5] (C: Carmichael, Hoagy; L: Adamson, Harold); That's Where I'm So Different [2] (C: Carmichael, Hoagy; L: Adamson, Harold); April Springs [2] (C: Carmichael, Hoagy; L: Adamson, Harold); Love Will Soon Be Here [2] (C: Carmichael, Hoagy; L: Adamson, Harold); Could You Love a Dreamer [2]

Notes [1] From Broadway production. [2] Not used. [3] Special lyrics by Ken Darby and Eliot Daniel. [4] Not used but recorded. [5] Recorded as a test by Monroe. [6] Some notes dubbed by Marni Nixon. [7] Jane Russell appeared on the MGM soundtrack album, but when Fox produced an album 10 years later they did not have the rights to the Russell tracks. Eileen Wilson sang her songs on the Marilyn compilation album. [8] Also in MAN IN THE ATTIC.

2044 ♦ GEORGE WHITE'S SCANDALS (1945)
RKO, 1945

Composer(s) Fain, Sammy
Lyricist(s) Yellen, Jack
Choreographer(s) Matray, Ernst

Producer(s) White, George
Director(s) Feist, Felix E.
Screenwriter(s) Wedlock Jr., Hugh; Snyder, Howard; Levy, Parke; Green, Howard J.

Cast Davis, Joan; Haley, Jack; Terry, Phillip; Holliday, Martha; Smith, Ethel; Hamilton, Margaret; Tryon, Glenn; Greer, Bettejane; Young, Audrey; Murphy, Rose; Feld, Fritz; Wills, Beverly [1]; Gene Krupa and His Band

Song(s) How'd You Get Out of My Dreams; Life Is Just a Bowl of Cherries (C: Henderson, Ray; L: Brown, Lew); Leave Us Leap (Inst.) (C: Krupa, Gene); Wishing (C/L: DeSylva, B.G.); I Want to Be a Drummer; I Wake Up in the Morning; E.M.S. (C/L: Krupa, Gene); Who Killed Vaudeville [2]; Bolero in the Jungle (C/L: Krupa, Gene); Bouquet and Lace Ballet (Inst.) (C: Harline, Leigh); The Parrot [3] (C: Abreu, Zequinha; L: Drake, Ervin)

Notes [1] Joan Davis' daughter plays her mother as a child. [2] Also in MAKE MINE LAUGHS.

2045 ♦ GEORGE WHITE'S SCANDALS OF 1934
Fox, 1934

Composer(s) Henderson, Ray
Lyricist(s) Caesar, Irving; Yellen, Jack
Choreographer(s) Hale, George

Producer(s) Kane, Robert T.
Director(s) White, George; Lachman, Harry; Freeland, Thornton
Screenwriter(s) White, George; Yellen, Jack

Cast Vallee, Rudy; Durante, Jimmy; Faye, Alice; Ratoff, Gregory; Ames, Adrienne

Song(s) Hold My Hand; Nasty Man; So Nice; Cabin in the Cotton & Cotton in the Cabin (C/L: Caesar, Irving); Cabin Dance (Inst.) [1]; Following in Mother's Footsteps; My Dog Loves Your Dog; Sweet & Simple; Six Women (Me and Henry the Eighth); Every Day Is Father's Day with Baby

Notes There are brief vocal renditions of "Sentimental Gentleman from Georgia" and "Cabin in the Cotton" by Mitchell Parish and Frank Perkins; "Carolina in the Morning" by Walter Donaldson and Gus Kahn; "River Stay 'Way from My Door" by Harry Woods and Mort Dixon; "Got the South in My Soul" by Victor Young and Lee Wiley; "Lawd You Made the Night too Long" by Victor Young and Sam M. Lewis; "That's Why Darkies Were Born" by Lew Brown and Ray Henderson; "Annie Doesn't Live Here Anymore" by Joe Young, Joe Burke and Harold Spina and "Did You Ever See a Dream Walking" by Harry Revel and Mack Gordon. Moshier's *The Alice Faye Movie Book* lists the song "Picking Cotton" by B.G. De Sylva, Lew Brown and Ray Henderson but does not list the song "Cabin in the Cotton & Cotton in the Cabin." From an advertisement: "Surpassing George White's greatest successes. more romance . . . bigger stars . . . greater spectacle . . . faster fun . . . peppier dancing . . . more beautiful girls—including a trainload of 300 GENUINE George White Scan-dolls from Broadway . . . and a bevy of sure-fire song hits by hit writers . . . the show of shows—IT'S TREMENDOUS!" [1] Also in STEAMBOAT ON THE RIVER.

2046 ♦ GEORGE WHITE'S SCANDALS OF 1935
Fox, 1935

Composer(s) Meyer, Joseph
Lyricist(s) Yellen, Jack; Friend, Cliff

Producer(s) White, George
Director(s) White, George
Screenwriter(s) Yellen, Jack; McNutt, Patterson

Cast Faye, Alice; Dunn, James; Sparks, Ned; Roberti, Lyda; Edwards, Cliff; Judge, Arline; Powell, Eleanor; Rubin, Benny; Dunn, Emma; Richman, Charles; Knight, Fuzzy; White, George

Song(s) It's Time to Say Goodnight [1]; It's an Old Southern Custom (L: Yellen, Jack); According to the Moonlight (L: Yellen, Jack; Magidson, Herb); I Got Shoes—You Got Shoesies; Oh I Didn't Know (You'd Get that Way); Hunkadola; I Was Born too Late (L: Yellen, Jack); You Belong to Me (C: Friend, Cliff; L: Yellen, Jack)

Notes Johnny Green and Edward Heymann were hired to write this score but their efforts were rejected. [1] Moshier in *The Alice Faye Movie Book* lists Cliff Friend alone as the lyricist.

2047 ✦ GEORGY GIRL
Columbia, 1966

Musical Score Faris, Alexander

Producer(s) Goldston, Robert; Plaschkes, Otto
Director(s) Narizzano, Silvio
Screenwriter(s) Nichols, Peter; Forster, Margaret
Source(s) *Georgy Girl* (novel) Forster, Margaret

Cast Mason, James; Bates, Alan; Rampling, Charlotte; Redgrave, Lynn; Kempson, Rachel

Song(s) Georgy Girl (C: Springfield, Tom; L: Dale, Jim); You Look a Little Lovelier Every Day (C/L: Bowen, William Hill); Deep in My Lonely Heart (C: Faris, Alexander; L: Faris, Alexander; Noble, Barry); Whole Lot of Woman [1] (C/L: Rainwater, Marvin)

Notes [1] Not written for picture.

2048 ✦ GERALDINE
Republic, 1953

Producer(s) Picker, Sidney
Director(s) Springsteen, R.G.
Screenwriter(s) Milne, Peter; Gill, Frank, Jr.

Cast Carroll, John; Powers, Mala; Freberg, Stan; Backus, Jim; Miller, Kristine; Belasco, Leon; Stossel, Ludwig; Lee, Earl; Reed, Alan; Bryant, Nana; Jones, Carolyn

Song(s) Flaming Lips (C/L: Freberg, Stan); Along the Colorado Trail (C: Traditional; L: Coster, Irwin); Rat Row (C/L: Knight, Fuzzy); I'm Looking for a Mommy for My Daddy (C/L: Gill Jr., Frank; Roberts, Gerald); I Caught Daddy Smooching the Easter Rabbit (C/L: Gill Jr., Frank; Roberts, Gerald); Black Is the Color (C: Traditional; L: Coster, Irwin); Geraldine (C: Young, Victor; L: Clare, Sidney); Wintertime of Love (C: Young, Victor; L: Heyman, Edward)

2049 ✦ GERONIMO'S REVENGE
Disney, 1964

Musical Score Wallace, Oliver; Bruns, George

Song(s) Song of the Texas Rangers [1] (C: Dubin, Joseph S.; L: Jackman, Bob); The Tired Cowhand (C: Baker, Buddy; L: Harmon, Dave); Rhythm of the Rain (C: Marks, Franklyn; L: Jackman, Bob)

Notes No other information available. [1] Also in GUNFIGHT AT SANDOVAL and TEXAS JOHN SLAUGHTER.

2050 ✦ GET CARTER
Metro–Goldwyn–Mayer, 1971

Musical Score Budd, Roy
Composer(s) Budd, Roy
Lyricist(s) Fishman, Jack

Producer(s) Klinger, Mike
Director(s) Hodges, Mike
Screenwriter(s) Hodges, Mike
Source(s) *Jack's Return Home* (novel) Lewis, Ted

Cast Caine, Michael; Osborne, John; Hendry, Ian; Ekland, Britt

Song(s) Lookin' for Someone; Gettin' Nowhere in a Hurry; Livin' Should Be That Way; Love Is a Four Letter Word; Something on My Mind [1]; Hallucination

Notes A British MGM release. The American remake is titled HIT MAN. There is also a vocal of "How About You" by Burton Lane and Ralph Freed. [1] Used instrumentally only.

2051 ✦ GET GOING
Universal, 1943

Musical Score Skinner, Frank
Composer(s) Rosen, Milton
Lyricist(s) Carter, Everett

Producer(s) Cowan, Will
Director(s) Yarbrough, Jean
Screenwriter(s) Wilson, Warren

Cast McDonald, Grace; Paige, Robert

Song(s) Hold That Line [2]; Got Love [1]; You're My Dish [3] (C: McHugh, Jimmy; L: Adamson, Harold)

Notes There is also a vocal of "Siboney" by Ernesto Lecuona and Dolly Morse. [1] Also in I'M NOBODY'S SWEETHEART NOW, MISSISSIPPI GAMBLER (1942) and SWING IT SOLDIER. [2] Also in SLIGHTLY TERRIFIC. [3] Also in MERRY-GO-ROUND OF 1938.

2052 ✦ GET HEP TO LOVE
Universal, 1942

Musical Score Previn, Charles

Producer(s) Burton, Bernard W.
Director(s) Lamont, Charles
Screenwriter(s) Dratler, Jay

Cast Jean, Gloria; Ryan, Peggy; Bryant, Nana; Frazee, Jane; Paige, Robert; O'Connor, Donald; Collins, Cora Sue; Bacon, Irving; Ryan, Tim; The Jivin' Jacks and Jills

Song(s) Let's Hitch a Horsie to the Automobile (C/L: Livingston, Jerry; Hoffman, Al; Curtis, Mann)

Notes Titled IT COMES UP LOVE in Great Britain. There are vocals of "Siboney" by Dolly Morse and Ernesto Lecuona; "Villanelle" by Eva Dell'Acqua and

Ralph Freed and "Ah, Fors'e Lui Che L'Anima" from Verdi's LA TRAVIATA.

2053 ✦ GET YOURSELF A COLLEGE GIRL
Metro–Goldwyn–Mayer, 1965

Musical Score Karger, Fred
Choreographer(s) Belfer, Hal

Producer(s) Katzman, Sam
Director(s) Miller, Sidney
Screenwriter(s) Kent, Robert E.

Cast The Dave Clark Five; Getz, Stan; Gilberto, Astrud; Jimmy Smith Trio; Bell, Freddie; Linn, Roberta; The Bell Boys; Waterman, Willard; Mioni, Fabrizio; Mobley, Mary Ann; O'Brien, Joan; Sinatra, Nancy; Noel, Chris

Song(s) The Swingin' Set (C: Karger, Fred; L: Miller, Sidney; Brooks, Donnie); Bony Moronie (C/L: Williams, Larry); Whenever You're Around (C/L: Clark, Dave; Smith, Mike); How Would You Like It (C/L: Brooks, Donnie); Blue Feeling (C/L: Henshaw, J.); Get Yourself a College Girl (C: Karger, Fred; L: Miller, Sidney); The Girl from Ipanema [1] (C: Jobim, Antonio Carlos; L: Gimbel, Norman); The Swim (C/L: Tamblyn, Larry); Talkin' About Love (C/L: Bell, Freddie; Linn, Roberta); Around and Around (C/L: Berry, Chuck)

Notes Released as THE SWINGIN' SET internationally. [1] Portuguese lyrics by Vinicious de Moraes.

2054 ✦ GHOSTBUSTERS
Columbia, 1984

Musical Score Bernstein, Elmer

Producer(s) Reitman, Ivan
Director(s) Reitman, Ivan
Screenwriter(s) Aykroyd, Dan; Ramis, Harold

Cast Murray, Bill; Aykroyd, Dan; Weaver, Sigourney; Ramis, Harold; Moranis, Rick; Potts, Annie; Atherton, William; Hudson, Ernie; Margulies, David

Song(s) Ghostbusters (C/L: Parker Jr., Ray); Cleanin' Up the Town (C/L: O'Neal, Kevin; O'Neal, Brian); Savin' the Day (C/L: Alessi, Bobby; Immer, Dave); Magic (C/L: Smiley, Mick)

Notes Only original songs listed.

2055 ✦ THE GHOST CATCHERS
Universal, 1944

Musical Score Ward, Edward
Composer(s) Revel, Harry
Lyricist(s) Webster, Paul Francis

Producer(s) Hartmann, Edmund L.
Director(s) Cline, Edward F.
Screenwriter(s) Hartmann, Edmund L.
Source(s) (story) Cline, Edward F.; Gross, Miton

Cast Olsen, Ole; Johnson, Chic; Jean, Gloria; O'Driscoll, Martha; Carrillo, Leo; Devine, Andy; Chaney Jr., Lon; Grant, Kirby; Catlett, Walter; Armetta, Henry; Downey, Morton

Song(s) Three Cheers for the Customer; Blue Candlelight and Red, Red Roses; Quoth the Raven; I'll Remember April [1] (C/L: de Paul, Gene; Johnston, Pat; Raye, Don); I'm Old Enough to Dream (C: Ward, Edward; L: Carter, Everett); Baltimore Oriole [2] (C: Carmichael, Hoagy); There'll Be a Yankee Christmas [2] (C: Alter, Louis); Livin' in My Own Sweet Way [2]; My American Creed [2]

Notes There are also vocals of "These Foolish Things Remind Me of You" by Holt Marvell, Jack Strachey and Harry Link and "Swanee River" by Stephen Foster. [1] Also in IDEA GIRL, I'LL REMEMBER APRIL and RIDE 'EM COWBOY. Not used in STRICTLY IN THE GROOVE. [2] Not used.

2056 ✦ GHOST IN THE INVISIBLE BIKINI
American International, 1966

Musical Score Baxter, Les
Composer(s) Hemric, Guy; Styner, Jerry
Lyricist(s) Hemric, Guy; Styner, Jerry

Producer(s) Nicholson, James H.; Arkoff, Samuel Z.
Director(s) Weis, Don
Screenwriter(s) Heyward, Louis M.; Ullman, Elwood

Cast Kirk, Tommy; Walley, Deborah; Kincaid, Aron; O'Hara, Quinn; White, Jesse; Lembeck, Harvey; Sinatra, Nancy; Martin, Claudia; Bushman, Francis X.; Rubin, Benny; Shaw, Bobbi; Rathbone, Basil; Kelly, Patsy; Karloff, Boris

Song(s) Geronimo; Sing A-Mal-Thing; Don't Try to Fight It Baby; Stand Up and Fight; Make the Music Pretty

Notes No cue sheet available.

2057 ✦ GHOST TOWN GOLD
Republic, 1937

Producer(s) Siegel, Sol C.
Director(s) Kane, Joseph
Screenwriter(s) Rathmell, John; Drake, Oliver

Cast Livingston, Bob; Corrigan, Ray; Terhune, Max; Hughes, Kay; Mason, LeRoy; Caruth, Burt; Canutt, Yakima

Song(s) Behind Those Swinging Doors (C/L: Allan, Fleming)

2058 ✦ GHOST TOWN RIDERS
Universal, 1939

Composer(s) Allan, Fleming
Lyricist(s) Allan, Fleming

Producer(s)   Carr, Trem
Director(s)   Waggner, George
Screenwriter(s)   West, Joseph

Cast   Baker, Bob; Shannon, Fay

Song(s)   Headin' Home; It Ain't So Rosy on the Range; Down That Old Home Trail

2059 ✦ GIANT
Warner Brothers, 1956

Musical Score   Tiomkin, Dimitri
Composer(s)   Tiomkin, Dimitri
Lyricist(s)   Webster, Paul Francis

Producer(s)   Stevens, George; Ginsberg, Henry
Director(s)   Stevens, George
Screenwriter(s)   Guiol, Fred; Moffat, Ivan
Source(s)   *Giant* (novel) Ferber, Edna

Cast   Taylor, Elizabeth; Hudson, Rock; Dean, James; Baker, Carroll; Withers, Jane; Wills, Chill; Dean, James; McCambridge, Mercedes; Hopper, Dennis; Mineo, Sal; Taylor, Rod; Evelyn, Judith; Holliman, Earl; Nichols, Robert; Scourby, Alexander

Song(s)   Giant (This Then Is Texas); There's Never Been Anyone Else But You [1]; Jeff Rink Ballad [2]

Notes   There is also a vocal of "Yellow Rose of Texas" by Don George. [1] Used as background instrumental only. [2] Sheet music only.

2060 ✦ G.I. BLUES
Paramount, 1960

Musical Score   Lilley, Joseph J.
Choreographer(s)   O'Curran, Charles

Producer(s)   Wallis, Hal B.
Director(s)   Taurog, Norman
Screenwriter(s)   Beloin, Edmund; Garson, Henry
Source(s)   *Sailor Beware* (play) Nicholson, Kenyon; Robinson, Charles

Cast   Presley, Elvis; Prowse, Juliet; Ivers, Robert; Roman, Leticia; The Jordanaires; Johnson, Arch

Song(s)   Wooden Heart [1] (C: Traditional; L: Wise, Fred; Weisman, Ben; Twomey, Kay; Kaempfert, Berthold); What's She Really Like (C/L: Wayne, Sid; Silver, Abner); G.I. Blues (C/L: Tepper, Sid; Bennett, Roy C.); Doin' the Best I Can (C: Pomus, Doc; L: Shuman, Mort); Blue Suede Shoes (C/L: Perkins, Carl); Frankfurt Special (C: Edwards, Sherman; L: Wayne, Sid); Shoppin' Around (C/L: Tepper, Sid; Bennett, Roy C.; Schroeder, Aaron); Tonight Is So Right for Love [2] (C: Offenbach, Jacques; L: Wayne, Sid; Silver, Abner); Pocketful of Rainbows (C/L: Wise, Fred; Weisman, Ben); Crawfish [3] (C: Weisman, Ben; L: Wise, Fred); Big Boots (C/L: Wayne, Sid; Edwards, Sherman); Didja' Ever! (C: Edwards, Sherman; L: Wayne, Sid)

Notes   [1] Based on "I Den Zum Stadtele Naus." [2] Based on "Barcarolle" from the TALES OF HOFFMAN. [3] Also in KID CREOLE.

2061 ✦ GIDGET
Columbia, 1959

Musical Score   Morton, Arthur

Producer(s)   Rachmil, Lewis J.
Director(s)   Wendkos, Paul
Screenwriter(s)   Upton, Gabrielle
Source(s)   *Gidget* (novel) Kohner, Frederick

Cast   Dee, Sandra; Robertson, Cliff; Darren, James; O'Connell, Arthur

Song(s)   Gidget (C: Karger, Fred; L: Washington, Patti); Next Best Thing to Love (C: Karger, Fred; L: Styne, Stanley); There's No Such Thing (C: Karger, Fred; L: Styne, Stanley)

2062 ✦ GIDGET GOES HAWAIIAN
Columbia, 1961

Musical Score   Duning, George
Composer(s)   Karger, Fred
Lyricist(s)   Styne, Stanley

Producer(s)   Bresler, Jerry
Director(s)   Wendkos, Paul
Screenwriter(s)   Flippen, Ruth Brooks
Source(s)   characters by Kohner, Frederick

Cast   Darren, James; Callan, Michael; Walley, Deborah; Reiner, Carl; Cass, Peggy; Foy Jr., Eddie; Donnell, Jeff

Song(s)   Gidget Goes Hawaiian; Wild About that Girl

Notes   No cue sheet available.

2063 ✦ GIDGET GOES TO ROME
Columbia, 1963

Musical Score   Williams, John
Composer(s)   Weiss, George David
Lyricist(s)   Kasha, Al

Producer(s)   Bresler, Jerry
Director(s)   Wendkos, Paul
Screenwriter(s)   Flippen, Ruth Brooks; Eunson, Katherine; Eunson, Dale
Source(s)   characters by Kohner, Frederick

Cast   Carol, Cindy; Darren, James; Landis, Jessie Royce; Danova, Cesare; de Metz, Danielle; Corcoran, Noreen; Donnell, Jeff; Porter, Don

Song(s)   Gegetta; Big Italian Moon

Notes   No cue sheet available.

2064 ✦ GIFT OF GAB
Universal, 1934

Composer(s) Conrad, Con
Lyricist(s) Magidson, Herb

Director(s) Freund, Karl
Screenwriter(s) James, Rian; Breslow, Lou

Cast Lowe, Edmund; Stuart, Gloria; Etting, Ruth; Baker, Phil; Waters, Ethel; White, Alice; Woollcott, Alexander; Moore, Victor; Vinson, Helen; Austin, Gene; Devine, Andy; Shaw, Winifred; Holloway, Sterling; Karloff, Boris; Lugosi, Bela; Lukas, Paul; Gus Arnheim and His Orchestra

Song(s) Talking to Myself; I Ain't Gonna Sin No More; Gift of Gab; Somebody Looks Good (C: Von Tilzer, Albert; L: Whiting, George); Don't Let This Waltz Mean Goodbye (C: Von Tilzer, Albert; L: Meskill, Jack); Walkin' on Air (C: Von Tilzer, Albert; L: Meskill, Jack); What a Wonderful Day (C: Sherman, Al; L: Tobias, Harry); Tomorrow - Who Cares (C/L: Mencher, Murray; Tobias, Charles); Blue Sky Avenue (C: Conrad, Con; L: Magidson, Herb)

Notes No cue sheet available.

2065 ✦ THE GIFT OF LOVE
Twentieth Century–Fox, 1958

Musical Score Mockridge, Cyril J.

Producer(s) Brackett, Charles
Director(s) Negulesco, Jean
Screenwriter(s) Davis, Luther

Cast Bacall, Lauren; Stack, Robert; Rudie, Evelyn; Greene, Lorne; Seymour, Anne; Platt, Edward

Song(s) The Gift of Love (C: Fain, Sammy; L: Webster, Paul Francis)

Notes This is a remake of the 1946 film SENTIMENTAL JOURNEY. "Preguntale a Las Estrellas" ("O Ask of the Stars Above") is also used vocally.

2066 ✦ GIGI
Metro–Goldwyn–Mayer, 1958

Composer(s) Loewe, Frederick
Lyricist(s) Lerner, Alan Jay

Producer(s) Freed, Arthur
Director(s) Minnelli, Vincente [4]
Screenwriter(s) Lerner, Alan Jay
Source(s) *Gigi* (novel) Colette

Cast Caron, Leslie [2]; Chevalier, Maurice; Jourdan, Louis; Gingold, Hermione; Gabor, Eva; Jeans, Isabel; Bergerac, Jacques; Abbott, John

Song(s) Thank Heaven for Little Girls; It's a Bore; The Parisians; Gossip; She Is Not Thinking of Me; The Night They Invented Champagne; I Remember It Well; Gaston's Soliloquy; Gigi; I'm Glad I'm Not Young Anymore; Say a Prayer for Me Tonight [1]; A Toujours [3]

Notes [1] Originally cut from MY FAIR LADY. [2] Dubbed by Betty Wand. [3] Used instrumentally only. [4] Charles Walters staged "The Night They Invented Champagne" (with Minnelli directing). Walters also directed all the retakes (which were extensive).

2067 ✦ GILDA
Columbia, 1946

Composer(s) Fisher, Doris
Lyricist(s) Roberts, Allan
Choreographer(s) Cole, Jack

Producer(s) Van Upp, Virginia
Director(s) Vidor, Charles
Screenwriter(s) Parsonnet, Marion

Cast Hayworth, Rita [2]; Ford, Glenn; Macready, George; Calleia, Joseph; Geray, Steven; Sawyer, Joe; Donath, Ludwig; Roman, Ruth

Song(s) Put the Blame on Mame [1]; Amado Mio [3]

Notes [1] Also in BETTY CO-ED and SENIOR PROM. [2] Dubbed by Anita Ellis except for reprise of "Put the Blame on Mame" where she accompanies herself on the guitar. Dubbing is erroniously credited to Nan Wynn in some sources. [3] Also in I SURRENDER DEAR.

2068 ✦ GILDA LIVE
Warner Brothers, 1980

Composer(s) Shaffer, Paul
Lyricist(s) Radner, Gilda

Producer(s) Michaels, Lorne
Director(s) Nichols, Mike
Screenwriter(s) Beatts, Anne; Michaels, Lorne; Miller, Marilyn Suzanne; Novello, Don; O'Donoghue, Michael; Radner, Gilda; Shaffer, Paul; Shuster, Rosie; Zweibel, Alan

Cast Radner, Gilda; Novello, Don; Shaffer, Paul; Kirshner, Don; Schnactman, Arnie; Nichols, Nils

Song(s) Let's Talk Dirty to the Animals (C/L: O'Donoghue, Michael); I Love to Be Unhappy; Goodbye Saccharine (C/L: Miller, Marilyn Suzanne; Hardwick, Cheryl; Shaffer, Paul); Gimme Mick; Auld Lang Syne (C: Traditional; L: Zweibel, Alan); Honey (Touch Me with My Clothes On)

Notes A rendition of "The Way We Were" by Marvin Hamlisch and Marilyn and Alan Bergman is also used.

2069 ✦ THE GILDED LILY
Paramount, 1935

Producer(s) Lewis, Albert
Director(s) Ruggles, Wesley
Screenwriter(s) Binyon, Claude

Cast Colbert, Claudette; MacMurray, Fred; Milland, Ray; Smith, C. Aubrey; Alberni, Luis; Meek, Donald; Hymer, Warren; Wilson, Charles

Song(s) Something About Romance (C: Johnston, Arthur; L: Coslow, Sam); Restless [1] (C: Satterfield, Tom; L: Coslow, Sam)

Notes [1] Based on an instrumental backing piece, "The Inquiring Reporter."

2070 ✦ GILDERSLEEVE ON BROADWAY
RKO, 1943

Producer(s) Schlom, Herman
Director(s) Douglas, Gordon M.
Screenwriter(s) Kent, Robert E.

Cast Peary, Harold; Burke, Billie; Carleton, Claire; LeGrand, Richard; Mercer, Freddie; Cavanaugh, Hobart; Kinskey, Leonid

Song(s) Touch of Texas [1] (C: McHugh, Jimmy; L: Loesser, Frank)

Notes [1] Also in SEVEN DAYS LEAVE and MOON OVER LAS VEGAS (Universal).

2071 ✦ THE GIRL AND THE GAMBLER
RKO, 1939

Musical Score Webb, Roy
Composer(s) Gonzales, Aaron
Lyricist(s) Gonzales, Aaron

Producer(s) Reid, Cliff
Director(s) Landers, Lew
Screenwriter(s) Fields, Joseph; Young, Clarence Upson
Source(s) *The Dove* (play) Mack, Willard

Cast Carrillo, Leo; Holt, Tim; Duna, Steffi; MacBride, Donald; Martin, Chris-Pin; Raquello, Edward; Fix, Paul

Song(s) Timbalero [1]; Mi Ultimo Adios; Palomita Mia [2]

Notes [1] May have also been in BACHELOR MOTHER. [2] Sheet music only.

2072 ✦ THE GIRL AND THE GENERAL
Metro–Goldwyn–Mayer, 1970

Musical Score Morricone, Ennio

Producer(s) Ponti, Carlo
Director(s) Campanile, Pasquale Festa
Screenwriter(s) Malerba, Luigi; Campanile, Pasquale Festa

Cast Steiger, Rod; Lisi, Virna; Orsini, Umberto

Song(s) La Licenza Premio (C: Morricone, Ennio; L: Nohra, Audrey); Ti Xe El Piu: Bel (C: Morricone, Ennio; L: Bardotti, Sergio)

2073 ✦ THE GIRL CAN'T HELP IT
Twentieth Century–Fox, 1956

Producer(s) Tashlin, Frank
Director(s) Tashlin, Frank
Screenwriter(s) Tashlin, Frank; Baker, Herbert

Cast Ewell, Tom; Mansfield, Jayne; O'Brien, Edmond; Jones, Henry; Emery, John; Moore, Juanita; London, Julie; Anthony, Ray; Gordon, Barry; Domino, Antoine "Fats"; The Platters; Little Richard and His Band; Gene Vincent and His Blue Caps; The Treniers; Fontaine, Eddie; The Chuckles; Lincoln, Abbey; Olenn, Johnny; Tempo, Nino; Cochran, Eddie

Song(s) The Girl Can't Help It (C/L: Troup, Bobby); I Wish I Could Shimmy Like My Sister Kate [1] (C/L: Pirion, A.J.); My Idea of Love (C/L: Glenn, Johnny); I Ain't Gonna Cry No More (C/L: Glenn, Johnny); Ready Teady (C/L: Blackwell, Robert; Marascalco, John); She's Got It [2] (C/L: Penniman, Richard; Marascalco, John); Cool It, Baby! [1] (C: Newman, Lionel; L: Coates, Carroll); Cinnamon Sinners (C/L: Chase, Lincoln); Spread the Word (C/L: Russell, Bob); Cry Me a River (C/L: Hamilton, Arthur); Be-Bop-A-Lula (C/L: Vincent, Gene; Davis, Tex); 20 Flight Rock (C/L: Fairchild, Ned); Rock Around the Rock Pile (C/L: Troup, Bobby); Rockin' Is Our Bizness (C/L: Trenier, Claude; Gilbeaux, Gene; Hill, Don; Trenier, Buddy); Blue Monday (C/L: Domino, Antoine "Fats"); You'll Never, Never Know I Care (C: Robi, Paul; Williams, Tony; L: Miles, Jean); Ev'ry Time (C: Iavello, Tony; L: Leven, Mel); Big Band Boogie (inst.) (C: Anthony, Ray)

Notes [1] Also in TEENAGE REBEL. [2] Richard Penniman is Little Richard.

2074 ✦ GIRL CRAZY (1932)
RKO, 1932

Composer(s) Gershwin, George
Lyricist(s) Gershwin, Ira

Producer(s) LeBaron, William
Director(s) Seiter, William A.
Screenwriter(s) Welch, Eddie; De Leon, Walter; Whelan, Tim
Source(s) *Girl Crazy* (musical) Gershwin, George; Gershwin, Ira; McGowan, Jack; Bolton, Guy

Cast Wheeler, Bert; Woolsey, Robert; Fields, Stanley; Quillan, Eddie; Green, Mitzi; Lee, Dorothy; Kelly, Kitty; Judge, Arline; Benedict, Brooks

Song(s) But Not For Me; Barbary Coast; I Got Rhythm; Bidin' My Time; You've Got What Gets Me [1]; Rhythm

Notes Cue sheet does not differentiate between vocals and instrumentals. [1] Also in FLYING DEVILS.

2075 ✦ GIRL CRAZY (1943)
Metro–Goldwyn–Mayer, 1943

Composer(s) Gershwin, George
Lyricist(s) Gershwin, Ira
Choreographer(s) Walters, Charles [2]

Producer(s) Freed, Arthur
Director(s) Taurog, Norman [1]
Screenwriter(s) Finklehoffe, Fred F.
Source(s) *Girl Crazy* (musical) Gershwin, George; Gershwin, Ira; Bolton, Guy; McGowan, Jack

Cast Garland, Judy; Rooney, Mickey; Stratton, Gil; Strickland, Robert; Allyson, June; Ragland, Rags; Walker, Nancy; Kibbee, Guy; Tommy Dorsey and His Orchestra

Song(s) Treat Me Rough; Bidin' My Time; Could You Use Me; Embraceable You; But Not for Me; I Got Rhythm; Broncho Busters [3]; Happy Birthday, Ginger (C/L: Edens, Roger)

Notes Dorsey's orchestra plays "Fascinating Rhythm." Judy Garland's dancing partner in "Embraceable You" is Charles Walters. [1] Busby Berkeley was replaced as director midway through filming. [2] Berkeley choreographed the "I've Got Rhythm" number. [3] Prerecorded but not used.

2076 ✦ THE GIRL DOWNSTAIRS
Metro–Goldwyn–Mayer, 1938

Musical Score Axt, William

Producer(s) Rapf, Harry
Director(s) Taurog, Norman
Screenwriter(s) Goldman, Harold; Jackson, Felix; Noti, Karl
Source(s) (story) Hunyady, Sandor

Cast Gaal, Franciska; Tone, Franchot; Connolly, Walter; Gardiner, Reginald; Johnson, Rita; Owen, Reginald; Pangborn, Franklin; Coote, Robert; Gilbert, Billy

Song(s) When You're in Love (C/L: Forrest, Chet; Wright, Robert)

2077 ✦ THE GIRL FRIEND
Columbia, 1935

Composer(s) Johnston, Arthur
Lyricist(s) Kahn, Gus
Choreographer(s) Felix, Seymour

Director(s) Buzzell, Edward
Screenwriter(s) Rubin, Benny; Purcell, Gertrude

Cast Sothern, Ann; Haley, Jack; Hall, Thurston; Killian, Victor; Pryor, Roger; Courtney, Inez; Wilson, Marie

Song(s) Two Together; What Is This Power?; Napoleon's Exile; Welcome to Napoleon; Girl Friend [1]

Notes There was no trace of the original musical comedy by the time the film was released. [1] This may be used as the main title music.

2078 ✦ THE GIRL FROM CALGARY
Monogram, 1932

Producer(s) Chadwick, I.E.
Director(s) Whiteman, Paul
Screenwriter(s) Chadwick, Lee

Cast D'Orsay, Fifi; Kelly, Paul; Warwick, Roobert; Maxwell, Edwin; Allwyn, Astrid; Featherstone, Eddie

Song(s) Maybe Perhaps (C/L: Malotte, Albert Hay)

Notes No cue sheet available. Contains footage from the Sono Art-World picture THE GREAT GABBO.

2079 ✦ THE GIRL FROM HAVANA (1929)
Fox, 1929

Director(s) Stoloff, Benjamin; Burke, Edwin
Screenwriter(s) Burke, Edwin

Cast Lane, Lola; Page, Paul; Thomson, Kenneth; Moorhead, Natalie; Hymer, Warren

Song(s) Time Will Tell (C: Baer, Abel; L: Gilbert, L. Wolfe)

2080 ✦ THE GIRL FROM HAVANA (1940)
Republic, 1940

Composer(s) Styne, Jule
Lyricist(s) Brown, George; Meyer, Sol

Producer(s) North, Robert
Director(s) Landers, Lew
Screenwriter(s) Boylan, Malcolm Stuart; Brown, Karl

Cast O'Keefe, Dennis; Jory, Victor; Carleton, Claire; Duna, Steffi; Jones, Gordon; Page, Bradley; Richards, Addison; Biberman, Abner

Song(s) The Girl from Havana; Querido

2081 ✦ THE GIRL FROM JONES BEACH
Warner Brothers, 1949

Musical Score Buttolph, David

Producer(s) Gottlieb, Alex
Director(s) Godfrey, Peter
Screenwriter(s) Diamond, I.A.L.
Source(s) "Fargo Girl" (story) Boretz, Allen

Cast Reagan, Ronald; Mayo, Virginia; Bracken, Eddie; Drake, Dona; Travers, Henry; Wilson, Lois; Bates,

Florence; Cowan, Jerome; Westcott, Helen; Harvey, Paul; Corrigan, Lloyd

Song(s)   The Girl From Jones Beach (C: Marcus, Sol; L: Seiler, Eddie)

Notes   "I Only Have Eyes for You" by Al Dubin and Harry Warren is also used as a background vocal.

2082 ✦ GIRL FROM MISSOURI
MGM, 1934

Producer(s)   Hyman, Bernard H.
Director(s)   Conway, Jack
Screenwriter(s)   Loos, Anita

Cast   Harlow, Jean; Kelly, Patsy; Tone, Franchot; Barrymore, Lionel; Stone, Lewis; Blandick, Clara; Pendleton, Nat

Song(s)   Born to Be Kissed (C: Schwartz, Arthur; L: Dietz, Howard)

Notes   Originally titled BORN TO BE KISSED.

2083 ✦ THE GIRL FROM PETROVKA
Universal, 1974

Musical Score   Mancini, Henry

Producer(s)   Zanuck, Richard D.; Brown, David
Director(s)   Miller, Robert Ellis
Screenwriter(s)   Scott, Allan; Bryant, Chris
Source(s)   (novel) Feifer, George

Cast   Hawn, Goldie; Holbrook, Hal; Aslan, Gregoire; Hopkins, Anthony; Dolin, Anton; Wintzell, Bruno; Andric, Zoran

Song(s)   Nyet Nyet Nyet (C: Budd, Roy; L: Fishman, Jack)

2084 ✦ THE GIRL FROM RIO
Monogram, 1939

Director(s)   Hillyer, Lambert
Screenwriter(s)   Raison, Milton; Neville, John Thomas

Cast   Movita; Hull, Warren; Baldwin, Alan; Linaker, Kay; Clement, Clay

Song(s)   The Singing Burro (C/L: De Recat, Emile); Romance in Rio (C: Lange, Johnny; L: Porter, Lew)

Notes   No cue sheet available.

2085 ✦ THE GIRL FROM SCOTLAND YARD
Paramount, 1937

Producer(s)   Cohen, Emanuel
Director(s)   Vignola, Robert
Screenwriter(s)   Anderson, Doris; Schary, Dore

Cast   Morley, Karen; Baldwin, Robert; Ciannelli, Eduardo; Alexander, Katherine; Monti, Milli; Crane, Lloyd; Flanagan, Bud

Song(s)   We Haven't a Moment to Lose (C: Johnston, Arthur; L: Burke, Johnny)

2086 ✦ THE GIRL FROM WOOLWORTH'S
Warner Brothers–First National, 1929

Composer(s)   Meyer, George W.
Lyricist(s)   Bryan, Alfred

Producer(s)   Rowland, Richard A.
Director(s)   Beaudine, William
Screenwriter(s)   Comandini, Adele; Weil, Richard; Luddy, Edward

Cast   White, Alice; Delaney, Charles; Oakman, Wheeler; Flynn, Rita; Hall, Ben; Orlamond, William

Song(s)   Crying for Love; Someone; What I Know About Love (C: Jerome, M.K.; L: Ruby, Herman); You Baby Me I'll Baby You

Notes   No cue sheet available.

2087 ✦ GIRL HAPPY
Metro–Goldwyn–Mayer, 1965

Musical Score   Stoll, George; Van Eps, Robert
Composer(s)   Giant, Bill; Baum, Bernie; Kaye, Florence
Lyricist(s)   Giant, Bill; Baum, Bernie; Kaye, Florence
Choreographer(s)   Winters, David

Producer(s)   Pasternak, Joe
Director(s)   Sagal, Boris
Screenwriter(s)   Bullock, Harvey; Allen, R.S.

Cast   Presley, Elvis; Fabares, Shelley; Stone, Harold J.; Crosby, Gary; Baker, Joby; Talbot, Nita; Mobley, Mary Ann; Mioni, Fabrizio; Coogan, Jackie; Fiedler, John

Song(s)   Girl Happy (C/L: Pomus, Doc; Meade, Norman); Spring Fever; Wolf Call; The Fort Lauderdale Chamber of Commerce (C/L: Tepper, Sid; Bennett, Roy C.); Startin' Tonight (C/L: Rosenblatt, Lenore; Millrose, Victor); Do Not Disturb; Cross My Heart and Hope to Die (C/L: Wayne, Sid; Wiseman, Ben); The Meanest Girl in Town (C/L: Byers, Joy); I've Got News for You (C/L: Wise, Fred; Starr, Randy); Do the Clam (C/L: Wayne, Sid; Wiseman, Ben; Fuller, Dolores); Puppet on a String (C/L: Tepper, Sid; Bennett, Roy C.); I've Got to Find My Baby (C/L: Byers, Joy)

2088 ✦ THE GIRL HE LEFT BEHIND (1943)

See THE GANG'S ALL HERE.

2089 ✦ THE GIRL HE LEFT BEHIND (1956)
Warner Brothers, 1956

Musical Score   Webb, Roy

Producer(s)   Rosenberg, Frank P.
Director(s)   Butler, David
Screenwriter(s)   Trosper, Guy

Source(s) *The Girl He Left Behind* (novel) Hargrove, Marion

Cast Hunter, Tab; Wood, Natalie; Landis, Jessie Royce; Backus, Jim; Jones, Henry; Hamilton, Murray; King, Alan; Garner, James; Janssen, David; Ames, Florenz

Song(s) Honey-Babe [1] (C: Steiner, Max; L: Webster, Paul Francis)

Notes [1] Also in BATTLE CRY.

2090 ◆ THE GIRL IN OVERALLS

See SWING SHIFT MAISIE.

2091 ◆ GIRL IN PAWN

See LITTLE MISS MARKER (1934).

2092 ◆ THE GIRL IN THE RED VELVET SWING
Twentieth Century–Fox, 1955

Musical Score Harline, Leigh
Composer(s) Newman, Lionel
Lyricist(s) Darby, Ken
Choreographer(s) Robel, David

Producer(s) Brackett, Charles
Director(s) Fleischer, Richard
Screenwriter(s) Reisch, Walter; Brackett, Charles

Cast Milland, Ray; Collins, Joan; Granger, Farley; Adler, Luther; Skinner, Cornelia Otis; Farrell, Glenda; Fuller, Frances; Robbins, Gale

Song(s) Men-Men-Men; It's the Same the Whole World Over [1] (L: Seymour, Harry); I Challenge You

Notes [1] Special lyrics by Harry Seymour.

2093 ◆ THE GIRL MOST LIKELY
RKO, 1957

Musical Score Riddle, Nelson
Composer(s) Blane, Ralph; Martin, Hugh
Lyricist(s) Blane, Ralph; Martin, Hugh
Choreographer(s) Champion, Gower

Producer(s) Rubin, Stanley
Director(s) Leisen, Mitchell
Screenwriter(s) Freeman, Devery

Cast Merkel, Una; Cady, Frank; Noonan, Tommy; Ballard, Kaye; Andes, Keith; Robertson, Cliff; Powell, Jane

Song(s) My Song [3]; I Don't Know What I Want; Balboa; The Girl Most Likely (C: Riddle, Nelson; L: Russell, Bob); We Gotta Keep Up with the Joneses [1] (L: Martin, Hugh; Blane, Ralph; Pribor, Richard); Wedding Fantasy (C/L: Pribor, Richard); Travelogue;

Crazy Horse; All the Colors of the Rainbow; I Like the Feeling [2]; Indecision [4]

Notes [1] Additional lyrics by Pribor. [2] Instrumental use only, but prerecorded and on the soundtrack album. [3] Not used in THE GIRL RUSH. [4] Not used.

2094 ◆ A GIRL NAMED TAMIKO
Paramount, 1963

Musical Score Bernstein, Elmer

Producer(s) Wallis, Hal B.
Director(s) Sturges, John
Screenwriter(s) Anhalt, Edward
Source(s) *A Girl Named Tamiko* (novel) Kirkbride, Ronald

Cast Harvey, Laurence; Nuyen, France; Hyer, Martha; Merrill, Gary; Umeki, Miyoshi; Brodie, Steve; Patrick, Lee; Loo, Richard; Ahn, Philip

Song(s) A Girl Named Tamiko (C: Bernstein, Elmer; L: David, Mack)

2095 ◆ THE GIRL NEXT DOOR
Twentieth Century–Fox, 1953

Musical Score Mockridge, Cyril J.
Composer(s) Myrow, Josef
Lyricist(s) Gordon, Mack
Choreographer(s) Barstow, Richard

Producer(s) Bassler, Robert
Director(s) Sale, Richard
Screenwriter(s) Lennart, Isobel

Cast Dailey, Dan; Haver, June [1]; Day, Dennis; Gray, Billy; Williams, Cara; Schafer, Natalie; Sundberg, Clinton; Rorke, Hayden; Sanders, Mary Jane

Song(s) We Girls of the Chorus; The Great White Way; (Ho Hum—Ho Hum) A Quiet Little Place in the Country; If I Love You a Mountain; I'd Rather Have a Pal than a Gal Anytime; You're Doin' All Right; Nowhere Guy; I'm Mad About the Girl Next Door; You; Shoot the Moon [3]; Count Your Calories [2]

Notes [1] Dubbed by Beryl Davis. [2] Not used. [3] Used instrumentally only.

2096 ◆ THE GIRL OF THE GOLDEN WEST
Metro–Goldwyn–Mayer, 1938

Musical Score Stothart, Herbert
Composer(s) Romberg, Sigmund
Lyricist(s) Kahn, Gus
Choreographer(s) Rasch, Albertina

Producer(s) McGuire, William Anthony
Director(s) Leonard, Robert Z.
Screenwriter(s) Dawn, Isabel; DeGaw, Boyce
Source(s) *The Girl of the Golden West* (play) Belasco, David

Cast MacDonald, Jeanette; Eddy, Nelson; Pidgeon, Walter; Carrillo, Leo; Ebsen, Buddy; Penn, Leonard; Lawson, Priscilla; Murphy, Bob; Howland, Olin; Edwards, Cliff; Bevan, Billy; Warner, H.B.; Woolley, Monty; Grapewin, Charley; Beery, Noah; Cody Jr., Bill

Song(s) Sunup to Sundown; Shadows on the Moon; Soldiers of Fortune; Gifts for Nina (C/L: Stothart, Herbert); The Wind in the Trees; Oh Dream of Love [1] (C: Stothart, Herbert); Senorita; Mariachie; The West Ain't Wild Anymore; Who Are We to Say; Girl of the Golden West [2]

Notes [1] Music after Liszt. [2] Instrumental use only.

2097 ✦ GIRL OF THE OZARKS
Paramount, 1936

Producer(s) Botsford, A.M.
Director(s) Shea, William
Screenwriter(s) Anthony, Stuart; Simmons, Michael L.

Cast Weidler, Virginia; Erickson, Leif; Russell, Elizabeth; Hall, Ben; Crosman, Henrietta

Song(s) I Got Time and I Got No Place to Go (C/L: Coslow, Sam); Old Dan Tucker [1] (C: Emmett, Dan; L: Coslow, Sam)

Notes Formerly titled THE GOOD FOR NOTHING. [1] Written in 1843.

2098 ✦ GIRL OF THE RIO
RKO, 1931

Musical Score Steiner, Max

Producer(s) LeBaron, William
Director(s) Brenon, Herbert
Screenwriter(s) Meehan, Elizabeth
Source(s) (play) Mack, Willard

Cast Del Rio, Dolores; Carrillo, Leo; Foster, Norman; Fields, Stanley; Campeau, Frank; Gleason, Lucille [1]; Ince, Ralph

Song(s) Querida (C/L: Schertzinger, Victor)

Notes [1] Billed as Lucille Webster Gleason.

2099 ✦ GIRL OF THE YEAR

See THE PETTY GIRL.

2100 ✦ GIRL ON THE BARGE
Universal, 1929

Director(s) Sloman, Edward
Screenwriter(s) Smith, Charles Henry; Reed, Tom
Source(s) "The The Girl on the Barge" (story) Hughes, Rupert

Cast Hersholt, Jean; O'Neil, Sally; McGregor, Malcolm; McIntosh, Morris; Kelly, Nancy

Song(s) When You Were in Love with No One but Me (C/L: Ahlert, Fred E.; Turk, Roy; Cherniavsky, Joseph [1]); To-Day and To-Morrow (C/L: Ahlert, Fred E.; Turk, Roy; Cherniavsky, Joseph)

Notes No cue sheet available. [1] Spelled Charniousky on sheet music.

2101 ✦ GIRL ON THE SPOT
Universal, 1946

Composer(s) Fairchild, Edgar
Lyricist(s) Brooks, Jack
Choreographer(s) Da Pron, Louis

Producer(s) Blake, George
Director(s) Beaudine, William
Screenwriter(s) Cochran, Dorcas; Warner, Jerry

Cast Collier, Lois; Lane, Richard; Brophy, Edward S.; Newell, Billy; Barker, Jess; Stossel, Ludwig

Song(s) To the Banquet We Go; We're All a Happy Lot (C: von Suppe, Franz); Poor Lonesome Maiden (C: von Suppe, Franz); A New Day [1]; Be Brave Men; Toast the Pirate King; Come Lonely Lover

Notes There are also vocals of "Happy and Light of Heart" and "I Dreamt I Dwelt in Marble Halls" by M.W. Balfe. [1] Not used in HERE COME THE CO-EDS.

2102 ✦ GIRL OVERBOARD
Universal, 1929

Producer(s) Decker, Harry
Director(s) Ruggles, Wesley
Screenwriter(s) Anthony, Walter; Smith, Charles Henry

Cast Philbin, Mary; Mackaye, Fred; Harlan, Otis; McDonald, Francis; Breese, Edmund; North, Wilfred

Song(s) Today and Tomorrow (C/L: Ahlert, Fred E.; Turk, Roy; Cherniavsky, Joseph)

Notes No cue sheet available.

2103 ✦ GIRL RUSH (1944)
RKO, 1944

Musical Score Harline, Leigh
Composer(s) Pollack, Lew
Lyricist(s) Harris, Harry
Choreographer(s) O'Curran, Charles

Director(s) Douglas, Gordon M.
Screenwriter(s) Kent, Robert E.
Source(s) "Petticoat Fever" (story) Vadnay, Laszlo; Laszlo, Aladar

Cast Langford, Frances; Brown, Wally; Vague, Vera; Carney, Alan; Mitchum, Robert; Hurst, Paul; Brill, Patti

Song(s) (When I'm) Walking Arm in Arm with Jim [1]; If Mother Could Only See Us Now; Anabella's Bustle [1]; Rainbow Valley [2]

Notes [1] Also in SUNSET PASS and THE HALF-BREED. [2] Also in CODE OF THE WEST.

2104 ✦ THE GIRL RUSH (1955)
Paramount, 1955

Musical Score Spencer-Hagen, M.S.I.
Composer(s) Martin, Hugh; Blane, Ralph
Lyricist(s) Martin, Hugh; Blane, Ralph
Choreographer(s) Alton, Robert

Producer(s) Brisson, Frederick
Director(s) Pirosh, Robert
Screenwriter(s) Pirosh, Robert; Davis, Jerome

Cast Russell, Rosalind; Lamas, Fernando; Albert, Eddie; De Haven, Gloria; Lorne, Marion; Fortier, Robert; Crichton, Don; White, Jesse; Mattox, Matt; Chakiris, George

Song(s) An Occasional Man; At Last We're Alone; Birmin'ham; Champagne [1]; It's June [1]; Homesick Hillbilly; If You'll Only Take a Chance; Out of Doors; The Girl Rush; I Take a Dim View of the West [2]; My Song [3] [6]; So Right for Me [3] [5]; Miss Jemima Walks By [3] [4] (C: Van Heusen, James; L: Burke, Johnny); Is It Really Me [3]

Notes [1] Same music. [2] Used instrumentally only though recorded with a vocal by Rosalind Russell and Marion Lorne. [3] Not used. [4] Written for DIXIE but used instrumentally only in that picture. [5] Recorded. [6] Used in THE GIRL MOST LIKELY.

2105 ✦ THE GIRL SAID NO
Metro–Goldwyn–Mayer, 1930

Director(s) Wood, Sam
Screenwriter(s) MacArthur, Charles

Cast Haines, William; Hyams, Leila; Moran, Polly; Dressler, Marie; Bushman Jr., Francis X.; Blandick, Clara

Song(s) I Don't Want Your Kisses If I Can't Have Your Love [1] (C/L: Broones, Martin; Fisher, Fred)

Notes No cue sheet available. [1] Also in SO THIS IS COLLEGE.

2106 ✦ A GIRL'S BEST YEARS
Metro–Goldwyn–Mayer, 1937

Composer(s) Jason, Will; Burton, Val
Lyricist(s) Jason, Will; Burton, Val

Director(s) LeBorg, Reginald
Screenwriter(s) Rauh, Stanley; Goldstone, Richard

Cast Doran, Mary; Warburton, John; Terry, Sheila; Parker, Barnett

Song(s) Here It Is; Wherever There's Smoke, There's Fire

Notes Short subject.

2107 ✦ GIRLS DEMAND EXCITEMENT
Fox, 1931

Director(s) Felix, Seymour
Screenwriter(s) Thompson, Harlan

Cast Cherrill, Virginia; Wayne, John; Churchill, Marguerite; Eddy, Helen Jerome

Song(s) (There's Something About An) Old Fashioned Girl [1] (C: Henderson, Ray; L: DeSylva, B.G.; Brown, Lew)

Notes [1] Also in JUST IMAGINE.

2108 ✦ GIRLS! GIRLS! GIRLS!
Paramount, 1962

Musical Score Lilley, Joseph J.
Choreographer(s) O'Curran, Charles

Producer(s) Wallis, Hal B.
Director(s) Taurog, Norman
Screenwriter(s) Anhalt, Edward; Weiss, Allan

Cast Stevens, Stella [1]; Presley, Elvis; Goodwin, Laurel; Slate, Jeremy; Fong, Benson; Strauss, Robert; Paiva, Nestor; Lee, Guy

Song(s) Girls! Girls! Girls! (C/L: Leiber, Jerry; Stoller, Mike); Never Let Me Go [4] (C/L: Livingston, Jay; Evans, Ray); I Don't Wanna Be Tied (C/L: Grant, Bill; Baum, Bernie; Kaye, Florence); Where Do You Come From? [3] (C/L: Batchelor, Ruth; Roberts, Bob); I Don't Want To (C/L: Spielman, Fred; Torre, Janice); Mama (C/L: O'Curran, Charles; Brooks, Dudley); We'll Be Together [2] (C: Traditional; L: O'Curran, Charles; Brooks, Dudley); A Boy Like Me, A Girl Like You (C/L: Tepper, Sid; Bennett, Roy C.); Earth Boy (C/L: Tepper, Sid; Bennett, Roy C.); The Nearness of You [3] (C: Carmichael, Hoagy; L: Washington, Ned); Return to Sender (C/L: Blackwell, Otis; Scott, Winfield); Because of Love (C/L: Batchelor, Ruth; Roberts, Bob); Thanks to the Rolling Sea (C/L: Batchelor, Ruth; Roberts, Bob); Song of the Shrimp (C/L: Bennett, Roy C.; Tepper, Sid); The Walls Have Ears (C/L: Bennett, Roy C.; Tepper, Sid); We're Coming in Loaded (C/L: Blackwell, Otis; Scott, Winfield); Baby, Baby, Baby (C/L: Livingston, Jay; Evans, Ray)

Notes Previously titled GUMBO YA-YA. [1] Dubbed by Gilda Maiken. [2] Music based on the Mexican folk song "Carmela." [3] Not used but recorded. Written for the unproduced film ROMANCE IN THE ROUGH. Also not used in ST. LOUIS BLUES (1939) and ASH WEDNESDAY. [4] Also in THE SCARLET HOUR.

2109 ✦ GIRLS IN THE STREET
Republic, 1937

Producer(s) Wilcox, Herbert
Director(s) Wilcox, Herbert
Screenwriter(s) Tranter, Florence; Hoffe, Monckton

Cast Neagle, Anna; Carminati, Tullio; Douglas, Robert; Hodges, Horace

Song(s) The Eyes of the World (C/L: Lerner, Sam; Goodhart, Al; Hoffman, Al); Jingle of the Jungle (C/L: Lerner, Sam; Goodhart, Al; Hoffman, Al)

Notes A British picture originally titled LONDON MELODY.

2110 ✦ THE GIRLS OF PLEASURE ISLAND
Paramount, 1953

Musical Score Murray, Lyn

Producer(s) Jones, Paul
Director(s) Herbert, F. Hugh; Ganzer, Alvin [2]
Screenwriter(s) Herbert, F. Hugh
Source(s) *Pleasure Island* (novel) Maier, William

Cast Bromiley, Dorothy; Dalton, Audrey; Elan, Joan; Taylor, Don; Barry, Gene; Genn, Leo; Ober, Philip; Lanchester, Elsa

Song(s) Fiji Fanny (C/L: Brown, Forman)

Notes [2] Ganzer took over when Herbert became ill.

2111 ✦ GIRLS OF THE BIG HOUSE
Republic, 1945

Producer(s) Abel, Rudolph E.
Director(s) Archainbaud, George
Screenwriter(s) Branch, Houston

Cast Roberts, Lynne; Christine, Virginia; Martin, Marion; Mara, Adele; Posers, Richard; Wall, Geraldine

Song(s) There's a Man in My Life (C/L: James, Inez; Elliott, Jack); Alma Mater (C: Green, Sanford; L: Carroll, June)

2112 ✦ THE GIRLS ON THE BEACH
Paramount, 1965

Musical Score Usher, Gary

Producer(s) Jacobson, Harvey
Director(s) Witney, William
Screenwriter(s) Malcolm, David
Source(s) (musical)

Cast West, Martin; Marshall, Linda; Corcoran, Noreen; Roger, Steven; Gore, Lesley; The Beach Boys; The Crickets; Bromley, Sheila

Song(s) Girls on the Beach (C/L: Wilson, Brian); Leave Me Alone (C/L: Gore, Lesley); Lonely Sea (C:

Usher, Gary; L: Wilson); Little Honda (C/L: Wilson, Brian); It's Gotta Be You (C: Ogerman, Claus; L: Raleigh, Ben); I Don't Want to Be a Loser (C/L: Raleigh, Ben; Barkan, Mark); Why Do I Love You So (C: Usher, Gary; L: Christian, Roger); I Want to Marry a Beatle (C/L: Connors, Carol; Taugman, Richard)

Notes Formerly titled BEACH GIRLS.

2113 ✦ GIRLS ON THE LOOSE
Universal, 1958

Producer(s) Rybnick, Harry; Kay, Richard
Director(s) Henreid, Paul
Screenwriter(s) Friedman, Alan; Raison, Dorothy; Rivkin, Allen

Cast Corday, Mara; Milan, Lita; Bostock, Barbara; Barker, Joyce; Dalton, Abby; Richman, Mark; Lormer, Jon; Green, Ronald; Kruger, Fred

Song(s) How Do You Learn to Love? (C/L: Philpott, Dixie; Whitaker, Ray; Hampton, Dolores); I Was a Little Too Lonely (C/L: Evans, Ray; Livingston, Jay)

Notes Originally titled TAKE FIVE FROM FIVE.

2114 ✦ GIRLS' TOWN
Metro–Goldwyn–Mayer, 1960

Musical Score Alexander, Van
Composer(s) Anka, Paul
Lyricist(s) Anka, Paul

Producer(s) Zugsmith, Albert
Director(s) Haas, Charles
Screenwriter(s) Smith, Robert

Cast Van Doren, Mamie; Torme, Mel; Anthony, Ray; Hayes, Margaret; Anka, Paul; Crosby, Cathy; Perreau, Gigi; Donahue, Elinor; Talbott, Gloria; Graham, Sheila; Mitchum, Jim; Contino, Dick; Lloyd Jr., Harold; Chaplin Jr., Charles; The Platters; Leeds, Peter

Song(s) Girls' Town; I Love You; I'm Just a Lonely Boy; Wish It Were Me (C/L: Ram, Buck); It's Time to Cry

2115 ✦ GIRL WITH GREEN EYES
United Artists, 1964

Musical Score Addison, John

Producer(s) Richardson, Tony
Director(s) Davis, Desmond
Screenwriter(s) O'Brien, Edna
Source(s) *The Lonely Girl* (novel) O'Brien, Edna

Cast Finch, Peter; Tushingham, Rita; Kean, Marie; O'Sullivan, Arthur; Redgrave, Lynn

Song(s) Dance Hall Fly Twist (C/L: Madara, John; White, David)

2116 ♦ THE GIRL WITHOUT A ROOM
Paramount, 1933

Composer(s) Burton, Val; Jason, Will
Lyricist(s) Burton, Val; Jason, Will
Choreographer(s) Ceballos, Larry

Producer(s) Rogers, Charles R.
Director(s) Murphy, Ralph
Screenwriter(s) Butler, Frank; Binyon, Claude
Source(s) (novel) Lait, Jack

Cast Churchill, Marguerite; Farrell, Charles; Ruggles, Charles; Ratoff, Gregory; Woolf, Walter; Bradley, Grace; Auer, Mischa; Kinskey, Leonid; Ash, Sam

Song(s) The Whistle Has A Blow; You Alone; Rooftop Serenade [3]; Art Award; What Did the Volga Boatman Do on Sunday [1]; He [1]; She Made Her Bed [1] [2]

Notes [1] Not used. [2] This number was filmed. [3] Same number as "Penthouse Serenade."

2117 ♦ GIT ALONG LITTLE DOGIES
Republic, 1937

Producer(s) Schaefer, Armand
Director(s) Kane, Joseph
Screenwriter(s) McGowan, Dorrell; McGowan, Stuart

Cast Autry, Gene; Burnette, Smiley; Maple City Four, The; Allen, Judith; Heyburn, Weldon; Farnum, William; Fung, Willie; Ahern, Will; Ahern, Gladys; The Cabin Kids

Song(s) Honey, Bringing Honey to You (C/L: Unknown); If You Want to Be a Cowboy (C/L: Allan, Fleming); Stock Selling Song (C/L: Unknown); Long Long Ago [1] (C/L: Unknown)

Notes No cue sheet available. It is not known if the above songs are public domain or written for the film. There are also vocals of "Git Along Little Dogies" and "Chinatown, My Chinatown" by Jean Schwartz and William Jerome, "Wait for the Wagon," "Red River Valley," "Comin' Round the Mountain," "In the Valley When the Sun Goes Down," "Oh, Suzanna" and "Good Night Ladies" by E.P. Christy and Ferd V.D. Garretson, "After You've Gone" by Henry Creamer and Turner Layton and "Happy Days Are Here Again" by Jack Yellen and Milton Ager. [1] May be the standard written by T.H. Bayley.

2118 ♦ GIVE A GIRL A BREAK
Metro–Goldwyn–Mayer, 1953

Musical Score Previn, Andre
Composer(s) Lane, Burton
Lyricist(s) Gershwin, Ira
Choreographer(s) Donen, Stanley; Champion, Gower

Producer(s) Cummings, Jack
Director(s) Donen, Stanley
Screenwriter(s) Hackett, Albert; Goodrich, Frances

Cast Champion, Gower [1]; Champion, Marge; Reynolds, Debbie; Wood, Helen; Fosse, Bob; Kasznar, Kurt; Anderson, Richard; Ching, William; Tuttle, Lurene; Keating, Larry

Song(s) Give a Girl a Break; Nothing Is Impossible; In Our United State; It Happens Ev'ry Time; Applause, Applause; Dream World [2]; Ach Du Lieber Oom-Pah-Pah [3]; Woman, There Is No Living with You [3]

Notes [1] Dubbed. [2] Used instrumentally only though recorded with lyrics. [3] Not used.

2119 ♦ GIVE 'EM THE AXE
Paramount, 1930 unproduced

Composer(s) Dreyer, Dave
Lyricist(s) Macdonald, Ballard

Song(s) You'll Do Until Somebody Comes Along; Spring Has Came; Hopeless, Helpless, Lovesick and Blue; Here Is My Heart; I've Made Up Your Mind for Me; Stop That Band; The Money I've Got to Get [1]; Not Tonight Josephine

Notes [1] Used in ONLY SAPS WORK.

2120 ♦ GIVE ME A SAILOR
Paramount, 1938

Composer(s) Rainger, Ralph
Lyricist(s) Robin, Leo
Choreographer(s) Prinz, LeRoy

Producer(s) Lazarus, Jeff
Director(s) Nugent, Elliott
Screenwriter(s) Anderson, Doris; Butler, Frank
Source(s) *Linger Longer Letty* (musical) Nichols, Anne

Cast Raye, Martha; Hope, Bob; Grable, Betty; Whiting, Jack; Kolb, Clarence; Nugent, J.C.; Churchill, Bonnie Jean

Song(s) The U.S.A. and You; What Goes On Here (in My Heart) [4]; A Little Kiss at Twilight; It Don't Make Sense [1] [2]; Give Me a Sailor (1) [1] (C/L: Coslow, Sam); Oh Baby, Obey [1] [3]; You're a Blessing to Me [1] [5]; Give Me a Sailor (2) [1] (C: Carmichael, Hoagy; L: Loesser, Frank); I'm in the Pink [1] (C: Lane, Burton; L: Loesser, Frank); Am I the Lucky One [1] (C: Lane, Burton; L: Loesser, Frank); I'm in Dreamland [1] (C: Lane, Burton; L: Loesser, Frank)

Notes [1] Not used. [2] Published though not used. Also not used in THE BIG BROADCAST OF 1937. [3] Written for unproduced film COME ON MARINES. Also not used in FOUR HOURS TO KILL. [4] Not used in THE BIG BROADCAST OF 1938 and COLLEGE SWING. [5] Also not used in COCOANUT GROVE, FOUR HOURS TO KILL, HERE IS MY HEART and WAIKIKI WEDDING.

2121 ◆ GIVE ME THE STARS
Republic, 1944

Musical Score Russell, Kennedy
Composer(s) Russell, Kennedy
Lyricist(s) O'Connor, Desmond

Producer(s) Zelnik, Fred
Director(s) Rogers, Maclean
Screenwriter(s) Rogers, Maclean; Melford, Austin

Cast Lynn, Leni; Fyffe, Will; Hunter, Jackie; Lindo, Olga

Song(s) Hap, Hap, Happy; Mary Brown; Through All the Changing Seasons; You Can Give Me the Stars; I Hate Songs (C/L: Hunter, Jackie)

Notes A British National picture.

2122 ◆ GIVE MY REGARDS TO BROAD STREET
Twentieth Century–Fox, 1984

Musical Score McCartney, Paul
Composer(s) McCartney, Paul
Lyricist(s) McCartney, Paul

Producer(s) Epaminondus, Andros
Director(s) Webb, Peter
Screenwriter(s) McCartney, Paul

Cast McCartney, Paul; McCartney, Linda; Brown, Bryan; Ullman, Tracey

Song(s) Wanderlust; No More Lonely Nights; Ballroom Dancing; Silly Love Songs; Not Such a Bad Boy; No Values

Notes Vocals are not differentiated from instrumentals on the cue sheet. There are also vocals of the John Lennon and Paul McCartney songs: "Good Day Sunshine;" "Yesterday;" "Here, There and Everywhere;" "For No One" and "Eleanor Rigby."

2123 ◆ GIVE MY REGARDS TO BROADWAY
Twentieth Century–Fox, 1948

Choreographer(s) Felix, Seymour

Producer(s) Morosco, Walter
Director(s) Bacon, Lloyd
Screenwriter(s) Hoffenstein, Samuel; Reinhardt, Elizabeth

Cast Dailey, Dan; Winninger, Charles; Guild, Nancy; Ruggles, Charles; Bainter, Fay; Lawrence, Barbara; Rumann, Sig

Song(s) Albert the Great (C: Henderson, Charles; L: Gordon, Mack)

Notes Featured as vocals are "Oh You Beautiful Doll" by Nat D. Ayer and A. Seymour Brown; "Let a Smile Be Your Umbrella on a Rainy, Rainy, Day" by Sammy Fain, Irving Kahal and Francis Wheeler; "Where Did You Get That Hat?" by Joseph J. Sullivan; "Give My Regards to Broadway" by George M. Cohan and "When Francis Dances with Me" by Sol Violinsky and Benny Ryan.

2124 ◆ GIVE OUT SISTERS
Universal, 1942

Choreographer(s) Mattison, John

Producer(s) Burton, Bernard W.
Director(s) Cline, Edward F.
Screenwriter(s) Smith, Paul Gerard; Wilson, Warren

Cast The Andrews Sisters; McDonald, Grace; Butterworth, Charles; Frawley, William; Catlett, Walter; Ryan, Peggy

Song(s) It's the New Generation (C/L: Donaldson, Walter); You're Just a Flower from an Old Bouquet (C/L: Denni, Gwynne; Denni, Lucien); Who Do You Think You're Foolin? (C/L: Stillwell, Ray; Gold, Ray); Jiggers, the Beat (C/L: Robins, Sid; Lerner, Al)

Notes There is also a vocal of the "Pennsylvania Polka" by Lester Lee and Zeke Manners.

2125 ◆ GIVE US THIS NIGHT
Paramount, 1936

Composer(s) Korngold, Erich Wolfgang
Lyricist(s) Hammerstein II, Oscar

Producer(s) LeBaron, William
Director(s) Hall, Alexander
Screenwriter(s) Mayer, Edwin Justus; Starling, Lynn

Cast Kiepura, Jan; Swarthout, Gladys; Mowbray, Alan [3]; Baker, Benny; Merivale, Philip; Toler, Sidney; Burani, Michelette; Collier Sr., William

Song(s) Sorrento Song [2]; Fisherman's Song [4]; Softly Through the Heart of Night; Processional; Sweet Melody of Night; Morning Song in Naples [2] (L: Tobias, Harry); My Love and I [7]; I Mean to Say I Love You; Opera—Part I; Opening Ballroom [1]; Opera—Part II; Opera—Part III; Give Us This Night (1) [1] (C: Korngold, Erich Wolfgang; Boutelje, Phil); Music in the Night (and Laughter in the Air) [1] [6]; Was There Ever a Voice [1]; Eager As a Bird [1]; Luigi [1] (C: Whiting, Richard A.); Give Us This Night [1] [5] (C: Lawnhurst, Vee; L: Seymour, Tot)

Notes In the "Wedding Song" Korngold is playing the piano on the soundtrack. [1] Not used. [2] Same music. [3] Dubbed by Allan Rogers. [4] Based on music by Offenbach. [5] Written for exploitation use only. [6] Published though not used. [7] Also in THE LOST WEEKEND.

2126 ◆ GIVE US WINGS
Universal, 1940

Producer(s) Goldsmith, Ken
Director(s) Lamont, Charles

Screenwriter(s)   Horman, Arthur T.; Johnson, Robert Lee

Cast   The Little Tough Guys; The Dead End Kids; Jory, Victor; Ford, Wallace; Gwynne, Walter

Song(s)   Come On Down (C/L: Reinhart, Dick); On a Blue Ridge Mountain Trail (C/L: Bond, Johnny; Marvin, Johnny)

2127 ✦ THE GLACIER FOX
Sanrio, 1979

Musical Score   Sato, Masaru; Takekawa, Yukihide
Composer(s)   Takekawa, Yukihide
Lyricist(s)   Bishop, Randy; Narahashi, Yoko

Producer(s)   Tsugawa, Hiromu
Director(s)   Kurahara, Koreyoshi
Screenwriter(s)   Kurahara, Koreyoshi
Narrator(s)   Bloch, Walter

Song(s)   In Quest of the Northern Sun; No Mercy; We've Come to the Crossroads; Vagabond; I Will Survive (L: Bishop, Randy); To Be Close (L: Gwinn, Marty; Narahashi, Yoko); Treasured Dreams (C: Sato, Masaru; L: Gwinn, Marty; Narahashi, Yoko; Bishop, Randy); The Wind Will Bring My Love (L: Gwinn, Marty; Narahashi, Yoko); Laughing in the Sunshine; Everything Is Mystery; Good Morning World; Big Adventure

Notes   A documentary. No cue sheet available.

2128 ✦ GLACIER TRAILS
Twentieth Century–Fox, 1941

Song(s)   Down the Glacier Trail [1] (C: Stept, Sam H.; L: Allvine, Earl F.)

Notes   This is a Lowell Thomas Magic Carpet of Movietone travelogue. [1] Based on "On the Sunset Trail" by Sam Stept and Sidney D. Mitchell.

2129 ✦ THE GLADIATOR
Columbia, 1938

Musical Score   Young, Victor

Producer(s)   Gross, Edward
Director(s)   Sedgwick, Edward
Screenwriter(s)   Melson, Charles; Sheekman, Arthur
Source(s)   *The Gladiator* (novel) Wylie, Philip

Cast   Brown, Joe E.; Dean, Man Mountain; Travis, June; Moore, Dickie; Littlefield, Lucien; Kent, Robert

Song(s)   On to Victory (C: Samuels, Walter G.; L: Newman, Charles)

2130 ✦ THE GLAD RAG DOLL
Warner Brothers, 1929

Director(s)   Curtiz, Michael
Screenwriter(s)   Baker, Graham

Cast   Costello, Dolores; Gillingwater, Claude; Ferris, Audrey; Ricketts, Thomas; Fuller, Dale; Beavers, Louise

Song(s)   Glad Rag Doll (C: Ager, Milton; Dougherty, Dan; L: Yellen, Jack)

Notes   No cue sheet available.

2131 ✦ GLAMOUR BOY
Paramount, 1941

Composer(s)   Schertzinger, Victor
Lyricist(s)   Loesser, Frank

Producer(s)   Clark, Colbert
Director(s)   Murphy, Ralph
Screenwriter(s)   Ropes, Bradford; Burton, Val; Herbert, F. Hugh

Cast   Cooper, Jackie; Hickman, Darryl; Foster, Susanna; Abel, Walter; Demarest, William; Gillis, Ann; Meiser, Edith; Searl, Jackie

Song(s)   Love Is Such an Old Fashioned Thing [2]; Magic of Magnolias [1]

Notes   The film was released as HEARTS IN SPRINGTIME in Great Britain. [1] This was originally titled MAGNOLIAS IN THE NIGHT but Schertzinger had previously written a song for Fox titled "Magnolias in the Moonlight," with Harry Tobias. [2] Not used in SWEATER GIRL but with Jule Styne music.

2132 ✦ GLAMOUR FOR SALE (1940)
Columbia, 1940

Composer(s)   Oakland, Ben

Director(s)   Lederman, D. Ross
Screenwriter(s)   Bright, John

Cast   Louise, Anita; Pryor, Roger; MacCloy, June; Robinson, Frances; Beddoe, Don; Borg, Veda Ann

Song(s)   Crazy Dreams (L: Magidson, Herb); If They Gave Me a Million [1] (L: Drake, Milton)

Notes   [1] First used in IT'S ALL YOURS.

2133 ✦ GLAMOUR GIRL
Columbia, 1947

Musical Score   Duning, George

Producer(s)   Katzman, Sam
Director(s)   Dreifuss, Arthur
Screenwriter(s)   Gold, Lee; Webster, M. Coates

Cast   Gene Krupa and His Orchestra; Duane, Michael; Lloyd, Jimmy; Leonard, Jack; Reed, Susan; Grey, Virginia; Neill, Noel; Watkin, Pierre; Borden, Eugene

Song(s)   Without Imagination [2] (C/L: Fisher, Doris; Roberts, Allan); Gene's Boogie Woogie (C/L: Ellis, Segar; Williams, George); Anywhere [1] (C: Styne, Jule; Cahn, Sammy)

Notes Susan Reed arranged and sang these traditional songs: "Turtle Dove," "Go Away from My Window," "Cockles and Mussels," "The Soldier and the Lady" and "Black, Black, Black." Krupa performed "Melody in 'F'." [1] From TONIGHT AND EVERY NIGHT. [2] Also in THE GUILT OF JANET AMES.

2134 ✦ THE GLASS BOTTOM BOAT
Metro–Goldwyn–Mayer, 1966

Musical Score De Vol, Frank

Producer(s) Melcher, Martin; Freeman, Everett
Director(s) Tashlin, Frank
Screenwriter(s) Freeman, Everett

Cast Day, Doris; Taylor, Rod; Godfrey, Arthur; McGiver, John; Lynde, Paul; Andrews, Edward; Fleming, Eric; DeLuise, Dom; Fraser, Elisabeth; Martin, Dick; Pearce, Alice; Tobias, George; Corby, Ellen

Song(s) Soft as the Starlight (C/L: Lubin, Joe; Howard, Jerome); Glass Bottom Boat (C/L: Lubin, Joe)

2135 ✦ THE GLASS SLIPPER
Metro–Goldwyn–Mayer, 1954

Musical Score Kaper, Bronislau
Choreographer(s) Petit, Roland

Producer(s) Knopf, Edwin H.
Director(s) Walters, Charles
Screenwriter(s) Deutsch, Helen

Cast Caron, Leslie; Wilding, Michael; Wynn, Keenan; Winwood, Estelle; Lanchester, Elsa; Jones, Barry; Blake, Amanda; Tuttle, Lurene; Daniels, Lisa

Song(s) Take My Love (C: Kaper, Bronislau; L: Deutsch, Helen)

2136 ✦ THE GLENN MILLER STORY
Universal, 1954

Musical Score Mancini, Henry
Choreographer(s) Williams, Kenny

Producer(s) Rosenberg, Aaron
Director(s) Mann, Anthony
Screenwriter(s) Davies, Valentine; Brodney, Oscar

Cast Stewart, James [1]; Allyson, June; Bacon, Irving; Lockhart, Kathleen; Morgan, Henry [2]; Drake, Charles; Tobias, George; Ross, Marion; MacLane, Barton; Rumann, Sig; Bell, James; Warren, Katharine; Armstrong, Louis; Krupa, Gene; Langford, Frances; Pollack, Ben; The Archie Savage Dancers; The Modernaires

Notes There are no original songs in this film. Vocals and instrumentals include: "Moonlight Serenade" by Mitchell Parish and Glenn Miller; "Looking at the World Through Rose Colored Glasses" by Tommy Malie and Jimmy Steiger; "Little Brown Jug" and "Bidin' My Time" by George and Ira Gershwin; "Basin Street Blues" by Spencer Williams; "Over the Rainbow" by Harold Arlen and E.Y. Harburg; "I Know Why," "Chattanooga Choo Choo" and "At Last" by Mack Gordon and Harry Warren; "A String of Pearls" by Eddie DeLange and Jerry Gray; "Pennsylvania 6-5000" by Carl Sigman and Jerry Gray; "Tuxedo Junction" by Buddy Feyne, Erskine Hawkins, William Johnson and Julian Dash; "St. Louis Blues" by W.C. Handy; "In the Mood" by Andy Razaf and Joe Garland; "American Patrol" by F.W. Meacham and "Adios" by Enrico Madriguera. [1] Trumpet dubbed by Joe Yuki. [2] Piano playing dubbed by Lyman Gandee.

2137 ✦ A GLOBAL AFFAIR
Metro–Goldwyn–Mayer, 1964

Musical Score Frontiere, Dominic
Composer(s) Frontiere, Dominic
Lyricist(s) Cochran, Dorcas

Producer(s) Bartlett, Hall
Director(s) Arnold, Jack
Screenwriter(s) Fisher, Bob; Lederer, Charles; Marx, Arthur

Cast Hope, Bob; Mercier, Michele; Andersen, Elga; De Carlo, Yvonne; Taka, Miiko; Sterling, Robert; Persoff, Nehemiah; McGiver, John; Bergerac, Jacques; Shaughnessy, Mickey; Pulver, Lilo; Shaw, Reta; Downs, Hugh

Song(s) So Wide the World; Fais-Do-Do Go to Sleep; A Global Affair [1]

Notes [1] Used instrumentally only.

2138 ✦ GLORIFYING THE AMERICAN GIRL
Paramount, 1929

Composer(s) Donaldson, Walter
Lyricist(s) Donaldson, Walter
Choreographer(s) Tours, Frank; Shawn, Ted; Harkrider, John

Producer(s) Ziegfeld, Florenz
Director(s) Webb, Millard; Harkrider, John
Screenwriter(s) McAvoy, J.P.; Webb, Millard

Cast Eaton, Mary; Cantor, Eddie; Vallee, Rudy; Morgan, Helen; Crandall, Edward; Shea, Olive; Healy, Dan; Renard, Kaye; Edwards, Sarah; Ziegfeld, Mr. and Mrs. Florenz; Lardner, Ring; Beery, Noah; Guinan, Texas; Weissmuller, Johnny; Brokenshire, Norman

Song(s) What Wouldn't I Do for that Man [1] (C: Gorney, Jay; L: Harburg, E.Y.)

Notes There are also vocals of "Blue Skies" by Irving Berlin (also in BLUE SKIES, ALEXANDER'S RAGTIME BAND and THE JAZZ SINGER); "I'm Just a Vagabond Lover" by Rudy Vallee and Leon Zimmerman (also in THE VAGABOND LOVER);

"Baby Face" by Benny Davis and Harry Akst and the Walter Donaldson songs "At Sundown," "Beautiful Changes," "Sam the Old Accordion Man" and "There Must Be Someone Waiting for Me." [1] Also in APPLAUSE.

2139 ◆ GLORY
RKO, 1936

Musical Score Perkins, Frank
Composer(s) Jerome, M.K.
Lyricist(s) Koehler, Ted

Producer(s) Butler, David
Director(s) Butler, David
Screenwriter(s) Milne, Peter

Cast O'Brien, Margaret; Brennan, Walter; Greenwood, Charlotte; Lupton, John; Palmer, Byron; Davis, Lisa; Kinskey, Leonid

Song(s) Calypso; Gettin' Nowhere Road; Happy Time Again; Glory; Kentucky Means Paradise [1]

Notes [1] Sheet music only.

2140 ◆ GLORY ALLEY
Metro–Goldwyn–Mayer, 1952

Musical Score Stoll, George; Rugolo, Pete
Choreographer(s) O'Curran, Charles

Producer(s) Nayfack, Nicholas
Director(s) Walsh, Raoul
Screenwriter(s) Cohn, Art

Cast Meeker, Ralph; Caron, Leslie; Roland, Gilbert; Kasznar, Kurt; Armstrong, Louis; McIntire, John; Seymour, Dan; Teagarden, Jack; Gates, Larry

Song(s) Glory Alley (C: Livingston, Jerry; L: David, Mack); Tail Gate (C/L: Alexander, Jeff); That's What the Man Said (C/L: Robison, Willard)

Notes There is also a vocal of "St. Louis Blues" by W.C. Handy.

2141 ◆ "G" MEN
Warner Brothers, 1935

Musical Score Kaun, Bernhard

Producer(s) Edelman, Louis F.
Director(s) Keighley, William
Screenwriter(s) Miller, Seton I.

Cast Cagney, James; Lindsay, Margaret; Dvorak, Ann; Armstrong, Robert; MacLane, Barton; Nolan, Lloyd; Harrigan, William; Blue, Monte; Toomey, Regis

Song(s) You Bother Me an Awful Lot (C: Fain, Sammy; L: Kahal, Irving)

Notes "Lullaby of Broadway" by Harry Warren and Al Dubin is also used.

2142 ◆ THE GNOME-MOBILE
Disney, 1967

Musical Score Baker, Buddy

Producer(s) Algar, James
Director(s) Stevenson, Robert
Screenwriter(s) Kadison, Ellis
Source(s) *Gnomemobile* (novel) Sinclair, Upton

Cast Brennan, Walter; Garber, Matthew; Dotrice, Karen; Deacon, Richard; Lowell, Tom; McClory, Sean; Wynn, Ed; Cowan, Jerome; Lane, Charles; Lamb, Gil; Prickett, Maudie

Song(s) The Gnome-Mobile Song (In Me Jaunting Car) (C/L: Sherman, Richard M.; Sherman, Robert B.)

2143 ◆ GOBS AND GALS
Republic, 1951

Musical Score Wilson, Stanley

Producer(s) Picker, Sidney
Director(s) Springsteen, R.G.
Screenwriter(s) Horman, Arthur T.

Cast Brothers, Bernard; Hutton, Robert; Downs, Cathy; Marly, Florence; Jones, Gordon; Belasco, Leon

Song(s) East Indian Polka (C/L: Elliott, Jack)

2144 ◆ GO CHASE YOURSELF
RKO, 1938

Producer(s) Sisk, Robert
Director(s) Cline, Edward F.
Screenwriter(s) Yawitz, Paul; Granet, Bert

Cast Penner, Joe; Ball, Lucille; Lane, Richard; Travis, June; Feld, Fritz; Kennedy, Tom; Bates, Granville; Page, Bradley; Irving, George; Carson, Jack

Song(s) The First Time I Saw You (C: Shilkret, Nathaniel; L: Wrubel, Allie); I'm from the City (C/L: Raynor, Hal; Penner, Joe)

2145 ◆ THE GODDESS
Columbia, 1958

Producer(s) Perlman, Milton
Director(s) Cromwell, John
Screenwriter(s) Chayefsky, Paddy

Cast Stanley, Kim; Holland, Betty; Bridges, Lloyd; Copeland, Joan; Hiken, Gerald; Hill, Steven; Brinkerhoff, Burt; Van Patten, Joyce; Beavers, Louise; Duke, Patty; Klemperer, Werner

Song(s) The Window of Dreams (C/L: Livingston, Jay; Evans, Ray)

2146 ✦ THE GODFATHER
Paramount, 1972

Musical Score   Rota, Nino; Coppola, Carmine

Producer(s)   Ruddy, Albert S.
Director(s)   Coppola, Francis Ford
Screenwriter(s)   Puzo, Mario
Source(s)   *The Godfather* (novel) Puzo, Mario

Cast   Brando, Marlon; Pacino, Al; Duvall, Robert; Caan, James; Keaton, Diane; Shire, Talia; Hayden, Sterling; Conte, Richard

Song(s)   I Have But One Heart (C: Farrow, Johnny; L: Symes, Marty); Speak Softly Love (C: Rota, Nino; L: Kusik, Larry); Non Ci Lasceremo Mai (We Will Never Never Part) [1] (C: Coppola, Carmine; L: Pennino, Italia); Many Different People [1] (C: Rota, Nino; L: Simon, Norman; Meshel, Billy); Come Live Your Life with Me [1] (C: Rota, Nino; L: Kusik, Larry; Meshel, Billy); The Godfather Waltz [2] (C: Rota, Nino; L: Pennino, Italia); Antico Canto Siciliano [3] (C/L: Coppola, Carmine)

Notes   [1] Lyric added for exploitation. [2] Lyric added for exploitation but used with a lyric in GODFATHER II. [3] Sheet music only.

2147 ✦ THE GODFATHER PART II
Paramount, 1974

Musical Score   Rota, Nino; Coppola, Carmine

Producer(s)   Coppola, Francis Ford
Director(s)   Coppola, Francis Ford
Screenwriter(s)   Coppola, Francis Ford; Puzo, Mario

Cast   De Niro, Robert; Pacino, Al; Keaton, Diane; Strasberg, Lee; Duvall, Robert; King, Morgana

Song(s)   Love Said Goodbye (C: Rota, Nino; L: Kusik, Larry); Sophia [1] (C: Coppola, Carmine; L: Pennino, Italia; Palomba, Salvatore); Napule Ve Salute (Goodbye to Naples) [2] (C: Pennino, Francesco; L: Pennino, Italia; Pennino, Francesco); Ho Bisogono Di Te (Gelosia) (When I'm with You) [3] (C: Coppola, Carmine; L: Pennino, Francesco); The Godfather Waltz [4] (C: Rota, Nino; L: Pennino, Italia); Senza Mamma (C/L: Pennino, Francesco)

Notes   There are also vocals of "Tu" by Fernan Sanchez and E. Sanchez Fuentes and "Guantanamera," a traditional song. [1] Lyric written for exploitation only. [2] Italia Pennino wrote the English lyrics. [3] Used instrumentally only. [4] Used instrumentally in THE GODFATHER.

2148 ✦ GODSPELL
Columbia, 1973

Composer(s)   Schwartz, Stephen
Lyricist(s)   Schwartz, Stephen
Choreographer(s)   Bayes, Sammy

Producer(s)   Lansbury, Edgar
Director(s)   Greene, David
Screenwriter(s)   Tebelak, John-Michael; Greene, David
Source(s)   *Godspell* (musical) Schwartz, Stephen; Tebelak, John-Michael

Cast   Garber, Victor; Haskell, David; Lamont, Robin; Sroka, Jerry; Thigpen, Lynne; Hanley, Katie; McCormick, Gilmer; Jonas, Joanne

Song(s)   Day By Day; All for the Best; O Bless the Lord My Soul; Prepare Ye the Way of the Lord; Turn Back, O Man; Beautiful City; Save the People; All Good Gifts; Light of the World; Alas for You; On the Willows; By My Side (C/L: Hamburger, Jay; Gordon, Peggy)

Notes   No cue sheet available. All songs written for off-Broadway production.

2149 ✦ GOD TOLD ME TO
New World, 1976

Musical Score   Cordell, Frank

Producer(s)   Cohen, Larry
Director(s)   Cohen, Larry
Screenwriter(s)   Cohen, Larry

Cast   Lo Bianco, Tony; Raffin, Deborah; Dennis, Sandy; Sidney, Sylvia; Levene, Sam; Drivas, Robert; Kellin, Mike; Nichols, Robert; Heffernan, John

Song(s)   Sweet Momma Sweetlove (C: Ragland, Robert O.; L: Webb, Janelle)

Notes   No cue sheet available.

2150 ✦ GODZILLA 1985
New World, 1985

Musical Score   Koroku, Reijiro

Producer(s)   Tanaka, Tomoyuki; Randel, Anthony
Director(s)   Hashimoto, Kohji; Kizer, R.J.
Screenwriter(s)   Nagahara, Shuichi; Tomei, Lisa

Cast   Burr, Raymond; Kobayashi, Keiju; Tanaka, Ken; Sawaguchi, Yasuka

Song(s)   Sayonara Till We Meet (C: Miki, Takashi; L: Araki, Toyohisa); Godzilla (C: Koroku, Reijiro; L: Henrick, Linda)

Notes   No cue sheet available.

2151 ✦ GO FOR BROKE!
Metro–Goldwyn–Mayer, 1951

Musical Score   Colombo, Alberto

Producer(s)   Schary, Dore
Director(s)   Pirosh, Robert
Screenwriter(s)   Pirosh, Robert

Cast Johnson, Van; Nakano, Lane; Fukunaga, Akira; Oyasato, Henry; Hamada, Harry; Okamoto, Ken K.; Miki, George; Nakamura, Henry; Haggerty, Don; Canale, Gianna Maria; Anderson, Warner; Riss, Dan

Song(s) The Meaning of Love (C: Colombo, Alberto; L: Pirosh, Robert; Okamoto, Ken K.)

Notes No cue sheet available.

2152 ◆ THE GO-GETTER
Warner Brothers, 1937

Producer(s) Wallis, Hal B.
Director(s) Berkeley, Busby
Screenwriter(s) Daves, Delmer

Cast Brent, George; Louise, Anita; Winninger, Charles; Eldredge, John; O'Neill, Henry; Crehan, Joseph; Oliver, Gordon; Acuff, Eddie

Song(s) It Shall Be Done [1] (C: Jerome, M.K.; L: Scholl, Jack)

Notes [1] No song listed on cue sheet but cited in Hirschhorn and Burton.

2153 ◆ GO GO MANIA
American International, 1965

Producer(s) Field, Barry
Director(s) Goode, Frederic

Cast Munro, Matt; Maughan, Susan; The Animals; The Honeycombs; The Rockin' Berries; Herman's Hermits; The Nashville Teens; The Four Pennies; Billy J. Kramer and the Dakotas; The Fourmost; Peter and Gordon; Sounds Incorporated; Tommy Quickly and the Remo Four; Davis, Billie; The Spencer Davis Group; The Beatles

Notes No cue sheet available. It is not known if there are any original songs in this film.

2154 ◆ GOING APE!
Paramount, 1981

Composer(s) Bernstein, Elmer
Lyricist(s) Kronsberg, Jeremy Joe

Producer(s) Rosen, Robert L.
Director(s) Kronsberg, Jeremy Joe
Screenwriter(s) Kronsberg, Jeremy Joe

Cast Danza, Tony; Nelkin, Stacey; Walter, Jessica; DeVito, Danny; Rusty

Song(s) Suddenly; Bittersweet; Grim Brother Grimm; It Ain't Who's Right It's What's Right; One Way Street

2155 ◆ GOING BERSERK
Universal, 1983

Musical Score Scott, Tom
Composer(s) Scott, Tom

Producer(s) Heroux, Claude
Director(s) Steinberg, David
Screenwriter(s) Olsen, Dana; Steinberg, David

Cast Candy, John; Levy, Eugene; Flaherty, Joe; Mills, Alley; Hingle, Pat; Bronston, Ann; Libertini, Richard; Carter, Dixie; Dooley, Paul; Hudson, Ernie; Gifford, Gloria; Donahue, Elinor

Song(s) Going Berserk (L: Preston, Rob); Mom Is Dead (L: Ving, Lee)

2156 ◆ GOING HIGHBROW
Warner Brothers, 1935

Composer(s) Alter, Louis
Lyricist(s) Scholl, Jack

Producer(s) Bischoff, Sam
Director(s) Florey, Robert
Screenwriter(s) Kaufman, Edward; Bartlett, Sy; Markson, Ben
Source(s) *Social Pirates* (play) Spence, Ralph

Cast Kibbee, Guy; Pitts, ZaSu; Horton, Edward Everett; Alexander, Ross; Martel, June; Westcott, Gordon; Canova, Judy; Walker, Nella; Norton, Jack; Treacher, Arthur

Song(s) One in a Million; Moon Crazy

Notes These are listed as instrumentals on cue sheets.

2157 ◆ GOING HOLLYWOOD
Metro–Goldwyn–Mayer, 1933

Composer(s) Brown, Nacio Herb
Lyricist(s) Freed, Arthur
Choreographer(s) Rasch, Albertina

Producer(s) Wanger, Walter
Director(s) Walsh, Raoul
Screenwriter(s) Stewart, Donald Ogden

Cast Davies, Marion; Crosby, Bing; D'Orsay, Fifi; Sparks, Ned; Erwin, Stuart; Kelly, Patsy; Watson, Bobby; Three Radio Rogues

Song(s) Our Big Love Scene; Beautiful Girl [1]; Grand Central Episode (C: Stothart, Herbert; Brown, Nacio Herb); Going Hollywood; We'll Make Hay While the Sun Shines; Cinderella's Fella; After Sundown; Temptation

Notes There are a few snippets of other popular songs. [1] Also in STAGE MOTHER and SINGIN' IN THE RAIN.

2158 ◆ GOING HOME
Metro–Goldwyn–Mayer, 1971

Musical Score Walker, Bill
Composer(s) Walker, Bill
Lyricist(s) Walker, Bill

Producer(s) Leonard, Herbert B.
Director(s) Leonard, Herbert B.
Screenwriter(s) Marcus, Lawrence B.

Cast Mitchum, Robert; Vaccaro, Brenda; Vincent, Jan-Michael; Bernard, Jason; Kirkland, Sally; Gilbert, Lou; Wilson, Mary Louise

Song(s) Tell Me About Love (C/L: Vic, Danny); Silver Bird (C/L: Lane, Red); Way Back Home in West Virginia; You'll Never Know How Much; The La La Song; Rope Around the Wind (C/L: Lane, Red; Henley, Larry); Singaree-Singaroh (C/L: Lane, Red; Henley, Larry)

Notes There is also a vocal of "Blue Moon" by Rodgers and Hart.

2159 ✦ GOING MY WAY
Paramount, 1944

Composer(s) Van Heusen, Jimmy
Lyricist(s) Burke, Johnny

Producer(s) McCarey, Leo
Director(s) McCarey, Leo
Screenwriter(s) Butler, Frank; Cavett, Frank

Cast Crosby, Bing; Fitzgerald, Barry; Stevens, Rise; Lockhart, Gene; McHugh, Frank; Frawley, William; Brown, James; Hall, Porter; Bonanova, Fortunio

Song(s) Hail Alma Mater; The Day After Forever; Too Ra Loo Ra Loo Ral [1] (C/L: Shannon, J.R.); Going My Way; Swinging on a Star (Would You Like to Swing on a Star?); The Flamingo and the Rose [2]; April Wants to Dance Again [2]; A Nickel's Worth of Sunshine [2]

Notes The movie was originally titled THE PADRE. The film was suggested by the life of Father Joe Connor who, under the name Pierre Norman, collaborated on several popular songs including "When I Take My Sugar to Tea" and "You Brought a New Kind of Love to Me." [1] Not written for film. [2] Not used.

2160 ✦ GOING PLACES
Warner Brothers–First National, 1938

Composer(s) Warren, Harry
Lyricist(s) Mercer, Johnny

Producer(s) Wallis, Hal B.
Director(s) Enright, Ray
Screenwriter(s) Herzig, Sig; Wald, Jerry; Leo, Maurice
Source(s) *The Hottentot* (play) Mapes, Victor; Collier Sr., William

Cast Powell, Dick; Louise, Anita; Jenkins, Allen; Reagan, Ronald; Catlett, Walter; Huber, Harold; Williams, Larry; Hall, Thurston; Gombell, Minna; Compton, Joyce; Anderson, Eddie "Rochester"; Armstrong, Louis; Sullivan, Maxine

Song(s) Jeepers Creepers; Oh What a Horse was Charlie [1]; Mutiny in the Nursery (C: Mercer, Johnny); Say It with a Kiss [1] [2]

Notes [1] The Al Dubin biography makes no mention of these songs. Tony Thomas' Warren bio credits the lyrics to Dubin alone. Roy Hemming's book on the songwriters of Hollywood credits both Dubin and Mercer. Hirschhorn's book only credits Mercer. Recordings of "Say It with a Kiss" credit only Mercer. [2] Recorded but not used as a vocal (only title words sung by Powell).

2161 ✦ GOING STEADY
Columbia, 1956

Producer(s) Katzman, Sam
Director(s) Sears, Fred F.
Screenwriter(s) Grossman, Budd

Cast Bee, Molly; Reed Jr., Alan; Goodwin, Bill; Hervey, Irene; Miller, Ken; Easter, Susan

Song(s) Going Steady with a Dream (C: Karger, Fred; L: Quine, Richard)

Notes No cue sheet available.

2162 ✦ GOIN' TO TOWN
Paramount, 1935

Composer(s) Fain, Sammy
Lyricist(s) Kahal, Irving

Producer(s) LeBaron, William
Director(s) Hall, Alexander
Screenwriter(s) West, Mae

Cast West, Mae; Cavanagh, Paul; Lebedeff, Ivan; Coral, Tim; Gateson, Marjorie; Withers, Grant; Alberni, Luis

Song(s) Now I'm a Lady [3] (L: Kahal, Irving; Coslow, Sam); He's a Bad Man; Love Is Love [1]; Easy Goin' Gal [2] (C: Rainger, Ralph; Whiting, Richard A.; L: Robin, Leo); Manana [2] (C: Rainger, Ralph; Whiting, Richard A.; L: Robin, Leo); Your Eyes [2] (C: Rainger, Ralph; Whiting, Richard A.; L: Robin, Leo); While the Night Is Young [2] [3] (C: Rainger, Ralph; Whiting, Richard A.; L: Robin, Leo); Bad Man [2] (C: Rainger, Ralph; Whiting, Richard A.; L: Robin, Leo); Got a Way of Doin' Things (C: Rainger, Ralph; Whiting, Richard A.; L: Robin, Leo); El Cubanito [2]; He's a Fox Hunting Polo Playing Son of a British Nobleman [2]

Notes Picture originally titled NOW I'M A LADY then HOW AM I DOING. [1] Apparently only used instrumentally in film although recorded by Mae West. [2] Not used. [3] The first set of lyrics was approved by Mae West but not by the censors. The second set by Kahal was approved by the censors but not by West. So Sam Coslow was brought in to provide a new set of lyrics agreeable to all parties. [3] Also not used in THE BIG BROADCAST OF 1936.

2163 ✦ GO INTO YOUR DANCE
Warner Brothers–First National, 1935

Composer(s) Warren, Harry
Lyricist(s) Dubin, Al
Choreographer(s) Connolly, Bobby

Producer(s) Bischoff, Sam
Director(s) Mayo, Archie
Screenwriter(s) Baldwin, Earl

Cast Jolson, Al; Keeler, Ruby; Morgan, Helen; Farrell, Glenda; Rubin, Benny; Regan, Phil; MacLane, Barton; Lynn, Sharon; Kelly, Patsy; Tamiroff, Akim; Cawthorn, Joseph; Dubin, Al; Warren, Harry

Song(s) A Good Old Fashioned Cocktail; Mammy, I'll Sing About You; About a Quarter to Nine; The Little Things You Used to Do; Go Into Your Dance; Casino De Paree; She's a Latin from Manhattan; Spain (Inst.); Pimiento [1]

Notes Released in Great Britain as CASINO DE PARIS. [1] Not on cue sheets; only on a list compiled by Danny Gould, head of Warners' music department.

2164 ✦ GOLD DIGGERS IN PARIS
Warner Brothers, 1938

Composer(s) Warren, Harry
Lyricist(s) Dubin, Al
Choreographer(s) Berkeley, Busby

Director(s) Enright, Ray
Screenwriter(s) Baldwin, Earl; Duff, Warren
Source(s) *Here Comes the Girls* (idea in a play) Horwin, Jerry; Seymour, James

Cast Vallee, Rudy; Herbert, Hugh; Jenkins, Allen; Dickson, Gloria; Lane, Rosemary; Cooper, Melville; Brophy, Edward S.; Anderson, Eddie "Rochester"; Freddie Fisher and His Schnickelfritz Band

Song(s) I Wanna Go Back to Bali; Day Dreaming All Night Long [3] (L: Mercer, Johnny); A Stranger in Paree; The Latin Quarter; Put that Down in Writing [1]; Waltz of the Flowers [2] (L: Mercer, Johnny); My Adventure [2] (L: Mercer, Johnny)

Notes Titled THE GAY IMPOSTORS in Great Britain. [1] Used only instrumentally according to cue sheets. [2] Not listed in cue sheets. [3] Some sources (including *New York Times* review, published music and Tony Thomas' Warren biography) list Mercer alone as lyricist. But cue sheets disagree and also credit Dubin.

2165 ✦ THE GOLD DIGGERS OF BROADWAY
Warner Brothers, 1929

Composer(s) Burke, Joe
Lyricist(s) Dubin, Al
Choreographer(s) Ceballos, Larry

Director(s) Del Ruth, Roy
Screenwriter(s) Lord, Robert
Source(s) *The Gold Diggers* (play) Hopwood, Avery

Cast Welford, Nancy; Pennington, Ann; Lightner, Winnie; Tearle, Conway; Tashman, Lilyan; Bakewell, William; Lucas, Nick

Song(s) Tip Toe Through the Tulips [2]; Painting the Clouds with Sunshine [1]; In a Kitchenette; Go to Bed; And Still They Fall in Love; What Will I Do Without You? [3]; Song of the Gold Diggers; Mechanical Man; Poison Kiss of That Spaniard; Keeping the Wolf from the Door; Pennington Pep

Notes No cue sheet available. A remake of THE GOLD DIGGERS (1923). [1] Also in LITTLE JOHNNY JONES and PAINTING THE CLOUDS WITH SUNSHINE. [2] Also in PAINTING THE CLOUDS WITH SUNSHINE. [3] Also in BIG BOY and SALLY.

2166 ✦ GOLD DIGGERS OF 1933
Warner Brothers, 1933

Composer(s) Warren, Harry
Lyricist(s) Dubin, Al
Choreographer(s) Berkeley, Busby

Producer(s) Lord, Robert
Director(s) LeRoy, Mervyn
Screenwriter(s) Gelsey, Erwin; Seymour, James; Boehm, David; Markson, Ben
Source(s) *The Gold Diggers* (play) Hopwood, Avery

Cast Moten, Etta; William, Warren; Blondell, Joan [1]; MacMahon, Aline; Keeler, Ruby; Powell, Dick; Kibbee, Guy; Sparks, Ned; Rogers, Ginger; Nordstrom, Clarence; Agnew, Robert; Young, Tammany; Holloway, Sterling

Song(s) Gold Diggers Song (We're in the Money); The Shadow Waltz; I've Got to Sing a Torch Song; Pettin' in the Park; Remember My Forgotten Man

Notes [1] Dubbed by Etta Moten for "Remember My Forgotten Man" (except spoken verse and chorus).

2167 ✦ GOLD DIGGERS OF 1935
Warner Brothers–First National, 1935

Composer(s) Warren, Harry
Lyricist(s) Dubin, Al
Choreographer(s) Berkeley, Busby

Producer(s) Lord, Robert
Director(s) Berkeley, Busby
Screenwriter(s) Seff, Manuel; Milne, Peter

Cast Powell, Dick; Menjou, Adolphe; Brady, Alice; Farrell, Glenda; McHugh, Frank; Herbert, Hugh; Stuart, Gloria

Song(s) I'm Going Shopping with You; The Words Are in My Heart; Dagger Dance (Inst.); Lullaby of

Broadway; Shadows of Yesterday's Stars (Inst.); Tell Me Again (Inst.); Moonlight and You (Inst.); Tell Me That You Care (Inst.)

Notes It is not known if the instrumentals were ever developed into songs.

2168 ◆ GOLD DIGGERS OF 1937
Warner Brothers–First National, 1936

Composer(s) Arlen, Harold
Lyricist(s) Harburg, E.Y.
Choreographer(s) Berkeley, Busby

Producer(s) Wallis, Hal B.
Director(s) Bacon, Lloyd
Screenwriter(s) Duff, Warren
Source(s) *Sweet Mystery of Life* (play) Maibaum, Richard; Wallach, Michael; Haight, George

Cast Powell, Dick; Perkins, Osgood; Brown, Charles; Moore, Victor; Blondell, Joan; Dixon, Lee; Howland, Olin; Marquis, Rosalind

Song(s) Speaking of the Weather; Let's Put Our Heads Together; With Plenty of Money and You [2] (C: Warren, Harry; L: Dubin, Al); Life Insurance Song; All's Fair in Love and War (C: Warren, Harry; L: Dubin, Al); Love What Are You Doing to My Heart [1] (C/L: Lewis, Barczi); Bermuda Buggyride [1] (C: Green, Sanford; L: David, Mack); Papa Tree-Top Tall [1] (C: Carmichael, Hoagy; L: Adams, Stanley); Swing for Sale [1] (C: Chaplin, Saul; L: Cahn, Sammy); Hush Mah Mouth

Notes [1] Used instrumentally only. It is not known if they were written for film or just interpolated as background music. [2] Also in MY DREAM IS YOURS and SHE'S WORKING HER WAY THROUGH COLLEGE.

2169 ◆ THE GOLDEN CALF
Fox, 1930

Composer(s) Monaco, James V.
Lyricist(s) Friend, Cliff
Choreographer(s) Lindsay, Earl

Producer(s) Marin, Ned
Director(s) Webb, Millard; Merlin, Frank
Screenwriter(s) Atteridge, Harold
Source(s) "The Golden Calf" (story) Davis, Aaron

Cast Carol, Sue; Mulhall, Jack; Brendel, El; White, Marjorie; Catlett, Walter; Chase, Ilka; Page, Paul; Keene, Richard

Song(s) You Gotta Be Modernistic; Maybe, Someday; Can I Help It (If I'm in Love with You)?; A Picture No Artist Can Paint; Horsey Keep Your Tail Up [1] (C/L: Hirsch; Kaplan); I'm Telling the World About You

Notes [1] Not written for picture.

2170 ◆ GOLDEN CALIFORNIA
Twentieth Century–Fox, 1938

Song(s) Sunset at the Abbey (C/L: Sellars, Gatty)

Notes This is a Lowell Thomas Magic Carpet of Movietone travelogue.

2171 ◆ THE GOLDEN CHILD
Paramount, 1986

Producer(s) Feldman, Edward S.; Wachs, Robert D.
Director(s) Ritchie, Michael
Screenwriter(s) Feldman, Dennis

Cast Murphy, Eddie; Lewis, Charlotte; Dance, Charles

Song(s) The Best Man in the World (C: Barry, John; L: Wilson, Ann; Wilson, Nancy; Ennis, Sue)

2172 ◆ THE GOLDEN CIRCLE
Paramount, 1951 unproduced

Composer(s) Van Heusen, James
Lyricist(s) Burke, Johnny

Song(s) Somewhere In a Corner of Your Heart; Good Night, Good Morning; The Dreamer Who Gets Things Done; It's Catching; The Story in Variety; This Is a Tree

2173 ◆ GOLDEN DAWN
Warner Brothers, 1930

Composer(s) Akst, Harry
Lyricist(s) Clarke, Grant
Choreographer(s) Ceballos, Larry; Cansino, Eduardo [2]

Director(s) Enright, Ray
Screenwriter(s) Anthony, Walter
Source(s) *Golden Dawn* (musical) Hammerstein II, Oscar; Harbach, Otto; Kalman, Emmerich; Stothart, Herbert

Cast Woolf, Walter; Segal, Vivienne; Beery, Noah; Gentle, Alice; Lane, Lupino; Byron, Marion; Henderson, Dick; Sojin; Matiesen, Otto; Martindel, Edward; Cansino, Eduardo [2]

Song(s) When I Crack My Whip [1] (C: Kalman, Emmerich; Stothart, Herbert; L: Harbach, Otto; Hammerstein II, Oscar); Dawn [1] (C: Stolz, Robert; Stothart, Herbert; L: Harbach, Otto; Hammerstein II, Oscar); My Bwana [1] (C: Kalman, Emmerich; Stothart, Herbert; L: Harbach, Otto; Hammerstein II, Oscar): We Two [1] (C: Kalman, Emmerich; Stothart, Herbert; L: Harbach, Otto; Hammerstein II, Oscar); My Heart's Love Call; Africa Smiles No More; Mooda's Song; In a Jungle Bungalow

Notes No cue sheet available. Robert Emmett Dolan and Walter O'Keefe are also credited by ASCAP carriage cards. [1] In original Broadway production. [2] Rita Hayworth's father.

2174 ✦ GOLDEN EARRINGS
Paramount, 1947

Composer(s) Young, Victor
Lyricist(s) Livingston, Jay; Evans, Ray

Producer(s) Tugend, Harry
Director(s) Leisen, Mitchell
Screenwriter(s) Polonsky, Abraham; Butler, Frank; Deutsch, Helen

Cast Dietrich, Marlene; Milland, Ray; Vye, Murvyn; Lester, Bruce; Hoey, Dennis; Reynolds, Quentin

Song(s) Golden Earrings; Chant [1] (C: Dietrich, Marlene; Manton, Maria)

Notes [1] The lyrics are in the script. This piece is not listed on the cue sheet.

2175 ✦ THE GOLDEN FLEECING
Metro–Goldwyn–Mayer, 1940

Musical Score Snell, Dave

Producer(s) Selwyn, Edgar
Director(s) Fenton, Leslie
Screenwriter(s) Perelman, S.J.; Perelman, Laura; Parsonnet, Marion

Cast Ayres, Lew; Nolan, Lloyd; Errol, Leon; Johnson, Rita; Grey, Virginia; Pendleton, Nat

Song(s) March, March, March the Boys Are Tramping (C: Snell, Dave; L: Kahn, Gus)

Notes The song lasts only around 30 seconds.

2176 ✦ GOLDEN GIRL (1951)
Twentieth Century–Fox, 1951

Composer(s) Daniel, Eliot; Darby, Ken
Lyricist(s) Darby, Ken; Daniel, Eliot
Choreographer(s) Felix, Seymour

Producer(s) Jessel, George
Director(s) Bacon, Lloyd
Screenwriter(s) Bullock, Walter; O'Neal, Charles; Lehman, Gladys

Cast Gaynor, Mitzi; Robertson, Dale; Day, Dennis; Barton, James; Merkel, Una; Walburn, Raymond; Sheldon, Gene

Song(s) California Moon [1] (C: Cooper, Joe; L: Jessel, George; Lerner, Sam); Parade Entrance to Quincy; Never (C: Newman, Lionel; L: Daniel, Eliot); Sunday Mornin'; Join the Party; A Pretty Dress (C: Daniel, Eliot; L: Jessel, George; Daniel, Eliot)

Notes Vocal renditions of "Carry Me Back to Old Virginny" and "Oh, Dem Golden Slippers" by James A. Bland; "San Francisco" by Bronislau Kaper and Walter Jurmann; "Shew! Fly Don't Bother Me" by Frank Campbell and Billy Reeves; the Mexican folk tune

"Cielito Lindo;" "Beautiful Dreamer" by Stephen Foster; "La Donna e Mobile" by Guiseppe Verdi; "Kiss Me Quick" by Fred Buckley; the Irish air "Believe Me If All Those Endearing Young Charms" by Thomas Moore; "When Johnny Comes Marching Home" by Louis Lambert (Patrick Sarsfield Gilmore); "Battle Hymn of the Republic" by William Steffe and Julia Ward Howe; "Dixie" by Dan Emmett and "The Battle Cry of Freedom" by George Frederick Root are also used. [1] Patter lyrics are by Eliot Daniel.

2177 ✦ GOLDENGIRL (1979)
Avco Embassy, 1979

Musical Score Conti, Bill

Producer(s) O'Donovan, Danny
Director(s) Sargent, Joseph
Screenwriter(s) Kohn, John
Source(s) (novel) Lear, Peter

Cast Anton, Susan; Coburn, James; Jurgens, Curt; Caron, Leslie; Culp, Robert; Watson Jr., James A.; Guardino, Harry; Costello, Ward; Lerner, Michael; Walter, Jessica

Song(s) Slow Down, I'll Find You (C: Conti, Bill; L: Conti, Bill; Connors, Carol)

Notes No cue sheet available.

2178 ✦ THE GOLDEN HEAD
Paramount, 1964

Musical Score Fenyes, Peter

Director(s) Thorpe, Richard
Screenwriter(s) Goulder, Stanley; Boldizsar, Ivan
Source(s) *Nepomuk of the River* (novel) Pilkington, Roger

Cast Sanders, George; Hackett, Buddy; Conrad, Jess; Power, Lorraine; Coote, Robert

Song(s) Things I'd Like to Say (C/L: Murray, Mitch)

Notes A British/Hungarian film released by Paramount.

2179 ✦ GOLDEN HOOFS
Twentieth Century–Fox, 1941

Musical Score Mockridge, Cyril J.

Producer(s) Morosco, Walter; Dietrich, Ralph
Director(s) Shores, Lynn
Screenwriter(s) Kohn, Ben Grauman

Cast Withers, Jane; Rogers, Charles "Buddy"; Aldridge, Katharine; Irving, George; Pepper, Buddy; Clark, Cliff; Hurlick, Philip; Ryan, Sheila

Song(s) Consider Yourself in Love (C: Spina, Harold; L: Bullock, Walter)

2180 ✦ THE GOLDEN HORN

See POT O' GOLD.

2181 ✦ THE GOLDEN SEAL
Goldwyn, 1983

Musical Score Barry, John

Producer(s) Thatcher, Russell
Director(s) Zuniga, Frank
Screenwriter(s) Grover, John
Source(s) *A River Rat Out of Eden* (novel) Marshall, James Vance

Cast Railsback, Steve; Beck, Michael; Milford, Penelope; Campbell, Torquil

Notes No cue sheet available.

2182 ✦ GOLDEN SLIPPERS
Paramount, 1946

Producer(s) Templeton, George
Director(s) Templeton, George

Cast Edwards, Mary [1]; Rasumny, Mikhail; Ryder, Alfred; Harris and Shaw

Song(s) There's Laughter After Tears [2] (C/L: Livingston, Jay; Evans, Ray)

Notes Short subject. "I Feel a Song Coming On" by Jimmy McHugh, Dorothy Fields and George Oppenheimer is also given a vocal treatment, as is "Moments Like This" by Frank Loesser and Burton Lane. [1] Dubbed by Mary Roche. [2] Sometimes referred to as "There's Laughter After the Blues."

2183 ✦ THE GOLDEN STALLION
Republic, 1949

Composer(s) Willing, Foy
Lyricist(s) Robin, Sid

Producer(s) White, Edward J.
Director(s) Witney, William
Screenwriter(s) Nibley, Sloan

Cast Rogers, Roy; Trigger; Evans, Dale; Rodriguez, Estelita; Brady, Pat; Evans, Douglas; Fenton, Frank; Conklin, Chester; Foy Willing and the Riders of the Purple Sage

Song(s) There's Always Time for a Song; The Golden Stallion; Night on the Prairie [1] (C/L: Gluck, Nate; Hamilton, Albert); Down Mexico Way [2] (C: Styne, Jule; L: Meyer, Sol; Cherkose, Eddie)

Notes [1] Spanish lyrics by Aaron Gonzalez. Also in COLORADO. [2] Also in DOWN MEXICO WAY, HOME IN WYOMING and YELLOW ROSE OF TEXAS.

2184 ✦ THE GOLDEN TIDE
Republic, 1953

Musical Score Young, Victor
Composer(s) Young, Victor
Lyricist(s) Heyman, Edward

Producer(s) O'Sullivan, William J.
Director(s) Springsteen, R.G.
Screenwriter(s) Wormser, Richard E.
Source(s) *The Golden Tide* (novel) Roe, Vingle E.

Cast Ralston, Vera Hruba; Brian, David; Brady, Scott; Winninger, Charles; Emerson, Hope

Song(s) Bon Soir; On the Rue de la Paix; California

2185 ✦ THE GOLDEN WEST
Fox, 1932

Director(s) Howard, David

Cast O'Brien, George; Chandler, Janet; Burns, Marion

Song(s) Home Folks (C/L: Hanley, James F.); As the Years Roll By [1] (C: Hanley, James F.; L: Mitchell, Sidney D.)

Notes [1] Not on cue sheet.

2186 ✦ GOLDFINGER
United Artists, 1964

Musical Score Barry, John

Producer(s) Saltzman, Harry; Broccoli, Albert R.
Director(s) Hamilton, Guy
Screenwriter(s) Maibaum, Richard; Dehn, Paul
Source(s) *Goldfinger* (novel) Fleming, Ian

Cast Connery, Sean; Frobe, Gert; Blackman, Honor; Eaton, Shirley

Song(s) Goldfinger (C: Barry, John; L: Bricusse, Leslie; Newley, Anthony)

2187 ✦ GOLD IS WHERE YOU FIND IT
Warner Brothers–First National, 1938

Musical Score Steiner, Max

Producer(s) Wallis, Hal B.
Director(s) Curtiz, Michael
Screenwriter(s) Duff, Warren; Buckner, Robert

Cast Brent, George; de Havilland, Olivia; Rains, Claude; Lindsay, Margaret; Litel, John; Ralston, Marcia; MacLane, Barton; Holt, Tim; Toler, Sidney; O'Neill, Henry; Best, Willie; McWade, Robert; Hayes, George "Gabby"; Davenport, Harry; Kolb, Clarence

Song(s) I Gotta Get Back To My Gal [1] (C: Jerome, M.K.; L: Scholl, Jack)

Notes [1] Also in EMPTY HOLSTERS, SONGS OF THE RANGE and WEST OF THE ROCKIES.

2188 ◆ GOLD MINE IN THE SKY
Republic, 1938

Producer(s) Ford, Charles E.
Director(s) Kane, Joseph
Screenwriter(s) Burbridge, Betty; Natteford, Jack

Cast Autry, Gene; Burnette, Smiley; Hughes, Carol; Reynolds, Craig; Ainsworth, Cupid; Mason, LeRoy; Marvin, Frankie; Cherkose, Eddie; Corbett, Ben; The Stafford Sisters

Song(s) Hummin' When We're Comin' Round the Bend (C: Colombo, Alberto; L: Cherkose, Eddie); There's a Gold Mine in the Sky (C/L: Kenny, Nick; Kenny, Charles); That's How Donkeys Were Born (C/L: Burnette, Smiley; Cherkose, Eddie); As Long As I Have My Horse [1] (C/L: Autry, Gene; Marvin, Johnny; Rose, Fred); Hike Yaa Move Along [3] (C/L: Burnette, Smiley); Dude Ranch Cowhands [2] (C/L: Autry, Gene; Marvin, Johnny; Rose, Fred); I'd Love to Call You My Sweetheart (C/L: Ash, Paul; Goodwin, Joe; Shay, Larry); Tumbleweed Tenor (C/L: Burnette, Smiley; Cherkose, Eddie)

Notes [1] Later in the Columbia picture WHIRLWIND but without the Johnny Marvin credit. [2] Also in EL RANCHO GRANDE. [3] Also in PUBLIC COWBOY NUMBER ONE.

2189 ◆ GOLD OF THE SEVEN SAINTS
Warner Brothers–First National, 1961

Musical Score Jackson, Howard

Producer(s) Freeman, Leonard
Director(s) Douglas, Gordon M.
Screenwriter(s) Brackett, Leigh; Freeman, Leonard
Source(s) *Desert Guns* (novel) Frazee, Steve

Cast Walker, Clint; Moore, Roger; Roman, Leticia; Middleton, Robert; Wills, Chill; Evans, Gene; Contreras, Roberto

Song(s) I'm a Lad (C/L: Miller, Sy)

2190 ◆ GOLDTOWN GHOST RAIDERS
Columbia, 1953

Producer(s) Schaefer, Armand
Director(s) Archainbaud, George
Screenwriter(s) Geraghty, Gerald

Cast Autry, Gene; Burnette, Smiley; Davis, Gail; Riley, Kirk; Champion

Song(s) There's a Gold Mine in Your Heart (C/L: Unknown); The Thieving Burro (C/L: Unknown); Pancho's Widow (C: Stept, Sam H.; L: Washington, Ned)

Notes No cue sheet available.

2191 ◆ THE GOLDWYN FOLLIES
United Artists, 1938

Composer(s) Gershwin, George
Lyricist(s) Gershwin, Ira
Choreographer(s) Balanchine, George; Lee, Sammy

Producer(s) Goldwyn, Samuel
Director(s) Marshall, George; Potter, H.C.
Screenwriter(s) Hecht, Ben

Cast Menjou, Adolphe; Leeds, Andrea [1]; Zorina, Vera; Bergen, Edgar; McCarthy, Charlie; Jepson, Helen; Kullman, Charles; Baker, Kenny; The Ritz Brothers; Baker, Phil; Logan, Ella; Clark, Bobby; Cowan, Jerome

Song(s) I'm Not Complaining [2] (C: Duke, Vernon); Love Walked In; Love Is Here to Stay; I Love to Rhyme; I Was Doing All Right; Spring Again (C: Duke, Vernon); Here Pussy Pussy (C/L: Golden, Ray; Kuller, Sid); Just Another Rhumba [2]

Notes No cue sheet available. A Goldwyn film distributed by United Artists. Vernon Duke (and Oscar Levant) helped put the music in order after George Gershwin's death. Most of the verses were written by Duke who helped Ira fill out the songs from George's lead sheets. [1] Dubbed by Virginia Verrill. [2] Not used.

2192 ◆ THE GONG SHOW MOVIE
Universal, 1980

Composer(s) Barris, Chuck
Lyricist(s) Barris, Chuck

Producer(s) Granoff, Budd
Director(s) Barris, Chuck
Screenwriter(s) Barris, Chuck; Downey, Robert
Source(s) "The Gong Show" (TV show) Barris, Chuck; Bearde, Chris

Cast Altman, Robin; Barris, Chuck; O'Mullin, Brian; Bernardi, Jack; Satisfaction; King, Mabel; Lembeck, Harvey; Langston, Murray; Garvey, Steve; Presar, Melvin; Farr, Jamie; Delugg, Milton; Stevens, Mark; McCormick, Pat; Andrews, Patty; Morgan, Jaye P.; Patton, Gene; Taylor, Rip; Grier, Rosey; Randall, Tony

Song(s) Sometimes It Just Don't Pay to Get Up; Why Me Oh Lord; Don't Get Up; I'm the Cook

Notes Only songs of over a minute listed.

2193 ◆ GOODBYE AGAIN
United Artists, 1961

Musical Score Auric, Georges
Composer(s) Auric, Georges
Lyricist(s) Langdon

Producer(s) Litvak, Anatole
Director(s) Litvak, Anatole

Screenwriter(s) Taylor, Samuel
Source(s) *Aimez-Vous Brahms?* (novel) Sagan, Francoise

Cast Bergman, Ingrid; Montand, Yves; Perkins, Anthony; Landis, Jessie Royce; Lane, Jackie; Clarke, Jean; Mercier, Michele; Carroll, Diahann

Song(s) Aimez-Vous; Goodbye Again; Love Is Just a Word

2194 ◆ GOODBYE CHARLIE
Twentieth Century–Fox, 1964

Musical Score Previn, Andre
Composer(s) Previn, Andre
Lyricist(s) Langdon, Dory

Producer(s) Weisbart, David
Director(s) Minnelli, Vincente
Screenwriter(s) Kurnitz, Harry
Source(s) *Goodbye Charlie* (play) Axelrod, George

Cast Curtis, Tony; Reynolds, Debbie; Boone, Pat; Matthau, Walter; Barnes, Joanna; McRae, Ellen; Gabel, Martin; Carmel, Roger C.; Romanoff, Michael; Devon, Laura

Song(s) Seven at Once; Goodbye Charlie

2195 ◆ GOODBYE, COLUMBUS
Paramount, 1969

Musical Score Fox, Charles

Producer(s) Jaffe, Stanley R.
Director(s) Peerce, Larry
Screenwriter(s) Schulman, Arnold
Source(s) "Goodbye, Columbus" (novella) Roth, Philip

Cast Benjamin, Richard; MacGraw, Ali; Klugman, Jack; Martin, Nan; Meyers, Michael; Shelle, Lori

Song(s) (Hello Life) Goodbye, Columbus (C/L: Yester, James); Carmen Ohio (C: Traditional; L: Cornell, Fred A.); It's Gotta Be Real (C/L: Ramos, Larry); So Kind to Me (C/L: Kirkman, Terry); Love Has a Way [1] (C: Fox, Charles; L: Darrow, Jay)

Notes [1] Sheet music only.

2196 ◆ GOODBYE LOVE
RKO, 1935

Composer(s) Gottler, Archie; Conrad, Con
Lyricist(s) Gottler, Archie; Mitchell, Sidney D.; Conrad, Con

Producer(s) Schnitzer, Joseph I.; Zierler, Samuel
Director(s) Humberstone, H. Bruce
Screenwriter(s) Del Ruth, Hampton; Rosener, George; Lawson, John Howard

Cast Ruggles, Charles; Teasdale, Verree; Blackmer, Sidney; Methot, Mayo; Barry, Phyllis; Walker, Ray; Kelly, John; Alberni, Luis

Song(s) Goodbye Love; Alimony Club

2197 ◆ GOODBYE, MR. CHIPS (1939)
Metro–Goldwyn–Mayer, 1939

Musical Score Addinsell, Richard

Producer(s) Saville, Victor
Director(s) Wood, Sam
Screenwriter(s) Sherriff, R.C.; West, Claudine; Maschwitz, Eric
Source(s) *Goodbye, Mr. Chips* (novel) Hilton, James

Cast Donat, Robert; Garson, Greer; Kilburn, Terry; Mills, John; Henreid, Paul [1]; Furse, Judith; Rosmer, Milton

Song(s) Brookfield School Song (C: Addinsell, Richard; L: Maschwitz, Eric)

Notes Greer Garson's screen debut. [1] Listed in script as Paul von Henried.

2198 ◆ GOODBYE, MR. CHIPS (1969)
Metro–Goldwyn–Mayer, 1969

Musical Score Williams, John
Composer(s) Bricusse, Leslie
Lyricist(s) Bricusse, Leslie
Choreographer(s) Kaye, Nora

Producer(s) Jacobs, Arthur P.
Director(s) Ross, Herbert
Screenwriter(s) Rattigan, Terence
Source(s) *Goodbye, Mr. Chips* (novel) Hilton, James

Cast O'Toole, Peter; Clark, Petula; Redgrave, Michael; Phillips, Sian; Baker, George; Bryant, Michael; Hedley, Jack; Leggatt, Alison; March, Elspeth

Song(s) Fill the World with Love; Where Did My Childhood Go; London Is London; And the Sky Smiled; Apollo; When I Am Older; The Perfect Man [1]; Walk Through the World; What Shall I Do with Today; What a Lot of Flowers; Schooldays; You and I

Notes [1] On cue sheet, but apparently not in any prints.

2199 ◆ GOODBYE MY FANCY
Warner Brothers–First National, 1951

Producer(s) Blanke, Henry
Director(s) Sherman, Vincent
Screenwriter(s) Goff, Ivan; Roberts, Ben
Source(s) *Goodbye My Fancy* (play) Kanin, Fay

Cast Crawford, Joan; Young, Robert; Lovejoy, Frank; Arden, Eve; Rule, Janice; Tuttle, Lurene; St. John, Howard; Corby, Ellen

Song(s) Alma Mater (C: Jerome, M.K.; L: Scholl, Jack); Glorious Month of June (C/L: Gilbert, J.L.; Gardner, William H.); Welcome to All Who Gather Here (C/L: Kountz, Richard; Hughes, Baxter)

2200 ✦ GOOD-BYE MY LADY
Warner Brothers, 1956

Musical Score Almeida, Laurindo; Field, George

Producer(s) Wellman, William A.
Director(s) Wellman, William A.
Screenwriter(s) Fleischman, Sid

Cast Brennan, Walter; Harris, Phil; de Wilde, Brandon; Poitier, Sidney; Hopper, William; Beavers, Louise

Song(s) When Your Boy Becomes a Man (C/L: Erby, Moris; Powell, Don)

2201 ✦ GOODBYE NEW YORK
Castle Hill, 1985

Musical Score Abene, Michael; Abene, Gretchen Hoffman

Producer(s) Kollek, Amos
Director(s) Kollek, Amos
Screenwriter(s) Kollek, Amos

Cast Hagerty, Julie; Kollek, Amos; Shiloh, Shmuel; Ger, Aviva; Topaz, David; Babtist, Jennifer; Goutman, Christopher

Song(s) Try Again (C: Kollman, Otto; L: Ithier, Hubert); I Want to Try (C/L: King, Gayle); Madeleine (C: Kollman, Otto; L: Bergdahl, Edith; May, Johnny)

Notes No cue sheet available.

2202 ✦ GOODBYE, NORMA JEAN
Filmways, 1978

Musical Score Beck, Joe

Producer(s) Buchanan, Larry
Director(s) Buchanan, Larry
Screenwriter(s) Shubert, Lynn; Buchanan, Larry

Cast Rowe, Misty; Locke, Terrence; Mackenzie, Patch; Hanson, Preston

Song(s) Norma Jean Wants to Be a Movie Star (C/L: Cunningham, Johnny)

Notes No cue sheet available.

2203 ✦ GOOD DAME
Paramount, 1934

Producer(s) Schulberg, B.P.
Director(s) Gering, Marion

Screenwriter(s) Lipman, William R.; Lawrence, Vincent; Partos, Frank; Hellman, Sam

Cast March, Fredric; Sidney, Sylvia; Farnum, William; LaRue, Jack; Brennan, Walter

Song(s) She's a Good Dame [1] (C: Rainger, Ralph; L: Robin, Leo)

Notes Titled GOOD GIRL in Great Britain. [1] The song was not used in the picture but was published.

2204 ✦ THE GOOD FELLOWS
Paramount, 1943

Producer(s) MacEwen, Walter
Director(s) Graham, Jo
Screenwriter(s) Wedlock Jr., Hugh; Snyder, Howard
Source(s) *The Good Fellow* (play) Kaufman, George S.; Mankiewicz, Herman

Cast Kellaway, Cecil; Paige, Mabel; Walker, Helen; Brown, James

Song(s) Brother Love, Eternal Be [1] (C/L: Lilley, Joseph J.)

Notes [1] Not used.

2205 ✦ GOOD GIRL

See GOOD DAME.

2206 ✦ THE GOOD GUYS AND THE BAD GUYS
Warner Brothers, 1969

Musical Score Lava, William

Producer(s) Cohen, Ronald M.; Shryack, Dennis
Director(s) Kennedy, Burt
Screenwriter(s) Cohen, Ronald M.; Shryack, Dennis

Cast Mitchum, Robert; Kennedy, George; Carradine, David; Louise, Tina; Fowley, Douglas; Balsam, Martin; Nettleton, Lois; Chandler, John Davis; Carradine, John; Windsor, Marie; Freeman, Kathleen

Song(s) The Ballad of Marshal Flagg (C: Lava, William; L: Washington, Ned)

2207 ✦ GOOD INTENTIONS
Fox, 1930

Director(s) Howard, William K.
Screenwriter(s) Howard, William K.; Watters, George Manker

Cast Lowe, Edmund; Churchill, Marguerite; Toomey, Regis; Foxe, Earle; Caine, Georgia; Davis Jr., Owen; Hamilton, Hale

Song(s) A Slave to Love (C: Monaco, James V.; L: Friend, Cliff)

Notes Originally titled THE FATAL WEDDING.

2208 ✦ GOOD LITTLE MONKEYS
Metro–Goldwyn–Mayer, 1935

Song(s) Speak No Evil (C/L: Bradley, Scott)

Notes Animated cartoon.

2209 ✦ GOOD MORNING, JUDGE
Universal, 1943

Musical Score Rosen, Milton

Producer(s) Malvern, Paul
Director(s) Yarbrough, Jean
Screenwriter(s) Geraghty, Maurice; Wilson, Warren

Cast Allbritton, Louise; Hughes, Mary Beth; Naish, J. Carrol; Beavers, Louise

Song(s) Spellbound [1] (C: Rosen, Milton; L: Carter, Everett); When Banana Blossoms Bloom [2] (C: Previn, Charles; L: Lerner, Sam)

Notes [1] Also in FOLLOW THE BAND. [2] Also in MARGIE (1940).

2210 ✦ GOOD MORNING, MISS DOVE
Twentieth Century–Fox, 1955

Musical Score Harline, Leigh

Producer(s) Engel, Samuel G.
Director(s) Koster, Henry
Screenwriter(s) Griffin, Eleanore
Source(s) *Good Morning, Miss Dove* (novel) Patton, Frances Gray

Cast Jones, Jennifer; Stack, Robert; Hamilton, Kipp; Thompson, Marshall; Connors, Chuck; Paris, Jerry; Wickes, Mary

Song(s) Cedar Grove (C: Newman, Lionel; L: Griffin, Eleanore; Patton, Francis Gray)

2211 ✦ THE GOOD MOTHER
Touchstone, 1989

Musical Score Bernstein, Elmer
Composer(s) Piccolo, Greg
Lyricist(s) Piccolo, Greg

Producer(s) Glimcher, Arnold
Director(s) Nimoy, Leonard
Screenwriter(s) Bortman, Michael
Source(s) *The Good Mother* (novel) Miller, Sue

Cast Keaton, Diane; Neeson, Liam; Robards Jr., Jason; Bellamy, Ralph; Wright, Teresa; Naughton, James; Vieira, Asia; Morton, Joe; Sagal, Katey

Song(s) Blues Times Blue; Whiplash

2212 ✦ GOOD NEWS (1930)
Metro–Goldwyn–Mayer, 1930

Composer(s) Henderson, Ray
Lyricist(s) Brown, Lew; DeSylva, B.G.
Choreographer(s) Lee, Sammy

Director(s) MacGregor, Edgar J.; Grinde, Nick
Screenwriter(s) Marion, Frances; Franham, Joe
Source(s) *Good News* (musical) DeSylva, B.G.; Henderson, Ray; Brown, Lew; Schwab, Laurence; Mandel, Frank

Cast Lawlor, Mary [1]; Smith, Stanley; Love, Bessie; Edwards, Cliff; Shy, Gus [1]; Lane, Lola; Daves, Delmer; McGlynn, Frank; McNulty, Dorothy [2]; Abe Lyman and His Band

Song(s) Football (C: Brown, Nacio Herb; L: Freed, Arthur); I Feel Pessimistic (C: Robinson, J. Russel; L: Waggner, George); If You're Not Kissing Me (C: Brown, Nacio Herb; L: Freed, Arthur); Varsity Drag; (Gee but) I'd Like to Make You Happy (C: Ward, Edward; L: Montgomery, Reggie); Tait Song; He's a Ladies' Man; The Best Things in Life Are Free; Good News; Students Are We [3] (C/L: Unknown); That's How You Know We're Co-eds [3] (C/L: Unknown); The Call to Arms [4] (C: Brown, Nacio Herb; L: Freed, Arthur); College Hymn [4] (C: Brown, Nacio Herb; L: Freed, Arthur); Fight 'Em [4] (C: Brown, Nacio Herb; L: Freed, Arthur); You're in a Class By Yourself [4] (C: Brown, Nacio Herb; L: Freed, Arthur)

Notes Titles list Felix F. Feist as also writing interpolations, but no song is credited to him. [1] From Broadway cast. [2] Changed name later to Penny Singleton. [3] Not on cue sheet. [4] Not used.

2213 ✦ GOOD NEWS (1947)
Metro–Goldwyn–Mayer, 1947

Composer(s) Henderson, Ray
Lyricist(s) DeSylva, B.G.; Brown, Lew
Choreographer(s) Alton, Robert

Producer(s) Freed, Arthur
Director(s) Walters, Charles
Screenwriter(s) Comden, Betty; Green, Adolph
Source(s) *Good News* (musical) DeSylva, B.G.; Brown, Lew; Henderson, Ray; Mandel, Frank; Schwab, Laurence

Cast Allyson, June; Lawford, Peter; Marshall, Patricia; McCracken, Joan; McDonald, Ray; Torme, Mel; Strickland, Robert; MacBride, Donald; Sundberg, Clinton; Dugan, Tom; Ankrum, Morris; Gilchrist, Connie; Green, Jane

Song(s) Tait Song; Good News [3]; Best Things in Life Are Free; He's a Ladies' Man [3]; Lucky in Love; French Lesson (C: Edens, Roger; L: Comden, Betty; Green, Adolph); Pass That Peace Pipe [2] (C/L: Edens, Roger; Blane, Ralph; Martin, Hugh); Just Imagine; Varsity Drag [3]; An Easier Way [1] (C: Edens, Roger; L: Comden, Betty; Green, Adolph)

Notes Walter's first directing assignment and Comden and Green's first screenplay. [1] Deleted from final print. [2] Written for ZIEGFELD FOLLIES OF 1944, which finally came to fruition in 1946, and part of score of unproduced HUCKLEBERRY FINN. [3] Roger Edens and Kay Thompson added material to these songs.

2214 ✦ GOODNIGHT SWEETHEART
Republic, 1944

Producer(s) White, Eddy
Director(s) Santley, Joseph
Screenwriter(s) Townley, Jack; Dawn, Isabel

Cast Livingston, Robert; Terry, Ruth; Hall, Thurston; Hull, Henry; Armstrong, Robert; Corrigan, Lloyd; Eburne, Maude; Littlefield, Lucien; Howland, Olin; Conklin, Chester; Lynn, Emmett

Song(s) I'm Not Myself Anymore [1] (C: Ohman, Phil; L: Washington, Ned)

Notes [1] Also in SLEEPY LAGOON.

2215 ✦ GOODNIGHT VIENNA

See MAGIC NIGHT.

2216 ✦ THE GOOD OLD SOAK
Metro–Goldwyn–Mayer, 1937

Musical Score Ward, Edward

Producer(s) Rapf, Harry
Director(s) Ruben, J. Walter
Screenwriter(s) Thomas, A.E.
Source(s) *The Old Soak* (play) Marquis, Don

Cast Beery, Wallace; Merkel, Una; Linden, Eric; Barnett, Judith; Furness, Betty; Healy, Ted; Beecher, Janet; Sidney, George; McWade, Robert

Song(s) You've Got a Certain Something (C: Donaldson, Walter; L: Wright, Bob; Forrest, Chet)

2217 ✦ GOOD SAM
RKO, 1948

Musical Score Dolan, Robert Emmett

Producer(s) McCarey, Leo
Director(s) McCarey, Leo
Screenwriter(s) Englund, Ken

Cast Cooper, Gary; Sheridan, Ann; Collins, Ray; Lowe, Edmund; Lorring, Joan; Sundberg, Clinton; Urecal, Minerva; Beavers, Louise; Dolan Jr., Bobby

Song(s) Eight to Five (C/L: McCarey, Leo); Call to Remembrance (C/L: Dolan, Robert Emmett); Daddy Dear (C/L: Dolan, Robert Emmett)

2218 ✦ GOOD SPORT
Fox, 1931

Director(s) MacKenna, Kenneth

Cast Watkins, Linda; Boles, John; Nissen, Greta; Hopper, Hedda; Dinehart, Alan

Song(s) We Gotta Find a New Kentucky Home (C/L: Hanley, James F.); Black and Tan Fantasy (Inst.) [1] (C: Miley, Bubba; Ellington, Duke)

Notes [1] Not written for this picture.

2219 ✦ THE GOOD, THE BAD AND THE UGLY
United Artists, 1967

Musical Score Morricone, Ennio

Producer(s) Grimaldi, Alberto
Director(s) Leone, Sergio
Screenwriter(s) Vincenzoni, Luciano; Leone, Sergio

Cast Eastwood, Clint; Wallach, Eli; Van Cleef, Lee

Song(s) Stori a di un Soldato (C: Morricone, Ennio; L: Connor, T.)

2220 ✦ GOOD TIME CHARLIE
Paramount, 1930 unproduced

Song(s) Spring Has Came (C: Dreyer, Dave; L: Macdonald, Ballard); Wopsy (C: Dreyer, Dave; L: Macdonald, Ballard)

Notes The picture appears to have been originally titled THE DUDE RANCH.

2221 ✦ GOOD TIMES
Columbia, 1967

Composer(s) Bono, Sonny
Lyricist(s) Bono, Sonny
Choreographer(s) Tayir, Andre

Producer(s) Parsons, Lindsley
Director(s) Friedkin, William
Screenwriter(s) Barrett, Tony

Cast Sonny and Cher; Sanders, George; Alden, Norman; Duran, Larry; Thorsden, Kelly; Weinrib, Lennie

Song(s) I Got You Babe; It's the Little Things; Good Times; Trust Me; Don't Talk to Strangers; I'm Gonna Love You; Just a Name

Notes No cue sheet available.

2222 ✦ GOOD WILL TO MEN
Metro–Goldwyn–Mayer, 1955

Song(s) Peace on Earth (C: Bradley, Scott; L: Wesley, Charles; Hanna, William; Barbera, Joseph)

Notes Animated cartoon.

2223 ✦ GOOFY CARTOONS
Disney

Cast Goofy

Song(s) The World Owes Me a Living [1] (C: Harline, Leigh; L: Morey, Larry)

Notes Animated shorts. [1] This song is also used in THE GRASSHOPPER AND THE ANT.

2224 ✦ GOOFY'S GLIDER
Disney, 1940

Musical Score Wolcott, Charles

Cast Goofy

Song(s) My Glider and I (C/L: Wolcott, Charles)

Notes Animated cartoon. No credit sheet available.

2225 ✦ THE GOONIES
Warner Brothers, 1985

Musical Score Grusin, Dave

Producer(s) Donner, Richard; Bernhard, Harvey
Director(s) Donner, Richard
Screenwriter(s) Columbus, Chris

Cast Astin, Sean; Brolin, Josh; Cohen, Jeff; Feldman, Corey; Green, Kerri; Plimpton, Martha; Quan, Ke Huy; Matuszak, John; Davi, Robert; Ramsey, Anne

Song(s) Wherever You're Goin' (It's All Right) (C/L: Cronin, Kevin); Red Hot (C/L: Williams, Joseph; Sembello, Danny); Goonies 'R' Good Enough (C/L: Lauper, Cyndi; Broughton, Stephen; Stead, Lunt-Arthur); Save the Night (C/L: Williams, Joseph; LaTelevision, Amy); What a Thrill (C/L: Lauper, Cyndi; Turi, John)

Notes All of these are background vocals.

2226 ✦ THE GORGEOUS HUSSY
Metro–Goldwyn–Mayer, 1936

Musical Score Stothart, Herbert
Choreographer(s) Raset, Val

Producer(s) Mankiewicz, Joseph L.
Director(s) Brown, Clarence
Screenwriter(s) Morgan, Ainsworth; Avery, Stephen Morehouse
Source(s) *The Gorgeous Hussy* (novel) Adams, Samuel Hopkins

Cast Crawford, Joan; Taylor, Robert; Barrymore, Lionel; Tone, Franchot; Douglas, Melvyn; Stewart, James; Skipworth, Alison; Bondi, Beulah

Song(s) The Hay Ride (C: Stothart, Herbert; Ward, Edward; L: Traditional)

Notes There are other vocals indicated, but I believe they were all humming or vocalizing.

2227 ✦ GOTCHA!
Universal, 1985

Musical Score Conti, Bill
Composer(s) Giuffria, Gregg; Eisley, David Glen
Lyricist(s) Giuffria, Gregg; Eisley, David Glen

Producer(s) Hensler, Paul
Director(s) Kanew, Jeff
Screenwriter(s) Gordon, Dan

Cast Edwards, Anthony; Fiorentino, Linda; Corri, Nick; Rocco, Alex; Adams, Marla; Rydell, Christopher; Leigh, Ayshea

Song(s) Gotcha (C/L: Sinnamon, Shandi); Never Too Late; What's Your Name; Say It Ain't True; Gotcha Where I Want Ya (C/L: Jett, Joan; Allen, J.; Laguna, Kenny)

2228 ✦ GO WEST
Metro–Goldwyn–Mayer, 1940

Composer(s) Kaper, Bronislau
Lyricist(s) Kahn, Gus

Producer(s) Cummings, Jack
Director(s) Buzzell, Edward
Screenwriter(s) Brecher, Irving

Cast Marx, Groucho; Marx, Harpo; Marx, Chico; Carroll, John; Lewis, Diana; Barrat, Robert; King, Walter Woolf

Song(s) You Can't Argue with Love; Ridin' the Range (C/L: Edens, Roger); As If I Didn't Know [1]

Notes [1] Used instrumentally only

2229 ✦ GO WEST, YOUNG LADY
Columbia, 1941

Composer(s) Chaplin, Saul
Lyricist(s) Cahn, Sammy
Choreographer(s) Da Pron, Louis

Producer(s) Sparks, Robert
Director(s) Strayer, Frank R.
Screenwriter(s) De Wolf, Karen; Flournoy, Richard

Cast Singleton, Penny; Ford, Glenn; Miller, Ann; Bob Wills and His Texas Playboys; Jenkins, Allen; Ruggles, Charles; Prouty, Jed; Meiser, Edith

Song(s) Go West Young Lady; Somewhere Along the Trail [1]; Doggie Take Your Time; I Wish That I Could

Be a Singing Cowboy; Most Gentlemen Don't Prefer a Lady; Rise to Arms [2]; Pots and Pans on Parade [2]

Notes [1] Also in ROCKIN' IN THE ROCKIES. [2] Sheet music only.

2230 ◆ GO WEST YOUNG MAN
Paramount, 1936

Composer(s) Johnston, Arthur
Lyricist(s) Burke, Johnny

Producer(s) Cohen, Emanuel
Director(s) Hathaway, Henry
Screenwriter(s) West, Mae
Source(s) *Personal Appearance* (play) Riley, Lawrence

Cast West, Mae; Scott, Randolph; Brady, Alice; William, Warren; Talbot, Lyle; LaRue, Jack; Jewell, Isabel; Xavier Cugat and His Orchestra

Song(s) On a Typical Tropical Night; I Was Saying to the Moon; Go West Young Man [1]; Moment [1]

Notes [1] Only used as instrumental background.

2231 ◆ THE GRACE MOORE STORY

See SO THIS IS LOVE.

2232 ◆ THE GRACIE ALLEN MURDER CASE
Paramount, 1939

Producer(s) Arthur, George M.
Director(s) Green, Alfred E.
Screenwriter(s) Perrin, Nat
Source(s) *The Gracie Allen Murder Case* (novel) Van Dine, S.S.

Cast Allen, Gracie; William, Warren; Drew, Ellen; Taylor, Kent; Prouty, Jed; Cowan, Jerome; Warner, H.B.; Demarest, William; Shaw, Al; Lee, Sammy; MacMahon, Horace

Song(s) Snug As a Bug in a Rug (C: Malneck, Matty; L: Loesser, Frank); A Flea Flew in My Flute [1] (C: Boutelje, Phil; L: Loesser, Frank)

Notes [1] Not used.

2233 ◆ THE GRADUATE
Avco Embassy, 1967

Musical Score Grusin, Dave
Composer(s) Simon, Paul
Lyricist(s) Simon, Paul

Producer(s) Turman, Lawrence
Director(s) Nichols, Mike
Screenwriter(s) Willingham, Calder; Henry, Buck
Source(s) *The Graduate* (novel) Webb, Charles

Cast Hoffman, Dustin; Bancroft, Anne; Ross, Katharine; Henry, Buck; Daniels, William; Hamilton, Murray; Wilson, Elizabeth; Lorne, Marion; Dreyfuss, Richard

Song(s) Sounds of Silence; April Come She Will; Big Bright Green Pleasure Machine; Scarborough Fair; Chase Theme; Mrs. Robinson

2234 ◆ GRADUATION DAY
IFI/Scope III, 1981

Musical Score Kembel, Arthur
Composer(s) Spry, Jeffrey; Spry, Joe
Lyricist(s) Burlison, Doug

Producer(s) Baughn, David; Freed, Herb
Director(s) Freed, Herb
Screenwriter(s) Marisse, Anne; Freed, Herb

Cast George, Christopher; Mackenzie, Patch; Murphy, E. Danny; Peaker, E.J.; Hufsey, Billy

Song(s) Gangster Rock; The Killer; Lucky Strike; Graduation Day Blues (C/L: Loud, Grant); The Winner (C: Ong, Lance; Rohels, Gabriel; L: Cole, David)

Notes No cue sheet available.

2235 ◆ GRAND CANARY
Fox, 1934

Composer(s) Mockridge, Cyril J.

Producer(s) Lasky, Jesse L.
Director(s) Cummings, Irving
Screenwriter(s) Pascal, Ernest
Source(s) *Grand Canary* (novel) Cronin, A.J.

Cast Baxter, Warner; Evans, Madge; Rambeau, Marjorie; Warner, H.B.

Song(s) Oh Ain't He Grand (L: Chandlee); El Amor Es Una Flor (L: Howard)

2236 ◆ GRAND CANYON TRAIL
Republic, 1949

Musical Score Scott, Nathan
Composer(s) Elliott, Jack
Lyricist(s) Elliott, Jack

Producer(s) White, Edward J.
Director(s) Witney, William
Screenwriter(s) Geraghty, Gerald

Cast Rogers, Roy; Trigger; Frazee, Jane; Devine, Andy; Foy Willing and the Riders of the Purple Sage; Livingston, Robert; Barcroft, Roy; Finlayson, James

Song(s) Colorado Joe; Grand Canyon Trail; Everything's Going My Way (C/L: Willing, Foy)

2237 ◆ GRAND CENTRAL MURDER
Metro–Goldwyn–Mayer, 1942

Musical Score Snell, Dave

Producer(s) Zeidman, B.F.
Director(s) Simon, S. Sylvan
Screenwriter(s) Ruric, Peter
Source(s) *Grand Central Murder* (novel) McVeigh, Sue

Cast   Heflin, Van; Parker, Cecilia; Hinds, Samuel S.; Gilchrist, Connie; Dane, Patricia; Grey, Virginia; Levene, Sam; Daniels, Mark; Conway, Tom

Song(s)   Broadway's Still Broadway [1] (C: Revel, Harry; L: Fetter, Ted)

Notes   [1] Also in TWO GIRLS ON BROADWAY.

2238 ♦ GRANDFATHER'S FOLLIES
Warner Brothers, 1944

Composer(s)   Jerome, M.K.
Lyricist(s)   Scholl, Jack

Song(s)   Grandfather's Follies; Let's Go Down to the Seaside

Notes   Short subject. There are also renditions of many turn of the century songs. It is not known if the above songs were written for this short.

2239 ♦ GRANDPA GOES TO TOWN
Republic, 1940

Producer(s)   Meins, Gus
Director(s)   Meins, Gus
Screenwriter(s)   Townley, Jack

Cast   Gleason, James; Gleason, Lucille; Gleason, Russell; Davenport, Harry; Ranson, Lois; Rosenbloom, Maxie; Ryan, Tommy; Beery, Noah; Meins, Douglas

Song(s)   Sunshine for Sale [1] (C: Styne, Jule; L: Barzman, Sol); Out Yonder (C/L: Samuels, Walter G.)

Notes   [1] Also in A MAN BETRAYED (WHEEL OF FORTUNE).

2240 ♦ THE GRAND PARADE
Pathe, 1930

Composer(s)   Goulding, Edmund; Dougherty, Dan
Lyricist(s)   Goulding, Edmund; Dougherty, Dan
Choreographer(s)   Boleslawski, Richard

Producer(s)   Goulding, Edmund
Director(s)   Newmayer, Fred; Reicher, Frank
Screenwriter(s)   Goulding, Edmund

Cast   Twelvetrees, Helen; Scott, Fred; Carle, Richard; Astaire, Marie; Powell, Russell; Jamison, Bud

Song(s)   Molly; Sweetheart; Grand Parade; Alone in the Rain; It's All in Me; Moanin' for You

Notes   No cue sheet available.

2241 ♦ GRAND PRIX
Metro–Goldwyn–Mayer, 1967

Musical Score   Jarre, Maurice

Producer(s)   Lewis, Edward
Director(s)   Frankenheimer, John
Screenwriter(s)   Aurthur, Robert Alan

Cast   Garner, James; Saint, Eva Marie; Montand, Yves; Mifune, Toshiro; Bedford, Brian; Walter, Jessica; Sabato, Antonio; Hardy, Francoise; Celi, Adolfo

Song(s)   Take a Chance (C/L: Kusik, Larry; Snyder, Eddie); Moi L'Accordeon (C/L: Di Maccio, Christian; Desbois, R.)

2242 ♦ GRAND SLAM
Paramount, 1968

Musical Score   Morricone, Ennio
Composer(s)   Morricone, Ennio
Lyricist(s)   Bardotti, Sergio [1]; Matarazzo, Maysa [2]

Producer(s)   Colombo, Harry; Papi, George
Director(s)   Montaldo, Giuliano
Screenwriter(s)   Poli, Mino

Cast   Robinson, Edward G.; Leigh, Janet; Kinski, Klaus; Celi, Adolfo

Song(s)   Go Away, Melancholy (Vai Via Malinconia); He and I (Dizer Somento Ciao)

Notes   No cue sheets available. [1] Italian lyricist. [2] Portuguese lyricist.

2243 ♦ THE GRASS IS GREENER
Universal, 1960

Producer(s)   Donen, Stanley
Director(s)   Donen, Stanley
Screenwriter(s)   Williams, Hugh; Williams, Margaret
Source(s)   *The Grass Is Greener* (play) Williams, Hugh; Williams, Margaret

Cast   Grant, Cary; Kerr, Deborah; Mitchum, Robert; Simmons, Jean; Watson, Moray

Notes   No cue sheet available. There are vocals of the following Noel Coward songs: "Mad Dogs and Englishmen," "Stately Homes of England" and "I'll Follow My Secret Heart."

2244 ♦ GREASE
Paramount, 1978

Composer(s)   Jacobs, Jim; Casey, Warren
Lyricist(s)   Jacobs, Jim; Casey, Warren
Choreographer(s)   Birch, Patricia

Producer(s)   Carr, Allan; Stigwood, Robert
Director(s)   Kleiser, Randal
Screenwriter(s)   Woodard, Bronte
Source(s)   *Grease* (musical) Jacobs, Jim; Casey, Warren

Cast   Newton-John, Olivia; Travolta, John; Channing, Stockard; Conaway, Jeff; Conn, Didi; Lamas, Lorenzo; Arden, Eve; Avalon, Frankie; Blondell, Joan; Caesar, Sid; Byrnes, Edward; Ghostley, Alice; Goodman, Dody

Song(s)   Love Is a Many-Splendored Thing [2] (C: Fain, Sammy; L: Webster, Paul Francis); Grease (C/L: Gibb, Barry); Alma Mater [1]; Summer Nights [1]; Rydell Fight Song; Look at Me, I'm Sandra Dee [1];

Hopelessly Devoted to You (C/L: Farrar, John);
Greased Lightin' [1]; It's Raining on Prom Night [1];
Beauty School Dropout [1]; Rock 'N' Roll Party Queen
[1]; Those Magic Changes [1]; Born to Hand Jive [1];
Sandy (C: St. Louis, Louis; L: Simon, Scott); There Are
Worse Things I Could Do [1]; You're the One That I
Want (C/L: Farrar, John); We Go Together [1]; Alone
at the Drive-In Movie [1] [3]; Freddy My Love [1] [3];
Mooning [1] [3]

Notes [1] From Broadway production. [2] Not written
for film. [3] Sheet music only.

2245 ◆ GREASE 2
Paramount, 1982

Composer(s) St. Louis, Louis
Lyricist(s) Greenfield, Howard

Producer(s) Stigwood, Robert; Carr, Allan
Director(s) Birch, Patricia
Screenwriter(s) Finkleman, Ken

Cast Caulfield, Maxwell; Pfeiffer, Michelle; Luft,
Lorna; Teefy, Maureen; Price, Alison; Segall, Pamela;
Zmed, Adrian; Frechette, Peter; McDonald, Christopher;
Conn, Didi; Arden, Eve; Caesar, Sid; Goodman, Dody;
Hunter, Tab; Patterson, Dick; Stevens, Connie; Lattanzi,
Matt

Song(s) Back to School Again; Who's That Guy; (Love
Will) Turn Back the Hands of Time; Charades (L:
Gibson, Michael); Prowlin' (C/L: Bugatti, Dominic;
Musker, Frank); Cool Rider (C/L: Linde, Dennis); Girl
for All Seasons (C/L: Bugatti, Dominic; Musker, Frank);
Rock-A-Hula-Luau (C/L: Bugatti, Dominic; Musker,
Frank); Brad (C/L: Cerf, Christopher); Score Tonight
(C/L: Bugatti, Dominic; Musker, Frank; St. Louis,
Louis); Do It for Our Country (C/L: Hegel, Rob;
Linde, Dennis); Reproduction (C/L: Morrison, Bob;
MacRae, Johnny)

Notes No cue sheet available.

2246 ◆ GREASED LIGHTNING
Warner Brothers, 1977

Musical Score Karlin, Fred
Composer(s) Karlin, Fred

Producer(s) Weinstein, Hannah
Director(s) Schultz, Michael
Screenwriter(s) Vose, Kenneth; DuKore, Lawrence;
Van Peebles, Melvin; Capetanos, Leon

Cast Pryor, Richard; Bridges, Beau; Little, Cleavon;
Grier, Pam; Gardenia, Vincent; Havens, Richie; Bond,
Julian; Jackson, Maynard

Song(s) All Come True (L: Gimbel, Norman); Maybe
Tomorrow (L: Craig, Bradford)

Notes "Here Comes Peter Cottontail" by Jack Rollins
and Steve Nelson was also used. The above songs were
used as background vocals.

2247 ◆ THE GREAT AMERICAN BROADCAST
Twentieth Century–Fox, 1941

Musical Score Newman, Alfred
Composer(s) Warren, Harry
Lyricist(s) Gordon, Mack

Producer(s) Zanuck, Darryl F.
Director(s) Mayo, Archie
Screenwriter(s) Ettlinger, Don; Blum, Edwin; Ellis,
Robert; Logan, Helen

Cast Faye, Alice; Oakie, Jack; Payne, John; Romero,
Cesar; The Ink Spots; Hughes, Mary Beth; Acuff, Eddie;
The Wiere Brothers; The Nicholas Brothers

Song(s) The Great American Broadcast; It's All in a
Lifetime; I Take to You; Where You Are; Long Ago Last
Night; I've Got a Bone to Pick with You; Run, Little
Raindrop, Run [1]; Chapman's Cheerful Cheese [2];
Chesterstrikes [3]

Notes "Give My Regards to Broadway" by George M.
Cohan; The "Sextette" from LUCIA by Donizetti; "If I
Didn't Care" by Jack Lawrence and "Alabamy Bound"
by Ray Henderson, Bud Green and B.G. DeSylva are also
performed vocally. [1] Cut; used in SPRINGTIME IN
THE ROCKIES (1942). [2] Not on cue sheets. [3] Not
used.

2248 ◆ THE GREAT BANK ROBBERY
Warner Brothers, 1969

Musical Score Riddle, Nelson
Composer(s) Van Heusen, James
Lyricist(s) Cahn, Sammy

Producer(s) Stuart, Malcolm
Director(s) Averback, Hy
Screenwriter(s) Blatty, William Peter
Source(s) (novel) O'Rourke, Frank

Cast Mostel, Zero; Novak, Kim; Walker, Clint; Akins,
Claude; Tamiroff, Akim; Storch, Larry; Anderson, John;
Jaffe, Sam; Mako; Cook Jr., Elisha; Warrick, Ruth

Song(s) The Rainbow Rider; Heaven Helps Him Who
Helps Himself

2249 ◆ THE GREAT CARUSO
Metro–Goldwyn–Mayer, 1951

Musical Score Green, Johnny
Choreographer(s) Adler, Peter Herman

Producer(s) Pasternak, Joe
Director(s) Thorpe, Richard
Screenwriter(s) Levien, Sonya; Ludwig, William
Source(s) *Enrico Caruso, His Life and Death*
(biography) Caruso, Dorothy

Cast Lanza, Mario; Blyth, Ann; Kirsten, Dorothy;
Novotna, Jarmila; Thebom, Blanche; Celli, Teresa;
Hageman, Richard; Reid, Carl Benton; Franz, Eduard;
Donath, Ludwig; Napier, Alan

Song(s)   The Loveliest Night of the Year [1] (C: Traditional; L: Webster, Paul Francis)

Notes   Vocals include "Magnificat;" "'A Vucchella" by Tosti and D'Annunzio; "La Danza" by Rossini; "The Consecration Scene," "The Trio Finale," "Celeste Aida" and "Numi Pieta" from Verdi's AIDA; "The Torture Scene" and "E Lucevan le Stelle" from Puccini's LA TOSCA; "The Villification Scene" and "Brindisi" from Mascagni's CAVALLERIA RUSTICANA; "Cielo e Mar" from Ponchielli's LA GIOCONDA; "La Donna e Mobile" from Verdi's RIGOLETTO; "Torna a Surriento" by De Curtis; "Che Celida Manina" from Puccini's LA BOHEME; "Mattinata" by Leoncavallo; "Miserere" from Verdi's IL TROVATORE; the "Quartette" from Verdi's RIGOLETTO; "Sweethearts" from SWEETHEARTS by Victor Herbert and Harry B. Smith; "Recitativo" and "Vesti la Giubba" from Leoncavallo's PAGLIACCI; "Ave Maria" by Bach and Gounod; the "Sextette" from LUCIA DI LAMMERMOOR by Donizetti; "Because" by Guy D'Hardelot and "M'Appari" and "The Finale" from MARTHA by Flotow. [1] Irving Aaronson credited with music on sheet music.

2250 ✦ THE GREAT DIVIDE
Warner Brothers–First National, 1929

Composer(s)   Ruby, Herman
Lyricist(s)   Perkins, Ray

Producer(s)   North, Robert
Director(s)   Barker, Reginald
Screenwriter(s)   Myton, Fred; Perez, Paul
Source(s)   *The Great Divide* (play) Moody, William Vaughn

Cast   Mackaill, Dorothy; Keith, Ian; Loy, Myrna; Fawcett, George; Hale, Creighton; Littlefield, Lucien; Gillingwater, Claude

Song(s)   The End of the Lonesome Trail; Si, Si, Senor

Notes   No cue sheet available.

2251 ✦ THE GREATEST
Columbia, 1977

Musical Score   Masser, Michael

Producer(s)   Marshall, Tom
Director(s)   Gries, Tom
Screenwriter(s)   Lardner Jr., Ring
Source(s)   *The Greatest: My Own Story* (autobiography) Ali, Muhammad; Muhammad, Herbert; Durham, Richard

Cast   Ali, Muhammad; Borgnine, Ernest; Haynes, Lloyd; Benson, Lucille; Merrill, Dina; Mosley, Roger E.; Duvall, Robert; Huddleston, David

Song(s)   The Greatest Love of All (C: Masser, Michael; L: Creed, Linda); I Always Knew I Had It in Me (C: Masser, Michael; L: Goffin, Gerry)

Notes   No cue sheet available.

2252 ✦ THE GREATEST SHOW ON EARTH
Paramount, 1952

Musical Score   Young, Victor
Composer(s)   Sullivan, Henry
Lyricist(s)   Anderson, John Murray
Choreographer(s)   Anderson, John Murray; Barstow, Richard

Producer(s)   De Mille, Cecil B.
Director(s)   De Mille, Cecil B.
Screenwriter(s)   Frank, Fredric M.; Lyndon, Barre; St. John, Theodore

Cast   Heston, Charlton; Stewart, James; Hutton, Betty; Lamour, Dorothy; Wilde, Cornel; Grahame, Gloria; Bettger, Lyle; Tierney, Lawrence; Kellogg, John; Wilcoxon, Henry

Song(s)   Popcorn and Lemonade [1]; Sing a Happy Song; Only a Rose [2] (C: Friml, Rudolf; L: Hooker, Brian); Lovely Luawana Lady (C: North, John Ringling; L: Goetz, E. Ray); A Picnic in the Park; Be a Jumping Jack (C: Young, Victor; L: Washington, Ned); The Greatest Show on Earth (C: Young, Victor; L: Washington, Ned)

Notes   [1] Not on cue sheets. [2] Not written for movie. Originally in Broadway score THE VAGABOND KING.

2253 ✦ THE GREATEST STORY EVER TOLD
United Artists, 1965

Musical Score   Newman, Alfred

Producer(s)   Stevens, George
Director(s)   Stevens, George
Screenwriter(s)   Stevens, George; Barrett, James Lee

Cast   Von Sydow, Max; McGuire, Dorothy; Rains, Claude; Ferrer, Jose; Heston, Charlton; Pleasence, Donald; McCallum, David; McDowall, Roddy; Farr, Jamie

Song(s)   Palm Sunday Hosanna (There Shall Come a Time to Enter) (C: Newman, Alfred; L: Darby, Ken)

Notes   There are several other liturgical songs.

2254 ✦ THE GREAT GABBO
Sono-Art, 1929

Composer(s)   Titsworth, Paul; Cowan, Lynn; McNamee, Donald; King Zany
Lyricist(s)   Titsworth, Paul; Cowan, Lynn; McNamee, Donald; King Zany
Choreographer(s)   Kusell, Maurice L.

Director(s)   Cruze, James
Screenwriter(s)   Herbert, Hugh

Cast   von Stroheim, Erich; Compson, Betty; Douglas, Donald; Kane, Marjorie "Babe"

Song(s) The New Step (C/L: Cowan, Lynn; Titsworth, Paul); I'm in Love with You (C/L: Cowan, Lynn; Titsworth, Paul); I'm Laughing; Ickey; Every Now and Then; The Web of Love (C/L: Cowan, Lynn; Titsworth, Paul); The Ga-Ga Bird (C/L: Cowan, Lynn; Titsworth, Paul)

Notes No cue sheet available. These songwriters did not collaborate. It is not known who wrote which songs.

2255 ◆ THE GREAT JOHN L
United Artists, 1945

Producer(s) Mastroly, Frank; Grant, James Edward
Director(s) Tuttle, Frank
Screenwriter(s) Grant, James Edward

Cast McClure, Greg; Darnell, Linda; Britton, Barbara; Kruger, Otto; Ford, Wallace; Mathews, George; Barrat, Robert; Kerrigan, J.M.; Calhoun, Rory; Sullivan, Lee

Song(s) A Friend of Yours (C: Van Heusen, James; L: Burke, Johnny); He Was a Perfect Gentleman (C: Van Heusen, James; L: Burke, Johnny)

Notes No cue sheet available. There is also a vocal of "When You Were Sweet Sixteen" by James Thornton.

2256 ◆ THE GREAT LOCOMOTIVE CHASE
Disney, 1956

Musical Score Smith, Paul J.

Producer(s) Watkin, Lawrence Edward
Director(s) Lyon, Francis D.
Screenwriter(s) Watkin, Lawrence Edward

Cast Parker, Fess; Hunter, Jeffrey; York, Jeff; Lupton, John; Firestone, Eddie; Tobey, Kenneth; Carey Jr., Harry; Pickens, Slim

Song(s) Sons of Old Aunt Dinah (C: Smith, Paul J.; Jones, Stan; L: Watkin, Lawrence Edward); Railroadin' Man (C/L: Jones, Stan)

2257 ◆ THE GREAT LOVER
Paramount, 1949

Musical Score Lilley, Joseph J.
Composer(s) Livingston, Jay; Evans, Ray
Lyricist(s) Livingston, Jay; Evans, Ray

Producer(s) Beloin, Edmund
Director(s) Hall, Alexander
Screenwriter(s) Beloin, Edmund; Shavelson, Melville; Rose, Jack

Cast Hope, Bob; Fleming, Rhonda; Young, Roland; Culver, Roland; Lyon, Richard; Gray, Gary; Backus, Jim

Song(s) A Thousand Violins; Lucky Us!

Notes First titled EASY DOES IT.

2258 ◆ THE GREAT MAN
Universal, 1956

Musical Score Mancini, Henry

Producer(s) Rosenberg, Aaron
Director(s) Ferrer, Jose
Screenwriter(s) Ferrer, Jose; Morgan, Al
Source(s) *The Great Man* (novel) Morgan, Al

Cast Ferrer, Jose; Jagger, Dean; Wynn, Keenan; London, Julie; Gilbert, Joanne; Wynn, Ed; Backus, Jim; Foulk, Robert; Morgan, Russ; Talbot, Lyle; Platt, Edward; Backus, Henny

Song(s) The Meaning of the Blues (C/L: Troup, Bobby; Worth, Leah)

2259 ◆ THE GREAT MORGAN
Metro–Goldwyn–Mayer, 1945

Musical Score Terr, Max

Producer(s) Bresler, Jerry
Director(s) Perrin, Nat
Screenwriter(s) Perrin, Nat

Cast Morgan, Frank; Ames, Leon

Song(s) Tales from the Vienna Woods (C: Strauss, Johann; L: Brent, Earl); Thank You Columbus [1] (C: Lane, Burton; L: Harburg, E.Y.); (I Fell in Love with) The Leader of the Band (C: Styne, Jule; L: Magidson, Herb)

Notes This film, not released in the United States, features outtakes from the MGM vaults. The cast list is of those original to this film. Among the stars whose clips were featured were Eleanor Powell (from HONOLULU), Carlos Ramirez, Lucille Norman, Virginia O'Brien and the King Sisters. There is also a vocal of "Donkey Serenade" by Rudolf Friml, Herbert Stothart, Robert Wright and George Forrest. [1] This number was written in 1941. Perhaps it was meant for BABES ON BROADWAY.

2260 ◆ THE GREAT MOUSE DETECTIVE
Disney, 1986

Musical Score Mancini, Henry
Composer(s) Mancini, Henry
Lyricist(s) Grossman, Larry; Fitzhugh, Ellen

Producer(s) Mattinson, Burny
Director(s) Musker, John; Clements, Ron; Michener, David; Mattinson, Burny
Screenwriter(s) Young, Pete; Hulett, Steve; Musker, John; O'Callaghan, Matthew; Michener, David; Gerry, Vance; Clements, Ron; Morris, Bruce M.; Mattinson, Burny; Shaw, Melvin
Source(s) Basil of Baker Street series (stories) Titus, Eve; Galdone, Paul

Voices Price, Vincent; Ingham, Barrie; Bettin, Val; Pollatschek, Susanne; Candido, Candy; Chesney, Diana; Brenner, Eve; Young, Alan

Supervising Animator(s) Henn, Mark; Keane, Glen; Minkoff, Robert; Butoy, Hendel

Song(s) The World's Greatest Criminal Mind; Goodbye, So Soon; Let Me Be Good to You (C/L: Manchester, Melissa); Are You the One Who Loves Me [1]

Notes Animated feature. [1] Not used.

2261 ✦ THE GREAT MUPPET CAPER
Universal, 1981

Musical Score Raposo, Joseph
Composer(s) Raposo, Joseph
Lyricist(s) Raposo, Joseph
Choreographer(s) Mann, Anita

Producer(s) Lazar, David; Oz, Frank
Director(s) Henson, Jim
Screenwriter(s) Patchett, Tom; Tarses, Jay; Juhl, Jerry; Rose, Jack

Puppeteer(s) Henson, Jim; Oz, Frank; Goelz, Dave; Nelson, Jerry; Hunt, Richard
Cast Grodin, Charles; Rigg, Diana; Cleese, John; Morley, Robert; Ustinov, Peter; Warden, Jack

Song(s) Hey, a Movie; Nightlife; Stepping Out—Nightclub Utility; The First Time; Couldn't We Ride; Miss Piggy Fantasy

2262 ✦ THE GREAT OUTDOORS
Universal, 1988

Musical Score Newman, Thomas
Composer(s) Newman, Thomas
Lyricist(s) Newman, Thomas

Producer(s) Schmidt, Arne L.
Director(s) Deutch, Howard
Screenwriter(s) Hughes, John

Cast Candy, John; Aykroyd, Dan; Faracy, Stephanie; Bening, Annette; Young, Chris; Giatti, Ian; Gordon, Hilary; Gordon, Rebecca; Prosky, Robert; Arquette, Lewis

Song(s) Undressing Connie; Raccoons; Land of a Thousand Dances (C/L: Kenner, Chris; Domino, Antoine "Fats"); Beaver Patrol (C/L: Archibald, Tim); Hot Fun in the Summertime (C/L: Stewart, Sylvester); Cabin Feaver (C/L: Sadia; Wilcox, David); Paul Bunyan Love (C/L: Kangas, Les); Dragboat [1] (C/L: Scott, Tom); Big Country [1] (C/L: Gowdy, Bruce; Sherwood, Billy; Aykroyd, Peter)

Notes [1] Not on cue sheet, but only songs listed in Academy Index.

2263 ✦ THE GREAT RACE
Warner Brothers, 1965

Musical Score Mancini, Henry
Composer(s) Mancini, Henry
Lyricist(s) Mercer, Johnny

Producer(s) Jurow, Martin
Director(s) Edwards, Blake
Screenwriter(s) Ross, Arthur

Cast Lemmon, Jack; Curtis, Tony; Wood, Natalie; Falk, Peter; Wynn, Keenan; O'Connell, Arthur; Vance, Vivian; Provine, Dorothy; Storch, Larry; Martin, Ross; Macready, George; Kaplan, Marvin; Pyle, Denver

Song(s) The Sweetheart Tree; He Shouldn't-A, Hadn't-A, Oughtn't-A Swang on Me

Notes Renditions of "The Desert Song" by Sigmund Romberg, Otto Harbach and Oscar Hammerstein II and "It Looks Like a Big Night Tonight" by Harry Williams and Egbert Van Alstyne are also used.

2264 ✦ THE GREAT SCHNOZZLE

See PALOOKA.

2265 ✦ THE GREAT VICTOR HERBERT
Paramount, 1939

Composer(s) Herbert, Victor
Choreographer(s) Prinz, LeRoy

Producer(s) Stone, Andrew L.
Director(s) Stone, Andrew L.
Screenwriter(s) Lively, Robert; Crouse, Russel

Cast Jones, Allan; Martin, Mary; West, Everett; Davis, Wynn; Foster, Susanna; Connolly, Walter; Cowan, Jerome; Finlayson, James; Tucker, Richard

Song(s) You Are Beautiful [1] (L: Loesser, Frank; Boutelje, Phil); Happy Days [2] (L: Loesser, Frank; Boutelje, Phil); Wonderful Dreams [3] (L: Loesser, Frank)

Notes Picture originally titled GAY DAYS OF VICTOR HERBERT. Only original songs listed above. Also heard in the film are "Rose of the World" and "Twilight in Barakeesh" from ROSE OF ALGERIA; "To the Land of My Own Romance" from THE ENCHANTRESS; "March of the Toys" from BABES IN TOYLAND; "Ah! Sweet Mystery of Life" from NAUGHTY MARIETTA; "There Once Was an Owl" from BABETTE; "A Kiss in the Dark" from ORANGE BLOSSOMS; "Absinthe Frappe" from IT HAPPENED IN NORDLAND; "Fleurette" (inst.); "Thine Alone" from EILEEN; "Serenade;" "Air de Ballet;" "All for You" from PRINCESS PAT; "Sweet Harp of the Days That Are Gone," "Lullaby" and "Chang the Lover" from WILLOW PLATE SUITE and "If I Were on the Stage" from MME. MODISTE. There is also a bicycle medley consisting of "I'm the Leader of Society" from THE VICEROY; "I'm Falling in Love with Someone" from NAUGHTY MARIETTA; "How Do You Get That Way" from ANGEL FACE; "I Love Thee" from THE SERENADE; "I Might Be Your Once-in-a-While" from ANGEL FACE; "Neopolitan Love Song" from PRINCESS PAT; "Ask Her While the Band Is Playing" from ROSE OF ALGERIA 'and "Beware of the Automobile" from MISS DOLLY DOLLARS. [1] From Herbert melody "Al Fresco." Probably not used in the film. [2] From Herbert melody "Punchinello." [3] From Herbert melody "Yesterthoughts." Also called "Beautiful Dreams."

2266 ♦ THE GREAT WALTZ (1938)
Metro–Goldwyn–Mayer, 1938

Musical Score   Tiomkin, Dimitri
Composer(s)   Strauss, Johann; Tiomkin, Dimitri
Lyricist(s)   Hammerstein II, Oscar
Choreographer(s)   Rasch, Albertina

Producer(s)   Hyman, Bernard H.
Director(s)   Duvivier, Julien
Screenwriter(s)   Hoffenstein, Samuel; Reisch, Walter

Cast   Rainer, Luise; Gravet, Fernand; Korjus, Miliza [1]; Herbert, Hugh; Atwill, Lionel; Bois, Curt; Kinskey, Leonid; Shean, Al; Gombell, Minna; Bing, Herman

Song(s)   I'm in Love with Vienna; Polka; There'll Come a Time; Artist's Life [2] (L: Tiomkin, Dimitri); Revolutionary March; Birth of the Vienna Woods [2] (L: Tiomkin, Dimitri); Tales from the Vienna Woods; One Day When We Were Young; Du Und Du (Only You); The Bat

Notes   Victor Fleming and Josef von Sternberg also helped (uncredited) on the direction. [1] U.S. film debut and finale. [2] I'm not sure about the Tiomkin lyric credits but Hammerstein's name was not on these cues. They may be instrumentals with vocalizing.

2267 ♦ THE GREAT WALTZ (1972)
Metro–Goldwyn–Mayer, 1972

Musical Score   Strauss Jr., Johann
Composer(s)   Strauss Jr., Johann
Lyricist(s)   Wright, Robert; Forrest, George
Choreographer(s)   White, Onna

Producer(s)   Stone, Andrew L.
Director(s)   Stone, Andrew L.
Screenwriter(s)   Stone, Andrew L.

Cast   Buchholz, Horst [19]; Patrick, Nigel; Mitchell, Yvonne; Brazzi, Rossano; Robinson, Susan; Howe, George; Lane, Lauri Lupino; Woolf, Vicki [20]; Faulkner, James; McKellar, Kenneth [21]; Costa, Mary

Song(s)   Crystal and Gold; Nightfall Choral [1] (C: Strauss, Johann); The King Is Dead [2]; Warm (1) [3];

Warm (2) [4]; Peace on Earth [5]; Letter of Love [6] (C: Offenbach, Jacques); Love Is Music [7]; Louder and Faster [8]; With You Gone [9] (C: Strauss, Josef); Through Jetty's Eyes (1) [10]; Through Jetty's Eyes (2) [11]; Through Jetty's Eyes (3) [12]; Through Jetty's Eyes (4) [7]; Father Assists [14]; Blue Danube Rehearsal [14]; Blue Danube Floods the World (1) [14]; Blue Danube Floods the World (2) [13]; Say Yes [15]; Six Drinks [16]; Die Fledermaus Is Born [17]; Who Are You? [18]; Die Fledermaus Finale; Great Waltz in Boston [14]

Notes   Music for songs adapted by Wright and Forrest. Incidental music and music score adapted by Robert Docker and Roland Shaw. [1] From "Lorelei, Rhein, Klange." [2] From "Vibrationen Waltz." [3] From "Die Extravaganten Waltz." [4] From "Medley for Prince Albert." [5] From "Der Lustige Krieg March." [6] From "La Perichole." [7] From "Wine, Woman and Song." [8] From "Leichtes Blut Polka." [9] From "Brennende Liebe." [10] From "Vienna Blood." [11] From "Roses from the South." [12] From "Voices of Spring." [13] From "Drolerie Polka." [14] From "The Blue Danube." [15] From "Gypsy Baron." [16] From "Armen Ball Polka." [17] From the "Die Fledermaus Overture." [18] From "Du Und Du." [19] Dubbed by Ken Barrie. [20] Dubbed by Joan Baxter. [21] Sings narration but does not appear on screen.

2268 ♦ THE GREAT WHITE HOPE
Twentieth Century–Fox, 1970

Producer(s)   Turman, Lawrence
Director(s)   Ritt, Martin
Screenwriter(s)   Sackler, Howard
Source(s)   *The Great White Hope* (play) Sackler, Howard

Cast   Jones, James Earl; Alexander, Jane; Gilbert, Lou; Morris, Chester; Holbrook, Hal; Richards, Beah

Song(s)   Let Me Hold You in My Arms Tonight (C/L: Fuller, Jesse); Breakfast Blues (C/L: Frazier, Thurston)

Notes   There are also vocals of "I'm So High" "The Royal Telephone" "Spirits Bright"—all public domain—and "I Always Think I'm Up in Heaven When I'm Down in Dixieland" by Maurice Abrahams, Sam M. Lewis and Joe Young. It is not known if the Fuller song was written for this production.

2269 ♦ THE GREAT ZIEGFELD
Metro–Goldwyn–Mayer, 1936

Composer(s)   Donaldson, Walter
Lyricist(s)   Adamson, Harold
Choreographer(s)   Felix, Seymour

Producer(s)   Stromberg, Hunt
Director(s)   Leonard, Robert Z.
Screenwriter(s)   McGuire, William Anthony

Cast Loy, Myrna; Powell, William; Rainer, Luise; Morgan, Frank; Brice, Fanny; Bruce, Virginia; Owen, Reginald; Bolger, Ray; Cossart, Ernest; Cawthorn, Joseph; Pendleton, Nat; Hoctor, Harriet; Chatburn, Jean; Irving, Paul; Bing, Herman; Judels, Charles; Corday, Marcelle; Walburn, Raymond; Trimble, A.A.; Doyle, Buddy; Morner, Stanley [1]

Song(s) You Gotta Pull Strings; She's a Follies Girl; You; You Never Looked So Beautiful [2]; Queen of the Jungle; It's Been So Long [3]

Notes Vocals also include "I Wish You'd Come and Play with Me" by Plumpton; "It's Delightful to Be Married" by Anna Held and Vincent Scotto; "If You Knew Susie" by B.G. DeSylva and Joseph Meyer; "Shine on Harvest Moon" by Jack Norworth and Nora Bayes; "A Pretty Girl Is Like a Melody" and "Yiddle on Your Fiddle" by Irving Berlin; "Un Bel Di Vedremo" by Puccini; "Vesti La Giubba" by Leoncavallo; George Gershwin's instrumental "Rhapsody in Blue;" "My Man" by Channing Pollock and Maurice Yvain; "Look for the Silver Lining" by Jerome Kern and B.G. DeSylva; "Ole Man River" by Jerome Kern and Oscar Hammerstein II; and a few snippets (under 15 seconds) of other show tunes presented by Ziegfeld. [1] Actually Dennis Morgan. He was dubbed singing "A Pretty Girl Is Like a Melody" by Allan Jones. [2] Also in Ziegfeld Girl. [3] Sheet music only.

2270 ✦ THE GREEK TYCOON
Universal, 1978

Producer(s) Klein, Allen; Landau, Ely
Director(s) Thompson, J. Lee
Screenwriter(s) Fine, Mort

Cast Quinn, Anthony; Bisset, Jacqueline; Albert, Edward; Vallone, Raf; Sparv, Camilla; Durning, Charles

Song(s) Funny Kind of Love Affair (C/L: Moran, Mike)

2271 ✦ THE GREEN BERETS
Warner Brothers, 1968

Musical Score Rozsa, Miklos

Producer(s) Wayne, Michael
Director(s) Wayne, John; Kellogg, Ray
Screenwriter(s) Barrett, James Lee
Source(s) *The Green Berets* (novel) Moore, Robin

Cast Wayne, John; Janssen, David; Hutton, Jim; Ray, Aldo; St. Jacques, Raymond; Cabot, Bruce; Soo, Jack; Takei, George; Wayne, Patrick; Askew, Luke; Tsu, Irene; Henry, Mike; Pryor, Richard "Cactus"

Song(s) The Ballad of the Green Berets (C/L: Sadler, Barry; Moore, Robin); The River Seine [1] (C/L: LaFarge, Guy; Monod, Flavien; Roberts, Allan; Holt, Arlan)

Notes The title number was used as a background vocal. *50th Anniversary* lists Wayne Kellogg as the director. [1] Roberts and Holt wrote English lyrics. In French the song is also in UNDER MY SKIN (20th).

2272 ✦ THE GREEN BUDDHA
Republic, 1958

Musical Score Williamson, Lambert
Composer(s) Williamson, Lambert
Lyricist(s) Breeze, Dennis

Producer(s) Springsteen, R.G.
Director(s) Springsteen, R.G.
Screenwriter(s) Erickson, Paul

Cast Morris, Wayne; Germaine, Mary; Ashton, Marcia; Merrall, Mary; Rilla, Walter

Song(s) Peace of Mind; Poet with a Punch

2273 ✦ GREEN DOLPHIN STREET
Metro–Goldwyn–Mayer, 1947

Musical Score Kaper, Bronislau

Producer(s) Wilson, Carey
Director(s) Saville, Victor
Screenwriter(s) Raphaelson, Samson
Source(s) *Green Dolphin Street* (novel) Goudge, Elizabeth

Cast Turner, Lana; Heflin, Van; Hart, Richard; Morgan, Frank; Gwenn, Edmund; Whitty, Dame May; Owen, Reginald; Cooper, Gladys; MacGill, Moyna; Christian, Linda

Song(s) On Green Dolphin Street [1] (C: Kaper, Bronislau; L: Washington, Ned)

Notes [1] Used instrumentally only.

2274 ✦ THE GREEN-EYED BLONDE
Warner Brothers, 1957

Musical Score Stevens, Leith
Composer(s) Singer, Guy
Lyricist(s) Singer, Guy

Producer(s) Melcher, Martin
Director(s) Girard, Bernard
Screenwriter(s) Stubblefield, Sally

Cast Oliver, Susan; Plowman, Linda; Long, Beverly; Nilsson, Norma Jean; Moore, Tommie; Merey, Carla; Brophy, Sallie

Song(s) The Green-Eyed Blonde (C/L: Lubin, Joe); Story of Young Love; When I Marry; Love, Love, Love; She'll Be Comin' Round (C/L: Lubin, Joe; Howard, Jerome); Hangin' Around (C/L: Lubin, Joe; Howard, Jerome); Buddy's Lullaby (C/L: Lubin, Joe; Howard, Jerome)

Notes Some of these are background vocal only.

2275 ✦ GREEN FIRE
Metro–Goldwyn–Mayer, 1954

Musical Score Rozsa, Miklos

Producer(s) Deutsch, Armand
Director(s) Marton, Andrew
Screenwriter(s) Goff, Ivan; Roberts, Ben
Source(s) *Green Fire* (novel) Rainier, Peter W.

Cast Granger, Stewart; Kelly, Grace; Douglas, Paul; Ericson, John; Vye, Murvyn; Torvay, Jose

Song(s) Green Fire (C: Rozsa, Miklos; L: Brooks, Jack)

2276 ✦ THE GREEN GLOVE
United Artists, 1952

Musical Score Kosma, Joseph
Composer(s) Kosma, Joseph
Lyricist(s) Bassis, H.

Producer(s) Maurer, George
Director(s) Mate, Rudolph
Screenwriter(s) Bennett, Charles

Cast Macready, George; Ford, Glenn; Brooks, Geraldine; Hardwicke, Sir Cedric; Andre, Gaby; Greco, Juliette

Song(s) L'Amour Est Parti Romance; No Regrets [1] (L: Morse, Jerry)

Notes [1] Sheet music only.

2277 ✦ GREEN GRASS OF WYOMING
Twentieth Century–Fox, 1948

Musical Score Mockridge, Cyril J.

Producer(s) Bassler, Robert
Director(s) King, Louis
Screenwriter(s) Berkeley, Martin
Source(s) *Green Grass of Wyoming* (novel) O'Hara, Mary [1]

Cast Cummins, Peggy; Coburn, Charles; Arthur, Robert; Nolan, Lloyd; Ives, Burl; Wall, Geraldine; Adler, Robert; Wright, Will

Song(s) The Ballad of Thunderhead (C/L: Ives, Burl)

Notes Ives also sings some traditional tunes. [1] Pseudonym of Mary Alsop Sture-Vasa.

2278 ✦ GREEN MANSIONS
Metro–Goldwyn–Mayer, 1959

Musical Score Kaper, Bronislau; Villa-Lobos, Heitor

Producer(s) Grainger, Edmund
Director(s) Ferrer, Mel
Screenwriter(s) Kingsley, Dorothy
Source(s) *Green Mansions* (novel) Hudson, William Henry

Cast Hepburn, Audrey; Perkins, Anthony; Cobb, Lee J.; Hayakawa, Sessue; Silva, Henry; Persoff, Nehemiah; Pate, Michael; Hemsley, Estelle

Song(s) Song of Green Mansions (C: Kaper, Bronislau; L: Webster, Paul Francis)

2279 ✦ THE GREEN PASTURES
Warner Brothers, 1936

Musical Score Korngold, Erich Wolfgang

Producer(s) Blanke, Henry
Director(s) Keighley, William; Connelly, Marc
Screenwriter(s) Bradford, Roark
Source(s) *The Green Pastures* (play) Connelly, Marc

Cast Ingram, Rex; Polk, Oscar; Anderson, Eddie "Rochester"; Wilson, Frank; Reed, George; Gleaves, Abraham; Anderson, Myrtle; Stokes, Al; Harris, Edna M.; Fuller, James

Notes It is not known if there are any original songs in this film. These are all traditional spirituals "Camp Meetin' in the Promised Land;" "Oh Rise and Shine;" "Certainly Lord;" "Hallelujah;" "In Bright Mansions Above;" "Don't Let Nobody Turn You Round;" "Run Sinner Run;" "Dere's No Hidin' Place Down Dere;" "De Ol' Arks's a-Moverin';" "Go Down Moses;" "Lord I'm No Ways Weary;" "Jashua Fit de Battle of Jericho;" "Death's Go'n' Ter Lay His Col' Icy Hands on Me;" "The Lamb's A-Cryin';" "March On" and "Hallelujah King Jesus."

2280 ✦ THE GREEN SLIME
Metro–Goldwyn–Mayer, 1968

Musical Score Fox, Charles; Tsushima, Toshiaki

Producer(s) Reiner, Ivan; Manley, Walter
Director(s) Fukasaku, Kinji
Screenwriter(s) Sinclair, Charles; Finger, William; Rowe, Tom

Cast Paluzzi, Luciana; Jaeckel, Richard; Widom, Bud; Gunther, Ted; Horton, Robert

Song(s) The Green Slime (C/L: Gaden, Sherry)

Notes Also known as BATTLE BEYOND THE STARS.

2281 ✦ GREENWICH VILLAGE
Twentieth Century–Fox, 1944

Composer(s) Brown, Nacio Herb
Lyricist(s) Robin, Leo
Choreographer(s) Felix, Seymour

Producer(s) LeBaron, William
Director(s) Lang, Walter
Screenwriter(s) Baldwin, Earl; Bullock, Walter

Cast Miranda, Carmen; Ameche, Don; Bendix, William; Blaine, Vivian; Bressart, Felix; De Marco, Tony; De Marco, Sally; The Revuers [2]; Pully, B.S.; The Four Step Brothers; Rameau, Emil; Orth, Frank; Meyer, Torben

Song(s) This Is Our Lucky Day (L: Brown, Nacio Herb); I Like to Be Loved By You [1] (C: Warren, Harry; L: Gordon, Mack); It Goes to Your Toes; Give Me a Band and a Bandana; It's All for Art's Sake; The Baroness Bazooka [3] (C/L: Comden, Betty; Green, Adolph; Holiday, Judy; Hammer, Alvin); Could It Be You [4] (C: Brown, Nacio Herb; L: Caesar, Irving)

Notes There are also vocals of "I'm Just Wild About Harry" by Eubie Blake and Noble Sissle; "Swingin' Down the Lane" by Isham Jones and Gus Kahn and "Whispering" by Vincent Rose, Richard Coburn and John Schonberger (sometimes credited to Malvin and John Schonberger). [1] Sequence filmed but not used in SPRINGTIME IN THE ROCKIES. [2] The Revuers consists of Betty Comden, Adolph Green, Judy Holiday, John Frank and Alvin Hammer. [3] Filmed but cut from final print. [4] Not used. Also not used in WINTERTIME.

2282 ✦ GREMLINS
Warner Brothers, 1984

Musical Score Goldsmith, Jerry

Producer(s) Finnell, Michael
Director(s) Dante, Joe
Screenwriter(s) Columbus, Chris

Cast Galligan, Zach; Cates, Phoebe; Axton, Hoyt; McCain, Frances Lee; Holliday, Polly; Luke, Keye; Brady, Scott; Carey Jr., Harry; Feldman, Corey; Turman, Glynn; Reinhold, Judge; Jones, Chuck

Song(s) The Little One (C/L: Goldsmith, Jerry); Christmas (Baby Please Come Home) (C/L: Greenwich, Ellie; Spector, Phil); Make It Shine (C/L: Ross, Marv); Out Out (C/L: Gabriel, Peter); Gremlins . . . Mega Madness (C/L: Sembello, Michael; Hudson, Mark; Freeman, Don)

Notes Ii is not known which of these was written for the picture. All are background vocal.

2283 ✦ GRENADEROS DEL AMOR
Fox, 1934

Composer(s) Kernell, William
Lyricist(s) Roulien, Raul

Producer(s) Stone, John
Director(s) Reinhardt, John

Cast Roulien, Raul; Montenegro, Conchita

Song(s) Ladies Who Come from Spain; Napoleon Bonaparte; Babette; Men Were Born to Rule the World; Dance Again; Austrian Marching Song (L: Reinhardt); The Fatherland (L: Reinhardt); Bailemos Pues [1]

Notes [1] Not on cue sheets.

2284 ✦ GREYFRIARS BOBBY
Disney, 1961

Musical Score Chagrin, Francis

Producer(s) Attwooll, Hugh
Director(s) Chaffey, Don
Screenwriter(s) Westerby, Robert
Source(s) "Story of Greyfriars Bobby" (story) Atkinson, Eleanor

Cast Crisp, Donald; Naismith, Laurence; MacKenzie, Alex; Walsh, Kay

Song(s) Greyfriars Bobby [1] (C/L: Sherman, Richard M.; Sherman, Robert B.)

Notes [1] Written for exploitation only.

2285 ✦ GRID RULES
Metro–Goldwyn–Mayer, 1938

Director(s) Cahn, Edward L.
Screenwriter(s) Adler, E. Maurice
Narrator(s) Smith, Pete

Song(s) Roll Up the Score (Inst.) (C: Lane, Burton)

Notes Short subject. A Pete Smith specialty.

2286 ✦ GRINGO
Kasba, 1984

Producer(s) Kowalski, Lech; Barish, Ann S.
Director(s) Kowalski, Lech

Cast Spacely, John; Shingles, Steven; du Sorbier, Claude

Song(s) C & D (C/L: Kentis, Chuck)

Notes No cue sheet available. Documentary.

2287 ✦ THE GROUP
United Artists, 1966

Musical Score Gross, Charles

Producer(s) Buchman, Sidney
Director(s) Lumet, Sidney
Screenwriter(s) Buchman, Sidney
Source(s) *The Group* (novel) McCarthy, Mary

Cast Bergen, Candice; Hackett, Joan; Hartman, Elizabeth; Knight, Shirley; Pettet, Joanna; Redd, Mary-Robin; Walter, Jessica; Widdoes, Kathleen

Song(s) Alma Mater (C: Purcell, Henry; L: Otto, Susan)

Notes There are also several public domain vocals and a vocal of "We'll Build a Bungalow" by Betty Mayhams and Norris Troubador.

2288 ◆ GUESS WHO'S COMING TO DINNER
Columbia, 1967

Musical Score   De Vol, Frank

Producer(s)   Kramer, Stanley
Director(s)   Kramer, Stanley
Screenwriter(s)   Rose, William

Cast   Tracy, Spencer; Hepburn, Katharine; Poitier, Sidney; Houghton, Katharine; Kellaway, Cecil; Richards, Beah; Sanford, Isabel

Song(s)   Guess Who's Coming to Dinner (C/L: Hill, Billy)

2289 ◆ A GUIDE FOR THE MARRIED MAN
Twentieth Century–Fox, 1967

Musical Score   Williams, John

Producer(s)   McCarthy, Frank
Director(s)   Kelly, Gene
Screenwriter(s)   Tarloff, Frank
Source(s)   *A Guide for the Married Man* (novel) Tarloff, Frank

Cast   Matthau, Walter; Morse, Robert; Stevens, Inger; Langdon, Sue Ane; Kelly, Claire; Ball, Lucille; Benny, Jack; Bergen, Polly; Bishop, Joey; Blue, Ben; Caesar, Sid; Carney, Art; Cox, Wally; Ingels, Marty; Guilbert, Ann Morgan; Hunter, Jeffrey; Jaffe, Sam; Mansfield, Jayne; March, Hal; Nye, Louis; Reiner, Carl; Silvers, Phil; Terry-Thomas

Song(s)   A Guide for the Married Man (C: Williams, John; L: Bricusse, Leslie)

2290 ◆ THE GUILT OF JANET AMES
Columbia, 1947

Musical Score   Duning, George

Director(s)   Levin, Henry
Screenwriter(s)   MacFarlane, Louella; Rivkin, Allen; Freeman, Devery

Cast   Caesar, Sid; Russell, Rosalind; Douglas, Melvyn; Foch, Nina; Cane, Charles; Von Zell, Harry; Converse, Peggy; Beaumont, Hugh

Song(s)   Without Imagination [1] (C/L: Roberts, Allan; Fisher, Doris)

Notes   [1] Also in GLAMOUR GIRL.

2291 ◆ GULLIVER'S TRAVELS
Paramount, 1939

Musical Score   Young, Victor
Composer(s)   Rainger, Ralph
Lyricist(s)   Robin, Leo

Producer(s)   Fleischer, Max
Director(s)   Fleischer, Dave

Screenwriter(s)   Gordon, Dan; Howard, Cal; Pierce, Ted; Sparber, Isadore; Seward, Edmond
Source(s)   *Gulliver's Travels* (novel) Swift, Jonathan
Voices   Dragonette, Jessica; Ross, Lanny; Hines, Margie; Warren, Lovey; Colvig, Pinto; Mercer, Jack; Howard, Cal

Directing Animator(s)   Kneitel, Seymour; Bowsky, William; Palmer, Tom; Natwick, Grim; Hennig, William; Crandall, Roland; Johnson, Tom; Leffingwell, Robert; Kelling, Frank; Hoskins, Winfield; Calpini, Orestes

Song(s)   Pussy-Footin' Around [2]; I Hear a Dream (Come Home Again); All's Well; Faithful Forever; Bluebirds in the Moonlight [3]; We're All Together Now; Cheerio [1]; It's a Hap-Hap-Happy Day (C: Timberg, Sammy; Sharples, Winston; L: Neiburg, Al J.); Faithful; Forever; Gabby's Exploits [1]; You Can Buy the Sun for a Song

Notes   Animated feature. [1] Not used. [2] Might be used instrumentally but not vocally. [3] Written for PARIS HONEYMOON and not used. Also not used in MAN ABOUT TOWN.

2292 ◆ GULLIVER'S TRAVELS BEYOND THE MOON
Continental Dist., 1966

Composer(s)   Delugg, Milton
Lyricist(s)   Delugg, Anne

Producer(s)   Okawa, Hiroshi
Director(s)   Kuroda, Yoshio
Screenwriter(s)   Sekizawa, Shinchi

Song(s)   The Earth Song; I Wanna Be Like Gulliver; That's the Way It Goes; Keep Your Hopes High

Notes   No cue sheet available. Animated feature produced in Japan where its original name is GULLIVER NO UCHU RYOKO.

2293 ◆ GUMBALL RALLY
Warner Brothers, 1976

Musical Score   Frontiere, Dominic

Producer(s)   Bail, Chuck
Director(s)   Bail, Chuck
Screenwriter(s)   Capetanos, Leon

Cast   Sarrazin, Michael; Burton, Norman; Busey, Gary; Durren, John; Flannery, Susan; Julia, Raul

Song(s)   Best Western Blues (C/L: Busey, Gary; Jason, Harvey)

2294 ◆ A GUNFIGHT
Paramount, 1971

Musical Score   Rosenthal, Laurence

Producer(s)   Rubin, A. Ronald; Bloom, Harold Jack
Director(s)   Johnson, Lamont
Screenwriter(s)   Bloom, Harold Jack

Cast Douglas, Kirk; Cash, Johnny; Alexander, Jane; Black, Karen; Carradine, Keith; Vallone, Raf

Song(s) Devil Wind (C/L: Cash, Johnny); My Mother Was a Lady (C/L: Marks, E.B.; Stern, Joseph)

2295 ✦ GUNFIGHT AT SANDOVAL
Disney, 1961

Musical Score Marks, Franklyn; Dubin, Joseph S.

Producer(s) Pratt, James
Director(s) Keller, Harry
Screenwriter(s) Gilroy, Frank D.; Tombragel, Maurice

Cast Tryon, Tom; Duryea, Dan; Garland, Beverly; Bettger, Lyle; Moore, Norma; Carey Jr., Harry; Pratt, Judson; Haggerty, Don

Song(s) Texas John Slaughter [2] (C/L: Jones, Stan); Song of the Texas Rangers [1] (C: Dubin, Joseph S.; L: Jackman, Bob)

Notes [1] Also in GERONIMO'S REVENGE and TEXAS JOHN SLAUGHTER. [2] Also in TEXAS JOHN SLAUGHTER.

2296 ✦ GUNFIGHT AT THE O.K. CORRAL
Paramount, 1957

Musical Score Tiomkin, Dimitri

Producer(s) Wallis, Hal B.
Director(s) Sturges, John
Screenwriter(s) Uris, Leon
Source(s) "The Killer" (article) Scullin, George

Cast Lancaster, Burt; Douglas, Kirk; Ireland, John; Fleming, Rhonda; Van Fleet, Jo; Faylen, Frank

Song(s) The Gunfight at the O.K. Corral (C: Tiomkin, Dimitri; L: Washington, Ned)

Notes Frankie Laine sings the song on the soundtrack.

2297 ✦ GUNFIGHTERS OF CASA GRANDE
Metro–Goldwyn–Mayer, 1965

Musical Score Douglas, Johnny
Composer(s) Mellin, Robert
Lyricist(s) Mellin, Robert

Producer(s) Welch, Lester
Director(s) Rowland, Roy
Screenwriter(s) Chase, Borden; Chase, Patricia; Reynolds, Clarke

Cast Nicol, Alex; Mistral, Jorge; Bentley, Dick; Rowland, Steve; Lorys, Diana; Posner, Phil

Song(s) Ride Pistoleros; Gunslingers of Casa Grande

Notes No cue sheet available.

2298 ✦ GUNFIGHT IN ABILENE
Universal, 1966

Musical Score Rogers, Milton "Shorty"

Producer(s) Christie, Howard
Director(s) Hale, William
Screenwriter(s) Giler, Berne; Black, John D.F.
Source(s) *Gun Shy* (novel) Young, Clarence Upson

Cast Darin, Bobby; Banks, Emily; Nielsen, Leslie; Rhodes, Donnelly; Galloway, Don; McGrath, Frank; Sarrazin, Michael

Song(s) Amy (C/L: Darin, Bobby)

2299 ✦ GUNG HO! (1943)
Universal, 1943

Musical Score Skinner, Frank

Producer(s) Wanger, Walter
Director(s) Enright, Ray
Screenwriter(s) Hubbard, Lucien

Cast Scott, Randolph; McDonald, Grace; Curtis, Alan; Beery Jr., Noah; Naish, J. Carrol; Bruce, David; Coe, Peter; Mitchum, Robert; Lane, Richard; Cameron, Rod; Levene, Sam

Song(s) Gung Ho (C: Skinner, Frank; L: Bibo, Irving)

2300 ✦ GUNG HO (1986)
Paramount, 1986

Musical Score Newman, Thomas

Producer(s) Ganz, Tony; Blum, Deborah
Director(s) Howard, Ron
Screenwriter(s) Ganz, Lowell; Mandel, Babaloo

Cast Keaton, Michael; Watanabe, Gedde; Wendt, George; Rogers, Mimi; Turturro, John; Shimono, Sab; Howard, Clint

Song(s) Don't Get Me Wrong [1] (C/L: Hynde, Chrissie); Breakin' the Ice [1] (C/L: Thomas, Ken; Wells, Matthew; Klein, Patrick; Anderson, Mike)

Notes [1] All background vocals.

2301 ✦ THE GUN HAWK
Allied Artists, 1963

Musical Score Haskell, Jimmie

Producer(s) Bernstein, Richard
Director(s) Ludwig, Edward
Screenwriter(s) Heims, Jo

Cast Calhoun, Rory; Cameron, Rod; Lee, Ruta; Lauren, Rod; Woodward, Morgan; Litel, John

Song(s) A Searcher for Love (C/L: Marcucci, Robert; Faith, Russell)

Notes No cue sheet available.

2302 ✦ GUN LAW
RKO, 1938

Musical Score   Webb, Roy; Steiner, Max

Producer(s)   Gilroy, Bert
Director(s)   Howard, David
Screenwriter(s)   Drake, Oliver

Cast   O'Brien, George; Oehmen, Rita; Whitley, Ray; Everton, Paul; Gleckler, Robert; Bond, Ward; McDonald, Francis; Pawley, Edward

Song(s)   So Long, Old Pinto (C/L: Drake, Oliver); Tumble on Tumble Weed [1] (C: Dreyer, Dave; L: Scholl, Jack)

Notes   Also known as WHEN THE LAW RIDES. [1] Also in THE FIGHTING GRINGO and SILLY BILLIES.

2303 ✦ GUNMAN'S CODE
Universal, 1946

Musical Score   Skinner, Frank; Salter, Hans J.
Composer(s)   Rosen, Milton
Lyricist(s)   Carter, Everett

Producer(s)   Fox, Wallace W.
Director(s)   Fox, Wallace W.
Screenwriter(s)   Lively, William

Cast   Grant, Kirby; Knight, Fuzzy; Adams, Jane; Thomas, Bernard

Song(s)   Those Happy Old Days; I'm Tying Up My Bridle to the Door of Your Heart [2]; The Call of the Range [1]

Notes   [1] Also in BEYOND THE PECOS, FRONTIER LAW and MAN FROM MONTANA (1941). [2] Also in RIDERS OF PASCO BASIN.

2304 ✦ GUNN
Paramount, 1967

Musical Score   Mancini, Henry
Composer(s)   Mancini, Henry

Producer(s)   Crump, Owen
Director(s)   Edwards, Blake
Screenwriter(s)   Edwards, Blake; Blatty, William Peter

Cast   Stevens, Craig; Devon, Laura; Asner, Edward; Traubel, Helen; O'Malley, J. Pat; Toomey, Regis

Song(s)   I Like the Look (L: Bricusse, Leslie); Dreamsville [1] (L: Livingston, Jay; Evans, Ray); Bye Bye [2] (L: Livingston, Jay; Evans, Ray); If Only I Could Fly (C/L: Weatherly, James D. [3])

Notes   Laura Devon sings "I Like the Look" and "Dreamsville" on the soundtrack. [1] Music written for television production PETER GUNN. [2] Based on Mancini's "Peter Gunn Theme" from the television show. [3] Of the group Gordian Knot.

2305 ✦ GUNPOINT
Universal, 1965

Producer(s)   Kay, Gordon
Director(s)   Bellamy, Earl
Screenwriter(s)   Willingham, Mary; Willingham, Willard

Cast   Murphy, Audie; Staley, Joan; Stevens, Warren; Buchanan, Edgar; Pyle, Denver; Dano, Royal

Song(s)   Far Away (C: Schwarzwald, Milton; L: Herbert, Frederick)

2306 ✦ THE GUN RUNNERS
United Artists, 1958

Musical Score   Stevens, Leith
Composer(s)   Lubin, Joe
Lyricist(s)   Lubin, Joe

Producer(s)   Greene, Clarence
Director(s)   Siegel, Don
Screenwriter(s)   Mainwaring, Daniel; Monash, Paul
Source(s)   *To Have and Have Not* (novel) Hemingway, Ernest

Cast   Murphy, Audie; Albert, Eddie; Owens, Patricia; Sloane, Everett; Hall, Gita; Elam, Jack

Song(s)   Havana Holiday; Beyond the Sea [1]; All the Way in Love [1]; They're Playing Our Song [1] (C/L: Lubin, Joe; Howard, Jerome)

Notes   [1] Used instrumentally only.

2307 ✦ GUNS AND GUITARS
Republic, 1936

Producer(s)   Levine, Nat
Director(s)   Kane, Joseph
Screenwriter(s)   McGowan, Dorrell; McGowan, Stuart

Cast   Autry, Gene; Dix, Dorothy; Burnette, Smiley; London, Tom; King, Charles; Champion; McGowan, J.P.; Burns, Bob

Song(s)   Ridin' All Day (C/L: Autry, Gene; Burnette, Smiley); The Cowboy Medicine Show (C/L: Burnette, Smiley; Autry, Gene); Guns and Guitars (C/L: Autry, Gene; Drake, Oliver); Dreamy Valley (C/L: Drake, Oliver; Grey, Harry)

Notes   No cue sheet available. Autry's participation in the above songs is doubtful.

2308 ✦ GUNS, GIRLS AND GANGSTERS
United Artists, 1958

Musical Score   Newman, Emil

Producer(s)   Kent, Robert E.
Director(s)   Cahn, Edward L.
Screenwriter(s)   Kent, Robert E.

Cast   Van Doren, Mamie; Mohr, Gerald; Van Cleef, Lee; Richards, Grant; Edwards, Elaine

Song(s)   Anything Your Heart Desires (C: Bregman, Buddy; L: Styne, Stanley); Meet Me Halfway (C: Bregman, Buddy; L: Styne, Stanley)

2309 ✦ GUNSIGHT RIDGE
United Artists, 1957

Musical Score   Raksin, David

Producer(s)   Bassler, Robert
Director(s)   Lyon, Francis D.
Screenwriter(s)   Jennings, Talbot; Jennings, Elizabeth

Cast   McCrea, Joel; Stevens, Mark; Weldon, Joan; Fields, Darlene; Richards, Addison

Song(s)   The Ballad of Gunsight Ridge (C: Raksin, David; L: Unknown)

2310 ✦ GUN SMOKE
Paramount, 1931

Director(s)   Sloman, Edward
Screenwriter(s)   Jones, Grover; McNutt, William Slavens

Cast   Arlen, Richard; Brian, Mary; Boyd, William; Pallette, Eugene

Song(s)   Lucky's Song [1] (C: Hayden, Russell; L: Houston, Norman)

Notes   [1] The song is not used in the movie.

2311 ✦ GUNSMOKE RANCH
Republic, 1937

Musical Score   Riesenfeld, Hugo

Producer(s)   Siegel, Sol C.
Director(s)   Kane, Joseph
Screenwriter(s)   Drake, Oliver

Cast   Livingston, Robert; Corrigan, Ray; Terhune, Max; Harlan, Kenneth; Thayer, Julia; Canutt, Yakima; Walker, Bob

Song(s)   Barn Dance (C/L: Allan, Fleming); When the Campfire Is Low on the Prairie [1] (C: Stept, Sam H.; L: Mitchell, Sidney D.)

Notes   [1] Also in INDIAN TERRITORY (Columbia) and COMIN' ROUND THE MOUNTAIN but without Sidney D. Mitchell credit.

2312 ✦ GUNS OF DARKNESS
Warner Brothers, 1962

Musical Score   Frankel, Benjamin

Producer(s)   Clyde, Thomas
Director(s)   Asquith, Anthony
Screenwriter(s)   Mortimer, John
Source(s)   *Act of Mercy* (novel) Clifford, Francis

Cast   Niven, David; Caron, Leslie; Opatoshu, David; Justice, James Robertson

Song(s)   Untitled on cue sheets (C: Frankel, Benjamin; L: Stellman, Marcel)

Notes   This is the first cue. It might be the title track.

2313 ✦ THE GUNS OF NAVARONE
Columbia, 1961

Musical Score   Tiomkin, Dimitri

Producer(s)   Foreman, Carl
Director(s)   Thompson, J. Lee
Screenwriter(s)   Foreman, Carl
Source(s)   *The Guns of Navarone* (novel) McLean, Alistair

Cast   Peck, Gregory; Niven, David; Quinn, Anthony; Baker, Stanley; Quayle, Anthony; Papas, Irene; Scala, Gia; Darren, James; Robertson, James; Harris, Richard; Forbes, Bryan

Song(s)   The Guns of Navarone (C: Tiomkin, Dimitri; L: Webster, Paul Francis); Ya SSU—The Wedding Song [1] (C: Tiomkin, Dimitri; L: Washington, Ned)

Notes   [1] Sheet music only.

2314 ✦ GUNS OF THE PECOS
Warner Brothers–First National, 1937

Musical Score   Jackson, Howard
Composer(s)   Jerome, M.K.
Lyricist(s)   Scholl, Jack

Producer(s)   Foy, Bryan
Director(s)   Smith, Noel
Screenwriter(s)   Buckley, Harold
Source(s)   "Lone Star Ranger" (story) Coldeway, Anthony

Cast   Foran, Dick; Nagel, Anne; Hart, Gordon; Crehan, Joseph; Acuff, Eddie; Middlemass, Robert

Song(s)   When a Cowboy Takes a Wife; The Prairie Is My Home [1]

Notes   [1] Also in EMPTY HOLSTERS, THE LAND BEYOND THE LAW and PRAIRIE THUNDER.

2315 ✦ GUNS OF THE TIMBERLAND
Warner Brothers, 1960

Musical Score   Buttolph, David
Composer(s)   Livingston, Jerry
Lyricist(s)   David, Mack

Producer(s)   Spelling, Aaron
Director(s)   Webb, Robert D.
Screenwriter(s)   Petracca, Joseph; Spelling, Aaron

Cast   Ladd, Alan; Crain, Jeanne; Roland, Gilbert; Avalon, Frankie; Bettger, Lyle; Beery Jr., Noah; Felton, Verna; Ladd, Alana; Toomey, Regis

Song(s)   Cry Timber! (C/L: Miller, Sy); Gee Whizz Whilikens Golly Gee; The Faithful Kind

2316 ✦ GUN TOWN
Universal, 1945

Producer(s) Fox, Wallace W.
Director(s) Fox, Wallace W.
Screenwriter(s) Lively, William

Cast Grant, Kirby; Knight, Fuzzy; Currie, Louise; Talbot, Lyle; Carleton, Claire; White, Dan

Song(s) A Cowboy Is Happy [1] (C: Rosen, Milton; L: Carter, Everett); I Just Got In [2] (C: Berens, Norman; L: Brooks, Jack)

Notes [1] Also in COWBOY IN MANHATTAN and RAWHIDE RANGERS. [2] Also in FRISCO SAL.

2317 ✦ THE GURU
Twentieth Century–Fox, 1969

Musical Score Khan, Vilayat
Composer(s) Kahn, Vilayat
Lyricist(s) Kahn, Vilayat

Producer(s) Merchant, Ismail
Director(s) Ivory, James
Screenwriter(s) Jhabvala, Ruth Prawer; Ivory, James

Cast York, Michael; Dutt, Utpal; Jaffrey, Madhur; Tushingham, Rita; Sen, Aparna; Foster, Barry; Palsikar, Nana

Song(s) Indian Song (C/L: Shankar, Ravi; Kishan, Jai); The Sea Through the Window; Where Did You Come From (C: London, Mark; L: Black, Don); With a Little Help From My Friends [1] (C/L: Lennon, John; McCartney, Paul); You Look a Lovely Couple (C: Khan, Imrat Hussein; Jhabvala, Ruth Prawer); She Stayed; Boat Song (C: Khan, Imrat Hussein; Jhabvala, Ruth Prawer); Ustad Looking at Newspapers; Beginning of Concert

Notes It is not known if the Khan works are songs or just humming vocals. [1] Not written for film.

2318 ✦ GUS EDWARDS' COLORTONE REVUE
Metro–Goldwyn–Mayer, 1928

Composer(s) Edwards, Gus
Lyricist(s) Edwards, Gus

Cast Armida; Harris, Georgie; Walker, Doris

Song(s) That International Melody (L: Rose, Billy); Zuyder Zee; Bide-A-Wee; Is He My Boy Friend

Notes Short subject.

2319 ✦ GUS EDWARDS' SONG REVUE
Metro–Goldwyn–Mayer, 1929

Composer(s) Edwards, Gus
Lyricist(s) Edwards, Gus

Cast Edwards, Gus

Notes There are no original songs in this short subject. It is subtitled: TABLOID REVUE OF HIS FAMOUS SONG HITS. These include "Stein Song;" "By the Light of the Silvery Moon;" "Jimmy Valentine;" "Sunbonnet Sue;" "If I Was a Millionaire" and "School Days."

2320 ✦ GUYANA—CULT OF THE DAMNED
Universal, 1980

Producer(s) Cardona Jr., Rene
Director(s) Cardona Jr., Rene
Screenwriter(s) Valdemar, Carlos; Cardona Jr., Rene

Cast Whitman, Stuart; Barry, Gene; Ireland, John; Cotten, Joseph; Dillman, Bradford; De Carlo, Yvonne; Ashley, Jennifer

Song(s) A Time to Love (C/L: Ordaz, Alfredo Diaz)

2321 ✦ GUYS AND DOLLS
Goldwyn, 1955

Composer(s) Loesser, Frank
Lyricist(s) Loesser, Frank
Choreographer(s) Kidd, Michael [2]

Producer(s) Goldwyn, Samuel
Director(s) Mankiewicz, Joseph L.
Screenwriter(s) Mankiewicz, Joseph L.
Source(s) *Guys and Dolls* (musical) Burrows, Abe; Swerling, Jo; Loesser, Frank

Cast Brando, Marlon; Simmons, Jean; Sinatra, Frank; Blaine, Vivian [2]; Keith, Robert; Kaye, Stubby [2]; Pully, B.S. [2]; Silver, Johnny; Toomey, Regis; Leonard, Sheldon; Dayton, Dan; Borg, Veda Ann; Givney, Kathryn

Song(s) Fugue for Tinhorns; Follow the Fold; The Oldest Established; I'll Know; Pet Me Poppa [1]; Adelaide's Lament; Guys and Dolls; Adelaide [1]; A Woman in Love [1]; If I Were a Bell; Luck Be a Lady; Sue Me; Sit Down You're Rockin' the Boat; Take Back Your Mink

Notes [1] Written for film. All other numbers are from the Broadway original. [2] From original Broadway production.

2322 ✦ THE GUY WHO CAME BACK
Twentieth Century–Fox, 1951

Musical Score Harline, Leigh

Producer(s) Blaustein, Julian
Director(s) Newman, Joseph
Screenwriter(s) Scott, Allan

Cast Douglas, Paul; Bennett, Joan; Darnell, Linda; DeFore, Don; Gray, Billy; Mostel, Zero; Ryan, Edmon

Song(s) Keep Your Eye on the Ball (C/L: Darby, Ken)

2323 ✦ GYPSY
Warner Brothers, 1962

Composer(s) Styne, Jule
Lyricist(s) Sondheim, Stephen
Choreographer(s) Tucker, Robert

Producer(s) LeRoy, Mervyn
Director(s) LeRoy, Mervyn
Screenwriter(s) Spigelgass, Leonard
Source(s) *Gypsy* (musical) Laurents, Arthur; Sondheim, Stephen; Styne, Jule

Cast Russell, Rosalind [4]; Wood, Natalie [3]; Malden, Karl; Wallace, Paul; Bruce, Betty; Baer, Parley; Shannon, Harry; Cupito, Suzanne; Jillian, Ann; Pace, Diane; Dane, Faith; Arlen, Roxanne; Willes, Jean

Song(s) Let Me Entertain You; Small World; Some People; Mr. Goldstone; Little Lamb; You'll Never Get Away from Me; Moo Cow [1]; Broadway; If Mama Was Married; All I Need Is the Girl; Everything's Coming Up Roses; You Gotta Have a Gimmick [2]; Rose's Turn

Notes There are additional short cues attributed to the songwriters. They include "La De Da," "Extra" (Actully one of the intros to "Let Me Entertain You"), "Vocal Fanfare" and "Toreadorables." [1] Called "Dainty June and Her Farmboys" in musical. [2] Titled "You Gotta Get a Gimmick" on cue sheet. [3] Dubbed by Marni Nixon. [4] Dubbed by Lisa Kirk though the vocals are in part Russell's.

2324 ✦ GYPSY COLT
Metro–Goldwyn–Mayer, 1954

Musical Score Kopp, Rudolph; Sendrey, Al

Producer(s) Grady, William, Jr.; Franklin Jr., Sidney
Director(s) Marton, Andrew
Screenwriter(s) Berkeley, Martin

Cast Corcoran, Donna; Bond, Ward; Dee, Frances; Keating, Larry; Van Cleef, Lee

Song(s) Pepito [1] (C/L: Wollcott, Charles)

Notes [1] Also in FAST COMPANY.

2325 ✦ GYPSY NIGHT
Metro–Goldwyn–Mayer, 1935

Composer(s) Lane, Burton
Lyricist(s) Adamson, Harold

Director(s) Hecht, Harold; Berne, Joseph
Screenwriter(s) Goldstone, Richard; Berne, Joseph

Cast Matthews, Mary Jo; Mario, Joseph; Khmara, Ilia; Askam, Perry

Song(s) Ivan's Song (L: Adamson, Harold; Goldstone, Richard); Yascha & Sascha

Notes Short subject.

2326 ✦ GYPSY WILDCAT
Universal, 1944

Musical Score Ward, Edward

Producer(s) Waggner, George
Director(s) Neill, Roy William
Screenwriter(s) Hogan, James; Lewis, Gene; Cain, James M.

Cast Montez, Maria; Hall, Jon; Dumbrille, Douglass; Coe, Peter; Carrillo, Leo; Sondergaard, Gale; Bois, Curt; Bruce, Nigel

Song(s) Gypsy Song of Love (C: Ward, Edward; L: Waggner, George); The Coach (C/L: Ward, Edward)

H

2327 ◆ HAIL, HERO!
National General, 1969

Musical Score   Moross, Jerome
Composer(s)   Lightfoot, Gordon
Lyricist(s)   Lightfoot, Gordon

Producer(s)   Cohen, Harold D.
Director(s)   Miller, David
Screenwriter(s)   Manber, David
Source(s)   (novel) Weston, John

Cast   Douglas, Michael; Kennedy, Arthur; Wright, Teresa; Larch, John; Drake, Charles; Strauss, Peter

Notes   No cue sheet available.

2328 ◆ HAIL THE CONQUERING HERO
Paramount, 1944

Musical Score   Heymann, Werner

Producer(s)   Sturges, Preston
Director(s)   Sturges, Preston
Screenwriter(s)   Sturges, Preston

Cast   Bracken, Eddie; Raines, Ella; Demarest, William; Walburn, Raymond; Pangborn, Franklin; Patterson, Elizabeth; Conlin, Jimmy; Caine, Georgia; Howard, Esther; Bridge, Alan

Song(s)   Home to the Arms of Mother (C/L: Sturges, Preston); We Want Woodrow (C/L: Sturges, Preston)

2329 ◆ HAIR
United Artists, 1979

Musical Score   MacDermot, Galt
Composer(s)   MacDermot, Galt
Lyricist(s)   Rado, James; Ragni, Gerome
Choreographer(s)   Tharp, Twyla

Producer(s)   Persky, Lester; Butler, Michael
Director(s)   Forman, Milos
Screenwriter(s)   Weller, Michael
Source(s)   *Hair* (musical) MacDermot, Galt; Rado, James; Ragni, Gerome

Cast   Savage, John; Williams, Treat; D'Angelo, Beverly; Golden, Annie; Ray, Nicholas; Rae, Charlotte; Wright, Dorsey; Dacus, Don; Barnes, Cheryl; Moore, Melba; Chapin, Miles; Jeter, Michael; Hall, Carl; Galloway, Leata; Carter, Nell; Beechman, Laurie; Foley, Ellen; Woodard, Charlaine; Dyson, Ronnie; The Twyla Tharp Dancers; American Ballet Theatre, The

Song(s)   Aquarius; Sodomy; Donna; Hashish; Colored Spade; Manchester England; I'm Black; Ain't Got No; I Got Life; Hair; Electric Blues; LBJ; Old Fashioned Melody; Wedding Ceremony (Twyla's Chant); Hare Krisna; Where Do I Go; Black Boys; White Boys; Walking in Space (My Body); Easy to Be Hard; 3500; Good Morning Starshine; Someone to Hold (Saddest Story); Flesh Failures (Let the Sunshine In)

2330 ◆ HAIR RAISING HARE
Warner Brothers, 1946

Musical Score   Stalling, Carl

Director(s)   Jones, Chuck
Screenwriter(s)   Pierce, Ted

Cast   Bunny, Bugs; Lorre, Peter

Song(s)   Headin' for My Beddin' (C/L: Blanc, Mel)

Notes   Merrie Melodie cartoon.

2331 ◆ HAIRSPRAY
New Line, 1988

Producer(s)   Talalay, Rachel
Director(s)   Waters, John
Screenwriter(s)   Waters, John

Cast   Bono, Sonny; Brown, Ruth; Divine; Fitzpatrick, Colleen; St. Gerard, Michael; Harry, Deborah; Lake, Ricki; Powers, Leslie Ann; Prince, Clayton; Stiller, Jerry; Mink Stole; Zadora, Pia

Song(s)   Hairspray (C/L: Sweet, Rachel; Battaglia, Anthony; Bassen, Willie)

Notes   No cue sheet available.

2332 ◆ HALF A HERO
Metro–Goldwyn–Mayer, 1953

Musical Score   Sawtell, Paul

Producer(s)   Rapf, Matthew
Director(s)   Weis, Don
Screenwriter(s)   Shulman, Max

Cast Skelton, Red; Hagen, Jean; Dingle, Charles; Waterman, Willard; Wickes, Mary; Bergen, Polly

Song(s) Love [1] (C/L: Martin, Hugh; Blane, Ralph)

Notes [1] Also in THE BEAT GENERATION and ZIEGFELD FOLLIES.

2333 ◆ HALF ANGEL
Twentieth Century–Fox, 1951

Musical Score Mockridge, Cyril J.

Producer(s) Blaustein, Julian
Director(s) Sale, Richard
Screenwriter(s) Riskin, Robert

Cast Young, Loretta; Cotten, Joseph; Kellaway, Cecil; Ruysdael, Basil; Backus, Jim; Ryan, Irene; Ridgely, John

Song(s) My Castle in the Sand (C: Newman, Alfred; L: Blane, Ralph)

2334 ◆ HALF A SIXPENCE
Paramount, 1968

Musical Score Kostal, Irwin
Composer(s) Heneker, David
Lyricist(s) Heneker, David
Choreographer(s) Lynne, Gillian

Producer(s) Schneer, Charles H.; Sidney, George
Director(s) Sidney, George
Screenwriter(s) Cross, Beverly
Source(s) *Half a Sixpence* (musical) Heneker, David; Cross, Beverly

Cast Steele, Tommy [1]; Foster, Julia [2]; Ritchard, Cyril; Horner, Penelope; Dale, Grover

Song(s) Long Ago [1]; All in the Cause of Economy [1]; Half a Sixpence [1]; Money to Burn [1]; I Don't Believe a Word of It [3]; I'm Not Talking to You [3]; A Proper Gentleman [1]; She's Too Far Above Me [1]; If the Rain's Got to Fall [1]; The Race [5] (C: Kostal, Irwin); Flash, Bang, Wallop! [1]; I Know What I Am [1]; This Is My World (C: Kostal, Irwin)

Notes To reduce running time the "Bandstand Sequence Composition" was removed from domestic prints only and a portion of "This Is My World" was substituted. [1] From Broadway production. [2] Dubbed by Marti Webb, the original star in London. [3] From London production (as are all the Broadway songs). [4] Used instrumentally only. [5] Also titled "Lady Botting's Boating Regatta Cup Racing Song" and "The Race Is On."

2335 ◆ THE HALF-BREED
RKO, 1951

Musical Score Sawtell, Paul; Webb, Roy

Producer(s) Schlom, Herman
Director(s) Gilmore, Stuart

Screenwriter(s) Shumate, Harold; Wormser, Richard E.; Hoffman, Charles

Cast Young, Robert; Carter, Janis; Buetel, Jack; MacLane, Barton; Hadley, Reed; Hall, Porter; Gilchrist, Connie; White, Sammy

Song(s) Walking Arm in Arm with Jim [2] (C: Harris, Harry; L: Pollack, Lew); Remember the Girl You Left Behind [1] (C: Revel, Harry; L: Greene, Mort)

Notes [1] Also in NEVADA. [2] Also in GIRL RUSH (1944) and SUNSET PASS.

2336 ◆ HALF-MARRIAGE
RKO, 1929

Composer(s) Levant, Oscar
Lyricist(s) Clare, Sidney

Producer(s) LeBaron, William
Director(s) Cowen, William J.
Screenwriter(s) Murfin, Jane
Source(s) "Half Marriage" (story) Turner, George Kibbe

Cast Murray, Ken; Borden, Olive; Farley, Morgan; Blane, Sally; Tucker, Richard; Greenway, Ann; Gus Arnheim and His Cocoanut Grove Ambassadors; Hopper, Hedda

Song(s) After the Clouds Roll By; To Me, She's Marvelous (L: Levant, Oscar)

Notes Cue sheets do not differentiate between vocals and instrumentals.

2337 ◆ THE HALF NAKED TRUTH
RKO, 1932

Producer(s) Berman, Pandro S.
Director(s) La Cava, Gregory
Screenwriter(s) La Cava, Gregory; Ford, Corey
Source(s) "Phantom Fame" (story) Freedman, David

Cast Velez, Lupe; Tracy, Lee; Morgan, Frank; Pallette, Eugene

Song(s) O! Mister Carpenter (C: Akst, Harry; L: Eliscu, Edward)

Notes Cue sheet does not differentiate between instrumental and vocal.

2338 ◆ HALF SHOT AT SUNRISE
RKO, 1930

Composer(s) Tierney, Harry
Lyricist(s) Caldwell, Anne
Choreographer(s) Read, Mary

Producer(s) Hobart, Henry
Director(s) Sloane, Paul
Screenwriter(s) Caldwell, Anne; Spence, Ralph

Cast Wheeler, Bert; Woolsey, Robert; Lee, Dorothy; McFarlane, George; Oliver, Edna May; Stengel, Leni; Trevor, Hugh; Robinson, Robert; The Tiller Sunshine Girls

Song(s) Springtime of Love; Kiss Me Cherie; Our Big Times Are Coming [1]; Whistling the Blues Away

Notes [1] Used instrumentally only.

2339 ◆ HALFWAY TO HEAVEN
Paramount, 1944

Cast Rhodes, Betty Jane; Johnston, Johnnie

Song(s) Halfway to Heaven (C: Lilley, Joseph J.; L: Seelen, Jerry)

Notes Short subject. "With My Eyes Wide Open I'm Dreaming" by Mack Gordon and Harry Revel; "Ain't Got a Dime to My Name" by Johnny Burke and James Van Heusen; and "Mama Don't Allow It" by Charles Davenport are also used vocally.

2340 ◆ HALLELUJAH!
Metro–Goldwyn–Mayer, 1929

Producer(s) Vidor, King
Director(s) Vidor, King
Screenwriter(s) Rideout, Ransom; Schayer, Richard

Cast Haynes, Daniel L.; McKinney, Nina Mae; Fountaine, William; Gray, Harry; DeKnight, Fannie Belle; McGarrity, Everett; Spivey, Victoria; Dixie Jubilee Singers

Song(s) Waiting At the End of the Road (C/L: Berlin, Irving); Cotton (C: Brown, Nacio Herb; L: Freed, Arthur); Swanee Shuffle (C/L: Berlin, Irving)

Notes There is also a vocal of "St. Louis Blues" by W.C. Handy and a lot of traditional spirituals and songs. The song "Cotton" lasts around 15 seconds.

2341 ◆ HALLELUJAH, I'M A BUM
United Artists, 1933

Composer(s) Rodgers, Richard
Lyricist(s) Hart, Lorenz

Producer(s) Milestone, Lewis
Director(s) Milestone, Lewis
Screenwriter(s) Behrman, S.N.

Cast Jolson, Al; Evans, Madge; Morgan, Frank; Langdon, Harry; Conklin, Chester; Brooke, Tyler; Young, Tammany; Roach, Bert; Connor, Edgar; Wolbert, Dorothy; Carver, Louise; Rodgers, Richard; Hart, Lorenz

Song(s) I Gotta Get Back to New York; My Pal Bumper (Bumper's Home Again); Tick-Tock; Hallelujah, I'm a Bum (1); Hallelujah, I'm a Bum (2); Laying the Cornerstone; Dear June; Bumper Found a Grand; What Do You Want with Money?; Kangaroo

Court (Bumper's Going to Court); I'd Do It Again; You Are Too Beautiful; Sleeping Beauty [1]

Notes No cue sheet available. Titled HALLELUJAH, I'M A TRAMP in Great Britain. Rodgers appears as the photographer; Hart appears as the bank teller. Roland Young had the Frank Morgan role but got sick and was replaced after filming had started. [1] Cut prior to release.

2342 ◆ HALLELUJAH, I'M A TRAMP

See HALLELUJAH, I'M A BUM.

2343 ◆ THE HALLELUJAH TRAIL
United Artists, 1965

Musical Score Bernstein, Elmer
Composer(s) Bernstein, Elmer
Lyricist(s) Sheldon, Ernie

Producer(s) Sturges, John
Director(s) Sturges, John
Screenwriter(s) Gay, John

Cast Lancaster, Burt; Remick, Lee; Hutton, Jim; Keith, Brian; Tiffin, Pamela; Pleasence, Donald; Landau, Martin

Song(s) Hallelujah Trail; Stand Up Hymn; Stand Up March; We Will Save

2344 ◆ HALLOWEEN III: SEASON OF THE WITCH
Universal, 1982

Musical Score Carpenter, John; Howarth, Alan

Producer(s) Hill, Debra; Carpenter, John
Director(s) Wallace, Tommy Lee
Screenwriter(s) Wallace, Tommy Lee

Cast Atkins, Tom; Nelkin, Stacey; O'Herlihy, Dan; Currie, Michael; Strait, Ralph; Barbor, Jadeen

Song(s) Silver Shamrock (C/L: Wallace, Tommy Lee; Howarth, Alan)

2345 ◆ HALLS OF ANGER
United Artists, 1970

Musical Score Grusin, Dave

Producer(s) Hirschman, Herbert
Director(s) Bogart, Paul
Screenwriter(s) Shaner, John; Ramrus, Al

Cast Lockhart, Calvin; Bridges, Jeff; Watson, James; Reiner, Rob; MacLachlan, Janet; Jesse, DeWayne

Song(s) Reachin' Out to You (C: Grusin, Dave; L: Gimbel, Norman); Cheerleaders Chant (C/L: Grusin, Dave)

2346 ✦ HAMMERHEAD
Columbia, 1968

Musical Score   Whitaker, David

Producer(s)   Allen, Irving
Director(s)   Miller, David
Screenwriter(s)   Bast, William; Baker, Herbert

Cast   Edwards, Vince; Geeson, Judy; Vaughan, Peter; Dors, Diana; Bates, Michael; Adams, Beverly; Cargill, Patrick

Song(s)   Hammerhead (C: Whitaker, David; L: Worsley, John); I'll Be Your Old-Fashioned Girl (C: Baker, Herbert; L: Worsley, John)

Notes   No cue sheet available.

2347 ✦ HAMMETT
Orion, 1983

Musical Score   Barry, John

Producer(s)   Roos, Fred; Colby, Ronald; Guest, Don
Director(s)   Wenders, Wim
Screenwriter(s)   Thomas, Ross; O'Flaherty, Dennis
Source(s)   *Hammett* (novel) Gores, Joe

Cast   Forrest, Frederic; Boyle, Peter; Henner, Marilu; Kinnear, Roy; Cook Jr., Elisha

Song(s)   I Wish That I Could Write a Song About You (C/L: Forrest, Fred); Punk's Tune (C/L: Kelly, David Patrick)

2348 ✦ HANDLE WITH CARE (1932)
Fox, 1932

Composer(s)   Whiting, Richard A.
Lyricist(s)   Robin, Leo

Director(s)   Butler, David
Screenwriter(s)   Craven, Frank; Mintz, Sam

Cast   Dunn, James; Mallory, Boots; Brendel, El; Phelps, Buster; Jory, Victor

Song(s)   Throw a Little Salt on the Blue Bird's Tail; Around You [1]; Enclosed Please Find [2]

Notes   [1] Used instrumentally only. [2] Not used. Also not used in Marie Galante.

2349 ✦ HANDLE WITH CARE (1977)

See CITIZEN'S BAND.

2350 ✦ HANDS ACROSS THE BORDER
Republic, 1943

Composer(s)   Ohman, Phil
Lyricist(s)   Washington, Ned
Choreographer(s)   Gould, Dave

Producer(s)   Grey, Harry
Director(s)   Kane, Joseph
Screenwriter(s)   Ropes, Bradford; Cheney, J. Benton

Cast   Rogers, Roy; Terry, Ruth; Brady, Pat; Farr, Hugh; Nolan, Bob; Spencer, Tim; Carson, Ken; Williams, Guinn "Big Boy"; Treen, Mary; Stevens, Onslow; Crehan, Joseph; Renaldo, Duncan; Mason, LeRoy; Barcroft, Roy; Duncan, Kenne

Song(s)   When Your Heart's on Easy Street [3]; Hey Hey (C/L: Nolan, Bob; Spencer, Tim); The Girl with the High Button Shoes; Hands Across the Border [2] (C: Carmichael, Hoagy); Cool Water [1] (C/L: Nolan, Bob); Dreaming to Music; Ay Jalisco No te Rajes (C/L: Esperon, Manuel; Cortazar, Ernesto M.)

Notes   [1] Also in ALONG THE NAVAJO TRAIL and DING DONG WILLIAMS (RKO). [2] Also in BRAZIL (1944). [3] Also in TIMBER TRAIL.

2351 ✦ HANDS ACROSS THE TABLE
Paramount, 1935

Producer(s)   Sheldon, E. Lloyd
Director(s)   Leisen, Mitchell
Screenwriter(s)   Krasna, Norman; Lawrence, Vincent; Fields, Herbert

Cast   Lombard, Carole; MacMurray, Fred; Bellamy, Ralph; Allwyn, Astrid; Donnelly, Ruth; Prevost, Marie; Demarest, William; Bing, Herman; Allen, Regi

Song(s)   The Morning After [1] [3] (C/L: Coslow, Sam); Hands Across the Table [1] [2] (C: Delettre, Jean; L: Parish, Mitchell)

Notes   [1] Used instrumentally only. [2] Not written for movie but bought along with title. [3] This was recorded to be sung but wasn't used in picture as vocal. Also not used in MANY HAPPY RETURNS but with composer credit to Arthur Johnston.

2352 ✦ HANDY ANDY
Fox, 1934

Producer(s)   Wurtzel, Sol M.
Director(s)   Butler, David
Screenwriter(s)   Glasmon, Kubec; Conselman, William; Johnson, Henry
Source(s)   *Merry Andrew* (play) Beach, Lewis

Cast   Rogers, Will; Wood, Peggy; Carlisle, Mary

Song(s)   My Song of Love for You [1] (C/L: Albers, Fred C.); Roses in the Rain (C: Whiting, Richard A.; L: Conselman, William)

Notes   [1] Not written for film.

2353 ✦ THE HANGED MAN
Universal, 1965

Musical Score   Carter, Benny

Song(s)   Only Trust Your Heart (C: Carter, Benny; L: Cahn, Sammy)

Notes This is a Universal Pictures release for foreign distribution. No other information available.

2354 ◆ THE HANGING TREE
Warner Brothers, 1959

Musical Score Steiner, Max

Producer(s) Jurow, Martin; Shepherd, Richard
Director(s) Daves, Delmer
Screenwriter(s) Mayes, Wendell; Welles, Halsted

Cast Cooper, Gary; Schell, Maria; Malden, Karl; Scott, George C.; Swenson, Karl; Gregg, Virginia; Dierkes, John; Donovan, King; Piazza, Ben

Song(s) The Hanging Tree [1] (C: Livingston, Jerry; L: David, Mack)

Notes [1] Used as a background vocal.

2355 ◆ THE HANGMAN
Paramount, 1959

Musical Score Sukman, Harry

Producer(s) Freeman Jr., Frank
Director(s) Curtiz, Michael
Screenwriter(s) Nichols, Dudley

Cast Taylor, Robert; Parker, Fess; Louise, Tina; Lord, Jack; Evans, Gene; Shaughnessy, Mickey; Harmer, Shirley; Westerfield, James

Song(s) Roll on the Wagon (C/L: Sanders, Troy); The Hangman (1) [1] (C: Sukman, Harry; Walton, Tom [2]); The Hangman (2) [3] (C: Bacharach, Burt; L: David, Hal)

Notes [1] Instrumental only. [2] Pseudonym for Walton T. Farrar. [3] Written for exploitation only.

2356 ◆ HANGOVER SQUARE
Twentieth Century–Fox, 1945

Musical Score Herrmann, Bernard
Composer(s) Newman, Lionel
Lyricist(s) Henderson, Charles

Producer(s) Bassler, Robert
Director(s) Brahm, John
Screenwriter(s) Lyndon, Barre
Source(s) (novel) Hamilton, Patrick

Cast Cregar, Laird; Darnell, Linda; Sanders, George; Napier, Alan

Song(s) Gay Love [1] (C: Herrmann, Bernard); So Close to Paradise [1]; All for You [1]; Have You Seen Joe?; Why Do They Wake Me Up So Early in the Morning

Notes [1] These last less then 20 seconds. They each consist of only three lines of lyrics. It is not known if they were actually developed into full-fledged songs.

2357 ◆ HANG YOUR HAT ON THE WIND
Disney, 1969

Musical Score Liebert, William E.; Sparks, Randy
Composer(s) Sparks, Randy
Lyricist(s) Sparks, Randy

Producer(s) Lansburgh, Larry
Director(s) Lansburgh, Larry
Screenwriter(s) West, Paul

Cast Natoli, Ric; Pratt, Judson; Tompkins, Angel; Faulkner, Edward

Song(s) Hang Your Hat on the Wind (L: Lansburgh, Larry; Sparks, Randy); Catch the Wind and Hold It; Elena Would Love Me Again [1]; Indian Cowboy [1]; Say Good Day [1]; Shadows of Eagles; Stay As Long As You Can; Them Flyin' Machines [1]; Time and Space [1]; Wind and Sand [1]

Notes [1] Used instrumentally only.

2358 ◆ THE HANOI HILTON
Cannon, 1987

Musical Score Webb, Jimmy

Producer(s) Golan, Menahem; Globus, Yoram
Director(s) Chetwynd, Lionel
Screenwriter(s) Chetwynd, Lionel

Cast Moriarty, Michael; Jones, Jeffrey; Le Mat, Paul; Davies, Stephen; Pressman, Lawrence; Aleong, Aki; Diehl, John; Soul, David

Song(s) Hero's Heart (C/L: Webb, Jimmy)

Notes No cue sheet available.

2359 ◆ HANS CHRISTIAN ANDERSEN
RKO, 1952

Musical Score Scharf, Walter
Composer(s) Loesser, Frank
Lyricist(s) Loesser, Frank
Choreographer(s) Petit, Roland

Producer(s) Goldwyn, Samuel
Director(s) Vidor, Charles
Screenwriter(s) Hart, Moss

Cast Kaye, Danny; Granger, Farley; Jeanmaire, Zizi; Walsh, Joey; Tonge, Philip; Bruhn, Erik; Petit, Roland; Brown, John; Quaylen, Jeanne; Malcolm, Robert

Song(s) The King's New Clothes; The Inch Worm; I'm Hans Christian Andersen; Wonderful Copenhagen; Street Voices; Thumbelina; Anywhere I Wander; No Two People; The Ugly Duckling

2360 ◆ THE HAPPENING
Columbia, 1967

Musical Score De Vol, Frank

Producer(s) Kinberg, Jud
Director(s) Silverstein, Elliott

Screenwriter(s)   Pierson, Frank R.; Buchanan, James David; Austin, Ronald

Cast   Dunaway, Faye; Berle, Milton; Walker, Robert; Hyer, Martha; Maharis, George; Parks, Michael; Quinn, Anthony; Homolka, Oscar; Roche, Eugene; Kruschen, Jack

Song(s)   The Happening (C: De Vol, Frank; L: Holland, Eddie; Dozier, Lamont; Holland, Brian); Early in the Morning (C: De Vol, Frank; L: Roy, William)

Notes   Also known as THE INNOCENT.

2361 ✦ THE HAPPIEST MILLIONAIRE
Disney, 1967

Musical Score   Elliott, Jack
Composer(s)   Sherman, Richard M.; Sherman, Robert B.
Lyricist(s)   Sherman, Richard M.; Sherman, Robert B.
Choreographer(s)   Breaux, Marc; Wood, Dee Dee

Producer(s)   Anderson, Bill
Director(s)   Tokar, Norman
Screenwriter(s)   Carothers, A.J.
Source(s)   (play) Crichton, Kyle

Cast   MacMurray, Fred; Steele, Tommy; Garson, Greer; Page, Geraldine; Cooper, Gladys; Baddeley, Hermione; Petersen, Paul; Hodges, Eddie; Warren, Lesley Ann; Davidson, John

Song(s)   Are We Dancing?; Bye-Yum Pum Pum; Detroit; Fortuosity; I'll Always Be Irish; Let's Have a Drink on It!; Strengthen the Dwelling; There Are Those; Valentine Candy [1]; Watch Your Footwork! [3]; (I Believe in This Country) What's Wrong with That?; It Won't Be Long 'Til Christmas [4]; Get Up and Go, Boys! [2]; When a Man Has a Daughter [5]

Notes   [1] Used instrumentally only except in premiere version. However, it was added to the home video release. [2] Not used. [3] Used instrumentally only in Continental, French and Latin American versions. [4] In version screened for critics but cut before premiere. [5] Sheet music only.

2362 ✦ HAPPILY BURIED
Metro–Goldwyn–Mayer, 1939

Musical Score   Snell, Dave

Director(s)   Feist, Felix E.
Screenwriter(s)   Woodford, Jack; Goldstone, Richard; Feist, Felix E.

Cast   Oehmen, Rita; Allan, Anthony; Rubin, Benny

Song(s)   Director's Recitative (C/L: Wright, Bob; Forrest, Chet); I'd Rather Have You (C/L: Wright, Bob; Forrest, Chet)

Notes   Short subject.

2363 ✦ HAPPILY EVER AFTER

See TONIGHT'S THE NIGHT.

2364 ✦ HAPPINESS AHEAD
Warner Brothers–First National, 1934

Composer(s)   Wrubel, Allie
Lyricist(s)   Dixon, Mort

Producer(s)   Bischoff, Sam
Director(s)   LeRoy, Mervyn
Screenwriter(s)   Sauber, Harry; Marlow, Brian

Cast   Powell, Dick; Hutchinson, Josephine; Halliday, John; McHugh, Frank; Jenkins, Allen; Donnelly, Ruth; Dare, Dorothy; Gateson, Marjorie; Gordon, Gavin; Hicks, Russell; Forbes, Mary; Treen, Mary

Song(s)   (There Must Be) Happiness Ahead; Pop Goes Your Heart; (All On Account of a) Strawberry Sundae; Window Cleaners Song (Massaging Window Panes) (C: Ruby, Harry; L: Kalmar, Bert); Beauty Must Be Loved (C: Fain, Sammy; L: Kahal, Irving); To Be or Not to Be in Love [1] (C/L: Grennard, Elliott; Wrubel, Allie)

Notes   [1] Used instrumentally only.

2365 ✦ HAPPY ANNIVERSARY
United Artists, 1959

Musical Score   Kaplan, Sol; Allen, Robert
Composer(s)   Allen, Robert
Lyricist(s)   Stillman, Al

Producer(s)   Fields, Ralph
Director(s)   Miller, David
Screenwriter(s)   Chodorov, Jerome; Fields, Joseph
Source(s)   *Anniversary Waltz* (play) Chodorov, Jerome; Fields, Joseph

Cast   Niven, David; Gaynor, Mitzi; Reiner, Carl; Duke, Patty; Smith, Loring; Povah, Phyllis; Van Vooren, Monique; Wilson, Elizabeth; Coughlin, Kevin

Song(s)   Happy Anniversary; I Don't Regret a Thing

2366 ✦ HAPPY BIRTHDAY, GEMINI
United Artists, 1980

Musical Score   Look, Rich

Producer(s)   Hitzig, Rupert
Director(s)   Benner, Richard
Screenwriter(s)   Benner, Richard
Source(s)   *Gemini* (play) Innaurato, Albert

Cast   Rosenberg, Alan; Moreno, Rita; Kahn, Madeline; Grant, David Marshall; Viharo, Robert

Song(s)   Happy B'Day Gemini (C: Look, Rich; L: Chamberlain, Cathy); Debbie's Song (C: Look, Rich; L: Monet, Kash)

2367 ◆ HAPPY BIRTHDAY TO ME
Columbia, 1981

Musical Score   Rubin, Lance

Producer(s)   Dunning, John; Link, Andre; Harding, Stewart
Director(s)   Thompson, J. Lee
Screenwriter(s)   Saxton, John; Jobin, Peter; Bond, Timothy

Cast   Anderson, Melissa Sue; Ford, Glenn; Dane, Lawrence; Acker, Sharon; Hyland, Frances; Craven, Matt

Song(s)   Happy Birthday to Me (C: Rubin, Lance; L: Leikin, Molly-Ann)

Notes   No cue sheet available.

2368 ◆ HAPPY DAYS
Fox, 1930

Composer(s)   Baer, Abel
Lyricist(s)   Gilbert, L. Wolfe
Choreographer(s)   Lindsay, Earl

Director(s)   Stoloff, Benjamin; Catlett, Walter
Screenwriter(s)   Burke, Edwin

Cast   Albertson, Frank; MacFarlane, George; Baxter, Warner; McLaglen, Victor; Brendel, El; Murray, J. Harold; Catlett, Walter; Olsen, George; Collier Sr., William; Page, Paul; Corbett, James J.; Patricola, Tom; Farrell, Charles; Pennington, Ann; Gaynor, Janet; Richardson, Frank; Keene, Richard; Rogers, Will; Lee, Dixie; Rollins, David; Lowe, Edmund; Smith, Jack; Lynn, Sharon; White, Marjorie

Song(s)   I'm on a Diet of Love; Sugar Foot Strut (C/L: Pierce; Myers; Schwab); Minstrel Memories; A Toast to the Girl I Love (C: Hanley, James F.; L: Brockman, James); Mona (C/L: Conrad, Con; Gottler, Archie; Mitchell, Sidney D.); Vic and Eddie [1] (C/L: Stoddard, Harry; Klauber, Marcy); Snake Hips (C/L: Conrad, Con; Gottler, Archie; Mitchell, Sidney D.); We'll Build a Little World of Our Own (C: Hanley, James F.; L: Brockman, James); Crazy Feet (C/L: Conrad, Con; Gottler, Archie; Mitchell, Sidney D.); Happy Days (C: Hanley, James F.; L: McCarthy, Joseph); Dream on a Piece of Wedding Cake [2] (C: Hanley, James F.; L: Brockman, James); Catch On [3]; Cotton Moon [3]; Drink to the Girl of My Dreams [3]

Notes   [1] Not in foreign prints. [2] Not on cue sheet. [3] Not used.

2369 ◆ THE HAPPY ENDING
United Artists, 1969

Musical Score   Legrand, Michel
Composer(s)   Legrand, Michel
Lyricist(s)   Bergman, Marilyn; Bergman, Alan

Producer(s)   Brooks, Richard
Director(s)   Brooks, Richard
Screenwriter(s)   Brooks, Richard

Cast   Simmons, Jean; Forsythe, John; Jones, Shirley; Bridges, Lloyd; Fabray, Nanette; Darin, Bobby

Song(s)   What Are You Doing the Rest of Your Life; Hurry Up 'N' Hurry Down; Something for Everybody; Happy Anniversary Baby

2370 ◆ HAPPY GO LOVELY
RKO, 1951

Musical Score   Spoliansky, Mischa
Choreographer(s)   Bilings, Jack; Grant, Pauline

Producer(s)   Hellman, Marcel
Director(s)   Humberstone, H. Bruce
Screenwriter(s)   Guest, Val

Cast   Niven, David; Vera-Ellen; Romero, Cesar; Howes, Bobby; Hart, Diane

Song(s)   Would You, Could You (C/L: Spoliansky, Mischa)

2371 ◆ HAPPY GO LUCKY (1937)
Republic, 1937

Composer(s)   Stept, Sam H.
Lyricist(s)   Washington, Ned

Producer(s)   Clark, Colbert
Director(s)   Bradbury, Robert N.
Screenwriter(s)   Schrock, Raymond; Cooper, Olive

Cast   Regan, Phil; Venable, Evelyn; Prouty, Jed; Newell, William; Hale, Jonathan; Briggs, Harlan

Song(s)   Call on the Marines; Interlude; Treat for the Eyes (L: Friend, Cliff); Right or Wrong (L: Koehler, Ted)

2372 ◆ HAPPY-GO-LUCKY (1943)
Paramount, 1943

Composer(s)   McHugh, Jimmy
Lyricist(s)   Loesser, Frank
Choreographer(s)   Oscard, Paul

Producer(s)   Wilson, Harold
Director(s)   Bernhardt, Curtis
Screenwriter(s)   de Leon, Walter; Panama, Norman; Frank, Melvin

Cast   Martin, Mary; Powell, Dick; Hutton, Betty; Vallee, Rudy; Bracken, Eddie; Paige, Mabel; Blore, Eric; Bevans, Clem

Song(s)   Sing a Tropical Song; Happy-Go-Lucky; Ugly Woman [2] (C: Charles, Hubert Rayfield; L: Charles, Hubert Rayfield; Sir Lancelot); "Murder" He Says; Let's Get Lost; Ta Ra Ra Boom Der E (C: Sayers, Henry J.; L: Willson, Meredith); The Fuddy Duddy Watchmaker; Jerry or Joe [1]

Notes [1] Not used. [2] Sir Lancelot, who sings the song in the film, rewrote the lyrics.

2373 ✦ HAPPY LANDING
Twentieth Century–Fox, 1938

Composer(s) Pokrass, Sam
Lyricist(s) Yellen, Jack
Choreographer(s) Losee, Harry

Producer(s) Zanuck, Darryl F.
Director(s) Del Ruth, Roy
Screenwriter(s) Sperling, Milton; Ingster, Boris

Cast Henie, Sonja; Ameche, Don; Romero, Cesar; Merman, Ethel

Song(s) The Loveliness of You (C: Revel, Harry; L: Gordon, Mack); You Are the Music to the Words in My Heart; A Gypsy Told Me; Hot and Happy; Yonny and His Oompah; You Appeal to Me (C: Spina, Harold; L: Bullock, Walter)

2374 ✦ THE HAPPY ROAD
Metro–Goldwyn–Mayer, 1957

Musical Score Van Parys, Georges

Producer(s) Kelly, Gene
Director(s) Kelly, Gene
Screenwriter(s) Julian, Arthur; Morhaim, Joseph; Kurnitz, Harry

Cast Kelly, Gene; Lang, Barbara; Clark, Bobby; Fossey, Brigitte; Treville, Roger; Redgrave, Michael

Song(s) The Happy Road (C: Van Parys, Georges; L: Kelly, Gene; Chevalier, Maurice)

Notes Kelly wrote the English lyrics; Chevalier, the French.

2375 ✦ THE HAPPY TIME
Columbia, 1952

Musical Score Tiomkin, Dimitri

Producer(s) Kramer, Stanley
Director(s) Fleischer, Richard
Screenwriter(s) Felton, Earl
Source(s) *The Happy Time* (play) Taylor, Samuel

Cast Boyer, Charles; Jourdan, Louis; Hunt, Marsha; Kasznar, Kurt; Christian, Linda; Dalio, Marcel; Nolan, Jeanette; Raine, Jack; Erdman, Richard; Cameron, Marlene; Collins, Gene; Driscoll, Bobby

Song(s) The Happy Time (C: Tiomkin, Dimitri; L: Washington, Ned)

Notes [1] Also based on the book *The Happy Time* by Robert Fontaine.

2376 ✦ THE HARDBOILED CANARY

See THERE'S MAGIC IN MUSIC.

2377 ✦ HARD CHOICES
Lorimar, 1986

Musical Score Chattaway, Jay

Producer(s) Mickelson, Robert
Director(s) King, Rick
Screenwriter(s) Mickelson, Robert; King, Rick

Cast Klenck, Margaret; McCleery, Gary; Seitz, John; Sayles, John; Walsh, J.T.; Curtis, Liane; Gray, Spalding

Song(s) Let It Go (C: Lyon, Richard; L: O'Donnell, Mark)

Notes No cue sheet available.

2378 ✦ HARD CONTRACT
Twentieth Century–Fox, 1969

Musical Score North, Alex

Producer(s) Schwartz, Marvin
Director(s) Pogostin, S. Lee
Screenwriter(s) Pogostin, S. Lee

Cast Coburn, James; Remick, Lee; Palmer, Lilli; Meredith, Burgess; Magee, Patrick; Hayden, Sterling; Dauphin, Claude; Cherry, Helen; Black, Karen

Song(s) Sebastopol (C/L: Collado, Francisco); Was It Really Love? [1] (C: North, Alex; L: Webster, Paul Francis)

Notes [1] Lyric written for exploitation only.

2379 ✦ HARD COUNTRY
Universal, 1981

Musical Score Haskell, Jimmie
Composer(s) Murphey, Michael Martin
Lyricist(s) Murphey, Michael Martin

Producer(s) Greene, David; Bing, Mack
Director(s) Greene, David
Screenwriter(s) Kane, Michael

Cast Vincent, Jan-Michael; Basinger, Kim; Parks, Michael; Sartain, Gailard; Tucker, Tanya; Hannah, Daryl; Neeley, Ted

Song(s) Cowboy Cadillac; Hard Country; Hard Partyin'; Country Darlin'; Ride Out the Hard Times; Take It As It Comes; Break My Mind

Notes No cue sheet available.

2380 ✦ A HARD DAY'S NIGHT
United Artists, 1964

Musical Score Martin, George
Composer(s) Lennon, John; McCartney, Paul
Lyricist(s) Lennon, John; McCartney, Paul

Producer(s) Shenson, Walter
Director(s) Lester, Richard
Screenwriter(s) Owen, Alun

Cast Lennon, John [1]; McCartney, Paul [1]; Harrison, George [1]; Starr, Ringo [1]; Brambell, Wilfrid; Rossington, Norman

Song(s) A Hard Day's Night; I Should Have Known Better; I Wanna Be Your Man; Don't Bother Me (C/L: Harrison, George); All My Loving; If I Fell; Can't Buy Me Love; And I Love Her; I'm Happy Just to Dance with You; Tell Me Why; She Loves You; I'll Cry Instead [2]; Ringo's Theme—This Boy [2]

Notes [1] Members of the Beatles. [2] Sheet music only.

2381 ◆ HARD TO GET (1929)
Warner Brothers–First National, 1929

Director(s) Beaudine, William
Screenwriter(s) Gruen, James; Weil, Richard
Source(s) "Classified" (story) Ferber, Edna

Cast Mackaill, Dorothy; Delaney, Charles; Finlayson, James; Fazenda, Louise; Oakie, Jack; Burns, Edmund; Selwynne, Clarissa

Song(s) The (Things We Want Most Are) Hard to Get (C: Meyer, George W.; L: Bryan, Alfred; McLaughlin, John)

Notes No cue sheet available.

2382 ◆ HARD TO GET (1938)
Warner Brothers, 1938

Composer(s) Warren, Harry
Lyricist(s) Mercer, Johnny

Producer(s) Wallis, Hal B.
Director(s) Enright, Ray
Screenwriter(s) Wald, Jerry; Leo, Maurice; Macaulay, Richard

Cast Powell, Dick; de Havilland, Olivia; Winninger, Charles; Jenkins, Allen; Granville, Bonita; Cooper, Melville; Jeans, Isabel; Sutton, Grady; Hall, Thurston; Ridgely, John; Singleton, Penny

Song(s) There's a Sunny Side to Every Situation; You Must Have Been a Beautiful Baby [1]

Notes [1] Also in DEEP ADVENTURE, THE HARD WAY, THE EDDIE CANTOR STORY, MILDRED PIERCE and MY DREAM IS YOURS.

2383 ◆ HARD TO HANDLE
Warner Brothers, 1933

Producer(s) Griffen, Ray
Director(s) LeRoy, Mervyn
Screenwriter(s) Mizner, Wilson; Lord, Robert

Cast Cagney, James; Brian, Mary; Jenkins, Allen; Donnelly, Ruth; Dodd, Claire; Gordon, Gavin; Dunn, Emma; McWade, Robert

Song(s) Grapefruit Acres (Inst.) (C: Warren, Harry)

Notes Previously titled A BAD BOY and THE INSIDE.

2384 ◆ HARD TO HOLD
Universal, 1984

Musical Score Scott, Tom
Composer(s) Springfield, Rick
Lyricist(s) Springfield, Rick

Producer(s) Conte, D. Constantine
Director(s) Peerce, Larry
Screenwriter(s) Hedley, Tom

Cast Springfield, Rick; Eilber, Janet; Hansen, Patti; Salmi, Albert; Mumy, Billy [1]

Song(s) Stand Up; Taxi Dancing; When the Lights Go Down (C/L: Parker, Graham); Eat Pizza and Work; Bop 'Til You Drop; Heart of a Woman (C: Scott, Tom; L: Parton, Candy); I Go Swimming (C/L: Gabriel, Peter); Don't Walk Away; The Great Lost Art of Conversation; You Better Love Somebody

Notes There is also a vocal of "I Left My Heart in San Francisco" by Douglass Cross and George Cory. [1] Billed as Bill Mumy.

2385 ◆ THE HARD WAY
Warner Brothers, 1943

Musical Score Roemheld, Heinz
Composer(s) Jerome, M.K.
Lyricist(s) Scholl, Jack

Producer(s) Wald, Jerry
Director(s) Sherman, Vincent
Screenwriter(s) Fuchs, Daniel; Viertel, Peter

Cast Lupino, Ida; Morgan, Dennis; Leslie, Joan; Carson, Jack; George, Gladys; Emerson, Faye; Maricle, Leona; Hall, Thurston; Judels, Charles

Song(s) Runkle & Carmody Act; Youth Must Have Its Fling [1]; Good Night Oh My Darling

Notes Brief renditions of "You Must Have Been a Beautiful Baby" by Harry Warren and Johnny Mercer (also in DEEP ADVENTURE, HARD TO GET, THE EDDIE CANTOR STORY, MILDRED PIERCE and MY DREAM IS YOURS); "With Plenty of Money and You" by Dubin and Warren (also in GOLD DIGGERS OF 1937 and SHE'S WORKING HER WAY THROUGH COLLEGE); "My Little Buckaroo" by Jerome and Scholl; "Jeepers Creepers" by Warren and Mercer; "She's a Latin from Manhattan" by Dubin and Warren; "Shuffle Off to Buffalo" by Dubin and Warren and "Am I Blue" by Harry Akst and Grant Clarke were used in medleys. The ON YOUR TOES overture is, strangely enough, heard on the soundtrack as the overture to the straight play in which Joan Leslie is making her Broadway "dramatic" debut. [1] Also in HOLLYWOOD CANTEEN.

2386 ✦ HARE-ABIAN NIGHTS
Warner Brothers, 1959

Director(s) Harris, Ken
Screenwriter(s) Maltese, Michael

Cast Bunny, Bugs; Yosemite Sam

Song(s) Next Performer (C/L: Maltese, Michael)

Notes Merrie Melodie cartoon.

2387 ✦ HARLOW (A) (1965)
Paramount, 1965

Producer(s) Levine, Joseph E.
Director(s) Douglas, Gordon M.
Screenwriter(s) Hayes, John Michael

Cast Baker, Carroll; Balsam, Martin; Lansbury, Angela; Lawford, Peter; Connors, Michael; Buttons, Red

Song(s) Girl Talk [1] (C: Hefti, Neal; L: Troup, Bobby); Lonely Girl (C: Hefti, Neal; L: Livingston, Jay; Evans, Ray); Harlow [2] (C: Bacharach, Burt; David, Hal); Say Goodbye [2] (C: Bacharach, Burt; L: David, Mack)

Notes [1] Used instrumentally only. Lyric added after film. [2] Not used.

2388 ✦ HARLOW (B) (1965)
Magna, 1965

Musical Score Ham, Al; Riddle, Nelson

Producer(s) Savin, Lee
Director(s) Segal, Alex
Screenwriter(s) Tunberg, Karl

Cast Linley, Carol; Zimbalist Jr., Efrem; Sullivan, Barry; Hatfield, Hurd; Rogers, Ginger

Song(s) I Believed It All [1] (C: Ham, Al; L: Bergman, Alan; Bergman, Marilyn); With Open Arms (C: Ham, Al; L: Bergman, Alan; Bergman, Marilyn)

Notes No cue sheet available. "Vocal solos and obligatos by Mary Mayo." [1] Also in STOP THE WORLD, I WANT TO GET OFF.

2389 ✦ HARMONY AT HOME
Fox, 1929

Director(s) MacFadden, Hamilton
Screenwriter(s) Kummer, Clare; Miller, Seton I.; Collier Sr., William; McGuirk, Charles J.; Burke, Edwin; Lester, Elliott
Source(s) *The Family Upstairs* (film) Delf, Harry

Cast Churchill, Marguerite; Bell, Rex; Henry, Charlotte; Eaton, Charles; Lee, Dixie; Collier Sr., William; Patterson, Elizabeth

Song(s) Good Bye (C/L: King, Robert A.); A Little House to Dream By a Mountain Stream (C: Hanley, James F.; L: Brockman, James)

Notes This is a sound version of the 1926 film THE FAMILY UPSTAIRS. Retitled SHE STEPS OUT in 1930.

2390 ✦ HARMONY LANE
Mascot, 1935

Producer(s) Levene, Nat
Director(s) Santley, Joseph
Screenwriter(s) Santley, Joseph

Cast Montgomery, Douglass; Venable, Evelyn; Frawley, William; Cawthorn, Joseph; Muse, Clarence; Emery, Gilbert; Roberts, Florence; Collins, Cora Sue

Notes No cue sheet available. There are no original songs in this film. This biopic of Stephen Foster featured the songwriters' work.

2391 ✦ HAROLD AND MAUDE
Paramount, 1971

Composer(s) Stevens, Cat
Lyricist(s) Stevens, Cat

Producer(s) Mulverhill, Charles; Higgins, Colin
Director(s) Ashby, Hal
Screenwriter(s) Higgins, Colin

Cast Gordon, Ruth; Cort, Bud; Pickles, Vivian; Cusack, Cyril; Tyner, Charles; Geer, Ellen

Song(s) Don't Be Shy; On the Road to Find Out; I Wish, I Wish; Miles from Nowhere; Tea for the Tillerman; I Think I See the Light; Where Do the Children Play; If You Want to Sing Out; Trouble

Notes All songs used as background vocals.

2392 ✦ HAROLD TEEN
Warner Brothers, 1934

Composer(s) Fain, Sammy
Lyricist(s) Kahal, Irving

Producer(s) Lord, Robert
Director(s) Roth, Murray
Screenwriter(s) Smith, Paul Gerard; Cohn, Alfred A.
Source(s) *Harold Teen* (comic strip) Ed, Carl

Cast LeRoy, Hal; Hudson, Rochelle; Ellis, Patricia; Kibbee, Guy; Herbert, Hugh; Cavanaugh, Hobart; Chandler, Chick; Tamblyn, Eddie; Dumbrille, Douglass; Blandick, Clara; Methot, Mayo; Carle, Richard; Wilson, Charles

Song(s) Farewell Covina; How Do I Know It's Sunday; Simple and Sweet; Two Little Flies on a Lump of Sugar; Collegiate Wedding

Notes Released in Great Britain as DANCING FOOL.

2393 ◆ HARPER
Warner Brothers, 1966

Musical Score Mandel, Johnny

Producer(s) Gershwin, Jerry; Kastner, Elliott
Director(s) Smight, Jack
Screenwriter(s) Goldman, William
Source(s) *The Moving Target* (novel) MacDonald, Ross

Cast Newman, Paul; Bacall, Lauren; Harris, Julie; Hill, Arthur; Leigh, Janet; Tiffin, Pamela; Wagner, Robert; Winters, Shelley; Gould, Harold; Martin, Strother; Jenson, Roy

Song(s) Livin' Alone (C: Previn, Andre; L: Previn, Dory); Quietly These [1] (C: Previn, Andre; L: Previn, Dory); Sure As You're Born [2] (C: Mandel, Johnny; L: Bergman, Marilyn; Bergman, Alan)

Notes Released in Great Britain as THE MOVING TARGET. [1] Sheet music only. [2] Lyric written for exploitation only.

2394 ◆ HARPER VALLEY PTA
April Fools, 1978

Musical Score Riddle, Nelson

Producer(s) Edwards, George
Director(s) Bennett, Richard
Screenwriter(s) Edwards, George; Schneider, Barry
Source(s) "Harper Valley PTA" (song) Hall, Tom

Cast Eden, Barbara; Cox, Ronny; Fabray, Nanette; Swift, Susan; Nye, Louis; Fiedler, John; Christie, Audrey; Masak, Ron; Paulsen, Pat; de Witt, Fay

Song(s) Shady Sadie (C/L: Edwards, George; Carver, Gary; Anders, Luana); Harper Valley PTA (C/L: Hall, Tom)

Notes No cue sheet available.

2395 ◆ HARRY AND THE HENDERSONS
Universal, 1987

Musical Score Broughton, Bruce

Producer(s) Vane, Richard; Dear, William
Director(s) Dear, William
Screenwriter(s) Dear, William; Martin, William E.; Rappaport, Ezra D.

Cast Lithgow, John; Dillon, Melinda; Langrick, Margaret; Ruddy, Joshua; Hall, Kevin Peter; Suchet, David; Kazan, Lainie; Ameche, Don; Walsh, M. Emmet

Song(s) Love Lives On (C: Broughton, Bruce; Mann, Barry; L: Weil, Cynthia; Jennings, Will)

2396 ◆ HARRY AND WALTER GO TO NEW YORK
Columbia, 1976

Musical Score Shire, David
Composer(s) Shire, David
Lyricist(s) Bergman, Alan; Bergman, Marilyn

Producer(s) Devlin, Don; Gittes, Harry
Director(s) Rydell, Mark
Screenwriter(s) Byrum, John; Kaufman, Robert

Cast Caan, James; Gould, Elliott; Caine, Michael; Keaton, Diane; Durning, Charles; Warren, Lesley Ann; Gilford, Jack; Kane, Carol; Young, Burt

Song(s) I'm Harry; I'm Walter; Nobody's Perfect; Kingdom of Love; Suitor Scene; Overture; Finale

2397 ◆ HARRY IN YOUR POCKET
United Artists, 1973

Musical Score Schifrin, Lalo

Producer(s) Geller, Bruce
Director(s) Geller, Bruce
Screenwriter(s) Buchanan, James David; Austin, Ronald

Cast Coburn, James; Pidgeon, Walter; Sarrazin, Michael; VanDevere, Trish

Song(s) Day By Day By Day (C: Schifrin, Lalo; L: Geller, Bruce)

Notes Originally titled HARRY NEVER HOLDS.

2398 ◆ HARUM SCARUM
Metro–Goldwyn–Mayer, 1966

Musical Score Karger, Fred
Composer(s) Giant, Bill; Baum, Bernie; Kaye, Florence
Lyricist(s) Giant, Bill; Baum, Bernie; Kaye, Florence
Choreographer(s) Barton, Earl

Producer(s) Katzman, Sam
Director(s) Nelson, Gene
Screenwriter(s) Adams, Gerald Drayson

Cast Presley, Elvis; Mobley, Mary Ann; Jeffries, Fran; Ansara, Michael; Novello, Jay; Barty, Billy

Song(s) Harem Holiday (C/L: Andreloli, Pete; Poncia Jr., Vincent; Crane, Jimmie); My Desert Serenade (C/L: Gelber, Stanley); Go East Young Man; Animal Instinct; Kismet (C/L: Tepper, Sid; Bennett, Roy C.); Shake That Tambourine; Hey Little Girl (C/L: Byers, Joy); Golden Coins; Wisdom of the Ages; So Close, Yet So Far (From Paradise) (C/L: Byers, Joy); Mirage [1]

Notes Originally titled HAREM HOLIDAY. [1] Sheet music only.

2399 ◆ HARVEST MELODY
PRC, 1943

Composer(s) Akst, Harry
Lyricist(s) Davis, Benny

Director(s) Newfield, Sam
Screenwriter(s) Gale, Allan

Cast Lane, Rosemary; Downs, Johnny; Leonard, Sheldon; Wynters, Charlotte; Alberni, Luis; Rochelle, Claire; Saylor, Syd; Eddie LeBaron and His Orchestra; The Radio Rogues

Song(s) You Could Have Knocked Me Over with a Feather; Put It in Reverse; Let's Drive Out to a Drive-In; Tenderly (C: Shuken, Leo; L: Combes, Walter)

Notes No cue sheet available.

2400 ✦ HARVEY
Universal, 1950

Musical Score Skinner, Frank

Producer(s) Beck, John
Director(s) Koster, Henry
Screenwriter(s) Chase, Mary; Brodney, Oscar
Source(s) *Harvey* (play) Chase, Mary

Cast Stewart, James; Hull, Josephine [1]; Horne, Victoria [1]; White, Jesse [1]; Lynn, William; Kellaway, Cecil; Dow, Peggy; Drake, Charles; Ford, Wallace; Bryant, Nana; Mills, Grace; Bevans, Clem; Moore, Ida

Song(s) My Love (C: Scharf, Walter; L: Brooks, Jack)

Notes [1] From original Broadway cast.

2401 ✦ THE HARVEY GIRLS
Metro–Goldwyn–Mayer, 1945

Composer(s) Warren, Harry
Lyricist(s) Mercer, Johnny
Choreographer(s) Alton, Robert

Producer(s) Freed, Arthur
Director(s) Sidney, George
Screenwriter(s) Beloin, Edmund; Curtis, Nathaniel; Crane, Harry; O'Hanlon, James; Raphaelson, Samson; Van Riper, Kay
Source(s) (novel) Adams, Samuel Hopkins

Cast Garland, Judy; Hodiak, John; Bolger, Ray; Lansbury, Angela [3]; Foster, Preston; O'Brien, Virginia; Baker, Kenny; Main, Marjorie; Wills, Chill; Charisse, Cyd [4]; Royle, Selena; Earle, Edward

Song(s) The Train Must Be Fed [6] (C/L: Edens, Roger); In the Valley (Where the Evening Sun Goes Down); Wait and See; On the Atchison Topeka and the Santa Fe (L: Mercer, Johnny; Thompson, Kay [1]; Blane, Ralph [1]); Oh, You Kid; It's a Great Big World; The Wild, Wild West; Swing Your Partner Round and Round; The March of the Doagies [2]; My Intuition [2]; Hayride [2] [5]

Notes [1] Additional lyrics. [2] Filmed but not used. [3] Dubbed by Virginia Rees. [4] Dubbed by Betty

Russell. [5] Same music as "The House of Singing Bamboo" in PAGAN LOVE SONG (1950). [6] Kay Thompson may have contributed to this number.

2402 ✦ HAS ANYBODY SEEN MY GAL?
Universal, 1952

Choreographer(s) Belfer, Hal

Producer(s) Richmond, Ted
Director(s) Sirk, Douglas
Screenwriter(s) Hoffman, Joseph

Cast Laurie, Piper; Hudson, Rock; Coburn, Charles; Bari, Lynn; Perreau, Gigi; Homeier, Skip; Gates, Larry; Dean, James

Notes There are no songs written for this film. Vocals include "Five Foot Two, Eyes of Blue" by Sam Lewis, Joe Young and Ray Henderson; "When the Red, Red Robin (Comes Bob, Bob, Bobbin' Along)" by Harry Woods and "Gimme a Little Kiss" by Roy Turk, Jack Smith and Maceo Pinkard.

2403 ✦ HATARI!
Paramount, 1962

Musical Score Mancini, Henry

Producer(s) Hawks, Howard
Director(s) Hawks, Howard
Screenwriter(s) Brackett, Leigh

Cast Wayne, John; Buttons, Red; Kruger, Hardy; Blain, Gerard; Cabot, Bruce; Martinelli, Elsa

Song(s) Just for Tonight [1] (C: Carmichael, Hoagy; L: Mercer, Johnny); Paraphrase [2] (C: Carmichael, Hoagy); Baby Elephant Walk [3] (C: Mancini, Henry; L: David, Hal); After One Kiss [3] (C: Mancini, Henry; L: Heyman, Edward)

Notes There is also a vocal of "Oh Brandy Leave Me Alone" by Joseph Marais. [1] Formerly titled "Paris Nights." Used instrumentally only. There was an alternate lyric written titled "All of Your Love" which was basically the same song. [2] Also titled "Bermuda." [3] Lyric written for exploitation only.

2404 ✦ HAT CHECK HONEY
Universal, 1944

Composer(s) Rosen, Milton
Lyricist(s) Carter, Everett

Producer(s) Cowan, Will
Director(s) Cline, Edward F.
Screenwriter(s) Leo, Maurice; Davis, Stanley

Cast Errol, Leon; Davies, Richard; McDonald, Grace

Song(s) A Dream Ago [1]; Slightly Sentimental [2]; Rockin' with You; Nice to Know You

Notes There are also instrumentals of "Drumola" by Ted Weems; "Rhythm of the Islands" by Leon Belasco,

Jacques Press and Eddie Cherkose; "It Happened in Kaloha" by Ralph Freed and Frank Skinner and "Loose Wig" by Charles Weintraub and Frank Davenport. Some of these might have been just background music. [1] Also in HI,'YA, SAILOR, MOON OVER LAS VEGAS and STARS AND VIOLINS. [2] Also in MELODY GARDEN.

2405 ✦ HATS OFF
Grand National, 1936

Composer(s)   Oakland, Ben
Lyricist(s)   Magidson, Herb
Choreographer(s)   Dreifuss, Arthur

Producer(s)   Petroff, Boris
Director(s)   Petroff, Boris
Screenwriter(s)   Fuller, Samuel; Joseph, Edmund

Cast   Clarke, Mae; Payne, John; Lynd, Helen; Gallagher, Skeets; Alberni, Luis

Song(s)   Where Have You Been All My Life?; Twinkle Twinkle Little Star; Let's Have Another; Little Odd Rhythm; Hats Off; The Fight

Notes   No cue sheet available.

2406 ✦ HATS OFF TO RHYTHM

See EARL CARROLL'S SKETCHBOOK.

2407 ✦ THE HAUNTED STRANGLER
Metro–Goldwyn–Mayer, 1959

Musical Score   Orr, Buxton

Producer(s)   Croydon, John
Director(s)   Day, Robert
Screenwriter(s)   Read, Jan; Cooper, John C.

Cast   Karloff, Boris; Kent, Jean; Allan, Elizabeth; Dawson, Anthony; Day, Vera

Song(s)   Cora's Song (C/L: Orr, Buxton)

2408 ✦ HAVANA ROSE
Republic, 1951

Producer(s)   Picker, Sidney
Director(s)   Beaudine, William
Screenwriter(s)   Roberts, Charles E.; Townley, Jack

Cast   Rodriguez, Estelita; Bates, Florence; Bonanova, Fortunio; Belasco, Leon; Williams, Bill; Herbert, Hugh

Song(s)   Babalu (C/L: Lecuona, Margarita); Noche de Ronda [1] (C: Lara, Maria Teresa; L: Skylar, Sunny; Lara, Maria Teresa); Repiquetera Timbalero (C: Wilson, Stanley; L: Galian, Geri)

Notes   [1] English lyrics by Sunny Skylar. Also used (with original lyrics) in SOMBRERO (MGM), Spanish language version of THE BIG BROADCAST OF 1938

(Paramount), MASQUERADE IN MEXICO (Paramount) and RIDE CLEAR OF DIABLO (Universal).

2409 ✦ HAVE A HEART
Metro–Goldwyn–Mayer, 1934

Producer(s)   Considine Jr., John W.
Director(s)   Butler, David
Screenwriter(s)   DeSylva, B.G.; Butler, David; Ryerson, Florence; Woolf, Edgar Allan

Cast   Parker, Jean; Dunn, James; Merkel, Una; Erwin, Stuart

Song(s)   Lost in a Fog [1] (C: McHugh, Jimmy; L: Fields, Dorothy); Thank You For a Lovely Evening [2] (C: McHugh, Jimmy; L: Fields, Dorothy)

Notes   [1] Not in cue sheet. [2] Used instrumentally only.

2410 ✦ HAVING A WILD WEEKEND
Warner Brothers, 1965

Composer(s)   Clark, Dave
Lyricist(s)   Clark, Dave

Producer(s)   Deutsch, David
Director(s)   Boorman, John
Screenwriter(s)   Nichols, Peter

Cast   The Dave Clark Five [1]; Ferris, Barbara; Swift, Clive; Walters, Hugh; Bailey, Robin; Joyce, Yootha; Lacey, Ronald

Song(s)   Sweet Memories; Time; When; I Can't Stand It; On the Move; Ol Sol; Catch Us If You Can (C/L: Clark, Dave; Davidson, Lenny)

Notes   No cue sheet available. Released in Great Britain as CATCH US IF YOU CAN. [1] Including: Dave Clark; Lenny Davidson; Rick Huxley; Mike Smith; and Dennis Payton.

2411 ✦ HAVING WONDERFUL TIME
RKO, 1938

Musical Score   Webb, Roy
Composer(s)   Stept, Sam H.
Lyricist(s)   Tobias, Charles

Producer(s)   Berman, Pandro S.
Director(s)   Santell, Alfred
Screenwriter(s)   Kober, Arthur
Source(s)   *Having Wonderful Time* (play) Kober, Arthur

Cast   Rogers, Ginger; Fairbanks Jr., Douglas; Conklin, Peggy; Ball, Lucille; Bowman, Lee; Arden, Eve; Kent, Dorothea; Skelton, Red [2]; Meek, Donald

Song(s)   My First Impression of You; Nighty Night; Carefree Camp [1]; The Band Played Out of Tune [3]

Notes There is also a vocal of "Heigh Ho" by Larry Morey and Frank Churchill. [1] Used instrumentally only. [2] Billed as Richard "Red" Skelton. [3] Sheet music only.

2412 ✦ HAWAII
United Artists, 1966

Musical Score Bernstein, Elmer
Composer(s) Bernstein, Elmer
Lyricist(s) David, Mack

Producer(s) Mirisch, Walter
Director(s) Hill, George Roy
Screenwriter(s) Trumbo, Dalton; Taradash, Daniel
Source(s) *Hawaii* (novel) Michener, James A.

Cast Andrews, Julie; Von Sydow, Max; Harris, Richard; Hackman, Gene; La Garde, Jocelyne; Tupoli, Manu; O'Connor, Carroll

Song(s) My Wishing Doll; I Am Hawaii [1]

Notes Bette Midler's (tiny) screen debut. [1] Lyric written for exploitation only.

2413 ✦ HAWAIIAN NIGHTS (1934)

See DOWN TO THEIR LAST YACHT.

2414 ✦ HAWAIIAN NIGHTS (1939)
Universal, 1939

Composer(s) Malneck, Matty
Lyricist(s) Loesser, Frank

Producer(s) Golden, Max H.
Director(s) Rogell, Albert S.
Screenwriter(s) Grayson, Charles; Loeb, Lee

Cast Downs, Johnny; Hall, Thurston; Carlisle, Mary; Moore, Constance; Quillan, Eddie; Girardot, Etienne; Hinds, Samuel S.; Luana, Princess

Song(s) I Found My Love; Hey, Good Lookin'; Hawaii Sang Me to Sleep; Then I Wrote the Minuet in G (C: Beethoven, Ludwig von)

2415 ✦ HAWAII CALLS
Principal/RKO, 1938

Director(s) Cline, Edward F.
Screenwriter(s) Tuchock, Wanda
Source(s) (novel) Blanding, Don

Cast Breen, Bobby; Lani, Pua; Sparks, Ned; Cobb, Irvin S.; Hull, Warren; Holden, Gloria; Quigley, Juanita

Song(s) Macushla (C: MacMurrough, Dermot; L: Rose, Josephine V.); Down Where the Trade Winds Blow (C/L: Owens, Harry); Hawaii Calls (C/L: Owens, Harry)

Notes No cue sheet available. There is also a vocal of "Aloha Oe" by Queen Lilluokalani.

2416 ✦ HAWK OF POWDER RIVER
Eagle Lion, 1948

Musical Score Greene, Walter

Producer(s) Thomas, Jerry
Director(s) Taylor, Ray
Screenwriter(s) Smith, George

Cast Dean, Eddie; Ates, Roscoe; Holt, Jennifer; Carlson, June

Song(s) Black Hills [1] (C/L: Dean, Eddie; Blair, Hal); Uncle Looks (C/L: Gates, Pete); Driver Haw (C/L: Gates, Pete); Wild Country (C/L: Dean, Eddie; Blair, Hal)

Notes The cue sheet doesn't differentiate between vocals and instrumentals. [1] Also in BLACK HILLS.

2417 ✦ THE HAWK OF THE RIVER
Columbia, 1951

Composer(s) Burnette, Smiley
Lyricist(s) Burnette, Smiley

Producer(s) Clark, Colbert
Director(s) Sears, Fred F.
Screenwriter(s) Green, Howard J.

Cast Starrett, Charles; Mahoney, Jock; Moore, Clayton; Parker, Edwin; Diehl, Jim; Burnette, Smiley

Song(s) Chief Pocatello; Pedro Enchilada

2418 ✦ HAWMPS!
Mulberry Square, 1976

Musical Score Box, Euel

Producer(s) Camp, Joe
Director(s) Camp, Joe
Screenwriter(s) Bickley, William; Warren, Michael

Cast Hampton, James; Connelly, Christopher; Camp, Joe; Pyle, Denver; Elam, Jack

Song(s) I Just Wanta Go Home (C/L: Box, Euel; Box, Betty)

Notes No cue sheet available.

2419 ✦ HAY QUE CASAR AL PRINCIPE
Fox, 1931

Composer(s) Kernell, William
Lyricist(s) Mojica, Jose

Song(s) Hammer Song (Inst.); Paid to Love; Thru the Green Country Side; Gypsy Love Song (Inst.); Mi Sueno De Amor; En La Vieja Sylvania; Regiment of Love

Notes No further information available. It is not known if Mojica, credited with Spanish lyrics, just translated Kernell's lyrics or composed the originals in Spanish.

2420 ◆ HEAD
Columbia, 1968

Musical Score Thorne, Ken

Producer(s) Rafelson, Bob; Nicholson, Jack
Director(s) Rafelson, Bob
Screenwriter(s) Rafelson, Bob; Nicholson, Jack

Cast The Monkees [1]; Mature, Victor; Funicello, Annette; Sofaer, Abraham; Scotti, Vito; Jones, T.C.; Liston, Sonny; Ramsey, Logan

Song(s) Porpoise Song (C/L: Goffin, Gerry; King, Carole); Ditty (C/L: Rafelson, Bob; Nicholson, Jack); Circle Sky (C/L: Nesmith, Michael); Can You Dig It? (C/L: Tork, Peter); As We Go Along (C/L: King, Carole; Stern, Toni); Get Tuff (C/L: Thorne, Ken; Rafelson, Bob); Daddy's Song (C/L: Nillson); Do I Have to Do This All Over Again? (C/L: Tork, Peter)

Notes [1] Consisted of Peter Tork, Davy Jones, Micky Dolenz and Michael Nesmith.

2421 ◆ HEADIN' FOR BROADWAY
Twentieth Century–Fox, 1980

Musical Score Brooks, Joseph
Composer(s) Brooks, Joseph
Lyricist(s) Brooks, Joseph

Producer(s) Brooks, Joseph
Director(s) Brooks, Joseph
Screenwriter(s) Brooks, Joseph; Henkin, Hilary; Gross, Larry

Cast Smith, Rex; Treas, Terri; Reed, Vivian; Foote, Gene; Carafotes, Paul

Song(s) Rhythm; Beautiful Day; I Will Shine On; Bright Lights; Woman; Broadway

2422 ◆ HEAD OFFICE
Tri-Star, 1986

Musical Score Howard, James Newton

Producer(s) Hill, Debra
Director(s) Finkleman, Ken
Screenwriter(s) Finkleman, Ken

Cast Reinhold, Judge; DeVito, Danny; Engler, Lori-Nan; Albert, Eddie; Butrick, Merritt; Frazier, Ron; Masur, Richard; Moranis, Rick; Novello, Don; O'Donoghue, Michael; Seymour, Jane; Shawn, Wallace; Coe, George; King, Don; Murray, Brian Doyle

Song(s) You're in My Dreams (C/L: Witkin, Bruce); Sly Times (C/L: Pearson, Dunn; Porrello, Joe); Music Lovers (C/L: Pearson, Dunn; Porrello, Joe); You Need Love (C/L: Witkin, Bruce; Gambone, Jimmy); Military Madness (C/L: Howarth, Alan); Goin' Down (C/L: Gibbs, Rich); Flyer (C/L: Geo)

Notes No cue sheet available.

2423 ◆ HEADS UP!
Paramount, 1930

Composer(s) Rodgers, Richard
Lyricist(s) Hart, Lorenz
Choreographer(s) Hale, George

Director(s) Schertzinger, Victor
Screenwriter(s) McGowan, Jack; Kirkland, Jack
Source(s) *Heads Up!* (musical) McGowan, Jack; Smith, Paul Gerard; Rodgers, Richard; Hart, Lorenz

Cast Rogers, Charles "Buddy"; Kane, Helen; Moore, Victor; Breen, Margaret; Gowing, Gene; Carrington, Helen

Song(s) A Ship Without a Sail [1]; My Man Is on the Make [1]; 'Readin' Ritin' Rhythm [2] (C: Schertzinger, Victor; L: Hartman, Don); If I Knew You Better (C: Schertzinger, Victor L: Hartman, Don); Until Today I Had No Tomorrow [4] (C: Duke, Vernon; L: Harburg, E.Y.); Heads Up [4] (C: Duke, Vernon; L: Harburg, E.Y.); I May Fall in Love Again [4] (C: Duke, Vernon; L: Harburg, E.Y.)

Notes [1] From original production. [2] Sheet music only. [3] Hartman not credited on cue sheet only sheet music. [4] Not used.

2424 ◆ HEALTH
Twentieth Century–Fox, 1980

Musical Score Byrd, Joseph
Composer(s) Nicholls, Allan; Steinettes, The
Lyricist(s) Nicholls, Allan; Steinettes, The

Producer(s) Altman, Robert
Director(s) Altman, Robert
Screenwriter(s) Barhydt, Frank; Dooley, Paul; Altman, Robert

Cast Jackson, Glenda; Burnett, Carol; Garner, James; Bacall, Lauren; Cavett, Dick; Dooley, Paul; Moffat, Donald; Gibson, Henry; Dixon, MacIntyre; Woodard, Alfre

Song(s) Health; Esther Brill; Welcome to Health; Sugar Fit; Fixation; Sweet Hawaiian Maiden; Vegetable Soup; Isabella Garnell; Vote; Multi-Vitamin

2425 ◆ HEAR ME GOOD
Paramount, 1957

Producer(s) McGuire, Don
Director(s) McGuire, Don
Screenwriter(s) McGuire, Don

Cast March, Hal; Ross, Joe E.; Anders, Merry; Willes, Jean; Frome, Milton; Faye, Joey

Song(s) Hear Me Good (C/L: McGuire, Don)

2426 ✦ HEARTACHES (1947)
PRC, 1947

Musical Score Cadkin, Emil
Composer(s) Kent, Walter
Lyricist(s) Gannon, Kim

Producer(s) Stahl, Marvin D.
Director(s) Wrangell, Basil
Screenwriter(s) Bricker, George

Cast Ryan, Sheila; Norris, Edward; Wills, Chill; Orth, Frank

Song(s) Heartaches (C/L: Klenner; Hoffman); Never Knew That I Could Sing [1]; I'm So in Love; Just Can't Get That Gal

Notes [1] Also in DOWN MISSOURI WAY.

2427 ✦ HEARTACHES (1982)
Motion Picture Marketing, 1982

Musical Score Martin, Michael

Producer(s) Patterson, David J.; Raibourn, Jerry
Director(s) Shebib, Donald
Screenwriter(s) Heffernan, Terrence

Cast Kidder, Margot; Potts, Annie; Carradine, Robert; Rekert, Winston

Song(s) Heartaches (C: Jenkins, Ron; L: Sixt, Frank)

Notes No cue sheet available.

2428 ✦ HEARTBEAT (1946)
RKO, 1946

Musical Score Misraki, Paul

Producer(s) Hakim, Robert; Hakim, Raymond
Director(s) Wood, Sam
Screenwriter(s) Ryskind, Morrie; Leigh, Rowland

Cast Rogers, Ginger; Aumont, Jean-Pierre; Menjou, Adolphe; Cooper, Mikhail; Ciannelli, Eduardo; Rathbone, Basil

Song(s) Can You Guess (C: Misraki, Paul; L: Drake, Ervin)

2429 ✦ HEART BEAT (1980)
Orion/Warner, 1980

Musical Score Nitzsche, Jack

Producer(s) Greisman, Alan; Shamberg, Michael
Director(s) Byrum, John
Screenwriter(s) Byrum, John

Source(s) *Heart Beat: My Life with Jack and Neal* (memoir) Cassady, Carolyn

Cast Nolte, Nick; Spacek, Sissy; Heard, John; Sharkey, Ray; Dusenberry, Ann; Bill, Tony; Larroquette, John; Allen, Steve

Song(s) I Love Her Too (C: Nitzsche, Jack; L: Sainte-Marie, Buffy)

Notes No cue sheet available.

2430 ✦ HEARTBREAKERS
Orion, 1984

Musical Score Tangerine Dream

Producer(s) Weis, Bob; Roth, Bobby
Director(s) Roth, Bobby
Screenwriter(s) Roth, Bobby

Cast Coyote, Peter; Mancuso, Nick; Laure, Carole; Gail, Max; Harrold, Kathryn

Song(s) The Blues Don't Care (C/L: James, Etta; Ray, Brian); You Want More (C: James, Etta; Ray, Brian; L: James, Etta; Ray, Brian; Legassick, Steve; Nocentelli, Leo)

Notes No cue sheet available.

2431 ✦ HEARTBREAK HOTEL
Touchstone, 1988

Musical Score Delerue, Georges

Producer(s) Obst, Lynda; Hill, Debra
Director(s) Columbus, Chris
Screenwriter(s) Columbus, Chris

Cast Keith, David; Weld, Tuesday; Schlatter, Charlie; Goethals, Angela; Landry, Karen; Mulkey, Chris

Song(s) Soul on Fire (C/L: Carillo, Frank; Byrd, Ricky; Craft, Robert)

2432 ✦ HEARTBREAK RIDGE
Warner Brothers, 1987

Musical Score Niehaus, Lennie
Composer(s) Van Peebles, Mario
Lyricist(s) Van Peebles, Mario

Producer(s) Eastwood, Clint
Director(s) Eastwood, Clint
Screenwriter(s) Carabatsos, James

Cast Eastwood, Clint; Mason, Marsha; Van Peebles, Mario; Heckart, Eileen; Svenson, Bo; Franco, Ramon; Gaines, Boyd; Gunn, Moses

Song(s) Sea of Heartbreak (C: Hampton, Paul; L: David, Hal); Fine Girl; I Love You, But I Ain't Stupid (C/L: Van Peebles, Mario; Nakano, Desmond); Recon Rap; Rock and Roll Star; A Very Precious Love [1] (C: Fain, Sammy; L: Webster, Paul Francis); How Much I

Care (C: Eastwood, Clint; L: Cahn, Sammy); Bionic Marine

Notes   It is not known which of these songs was written for the picture. [1] Also in MARJORIE MORNINGSTAR.

2433 ✦ HEARTBURN
Paramount, 1986

Musical Score   Simon, Carly

Producer(s)   Nichols, Mike; Greenhut, Robert
Director(s)   Nichols, Mike
Screenwriter(s)   Ephron, Nora
Source(s)   *Heartburn* (novel) Ephron, Nora

Cast   Streep, Meryl; Nicholson, Jack; Daniels, Jeff; Stapleton, Maureen; Channing, Stockard; Masur, Richard; O'Hara, Catherine; Hill, Steven; Forman, Milos; Stern, Natalie

Song(s)   Coming Around Again (C/L: Simon, Carly)

2434 ✦ THE HEART IS A LONELY HUNTER
Warner Brothers, 1968

Musical Score   Grusin, Dave
Composer(s)   Grusin, Dave
Lyricist(s)   Hilton, Hermine

Producer(s)   Ryan, Thomas C.; Merson, Marc
Director(s)   Miller, Robert Ellis
Screenwriter(s)   Ryan, Thomas C.
Source(s)   *The Heart Is a Lonely Hunter* (novel) McCullers, Carson

Cast   Arkin, Alan; Barrett, Laurinda; Keach, Stacy; McCann, Chuck; McGuire, Biff; Rodriguez, Percy; Tyson, Cicely; Locke, Sondra

Song(s)   Beyond the Reach of Love; The Color of the Wind Is Cold; Elizabeth (L: Wilson, Dave); The Pipes of Pan (L: Wilson, Dave); The Heart Is a Lonely Hunter [1] (C: Grusin, Dave; L: Lee, Peggy)

Notes   [1] Lyric written for exploitation only.

2435 ✦ HEART LIKE A WHEEL
Twentieth Century–Fox, 1983

Musical Score   Rosenthal, Laurence

Producer(s)   Roven, Charles
Director(s)   Kaplan, Jonathan
Screenwriter(s)   Friedman, Ken

Cast   Bedelia, Bonnie; Bridges, Beau; Rossi, Leo; Axton, Hoyt; Edwards, Anthony; Martin, Dean Paul; Geer, Ellen; Evans, Steve

Song(s)   Born to Win (C/L: Snow, Tom); Gimme This Moment (C/L: Bratton, Creed)

Notes   No cue sheet available.

2436 ✦ HEART OF ARIZONA
Paramount, 1938

Producer(s)   Sherman, Harry
Director(s)   Selander, Lesley
Screenwriter(s)   Houston, Norman

Cast   Boyd, William; Hayden, Russell; Moorhead, Natalie; Hayes, George "Gabby"; King, Billy

Song(s)   Lucky's Song (C: Hayden, Russell; L: Houston, Norman)

Notes   Title changed from GUNSMOKE.

2437 ✦ HEART OF THE GOLDEN WEST
Republic, 1942

Producer(s)   Kane, Joseph
Director(s)   Kane, Joseph
Screenwriter(s)   Felton, Earl

Cast   Rogers, Roy; Hayes, George "Gabby"; Catlett, Walter; Terry, Ruth; Harvey, Paul; MacDonald, Edmund; Haade, William; Taliaferro, Hal; Whipper, Leigh; The Sons of the Pioneers; The Hall Johnson Choir; Burnette, Smiley

Song(s)   River Robin (C/L: Nolan, Bob); River Chant (C/L: Johnson, Hall); Cowboys and Indians (C/L: Spencer, Tim); Make Yourself at Home [1] (C: Styne, Jule; L: Bullock, Walter); Night Falls on the Prairie (C/L: Nolan, Bob); Who's Gonna Help Me Sing (C/L: Nolan, Bob)

Notes   There are also vocals of "Every Time I Feel the Spirit" and "Carry Me Back to Old Virginny." [1] Also in HIT PARADE OF 1941 and IDAHO.

2438 ✦ HEART OF THE NORTH
Warner Brothers–First National, 1938

Musical Score   Deutsch, Adolph

Producer(s)   Foy, Bryan
Director(s)   Seiler, Lewis
Screenwriter(s)   Katz, Lee; Sherman, Vincent

Cast   Foran, Dick; Dickson, Gloria; Knowles, Patric; Jenkins, Allen; Chapman, Janet; Stephenson, James

Song(s)   Song of the Mounted Police [1] (C: Jerome, M.K.; L: Scholl, Jack)

Notes   [1] Also in MUSICAL MOVIELAND.

2439 ✦ HEART OF THE RIO GRANDE
Republic, 1942

Producer(s)   Grey, Harry
Director(s)   Morgan, William
Screenwriter(s)   Miller, Winston; Hayward, Lillie
Source(s)   "Sure Money Talks But . . ." (story) Wildes, Newlin B.

Cast Autry, Gene; Burnette, Smiley; McKenzie, Fay; Fellows, Edith; Watkin, Pierre; Porter, Jimmy; The Jimmy Wakely Trio

Song(s) Let Me Ride Down Rocky Canyon (C/L: Whitley, Ray; Autry, Gene; Rose, Fred); Deep in the Heart of Texas [2] (C: Swander, Don; L: Hershey, June); Dusk on the Painted Desert (C/L: George, Don; Bernard, Helen; Frisch, Al); A Rumble Seat for Two (C/L: Marvin, Johnny; Marvin, Frankie); Rancho Pillow [3] (C/L: Newman, Charles; Wrubel, Allie); Rainbow in the Night (C: Styne, Jule; L: Meyer, Sol); Cimarron [1] (C/L: Bond, Johnny); I'll Wait for You (C/L: Autry, Gene; Rose, Fred); Saddle Your Blues to a Wild Mustang (C/L: Whiting, George; Bernier, Buddy; Haid, Billy); Oh, Woe Is Me (C/L: Burnette, Smiley); Painted Desert (C/L: Autry, Gene; Whitley, Ray)

Notes [1] Also in TWILIGHT ON THE TRAIL (Paramount). [2] Also in HI, NEIGHBOR, KING OF THE COWBOYS, DEEP IN THE HEART OF TEXAS (Universal) and I'LL GET BY (20th). [3] Also in THE BIG SOMBRERO (Columbia).

2440 ✦ HEART OF THE ROCKIES
Republic, 1951

Composer(s) Elliott, Jack
Lyricist(s) Elliott, Jack

Producer(s) White, Edward J.
Director(s) Witney, William
Screenwriter(s) Taylor, Eric

Cast Rogers, Roy; Trigger; Edwards, Penny; Jones, Gordon; Morgan, Ralph; Graham, Fred; Henry, Robert "Buzz"; Foy Willing and the Riders of the Purple Sage

Song(s) Heart of the Rockies; Prairie Country [1] (C/L: Willing, Foy); Wanderin' (C: Traditional); Rodeo Square Dance

Notes [1] Spanish lyrics by Geri Galian.

2441 ✦ HEART OF THE WEST
Paramount, 1936

Producer(s) Sherman, Harry
Director(s) Bretherton, Howard
Screenwriter(s) Schroeder, Doris

Cast Boyd, William; Ellison, James; Hayes, George "Gabby"; Gabriel, Lynn; Blackmer, Sidney

Song(s) My Heart's in the Heart of the West (C: Young, Victor; L: Coslow, Sam)

2442 ✦ HEARTS DIVIDED
Warner Brothers–First National, 1936

Musical Score Roemheld, Heinz
Composer(s) Warren, Harry
Lyricist(s) Dubin, Al

Producer(s) Brown, Harry Joe
Director(s) Borzage, Frank

Screenwriter(s) Doyle, Laird; Robinson, Casey
Source(s) *Glorious Betsy* (play) Young, Rida Johnson

Cast Davies, Marion; Powell, Dick; Ruggles, Charles; Rains, Claude; Horton, Edward Everett; Treacher, Arthur; Stephenson, Henry; Blandick, Clara; Larkin, John; McDaniel, Hattie; Girardot, Etienne; Bondi, Beulah; The Hall Johnson Choir

Song(s) My Kingdom for a Kiss; Two Hearts Divided

2443 ✦ HEARTS IN DIXIE
Fox, 1929

Composer(s) Jackson, Howard
Lyricist(s) Weems, Walter
Choreographer(s) Fanchon and Marco

Director(s) Sloane, Paul; Van Buren, A.H.
Screenwriter(s) Weems, Walter

Cast Fetchit, Stepin; Muse, Clarence; Jackson, Eugene; Morrison, Dorothy; Pilot, Bernice; Ingram, Clifford

Song(s) Here Comes the Bride; Jubilatin'; Hearts in Dixie; Trouble Goes By; Lazy Song; Lullaby (C/L: Weems, Walter; Muse, Clarence)

2444 ✦ HEARTS IN EXILE
Warner Brothers, 1929

Director(s) Curtiz, Michael
Screenwriter(s) Gates, Harvey
Source(s) *Hearts in Exile* (play) Oxenham, John

Cast Costello, Dolores; Withers, Grant; Kirkwood, James; Tell, Olive; Torrence, David; Fawcett, George; Irving, William; Dugan, Tom; Dione, Rose

Song(s) Like a Breath of Springtime (C: Burke, Joe; L: Dubin, Al)

Notes No cue sheet available.

2445 ✦ HEARTS IN SPRINGTIME

See GLAMOUR BOY.

2446 ✦ HEARTS OF THE WEST
Metro–Goldwyn–Mayer, 1975

Musical Score Lauber, Ken
Composer(s) Lauber, Ken
Lyricist(s) Rogers, Jack

Producer(s) Bill, Tony
Director(s) Zieff, Howard
Screenwriter(s) Thompson, Rob

Cast Bridges, Jeff; Griffith, Andy; Pleasence, Donald; Danner, Blythe; Shull, Richard B.; Edelman, Herb; Cady, Frank; James, Anthony; Gilliam, Burton; Clark, Matt; Arkin, Alan

Song(s) Yellow Yodel; Move 'Em Out

Notes Only original songs listed. Titled HOLLYWOOD COWBOY internationally.

2447 ◆ THE HEAT'S ON
Columbia, 1943

Composer(s) Gorney, Jay
Lyricist(s) Myers, Henry; Eliscu, Edward
Choreographer(s) Lichine, David

Producer(s) Carter, Milton
Director(s) Ratoff, Gregory
Screenwriter(s) Davis, Fitzroy; George, George W.; Schiller, Fred

Cast West, Mae; Moore, Victor; Gaxton, William; Bridges, Lloyd; Xavier Cugat and His Orchestra; Lichine, David; Scott, Hazel; Allen, Lester; Ash, Sam; Sues, Leonard; Romay, Lina

Song(s) (I'm Just a) Stranger in Town; Negra Leono [1] (C/L: Fernandez, Antonio); There Goes That Guitar; Antonio (C/L: Andre, Fabian; Huntley, Leo; Blackburn, John); The White Keys and the Black Keys; Thinkin' About the Wabash [2] (C: Styne, Jule; L: Cahn, Sammy; Bullock, Walter); They Looked So Pretty on the Envelope; Hello Mi Amigo

Notes Originally titled TROPICANA, by which name it was released in Great Britain. [1] Also in PAN AMERICANA (RKO) and SLIGHTLY SCANDALOUS (Universal). In GAY SENORITA and credited to Don George and Serge Walter. [2] Bullock not credited on sheet music.

2448 ◆ HEAVEN IS ROUND THE CORNER
Republic, 1944

Musical Score Russell, Kennedy
Composer(s) Russell, Kennedy
Lyricist(s) O'Connor, Desmond

Producer(s) Zelnik, Fred
Director(s) Rogers, Maclean
Screenwriter(s) Melford, Austin

Cast Fyffe, Will; Lynn, Leni; Trevor, Austin; Kun, Magda; Glenville, Peter

Song(s) Song of the Birds (L: Russell, Kennedy); Heaven Is Round the Corner; Ticking Your Cares Away

Notes A British National picture. There are also vocals of "Pour Etre Heureux" by Oberfeld and "Romeo and Juliet" waltz by Gounod.

2449 ◆ HEAVENLY DAYS
RKO, 1944

Musical Score Harline, Leigh

Producer(s) Fellows, Robert
Director(s) Estabrook, Howard
Screenwriter(s) Estabrook, Howard; Quinn, Don

Cast Fibber McGee and Molly [2]; Pallette, Eugene; Oliver, Gordon; Walburn, Raymond; Hale, Barbara; Douglas, Don; Inescort, Frieda; Bacon, Irving; The King's Men

Song(s) Please Won't You Leave My Girl Alone [1] (C: McHugh, Jimmy; L: Loesser, Frank); Raggedy Ann (C/L: Woodin, Will; Gruelle, Johnny)

Notes There are also vocals of "I'm Always Chasing Rainbows" by Joseph McCarthy and Harry Carroll; "Red Wing" by Kerry Mills and Thurland Chattaway and "Go Tell Aunt Rhody." [1] Also in SEVEN DAYS LEAVE. [2] Jim and Marion Jordan.

2450 ◆ THE HEAVENLY KID
Orion, 1985

Musical Score Ramsey, Kennard

Producer(s) Engelberg, Mort
Director(s) Medoway, Cary
Screenwriter(s) Medoway, Cary; Copeland, Martin

Cast Smith, Lewis; Gedrick, Jason; Kaczmarek, Jane; Mulligan, Richard; Metcalf, Mark

Song(s) Hamburgers (C/L: Duke, George); Dream Machine (C/L: Goodrum, Randy); Crusin' Tonight (C/L: Goodrum, Randy; Duke, George); Mean to Me (C/L: Duke, George); So Far Away (C/L: Sinnamon, Shandi); The Heavenly Kid (Out on the Edge) (C/L: Goodrum, Randy; Duke, George)

Notes No cue sheet available.

2451 ◆ HEAVEN WITH A GUN
Metro–Goldwyn–Mayer, 1969

Musical Score Mandel, Johnny

Producer(s) King, Frank; King, Maurice
Director(s) Katzin, Lee H.
Screenwriter(s) Carr, Richard

Cast Ford, Glenn; Jones, Carolyn; Hershey, Barbara; Anderson, John; Carradine, David; Beery Jr., Noah; Townes, Harry; Cannon, J.D.

Song(s) A Lonely Place (C: Mandel, Johnny; L: Webster, Paul Francis)

2452 ◆ HEAVY METAL
Columbia, 1981

Musical Score Bernstein, Elmer

Producer(s) Reitman, Ivan; Vogel, Leonard
Director(s) Potterton, Gerald
Screenwriter(s) Goldberg, Dan; Blum, Len
Source(s) stories and original art by Corben, Richard; McKie, Angus; O'Bannon, Dan; Warkentin, Thomas; Wrightson, Berni
Voices Bumpass, Roger; Burroughs, Jackie; Candy, John; Flaherty, Joe; Francks, Don; Lavut, Martin; Levy,

Eugene; Playten, Alice; Ramis, Harold; Lightstone, Marilyn; Vernon, John

Song(s) All of You (C/L: Felder, Don); Heavy Metal (Takin' a Ride) (C/L: Felder, Don); Heavy Metal (C/L: Hagar, Sammy; Peterik, Jim); The Mog Rulse (C/L: Butler, Terence; Dio, Ronnie James; Iommi, Anthony); Veteran of the Sychic Wars (C/L: Bloom, Eric; Moorcock, Michael); Reach Out (C/L: James, Robert; Comita, Pete); I Must Be Dreamin' (C/L: Nielsen, Rick); True Companion (C/L: Fagen, Donald); Radar Rider (C/L: Riggs, Jerry; Jordan, Marc); Heartbeat (C/L: Riggs, Jerry); Crazy? (A Suitable Cast for Treatment) (C/L: McCafferty, Dan; Agnew, Pete; Charlton, Manny; Sweet, Darrel)

Notes No cue sheet available. An animated feature.

2453 ✦ HEDDA HOPPER'S HOLLYWOOD (NO. 1)
Paramount, 1941

Cast Kay Kyser and His Orchestra

Song(s) Alexander the Swoose (C/L: Forrest, Ben; Loon; Keller)

Notes Short subject.

2454 ✦ HEDDA HOPPER'S HOLLYWOOD (NO. 2)
Paramount, 1941

Song(s) Mocambo (C: Ohman, Phil; L: Carling, Foster)

Notes Short subject.

2455 ✦ HEIDI (1937)
Twentieth Century–Fox, 1937

Composer(s) Pollack, Lew
Lyricist(s) Mitchell, Sidney D.

Producer(s) Zanuck, Darryl F.
Director(s) Dwan, Allan
Screenwriter(s) Ferris, Walter; Josephson, Julien
Source(s) *Heidi* (novel) Spyri, Johanna

Cast Temple, Shirley; Hersholt, Jean; Treacher, Arthur; Westley, Helen; Moore, Pauline; Nash, Mary; Blackmer, Sidney; Christians, Mady; Rumann, Sig

Song(s) In Our Little Wooden Shoes

2456 ✦ HEIDI (1968)
Warner Brothers, 1968

Musical Score Grothe, Franz

Producer(s) Schwetter, Karl; Deutsch, Richard
Director(s) Jacobs, Werner
Screenwriter(s) Schweitzer, Richard
Source(s) *Heidi* (novel) Spyri, Johanna

Cast Singhammer, Eva Maria; Mittermayr, Gertraud; Knuth, Gustav; Ledl, Lotte; Schroder, Ernst; Throoger, Margot

Song(s) Heidi (C: Grothe, Franz; L: Styne, Stanley); Echo Mountain Song (C: Charlap, Moose; L: Styne, Stanley)

Notes English dubbing by Michael Haller.

2457 ✦ HEIDI'S SONG
Paramount, 1982

Musical Score Curtin, Hoyt S.
Composer(s) Lane, Burton
Lyricist(s) Cahn, Sammy

Producer(s) Barbera, Joseph; Hanna, William
Director(s) Taylor, Robert
Screenwriter(s) Barbera, Joseph; Brewer, Jameson; Taylor, Robert
Voices Greene, Lorne; Davis Jr., Sammy; Gray, Margery; Bell, Michael; Cullen, Peter; Feld, Fritz

Song(s) Wunderhorn; Heidi; Good At Making Friends; A Christmas-y Day; She's a Nothing; An Armful of Sunshine; Can You Imagine?; An Un-kind Word; That's What Friends Are For; Ode to a Rat; Nightmare Ballet (inst.)

Notes Animated feature.

2458 ✦ THE HEIRESS
Paramount, 1949

Musical Score Copland, Aaron

Producer(s) Wyler, William
Director(s) Wyler, William
Screenwriter(s) Goetz, Ruth; Goetz, Augustus
Source(s) *The Heiress* (play) Goetz, Ruth; Goetz, Augustus

Cast de Havilland, Olivia; Clift, Montgomery; Richardson, Ralph; Hopkins, Miriam; Brown, Vanessa; Freeman, Mona

Song(s) My Love Loves Me [1] (C/L: Livingston, Jay; Evans, Ray); Plaisir D'Amour [2] (C/L: Martini, G.B.)

Notes [1] Song written for exploitation only. Based on "Plasir D'Amour." [2] Sung by Montgomery Clift's character. This is a public domain song.

2459 ✦ HE KNOWS YOU'RE ALONE
Metro–Goldwyn–Mayer, 1980

Musical Score Peskanov, Mark; Peskanov, Alexander
Composer(s) Peskanov, Mark; Peskanov, Alexander
Lyricist(s) Napoli, Jeanne; Roggeman, deBorge

Producer(s) Manasse, George
Director(s) Mastroianni, Armand
Screenwriter(s) Parker, Scott

Cast Scardino, Don; O'Heaney, Caitlin; Kemp, Elizabeth; Pease, Patsy; Rebhorn, James; Hanks, Tom; Barron, Dana; Rolfing, Tom

Song(s) Mysterious Lover; I'll Never Tie You Down; It's the Night Again (L: Wells, Brooksie)

Notes Originally titled BLOOD WEDDING.

2460 ◆ HE LAUGHED LAST
Columbia, 1956

Musical Score Morton, Arthur

Producer(s) Taps, Jonie
Director(s) Edwards, Blake
Screenwriter(s) Edwards, Blake

Cast Laine, Frankie; Marlow, Lucy; Dexter, Anthony; Long, Dick; Reed, Alan; White, Jesse; Ames, Florenz

Song(s) Save Your Sorrows (C/L: Morton, Arthur); Strike Me Pink (C/L: Morton, Arthur)

Notes No cue sheet available. There is also a vocal of "Danny Boy."

2461 ◆ HELDORADO
Republic, 1946

Composer(s) Elliott, Jack
Lyricist(s) Elliott, Jack

Producer(s) White, Edward J.
Director(s) Witney, William
Screenwriter(s) Geraghty, Gerald; Zimet, Julian

Cast Rogers, Roy; Trigger; Hayes, George "Gabby"; Evans, Dale; Bob Nolan and the Sons of the Pioneers

Song(s) Heldorado; Silver Stars, Purple Sage, Eyes of Blue (C/L: Darling, Denver); My Saddle Pals and I (C/L: Rogers, Roy); Good Neighbor; You Ain't Heard Nothin' Till You Hear Him Roar [1] (C/L: Nolan, Bob)

Notes [1] BMI list only.

2462 ◆ THE HELEN MORGAN STORY
Warner Brothers, 1957

Choreographer(s) Prinz, LeRoy

Producer(s) Rackin, Martin
Director(s) Curtiz, Michael
Screenwriter(s) Saul, Oscar; Riesner, Dean; Longstreet, Stephen; Gidding, Nelson

Cast Blyth, Ann [1]; Newman, Paul; Carlson, Richard; Evans, Gene; Williams, Cara; Vincent, Virginia; King, Walter Woolf; Green, Dorothy; Platt, Edward; Douglas, Warren; White, Sammy; The DeCastro Sisters; McHugh, Jimmy; Vallee, Rudy; Winchell, Walter

Notes Released in Great Britain as BOTH ENDS OF THE CANDLE. None of the songs were written for the movie. Some are briefly included in medleys. Vocals include: "If You Were the Only Girl in the World" by Clifford Grey and Nat D. Ayer; "Avalon" by Vincent Rose, Al Jolson and B.G. DeSylva; "The Girl Friend" by Richard Rodgers and Lorenz Hart; "The One I Love Belongs to Somebody Else" by Isham Jones and Gus Kahn (also in the Republic picture THE LAST CROOKED MILE); "Love Nest" by Louis A. Hirsch and Otto Harbach; "Bye Bye Blackbird" by Ray Henderson and Mort Dixon; "Do Do Do," "Someone to Watch Over Me," "Somebody Loves Me" and "The Man I Love" by George and Ira Gershwin; "Breezin' Along with the Breeze" by Richard A. Whiting, Haven Gillespie and Seymour Simons; "My Time Is Your Time" by Eric Little and Leo Dance; "On the Sunny Side of the Street" by Jimmy McHugh and Dorothy Fields; "I Want to Be Happy" by Vincent Youmans and Irving Caesar; "Charleston" by Cecil Mack and Jimmy Johnson: "Why Was I Born" and "Can't Help Lovin Dat Man" by Jerome Kern and Oscar Hammerstein II; "Deep Night" by Rudy Vallee and Charles Henderson; "April in Paris" by Vernon Duke and E.Y. Harburg; "Sweet Georgia Brown" by Ben Bernie, Maceo Pinkard and Kenneth Casey; "Bill" by Jerome Kern, Oscar Hammerstein II and P.G. Wodehouse and "You Do Something to Me" by Cole Porter. [1] Dubbed by Gogi Grant.

2463 ◆ HELL AND HIGH WATER
Paramount, 1933

Director(s) Jones, Grover; McNutt, William Slavens
Screenwriter(s) Leahy, Agnes Brand

Cast Arlen, Richard; Allen, Judith; Standing, Sir Guy; Grapewin, Charley; Frawley, William

Song(s) Hell and High Water [2] (C: Johnston, Arthur; L: Coslow, Sam); Learn to Croon [1] (C: Johnston, Arthur; L: Coslow, Sam; Holden, Eddie); You Threw Me Overboard [2] (C/L: Coslow, Sam)

Notes Titled CAP'N JERICHO in Great Britain. [1] There were comedy lyrics by Eddie Holden. Also in COLLEGE HUMOR and TOO MUCH HARMONY. [2] Not used.

2464 ◆ HELL CANYON OUTLAWS
Allied Artists, 1957

Director(s) Landres, Paul

Cast Robertson, Dale; Keith, Brian; Rossana, Rory; Kallman, Dick; Baer, Buddy

Song(s) Tall Trouble (C/L: Kallman, Dick)

Notes Originally titled STORM OUT OF THE WEST.

2465 ◆ HELLER IN PINK TIGHTS
Paramount, 1960

Musical Score Amfitheatrof, Daniele

Producer(s) Ponti, Carlo; Girosi, Marcello
Director(s) Cukor, George
Screenwriter(s) Bernstein, Walter; Nichols, Dudley
Source(s) *Heller with a Gun* (novel) L'Amour, Louis

2472 ✦ HELLO, EVERYBODY

Cast Loren, Sophia; Quinn, Anthony; Forrest, Steve; Heckart, Eileen; O'Brien, Margaret; Novarro, Ramon; Lowe, Edmund

Song(s) Angela (C: Amfitheatrof, Daniele); Beware [1] (C: Offenbach, Jacques; L: Brooks, Jack); Love, Lovely Love [3] (C/L: Deutsch, Adolph)

Notes Formerly titled HELLER WITH A GUN. [1] Music from LA BELLE HELENE. [3] Not used. Also not used in THE MATCHMAKER.

2466 ✦ THE HELLIONS
Columbia, 1962

Musical Score Adler, Larry

Producer(s) Huth, Harold
Director(s) Annakin, Ken
Screenwriter(s) Swanton, Harold; Kirwan, Patrick; Huth, Harold

Cast Todd, Richard; Aubrey, Anne; Uys, Jamie; Wilde, Marty; Jeffries, Lionel; Walker, Zena; Blakely, Colin

Song(s) The Hellions (C: Adler, Larry; L: Kretzmer, Herbert; Adler, Larry)

Notes No cue sheet available.

2467 ✦ HELL NIGHT
Compass International, 1981

Musical Score Wyman, Dan

Producer(s) Yablans, Irwin; Curtis, Bruce Cohn
Director(s) DeSimone, Tom
Screenwriter(s) Feldman, Randolph

Cast Blair, Linda; Van Patten, Vincent; Barton, Peter; Brophy, Kevin; Neumann, Jenny; Goodwin, Suki; Sturtevant, Jimmy

Song(s) Look Out (C: Wyman, Dan; L: Walter, Bob)

Notes No cue sheet available.

2468 ✦ HELLO ANNAPOLIS
Columbia, 1942

Director(s) Barton, Charles
Screenwriter(s) Davis, Donald; Reed, Tom; Wisberg, Aubrey

Cast Parks, Larry; Stevens, Robert; Brown, Stanley; Brown, Tom; Parker, Jean; Hall, Thurston; Caine, Georgia; Busch, Mae

Song(s) Captain My Captain (L: Stoloff, Morris)

Notes The song is based on a traditional work. Nico Grigor is credited on the cue sheets and some sources for this and other works. However, in each case an addendum on the cue sheet states: "Grigor actually had nothing to do with writing these works but his name was placed on the cue sheet to facilitate collection of performance royalties."

2469 ✦ HELLO BEAUTIFUL

See THE POWERS GIRL.

2470 ✦ HELLO, DOLLY!
Twentieth Century–Fox, 1969

Composer(s) Herman, Jerry
Lyricist(s) Herman, Jerry
Choreographer(s) Kidd, Michael

Producer(s) Lehman, Ernest
Director(s) Kelly, Gene
Screenwriter(s) Lehman, Ernest
Source(s) *Hello, Dolly!* (musical) Herman, Jerry; Stewart, Michael

Cast Streisand, Barbra; Matthau, Walter; Crawford, Michael; Armstrong, Louis; McAndrew, Marianne; Peaker, E.J.; Lockin, Danny; Tune, Tommy; Feld, Fritz; O'Malley, J. Pat

Song(s) Call on Dolly [1]; Just Leave Everything to Me; It Takes a Woman [1]; Put On Your Sunday Clothes [1]; Ribbons Down My Back [1]; Dancing [1]; Before the Parade Passes By [1]; Elegance [1]; Love Is Only Love; Hello, Dolly [1]; It Only Takes a Moment [1]; So Long, Dearie [1]

Notes [1] From original musical.

2471 ✦ HELLO, DOWN THERE
Paramount, 1969

Musical Score Barry, Jeff
Composer(s) Barry, Jeff
Lyricist(s) Barry, Jeff

Producer(s) Sherman, George
Director(s) Arnold, Jack
Screenwriter(s) McGreevey, John; Telford, Frank

Cast Randall, Tony; Leigh, Janet; Backus, Jim; McDowall, Roddy; Dreyfuss, Richard; Berry, Ken; Rae, Charlotte; Cole, Kay; Stang, Arnold; Lembeck, Harvey; Griffin, Merv; Meredith, Lee; Backus, Henny; Henning, Pat

Song(s) I Can Love You; Hey, Little Goldfish; Glub; Hello, Down There

Notes Re-released as SUB-A-DUB-DUB in 1974.

2472 ✦ HELLO, EVERYBODY
Paramount, 1933

Composer(s) Johnston, Arthur
Lyricist(s) Coslow, Sam

Director(s) Seiter, William A.
Screenwriter(s) Yost, Dorothy; Hazard, Lawrence

Cast Smith, Kate; Scott, Randolph; Blane, Sally; Gordon, Julia Swayne; Barbier, George; Grapewin, Charley; Collins, Ted [2]

THE COMPLETE MUSICAL COMPANION

Song(s) When the Moon Comes Over the Mountain [1] (C: Woods, Harry; L: Johnson, Howard); Moon Song (That Wasn't Meant for Me); Out in the Great Open Spaces; Twenty Million People; Pickaninnies' Heaven; My Queen of Lullaby Land

Notes Originally titled QUEEN OF THE AIR and later MOON SONG. "Dinah" by Harry Akst, Joe Lewis and Joe Young is also interpolated into the score. [1] Also in THE BIG BROADCAST and DINNER AT EIGHT (MGM) and was Kate Smith's radio theme song. Smith later took partial credit for writing this song. She had nothing to do with its writing. [2] This was Smith's business manager, the same part he played in the film.

2473 ✦ HELLO, FRISCO, HELLO
Twentieth Century–Fox, 1943

Choreographer(s) Raset, Val

Producer(s) Sperling, Milton
Director(s) Humberstone, H. Bruce
Screenwriter(s) Ellis, Robert; Logan, Helen; Macaulay, Richard

Cast Faye, Alice; Payne, John; Oakie, Jack; Bari, Lynn; Cregar, Laird; Havoc, June; Bond, Ward; Mather, Aubrey; Barbier, George; Bonanova, Fortunio

Song(s) You'll Never Know (C: Warren, Harry; L: Gordon, Mack); I've Got a Gal in Ev'ry Port (C: Henderson, Charles; L: Gordon, Mack); Grizzly Bear [1] (C: Botsford, George; L: Botsford, George; Gordon, Mack); I Gotta Have You [2] (C: Warren, Harry; L: Gordon, Mack)

Notes Vocals of over a minute include "Hello, Frisco! I Called You Up to Say 'Hello!'" by Louis A. Hirsch and Gene Buck; "By the Watermelon Vine (Lindy Lou)" by Thomas S. Allen; "Yield Not to Temptation" by Horatio R. Palmer; "Ragtime Cowboy Joe" by Maurice Abrahams, Lewis F. Muir and Grant Clarke; "Sweet Cider Time When You Were Mine" by Percy Wenrich; "In the Shade of the Old Apple Tree" by Egbert Van Alstyne and Harry Williams; "It's Tulip Time in Holland (Two Lips Are Calling Me)" by Richard A. Whiting and Dave Radford; "They Always Pick on Me" by Harry Von Tilzer and Stanley Murphy; "Bedelia" by Jean Schwartz and William Jerome; "By the Light of the Silvery Moon" by Gus Edwards and Edward Madden and "Gee, But It's Great to Meet a Friend from Your Home Town" by James McGavisk and William Tracey. [1] Special lyrics by Gordon. [2] Recorded but not used.

2474 ✦ HELLO—GOODBYE
Twentieth Century–Fox, 1970

Musical Score Lai, Francis

Producer(s) Hakim, Andre
Director(s) Negulesco, Jean
Screenwriter(s) Marshall, Roger

Cast Crawford, Michael; Jurgens, Curt; Gilles, Genevieve; Furstenberg, Ira; Pickles, Vivian

Song(s) No Need to Cry (C: Lai, Francis; Leggert, A.); Hello—Goodbye [1] (C: Lai, Francis; L: Dugati, Giovanni)

Notes Titled HELLO GOODBYE in some sources. [1] Lyric written for exploitation only.

2475 ✦ HELLO SISTER
Sono-Art World Wide Pictures, 1930

Composer(s) Columbo, Russ; Gordean, Jack
Lyricist(s) Columbo, Russ; Gordean, Jack
Choreographer(s) Kusell, Maurice L.

Producer(s) Cruze, James
Director(s) Lang, Walter
Screenwriter(s) Marlow, Brian
Source(s) "Clipped Wings" (story) Lambert, Rita

Cast Borden, Olive; Hughes, Lloyd; Fawcett, George; Rosing, Bodil; Peck, Norman

Song(s) What Good Am I Without You

Notes No cue sheet available.

2476 ✦ HELL'S BELLS
Fox, 1930

Composer(s) Monaco, James V.
Lyricist(s) Friend, Cliff

Song(s) I Do It with My Oo-La-La-La-La; A Song of Love Is Singing in My Heart

Notes Short subject.

2477 ✦ HELL'S HALF ACRE
Republic, 1953

Producer(s) Auer, John H.
Director(s) Auer, John H.
Screenwriter(s) Fisher, Steve

Cast Corey, Wendell; Keyes, Evelyn; Lanchester, Elsa; Windsor, Marie; Luke, Keye

Song(s) Polynesian Rhapsody [1] (C/L: Fisher, Steve; Pitman, Jack); Lani (C/L: Pitman, Jack)

Notes [1] Fisher not credited on sheet music.

2478 ✦ HELL'S HIGHWAY
RKO, 1932

Director(s) Brown, Rowland
Screenwriter(s) Ornitz, Samuel; Tasker, Robert; Brown, Rowland

Cast Dix, Richard; Brown, Tom; Hudson, Rochelle; Gordon, C. Henry; Apfel, Oscar; Fields, Stanley; Middleton, Charles; Muse, Clarence; Knight, Fuzzy

Song(s) Liberty Road (C/L: Muse, Clarence); The Load Is Heavy (C/L: Snyder, Ted)

Notes Cue sheet does not differentiate between vocals and instrumentals.

2479 ✦ HELL'S OUTPOST
Republic, 1954

Musical Score Butts, Dale

Producer(s) Kane, Joseph
Director(s) Kane, Joseph
Screenwriter(s) Gamet, Kenneth
Source(s) *Silver Rock* (novel) Short, Luke [1]

Cast Cameron, Rod; Leslie, Joan; Wills, Chill; Russell, John; Davis, Jim; MacLane, Barton

Song(s) Packin' the Mail (C/L: Wills, Chill)

Notes [1] Pseudonym of Frederick Dilley Glidden.

2480 ✦ THE HELL WITH HEROES
Universal, 1968

Musical Score Jones, Quincy

Producer(s) Chase, Stanley
Director(s) Sargent, Joseph
Screenwriter(s) Welles, Halsted; Livingston, Harold

Cast Taylor, Rod; Deuel, Peter; Guardino, Harry; McCarthy, Kevin; Cardinale, Claudia

Song(s) Where There Is Love (C: Jones, Quincy; L: Fields, Dorothy)

2481 ✦ HELLZAPOPPIN'
Universal, 1941

Musical Score Skinner, Frank
Composer(s) de Paul, Gene
Lyricist(s) Raye, Don
Choreographer(s) Castle, Nick

Producer(s) Levey, Jules
Director(s) Potter, H.C.
Screenwriter(s) Perrin, Nat; Wilson, Warren
Source(s) *Hellzapoppin'* (musical) Tobias, Charles; Olsen, Ole; Johnson, Chic

Cast Johnson, Chic; Olsen, Ole; Lane, Richard; Slim and Slam; Raye, Martha; Paige, Robert; Frazee, Jane; Howard, Lewis; Auer, Mischa; Herbert, Hugh; Howard, Shemp; Kolb, Clarence; Cook Jr., Elisha

Song(s) You Were There (C: de Paul, Gene; Schoen, Vic); Hellzapoppin'; What Kind of Love Is This?; Heaven for Two; Watch the Birdie; Congeroo; Puttin' on the Dog; Conga Beso

Notes There is also a vocal of "Waiting for the Robert E. Lee" by L. Wolfe Gilbert and Lewis F. Muir.

2482 ✦ HELP!
United Artists, 1965

Musical Score Thorne, Ken
Composer(s) McCartney, Paul; Lennon, John
Lyricist(s) McCartney, Paul; Lennon, John

Producer(s) Shenson, Walter
Director(s) Lester, Richard
Screenwriter(s) Wood, Charles; Behm, Marc

Cast McCartney, Paul [1]; Lennon, John [1]; Harrison, George [1]; Starr, Ringo [1]; McKern, Leo; Bron, Eleanor; Spinetti, Victor

Song(s) Help; You're Gonna Lose That Girl; You've Got to Hide Your Love Away; Ticket to Ride; I Need You (C/L: Harrison, George); She's a Woman; The Night Before; Another Girl; From Me to You; You Can't Do That; Can't Buy Me Love; Hard Day's Night; Happy Just to Dance with You; Tell Me What You See [2]

Notes This cue sheet is very confusing. Vocals and instrumentals are not delineated. [1] Members of the Beatles. [2] Sheet music only.

2483 ✦ HE MARRIED HIS WIFE
Twentieth Century–Fox, 1939

Producer(s) Zanuck, Darryl F.
Director(s) Del Ruth, Roy
Screenwriter(s) Hellman, Sam; Ware, Darrell

Cast McCrea, Joel; Kelly, Nancy; Young, Roland; Boland, Mary; Romero, Cesar; Healy, Mary; Talbot, Lyle; Cook Jr., Elisha

Song(s) Was It You There in My Arms (C/L: Burton, Val; Jason, Will)

2484 ✦ HENRY ALDRICH—BOY SCOUT
Paramount, 1944

Composer(s) Lee, Lester
Lyricist(s) Seelen, Jerry

Producer(s) Kraike, Michel
Director(s) Bennett, Hugh
Screenwriter(s) Bolton, Muriel Roy

Cast Lydon, Jimmy; Smith, Charles; Blakeney, Olive; Litel, John; Watson, Minor; Hickman, Darryl

Song(s) Campfire; Marching Along; Our Daily Deed [1]

Notes Originally called HENRY ALDRICH'S CODE OF HONOR. [1] Not included.

2485 ✦ HENRY ALDRICH, EDITOR
Paramount, 1942

Musical Score Shuken, Leo

Producer(s) Schermer, Jules
Director(s) Bennett, Hugh
Screenwriter(s) Burton, Val; Bolton, Muriel Roy

Cast Lydon, Jimmy; Smith, Charles; Quigley, Rita; Litel, John; Blakeney, Olive

Song(s) Centerville High Alma Mater [1] (C: Young, Victor; L: Burton, Val)

Notes [1] Also in HENRY ALDRICH FOR PRESIDENT.

2486 ✦ HENRY ALDRICH FOR PRESIDENT

See HENRY FOR PRESIDENT.

2487 ✦ HENRY ALDRICH SWINGS IT
Paramount, 1943

Producer(s) Kraike, Michel
Director(s) Bennett, Hugh
Screenwriter(s) Burton, Val; Bolton, Muriel Roy; Leslie, Aleen

Cast Lydon, Jimmy; Smith, Charles; Blakeney, Olive; Litel, John; Feld, Fritz; Chandler, Mimi; Hudson, Beverly

Song(s) Ding Dong, Sing a Song [1] (C: Styne, Jule; L: Gannon, Kim)

Notes [1] Written for but not used in SALUTE FOR THREE.

2488 ✦ HENRY AND DIZZY
Paramount, 1942

Musical Score Harline, Leigh

Producer(s) Siegel, Sol C.
Director(s) Bennett, Hugh
Screenwriter(s) Burton, Val

Cast Lydon, Jimmy; Smith, Charles; Anderson, Mary; Litel, John; Blakeney, Olive; Howland, Olin; Switzer, Carl "Alfalfa"; Neill, Noel

Song(s) Sailing Along on Lake Wapacotapotalong (C/L: Burton, Val)

Notes Originally titled HERE COMES HENRY ALDRICH and MR. ALDRICH'S BOY.

2489 ✦ HENRY FOR PRESIDENT
Paramount, 1941

Producer(s) Siegel, Sol C.
Director(s) Bennett, Hugh
Screenwriter(s) Burton, Val

Cast Lydon, Jimmy; Preisser, June; Anderson, Mary; Smith, Charles; Litel, John; Peterson, Dorothy; Bacon, Irving

Song(s) Johnny Jones (C: Barris, Harry; L: Loesser, Frank); Battle Hymn of the Republic (C: Howe, Julia Ward; L: Sistrom, Joe); Centerville Alma Mater [1] (C: Young, Victor; L: Burton, Val)

Notes Also titled HENRY ALDRICH FOR PRESIDENT. [1] Also in HENRY ALDRICH, EDITOR.

2490 ✦ HERBIE GOES BANANAS
Disney, 1980

Musical Score De Vol, Frank; Steiner, Fred; Pleis, Jack
Composer(s) De Vol, Frank
Lyricist(s) De Vol, Frank

Producer(s) Miller, Ron
Director(s) McEveety, Vincent
Screenwriter(s) Tait, Don

Cast Leachman, Cloris; Smith, Charles Martin; Vernon, John; Burns, Stephan W.; Davalos, Elyssa; Garay III, Joaquin; Korman, Harvey; Jaeckel, Richard; Rocco, Alex

Song(s) I Found a New Friend; Look at Me (One Look at Me)

2491 ✦ HER BODYGUARD
Paramount, 1933

Composer(s) Johnston, Arthur
Lyricist(s) Coslow, Sam

Producer(s) Schulberg, B.P.
Director(s) Beaudine, William
Screenwriter(s) Spence, Ralph; De Leon, Walter; Partos, Frank; Martin, Francis

Cast Arnold, Edward; Gibson, Wynne; Lowe, Edmund; Hines, Johnny; Dinehart, Alan; Knight, Fuzzy; White, Marjorie

Song(s) Opening of Act; Where Have I Heard that Melody [1]; Her Bodyguard [2]

Notes [1] Based on a melody by Shubert. Also in TOO MUCH HARMONY. [2] Not used.

2492 ✦ HER CARDBOARD LOVER
Metro–Goldwyn–Mayer, 1942

Musical Score Waxman, Franz

Producer(s) Ruben, J. Walter
Director(s) Cukor, George
Screenwriter(s) Deval, Jacques; Collier, John; Veiller, Anthony; Wright, William H.
Source(s) (play) Deval, Jacques

Cast Shearer, Norma; Taylor, Robert; Sanders, George; McHugh, Frank; Patterson, Elizabeth; Wills, Chill

Song(s) Casino Sequence (C: Waxman, Franz; L: Ruffino, Carlos; Ruffino, Mercedes); I Dare You (C: Lane, Burton; L: Freed, Ralph); Always and Always [1] (C/L: Ward, Edward; L: Forrest, Chet; Wright, Bob); With Your Looks and My Brains [2] (C: Lane, Burton; L: Freed, Ralph)

Notes The source was first translated and given its title by Valerie Wyngate. A later revision was by P.G. Wodehouse. The play had been filmed twice before, in 1928 and 1932. This was Norma Shearer's last film appearance. [1] Also in MANNEQUIN (1938). [2] Not used.

2493 ✦ HER DILEMMA

See CONFESSIONS OF A CO-ED.

2494 ✦ HERE COMES CARTER
Warner Brothers (First National), 1936

Composer(s) Jerome, M.K.
Lyricist(s) Scholl, Jack

Producer(s) Foy, Bryan
Director(s) Clemens, William
Screenwriter(s) Chanslor, Roy
Source(s) "The Lowdown" (story) Jacoby, Michel

Cast Alexander, Ross; Farrell, Glenda; Nagel, Anne; Cavanaugh, Hobart; Reynolds, Craig; Stone, George E.; Sheehan, John; Crehan, Joseph

Song(s) You on My Mind [1]; Through the Courtesy of Love [1]

Notes No cue sheet available. Released in Great Britain as THE VOICE OF SCANDAL. [1] Also in THE TATTLER.

2495 ✦ HERE COMES COOKIE
Paramount, 1935

Producer(s) LeBaron, William
Director(s) McLeod, Norman Z.
Screenwriter(s) Mintz, Sam; Hartman, Don

Cast Allen, Gracie; Burns, George; Barbier, George; Furness, Betty; Tombes, Andrew; Bacon, Irving; Powell, Jack

Song(s) Here Comes Cookie [2] (C/L: Gordon, Mack); The Vamp of the Pampas [1] (C: Whiting, Richard A.; L: Robin, Leo)

Notes The production was titled THE PLOT THICKENS and SOUP TO NUTS. It was released as THE PLOT THICKENS in Great Britain. [1] Not used except as background, but it was recorded with Gracie Allen and published. *Variety* does review the song. [2] Also in LOVE IN BLOOM.

2496 ✦ HERE COMES ELMER
Republic, 1943

Producer(s) Schaefer, Armand
Director(s) Santley, Joseph
Screenwriter(s) Davis, Stanley; Townley, Jack

Cast Pearce, Al; Stuart, Gloria; Harris, Arlene; Albertson, Frank; Wright, Will; Cochrane, Nick; Tomlin, Pinky; Vernon, Wally; Comstock, William; Evans, Dale; Auerbach, Arthur [1]; Jan Garber and His Band; The King Cole Trio; Greene, Harrison

Song(s) Egga Dagga [2] (C/L: Cochrane, Nick C.); Straighten Up and Fly Right (C/L: Cole, Nat "King"); You're So Good to Me (C: Styne, Jule; L: Cahn, Sammy); Don't Be Afraid to Tell Your Mother (C/L: Tomlin, Pinky; Grier, Jesse; Poe, Coy); Hitch Old Dobbin to the Shay Again (C/L: Lewis Jr., J.C.; Conlon, Jud)

Notes There are also vocals of "Put on Your Old Grey Bonnet" by Stanley Murphy and Percy Wenrich and "Your Eyes Have Told Me So" by Gus Kahn, Egbert van Alstyne and Walter Blaufuss. [1] Billed as Artie. [2] Also in SEVEN SINNERS (Universal) and HOLY TERROR (20th) both also credited to Nick Cochrane and in MGM's HOLLYWOOD PARTY IN TECHNICOLOR where it's credited to Jean Bouquet and Dorcas Cochrane.

2497 ✦ HERE COMES THE BAND
Metro–Goldwyn–Mayer, 1935

Musical Score Ward, Edward
Composer(s) Lane, Burton
Lyricist(s) Adamson, Harold
Choreographer(s) Hale, Chester

Producer(s) Hubbard, Lucien
Director(s) Sloane, Paul
Screenwriter(s) Sloane, Paul; Spence, Ralph; Mansfield, Victor

Cast Ted Lewis and His Orchestra; Bruce, Virginia; Stockwell, Harry; Healy, Ted; Richards, Addison; McFarland, George "Spanky"; Roach, Bert; Gilbert, Billy

Song(s) Headin' Home (C: Stothart, Herbert; L: Washington, Ned); I'm Bound for Heaven; The Army Band; You're My Thrill (L: Washington, Ned); Tender Is the Night (C: Donaldson, Walter); Court Room Sequence (C/L: Stothart, Herbert); Here Comes the Band [1]

Notes There are also vocals of "Me and My Shadow" by Al Jolson, Billy Rose and Dave Dreyer; "Roll Along Prairie Moon" by Ted Fiorito, Albert Von Tilzer and Harry MacPherson (also in KING OF THE COWBOYS), as well as snippets of other twenties tunes. [1] Not used.

2498 ✦ HERE COMES THE GROOM (1934)
Paramount, 1934

Producer(s) Rogers, Charles R.
Director(s) Sedgwick, Edward
Screenwriter(s) Praskins, Leonard; Robinson, Casey

Cast Haley, Jack; Boland, Mary; Hamilton, Neil; Ellis, Patricia; Jewell, Isabel; Gray, Lawrence; Toler, Sidney; Bond, Ward; Treacher, Arthur

Song(s) I'll Blame the Waltz (Not You) (C: Revel, Harry; L: Gordon, Mack)

2499 ✦ HERE COMES THE GROOM (1951)
Paramount, 1951

Composer(s) Livingston, Jay; Evans, Ray
Lyricist(s) Livingston, Jay; Evans, Ray
Choreographer(s) O'Curran, Charles

Producer(s) Capra, Frank
Director(s) Capra, Frank
Screenwriter(s) Van Upp, Virginia; O'Brien, Liam; Connolly, Myles

Cast Crosby, Bing; Wyman, Jane; Smith, Alexis; Tone, Franchot; Barton, James; Alberghetti, Anna Maria; Keith, Robert; Gilchrist, Connie; Catlett, Walter; Reed, Alan; Warner, H.B.; Joy, Nicholas; Corby, Ellen; Bacon, Irving

Song(s) Your Own Little House; Misto Cristofo Columbo; What Shall We Do with the Drunken Sailor (C: Traditional); In the Cool, Cool, Cool of the Evening [2] (C: Carmichael, Hoagy; L: Mercer, Johnny); Bonne Nuit (Good Night); Haul Away, My Lou [1]; Lovely Weather for Ducks [1] [3]; Fa La Nana Bambin [1] (C: Sadero, Gini)

Notes First titled YOU BELONG TO ME. [1] Not used. [2] Written for unproduced film THE KEYSTONE GIRL. [3] Used in THE STARS ARE SINGING.

2500 ✦ HERE COMES THE NAVY
Warner Brothers, 1934

Producer(s) Edelman, Louis F.
Director(s) Bacon, Lloyd
Screenwriter(s) Baldwin, Karl; Markson, Ben

Cast Cagney, James; O'Brien, Pat; Stuart, Gloria; McHugh, Frank; Tree, Dorothy; Barrat, Robert

Song(s) Hey Sailor [1] (C: Fain, Sammy; L: Kahal, Irving)

Notes Originally titled HEY SAILOR. [1] Cue sheet indicates instrumental use only.

2501 ✦ HERE COME THE CO-EDS
Universal, 1945

Composer(s) Fairchild, Edgar
Lyricist(s) Brooks, Jack
Choreographer(s) Da Pron, Louis

Producer(s) Grant, John
Director(s) Yarbrough, Jean
Screenwriter(s) Horman, Arthur T.; Grant, John

Cast Abbott, Bud; Costello, Lou; Chaney Jr., Lon; Ryan, Peggy; Phil Spitalny and His All-Girl Orchestra; Evelyn Kaye and Her Magic Violin; O'Driscoll, Martha; Vincent, June; Cook, Donald; Dingle, Charles; Lane, Richard; Kirk, Joe

Song(s) Someday, We Will Remember; Let's Play House; I Don't Care If I Never Dream Again; Hooray for Our Side; Jumpin' on Saturday Night; A New Day [1]

Notes [1] Not used. Heard as background instrumental. Used in GIRL ON THE SPOT.

2502 ✦ HERE COME THE GIRLS
Paramount, 1953

Composer(s) Livingston, Jay; Evans, Ray
Lyricist(s) Livingston, Jay; Evans, Ray
Choreographer(s) Castle, Nick

Producer(s) Jones, Paul
Director(s) Binyon, Claude
Screenwriter(s) Hartmann, Edmund L.; Kanter, Hal

Cast Hope, Bob; Martin, Tony; Dahl, Arlene; Clooney, Rosemary; Mitchell, Millard; Demarest, William; Clark, Fred

Song(s) Girls; Ya Got Class; It's Tomorrow; When You Love Someone; Ali Baba (Be My Baby); Heavenly Days; See the Circus; Never So Beautiful; It's Torment; Who Sir, Me Sir? [1]; Laughs [2]; La-La-Lalapalooza [2]; The Show Starts Right Away [2]

Notes First titled GIRLS ARE HERE TO STAY and CHAMPAGNE FOR EVERYBODY. [1] Not used but was recorded by Bob Hope. [2] Not used.

2503 ✦ HERE COME THE TIGERS
American International, 1978

Musical Score Manfredini, Harry

Producer(s) Cunningham, Sean S.; Miner, Stephen
Director(s) Cunningham, Sean S.
Screenwriter(s) McCoy, Arch

Cast Lincoln, Richard; Zvanut, James; Grey, Samantha; Caldwell, William; Lieberman, Manny

Song(s) You Gotta Believe It (C/L: Manfredini, Harry); Buster's Theme (C: Manfredini, Harry; L: Briggs, John)

Notes No cue sheet available.

2504 ✦ HERE COME THE WAVES
Paramount, 1944

Composer(s) Arlen, Harold
Lyricist(s) Mercer, Johnny
Choreographer(s) Dare, Danny

Producer(s) Sandrich, Mark
Director(s) Sandrich, Mark

Screenwriter(s)   Scott, Allan; Englund, Ken; Myers, Zion

Cast   Crosby, Bing; Hutton, Betty; Tufts, Sonny; Doran, Ann; Neill, Noel; Clarke, Mae; Barris, Harry; Crawford, Gwen; Watson, Minor

Song(s)   Join the Navy; That Old Black Magic [3]; Let's Take the Long Way Home [2]; There's a Fella Waitin' in Poughkeepsie; I Promise You; Here Come the Waves; Ac-cent-tchu-ate the Positive; My Mama Thinks I'm a Star [1]; Got To Wear You Off My Weary Mind [1]; A Woman's Work Is Never Done [1]

Notes   First called SONG OF THE WAVES. There is also a rendition of the Burke and Van Heusen song "Moonlight Becomes You." [1] Not used but recorded. [2] Not used in OUT OF THIS WORLD. [3] Also in STAR-SPANGLED RHYTHM, RADIO STARS ON PARADE (RKO) and SENIOR PROM (Columbia).

2505 ✦ HERE IS MY HEART
Paramount, 1934

Composer(s)   Rainger, Ralph
Lyricist(s)   Robin, Leo

Producer(s)   Lighton, Louis D.
Director(s)   Tuttle, Frank
Screenwriter(s)   Mayer, Edwin Justus; Thompson, Harlan
Source(s)   *The Grand Duchess and the Waiter* (play) Savoir, Alfred

Cast   Crosby, Bing; Carlisle, Kitty; Young, Roland; Owen, Reginald; Parker, Cecilia; Skipworth, Alison; Frawley, William; Tamiroff, Akim

Song(s)   June in January; Love Is Just Around the Corner [4] (C: Gensler, Lewis E.); With Every Breath I Take [1]; (I Can't Imagine) Me Without You [2] [3] (C: Gensler, Lewis E.); I Knew [2] [3] (C: Gensler, Lewis E.); Here You Are [3]; We Can't Make a Monkey of the Moon [3]; You're a Blessing to Me [3] [5]

Notes   This is a remake of THE GRAND DUCHESS AND THE WAITER. [1] Rainger actually plays the piano for Crosby in music salon scene and for Kitty Carlisle in the hotel room scene. [2] Written for but not used in HER MASTER'S VOICE. Also not used in FOUR HOURS TO KILL and IT'S A GREAT LIFE. [3] Not used. [4] Not used in HER MASTER'S VOICE but also used in MILLIONS IN THE AIR. [5] Also not used in the following films: COCOANUT GROVE, FOUR HOURS TO KILL, GIVE ME A SAILOR and WAIKIKI WEDDING.

2506 ✦ HERE'S TO ROMANCE
Fox, 1935

Composer(s)   Conrad, Con
Lyricist(s)   Conrad, Con; Magidson, Herb

Producer(s)   Lasky, Jesse L.
Director(s)   Cruze, James
Screenwriter(s)   Pascal, Ernest; Levien, Sonya

Cast   Martini, Nino; Tobin, Genevieve; Louise, Anita

Song(s)   Here's to Romance; Midnight in Paris; Delusione (C/L: Sandoval, Miguel); I Carry You in My Pocket [1] (C/L: Grosvenor, Ralph); Midnight in Paris [1] (C: Conrad, Con; L: Magidson, Herb)

Notes   There is also a vocal of "Hunkadola" by Jack Yellen, Cliff Friend and Joseph Meyer from GEORGE WHITE'S SCANDALS OF 1935. Many classical pieces were also sung. [1] Sheet music only.

2507 ✦ HERE WE GO AGAIN
RKO, 1942

Composer(s)   Revel, Harry
Lyricist(s)   Greene, Mort

Producer(s)   Dwan, Allan
Director(s)   Dwan, Allan
Screenwriter(s)   Smith, Paul Gerard; Bigelow, Joe; Quinn, Don [1]; Klinker, Zeno [2]; Kingsley, Dorothy [2]; Foster, Royal [2]

Cast   Bergen, Edgar; McCarthy, Charlie; Fibber McGee and Molly; Peary, Harold; Simms, Ginny; Thompson, Bill; Gordon, Gale; Randolph, Isabel; Snerd, Mortimer

Song(s)   Delicious Delirium; Until I Live Again

Notes   [1] Material for Fibber McGee and Molly. [2] Material for Edgar Bergen.

2508 ✦ HERE WE GO ROUND THE MULBERRY BUSH
Lopert, 1968

Composer(s)   Spencer Davis Group, The
Lyricist(s)   Spencer Davis Group, The

Producer(s)   Donner, Clive
Director(s)   Donner, Clive
Screenwriter(s)   Davies, Hunter

Cast   Evans, Barry; Geeson, Judy; Scoular, Angela; White, Sheila; Audley, Maxine; Elliott, Denholm

Song(s)   Here We Go Round the Mulberry Bush (C/L: Winwood, Stevie; Traffic); Am I What I Was or Was I What I Am? (C/L: Winwood, Stevie; Traffic); Utterly Simple (C/L: Winwood, Stevie; Traffic); Possession; Every Little Thing; Taking Out Time; Pictures of Her; Just Like Me; Looking Back; Waltz for Caroline

Notes   No cue sheet available.

2509 ✦ HER FIRST ROMANCE
Monogram, 1940

Producer(s)   Chadwick, I.E.
Director(s)   Dmytryk, Edward

Screenwriter(s) Comandini, Adele
Source(s) *His First Daughter* (novel) Stratton-Porter, Gene

Cast Fellows, Edith; Evans, Wilbur; Wells, Jacqueline [1]; Ladd, Alan; Daniel, Roger; Linden, Judith; Kerby, Marion; Moreland, Alexandria; Sheldon, Julie

Song(s) Star of Love (C: Stone, Gregory; L: Caine, Charles)

Notes No cue sheet available. [1] Also known as Julie Bishop.

2510 ✦ HER HIGHNESS AND THE BELLBOY
Metro–Goldwyn–Mayer, 1945

Musical Score Stoll, George; Jackson, Calvin
Choreographer(s) Walters, Charles

Producer(s) Pasternak, Joe
Director(s) Thorpe, Richard
Screenwriter(s) Connell, Richard; Lehman, Gladys

Cast Lamarr, Hedy; Walker, Robert; Allyson, June; Esmond, Carl; Moorehead, Agnes; Ragland, Rags; Stossel, Ludwig; Cleveland, George

Song(s) Honey [1] (C/L: Whiting, Richard A.; Simons, Seymour; Gillespie, Haven); Dream (C: Stoll, George; Jackson, Calvin; L: Stoll, George; Connell, Richard; Lessy, Ben)

Notes There is also a vocal of "Wait Till the Sun Shines Nellie" by Harry Von Tilzer and Andrew B. Sterling. [1] Written in 1931.

2511 ✦ HER HUSBAND LIES
Paramount, 1937

Producer(s) Schulberg, B.P.
Director(s) Ludwig, Edward
Screenwriter(s) Smith, Wallace; Greene, Eve

Cast Cortez, Ricardo; Patrick, Gail; Brown, Tom; Tamiroff, Akim; Calhern, Louis; LaRue, Jack

Song(s) You Gambled with Love (C: Lane, Burton; L: Freed, Ralph); No More Tears [1] (C: Lane, Burton; L: Freed, Ralph)

Notes Previously titled BROADWAY GALLANT and later, LOVE TRAP. [1] Also in NIGHT CLUB SCANDAL.

2512 ✦ HERITAGE OF THE DESERT
Paramount, 1939

Producer(s) Sherman, Lowell
Director(s) Selander, Lesley
Screenwriter(s) Huston, Norman; Jacobs, Harrison
Source(s) *Heritage of the Desert* (novel) Grey, Zane

Cast Woods, Donald; Venable, Evelyn; Hayden, Russell; Barrat, Robert; Toler, Sidney

Song(s) Here's a Heart [1] (C: Young, Victor; L: Loesser, Frank)

Notes [1] The song is not used in the movie.

2513 ✦ HER JUNGLE LOVE
Paramount, 1938

Musical Score Stone, Gregory
Composer(s) Hollander, Frederick
Lyricist(s) Freed, Ralph

Producer(s) Arthur, George M.
Director(s) Archainbaud, George
Screenwriter(s) March, Joseph Moncure; Hayward, Lillie; Welch, Eddie

Cast Lamour, Dorothy; Milland, Ray; Overman, Lynne; Naish, J. Carrol; Hale, Jonathan; Earle, Edward

Song(s) Lovelight in the Starlight; Coffee and Kisses; Jungle Love (1) [1] [2] (C: Rainger, Ralph; L: Robin, Leo); Jungle Love (2) [1]

Notes [1] Not used. [2] Published though not used.

2514 ✦ HER KIND OF MAN
Warner Brothers, 1946

Musical Score Waxman, Franz

Producer(s) Gottlieb, Alex
Director(s) de Cordova, Frederick
Screenwriter(s) Kahn, Gordon; Atlas, Leopold
Source(s) "Melancholy" (story) Kern, James V.; Hoffman, Charles

Cast Clark, Dane; Paige, Janis; Scott, Zachary; Emerson, Faye; Tobias, George; Leonard, Sheldon

Song(s) Speak to Me of Love (C/L: Lenoir, Jean; Siever, Bruce)

Notes There are also vocals of "Something to Remember You By" by Arthur Schwartz and Howard Dietz (also in MGM's THE BAND WAGON and Fox's DANCING IN THE DARK) and "Body and Soul" by Johnny Green, Edward Heyman, Robert Sour, Frank Eyton and Howard Dietz (also in THE MAN I LOVE). It is not known if "Speak to Me of Love" was written for this film.

2515 ✦ HER LUCKY NIGHT
Universal, 1945

Producer(s) Wilson, Warren
Director(s) Lilley, Edward
Screenwriter(s) Bruckman, Clyde

Cast O'Driscoll, Martha; The Andrews Sisters; Beery Jr., Noah

Song(s) The Polka Polka (C/L: Manners, Maxine)

Notes There are also vocals of "Straighten Up and Fly Right" by Nat "King" Cole and Irving Mills; "Sing a

Tropical Song" by Frank Loesser and Jimmy McHugh; "Is You Is, Or Is You Ain't My Baby" by Louis Jordan and Billy Austin and "Dance with a Dolly" by Terry Shand, Jimmy Eaton and Mickey Leader.

2516 ✦ HER MAJESTY LOVE
Warner Brothers–First National, 1931

Composer(s) Jurmann, Walter
Lyricist(s) Dubin, Al

Director(s) Dieterle, William
Screenwriter(s) Lord, Robert; Caesar, Arthur; Blanke, Henry; Jackson, Joseph
Source(s) (play) Bernauer, R.; Oesterreicher, R.

Cast Miller, Marilyn; Lyon, Ben; Fields, W.C.; Errol, Leon; Sterling, Ford; Conklin, Chester; Stubbs, Harry; Wilson, Clarence; Holman, Harry

Song(s) You're Baby Minded Now; Because of You; Don't Ever Be Blue; Though You're Not the First One

Notes No cue sheet available.

2517 ✦ HERMAN AND KATNIP CARTOONS
Paramount, 1952

Composer(s) Carr, Leon
Lyricist(s) David, Hal

Song(s) Skiddle Diddle Dee—Skiddle Diddle Dey; Herman the Mouse

Notes Animated short subjects.

2518 ✦ HER MASTER'S VOICE
Paramount, 1936

Composer(s) Gensler, Lewis E. [1]
Lyricist(s) Robin, Leo [1]

Producer(s) Wanger, Walter
Director(s) Santley, Joseph
Screenwriter(s) Schary, Dore; Sauber, Harry
Source(s) *Her Master's Voice* (play) Kummer, Clare

Cast Horton, Edward Everett; Conklin, Peggy; Crews, Laura Hope [2]; Patterson, Elizabeth [2]; Mitchell, Grant; Coleman, Charles

Song(s) With All My Heart (C: McHugh, Jimmy; L: Kahn, Gus); I Knew [1] [3]; Lazy Bones Gotta Job Now [1] [4]; I Lost My Heart (and Found My Heart's Desire) [1] [4]; Minerva [1]; I Welcome You [1]; Honolulu Lulu [1]; Her Master's Voice [1]; Love Commands [1]; Completely [1]; You're Guilty [1]; No Account Noah [1]; Love Is Just Around the Corner [1] [5]; (I Can't Imagine) Me without You [1]

Notes "Down By the Old Mill Stream" by Dell Taylor is used extensively in the score. The movie was taken out of production in June of 1934, and the Robin and Gensler tunes were dropped. When it went back into production it was no long a musical film. [1] Not used.

[2] In original Broadway production. [3] Also not used in FOUR HOURS TO KILL, HERE IS MY HEART and IT'S A GREAT LIFE. [4] Used in IT'S A GREAT LIFE. [5] Used in HERE IS MY HEART and MILLIONS IN THE AIR.

2519 ✦ HERO AND THE TERROR
Cannon, 1988

Musical Score Frank, David

Producer(s) Wagner, Raymond
Director(s) Tannen, William
Screenwriter(s) Shyack, Dennis; Blodgett, Michael
Source(s) (novel) Blodgett, Michael

Cast Norris, Chuck; Thayer, Brynn; O'Halloran, Jack; James, Steve; Kramer, Jeffrey; O'Neal, Ron

Song(s) Two Can Be One (C: Frank, David; L: Jason, Robert; Osso, Denise)

Notes No cue sheet available.

2520 ✦ HEROES OF THE HILLS
Republic, 1938

Producer(s) Berke, William
Director(s) Sherman, George
Screenwriter(s) Roberts, Stanley; Burbridge, Betty

Cast Livingston, Robert; Corrigan, Ray; Terhune, Max; Lawson, Priscilla; Mason, LeRoy; Eagles, James; Barcroft, Roy; Hays, Barry

Song(s) Back to the Soil (C: Colombo, Alberto; L: Cherkose, Eddie)

2521 ✦ HER PRIMITIVE MAN
Universal, 1944

Musical Score Ward, Edward

Producer(s) Fessier, Michael; Pagano, Ernest
Director(s) Lamont, Charles
Screenwriter(s) Fessier, Michael; Pagano, Ernest

Cast Allbritton, Louise; Paige, Robert; Benchley, Robert; Broderick, Helen; Bachelor, Stephanie; Truex, Ernest; O'Shea, Oscar; Catlett, Walter; Heydt, Louis Jean

Song(s) What Now? (C/L: Durant, Eddie; Joyant, Elena)

2522 ✦ HER PRIVATE LIFE
Warner Brothers–First National, 1929

Producer(s) Marin, Ned
Director(s) Korda, Alexander
Screenwriter(s) Halsey, Forrest
Source(s) *Declasse* (play) Akins, Zoe

Cast Dove, Billie; Pidgeon, Walter; Herbert, Holmes; Love, Montagu; Young, Roland; Todd, Thelma; Pitts, ZaSu

Song(s) Love Is Like a Rose (C: Meyer, George W.; L: Bryan, Alfred)

Notes No cue sheet available. A remake of the 1925 film DECLASSE.

2523 ✦ HERS TO HOLD
Universal, 1943

Producer(s) Jackson, Felix
Director(s) Ryan, Frank
Screenwriter(s) Soter, Lewis R.

Cast Durbin, Deanna; Cotten, Joseph; Winninger, Charles; Walker, Nella; Schilling, Gus; Stossel, Ludwig; Bacon, Irving; Westman, Nydia; Hinds, Samuel S.; Adrian, Iris; Ankers, Evelyn

Song(s) Say a Prayer for the Boys Over There (C: McHugh, Jimmy; L: Magidson, Herb)

Notes No cue sheet available. Vocals include "Begin the Beguine" by Cole Porter; "God Bless America" by Irving Berlin; "Kashmiri Love Song" by Lawrence Hope and Amy Woodforde-Finden; and "Seguidilla" from Bizet's CARMEN.

2524 ✦ HER TWELVE MEN
Metro–Goldwyn–Mayer, 1954

Musical Score Kaper, Bronislau

Producer(s) Houseman, John
Director(s) Leonard, Robert Z.
Screenwriter(s) Roberts, William; Hobson, Laura Z.

Cast Garson, Greer; Ryan, Robert; Sullivan, Barry; Haydn, Richard; Lawrence, Barbara; Arness, James; Thompson, Rex; Considine, Tim; Stollery, David; Bergen, Frances; Wolfe, Ian

Song(s) Oh! Mighty Oaks! (C: Kaper, Bronislau; L: Wolcott, Charles)

2525 ✦ HE'S MY GUY
Universal, 1943

Producer(s) Cowan, Will
Director(s) Cline, Edward F.
Screenwriter(s) Webster, M. Coates; Garrett, Grant

Cast Foran, Dick; Hervey, Irene; Davis, Joan; Knight, Fuzzy; Douglas, Lon; Niesen, Gertrude; The Diamond Brothers; The Mills Brothers; Da Pron, Louis; The Dovene Sisters; Krueger, Lorraine

Song(s) He's My Guy [1] (C: de Paul, Gene; L: Raye, Don); How Am I to Know [2] (C: King, Jack; L: Parker, Dorothy); Everything Is Talent Today (C: Chaplin, Saul; L: Cahn, Sammy); Heads Up (C: Rosen, Milton; L: Carter, Everett); On the Old Assembly Line (C: Henderson, Ray; L: Green, Bud); Cielito Lindo (C: Fernandez, C.; L: Redmond, John; Cavanaugh, Jimmy)

Notes It is not known which of the above were written for this film. There is also a vocal of "Two Guitars" by A. Salama. [1] Also in HI' YA CHUM and UNDERCOVER GIRL. [2] Also in the MGM films DYNAMITE and THE HOODLUM SAINT.

2526 ✦ HE STAYED FOR BREAKFAST
Columbia, 1939

Producer(s) Schulberg, B.P.
Director(s) Hall, Alexander
Screenwriter(s) Wolfson, P.J.; Fessier, Michael; Vajda, Ernest
Source(s) *Ode to Liberty* (play) Howard, Sidney

Cast Young, Loretta; Douglas, Melvyn; Marshal, Alan; Pallette, Eugene; O'Connor, Una; Kinskey, Leonid; Bois, Curt

Song(s) Worker's Song [2] (C: Mertz, Paul; L: Drake, Milton)

Notes [1] This play is based on LIBERTE PROVISOIRE by Michel Duran. [2] Based on "Old School."

2527 ✦ HEY BOY! HEY GIRL!
Columbia, 1959

Producer(s) Romm, Harry
Director(s) Lowell, David
Screenwriter(s) Hayes, Raphael; West, James

Cast Prima, Louis; Smith, Keely; Sam Butera and the Witnesses; Gregory, James; Slatem, Henry; Heller, Barbara; Charney, Kim

Notes No cue sheet available. It is not clear if there were any songs written for this film. Vocals include "Oh Marie;" "Autmun Leaves" by Joseph Kosma, Johnny Mercer and Jacques Prevert; "Hey Boy, Hey Girl" by J. Thomas and C.McLollie and "Lazy River" by Hoagy Carmichael and Sidney Arodin; "When the Saints Go Marching In" and "Fever" by J.R. Davenport and Eddie Cooley; "Nighty Nite," "A Banana Split for My Baby" and "You Are My Love" by Joe Sauter and Weiss Barry.

2528 ✦ HEY GOOD LOOKIN'
Warner Brothers, 1983

Composer(s) Madara, John; Sandler, Ric
Lyricist(s) Madara, John; Sandler, Ric

Producer(s) Bakshi, Ralph
Director(s) Bakshi, Ralph
Screenwriter(s) Bakshi, Ralph
Voices Romanus, Richard; Proval, David; Bowman, Tina; Welles, Jesse; Grisanti, Angelo

Song(s) Hey, Good Lookin'; Burnin' You Gave Your Love to Me; This Could Be Love; Crazy's Theme; Our Love; South Street Walk; I'm Cryin'; Get It While the Gettin' Is Hot; Movin'; Don't Say Goodbye; That Girl

Was Mine; Just One Night; Playin' to Win; I'll Come Back

Notes Animated feature. All background vocals. Most are under two minutes in length.

2529 ◆ HEY HEY U.S.A.

See CHICAGO BEN.

2530 ◆ HEY, LET'S TWIST
Paramount, 1961

Musical Score Glover, Henry
Composer(s) Glover, Henry; Dee, Joey; Levy, Morris
Lyricist(s) Dee, Joey; Levy, Morris

Producer(s) Romm, Harry
Director(s) Garrison, Greg
Screenwriter(s) Hackady, Hal

Cast Joey Dee and the Starlighters; Campbell, Jo Ann; Armen, Kay; Randazzo, Teddy; Lampert, Zohra; di Luca, Dino; Dickens, Richard; The Peppermint Loungers; Arbus, Alan

Song(s) Hey, Let's Twist; Joey's Blues; Na Voce 'Nachitarra E'O Poco' Luna (C/L: Stillman, Al; Rossi, C.A.; Calise, Ugo); Roly Poly; It's a Pity to Say Goodnight (C/L: Reid, Billy); Mother Goose Twist (C/L: Barberis, Billy; Weinstein, Bobby; Randazzo, Teddy); I Wanna Twist; Shout (C/L: Isley Brothers, The); Let Me Do My Twist; Peppermint Twist (C: Glover, Henry; L: Dee, Joey)

Notes Not all these were written for this production. Morris Levy's contributions to these songs is doubtful.

2531 ◆ HEY, ROOKIE
Columbia, 1944

Composer(s) Gorney, Jay
Lyricist(s) Myers, Henry; Eliscu, Edward
Choreographer(s) Raset, Val; Donen, Stanley

Producer(s) Briskin, Irving
Director(s) Barton, Charles
Screenwriter(s) Myers, Henry; Eliscu, Edward; Gorney, Jay
Source(s) *Hey, Rookie* (musical) Myers, Henry; Eliscu, Edward; Gorney, Jay

Cast Miller, Ann; Parks, Larry; Besser, Joe; Dupree, Roland; Gilford, Jack; Weaver, Doodles; The Six Solid Senders; Hal McIntyre and His Orchestra; O'Leary, Jerry; Clark, Judy; The Vagabonds [1]; Hi-Lo-Jack and a Dame [2]; The Condos Brothers

Song(s) Hey, Rookie; Streamlined Sheik; You're Good for My Morale; Keep 'Em Happy [3] (C: Chaplin, Saul; L: Unknown); There Goes Taps [4]; When the Jailbirds Come to Town [4]; It's Great to Be in Uniform [4]; It's a Swelluva Life in the Army [4]

Notes Vocals also include "American Boy" by James V. Monaco and Al Dubin (originally in STAGE DOOR CANTEEN); "Take a Chance" by J.C. Lewis Jr.; "He's Got a Wave in His Hair (And a WAAC on His Hands)" by Hughie Prince and Sonny Burke; "So What Serenade" by James Cavanaugh, John Redmond and Nat Simon; and "When Irish Eyes Are Smiling" by Chauncey Olcott, Ernest R. Ball and George Graff Jr. [1] Consisted of Pete Peterson, Attilio Risso, Dominic Germano and Albert Torrieri. [2] Consisted of Charles D. King Jr., Robert Evans, Carter Ferriss and Vera Deane. [3] Not used. Referred to in some sources. [4] Not on cue sheet but referred to in some sources. These might have been in the original stage score.

2532 ◆ HEY THERE IT'S YOGI BEAR
Columbia, 1964

Musical Score Paich, Marty
Composer(s) Gilbert, Ray
Lyricist(s) Goodwin, Doug

Producer(s) Hanna, William; Barbera, Joseph
Director(s) Hanna, William; Barbera, Joseph
Screenwriter(s) Barbera, Joseph; Foster, Warren; Hanna, William
Voices Butler, Daws; Messick, Don; Bennett, Julie; Blanc, Mel; Vander Pyl, Jean; Smith, Hal; O'Malley, J. Pat

Song(s) Hey There It's Yogi Bear (C/L: Gates, David)

Notes No cue sheet available. Animated feature.

2533 ◆ HI, BEAUTIFUL
Universal, 1944

Composer(s) McHugh, Jimmy
Lyricist(s) Adamson, Harold

Producer(s) Hyland, Dick Irving
Director(s) Goodwins, Leslie
Screenwriter(s) Hyland, Dick Irving
Source(s) "Be It Ever So Humble" (story) Griffin, Eleanore; Rankin, William

Cast O'Driscoll, Martha; Beery Jr., Noah; McDaniel, Hattie; Catlett, Walter; Ryan, Tim

Song(s) I Love to Whistle [2]; Sing Everybody Sing [1] (C/L: Long, J.P.; Stillman, Al); Don't Sweetheart Me (C/L: Tobias, Charles; Friend, Cliff); Best of All! (C/L: Wrubel, Allie); Hi Beautiful [3] (C/L: Newell, Roy; Herscher, Louis; Jan, Dorothy)

Notes This is a remake of LOVE IN A BUNGALOW (1937). It is not known which, if any, of the above were written for this film. There is also a vocal of "Tiger Rag" by D.J. LaRocca. [1] American version by Al Stillman. Also in THE DAM BUSTERS (Warner) but without Stillman credit. [2] Also used in MAD ABOUT MUSIC. [3] Sheet music only.

2534 ✦ HI, BUDDY!
Universal, 1943

Composer(s) Rosen, Milton
Lyricist(s) Carter, Everett

Producer(s) Malvern, Paul
Director(s) Young, Harold
Screenwriter(s) Wilson, Warren

Cast Foran, Dick; Hilliard, Harriet; Paige, Robert; The King's Men; The Step Brothers; The Four Sweethearts

Song(s) Here's To Tomorrow (C: Pollack, Lew; L: Newman, Charles); Hi, Buddy Hi; We're in the Navy [2] (C: de Paul, Gene; L: Raye, Don); We're the Marines; Mister Yankee Doodle [1]

Notes Vocals also include "Huckleberry Finn" by Cliff Hess, Sam Lewis and Joe Young; "Mickey" by Harry Williams and Neil Moret; "School Days" by Will D. Cobb and Gus Edwards; "Star Dust" by Hoagy Carmichael and Mitchell Parish; "Take Me In Your Arms" by Fred Markush and Mitchell Parish; "Camptown Races" and "Old Folks at Home" by Stephen Foster; "Rock-A-Bye Your Baby with a Dixie Melody" by Sam Lewis, Joe Young and Jean Schwartz; "They Go Wild, Simply Wild Over Me" by Joe McCarthy and Fred Fisher; "We-All Together" by Louis Ahlert and Sammy Cahn; "How Ya Gonna Keep 'Em Down on the Farm?" by Sam Lewis, Joe Young and Walter Donaldson and "Oui, Oui, Marie" by Alfred Bryan, Joseph McCarthy and Fred Fisher. [1] Also in SING ANOTHER CHORUS. [2] Also in ABBOTT & COSTELLO & DICK POWELL IN THE NAVY.

2535 ✦ HIDDEN GUNS
Republic, 1956

Musical Score Idriss, Ramez
Composer(s) Gannaway, Albert C.
Lyricist(s) Levy, Hal

Producer(s) Gannaway, Albert C.; Ver Halen Jr., C.J.
Director(s) Gannaway, Albert C.
Screenwriter(s) Gannaway, Albert C.; Roeca, Sam

Cast Bennett, Bruce; Arlen, Richard; Carradine, John; Young, Faron; Corrigan, Lloyd; Dickinson, Angie; Bacon, Irving; Williams, Guinn "Big Boy"

Song(s) The Sherriff; Vice Versa; Hidden Guns (C: Idriss, Ramez)

Notes No cue sheet available.

2536 ✦ HIDEAWAY GIRL
Paramount, 1937

Producer(s) Botsford, A.M.
Director(s) Archainbaud, George
Screenwriter(s) March, Joseph Moncure; Welch, Eddie

Cast Ross, Shirley; Cummings, Robert; Raye, Martha; Da Pron, Louis

Song(s) Beethoven, Mendelssohn and Liszt [3] (C/L: Coslow, Sam); Dancing Into My Heart (C: Lane, Burton; L: Freed, Ralph); Two Birdies Up a Tree [1] (C: Lane, Burton; L: Freed, Ralph); What Is Love? [2] (C: Young, Victor; Rainger, Ralph; L: Robin, Leo)

Notes [1] Irving Kahal wrote some special lyrics for the Captain and Martha Raye and for the sailors' chorus. [2] Not used but published. [3] Originally titled "Beethoven, Rubenstein and Brahms."

2537 ✦ HIDE IN PLAIN SIGHT
Metro–Goldwyn–Mayer, 1980

Musical Score Rosenman, Leonard

Producer(s) Christiansen, Robert; Rosenberg, Rick
Director(s) Caan, James
Screenwriter(s) Eastman, Spencer
Source(s) (novel) Waller, Leslie

Cast Caan, James; Eikenberry, Jill; Viharo, Robert; Grifasi, Joe; Rae, Barbara; McMillan, Kenneth; Sommer, Josef; Aiello, Danny

Song(s) Petronella Mazurka (C/L: Petronella, Victor); Here's Looking at You (C/L: Costa, Joe; Pace, Gary; McKay, Lindsay); You've Got to Change Your Evil Ways (C/L: Henry, Sonny)

Notes There is also a vocal of "The Shadow of Your Smile" by Johnny Mandel and Paul Francis Webster.

2538 ✦ HIDE-OUT (1930)
Universal, 1930

Director(s) Barker, Reginald
Screenwriter(s) Taylor, Matt; Ripley, Arthur; Hillyer, Lambert

Cast Murray, James; Crawford, Kathryn; Stockdale, Carl; Moran, Lee; Hearn, Edward; Elliott, Robert

Song(s) Just You and I (C: Perry, Sam; L: Marks, Clarence)

Notes No cue sheet available.

2539 ✦ HIDE-OUT (1934)
Metro–Goldwyn–Mayer, 1934

Musical Score Axt, William
Composer(s) Brown, Nacio Herb
Lyricist(s) Freed, Arthur

Producer(s) Stromberg, Hunt
Director(s) Van Dyke, W.S.
Screenwriter(s) Goodrich, Frances; Hackett, Albert

Cast Montgomery, Robert; O'Sullivan, Maureen; Arnold, Edward; Patterson, Elizabeth; Rooney, Mickey; Kane, Whitford

Song(s) The Dream Was So Beautiful; All I Do Is Dream of You

2540 ✦ HIDEOUT (1949)
Republic, 1949

Producer(s) Picker, Sidney
Director(s) Ford, Philip
Screenwriter(s) Butler, John K.

Cast Booth, Adrian; Bridges, Lloyd; Collins, Ray; Ryan, Sheila; Carney, Alan; Corey, Jeff; Chandler, Fletcher; Beddoe, Don; Bryant, Nana

Song(s) Alma Mater (C: Green, Sanford; L: Carroll, June)

2541 ✦ HI, GAUCHO!
RKO, 1935

Composer(s) Malotte, Albert Hay
Lyricist(s) Malotte, Albert Hay

Producer(s) Burch, John E.
Director(s) Atkins, Tommy
Screenwriter(s) Ruffington, Adele

Cast Carroll, John; Duna, Steffi; La Rocque, Rod; Love, Montagu; Oodie, Ann

Song(s) Song of the Open Road; Bandit Song; Panchita; Serenade; Little White Rose

2542 ✦ HIGH AND HAPPY

See HIT PARADE OF 1947.

2543 ✦ HIGH ANXIETY
Twentieth Century–Fox, 1977

Musical Score Morris, John
Composer(s) Brooks, Mel
Lyricist(s) Brooks, Mel

Producer(s) Brooks, Mel
Director(s) Brooks, Mel
Screenwriter(s) Brooks, Mel; Clark, Ron; DeLuca, Rudy; Levinson, Barry

Cast Brooks, Mel; Kahn, Madeline; Leachman, Cloris; Korman, Harvey; Carey, Ron; Morris, Howard; Van Patten, Dick; Riley, Jack; Clark, Ron; DeLuca, Rudy; Levinson, Barry

Song(s) If You Love Me Baby Tell Me Loud; High Anxiety

2544 ✦ HIGH-BALLIN'
American International, 1978

Musical Score Hoffert, Paul

Producer(s) Slan, Jon
Director(s) Carter, Peter
Screenwriter(s) Edwards, Paul

Cast Fonda, Peter; Reed, Jerry; Shaver, Helen; Wiggins, Chris; Langevin, Christopher; Ferry, David

Song(s) High Rollin' (C/L: Reed, Jerry; Feller, Dick)

Notes No cue sheet available.

2545 ✦ HIGHER AND HIGHER
RKO, 1943

Composer(s) McHugh, Jimmy
Lyricist(s) Adamson, Harold
Choreographer(s) Matray, Ernst

Producer(s) Whelan, Tim
Director(s) Whelan, Tim
Screenwriter(s) Dratler, Jay; Spence, Ralph; Bowers, William; Harris, Howard
Source(s) *Higher and Higher* (musical) Hurlbut, Gladys; Logan, Joshua; Rodgers, Richard; Hart, Lorenz

Cast Morgan, Michele; Haley, Jack [2]; Sinatra, Frank; Errol, Leon; McGuire, Marcy; Borge, Victor; Wickes, Mary; Risdon, Elizabeth; Hale, Barbara; Torme, Mel; Hartman, Paul; Hartman, Grace; Wilson, Dooley; Scott, Ivy; Evans, Rex

Song(s) It's a Most Important Affair; Disgustingly Rich [2] (C: Rodgers, Richard; L: Hart, Lorenz); Today I'm a Debutante; I Couldn't Sleep a Wink Last Night [4]; The Music Stopped; A Lovely Way to Spend an Evening [6]; I Saw You First [5]; You're on Your Own; Minuet in Boogie [1]; Higher and Higher [3]

Notes [1] Based on Paderewski's "Minuet in G." [2] From Broadway original. [3] Listed in the *Rodgers and Hammerstein Fact Book* but nowhere else. [4] Also in BEAT THE BAND and RADIO STARS ON PARADE. [5] Also in DING DONG WILLIAMS and RACE STREET. [6] Also in THE RACKET.

2546 ✦ HIGH FLYERS
RKO, 1937

Composer(s) Dreyer, Dave
Lyricist(s) Ruby, Herman

Producer(s) Marcus, Lee
Director(s) Cline, Edward F.
Screenwriter(s) Rubin, Benny; Granet, Bert; Morgan, Byron
Source(s) *The Kangaroos* (play) Mapes, Victor

Cast Wheeler, Bert; Woolsey, Robert; Velez, Lupe; Lord, Marjorie; Dumont, Margaret; Carson, Jack

Song(s) Keep Your Head Above Water; I Always Get My Man; I'm a Gaucho

2547 ✦ HIGH HAT
Publix, 1928

Song(s) Sally's Coming Home (C/L: Hess, Cliff; Santley, Joseph)

2548 ◆ HIGH HELL

Notes No cue sheet available. Sheet music only. This might have been a theme of the silent film HIGH HAT which was released by First National in April 1927 and starred Sam Hardy and Mary Blane. However, none of the characters in that film are named Sally.

2548 ◆ HIGH HELL
Paramount, 1958

Producer(s) Balaban, Burt; Mayer, Arthur
Director(s) Balaban, Burt
Screenwriter(s) Tunick, Irv
Source(s) *High Cage* (novel) Frazee, Steve

Cast Derek, John; Stewart, Elaine; Allen, Patrick; Burke, Rodney; Wells, Jerold

Song(s) A Man's a Man (C/L: Miller, Sonny; Cardew, Phil)

2549 ◆ HIGH NOON
United Artists, 1952

Musical Score Tiomkin, Dimitri

Producer(s) Kramer, Stanley
Director(s) Zinnemann, Fred
Screenwriter(s) Foreman, Carl
Source(s) *Tin Star* (novel) Cunningham, John W.

Cast Cooper, Gary; Kelly, Grace; Jurado, Katy; Mitchell, Thomas; Bridges, Lloyd; Kruger, Otto; Chaney Jr., Lon; Morgan, Henry; Wooley, Sheb; Van Cleef, Lee

Song(s) High Noon (C: Tiomkin, Dimitri; L: Washington, Ned)

Notes No cue sheet available.

2550 ◆ HIGH SCHOOL
Twentieth Century–Fox, 1939

Producer(s) Zanuck, Darryl F.
Director(s) Del Ruth, Roy
Screenwriter(s) Hellman, Sam; Ware, Darrell; Starling, Lynn; O'Hara, John

Cast McCrea, Joel; Kelly, Nancy; Young, Roland; Boland, Mary; Romero, Cesar; Healy, Mary; Talbot, Lyle; Cook Jr., Elisha; Parker, Barnett

Song(s) Thomas Jefferson High School Alma Mater Song (C/L: Abbott, Frederick)

2551 ◆ HIGH SCHOOL CONFIDENTIAL
Metro–Goldwyn–Mayer, 1958

Musical Score Glasser, Albert

Producer(s) Zugsmith, Albert
Director(s) Arnold, Jack
Screenwriter(s) Blees, Robert; Meltzer, Lewis

Cast Barrymore, John Drew; Jergens, Diane; Douglas, Burt; Sterling, Jan; Tamblyn, Russ; Van Doren, Mamie;

Lewis, Jerry Lee; Anthony, Ray; Coogan, Jackie; Chaplin Jr., Charles; Raymond, Robin; Talbot, Lyle

Song(s) High School Confidential (C/L: Lewis, Jerry Lee; Hargrave, Ron)

2552 ◆ HIGH SCHOOL HERO
Monogram, 1946

Musical Score Kay, Edward J.
Composer(s) Kay, Edward J.
Lyricist(s) Kay, Edward J.
Choreographer(s) Boyle, Jack

Producer(s) Katzman, Sam
Director(s) Dreifuss, Arthur
Screenwriter(s) Collins, Hal; Dreifuss, Arthur

Cast Stewart, Freddie; Preisser, June; Neill, Noel; Rooney, Anne; Mills, Warren; Moran, Jackie; Darro, Frankie; Isabelita; Savitt, Jan; Slack, Freddie; Derita, Joe

Song(s) You're For Me; Come to My Arms; Whitney High; Night Time and You; You're Just What I Crave (C/L: Alexander, Arthur); Fairview High (C/L: Grayson, Phil); Southpaw Serenade (C/L: Slack, Freddie)

Notes No cue sheet available.

2553 ◆ HIGH SOCIETY
Metro–Goldwyn–Mayer, 1956

Composer(s) Porter, Cole
Lyricist(s) Porter, Cole
Choreographer(s) Walters, Charles

Producer(s) Siegel, Sol C.
Director(s) Walters, Charles
Screenwriter(s) Patrick, John
Source(s) *The Philadelphia Story* (play) Barry, Philip

Cast Crosby, Bing; Kelly, Grace; Sinatra, Frank; Holm, Celeste; Lund, John; Calhern, Louis; Blackmer, Sidney; Louis Armstrong and His Band; Gillmore, Margalo; Reed, Lydia

Song(s) High Society Calypso; Little One; Who Wants to Be a Millionaire; True Love; You're Sensational; I Love You Samantha; Now You Has Jazz; Well, Did You Evah [1]; Mind If I Make Love to You; Let's Vocalize [2]; Caroline [2]; So What? [2]; Who Has? [2]; How Could I? [2]

Notes [1] Written for stage version of DUBARRY WAS A LADY (1939). Later in AT LONG LAST LOVE (20th). [2] Not used.

2554 ◆ HIGH SOCIETY BLUES
Fox, 1930

Musical Score Kaylin, Samuel
Composer(s) Hanley, James F.
Lyricist(s) McCarthy, Joseph

Producer(s) Rockett, Al
Director(s) Butler, David
Screenwriter(s) Green, Howard J.
Source(s) "Those High Society Blues" (story) Burnet, Dana

Cast Gaynor, Janet; Farrell, Charles; Collier Sr., William; Hopper, Hedda; Fazenda, Louise; Littlefield, Lucien; Compton, Joyce; Hurst, Brandon; Gaye, Gregory

Song(s) Breakaway [1] (C/L: Gottler, Archie; Conrad, Con; Mitchell, Sidney D.); I'm in the Market for You; Serenade; High Society Blues; Just Like in A Story Book; Eleanor (The Song That I Sing in My Dreams) [2]

Notes Some sources claim "Eleanor" is a different song from "The Song That I Sing in My Dreams," but the cue sheet doesn't indicate this. [1] Originally in the FOLLIES OF 1929. [2] Only used in foreign release.

2555 ✦ HIGH TENSION
Twentieth Century–Fox, 1936

Producer(s) Wurtzel, Sol M.
Director(s) Dwan, Allan
Screenwriter(s) Breslow, Lou; Eliscu, Edward; Patrick, John

Cast Donlevy, Brian; Farrell, Glenda; Foster, Norman; Wood, Helen; McWade, Robert; McDaniel, Hattie; Alper, Murray

Song(s) In Trinity Church (C/L: Rogers, John); And That Woman Made a Monkey Out of Me (C/L: Clare, Sidney)

2556 ✦ HIGH TIME
Twentieth Century–Fox, 1960

Musical Score Mancini, Henry
Composer(s) Van Heusen, James
Lyricist(s) Cahn, Sammy

Producer(s) Brackett, Charles
Director(s) Edwards, Blake
Screenwriter(s) Waldman, Frank; Waldman, Tom

Cast Crosby, Bing; Fabian; Weld, Tuesday; Maurey, Nicole; Beymer, Richard; Adiarte, Patrick; Craig, Yvonne; MacLeod, Gavin; Schreiber, Paul

Song(s) You Tell Me Your Dream, I'll Tell You Mine (C: Daniels, Charles; L: Rice, Seymour; Brown, Albert H.); The Second Time Around; Go, Go, Go [1]; Nobody's Perfect [1]; Showmanship [1]

Notes [1] Not used.

2557 ✦ HIGH VOLTAGE
Pathe, 1929

Producer(s) Block, Ralph
Director(s) Higgin, Howard

Screenwriter(s) Clawson, Elliott; Gleason, James; Nicholson, Kenyon

Cast Boyd, William; Moore, Owen; Lombard, Carole; Ellis, Diane; Bevan, Billy; Smalley, Phillips

Song(s) Colleen O'Dare (C: Green, George; L: Waggner, George)

Notes No cue sheet available.

2558 ✦ HIGHWAY QUEEN
Metro–Goldwyn–Mayer, 1972

Musical Score Seltzer, Dov
Composer(s) Seltzer, Dov
Lyricist(s) Manor, Ehud

Producer(s) Golan, Menahem
Director(s) Golan, Menahem
Screenwriter(s) Golan, Menahem; Almagor, Gila

Cast Almagor, Gila; Barkan, Yuda; Bernstein-Cohen, Miriam; Koenig, Lea; Yishai, Galia

Song(s) Highway Queen; Discoteque; Trip Song

2559 ✦ HIGH, WIDE AND HANDSOME
Paramount, 1937

Musical Score Kern, Jerome
Composer(s) Kern, Jerome
Lyricist(s) Hammerstein II, Oscar
Choreographer(s) Prinz, LeRoy

Producer(s) Hornblow Jr., Arthur
Director(s) Mamoulian, Rouben
Screenwriter(s) Hammerstein II, Oscar; O'Neil, George

Cast Dunne, Irene; Scott, Randolph; Lamour, Dorothy; Walburn, Raymond; Tamiroff, Akim; Bickford, Charles; Blue, Ben; Patterson, Elizabeth; Frawley, William; Hale, Alan; Pichel, Irving; Littlefield, Lucien; Andrews, Stanley; Sedan, Rolfe

Song(s) High, Wide and Handsome; Can I Forget You; Titusville Square and Shanty Boat (Jenny Dear); The Things I Want; Allegheny Al; The Folks Who Live on the Hill; Workmen's Chorus; Governor's Ball Solo; Go Choose Your East (L: Traditional); The Fields [1]; Water Pitcher Episode (L: Bennett, Robert Russell; Kern, Jerome); Will You Marry Me Tomorrow, Maria?

Notes Jerome Kern also wrote the following themes (or they were based on music from songs in this film) for the scoring: "Sally's Dance," "Fire Scene," "Awake and Bathe," "Hayloft Awakening," "Added Barn Dance," "Apple Orchard Scene," "Apple Orchard Coda," "Sally's Departure," "Folks" and "Prelude to House on Hill", "Oil Well Comes In," "The Interrupted House," "Sally Waiting," "Hunky Dory," "Sally Runs After Circus," "Peter's Hallucination," "The Fight," "Finale Ultimo," "Prelude to Part II," "Finale," "Doc and Mac," "Tonic Distribution," "Barnyard Scene," "Wagon and Hilltop

Scene," "Kissing Game Tag," "Coda to Orchard," "Stairway Scene," "Sally's Dance Revised," "Grandma's Polka" and "Harangue No. 1." [1] Not used.

2560 ✦ A HIGH WIND IN JAMAICA
Twentieth Century–Fox, 1965

Musical Score Adler, Larry

Producer(s) Croydon, John
Director(s) Mackendrick, Alexander
Screenwriter(s) Harwood, Ronald; Cannan, Denis; Mann, Stanley
Source(s) *A High Wind in Jamaica* (novel) Hughes, Richard

Cast Quinn, Anthony; Coburn, James; Price, Dennis; Frobe, Gert; Kedrova, Lila; Amis, Martin

Song(s) A High Wind in Jamaica (C: Adler, Larry; L: Logue, Christopher)

2561 ✦ HI, GOOD LOOKIN'!
Universal, 1944

Producer(s) Gross, Frank
Director(s) Lilley, Edward
Screenwriter(s) Smith, Paul Gerard; Ropes, Bradford; Conrad, Eugene

Cast Hilliard, Harriet; Grant, Kirby; Quillan, Eddie; Kean, Betty; Knight, Fuzzy; The Delta Rhythm Boys

Song(s) I Won't Forget the Dawn (C: de Paul, Gene; L: Raye, Don); By Mistake (C/L: James, Inez; Miller, Sidney); You're Just the Sweetest Thing (C/L: Bishop, Arthur; Adlam, Buzz); A Slight Case of Love (C/L: Adlam, Buzz)

Notes Vocals also include "For Dancers Only" by Sy Oliver; "Paper Doll" by Johnny S. Black; "For All We Know" by J. Fred Coots and Sam Lewis; "Deacon Jones" by Johnny Lange, Hy Heath and Richard Loring; "Aunt Hagar's Blues" by W.C. Handy and "Just a Stowaway" by Vick Knight.

2562 ✦ HILLBILLY HARE
Warner Brothers, 1950

Musical Score Stalling, Carl

Director(s) McKimson, Robert
Source(s) (short subject)

Cast Bunny, Bugs

Song(s) Square Dancin' (C/L: Blanc, Mel)

Notes Merrie Melodie cartoon.

2563 ✦ HILLS OF OLD WYOMING
Paramount, 1937

Producer(s) Sherman, Harry
Director(s) Watt, Nate
Screenwriter(s) Geraghty, Maurice

Cast Boyd, William; Hayden, Russell; Hayes, George "Gabby"; Morris, Stephen; Young, Clara Kimball; Sheridan, Gail

Song(s) Hills of Old Wyoming [1] (C: Rainger, Ralph; L: Robin, Leo)

Notes [1] Also in PALM SPRINGS.

2564 ✦ HILLS OF UTAH
Columbia, 1951

Producer(s) Schaefer, Armand
Director(s) English, John
Screenwriter(s) Geraghty, Gerald

Cast Autry, Gene; Buttram, Pat; Riley, Elaine; Stevens, Onslow; Champion

Song(s) Peter Cottontail (C/L: Nelson, Steve; Rollins, Jack); Utah [1] (C/L: Unknown)

Notes No cue sheet avaiable. [1] Might be the same song as that written by Charles Henderson for the Roy Rogers Republic picture UTAH.

2565 ✦ THE HINDENBURG
Universal, 1975

Musical Score Shire, David

Director(s) Wise, Robert
Screenwriter(s) Gidding, Nelson
Source(s) (book) Mooney, Michael M.

Cast Scott, George C.; Bancroft, Anne; Thinnes, Roy; Young, Gig; Meredith, Burgess; Auberjonois, Rene; Atherton, William; Durning, Charles; Dysart, Richard; Clary, Robert; Donat, Peter

Song(s) There's a Lot to Be Said for the Fuehrer (C: Shire, David; L: Kleban, Edward)

2566 ✦ HI, NEIGHBOR
Republic, 1942

Composer(s) Kraushaar, Raoul
Lyricist(s) Magowan, S.; Magowan, B.

Producer(s) Schaefer, Armand
Director(s) Lamont, Charles
Screenwriter(s) McGowan, Dorrell; McGowan, Stuart

Cast Parker, Jean; Archer, John; Beecher, Janet; Hare, Marilyn; Shirley, Bill; Drake, Pauline; Sherman, Fred; Lulu Belle and Scotty; Roy Acuff and His Smoky Mountain Boys and Girls; Randolph, Lillian

Song(s) Graduation Routine; Professor Routine; Hail to Greenfield; Hi, Neighbor [2] (C/L: Owens, Jack); When a Fella's Got a Girl [4] (C: Styne, Jule; L: Meyer, Sol; Brown, George); Moo Woo Woo (C/L: Hoefle, Carl; Porter, Del); Stuck Up Blues (C/L: Acuff, Roy); Pass the Biscuits Mirandy [3] (C/L: Hoefle, Carl; Porter, Del); Deep in the Heart of Texas [1] (C: Swander, Don; L: Hershey, June); I Know We Are Saying Goodbye (C/L: Acuff, Roy)

Notes Originally titled COLLEGE IN THE PINES. [1] Also in HEART OF THE RIO GRANDE, KING OF THE COWBOYS, I'LL GET BY (20th) and DEEP IN THE HEART OF TEXAS (Universal). [2] Also in SAN ANTONIO ROSE (Universal). [3] Also in I'M FROM ARKANSAS (PRC). [4] Also in SING, DANCE, PLENTY HOT.

2567 ✦ HI, NELLIE!
Warner Brothers, 1934

Producer(s) Presnell, Robert
Director(s) LeRoy, Mervyn
Screenwriter(s) Finkel, Abem; Sutherland, Sidney

Cast Muni, Paul; Farrell, Glenda; Dumbrille, Douglass; Barrat, Robert; Sparks, Ned; Cavanaugh, Hobart

Song(s) Hi Nellie [1] (C: Wrubel, Allie; L: Dixon, Mort)

Notes No cue sheet available. The song might have been written for exploitation only.

2568 ✦ HIPS HIPS HOORAY
RKO, 1934

Musical Score Webb, Roy
Composer(s) Ruby, Harry
Lyricist(s) Kalmar, Bert
Choreographer(s) Gould, Dave

Producer(s) Swanson, H.N.
Director(s) Sandrich, Mark
Screenwriter(s) Kalmar, Bert; Ruby, Harry; Kaufman, Edward

Cast Wheeler, Bert; Woolsey, Robert; Etting, Ruth; Todd, Thelma; Lee, Dorothy; Meeker, George; Barry, Phyllis; Burtis, James; Briggs, Matt; Charters, Spencer

Song(s) Keep Romance Alive; Keep on Doin' What You're Doin'; Tired of It All [1]

Notes Cue sheet does not differentiate between vocals from instrumentals. [1] Used instrumentally only.

2569 ✦ THE HIRED KILLER
Paramount, 1967

Musical Score Poitevin, Robert

Producer(s) Gay, Frank
Director(s) Shannon, Frank
Screenwriter(s) Shannon, Frank

Cast Webber, Robert; Nero, Franco; Valerie, Jeanne

Song(s) The Wind Will Carry Them By (C/L: Shapiro, D.); Just Can't Stand It No More (C/L: Fowlkes, D.; Johnson, W.; King, J.); When You Are Gone (C/L: Shapiro, D.); Take a Heart (C/L: Dallon, M.); I'll Love Again (C/L: Fowlkes, D.; Johnson, W.; King, J.); My Man (C/L: Poitevin, Robert; Di Giannantonio, L.); Don't Be Ashamed (C/L: Fowlkes, D.; Johnson, W.; King, J.)

Notes Previously titled TECHNIQUE OF A MURDER.

2570 ✦ HIS BROTHER'S WIFE
Metro–Goldwyn–Mayer, 1936

Musical Score Waxman, Franz

Producer(s) Weingarten, Lawrence
Director(s) Van Dyke, W.S.
Screenwriter(s) Gordon, Leon; Meehan, John

Cast Stanwyck, Barbara; Taylor, Robert; Hersholt, Jean; Calleia, Joseph; Hinds, Samuel S.

Song(s) Can't We Fall in Love (C: Donaldson, Walter; L: Adamson, Harold)

2571 ✦ HIS BUTLER'S SISTER
Universal, 1943

Musical Score Salter, Hans J.

Producer(s) Jackson, Felix
Director(s) Borzage, Frank
Screenwriter(s) Hoffenstein, Samuel; Rheinhardt, Betty

Cast Durbin, Deanna; Tone, Franchot; O'Brien, Pat; Tamiroff, Akim; Mowbray, Alan; Jenks, Frank; Conried, Hans; Arno, Sig; Catlett, Walter; Janssen, Elsa; Bates, Florence; Ankers, Evelyn; Karns, Roscoe; Hicks, Russell

Song(s) In the Spirit of the Moment (C: Jurmann, Walter; L: Grossman, Bernie); Turandot—3rd Act (C: Puccini, Giacomo; L: Lerner, Sam)

Notes There are also vocals of "Is It True What They Say About Dixie" by Irving Caesar, Sammy Lerner and Gerald Marks and "When You're Away" by Henry M. Blossom and Victor Herbert.

2572 ✦ HIS GLORIOUS NIGHT
Metro–Goldwyn–Mayer, 1929

Musical Score Barrymore, Lionel

Director(s) Barrymore, Lionel
Screenwriter(s) Mack, Willard
Source(s) *Olympia* (play) Molnar, Ferenc

Cast Gilbert, John; Owen, Catherine Dale; O'Neil, Nance; Von Seyffertitz, Gustav; Hopper, Hedda; Hill, Doris; Davis, Tyrrell; Carle, Richard

Song(s) The Old Love Song (C: Barrymore, Lionel; L: Unknown)

Notes John Gilbert's first all-talkie.

2573 ✦ HIS KIND OF WOMAN
RKO, 1951

Musical Score Harline, Leigh

Producer(s) Sparks, Robert
Director(s) Farrow, John
Screenwriter(s) Fenton, Frank; Leonard, Jack

Cast Mitchum, Robert; Russell, Jane; Price, Vincent; Holt, Tim; McGraw, Charles; Reynolds, Marjorie; Burr, Raymond; Banning, Leslye; Backus, Jim; Van Zandt, Philip

Song(s) Five Little Miles from San Berdoo (C/L: Coslow, Sam); You'll Know (C: McHugh, Jimmy; L: Adamson, Harold)

2574 ✦ HIS MAJESTY O'KEEFE
Warner Brothers, 1954

Musical Score Tiomkin, Dimitri
Composer(s) Tiomkin, Dimitri
Lyricist(s) Webster, Paul Francis

Producer(s) Hecht, Harold
Director(s) Haskin, Byron
Screenwriter(s) Chase, Borden; Hill, James
Source(s) *His Majesty O'Keefe* (novel) Green, Gerald; Klingman, Lawrence

Cast Lancaster, Burt; Rice, Joan; Morell, Andre; Sofaer, Abraham; Savage, Archie; Fong, Benson; Prendergast, Tessa; Ahn, Philip

Song(s) Emerald Isle; Fiji Islands [1]

Notes [1] Used instrumentally only.

2575 ✦ HISTORY OF THE WORLD, PART 1
Twentieth Century–Fox, 1981

Musical Score Morris, John

Producer(s) Brooks, Mel
Director(s) Brooks, Mel
Screenwriter(s) Brooks, Mel

Cast Brooks, Mel; DeLuise, Dom; Kahn, Madeline; Korman, Harvey; Leachman, Cloris; Carey, Ron; Hines, Gregory; Stephenson, Pamela; Greene, Shecky; Caesar, Sid; Humes, Mary-Margaret; Welles, Orson; Arthur, Beatrice; Callas, Charlie; Mazursky, Paul; Clark, Ron; Youngman, Henny; Feld, Fritz; McCormick, Pat; Graham, Ronny; Mason, Jackie; Leeds, Phil; Carter, Jack; Murray, Jan; Milligan, Spike; Hillerman, John; Gavin, John

Song(s) The Inquisition (C/L: Brooks, Mel; Graham, Ronny); Jews in Space (C/L: Brooks, Mel)

2576 ✦ HIT!
Paramount, 1973

Musical Score Schifrin, Lalo

Producer(s) Korshak, Harry
Director(s) Furie, Sidney J.
Screenwriter(s) Trustman, Alan R.; Wolf, David

Cast Williams, Billy Dee; Pryor, Richard; Hampton, Paul; Welles, Gwen; Melton, Sid

Song(s) Pages of Life [1] (C: Schifrin, Lalo; L: Kusik, Larry)

Notes [1] Not used in picture.

2577 ✦ HIT AND RUN
United Artists, 1957

Musical Score Steininger, Franz

Producer(s) Haas, Hugo
Director(s) Haas, Hugo
Screenwriter(s) Haas, Hugo

Cast Haas, Hugo; Moore, Cleo; Edwards, Vince; Mitchum, Julie

Song(s) What Good'll It Do Me? (C: Steininger, Franz; L: Unknown)

2578 ✦ HITCH HIKE LADY
Republic, 1935

Producer(s) Levine, Nat
Director(s) Scotto, Aubrey
Screenwriter(s) Rigby, Gordon; Cole, Lester

Cast Skipworth, Alison; Clarke, Mae; Treacher, Arthur; Ellison, James; Hymer, Warren; Mercer, Beryl; Henderson, Del; Belmore, Lionel; Hayes, George "Gabby"; Harlan, Otis

Song(s) Song of the Highway (C/L: Drake, Oliver; Burnette, Smiley)

2579 ✦ HITCH HIKE TO HAPPINESS
Republic, 1944

Composer(s) Kent, Walter
Lyricist(s) Gannon, Kim

Producer(s) Brown, Donald H.
Director(s) Santley, Joseph
Screenwriter(s) Townley, Jack

Cast Pearce, Al; Evans, Dale; Taylor, Brad; Frawley, William; Cowan, Jerome; Trenk, Willy; Harris, Harlene; Compton, Joyce; Bacon, Irving; Eburne, Maude

Song(s) Hitch Hike to Happiness; My Pushover Heart [2]; Sentimental [3]; For You and Me [1]

Notes [1] Also in MAN FROM OKLAHOMA and SWINGIN' ON A RAINBOW. [2] Also in MURDER IN THE MUSIC HALL and RENDEZVOUS WITH ANNIE. [3] Also in MILLION DOLLAR PURSUIT.

2580 ✦ HIT MAN
Metro–Goldwyn–Mayer, 1973

Musical Score Barnum, H.B.
Composer(s) Barnum, H.B.

Lyricist(s) Barnum, H.B.; Sharpe, Joyce; Cobbin, James D.; Murray, Ronald L.; Wilson, Jerome L.

Producer(s) Corman, Gene
Director(s) Armitage, George
Screenwriter(s) Armitage, George
Source(s) *Jack's Return Home* (novel) Lewis, Ted

Cast Casey, Bernie; Grier, Pam; Moore, Lisa

Song(s) Hit Man; I'll Always Love You; Youngblood (L: Barnum, H.B.)

Notes A remake of the British MGM film, GET CARTER.

2581 ✦ HIT OF THE SHOW
FBO Pictures, 1928

Director(s) Ince, Ralph
Screenwriter(s) Wolf, Edgar Allan

Cast Brown, Joe E.; Olmstead, Gertrude; Bailey, William Norton; Astor, Gertrude; Ness, Ole M.; Shumway, Lee; Pollard, Daphne

Song(s) You're in Love and I'm in Love (C/L: Donaldson, Walter); Waitin' for Katie (C: Shapiro, Ted; L: Kahn, Gus)

Notes No cue sheet available.

2582 ✦ HIT PARADE
Republic, 1936

Musical Score Colombo, Alberto
Composer(s) Stept, Sam H.
Lyricist(s) Washington, Ned

Producer(s) Clark, Colbert
Director(s) Meins, Gus
Screenwriter(s) Ropes, Bradford; Ornitz, Samuel

Cast Langford, Frances; Regan, Phil; Henry, Louise; Kelton, Pert; Brophy, Edward S.; Terhune, Max; Courtney, Inez; Owsley, Monroe; Watkin, Pierre; Givot, George; White, Sammy; Demarest, William

Song(s) I've Got to Be a Rug Cutter (C/L: Ellington, Duke); It Don't Mean a Thing (C/L: Ellington, Duke); Along Came Pete; Hail Alma Mater; Sweet Heartache; Last Night I Dreamed of You; Was It Rain? (C: Handman, Lou; L: Hirsch, Walter); Evolution; I'll Reach for a Star (C: Handman, Lou; L: Hirsch, Walter); Love Is Good for Anything that Ails You (C/L: Friend, Cliff; Malneck, Matty)

Notes This was reissued as I'LL REACH FOR A STAR. This might be an incomplete cue sheet.

2583 ✦ HIT PARADE OF 1941
Republic, 1940

Composer(s) Styne, Jule
Lyricist(s) Bullock, Walter

Producer(s) Siegel, Sol C.
Director(s) Auer, John H.
Screenwriter(s) Ropes, Bradford; Herbert, F. Hugh; Leo, Maurice

Cast Baker, Kenny; Langford, Frances; Herbert, Hugh; Boland, Mary; Miller, Ann; Kelly, Patsy; Silvers, Phil; Holloway, Sterling; MacBride, Donald; Parker, Barnett; Pangborn, Franklin; Six Hits and a Miss; Borrah Minnevitch and His Harmonica Rascals

Song(s) Make Yourself at Home [3]; Swap Shop; Trading Post of the Air; Who Am I [4]; Swing Low Sweet Rhythm; In the Cool of the Evening [2]; Hit Parade Finale [1]

Notes [1] Includes vocals of "Margie" by Con Conrad, Benny Davis and J. Russel Robinson; "Mary Lou" by Abe Lyman, George Waggner and J. Russel Robinson and "Dinah" by Harry Akst, Sam Lewis and Joe Young. [2] Also in SWING YOUR PARTNER. [3] Also in HEART OF THE GOLDEN WEST and IDAHO. [4] Also in RIDIN' DOWN THE CANYON and THE TIGER WOMAN.

2584 ✦ HIT PARADE OF 1943
Republic, 1943

Composer(s) Styne, Jule
Lyricist(s) Adamson, Harold

Producer(s) Cohen, Albert J.
Director(s) Rogell, Albert S.
Screenwriter(s) Hyland, Frances; Gill, Frank, Jr.

Cast Carroll, John; Hayward, Susan; Patrick, Gail; Catlett, Walter; Arden, Eve; Freddy Martin and His Orchestra; Count Basie and His Orchestra; Ray McKinley and His Orchestra; The Golden Gate Quartette; Pops and Louis; The Three Cheers; The Music Maids

Song(s) Do These Old Eyes Deceive Me; Limpwitz Little Liver Pills (C/L: Newman, Albert; Gill, F.); Tahm Boom Bah; That's How to Write a Song; Who Took Me Home Last Night [2]; Harlem Sandman; A Change of Heart [1]; Yankee Doodle Tan (C: Johnson, J.C.; L: Razaf, Andy)

Notes Reissued as CHANGE OF HEART. [1] Also in BEHIND CITY LIGHTS. [2] Also in CASANOVA IN BURLESQUE, THE PHANTOM SPEAKS and THUMBS UP.

2585 ✦ HIT PARADE OF 1947
Republic, 1947

Composer(s) McHugh, Jimmy
Lyricist(s) Adamson, Harold
Choreographer(s) Fanchon

Producer(s) McDonald, Frank
Director(s) McDonald, Frank
Screenwriter(s) Loos, Mary

Cast Albert, Eddie; Moore, Constance; Edwards, Joan; Lamb, Gil; Goodwin, Bill; Frawley, William; Lane, Richard; Fenton, Frank; Sanford, Ralph; Scannell, Frank; Woody Herman and His Orchestra; Bob Nolan and the Sons of the Pioneers; Rogers, Roy; Trigger

Song(s) Couldn't Be More in Love; The Cats Are Going to the Dogs; I Guess I'll Have That Dream Right Now; The Customer Is Always Wrong; Brooklyn Buckaroo (C/L: Spencer, Tim); Out California Way [1] (C/L: Carling, Foster; Meskin, Jack); Chiquita from Santa Anita; It Could Happen to Me; Is There Anyone Here from Texas

Notes Also released as HIGH AND HAPPY. [1] Also in OUT CALIFORNIA WAY.

2586 ✦ HIT PARADE OF 1951
Republic, 1950

Composer(s) Rinker, Al; Huddleston, Floyd
Lyricist(s) Rinker, Al; Huddleston, Floyd

Producer(s) Auer, John H.
Director(s) Auer, John H.
Screenwriter(s) Wilson, Warren; Wisberg, Aubrey; Reinhardt, Elizabeth; Kimble, Lawrence

Cast Carroll, John; McDonald, Marie; Rodriguez, Estelita; Fontaine, Frank; Withers, Grant; Rasumny, Mikhail; Flagg, Steve; Cavanagh, Paul; Rosett, Rose; The Firehouse Five Plus Two; Bobby Ramos and His Rhumba Band

Song(s) Boca Chica (C/L: Miller, Sy; Garrett, Betty); How Would I Know; You Don't Know the Other Side of Me; Wishes Come True; You're So Nice; A Very Happy Character Am I; Square Dance Samba

Notes This film was also released under the title SONG PARADE.

2587 ✦ THE HITTER
Peppercorn-Wormser, 1980

Musical Score Ruff, Garfeel

Producer(s) Herman, Gary; Leitch, Christopher
Director(s) Leitch, Christopher
Screenwriter(s) Leitch, Christopher; Harris, Ben

Cast O'Neal, Ron; Caesar, Adolph; Frazier, Sheila; Cobbs, Bill; Brown, Alfie

Song(s) The Hitter (C/L: Pearson, Al); Can't Quit (C/L: Wilkie, Frank); Don't Count on Me (C/L: Godfrey, Ronnie); Street Hustlin' (C/L: Strong, Buddy); Layback (One Nighter) (C/L: Pearson, Al)

Notes No cue sheet available.

2588 ✦ HIT THE DECK (1930)
Radio, 1930

Composer(s) Youmans, Vincent
Lyricist(s) Grey, Clifford; Robin, Leo
Choreographer(s) Eaton, Pearl

Director(s) Reed, Luther
Screenwriter(s) Reed, Luther
Source(s) *Hit the Deck* (musical) Youmans, Vincent

Cast The Brox Sisters; Oakie, Jack; Walker, Polly; Gray, Roger [1]; Woods, Franker [1]; Sweet, Harry; Padula, Marguerita; Clyde, June; Clayton, Ethel

Song(s) Why Oh Why? [1]; Join the Navy [1]; Loo-Loo [1]; Sailors Have Sweethearts in Ev'ry Port (C: Tierney, Harry; L: Caldwell, Anne); Harbor of My Heart [1]; Hallelujah [1]; Quite the Thing [2] [1]; Smith (C: Tierney, Harry; L: Caldwell, Anne); Keepin' Myself for You (L: Clare, Sidney); Sometimes I'm Happy [1] (L: Caesar, Irving); Shore Leave [1]; Lucky Bird [1]

Notes [1] From Broadway production. [2] Used instrumentally only. [3] Sometimes titled "Nothing Could Be Sweeter."

2589 ✦ HIT THE DECK (1955)
Metro–Goldwyn–Mayer, 1955

Composer(s) Youmans, Vincent
Lyricist(s) Grey, Clifford; Robin, Leo
Choreographer(s) Pan, Hermes

Producer(s) Pasternak, Joe
Director(s) Rowland, Roy
Screenwriter(s) Levien, Sonya; Ludwig, William
Source(s) *Hit the Deck* (musical) Youmans, Vincent; Robin, Leo; Fields, Herbert; Grey, Clifford

Cast Powell, Jane; Martin, Tony; Reynolds, Debbie; Pidgeon, Walter; Damone, Vic; Raymond, Gene; Miller, Ann; Tamblyn, Russ; Naish, J. Carrol; Armen, Kay; Anderson, Richard; Darwell, Jane; King, Alan; Slate, Henry

Song(s) Join the Navy [1]; Hallelujah [1]; Keepin' Myself for You (L: Clare, Sidney); Sometimes I'm Happy [1] (L: Caesar, Irving); Lucky Bird [1]; A Kiss or Two (L: Robin, Leo); Why Oh Why? [1]; I Know that You Know (L: Caldwell, Anne); The Lady from the Bayou (L: Robin, Leo); Ciribiribin (C: Pestalozza, Alberto; L: Johnson); More Than You Know (L: Rose, Billy; Eliscu, Edward); Loo-Loo [1]; Drums and Drill (C/L: Robin, Leo)

Notes [1] From Broadway original.

2590 ✦ HIT THE HAY
Columbia, 1946

Producer(s) Richmond, Ted
Director(s) Lord, Del
Screenwriter(s) Weil, Richard; Marion, Charles R.

Cast   Canova, Judy; Hunter, Ross; Bonanova, Fortunio; Merrick, Doris; Holden, Gloria; Perlot, Francis; Sutton, Grady; Mason, Louis

Notes   No cue sheet available. There are no original songs in this film. There are excerpts from Flotow's MARTHA and a jazz version of Rossini's WILLIAM TELL.

2591 ✦ HIT THE ICE
Universal, 1943

Composer(s)   Revel, Harry
Lyricist(s)   Webster, Paul Francis

Producer(s)   Gottlieb, Alex
Director(s)   Lamont, Charles
Screenwriter(s)   Lees, Robert; Rinaldo, Frederic I.; Grant, John

Cast   Abbott, Bud; Costello, Lou; Simms, Ginny; Knowles, Patric; Knox, Elyse; Leonard, Sheldon; Johnny Long and His Orchestra; The Four Teens; Lawrence, Marc

Song(s)   I'm Like a Fish Out of Water; I'd Like to Set You to Music; The Slap Polka [1]; Happiness Ahead [2]

Notes   [1] Also in I'LL TELL THE WORLD. [2] On cue sheet as "Happiness Bound."

2592 ✦ HITTING A NEW HIGH
RKO, 1938

Composer(s)   McHugh, Jimmy
Lyricist(s)   Adamson, Harold

Producer(s)   Lasky, Jesse L.
Director(s)   Walsh, Raoul
Screenwriter(s)   Purcell, Gertrude; Twist, John

Cast   Pons, Lily; Oakie, Jack; Howard, John; Blore, Eric; Horton, Edward Everett; Ciannelli, Eduardo

Song(s)   Let's Give Love Another Chance; This Never Happened Before; I Hit a New High; You'e Like a Song [1]

Notes   There are also vocals of "Nightingale of Parisatte" by Saint-Saens; "Andon Gl'Incensi" from LUCIA by Donizetti and "Je Suis Titania" from MIGNON by A. Thomas. [1] Not used.

2593 ✦ HITTING THE HEADLINES

See YOKEL BOY.

2594 ✦ HIT TUNE JAMBOREE
Universal, 1942

Source(s)   Short story

Song(s)   Heart of Harlem [1] (C/L: Actman, Irving; Loesser, Frank)

Notes   There are other songs in this short. [1] Performed instrumentally only.

2595 ✦ HI' YA CHUM
Universal, 1943

Composer(s)   de Paul, Gene
Lyricist(s)   Raye, Don
Choreographer(s)   Prinz, Eddie

Producer(s)   Benedict, Howard
Director(s)   Young, Harold
Screenwriter(s)   Hartmann, Edmund L.

Cast   The Ritz Brothers; Frazee, Jane; Paige, Robert; Clyde, June; Hurst, Paul; McDonald, Edmund

Song(s)   The Doo Dat; You're a Lucky Fellow, Mr. Smith [2] (C: Burke, Sonny; Prince, Hughie); Two on a Bike; He's My Guy [1]; Cactus Pete for Sheriff (C: Press, Jacques; L: Cherkose, Eddie); I'm Hitting a High Spot; You've Gotta Have Personality

Notes   Released as EVERYTHING HAPPENS TO US in Great Britain. Originally titled PASSING THE BUCK. [1] Also in HE'S MY GUY and UNDERCOVER GIRL. [2] Also in ABBOTT & COSTELLO & DICK POWELL IN THE NAVY, BUCK PRIVATES (1941) and YOU'RE A LUCKY FELLOW, MR. SMITH.

2596 ✦ HI' YA, SAILOR
Universal, 1943

Composer(s)   Rosen, Milton
Lyricist(s)   Carter, Everett

Producer(s)   Yarbrough, Jean
Director(s)   Yarbrough, Jean
Screenwriter(s)   Roberts, Stanley

Cast   Woods, Donald; Knox, Elyse; Quillan, Eddie; Willis, Matt

Song(s)   Hi 'Ya Sailor; How's About It; Oh, Brother! (C/L: Manners, Maxine; Miller, Joan); Tattooed Woman (C/L: Beatty, George); So Good Night [3]; Spell of the Moon; Just a Step Away from Heaven [2]; A Dream Ago [1]

Notes   There are also vocals of "One O' Clock Jump" by Count Basie and "The More I Go Out with Somebody Else" by Billy Post and Norman Pierce. [1] Also in HAT CHECK HONEY; MOON OVER LAS VEGAS and STARS AND VIOLINS. [2] Also in SWEET SWING. [3]Also in SUMMER LOVE.

2597 ✦ HOG WILD
Avco Embassy, 1980

Musical Score   Zaza, Paul
Composer(s)   Ford, Dwayne
Lyricist(s)   Ford, Dwayne

Producer(s)   Heroux, Claude
Director(s)   Rose, Les
Screenwriter(s)   Marin, Andrew Peter

Cast   Biehn, Michael; D'Arbanville, Patti; Rosato, Tony; Rizacos, Angelo; Doyle, Martin; Craven, Matt

Song(s)   Let the Bad Boys Come; Darling, It's You; Pick You Up and Set You Down Easy; I Want to Be Loving You Forever; Life Is Just a Silly Game; Cowboys and Rustlers; You and Me; Is It for Me

Notes   No cue sheet available.

2598 ✦ HOLD BACK THE DAWN
Paramount, 1941

Musical Score   Young, Victor

Producer(s)   Hornblow Jr., Arthur
Director(s)   Leisen, Mitchell
Screenwriter(s)   Brackett, Charles; Wilder, Billy
Source(s)   *Hold Back the Dawn* (novel) Frings, Ketti

Cast   Boyer, Charles; de Havilland, Olivia; Goddard, Paulette; Abel, Walter; De Camp, Rosemary; Leisen, Mitchell; Donlevy, Brian; Lake, Veronica

Song(s)   My Boy, My Boy [1] (C: Spielman, Fred; L: Berg, Jimmy; Loesser, Frank; Jacobson, Fred); Hold Back the Dawn [2] (C/L: Loring, Richard; Cross, Steven); A Sinner Kissed an Angel [2] (C: Joseph, Ray; L: David, Mack)

Notes   [1] This is performed instrumentally only.

2599 ✦ HOLD BACK TOMORROW
Universal, 1955

Musical Score   Cutner, Sidney

Producer(s)   Haas, Hugo
Director(s)   Haas, Hugo
Screenwriter(s)   Haas, Hugo

Cast   Moore, Cleo; Agar, John; De Kova, Frank; Boyd, Dallas

Song(s)   Hold Back Tomorrow (C/L: Steininger, Franz; Rotella, Johnny)

2600 ✦ HOLD EVERYTHING
Warner Brothers, 1930

Composer(s)   Burke, Joe
Lyricist(s)   Dubin, Al

Director(s)   Del Ruth, Roy
Screenwriter(s)   Lord, Robert
Source(s)   *Hold Everything* (musical) DeSylva, B.G.; McGowan, Jack; Henderson, Ray; Brown, Lew

Cast   Brown, Joe E.; Lightner, Winnie; Carpentier, Georges; O'Neil, Sally; Breese, Edmund; Roach, Bert; Revier, Dorothy

Song(s)   Take It on the Chin; When Little Red Roses Get the Blues for You; Sing a Little Theme Song; Physically Fit; Girls We Remember [2]; All Alone Together; Isn't This a Cockeyed World; You're the Cream in My Coffee [1] (C: Henderson, Ray; L: Brown, Lew; DeSylva, B.G.); I'm All Burned Up; I'm Screwy Over Looey; To Know You Is to Love You

Notes   No cue sheet available. [1] From original stage musical. [2] Also in SIDE SHOW.

2601 ✦ HOLD ON!
Metro–Goldwyn–Mayer, 1966

Musical Score   Karger, Fred
Composer(s)   Karger, Fred; Weisman, Ben; Wayne, Sid
Lyricist(s)   Karger, Fred; Weisman, Ben; Wayne, Sid
Choreographer(s)   Taylor, Wilda

Producer(s)   Katzman, Sam
Director(s)   Lubin, Arthur
Screenwriter(s)   Gordon, James B.

Cast   Herman's Hermits; Fabares, Shelley; Langdon, Sue Ane; Anderson, Herbert; Fox, Bernard; Hickox, Harry; Petra, Hortense; Deems, Mickey; Kellogg, Ray; Hart, John; Arnold, Phil

Song(s)   Hold On [2] (C/L: Sloan, P.F.); We Want You, Herman; Linquist (C/L: Karger, Fred); A Must to Avoid [2] (C/L: Sloan, P.F.); Where Were You When I Needed You (C/L: Sloan, P.F.; Barri, Steve); Make Me Happy; The George and Dragon; Got a Feeling; All the Things I Do For You, Baby (C/L: Sloan, P.F.; Barri, Steve); Leaning on the Lamppost [3] (C/L: Gay, Noel); Wild Love; Gotta Get Away [1]

Notes   [1] Used instrumentally only. [2] Credited to Sloane and Barri on cue sheets. [3] This is "Leaning on the Lamp Post" from ME AND MY GIRL by Noel Gay. The cue sheets and credits both spelled his name wrong as Noel Tay.

2602 ✦ HOLD THAT CO-ED
Twentieth Century–Fox, 1938

Composer(s)   Revel, Harry
Lyricist(s)   Gordon, Mack
Choreographer(s)   Castle, Nick; Sawyer, Geneva

Producer(s)   Zanuck, Darryl F.
Director(s)   Marshall, George
Screenwriter(s)   Tunberg, Karl; Ettlinger, Don; Yellen, Jack

Cast   Barrymore, John; Murphy, George; Weaver, Marjorie; Davis, Joan; Haley, Jack; Barbier, George; Terry, Ruth; Meek, Donald; Downs, Johnny; Sully, Frank

Song(s)   Heads High (C: Pollack, Lew; L: Brown, Lew); Limpy Dimpy (C/L: Styne, Jule; Castle, Nick; Clare, Sidney); Here I Am Doing It; Hold That Co-Ed; The All-American Swing [1]

Notes There are also vocals of "Harrigan" by George M. Cohan. [1] Not used. Also not used in MY LUCKY STAR.

2603 ✦ HOLD THAT GHOST
Universal, 1941

Choreographer(s) Castle, Nick

Producer(s) Kelly, Burt; Tryon, Glenn
Director(s) Lubin, Arthur
Screenwriter(s) Grant, John; Lees, Robert; Rinaldo, Frederic I.

Cast Ted Lewis and His Entertainers; The Andrews Sisters; Abbott, Bud; Costello, Lou; Davis, Joan; Carlson, Richard; Auer, Mischa; Ankers, Evelyn; Lawrence, Marc; Howard, Shemp; Hicks, Russell

Song(s) Sleepy Serenade (C: Singer, Lou; L: Greene, Mort); Aurora [1] (C: Lago, Mario; Roberti, Roberto; L: Adamson, Harold)

Notes There are also vocals of "When My Baby Smiles At Me" by Andrew B. Sterling, Ted Lewis and Bill Monro and "Me and My Shadow" by Al Jolson, Billy Rose and Dave Dreyer. [1] English lyrics by Adamson.

2604 ✦ HOLD THAT GIRL
Fox, 1934

Producer(s) Wurtzel, Sol M.
Director(s) MacFadden, Hamilton
Screenwriter(s) Nichols, Dudley; Trotti, Lamar

Cast Dunn, James; Trevor, Claire; Michael, Gertrude

Song(s) It's All for the Best (C/L: Whiting, Richard A.); Fan Dance [1] (C: Hollander, Frederick; L: Brown, Forman)

Notes [1] Sheet music only.

2605 ✦ HOLD YOUR MAN
Metro–Goldwyn–Mayer, 1933

Director(s) Wood, Sam
Screenwriter(s) Loos, Anita; Rogers, Howard Emmett

Cast Harlow, Jean; Gable, Clark; Erwin, Stuart; Burgess, Dorothy; Kirkland, Muriel; Courtney, Inez

Song(s) Hold Your Man [1] (C: Brown, Nacio Herb; L: Freed, Arthur)

Notes [1] Also in DANCING LADY.

2606 ✦ A HOLE IN THE HEAD
United Artists, 1959

Musical Score Riddle, Nelson
Composer(s) Van Heusen, James
Lyricist(s) Cahn, Sammy

Producer(s) Capra, Frank
Director(s) Capra, Frank
Screenwriter(s) Schulman, Arnold
Source(s) *A Hole in the Head* (play) Schulman, Arnold

Cast Sinatra, Frank; Robinson, Edward G.; Hodges, Eddie; Jones, Carolyn; Parker, Eleanor; Wynn, Keenan

Song(s) All My Tomorrows; High Hopes; Shirl's Theme (C: Riddle, Nelson)

2607 ✦ HOLIDAY FOR LOVERS
Twentieth Century–Fox, 1959

Producer(s) Weisbart, David
Director(s) Levin, Henry
Screenwriter(s) Davis, Luther
Source(s) (play) Alexander, Ronald

Cast Webb, Clifton; St. John, Jill; Henreid, Paul; Greco, Jose; Wyman, Jane; Lynley, Carol; Crosby, Gary

Song(s) Holiday for Lovers (C: Van Heusen, James; L: Cahn, Sammy); Rio [1] (C/L: Barroso, Ary); Accorda Escola de Samba (C/L: Martins, Herivelto; Lacerda, Benedito); Samby Ya' Ya' (C/L: Amaral, Nestor); Quererte Tientos Gitanos (C/L: Greco, Jose; Machado, Roger)

Notes [1] Not used in THREE LITTLE GIRLS IN BLUE.

2608 ✦ HOLIDAY FOR SINNERS
Metro–Goldwyn–Mayer, 1952

Musical Score Previn, Andre

Producer(s) Houseman, John
Director(s) Mayer, Gerald
Screenwriter(s) Bezzerides, A.I.
Source(s) *The Days Before Lent* (novel) Basso, Hamilton

Cast Young, Gig; Wynn, Keenan; Rule, Janice; Campbell, William; Anderson, Richard; Chekhov, Michael; Giglio, Sandro; Brett, Edith; Hall, Porter

Song(s) Wonder Why [1] (C: Brodszky, Nicholas; L: Cahn, Sammy)

Notes [1] Also in RICH, YOUNG AND PRETTY and SMALL TOWN GIRL (1953).

2609 ✦ HOLIDAY IN HAVANA
Columbia, 1949

Producer(s) Richmond, Ted
Director(s) Yarbrough, Jean
Screenwriter(s) Lees, Robert; Rinaldo, Frederic I.; De Wolf, Karen

Cast Arnaz, Desi; Hatcher, Mary; Arno, Sig; Doran, Ann; Geray, Steven; Urecal, Minerva; Walker, Ray

Song(s) Copacabana [1] (C/L: Roberts, Allan; Fisher, Doris); The Straw Hat Song (C: Karger, Fred; L: Roberts, Allan)

Notes There are also vocals of "Rumba Rumbero" by Albert Gasso and Miguelito Valdez; "I'll Take Romance" by Ben Oakland and Oscar Hammerstein II (Also used in MANHATTAN ANGEL and I'LL TAKE ROMANCE); "Made for Each Other (Tu Felicidad)" by Rene Touzet, Ervin Drake and Jimmy Shirl; and "Holiday in Havana" and "Arnaz Jam" (inst.) by Desi Arnaz. [1] Also in THRILL OF BRAZIL.

2610 ♦ HOLIDAY IN MEXICO
Metro–Goldwyn–Mayer, 1946

Choreographer(s) Donen, Stanley

Producer(s) Pasternak, Joe
Director(s) Sidney, George
Screenwriter(s) Lennart, Isobel

Cast Pidgeon, Walter; Iturbi, Jose; McDowall, Roddy; Massey, Ilona; Xavier Cugat and His Orchestra; Powell, Jane; Haas, Hugo

Song(s) Holiday in Mexico (C: Fain, Sammy; L: Freed, Ralph); Main Title (C: Stoll, George; Jackson, Calvin; L: Freed, Ralph); (You Te Amo Much) And That's That (C: Stept, Sam H.; Cugat, Xavier; L: Drake, Ervin); Someone to Love (C: Abraham; L: Freed, Ralph); You, So It's You (C/L: Brown, Nacio Herb; Brent, Earl); And Dreams Remain (C: Soler, Raoul; L: Freed, Ralph); Csak Egy Szep Lany (C/L: Janos); I Think of You [2] (C/L: Elliott, Jack; Marcotte, Don); Walter Winchell Rhumba [1] (C: Morales, Noro; L: Sigman, Carl); Impatient Years [3] (C: Fain, Sammy; L: Freed, Ralph); These Patient Years [3] (C: Fain, Sammy; L: Freed, Ralph); Ave Maria and Finale (C: Previn, Charles); Poco a Poco (C: Fain, Sammy; L: Freed, Ralph)

Notes [1] Sheet music only. Also not used in NO LEAVE, NO LOVE (MGM). [2] Music based on 2nd theme of 1st movement of Rachmaninov's "Piano Concerto #2." [3] Not used.

2611 ♦ HOLIDAY INN
Paramount, 1942

Composer(s) Berlin, Irving
Lyricist(s) Berlin, Irving
Choreographer(s) Dare, Danny

Producer(s) Sandrich, Mark
Director(s) Sandrich, Mark
Screenwriter(s) Binyon, Claude

Cast Astaire, Fred; Crosby, Bing; Reynolds, Marjorie [3]; Dale, Virginia; Abel, Walter; Beavers, Louise; Barris, Harry; Bob Crosby's Bobcats

Song(s) Happy Holiday; I'll Capture Her Heart Singing; You're Easy to Dance With; White Christmas [4]; Let's Start the New Year Right; Abraham; Be Careful, It's My Heart; I Can't Tell a Lie; Easter Parade [2]; Let's Say It with Firecrackers; Song of Freedom;

Plenty to Be Thankful For; This Is a Great Country [1]; I Pledge Allegiance [1]

Notes There are also brief renditions of "Lazy" and "All God's Chillun Got Wings." "The Jitterbug Dance" to the tune of "You're Easy to Dance With" was written by Bob Haggart and Paul Wettstein. [1] Not used. [2] Originally in Broadway musical AS THOUSANDS CHEER. Also in EASTER PARADE and ALEXANDER'S RAGTIME BAND. [3] Dubbed by Martha Mears. [4] Also in WHITE CHRISTMAS.

2612 ♦ HOLLYWOOD BOND CARAVAN
Paramount, 1945

Screenwriter(s) Shavelson, Melville

Cast Pangborn, Franklin; Welles, Virginia; Demarest, William; Benchley, Robert; Hutton, Betty; Weaver, Marjorie; Drake, Dona; Ladd, Alan; Crosby, Bing; Cavallaro, Carmen; Hope, Bob; San Juan, Olga; Bogart, Humphrey

Song(s) Rhumba Matumba [4] (C/L: Collazo, Bobby); Buy a Piece of the Peace [2] (C: Styne, Jule; L: Cahn, Sammy); We've Got Another Bond to Buy [1] (C: McHugh, Jimmy; L: Adamson, Harold); Left - Right [3] (C: Styne, Jule; L: Gannon, Kim; Meyer, Sol)

Notes Short subject. No cue sheet available. Much of this material was used in another short called CANADIAN BOND SHORT SUBJECT, maybe also titled HAPPY GANG. The cast is an approximation based on Shavelson's script. [1] The number was written for the Victory Loan Drive and given to the government. [2] This may not appear in the movie. It was written for Frank Sinatra. [3] Originally in SALUTE FOR THREE this might not be in this picture. [4] Also in the Universal films CUBAN PETE and MY GAL LOVES MUSIC.

2613 ♦ HOLLYWOOD BOULEVARD
New World, 1976

Musical Score Stein, Andrew

Producer(s) Davison, Jon
Director(s) Dante, Joe; Arkush, Allan
Screenwriter(s) Hobby, Patrick

Cast Rialson, Candice; Woronov, Mary; George, Rita; Kramer, Jeffrey; Bartel, Paul; Kaplan, Jonathan; Commander Cody and the Lost Planet Airmen

Song(s) Hello Hollywood! (C/L: Frayne, George; Stein, Andrew)

Notes No cue sheet available.

2614 ♦ HOLLYWOOD BREVITIES
Warner Brothers, 1949

Composer(s) Coslow, Sam
Lyricist(s) Coslow, Sam

Song(s) Main Title; Mr. Broadway; Moonlight Silhouette; The Majarajah; Guadalajara Hop

Notes Short subject.

2615 ✦ HOLLYWOOD CANTEEN
Warner Brothers, 1944

Lyricist(s) Koehler, Ted
Choreographer(s) Prinz, LeRoy

Producer(s) Gottlieb, Alex
Director(s) Daves, Delmer
Screenwriter(s) Daves, Delmer

Cast Hutton, Robert; Clark, Dane; The Andrews Sisters; Benny, Jack; Brown, Joe E.; Cantor, Eddie; Carlisle, Kitty; Carson, Jack; Crawford, Joan; Dantine, Helmut; Davis, Bette; Emerson, Faye; Francen, Victor; Garfield, John; Greenstreet, Sydney; Hale, Alan; Henreid, Paul; King, Andrea; Lorre, Peter; Lupino, Ida; Manning, Irene; Martin, Nora; McCracken, Joan; Moran, Dolores; Morgan, Dennis; Parker, Eleanor; Prince, William; Reynolds, Joyce; Ridgely, John; Rogers, Roy; Trigger; Sakall, S.Z.; Smith, Alexis; Scott, Zachary; Stanwyck, Barbara; Stevens, Craig; Szigeti, Joseph; Woods, Donald; Wyman, Jane; Jimmey Dorsey and His Band; Carmen Cavallaro and His Orchestra

Song(s) Hollywood Canteen (C: Jerome, M.K.; Heindorf, Ray); Youth Must Have Its Fling [6] (C: Jerome, M.K.; L: Scholl, Jack); What Are You Doin' the Rest of Your Life (C: Lane, Burton); The General Jumped at Dawn (C/L: Mundy, Jimmy); We're Staying Home Tonight (My Baby and Me) [3] (C: Schwartz, Arthur; L: Loesser, Frank); We're Having a Baby My Baby and Me (C: Duke, Vernon; L: Adamson, Harold); Tumbling Tumbleweeds [5] (C/L: Nolan, Bob); Don't Fence Me In [4] (C/L: Porter, Cole); I'm Getting Corns for My Country [1] (C/L: Charles, Dick; Barry, Jean); You Can Always Tell a Yank (C: Lane, Burton; L: Harburg, E.Y.); Sweet Dreams, Sweetheart (C: Jerome, M.K.); Ballet in Jive (Inst.) (C: Heindorf, Ray); (Enlloro) Voodoo Moon Enduro [2] (C: Morales, Obdulio; Blanco, Julio; L: Sunshine, Marion)

Notes [1] With interpolated material by Leah Worth. [2] Presented instrumentally. Harold Rome is credited with lyrics on cue sheet—not Marion Sunshine. [3] 4 seconds of screen time. Also in THANK YOUR LUCKY STARS. [4] Also in DON'T FENCE ME IN (Republic) and ADIOS ARGENTINA (Fox). [5] Also in RHYTHM ROUND-UP (Columbia) and the Republic pictures DON'T FENCE ME IN, IN OLD MONTEREY, SILVER SPURS and TUMBLING TUMBLEWEEDS. [6] Also in THE HARD WAY.

2616 ✦ HOLLYWOOD HOTEL
Warner Brothers, 1938

Musical Score Roemheld, Heinz
Composer(s) Whiting, Richard A.

Lyricist(s) Mercer, Johnny
Choreographer(s) Berkeley, Busby

Producer(s) Wallis, Hal B.
Director(s) Berkeley, Busby; Lewis, Gene [1]
Screenwriter(s) Wald, Jerry; Leo, Maurice; Macaulay, Richard

Cast Powell, Dick; Lane, Rosemary; Lane, Lola; Healy, Ted; Davis, Johnnie; Mowbray, Alan; Langford, Frances; Herbert, Hugh; Farrell, Glenda; Joslyn, Allyn; Benny Goodman and His Orchestra; James, Harry; Parsons, Louella

Song(s) I'm Like a Fish Out of Water; Silhouetted in the Moonlight; Let That Be a Lesson to You; I've Hitched My Wagon to a Star; Sing You Son-Of-A- Gun; Hooray for Hollywood; Can't Teach My Heart New Tricks

Notes There is also a rendition of "Old Black Joe" by Stephen Foster. "Hooray for Hollywood" is the most famous song of the decade of which no commercial 78 rpm recording was ever made. [1] Lewis is credited as Dialogue Director.

2617 ✦ THE HOLLYWOOD KNIGHTS
Columbia, 1980

Producer(s) Lederer, Richard
Director(s) Mutrux, Floyd
Screenwriter(s) Mutrux, Floyd

Cast Danza, Tony; Averitt, Julius; Ballard, Steve; Drier, Moosie; Kolb, Mina; Pankin, Stuart; Pfeiffer, Michelle; Schaal, Richard; Weaver, Carl Earl; Wuhl, Robert

Song(s) Hollywood Knights (C/L: Hockensen, Ed; Sudano, Bruce; Esposito, Joseph)

Notes No cue sheet available.

2618 ✦ HOLLYWOOD ON PARADE
Paramount, 1933

Producer(s) Lewyn, Louis

Cast Edwards, Cliff; Muse, Clarence; Harlow, Jean; Bennett, Constance; Bennett, Joan; Lombard, Carole; Powell, William; Wheeler, Bert; Woolsey, Robert; Langdon, Harry; Moran, Polly; Velez, Lupe; Cooper, Gary

Song(s) Hollywood on Parade (C: Grayson, Harold; Beelby, Malcolm; L: Bow, Clara); Lupe (C: Amador, Martha Benito; L: Hustwick, Al)

Notes Short subject. No cue sheet available.

2619 ✦ HOLLYWOOD OR BUST
Paramount, 1956

Composer(s) Fain, Sammy
Lyricist(s) Webster, Paul Francis
Choreographer(s) O'Curran, Charles

Producer(s)   Wallis, Hal B.
Director(s)   Tashlin, Frank
Screenwriter(s)   Lazarus, Erna

Cast   Martin, Dean; Lewis, Jerry; Crowley, Pat; Rosenbloom, Maxie; Ekberg, Anita; Waterman, Willard

Song(s)   A Day in the Country; Hollywood or Bust; It Looks Like Love; Let's Be Friendly; That Fortunate Feeling [1]; The Wild and Woolly West; My New Car [2] (C: Traditional; L: Lazarus, Erna); I Eat Poochy Pup Dog Food [3] (C: Traditional; L: Lazarus, Erna)

Notes   [1] Not used. [2] To the tune of "Three Blind Mice." [3] To the tune of "Rock-a-Bye Baby."

2620 ♦ HOLLYWOOD PARTY
Metro–Goldwyn–Mayer, 1934

Composer(s)   Rodgers, Richard
Lyricist(s)   Hart, Lorenz
Choreographer(s)   Felix, Seymour; Hale, George; Gould, Dave

Producer(s)   Rapf, Harry
Director(s)   Rowland, Roy; Goulding, Edmund; Mack, Russell; Boleslawski, Richard; Dwan, Allan
Screenwriter(s)   Dietz, Howard; Kober, Arthur

Cast   Laurel, Stan; Hardy, Oliver; Durante, Jimmy; Pearl, Jack; Moran, Polly; Butterworth, Charles; Quillan, Eddie; Clyde, June; Mouse, Mickey; Velez, Lupe; Givot, George; Carle, Richard; Williams, Frances; Ted Healy and His Stooges; Ross, Shirley; Barris, Harry; Treacher, Arthur; Young, Robert; Kennedy, Tom; Kinskey, Leonid; Durante, Jean Olsen

Song(s)   I've Had My Moments (C: Donaldson, Walter; L: Kahn, Gus); (I'm) Feelin' High (C: Donaldson, Walter; L: Dietz, Howard); Hot Choc'late Soldiers (C: Brown, Nacio Herb; L: Freed, Arthur); Hollywood Party (1); Reincarnation (C: Rodgers, Richard; Durante, Jimmy); Hollywood Party (2); Hello; The Mahster's Coming [1]; You Are [1] [2]; Black Diamond [1]; Prayer [1] [3]; The Pots; I'm One of the Boys [1]; Burning! [1]; Baby Stars [1]; You've Got That [1] [4]; Fly Away to Ioway [1] [5]; Give a Man a Job [1]; I'm a Queen in My Own Domain [1]; My Friend the Night [1]; Keep Away from the Moonlight [1]; The Night Was Made for Dancing [1]; Hollywood Waltz (Inst.) [6]

Notes   No cue sheet available. The film was originally to be titled HOLLYWOOD REVUE OF 1933. [1] Not used. [2] Possibly revised for MEET THE BARON (1933). [3] Same music as "Blue Moon." Later became the title tune for the film MANHATTAN MELODRAMA (1934) but not used in that film. Instead another lyric was written and the sung in MANHATTAN MELODRAMA as "The Bad in Every Man." [4] There were two sets of lyrics written to this tune. [5] A satire on "Shuffle Off to Buffalo." [6] Music later used as basis for "Over and Over Again" in Broadway musical JUMBO (1935).

2621 ♦ HOLLYWOOD PARTY IN TECHNICOLOR
Metro–Goldwyn–Mayer, 1937

Choreographer(s)   Romero, Carlos

Producer(s)   Lewyn, Louis
Director(s)   Rowland, Roy
Screenwriter(s)   Krafft, John

Cast   Landi, Elissa; Morrison, Joe; Errol, Leon; The Al Lyons Band; Jones Boys; The Ahern Sisters; The Marcus Show Girls

Song(s)   Egga Dagga [1] (C: Bouquet, Jean; L: Cochran, Dorcas); South Sea Island Magic (C/L: Long; Tomerlin)

Notes   Short subject. There is also a vocal of "Chinatown My Chinatown" by Jean Schwartz and William Jerome. [1] Also used in SEVEN SINNERS (Universal), HERE COMES ELMER (Republic) and HOLY TERROR (Fox) with credit to Nick C. Cochrane.

2622 ♦ HOLLYWOOD PREMIER
Metro–Goldwyn–Mayer, 1933

Composer(s)   Rubens, George Frank
Lyricist(s)   Rubens, George Frank
Choreographer(s)   Prinz, LeRoy

Director(s)   Roth, Murray
Screenwriter(s)   Roth, Murray; Rauh, Stanley

Cast   Garr, Eddie; Barry, Phyllis; Bing, Herman; The M-G-M Dancing Girls

Song(s)   Market Opening; Young and Tender; Making Hi-De-Hi; Can Broadway Do Without Me [1] (C/L: Durante, Jimmy)

Notes   Short subject. [1] Also in SPEAK EASILY.

2623 ♦ HOLLYWOOD REVUE OF 1929
Metro–Goldwyn–Mayer, 1929

Composer(s)   Edwards, Gus
Lyricist(s)   Goodwin, Joe
Choreographer(s)   Lee, Sammy

Producer(s)   Rapf, Harry
Director(s)   Reisner, Charles
Screenwriter(s)   Boasberg, Al; Hopkins, Robert E.

Cast   Benny, Jack; Nagel, Conrad; Gilbert, John; Shearer, Norma; Crawford, Joan; Love, Bessie; Barrymore, Lionel; Edwards, Cliff; Laurel, Stan; Hardy, Oliver; Page, Anita; Asther, Nils; The Brox Sisters; Davies, Marion; Keaton, Buster; Haines, William;

Dressler, Marie; King, Charles; Moran, Polly; Edwards, Gus; Kane, Karl; Arthur, George K.; Wee, Gwen; Alberta Rasch Ballet; The Rounders; Biltmore Quartet

Song(s) Bones and Tambourine (C/L: Fisher, Fred); Gotta Feelin' for You (C: Alter, Louis; L: Trent, Jo); Minstrel Days (C/L: Snell, Dave; Edwards, Gus); Low Down Rhythm (C: Greer, Jesse; L: Klages, Raymond); Your Mother and Mine [3]; You Were Meant for Me [1] (C: Brown, Nacio Herb; L: Freed, Arthur); Nobody But You; I Never Knew I Could Do Anything Like That; For I'm the Queen (C/L: Rice, Andy; Broones, Martin); Tommy Atkins on Parade (C: Brown, Nacio Herb; L: Freed, Arthur); Strike Up the Band (C/L: Fisher, Fred); You're the Jewel in My Heart (Tableaux of Jewels) (C/L: Fisher, Fred); Lon Chaney's Gonna Get You If You Don't Watch Out (L: Murray, John T.); Singin' in the Rain [2] [4] (C: Brown, Nacio Herb; L: Freed, Arthur); Charlie, Ike and Gus; Orange Blossom Time

Notes Ann Dvorak is a chorus girl in this film. There are also vocals of "Ciribiribin" by Rudolf Thaler and Alberto Pestalozza; "Oh Marie" and "O Sole Mio" by Di Capua; "A Frangesa" by Costa and "Funiculi, Funicula" by Luigi Denza; "Sonny Boy" by Al Jolson, B.G. DeSylva, Lew Brown and Ray Henderson and "Strolling Through the Park One Day." [1] Also in BROADWAY MELODY, DOUGHBOYS; SINGIN' IN THE RAIN and THE SHOW OF SHOWS (Warner). [2] Also in LITTLE NELLIE KELLY, SINGIN' IN THE RAIN and A CLOCKWORK ORANGE. [3] Also in THE SHOW OF SHOWS (Warner). [4] This sequence and the one featuring the Brox Sisters were interpolated into the 1930 short subject DOGWAY MELODY.

2624 ✦ HOLLYWOOD WONDERLAND
Warner Brothers, 1946

Composer(s) Jerome, M.K.
Lyricist(s) Scholl, Jack

Song(s) Hollywood Wonderland; Drifting on the Rio Grand; Swinging Thru the Kitchen Doors; Dancin' is the Darndest Fun; The Open Road

Notes Short subject.

2625 ✦ A HOLY TERROR (1931)
Fox, 1931

Composer(s) Henderson, Ray
Lyricist(s) Brown, Lew; DeSylva, B.G.

Producer(s) Grainger, Edmund
Director(s) Cummings, Irving
Screenwriter(s) Cohn, Alfred A.
Source(s) *Trailin'* (novel) Brand, Max

Cast O'Brien, George; Eilers, Sally; La Roy, Rita; Fields, Stanley; Bogart, Humphrey; Kirkwood, James

Song(s) Aren't We All; I Am the Words [1]

Notes [1] Previously in JUST IMAGINE.

2626 ✦ HOLY TERROR (1936)
Twentieth Century–Fox, 1936

Composer(s) Akst, Harry
Lyricist(s) Clare, Sidney

Producer(s) Stone, John
Director(s) Tinling, James
Screenwriter(s) Breslow, Lou; Patrick, John

Cast Withers, Jane; Martin, Anthony; Ray, Leah; Brendel, El; Lewis, Joe; Eldredge, John; Roy, Gloria; Tombes, Andrew; Davis, Joan

Song(s) Don't Sing—Everybody Swing; I Don't Know Myself Since I Know You; There I Go Again; Call of the Siren; Egga Dagga Pfht [1] (C/L: Cochrane, Nick C.)

Notes [1] Also in MGM's HOLLYWOOD PARTY IN TECHNICOLOR where the song is credited to Jean Bouquet and Dorcas Cochrane and also in Universal's SEVEN SINNERS and Republic's HERE COMES ELMER where it is credited as above.

2627 ✦ HOMBRE
Twentieth Century–Fox, 1967

Musical Score Rose, David

Producer(s) Ritt, Martin; Ravetch, Irving
Director(s) Ritt, Martin
Screenwriter(s) Ravetch, Irving; Frank Jr., Harriet
Source(s) *Hombre* (novel) Leonard, Elmore

Cast Newman, Paul; Boone, Richard; March, Fredric; Cilento, Diane; Mitchell, Cameron; Rush, Barbara; Lazer, Peter; Balsam, Martin; Silvera, Frank

Song(s) Days of Love [1] (C: Rose, David; L: Webster, Paul Francis)

Notes [1] Presented instrumentally only.

2628 ✦ HOME BEFORE DARK
Warner Brothers, 1958

Musical Score Steiner, Max

Producer(s) LeRoy, Mervyn
Director(s) LeRoy, Mervyn
Screenwriter(s) Bassing, Eileen; Bassing, Robert

Cast Simmons, Jean; O'Herlihy, Dan; Zimbalist Jr., Efrem; Albertson, Mabel; Dunne, Stephen; Weldon, Joan; Barnes, Joanna; Card, Kathryn

Song(s) Home Before Dark (C: McHugh, Jimmy; L: Cahn, Sammy)

Notes Used as background instrumental only.

2629 ✦ HOME IN OKLAHOMA
Republic, 1946

Composer(s) Elliott, Jack
Lyricist(s) Elliott, Jack

Producer(s) White, Edward J.
Director(s) Witney, William
Screenwriter(s) Geraghty, Gerald

Cast Rogers, Roy; Hayes, George "Gabby"; Evans, Dale; Hughes, Carol; Meeker, George; Rees, Lanny; Dandridge, Ruby; AThe Flying "L" Ranch Quartette

Song(s) Home in Oklahoma; The Everlasting Hills of Oklahoma (C/L: Spencer, Tim); Jailhouse Sequence; Breakfast Club Song; Cowboy Ham and Eggs (C/L: Spencer, Tim); Miguelito [1]; Hereford Heaven (C/L: Turner, Roy J.)

Notes [1] Also in FEDERAL AGENT AT LARGE.

2630 ✦ HOME IN WYOMING
Republic, 1942

Producer(s) Grey, Harry
Director(s) Morgan, William
Screenwriter(s) Tasker, Robert; Webster, M. Coates

Cast Autry, Gene; Burnette, Smiley; McKenzie, Fay; Howland, Olin; Chandler, Chick; Taylor, Forrest

Song(s) Tweedle O' Twill [2] (C/L: Rose, Fred); Down Mexico Way [1] (C: Styne, Jule; L: Cherkose, Eddie; Meyer, Sol)

Notes No cue sheet available. [1] Also in DOWN MEXICO WAY; THE GOLDEN STALLION and YELLOW ROSE OF TEXAS. [2] Gene Autry also credited on sheet.

2631 ✦ HOME IS WHERE THE HEART IS
Atlantic, 1987

Musical Score Robertson, Eric N.

Producer(s) Eckert, John M.
Director(s) Bromfield, Rex
Screenwriter(s) Bromfield, Rex

Cast Bromfield, Valri; Miller, Stephen E.; Henry, Deanne; Mull, Martin; Nielsen, Leslie

Song(s) The Luckiest Man Alive (C/L: Baldry, Long John); Don't Lock Me Up (C/L: Horowitz, Dalbello; Horowitz, Asher)

Notes No cue sheet available.

2632 ✦ HOME ON THE PRAIRIE
Republic, 1939

Producer(s) Grey, Harry
Director(s) Townley, Jack
Screenwriter(s) Powell, Charles; Franklin, Paul

Cast Autry, Gene; Burnette, Smiley; Storey, June; Cleveland, George; Mulhall, Jack; Miller, Walter

Song(s) I'm Gonna Round Up My Blues [1] (C/L: Marvin, Johnny); There's Nothin' Like Work (C/L: Burnette, Smiley; Cherkose, Eddie); I'd Rather Be on the Outside (C/L: Marvin, Johnny); Home (C/L: Van Steeden, Peter; Clarkson, Harry; Clarkson, Jeff); Moonlight on the Ranch House (C/L: Samuels, Walter G. G.); Big Bullfrog (C/L: Samuels, Walter G.)

Notes No cue sheet available. [1] Gene Autry also credited on sheet music.

2633 ✦ HOME ON THE RANGE
Republic, 1946

Producer(s) Gray, Louis
Director(s) Springsteen, R.G.
Screenwriter(s) Burbridge, Betty

Cast Hale, Monte; Booth, Adrian; Bob Nolan and the Sons of the Pioneers

Song(s) Happy Go Lucky Cowboy (C/L: Forster, Gordon); Over the Rainbow Trail We'll Ride [1] (C/L: Carson, Ken); Take Your Time (C/L: Spencer, Glenn); Down at the Old Hoe-Down (C/L: Forster, Gordon); Square Dance Call (C/L: Gotcher, Les)

Notes [1] Also in SAN FERNANDO VALLEY.

2634 ✦ HOMEWORK
Jensen Farley, 1982

Musical Score Jones, Tony; Wetzel, Jim
Composer(s) Murray, Larry
Lyricist(s) Murray, Larry

Producer(s) Beshears, James
Director(s) Beshears, James
Screenwriter(s) Peterson, Maurice; Safran, Don

Cast Collins, Joan; Morgan, Michael; Kepler, Shell; Horn, Lanny; Donovan, Erin; Snodgress, Carrie

Song(s) Friend and Faces; Who Do You Do It To; One Step Out of Time; Alice (C/L: Jack, Ian); Victim of Romance (C/L: Martin, John Moon); Totally Hip (C/L: Wippo; Jaye, Michael); Lovers (C/L: Jones, Tony); School Days (C/L: Jones, Tony)

Notes No cue sheet available.

2635 ✦ HONDO
Warner Brothers, 1956

Musical Score Friedhofer, Hugo

Producer(s) Fellows, Robert
Director(s) Farrow, John
Screenwriter(s) Grant, James Edward
Source(s) "The Gift of Cochise" (story) L'Amour, Louis

Cast   Wayne, John; Page, Geraldine; Bond, Ward; Pate, Michael; Arness, James; Acosta, Rodolfo; Gordon, Leo

Song(s)   Hondo, Hondo [1] (C: Friedhofer, Hugo; L: Ronell, Ann)

Notes   [1] Used as instrumental only.

2636 ✦ HONEY
Paramount, 1930

Composer(s)   Harling, W. Franke
Lyricist(s)   Coslow, Sam
Choreographer(s)   Bennett, David

Producer(s)   Selznick, David O.
Director(s)   Ruggles, Wesley
Screenwriter(s)   Mankiewicz, Herman J.
Source(s)   *Come Out of the Kitchen* (play) Thomas, A.E.; Miller, Alice Duer

Cast   Carroll, Nancy; Smith, Stanley; Roth, Lillian; Gallagher, Skeets; Green, Harry; Pitts, ZaSu; Howland, Jobyna; Green, Mitzi

Song(s)   In My Little Hope Chest; Let's Be Domestic; I Don't Need Atmosphere (To Fall in Love); Sing, You Sinners; My Sweeter Than Sweet [4] (C: Whiting, Richard A.; L: Marion Jr., George); Dames [1]; The Prisoner's Song [5] (C/L: Massey, Guy); What Is This Power I Have? [1] [3]; My Lover [1] [2] (L: Smith, Paul Gerard; Coslow, Sam); If This Is Love [1] [2] (L: Smith, Paul Gerard; Coslow, Sam); Give a Guy a Kiss [1] [2] (L: Smith, Paul Gerard; Coslow, Sam); Help Help [1]

Notes   Originally titled COME OUT OF THE KITCHEN. [1] Cut. [2] Smith wrote the lyrics for the chorus and Coslow the lyrics for the verse. [3] Published. Some sources list this as being in the picture, however the cue sheet disagrees. [4] Also in SWEETIE and not used in SAFETY IN NUMBERS. [5] Also in THE DANGEROUS NAN MCGREW.

2637 ✦ HONEYCHILE
Republic, 1951

Musical Score   Young, Victor

Producer(s)   Picker, Sidney
Director(s)   Springsteen, R.G.
Screenwriter(s)   Trivers, Barry; Roberts, Charles E.; Townley, Jack

Cast   Canova, Judy; Foy Jr., Eddie; Hale Jr., Alan; Catlett, Walter; Kinskey, Leonid; Ates, Roscoe; Knight, Fuzzy

Song(s)   Honeychile (C: Spina, Harold; L: Elliott, Jack); Rag Mop (C/L: Wills, Johnnie; Anderson, Deacon); More Than I Care to Remember (C/L: Terry, Matt; Johnson, Ted); Tutti Frutti (C: Canova, Ann; L: Elliott, Jack)

2638 ✦ HONEYLAND
Metro–Goldwyn–Mayer, 1935

Musical Score   Bradley, Scott

Song(s)   Honeyland (C/L: Bradley, Scott); We's Bees (C/L: Bradley, Scott; Keyes, Baron)

Notes   Animated cartoon.

2639 ✦ HONEYMOON
RKO, 1947

Composer(s)   Harline, Leigh
Lyricist(s)   Greene, Mort
Choreographer(s)   O'Curran, Charles

Producer(s)   Duff, Warren
Director(s)   Keighley, William
Screenwriter(s)   Kanin, Michael

Cast   Temple, Shirley; Tone, Franchot; Madison, Guy; Romay, Lina; Lockhart, Gene; Mura, Corinna; Mitchell, Grant

Song(s)   Ven Aqui; I Love Geraniums

2640 ✦ HONEYMOON AHEAD
Universal, 1945

Composer(s)   Rosen, Milton
Lyricist(s)   Carter, Everett

Producer(s)   Cowan, Will
Director(s)   LeBorg, Reginald
Screenwriter(s)   Burton, Val; Ullman, Elwood

Cast   Jones, Allan; McDonald, Grace; Walburn, Raymond

Song(s)   'Round the Bend; Time Will Tell; Now and Always; How Lovely

2641 ✦ HONEYMOON HATE
Paramount, 1930 unproduced

Composer(s)   Harling, W. Franke
Lyricist(s)   Coslow, Sam

Cast   MacDonald, Jeanette; Ruggles, Charles; Martini, Nino

Song(s)   To Fall in Love in Venice; I'm on My Way to Berlin; It's Only a Song Tonight; I Am Afraid to Waltz with You; I Understand Tonight; Want a Good Time Bad; Here's to Aunt Octavia; Lament; Pharoah Had a Daughter and Her Name was Cleopatra

2642 ✦ HONEYMOON HOTEL
Metro–Goldwyn–Mayer, 1964

Musical Score   Scharf, Walter
Composer(s)   Van Heusen, James
Lyricist(s)   Cahn, Sammy
Choreographer(s)   Nelson, Miriam

Producer(s) Berman, Pandro S.
Director(s) Levin, Henry
Screenwriter(s) Allen, R.S.; Bullock, Harvey

Cast Goulet, Robert; Kwan, Nancy; Morse, Robert; St. John, Jill; Helm, Anne; Lanchester, Elsa; Fox, Bernard; Allman, Elvia; Wynn, Keenan

Song(s) Honeymoon Hotel; You're It; Love Is Oh So Easy [1]

Notes [1] Used instrumentally only.

2643 ◆ HONEYMOON LANE
Paramount, 1931

Composer(s) Hanley, James F.
Lyricist(s) Dowling, Eddie

Producer(s) Sono-Art Productions
Director(s) Craft, William James
Screenwriter(s) Sarecky, Barney; Jevne, Jack
Source(s) *Honeymoon Lane* (musical) Dowling, Eddie; Hanley, James F.

Cast Dowling, Eddie; Dooley, Ray; Collyer, June; Hatton, Raymond; Beery, Noah; Kaliz, Armand; Carr, Mary

Song(s) Little White House at the End of Honeymoon Lane [1]; Honeymoon Lane; Royal March (inst.)

Notes [1] Performed instrumentally only. The song is from the stage musical. Billy Moll is also credited on sheet music.

2644 ◆ HONEYMOON LODGE
Universal, 1943

Producer(s) Wilson, Warren
Director(s) Lilley, Edward
Screenwriter(s) Bruckman, Clyde

Cast Bruce, David; Vincent, June; Hilliard, Harriet

Notes It is not known if any of the vocals were written for this film. They include: "Do I Worry" by Stanley Cowan and Bobby Worth; "I Never Knew" by Tom Pitts, Ray Egan and Roy K. Marsh; "I'm Thru with Love" by Matty Malneck, Fred Livingston and Gus Kahn and "Why Don't You Fall in Love with Me?" by Mabel Wayne and Al Lewis.

2645 ◆ THE HONEYMOON MACHINE
Metro–Goldwyn–Mayer, 1961

Musical Score Harline, Leigh

Producer(s) Weingarten, Lawrence
Director(s) Thorpe, Richard
Screenwriter(s) Wells, George
Source(s) *The Golden Fleecing* (play) Semple Jr., Lorenzo

Cast McQueen, Steve; Bazlen, Brigid; Hutton, Jim; Prentiss, Paula; Jagger, Dean; Weston, Jack; Mullaney, Jack

Song(s) Love Is Crazy (C: Harline, Leigh; L: Brooks, Jack)

2646 ◆ HONEYSUCKLE ROSE
Warner Brothers, 1980

Composer(s) Nelson, Willie
Lyricist(s) Nelson, Willie

Producer(s) Taft, Gene
Director(s) Schatzberg, Jerry
Screenwriter(s) Sobieski, Carol; Wittliff, William D.; Binder, John
Source(s) "Intermezzo" (story) Stevens, Gosta; Molander, Gustave

Cast Nelson, Willie; Cannon, Dyan; Irving, Amy; Pickens, Slim; Floyd, Joey; Pointer, Priscilla; Levin, Charles; Rooney Jr., Mickey; Harris, Emmylou; Scarwid, Diana

Song(s) On the Road Again; So You Think You're a Cowboy (C/L: Nelson, Willie; Cochran, Hank); Singing the Yodelling Blues (C/L: Joyce, Chuck; Threadgill, Kenneth; Paul, Julie); Crazy; Coming Back to Texas (C/L: Threadgill, Kenneth; Joyce, Chuck; Paul, Julie); Loving Her Was Easier (Than Anything I'll Ever Do Again) [1] (C/L: Kristofferson, Kris); Under the 'X' in Texas (C/L: Gimble, Johnny); My Own Peculiar Way; Whiskey River (C/L: Shinn, John Bush); Till I Gain Control Again (C/L: Crowell, Rodney); If You Could Touch Her at All (C/L: Clayton, Lee); Angel Eyes (C/L: Crowell, Rodney); Yesterday's Wine; I Didn't Write the Music (C/L: Rooney Jr., Mickey); Angels Flying Too Close to the Ground; You Show Me Yours (And I'll Show You Mine) (C/L: Kristofferson, Kris); Make the World Go Away (C/L: Cochran, Hank); There's Two Sides to Every Story; A Song for You (C/L: Russell, Leon); Uncloudy Day

Notes It is unclear from the records which were written for the picture. [1] Also in CISCO PIKE (Columbia).

2647 ◆ HONG KONG AFFAIR
Allied Artists, 1958

Musical Score Forbes, Louis

Producer(s) Heard, Paul F.; Friedgen, J. Raymond
Director(s) Heard, Paul F.
Screenwriter(s) Luft, Herbert G.; Heard, Paul F.; Friedgen, J. Raymond; Turner, Helene

Cast Kelly, Jack; Wynn, May; Loo, Richard

Song(s) Hong Kong Affair (C: Forbes, Louis; L: Herrick, Paul)

2648 ◆ THE HONKERS
United Artists, 1972

Musical Score   Haskell, Jimmie

Producer(s)   Gardner, Arthur; Levy, Jules V.
Director(s)   Ihnat, Steve
Screenwriter(s)   Ihnat, Steve; Lodge, Stephen

Cast   Coburn, James; Pickens, Slim; Nettleton, Lois; Archer, Anne; Eccles, Ted

Song(s)   Love's Satisfaction (C/L: Lewis, Bobby; Turner, Scott); I'm a Rodeo Cowboy (C/L: Pickens, Slim); All I Ever Need Is You (C/L: Holiday, Jimmy; Reeves, Eddie); That's Just the Way I Am (C/L: Turner, Scott; DeHaven, Penny); Blowin' on Cold Ashes (C/L: Mize, Billy); My Special Day (C/L: Russell, Bobby); All Together Now Cry (C/L: Mize, Billy); Doggone This Heartache (C/L: Lewis, Bobby; Parker, Billy); Easy Made for Lovin' (C/L: Russell, Bobby)

2649 ◆ HONKY TONK
Warner Brothers, 1929

Composer(s)   Ager, Milton
Lyricist(s)   Yellen, Jack
Choreographer(s)   Ceballos, Larry

Director(s)   Bacon, Lloyd
Screenwriter(s)   Yellen, Jack; Baker, V.C. Graham

Cast   Tucker, Sophie; Lee, Lila; Ferris, Audrey; Duryea, George; Hamilton, Mahlon; Murray, John T.; Mack, Willard

Song(s)   I'm the Last of the Red Hot Mommas; I'm Doin' What I'm Doin' for Love; He's a Good Man to Have Around; I'm Feathering a Nest (for a Little Bluebird); I Don't Want to Get Thin; Some of These Days [1] (C/L: Brooks, Shelton)

Notes   No cue sheet available. Yellen only contributed Sophie Tucker's dialogue. *Variety* review cites a song titled "Take Off Your Mask." [1] Also in READY FOR LOVE (Paramount).

2650 ◆ HONKY TONK FREEWAY
Universal, 1981

Musical Score   Martin, George; Bernstein, Elmer

Producer(s)   Koch, Howard W.; Boyd, Don
Director(s)   Schlesinger, John
Screenwriter(s)   Clinton, Edward

Cast   Bridges, Beau; Cronyn, Hume; D'Angelo, Beverly; Devane, William; Dzundza, George; Garr, Teri; Grifasi, Joe; Hesseman, Howard; Jabara, Paul; Page, Geraldine; Stern, Daniel; Tandy, Jessica; Frazier, Ron; Rush, Deborah; Billingsley, Peter; Beardsley, Alice; Hanft, Helen; Burmeister, Leo; LeRoy, Gloria

Song(s)   Honky Tonk Freeway (C: Dorff, Stephen H.; L: Brown, Milton); My Man Ain't Man Enough for Me (C/L: Jabara, Paul; Lee, Jennifer); Years from Now (C/L: Cook, Roger; Cochran, Charles Lincoln); Ticlaw Anthem (C/L: Martin, George; Musker, Frank); Years from Now (C/L: Cook, Roger); You're Crazy But I Like You (C/L: Musker, Frank; Bugatti, Dominic); Diamond Trinkets (C: Bernstein, Elmer; L: Black, Don); Faster Faster (C/L: Jabara, Paul); Love Keeps Bringing Me Down (C/L: Martin, George)

2651 ◆ HONKYTONK MAN
Warner Brothers, 1982

Musical Score   Dorff, Stephen H.

Producer(s)   Eastwood, Clint
Director(s)   Eastwood, Clint
Screenwriter(s)   Carlille, Clancy
Source(s)   *Honkytonk Man* (novel) Carlille, Clancy

Cast   Eastwood, Clint; Eastwood, Kyle; McIntire, John; Bloom, Verna; Clark, Matt; Corbin, Barry

Song(s)   When I Sing About You (C/L: Blackwell, DeWayne); In the Jailhouse Now (C/L: Rodgers, Jimmie); No Sweeter Cheater than You (C/L: Tork, Mitch; Redd, Ramona); Honkytonk Man (C/L: Blackwell, DeWayne); One Fiddle, Two Fiddle (C/L: Crofford, Cliff; Durrill, John; Garrett, Snuff); San Antonio Rose [1] (C/L: Wills, Bob); Whorehouse Piano (Inst.) (C: Dorff, Stephen H.; Garrett, Snuff); When the Blues Come Around This Evening (C/L: Crofford, Cliff; Durrill, John); Turn the Pencil Over (C/L: Blackwell, DeWayne); Texas Moonbeam Waltz (Inst.) (C: Crofford, Cliff; Dorff, Stephen H.; Garrett, Snuff); Please Surrender (C/L: Crofford, Cliff; Durrill, John; Garrett, Snuff)

Notes   [1] Also in RHYTHM ROUND-UP (Columbia), UNDER COLORADO SKIES (Republic), SAN ANTONIO ROSE (Universal) and BOB WILLS AND HIS TEXAS PLAYBOYS.

2652 ◆ HONOLULU
Metro–Goldwyn–Mayer, 1939

Musical Score   Waxman, Franz
Composer(s)   Warren, Harry
Lyricist(s)   Kahn, Gus
Choreographer(s)   Connolly, Bobby; Lee, Sammy

Producer(s)   Cummings, Jack
Director(s)   Buzzell, Edward
Screenwriter(s)   Fields, Herbert; Partos, Frank

Cast   Powell, Eleanor; Young, Robert; Burns, George; Allen, Gracie; Johnson, Rita; Kolb, Clarence; Sayers, Jo Ann; Morriss, Ann; Gargan, Edward; Anderson, Eddie "Rochester"; Hussey, Ruth; Rumann, Sig

Song(s) Honolulu; This Night (Will Be My Souvenir); The Leader Doesn't Like Music; Liliu E (C/L: Kaulia); The Beauty Hula [1] (C/L: Noble, Ray); Kukuna Aka La (C: Noble, Ray; L: Wright, Bob; Forrest, Chet); Hola E Pae (C/L: Noble, Ray); What Makes the World Go 'Round [2]

Notes One of Eleanor Powell's numbers was cut and inserted into THE GREAT MORGAN. See that film for possible titles of the number. [1] Later in ON AN ISLAND WITH YOU with additional credit of Almeida. [2] Not used.

2653 ◆ HONOLULU LU
Columbia, 1941

Composer(s) Chaplin, Saul
Lyricist(s) Cahn, Sammy

Producer(s) MacDonald, Wallace
Director(s) Barton, Charles
Screenwriter(s) Gibbons, Eliot; Yawitz, Paul

Cast Velez, Lupe; Carrillo, Leo; Bennett, Bruce; Beddoe, Don; Tucker, Forrest; Clark, Roger; Gateson, Marjorie

Song(s) Sailor Boy; That's the Kind of Work I Do; Honolulu Lu

2654 ◆ HONOR OF THE WEST
Universal, 1939

Composer(s) Allan, Fleming
Lyricist(s) Allan, Fleming

Producer(s) Carr, Trem
Director(s) Waggner, George
Screenwriter(s) West, Joseph

Cast Baker, Bob; Bell, Marjorie; Young, Carleton; Kirk, Jack; Strange, Glenn

Song(s) As the Old Chuckwagon Rolls Along; Pride of the Prairie; Headin' for the Old Corral; Dry and Dusty [1]

Notes [1] BMI list only.

2655 ◆ THE HOODLUM SAINT
Metro–Goldwyn–Mayer, 1945

Musical Score Shilkret, Nathaniel

Producer(s) Reid, Cliff
Director(s) Taurog, Norman
Screenwriter(s) Wead, Frank; Hill, James

Cast Powell, William; Williams, Esther; Lansbury, Angela [1]; Gleason, James; Stone, Lewis; Ragland, Rags; McHugh, Frank; Summerville, Slim

Song(s) Sweetheart (C: Johnson, Arnold; L: Davis, Benny); If I Had You (C/L: Shapiro, Ted; Campbell, Jimmy; Connelly, Reg); How Am I To Know [2] (C: King, Jack; L: Parker, Dorothy)

Notes [1] Dubbed by Doreen Tryden. [2] Also in DYNAMITE and HE'S MY GUY (Universal).

2656 ◆ HOOPER
Warner Brothers, 1978

Musical Score Justis, Bill

Producer(s) Moonjean, Hank
Director(s) Needham, Hal
Screenwriter(s) Rickman, Tom; Kerby, Bill

Cast Reynolds, Burt; Vincent, Jan-Michael; Field, Sally; Keith, Brian; Marley, John; Klein, Robert

Song(s) Hooper (C/L: Myggen, Bent); Move Over Mama (C/L: Mahoney, James A.); A Player, A Pawn, A Hero, A King (C/L: Harris, Stewart)

2657 ◆ HOORAY FOR LOVE
RKO, 1935

Composer(s) McHugh, Jimmy
Lyricist(s) Fields, Dorothy
Choreographer(s) Lee, Sammy

Producer(s) Young, Felix
Director(s) Lang, Walter
Screenwriter(s) Hazard, Lawrence; Harris, Ray

Cast Sothern, Ann; Raymond, Gene; Robinson, Bill; Gambarelli, Maria; Hall, Thurston; Kelton, Pert; Caine, Georgia; Stander, Lionel; Waller, Thomas "Fats"; Hardy, Sam; Legon, Jeni; Girardot, Etienne

Song(s) I'm in Love All Over Again; Palsie Walsie; You're an Angel; I'm Living in a Great Big Way [1]; Hooray for Love [2]

Notes Strangely enough two of the song titles, "Hooray for Love" and "Palsy Walsy," were later used for Harold Arlen melodies. [1] Also in WHERE DANGER LIES. [2] Also in FORTY NAUGHTY GIRLS.

2658 ◆ HOOSIER HOLIDAY
Republic, 1943

Producer(s) Schaefer, Armand
Director(s) McDonald, Frank
Screenwriter(s) McGowan, Dorrell; McGowan, Stuart

Cast Byron, George; Kettering, Frank; Trietsch, Paul; Ward, Charles O.; Trietsch, Kenneth H.; Evans, Dale; Ludes, Alice; Hall, Thurston

Song(s) Long Boy (C/L: Walker, Barclay; Herschell, William); The K.P. Serenade (C/L: Twomey, Kay; Goodhart, Al); Who's Your Little Hoosier (C/L: Marvin, Johnny); Boogie Woogie Hoedown (C/L: Henderson, Charles); Giddap Mule (C/L: Ware, L.)

Notes There are also vocals of "Back Home Again in Indiana" by Ballard Macdonald and James F. Hanley; "Crawdad Hole" and "Buffalo Gals."

2659 ✦ HOOTENANNY HOOT
Metro–Goldwyn–Mayer, 1964

Musical Score Karger, Fred
Choreographer(s) Belfer, Hal

Producer(s) Katzman, Sam
Director(s) Nelson, Gene
Screenwriter(s) Gordon, James B.

Cast The Brothers Four; Wooley, Sheb; Cash, Johnny; The Gateway Trio; Henske, Judy; Hamilton IV, George; Joe and Eddie; Taylor, Cathie; Crosby, Chris; Breck, Peter; Lewis, Bobo

Song(s) Hootenanny Hoot (C: Karger, Fred; L: Wooley, Sheb); Puttin' on the Style (C: Regis, Fred; L: Regis, Fred; Reynolds, Malvina); Abilene (C: Brown, Les; L: Loudermilk, John); Frankie's Man Johnnie (C: Traditional; L: Cash, Johnny); There's a Meetin' Here Tonight (C: Traditional; L: Gibson, Bob); The Frozen Logger (C: Traditional; L: Fascinato, Jack); Frog (C/L: Traditional; Foley, Dick; Flick, Bob; Kirkland, Mike; Paine, John); Sweet, Sweet Love (C/L: Turnbull, Graham; Lampert, Diane; Farrow, Peter); Ballad of Little Romy (C/L: Henske, Judy); Building a Railroad (C/L: Wooley, Sheb); Foolish Questions (C/L: Walton, Jerry); Darling Corey (C/L: Gotz, Stuart)

Notes There is also a vocal of "Wading in the Water."

2660 ✦ HOPALONG RIDES AGAIN
Paramount, 1937

Producer(s) Sherman, Harry
Director(s) Selander, Lesley
Screenwriter(s) Houston, Norman

Cast Boyd, William; Hayden, Russell; Hayes, George "Gabby"; Duncan, William; Wilde, Lois

Song(s) I Still Remember [1] (C/L: Roberts, Carleton; Dixon, Cliff)

Notes [1] Not used.

2661 ✦ HOPPITY GOES TO TOWN

See MR. BUG GOES TO TOWN.

2662 ✦ HOPPY'S HOLIDAY
Paramount, 1941 unproduced

Song(s) Drifting Smoke (C/L: Burnette, Smiley)

2663 ✦ HOPSCOTCH
Avco Embassy, 1980

Producer(s) Landau, Edie; Landau, Ely
Director(s) Neame, Ronald
Screenwriter(s) Garfield, Brian; Forbes, Bryan
Source(s) (novel) Garfield, Brian

Cast Matthau, Walter; Jackson, Glenda; Waterston, Sam; Lom, Herbert; Beatty, Ned; Matthau, David; Darden, Severn

Song(s) Once a Night (C/L: English, Jackie; Bremers, Beverly)

Notes No cue sheet available.

2664 ✦ HORIZONS WEST
Universal, 1952

Musical Score Stein, Herman

Producer(s) Cohen, Albert J.
Director(s) Boetticher, Budd
Screenwriter(s) Stevens, Louis

Cast Hudson, Rock; Arness, James; Ryan, Robert; Adams, Julia; Burr, Raymond; Weaver, Dennis; McIntire, John; Bavier, Frances; Clarke, Mae

Song(s) Daddy, Surprise Me! [1] (C/L: James, Inez; Miller, Sidney)

Notes [1] Also in ARE YOU WITH IT?

2665 ✦ THE HORIZONTAL LIEUTENANT
Metro–Goldwyn–Mayer, 1962

Musical Score Stoll, George

Producer(s) Pasternak, Joe
Director(s) Thorpe, Richard
Screenwriter(s) Wells, George
Source(s) *The Bottletop Affair* (novel) Cotler, Gordon

Cast Hutton, Jim; Prentiss, Paula; Carter, Jack; Backus, Jim; McGraw, Charles; Umeki, Miyoshi; Ingels, Marty

Song(s) The Horizontal Lieutenant [1] (C/L: Stoll, George; Unger, Stella; Pasternak, Joe)

Notes There is also a vocal of "How About You" by Burton Lane and Ralph Freed. [1] Pasternak only listed on cue sheet not on credits.

2666 ✦ HORROR HOSPITAL
Scope III, 1979

Musical Score Edwards, Ann; De Wolfe

Producer(s) Gordon, Richard
Director(s) Balch, Anthony
Screenwriter(s) Balch, Anthony; Balch, Alan Watson

Cast Gough, Michael; Askwith, Robin; Shaw, Vanessa; Pollock, Ellen

Song(s) Mark of Death (C/L: de Havilland, Jason)

Notes No cue sheet available. Also known as COMPUTER KILLERS.

2667 ◆ HORSE AND BUGGY DAYS
Warner Brothers, 1950

Musical Score Jackson, Howard
Composer(s) Jerome, M.K.
Lyricist(s) Scholl, Jack

Song(s) Seaside Finale [2]; Minstrel Days [1]

Notes Short subject. There are also renditions of several turn-of-the-century songs. [1] Also in MINSTREL DAYS and MY WILD IRISH ROSE. [2] Also in THOSE GOOD OLD DAYS.

2668 ◆ HORSE FEATHERS
Paramount, 1932

Composer(s) Ruby, Harry
Lyricist(s) Kalmar, Bert

Director(s) McLeod, Norman Z.
Screenwriter(s) Perelman, S.J.; Kalmar, Bert; Ruby, Harry

Cast Marx, Groucho; Marx, Chico; Marx, Harpo; Marx, Zeppo; Todd, Thelma

Song(s) I'm Against It; Everyone Says "I Love You"; I'm Daffy Over You [1] (C: Marx, Chico; L: Violinsky, Sol)

Notes [1] Used instrumentally here and also in MONKEY BUSINESS. With an additional lyric by Benny Davis the song became known as "Lucky Little Penny."

2669 ◆ A HORSEFLY FLEAS
Warner Brothers, 1948

Musical Score Stalling, Carl

Director(s) McKimson, Robert
Screenwriter(s) Foster, Warren

Cast Flea, Anthony

Song(s) Food Around the Corner [1] (C/L: Clampett, Robert)

Notes Looney Tune. [1] Also in AN ITCH IN TIME.

2670 ◆ THE HORSE IN THE GRAY FLANNEL SUIT
Disney, 1968

Musical Score Bruns, George

Producer(s) Hibler, Winston
Director(s) Tokar, Norman
Screenwriter(s) Pelletier, Louis
Source(s) *The Year of the Horse* (novel) Hatch, Eric

Cast Jones, Dean; Baker, Diane; Bochner, Lloyd; Clark, Fred; Janov, Ellen; Amsterdam, Morey; Russell, Kurt; Tuttle, Lurene; Hewitt, Alan; Albarado

Song(s) Aspercel (C/L: Bruns, George)

2671 ◆ HORSE PLAY
Universal, 1933

Director(s) Sedgwick, Edward
Screenwriter(s) Walker, H.M.; Van Every, Dale

Cast Summerville, Slim; Devine, Andy; Hyams, Leila; Keefe, Cornelius; O'Connor, Una; Griffies, Ethel

Song(s) Blood on the Saddle [1] (C/L: Johnston, Gene; L: Cheatman, E.)

Notes Also in BOYS' RANCH.

2672 ◆ THE HORSE SOLDIERS
United Artists, 1959

Musical Score Buttolph, David

Producer(s) Mahin, John Lee; Rackin, Martin
Director(s) Ford, John
Screenwriter(s) Mahin, John Lee; Rackin, Martin
Source(s) *The Horse Soldiers* (novel) Sinclair, Harold

Cast Wayne, John; Holden, William; Towers, Constance; Jones, Stan; Gibson, Althea; Gibson, Hoot [1]; Pratt, Judson; Ruysdael, Basil; Whitehead, O.Z.; Pyle, Denver; Martin, Strother

Song(s) I Left My Love (C/L: Jones, Stan)

Notes [1] Last film appearance.

2673 ◆ THE HORSE WITH THE FLYING TAIL
Disney, 1961

Musical Score Lava, William

Producer(s) Lansburgh, Larry
Director(s) Lansburgh, Larry
Screenwriter(s) Lansburgh, Janet; Bryan, Bill

Cast Fenneman, George; Williams, Dorian; Nautical

Song(s) The Horse with the Flying Tail (C: Lava, William; L: Jackman, Bob)

2674 ◆ HOT BLOOD
Columbia, 1956

Musical Score Baxter, Les
Composer(s) Baxter, Les
Lyricist(s) Bagdasarian, Ross
Choreographer(s) Mattox, Matt

Producer(s) Welsch, Howard; Tatelman, Harry
Director(s) Ray, Nicholas
Screenwriter(s) Lasky Jr., Jesse

Cast Russell, Jane; Wilde, Cornel; Adler, Luther; Calleia, Joseph; Rasumny, Mikhail; Deacon, Richard

Song(s) Tsara, Tsara; I Could Learn to Love You

Notes No cue sheet available.

2675 ✦ HOT CURVES
Tiffany, 1930

Composer(s) Violinsky, Sol
Lyricist(s) Ryan, Ben

Director(s) Taurog, Norman
Screenwriter(s) Snell, Earle; Mortimer, Frank; Rubin, Benny

Cast Day, Marceline; Rubin, Benny; Kelton, Pert; Moorhead, Natalie; Lease, Rex; Carr, Mary; Ince, John

Song(s) If I Only Knew That You Could Care for Me; My Son-ny; Tum Tum Tumble Into Love

Notes No cue sheet available.

2676 ✦ HOT DOG . . . THE MOVIE
MGM/UA, 1984

Musical Score Bernstein, Peter

Producer(s) Feldman, Edward S.
Director(s) Markle, Peter
Screenwriter(s) Marvin, Mike

Cast Naughton, David; Houser, Patrick; Smith, Tracy; Reger, John Patrick

Song(s) Top of the Hill (C: Bernstein, Peter; L: Goldenberg, Mark); Hold On (C: Bernstein, Peter; L: Goldenberg, Mark); Dreamers on the Rise (C/L: Stewart, John); Bringing Down the Moon (C/L: Stewart, John); Rudi's Victory Song (C/L: Reger, John Patrick)

Notes No cue sheet available.

2677 ✦ HOTEL
Warner Brothers, 1967

Musical Score Keating, John

Producer(s) Mayes, Wendell
Director(s) Quire, Richard
Screenwriter(s) Mayes, Wendell
Source(s) *Hotel* (novel) Hailey, Arthur

Cast Taylor, Rod; Spaak, Catherine; Malden, Karl; Douglas, Melvyn; Conte, Richard; Rennie, Michael; Oberon, Merle; McCarthy, Kevin; MacRae, Carmen; Ryder, Alfred; Roberts, Roy

Song(s) This Year (C: Keating, John; L: Worth, John); The Hotel [1] (C: Keating, John; L: Quine, Richard)

Notes "The Very Thought of You" by Ray Noble; "Alone Together" by Howard Dietz and Arthur Schwartz; "As Time Goes By" by Herman Hupfeld and "Why Shouldn't I" by Cole Porter are also presented as visual vocals. [1] Lyric written for exploitation only.

2678 ✦ HOTEL HAYWIRE
Paramount, 1937

Producer(s) Jones, Paul
Director(s) Archainbaud, George
Screenwriter(s) Sturges, Preston

Cast Carrillo, Leo; Carlisle, Mary; Overman, Lynne; Byington, Spring; Baker, Benny; Hall, Porter; Conklin, Chester

Song(s) Double Trouble (C: Rainger, Ralph; L: Robin, Leo)

2679 ✦ HOTEL IMPERIAL
Paramount, 1939

Director(s) Florey, Robert
Screenwriter(s) Gabriel, Gilbert; Thoeren, Robert

Cast Miranda, Isa; Milland, Ray; Owen, Reginald; Lockhart, Gene; Naish, J. Carrol; Bois, Curt; Dekker, Albert

Song(s) There's Something Magic Saying 'Nitchevo' (C: Hollander, Frederick; L: Freed, Ralph)

Notes No cue sheet available.

2680 ✦ HOT FOR PARIS
Fox, 1929

Composer(s) Donaldson, Walter
Lyricist(s) Leslie, Edgar

Director(s) Walsh, Raoul
Screenwriter(s) McGuirk, Charles J.; Wells, William K.

Cast McLaglen, Victor; D'Orsay, Fifi; Brendel, El; Moran, Polly; Pawle, Lennox; Tollaire, August; Judels, Charles

Song(s) If You Want to See Paree, Look in My Eyes; Sweet Nothings of Love; I'm the Duke of Kakiyak; The Shelter of My Baby's Arms [1]; Volga Boat Song [1]; Cuckoo Song [1]; Sing Me a Little Folk Song [2]

Notes [1] Not used. [2] Used instrumentally only.

2681 ✦ THE HOT HEIRESS
Warner Brothers–First National, 1931

Composer(s) Rodgers, Richard
Lyricist(s) Hart, Lorenz

Director(s) Badger, Clarence
Screenwriter(s) Fields, Herbert

Cast Lyon, Ben; Munson, Ona; Pidgeon, Walter; Todd, Thelma; Dugan, Tom; Courtney, Inez; Bartlett, Elsie; Herbert, Holmes; Walker, Nella; Irving, George

Song(s) You're the Cats; Nobody Loves a Riveter; Like Ordinary People Do; He Looks So Good to Me [1]

Notes No cue sheet available. [1] Cut before release.

2682 ♦ HOT LEAD AND COLD FEET
Disney, 1978

Musical Score Baker, Buddy

Producer(s) Miller, Ron
Director(s) Butler, Robert
Screenwriter(s) McEveety, Joseph L.; Alsberg, Arthur; Nelson, Don

Cast Dale, Jim; Valentine, Karen; Knotts, Don; Elam, Jack; McGavin, Darren

Song(s) May the Best Man Win (C/L: Kasha, Al; Hirschhorn, Joel); Something Good Is Bound to Happen (C: Baker, Buddy; L: Alsberg, Arthur; Nelson, Don)

2683 ♦ HOT MILLIONS
Metro–Goldwyn–Mayer, 1969

Musical Score Johnson, Laurie

Producer(s) Alberg, Mildred Freed
Director(s) Till, Eric
Screenwriter(s) Wallach, Ira; Ustinov, Peter

Cast Romero, Cesar; Morley, Robert; Newhart, Bob; Malden, Karl; Smith, Maggie; Ustinov, Peter

Song(s) This Time (C: Johnson, Laurie; L: Black, Don); There Is Another Song [1] (C: Johnson, Laurie; L: Kretzmer, Herbert)

Notes [1] Lyric written for exploitation only.

2684 ♦ HOT MONEY
Warner Brothers, 1936

Producer(s) Foy, Bryan
Director(s) McGann, William
Screenwriter(s) Jacobs, William

Cast Alexander, Ross; Roberts, Beverly; Cawthorn, Joseph; Graetz, Paul; Tombes, Andrew; Nagel, Anne

Song(s) What Can I Do? I Love Him (C/L: Herscher, Ruth; Herscher, Louis)

Notes No song indicated on cue sheet.

2685 ♦ THE HOT ONE

See CORVETTE SUMMER.

2686 ♦ HOT PEPPER
Fox, 1933

Composer(s) Burton, Val; Jason, Will
Lyricist(s) Burton, Val; Jason, Will

Director(s) Blystone, John
Screenwriter(s) Connors, Barry; Klein, Philip; Nichols, Dudley

Source(s) characters by Anderson, Maxwell; Stallings, Laurence

Cast Lowe, Edmund; McLaglen, Victor; Velez, Lupe; Brendel, El

Song(s) Ain't It Gonna Ring No More; Metropomania [1]; Mon Papa—A French Can-Can [2]

Notes [1] Used instrumentally only. [2] Sheet music only.

2687 ♦ HOT PURSUIT
RKO/Paramount, 1987

Musical Score Rareview

Producer(s) David, Pierre; Parvin, Theodore R.
Director(s) Lisberger, Steven
Screenwriter(s) Lisberger, Steven; Carabatsos, Steven W.

Cast Cusack, John; Loggia, Robert; Stiller, Jerry; Gazelle, Wendy; Markham, Monte; Fabares, Shelley

Song(s) Do De Lo (C: Scott, Thomas W.; Conlan, Joseph; L: Sinnamon, Shandi)

Notes No cue sheet available.

2688 ♦ HOT RHYTHM
Monogram, 1944

Composer(s) Kay, Edward J.; Brown, N.; Wicks, Virginia; Herscher, Louis

Producer(s) Parsons, Lindsley
Director(s) Beaudine, William
Screenwriter(s) Ryan, Tim; Marion, Charles R.

Cast Lowery, Robert; Drake, Dona; Ryan, Tim; Ryan, Irene; Miller, Sidney; Cooper, Jerry; Kent, Robert; Langdon, Harry

Song(s) Where Were You? (C: Herscher, Louis; L: Herscher, Ruth); Talk Me Into It; Happiest Girl in Town; Right Under My Nose; Say It with Your Heart

Notes No cue sheet available.

2689 ♦ THE HOT ROCK
Twentieth Century–Fox, 1972

Musical Score Jones, Quincy

Producer(s) Landers, Hal; Roberts, Bobby
Director(s) Yates, Peter
Screenwriter(s) Goldman, William
Source(s) (novel) Westlake, Donald E.

Cast Redford, Robert; Segal, George; Leibman, Ron; Sand, Paul; Gunn, Moses; Redfield, William; Rae, Charlotte; Mostel, Zero; Bellaver, Harry; Allen, Seth

Song(s) When You Believe (C/L: Rinehart, Bill); Listen to the Melody [1] (C: Jones, Quincy; L: Lihler, Tay; Rinehart, Bill)

Notes Sheet music only.

2690 ✦ HOT RODS TO HELL
Metro–Goldwyn–Mayer, 1966

Musical Score Karger, Fred
Composer(s) Karger, Fred; Wayne, Sid; Weisman, Ben
Lyricist(s) Karger, Fred; Wayne, Sid; Weisman, Ben

Producer(s) Katzman, Sam
Director(s) Brahm, John
Screenwriter(s) Kent, Robert E.
Source(s) "The Red Car" (story) Gaby, Alex

Cast Andrews, Dana; Crain, Jeanne; Farmer, Mimsy; Mock, Laurie; Bertoya, Paul; Kirkwood, Gene

Song(s) So Close to Love [2]; Chicken Walk; Blue Lou [2]; Back Street [1]

Notes International title 52 MILES TO TERROR. [1] Used instrumentally only. [2] Also in THE YOUNG RUNAWAYS.

2691 ✦ H.O.T.S.
Derio Productions, 1979

Musical Score Davis, David

Producer(s) Davis, W. Terry; Schain, Don
Director(s) Sindell, Gerald Seth
Screenwriter(s) Caffaro, Cheri; Buchanan, Joan

Cast Kiger, Susan; London, Lisa; Bryant, Pamela Jean; Cameron, Kimberley; Olfson, Ken; Steelsmith, Mary

Song(s) How Hot Can You Get (C/L: Brown, Ted)

Notes No cue sheet available.

2692 ✦ HOT SATURDAY
Paramount, 1932

Lyricist(s) Coslow, Sam

Director(s) Seiter, William A.
Screenwriter(s) Lovett, Josephine; March, Joseph Moncure
Source(s) (novel) Ferguson, Harvey

Cast Carroll, Nancy; Grant, Cary; Scott, Randolph; Bond, Lillian; Darwell, Jane; Sutton, Grady

Song(s) This Is the Night [1] (C: Rainger, Ralph); I'm Burning for You (C: Johnston, Arthur)

Notes [1] Also in INTERNATIONAL HOUSE and THIS IS THE NIGHT.

2693 ✦ HOT SPELL
Paramount, 1958

Producer(s) Wallis, Hal B.
Director(s) Mann, Daniel
Screenwriter(s) Poe, James
Source(s) *Next of Kin* (play) Coleman, Lonnie

Cast Booth, Shirley; Quinn, Anthony; MacLaine, Shirley; Holliman, Earl; Heckart, Eileen

Song(s) Hot Spell [1] (C: Bacharach, Burt; L: David, Mack)

Notes [1] Written for exploitation only. Yes, Mack David is correct.

2694 ✦ HOT SPOT

See I WAKE UP SCREAMING.

2695 ✦ HOT STREAK

See JINXED.

2696 ✦ HOT STUFF
Columbia, 1979

Musical Score Williams, Patrick

Producer(s) Engelberg, Mort
Director(s) DeLuise, Dom
Screenwriter(s) Kane, Michael; Westlake, Donald E.

Cast DeLuise, Dom; Pleshette, Suzanne; Reed, Jerry; Davis, Ossie; Avalos, Luis; Lawrence, Marc; McCutcheon, Bill; Martin, Barney; McCormick, Pat; Halpin, Luke

Song(s) Hot Stuff (C/L: Reed, Jerry); Keep It Loose (C: Williams, Patrick; L: Jennings, Will)

2697 ✦ HOT SUMMER NIGHT
Metro–Goldwyn–Mayer, 1957

Musical Score Previn, Andre

Producer(s) Fine, Mort
Director(s) Friedkin, David
Screenwriter(s) Fine, Mort; Friedkin, David

Cast Nielsen, Leslie; Miller, Colleen; Andrews, Edward; Flippen, Jay C.; Best, James; Richards, Paul; Wilke, Robert J.; Akins, Claude

Song(s) Hot Summer Night [1] (C: Previn, Andre; L: Russell, Bob)

Notes Originally titled CAPITAL OFFENSE. [1] Used instrumentally only.

2698 ✦ HOUDINI
Paramount, 1953

Musical Score Webb, Roy

Producer(s) Pal, George
Director(s) Marshall, George
Screenwriter(s) Yordan, Philip

Cast Curtis, Tony; Leigh, Janet; Thatcher, Torin; Rumann, Sig; Clarke, Angela; Schnabel, Stefan; Gilchrist, Connie

Song(s) The Golden Years [1] (C/L: Livingston, Jay; Evans, Ray)

Notes [1] Music adapted by Von Suppe's "Poet and Peasant Overture." Song used instrumentally only.

2699 ✦ HOUND-DOG MAN
Twentieth Century–Fox, 1959

Musical Score Mockridge, Cyril J.
Composer(s) Darby, Ken
Lyricist(s) Darby, Ken
Choreographer(s) Earl, Josephine

Producer(s) Wald, Jerry
Director(s) Siegel, Don
Screenwriter(s) Gipson, Fred; Miller, Winston
Source(s) *Circles Round the Wagon* (novel) Gipson, Fred

Cast Fabian; Lynley, Carol; Whitman, Stuart; O'Connell, Arthur; Stevens, Dodie

Song(s) Hound-Dog Man (C/L: Pomus, Doc; Shuman, Mort); I'm Growin' Up (C/L: Marcucci, Robert; DeAngelis, Pete); Single; This Friendly World; Pretty Little Girl (C/L: Marcucci, Robert; DeAngelis, Pete); What Big Boy? (C/L: Ponti, Sal; Avalon, Frankie); Hayfoot, Strawfoot; Got the Feelin' [1] (C/L: Sherman, Richard M.; Sherman, Robert B.)

Notes [1] Sheet music only.

2700 ✦ HOUND FOR TROUBLE
Warner Brothers, 1951

Musical Score Stalling, Carl

Director(s) Jones, Chuck
Screenwriter(s) Maltese, Michael

Cast Dog, Charlie

Song(s) Attsa Matta for You (C/L: Maltese, Michael)

Notes Animated cartoon.

2701 ✦ THE HOURS BETWEEN

See TWENTY-FOUR HOURS.

2702 ✦ HOUSEBOAT
Paramount, 1958

Musical Score Duning, George

Producer(s) Rose, Jack
Director(s) Shavelson, Melville
Screenwriter(s) Rose, Jack; Shavelson, Melville

Cast Grant, Cary; Loren, Sophia; Guardino, Harry; Hyer, Martha; Ciannelli, Eduardo; Hamilton, Murray; Kennedy, Madge; Litel, John; Klemperer, Werner; Petersen, Paul

Song(s) Bing! Bang! Bong! (C/L: Livingston, Jay; Evans, Ray); Almost in Your Arms (Love Song from Houseboat) (C/L: Livingston, Jay; Evans, Ray); Houseboat [1] (C: Duning, George; L: Allen, Steve)

Notes [1] Lyrics added for exploitation only.

2703 ✦ A HOUSE IS NOT A HOME
Embassy, 1964

Musical Score Weiss, Joseph

Producer(s) Greene, Clarence
Director(s) Rouse, Russell
Screenwriter(s) Rouse, Russell; Greene, Clarence
Source(s) *A House Is Not a Home* (book) Adler, Polly

Cast Winters, Shelley; Crawford, Broderick; Romero, Cesar; Taylor, Robert; Taeger, Ralph; Ballard, Kaye; Shaughnessy, Mickey; Seagram, Lisa; White, Jesse; Gilchrist, Connie

Song(s) A House Is Not a Home (C: Bacharach, Burt; L: David, Hal)

2704 ✦ HOUSE OF CARDS
Universal, 1968

Musical Score Lai, Francis

Producer(s) Berg, Dick
Director(s) Guillermin, John
Screenwriter(s) Bonner, James P.
Source(s) (novel) Ellin, Stanley

Cast Peppard, George; Michell, Keith; Welles, Orson; Michael, Ralph; Stevens, Inger; Audley, Maxine; Bayliss, Peter

Song(s) Chateau de Cartes (C: Lai, Francis; L: Barouh, Pierre)

2705 ✦ HOUSE OF SECRETS

See TRIPLE DECEPTION.

2706 ✦ HOUSE OF STRANGERS
Twentieth Century–Fox, 1949

Musical Score Amfitheatrof, Daniele

Producer(s) Siegel, Sol C.
Director(s) Mankiewicz, Joseph L.
Screenwriter(s) Yordan, Philip
Source(s) (novel) Weidman, Jerome

Cast Robinson, Edward G.; Hayward, Susan; Conte, Richard; Adler, Luther; Valentine, Paul; Zimbalist Jr., Efrem; Paget, Debra; Emerson, Hope

Song(s) Can't We Talk It Over (C: Young, Victor; L: Washington, Ned)

Notes   There are also vocals of "Please Don't Talk About Me When I'm Gone" by Sidney Clare, Sam H. Stept and Bee Palmer and "Was That the Human Thing to Do" by Sammy Fain and Joe Young.

2707   ◆   THE HOUSE OF THE SEVEN GABLES
Universal, 1940

Musical Score   Skinner, Frank

Producer(s)   Kelly, Burt
Director(s)   May, Joe
Screenwriter(s)   Cole, Lester; Greene, Harold
Source(s)   *The House of the Seven Gables* (novel) Hawthorne, Nathaniel

Cast   Sanders, George; Price, Vincent; Lindsay, Margaret; Foran, Dick; Grey, Nan; Kellaway, Cecil; Napier, Alan; Emery, Gilbert; Mander, Miles

Song(s)   The Color of Your Eyes (C: Skinner, Frank; L: Freed, Ralph)

2708   ◆   THE HOUSE ON SKULL MOUNTAIN
Twentieth Century–Fox, 1974

Musical Score   Immel, Jerrold

Producer(s)   Storey, Ray
Director(s)   Honthaner, Ron
Screenwriter(s)   Pares, Mildred

Cast   French, Victor; Michelle, Janee; McKenzie, Mary J. Todd; Durand, Jean; Woods, Ella

Song(s)   My Hometown Is Just a Stranger Now (C: Freeman, Art; L: Talmadge, Ruth); Love Has Gently Come This Morning (C: Mendoza-Nava, Jaime; L: Welsh, John; Welsh, Susan)

2709   ◆   HOUSEWIFE
Warner Brothers, 1934

Producer(s)   Lord, Robert
Director(s)   Green, Alfred E.
Screenwriter(s)   Seff, Manuel; Hayward, Lillie

Cast   Brent, George; Davis, Bette; Dvorak, Ann; Halliday, John; Donnelly, Ruth; Cavanaugh, Hobart; Barrat, Robert; Cawthorn, Joseph; Regan, Phil; Robertson, Willard

Song(s)   Cosmetics by Dupree (C: Wrubel, Allie; L: Dixon, Mort)

2710   ◆   HOWARD THE DUCK
Universal, 1989

Musical Score   Barry, John; Dolby, Thomas
Composer(s)   Dolby, Thomas
Lyricist(s)   Willis, Allee

Producer(s)   Katz, Gloria
Director(s)   Huyck, Willard
Screenwriter(s)   Huyck, Willard; Katz, Gloria
Source(s)   *Howard the Duck* (comic book) Gerber, Steve

Cast   Thompson, Lea; Jones, Jeffrey; Robbins, Tim; Zien, Chip; Guilfoyle, Paul; Sagal, Liz; Davalos, Dominque; Robinson, Holly; Chapin, Miles

Song(s)   Hunger City; Don't Turn Away; Ducktor Dread Dub (L: Dolby, Thomas); Ultralight (C/L: Levay, Sylvester; Barry, John; McClinton, George); Howard the Duck [1]

Notes   [1] Used instrumentally—except for seven seconds.

2711   ◆   HOW COME NOBODY'S ON OUR SIDE
American Films, 1977

Musical Score   Johnson, Lamont
Composer(s)   Johnson, Lamont

Producer(s)   Smith, Maurice
Director(s)   Michaels, Richard
Screenwriter(s)   Chapman, Leigh

Cast   Roarke, Adam; Pishop, Larry; Hay, Alexandra

Song(s)   How Come Nobody's On Our Side? (L: Johnson, Arthur); West Coast Wind Song (Inst.); Person That I Know (C/L: Keakle, Gordon); I Don't Know but I'll Get There (L: Judd, Carolyn)

Notes   No cue sheet available.

2712   ◆   HOW DO YOU DO
PRC, 1946

Musical Score   Jackson, Howard
Composer(s)   Borne, Hal
Lyricist(s)   Borne, Hal

Director(s)   Murphy, Ralph
Screenwriter(s)   Sauber, Harry; Carole, Joseph

Cast   Gordon, Bert; Von Zell, Harry; Walker, Cheryl; Albertson, Frank; Morse, Ella Mae; Windsor, Claire; Luke, Keye; Middleton, Charles; McHugh, Matt

Song(s)   Twelve Hour Pass; Boogie Woogie Cindy; Drink to Me

2713   ◆   HOWDY BROADWAY
Rayart Pictures, 1929

Cast   Ruby, Ellalee; Ennis, Lucy; Clark, Jack J.; Tommy Christian and His Band

Song(s)   Atta Boy, Ole Kid (C/L: Moll, Billy; Christian, Tommy); I Want You to Know I Love You (C/L: Terker, Arthur; Christian, Tommy); Gazoozalum Gazoo; You're Gonna Be Blue; Somebody's Sweetheart—Not

Mine; Howdy Broadway; Gypsy Love; Sophomore Strut

Notes   No cue sheet available.

2714 ◆ HOW GREEN WAS MY VALLEY
Twentieth Century–Fox, 1941

Musical Score   Newman, Alfred

Producer(s)   Zanuck, Darryl F.
Director(s)   Ford, John
Screenwriter(s)   Dunne, Philip
Source(s)   *How Green Was My Valley* (novel) Llewellyn, Richard

Cast   Pidgeon, Walter; O'Hara, Maureen; Crisp, Donald; Lee, Anna; McDowall, Roddy; Loder, John; Allgood, Sara; Fitzgerald, Barry; Knowles, Patric; Lowry, Morton; Todd, Ann; Williams, Rhys; Griffies, Ethel; Pichel, Irving

Song(s)   How Green Was My Valley [1] (C: Newman, Alfred; L: Webster, Paul Francis)

Notes   [1] Lyric added for exploitation only.

2715 ◆ HOW'S ABOUT IT
Universal, 1943

Producer(s)   Goldsmith, Ken
Director(s)   Kenton, Erle C.
Screenwriter(s)   Ronson, Mel

Cast   Paige, Robert; McDonald, Grace

Song(s)   Going Up (C/L: Roth, Allen; Gordon, Irving); I'm On My Way (C/L: Pepper, Buddy; James, Inez); East of the Rockies (C/L: Robins, Sid); Don't Mind the Rain (C/L: Miller, Ned; Cohn, Chester); You're a Sweetheart [2] (C: McHugh, Jimmy; L: Adamson, Harold); Take It and Git [1] (C/L: Chapman, William; Chapman, Melvin; Marshall, James T.; Green, Johnny); Here Comes the Navy [3] (C: Vejvoda, Jaromir; L: Brown, Lew; Timm, W.A.; Vejvoda, Jaromir; Oakes, C.P.)

Notes   [1] Also in GALS, INCORPORATED. [2] Also in MEET DANNY WILSON and YOU'RE A SWEETHEART. [3] To tune of "Beer Barrel Polka."

2716 ◆ HOW SWEET IT IS!
National General, 1968

Musical Score   Williams, Patrick

Producer(s)   Marshall, Garry
Director(s)   Paris, Jerry
Screenwriter(s)   Marshall, Garry; Belson, Jerry
Source(s)   *The Girl in the Turqoise Bikini* (novel) Resnik, Muriel

Cast   Garner, James; Reynolds, Debbie; Ronet, Maurice; Lynde, Paul; Dalio, Marcel; Conforti, Gino; Scotti, Vito; Terry-Thomas

Song(s)   How Sweet It Is (C/L: Webb, Jimmy)

Notes   No cue sheet available.

2717 ◆ HOW THE WEST WAS WON
Metro–Goldwyn–Mayer, 1962

Musical Score   Newman, Alfred
Composer(s)   Traditional
Lyricist(s)   Mercer, Johnny

Producer(s)   Smith, Bernard
Director(s)   Ford, John [3]; Marshall, George [4]; Hathaway, Henry [5]
Screenwriter(s)   Webb, James R.
Source(s)   "How the West Was Won" (magazine series)
Narrator(s)   Tracy, Spencer

Cast   Brian, David; Brennan, Walter; Bazlen, Brigid; Widmark, Richard; Wayne, John; Wallach, Eli; Stewart, James; Baker, Carroll; Cobb, Lee J.; Fonda, Henry; Jones, Carolyn; Malden, Karl; Peck, Gregory; Peppard, George; Preston, Robert; Reynolds, Debbie; Brian, David; Massey, Raymond; Moorehead, Agnes; Morgan, Harry; Ritter, Thelma; Shaughnessy, Mickey; Tamblyn, Russ; Van Cleef, Lee; Flippen, Jay C.; Sundberg, Clinton

Song(s)   Home in the Meadow [1] (L: Cahn, Sammy); How the West Was Won (C: Newman, Alfred; L: Darby, Ken); Wait for the Wagon [1] [6]; Raise a Ruckus Tonight [1]; What Was Your Name in the States; A Thousand, Thousand Miles (C/L: Darby, Ken); No Goodbye [2] (C: Newman, Alfred; L: Darby, Ken)

Notes   This film was shot in Cinerama. There are also traditional American folk songs arranged and adapted by Ken Darby or Joseph Lilley or Alfred Newman. Robert Dolan is credited on sheet music for the music to the Johnny Mercer songs. [1] Music arranged and adapted by Robert Emmet Dolan. [2] Used instrumentally only. [3] Director of THE CIVIL WAR. [4] Director of THE RAILROAD. [5] Director of THE RIVERS, THE PLAINS, THE OUTLAWS. [6] Traditional song also used for the Republic picture UNDER WESTERN SKIES with new lyrics by Sid Robin.

2718 ◆ HOW TO BE VERY, VERY POPULAR
Twentieth Century–Fox, 1955

Musical Score   Mockridge, Cyril J.
Choreographer(s)   Godkin, Paul

Producer(s)   Johnson, Nunnally
Director(s)   Johnson, Nunnally

Screenwriter(s)   Johnson, Nunnally
Source(s)   (play) Lindsay, Howard

Cast   Grable, Betty; North, Sheree; Cummings, Robert; Coburn, Charles; Noonan, Tommy; Bean, Orson; Clark, Fred; Pearce, Alice; Williams, Rhys; Tombes, Andrew

Song(s)   How to Be Very, Very Popular (C: Styne, Jule; L: Cahn, Sammy); Bristol Bell Song (C: Newman, Lionel; L: Darby, Ken)

2719 ✦ HOW TO MARRY A MILLIONAIRE
Twentieth Century–Fox, 1953

Producer(s)   Johnson, Nunnally
Director(s)   Negulesco, Jean
Screenwriter(s)   Johnson, Nunnally
Source(s)   (plays) Akins, Zoe; Eunson, Dale; Albert, Katherine

Cast   Grable, Betty; Monroe, Marilyn; Bacall, Lauren; Wayne, David; Calhoun, Rory; Mitchell, Cameron; Clark, Fred; Powell, William [1]

Song(s)   New York (C: Newman, Lionel; L: Darby, Ken)

Notes   There is also a long instrumental piece titled "Street Scene" which is comprised of music Newman wrote for the film STREET SCENE. [1] Dubbed by Manuel de Juan (maybe Spanish version).

2720 ✦ HOW TO SAVE A MARRIAGE—AND RUIN YOUR LIFE
Columbia, 1968

Musical Score   Legrand, Michel
Composer(s)   Bernstein, Elmer
Lyricist(s)   David, Mack

Producer(s)   Shapiro, Stanley
Director(s)   Cook, Fielder
Screenwriter(s)   Shapiro, Stanley; Monaster, Nate

Cast   Martin, Dean; Stevens, Stella; Wallach, Eli; Jackson, Anne; Field, Betty; Albertson, Jack

Song(s)   The Winds of Change; How to Save a Marriage and Ruin Your Life [1]

Notes   No cue sheet available. [1] Written for exploitation only.

2721 ✦ HOW TO STEAL A MILLION
Twentieth Century–Fox, 1966

Musical Score   Williams, John

Producer(s)   Kohlmar, Fred
Director(s)   Wyler, William
Screenwriter(s)   Kurnitz, Harry

Cast   Hepburn, Audrey; O'Toole, Peter; Wallach, Eli; Griffith, Hugh; Boyer, Charles; Gravet, Fernand

Song(s)   Two Lovers (C: Williams, John; L: Bricusse, Leslie)

2722 ✦ HOW TO STUFF A WILD BIKINI
American International, 1965

Musical Score   Baxter, Les
Composer(s)   Hemric, Guy; Styner, Jerry
Lyricist(s)   Hemric, Guy; Styner, Jerry

Producer(s)   Nicholson, James H.; Arkoff, Samuel Z.
Director(s)   Asher, William
Screenwriter(s)   Asher, William; Townsend, Leo

Cast   Funicello, Annette; Hickman, Dwayne; Donlevy, Brian; Lembeck, Harvey; Adams, Beverly; McCrea, Jody; Keaton, Buster; Rooney, Mickey; Shaw, Bobbi

Song(s)   Give Her Lovin' (C/L: Easton, Lynn)

Notes   No cue sheet available.

2723 ✦ HOW TO SUCCEED IN BUSINESS WITHOUT REALLY TRYING
United Artists, 1967

Musical Score   Loesser, Frank
Composer(s)   Loesser, Frank
Lyricist(s)   Loesser, Frank
Choreographer(s)   Moreda, Dale

Producer(s)   Swift, David
Director(s)   Swift, David
Screenwriter(s)   Swift, David
Source(s)   *How to Succeed in Business Without Really Trying* (musical) Burrows, Abe; Loesser, Frank; Weinstock, Jack; Gilbert, Willie

Cast   Morse, Robert [1]; Lee, Michele; Vallee, Rudy [1]; Teague, Anthony "Scooter"; Arthur, Maureen; Matheson, Murray; Reynolds, Kay; Lewis, Robert Q.

Song(s)   Hot to Succeed; Company Way; A Secretary Is Not a Toy; Been a Long Day; I Believe in You; Grand Old Ivy; Rosemary; Brotherhood of Man; Coffee Break [2]

Notes   All songs are from the Broadway musical. [1] Members of the original Broadway cast. [2] Filmed but cut before opening.

2724 ✦ HUCKLEBERRY FINN (1945)
Metro–Goldwyn–Mayer, 1945 unproduced

Composer(s)   Martin, Hugh; Blane, Ralph
Lyricist(s)   Martin, Hugh; Blane, Ralph

Producer(s)   Freed, Arthur
Screenwriter(s)   Benson, Sally
Source(s)   *Huckleberry Finn* (novel) Twain, Mark

Song(s) The Cockebur Song; Ah' Bin Rich; There Were Others Passing By; It Must Be Spring; I'm the First Man; My Old Home Town; Pass That Peace Pipe [2] (C/L: Edens, Roger; Martin, Hugh; Blane, Ralph); Puttin' on Airs [1] (C/L: Blane, Ralph)

Notes [1] Later also in score of unproduced TAKE ME OUT TO THE BALL GAME. [2] Also not used in ZIEGFELD FOLLIES (1946). Used in GOOD NEWS (1947).

2725 ✦ HUCKLEBERRY FINN (1950)
Metro–Goldwyn–Mayer, 1950 unproduced

Composer(s) Lane, Burton
Lyricist(s) Harburg, E.Y.

Producer(s) Freed, Arthur
Screenwriter(s) Stewart, Donald Ogden
Source(s) *Huckleberry Finn* (novel) Twain, Mark

Song(s) That Real Sunday Feeling; Don't Run Mirandy; Jumpin' Jubilee

2726 ✦ HUCKLEBERRY FINN (1951)
Metro–Goldwyn–Mayer, 1951 unproduced

Composer(s) Lane, Burton
Lyricist(s) Lerner, Alan Jay

Producer(s) Freed, Arthur
Screenwriter(s) Lerner, Alan Jay
Source(s) *Huckleberry Finn* (novel) Twain, Mark

Song(s) I'm from Missouri; Huckleberry Finn; The World's Full o' Suckers; I'll Wait for You by the River; I'll Meet You Down by the River; Pittsburgh Blue; Asparagus Is Served; When You Grown Up You'll Know

Notes Some of this score was used in the 1960 Samuel Goldwyn HUCKLEBERRY FINN.

2727 ✦ HUCKLEBERRY FINN (1974)
United Artists, 1974

Composer(s) Sherman, Robert B.; Sherman, Richard M.
Lyricist(s) Sherman, Robert B.; Sherman, Richard M.
Choreographer(s) Breaux, Marc

Producer(s) Jacobs, Arthur P.
Director(s) Thompson, J. Lee
Screenwriter(s) Sherman, Richard M.; Sherman, Robert B.
Source(s) *Huckleberry Finn* (novel) Twain, Mark

Cast East, Jeff; Winfield, Paul; Korman, Harvey; Wayne, David; O'Connell, Arthur; Merrill, Gary; Benson, Lucille

Song(s) Freedom; Huckleberry Finn; Someday Honey Darling; Rotten Luck; Cairo, Ill.; Royalty; Rose in a Bible; Royal Nonesuch; Into His Hands [1]; What's Right, What's Wrong

Notes [1] Music based on "Three Blind Mice."

2728 ✦ THE HUCKSTERS
Metro–Goldwyn–Mayer, 1947

Musical Score Hayton, Lennie

Producer(s) Hornblow Jr., Arthur
Director(s) Conway, Jack
Screenwriter(s) Davis, Luther
Source(s) *The Hucksters* (novel) Wakeman, Frederick

Cast Gable, Clark; Kerr, Deborah; Greenstreet, Sydney; Menjou, Adolphe; Gardner, Ava [1]; Wynn, Keenan; Arnold, Edward; Mather, Aubrey

Song(s) Jingle #3 (C/L: Thompson, Kay); Don't Tell Me (C/L: Pepper, Buddy)); Beauty Jingle (C/L: Thompson, Kay)

Notes [1] Dubbed by Eileen Wilson.

2729 ✦ HUD
Paramount, 1963

Producer(s) Ritt, Martin; Ravetch, Irving
Director(s) Ritt, Martin
Screenwriter(s) Ravetch, Irving; Frank Jr., Harriet
Source(s) *Horseman Pass By* (novel) McMurty, Larry

Cast Newman, Paul; Douglas, Melvyn; de Wilde, Brandon; Neal, Patricia

Song(s) Hud [1] (C: Bernstein, Elmer; L: David, Mack)

Notes [1] Not used. Written for exploitation use only.

2730 ✦ HULLABALOO
Metro–Goldwyn–Mayer, 1940

Choreographer(s) Lee, Sammy

Producer(s) Sidney, Louis K.
Director(s) Marin, Edwin L.
Screenwriter(s) Perrin, Nat

Cast Morgan, Frank; Grey, Virginia; Dailey, Dan [2]; Burke, Billie; Morriss, Ann; Owen, Reginald; Lynn, Leni; Westman, Nydia; Meek, Donald; O'Brien, Virginia; Holland, Charles

Song(s) We've Come a Long Way Together (C: Stept, Sam H.; L: Koehler, Ted); A Handful of Stars (C: Shapiro, Ted; L: Lawrence, Jack); Hullabaloo [1] (C/L: Brent, Earl); Rehearsal Routine (C/L: Brent, Earl)

Notes There are other brief vocals of popular tunes and folk songs of the day. [1] Used instrumentally only. [2] Billed as Dan Dailey Jr.

2731 ✦ THE HUMAN JUNGLE
Allied Artists, 1954

Musical Score Salter, Hans J.

Producer(s) Goetz, Hayes
Director(s) Newman, Joseph
Screenwriter(s) Sackheim, William; Fuchs, Daniel

Cast Merrill, Gary; Sterling, Jan; Raymond, Paula; Meyer, Emile; Toomey, Regis; Connors, Chuck

Song(s) It Ain't Gonna Be You (C/L: Rich, Max)

2732 ✦ HUMONGOUS
Embassy, 1982

Musical Score Cockell, John Mills

Producer(s) Kramreither, Anthony
Director(s) Lynch, Paul
Screenwriter(s) Gray, William

Cast Julian, Janet; Wallace, David; Baldwin, Janet

Song(s) Magic to Me (C: Cockell, John Mills; L: Sweeting, Lisa J.)

Notes No cue sheet available.

2733 ✦ THE HUNCHBACK OF NOTRE DAME
Allied Artists, 1957

Musical Score Auric, Georges
Composer(s) Auric, Georges
Lyricist(s) Prevert, Jacques

Producer(s) Hakim, Robert; Hakim, Raymond
Director(s) Delannoy, Jean
Screenwriter(s) Aurenche, Jean; Prevert, Jacques
Source(s) *The Hunchback of Notre Dame* (novel) Hugo, Victor

Cast Quinn, Anthony; Lollobrigida, Gina; Daney, Jean; Cuny, Alain

Song(s) Fools Procession; Life Is Sweet; A Halter for the Gallows Birds; Old Woman Lament (L: Hugo, Victor); Esmeralda Dance (C: Lavagnino, Angelo Francesco; L: Sidoni, Sylvana)

2734 ✦ THE HUNGER
Metro–Goldwyn–Mayer, 1983

Musical Score Lawson, David

Producer(s) Shepherd, Richard
Director(s) Scott, Tony
Screenwriter(s) Davis, Ivan; Thomas, Michael

Cast Deneuve, Catherine; Bowie, David; Sarandon, Susan; De Young, Cliff; Hedaya, Dan; Ehlers, Beth

Song(s) Bela Lugosi's Dead (C/L: Haskins, David; Haskins, Kevin; Murphy, Peter; Ash, Daniel); Funtime (C/L: Pop, Iggy; Bowie, David)

2735 ✦ HUNK
Crown, 1987

Musical Score Kurtz, David

Producer(s) Tenser, Marilyn J.
Director(s) Bassoff, Lawrence
Screenwriter(s) Bassoff, Lawrence

Cast Nelson, John Allen; Levitt, Steve; Shelton, Deborah; Bush, Rebeccah; Coco, James; Morse, Robert; Schreiber, Avery

Song(s) Take a Second Look (C: Kurtz, David; L: Monday)

Notes No cue sheet available.

2736 ✦ THE HUNTER
Paramount, 1980

Producer(s) Engelberg, Mort
Director(s) Kulik, Buzz
Screenwriter(s) Leighton, Ted; Hyams, Peter
Source(s) (book) Keane, Christopher

Cast McQueen, Steve; Wallach, Eli; Rosales, Tom; Harrold, Kathryn; Walter, Tracey; Burton, LeVar

Song(s) Lonesome Fellow from Texas (C/L: Legrand, Michel); Train in the Rain (C/L: Legrand, Michel)

2737 ✦ THE HUNTERS
Twentieth Century–Fox, 1958

Musical Score Sawtell, Paul

Producer(s) Powell, Dick
Director(s) Powell, Dick
Screenwriter(s) Mayes, Wendell
Source(s) *The Hunters* (novel) Salter, James

Cast Mitchum, Robert; Wagner, Robert; Egan, Richard; Britt, May; Philips, Lee; Gabriel, John

Song(s) The Hunters [1] (C/L: Gabriel, John)

Notes [1] Not used.

2738 ✦ HURRICANE
Goldwyn, 1937

Musical Score Newman, Alfred

Director(s) Ford, John; Heisler, Stuart
Screenwriter(s) Nichols, Dudley; Garrett, Oliver H.P.
Source(s) *Hurricane* (novel) Nordhoff, Charles; Hall, James Norman

Cast Lamour, Dorothy; Hall, Jon; Smith, C. Aubrey; Astor, Mary; Massey, Raymond; Mitchell, Thomas; Carradine, John; Cowan, Jerome

Song(s) Moon of Manakoora [1] (C: Newman, Alfred; L: Loesser, Frank)

Notes No cue sheet available. Remade in 1979. There was a previous film of the same title in 1929. [1] Used instrumentally only, the song might have been written for exploitation only.

2739 ✦ HURRY SUNDOWN
Paramount, 1967

Musical Score Montenegro, Hugo
Composer(s) Montenegro, Hugo

Producer(s)   Preminger, Otto
Director(s)   Preminger, Otto
Screenwriter(s)   Ryan, Thomas C.; Foote, Horton
Source(s)   *Hurry Sundown* (novel) Gilden, K.B.

Cast   Caine, Michael; Fonda, Jane; Carroll, Diahann; Hooks, Robert; Ingram, Rex; Dunaway, Faye; Meredith, Burgess; Kennedy, George

Song(s)   Come Holy Ghost; Don't Bother (C/L: Caruso, Fred); Hurry Sundown (L: Kaye, Buddy)

2740 ◆ HUSH HUSH SWEET CHARLOTTE
Twentieth Century–Fox, 1964

Musical Score   De Vol, Frank

Producer(s)   Aldrich, Robert
Director(s)   Aldrich, Robert
Screenwriter(s)   Farrell, Henry; Heller, Lukas

Cast   Davis, Bette; de Havilland, Olivia; Cotten, Joseph; Moorehead, Agnes; Kellaway, Cecil; Buono, Victor; Astor, Mary; Addy, Wesley; Dern, Bruce; Kennedy, George; Corby, Ellen

Song(s)   Hush Hush Sweet Charlotte (C: De Vol, Frank; L: David, Mack)

2741 ◆ HUSTLE
Paramount, 1975

Musical Score   De Vol, Frank

Producer(s)   Aldrich, Robert
Director(s)   Aldrich, Robert
Screenwriter(s)   Shagan, Steve

Cast   Reynolds, Burt; Johnson, Ben; Brennan, Eileen; Albert, Eddie; Winfield, Paul; Deneuve, Catherine; Borgnine, Ernest; Carter, Jack; Bach, Catherine

Song(s)   I Never Loved [1] (C: De Vol, Frank; L: Hilton, Hermine)

Notes   Previously titled HOME FREE and CITY OF ANGELS. [1] Lyrics added for exploitation only not used in film.

2742 ◆ HYDE PARK CORNER
Republic, 1935

Musical Score   Lucas

Producer(s)   Templeman, Harcourt
Director(s)   Hill, Sinclair
Screenwriter(s)   Wyndham-Lewis, D.B.

Cast   Hale, Binnie; Harker, Gordon; McLaughlin, Gibb; Portman, Eric; Tate, Harry; Wolfit, Donald

Song(s)   You Don't Know the Half of It (C/L: Sigler, Maurice; Hoffman, Al; Goodhart, Al); Did You Get that Out of a Book (C/L: Sigler; Hoffman, Al; Goodhart, Al)

Notes   A Grosvenor films British release.

2743 ◆ HYPNOTIZED
World Wide Pictures, 1932

Musical Score   Ward, Edward
Composer(s)   Vescei, Josef
Lyricist(s)   Grossman, Bernie

Producer(s)   Hammons, E.W.
Director(s)   Sennett, Mack
Screenwriter(s)   Sennett, Mack; Ripley, Arthur; Waldron, John; McCoy, Harry; Rodney, Earle

Cast   Moran, George; Mack, Charles; Torrence, Ernest; Murray, Charles; Ford, Wallace; Alba, Maria; Bing, Herman; Alberni, Luis

Song(s)   In a Gypsy's Heart; Anywhere with You; Love Bring My Love Back to Me

Notes   No cue sheet available. Sheet music only. Joseph Vescei is credited on sheet music as Desider Vescei.

I

2744 ✦ I ACCUSE MY PARENTS
PRC, 1944

Musical Score Zahler, Lee
Composer(s) Livingston, Jay; Evans, Ray
Lyricist(s) Livingston, Jay; Evans, Ray

Producer(s) Alexander, Max
Director(s) Newfield, Sam
Screenwriter(s) Fraser, Harry; Dudley, Marjorie

Cast Lowell, Robert; Hughes, Mary Beth

Song(s) Are You Happy in Your Work?; Love Came Between Us; Where Can You Be?

Notes Cue sheet does not give titles.

2745 ✦ I AM AN AMERICAN
Warner Brothers, 1944

Song(s) Shout Wherever You May Be (I Am an American) (C: Lava, William; L: Shuster, Ira; Cunningham, Paul; Whitcup, Leonard)

Notes Short subject.

2746 ✦ I AM SUZANNE
Fox, 1934

Musical Score Hollander, Frederick
Composer(s) Hollander, Frederick
Lyricist(s) Brown, Forman

Producer(s) Lasky, Jesse L.
Director(s) Lee, Rowland V.
Screenwriter(s) Mayer, Edwin Justus; Lee, Rowland V.

Cast Harvey, Lillian; Raymond, Gene; Banks, Leslie

Song(s) St. Moritz Waltz; Eski-O-Lay-Li-O-Mo!; Just a Little Garret; Chant of the Sinners [1] (C/L: Burton, Val; Jason, Will)

Notes There is also a vocal of "You Brought a New Kind of Love to Me" by Sammy Fain, Irving Kahal and Pierre Norman. [1] Not used.

2747 ✦ I BECAME A CRIMINAL
Warner Brothers, 1948

Musical Score Galliard, M.F.

Producer(s) Bronsten, N.A.
Director(s) Cavalcanti, (Alberto)
Screenwriter(s) Langley, Noel
Source(s) "A Convict Has Escaped" (story) Budd, Jackson

Cast Gray, Sally; Howard, Trevor; Jones, Griffith; Ray, Rene; Merrall, Mary; Farrell, Charles; Smith, Cyril; Robins, Phyllis; Hope, Vida

Song(s) Caress Me (C/L: Langley, Noel; Smith, Norman)

Notes Released in Great Britain as THEY MADE ME A FUGITIVE.

2748 ✦ I BELIEVED IN YOU
Fox, 1934

Producer(s) Wurtzel, Sol M.
Director(s) Cummings, Irving
Screenwriter(s) Conselman, William

Cast Ames, Rosemary; Boles, John; Michael, Gertrude

Song(s) Out of a Blue Sky (C/L: Kernell, William); Down South in Greenwich Village (C: O'Keefe [1]; L: Conselman, William)

Notes [1] Pseudonym for Allan Stuart.

2749 ✦ I CAN'T GIVE YOU ANYTHING BUT LOVE, BABY
Universal, 1940

Composer(s) Skinner, Frank
Lyricist(s) Smith, Paul Gerard

Producer(s) Goldsmith, Ken
Director(s) Rogell, Albert S.
Screenwriter(s) Horman, Arthur T.

Cast Crawford, Broderick; Downs, Johnny; Moran, Peggy

Song(s) Tomato Juice Song; Sweetheart of School Fifty Nine [1]; Day By Day [2]

Notes There is also a vocal of "I Can't Give You Anything but Love, Baby" by Dorothy Fields and Jimmy McHugh. [1] Also in JAILHOUSE BLUES. [2] Sheet music only.

2750 ◆ ICE CAPADES
Republic, 1941

Composer(s) Styne, Jule
Lyricist(s) Meyer, Sol

Producer(s) North, Robert
Director(s) Santley, Jack
Screenwriter(s) Townley, Jack; Harari, Robert; Cooper, Olive

Cast Lewis, Dorothy; Ellison, James; Colonna, Jerry; Allen, Barbara Jo; Mowbray, Alan; Silvers, Phil; Schilling, Gus; Ryan, Tim; Clork, Harry; Belita; Dworshak, Lois; Taylor, Megan; Hruba, Vera; McCarthy, Red; The Ice Capades Company

Song(s) After All (C: Scharf, Walter); Tequila [1] (L: Brown, George; Meyer, Sol); The Guy with the Polka Dotted Tie; Johnny Doughboy Found a Rose in Ireland (C/L: Twomey, Kay; Goodhart, Al); Forever and Ever [2] (L: Brown, George; Meyer, Sol)

Notes Reedited as MUSIC IN THE MOONLIGHT with some changes. There are also vocals of "Song of the Islands" by Charles King; "Anchors Aweigh" by Charles Zimmerman; "The Caissons Go Rolling Along" by Edmund L. Gruber; "Army Air Corps" by Robert Crawford and "The Marine Hymn." [1] Also in SING, DANCE, PLENTY HOT. [2] Sheet music only.

2751 ◆ ICE CASTLES
Columbia, 1978

Musical Score Hamlisch, Marvin

Producer(s) Kemeny, John
Director(s) Wrye, Donald
Screenwriter(s) Wrye, Donald; Baim, Gary L.

Cast Benson, Robby; Dewhurst, Colleen; Skerritt, Tom; Warren, Jennifer; Huffman, David; Johnson, Lynn-Holly

Song(s) Through the Eyes of Love (C: Hamlisch, Marvin; L: Sager, Carole Bayer)

2752 ◆ ICE FOLLIES OF 1939
Metro–Goldwyn–Mayer, 1939

Musical Score Edens, Roger
Choreographer(s) Claudet, Frances; Raset, Val; Connolly, Bobby

Producer(s) Rapf, Harry
Director(s) Schunzel, Reinhold

Screenwriter(s) Praskins, Leonard; Ryerson, Florence; Woolf, Edgar Allan

Cast Crawford, Joan; Stewart, James; Ayres, Lew; Stone, Lewis; Ehrhardt, Bess; Shipstad, Roy; Johnson, Oscar; Shipstad, Eddie

Song(s) It's All So New to Me (C: Petkere, Bernice; L: Symes, Marty); Cinderella Reel (C/L: Edens, Roger); Blackbirds (C/L: Edens, Roger); Something's Gotta Happen Soon [1] (C: Brown, Nacio Herb; L: Freed, Arthur)

Notes [1] Sheet music only.

2753 ◆ ICELAND
Twentieth Century–Fox, 1942

Composer(s) Warren, Harry
Lyricist(s) Gordon, Mack
Choreographer(s) Gonzales, James [2]; Pan, Hermes

Producer(s) LeBaron, William
Director(s) Humberstone, H. Bruce
Screenwriter(s) Ellis, Robert; Logan, Helen

Cast Sammy Kaye and His Band; Merrill, Joan; Henie, Sonja; Payne, John; Oakie, Jack; Bressart, Felix; Maasen, Osa; Merrill, John; Feld, Fritz; Holloway, Sterling

Song(s) Let's Bring New Glory to Old Glory; You Can't Say No to a Soldier; There Will Never Be Another You; It's the Lovers' Knot; Panama [1]; Hawaiian Prelude [1]; I Like a Military Tune; Kaye's Melody (Inst.) (C: Kaye, Sammy)

Notes Titled KATINA internationally. There are also a vocals to Robert Hood Bowers' "Chinese Lullaby;" "A Song of Old Hawaii" by Johnny Noble and Gordon Beecher; "Hawaiian War Chant" by Johnny Noble and Leleichaku and "Aloha Oe" by Queen Liliuokalani. [1] About four lines each. [2] Choreographed skating sequences.

2754 ◆ ICEMAN
Universal, 1984

Musical Score Smeaton, Bruce

Producer(s) Palmer, Patrick; Jewison, Norman
Director(s) Schepisi, Fred
Screenwriter(s) Proser, Chip; Drummer, John

Cast Hutton, Timothy; Crouse, Lindsay; Lone, John; Sommer, Josef; Strathairn, David; Akin, Philip; Glover, Danny

Song(s) Heart of Gold (C/L: Young, Neil)

2755 ◆ I CONFESS
Warner Brothers, 1953

Musical Score Tiomkin, Dimitri

Producer(s) Hitchcock, Alfred
Director(s) Hitchcock, Alfred

Screenwriter(s) Tabori, George; Archibald, William
Source(s) *Nos Deux Consciences* (play) Anthelme, Paul

Cast Clift, Montgomery; Baxter, Anne; Malden, Karl; Aherne, Brian; Hasse, O.E.; Dann, Roger; Haas, Dolly; Andre, Charles; Pratt, Judson; Legare, Ovila

Song(s) Love, Look What You've Done to Me (C: Tiomkin, Dimitri; L: Washington, Ned)

2756 ✦ I COULD GO ON SINGING
United Artists, 1963

Musical Score Lindsey, Mort

Producer(s) Miller, Stuart; Turman, Ronald
Director(s) Neame, Ronald
Screenwriter(s) Simon, Mayo

Cast Garland, Judy; Bogarde, Dirk; Klugman, Jack; MacMahon, Aline

Song(s) I Could Go on Singing (C: Arlen, Harold; L: Harburg, E.Y.)

Notes There are also vocals of "Hello Bluebird" by Cliff Friend and "It Never Was You" by Kurt Weill and Maxwell Anderson.

2757 ✦ I COVER THE UNDERWORLD
Republic, 1954

Musical Score Young, Victor

Producer(s) O'Sullivan, William J.
Director(s) Springsteen, R.G.
Screenwriter(s) Butler, John K.

Cast McClory, Sean; Jordan, Joanne; Middleton, Ray; Greene, Jaclynne; Van Cleef, Lee; Griffith, James; Roberts, Roy; Van Zandt, Philip

Song(s) It's Not the First Love [1] (C/L: Maxwell, Eddie; Scott, Nathan)

Notes A remake of GANGS OF NEW YORK. [1] Also in ROSE OF THE YUKON and THE TRESPASSER.

2758 ✦ IDAHO
Republic, 1943

Producer(s) Kane, Joseph
Director(s) Kane, Joseph
Screenwriter(s) Chanslor, Roy; Cooper, Olive

Cast Rogers, Roy; Grey, Virginia; Munson, Ona; Burnette, Smiley; Shannon, Harry; Purcell, Dick; Stevens, Onslow; Taliaferro, Hal; Sons of the Pioneers; St. Brendan's Choir

Song(s) Idaho [2] (C/L: Stone, Jesse); Don Juan [1] (C/L: Spencer, Tim); Lone Buckaroo (C/L: Nolan, Bob); Stop (C/L: Nolan, Bob); Make Yourself at Home [3] (C: Styne, Jule; L: Bullock, Walter)

Notes [1] Also in SUNSET ON THE DESERT. [2] May be used in SONG OF IDAHO (Columbia). [3] Also in HEART OF THE GOLDEN WEST and HIT PARADE OF 1941.

2759 ✦ IDEA GIRL
Universal, 1946

Composer(s) Fairchild, Edgar
Lyricist(s) Brooks, Jack

Producer(s) Cowan, Will
Director(s) Jason, Will
Screenwriter(s) Marion, Charles R.

Cast Bishop, Julie; Barker, Jess; Dolenz, George; Mowbray, Alan; Fulton, Joan; Ryan, Tim

Song(s) How Would You Feel (C: Brooks, Jack); I Can't Get You Out of My Mind [1]; I'll Remember April [2] (C/L: de Paul, Gene; Raye, Don; Johnston, Pat); I Don't Care If I Never Dream Again; Set 'Em Up Joe [3]

Notes [1] Also in THE NAUGHTY NINETIES. [2] Also in THE GHOST CATCHERS, I'LL REMEMBER APRIL and RIDE 'EM COWBOY. Not used in STRICTLY IN THE GROOVE. [3] Also in FRONTIER GAL and THE WISTFUL WIDOW OF WAGON GAP.

2760 ✦ I'D GIVE MY LIFE
Paramount, 1936

Producer(s) Rowland, Richard A.
Director(s) Marin, Edwin L.
Screenwriter(s) O'Neil, George; Ryan, Ben
Source(s) *The Noose* (play) Van Loan, H.H.; Mack, Willard

Cast Standing, Sir Guy; Brown, Tom; Drake, Frances; Beecher, Janet; Judels, Charles

Song(s) Some Day We'll Meet Again (C/L: Magidson, Herb; Conrad, Con)

2761 ✦ IDIOT'S DELIGHT
Metro–Goldwyn–Mayer, 1939

Musical Score Stothart, Herbert
Choreographer(s) King, George

Producer(s) Stromberg, Hunt
Director(s) Brown, Clarence
Screenwriter(s) Sherwood, Robert E.
Source(s) *Idiot's Delight* (play) Sherwood, Robert E.

Cast Shearer, Norma; Gable, Clark; Arnold, Edward; Coburn, Charles; Schildkraut, Joseph; Meredith, Burgess; Crews, Laura Hope; Gallagher, Skeets; Willes, Peter; Feld, Fritz; Stone, Paula; Grey, Virginia; Marsh, Joan; Dale, Virginia; Hayes, Bernadene; Krueger, Lorraine

Song(s) How Strange [1] (C: Stothart, Herbert; L: Kahn, Gus)

Notes [1] Based on the song "Kak Stranno" by B.A. Prozorovsky. Earl Brent also credited by ASCAP with music.

2762 ♦ THE IDOLMAKER
United Artists, 1980

Composer(s) Barry, Jeff
Lyricist(s) Barry, Jeff

Producer(s) Kirkwood, Gene; Koch Jr., Howard W.
Director(s) Hackford, Taylor
Screenwriter(s) Di Lorenzo, Edward

Cast Sharkey, Ray; Feldshuh, Tovah; Gallagher, Peter; Land, Paul; Pantoliano, Joe; McCormick, Maureen; Aprea, John

Song(s) Ooo-Wee Baby; Here Is My Love; Come and Get It; Shelley; I Can't Tell If You Love Me, Baby; A Boy and a Girl; Sweet Little Lover; I Know Where You're Goin'; Shelley; It's Never Been Tonight Before; Baby; However Dark the Night; I Believe It Can Be Done

2763 ♦ THE I DON'T CARE GIRL
Twentieth Century–Fox, 1952

Composer(s) Jessel, George; Daniel, Eliot
Lyricist(s) Jessel, George; Daniel, Eliot
Choreographer(s) Cole, Jack [1]; Felix, Seymour

Producer(s) Jessel, George
Director(s) Bacon, Lloyd
Screenwriter(s) Bullock, Walter

Cast Gaynor, Mitzi; Wayne, David; Levant, Oscar; Graham, Bob; Hill, Craig; Stevens, Warren; Brooks, Hazel

Song(s) As Long As You Care (I Don't Care) (C: Cooper, Joe; L: Jessel, George); The Ziegfeld Touch; Here Comes Love Again

Notes Based on the life of Eva Tanguay. Vocals include "Kiss Me, My Honey, Kiss Me" by Ted Snyder and Irving Berlin; "I Don't Care" by Harry O. Sutton and Jean Lenox; "This Is My Favorite City" by Josef Myrow and Mack Gordon; "Oh! You Beautiful Doll" by Nat D. Ayer and A. Seymour Brown; "On the Mississippi" by Harry Carroll, Arthur Fields and Ballard Macdonald; "Pretty Baby" by Tony Jackson, Egbert Van Alstyne and Gus Kahn; "Hello, Frisco! (I Called You Up to Say Hello)" by Gene Buck and Louis A. Hirsch; "Johnson Rag" by Guy Hall, Henry Kleinkauf and Jack Lawrence; "Funiculi Funicula" by Luigi Denza and "Beale Street Blues" by W.C. Handy. [1] Cole staged "The Beale Street Blues," "I Don't Care" and "The Johnson Rag."

2764 ♦ I DOOD IT
Metro–Goldwyn–Mayer, 1943

Composer(s) Fain, Sammy
Lyricist(s) Brown, Lew; Freed, Ralph
Choreographer(s) Connolly, Bobby

Producer(s) Cummings, Jack
Director(s) Minnelli, Vincente
Screenwriter(s) Herzig, Sig; Saidy, Fred

Cast Skelton, Red; Powell, Eleanor; Ainley, Richard; Dane, Patricia; Levene, Sam; Hall, Thurston; Horne, Lena; Scott, Hazel; Jimmy Dorsey and His Orchestra; O'Connell, Helen; Eberly, Bob

Song(s) So Long, Sarah Jane; Star Eyes (C: de Paul, Gene; L: Raye, Don); Jericho [2] (C: Myers, Richard; L: Robin, Leo); Swingin' the Jinx Away [3] (C/L: Porter, Cole); Lord and Lady Gate [1] (C: de Paul, Gene; L: Raye, Don); One O'Clock Jump (Inst.) (C: Basie, Count); Shorter than Me [4] (C: de Paul, Gene; L: Raye, Don); There's a Fly on My Music [5]; I've Forgotten You [5]; Petunia [5] (C: Brown, Nacio Herb); Beale Street Trolley [5]

Notes Released internationally as BY HOOK OR BY CROOK. This is a remake of SPITE MARRIAGE. There is also a vocal of "Hola e Pae" by Ray Noble and an instrumental of "Taking a Chance on Love" by Vernon Duke, John Latouche and Ted Fetter. [1] Used instrumentally only. [2] Also in SYNCOPATION (RKO). [3] Also in BORN TO DANCE. [4] Sheet music only. [5] Not used.

2765 ♦ I'D RATHER BE RICH
Universal, 1964

Musical Score Faith, Percy

Producer(s) Hunter, Ross
Director(s) Smight, Jack
Screenwriter(s) Brodney, Oscar; Krasna, Norman; Townsend, Leo

Cast Chevalier, Maurice; Goulet, Robert; Dee, Sandra; Williams, Andy; Raymond, Gene; Ruggles, Charles; Gingold, Hermione; Main, Laurie

Song(s) I'd Rather Be Rich (C: Shire, David; L: Maltby Jr., Richard); Almost There (C/L: Keller, Jerry; Shayne, Gloria)

Notes This is a remake of IT STARTED WITH EVE (1941). There are also vocals of "It Had to Be You" by Gus Kahn and Isham Jones and "Where Are You" (from TOP OF THE TOWN) by Harold Adamson and Jimmy McHugh.

2766 ✦ I DREAM OF JEANNIE
Republic, 1951

Producer(s) Yates, Herbert J.
Director(s) Dwan, Allan
Screenwriter(s) LeMay, Alan

Cast Shirley, Bill; Lawrence, Muriel; Middleton, Ray; Christie, Eileen; Bari, Lynn; Allen, Rex

Song(s) Oh Susanna (C: Foster, Stephen; L: Dwan, Allan); On Wings of Song (C: Mendelssohn, Felix; L: Armbruster, Robert); Head Over Heels (C: Foster, Stephen; L: Dwan, Allan; Armbruster, Robert); A Ribbon in Your Hair (C: Foster, Stephen; L: Armbruster, Robert); I See Her Still in My Dreams (C: Foster, Stephen; L: Armbruster, Robert; Dwan, Allan)

Notes Other vocals include these songs by Stephen Foster unless otherwise indicated; "Oh Boys, Carry Me 'Long;" "Camptown Races;" "Old Dog Tray;" "Lo I Hear the Gentle Lark" by William Shakespeare and Bishop; "The Glendy Burke;" "Nelly Bly;" "Gentle Annie;" "Melinda May;" "My Old Kentucky Home;" "Massa's in de Cold Cold Ground;" "Ring Ring de Banjo;" "Old Folks at Home;" "Beautiful Dreamer;" "Come Where My Love Lies Dreaming;" "Some Folks;" "Old Black Joe" and "Jeanie with the Light Brown Hair."

2767 ✦ I DREAM TOO MUCH
RKO, 1935

Composer(s) Kern, Jerome
Lyricist(s) Fields, Dorothy
Choreographer(s) Pan, Hermes

Producer(s) Berman, Pandro S.
Director(s) Cromwell, John
Screenwriter(s) North, Edmund; Gow, James

Cast Pons, Lily; Fonda, Henry; Blore, Eric; Perkins, Osgood; Littlefield, Lucien; Ball, Lucille; Auer, Mischa; Porcasi, Paul; Beckett, Scotty

Song(s) I'm the Echo; Street Music (Inst.); Buffo Terzetto (L: Kern, Jerome); The Jockey on the Carousel; I Got Love; I Dream Too Much

Notes There is also a vocal of the "Bell Song" from LAKME by Delibes.

2768 ✦ IF . . .
Paramount, 1969

Producer(s) Anderson, Lindsay; Medwin, Michael
Director(s) Anderson, Lindsay
Screenwriter(s) Anderson, Lindsay; Sherwin, David

Cast McDowell, Malcolm; Wood, David; Warwick, Richard; Washbourne, Mona

Song(s) College Song [1] (C: Gesangbuch, Mainz; L: Anderson, Lindsay)

Notes [1] Based on "Ellacombe."

2769 ✦ IF A MAN ANSWERS
Universal, 1962

Musical Score Salter, Hans J.

Producer(s) Hunter, Ross
Director(s) Levin, Henry
Screenwriter(s) Morris, Richard
Source(s) *If a Man Answers* (novel) Wolfe, Winifred

Cast Dee, Sandra; Darin, Bobby; Romero, Cesar; Presle, Micheline; Lund, John; Powers, Stefanie

Song(s) If a Man Answers (C/L: Darin, Bobby); True True Love [1] (C/L: Darin, Bobby)

Notes [1] Sheet music only.

2770 ✦ IF HE HOLLERS, LET HIM GO!
Cinerama Releasing, 1968

Musical Score Sukman, Harry

Producer(s) Martin, Charles
Director(s) Martin, Charles
Screenwriter(s) Martin, Charles

Cast Wynter, Dana; St. Jacques, Raymond; McCarthy, Kevin; McNair, Barbara; O'Connell, Arthur; Russell, John

Song(s) So Tired (C/L: Perkinson, Coleridge-Taylor); A Man Has to Love (C: Fain, Sammy; L: Martin, Charles); Can't Make It with the Same Man Twice (C: Fain, Sammy; L: Martin, Charles)

Notes No cue sheet available.

2771 ✦ IF I HAD MY WAY
Universal, 1940

Musical Score Skinner, Frank
Composer(s) Monaco, James V.
Lyricist(s) Burke, Johnny

Producer(s) Butler, David
Director(s) Butler, David
Screenwriter(s) Conselman, William; Kern, James V.

Cast Jean, Gloria; Crosby, Bing; Brendel, El; Winninger, Charles; Leonard, Eddie; Ring, Blanche; Joslyn, Allyn; Woods, David; Dodd, Claire; Bryant, Nana; Olsen, Moroni; Friganza, Trixie; Eltinge, Julian

Song(s) Meet the Sun Halfway; Doodle Dum Da (C/L: Sooter, Rudy); I Haven't Time to Be a Millionaire; The Pessimistic Character (with the Crab Apple Face); April Played the Fiddle

Notes There are also vocals of "Little Grey Home in the West" by D. Eardley Wilmott and Hermann Lohr and "Ida, Sweet As Apple Cider" by Eddie Leonard and "Rings on My Fingers" by George W. Meyer and Jack Mahone.

2772 ◆ IF I'M LUCKY
Twentieth Century–Fox, 1946

Composer(s) Myrow, Josef
Lyricist(s) DeLange, Eddie [1]
Choreographer(s) Williams, Kenny

Producer(s) Foy, Bryan
Director(s) Seiler, Lewis
Screenwriter(s) Ling, Eugene; Gabrielson, Frank

Cast Blaine, Vivian; Como, Perry; James, Harry; Miranda, Carmen; Silvers, Phil; Buchanan, Edgar; Hadley, Reed

Song(s) Follow the Band; If I'm Lucky; One More Kiss; Bet Your Bottom Dollar; One More Vote; Jam Session in Brazil (The Batacada); That Mexican Look [2]

Notes A remake of THANKS A MILLION (1937). The Harry James Orchestra plays the "King Porter Stomp" by Jelly Roll Morton. [1] Billed as Edgar DeLange. [2] Not used.

2773 ◆ IF IT'S TUESDAY, THIS MUST BE BELGIUM
United Artists, 1969

Musical Score Scharf, Walter

Producer(s) Margulies, Stan
Director(s) Stuart, Mel
Screenwriter(s) Shaw, David

Cast Pleshette, Suzanne; McShane, Ian; Natwick, Mildred; Cass, Peggy; Constantine, Michael; Fell, Norman; Rose, Reva; Ingels, Marty; Britton, Pamela

Song(s) If It's Tuesday, This Must Be Belgium (C/L: Leitch, Donovan); I'd Be Satisfied for Life (C/L: Wright, Lawrence); Lord of the Reedy River (C/L: Leitch, Donovan)

2774 ◆ I FOUND STELLA PARRISH
Warner Brothers, 1935

Musical Score Roemheld, Heinz
Composer(s) Warren, Harry
Lyricist(s) Dubin, Al

Producer(s) Brown, Harry Joe
Director(s) LeRoy, Mervyn
Screenwriter(s) Robinson, Casey

Cast Francis, Kay; Hunter, Ian; Lukas, Paul; Jason, Sybil; Ralph, Jessie; MacLane, Barton; Acuff, Eddie;

Sawyer, Joe; Kingsford, Walter; Beresford, Harry; Strange, Robert

Song(s) The Pig and the Cow, and the Dog and the Cat [1]; Powder My Back

Notes [1] Also in BROADWAY GONDOLIER.

2775 ◆ IF THIS ISN'T LOVE
RKO, 1934

Cast Lee, Dorothy; Woolf, Walter

Song(s) If It Isn't Love (C/L: Burton, Val; Jason, Will)

Notes No cue sheet available. No other information available.

2776 ◆ IF WINTER COMES
Metro–Goldwyn–Mayer, 1947

Musical Score Stothart, Herbert

Producer(s) Berman, Pandro S.
Director(s) Saville, Victor
Screenwriter(s) Roberts, Marguerite; Wimperis, Arthur
Source(s) *If Winter Comes* (novel) Hutchinson, A.S.M.

Cast Pidgeon, Walter; Kerr, Deborah; Lansbury, Angela; Barnes, Binnie; Leigh, Janet; Whitty, Dame May; Ray, Rene; Owen, Reginald; Williams, Rhys

Song(s) If Winter Comes (C: Carpenter, Imogene; L: Gannon, Kim)

Notes First filmed in 1923 by Fox.

2777 ◆ IF YOU COULD SEE WHAT I HEAR
Jensen Farley, 1982

Musical Score Robertson, Eric N.

Producer(s) Till, Eric
Director(s) Till, Eric
Screenwriter(s) Gillard, Stuart
Source(s) *If You Could See What I Hear* (novel) Sullivan, Tom; Gill, Derek

Cast Singer, Marc; Thompson, R.H.; Torgov, Sarah; Harper, Shari Belafonte

Song(s) If You Could See What I Hear (C/L: Sullivan, Tom; Lloyd, Michael; Greenfield, Howard); You're the One (C/L: Lloyd, Michael); I Hear Love (C/L: Lloyd, Michael; Fleischer, Mark); Just Another Heartbreak (C/L: Berardi, Michael; Berardi, Richard); Let Me Begin to Love You (C/L: Sullivan, Tom); Carry On and Something Else Again (C/L: deBurgh, Chris); Rainfall (C: Robertson, Eric N.; L: Norman, Marek)

Notes No cue sheet available.

2778 ◆ IF YOU FEEL LIKE SINGING

See SUMMER STOCK.

2779 ◆ IF YOU KNEW SUSIE
RKO, 1942

Musical Score Fairchild, Edgar [1]
Choreographer(s) O'Curran, Charles

Producer(s) Cantor, Eddie
Director(s) Douglas, Gordon M.
Screenwriter(s) Wilson, Warren; Brodney, Oscar; Pearson, Bud; White, Lester A.

Cast Cantor, Eddie; Davis, Joan; Joslyn, Allyn; Dingle, Charles; Brown, Phil; Leonard, Sheldon; Sawyer, Joe; Fowley, Douglas; Kerry, Margaret; Rumann, Sig; Feld, Fritz; Driscoll, Bobby

Song(s) My, How the Time Goes By (C: McHugh, Jimmy; L: Adamson, Harold); My Brooklyn Love Song (C/L: Idriss, Ramez; Tibbels, George); What Do I Want with Money (C: McHugh, Jimmy; L: Adamson, Harold)

Notes There is also a vocal of "If You Knew Susie" by B.G. DeSylva and Joseph Meyer. [1] Billed as Edgar "Cookie" Fairchild.

2780 ◆ I, JAMES LEWIS
Paramount, 1937 unproduced

Song(s) The Days of Philand'ring Are Over (C: Mozart; L: unknown)

2781 ◆ I LIKE IT THAT WAY
Universal, 1934

Composer(s) Gottler, Archie
Lyricist(s) Mitchell, Sidney D.

Director(s) Lachman, Harry
Screenwriter(s) Sprague, Chandler; Santley, Joseph

Cast Stuart, Gloria; Pryor, Roger; Marsh, Marian; Grey, Shirley; Gleason, Lucille; Madison, Noel; Shea, Gloria; Busch, Mae; Kennedy, Merna; Rooney, Mickey

Song(s) Blue Sky Avenue (C: Conrad, Con; L: Magidson, Herb); Let's Put Two and Two Together; I Like It That Way; Goin' to Town; Miss 1934; Good Old Days

Notes No cue sheet available.

2782 ◆ I LIKE MONEY

See MR. TOPAZE.

2783 ◆ I LIVE FOR LOVE
Warner Brothers, 1935

Musical Score Roemheld, Heinz
Composer(s) Wrubel, Allie
Lyricist(s) Dixon, Mort

Producer(s) Foy, Bryan
Director(s) Berkeley, Busby
Screenwriter(s) Wald, Jerry; Epstein, Julius J.; Andrews, Robert

Cast Del Rio, Dolores; Marshall, Everett; Kibbee, Guy; Jenkins, Allen; Churchill, Berton; Cavanaugh, Hobart; Treen, Mary; Shaw and Lee; Alvarado, Don

Song(s) Mine Alone; I Live for Love; Shaving Song (A Man Must Shave); Silver Wings; You're An Eyeful of Heaven [1]; I Wanna Play House with You [1]

Notes [1] Used instrumentally only. Some sources, however, say these are used vocally.

2784 ◆ I'LL BE YOURS
Universal, 1947

Musical Score Skinner, Frank

Producer(s) Jackson, Felix
Director(s) Seiter, William A.
Screenwriter(s) Sturges, Preston
Source(s) *The Good Fairy* (play) Molnar, Ferenc

Cast Durbin, Deanna; Menjou, Adolphe; Drake, Tom; Bendix, William; Fulton, Joan; Brooks, William

Song(s) It's Dreamtime (C: Schumann, Walter; L: Brooks, Jack); Cobleskill School Song [1] (C/L: Brooks, Jack)

Notes There are also vocals of "Daddy" by Bobby Troup; "Granada" by Augustin Lara; "Home on the Range" and "Love's Own Sweet Song" by C.C.S. Cushing, E.P. Heath and Emmerich Kalman. [1] Used instrumentally only.

2785 ◆ I'LL CRY TOMORROW
Metro–Goldwyn–Mayer, 1956

Musical Score North, Alex

Producer(s) Weingarten, Lawrence
Director(s) Mann, Daniel
Screenwriter(s) Deutsch, Helen; Kennedy, Jay Richard
Source(s) *I'll Cry Tomorrow* (book) Roth, Lillian; Connolly, Mike; Frank, Gerold

Cast Hayward, Susan; Conte, Richard; Albert, Eddie; Van Fleet, Jo; Taylor, Don; Danton, Ray; Margo; Gregg, Virginia; Barry, Donald; Kasday, David

Song(s) I'll Cry Tomorrow [1] (C: North, Alex; L: Mercer, Johnny)

Notes There were no songs written for this picture. There are vocals of "Sing You Sinners" by Sam Coslow and Franke Harling; "When the Red, Red Robin Comes Bob, Bob Bobbin' Along" by Harry Woods; "Happiness Is a Thing Called Joe" by Harold Arlen and E.Y. Harburg and "Valse Hugette" by Rudolf Friml and Brian Hooker. "I'm Sittin' on Top of the World" by Ray Henderson, Sam Lewis and Joe Young is not on the cue sheet but is sung by Hayward on the soundtrack album. [1] Not on cue sheet but on soundtrack album sung by Susan Hayward.

2786 ◆ I'LL GET BY
Twentieth Century–Fox, 1950

Choreographer(s) Ceballos, Larry

Producer(s) Perlberg, William
Director(s) Sale, Richard
Screenwriter(s) Loos, Mary; Sale, Richard

Cast Haver, June; Lundigan, William; De Haven, Gloria; Day, Dennis; James, Harry; Ritter, Thelma; Allen, Steve; Davenport, Danny; Hanlon, Tom

Song(s) Chi-Chi Club (C/L: Gordon, Mack); Fifth Avenue [1] (C: Warren, Harry; L: Gordon, Mack; Darby, Ken); Mac Namara's Band [2] (C: O'Conner, Shamus; L: Stamford, John J.; Latham, Red; Carlson, Wamp; Bonman, Guy)

Notes There are also vocal renditions of "Once in a While" by Michael Edwards and Bud Green; "I'll Get By (As Long As I Have You)" by Fred Ahlert and Roy Turk; "You Say the Sweetest Things Baby" and "There Will Never Be Another You" by Harry Warren and Mack Gordon; "Taking a Chance on Love" by Vernon Duke, John Latouche and Ted Fetter; "You Make Me Feel So Young" by Josef Myrow and Mack Gordon; "The Yankee Doodle Blues" by George Gershwin, Irving Caesar and B.G. De Sylva; "No Love, No Nothin'" by Harry Warren and Leo Robin; "It's Been a Long, Long Time" by Jule Styne and Sammy Cahn; "Deep in the Heart of Texas" by Don Swander and June Hershey and "I've Got the World on a String" by Harold Arlen and Ted Koehler as well as an instrumental of "I've Got a Gal in Kalamazoo" played by the Harry James Band. [1] Song written for YOUNG PEOPLE. New lyrics by Ken Darby were added to this version. [2] This song also wasn't written for this film. New lyrics by Latham, Carlson and Bonman were.

2787 ◆ I'LL NEVER FORGET WHAT'S 'IS NAME
Universal, 1967

Musical Score Lai, Francis
Composer(s) Lai, Francis
Lyricist(s) Pratt, Mike

Producer(s) Winner, Michael
Director(s) Winner, Michael
Screenwriter(s) Draper, Peter

Cast Welles, Orson; Reed, Oliver; White, Carol; Andrews, Harry; Hordern, Michael; Craig, Wendy; Finlay, Frank

Song(s) Keep It Cool; Party Music

2788 ◆ I'LL REACH FOR A STAR

See HIT PARADE.

2789 ◆ I'LL REMEMBER APRIL
Universal, 1944

Producer(s) Lewis, Gene
Director(s) Young, Harold
Screenwriter(s) Webster, M. Coates

Cast Jean, Gloria; Grant, Kirby

Song(s) A Half Moon in Three Quarter Time (C: Revel, Harry; L: Webster, Paul Francis); I'll Remember April [1] (C/L: de Paul, Gene; Raye, Don; Johnston, Pat); Hittin' the Beach Tonite (C/L: Roberts, Marty; Dornisch, Chic); There Is So Much to Wish For (C/L: Franklin, Dave); Dawn [2] (C/L: Roberts, Gil; del Moral, Jorge); Cha-da-Boom [3] (C: Sherman, Al; L: Tobias, Harry)

Notes [1] Also in THE GHOST CATCHERS; IDEA GIRL and RIDE 'EM COWBOY. Not used in STRICTLY IN THE GROOVE. [2] Sheet music credits Al Sherman and Harry Tobias. It may be different song with the same title. [3] Sheet music only.

2790 ◆ I'LL SEE YOU IN MY DREAMS
Warner Brothers, 1952

Lyricist(s) Kahn, Gus
Choreographer(s) Prinz, LeRoy

Producer(s) Edelman, Louis F.
Director(s) Curtiz, Michael
Screenwriter(s) Shavelson, Melville; Rose, Jack
Source(s) *The Gus Kahn Story* (book) Kahn, Grace; Edelman, Louis F.

Cast Day, Doris; Thomas, Danny; Lovejoy, Frank; Wymore, Patrice; Gleason, James; Wickes, Mary; Oshins, Julie; Backus, Jim; Gombell, Minna

Notes There are also vocals of "'ll See You in My Dreams," "The One I Love Belongs to Somebody Else," "It Had to Be You," and "Swinging Down the Lane" by Kahn and Isham Jones; "It Looks Like a Big Night Tonight" by Egbert Van Alstyne and Harry Williams; "Shine on Harvest Moon" by Jack Norworth and Nora Bayes (also in ALONG CAME RUTH; and both the Republic and Warner pictures titled SHINE ON HARVEST MOON); "I Wish I Had a Girl" and "The Month of June Is a Song of Love" by Kahn and Grace LeRoy; "Memories" by Kahn and Egbert Van Alstyne; "Pretty Baby" (also in APPLAUSE and THE EDDIE

CANTOR STORY) by Kahn, Van Alstyne and Tony Jackson; "Nobody's Sweetheart" by Kahn, Ernie Erdman, Billy Meyers and Elmer Schoebel; "My Buddy," "Carolina in the Morning," "Love Me or Leave Me," "Yes Sir, That's My Baby" (also in THE DANCE OF LIFE and THE EDDIE CANTOR STORY) and "Makin' Whoopee" by Kahn and Walter Donaldson; "Toot Toot Tootsie" by Kahn, Ernie Erdman and Dan Russo (Also in THE JAZZ SINGER and ROSE OF WASHINGTON SQUARE; THE JOLSON STORY and JOLSON SINGS AGAIN); "No No Nora" by Kahn, Erdman and Ted Fiorito; "Your Eyes Have Told Me So" by Kahn, Van Alstyne and Walter Blaufuss and "Ukelele Lady" by Kahn and Richard A. Whiting. Some of these songs are included briefly in medleys.

2791 ✦ I'LL TAKE ROMANCE
Universal, 1937

Director(s) Griffith, Edward H.
Screenwriter(s) Oppenheimer, George; Murfin, Jane

Cast Moore, Grace; Douglas, Melvyn; Westley, Helen; Erwin, Stuart; Hamilton, Margaret; Muir, Esther

Song(s) I'll Take Romance [1] (C: Oakland, Ben; L: Hammerstein II, Oscar)

Notes No cue sheet available. There are also operatic selections from LA TRAVIATA; MARTHA; MANON and MADAME BUTTERFLY. Also "Gavotte" by Massenet and "She'll Be Comin' Round the Mountain." [1] Also used in HOLIDAY IN HAVANA.

2792 ✦ I'LL TAKE SWEDEN
United Artists, 1965

Musical Score Haskell, Jimmie; Dunham, "By"
Composer(s) Lauber, Ken
Lyricist(s) Lampert, Diane

Producer(s) Small, Edward
Director(s) De Cordova, Frederick
Screenwriter(s) Perrin, Nat; Fisher, Bob; Marx, Arthur

Cast Hope, Bob; Weld, Tuesday; Avalon, Frankie; Merrill, Dina; Slate, Jeremy

Song(s) Nothing Can Compare with You (C/L: Dunham, "By"); I'll Take Sweden; Would You Like My Last Name; The Bells Keep Ringin' (C/L: Dunham, "By"; Beverly, Bobby); Hildegarde (C/L: Haskell, Jimmie; Dunham, "By"); There'll Be Rainbows Again (C/L: Dunham, "By"; Beverly, Bobby); I'm Gonna Go to Sweden (C/L: Haskell, Jimmie; Dunham, "By")

2793 ✦ I'LL TELL THE WORLD
Universal, 1945

Producer(s) Gross, Frank
Director(s) Goodwins, Leslie
Screenwriter(s) Blankfort, Henry; Pine, Lester

Cast Tracy, Lee; Walburn, Raymond; Joyce, Brenda; Preisser, June; Gomez, Thomas

Song(s) Where the Prairie Meets the Sky [2] (C: Rosen, Milton; L: Carter, Everett); Song of the Steamboat (C/L: Travis, Merle); Walk a Little, Talk a Little (C/L: Franklin, Don; George, Don); The Slap Polka [1] (C: Revel, Harry; L: Webster, Paul Francis); Moonlight Fiesta (C/L: Sherman, Al; Tobias, Harry)

Notes It is not known if any of these were written for this film. [1] Also in HIT THE ICE. [2] Also in BAD MAN FROM RED BUTTE, ESCAPE FROM HONG KONG, FRONTIER LAW and TWILIGHT ON THE PRAIRIE.

2794 ✦ ILLUSION
Paramount, 1929

Composer(s) Spier, Larry; Coots, J. Fred
Lyricist(s) Davis, Lou

Director(s) Mendes, Lothar
Screenwriter(s) Sheldon, E. Lloyd
Source(s) *Illusion* (novel) Train, Arthur Chesney

Cast Rogers, Charles "Buddy"; Carroll, Nancy; Collyer, June; Francis, Kay; Toomey, Regis

Song(s) With You In My Arms [2]; Revolutionary Rhythm [3]; Levee Love; I'll Be There; Illusion [1] (C: Spier, Larry; L: Coslow, Sam)

Notes No cue sheet available. [1] Also known as "Do You Mind If I Fall in Love," without Coslow lyrics and "When the Real Thing Comes Your Way" with Coslow lyrics. However, "When the Real Thing Comes Your Way" was published with music and lyrics credited to Larry Spier alone. [2] Coslow might have had something to do with this song. The documentation isn't clear. However a memo reads: "After much discussion and many changes with our Music Committee and the organization, the lyric—that is, the new lyric by Sam Coslow, has been accepted for the purpose necessary in ILLUSION.

"It is very unpleasant to have to write five or six different lyrics for a tune but Mr. Davis should be made to see the light that, after all, the Production requirements have also to be considered. I am writing this to you to have you definitely advise all those concerned that Coslow did not wish himself in on this new lyric but rather came to save a taut situation. Mr. Coslow is writing to Spier along similar lines, advising him of the problems attending the acceptance of this song. It seems Spier will discuss with Davis the advisability of playing ball, and it must be strictly understood that Davis is no more independent of this concern than this concern can afford to be with regard to his work.

"There are other pictures, and other opportunities, and if he cannot see it, you can give him for me the 'grand razoo', and as far as I'm concerned, he can be out of the picture or as long as that will be necessary."

Coslow wrote: "The next tune played was 'DO YOU MIND IF I FALL IN LOVE' which Mr. Mendes immediately insisted was just the type of tune he wanted for the theme spot, as he wanted something with a swing to it. Of course those horrible lyrics about cabbage and ham were turned down cold and ridiculed by everyone who heard them here . . . I'm sure that almost any lyric Lou Davis turns out will be a mess. My opinion of him as a lyric writer is that he is a great butcher. For instance, 'DO YOU MIND IF I FALL IN LOVE' is a rank imitation of 'YOU'RE THE CREAM IN MY COFFEE' and 'WITH YOU IN MY ARMS', his big punch line was the title of a current popular hit, 'I'LL GET BY.'. . ." [3] A memo of 9/12/29 reads "I am of the opinion that Spier & Coslow are entitled to mechanical instruments credit in reports made the Mills, as the numbers ('Revolutionary Rag' and 'When the Real Thing Comes Your Way') are entirely written by them." All three are credited on sheet music.

2795 ✦ I'LL WAIT FOR YOU
Metro–Goldwyn–Mayer, 1941

Musical Score   Kaper, Bronislau

Producer(s)   Knopf, Edwin H.
Director(s)   Sinclair, Robert B.
Screenwriter(s)   Trosper, Guy

Cast   Sterling, Robert; Hunt, Marsha; Weidler, Virginia; Kelly, Paul; Holden, Fay; Travers, Henry

Song(s)   A Lesson in Latin (C: Siegel, Al; L: Freed, Ralph)

Notes   A remake of HIDEOUT (1934).

2796 ✦ I LOVE A BANDLEADER
Columbia, 1945

Producer(s)   Kraike, Michel
Director(s)   Lord, Del
Screenwriter(s)   Yawitz, Paul

Cast   Harris, Phil; Brooks, Leslie; Catlett, Walter; Sully, Frank; The Four V's

Song(s)   Good Good Good (C/L: Roberts, Allan; Fisher, Doris)

Notes   No cue sheet available. Titled MEMORY FOR TWO in Great Britain.

2797 ✦ I LOVE A SOLDIER
Paramount, 1944

Musical Score   Dolan, Robert Emmett

Producer(s)   Sandrich, Mark
Director(s)   Sandrich, Mark
Screenwriter(s)   Scott, Allan

Cast   Goddard, Paulette; Tufts, Sonny; Bondi, Beulah; Fitzgerald, Barry; Treen, Mary; Doran, Ann

Song(s)   Song of the Ski-Troops (C: Dolan, Robert Emmett; L: Coslow, Sam)

Notes   Previously titled WHEN I COME BACK.

2798 ✦ I LOVED A WOMAN
Warner Brothers–First National, 1933

Producer(s)   Blanke, Henry
Director(s)   Green, Alfred E.
Screenwriter(s)   Wallace, Edgar; Sutherland, Sidney
Source(s)   (novel) Karsner, David

Cast   Tobin, Genevieve; Francis, Kay; Robinson, Edward G.; MacDonald, J. Farrell; Kolker, Henry; Barrat, Robert; Blackwood, George; Kinnell, Murray

Song(s)   "Original Song" [2] (C/L: Rayon, Ami); Tramp Tramp Tramp the Boys Are Marching (C: Traditional; L: Kahal, Irving)

Notes   [2] The original song was not named. It is sung on the soundtrack by Ami Rayon. There is also a vocal of "Home on the Range" and one of "Little Annie Rooney" by Nolan.

2799 ✦ I LOVED YOU WEDNESDAY
Fox, 1933

Composer(s)   Whiting, Richard A.
Lyricist(s)   Marion Jr., George

Director(s)   Menzies, William Cameron; King, Henry
Screenwriter(s)   Klein, Philip; Jackson, Horace
Source(s)   *I Loved You Wednesday* (play) Ricardel, Molly; DuBois, William

Cast   Baxter, Warner; Landi, Elissa; Jory, Victor; Jordan, Miriam; Crews, Laura Hope

Song(s)   Romantic [2] (C: DeFrancesco, Louis E.; L: Burton, Val; Jason, Will); My First Love to Last [1]; It's All for the Best (L: Whiting, Richard A.); I Found You—I Lost You (C: Kornblum, I.B.; L: Gilbert, L. Wolfe)

Notes   Also used vocally are "Les Temps De Grisettes" by Dardany; "La Margot" by Pares and Parys and "Petite Tonkinoise" by Scotto. [1] Also in ADORABLE. [2] Also in STATE FAIR (1933).

2800 ✦ I LOVE MELVIN
Metro–Goldwyn–Mayer, 1953

Musical Score   Stoll, George
Composer(s)   Myrow, Josef
Lyricist(s)   Gordon, Mack
Choreographer(s)   Alton, Robert

Producer(s)   Wells, George
Director(s)   Weis, Don
Screenwriter(s)   Wells, George; Flippen, Ruth Brooks

Cast Reynolds, Debbie; O'Connor, Donald; Merkel, Una; Anderson, Richard; Joslyn, Allyn; Tremayne, Les; Taylor, Robert

Song(s) A Lady Loves; We Have Never Met As Yet; Saturday Afternoon Before the Game; Where Did You Learn to Dance; Life Has Its Funny Little Ups and Downs; I Wanna Wander; And There You Are [1]

Notes [1] Used instrumentally only.

2801 ✦ I LOVE YOU, ALICE B. TOKLAS
Warner Brothers, 1968

Musical Score Bernstein, Elmer

Producer(s) Maguire, Charles
Director(s) Averback, Hy
Screenwriter(s) Mazursky, Paul

Cast Sellers, Peter; Van Fleet, Jo; Van Patten, Joyce; Arkin, David; Edelman, Herb; Taylor-Young, Leigh; Ludwig, Salem; Sutton, Grady

Song(s) I Love You, Alice B. Toklas Theme (C: Bernstein, Elmer; L: Tucker, Larry; Mazursky, Paul)

2802 ✦ IMAGE OF LOVE
Green Releasing Organization, 1965

Musical Score Laderman, Ezra

Producer(s) Stoumen, Lou
Director(s) Stoumen, Lou
Screenwriter(s) Stoumen, Lou
Narrator(s) Newley, Anthony

Song(s) Image of Love (C: Laderman, Ezra; L: Stoumen, Lou)

Notes No cue sheet available.

2803 ✦ IMAGINE: JOHN LENNON
Warner Brothers, 1988

Composer(s) Lennon, John; McCartney, Paul
Lyricist(s) Lennon, John; McCartney, Paul

Producer(s) Wolper, David L.; Solt, Andrew
Director(s) Solt, Andrew
Screenwriter(s) Eagan, Sam; Solt, Andrew

Song(s) Real Love (C/L: Lennon, John); Imagine (C/L: Lennon, John); How (C/L: Lennon, John); Julia; Mother (C/L: Lennon, John); Be-Bop-A-Lula (C/L: Vincent, Gene; Davis, Sheriff Tex); Rip It Up (C/L: Blackwell, Robert; Marascalco, John); Some Other Guy (C/L: Leiber, Jerry; Stoller, Mike; Barrett, Richard); Love Me Do; Twist and Shout (C/L: Medley, Bill; Russell, Bert); From Me to You; Jealous Guy (C/L: Lennon, John); Help; Nowhere Man; Strawberry Fields Forever; A Day in the Life; Lucy in the Sky with Diamonds; I've Got a Feeling; Revolution; Ballad of John and Yoko; Oh, Yoko (C/L: Lennon, John); Hold On, John (C/L: Lennon, John); Give Peace a Chance; Don't Let Me Down; God (C/L: Lennon, John); How Do You Sleep? (C/L: Lennon, John); Happy Xmas (War Is Over) (C/L: Lennon, John); Across the Universe; Come Together; Stand By Me (C/L: King, Ben E.; Leiber, Jerry; Stoller, Mike); Woman (C/L: Lennon, John); Beautiful Boy (C/L: Lennon, John); (Just Like) Starting Over (C/L: Lennon, John); All You Need is Love; In My Life

Notes None of these were written for the picture, which is a documentary of the life of John Lennon. Many of these songs last less than one minute.

2804 ✦ I MARRIED AN ANGEL (1933)
Metro–Goldwyn–Mayer, 1933 unproduced

Composer(s) Rodgers, Richard
Lyricist(s) Hart, Lorenz

Screenwriter(s) Hart, Lorenz

Song(s) Love Is Queen, Love Is King; Face the Facts; Tell Me I Know How to Love; Animated Objects; Why Have You Eyes?; I Married an Angel [1]; Bath and Dressmaking Sequence [2]

Notes Unproduced musical. The idea was later used for the Broadway musical of the same name. [1] Used subsequently in Broadway musical. [2] Used as basis for song "The Modiste" in the Broadway incarnation.

2805 ✦ I MARRIED AN ANGEL (1942)
Metro–Goldwyn–Mayer, 1942

Musical Score Stothart, Herbert
Composer(s) Stothart, Herbert
Lyricist(s) Wright, Bob; Forrest, Chet
Choreographer(s) Matray, Ernst

Producer(s) Stromberg, Hunt
Director(s) Van Dyke II, W.S.
Screenwriter(s) Loos, Anita
Source(s) *I Married an Angel* (musical) Rodgers, Richard; Hart, Lorenz

Cast MacDonald, Jeanette; Eddy, Nelson; Horton, Edward Everett; Barnes, Binnie; Owen, Reginald; Dumbrille, Douglass; Maris, Mona; Carter, Janis; Cooper, Inez

Song(s) Surprise at Party; Tira Lira La [4] (C: Rodgers, Richard); I Married an Angel [2] (C: Rodgers, Richard; Stothart, Herbert; L: Hart, Lorenz; Wright, Bob; Forrest, Chet); I'll Tell the Man in the Street [1] (C: Rodgers, Richard; L: Hart, Lorenz); Hey Butcher; Spring Is Here [2] (C: Rodgers, Richard; Stothart, Herbert; L: Hart, Lorenz; Wright, Bob; Forrest, Chet); May I Present the Girl; Willy's Former Girl Friends; Now You've Met the Angel; A Twinkle In Your Eye [2] (C: Rodgers, Richard; Stothart, Herbert; L: Hart, Lorenz; Wright, Bob; Forrest, Chet); But What of Truth; Little Work-a-Day World [3] (C: Rodgers,

Richard); Chanson Boheme [5] (C: Bizet, Georges); There Comes a Time [6]; To Count Palaffi [6]

Notes There are also vocals of "Villanelle" by Dell'Acqua; and "Anges Purs, Anges Radieux" from Gounod's FAUST. [1] In Broadway original. [2] Rodgers and Hart contribution in Broadway original. [3] Not on cue sheet. This is only listed by Stanley Green in *The Rodgers and Hammerstein Fact Book*. The music is that of "Did You Ever Get Stung?" from the Broadway original. Hart's lyric was discarded and another was written by Wright and Forrest. [4] The music is that of "At the Roxy Music Hall" from the Broadway original. The cue sheet still lists it as that and does not mention Wright and Forrest. [5] Based on the music of "Les Tringle des Sistres Tintainent" from Bizet's CARMEN, though Wright and Forrest are not mentioned on the cue sheet. [6] Listed in Hirschhorn's *The Hollywood Musical* but not on cue sheets.

2806 ◆ I MET HIM IN PARIS
Paramount, 1937

Musical Score Leipold, John

Producer(s) Ruggles, Wesley
Director(s) Ruggles, Wesley
Screenwriter(s) Binyon, Claude

Cast Colbert, Claudette; Douglas, Melvyn; Young, Robert; Bowman, Lee; Barrie, Mona; Feld, Fritz

Song(s) I Met Him in Paris [1] (C: Carmichael, Hoagy; L: Meinardi, Helen)

Notes [1] This song is not used vocally in the film. It might appear instrumentally but is not indicated on the cue sheets. It was, however, written for the film or at least for exploitation. Used in PACIFIC BLACKOUT.

2807 ◆ I'M FROM ARKANSAS
PRC, 1944

Musical Score Wheeler, Clarence

Producer(s) Kleinert, E.H.; Vershel, Irving
Director(s) Landers, Lew
Screenwriter(s) Klauber, Marcy; Carole, Joseph

Cast Summerville, Slim; Brendel, El

Song(s) Pass the Biscuits Mirandy [1] (C/L: Hoefle, Carl; Porter, Del); Pitchfork Polka (Topeka Polka) (C/L: Cooley, Spade; Hoefle, Carl; Porter, Del); Whistlin' Down the Lane with You (C/L: Whelan, Ekko; Romero, Garet); You Are My Sunshine [3] (C/L: Davis, Jimmie; Mitchell, Charles); Don't Turn Me Down Little Darlin' [4] (C/L: Dean, Eddie; Tobias, Harry; Canova, Judy); Yodel Mountain (C/L: Martin, Dude); Stay Away from My Heart [2] (C/L: Marvin, Johnny)

Notes Cue sheet doesn't differentiate between vocals and instrumentals. [1] Also in HI, NEIGHBOR

(Republic). [2] Also in ARIZONA TRAIL (Universal). [3] Also in COWBOY SERENADE, RIDIN' ON A RAINBOW and STRICTLY IN THE GROOVE (Universal). Jimmie Davis became Governor of Louisiana in 1944. [4] Zeke Canova also credited on sheet music.

2808 ◆ I'M FROM THE CITY
RKO, 1938

Musical Score Webb, Roy

Producer(s) Sistrom, William
Director(s) Holmes, Ben
Screenwriter(s) Barrows, Nicholas T.; St. Clair, Robert; Grey, John

Cast Penner, Joe; Lane, Richard; Kureger, Lorraine; Guilfoyle, Paul; Sutton, Kay

Song(s) I'm a Tough Coyote [1] (C/L: Raynor, Hal); I'm from the City [2] (C/L: Raynor, Hal; Penner, Joe)

Notes [1] Used instrumentally only. [2] Not on cue sheet.

2809 ◆ IMITATION OF LIFE
Universal, 1959

Producer(s) Hunter, Ross
Director(s) Sirk, Douglas
Screenwriter(s) Griffin, Eleanore; Scott, Allan
Source(s) *Imitation of Life* (novel) Hurst, Fannie

Cast Turner, Lana; Dee, Sandra; Moore, Juanita; Kohner, Susan [1]; Gavin, John; Alda, Robert; O'Herlihy, Dan; Jackson, Mahalia; Vivyan, John; Goodman, Lee; Donahue, Troy; Dicker, Karen; Burnham, Terry

Song(s) Imitation of Life (C: Fain, Sammy; L: Webster, Paul Francis); Empty Arms [2] (C: Hughes, Arnold; L: Herbert, Frederick)

Notes Originally filmed in 1934. There is also a rendition of the traditional song "Soon I Will Be Done with the Trouble of the World." [1] Dubbed by Jo Ann Greer. [2] Also in DESTRY.

2810 ◆ I'M NO ANGEL
Paramount, 1933

Composer(s) Brooks, Harvey
Lyricist(s) Ellison, Ben; DuBois, Gladys

Producer(s) LeBaron, William
Director(s) Ruggles, Wesley
Screenwriter(s) Thompson, Harlan; West, Mae

Song(s) I'm No Angel (L: Ellison, Ben); They Call Me Sister Honky Tonk; (No One Loves Me Like) That Dallas Man [1]; I've Found a New Way to Go To Town [4]; I Want You, I Need You [3] (L: Ellison, Ben); Lion Tamer's Blues [2]

Notes [1] Originally titled "There Is No One Like My Dallas Man." [2] Not used. [3] Was once titled "Take Me" but the Hays Office objected. [4] Glady DuBois not credited on sheet music.

2811 ✦ I'M NOBODY'S SWEETHEART NOW
Universal, 1940

Musical Score Skinner, Frank
Composer(s) Rosen, Milton
Lyricist(s) Carter, Everett

Producer(s) Sandford, Joseph G.
Director(s) Lubin, Arthur
Screenwriter(s) Darling, W. Scott; Lazarus, Erna; Block, Hal

Cast O'Keefe, Dennis; Parrish, Helen; Howard, Lewis; Moore, Constance; Crews, Laura Hope; Hinds, Samuel S.; Gateson, Marjorie; The Dancing Cansinos

Song(s) There Goes My Romance [2]; Got Love [1]

Notes There is also a vocal of "Nobody's Sweetheart" by Gus Kahn, Ernie Erdman, Billy Meyers and Elmer Schoebel. [1] Also in GET GOING, MISSISSIPPI GAMBLER (1942) and SWING IT SOLDIER. [2] Also in MISSISSIPPI GAMBLER (1942).

2812 ✦ I, MOBSTER
Twentieth Century–Fox, 1958

Musical Score Alperson Jr., Edward L.
Composer(s) Alperson Jr., Edward L.
Lyricist(s) Winn, Jerry

Producer(s) Alperson Jr., Edward L.
Director(s) Corman, Roger
Screenwriter(s) Fisher, Steve

Cast Cochran, Steve; Milan, Lita; Strauss, Robert; Lovesky, Celia; St. Cyr, Lili; Brinkley, John; Withers, Grant; Mylong, John

Song(s) Lost, Lonely and Looking for Love; Give Me Love

2813 ✦ IMPASSE
United Artists, 1969

Musical Score Springer, Phil

Producer(s) Klein, Hal
Director(s) Benedict, Richard
Screenwriter(s) Higgins, John C.

Cast Reynolds, Burt; Francis, Anne; Diaz, Vic; Acosta, Rodolfo; Bettger, Lyle; Gordon, Clarke; Daissas, Joanne; Corey, Jeff; Mayama, Miko

Song(s) Penny's Ballade (C: Springer, Phil; L: Higgins, John C.); Dear Sweet Miss Jones [1] (C: Springer, Phil; L: Levine, Irwin)

Notes [1] Used instrumentally only.

2814 ✦ THE IMPATIENT YEARS
Columbia, 1944

Producer(s) Van Upp, Virginia; Cummings, Irving
Director(s) Cummings, Irving
Screenwriter(s) Van Upp, Virginia

Cast Arthur, Jean; Coburn, Charles; Bowman, Lee; Buchanan, Edgar; Grapewin, Charley; Mitchell, Grant; Darwell, Jane; Davenport, Harry

Song(s) Who Said Dreams Don't Come True [1] (C: Akst, Harry; L: Davis, Benny; Jolson, Al)

Notes [1] Not written for picture. Not used in SHE'S A SWEETHEART.

2815 ✦ THE IMPERFECT GENTLEMAN

See THE PERFECT GENTLEMAN.

2816 ✦ IMPERFECT LADY
Paramount, 1947

Musical Score Young, Victor
Choreographer(s) Daniels, Billy; Earl, Josephine

Producer(s) Tunberg, Karl
Director(s) Allen, Lewis
Screenwriter(s) Tunberg, Karl

Cast Wright, Teresa [2]; Milland, Ray; Hardwicke, Sir Cedric; Field, Virginia; Owen, Reginald; Quinn, Anthony; Cooper, Melville; Mander, Miles

Song(s) Piccadilly Tilly (C/L: Livingston, Jay; Evans, Ray); Tonight [1] (C/L: Livingston, Jay; Evans, Ray)

Notes Previously known as LADY 17 and TAKE THIS WOMAN. Released as MRS. LORING'S SECRET in Great Britain. [1] Not used. Music based on Chopin's "Nocturne, Op. 9, No. 2." [2] Dubbed by Virginia Fields.

2817 ✦ THE IMPOSSIBLE POSSUM
Metro–Goldwyn–Mayer, 1952

Musical Score Bradley, Scott

Song(s) The Impossible Possum (C/L: Bradley, Scott)

Notes Cartoon.

2818 ✦ THE IMPOSSIBLE YEARS
Metro–Goldwyn–Mayer, 1968

Musical Score Costa, Don

Producer(s) Weingarten, Lawrence
Director(s) Gordon, Michael
Screenwriter(s) Wells, George
Source(s) *The Impossible Years* (play) Fisher, Bob; Marx, Arthur

Cast Niven, David; Albright, Lola; Everett, Chad; Nelson, Ozzie; Ferrare, Christina; Cooper, Jeff

Song(s) The Impossible Years [1] (C/L: Margo, Mitch; Margo, Phil; Medress, Hand; Siegel, Jay)

Notes [1] Members of The Tokens.

2819 ◆ THE IMPOSTER
Universal, 1944

Musical Score Tiomkin, Dimitri

Producer(s) Duvivier, Julien
Director(s) Duvivier, Julien
Screenwriter(s) Duvivier, Julien

Cast Gabin, Jean; Whorf, Richard; Joslyn, Allyn; Drew, Ellen; Van Eyck, Peter; Morgan, Ralph; Quillan, Eddie; Qualen, John; Moore, Dennis; McGraw, Charles; Stone, Milburn

Song(s) In Sweet Cherry Time (C: Renard, A.; L: Lerner, Sam)

Notes No cue sheet available.

2820 ◆ IMPULSE
Twentieth Century–Fox, 1984

Musical Score Chihara, Paul

Producer(s) Zinnemann, Tim
Director(s) Baker, Graham
Screenwriter(s) Davis, Bart; Dunaway, Don Carlos

Cast Matheson, Tim; Tilly, Meg; Cronyn, Hume; Karlen, John; Jones, Claude Earl; Jason, Peter

Song(s) The Highway of Love (C: Chihara, Paul; L: Landon, Carol); Before the Next Teardrop Falls (C/L: Peters, Ben; Keith, Vivian)

2821 ◆ INADMISSIBLE EVIDENCE
Paramount, 1968

Producer(s) Kinnoch, Ronald
Director(s) Page, Anthony
Screenwriter(s) Osborne, John
Source(s) *Inadmissable Evidence* (play) Osborne, John

Cast Williamson, Nicol; Bennett, Jill; Atkins, Eileen; Dean, Isabel

Song(s) Keep It Up (C: Moore, Dudley; L: Hastings, George)

2822 ◆ IN BEAVER VALLEY
Disney, 1950

Musical Score Smith, Paul J.

Director(s) Algar, James
Screenwriter(s) Watkin, Lawrence Edward; Sears, Ted
Narrator(s) Hibler, Winston

Song(s) Jing-A-Ling, Jing-A-Ling [1] (C: Smith, Paul J.; L: Raye, Don)

Notes Nature semi-documentary. [1] Used instrumentally only. Lyric added for exploitation.

2823 ◆ IN CALIENTE
Warner Brothers–First National, 1935

Composer(s) Wrubel, Allie
Lyricist(s) Dixon, Mort
Choreographer(s) Berkeley, Busby

Producer(s) Chodorov, Edward
Director(s) Bacon, Lloyd
Screenwriter(s) Wald, Jerry; Epstein, Julius J.
Source(s) "Caliente" (story) Duff, Warren; Block, Ralph

Cast O'Brien, Pat; Del Rio, Dolores; Carrillo, Leo; Horton, Edward Everett; Farrell, Glenda; The Canova Family; Regan, Phil; Shaw, Winifred; Bing, Herman

Song(s) Mexicana; In Caliente; To Call You My Own; The Lady in Red [1]; Muchacha (C: Warren, Harry; L: Dubin, Al)

Notes [1] Also in BROADWAY HOSTESS.

2824 ◆ INCENDIARY BLONDE
Paramount, 1945

Choreographer(s) Dare, Danny

Producer(s) Sistrom, Joseph
Director(s) Marshall, George
Screenwriter(s) Binyon, Claude; Butler, Frank

Cast Hutton, Betty; de Cordova, Arturo; Ruggles, Charles; Fitzgerald, Barry; Philips, Mary; Ciannelli, Eduardo; Dekker, Albert

Notes No original numbers. The numbers performed include "It Had to Be You" by Gus Kahn and Isham Jones; "Ragtime Cowboy Joe" by Maurice Abrahams, Lewis F. Muir and Grant Clarke; "Oh By Jingo" by Lew Brown and Albert von Tilzer; "Sweet Genevieve" by Henry Tucker and George Cooper; "Row Row Row" by William Jerome and James V. Monaco; "Darktown Strutters' Ball" by Shelton Brooks; "What Do You Want to Make Those Eyes at Me For?" by Howard Johnson, James V. Monaco and Joseph McCarthy and "Ida, Sweet As Apple Cider" by Eddie Leonard and Eddie Munson. "The Bugle Call Rag" by Jack Pettis, Billy Meyers and Elmer Schoebel is used for a dance routine.

2825 ◆ THE INCIDENT
Twentieth Century–Fox, 1968

Musical Score Knight, Terry

Producer(s) Sachson, Monroe; Meadow, Edward
Director(s) Peerce, Larry

Screenwriter(s) Baehr, Nicholas E.
Source(s) (teleplay) Baehr, Nicholas E.

Cast Musante, Tony; Sheen, Martin; Bridges, Beau; Bannard, Bob; McMahon, Ed; Mills, Donna; Gilford, Jack; Ritter, Thelma; Kellin, Mike; Sterling, Jan; Merrill, Gary; Peters, Brock; Dee, Ruby

Song(s) Is It Over Now (C/L: Knight, Terry)

2826 ✦ THE INCREDIBLE MR. LIMPET
Warner Brothers, 1964

Musical Score Perkins, Frank
Composer(s) Fain, Sammy
Lyricist(s) Adamson, Harold

Producer(s) Rose, John C.
Director(s) Lubin, Arthur
Screenwriter(s) Brewer, Jameson; Rose, John C.
Source(s) "Mr. Limpet" (story) Pratt, Theodore

Cast Knotts, Don; Cook, Carole; Weston, Jack; Duggan, Andrew; Keating, Larry; Beregi, Oscar; Frees, Paul

Song(s) Super Doodle Dandy; I Wish I Were a Fish; Be Careful How You Wish; Deep Rapture

2827 ✦ THE INCREDIBLE SHRINKING MAN
Universal, 1957

Producer(s) Zugsmith, Albert
Director(s) Arnold, Jack
Screenwriter(s) Matheson, Richard
Source(s) *The Incredible Shrinking Man* (novel) Matheson, Richard

Cast Williams, Grant; Stuart, Randy; Kent, April; Bailey, Raymond; Schallert, William

Song(s) The Girl in a Lonely Room [1] (C: Lawrence, Earl E.; L: Carling, Foster)

Notes [1] Used instrumentally only.

2828 ✦ THE INCREDIBLE SHRINKING WOMAN
Universal, 1981

Musical Score Ciani, Suzanne
Composer(s) Ciani, Suzanne
Lyricist(s) Ciani, Suzanne

Producer(s) Moonjean, Hank
Director(s) Schumacher, Joel
Screenwriter(s) Wagner, Jane
Source(s) *The Incredible Shrinking Man* (novel) Matheson, Richard

Cast Tomlin, Lily; Grodin, Charles; Beatty, Ned; Gibson, Henry; Wilson, Elizabeth; Smith, Maria; Bellwood, Pamela

Song(s) Cheese Tease Commercial; Try Our Glue; Cosmos Cleaner Commercial; Galaxy Glue; Galaxy Glue Sticks By You; Up Up Love; Pat & Stan; Que Pequena [1]; Don't Tell Me Why; Ayudame

Notes [1] Also in CRACKERS.

2829 ✦ INDEPENDENCE DAY
Warner Brothers, 1983

Musical Score Bernstein, Charles

Producer(s) Blatt, Daniel H.; Singer, Robert
Director(s) Mandel, Robert
Screenwriter(s) Hoffman, Alice

Cast Quinlan, Kathleen; Keith, David; Sternhagen, Frances; De Young, Cliff; Wiest, Dianne; Sommer, Josef; Farnsworth, Richard

Song(s) Follow Your Dreams (C/L: Messina, James); Looking for Love (C/L: Messina, James)

Notes Both are background vocal only.

2830 ✦ INDIAN AGENT
RKO, 1948

Musical Score Sawtell, Paul; Webb, Roy

Producer(s) Schlom, Herman
Director(s) Selander, Lesley
Screenwriter(s) Houston, Norman

Cast Holt, Tim; Beery Jr., Noah; Martin, Richard; Leslie, Nan; Woods, Harry; Powers, Richard; Cody, Iron Eyes

Song(s) Back to Texas (C/L: Bennett, Norman)

2831 ✦ THE INDIAN FIGHTER
United Artists, 1955

Musical Score Waxman, Franz
Composer(s) Gordon, Irving
Lyricist(s) Gordon, Irving

Producer(s) Schorr, William W.
Director(s) De Toth, Andre
Screenwriter(s) Davis, Frank; Hecht, Ben

Cast Douglas, Kirk; Martinelli, Elsa; Abel, Walter; Matthau, Walter; Chaney, Lon; Hale Jr., Alan; Cook Jr., Elisha; Cady, Frank

Song(s) I Give It All to You; Two Brothers; Indian Fighter Theme [1] (C: Waxman, Franz)

Notes [1] Sheet music only.

2832 ✦ INDIAN TERRITORY
Columbia, 1950

Producer(s) Autry, Gene
Director(s) English, John
Screenwriter(s) Hall, Norman S.

Cast   Autry, Gene; Champion; Stockman, Boyd; Buttram, Pat; Grant, Kirby; Davis, Gail; Van Zandt, Philip

Song(s)   Chattanooga Shoe Shine Boy (C/L: Stone, Harry; Stapp, Jack); When the Campfire Is Low on the Prairie [1] (C/L: Stept, Sam H.)

Notes   [1] Also in the Republic films COMIN' ROUND THE MOUNTAIN (1936) and GUNSMOKE RANCH.

2833 ✦ INDISCREET (1931)
United Artists, 1931

Composer(s)   Henderson, Ray
Lyricist(s)   DeSylva, B.G.; Brown, Lew

Producer(s)   Schenck, Joseph M.
Director(s)   McCarey, Leo
Screenwriter(s)   McCarey, Leo; DeSylva, B.G.; Brown, Lew; Henderson, Ray

Cast   Swanson, Gloria; Lyon, Ben; Lake, Arthur; Kent, Barbara; Owsley, Monroe; Eburne, Maude; Kolker, Henry; Walker, Nella

Song(s)   Come to Me; If You Haven't Got Love

Notes   No cue sheet available.

2834 ✦ INDISCREET (1958)
United Artists, 1958

Musical Score   Bennett, Richard Rodney

Producer(s)   Donen, Stanley
Director(s)   Donen, Stanley
Screenwriter(s)   Krasna, Norman
Source(s)   *Kind Sir* (play) Krasna, Norman

Cast   Grant, Cary; Bergman, Ingrid; Parker, Cecil; Calvert, Phyllis; Kossoff, David; Jenkins, Megs; Johnston, Oliver;

Song(s)   Indiscreet [1] (C: Van Heusen, James; L: Cahn, Sammy)

Notes   [1] Used as background orchestral only.

2835 ✦ INFORMATION RECEIVED
Universal, 1962

Musical Score   Slavin, Martin

Director(s)   Lynn, Robert
Screenwriter(s)   Ryder, Paul

Cast   Sesselman, Sabrina; Sylvester, William; Baddeley, Hermione; Underdown, Edward

Song(s)   Sabrina (C: Slavin, Martin; L: Gail, Abbe)

Notes   No cue sheet available.

2836 ✦ IN GAY MADRID
Metro–Goldwyn–Mayer, 1930

Musical Score   Stothart, Herbert
Composer(s)   Stothart, Herbert; Cugat, Xavier
Lyricist(s)   Grey, Clifford

Director(s)   Leonard, Robert Z.
Screenwriter(s)   Meredyth, Bess; Field, Salisbury; Mayer, Edwin Justus
Source(s)   *La Casa de la Troya* (novel) Lugin, Alejandro Perez

Cast   Novarro, Ramon; Jordan, Dorothy; Howell, Lottice; King, Claude; Besserer, Eugenie; Mong, William V.; Mercer, Beryl; Chandler, George

Song(s)   Let Me Give You My Love; Santiago; Smile, Comrades (Smile While We May) (C: Ahlert, Fred E.; L: Turk, Roy); Into My Heart (C: Ahlert, Fred E.; L: Turk, Roy); Dark Night; I Won't Go Away! (C/L: Novarro, Ramon)

2837 ✦ IN GOD WE TRUST
Universal, 1980

Musical Score   Morris, John
Composer(s)   Morris, John
Lyricist(s)   Morris, John

Producer(s)   West, Howard; Shapiro, George
Director(s)   Feldman, Marty
Screenwriter(s)   Feldman, Marty; Allen, Chris

Cast   Feldman, Marty; Kaufman, Andy; Lasser, Louise; Pryor, Richard; Boyle, Peter; Hyde-White, Wilfrid; Darden, Severn

Song(s)   Gregorian Chant; In God We Trust (L: Feldman, Marty); Hands to Hallelujah; God Gave Us His Son for Xmas (L: Feldman, Marty)

Notes   There is also a vocal of "Good for God" by Harry Nilsson.

2838 ✦ INHERIT THE WIND
United Artists, 1960

Musical Score   Gold, Ernest
Composer(s)   Traditional
Lyricist(s)   Gold, Ernest

Producer(s)   Kramer, Stanley
Director(s)   Kramer, Stanley
Screenwriter(s)   Douglas, Nathan E.; Smith, Harold Jacob
Source(s)   *Inherit the Wind* (play) Lee, Robert E.; Lawrence, Jerome

Cast   Tracy, Spencer; March, Fredric; Kelly, Gene; Eldridge, Florence; Work, Dick; Morgan, Harry; Akins, Claude; Anderson, Donna

Song(s) Old Time Religion; Good Enough for Brady; We'll Hang Bert Cates (and Drummond) [1] (C: Steffe, William)

Notes [1] Music based on "Battle Hymn of the Republic."

2839 ✦ IN LIKE FLINT
Twentieth Century–Fox, 1967

Musical Score Goldsmith, Jerry
Composer(s) Goldsmith, Jerry
Lyricist(s) Bricusse, Leslie

Producer(s) David, Saul
Director(s) Douglas, Gordon M.
Screenwriter(s) Fimberg, Hal

Cast Coburn, James; Cobb, Lee J.; Hale, Jean; Duggan, Andrew; Lee, Anna

Song(s) Your Zowie Face; Who Was That Lady? [1]; Ladies Will Kindly Remove Their Hats [1]; Westward Ho-o-o [1]; Where the Bad Guys Are Girls [2]

Notes [1] Used instrumentally only. [2] Not used.

2840 ✦ INNERSPACE
Warner Brothers, 1987

Musical Score Goldsmith, Jerry

Producer(s) Finnell, Michael
Director(s) Dante, Joe
Screenwriter(s) Boan, Jeffrey; Proser, Chip

Cast Quaid, Dennis; Short, Martin; Ryan, Meg; McCarthy, Kevin; Lewis, Fiona; Schallert, William; Freeman, Kathleen; Bean, Orson; Hooks, Kevin; Flaherty, Joe; Martin, Andrea; Jones, Chuck; Waterbury, Laura

Song(s) Is It Really Love (C/L: Walden, Narada Michael)

Notes No cue sheet available.

2841 ✦ THE INNOCENT

See THE HAPPENING.

2842 ✦ INNOCENT BYSTANDERS
Paramount, 1973

Musical Score Keating, John

Producer(s) Brown, George H.
Director(s) Collinson, Peter
Screenwriter(s) Mitchell, James
Source(s) *Innocent Bystanders* (novel) Munro, James

Cast Baker, Stanley; Sheybal, Vladek; Chaplin, Geraldine; Pleasence, Donald; Andrews, Dana; Lloyd, Sue

Song(s) What Makes the Man? (C: Keating, John; L: Smith, Norman)

2843 ✦ THE INNOCENTS
Twentieth Century–Fox, 1961

Musical Score Auric, Georges; Jones, Kenneth V.

Producer(s) Clayton, Jack
Director(s) Clayton, Jack
Screenwriter(s) Archibald, William; Capote, Truman
Source(s) *The Turn of the Screw* (novel) James, Henry

Cast Kerr, Deborah; Wyngarde, Peter; Jenkins, Megs; Redgrave, Michael; Stephens, Martin

Song(s) The Innocents (C: Auric, Georges; L: Dehn, Paul); O Willow Waly [1] (C: Auric, Georges; L: Dehn, Paul)

Notes [1] Sheet music only.

2844 ✦ INNOCENTS OF PARIS
Paramount, 1929

Composer(s) Whiting, Richard A.
Lyricist(s) Robin, Leo

Director(s) Wallace, Richard
Screenwriter(s) Vajda, Ernest; Doherty, Ethel

Cast Chevalier, Maurice; Durand, David; Beecher, Sylvia; Miljan, John; Livingston, Margaret; Simpson, Russell

Song(s) Dites Moi [1] [2] (C: Yvain, Maurice; L: Willemetz, Albert); Les Ananas [1] (C: Pearly, Fred; L: Eddy); Louise [3]; Valentine [1] (C: Christine, Henri Marius; L: Willemetz, Albert); On Top of the World Alone; Ca M'est Egal [1] (C: Oberfeld; L: Willemetz, Albert); It's a Habit of Mine; Wait Till You See My Cherie [4]

Notes [1] Not written for the picture. [2] Also in PLAYBOY OF PARIS. [3] Also in THE LOST WEEKEND and YOU CAN'T RATION LOVE. [4] Also in THE LOVE DOCTOR.

2845 ✦ THE INN OF THE SIXTH HAPPINESS
Twentieth Century–Fox, 1958

Musical Score Arnold, Malcolm

Producer(s) Adler, Buddy
Director(s) Robson, Mark
Screenwriter(s) Lennart, Isobel
Source(s) *The Inn of the Sixth Happiness* (novel) Rubgess, Alan

Cast Bergman, Ingrid; Jurgens, Curt; Donat, Robert; David, Michael; Seyler, Athene; Squire, Ronald

Song(s) The Inn of the Sixth Happiness [1] (C: Arnold, Malcolm; L: Webster, Paul Francis)

Notes Robert Donat's last film. [1] Lyric written for exploitation only.

2846 ✦ IN OLD AMARILLO
Republic, 1951

Composer(s) Elliott, Jack
Lyricist(s) Elliott, Jack

Producer(s) White, Edward J.
Director(s) Whitney, William
Screenwriter(s) Nibley, Sloan

Cast Rogers, Roy; Trigger; Rodriguez, Estelita; Edwards, Penny; Lee, Pinky; Barcroft, Roy; The Roy Rogers Riders

Song(s) If I Ever Fall in Love; Under the Lone Star Moon; In Old Amarillo [1]; Poor Lonesome Cowboy (C: Traditional; L: Lee, Pinky); Wasteland (C/L: Willing, Foy)

Notes [1] Spanish lyric by Geri Galian.

2847 ✦ IN OLD ARIZONA
Fox, 1929

Director(s) Walsh, Raoul; Cummings, Irving
Screenwriter(s) Barry, Tom

Cast Lowe, Edmund; Burgess, Dorothy; Baxter, Warner; MacDonald, J. Farrell; Warren, Fred; Armetta, Henry

Song(s) My Tonia (C: Henderson, Ray; L: DeSylva, B.G.; Brown, Lew); Caballero Song [1] (C: Stamper, Dave; L: Barry, Tom)

Notes No cue sheet available. [1] Not used.

2848 ✦ IN OLD CALIENTE
Republic, 1939

Producer(s) Kane, Joseph
Director(s) Kane, Joseph
Screenwriter(s) Geraghty, Gerald; Houston, Norman

Cast Rogers, Roy; Hart, Mary; Hayes, George "Gabby"; LaRue, Jack; de Mille, Katherine; Puglia, Frank; Wales, Ethel

Song(s) The Moon, She Will Be Shining Tonight (C/L: Samuels, Walter G.); Ride On Vaquero [1] (C: Baer, Abel; L: Gilbert, L. Wolfe); Sundown on the Rangeland [2] (C/L: Rogers, Roy; Rose, Fred); We're Not Comin' Out Tonight (C/L: Samuels, Walter G.)

Notes [1] Also in ROMANCE OF THE RIO GRANDE (1929) and (1940), both Fox pictures, and in OH SUSANNA! (1936). [2] Also in BAD MEN OF DEADWOOD.

2849 ✦ IN OLD CALIFORNIA
Republic, 1942

Musical Score Buttolph, David

Producer(s) North, Robert
Director(s) McGann, William
Screenwriter(s) Purcell, Gertrude; Hyland, Frances

Cast Wayne, John; Barnes, Binnie; Dekker, Albert; Parrish, Helen; Kennedy, Edgar; Kelly, Patsy; Purcell, Dick; Shannon, Harry; Halton, Charles

Song(s) There's Gold in the Hills (C: Buttolph, David; L: Meyer, Sol); California Joe (C/L: Rose, Fred; Marvin, Johnny)

2850 ✦ IN OLD CHEYENNE
Republic, 1941

Producer(s) Kane, Joseph
Director(s) Kane, Joseph
Screenwriter(s) Cooper, Olive
Source(s) "Frontier Feud" (story) Sprague, Chandler

Cast Rogers, Roy; Hayes, George "Gabby"; Woodbury, Joan; MacDonald, J. Farrell; Payne, Sally; Taliaferro, Hal; Haade, William

Song(s) Bonita (C: Styne, Jule; L: Meyer, Sol); Haunting Melodies (C/L: Sooter, Rudy)

2851 ✦ IN OLD CHICAGO
Twentieth Century–Fox, 1938

Composer(s) Pollack, Lew
Lyricist(s) Mitchell, Sidney

Producer(s) Zanuck, Darryl F.
Director(s) King, Henry
Screenwriter(s) Trotti, Lamar; Levien, Sonya

Cast Power, Tyrone; Faye, Alice; Ameche, Don; Brady, Alice; Devine, Andy; Donlevy, Brian; Brooks, Phyllis; Brown, Tom; Reynolds, Gene; Watson, Bobs; Hicks, Russell

Song(s) In Old Chicago (C: Revel, Harry; L: Gordon, Mack); How Many Miles to Dublin Town (C/L: Hughes, Anthony); I've Taken a Fancy to You [1]; I'll Never Let You Cry; Take a Dip in the Sea

Notes There are also renditions of "Carry Me Back to Old Virginny" by James A. Bland and "Sweet Genevieve" by Henry Tucker and George Cooper. [1] Also in FRONTIER MARSHALL (1939) and WILD GEESE CALLING.

2852 ✦ IN OLD KENTUCKY
Fox, 1935

Producer(s) Butcher, Edward
Director(s) Marshall, George

Screenwriter(s) Johnson, Henry; Hellman, Sam; Lehman, Gladys
Source(s) *In Old Kentucky* (play) Dazey, Charles T.

Cast Rogers, Will; Wilson, Dorothy; Hardie, Russell

Song(s) Bill Robinson's Table Setting Step (C/L: Robinson, Bill)

2853 ✦ IN OLD MONTEREY
Republic, 1939

Producer(s) Schaefer, Armand
Director(s) Kane, Joseph
Screenwriter(s) McGowan, Dorrell; McGowan, Stuart; Geraghty, Gerald

Cast Autry, Gene; Burnette, Smiley; Storey, June; Hayes, George "Gabby"; Hamblen, Stuart; The Ranch Boys; The Hoosier Hotshots; Hale, Jonathan

Song(s) Little Pardner (C/L: Marvin, Johnny; Autry, Gene; Rose, Fred); Born in the Saddle (C/L: Autry, Gene; Marvin, Johnny); Tumbling Tumbleweeds [1] (C/L: Nolan, Bob); It Looks Like Rain (C/L: Unknown)

Notes No cue sheet available. There seems to be vocals of "Columbia the Gem of the Ocean" by David T. Shaw and T.A. Beckett and "My Buddy" by Gus Kahn and Walter Donaldson. [1] Also in RHYTHM ROUND-UP (Columbia), DON'T FENCE ME IN, SILVER SPURS, TUMBLING TUMBLEWEEDS and HOLLYWOOD CANTEEN (Warner).

2854 ✦ IN OLD NEW YORK
Warner Brothers, 1951

Composer(s) Jerome, M.K.
Lyricist(s) Scholl, Jack

Song(s) Memories From Melody Lane [1]; When Little Old New York Was Young; Days of Maryland (C/L: Scholl, Jack); Musical Memories (C/L: Scholl, Jack); Svengali (C/L: Scholl, Jack); Old Beer Garden (C/L: Scholl, Jack)

Notes Short subject. [1] Also in MUSICAL MEMORIES.

2855 ✦ IN OLD SANTA FE
Mascot, 1935

Musical Score Roemheld, Heinz
Composer(s) Lewis, Harold
Lyricist(s) Grossman, Bernie

Producer(s) Levine, Nat
Director(s) Howard, David
Screenwriter(s) MacDonald, Wallace; Rathmell, John

Cast Maynard, Ken; Knapp, Evalyn; Warner, H.B.; Thomson, Kenneth

Song(s) As Long As I've Got My Dog [1]; Down in Old Santa Fe

Notes [1] Used instrumentally only. Sheet music credits Wallace MacDonald as lyricist and Lewis and Grossman with music.

2856 ✦ IN PERSON
RKO, 1935

Composer(s) Levant, Oscar
Lyricist(s) Fields, Dorothy
Choreographer(s) Pan, Hermes

Producer(s) Berman, Pandro S.
Director(s) Seiter, William A.
Screenwriter(s) Scott, Allan
Source(s) *In Person* (novel) Adams, Samuel Hopkins

Cast Rogers, Ginger; Brent, George; Mowbray, Alan; Mitchell, Grant; Hinds, Samuel S.

Song(s) Don't Mention Love to Me; Got a New Lease on Life; Out of Sight, Out of Mind

Notes There is also a vocal of "I Don't Care If She's Not Good-Looking" by Benjamin Hapgood Burt.

2857 ✦ IN SEARCH OF GREGORY
Universal, 1970

Musical Score Grainer, Ron

Producer(s) Janni, Joseph; Senatore, Daniele
Director(s) Wood, Peter
Screenwriter(s) Guerra, Tonino; Laks, Lucille

Cast Christie, Julie; Sarrazin, Michael; Hurt, John; Pitagora, Paola; Culver, Roland

Song(s) Dreams (C: Grainer, Ron; L: Black, Don); Close (C/L: Howard, Ken; Blaikley, Alan)

2858 ✦ IN SEARCH OF THE CASTAWAYS
Disney, 1962

Musical Score Alwyn, William
Composer(s) Sherman, Richard M.; Sherman, Robert B.
Lyricist(s) Sherman, Richard M.; Sherman, Robert B.

Producer(s) Attwooll, Hugh
Director(s) Stevenson, Robert
Screenwriter(s) Hawley, Lowell S.
Source(s) *Captain Grant's Children* (novel) Verne, Jules

Cast Chevalier, Maurice; Mills, Hayley; Sanders, George; Hyde-White, Wilfrid; Anderson Jr., Michael; Fraser, Ronald

Song(s) Castaway; Enjoy It!; Grompons! (Let's Climb); Merci Beaucoup; Guardian Star [1]

Notes [1] Not used.

2859 ✦ INSIDE DAISY CLOVER
Warner Brothers, 1966

Musical Score Previn, Andre
Composer(s) Previn, Andre
Lyricist(s) Previn, Dory

Producer(s) Pakula, Alan J.
Director(s) Mulligan, Robert
Screenwriter(s) Lambert, Gavin
Source(s) *Inside Daisy Clover* (novel) Lambert, Gavin

Cast Wood, Natalie; Plummer, Christopher; Redford, Robert; McDowall, Roddy; Gordon, Ruth; Bard, Katharine; Hartman, Paul

Song(s) You're Gonna Hear From Me; The Circus Is a Wacky World

2860 ✦ INSIDE JOB
Universal, 1946

Musical Score Skinner, Frank

Producer(s) Yarbrough, Jean
Director(s) Yarbrough, Jean
Screenwriter(s) Bricker, George; Warner, Jerry

Cast Curtis, Alan; Rutherford, Ann; Foster, Preston; Moss, Jimmie; Sawyer, Joe; Hinds, Samuel S.

Song(s) Do You Believe in Loving, Honey (C/L: Courtney, Del)

2861 ✦ INSIDE MOVES
AFD, 1980

Musical Score Barry, John

Producer(s) Tanz, Mark M.; Goodwin, R.W.
Director(s) Donner, Richard
Screenwriter(s) Curtin, Valerie; Levinson, Barry
Source(s) (novel) Walton, Todd

Cast Savage, John; Morse, David; Scarwid, Diana; Wright, Amy; Burton, Tony; Henderson, Bill; Russell, Harold

Song(s) What Have You Got to Lose (C/L: Kaz, Eric; Loring, Gloria); It's Your Move (C/L: Omartian, Michael; Price, Michael; Walsh, Dan); Outside (C/L: McDonald, Michael; Pack, David); Something's Missing (In My Life) (C/L: Jabara, Paul; Asher, Jay); Just Be Free (C/L: Fields, Alvin; Zager, Michael); Beautiful Dreamer (C/L: Jabara, Paul; Asher, Jay)

Notes No cue sheet available.

2862 ✦ INSIDE STRAIGHT
Metro–Goldwyn–Mayer, 1951

Musical Score Hayton, Lennie

Producer(s) Goldstone, Richard
Director(s) Mayer, Gerald
Screenwriter(s) Trosper, Guy

Cast Brian, David; Sullivan, Barry; Dahl, Arlene; McCambridge, Mercedes; Raymond, Paula; Jarman Jr., Claude; Chaney, Lon; Winters, Roland; Hoyt, John; Lewis, Monica

Song(s) What Can a Poor Maiden Do (C: Horn, Charles E.; L: Brent, Earl); Up in a Balloon (C/L: Farnie, H.B.)

2863 ✦ IN SOCIETY
Universal, 1944

Composer(s) Mizzy, Vic
Lyricist(s) Curtis, Mann

Producer(s) Hartmann, Edmund L.
Director(s) Yarbrough, Jean
Screenwriter(s) Grant, John; Hartmann, Edmund L.; Fimberg, Hal

Cast Abbott, Bud; Costello, Lou; Hutton, Marion; Grant, Kirby; Gillis, Ann; Hall, Thurston; Treacher, Arthur

Song(s) No Bout Adoubt It; Rehearsin' (C/L: Worth, Bobby; Cowan, Stanley); My Dreams Are Getting Better All the Time; What a Change in the Weather [1] (C/L: Kent, Walter; Gannon, Kim)

Notes [1] Also in SENORITA FROM THE WEST.

2864 ✦ THE INSPECTOR GENERAL
Warner Brothers, 1949

Musical Score Green, Johnny
Composer(s) Fine, Sylvia
Lyricist(s) Fine, Sylvia
Choreographer(s) Loring, Eugene

Producer(s) Wald, Jerry
Director(s) Koster, Henry
Screenwriter(s) Rapp, Philip; Kurnitz, Harry
Source(s) *The Inspector General* (play) Gogol, Nikolai

Cast Kaye, Danny; Slezak, Walter; Bates, Barbara; Lanchester, Elsa; Lockhart, Gene; Hale, Alan; Catlett, Walter; Williams, Rhys; Baker, Benny; Leavitt, Norman; Hearn, Sam; Learn, Lew; Paiva, Nestor

Song(s) Yakov's Elixir; Second Hungarian Rhapsody (C: Liszt, Franz); Medicine Show; Spring Song (C: Mendelssohn, Felix); Road Song; Brodny; Soliloquy for Three Heads; Tales from the Vienna Woods (C: Strauss, Johann); Lucia D'Lammermoor (C: Donizetti, G.); Happy Times; Onward, Onward; Drink Gypsy; Drink to Me Only with Thine Eyes (C: Traditional); Lonely Heart [1]; The Inspector General [1]

Notes Originally titled HAPPY TIMES. The classical pieces were arranged by Sylvia Fine with lyrics by her. Johnny Mercer is credited in some sources but not on cue sheets. [1] Listed in some sources but not on cue sheets.

2865 ◆ INSPECTOR HORNLEIGH GOES TO IT

See MAIL TRAIN.

2866 ◆ INSTANT JUSTICE
Warner Brothers, 1987

Musical Score   Kurtz, David

Song(s)   One for One (C: Kurtz, David; L: Mariano, Monday Michiru); How Does Love Go Wrong (C/L: Russell, Brenda; Caldwell, Bobby); Victim of Paradise (C/L: Lorber, Sam; Innis, Dave); Manhunt (C/L: Wirrick, James); Shake Me Up (C/L: Wright, Gary); Looking for Trouble [1] (C/L: Lorber, Sam; Innis, Dave)

Notes   Originally titled MARINE ISSUE. No other information available. [1] Also in RATBOY.

2867 ◆ INSURANCE INVESTIGATOR
Republic, 1951

Producer(s)   Lackey, William
Director(s)   Blair, George
Screenwriter(s)   Walker, Gertrude

Cast   Denning, Richard; Long, Audrey; Eldredge, John; Brooke, Hillary; Hale, Jonathan; Hadley, Reed

Song(s)   C'est Vous [1] (C/L: Newman, Albert; Cherwin, Richard; Washington, Ned)

Notes   [1] Also in ALIAS THE CHAMP.

2868 ◆ INTERLUDE
Universal, 1957

Musical Score   Skinner, Frank

Producer(s)   Hunter, Ross
Director(s)   Sirk, Douglas
Screenwriter(s)   Fuchs, Daniel; Coen, Franklin

Cast   Allyson, June; Brazzi, Rossano; Cook, Marianne; Andes, Keith; Rosay, Francoise; Wyatt, Jane; Bergen, Frances

Song(s)   Interlude (C: Skinner, Frank; L: Webster, Paul Francis)

Notes   This is a remake of WHEN TOMORROW COMES (1939).

2869 ◆ INTERMEZZO
United Artists, 1939

Producer(s)   Selznick, David O.
Director(s)   Ratoff, Gregory
Screenwriter(s)   Stevens, Gosta; Molander, Gustave

Cast   Bergman, Ingrid; Howard, Leslie; Best, Edna; Todd, Ann; Halliday, John; Kellaway, Cecil; Scott, Douglas; Wesselhoeft, Eleanor; Bennett, Enid

Song(s)   Intermezzo (C: Provost, Heinz; L: Henning, Robert)

Notes   No cue sheet available. Released internationally as ESCAPE TO HAPPINESS.

2870 ◆ INTERNATIONAL HOUSE
Paramount, 1933

Composer(s)   Rainger, Ralph
Lyricist(s)   Robin, Leo

Producer(s)   Lewis, Albert
Director(s)   Sutherland, Edward
Screenwriter(s)   Heifetz, Lou; Brant, Neil; Martin, Francis; De Leon, Walter

Cast   Fields, W.C.; Burns, George; Allen, Gracie; Erwin, Stuart; Maritza, Sari; Joyce, Peggy Hopkins; Pangborn, Franklin; Hare, Lumsden; Lugosi, Bela; Vallee, Rudy; Calloway, Cab; Baby Rose Marie

Song(s)   This is the Night [3] (L: Coslow, Sam); Thank Heaven for You; My Blue Bird's Singing the Blues; Reefer Man [1] (C: Robinson, J. Russel; L: Razaf, Andy); Here Lies Love [2]; She Was a China Tea Cup

Notes   [1] Not written for picture. This was filmed but not used in THE BIG BROADCAST and the whole sequence was interpolated into INTERNATIONAL HOUSE. [2] Also in BIG BROADCAST OF 1932 and TORCH SINGER. [3] Also in THIS IS THE NIGHT and HOT SATURDAY.

2871 ◆ INTERNATIONAL SETTLEMENT
Twentieth Century–Fox, 1938

Composer(s)   Akst, Harry
Lyricist(s)   Clare, Sidney

Producer(s)   Zanuck, Darryl F.
Director(s)   Forde, Eugene
Screenwriter(s)   Breslow, Lou; Patrick, John

Cast   Del Rio, Dolores; Sanders, George; Lang, June; Baldwin, Dick; Terry, Ruth; Carradine, John; Luke, Keye; Huber, Harold; Ames, Leon; de Cordoba, Pedro

Song(s)   The Shrug; You Make Me That Way

2872 ◆ INTERRUPTED MELODY
Metro–Goldwyn–Mayer, 1955

Producer(s)   Cummings, Jack
Director(s)   Bernhardt, Curtis
Screenwriter(s)   Ludwig, William; Levien, Sonya

Cast   Ford, Glenn; Parker, Eleanor [1]; Moore, Roger; Kellaway, Cecil; Leeds, Peter; Ellis, Evelyn; Baldwin, Walter

Notes   Based on the life story of Marjorie Lawrence. There were no original songs written for this picture. There are vocals of "Non Piu Andrai" from MARRIAGE OF FIGARO by Mozart; "O Don Fatale" from DON

CARLO and an excerpt from the Act I Finale of IL TROVATORE by Verdi; "Vissi D'Arte" from TOSCA and "Un Bel Di Vedremo" from MADAMA BUTTERFLY by Puccini; "Habanera" and "Seguedille" and "Duet" from Bizet's CARMEN; "Quando Me'n Vo' "from LA BOHEME by Puccini; "Mon Coeur S'Ouvre a ta Voix" from SAMSON AND DELILAH by Saint-Saens; the "Immolation Scene" from GOETTERDAEMMERUNG and "Liebestod" from TRISTAN AND ISOLDE by Wagner; "Annie Laurie" by William Douglas and Lady John Scott; "Over the Rainbow" from THE WIZARD OF OZ by Harold Arlen and E.Y. Harburg and "Waltzing Matilda" by Marie Cowan and A.B. "Banjo" Patterson. [1] Dubbed by Eileen Farrell.

2873 ◆ IN THE COOL OF THE DAY
Metro–Goldwyn–Mayer, 1963

Musical Score Chagrin, Francis

Producer(s) Houseman, John
Director(s) Stevens, Robert
Screenwriter(s) Roberts, Meade
Source(s) *In the Cool of the Day* (novel) Ertz, Susan

Cast Finch, Peter; Fonda, Jane; Lansbury, Angela; Hill, Arthur; Cummings, Constance; Knox, Alexander; Davenport, Nigel; Le Mesurier, John

Song(s) In the Cool of the Day [1] (C: Hadjidakis, Manos; L: Sullivan, Liam; Gatsos, Nikos); The Lemon Tree (C: Hadjidakis, Manos; L: Gatsos, Nikos)

Notes [1] English lyrics by Sullivan.

2874 ◆ IN THE GOOD OLD SUMMERTIME
Metro–Goldwyn–Mayer, 1949

Musical Score Stoll, George
Choreographer(s) Alton, Robert

Producer(s) Pasternak, Joe
Director(s) Leonard, Robert Z.
Screenwriter(s) Hackett, Albert; Goodrich, Frances; Tors, Ivan
Source(s) *The Shop Around the Corner* (play) Laszlo, Miklos

Cast Garland, Judy; Johnson, Van; Sakall, S.Z.; Byington, Spring; Sundberg, Clinton; Keaton, Buster; Van Dyke, Marcia

Song(s) Merry Christmas (C: Spielman, Fred; L: Torre, Janice)

Notes There are also vocals of "In the Good Old Summertime" by George Evans and Ren Shields; "Meet Me Tonight in Dreamland" by Beth Slater Whitson and Leo Friedman; "Put Your Arms Around Me, Honey" by Albert Von Tilzer and Junie McCree; "Wait 'Till the Sun Shines Nellie" by Harry Von Tilzer and Andrew B.

Sterling; "In the Evening" and "Play That Barber Shop Chord" by Lewis F. Muir, William Tracey and Ballard Macdonald and "I Don't Care" by Harry Sutton and Jean Lenox. "Last Night When We Were Young" by Harold Arlen and E.Y. Harburg was prerecorded but not used.

2875 ◆ IN THE GROOVE
Universal, 1941

Composer(s) Rosen, Milton
Lyricist(s) Carter, Everett

Song(s) The Boogie Woogie Man [1]; Rug Cuttin' Romeo [3]; Whistle Your Blues to a Bluebird [2]; Do I Worry? (C/L: Cowan, Stanley; Worth, Bob)

Notes It is not known if any of these were written for this short. [1] Also in MURDER IN THE BLUE ROOM and SING ANOTHER CHORUS. [2] Also in TOO MANY BLONDES and COWBOY IN MANHATTAN. [3] Also in SING ANOTHER CHORUS, SWING IT SOLDIER and WHERE DID YOU GET THAT GIRL.

2876 ◆ IN THE HEADLINES
Warner Brothers, 1929

Director(s) Adolfi, John
Screenwriter(s) Jackson, Joseph

Cast Withers, Grant; Nixon, Marion; Cook, Clyde; Breese, Edmund; Garon, Pauline; Oakland, Vivian

Song(s) Love Will Find a Way (C: Burke, Joe; L: Dubin, Al)

Notes No cue sheet available.

2877 ◆ IN THE HEAT OF THE NIGHT
United Artists, 1967

Musical Score Jones, Quincy
Composer(s) Jones, Quincy
Lyricist(s) Bergman, Alan; Bergman, Marilyn

Producer(s) Mirisch, Walter
Director(s) Jewison, Norman
Screenwriter(s) Silliphant, Stirling

Cast Poitier, Sidney; Steiger, Rod; Oates, Warren; Grant, Lee; Patterson, James; Dean, Quentin

Song(s) In the Heat of the Night; Bowlegged Polly; It Sure Is Groovy; Fowl Owl

2878 ◆ IN THE MEANTIME DARLING
Twentieth Century–Fox, 1944

Musical Score Buttolph, David
Choreographer(s) Sawyer, Geneva

Producer(s) Preminger, Otto
Director(s) Preminger, Otto
Screenwriter(s) Kober, Arthur; Uris, Michael

Cast Crain, Jeanne; Latimore, Frank; Pallette, Eugene; Nash, Mary; Prager, Stanley; Robbins, Gale; Randolph, Jane; Williams, Cara

Song(s) How Many Times Do I Have to Tell You [1] (C: McHugh, Jimmy; L: Adamson, Harold)

Notes [1] Also in FOUR JILLS IN A JEEP.

2879 ✦ IN THE MOOD
Lorimar, 1987

Musical Score Burns, Ralph

Producer(s) Adelson, Gary; Mack, Karen
Director(s) Robinson, Phil Alden
Screenwriter(s) Robinson, Phil Alden

Cast Dempsey, Patrick; Balsam, Talia; D'Angelo, Beverly; Constantine, Michael; Freeman, Kathleen

Song(s) Baby Blues (C: Burns, Ralph; L: Robinson, Phil Alden)

Notes No cue sheet available.

2880 ✦ IN THE NAVY

See ABBOTT & COSTELLO & DICK POWELL IN THE NAVY.

2881 ✦ IN THE SHADOW OF KILIMANJARO
Scotti Brothers, 1986

Musical Score Ober, Arlon

Producer(s) Das, Gautam; Sneller, Jeffrey M.
Director(s) Patel, Raju
Screenwriter(s) Sneller, Jeffrey M.; Harry, T. Michael

Cast Rhys-Davies, John; Bottoms, Timothy; Miracle, Irene; Carey, Michele; Trolley, Leonard

Song(s) In the Shadow of the Kilimanjaro (C/L: Smallwood, Allan; Minuci, Chieli)

Notes No cue sheet available.

2882 ✦ IN THE WAKE OF A STRANGER
Paramount, 1960

Musical Score Astley, Edwin

Producer(s) Penington, Jon
Director(s) Eady, David
Screenwriter(s) Tully, John
Source(s) *In the Wake of a Stranger* (novel) Black, Ian Stuart

Cast Wright, Tony; Eaton, Shirley; Green, Danny; Corbett, Harry H.

Song(s) Maggie May (C: Traditional; L: Astley, Edwin)

2883 ✦ IN THIS CORNER
Eagle Lion, 1948

Producer(s) Stephenson, David L.
Director(s) Riesner, Charles F.
Screenwriter(s) Symon, Buck; Niblo Jr., Fred

Cast Brady, Scott; Shaw, Anabel; Brown, Charles D.; Millcan, Jimmy

Song(s) Out of the Blue [1] (C/L: Nemo, Henry; Jason, Will)

Notes [1] Also in OUT OF THE BLUE (1947).

2884 ✦ INTO THE NIGHT
Universal, 1985

Musical Score Newborn, Ira
Composer(s) Newborn, Ira
Lyricist(s) Newborn, Ira

Producer(s) Folsey Jr., George; Koslow, Ron
Director(s) Landis, John
Screenwriter(s) Koslow, Ron

Cast Goldblum, Jeff; Pfeiffer, Michelle; Farnsworth, Richard; Papas, Irene; Harrold, Kathryn; Mazursky, Paul; Miles, Vera; Vadim, Roger; Gulager, Clu; Bowie, David; Aykroyd, Dan; Perkins, Carl; McGill, Bruce; Cronenberg, David; Evans, Art; Marton, Andrew; George, Christopher; Landis, John; Higgins, Colin; Petrie, Daniel; Bartel, Paul; Henson, Jim; Heckerling, Amy; Kasdan, Lawrence; Demme, Jonathan; Gottlieb, Carl; Siegel, Don; Arnold, Jack

Song(s) Into the Night; My Lucille

Notes There are also pop tunes on the soundtrack.

2885 ✦ INTRIGUE
United Artists, 1947

Musical Score Forbes, Louis

Producer(s) Bischoff, Sam
Director(s) Marin, Edwin L.
Screenwriter(s) Trivers, Barry; Slavin, George F.

Cast Raft, George; Havoc, June; Carter, Helena; Tully, Tom

Song(s) Intrigue (C: Akst, Harry; L: Lerner, Sam)

2886 ✦ INVITATION TO A GUNFIGHTER
United Artists, 1964

Musical Score Raksin, David

Producer(s) Wilson, Richard
Director(s) Wilson, Richard
Screenwriter(s) Wilson, Richard; Wilson, Elizabeth

Cast Brynner, Yul; Rule, Janice; Dexter, Brad; Ryder, Alfred; Kellin, Mike; Segal, George; David, Clifford;

Hingle, Pat; James, Clifton; Martin, Strother; Hiken, Gerald; Hickey, William

Song(s) Invitation to a Gunfighter (C: Raksin, David; L: David, Mack); Lullabye (C: Raksin, David; L: Raksin, David; Wilson, Elizabeth)

2887 ♦ INVITATION TO THE DANCE
Metro–Goldwyn–Mayer, 1956

Choreographer(s) Kelly, Gene

Producer(s) Freed, Arthur
Director(s) Kelly, Gene

Cast Kelly, Gene; Youskevitch, Igor; Sombert, Claire; Haney, Carol; Kasday, David; Toumanova, Tamara; Adams, Diana; Belita; Dale, Daphne; Davies, Irving; Bessy, Claude; Paltenghi, David; Rall, Tommy

Notes There are no vocals in this picture. There are three ballets in the film: "Circus," with music by Jacques Ibert; "Ring Around the Rosie," written for the film by Andre Previn and the animated cartoon "Sinbad the Sailor," based on music by Rimsky-Korsakov.

2888 ♦ I OUGHT TO BE IN PICTURES
Twentieth Century–Fox, 1982

Producer(s) Ross, Herbert; Simon, Neil
Director(s) Ross, Herbert
Screenwriter(s) Simon, Neil
Source(s) *I Ought to Be in Pictures* (play) Simon, Neil

Cast Matthau, Walter; Ann-Margaret; Manoff, Dinah [1]; Guest, Lance; Morales, Santos

Song(s) In Hollywood (Everybody Is a Star) (C/L: Belolo, Henri; Hurtt, Phil; Morali, Jacques); One Hello (C: Hamlisch, Marvin; L: Sager, Carole Bayer)

Notes [1] Repeating Broadway role.

2889 ♦ IRENE
RKO, 1940

Composer(s) Tierney, Harry
Lyricist(s) McCarthy, Joseph
Choreographer(s) Broadbent, Aida

Producer(s) Wilcox, Herbert
Director(s) Wilcox, Herbert
Screenwriter(s) Miller, Alice Duer
Source(s) *Irene* (musical) Montgomery, James H.; Tierney, Harry; McCarthy, Joseph

Cast Neagle, Anna; Milland, Ray; Young, Roland; Robson, May; Treacher, Arthur; Jewell, Isabel; Marshal, Alan; Burke, Billie; Hunt, Marsha; Nolan, Doris

Song(s) Castle of Dreams; You've Got Me Out on a Limb; Alice Blue Gown; Sweet Vermosa Brown; Irene; Alicia [1]

Notes Sheet music only.

2890 ♦ IRISH EYES ARE SMILING
Twentieth Century–Fox, 1944

Composer(s) Monaco, James V.
Lyricist(s) Gordon, Mack
Choreographer(s) Pan, Hermes

Producer(s) Runyon, Damon
Director(s) Ratoff, Gregory
Screenwriter(s) Baldwin, Earl; Battle, John Tucker

Cast Haver, June; Haymes, Dick; Woolley, Monty; Quinn, Anthony; Whitney, Beverly; Rosenbloom, Maxie; Borg, Veda Ann; Kolb, Clarence

Song(s) I Don't Want a Million Dollars; Bessie in a Bustle

Notes Vocals include: "Mother Machree" by Ernest R. Ball and Chauncy Olcott; "Strut Miss Lizzy" by Henry Creamer and Turner Layton; "Be My Little Baby Bumble Bee" by Henry Marshall and Stanley Murphy; and the following songs with music by Ernest R. Ball and lyrics by J. Keirn Brennan: "Dear Little Boy of Mine," "Let the Rest of the World Go By," "Turn Back the Universe and Give Me Yesterday," "A Little Bit of Heaven," "I'll Forget You" with lyrics by Annalu Burns and "When Irish Eyes Are Smiling" with lyrics by George Graff Jr. and Chauncey Olcott.

2891 ♦ IRMA LA DOUCE
United Artists, 1963

Musical Score Previn, Andre

Producer(s) Wilder, Billy
Director(s) Wilder, Billy
Screenwriter(s) Wilder, Billy; Diamond, I.A.L.
Source(s) *Irma La Douce* (musical) Monnot, Marguerite; Heneker, David; More, Julian; Norman, Monty

Cast Lemmon, Jack; MacLaine, Shirley; Jacobi, Lou; Yarnell, Bruce; Bernardi, Herschel; Holiday, Hope; McNear, Howard

Song(s) Little Birdie (C: Previn, Andre; L: Diamond, I.A.L.); Dis Donc [1] (C: Monnot, Marguerite; L: Norman, Monty; More, Julian; Heneker, David); Irma La Douce Theme [2] (C: Previn, Andre; L: Previn, Dory)

Notes [1] From Broadway musical. [2] Lyric written for exploitation only.

2892 ♦ IRON EAGLE
Tri-Star, 1986

Musical Score Poledouris, Basil

Producer(s) Samuels, Ron; Wizan, Joe
Director(s) Furie, Sidney J.
Screenwriter(s) Elders, Kevin; Furie, Sidney J.

Cast Gossett, Lou; Gedrick, Jason; Suchet, David; Thomerson, Tim; Scott, Larry B.; Lagerfelt, Caroline; Levine, Jerry; Rist, Robbie

Song(s) Iron Eagle (Never Say Die) (C/L: Hitchings, Duane; Hooker, Jake); This Raging Fire (C/L: Halligan Jr., Bob); One Vision (C/L: Mercury, Fred; Deacon, Joan; May, Brian; Taylor, Roger); Hide in the Rainbow (C/L: Dio, Ronnie James); Intense (C/L: Clinton, George S.); It's Too Late (C/L: Dexter, John; Hackman, Paul); Love Can Make You Cry (C/L: Kehr, Steve; Hunter, Ian; Kehr, Michael); Maniac House (C/L: Rew, Kimberly); Road of the Gypsy (C/L: Pastoria, Mark; Pastoria, Brian); These Are the Good Times (C/L: Hunter, Miles)

Notes No cue sheet available.

2893 ✦ IRON EAGLE II
Tri-Star, 1988

Musical Score Bhatia, Amin

Producer(s) Kotzky, Jacob; Harel, Sharon; Kemeny, John
Director(s) Furie, Sidney J.
Screenwriter(s) Elders, Kevin; Furie, Sidney J.

Cast Gossett, Lou; Humphrey, Mark; Margolin, Stuart; Scarfe, Alan; Brandon, Sharon H.

Song(s) Enemies Like You & Me (C/L: Janz, Elizabeth; Janz, Paul); Chasing the Angels (C/L: Parker, John); If You Were My Girl (C/L: Price, Michael; Scher, Richard; Holden, Mark); I Need You (C/L: Buckingham, Jan; Scott, Alan Roy; Autograf)

Notes No cue sheet available.

2894 ✦ IRONWEED
Tri-Star, 1987

Musical Score Morris, John

Producer(s) Barish, Keith; Nasatir, Marcia
Director(s) Babenco, Hector
Screenwriter(s) Kennedy, William
Source(s) *Ironweed* (novel) Kennedy, William

Cast Nicholson, Jack; Streep, Meryl; Baker, Carroll; O'Keefe, Michael; Venora, Diane; Gwynne, Fred; Waits, Tom; Whitton, Margaret

Song(s) Poor Little Lamb (C: Waits, Tom; L: Kennedy, William)

Notes No cue sheet available.

2895 ✦ IRRECONCILABLE DIFFERENCES
Warner Brothers, 1984

Musical Score Toussaint, Oliver

Producer(s) Sellers, Arlene; Winitsky, Alex
Director(s) Shyer, Charles
Screenwriter(s) Shyer, Charles; Meyers, Nancy

Cast O'Neal, Ryan; Long, Shelley; Barrymore, Drew; Wanamaker, Sam; Garfield, Allen; Stone, Sharon

Song(s) This Belle (Blake's Song) (C/L: Belson, Jerry; Miller, Harvey); Harmony [1] (C/L: De Sennerville, Paul); The Way I Loved You [1] (C/L: Toussaint, Oliver)

Notes [1] Sheet music only.

2896 ✦ ISABEL
Paramount, 1968

Composer(s) Strange, Mark
Lyricist(s) Strange, Mark

Producer(s) Almond, Paul
Director(s) Almond, Paul
Screenwriter(s) Almond, Paul

Cast Bujold, Genevieve; Strange, Mark; Hayes, Elton

Song(s) Isabel; Maybe Tomorrow

2897 ✦ IS EVERYBODY HAPPY? (1929)
Warner Brothers, 1929

Composer(s) Akst, Harry
Lyricist(s) Clarke, Grant
Choreographer(s) Ceballos, Larry

Director(s) Mayo, Archie
Screenwriter(s) Jackson, Joseph; Starr, James A.

Cast Lewis, Ted; Day, Alice; Pennington, Ann; Grant, Lawrence; Gordon, Julia Swayne; Hoffman, Otto

Song(s) Wouldn't It Be Wonderful?; I'm the Medicine Man for the Blues; Samoa; I'm Blue for You New Orleans; In the Land of Jazz (C: Perkins, Ray; L: Brennan, J. Keirn); Start the Band (C/L: Lewis, Ted)

Notes No cue sheet available. There are also renditions of W.C. Handy's "St. Louis Blues" and the "Tiger Rag" by the Original Dixieland Jazz Band.

2898 ✦ IS EVERYBODY HAPPY (1943)
Columbia, 1943

Producer(s) Briskin, Irving
Director(s) Barton, Charles
Screenwriter(s) Brice, Monte

Cast Lewis, Ted; Wynn, Nan; Duane, Michael; Parks, Larry; Merrick, Lynn; Haymes, Bob; Stanford, Robert; Barris, Harry; Winslow, Dick

Notes Based on the life of Ted Lewis. There are no original songs in this picture. Included in the score are "Just Around the Corner" by Dolph Singer and Harry Von Tilzer; "On the Sunny Side of the Street" by Dorothy Fields and Jimmy McHugh; "Be Yourself" by Harry Harris; "Cuddle Up a Little Closer" by Otto Harbach and Karl Hoschna; "By the Light of the Silvery Moon" by Gus Edwards and Edward Madden; "Way Down Yonder in New Orleans" by Henry Creamer and Turner Layton; "I'm Just Wild About Harry" by Noble Sissle and Eubie Blake; "Pretty Baby" by Gus Kahn,

Tony Jackson and Egbert Van Alstyne; "Am I Blue" by Grant Clarke and Harry Akst; "More Than Anything in the World" by Ruth Lowe; "St. Louis Blues" by W.C. Handy; and "Tell Me Why Nights Are Lonesome" by Will Callahan and Max Kortlander.

2899 ✦ ISHTAR
Columbia, 1987

Musical Score   Grusin, Dave
Composer(s)   Williams, Paul
Lyricist(s)   May, Elaine

Producer(s)   Beatty, Warren
Director(s)   May, Elaine
Screenwriter(s)   May, Elaine

Cast   Beatty, Warren; Hoffman, Dustin; Adjani, Isabelle; Grodin, Charles; Weston, Jack; Harper, Tess; Kane, Carol; Margulies, David

Song(s)   Dangerous Business (L: Williams, Paul); What's Wrong with That? (C/L: Gordon, Bruce); You Took My Love (C/L: Standig, Paul; Gmerek, Joseph; Trumpbour, John; May, Elaine); I'm Quitting High School (C: Strauss, John); Little Darlin' [1] (C/L: Williams, Maurice); Portable Picnic; Love In My Will; Hello Heartbreak; Software; The Echo Song; Carol (L: Williams, Paul); That a Lawnmower Can Do All That (L: Williams, Paul); Wardrobe of Love (L: Williams, Paul); Half Hour Song (L: Beatty, Warren; Hoffman, Dustin; Williams, Paul); Kiss Every Inch of You (C/L: Hoffman, Dustin); Sitting on the Edge of My Life (C/L: Hoffman, Dustin); Hello Ishtar (L: Williams, Paul); Harem Girl (C/L: Hoffman, Dustin); Vamp (C/L: Beatty, Warren); My Lips on Fire (C/L: Beatty, Warren; May, Elaine); Have-Not Blues (C/L: Beatty, Warren; May, Elaine); I Look to Mecca; How Big Am I

Notes   There are also popular songs interpolated into the score. John Strauss credited in *New York Times* for music score. [1] Sheet music only.

2900 ✦ ISLAND IN THE SKY (1938)
Twentieth Century–Fox, 1938

Producer(s)   Wurtzel, Sol M.
Director(s)   Leeds, Herbert I.
Screenwriter(s)   Hyland, Frances; Ray, Albert

Cast   Stuart, Gloria; Whalen, Michael; Kelly, Paul; Kellard, Robert; Storey, June; Hurst, Paul; Ames, Leon; Robertson, Willard

Song(s)   Living on the Town [1] (C: Akst, Harry; L: Clare, Sidney)

Notes   [1] Also in SHE HAD TO EAT.

2901 ✦ ISLAND IN THE SKY (1953)
Warner Brothers, 1953

Composer(s)   Friedhofer, Hugo; Newman, Emil
Lyricist(s)   Friedhofer, Hugo; Newman, Emil

Producer(s)   Wayne, John; Fellows, Robert
Director(s)   Wellman, William A.
Screenwriter(s)   Gann, Ernest K.
Source(s)   *Island in the Sky* (novel) Gann, Ernest K.

Cast   Wayne, John; Nolan, Lloyd; Abel, Walter; Arness, James; Devine, Andy; Joslyn, Allyn; Lydon, Jimmy [1]; Carey Jr., Harry; Toomey, Regis; Switzer, Carl "Alfalfa"

Song(s)   Heroic Island; Island in the Sky [2]; Family (C/L: Newman, Emil; Spencer, Herbert); Blue Waters (C/L: Newman, Emil; Newman, I.C.); S.O.S.

Notes   All background vocals. They may just contain humming not words. [1] Billed as James Lydon. [2] John Lehman added lyrics for exploitation only.

2902 ✦ ISLAND IN THE SUN
Twentieth Century–Fox, 1957

Musical Score   Arnold, Malcolm
Composer(s)   Belafonte, Harry; Burgess, Irving
Lyricist(s)   Belafonte, Harry; Burgess, Irving

Producer(s)   Zanuck, Darryl F.
Director(s)   Rossen, Robert
Screenwriter(s)   Hayes, Alfred
Source(s)   *Island in the Sun* (novel) Waugh, Alex

Cast   Mason, James; Fontaine, Joan; Dandridge, Dorothy; Collins, Joan; Rennie, Michael; Belafonte, Harry; Wynard, Diana; Williams, John; Boyd, Stephen; Owens, Patricia; Sydney, Basil

Song(s)   Island in the Sun; Lead Man Holler; You're Never Too Young to Be Old (C: Arnold, Malcolm; L: Mullan, Richard); Cocoanut Woman [1]; Don't Ever Love Me [1]

Notes   [1] Sheet music only.

2903 ✦ ISLAND OF LOST MEN
Paramount, 1939

Producer(s)   Zukor, Eugene
Director(s)   Neumann, Kurt
Screenwriter(s)   Lipman, William R.; McCoy, Horace

Cast   Wong, Anna May; Naish, J. Carrol; Quinn, Anthony

Song(s)   Music on the Shore (C: Hollander, Frederick; L: Loesser, Frank)

2904 ✦ ISLAND OF LOVE
Warner Brothers, 1963

Musical Score   Duning, George
Composer(s)   Fain, Sammy
Lyricist(s)   Adamson, Harold

Producer(s)   DaCosta, Morton
Director(s)   DaCosta, Morton
Screenwriter(s)   Schwartz, David R.
Source(s)   "Not on Your Life" (story) Katcher, Leo

Cast Preston, Robert; Randall, Tony; Moll, Georgia; Matthau, Walter; Bruce, Betty; Lambrinos, Vassili; Constantine, Michael; Vandis, Titos

Song(s) Speak Not a Word; Sailor's Song

2905 ✦ ISLE OF ESCAPE
Warner Brothers, 1930

Director(s) Bretherton, Howard
Screenwriter(s) Hubbard, Lucien; Alexander, J. Grubb
Source(s) (play) Dixon, G.C.

Cast Blue, Monte; Compson, Betty; Loy, Myrna; Beery, Noah; Simpson, Ivan L.; Ackroyd, Jack; Quartero, Nena

Song(s) My Kalua Rose (C: Ward, Edward; L: Bryan, Alfred)

Notes No cue sheet available.

2906 ✦ THE ISLE OF FURY
Warner Brothers, 1936

Producer(s) Foy, Bryan
Director(s) McDonald, Frank
Screenwriter(s) Andrews, Robert; Jacobs, William
Source(s) *The Narrow Corner* (novel) Maugham, W. Somerset

Cast Bogart, Humphrey; Lindsay, Margaret; Woods, Donald; Graetz, Paul; Hart, Gordon; Clive, E.E.

Song(s) Cottage in Killarney (C: Wrubel, Allie; L: Dixon, Mort)

2907 ✦ THE ISLE OF LOST SHIPS
Warner Brothers–First National, 1929

Director(s) Willat, Irvin
Screenwriter(s) Myton, Fred; Perez, Paul
Source(s) *The Isle of Dead Ships* (novel) Marriott, Crittenden

Cast Valli, Virginia; Robards, Jason; Selwynne, Clarissa; Beery, Noah; O'Connor, Robert Emmett

Song(s) Ship of My Dreams (C: Meyer, George W.; L: Bryan, Alfred)

Notes No cue sheet available. A remake of the 1929 silent film of the same name. It starred Anna Q. Nilsson, Milton Sills and Frank Campeau.

2908 ✦ ISLE OF TABU
Paramount, 1945

Composer(s) Wayne, Bernie
Lyricist(s) Raleigh, Ben
Choreographer(s) Earl, Josephine

Producer(s) Harris, Lou
Director(s) Shea, William
Screenwriter(s) Gruskin, Jerry

Cast Porter, Nancy; Quigley, Charles

Song(s) Dawn of a Bright New Day (C: Wayne, Bernie; L: Raleigh, Ben); White Blossoms of Tah-Ni [2] (C: Hollander, Frederick; L: Loesser, Frank); The Hula Oni Oni E [1] (C: Bernal, Cliff; Woodd, Napua; L: Cambria, Joaquin; Woodd, Napua); Pau-Kau Lana-Kua

Notes [1] Not written for film. [2] Also in ALOMA OF THE SOUTH SEAS.

2909 ✦ ISLE OF THE DEAD
RKO, 1945

Musical Score Harline, Leigh

Producer(s) Lewton, Val
Director(s) Robson, Mark
Screenwriter(s) Wray, Ardel; Mischel, Josef

Cast Karloff, Boris; Cramer, Marc; Robards, Jason; Napier, Alan; Emery, Katherine; Dorian, Ernest; Knaggs, Skelton; Thimig, Helene; Drew, Ellen

Song(s) Grecian Song (C/L: Lewton, Val; Robson, Mark)

2910 ✦ IS MY FACE RED?
RKO, 1932

Musical Score Steiner, Max

Producer(s) Brown, Harry Joe
Director(s) Seiter, William A.
Screenwriter(s) Robinson, Casey; Markson, Ben
Source(s) (play) Markson, Ben; Rivkin, Allen

Cast Cortez, Ricardo; Twelvetrees, Helen; Esmond, Jill; Judge, Arline; Armstrong, Robert; Pitts, ZaSu

Song(s) You Bunch of Fun (C/L: Grossman, Bernie; Lewis, Harold)

2911 ✦ ISN'T IT ROMANTIC
Paramount, 1948

Composer(s) Livingston, Jay
Lyricist(s) Evans, Ray
Choreographer(s) Earl, Josephine

Producer(s) Dare, Danny [4]
Director(s) McLeod, Norman Z.
Screenwriter(s) Strauss, Theodore; Mischel, Josef; Breen, Richard L.

Cast Lake, Veronica [3]; De Wolfe, Billy; Knowles, Patric; Freeman, Mona; Hatcher, Mary; Culver, Roland; Bailey, Pearl

Song(s) Indiana Dinner; Miss Julie July; Wond'rin' When [2]; At the Nickleodeon; I Shoulda Quit When I Was Ahead; Two-Time, Hot-Time, Ragtime Daddy [1]

Notes Movie first titled IT'S ALWAYS SPRING and FATHER'S DAY. [1] Not used. [2] Original title was "Who? Where? When?" but changed because of the similarity to the title of Rodgers and Hart's song "Where or When." [3] Dubbed by Martha Mears. [4] Billed as Daniel Dare.

2912 ◆ IS PARIS BURNING?
Paramount, 1966

Musical Score Jarre, Maurice

Producer(s) Graetz, Paul
Director(s) Clement, Rene
Screenwriter(s) Coppola, Francis Ford; Vidal, Gore; Aurenche, Jean; Bost, Pierre; Brule, Claude
Source(s) *Is Paris Burning?* (novel) Collins, Larry; Lapierre, Dominique

Cast Caron, Leslie; Welles, Orson; Ford, Glenn; Douglas, Kirk; Delon, Alain; Boyer, Charles; Perkins, Anthony; Belmondo, Jean-Paul; Signoret, Simone; Montand, Yves; Chakiris, George; Stack, Robert; Frobe, Gert; Dauphin, Claude; Gelin, Daniel

Song(s) Paris Smiles [1] (C: Jarre, Maurice; L: Livingston, Jay; Evans, Ray)

Notes [1] Lyrics added for exploitation.

2913 ◆ ISRAEL
Warner Brothers, 1960

Musical Score Bernstein, Elmer

Producer(s) Uris, Leon
Director(s) Zebba, Sam
Screenwriter(s) Uris, Leon
Narrator(s) Robinson, Edward G.

Song(s) Hatikvah (C/L: Traditional); David Melech Israel (C/L: Zeira, M.); Orcha BaMidbar (C/L: Zahavi, D.; Feichman, Y.); Ken Yovedu (C/L: Givon, A.); Eretz Zvat Halev U'Dvash (C/L: Gamliel, A.); Hey Daroma (C/L: Noy, M.; Hefer, Haim)

Notes It is not known if any of these were written for the film.

2914 ◆ ISTANBUL
Universal, 1956

Producer(s) Cohen, Albert J.
Director(s) Pevney, Joseph
Screenwriter(s) Miller, Seton I.; Gray, Barbara; Simmons, Richard Alan

Cast Flynn, Errol; Thatcher, Torin; Erickson, Leif; Bentley, John; Cole, Nat "King"; Klemperer, Werner

Song(s) When I Fall in Love [1] (C: Young, Victor; L: Heyman, Edward); I Was a Little Too Lonely (C/L: Livingston, Jay; Evans, Ray)

Notes A remake of SINGAPORE (1947). [1] Originally in ONE MINUTE TO ZERO.

2915 ◆ I START COUNTING
United Artists, 1970

Composer(s) Kirchin, Basil; Coleman; Nathan
Lyricist(s) Ryan

Producer(s) Greene, David
Director(s) Greene, David
Screenwriter(s) Harris, Richard

Cast Agutter, Jenny; Marshall, Bryan; Sutcliffe, Clare; Morris, Lana

Song(s) I Start Counting; Blue Coat (C/L: Trombey); Lawdy Lawdy (L: Kirchin, Basil; Coleman; Nathan); It'll Never Be Me (C/L: May; Waller; Taylor); They Want Love; Danger Signs (C/L: May; Waller; Taylor); Roar-Up (L: Kirchin, Basil; Coleman; Nathan); Who's Gonna Buy (C/L: Reno); If I Needed Somebody (C/L: May; Waller; Taylor); Home Made Aeroplane (C: Taylor); Children (C: Taylor)

Notes There is also a vocal of "The Last Charge" by DeWolfe.

2916 ◆ I SURRENDER DEAR
Columbia, 1948

Composer(s) Roberts, Allan; Fisher, Doris
Lyricist(s) Roberts, Allan; Fisher, Doris

Producer(s) Katzman, Sam
Director(s) Dreifuss, Arthur
Screenwriter(s) Webster, M. Coates; Collins, Hal

Cast Jean, Gloria; McGuire, Don; Tyrrell, Alice; Wood, Douglas; The Disc Jockeys [1]; The Novelites [2]; Street, David; Garroway, Dave

Song(s) Five o' the Best [4]; How Can You Tell [5]; Figaro Routine (C/L: Novelites, The [2]); Amado Mio [3]

Notes Note Dave Garroway's inclusion in the cast. There are also vocals of "There Is Nobody Else but Elsie" by Allie Wrubel; "When You're in the Room" by Ben Oakland and Oscar Hammerstein II and "I Surrender Dear" by Gordon Clifford and Harry Barris (also in the Paramount film COLLEGE HUMOR). [1] Consisted of Jack Eigen, Dave Garroway and Peter Potter. [2] Consisted of Frank Carozza, Joe Mayer, Arthur Tirabassi and Dick Winslow. [3] Originally in GILDA. [4] Also in SWEET GENEVIEVE. [5] Also in CIGARETTE GIRL.

2917 ◆ IT AIN'T HAY
Universal, 1943

Composer(s) Revel, Harry
Lyricist(s) Webster, Paul Francis

Producer(s) Gottlieb, Alex
Director(s) Kenton, Erle C.
Screenwriter(s) Boretz, Allen; Grant, John
Source(s) (story) Runyon, Damon

Cast Abbott, Bud; Costello, Lou; Kellaway, Cecil; McDonald, Grace; Noble, Leighton; Pallette, Eugene; Quillan, Eddie; Howard, Shemp; Hinds, Samuel S.; Jackson, Selmer; The Vagabonds; The Step Brothers; The Hollywood Blondes

Song(s) Sunbeam Serenade; Old Timer; Glory Be; Hang Your Troubles on a Rainbow

Notes A remake of PRINCESS O'HARA (1935).

2918 ✦ THE ITALIAN JOB
Paramount, 1969

Musical Score Jones, Quincy

Producer(s) Deeley, Michael
Director(s) Collinson, Peter
Screenwriter(s) Martin, Troy Kennedy

Cast Coward, Noel; Caine, Michael; Vallone, Raf; Beckley, Tony; Brazzi, Rossano; Hill, Benny; Blye, Maggie; Ware, Derek

Song(s) On Days Like These (C: Jones, Quincy; L: Black, Don); Getta Bloomin' Move On! (C: Jones, Quincy; L: Black, Don)

2919 ✦ IT ALL CAME TRUE
Warner Brothers, 1940

Producer(s) Warner, Jack L.; Wallis, Hal B.
Director(s) Seiler, Lewis
Screenwriter(s) Fessier, Michael; Kimble, Lawrence
Source(s) *Better Than Life* (novel) Bromfield, Louis

Cast Sheridan, Ann; Bogart, Humphrey; Lynn, Jeffrey; Pitts, ZaSu; Busley, Jesse; O'Connor, Una; Litel, John; Mitchell, Grant

Song(s) Angel in Disguise (C: Mann, Paul; L: Gannon, Kim; Weiss, Stephen)

Notes No cue sheet available but this is from trailer sheet. Other songs include "The Gaucho Serenade" by James Cavanaugh, John Redmond and Nat Simon; "Pretty Baby" and "Memories" by Gus Kahn and Egbert Van Alstyne; "Ain't We Got Fun" by Richard A. Whiting; "Put on Your Old Grey Bonnet" by Stanley Murphy and Percy Wenrich and "When Irish Eyes Are Smiling" by Chauncey Olcott and George Graff Jr.

2920 ✦ IT CAN'T LAST FOREVER
Columbia, 1937

Producer(s) Decker, Harry
Director(s) MacFadden, Hamilton
Screenwriter(s) Loeb, Lee; Buchman, Harold

Cast Bellamy, Ralph; Furness, Betty; Armstrong, Robert; Walburn, Raymond; Hall, Thurston; Judels, Charles

Song(s) Crazy Dreams (C: Oakland, Ben; L: Magidson, Herb); Lazy Rhythm (C: Oakland, Ben; L: Magidson, Herb)

Notes No cue sheet available.

2921 ✦ AN ITCH IN TIME
Warner Brothers, 1943

Musical Score Stalling, Carl

Director(s) Clampett, Bob

Cast Fudd, Elmer; Flea, Anthony

Song(s) Food Around the Corner [1] (C/L: Clampett, Robert)

Notes Animated short. [1] Also in A HORSEFLY FLEAS.

2922 ✦ IT COMES UP LOVE (1942)

See GET HEP TO LOVE.

2923 ✦ IT COMES UP LOVE (1943)
Universal, 1943

Producer(s) Goldsmith, Ken
Director(s) Lamont, Charles
Screenwriter(s) Bennett, Dorothy; Kenyon, Charles

Cast Jean, Gloria; Hunter, Ian; O'Connor, Donald; Inescort, Frieda; Allbritton, Louise

Notes There are vocals of "That's What the Rose Said to Me" by B.F. Barnett and Leo Edwards; "Love's Old Sweet Song" by J.L. Molloy; "Vamos a Ver" by Ruben Guevera and "Say Si Si" by Ernesto Lecuona.

2924 ✦ IT HAPPENED AT THE WORLD'S FAIR
Metro–Goldwyn–Mayer, 1963

Musical Score Stevens, Leith
Choreographer(s) Baker, Jack

Producer(s) Richmond, Ted
Director(s) Taurog, Norman
Screenwriter(s) Rose, Si; Jacobs, Seaman

Cast Presley, Elvis; O'Brien, Joan; Lockwood, Gary; Tiu, Vicky; Wynant, H.M.; Atwater, Edith; Raymond, Guy; Green, Dorothy; Tong, Kam; Craig, Yvonne

Song(s) Beyond the Bend (C/L: Wiseman, Ben; Wise, Fred; Fuller, Dee); Relax (C/L: Tepper, Sid; Bennett, Roy C.); Take Me to the Fair (C/L: Tepper, Sid; Bennett, Roy C.); They Remind Me Too Much of You (C/L: Robertson, Don); One Broken Heart for Sale

(C/L: Blackwell, Otis; Scott, Winfield); I'm Falling in Love Tonight (C/L: Robertson, Don); Cotton Candy Land (C/L: Batchelor, Ruth; Roberts, Bob); A World of Our Own (C/L: Giant, Bill; Baum, Bernie; Kaye, Florence); How Would You Like to Be (C: Raleigh, Ben; L: Barkan, Mark); Happy Ending (C/L: Wayne, Sid; Weisman, Ben)

2925 ◆ IT HAPPENED IN ATHENS
Twentieth Century–Fox, 1962

Producer(s) Elliott, James S.
Director(s) Marton, Andrew
Screenwriter(s) Vadnay, Laslo

Cast Mansfield, Jayne; Colton, Trax; Minardos, Nico; Mathias, Bob; Xenia, Maria

Song(s) It Happened in Athens [1] (C: Hadjidakis, Manos; L: Haldeman, Charles)

Notes [1] Lyric written for exploitation only.

2926 ◆ IT HAPPENED IN BROOKLYN
Metro–Goldwyn–Mayer, 1947

Musical Score Green, Johnny
Composer(s) Styne, Jule
Lyricist(s) Cahn, Sammy
Choreographer(s) Donohue, Jack

Producer(s) Cummings, Jack
Director(s) Whorf, Richard
Screenwriter(s) Lennart, Isobel

Cast Sinatra, Frank [1]; Grayson, Kathryn; Lawford, Peter; Durante, Jimmy; Grahame, Gloria; McGuire, Nancy

Song(s) Whose Baby Are You; Brooklyn Bridge; Bach Invention #1 (C: Bach, J.S.; Styne, Jule); I Believe; Time After Time; The Song's Gotta Come from the Heart; It's the Same Old Dream

Notes There are also vocals of "La Danza" by Rossini, "La Ci Darem La Mano" by Mozart and "Ou Va La Jeune Indone" by Delibes. [1] Piano playing dubbed by Andre Previn.

2927 ◆ IT HAPPENED ON FIFTH AVENUE
Allied Artists, 1947

Musical Score Ward, Edward
Composer(s) Revel, Harry
Lyricist(s) Revel, Harry

Producer(s) Del Ruth, Roy
Director(s) Del Ruth, Roy
Screenwriter(s) Freeman, Everett

Cast DeFore, Don; Harding, Ann; Ruggles, Charles; Moore, Victor; Storm, Gale; Mitchell, Grant; Brophy, Edward S.; Hale Jr., Alan; Kent, Dorothea; The King's Men

Song(s) That's What Christmas Means to Me; It's a Wonderful Wonderful Feeling; You're Everywhere (L: Webster, Paul Francis); Speak My Heart

Notes No cue sheet available.

2928 ◆ IT HAPPENED TO JANE
Columbia, 1959

Musical Score Duning, George
Composer(s) Lubin, Joe; Roth, I.J.
Lyricist(s) Lubin, Joe; Roth, I.J.

Producer(s) Quine, Richard
Director(s) Quine, Richard
Screenwriter(s) Katkov, Norman

Cast Lemmon, Jack; Day, Doris; Kovacs, Ernie; Cullen, Bill; Garroway, Dave; McCormick, Steve; Meadows, Jayne; Morgan, Henry; Moore, Garry; Paige, Bob; Palmer, Betsy; Wickes, Mary; Fennelly, Parker; Holm, John Cecil

Song(s) It Happened to Jane; That Jane from Maine; Be Prepared (C: Karger, Fred; L: Quine, Richard); Twinkle and Shine [1] (C/L: Dunham, "By")

Notes Reissued as TWINKLE AND SHINE in 1961 with some song changes (see [1] below). It was previously known as THE JANE FROM MAINE and THE WRECK OF THE OLD 97. [1] This was added to and was the only song in TWINKLE AND SHINE.

2929 ◆ IT HAPPENS EVERY SPRING
Twentieth Century–Fox, 1949

Producer(s) Siegel, Sol C.
Director(s) Hawks, Howard
Screenwriter(s) Lederer, Charles; Spigelgass, Leonard; Wilde, Hagar

Cast Grant, Cary; Sheridan, Ann; Marshall, Marion; Stuart, Randy

Song(s) It Happens Every Spring (C: Myrow, Josef; L: Gordon, Mack)

2930 ◆ IT'S A DATE
Universal, 1940

Producer(s) Pasternak, Joe
Director(s) Seiter, William A.
Screenwriter(s) Krasna, Norman

Cast Durbin, Deanna; Francis, Kay; Pidgeon, Walter; Pallette, Eugene; Howard, Lewis; Hinds, Samuel S.; Stephenson, Henry; Brissac, Virginia; Sakall, S.Z.; Harry Owens and His Royal Hawaiians

Song(s) Gypsy Lullaby (Csak Egy Szep Lany Van E Vilagon) (C: Traditional L: Freed, Ralph); Rhythm of the Islands (C/L: Belasco, Leon; Press, Jacques; Cherkose, Eddie); Love Is All (C: Tomlin, Pinky; L: Tobias, Harry); It Happened in Kaloha [1] (C: Skinner,

Frank; L: Freed, Ralph); Loch Lomond [1] (C/L: Skinner, Frank)

Notes Later remade as NANCY GOES TO RIO (1940). There are also vocals of "Musetta's Waltz" from Puccini's LA BOHEME and "Ave Maria" by Franz Schubert. [1] Sheet music only.

2931 ✦ IT'S A DATE AT REVEILLE WITH BEVERLY

See REVEILLE WITH BEVERLY.

2932 ✦ IT'S A GRAND OLD NAG
Republic, 1947

Musical Score Alexander, Jeff

Producer(s) Clampett, Bob
Director(s) Clampett, Bob

Song(s) The Filly with a Twinkle in Her Eye (C/L: Palmer, James L.)

Notes A cartoon short.

2933 ✦ IT'S A GREAT FEELING
Warner Brothers, 1949

Composer(s) Styne, Jule
Lyricist(s) Cahn, Sammy
Choreographer(s) Prinz, LeRoy

Producer(s) Gottlieb, Alex
Director(s) Butler, David
Screenwriter(s) Rose, Jack; Shavelson, Melville
Source(s) "Two Guys and a Gal" (story) Diamond, I.A.L.

Cast Morgan, Dennis; Day, Doris; Carson, Jack; Goodwin, Bill; Bacon, Irving; Carleton, Claire; de Wit, Jacqueline; Warde, Harlan

Song(s) It's a Great Feeling; Give Me a Song with a Beautiful Melody; Blame My Absent-Minded Heart; That Was a Big Fat Lie; Fiddle Dee Dee; At the Cafe Rendezvous; There's Nothin' Rougher than Love

Notes Also making cameo appearances are Gary Cooper, Joan Crawford, Errol Flynn, Sydney Greenstreet, Danny Kaye, Patricia Neal, Eleanor Parker, Ronald Reagan, Edward G. Robinson, and Jane Wyman as well as directors Michael Curtiz, King Vidor, Raoul Walsh and David Butler.

2934 ✦ IT'S A GREAT LIFE (1929)
Metro–Goldwyn–Mayer, 1929

Composer(s) Dreyer, Dave
Lyricist(s) Macdonald, Ballard
Choreographer(s) Lee, Sammy

Director(s) Wood, Sam
Screenwriter(s) Boasberg, Al; Mack, Willard

Cast The Duncan Sisters [1]; Gray, Lawrence; Rubin, Benny; Prouty, Jed

Song(s) Smile, Smile, Smile; Won't You Be My Lady Love; Fashion Show; The Sun of a May Morning [2]; I'm Following You; It Must Be an Old Spanish Custom; Let a Smile Be Your Umbrella [3] (C: Fain, Sammy; L: Wheeler, Francis; Kahal, Irving); Hoosier Hop; I'm Sailing on a Sunbeam; Rainbow Round My Shoulder

Notes First released as IMPERFICT LADIES. [1] Rosetta and Vivian. [2] Listed in some sources (but not cue sheet) as "I'm the Son of a —-." [3] Written in 1927.

2935 ✦ IT'S A GREAT LIFE (1936)
Paramount, 1936

Composer(s) Gensler, Lewis E.
Lyricist(s) Robin, Leo

Producer(s) Hurley, Harold
Director(s) Cline, Edward F.
Screenwriter(s) Smith, Paul Gerard; Thompson, Harlan

Cast Morrison, Joe; Kelly, Paul; Keith, Rosalind; Sale, Charles "Chic"; LeRoy, Baby; Jagger, Dean; Frawley, William; Polk, Oscar

Song(s) Lazy Bones Gotta Job Now [2]; I Lost My Heart (And Found My Heart's Desire) [2]; Liebestraume (C: Liszt, Franz); I Knew [1]

Notes Film first titled FROM LITTLE ACORNS. William Frawley also sings a chorus of "When Irish Eyes Are Smiling." [1] Not used. Also not used in FOUR HOURS TO KILL, HER MASTER'S VOICE and HERE IS MY HEART. [2] Written for HER MASTER'S VOICE.

2936 ✦ IT'S ALWAYS FAIR WEATHER
Metro–Goldwyn–Mayer, 1955

Musical Score Previn, Andre
Composer(s) Previn, Andre
Lyricist(s) Comden, Betty; Green, Adolph
Choreographer(s) Kelly, Gene; Donen, Stanley

Producer(s) Freed, Arthur
Director(s) Kelly, Gene; Donen, Stanley
Screenwriter(s) Comden, Betty; Green, Adolph

Cast Kelly, Gene; Dailey, Dan; Charisse, Cyd [2]; Gray, Dolores; Kidd, Michael [1]; Burns, David; Flippen, Jay C.

Song(s) March, March; Time for Parting; Blue Danube (C: Strauss, Johann); Music Is Better Than Words [5] (L: Comden, Betty; Green, Adolph; Edens, Roger); Stillman's Gym; Baby You Knock Me Out; Situation Wise; Once Upon a Time; Dan Dailey's Solo (C: Traditional); I Like Myself; Madeline's Commercial (C: Liszt, Franz); Thanks a Lot but No Thanks; I Thought

They'd Never Leave [3]; Love Is Nothing but a Racket [3]; Jack and the Space Giants [4] (Inst.)

Notes [1] Dubbed by Clark Burroughs. [2] Dubbed by Carole Richards. [3] Not used. [4] Ballet deleted from final print. [5] Also in DESIGNING WOMAN but without Edens credit. Possibly the same music track.

2937 ◆ IT'S A MAD, MAD, MAD, MAD WORLD
United Artists, 1964

Musical Score Gold, Ernest
Composer(s) Gold, Ernest
Lyricist(s) David, Mack

Producer(s) Kramer, Stanley
Director(s) Kramer, Stanley
Screenwriter(s) Rose, William; Rose, Tania

Cast Caesar, Sid; Berle, Milton; Provine, Dorothy; Rooney, Mickey; Tracy, Spencer; Durante, Jimmy; Silvers, Phil; Adams, Edie; Falk, Peter; Anderson, Eddie "Rochester"; Knotts, Don; Devine, Andy; The Three Stooges; Terry-Thomas; Keaton, Buster; Horton, Edward Everett

Song(s) It's a Mad, Mad, Mad, Mad World; Thirty One Flavors [1]; The Man with the Golden Dreams [1]; What a Day [1]; You Satisfy My Soul [1]

Notes [1] Not used.

2938 ◆ IT'S A PLEASURE
RKO, 1945

Musical Score Lange, Arthur; Roemheld, Heinz

Producer(s) Lewis, David
Director(s) Seiter, William A.
Screenwriter(s) Starling, Lynn; Paul, Elliot

Cast Henie, Sonja; O'Shea, Michael; Johnson, Bill; McDonald, Marie; Schilling, Gus; Adrian, Iris; Walker, Cheryl; O'Neill, Peggy; Loper, Don

Song(s) Romance (C: Donaldson, Walter; L: Leslie, Edgar); Tico Tico No Fuba [1] (C: Abreu, Zequinha; L: Oliveira, Aloysio; Drake, Ervin)

Notes [1] Also in BOMBALERA (Paramount); Columbia's GAY SENORITA and KANSAS CITY KITTY; BATHING BEAUTY (MGM) and COPACABANA (UA). Drake wrote the English lyrics.

2939 ◆ IT'S A WONDERFUL LIFE
RKO, 1946

Producer(s) Capra, Frank
Director(s) Capra, Frank
Screenwriter(s) Goodrich, Frances; Hackett, Albert; Capra, Frank
Source(s) "The Greatest Gift" (story) Stern, Philip Van Doren

Cast Stewart, James; Reed, Donna; Barrymore, Lionel

Song(s) It's a Wonderful Life (1) [1] (C: Tiomkin, Dimitri; L: Herbert, Frederick); It's a Wonderful Life (2) [1] (C: Shaw, Artie; L: Losey, Louis)

Notes [1] Not used.

2940 ◆ IT'S GREAT TO BE ALIVE
Fox, 1933

Composer(s) Kernell, William
Lyricist(s) Kernell, William

Director(s) Werker, Alfred
Screenwriter(s) Kober, Arthur

Cast Roulien, Raul; Stuart, Gloria; Oliver, Edna May; Mundin, Herbert; March, Joan; Dunn, Emma

Song(s) Goodbye Ladies; I'll Build a Nest [1]; Women; It's Great to Be the Only Man Alive; World Congress; Another Mother Song (C/L: Friedhofer, Hugo); Muddy Mississippi Water (C/L: Friedhofer, Hugo)

Notes Produced in a Spanish language version originally with the title EL ULTIMO VARON SOBRE LA TIERRA (THE LAST MAN ON EARTH). [1] Also in MY LIPS BETRAY.

2941 ◆ IT'S GREAT TO BE YOUNG
Columbia, 1946

Composer(s) Fisher, Doris; Roberts, Allan
Lyricist(s) Fisher, Doris; Roberts, Allan

Producer(s) Richmond, Ted
Director(s) Lord, Del
Screenwriter(s) Henley, Jack

Cast Brooks, Leslie; Lloyd, Jimmy; Donnell, Jeff; Stanton, Robert; Williams, Jack; Fina, Jack; Orth, Frank; Sutton, Grady; Milton Delugg and His Swing Wing

Song(s) It's Great to Be Young; A Thousand and One Sweet Dreams; Five of the Best; That Went Out with High-Button Shoes; Frankie Boogie; Bumble Boogie [1] (C: Rimsky-Korsakov, Nicholas; L: Fina, Jack)

Notes No cue sheet available. [1] Music based on "The Flight of the Bumble Bee."

2942 ◆ IT'S MAGIC

See ROMANCE ON THE HIGH SEAS.

2943 ◆ IT'S MY TURN
Columbia, 1980

Musical Score Williams, Patrick

Producer(s) Elfand, Martin
Director(s) Weill, Claudia
Screenwriter(s) Bergstein, Eleanor

Cast Clayburgh, Jill; Douglas, Michael; Grodin, Charles; Garland, Beverly; Hill, Steven; Copeland, Joan; Kimbrough, Charles; Stern, Daniel

Song(s) It's My Turn (C: Masser, Michael; L: Sager, Carole Bayer)

Notes The following people play themselves: Larry Doby, Bob Feller, Tony Ferrara, Whitey Ford, Al Forman, Tom Gorman, Bud Harrelson, Gene Hermanski, Elston Howard, Monte Irvin, Ed Kranepool, John Kuchs, Hector Lopez, Frank McCormick, Sal Maglie, Mickey Mantle, Roger Maris, Willard Marshall, Frank Messer, Johnny Orsino, Dusty Rhodes, Specs Shea, Ron Tellfsen, Bobby Thomson, Bill White, Sal Yvars.

2944 ✦ IT STARTED IN NAPLES
Paramount, 1960

Musical Score Cicognini, Alessandro; Savina, Carlo
Choreographer(s) Coleman, Leo

Producer(s) Rose, Jack
Director(s) Shavelson, Melville
Screenwriter(s) Shavelson, Melville; Rose, Jack; D'Amico, Suso Cecchi

Cast Loren, Sophia; Gable, Clark; De Sica, Vittorio; Marietto; Carlini, Paolo

Song(s) It Started in Naples (Bay of Naples) [1] (C: Cicognini, Alessandro; Savina, Carlo; L: Simoni, Sylvana); Stay Here with Me (Resta Cu'mme) [1] (C/L: Modugno, Domenico; Verde); Tu Vuo' Fa' L'Americano [2] (C/L: Carosone, Renato; Nisa); Carina [2] (C/L: Testa, A.; Poes, R.); The Bay of Naples [1] [3] (C: Cicognini, Alessandro; L: Simoni, Sylvana)

Notes [1] English lyrics by Milt Gabler. [2] English lyrics by Carol Danell. [3] Not used.

2945 ✦ IT STARTED WITH A KISS
Metro–Goldwyn–Mayer, 1960

Musical Score Alexander, Jeff

Producer(s) Rosenberg, Aaron
Director(s) Marshall, George
Screenwriter(s) Lederer, Charles

Cast Reynolds, Debbie; Ford, Glenn; Gabor, Eva; Rojo, Gustavo; Clark, Fred; Bavier, Frances; Buchanan, Edgar; Morgan, Henry (Harry); Warwick, Robert

Song(s) It Started with a Kiss (C: Render, Rudy; L: Lederer, Charles)

2946 ✦ IT STARTED WITH EVE
Universal, 1941

Producer(s) Pasternak, Joe
Director(s) Koster, Henry
Screenwriter(s) Krasna, Norman; Townsend, Leo

Cast Laughton, Charles; Durbin, Deanna; Cummings, Robert; Tallichet, Margaret; Catlett, Walter; Coleman, Charles; Bacon, Irving; Schilling, Gus; Blandick, Clara

Song(s) When I Sing [1] (C: Tchaikovsky, Peter; L: Lerner, Sam); Goin' Home [2] (C: Dvorak, Anton; L: Fisher, W. Arms)

Notes Later remade as I'D RATHER BE RICH (1964). There is also a vocal of "Clavelitos" by M. Sandwith and J. Valverde. [1] Based on the waltz from SLEEPING BEAUTY arranged by Charles Previn. [2] Based on the largo of the "New World Symphony."

2947 ✦ IT'S TOUGH TO BE A BIRD
Disney, 1969

Musical Score Bruns, George
Composer(s) Leven, Mel
Lyricist(s) Leven, Mel

Director(s) Kimball, Ward
Screenwriter(s) Berman, Ted; Kimball, Ward

Cast Buzzi, Ruth; Bakalyan, Richard

Song(s) It Is Tough to Be a Bird; When the Buzzards Return to Hinkley Ridge

2948 ✦ IVANHOE
Metro–Goldwyn–Mayer, 1952

Musical Score Rozsa, Miklos

Producer(s) Berman, Pandro S.
Director(s) Thorpe, Richard
Screenwriter(s) Roberts, Marguerite; Langley, Noel
Source(s) *Ivanhoe* (novel) Scott, Sir Walter

Cast Taylor, Robert; Taylor, Elizabeth; Fontaine, Joan; Sanders, George; Williams, Emlyn; Douglas, Robert; Currie, Finlay

Song(s) Song of Ivanhoe (C: Rozsa, Miklos; L: Roberts, Marguerite)

2949 ✦ I WAKE UP SCREAMING
Twentieth Century–Fox, 1941

Producer(s) Sperling, Milton
Director(s) Humberstone, H. Bruce
Screenwriter(s) Taylor, Dwight
Source(s) *I Wake Up Screaming* (novel) Fisher, Steve

Cast Grable, Betty; Mature, Victor; Landis, Carole; Cregar, Laird; Gargan, William; Mowbray, Alan; Joslyn, Allyn; Cook Jr., Elisha; Chandler, Chick; Ring, Cyril; Lane, Charles

Song(s) The Things I Love (C: Harris, Lewis; L: Barlow, Harold)

Notes This film's alternate title is HOT SPOT.

2950 ✦ I WALK ALONE
Paramount, 1947

Musical Score   Young, Victor

Producer(s)   Wallis, Hal B.
Director(s)   Haskin, Byron
Screenwriter(s)   Schnee, Charles
Source(s)   *Beggars Are Coming to Town* (play) Reeves, Theodore

Cast   Scott, Lizabeth [2]; Lancaster, Burt; Corey, Wendell; Douglas, Kirk; Lawrence, Marc; Miller, Kristine

Song(s)   In Love At Last [1] (C: Wrubel, Allie; L: Washington, Ned); Don't Call It Love (C: Wrubel, Allie; Washington, Ned)

Notes   Rights to the title of the Jule Styne and Sammy Cahn song "I'll Walk Alone" were bought for this picture. [1] Not used. [2] Dubbed by Judy Stevens.

2951 ✦ I WALKED WITH A ZOMBIE
RKO, 1943

Musical Score   Webb, Roy

Producer(s)   Lewton, Val
Director(s)   Tourneur, Jacques
Screenwriter(s)   Siodmak, Curt; Wray, Ardel

Cast   Ellison, James; Dee, Frances; Barrett, Edith; Bell, James; Gordon, Christine; Harris, Theresa; Sir Lancelot

Song(s)   O Marie Conga (C/L: Antoine, Leroy); Holland Calypso Song (C/L: Wray, Ardel); Wale (C/L: Antoine, Leroy)

2952 ✦ I WANTED WINGS
Paramount, 1941

Producer(s)   Hornblow Jr., Arthur
Director(s)   Leisen, Mitchell
Screenwriter(s)   Wead, Frank; Griffin, Eleanore; Lay Jr., Beirne; Maibaum, Richard; Herzig, Sig
Source(s)   *I Wanted Wings* (book) Lay Jr., Beirne [1]

Cast   Milland, Ray; Holden, William; Morris, Wayne; Lake, Veronica; Donlevy, Brian; Moore, Constance; Davenport, Harry; Hopper, Hedda

Song(s)   Born to Love (C: Young, Victor; L: Washington, Ned)

Notes   [1] Written as Lieutenant Beirne Lay Jr.

2953 ✦ I WAS FRAMED
Warner Brothers, 1942

Musical Score   Jackson, Howard

Producer(s)   Jacobs, William
Director(s)   Lederman, D. Ross
Screenwriter(s)   Kent, Robert E.
Source(s)   "Dust Be My Destiny" (story) Odlum, Jerome

Cast   Ames, Michael; Bishop, Julie; Toomey, Regis; Bowker, Aldrich; McDaniel, Sam

Song(s)   Stories My Mommie Told Me (C/L: Seymour, Harry)

2954 ✦ I WONDER WHO'S KISSING HER NOW
Twentieth Century–Fox, 1947

Composer(s)   Henderson, Charles; Jessel, George
Lyricist(s)   Henderson, Charles; Jessel, George
Choreographer(s)   Pan, Hermes

Producer(s)   Jessel, George
Director(s)   Bacon, Lloyd
Screenwriter(s)   Foster, Lewis R.

Cast   Haver, June; Stevens, Mark [1]; Stewart, Martha; Gardiner, Reginald; Aubert, Lenore; Frawley, William; Nelson, Gene; Bradley, Truman; Cleveland, George

Song(s)   Madame Du Barry; The Sentry Song; Come to the Saint Louis Fair; Annabelle Brown; Songs of Love; The Sad King

Notes   This is a film biography of the life of Joseph E. Howard. Vocals also include "I Wonder Who's Kissing Her Now," "Honeymoon" and "Be Sweet to Me Kid" by Joseph E. Howard, Will M. Hough and Frank R. Adams; "In the Sweet By and By" by J.P. Webster; "Wait Till the Sun Shines Nellie" by Harry Von Tilzer and Andrew B. Sterling; "Hello! My Baby" by Joseph E. Howard and Ida Emerson; "In the Evening By the Moonlight" by James A. Bland; "Love's Old Sweet Song" ("Sari Waltz") by Emmerich Kalman, C.C.S. Cushing and E.P. Heath; "Glow Worm" by Paul Lincke and Lilla Cayle Robinson; "What's the Use of Dreaming" and "Good Bye My Lady Love" by Joseph E. Howard. [1] Dubbed by Buddy Clark.

J

2955 ✦ JACK AND THE BEANSTALK
Warner Brothers, 1952

Musical Score Roemheld, Heinz
Composer(s) Lee, Lester
Lyricist(s) Russell, Bob
Choreographer(s) Conrad, Johnny

Producer(s) Gottlieb, Alex
Director(s) Yarbrough, Jean
Screenwriter(s) Curtis, Nathaniel

Cast Abbott, Bud; Costello, Lou; Baer, Buddy; Ford, Dorothy; Brown, Barbara; Stollery, David; Farnum, William; Johnny Conrad and His Dancers; Cogan, Shaye; Alexander, James; Patrick the Harp

Song(s) Jack and the Beanstalk; I Fear Nothing; Darlene; Dreamer's Cloth; He Never Looked Better in His Life

2956 ✦ JACKASS MAIL
Metro–Goldwyn–Mayer, 1942

Musical Score Brent, Earl; Snell, Dave
Composer(s) Brent, Earl
Lyricist(s) Brent, Earl
Choreographer(s) Lee, Sammy

Producer(s) Considine Jr., John W.
Director(s) McLeod, Norman Z.
Screenwriter(s) Hazard, Lawrence

Cast Beery, Wallace; Main, Marjorie; Naish, J. Carrol; Yule, Joe; Howard, Esther; Hickman, Darryl; Haade, William; Cavanaugh, Hobart

Song(s) Come Sing a Song of Gladness; Girls of the Golden West; It Is Sad in the Forest Today; O'Sullivan's Serenade

2957 ✦ THE JACKPOT
Twentieth Century–Fox, 1950

Musical Score Newman, Lionel
Composer(s) Traditional
Lyricist(s) Darby, Ken

Producer(s) Engel, Samuel G.
Director(s) Lang, Walter

Screenwriter(s) Ephron, Phoebe; Ephron, Henry
Source(s) article by McNulty, John

Cast Stewart, James; Hale, Barbara; Gleason, James; Clark, Fred; Mowbray, Alan; Medina, Patricia; Wood, Natalie; Rettig, Tommy; Talbot, Lyle

Song(s) Mary Had a Little Lamb; The Alphabet Song; A Candle (C: Darby, Ken; L: Traditional); Little Brown Jug (C: Winner, J.E.)

2958 ✦ JAILHOUSE BLUES
Universal, 1941

Composer(s) Skinner, Frank
Lyricist(s) Smith, Paul Gerard

Producer(s) Goldsmith, Ken
Director(s) Rogell, Albert S.
Screenwriter(s) Smith, Paul Gerard; Tarshis, Harold
Source(s) "Rhapsody in Stripes" (story) Tarshis, Harold

Cast Pendleton, Nat; Paige, Robert; Risdon, Elizabeth; Gwynne, Anne; McMahon, Horace; Hymer, Warren; Hinds, Samuel S.

Song(s) Sweetheart of School Fifty Nine [2]; Stick 'Em Up; Heart of Mine [1] (L: Skinner, Frank)

Notes There are also vocals of "M-O-T-H-E-R" by Howard Johnson and Theodore Morse and "M'Appari Tutt' Amor" by Flotow. [1] Also in RIO with lyrics credited to Ralph Freed. [2] Also in I CAN'T GIVE YOU ANYTHING BUT LOVE, BABY.

2959 ✦ JAILHOUSE ROCK
Metro–Goldwyn–Mayer, 1957

Musical Score Alexander, Jeff
Composer(s) Leiber, Jerry; Stoller, Mike
Lyricist(s) Leiber, Jerry; Stoller, Mike

Producer(s) Berman, Pandro S.
Director(s) Thorpe, Richard
Screenwriter(s) Trosper, Guy

Cast Presley, Elvis; Tyler, Judy; Shaughnessy, Mickey; Taylor, Vaughn; Holden, Jennifer; Jones, Dean; Neyland, Anne

Song(s) One More Day (C/L: Tepper, Sid; Bennett, Roy C.); Young and Beautiful (C/L: Silver, Fred; Schroeder, Aaron); I Wanna Be Free (I Want to Be Free); Don't Leave Me Now (C/L: Schroeder, Aaron; Weisman, Ben); Treat Me Nice; Jailhouse Rock; Baby, I Don't Care

2960 ✦ JAMAICA RUN
Paramount, 1953

Musical Score Cailliet, Lucien

Producer(s) Pine, William; Thomas, William
Director(s) Foster, Lewis R.
Screenwriter(s) Foster, Lewis R.
Source(s) (novel) Murray, Max

Cast Milland, Ray; Dahl, Arlene; Corey, Wendell; Knowles, Patric; Elliot, Laura

Song(s) Chanter La Poisson (Fishing Chant) [1] (C: Niles, Mac; L: Fahie, G.; Niles, Mac)

Notes [1] Only used instrumentally in film.

2961 ✦ JAMBOREE (1944)
Republic, 1944

Composer(s) Fisher, Fred
Lyricist(s) Fisher, Fred

Producer(s) Schaefer, Armand
Director(s) Santley, Joseph
Screenwriter(s) Townley, Jack; Caven, Taylor

Cast Terry, Ruth; Byron, George; Fisher, Freddie; Roth, Walter; Fisher, Darrell; Fox, Allen; Ludes, Alice

Song(s) Colonel Corn; You Nearly Lose Your Mind (C/L: Tubb, Ernest); Maggie Went to Aggie (C/L: Henderson, Charles); Jamboree; Merry Go Round; Walkin' the Floor Over You (C/L: Tubb, Ernest); Whittle Out a Whistle [1] (C/L: Hoefle, Carl)

Notes [1] Del Porter also credited on cue sheets.

2962 ✦ JAMBOREE (1957)
Warner Brothers, 1957

Musical Score Hefti, Neal; Blackwell, Otis
Composer(s) Unknown
Lyricist(s) Unknown

Producer(s) Rosenberg, Max J.; Subotsky, Milton
Director(s) Lockwood, Roy
Screenwriter(s) Kantor, Leonard

Cast Medford, Kay; Pastine, Robert; Halloway, Freda; Carr, Paul; Domino, Antoine "Fats"; Count Basie and His Orchestra; Whitman, Slim; Lewis, Jerry Lee; The Four Coins; Williams, Joe; Perkins, Carl; Lewis Lymon & the Teenchords; Francis, Connie; Rocco & His Saints; Smith, Joe; Avalon, Frankie; Grant, Milt; Clark, Dick; Perkins, Ray

Song(s) Jamboree; Great Balls of Fire (C/L: Hammer, Jack; Blackwell, Otis); Record Hop Tonight; For Children of All Ages; Glad All Over; Who Are We to Say (C/L: Kosloff, I.; Pray, T.); Teacher's Pet; Siempre; Cool Baby (C/L: Blackwell, Otis); Sayonara; Toreador (C/L: Colacrai, Cirino; Randazzo, Teddy); Your Last Chance (C/L: Robinson, M.; Cooper, L.); If Not for You; Unchain My Heart (C/L: Richards, L.M.); A Broken Promise; One O'Clock Jump; I Don't Like You No More (C/L: Colacrai, Cirino; Randazzo, Teddy); Cross Over (C/L: Jones, Ollie; Smith, B.); Hula Love (C/L: Knox, B.); Wait and See (C/L: Domino, Antoine "Fats"; Bartholomew, Dave); Twenty-Four Hours a Day; Every Night at Midnight (C/L: Subotsky, Milton)

Notes No cue sheet available. Released in Great Britain as DISC JOCKEY JAMBOREE. It is not known if there are any original songs in this film.

2963 ✦ THE JAMES DEAN STORY
Warner Brothers, 1957

Musical Score Stevens, Leith

Producer(s) George, George W.; Altman, Robert
Director(s) George, George W.; Altman, Robert
Screenwriter(s) Stern, Stewart
Narrator(s) Gabel, Martin

Song(s) Let Me Be Loved (C/L: Livingston, Jay; Evans, Ray)

Notes A documentary on James Dean. No cue sheet available.

2964 ✦ JAM SESSION
Columbia, 1944

Choreographer(s) Donen, Stanley

Producer(s) Briskin, Irving
Director(s) Barton, Charles
Screenwriter(s) Seff, Manuel

Cast Miller, Ann; Barker, Jess; Wynn, Nan; Charles Barnet and His Orchestra; Louis Armstrong and His Orchestra; Alvino Rey and His Orchestra; Jan Garber and His Orchestra; Glen Gray and His Casa Loma Orchestra; Teddy Powell and His Orchestra; Shawn, Bill; Loos, Anita

Song(s) Vict'ry Polka (C: Styne, Jule; L: Cahn, Sammy)

Notes Songs include "I Can't Give You Anything But Love, Baby" by Jimmy McHugh and Dorothy Fields; "I Lost My Sugar in Salt Lake City" by Leon Rene and Johnny Lange; "No Name Jive" (inst.) by Larry Wagner; "Jive Bomber" (inst.) by Spud Murphy; "St. Louis Blues" by W.C. Handy; "Murder He Says" by Frank Loesser and Jimmy McHugh; "It Started All Over Again" by Carey and Fisher; "Brazil" by S.K. Russell and Ary Barroso and "Cherokee" (inst.) by Ray Noble.

2965 ◆ JANIE
Warner Brothers, 1944

Musical Score Roemheld, Heinz

Producer(s) Gottlieb, Alex
Director(s) Curtiz, Michael
Screenwriter(s) Johnston, Agnes Christine; Hoffman, Charles
Source(s) *Janie* (play) Bentham, Josephine; Williams, Herschel

Cast Reynolds, Joyce; Hutton, Robert; Arnold, Edward; Harding, Ann; Benchley, Robert; Hale, Alan; Foley, Clare; Brown, Barbara; McDaniel, Hattie

Song(s) Janie (C/L: David, Lee); Keep Your Powder Dry (C: Styne, Jule; L: Cahn, Sammy)

2966 ◆ JANIE GETS MARRIED
Warner Brothers, 1946

Musical Score Hollander, Frederick

Producer(s) Gottlieb, Alex
Director(s) Sherman, Vincent
Screenwriter(s) Johnston, Agnes Christine

Cast Leslie, Joan; Hutton, Robert; Arnold, Edward; Harding, Ann; Benchley, Robert; Malone, Dorothy; McDaniel, Hattie; Erdman, Richard; Foley, Clare; Meek, Donald; Brown, Barbara; Hamilton, Margaret; Torme, Mel

Song(s) G.I. Song (C: Jerome, M.K.; L: Koehler, Ted)

2967 ◆ JASPER GOES FISHING
Paramount, 1943

Musical Score de Packh, Maurice

Producer(s) Pal, George
Director(s) Pal, George

Song(s) Going to the River (C/L: de Packh, Maurice)

Notes This is a George Pal Puppetoon short subject. De Packh also wrote the signature tune that preceeded all the Puppetoons.

2968 ◆ JAWS 2
Universal, 1978

Musical Score Williams, John

Producer(s) Zanuck, Richard D.; Brown, David
Director(s) Szwarc, Jeannot
Screenwriter(s) Gottlieb, Carl; Sackler, Howard

Cast Scheider, Roy; Gary, Lorraine; Hamilton, Murray; Mascolo, Joseph; Kramer, Jeffrey; Coe, Barry; Grover, Cindy

Song(s) You're the Force in My Life (C: Williams, John; L: Stanley, Joe)

2969 ◆ THE JAYHAWKERS
Paramount, 1959

Musical Score Moross, Jerome

Producer(s) Frank, Melvin; Panama, Norman
Director(s) Frank, Melvin
Screenwriter(s) Frank, Melvin; Bezzerides, A.I.; Petracca, Joseph; Fenton, Frank

Cast Chandler, Jeff; Parker, Fess; Silva, Henry; Maurey, Nicole

Song(s) Hippy-Happy-Henry (C/L: Boutelje, Phil); The Jayhawkers [1] (C/L: Wolfson, Mark; White, Eddie)

Notes [1] Written for exploitation only.

2970 ◆ JAZZ BOAT
Columbia, 1960

Musical Score Jones, Kenneth V.
Composer(s) Henderson, Joe
Lyricist(s) Henderson, Joe

Producer(s) Broccoli, Albert R.; Allen, Irving
Director(s) Hughes, Ken
Screenwriter(s) Hughes, Ken; Antrobus, John

Cast Newley, Anthony; Aubrey, Anne; Jeffries, Lionel; Lodge, David; McKern, Leo; Blair, Joyce; Ted Heath and His Music

Song(s) Don't Talk to Me About Love (L: Newley, Anthony); Jazz Boat; Someone to Love; I Wanna Jive Easy (L: Henderson, Joe; Hughes, Ken); Oui Oui Oui (C: Giraud, Hubert; L: Julian, Michael)

Notes No cue sheet available.

2971 ◆ JAZZ CINDERELLA
Chesterfield, 1930

Composer(s) Greer, Jesse
Lyricist(s) Klages, Raymond

Producer(s) Batcheller, George R.
Director(s) Pembroke, Scott
Screenwriter(s) Johnson, Adrien; Howell, Arthur [1]; Pembroke, Scott

Cast Robards, Jason; Loy, Myrna; Welford, Nancy; Phillips, Dorothy

Song(s) You're Too Good to Be True; Hot and Bothered Baby; True Love

Notes No cue sheet available. [1] This credit appears in *Variety* review but not other sources.

2972 ◆ JAZZ HEAVEN
RKO, 1929

Producer(s) Connolly, Myles
Director(s) Brown, Melville
Screenwriter(s) Ruben, J. Walter; Wood, Cyrus

Cast   Brown, Johnny Mack [1]; Cook, Clyde; Frederici, Blanche; O'Neil, Sally; Cawthorn, Joseph; Conti, Albert; Armetta, Henry

Song(s)   Someone [2] (C: Levant, Oscar; L: Clare, Sidney)

Notes   [1] Billed as John Mack Brown. [2] Also in DANCE HALL.

2973 ◆ THE JAZZ SINGER (1927)
Warner Brothers, 1927

Director(s)   Crosland, Alan
Screenwriter(s)   Cohn, Alfred A.
Source(s)   *The Jazz Singer* (play) Raphaelson, Samson

Cast   Jolson, Al; McAvoy, May; Oland, Warner [1]; Besserer, Eugenie; Rosenblatt, Cantor Joseph; Lederer, Otto; Demarest, William; Gordon, Bobby [1]

Notes   No cue sheet available. There are no original songs in this film. Vocals include "Blue Skies" by Irving Berlin (also in BLUE SKIES, GLORIFYING THE AMERICAN GIRL and ALEXANDER'S RAGTIME BAND); "Mother I Still Have You" by Louis Silvers and Al Jolson; "My Mammy" by Walter Donaldson, Sam Lewis and Joe Young; "Toot Toot Tootsie Goodbye" by Ernie Erdman, Dan Russo and Gus Kahn (From the stage musical BOMBO. Also in I'LL SEE YOU IN MY DREAMS, THE JOLSON STORY, JOLSON SINGS AGAIN and ROSE OF WASHINGTON SQUARE); "Dirty Hands Dirty Face" by James V. Monaco, Grant Clarke, Al Jolson and Edgar Leslie and the traditional prayer "Kol Nidre." Myrna Loy appeared as a chorus girl in this film. [1] Dubbed.

2974 ◆ THE JAZZ SINGER (1953)
Warner Brothers, 1953

Composer(s)   Fain, Sammy
Lyricist(s)   Seelen, Jerry
Choreographer(s)   Prinz, LeRoy

Producer(s)   Edelman, Louis F.
Director(s)   Curtiz, Michael
Screenwriter(s)   Davis, Frank; Stern, Leonard; Meltzer, Lewis
Source(s)   *The Jazz Singer* (play) Raphaelson, Samson

Cast   Thomas, Danny; Lee, Peggy; Dunnock, Mildred; Franz, Eduard [2]; Tully, Tom; Gerry, Alex; Joslyn, Allyn; Gordon, Harold

Song(s)   Living the Life I Love; Haskivenu (C/L: Lamkoff, Paul); Hush-A-Bye [1] (C: Thomas, Ambrose; Fain, Sammy); This Is a Very Special Day (C/L: Lee, Peggy); Odom Yesody Meyofor (C/L: Lamkoff, Paul); Oh, Moon (C/L: Jacobs, Ray); I Hear the Music Now [1] (C: Thomas, Ambrose; Fain, Sammy); Velvo Suds Commercial; What Are New Yorkers Made Of

Notes   There are also vocals of "Just One of Those Things" by Cole Porter; "Lover" by Richard Rodgers and Lorenz Hart and "Birth of the Blues" by B.G. DeSylva, Ray Henderson and Lew Brown. [1] Based on the "Raymond Overture." [2] Dubbed.

2975 ◆ THE JAZZ SINGER (1980)
AFD, 1980

Musical Score   Diamond, Neil; Rosenman, Leonard
Composer(s)   Diamond, Neil
Lyricist(s)   Diamond, Neil
Choreographer(s)   McKayle, Donald

Producer(s)   Leider, Jerry
Director(s)   Fleischer, Richard
Screenwriter(s)   Baker, Herbert
Source(s)   *The Jazz Singer* (play) Raphaelson, Samson

Cast   Diamond, Neil; Olivier, Laurence; Arnaz, Lucie; Adams, Catlin; Ajaye, Franklyn; Nicholas, Paul; Kellin, Mike

Song(s)   You Baby; America; Jerusalem; Love on the Rocks (C/L: Diamond, Neil; Becaud, Gilbert); On the Robert E. Lee (C/L: Diamond, Neil; Becaud, Gilbert); Summer Love (C/L: Diamond, Neil; Becaud, Gilbert); Hey Louise (C/L: Diamond, Neil; Becaud, Gilbert); Songs of Life (C/L: Diamond, Neil; Becaud, Gilbert); Hello Again (C: Diamond, Neil; Lindgren, Alan); Amazed and Confused (C: Diamond, Neil; Bennett, Richard); Acapulco (C: Diamond, Neil; Rhone, Doug); My Name Is Yussel

Notes   No cue sheet available.

2976 ◆ JEANNE EAGELS
Columbia, 1957

Musical Score   Duning, George

Producer(s)   Sidney, George
Director(s)   Sidney, George
Screenwriter(s)   Fuchs, Daniel; Levien, Sonya; Fante, John

Cast   Novak, Kim [1]; Chandler, Jeff; Moorehead, Agnes; Drake, Charles; Gates, Larry; Grey, Virginia; Lockhart, Gene; DeSantis, Joe; Hamilton, Murray

Song(s)   Half of My Heart (C: Duning, George; L: Washington, Ned)

Notes   [1] Dubbed by Eileen Wilson.

2977 ◆ JEEPERS CREEPERS
Republic, 1939

Producer(s)   Schaefer, Armand
Director(s)   MacDonald, Frank
Screenwriter(s)   McGowan, Stuart; McGowan, Dorrell

Cast Weaver, Leon; Rogers, Roy; Weaver, Frank; Elviry; Weaver, Loretta; Wrixon, Maris; Lee, Billy; Littlefield, Lucien; Hall, Thurston; Arthur, John

Song(s) Lily White Hands (C/L: Marvin, Johnny)

Notes Other vocals include "Jeepers Creepers" by Harry Warren and Johnny Mercer; "Little Brown Jug" and "In the Good Old Summertime" by George "Honey Boy" Evans and Ren Shields; "Wait for the Wagon," "Glory" and "Some Folks Do" by Stephen Foster and "Listen to the Mocking Bird."

2978 ✦ JEKYLL AND HYDE . . . TOGETHER AGAIN
Paramount, 1982

Composer(s) Ivers, Peter
Lyricist(s) Ivers, Peter

Producer(s) Gordon, Lawrence
Director(s) Belson, Jerry
Screenwriter(s) Johnson, Monica; Miller, Harvey; Belson, Jerry; Lesson, Michael

Cast Blankfield, Mark; Armstrong, Bess; Errickson, Krista

Song(s) Wham It; Light Up My Body; Hyde's Got Nothing to Hide (C: De Vorzon, Barry; L: Belson, Jerry)

2979 ✦ JENNIFER
American International, 1978

Producer(s) Krantz, Steve
Director(s) Mack, Brick
Screenwriter(s) Johnson, Kay Cousins

Cast Pelikan, Lisa; Convy, Bert; Foch, Nina; Johnston, Amy; Gavin, John; Corey, Jeff

Song(s) Jennifer (C/L: Jordan, Peter)

Notes No cue sheet available.

2980 ✦ JENNIFER ON MY MIND
United Artists, 1971

Musical Score Lawrence, Stephen

Producer(s) Schwartz, Bernard
Director(s) Black, Noel
Screenwriter(s) Segal, Erich
Source(s) (novel) Simon, Roger L.

Cast Brandon, Michael; Walker, Tippy; Gilbert, Lou; Vinovich, Stephen

Song(s) Where the Good Songs Go (C: Lawrence, Stephen; L: Paxton, Tom); Don't Lose a Minute (C/L: Bostwick, Barry; Conway, Jeff); Going Down Words (C/L: Bostwick, Barry; Conway, Jeff)

2981 ✦ JENNY LIND

See A LADY'S MORALS.

2982 ✦ JEREMIAH JOHNSON
Warner Brothers, 1972

Musical Score Rubinstein, John; McIntire, Tim
Composer(s) Rubinstein, John; McIntire, Tim
Lyricist(s) Rubinstein, John; McIntire, Tim

Producer(s) Wizan, Joe
Director(s) Pollack, Sydney
Screenwriter(s) Milius, John; Anhalt, Edward
Source(s) "The Crow Killer" (story) Thorp, Raymond; Bunker, Robert

Cast Redford, Robert; Geer, Will; Gierasch, Stefan; McLerie, Allyn Ann; Tyner, Charles; Bolton, Delle; Albee, Josh; Martinez, Joaquin

Song(s) Jeremiah Johnson; The Way That You Wander

2983 ✦ JEREMY
United Artists, 1973

Musical Score Holdridge, Lee

Producer(s) Pappas, George
Director(s) Barron, Arthur
Screenwriter(s) Barron, Arthur

Cast Benson, Robby; O'Connor, Glynnis; Bari, Len; Cimino, Leonard; Wilson, Ned; Bohn, Chris

Song(s) Blue Balloon (The Hourglass Song) (C/L: Brooks, Joseph); Jeremy (C: Holdridge, Lee; L: Joyce, Dorothea)

2984 ✦ JESSE JAMES
Twentieth Century–Fox, 1938

Producer(s) Zanuck, Darryl F.
Director(s) King, Henry
Screenwriter(s) Johnson, Nunnally
Source(s) research by Shaffer, Rosalind; James, Jo Frances

Cast Power, Tyrone; Fonda, Henry; Kelly, Nancy; Scott, Randolph; Hull, Henry; Summerville, Slim; Bromberg, J. Edward; Donlevy, Brian; Carradine, John; Meek, Donald; Russell, John; Darwell, Jane; Middleton, Charles; Chaney Jr., Lon; Chandler, George; Robertson, Willard

Song(s) Tavern Song [1] (C: Sanders, Troy; L: Mojica, Jose)

Notes [1] Used for 32 bars only. Also in ARIZONA WILDCAT but without Mojica credit.

2985 ✦ JESSE JAMES' WOMEN
United Artists, 1954

Musical Score Greene, Walter

Producer(s) Royal, Lloyd; Garraway, T.V.
Director(s) Barry, Donald
Screenwriter(s) Beauchamp, D.D.

Cast Barry, Donald; Beutel, Jack; Castle, Peggie; Baron, Lita; Rhed, Joyce; Brueck, Betty; Lee, Laura

Song(s) Careless Lover (C/L: Antheil, George); In the Shadow of My Heart (C/L: Jones, Stan)

2986 ✦ JESSICA
United Artists, 1961

Musical Score Nascimbene, Mario
Composer(s) Monnot, Marguerite
Lyricist(s) Nequlesco, Dusty

Producer(s) Negulesco, Jean
Director(s) Negulesco, Jean
Screenwriter(s) Sommer, Edith
Source(s) *The Midwife of Pont Clery* (novel) Sandstrom, Flora

Cast Dickinson, Angie; Chevalier, Maurice; Noel-Noel; Ferzetti, Gabriele; Koscina, Sylva; Moorehead, Agnes

Song(s) It Is Better to Love; Jessica; Vespa Song [1]; Will You Remember [1]

Notes [1] Sheet music only.

2987 ✦ JESUS CHRIST SUPERSTAR
Universal, 1973

Composer(s) Lloyd Webber, Andrew
Lyricist(s) Rice, Tim
Choreographer(s) Iscove, Rob

Producer(s) Stigwood, Robert; Jewison, Norman
Director(s) Jewison, Norman
Screenwriter(s) Bragg, Melvyn; Jewison, Norman
Source(s) *Jesus Christ Superstar* (musical) Rice, Tim; Lloyd Webber, Andrew

Cast Elliman, Yvonne; Neeley, Ted; Anderson, Carl; Dennen, Barry; Mostel, Josh; Bingham, Bob; Marshall, Larry

Song(s) Heaven on Their Minds; What's the Buzz; Strange Things Mystifying; Then We Are Decided; Everything's Alright; This Jesus Must Die; Hosanna; Simon Zealotes; Poor Jerusalem; Pilate's Dream; Mentioning My Name; The Temple; My Temple Should Be; I Don't Know How to Love Him; Damned for All Time; Blood Money; The Last Supper; Gethsemane; The Arrest; Peter's Denial; The Campsite (Inst.); Pilate and Christ; King Herod's Song; Could We Start Again Please; J.C. and Soldiers (Inst.); Judas' Death; Trial Before Pilate; Superstar; The Crucifixion; John Nineteen Forty-One (Inst.)

2988 ✦ JET OVER THE ATLANTIC
Warner Brothers, 1960

Musical Score Forbes, Louis

Producer(s) Bogeaus, Benedict
Director(s) Haskin, Byron
Screenwriter(s) Cooper, Irving H.

Cast Mayo, Virginia; Madison, Guy; Raft, George; Massey, Ilona; Macready, George; Lee, Anna

Song(s) What Would I Do Without You (C: Forbes, Louis; L: Hoffman, Jack)

2989 ✦ THE JEWEL OF THE NILE
Twentieth Century–Fox, 1985

Musical Score Nitzsche, Jack

Producer(s) Douglas, Michael
Director(s) Teague, Lewis
Screenwriter(s) Rosenthal, Mark; Konner, Lawrence

Cast Douglas, Michael; Turner, Kathleen; DeVito, Danny; Focas, Spiros; Patterson, Howard Jay; Nelson, Randall Edwin; Taylor, Holland

Song(s) When the Going Gets Tough, the Tough Get Going (C/L: Brathwaite, Wayne; Eastmond, Barry J.; Lange, Robert John; Ocean, Billy); The Jewel of the Nile (C: Britten, Terry; L: Lyle, Graham); I'm in Love (C: Butler, Jonathan; L: May, Simon)

Notes No cue sheet available.

2990 ✦ JEZEBEL
Warner Brothers, 1938

Musical Score Steiner, Max

Producer(s) Blanke, Henry
Director(s) Wyler, William
Screenwriter(s) Ripley, Clements; Finkel, Abem; Huston, John
Source(s) *Jezebel* (play) Davis, Owen

Cast Davis, Bette; Fonda, Henry; Brent, George; Lindsay, Margaret; Crisp, Donald; Bainter, Fay; Cromwell, Richard; O'Neill, Henry; Byington, Spring; Litel, John; Oliver, Gordon; Shaw, Janet; Harris, Theresa; Early, Margaret; Pichel, Irving; Anderson, Eddie "Rochester"; Beard, Stymie

Song(s) Jezebel [1] (C: Warren, Harry; L: Mercer, Johnny); Pretty Quadroon [2] (C/L: Vincent, Nat; Howard, Fred)

Notes [1] Not used in picture. Used for promotional use only (including trailer).

2991 ✦ JIGSAW
Universal, 1968

Musical Score Jones, Quincy
Composer(s) Kane, Barry; Greenbaum, Norman
Lyricist(s) Kane, Barry; Greenbaum, Norman

Producer(s)   MacDougall, Ranald
Director(s)   Goldstone, James
Screenwriter(s)   Werty, Quentin
Source(s)   *Fallen Angel* (novel) Fast, Howard

Cast   Dillman, Bradford; Guardino, Harry; Hyland, Diana; Hingle, Pat; Lange, Hope; Jory, Victor; Stewart, Paul; Pollard, Michael J.

Song(s)   Jigsaw; Bullets Laverne

2992 ✦ THE JIGSAW MAN
United Film Distribution, 1985

Musical Score   Cameron, John

Producer(s)   Fisz, S. Benjamin
Director(s)   Young, Terence
Screenwriter(s)   Eisinger, Jo
Source(s)   *The Jigsaw Man* (novel) Bennett, Dorthea

Cast   Caine, Michael; Olivier, Laurence; George, Susan; Powell, Robert; Gray, Charles; Medwin, Michael

Song(s)   Only You and I (C: Garvarentz, Georges; L: Sifre, Labi; English, S.)

Notes   No cue sheet available.

2993 ✦ JIMMY AND SALLY
Fox, 1933

Composer(s)   Gorney, Jay
Lyricist(s)   Clare, Sidney

Director(s)   Tinling, James
Screenwriter(s)   Conselman, William

Cast   Dunn, James; Trevor, Claire; Stephens, Harvey; Prouty, Jed; Roy, Gloria

Song(s)   It's the Irish in Me; Eat Marlowe's Meat; You're My Thrill

2994 ✦ JIMMY DORSEY AND HIS ORCHESTRA
Universal, 1948

Song(s)   We Hate Cowboy Songs (C/L: Tibbles, George; Ramos, Idriss)

Notes   Short subject. It is not known if this was written for this short. There are other vocals also.

2995 ✦ JIM, THE WORLD'S GREATEST
Universal, 1975

Musical Score   Myrow, Fred

Producer(s)   Coscarelli, Don
Director(s)   Coscarelli, Don; Mitchell, Craig
Screenwriter(s)   Coscarelli, Don; Mitchell, Craig

Cast   Harrison, Gregory; Guy, Rory; Wolcott, Robbie; Pennington, Marla; McClain, Karen

Song(s)   Love, Let's Say So Long (C: Myrow, Fred; L: Martin, Frederick); All Night Long (C: Myrow, Fred; L: Fleischer, Mark); Story of a Teen-ager [1] (C/L: Peek, Dan; Beckley, Gerry)

Notes   Also known as STORY OF A TEENAGER. [1] Sheet music only.

2996 ✦ JIM THORPE - ALL-AMERICAN
Warner Brothers, 1951

Musical Score   Steiner, Max

Producer(s)   Freeman, Everett
Director(s)   Curtiz, Michael
Screenwriter(s)   Morrow, Douglas; Freeman, Everett; Davis, Frank
Source(s)   "Bright Path" (story) Morrow, Douglas; Flaherty, Vincent; (biography) Birdwell, Russell J.; Thorpe, James

Cast   Lancaster, Burt; Bickford, Charles; Cochran, Steve; Thaxter, Phyllis; Wesson, Dick; Bighead, Jack; Warcloud, Suni; Paiva, Nestor

Song(s)   Old Carlisle (C/L: Warner, Glenn)

Notes   Released in Great Britain as MAN OF BRONZE.

2997 ✦ JINGLE JANGLE JINGLE
Paramount, 1947

Cast   The Page Cavanaugh Trio; Field, Margaret

Song(s)   Jingle Jangle Jingle [1] (C: Lilley, Joseph; L: Loesser, Frank); Walking My Baby Back Home [2] (C/L: Ahlert, Fred E.; Turk, Roy; Richman, Harry); That's Not the Knot (C/L: Livingston, Jay; Evans, Ray)

Notes   Short subject. [1] Also in AND THE ANGELS SING and THE FOREST RANGERS. [2] Written in 1930.

2998 ✦ JINXED
Metro–Goldwyn–Mayer/United Artists, 1982

Musical Score   Roberts, Bruce; Goodman, Miles

Producer(s)   Jaffe, Herb
Director(s)   Siegel, Don
Screenwriter(s)   Blessing, Bert; Newman, David

Cast   Midler, Bette; Wahl, Ken; Torn, Rip; Avery, Val

Song(s)   Cowgirl's Dream (C/L: Crofford, Cliff; Durrill, John; Garrett, Snuff); Easy Street (C/L: Piccirillo, Mike); Slippin' Down (C/L: Goetzman, Gary); No Jinx (C: Roberts, Bruce; Goodman, Miles; L: Willis, Allee; Walsh, Brock)

Notes   Also known as STRYKE AND HYDE and HOT STREAK. There are also vocals of "Cherry Pink and Apple Blossom White" by Louiguy and Mack David;

"The Bunny Hop" by Ray Anthony and Leonard Auletti and "Papa Loves Mambo" by Al Hoffman, Dick Manning and Bix Reichner.

2999 ✦ JITTERBUG FOLLIES
Metro–Goldwyn–Mayer, 1939

Musical Score   Lewis, Elbert C.

Song(s)   Jitterbug Follies (C/L: Lewis, Elbert C.)

Notes   Animated cartoon.

3000 ✦ JITTERBUGS
Twentieth Century–Fox, 1943

Composer(s)   Pollack, Lew
Lyricist(s)   Newman, Charles

Producer(s)   Wurtzel, Sol M.
Director(s)   St. Clair, Malcolm
Screenwriter(s)   Darling, W. Scott

Cast   Laurel, Stan; Hardy, Oliver; Blaine, Vivian; Bailey, Bob; Patrick, Lee; Keane, Robert Emmett

Song(s)   The Moon Kissed the Mississippi; I've Gotta See for Myself; If the Shoe Fits You, Wear It

Notes   Vivian Blaine's first film.

3001 ✦ JIVE BUSTERS
Universal, 1944

Song(s)   I'm A-Fixin' for to Be A-Headin' South [1] (C: Rosen, Milton; L: Carter, Everett)

Notes   There are other vocals in this short subject. [1] Also in SOUTH OF DIXIE.

3002 ✦ JIVE JUNCTION
PRC, 1943

Musical Score   Erdody, Leo
Composer(s)   Erdody, Leo; Porter, Lew; Stillman, June; Tableporter, F.J.
Lyricist(s)   Erdody, Leo; Porter, Lew; Stillman, June; Tableporter, F.J.
Choreographer(s)   Gallagher, Don

Producer(s)   Fromkess, Leon
Director(s)   Ulmer, Edgar G.
Screenwriter(s)   Wallace, Irving; Doniger, Walter; Wald, Malvin

Cast   Moore, Dickie; Thayer, Tina; Young, Gerra; Michaels, Johnny

Song(s)   A-Doo-Dee-Doo-Doo [1]; Cock a Doodle Doo; In a Little Music Shop; Jive Junction; Mother Earth; We're Just In Between; Where Is Love

Notes   No cue sheet available. There is also a vocal of "The Bell Song" from LAMKE by Leo Delibes. [1] Also

in MURDER IN THE BLUE ROOM (Univ.) but without Stillman credit.

3003 ✦ JOANNA
Twentieth Century–Fox, 1968

Musical Score   McKuen, Rod
Composer(s)   McKuen, Rod
Lyricist(s)   McKuen, Rod

Producer(s)   Laughlin, Michael S.
Director(s)   Sarne, Michael
Screenwriter(s)   Sarne, Michael

Cast   Waite, Genevieve; Doermer, Christian; Lockhart, Calvin; Sutherland, Donald; Forster-Jones, Glenna

Song(s)   When Joanna Loved Me (C/L: Wells, Robert; Segal, Jack); I'll Catch the Sun; Ain't You Glad You're Livin'Joe; Hello, Heartaches; Joanna [1]; I'm Only Me (Two Girls Bathing) [1]; Till We're Together Again [2]; Saturday Night in Knightsbridge [1]; When Am I Ever Going Home [1]; Some August Day [1]; Run to Me, Fly to Me [1]

Notes   [1] Used instrumentally only. [2] Not used.

3004 ✦ JOAN OF OZARK
Republic, 1942

Composer(s)   Revel, Harry
Lyricist(s)   Greene, Mort

Producer(s)   Parsons, Harriet
Director(s)   Santley, Joseph
Screenwriter(s)   Brice, Monte; Ropes, Bradford; Harari, Robert; Greene, Eve; Townley, Jack

Cast   Canova, Judy; Brown, Joe E.; Foy Jr., Eddie; Cowan, Jerome; Jeffreys, Anne

Song(s)   Pull the Trigger; Backwoods Barbecue; Lady at Lockheed; Dixie [1]

Notes   Titled QUEEN OF SPIES internationally. There is also a vocal of "Wabash Blues" by Dave Ringle and Fred Meinken. [1] Used instrumentally only.

3005 ✦ JOAN OF PARIS
RKO, 1943

Musical Score   Webb, Roy

Producer(s)   Hempstead, David
Director(s)   Stevenson, Robert
Screenwriter(s)   Bennett, Charles; St. Joseph, Ellis

Cast   Morgan, Michele; Henreid, Paul; Mitchell, Thomas; Cregar, Laird

Song(s)   Don't Let It Bother You [1] (C: Revel, Harry; L: Gordon, Mack)

Notes   [1] Also in THE GAY DIVORCEE.

3006 ✦ JOE DAKOTA
Universal, 1957

Musical Score   Mancini, Henry

Producer(s)   Christie, Howard
Director(s)   Bartlett, Richard
Screenwriter(s)   Talman, William; Jolley, Norman

Cast   Mahoney, Jock; McGraw, Charles; Patten, Luana; Weaver, Frank; Lawrence, Barbara; Akins, Claude; Van Cleef, Lee; Caruso, Anthony

Song(s)   The Flower of San Antone (C: Ray, Joseph; L: David, Mack)

3007 ✦ JOE PALOOKA

See PALOOKA.

3008 ✦ JOE PANTHER
Artists Creation, 1976

Musical Score   Karlin, Fred

Producer(s)   Beveridge, Stewart H.
Director(s)   Krasny, Paul
Screenwriter(s)   Eunson, Dale
Source(s)   (novel) Ball, Zachary

Cast   Keith, Brian; Montalban, Ricardo; Feinstein, Alan; Osmond, Cliff

Song(s)   The Time Has Come (C: Karlin, Fred; L: Gimbel, Norman)

Notes   No cue sheet available.

3009 ✦ JOHN AND MARY
Twentieth Century–Fox, 1969

Musical Score   Jones, Quincy

Producer(s)   Kadish, Ben
Director(s)   Yates, Peter
Screenwriter(s)   Mortimer, John
Source(s)   (novel) Jones, Mervyn

Cast   Hoffman, Dustin; Farrow, Mia; Tolan, Michael; Daly, Tyne; Mercer, Marian; Dukakis, Olympia

Song(s)   Lost in Space (C/L: Bridges, Jeff); Bump in the Night (C/L: Jones, Quincy); Maybe Tomorrow (C: Jones, Quincy; L: Bergman, Marilyn; Bergman, Alan)

3010 ✦ JOHN GOLDFARB, PLEASE COME HOME
Twentieth Century–Fox, 1965

Musical Score   Williams, John

Producer(s)   Parker, Steve
Director(s)   Thompson, J. Lee
Screenwriter(s)   Blatty, William Peter

Cast   MacLaine, Shirley; Ustinov, Peter; Crenna, Richard; Backus, Jim; Brady, Scott; Clark, Fred; Morgan, Harry; Hyde-White, Wilfrid; Adiarte, Patrick; Deacon, Richard; Cowan, Jerome

Song(s)   John Goldfarb, Please Come Home (C: Williams, John; L: Wolf, Don)

3011 ✦ JOHNNY ANGEL
RKO, 1945

Musical Score   Harline, Leigh

Producer(s)   Pereira, William L.
Director(s)   Marin, Edwin L.
Screenwriter(s)   Fisher, Steve
Source(s)   *Mr. Angel Comes Aboard* (novel) Booth, Charles Gordon

Cast   Trevor, Claire; Hasso, Signe; Gilmore, Lowell; Carmichael, Hoagy; Miller, Marvin; Wycherly, Margaret

Song(s)   Memphis in June (C: Carmichael, Hoagy; L: Webster, Paul Francis)

3012 ✦ JOHNNY APOLLO
Twentieth Century–Fox, 1940

Producer(s)   Zanuck, Darryl F.
Director(s)   Hathaway, Henry
Screenwriter(s)   Dunne, Philip; Brown, Rowland

Cast   Power, Tyrone; Lamour, Dorothy; Arnold, Edward; Nolan, Lloyd; Grapewin, Charley; Atwill, Lionel; Lawrence, Marc; Hale, Jonathan; Rosenthal, Harry; Hicks, Russell; Knight, Fuzzy; Lane, Charles

Song(s)   They Say [2] (C: Mann, Paul; Weiss, Stephan; L: Heyman, Edward); This Is the Beginning of the End (C/L: Gordon, Mack); Dancing for Nickels and Dimes [1] (C: Newman, Lionel; L: Loesser, Frank); Your Kiss [3] (C: Newman, Alfred; L: Loesser, Frank)

Notes   [1] Also in RIDE, KELLY, RIDE. [2] Also in DAUGHTERS COURAGEOUS (Warner). [3] Sheet music only.

3013 ✦ JOHNNY APPLESEED
Disney, 1948

Musical Score   Smith, Paul J.
Composer(s)   Kent, Walter; Gannon, Kim
Lyricist(s)   Kent, Walter; Gannon, Kim

Director(s)   Jaxon, Wilfred
Screenwriter(s)   Hibler, Winston; Rinaldi, Joe; Penner, Erdman; Marsh, Jesse

Song(s)   The Apple Song; The Lord Is Good to Me; The Pioneer Song; Walking Chorus [1]

Notes   This cartoon is a part of MELODY TIME. [1] Not used.

3014 ✦ JOHNNY COOL
United Artists, 1963

Musical Score May, Billy

Producer(s) Asher, William
Director(s) Asher, William
Screenwriter(s) Landon, Joseph
Source(s) *The Kingdom of Johnny Cool* (novel)
McPartland, John

Cast Silva, Henry; Montgomery, Elizabeth; Savalas, Telly; Davis Jr., Sammy; Lawrence, Marc

Song(s) Johnny Cool (C: Van Heusen, James; L: Cahn, Sammy)

Notes There is also a vocal of "Bee Bom" by Les Vandyke.

3015 ✦ JOHNNY DANGEROUSLY
Twentieth Century–Fox, 1984

Musical Score Morris, John

Producer(s) Hertzberg, Michael
Director(s) Heckerling, Amy
Screenwriter(s) Steinberg, Norman; Kukoff, Bernie; Colomby, Harry; Harris, Jeff

Cast Keaton, Michael; Piscopo, Joe; Henner, Marilu; Stapleton, Maureen; Boyle, Peter; Dunne, Griffin; O'Connor, Glynnis; DeLuise, Dom; DeVito, Danny; Walston, Ray

Song(s) This Is the Life (C/L: Yankovic, "Weird" Al); Johnny Dangerously (C: Morris, John; L: Gimbel, Norman)

3016 ✦ JOHNNY DOUGHBOY
Republic, 1942

Composer(s) Styne, Jule
Lyricist(s) Cahn, Sammy

Producer(s) Auer, John H.
Director(s) Auer, John H.
Screenwriter(s) Kimble, Lawrence

Cast Withers, Jane; Wilcoxon, Henry; Brook, Patrick; Demarest, William; Donnelly, Ruth; Switzer, Carl "Alfalfa"; Baby Sandy; Collins, Cora Sue; McFarland, George "Spanky"; Breen, Bobby

Song(s) Baby's a Big Girl Now; All Done All Through; All My Life (C: Stept, Sam H.; L: Mitchell, Sidney D.); It Takes a Guy Like I; You Do My Eyes a Favor; Better Not Roll Those Blue Blue Eyes (C/L: Twomey, Ann; Goodhart, Al); Victory Caravan; Give the Kids a Chance [1]

Notes [1] Used instrumentally only.

3017 ✦ JOHNNY FEDORA
Disney, 1954

Song(s) Johnny Fedora and Alice Blue Bonnet (C/L: Wrubel, Allie; Wolcott, Charles; Schoen, Vic)

Notes Cartoon. No credit sheet available. This is part of MAKE MINE MUSIC.

3018 ✦ JOHNNY GUITAR
Republic, 1954

Musical Score Young, Victor

Producer(s) Ray, Nicholas
Director(s) Ray, Nicholas
Screenwriter(s) Yordan, Philip
Source(s) *Johnny Guitar* (novel) Chanslor, Roy

Cast Crawford, Joan; Hayden, Sterling; McCambridge, Mercedes; Brady, Scott; Bond, Ward; Borgnine, Ernest; Carradine, John; Dano, Royal; Williams, Rhys

Song(s) Johnny Guitar (C: Young, Victor; L: Lee, Peggy)

3019 ✦ JOHNNY HOLIDAY
United Artists, 1950

Producer(s) Alcorn, Roland
Director(s) Goldbeck, Willis
Screenwriter(s) Andrews, Jack; Stephens, Frederick

Cast Stephens, Frederick; Martin Jr., Allen; Clements, Stanley; Bendix, William; Gallagher, Donald; Hagen, Jack; Granstedt, Greta; Carmichael, Hoagy

Song(s) My Christmas Song for You (C: Carmichael, Hoagy; L: Peterson, Furniss T.)

Notes No cue sheet available.

3020 ✦ JOHNNY RENO
Paramount, 1966

Musical Score Haskell, Jimmie

Producer(s) Lyles, A.C.
Director(s) Springsteen, R.G.
Screenwriter(s) Fisher, Steve

Cast Andrews, Dana; Russell, Jane; Chaney Jr., Lon; Arlen, Richard; Agar, John; Bettger, Lyle; Drake, Tom; Lowery, Robert

Song(s) Johnny Reno (C: Haskell, Jimmie; L: Dunham, "By")

3021 ✦ JOHNNY SHILOH
Disney, 1962

Musical Score Baker, Buddy

Cast Corcoran, Kevin; Keith, Brian

Song(s) Johnny Shiloh (C/L: Sherman, Richard M.; Sherman, Robert B.)

Notes No credit sheet available.

3022 ✦ JOHNNY TREMAIN
Disney, 1957

Musical Score Bruns, George
Composer(s) Bruns, George
Lyricist(s) Blackburn, Tom

Director(s) Stevenson, Robert
Screenwriter(s) Blackburn, Tom
Source(s) *Johnny Tremain* (novel) Forbes, Esther

Cast Stalmaster, Hal; Patten, Luana; York, Jeff; Cabot, Sebastian; Beymer, Richard [1]; Lane, Rusty; Bissell, Whit; Hare, Lumsden

Song(s) Johnny Tremain; Liberty Tree

Notes [1] Billed as Dick Beymer.

3023 ✦ JOHNNY TROUBLE
Warner Brothers, 1957

Musical Score De Vol, Frank

Producer(s) Auer, John H.
Director(s) Auer, John H.
Screenwriter(s) O'Neal, Charles; Lord, David
Source(s) "Prodigal's Mother" (story) Williams, Ben Ames

Cast Barrymore, Ethel; Kellaway, Cecil; Jones, Carolyn; White, Jesse; Harper, Rand; Whitman, Stuart; Larson, Jack; Wallace, Paul; Byrnes, Edward; Tempo, Nino; King, Kip

Song(s) Johnny Trouble (C/L: Lee, Peggy)

3024 ✦ THE JOKER IS WILD
Paramount, 1957

Musical Score Scharf, Walter
Composer(s) Van Heusen, James
Lyricist(s) Cahn, Sammy
Choreographer(s) Earl, Josephine

Producer(s) Briskin, Samuel J.
Director(s) Vidor, Charles
Screenwriter(s) Saul, Oscar
Source(s) *The Joker Is Wild* (book) Cohn, Art

Cast Sinatra, Frank; Gaynor, Mitzi; Crain, Jeanne; Albert, Eddie; Garland, Beverly; De Corsia, Ted; Coogan, Jackie

Song(s) The Greatest Little Sign in the World [1]; All the Way; Simple Little Things (C/L: Harris, Harry); My Favorite Dream [1] (C/L: Harris, Harry); Buddy [1] (C/L: Harris, Harry); Naturally (C/L: Harris, Harry); My Dream Girl [1] (C/L: Harris, Harry)

Notes Also used vocally are "At Sundown" by Walter Donaldson; "I Cried for You" by Arthur Freed, Gus Arnheim and Abe Lyman; "Chicago" by Fred Fisher; "June in January" by Leo Robin and Ralph Rainger; "Out of Nowhere" by Edward Heyman and John W. Green and "Swinging on a Star" by Burke and Van Heusen. Harris also wrote parodies to "My Old Flame" (not used); "Swinging on a Star" (used); "All the Way" (used) and "Out of Nowhere" (used). [1] Not used.

3025 ✦ THE JOKERS
Universal, 1967

Musical Score Pearson, Johnny

Producer(s) Foster, Maurice
Director(s) Winner, Michael
Screenwriter(s) Clement, Dick; La Frenais, Ian

Cast Crawford, Michael; Reed, Oliver; Andrews, Harry; Donald, James; Massey, Daniel; Hordern, Michael; Finlay, Frank; Kempson, Rachel; Graves, Peter; Fox, Edward

Song(s) The Jokers (C/L: Mills, Charles; Leander, Mike)

3026 ✦ JOLSON SINGS AGAIN
Columbia, 1949

Musical Score Duning, George
Choreographer(s) Brier, Audrene

Producer(s) Buchman, Sidney
Director(s) Levin, Henry
Screenwriter(s) Buchman, Sidney

Cast Parks, Larry [1]; Hale, Barbara; Demarest, William; Donath, Ludwig; McCormick, Myron

Notes There are no original songs in this picture. Vocals include "Rock-A-Bye Your Baby with a Dixie Melody" by Jean Schwartz, Joe Young and Sam Lewis; "Is It True What They Say About Dixie" by Gerald Marks, Irving Caesar and Sammy Lerner; "For Me and My Gal" by George W. Meyer, Edgar Leslie and E. Ray Goetz; "Learn to Croon" by Sam Coslow and Arthur Johnston; the Hebrew traditional prayer "Eyl Moleh Rachamin"; "Back in Your Own Backyard" by Al Jolson, Dave Dreyer and Billy Rose; a war medley consisting of "I'm Looking Over a Four Leaf Clover" by Harry Woods and Mort Dixon; "When the Red, Red Robin Comes Bob Bob Bobbin' Along" by Harry Woods; "Give My Regards to Broadway" by George M. Cohan; "Chinatown, My Chinatown" by William Jerome and Jean Schwartz; "I'm Just Wild About Harry" by Noble Sissle and Eubie Blake; "Baby Face" by Benny Davis and Harry Akst; "After You've Gone" by Turner Layton and Henry Creamer; "I Only Have Eyes for You" by Al Dubin and Harry Warren; "Sonny Boy" by B.G. DeSylva, Lew Brown, Ray Henderson and Al Jolson;

"Toot Toot Tootsie" by Gus Kahn, Ernie Erdman and Dan Russo (Written for stage musical BOMBO and also in I'LL SEE YOU IN MY DREAMS, THE JAZZ SINGER, ROSE OF WASHINGTON SQUARE and THE JOLSON STORY); "California Here I Come" by Al Jolson, B.G. DeSylva and Joseph Meyer; "You Made Me Love You" by Joseph McCarthy and James V. Monaco; "Let Me Sing and I'm Happy" by Irving Berlin; "My Blushin' Rosie" by Edgar Smith and John Stromberg; "My Mammy" by Walter Donaldson, Sam Lewis and Joe Young; "Swanee" by George Gershwin and Irving Caesar; "The Spaniard That Blighted My Life" by Billy Merson; "About a Quarter to Nine" by Al Dubin and Harry Warren; "Anniversary Song" by Saul Chaplin and Al Jolson; "Waiting for the Robert E. Lee" by L. Wolfe Gilbert and Lewis F. Muir; "April Showers" by Louis Silvers and B.G. DeSylva; and "Carolina in the Morning" by Walter Donaldson and Gus Kahn. [1] Dubbed by Al Jolson.

3027 ◆ THE JOLSON STORY
Columbia, 1946

Choreographer(s)   Cole, Jack

Producer(s)   Skolsky, Sidney
Director(s)   Green, Alfred E.
Screenwriter(s)   Longstreet, Stephen

Cast   Parks, Larry [1]; Keyes, Evelyn [2]; Demarest, William; Goodwin, Bill; Donath, Ludwig; Shayne, Tamara; Alexander, John; Cossart, Ernest; Beckett, Scotty; Todd, Ann

Notes   Interpolated songs include "Let Me Sing and I'm Happy" by Irving Berlin; "On the Banks of the Wabash" by Paul Dresser; "Ahavas Olom," a traditional Jewish hymn; "Ave Maria" and "Oh Lord, I'm Not Worthy" traditional Catholic hymns; "When You Were Sweet Sixteen" by James Thornton; "After the Ball" by Charles K. Harris; "By the Light of the Silvery Moon" by Edward Madden and Gus Edwards; "Blue Bell" by Edward Madden and Theodore Morse; "My Blushing Rosie" by Edgar Smith and John Stromberg; "I Want a Girl" by Harry Von Tilzer and William Dillon; "My Mammy" by Sam Lewis, Joe Young and Walter Donaldson; "I'm Sitting on Top of the World" by Ray Henderson, Sam Lewis and Joe Young; "You Made Me Love You" by Joseph McCarthy and James V. Monaco; "Swanee" by Irving Caesar and George Gershwin; "Toot Toot Tootsie" by Gus Kahn, Ernie Erdman and Dan Russo (also in I'LL SEE YOU IN MY DREAMS, THE JAZZ SINGER, JOLSON SINGS AGAIN and ROSE OF WASHINGTON SQUARE. Originally in stage musical BOMBO); "The Spaniard that Blighted My Life" by Billy Merson; "April Showers" by B.G. DeSylva and Louis Silvers; "California Here I Come" by Al Jolson, Joseph Meyer and B.G. DeSylva; "Liza (All the Clouds Will Roll Away)" by George and Ira Gershwin;

"There's a Rainbow 'Round My Shoulder" by Al Jolson, Billy Rose and Dave Dreyer; "She's a Latin from Manhattan" by Harry Warren and Al Dubin; "Avalon" by Al Jolson, B.G. DeSylva and Vincent Rose; "About a Quarter to Nine" by Harry Warren and Al Dubin; "Anniversary Song" by Al Jolson and Saul Chaplin; "Waitin' for the Robert E. Lee" by L. Wolfe Gilbert and Lewis Muir; and "Rock-A-Bye Your Baby with a Dixie Melody" by Sam Lewis, Joe Young and Jean Schwartz. [1] Dubbed by Al Jolson. And then when Jolson refused to do redubbing, he was dubbed by Walter Craig. [2] Dubbed by Virginia Rees.

3028 ◆ JONATHAN LIVINGSTON SEAGULL
Paramount, 1973

Composer(s)   Diamond, Neil
Lyricist(s)   Diamond, Neil

Producer(s)   Bartlett, Hall
Director(s)   Bartlett, Hall
Screenwriter(s)   Bach, Richard
Source(s)   *Jonathan Livingston Seagull* (novel) Bach, Richard
Voices   Franciscus, James; Mills, Juliet; Holbrook, Hal; McGuire, Dorothy; Crenna, Richard

Song(s)   Be; Dear Father; Lonely Looking Sky; Anthem (Sanctus); Skybird

3029 ◆ JONES FAMILY IN TOO BUSY TO WORK
Twentieth Century–Fox, 1939

Producer(s)   Wurtzel, Sol M.
Director(s)   Brower, Otto
Screenwriter(s)   Ellis, Robert; Logan, Helen; Rauh, Stanley
Source(s)   *The Torchbearers* (play) Kelly, George; *Your Uncle Dudley* (play) Lindsay, Howard; Robinson, Bertrand

Cast   Prouty, Jed; Byington, Spring; Howell, Kenneth; Ernest, George; Carlson, June; Davis, Joan; Chandler, Chick; Gateson, Marjorie; Tombes, Andrew; Bacon, Irving

Song(s)   Arbor Day (C: Tresselt, Frank; L: Clare, Sidney)

Notes   Also titled TOO BUSY TO WORK.

3030 ◆ JOSEPH ANDREWS
United Artists/Paramount, 1977

Musical Score   Addison, John

Producer(s)   Hartley, Neil
Director(s)   Richardson, Tony
Screenwriter(s)   Scott, Allan; Bryant, Chris
Source(s)   *Joseph Andrews* (novel) Fielding, Henry

Cast Firth, Peter; Ogle, Natalie; Ann-Margaret; Dale, Jim; Reid, Beryl; Rossington, Norman; Rowlands, Patsy; Gielgud, John; Breslaw, Bernard

Song(s) He Was Such a Gentle Boy (C/L: Stewart, Bob); Pedlar's Life (C: Traditional; L: Stewart, Bob); Nun's Chant (C: Stewart, Bob; L: Scott, A.; Bryant, C.)

3031 ✦ JOSETTE
Twentieth Century–Fox, 1938

Composer(s) Revel, Harry
Lyricist(s) Gordon, Mack
Choreographer(s) Castle, Nick; Sawyer, Geneva

Producer(s) Markey, Gene
Director(s) Dwan, Allan
Screenwriter(s) Grant, James Edward

Cast Ameche, Don; Simon, Simone; Young, Robert; Davis, Joan; Lahr, Bert; Hurst, Paul; Collier Sr., William; Bari, Lynn; Demarest, William; Gillette, Ruth; Kaliz, Armand; Gottschalk, Ferdinand

Song(s) May I Drop a Petal in Your Glass of Wine; In Any Language; Where in the World [1]

Notes [1] Sheet music only.

3032 ✦ JOURNAL OF CRIME
Warner Brothers–First National, 1934

Producer(s) Blanke, Henry
Director(s) Keighley, William
Screenwriter(s) Herbert, F. Hugh; Kenyon, Charles

Cast Dodd, Claire; Barbier, George; Dumbrille, Douglass; Madison, Noel; O'Neill, Henry; Reed, Philip; Chatterton, Ruth; Menjou, Adolphe

Song(s) "Original" [1] (C/L: Stewart)

Notes [1] Song not identified on cue sheet.

3033 ✦ THE JOURNEY
Metro–Goldwyn–Mayer, 1972

Musical Score Auric, Georges

Producer(s) Litvak, Anatole
Director(s) Litvak, Anatole
Screenwriter(s) Tabori, George

Cast Kerr, Deborah; Brynner, Yul; Morley, Robert; Marshall, E.G.; Kasznar, Kurt; Jackson, Anne; Aimee, Anouk; Robards Jr., Jason

Song(s) Ou Kosta (Golden Evening) (C: Michelet, Michel; L: Budberg, Mura); Setet-Axeg (C: Michelet, Michel; L: Symanye, Tibor)

Notes Only original songs listed.

3034 ✦ JOURNEY INTO FEAR
RKO, 1943

Musical Score Webb, Roy

Producer(s) Welles, Orson
Director(s) Foster, Norman
Screenwriter(s) Cotten, Joseph
Source(s) *Journey Into Fear* (novel) Ambler, Eric

Cast Cotten, Joseph; Del Rio, Dolores; Warrick, Ruth; Moorehead, Agnes; Durant, Jack; Sloane, Everett; Wyatt, Eustace; Readick, Frank; Conried, Hans; Welles, Orson; Bennett, Richard; Meltzer, Robert; Schnabel, Stefan; Moss, Jack; Barrier, Edgar

Song(s) C'est Mon Couer [1] (C/L: Morgan, Stephen)

Notes [1] Also in GANGWAY FOR TOMORROW and VARIETY TIME.

3035 ✦ JOURNEY INTO LIGHT
Twentieth Century–Fox, 1951

Musical Score Newman, Emil

Producer(s) Bernhard, Joseph; Bond, Anson
Director(s) Heisler, Stuart
Screenwriter(s) Nordi, Stephani; Shulman, Irving

Cast Hayden, Sterling; Lindfors, Viveca; Mitchell, Thomas; Donath, Ludwig; Warner, H.B.; Darwell, Jane; Webster, Peggy; Bird, Billie

Song(s) If I Had a Million Dreams (C/L: Newman, Emil)

3036 ✦ JOURNEY TO SHILOH
Universal, 1968

Musical Score Gates, David

Producer(s) Christie, Howard
Director(s) Hale, William
Screenwriter(s) Coon, Gene
Source(s) *Field of Honor* (novel) Henry, Will

Cast Caan, James; Sarrazin, Michael; Scott, Brenda; Stroud, Don; Petersen, Paul; Burns, Michael; Vincent, Jan-Michael; Ford, Harrison; Beery Jr., Noah

Song(s) Journey to Shiloh [1] (C: Gates, David; L: Coon, Gene)

Notes [1] Based on "Yellow Rose of Texas."

3037 ✦ JOURNEY TO THE CENTER OF THE EARTH
Twentieth Century–Fox, 1959

Musical Score Herrmann, Bernard
Composer(s) Van Heusen, James
Lyricist(s) Cahn, Sammy

Producer(s) Brackett, Charles
Director(s) Levin, Henry
Screenwriter(s) Reisch, Walter; Brackett, Charles
Source(s) *Journey to the Center of the Earth* (novel) Verne, Jules

Cast Boone, Pat; Mason, James; Dahl, Arlene; Baker, Diane; David, Thayer; Napier, Alan

Song(s) The Faithful Heart [1]; My Love Is Like a Red, Red Rose (L: Burns, Robert); Twice as Tall; To the Center of the Earth [2] (C/L: Boone, Pat); Come Spring [3]; I'm Never Alone [3]

Notes [1] Instrumental use only. [2] Sheet music only. [3] Not used.

3038 ♦ JOY IN THE MORNING
Metro–Goldwyn–Mayer, 1965

Musical Score Herrmann, Bernard

Producer(s) Weinstein, Henry T.
Director(s) Segal, Alex
Screenwriter(s) Benson, Sally; Hayes, Alfred; Lessing, Norman
Source(s) *Joy in the Morning* (novel) Smith, Betty

Cast Kennedy, Arthur; Homolka, Oscar; Davis, Donald; Tetzel, Joan; Blackmer, Sidney; Gregg, Virginia; Mimieux, Yvette; Chamberlain, Richard

Song(s) Joy in the Morning (C: Fain, Sammy; L: Webster, Paul Francis)

3039 ♦ THE JOY OF LIVING
RKO, 1938

Composer(s) Kern, Jerome
Lyricist(s) Fields, Dorothy

Producer(s) Young, Felix
Director(s) Garnett, Tay
Screenwriter(s) Towne, Gene; Baker, Graham; Scott, Allan

Cast Dunne, Irene; Fairbanks Jr., Douglas; Brady, Alice; Kibbee, Guy; Dixon, Jean; Blore, Eric; Ball, Lucille; Hymer, Warren

Song(s) What's Good About Goodnight; You Couldn't Be Cuter; Just Let Me Look at You; A Heavenly Party

3040 ♦ THE JOY OF SEX
Paramount, 1984

Composer(s) Holiday, Bishop; Lipsker, Scott; Payne, Harold
Lyricist(s) Holiday, Bishop; Lipsker, Scott; Payne, Harold

Producer(s) Koningsberg, Frank
Director(s) Coolidge, Martha
Screenwriter(s) Rowell, Kathleen Knutson; Salter, J.J.
Source(s) *The Joy of Sex* (reference)

Cast Hudson, Ernie; Camp, Colleen; Lloyd, Christopher

Song(s) Experience; Jingle; Cross the Line; Can't Get Through to You; Hang Up; I'm a Hot Blooded Man; Why; Don't Fight It; Dreams (C/L: Payne, Harold; Jackson, Clydene)

Notes Joey Harris' "Don't Say Love" was used, though not written for the film.

3041 ♦ JOYRIDE
American International, 1977

Musical Score Haskell, Jimmie

Producer(s) Curtis, Bruce Cohn
Director(s) Ruben, Joseph
Screenwriter(s) Ruben, Joseph; Rainer, Peter

Cast Arnaz Jr., Desi; Carradine, Robert; Lockhart, Anne; Ligon, Tom; Griffith, Melanie

Song(s) The Best That I Know How (C/L: Mann, Barry; Weil, Cynthia)

Notes No cue sheet available.

3042 ♦ JOY STREET
Fox, 1929

Director(s) Cannon, Raymond
Screenwriter(s) Condon, Charles; Gay, Frank

Cast Moran, Lois; Stuart, Nick; Bell, Rex; Phipps, Sally; Crespo, Jose

Song(s) Lonely (C: Hirsch, Louis A.; L: Unknown)

3043 ♦ JUBILEE TRAIL
Republic, 1953

Musical Score Young, Victor
Composer(s) Young, Victor
Lyricist(s) Clare, Sidney
Choreographer(s) Baker, Jack

Producer(s) Kane, Joseph
Director(s) Kane, Joseph
Screenwriter(s) Manning, Bruce

Cast Ralston, Vera Hruba; Leslie, Joan; Tucker, Forrest; Russell, John; Middleton, Ray; O'Brien, Pat; Baer, Buddy; Davis, Jim; MacLane, Barton

Song(s) Saying No (C: Bristow, Owen; Young, Victor); Jubilee Trail; A Man Is a Man; Clap Your Hands

3044 ♦ JUDGEMENT AT NUREMBERG
United Artists, 1961

Musical Score Gold, Ernest

Producer(s) Kramer, Stanley
Director(s) Kramer, Stanley
Screenwriter(s) Mann, Abby

Source(s)   "Judgement at Nuremberg" (teleplay)
Mann, Abby

Cast   Tracy, Spencer; Lancaster, Burt; Dietrich, Marlene; Schell, Maximilian; Widmark, Richard; Garland, Judy; Clift, Montgomery; Klemperer, Werner; Brandt, Martin; Meyer, Torben; Shatner, William

Song(s)   Liebeslied (C: Gold, Ernest; L: Perry, Alfred); Care for Me [1] (C: Gold, Ernest; L: Stillman, Al)

Notes   There were several vocals of German folksongs. [1] Sheet music only.

3045 ✦ JUDGE PRIEST
Fox, 1934

Composer(s)   Mockridge, Cyril J.
Lyricist(s)   Trotti, Lamar; Nichols, Dudley

Producer(s)   Wurtzel, Sol M.
Director(s)   Ford, John
Screenwriter(s)   Nichols, Dudley; Trotti, Lamar
Source(s)   "Tree Full of Hoot Owls"; "Br'er Fox and the Briar Patch"; "Words and Music" (stories) Cobb, Irvin S.

Cast   Rogers, Will; Brown, Tom; Louise, Anita; Hudson, Rochelle

Song(s)   Spirituals; Massa Jesus Wrote Me a Song

3046 ✦ THE JUDGE STEPS OUT
RKO, 1947

Musical Score   Harline, Leigh

Producer(s)   Kraike, Michel
Director(s)   Ingster, Boris
Screenwriter(s)   Ingster, Boris; Knox, Alexander

Cast   Knox, Alexander; Sothern, Ann; Tobias, George; Moffett, Sharyn; Bates, Florence; Inescort, Frieda; Dell, Myrna; Wolfe, Ian; Warner, H.B.; Hyer, Martha; Warren, James

Song(s)   Moonlight Over the Islands [1] (C: Pollack, Lew; L: Greene, Mort)

Notes   [1] Also in BAMBOO BLONDE and MAKE MINE LAUGHS.

3047 ✦ JUDITH
Paramount, 1966

Musical Score   Kaplan, Sol

Producer(s)   Unger, Kurt
Director(s)   Mann, Daniel
Screenwriter(s)   Hayes, John Michael
Source(s)   (story) Durrell, Lawrence

Cast   Loren, Sophia; Finch, Peter; Hawkins, Jack

Song(s)   Kibbutz Hora (C/L: Kaplan, Sol); Judith [1] (C: Kaplan, Sol; L: Shuman, Earl)

Notes   [1] Lyrics added after film for exploitation purposes only.

3048 ✦ JUDY GOES TO TOWN

See PUDDIN' HEAD.

3049 ✦ JUKE BOX JENNY
Universal, 1942

Composer(s)   Rosen, Milton
Lyricist(s)   Carter, Everett

Producer(s)   Sandford, Joseph G.
Director(s)   Young, Harold
Screenwriter(s)   Lees, Robert; Rinaldo, Frederic I.

Cast   Hilliard, Harriet; Murray, Ken; Douglas, Don; Adrian, Iris; Barnet, Charlie; Wingy Manone and His Orchestra; The King's Men

Song(s)   Swing It Mother Goose; Give Out [1]; Macumba [2]

Notes   Other vocals included "Fifty Million Nickels" by Charlie Barnet; "Then You'll Remember Me" by M.W. Balfe; "Carry Me Back to Old Virginny" by James A. Bland and "Sweet Genevieve" by G. Cooper and H. Tucker. [1] Also in MY GAL LOVES MUSIC. [2] Sheet music only.

3050 ✦ JUKE BOX RHYTHM
Columbia, 1959

Musical Score   Morton, Arthur
Choreographer(s)   Belfer, Hal

Producer(s)   Katzman, Sam
Director(s)   Dreifuss, Arthur
Screenwriter(s)   McCall Jr., Mary C.; Baldwin, Earl

Cast   Jessel, George; Morrow, Beverly Jo; Earl Grant Trio [1]; The Nitwits [2]; Otis, Johnny; The Treniers [3]; Jones, Jack; Conried, Hans; Inescort, Frieda; Donlevy, Brian; Feld, Fritz

Song(s)   Juke Box Jamboree (C: Karger, Fred; L: Quine, Richard; Styne, Stanley); I Feel It Right Here (C/L: Graham, Steve; Pober, Leon); The Freeze (C/L: Savoe, Tony; Saraceno, Joe); Make Room for the Joy (C: Bacharach, Burt; L: David, Hal); Spring Is the Season for Remembering (C: Oakland, Ben; L: Jessel, George); Let's Fall in Love [4] (C: Arlen, Harold; L: Koehler, Ted); Get Out of the Car (C/L: Trenier, Claude; Trenier, Cliff; Gilbeaux, Gene); Willie and the Hand Jive (C/L: Otis, Johnny); Last Night (C/L: Lampert, Diane; Pober, Leon)

Notes   It is not known if any of these were written for the film. [1] Consisted of Earl Grant, Edward W. Hunton and Fred Clark. [2] Consisted of Sid Millward and Wally Stewart. [3] Consisted of Claude Clifton and Milton Trenier, Eugene Gilbeaux, James Johnson,

Donald Hill and Henry Green. [4] Also in LET'S FALL IN LOVE, ON THE SUNNY SIDE OF THE STREET, SENIOR PROM and SLIGHTLY FRENCH.

3051 ✦ JUKE GIRL
Warner Brothers, 1942

Musical Score   Deutsch, Adolph
Composer(s)   Jerome, M.K.
Lyricist(s)   Scholl, Jack

Producer(s)   Wallis, Hal B.
Director(s)   Bernhardt, Curtis
Screenwriter(s)   Bezzerides, A.I.
Source(s)   "Jook Girl" (story) Pratt, Theodore

Cast   Sheridan, Ann; Reagan, Ronald; Whorf, Richard; Lockhart, Gene; Brewer, Betty; Emerson, Faye; Tobias, George; Hale, Alan; Da Silva, Howard; McBride, Donald; Knight, Fuzzy; Best, Willie; Bacon, Irving; Robertson, Willard

Song(s)   I Hates Love; I Got Me a Blue Bell

3052 ✦ JULIA MISBEHAVES
Metro–Goldwyn–Mayer, 1948

Musical Score   Deutsch, Adolph

Producer(s)   Riskin, Everett
Director(s)   Conway, Jack
Screenwriter(s)   Ludwig, William; Ruskin, Harry; Wimperis, Arthur
Source(s)   *The Nutmeg Tree* (novel) Sharp, Margery

Cast   Garson, Greer; Pidgeon, Walter; Lawford, Peter; Taylor, Elizabeth; Romero, Cesar; Watson, Lucile; Bruce, Nigel; Boland, Mary; Owen, Reginald; Stephenson, Henry; Mather, Aubrey; Borg, Veda Ann

Song(s)   When You're Playing with Fire (C: Borne, Hal; Deutsch, Adolph; L: Seelen, Jerry) [1]

Notes   Originally titled SPEAK TO ME OF LOVE. There is also a vocal of "Oh! What a Difference the Navy's Meant to Me" by Alleyn and Stanley. [1] Deutsch not credited on sheet music.

3053 ✦ JULIE
Metro–Goldwyn–Mayer, 1956

Musical Score   Stevens, Leith

Producer(s)   Melcher, Martin
Director(s)   Stone, Andrew L.
Screenwriter(s)   Stone, Andrew L.

Cast   Day, Doris; Jourdan, Louis; Sullivan, Barry; Lovejoy, Frank; Kelly, Jack; Kruschen, Jack; Marsh, Mae; Robinson, Ann; Phillips, Barney

Song(s)   Julie (C: Stevens, Leith; L: Adair, Tom); Midnight on the Cliff (Inst.) (C: Pennario, Leonard)

3054 ✦ JUMBO

See BILLY ROSE'S JUMBO.

3055 ✦ JUMPING JACKS
Paramount, 1952

Composer(s)   Livingston, Jerry
Lyricist(s)   David, Mack
Choreographer(s)   Sidney, Robert

Producer(s)   Wallis, Hal B.
Director(s)   Taurog, Norman
Screenwriter(s)   Lees, Robert; Rinaldo, Frederic I.; Baker, Herbert; Allardice, James B.; Weil, Richard

Cast   Martin, Dean; Lewis, Jerry; Freeman, Mona; DeFore, Don; Strauss, Robert

Song(s)   I Can't Resist a Boy in a Uniform; Keep a Little Dream Handy; The Parachute Jump; The Big Blue Sky (Is the Place for Me); I Know a Dream When I See One; An Old Fashioned Song for an Old Fashioned Girl [1]; The Lonesome Coyote [1]; What Have You Done for Me Lately? [2]

Notes   Originally titled READY, WILLING AND ABLE. [1] Not used. [2] Only in film for 12 seconds and 8 of those were only whistling. Not used in SCARED STIFF.

3056 ✦ JUMPIN' JACK FLASH
Twentieth Century–Fox, 1986

Musical Score   Newman, Thomas

Producer(s)   Gordon, Lawrence; Silver, Joel
Director(s)   Marshall, Penny
Screenwriter(s)   Franzoni, David H.; Melville, J.W.; Irving, Patricia; Thompson, Christopher

Cast   Goldberg, Whoopi; Collins, Stephen; Wood, John; Kane, Carol; Potts, Annie; Goetz, Peter Michael; Browne, Roscoe Lee; Botsford, Sara; Pryce, Jonathan; Hendra, Tony; Lovitz, Jon; Woods, Ren; Belushi, James; Whitehead, Paxton; Ullman, Tracey; Landers, Matt; Nunez Jr., Angel; Marshall, Garry

Song(s)   Set Me Free (C/L: Willis, Allee; Sembello, Danny; Weil, Cynthia); Jumpin' Jack Flash (C/L: Jagger, Mick; Richards, Keith); A Trick of the Night (C/L: Jolley, Steve; Swain, Tony); Window to the World (C/L: Sargent, Laurie); You Can't Hurry Love (C/L: Holland, Eddie; Dozier, Lamont; Holland, Brian); Hold On (C/L: Branigan, Billy); Misled (C/L: Bell, Ronald; Taylor, James; Kool & the Gang); Rescue Me (C/L: Smith, Carl William; Minor, Raynard)

Notes   It is not known if any of these were written for this production.

3057 ✦ JUNCTION CITY
Columbia, 1952

Director(s) Nazarro, Ray
Screenwriter(s) Shipman, Barry

Cast Starrett, Charles; Burnette, Smiley; Mahoney, Jock; Castle, Anita; Case, Kathleen

Song(s) The Glory Train (C/L: Richman, Ace; Smith, J.O.; Wallace, Eddie; Smith, Audrey Lee); Little Injun [1] (C/L: Burnette, Smiley)

Notes [1] Written in 1949 as "Li'l Indian."

3058 ✦ JUNE MOON
Paramount, 1931

Composer(s) Kaufman, George S.; Lardner, Ring
Lyricist(s) Kaufman, George S.; Lardner, Ring

Director(s) Sutherland, Edward
Screenwriter(s) Mankiewicz, Joseph L.; Lawrence, Vincent; Thompson, Keene
Source(s) *June Moon* (play) Kaufman, George S.; Lardner, Ring

Cast Oakie, Jack; Dee, Frances; Gibson, Wynne; Akst, Harry; MacCloy, June; Hardy, Sam

Song(s) Hello Tokio [3]; June Moon; Give Our Child a Name; Montana Moon; Got a Man on My Mind (Worryin' Away) [1] (C: Rainger, Ralph; L: Howard, Dick [2])

Notes See notes for the 1937 film BLONDE TROUBLE. [1] Also in ANYBODY'S WOMAN. [2] Pseudonym for Howard Dietz. [3] Also in BLONDE TROUBLE.

3059 ✦ THE JUNGLE BOOK
Disney, 1967

Musical Score Bruns, George
Composer(s) Sherman, Richard M.; Sherman, Robert B.
Lyricist(s) Sherman, Richard M.; Sherman, Robert B.

Director(s) Reitherman, Wolfgang
Screenwriter(s) Clemmons, Larry; Wright, Ralph; Anderson, Ken; Gerry, Vance
Source(s) Mowgli stories (stories) Kipling, Rudyard
Voices Harris, Phil; Cabot, Sebastian; Prima, Louis; Sanders, George; Holloway, Sterling; O'Malley, J. Pat; Reitherman, Bruce; Felton, Verna; Howard, Clint; Stuart, Chad; Hudson, Lord Tim; Abbott, John; Wright, Ben; Carr, Darleen

Directing Animator(s) Kahl, Milt; Thomas, Franklin; Johnston, Ollie; Lounsbery, John

Song(s) The Bare Necessities (C/L: Gilkyson, Terry); Colonel Hathi's March; I Wan'na Be Like You; My Own Home; That's What Friends Are For; Trust in Me [3]; Baloo's Blues [1]; Kalaweeta Kaliana [1] (C/L: Gilkyson, Terry); What'cha Wanna Do? [2] (C: Bruns, George; L: Clemmons, Larry); Song of the Seeonee [1] (C/L: Gilkyson, Terry); I Knew I Belonged to Her [1] (C/L: Gilkyson, Terry); In a Day's Work [1] (C/L: Gilkyson, Terry)

Notes Animated feature. [1] Not used. [2] Lyric written for exploitation only. [3] Music from "Land and Sand," cut from MARY POPPINS.

3060 ✦ JUNGLE PATROL
Twentieth Century–Fox, 1948

Musical Score Newman, Emil; Lange, Arthur

Producer(s) Seltzer, Frank N.
Director(s) Newman, Joseph
Screenwriter(s) Swann, Francis

Cast Miller, Kristine; Franz, Arthur; Ford, Ross; Noonan, Tommy [1]; Reynolds, Gene; Jaeckel, Richard; Lauter, Harry

Song(s) Forever and Always (C/L: Rinker, Al; Huddleston, Floyd)

Notes Originally titled WEST OF TOMORROW. [1] Billed as Tom Noonan.

3061 ✦ THE JUNGLE PRINCESS
Paramount, 1936

Producer(s) Sheldon, E. Lloyd
Director(s) Thiele, William
Screenwriter(s) Hume, Cyril; Morris, Gouverneur; Geraghty, Gerald

Cast Lamour, Dorothy; Milland, Ray; Tamiroff, Akim; Overman, Lynne

Song(s) Moonlight and Shadows (C: Hollander, Frederick; L: Robin, Leo)

3062 ✦ JUNIOR PROM
Monogram, 1946

Choreographer(s) Collins, Dean

Producer(s) Katzman, Sam
Director(s) Dreifuss, Arthur
Screenwriter(s) Lazarus, Erna; Collins, Hal

Cast Stewart, Frankie; Preisser, June; Clark, Judy; Neill, Noel; Moran, Jackie; Darro, Frankie; Lyman, Abe; Heywood, Eddie; The Airliners

Song(s) Keep the Beat (C/L: Robin, Sid); Teen Canteen (C/L: Robin, Sid); Trumbull for President (C/L: Cowan, Stanley)

Notes No cue sheet available. There are also vocals of "Loch Lomond," "It's Me Oh Lawd" and "(All of a Sudden) My Heart Sings" by Herpin and Jamblan with English lyrics by Harold Rome.

3063 ✦ JUPITER'S DARLING
Metro–Goldwyn–Mayer, 1955

Musical Score   Rose, David
Composer(s)   Lane, Burton
Lyricist(s)   Adamson, Harold
Choreographer(s)   Pan, Hermes

Producer(s)   Wells, George
Director(s)   Sidney, George
Screenwriter(s)   Kingsley, Dorothy
Source(s)   *Road to Rome* (play) Sherwood, Robert E.

Cast   Williams, Esther [1]; Keel, Howard; Champion, Marge; Champion, Gower; Sanders, George; Haydn, Richard; Demarest, William; Varden, Norma; Dumbrille, Douglass; Corden, Henry; Ansara, Michael

Song(s)   Horatio's Narration (C: Chaplin, Saul; L: Wells, George; Sidney, George; Kingsley, Dorothy; Adamson, Harold; Chaplin, Saul); If This Be Slav'ry; I Have a Dream; Hannibal's Victory March; I Never Trust a Woman; Don't Let This Night Get Away; The Life of an Elephant

Notes   The last MGM film for Esther Williams, Marge and Gower Champion and George Sidney. [1] Dubbed by Jo Ann Greer.

3064 ✦ JUST AROUND THE CORNER
Twentieth Century–Fox, 1938

Composer(s)   Spina, Harold
Lyricist(s)   Bullock, Walter
Choreographer(s)   Castle, Nick; Sawyer, Geneva

Producer(s)   Zanuck, Darryl F.
Director(s)   Cummings, Irving
Screenwriter(s)   Hill, Ethel; McEvoy, J.P.; Wise, Darrell

Cast   Temple, Shirley; Davis, Joan; Farrell, Charles; Duff, Amanda; Robinson, Bill; Lahr, Bert; Pangborn, Franklin; Witherspoon, Cora; Gillingwater, Claude

Song(s)   This Is a Happy Little Ditty; Brass Buttons and Epaulets; I Love to Walk in the Rain

3065 ✦ JUST FOR YOU
Paramount, 1952

Composer(s)   Warren, Harry
Lyricist(s)   Robin, Leo
Choreographer(s)   Tamiris, Helen

Producer(s)   Duggan, Pat
Director(s)   Nugent, Elliott
Screenwriter(s)   Carson, Robert
Source(s)   *Famous* (novel) Benet, Stephen Vincent

Cast   Crosby, Bing; Wyman, Jane; Barrymore, Ethel; Arthur, Bob; Wood, Natalie

Song(s)   Just for You; Zing a Little Zong; I'll Si-Si Ya in Bahia; He's Just Crazy for Me; Call Me Tonight; Checkin' My Heart; The Live Oak Tree; The Maiden of Guadalupe; On the 10:10 (From Ten-Ten-Tennessee); The Ol' Spring Fever [1]; A Flight of Fancy [1]

Notes   [1] Not used. These numbers appear as instrumental backgrounds.

3066 ✦ JUST IMAGINE
Fox, 1930

Composer(s)   Henderson, Ray
Lyricist(s)   DeSylva, B.G.; Brown, Lew
Choreographer(s)   Felix, Seymour

Producer(s)   DeSylva, B.G.; Brown, Lew; Henderson, Ray
Director(s)   Butler, David
Screenwriter(s)   DeSylva, B.G.; Brown, Lew; Henderson, Ray

Cast   Brendel, El; O'Sullivan, Maureen; Garrick, John; White, Marjorie; Albertson, Frank

Song(s)   (There's Something About An) Old Fashioned Girl [3]; Mothers Ought to Tell Their Daughters; Tain't No Sin (C: Donaldson, Walter; L: Leslie, Edgar); Sunny Side Up [4]; I Am the Words (You Are the Melody); Drinking Song; Never Swat a Fly [1]; The Romance of Elmer Stremingway; Monkey Dance (inst.); Dance of Victory (Inst.); Mars Sequence (Inst.); Never Never Wed [2]

Notes   [1] *Variety* reviewed a print in which this number had been cut. [2] This song appears in some sources but not on cue sheet. [3] Also in GIRLS DEMAND EXCITEMENT. [4] Also in SUNNY SIDE UP.

3067 ✦ JUSTINE
Twentieth Century–Fox, 1970

Musical Score   Goldsmith, Jerry
Composer(s)   Goldsmith, Jerry
Lyricist(s)   Shaper, Hal

Producer(s)   Berman, Pandro S.
Director(s)   Cukor, George
Screenwriter(s)   Marcus, Lawrence B.
Source(s)   *The Alexandria Quartet* (novels) Durrell, Lawrence

Cast   Aimee, Anouk; Bogarde, Dirk; Forster, Robert; Karina, Anna; Noiret, Philippe; York, Michael; Vernon, John; Albertson, Jack; Gorman, Cliff; Constantine, Michael

Song(s)   Justine [1]; Melissa [1]

Notes   [1] Presented instrumentally only.

3068 ✦ JUST ONE OF THE GUYS
Columbia, 1985

Musical Score Scott, Tom

Producer(s) Fogelson, Andrew
Director(s) Gottlieb, Lisa
Screenwriter(s) Feldman, Dennis; Franklin, Jeff

Cast Hyser, Joyce; Rohner, Clayton; Jacoby, Billy; Hudson, Tom; Zabka, William; McCloskey, Leigh

Song(s) Girl Got Something Boys Ain't Got (C/L: Morrow, Marvin; Geyer, Stephen); Comb My Hair (C/L: Lyon, John; Firestone, Rod); Thrills (C/L: Tanner, Marc; Reede, Jon; Aniello, Ron); Gone too Far (C/L: Piccirillo, Mike; Goetzman, Gary); Just One of the Guys (C/L: Tanner, Marc; Reede, Jon); Bones (C/L: Lacques, Paul); Prove It to You (C/L: Tanner, Marc; Romersa, Joe; Edwards, Ron E.); Tonight You're Mine Baby (C/L: Walden, Narada Michael; Glass, Preston); Turn Out Right (C/L: Shaffer, Paul; Butler, Jack); Way Down (C/L: Burnette, Billy; Johnson, Danny)

3069 ✦ JUST THE WAY YOU ARE
Metro–Goldwyn–Mayer, 1984

Musical Score Cosma, Vladimir

Producer(s) Fuchs, Leo L.
Director(s) Molinaro, Edouard
Screenwriter(s) Burns, Allan

Cast McNichol, Kristy; Ontkean, Michael; Hunter, Kaki; Guest, Lance; Paul, Alexandra; Dussollier, Andre; Daly, Timothy; Cassidy, Patrick; Salviat, Catherine; Carradine, Robert

Song(s) Whirly Girl (C/L: Angel, I.); Dance All Night (C/L: Angel, I.; Orlando; Alway, F.; Childs, C.); I Know There's Something Going On (C/L: Ballard, Russ); My Ride (C/L: Angel, I.; Orlando); Voulez-Vous (C/L: Anderson, Benny; Ulvaeus, Bjorn); Just the Way You Are [1] (C/L: Cosma, Vladimir)

Notes It is not known if any of these were written for this film. [1] Sheet music only.

K

3070 ✦ KALEIDOSCOPE
Warner Brothers, 1966

Musical Score   Myers, Stanley

Producer(s)   Kastner, Elliott
Director(s)   Smight, Jack
Screenwriter(s)   Carrington, Robert; Carrington, Jane-Howard

Cast   Beatty, Warren; York, Susannah; Revill, Clive; Porter, Eric; Melvin, Murray; Sewell, George

Song(s)   Mein Baby Komm (C/L: Myers, Stanley)

3071 ✦ THE KANSAN
United Artists, 1943

Producer(s)   Sherman, Harry
Director(s)   Archainbaud, George
Screenwriter(s)   Shumate, Harold
Source(s)   *Peace Marshall* (novel) Gruber, Frank

Cast   Dix, Richard; Wyatt, Jane; Dekker, Albert; Pallette, Eugene; Jory, Victor; Armstrong, Robert; Wallace, Beryl; Cavanaugh, Hobart; Best, Willie; Cameron, Rod

Song(s)   Lullaby of the Herd [1] (C: Ohman, Phil; L: Carling, Foster)

Notes   [1] Not used in the Paramount film THE RENEGADE TRAIL.

3072 ✦ KANSAS CITY BOMBER
Metro–Goldwyn–Mayer, 1972

Musical Score   Ellis, Don
Composer(s)   Ellis, Don

Producer(s)   Elfand, Martin
Director(s)   Freedman, Jerrold
Screenwriter(s)   Rickman, Tom; Clements, Calvin

Cast   Welch, Raquel; McCarthy, Kevin; Kallianiotes, Helena; Alden, Norman; Cooper, Jeanne; Pass, Mary Kay; Bartlett, Martine; Foster, Jodie

Song(s)   Your Way Ain't My Way, Baby (L: Liebling, Howard; Thomas, Jeff); Rounds and Spheres [1] (L: Eckstein, Maria); All Night Market [1] (L: Liebling, Howard)

Notes   [1] Used instrumentally only.

3073 ✦ KANSAS CITY KITTY
Columbia, 1944

Producer(s)   Richmond, Ted
Director(s)   Lord, Del
Screenwriter(s)   Seff, Manuel; Brice, Monte

Cast   Davis, Joan; Crosby, Bob; Frazee, Jane; Rolf, Erik; Ryan, Tim; Keane, Robert Emmett; The Williams Brothers; Willis, Matt

Song(s)   Take It From Me (C/L: Chaplin, Saul); Kansas City Kitty (C: Donaldson, Walter; L: Leslie, Edgar); Tico Tico No Fuba [1] (C: Abreu, Zequinha; L: Oliveira, Aloysio; Drake, Ervin); Pretty Kitty Blues Eyes (C/L: Mizzy, Vic; Curtis, Mann); Nothin' Boogie from Nowhere [2] (C/L: Chaplin, Saul)

Notes   [1] Also in GAY SENORITA, BOMBALERA (Paramount), BATHING BEAUTY (MGM), COPACABANA (UA) and IT'S A PLEASURE (RKO). Drake wrote the English lyrics. [2] Also in TWO BLONDES AND A REDHEAD.

3074 ✦ KARATE KID
Columbia, 1984

Musical Score   Conti, Bill

Producer(s)   Weintraub, Jerry
Director(s)   Avildsen, John G.
Screenwriter(s)   Kamen, Robert Mark

Cast   Macchio, Ralph; Morita, Pat [2]; Shue, Elisabeth; Kove, Martin; Heller, Randee; Zabka, William; Thomas, Ron; Garrison, Rob; McQueen, Chad; O'Dell, Tony; Juarbe, Israel

Song(s)   (Bop Bop) On the Beach (C/L: Love, Mike); (It Takes) Two to Tango (C/L: Lambert, Dennis; Beckett, Peter); The Ride (C/L: Rose, Geoffrey; Rose, Sam); Rhythm Man (C/L: St. Regis, M.; St. Regis, G.; Peters, J.; Adams, R.; Flashman, A.; Hutt, A.; Challen, G.); Please Answer Me (C/L: Mark, John; Fenton, Richard); No Shelter (C/L: Mark, John; Fenton, Richard); Desire (C/L: Gill, Andy; King, Jon); Young Hearts (C/L: Merenda, David); You're the Best (C: Conti, Bill; L: Willis, Allee); Moment of Truth (C: Conti, Bill; L: Lambert, Dennis; Beckett, Peter); Feel the Night [1] (C: Conti, Bill; L: Robertson, Baxter)

Notes [1] Instrumental use only. Most of these are background vocals. [2] Billed as Noriyuki "Pat" Morita.

3075 ✦ THE KARATE KID PART II
Columbia, 1986

Musical Score Conti, Bill

Producer(s) Weintraub, Jerry
Director(s) Avildsen, John G.
Screenwriter(s) Kamen, Robert Mark

Cast Morita, Pat; Macchio, Ralph; McCarthy, Nobu; Kamekona, Danny; Tomita, Tamlyn; Okumoto, Yuji; Tanimoto, Charlie

Song(s) Glory of Love (Theme from the Karate Kid II) (C/L: Cetera, Peter; Foster, David; Nini, Diane); Two Looking at One (C/L: Conti, Bill; Simon, Carly; Brackman, Jacob)

3076 ✦ THE KARATE KILLERS
Metro–Goldwyn–Mayer, 1967

Musical Score Riddle, Nelson; Fried, Gerald [1]

Producer(s) Ingster, Boris
Director(s) Shear, Barry
Screenwriter(s) Ingster, Boris

Cast Vaughn, Robert; McCallum, David; Jurgens, Curt; Lom, Herbert; Savalas, Telly; Terry-Thomas; Carroll, Leo G.; Darby, Kim; McBain, Diane; Ireland, Jill; de Metz, Danielle; Tsu, Irene; Crawford, Joan

Song(s) Come on Down to My Boat (C/L: Farrell, Wes; Goldstein, Jerry)

Notes This is a MAN FROM U.N.C.L.E. movie. [1] Theme by Gerald Fried.

3077 ✦ KATHLEEN
Metro–Goldwyn–Mayer, 1941

Musical Score Waxman, Franz

Producer(s) Haight, George
Director(s) Bucquet, Harold S.
Screenwriter(s) McCall Jr., Mary C.

Cast Temple, Shirley; Marshall, Herbert; Day, Laraine; Patrick, Gail; Bressart, Felix

Song(s) Around the Corner (C/L: Edens, Roger; Brent, Earl)

Notes Shirley Temple's only MGM film.

3078 ✦ KATHY O
Universal, 1958

Producer(s) Gomberg, Sy
Director(s) Sher, Jack
Screenwriter(s) Sher, Jack; Gomberg, Sy

Source(s) "Memo on Kathy O'Rourke" (story) Sher, Jack

Cast McCormack, Patty; Duryea, Dan; Sterling, Jan; Croft, Mary Jane; Fickett, Mary; Levene, Sam

Song(s) Kathy-O (C/L: Tobias, Charles; Sher, Jack; Joseph, Ray)

Notes Originally titled THE MAGNIFICENT BRAT.

3079 ✦ KATIE DID IT
Universal, 1950

Musical Score Skinner, Frank

Producer(s) Goldstein, Leonard
Director(s) de Cordova, Frederick
Screenwriter(s) Brodney, Oscar; Henley, Jack

Cast Blyth, Ann; Kellaway, Cecil; Stevens, Mark; Stevens, Craig; White, Jesse; Bacon, Irving

Song(s) A Little Old Cape Cod Cottage (C/L: Shapiro, Dan; Lee, Lester)

3080 ✦ KATINA

See ICELAND.

3081 ✦ KAZABLAN
Metro–Goldwyn–Mayer, 1974

Musical Score Seltzer, Dov
Composer(s) Seltzer, Dov
Lyricist(s) Ettinger, Amos [1]
Choreographer(s) Braun, Shimon

Producer(s) Golan, Menahem
Director(s) Golan, Menahem
Screenwriter(s) Golan, Menahem; Hefer, Haim [1]
Source(s) (musical) Mossinson, Yigal; Silberg, Yoel; Hefer, Haim; Almagor, Dan; Ettinger, Amos

Cast Gaon, Yehoram; Elias, Arie; Lavie, Efrat; Efroni, Yehudah; Grotes, Esther

Song(s) Man of Respect (L: Almagor, Dan); We Are All Jews (L: Hefer, Haim); There's a Place; Democracy; Hey, What's Up! (L: Hefer, Haim); Jaffa; Rosa, Rosa (L: Hefer, Haim); Kazablan (Get Off My Back) (L: Ettinger, Amos; Almagor, Dan); Brith Milah Pageant (L: Hefer, Haim); This Little Boy Will Be a Great Man (L: Hefer, Haim); Who Will Make Me Fly Away (L: Hefer, Haim)

Notes [1] English adaptation of script and all lyrics by David Paulsen.

3082 ✦ KEEP 'EM FLYING
Universal, 1941

Composer(s) de Paul, Gene
Lyricist(s) Raye, Don

Producer(s) Tryon, Glenn
Director(s) Lubin, Arthur
Screenwriter(s) Boardman, True; Perrin, Nat; Grant, John

Cast Abbott, Bud; Costello, Lou; Raye, Martha; Foran, Dick; Bruce, Carol; Gargan, William; Lang, Charles; Smith, Loring

Song(s) Pig Foot Pete; Let's Keep 'Em Flying; The Boy with the Wistful Eyes [1]; Together [2]; You Don't Know What Love Is [3]

Notes There is also a rendition of "I'm Gettin' Sentimental Over You" by Ned Washington and George Bassman. "Time on My Hands" by Vincent Youmans, Harold Adamson and Mack Gordon is recorded but not used. [1] Later in "KEEP 'EM SLUGGING" and also in BUTCH MINDS THE BABY. [2] Not used but recorded. [3] Sheet music only.

3083 ◆ KEEP 'EM ROLLING

Universal, 1942

Cast Peerce, Jan

Song(s) Keep 'Em Rolling (C: Rodgers, Richard; L: Hart, Lorenz)

Notes No cue sheet available. Short subject.

3084 ◆ KELLY'S HEROES

Metro–Goldwyn–Mayer, 1970

Musical Score Schifrin, Lalo
Composer(s) Schifrin, Lalo

Producer(s) Katzka, Gabriel; Beckerman, Sidney
Director(s) Hutton, Brian G.
Screenwriter(s) Martin, Troy Kennedy

Cast Eastwood, Clint; Savalas, Telly; Rickles, Don; O'Connor, Carroll; Sutherland, Donald

Song(s) Burning Bridges (L: Curb, Mike); All for the Love of Sunshine (L: Curb, Mike; Hatcher, Harley); Si Tu Me Dis (L: Lees, Gene)

3085 ◆ THE KENTUCKIAN

United Artists, 1955

Musical Score Herrmann, Bernard
Composer(s) Gordon, Irving
Lyricist(s) Gordon, Irving

Producer(s) Hecht, Harold
Director(s) Lancaster, Burt
Screenwriter(s) Guthrie Jr., A.B.
Source(s) *The Gabriel Horn* (novel) Holt, Felix

Cast Lancaster, Burt; McIntire, John; Matthau, Walter; Carradine, John; Foster, Dianne

Song(s) Possum Up a Gum Tree; I See My Darlin'; Land of Promise; The Texas Song; Where, Oh, Where Is Dear Little Jennie

3086 ◆ KENTUCKY KERNALS

RKO, 1934

Composer(s) Ruby, Harry
Lyricist(s) Kalmar, Bert

Producer(s) Swanson, H.N.
Director(s) Stevens, George
Screenwriter(s) Kalmar, Bert; Ruby, Harry; Guiol, Fred

Cast Wheeler, Bert; Woolsey, Robert; Carlisle, Mary; McFarland, George "Spanky"; Beery, Noah; LaVerne, Lucille; Sleep 'N' Eat; Dumont, Margaret

Song(s) One Little Kiss; Supper Song

3087 ◆ KENTUCKY MOONSHINE

Twentieth Century–Fox, 1938

Composer(s) Pollack, Lew
Lyricist(s) Mitchell, Sidney D.

Producer(s) Zanuck, Darryl F.
Director(s) Butler, David
Screenwriter(s) Arthur, Art; Musselman, M.M.

Cast The Ritz Brothers; Martin, Tony; Weaver, Marjorie; Summerville, Slim; Carradine, John; Vernon, Wally; Treen, Mary

Song(s) Reuben, Reuben I've Been Swingin'(L: Mitchell, Sidney D.; Kuller, Sid; Golden, Ray); Moonshine Over Kentucky; Sing a Song of Harvest [1]; Kentucky in the Moonlight (C/L: Styne, Jule; Kuller, Sid; Golden, Ray); Kentucky Opera (C/L: Styne, Jule; Kuller, Sid; Golden, Ray); Pagliacci—Prologue [2] (C: Leoncavallo, Ruggiero; Styne, Jule; L: Styne, Jule); Isn't It Wonderful Isn't It Swell [3]; Shall We Dance [3]

Notes Titled THREE MEN AND A GIRL overseas. [1] Arrangement by Jule Styne and David Raksin for Andrea Marsh and the Brian Sisters. [2] Based on "Pagliacci" by Leoncavallo. [3] Sheet music only.

3088 ◆ KETTLES ON OLD MACDONALD'S FARM

Universal, 1957

Musical Score Mancini, Henry

Producer(s) Christie, Howard
Director(s) Vogel, Virgil
Screenwriter(s) Raynor, William; Margolis, Herbert

Cast Main, Marjorie; Fennelly, Parker; Talbot, Gloria; Smith, John; Akins, Claude; Dunn, George

Song(s) Where Is My Little Dog Gone (C: Traditional; L: Ashurn, Harris)

3089 ✦ THE KEY
Warner Brothers, 1934

Producer(s) Presnell, Robert
Director(s) Curtiz, Michael; McDonald, Frank
Screenwriter(s) Doyle, Laird
Source(s) *The Key* (play) Gore-Browne, R.; Hardy, J.L.

Cast Powell, William; Best, Edna; Clive, Colin; Cavanaugh, Hobart; Hobbes, Halliwell; Crisp, Donald; Kerrigan, J.M.; O'Neill, Henry; Regan, Phil; Treacher, Arthur

Song(s) There's a Cottage in Killarney (C: Wrubel, Allie; L: Dixon, Mort)

Notes No cue sheet available.

3090 ✦ KEY EXCHANGE
Twentieth Century–Fox, 1985

Musical Score Daring, Mason

Producer(s) Maxwell, Mitchell; Kurta, Paul
Director(s) Kellman, Barnet
Screenwriter(s) Scott, Kevin; Kurta, Paul
Source(s) *Key Exchange* (play) Wade, Kevin

Cast Adams, Brooke; Masters, Ben; Stern, Daniel; Aiello, Danny; Roberts, Tony; Allen, Seth; Armstrong, Kerry; Charles, Keith; Cunningham, John; Golden, Annie; Kellman, Barnet; Koch, Edward I.; Robbins, Rex

Song(s) Built for Speed (C/L: Jay, Michael; Chlanda, Ryche); People Are Talking (C/L: Daring, Mason); Lifeline (C/L: Daring, Mason; White, Kenny); Burnin' My Heart Out (C/L: Daring, Mason); One Hundred Ways (C/L: Wakefield, Kathy; Wright, Ben; Coleman, Tony); Throwdown (C/L: Guthrie, Gwen); Only Joking (C/L: Daring, Mason); Dinero [1] (C: London, Frank; Daring, Mason; L: Salgado, Efrain); What You Need Tonight (C/L: Daring, Mason; White, Kenny); Right from the Heart (C/L: Daring, Mason; O'Neill, Dennis)

Notes [1] Also in BROTHER FROM ANOTHER PLANET.

3091 ✦ THE KEYSTONE GIRL
Paramount, 1950 unproduced

Composer(s) Carmichael, Hoagy
Lyricist(s) Mercer, Johnny

Song(s) Queenie, the Quick Change Artist; He's Dead but He Won't Lie Down [1]; All Tied Up; But They Better Not Wait Too Long!; My Cadill-liddle-ol-lac; Any Similarity Is Just Coincidental; Don't Care—For the Heck of It; I Guess It Was You All the Time [3]; In the Cool, Cool, Cool of the Evening [2]

Notes This story is based on the life of Mack Sennett. [1] Later used in the Republic picture TIMBERJACK.

[2] Later used in HERE COMES THE GROOM. [3] Later used in THOSE REDHEADS FROM SEATTLE.

3092 ✦ THE KIBITZER
Paramount, 1929

Director(s) Sloman, Edward
Screenwriter(s) Mintz, Sam; Shore, Viola Brothers
Source(s) *The Kibitzer* (play) Swerling, Jo; Robinson, Edward G.

Cast Green, Harry; Brian, Mary; Hamilton, Neil; Gran, Albert; Newell, David

Song(s) Just Wait and See Sweetheart (C: Whiting, Richard A.; L: Robin, Leo)

Notes Released as THE BUSYBODY in Great Britain.

3093 ✦ KID BLUE
Twentieth Century–Fox, 1973

Musical Score Rubinstein, John; McIntire, Tim

Producer(s) Schwartz, Marvin
Director(s) Frawley, James
Screenwriter(s) Shrake, Edwin

Cast Hopper, Dennis; Oates, Warren; Boyle, Peter; Johnson, Ben; Rule, Janice; James, Clifton; Waite, Ralph

Song(s) Kid Blue Main Title (C/L: Rubinstein, John; McIntire, Tim)

Notes Originally titled DIME BOX.

3094 ✦ KIDDIE REVUE
Metro–Goldwyn–Mayer, 1930

Composer(s) Edwards, Gus

Director(s) Edwards, Gus
Screenwriter(s) Hopkins, Robert E.

Song(s) Booperaboop [1]; A Little Bit of Opera (L: Waggner, George; Cobb, Will D.); Babies a la Mode (Frocks and Frills) (C/L: Edwards, Gus)

Notes Short subject. [1] Also in BABY FOLLIES though credited to Edwards, Waggner and Howard Johnson.

3095 ✦ THE KID FROM AMARILLO
Columbia, 1951

Producer(s) Clark, Colbert
Director(s) Nazarro, Ray
Screenwriter(s) Shipman, Barry

Cast Starrett, Charles; Lauter, Harry; Sears, Fred F.; Megowan, Don; The Cass County Boys; Burnette, Smiley

Song(s) Old Coleville Jail [1] (L: Mertz, Paul); Zekiel Saw the Wheel (L: Scoggins, Jerry); Great Burnette from Chihuahua (C/L: Burnette, Smiley)

Notes [1] Based on "Down in the Valley."

3096 ✦ THE KID FROM BROKEN GUN
Columbia, 1952

Producer(s) Clark, Colbert
Director(s) Sears, Fred F.
Screenwriter(s) Shipman, Barry; Repp, Ed Earl

Cast Starrett, Charles; Burnette, Smiley; Mahoney, Jock [1]; Stevens, Angela; Coffin, Tristram; O'Malley, Pat

Song(s) It's the Law (C/L: Burnette, Smiley)

Notes [1] Billed as Jack Mahoney.

3097 ✦ KID FROM BROOKLYN
Goldwyn, 1945

Musical Score Dragon, Carmen
Composer(s) Styne, Jule
Lyricist(s) Cahn, Sammy
Choreographer(s) Pearce, Bernard

Producer(s) Goldwyn, Samuel
Director(s) McLeod, Norman Z.
Screenwriter(s) Hartman, Don; Shavelson, Melville
Source(s) *The Milky Way* (play) Root, Lynn; Clork, Harry

Cast Kaye, Danny; Mayo, Virginia [2]; Vera-Ellen [1]; Cochran, Steve; Arden, Eve; Abel, Walter; Stander, Lionel; Bainter, Fay; Kolb, Clarence; Cutner, Victor; Cane, Charles; Cowan, Jerome; Wilson, Don; Thompson, Kay; Downs, Johnny

Song(s) Sunflower Song; Hey, What's Your Name?; You're the Cause of It All; Welcome Burleigh; I Love an Old Fashioned Song; Josie; Pavlova (C/L: Fine, Sylvia; Liebman, Max)

Notes [1] Dubbed by Dorothy Ellers. [2] Dubbed by Betty Russell.

3098 ✦ THE KID FROM SPAIN
United Artists, 1933

Composer(s) Ruby, Harry
Lyricist(s) Kalmar, Bert
Choreographer(s) Berkeley, Busby

Producer(s) Goldwyn, Samuel
Director(s) McCarey, Leo
Screenwriter(s) Kalmar, Bert; Ruby, Harry; McGuire, William Anthony

Cast Cantor, Eddie; Roberti, Lyda; Conover, Theresa Maxwell; Young, Robert; Hall, Ruth; Miljan, John; Beery, Noah; Naish, J. Carrol; O'Connor, Robert Emmett

Song(s) In the Moonlight; Look What You've Done; What a Perfect Combination (C: Akst, Harry; Ruby, Harry; Kalmar, Bert; Caesar, Irving); The College Song

Notes No cue sheet available. In the chorus of Goldwyn Girls are Lucille Ball, Paulette Goddard, Betty Grable and Virginia Bruce.

3099 ✦ KID FROM TEXAS
Metro–Goldwyn–Mayer, 1939

Musical Score Axt, William

Producer(s) Selwyn, Edgar
Director(s) Simon, S. Sylvan
Screenwriter(s) Ryerson, Florence; Woolf, Edgar Allan; Mannheimer, Albert

Cast O'Keefe, Dennis; Rice, Florence; Allan, Anthony; Ralph, Jessie; Ebsen, Buddy; Carson, Jack; Dale, Virginia

Song(s) Right in the Middle of Texas (C: Ruthven, Ormond B.; L: Mannheimer, Albert; Merlin, Milton)

3100 ✦ KID GALAHAD (1937)
Warner Brothers–First National, 1937

Musical Score Roemheld, Heinz

Producer(s) Wallis, Hal B.
Director(s) Curtiz, Michael
Screenwriter(s) Miller, Seton I.

Cast Robinson, Edward G.; Davis, Bette; Bogart, Humphrey; Morris, Wayne; Bryan, Jane; Carey, Harry; Borg, Veda Ann; Faylen, Frank

Song(s) The Moon Is in Tears Tonight [1] (C: Jerome, M.K.; L: Scholl, Jack)

Notes Now titled THE BATTLING BELLHOP. Remade in 1941 as THE WAGONS ROLL AT NIGHT. [1] Used for six seconds in LOVE AND LEARN.

3101 ✦ KID GALAHAD (1962)
United Artists, 1962

Musical Score Alexander, Jeff

Producer(s) Weisbart, David
Director(s) Karlson, Phil
Screenwriter(s) Fay, William
Source(s) *Kid Galahad* (novel) Wallace, Francis

Cast Presley, Elvis; Young, Gig; Blackman, Joan; Bronson, Charles; Albright, Lola; Lewis, David; Glass, Ned

Song(s) King of the Whole Wide World (C: Roberts, Bob; L: Batchelor, Ruth); This Is Living (C: Weisman, Ben; L: Wise, Fred); Home Is Where the Heart Is (C: Edwards, Sherman; L: David, Hal); Riding the Rainbow (C: Weisman, Ben; L: Wise, Fred); I Got Lucky (C: Fuller, Dee; Weisman, Ben; L: Wise, Fred); A Whistling Tune (C: Edwards, Sherman; L: David, Hal)

3102 ✦ KID MILLIONS
United Artists, 1934

Composer(s)   Donaldson, Walter
Lyricist(s)   Kahn, Gus
Choreographer(s)   Felix, Seymour

Producer(s)   Goldwyn, Samuel
Director(s)   Del Ruth, Roy
Screenwriter(s)   Sheekman, Arthur; Perrin, Nat; Johnson, Nunnally

Cast   Cantor, Eddie; Merman, Ethel; Sothern, Ann; Murphy, George; Block, Jesse; Sully, Eve; Churchill, Berton; Hymer, Warren; Harvey, Paul; Kennedy, Edgar

Song(s)   Okay Toots; An Earful of Music; When My Ship Comes In; Ice Cream Fantasy; Your Head on My Shoulder (C: Lane, Burton; L: Adamson, Harold); I Want to Be a Minstrel Man [1] (C: Lane, Burton; L: Adamson, Harold)

Notes   No cue sheet available. There is also a vocal of "Mandy" by Irving Berlin. Originally in the ZIEGFELD FOLLIES OF 1919, the song was also used in the films THIS IS THE ARMY (also stage show), KID BOOTS and WHITE CHRISTMAS. [1] Same music as "You're All the World to Me" in ROYAL WEDDING.

3103 ✦ KID NIGHTINGALE
Warner Brothers, 1939

Producer(s)   Foy, Bryan
Director(s)   Amy, George
Screenwriter(s)   Belden, Charles; Schrock, Raymond
Source(s)   "Singing Swinger" (story) Katz, Lee

Cast   Payne, John; Wyman, Jane; Burns, Harry; Catlett, Walter; Brophy, Edward S.; Brown, Charles

Song(s)   Hark Hark the Meadowlark (C: Jerome, M.K.; L: Scholl, Jack); Who Told You I Cared [1] (C: Reisfeld, Burt; L: Whiting, George)

Notes   There is also a vocal of "I'm Dancing with Tears in My Eyes" by Joe Burke and Al Dubin. This 1930 song is also listed under A DANGEROUS BRUNETTE, a film there is no information about. [1] Background vocal use only.

3104 ✦ KID RODELO
Paramount, 1966

Musical Score   Douglas, Johnny

Producer(s)   Lamont, Jack; Storrow Jr., James J.
Director(s)   Carlson, Richard
Screenwriter(s)   Natteford, Jack

Cast   Murray, Don; Leigh, Janet; Crawford, Broderick; Carlson, Richard

Song(s)   Love Is Trouble (C/L: Glaser, Tom)

3105 ✦ KID'S LAST RIDE
Monogram, 1941

Musical Score   Sanucci, Frank

Producer(s)   Weeks, George W.
Director(s)   Luby, S. Roy
Screenwriter(s)   Snell, Earle

Cast   Corrigan, Ray; King, John; Terhune, Max; Walters, Luana; Brian, Edwin; Strange, Glenn

Song(s)   It's All Part of the Game (C: George, Jean [1]; L: Tobias, Harry); The Call of the Wild (C: George, Jean [1]; L: Tobias, Harry)

Notes   [1] Pseudonym for Lucille Nolte.

3106 ✦ KIKI
United Artists, 1931

Choreographer(s)   Berkeley, Busby

Producer(s)   Pickford, Mary
Director(s)   Taylor, Sam
Screenwriter(s)   Taylor, Sam
Source(s)   *Kiki* (play) Belasco, David

Cast   Pickford, Mary; Denny, Reginald; Cawthorn, Joseph; Livingston, Margaret; Tead, Phil; Walton, Fred

Notes   No cue sheet available.

3107 ✦ KILL A DRAGON
United Artists, 1957

Musical Score   Springer, Phil
Composer(s)   Springer, Phil
Lyricist(s)   Kay, Buddy

Producer(s)   Klein, Hal
Director(s)   Moore, Michael
Screenwriter(s)   Schenck, George; Marks, William

Cast   Palance, Jack; Lamas, Fernando; Ray, Aldo; Gur, Alizia; Tong, Kam; Knight, Don; Lee, Hans; Dan, Judy

Song(s)   Kill a Dragon; There's Love in Your Eyes

3108 ✦ THE KILLER ELITE
United Artists, 1975

Musical Score   Fielding, Jerry

Producer(s)   Baum, Martin; Lewis, Arthur
Director(s)   Peckinpah, Sam
Screenwriter(s)   Silliphant, Stirling; Norman, Marc
Source(s)   *Monkey in the Middle* (novel) Rostand, Robert

Cast   Caan, James; Duvall, Robert; Hill, Arthur; Hopkins, Bo; Mako; Young, Burt; Young, Gig; Heflin, Kate; Blake, Sondra

Song(s)   Nutbush City Limits (C/L: Turner, Tina)

Notes   There are a few more very brief vocals.

3109 ✦ KILLER FISH
AFD, 1979

Musical Score De Angelis, Guido; De Angelis, Maurizio

Producer(s) Ponti, Alex
Director(s) Dawson, Anthony M.
Screenwriter(s) Rogers, Michael

Cast Majors, Lee; Black, Karen; Franciscus, James; Hemingway, Margaux; Berenson, Marisa; Collins, Gary

Song(s) The Winner Takes All (C/L: Lang, Barry; May, Simon; De Angelis, Guido; De Angelis, Maurizio)

Notes No cue sheet available.

3110 ✦ KILLER PARTY
Metro–Goldwyn–Mayer, 1986

Musical Score Beal, John
Composer(s) Brackett, Alan; Shelly, Scott
Lyricist(s) Brackett, Alan; Shelly, Scott

Producer(s) Lepiner, Michael
Director(s) Fruet, William
Screenwriter(s) Cohen, Barney

Cast Hewitt, Martin; Seymour, Ralph; Wilkes, Elaine; Bartel, Paul; Willis-Burch, Sherry; Fleer, Alicia; Brown, Woody

Song(s) You're No Fool (C/L: Churchill, Brandon; Chadock, Wright); Give It Up (C/L: Casey, H.; Carter, D.); Best Times; Jump In; I Lose It; Such an Evil Woman; The Lucky One (C/L: Roberts, Bruce)

3111 ✦ THE KILLERS (1946)
Universal, 1946

Musical Score Rozsa, Miklos

Producer(s) Hellinger, Mark
Director(s) Siodmak, Robert
Screenwriter(s) Veiller, Anthony
Source(s) "The Killers" (story) Hemingway, Ernest

Cast Lancaster, Burt; McGraw, Charles; Conrad, William; O'Brien, Edmond; Gardner, Ava; Dekker, Albert; Levene, Sam; Barnett, Vince; Corey, Jeff; Christine, Virginia; Smith, Queenie

Song(s) The More I Know of Love (C: Rozsa, Miklos; L: Brooks, Jack)

3112 ✦ THE KILLERS (1964)
Universal, 1964

Musical Score Mancini, Henry; Steiner, Fred

Producer(s) Siegel, Don
Director(s) Siegel, Don
Screenwriter(s) Coon, Gene
Source(s) "The Killers" (story) Hemingway, Ernest

Cast Cassavetes, John; Marvin, Lee; Gulager, Clu; Dickinson, Angie; Reagan, Ronald; Akins, Claude; Fell, Norman

Song(s) Too Little Time (C: Mancini, Henry; L: Raye, Don)

Notes Also known as ERNEST HEMINGWAY'S THE KILLERS.

3113 ✦ KILLER'S KISS
United Artists, 1955

Musical Score Fried, Gerald

Producer(s) Bousel, Morris; Kubrick, Stanley
Director(s) Kubrick, Stanley
Screenwriter(s) Sackler, Howard; Kubrick, Stanley

Cast Sobotka, Ruth; Smith, Jamie; Kane, Irene; Silvera, Frank; Jarret, Jerry; Dana, Mike

Song(s) Unknown (C: Fried, Gerald; L: Gimbel, Norman)

3114 ✦ THE KILLING OF A CHINESE BOOKIE
Faces, 1976

Musical Score Harwood, Bo

Producer(s) Ruban, Al
Director(s) Cassavetes, John
Screenwriter(s) Cassavetes, John

Cast Gazzara, Ben; Carey, Timothy Agoglia; Johari, Azizi; Roberts, Meade

Song(s) Almost (C: Harwood, Bo; Harris, Anthony; L: Cassavetes, John); Rainy Fields of Frost and Magic (C/L: Harwood, Bo); You Are There (C: Harwood, Bo; L: Cassavetes, John); No One Around to Hear (C/L: Harwood, Bo)

Notes No cue sheet available.

3115 ✦ A KILLING SUCCESS

See CARAMBOLAGES.

3116 ✦ KILLPOINT
Crown International, 1984

Composer(s) Stevenett, Daryl
Lyricist(s) Stevenett, Daryl

Producer(s) Harris, Frank; Stevenett, Diane
Director(s) Harris, Frank
Screenwriter(s) Harris, Frank

Cast Fong, Leo; Roundtree, Richard; Mitchell, Cameron; Pierce, Stack; Holiday, Hope

Song(s) I'm Getting Old; Truck Drivin' Man; Cheatin' on Yer Daddy; Good Me Die Young; Livin' on the Inside (C/L: Jeffreys, Herman)

Notes No cue sheet available.

3117 ✦ KIM
Metro–Goldwyn–Mayer, 1950

Musical Score Previn, Andre; Kaper, Bronislau

Producer(s) Gordon, Leon
Director(s) Saville, Victor
Screenwriter(s) Gordon, Leon; Deutsch, Helen; Schayer, Richard
Source(s) "Kim" (story) Kipling, Rudyard

Cast Flynn, Errol; Stockwell, Dean; Douglas, Paul; Lukas, Paul; Gomez, Thomas; Kellaway, Cecil; Moss, Arnold; Owen, Reginald; Luez, Laurette

Song(s) The Sky's the Same Color [1] (C: Previn, Andre; L: Deutsch, Helen)

Notes [1] Only a 15 second vocal.

3118 ✦ KIND LADY
Metro–Goldwyn–Mayer, 1935

Musical Score Ward, Edward

Producer(s) Hubbard, Lucien
Director(s) Seitz, George B.
Screenwriter(s) Schubert, Bernard
Source(s) Kind Lady (play) Chodorov, Edward

Cast MacMahon, Aline; Rothbone, Basil; Carlisle, Mary; Digges, Dudley; Albertson, Frank

Song(s) The Duchess Has a Twinkle in Her Eye (C: Kaper, Bronislau; Jurmann, Walter; L: Washington, Ned)

Notes The source is based on Hugh Walpole's THE SILVER CASKET.

3119 ✦ THE KING AND I
Twentieth Century–Fox, 1956

Musical Score Newman, Alfred
Composer(s) Rodgers, Richard
Lyricist(s) Hammerstein II, Oscar
Choreographer(s) Robbins, Jerome

Producer(s) Brackett, Charles
Director(s) Lang, Walter
Screenwriter(s) Lehman, Ernest
Source(s) The King and I (musical) Hammerstein II, Oscar; Rodgers, Richard

Cast Kerr, Deborah [3]; Brynner, Yul [2]; Moreno, Rita [4]; Benson, Martin; Saunders, Terry; Thompson, Rex; Adiarte, Patrick; Mowbray, Alan; Rivas, Carlos [5]; Yuriko; Toone, Geoffrey; de Lappe, Gemze; Michiko

Song(s) Native Chant (Inst.); I Whistle a Happy Tune [1]; March of the Siamese Children [1] (Inst.); Hello, Young Lovers [1]; A Puzzlement [1]; Getting to Know You [1]; We Kiss in a Shadow [1]; Something Wonderful [1]; The Small House of Uncle Thomas [1]; Song of the King; Shall We Dance [1]; Dance of Anna and Sir Edward (Inst.); Finale Act I [1]; My Lord and Master [6]; Shall I Tell You What I Think of You [6]; I Have Dreamed [6]

Notes There are background instrumental uses of many of the other songs from the score. [1] From Broadway musical. [2] Repeating Broadway role. [3] Dubbed by Marni Nixon. [4] Dubbed by Cleone Duncan but those tracks were probably not used. [5] Dubbed by Reuben Fuentes. [6] Prerecorded but not used.

3120 ✦ THE KING AND THE CHORUS GIRL
Warner Brothers, 1937

Musical Score Heymann, Werner [1]
Composer(s) Heymann, Werner [1]
Lyricist(s) Koehler, Ted

Producer(s) LeRoy, Mervyn
Director(s) LeRoy, Mervyn
Screenwriter(s) Krasna, Norman; Marx, Groucho
Source(s) "Grand Passion" (story) Krasna, Norman; Marx, Groucho

Cast Gravet, Fernand; Blondell, Joan; Horton, Edward Everett; Mowbray, Alan; Nash, Mary; Wyman, Jane; Alberni, Luis; Baker, Kenny; Shaw and Lee

Song(s) Rue De La Paix; For You

Notes Released in Great Britain as ROMANCE IS SACRED. [1] Billed as Werner Richard Heymann.

3121 ✦ KING CREOLE
Paramount, 1958

Musical Score Scharf, Walter
Composer(s) Weisman, Ben
Lyricist(s) Wise, Fred
Choreographer(s) O'Curran, Charles

Producer(s) Wallis, Hal B.
Director(s) Curtiz, Michael
Screenwriter(s) Baker, Herbert; Gazzo, Michael Vincente
Source(s) A Stone for Danny Fisher (novel) Robbins, Harold

Cast Presley, Elvis; Montevecchi, Liliane; Jones, Carolyn; Matthau, Walter; Hart, Dolores; Jagger, Dean; Morrow, Vic

Song(s) As Long As I Have You; Banana (C/L: Bennett, Roy C.; Tepper, Sid); Crawfish [2]; Danny [1]; Dixieland Rock (C/L: Schroeder, Aaron; Frank, Rachael); Don't Ask Me Why; Hard Headed Woman

(C/L: DeMetrius, Claude); Trouble (I'm Evil) (C/L: Leiber, Jerry; Stoller, Mike); King Creole (C/L: Leiber, Jerry; Stoller, Mike); Lover Doll (C: Silver, Abner; L: Wayne, Sid); New Orleans (C/L: Bennett, Roy C.; Tepper, Sid); Steadfast, Loyal and True (C/L: Leiber, Jerry; Stoller, Mike); Turtles, Berries and Gumbo (C/L: Wood, Al; Twomey, Kay); Young Dreams (C/L: Schroeder, Aaron; Kalmanoff, Martin)

Notes   [1] Instrumentally only. [2] Also in G.I. BLUES.

3122 ✦ KINGDOM OF THE SPIDERS
Arachnid Productions, 1978

Producer(s)   Kantor, Igo; Sneller, Jeffrey M.
Director(s)   Cardos, John "Bud"
Screenwriter(s)   Robinson, Richard; Caillou, Alan

Cast   Shatner, William; Bolling, Tiffany; Strode, Woody; Davis, Altovise; Dressler, Leiux; McLean, David

Song(s)   Peaceful Verde Valley (C/L: Burnette, Dorsey)

3123 ✦ KING KELLY OF THE U.S.A.
Monogram, 1934

Composer(s)   Sanders, Joe
Lyricist(s)   Grossman, Bernie

Producer(s)   Bertholon, George
Director(s)   Fields, Leonard
Screenwriter(s)   Fields, Leonard; Silverstein, David

Cast   Robertson, Guy; Ware, Irene; Kennedy, Edgar; Pangborn, Franklin; Compton, Joyce; Gottschalk, Ferdinand; von Brincken, William; Harlan, Otis

Song(s)   Believe Me; Right Next Door to Love; There's a Love Song in the Air

Notes   No cue sheet available.

3124 ✦ KING KONG
Paramount, 1976

Musical Score   Barry, John

Producer(s)   De Laurentiis, Dino
Director(s)   Guillermin, John
Screenwriter(s)   Semple Jr., Lorenzo

Cast   Bridges, Jeff; Grodin, Charles; Lange, Jessica

Song(s)   Are You in There? [1] (C: Barry, John; L: Pomeranz, David)

Notes   [1] Lyrics added for exploitation only.

3125 ✦ KING OF BURLESQUE
Twentieth Century–Fox, 1935

Composer(s)   McHugh, Jimmy
Lyricist(s)   Koehler, Ted
Choreographer(s)   Lee, Sammy

Producer(s)   Zanuck, Darryl F.
Director(s)   Lanfield, Sidney
Screenwriter(s)   Markey, Gene; Tugend, Harry

Cast   Baxter, Warner; Faye, Alice; Oakie, Jack; Judge, Arline; Barrie, Mona; Ratoff, Gregory; Dunbar, Dixie; Waller, Thomas "Fats"; Long Jr., Nick; Baker, Kenny; Luke, Keye

Song(s)   Whose Big Baby Are You; Spreadin' Rhythm Around; I've Got My Fingers Crossed; I'm Shooting High; I Love to Ride the Horses on a Merry-Go-Round (C: Pollack, Lew; L: Yellen, Jack); Lovely Lady

Notes   There is also a vocal of "Alabamy Bound" by Ray Henderson, B.G. DeSylva and Bud Green.

3126 ✦ KING OF GAMBLERS
Paramount, 1937

Producer(s)   Jones, Paul
Director(s)   Florey, Robert
Screenwriter(s)   Anderson, Doris

Cast   Trevor, Claire [1]; Tamiroff, Akim; Nolan, Lloyd; Brent, Evelyn; Crabbe, Buster; Hall, Porter

Song(s)   I Hate to Talk About Myself (C: Rainger, Ralph; Whiting, Richard A.; L: Robin, Leo); I'm Feelin' High (C: Lane, Burton; L: Freed, Ralph)

Notes   First titled KID FROM PARADISE. [1] Dubbed by Miss Saxon.

3127 ✦ KING OF HEARTS
United Artists, 1967

Musical Score   Delerue, Georges

Producer(s)   de Broca, Philippe
Director(s)   de Broca, Philippe
Screenwriter(s)   Boulanger, Daniel

Cast   Bates, Alan; Bujold, Genevieve; Brialy, Jean-Claude; Presle, Micheline

Song(s)   La Cantique (C: Delerue, Georges; L: Boulanger, Daniel)

Notes   French title: LE ROI DE COEUR.

3128 ✦ KING OF JAZZ
Universal, 1930

Composer(s)   Ager, Milton
Lyricist(s)   Yellen, Jack
Choreographer(s)   Markert, Russell

Producer(s)   Laemmle Jr., Carl
Director(s)   Anderson, John Murray
Screenwriter(s)   Lowe, Edward T.; Ruskin, Harry; MacArthur, Charles

Cast   Paul Whiteman and His Orchestra; Boles, John; La Plante, Laura; Loff, Jeanette; Tryon, Glenn; Kennedy, Merna; Crawford, Kathryn; Summerville, Slim [3];

Smith, Stanley; Harlan, Otis; Kent, Billy; Hayes, Grace; Rhythm Boys, The [1]; The Brox Sisters; Irwin, Charles; Rose, Don; The Tommy Atkins Sextet; Russell Markert Dancers; Sisters G

Song(s) Music Hath Charms; It Happened in Monterey (C: Wayne, Mabel; L: Rose, Billy); Rhapsody in Blue (Inst.) (C: Gershwin, George); My Bridal Veil (L: Yellen, Jack; Anderson, John Murray); Oh Happy Bride; So the Bluebirds and the Blackbirds Get Together (C/L: Barris, Harry; Moll, Billy); Mississippi Mud (C/L: Barris, Harry; Cavanaugh, James); How I'd Like to Own a Fish Store (C/L: Stone, Billy); A Bench in the Park; Ragamuffin Romeo (C: Wayne, Mabel; L: DeCosta, Harry); Happy Feet; Has Anybody Seen Our Nellie; The Song of the Dawn; My Lover [2] (C: Dietrich, James; L: Yellen, Jack; Hayes, Grace); I Like to Do Things for You [2]

Notes There are also vocals of the spiritual "The Lord Delivered Daniel;" "Long, Long Ago" by Bayly; "Old Black Joe" and "La Paloma" by Yradier; "Asleep in the Deep" by Lamb; "John Peel," "Santa Lucia" and "Comin' Thru the Rye" by Robert Burns; "Die Lorelei" by Silcher; "Killarney," "Ay Ay Ay" (a Creole song) and "Black Eyes" by Harry Horlick and Stone (may be same as "Dark Eyes") and the French folksong "The Three Captains." [1] Bing Crosby, Harry Barris and Al Rinker. [2] Not on cue sheet. [3] Billed as George "Slim" Summerville.

3129 ✦ KING OF THE COWBOYS
Republic, 1943

Producer(s) Grey, Harry
Director(s) Kane, Joseph
Screenwriter(s) Cooper, Olive; Cheney, J. Benton

Cast Rogers, Roy; Burnette, Smiley; Bob Nolan and the Sons of the Pioneers; Moran, Peggy; Mohr, Gerald; Kent, Dorothea; Corrigan, Lloyd; Bacon, Irving

Song(s) Ride 'Em Cowboy (King of the Range) [4] (C/L: Spencer, Tim); Deep in the Heart of Texas [1] (C: Swander, Don; L: Hershey, June); I'm an Old Cowhand [3] (C/L: Mercer, Johnny); Gay Ranchero (Las Altenitas) [2] (C: Espinosa, J.J.; L: Tuvim, Abe; Luban, Francia); They Cut Down the Old Pine Tree [6] (C: Brown, George; L: Raskin, Willie; Eliscu, Edward); Ride, Ranger, Ride [5] (C/L: Spencer, Tim)

Notes There is also a vocal of "Roll Along Prairie Moon" by Ted Fiorito, Harry MacPherson and Albert Von Tilzer (also in HERE COMES THE BAND). [1] Also in HEART OF THE RIO GRANDE, HI, NEIGHBOR, I'LL GET BY (20th) and DEEP IN THE HEART OF TEXAS (Universal). [2] Also in THE GAY RANCHERO. [3] Also in RHYTHM ON THE RANGE (Paramount). [4] Also in RIDE 'EM COWBOY with additional writing credit to Roy Rogers. [5] Also in GANGSTERS OF THE FRONTIER (PRC), THE BIG SHOW, RIDE, RANGER, RIDE and TEXANS NEVER CRY (Columbia). [6] Written in 1929.

3130 ✦ KING OF THE GRIZZLIES
Disney, 1969

Musical Score Baker, Buddy

Producer(s) Hibler, Winston
Director(s) Kelly, Ron
Screenwriter(s) Speirs, Jack
Source(s) *The Biography of a Grizzly* (book) Seton, Ernest Thompson

Cast Yesno, John; Wiggins, Chris; Webster, Hugh; Van Evera, Jack

Song(s) The Campfire Is Home (C/L: Speirs, Jack); Lonely Trail [1] (C: Baker, Buddy; L: Jackman, Bob)

Notes [1] Used instrumentally only.

3131 ✦ KING OF THE KHYBER RIFLES
Twentieth Century–Fox, 1954

Musical Score Herrmann, Bernard

Producer(s) Rosenberg, Frank P.
Director(s) King, Henry
Screenwriter(s) Goff, Ivan; Roberts, Ben
Source(s) (novel) Mundy, Talbot

Cast Power, Tyrone; Moore, Terry; Rennie, Michael; Justin, John; Rolfe, Guy

Song(s) Khyber Love Song [1] (C: Mehra, Lal Chand; L: Wassil, Aly)

Notes [1] Music same as "Hindu Song of Love."

3132 ✦ KING OF THE MOUNTAIN
Universal, 1981

Musical Score Melvoin, Michael

Producer(s) Sanders, Jack Frost
Director(s) Nosseck, Noel
Screenwriter(s) Christian, H.A.

Cast Hamlin, Harry; Bottoms, Joseph; Van Valkenburg, Deborah; Cox, Richard; Hopper, Dennis; Haggerty, Dan; Cassel, Seymour

Song(s) Dangerous Strangers (C/L: Riopelle, Jerry; Hall, Tamara); Where Do I Fit In? (C/L: Kerr, Richard; Seals, Troy); Someday (C/L: Champlin, Bill; Craig, Pat)

Notes No cue sheet available.

3133 ✦ KING RICHARD AND THE CRUSADERS
Warner Brothers, 1954

Musical Score Steiner, Max

Producer(s) Blanke, Henry
Director(s) Butler, David

Screenwriter(s)   Twist, John
Source(s)   *The Talisman* (novel) Scott, Sir Walter

Cast   Harrison, Rex; Mayo, Virginia; Sanders, George; Harvey, Laurence; Douglas, Robert; Pate, Michael; Raymond, Paula

Song(s)   Ilderim's Song (C: Heindorf, Ray; L: Twist, John)

3134 ✦ KING SOLOMON OF BROADWAY
Universal, 1935

Producer(s)   Bernheim, Julius
Director(s)   Crosland, Alan
Screenwriter(s)   Clork, Harry; Malloy, Doris

Cast   Page, Dorothy; Henry, Louise; Pawley, Edward

Song(s)   Flower in My Lapel (C/L: Conrad, Con; Magidson, Herb); That's What You Think (C/L: Tomlin, Pinky; Jasper, Raymond; Poe, Coy); Everything Will Be All Right (C/L: Tomlin, Pinky); Moaning in the Moonlight (C/L: Conrad, Con; Magidson, Herb)

3135 ✦ KING SOLOMON'S MINES
Metro–Goldwyn–Mayer, 1950

Producer(s)   Zimbalist, Sam
Director(s)   Bennett, Compton; Marton, Andrew
Screenwriter(s)   Deutsch, Helen
Source(s)   *King Solomon's Mines* (novel) Haggard, H. Rider

Cast   Kerr, Deborah; Granger, Stewart; Carlson, Richard; Haas, Hugo; Kimursi; Gilmore, Lowell

Song(s)   Climbing Up, Climbing Up (C: Spoliansky, Mischa; L: Maschwitz, Eric); Ho! Ho! (C: Spoliansky, Mischa; L: Maschwitz, Eric)

Notes   No cue sheet available.

3136 ✦ KING'S RHAPSODY
United Artists, 1955

Musical Score   Novello, Ivor
Composer(s)   Novello, Ivor
Lyricist(s)   Novello, Ivor

Producer(s)   Wilcox, Herbert
Director(s)   Wilcox, Herbert
Screenwriter(s)   Hassall, Christopher; Bower, Pamela; Herbert, A.P.
Source(s)   *King's Rhapsody* (musical) Novello, Ivor

Cast   Flynn, Errol; Neagle, Anna; Wymore, Patrice; Hunt, Martita; Currie, Finlay; Hockridge, Edmund

Song(s)   King's Rhapsody; Someday My Heart Will Awake; The Years Together; Gates of Paradise; Take Your Girl; If This Were Love; Proxy Ballet; The Violin Began to Play

3137 ✦ THE KING STEPS OUT
Columbia, 1936

Composer(s)   Kreisler, Fritz
Lyricist(s)   Fields, Dorothy

Producer(s)   Perlberg, William
Director(s)   von Sternberg, Josef
Screenwriter(s)   Buchman, Sidney
Source(s)   *Sissy* (musical) Marischka, Hubert; Marischka, Ernst; Kreisler, Fritz; Holm, Gustav; Decsey, Ernest

Cast   Moore, Grace; Tone, Franchot; Connolly, Walter; Walburn, Raymond; Jory, Victor; Inescort, Frieda; Hall, Thurston; Bing, Herman; Hassell, George

Song(s)   Learn How to Love [1]; Stars in My Eyes [2]; Toy Soldier's March [3]; Madly in Love [4]; What Shall Remain [6]; Liebesfreud [5] (inst.); Schoen Rosmarin [5] (inst.); The End Begins [7]

Notes   *Variety* spells the source names "Marieschka." [1] Based on "Caprice Viennois" in musical SISSY. [2] Rewrite of "Who Can Tell" from APPLE BLOSSOMS, later used in SISSY. [3] Based on "Second Violin" from APPLE BLOSSOMS later used in SISSY. [4] Rewrite of "Ein Stilles Gluck" from SISSY. [5] From SISSY. [6] Transcribed from an old Austrian folk song by Fritz Kreisler with new lyrics by Fields. [7] Sheet music only.

3138 ✦ KISMET (1944)
Metro–Goldwyn–Mayer, 1944

Musical Score   Stothart, Herbert
Composer(s)   Arlen, Harold
Lyricist(s)   Harburg, E.Y.

Producer(s)   Riskin, Everett
Director(s)   Dieterle, William
Screenwriter(s)   Meehan, John
Source(s)   *Kismet* (play) Knoblock, Edward

Cast   Colman, Ronald; Dietrich, Marlene; Craig, James; Arnold, Edward; Herbert, Hugh; Page, Joy [1]; Bates, Florence; Davenport, Harry

Song(s)   Tell Me, Tell Me, Evening Star; Willow in the Wind; I See a Morning Star [2]

Notes   Previously filmed in 1920 and 1930. [1] Dubbed by Doreen Tryden. [2] Not used.

3139 ✦ KISMET (1956)
Metro–Goldwyn–Mayer, 1956

Composer(s)   Wright, Robert; Forrest, George; Borodin, Alexander [1]
Lyricist(s)   Wright, Robert; Forrest, George
Choreographer(s)   Cole, Jack

Producer(s)   Freed, Arthur
Director(s)   Minnelli, Vincente

Screenwriter(s) Lederer, Charles; Davis, Luther; Wright, Robert; Forrest, George
Source(s) *Kismet* (musical) Lederer, Charles; Davis, Luther; Wright, Robert; Forrest, George

Cast Keel, Howard; Blyth, Ann; Gray, Dolores; Damone, Vic; Woolley, Monty; Cabot, Sebastian; Flippen, Jay C.; Mazurki, Mike; Elam, Jack; De Corsia, Ted

Song(s) Rhymes Have I [2]; Fate [5]; Not Since Nineveh [10]; Baubles, Bangles and Beads [11]; Stranger in Paradise [12]; Gesticulate [6]; Bored [3] (C: Wright, Robert; Forrest, George); Night of My Nights [9]; The Olive Tree [4]; Rahadlakum; And This Is My Beloved [7]; Sands of Time [8]

Notes All songs but [3] from Broadway original. [1] Most music based on themes by Borodin. [2] Filmed but only a few lines were used. [3] Not in Broadway musical. No Borodin material used in music. [4] Based on music from PRINCE IGOR Act III and the song "Rich and Poor." [5] Based on the first movement of the "Symphony No. 2 in B Minor." [6] Based on the first movement of the "Symphony No. 1" and PRINCE IGOR Act II. [7] Based on the third movement of the "String Quartet No. 2 in D." [8] Based on the tone-poem "The Steppes of Central Asia." [9] Based on the piano piece "Petite Suite," also known as "Serenade." [10] From the "Polovetsian Dances - PRINCE IGOR Act III." [11] Based on PRINCE IGOR Act I; Symphony No. 2 in B Minor; String Quartet No. 2, D Major. [12] from PRINCE IGOR Act II.

3140 ✦ THE KISS
Tri-Star, 1988

Musical Score Robinson, J. Peter

Producer(s) Densham, Pen; Watson, John
Director(s) Densham, Pen
Screenwriter(s) Volk, Stephen; Ropelewski, Tom

Cast Pacula, Joanna; Salenger, Meredith; Kuzyk, Mimi

Song(s) Under My Skin (C: Robinson, J. Peter; Canning, Tom; L: Densham, Pen; Lewis, Richard B.); Poolside Blues (C/L: Williams, Larry; Canning, Tom)

Notes No cue sheet available.

3141 ✦ KISS AND MAKE UP
Paramount, 1934

Composer(s) Rainger, Ralph
Lyricist(s) Robin, Leo

Producer(s) Schulberg, B.P.
Director(s) Thompson, Harlan
Screenwriter(s) Thompson, Harlan; Marion Jr., George; Hinton, Jane
Source(s) *Kozmetika* (play) Bekeffi, Stephen

Cast Grant, Cary; Tobin, Genevieve; Mack, Helen; Horton, Edward Everett; Littlefield, Lucien; Maris, Mona; Storm, Rafael; The Wampas Baby Stars

Song(s) Love Divided by Two; Corn Bec and Cabbage I Love You; Kiss and Make-Up [1]; The Mirror Song (Scene) [2]; Love in Bloom [3] [5]; There Never Was a Night Like This [4]; The Night Shall Be Filled with Love [3]

Notes [1] Originally a song, it is used instrumentally only. [2] Not used but recorded with Billie Lowe dubbing for Helen Mack. [3] Not used. [4] Not used but recorded. [5] Used in THE BIG BROADCAST OF 1938, NEW YORK TOWN, $1,000 A TOUCHDOWN and SHE LOVES ME NOT.

3142 ✦ THE KISS BEFORE THE MIRROR
Universal, 1933

Musical Score Harling, W. Franke
Composer(s) Harling, W. Franke
Lyricist(s) Harling, W. Franke

Director(s) Whale, James
Screenwriter(s) McGuire, William Anthony
Source(s) (play) Fodor, Laszlo

Cast Morgan, Frank; Lukas, Paul; Carroll, Nancy; Stuart, Gloria; Grapewin, Charley; Dixon, Jean; Pidgeon, Walter; Cook, Donald

Song(s) The Kiss Before the Mirror; A Little Bit of Love

Notes Remade as WIVES UNDER SUSPICION (1938).

3143 ✦ KISSES FOR BREAKFAST
Warner Brothers, 1941

Musical Score Deutsch, Adolph
Composer(s) Strauss, Josef
Lyricist(s) Scholl, Jack

Producer(s) Thompson, Harlan
Director(s) Seiler, Lewis
Screenwriter(s) Gamet, Kenneth
Source(s) *Matrimonial Bed* (play) Mirande, Yves; Mouezy-Eon, Andre; Hicks, Seymour

Cast Morgan, Dennis; Wyatt, Jane; Patrick, Lee; Ross, Shirley; Cowan, Jerome; O'Connor, Una; Parker, Barnett; Wilde, Cornel; Best, Willie; Beavers, Louise

Song(s) Sing with Your Heart; In Time; Roll Out-Heave Dat Cotton (C/L: Hays, Will S.)

Notes A remake of the 1930 film MATRIMONIAL BED.

3144 ✦ KISSIN' COUSINS
Metro–Goldwyn–Mayer, 1964

Musical Score Karger, Fred
Composer(s) Giant, Bill; Baum, Bernie; Kaye, Florence

3145 ◆ THE KISSING BANDIT

Lyricist(s) Giant, Bill; Baum, Bernie; Kaye, Florence
Choreographer(s) Belfer, Hal

Producer(s) Katzman, Sam
Director(s) Nelson, Gene
Screenwriter(s) Nelson, Gene; Adams, Gerald Drayson

Cast Presley, Elvis; O'Connell, Arthur; Farrell, Glenda; Albertson, Jack; Austin, Pamela; Pepper, Cynthia; Craig, Yvonne; Woods, Donald

Song(s) Kissin' Cousins #2; Smokey Mountain Boy (C/L: Rosenblatt, Lenore; Millrose, Victor); There's Gold in the Mountains; One Boy—Two Little Girls; Catchin' on Fast; Tender Feeling; Pappy Won't You Please Come Home (C/L: Tepper, Sid; Bennett, Roy C.); Barefoot Ballad (C/L: Fuller, Dolores; Morris, Lee); Once Is Enough (C/L: Tepper, Sid; Bennett, Roy C.); Kissin' Cousins #1 (C/L: Wise, Fred; Starr, Randy); Anyone [1] (C/L: Benjamin, Bernie; Marcus, Sol; DeJesus, Louis); Echoes of Love [1] (C/L: Roberts, Bob; McMains, Patty); It's a Long, Lonely Highway (C/L: Pomus, Doc; Shuman, Mort)

Notes [1] Sheet music only.

3145 ◆ THE KISSING BANDIT
Metro–Goldwyn–Mayer, 1948

Composer(s) Brown, Nacio Herb
Lyricist(s) Brent, Earl
Choreographer(s) Alton, Robert

Producer(s) Pasternak, Joe
Director(s) Benedek, Laslo
Screenwriter(s) Lennart, Isobel; Harding, John Briard

Cast Sinatra, Frank; Grayson, Kathryn; Naish, J. Carrol; Natwick, Mildred; Rasumny, Mikhail; Gilbert, Billy; Osato, Sono; Sundberg, Clinton; Young, Carleton; Montalban, Ricardo; Miller, Ann; Charisse, Cyd

Song(s) Tomorrow Means Romance (L: Katz, William); What's Wrong with Me? (L: Heyman, Edward); If I Steal a Kiss (L: Heyman, Edward); I Like You (The Whip Dance) (C/L: Brown, Nacio Herb); Siesta; Dance of Fury [2] (Inst.); Senorita (L: Heyman, Edward); Love Is Where You Find It [3]; We're On Our Way [1]

Notes [1] Used instrumentally only. [2] Choreographed by Stanley Donen after principal photography had finished. [3] Also in A DATE WITH JUDY.

3146 ◆ KISS ME AGAIN
Warner Brothers–First National, 1931

Composer(s) Herbert, Victor
Lyricist(s) Blossom, Henry

Director(s) Seiter, William A.
Screenwriter(s) Josephson, Julien; Perez, Paul

Source(s) *Mlle. Modiste* (musical) Blossom, Henry; Herbert, Victor

Cast Claire, Bernice; Pidgeon, Walter; Collyer, June; Horton, Edward Everett; Vosselli, Judith; Gillingwater, Claude [1]; McHugh, Frank

Song(s) Kiss Me Again; The Mascot of the Troop; The Time, the Place and the Girl

Notes No cue sheet available. Released in Great Britain as TOAST OF THE LEGION. All these songs are from the original production. [1] Gillingwater was in the original 1905 production.

3147 ◆ KISS ME DEADLY
United Artists, 1955

Musical Score De Vol, Frank

Producer(s) Aldrich, Robert
Director(s) Aldrich, Robert
Screenwriter(s) Bezzerides, A.I.
Source(s) *Kiss Me Deadly* (novel) Spillane, Mickey

Cast Meeker, Ralph; Leachman, Cloris; Cooper, Maxine; Rodgers, Gaby; Dekker, Albert

Song(s) I'd Rather Have the Blues (C/L: De Vol, Frank)

3148 ◆ KISS ME GOODBYE
Twentieth Century–Fox, 1982

Musical Score Burns, Ralph

Producer(s) Mulligan, Robert
Director(s) Mulligan, Robert
Screenwriter(s) Peters, Charlie
Source(s) *Dona Flor and Her Two Husbands* (movie) Amado, Jorge; Baretto, Bruno

Cast Field, Sally; Caan, James; Bridges, Jeff; Dooley, Paul; Trevor, Claire; Natwick, Mildred; Burrell, Maryedith

Song(s) Nice Dream (C/L: Allen, Peter)

3149 ◆ KISS ME KATE
Metro–Goldwyn–Mayer, 1953

Composer(s) Porter, Cole
Lyricist(s) Porter, Cole
Choreographer(s) Pan, Hermes

Producer(s) Cummings, Jack
Director(s) Sidney, George
Screenwriter(s) Kingsley, Dorothy
Source(s) *Kiss Me Kate* (musical) Porter, Cole; Spewack, Sam; Spewack, Bella

Cast Grayson, Kathryn; Keel, Howard; Miller, Ann; Wynn, Keenan; Van, Bobby; Rall, Tommy; Whitmore,

James; Kasznar, Kurt; Fosse, Bob; Randell, Ron; Parker, Willard

Song(s) So in Love; Too Darn Hot; So Kiss Me Kate; Why Can't You Behave; Wunderbar; We Open in Venice; Tom, Dick or Harry; I've Come to Wive It Wealthily in Padua; I Hate Men; Were Thine That Special Face; Where Is the Life that Late I Led?; Always True to You in My Fashion; Brush Up Your Shakespeare; From This Moment On [1]

Notes All songs but [1] from original Broadway show. Bob Fosse choreographed his own dances. [1] Cut from stage musical OUT OF THIS WORLD.

3150 ✦ KISS ME, STUPID
United Artists, 1964

Musical Score Previn, Andre
Composer(s) Gershwin, George
Lyricist(s) Gershwin, Ira

Producer(s) Wilder, Billy
Director(s) Wilder, Billy
Screenwriter(s) Wilder, Billy; Diamond, I.A.L.
Source(s) *L'Ora Della Fantasia* (play) Bonacci, Anna

Cast Martin, Dean; Novak, Kim; Walston, Ray; Farr, Felicia; Osmond, Cliff; Blanc, Mel; Gibson, Henry; Pearce, Alice

Song(s) I'm a Poached Egg; Sophia [1]; All the Live Long Day [2]

Notes "'S Wonderful" by the Gershwins is also sung. [1] A revision of "Wake Up Brother" from SHALL WE DANCE. [2] A combination of two fragments from the songs "Phoebe" and "All the Livelong Day."

3151 ✦ KISS THE BOYS GOODBYE
Paramount, 1941

Composer(s) Schertzinger, Victor
Lyricist(s) Loesser, Frank

Producer(s) LeBaron, William
Director(s) Schertzinger, Victor
Screenwriter(s) Taylor, Dwight; Tugend, Harry
Source(s) *Kiss the Boys Goodbye* (play) Boothe, Clare [3]

Cast Ameche, Don; Martin, Don; Boswell, Connee; Walburn, Raymond; Levant, Oscar; Anderson, Eddie "Rochester"; Allen, Barbara Jo [4]; Cowan, Jerome; Patterson, Elizabeth; Trotter, John Scott; Watson, Minor; Barris, Harry

Song(s) Kiss the Boys Goodbye; Find Yourself a Melody; Sand in My Shoes; I'll Never Let a Day Pass By; My Start [2]; We've Met Somewhere Before [1]; There's No Forgetting You [1]

Notes [1] Not used. [2] First titled "That's How I Got My Start" but Gene Autry owned the title for an earlier

song so it was retitled "Once I Met . . . " then it was retitled again as "My Start." It was published initially as "That's How I Got My Start" but the correct title is "My Start." [3] Later known as Clare Boothe Luce. [4] Also known as Vera Vague.

3152 ✦ KISS THEM FOR ME
Twentieth Century–Fox, 1957

Producer(s) Wald, Jerry
Director(s) Donen, Stanley
Screenwriter(s) Epstein, Julius J.
Source(s) *Shore Leave* (play) Davis, Luther

Cast Grant, Cary; Parker, Suzy; Mansfield, Jayne; Erickson, Leif; Walston, Ray; Blyden, Larry; Frey, Nathaniel; Klemperer, Werner; Wright, Ben

Song(s) Kiss Them for Me (C: Newman, Lionel; L: Coates, Carroll)

3153 ✦ KIT CARSON
United Artists, 1940

Composer(s) Ward, Edward
Lyricist(s) Forrest, Chet; Wright, Bob

Producer(s) Small, Edward
Director(s) Seitz, George B.
Screenwriter(s) Bruce, George

Cast Hall, Jon; Bond, Ward; Huber, Harold; Andrews, Dana; Bari, Lynn; Riano, Renie; Moore, Clayton; Hatton, Raymond

Song(s) With My Concertina; Prairie Schooner (Sail Away)

Notes No cue sheet available.

3154 ✦ KITTY
Paramount, 1945

Choreographer(s) Daniels, Billy

Producer(s) Tunberg, Karl; Ware, Darrell
Director(s) Leisen, Mitchell
Screenwriter(s) Tunberg, Karl; Ware, Darrell
Source(s) *Kitty* (novel) Marshall, Rosamund

Cast Milland, Ray; Goddard, Paulette; Owen, Reginald; Collier, Constance; Knowles, Patric; Kellaway, Cecil; Blore, Eric

Song(s) Kitty [1] (C/L: Livingston, Jay; Evans, Ray)

Notes [1] Written for exploitation only.

3155 ✦ THE KLANSMAN
Paramount, 1974

Composer(s) Rice, Mack; Crutcher, Bettye
Lyricist(s) Rice, Mack; Crutcher, Bettye

Producer(s)   Alexander, William
Director(s)   Young, Terence
Source(s)   (novel) Hule, William Bradford

Cast   Burton, Richard; Marvin, Lee; Mitchell, Cameron; Simpson, O.J.; Evans, Linda; Falana, Lola; Huddleston, David

Song(s)   Good Christian People; How Do You Feel This Morning; Weak Spot (C/L: Rice, Mack; Crutcher, Bettye; Gardner, Stu); Little Blue Boy (C/L: Warren, Dale; Gardner, Stu); Marching to Victory (C/L: Warren, Dale; Gardner, Stu); Little Boy Blue (C/L: Warren, Dale; Gardner, Stu)

3156 ◆ KLONDIKE ANNIE
Paramount, 1936

Composer(s)   Austin, Gene
Lyricist(s)   Austin, Gene

Producer(s)   LeBaron, William
Director(s)   Walsh, Raoul
Screenwriter(s)   West, Mae

Cast   West, Mae; Huber, Harold; McLaglen, Victor; Reed, Philip; Eddy, Helen Jerome; Austin, Gene

Song(s)   I'm an Occidental Woman; Mister Deep Blue Sea (C/L: Austin, Gene; Johnson, James P.); Little Bar Butterfly; Cheer Up Little Sister; It's Better to Give than To Receive; It's Never Too Late to Say No [1]; That May Not Be Love (But It's Wonderful) [1] (C/L: Austin, Gene; Bates, Charles); I Hear You Knocking (But You Can't Come In) [1]; Open Up Your Heart and Let the Sunshine In [1]; I Want a Red Blooded Papa to Chase My Blues Away [1] (C/L: Coslow, Sam); It Must Be Love or Something [1] (C: Rainger, Ralph; L: Coslow, Sam); My Medicine Man [1] [2] (C/L: Coslow, Sam)

Notes   The picture was first titled KLONDIKE LOU. There are also renditions of "There'll Be a Hot Time in the Old Town Tonight" by T.A. Metz and J. Hayden, "Now the Day Is Over" by Sabine Baring Gould and Joseph Barnby and "Auld Lang Syne." Gene Austin appears as the piano player. [1] Not used. [2] Recorded. On February 28, 1926 the Hearst Papers ran the following editorial:

THE SCREEN MUST NOT RELAPSE TO LEWDNESS

In 1927 Mae West wrote and produced a play called "Sex" in New York City.

In March, 1927, the play was raided as obscene by the New York police. Mae West was indicted with her producer and members of the cast. She was convicted and sentenced to ten days in the workhouse on Welfare Island and fined five hundred dollars. She served the ten days and paid the fine. In 1928, Mae West wrote, and acted in a play called "The Drag," which opened in suburban cities. It was branded as sheer filth and

scourged from the stage. Rewritten by Mae West, it was produced on Broadway as "The Pleasure Man." The play was raided on the opening night and Mae West, the cast and producer were arrested. The trial which took place in April, 1930, resulted in a hung jury.

3157 ◆ KLUTE
Warner Brothers, 1971

Musical Score   Small, Michael

Producer(s)   Pakula, Alan J.
Director(s)   Pakula, Alan J.
Screenwriter(s)   Lewis, Andy; Lewis, Dave

Cast   Fonda, Jane; Sutherland, Donald; Cioffi, Charles; Schneider, Roy R.; Tristan, Dorothy; Gam, Rita; Nathan, Vivian; Nathan, George; Holland, Anthony; Shull, Richard B.; White, Jane; Stapleton, Jean

Song(s)   Take Me High, Take Me Higher (C/L: Small, Michael)

3158 ◆ KNICKERBOCKER HOLIDAY
United Artists, 1944

Composer(s)   Weill, Kurt
Lyricist(s)   Anderson, Maxwell

Producer(s)   Brown, Harry Joe
Director(s)   Brown, Harry Joe
Screenwriter(s)   Boehm, David; Goldman, Harold; Leigh, Rowland
Source(s)   *Knickerbocker Holiday* (musical) Weill, Kurt; Anderson, Maxwell

Cast   Coburn, Charles; Dowling, Constance; Eddy, Nelson; Cossart, Ernest; Winters, Shelley; Strange, Glenn; Kruger, Otto; Kilbride, Percy; Conklin, Chester; Feld, Fritz

Song(s)   There's Nowhere to Go but Up; September Song [1]; Indispensable Man; Holiday (C/L: Paxton, Theodore; Eddy, Nelson); Let's Make Tomorrow Today (C: Heymann, Werner; L: Brown, Forman); Jail Song (C: Weill, Kurt; L: Brown, Forman; Eddy, Nelson); Be Not Hasty Maiden Fair (C/L: Paxton, Theodore; Eddy, Nelson); Sing Out (C: Steininger, Franz; L: Brown, Forman); Love Has Made This Such a Lovely Day (C: Styne, Jule; L: Cahn, Sammy); Zuyder Zee (C: Styne, Jule; L: Cahn, Sammy); One More Smile [2] (C: Styne, Jule; Cahn, Sammy)

Notes   No cue sheet available. [1] From original stage show. Also heard in SEPTEMBER AFFAIR and PEPE. [2] Not used.

3159 ◆ KNIGHTS OF THE RANGE
Paramount, 1940

Composer(s)   Ohman, Phil
Lyricist(s)   Carling, Foster

Producer(s)   Sherman, Harry
Director(s)   Selander, Lesley
Screenwriter(s)   Huston, Norman
Source(s)   *Knights of the Range* (novel) Grey, Zane

Cast   The King's Men; Robinson, Rad; Hayden, Russell; Jory, Victor; Parker, Jean; Ankrum, Morris

Song(s)   Where the Cimarron Flows; Prayer on the Prairie; Roll Along, Covered Wagon; Mornin' on the Trail; The Covered Wagon Rolled Right Along [1] (C: Heath, Hy; L: Wood, Britt)

Notes   [1] Sheet music only.

3160 ✦ KNOCK ON WOOD
Paramount, 1954

Composer(s)   Fine, Sylvia
Lyricist(s)   Fine, Sylvia
Choreographer(s)   Kidd, Michael

Producer(s)   Frank, Melvin; Panama, Norman
Director(s)   Frank, Melvin; Panama, Norman
Screenwriter(s)   Frank, Melvin; Panama, Norman

Cast   Kaye, Danny; Zetterling, Mai; Thatcher, Torin; Burns, David

Song(s)   Chacun a Son Gout; Knock on Wood; All About You; (The Drastic, Livid History of) Monahan O'Han

3161 ✦ KRAKATOA, EAST OF JAVA
Cinerama Releasing, 1969

Musical Score   de Vol, Frank
Composer(s)   de Vol, Frank
Lyricist(s)   David, Mack

Producer(s)   Forman, William R.
Director(s)   Kowalski, Bernard L.
Screenwriter(s)   Gould, Clifford; Gordon, Bernard

Cast   Schell, Maximilian; Baker, Diane; Keith, Brian; Werle, Barbara; Leyton, John; Brazzi, Rossano; Mineo, Sal; Cannon, J.D.; Holder, Geoffrey; Lawrence, Marc

Song(s)   East of Java; A Nice Old Fashioned Girl; Just Before Sunrise; Kee Kana Lu

Notes   No cue sheet available.

3162 ✦ KRUSH GROOVE
Warner Brothers, 1985

Producer(s)   McHenry, Doug; Schultz, Michael
Director(s)   Schultz, Michael
Screenwriter(s)   Farquhar, Ralph

Cast   Underwood, Blair; The Fat Boys; Run-D.M.C.; Sheila E.; Blow, Kurtis; New Edition

Song(s)   King of Rock (C/L: Smith, Larry; Simmons, J.; McDaniels, D.); Don't You Dog Me (C/L: Blow, Kurtis); Love Bizarre (C/L: Sheila E.; Prince); Holly Rock (C/L: Sheila E.); If I Ruled the World (C/L: Blow, Kurtis); It's Like That (C/L: Smith, Larry; Simmons, J.; McDaniels, D.); Feel the Spin (C/L: Harry, Deborah; Jellybean; Colandreo, Toni); Please Don't Go (C/L: Tripoli, Andy "Panda"); My Secret (C/L: Eastman, Dick; Hart, Bobby); She's on It (C/L: Rubin, Rick; Horivitz, Adam); Radio (C/L: Rubin, Rick; Smith, James); Pump It Up (Let's Get Funky) (C/L: Blow, Kurtis; Morales, Mark; Robinson, Darren; Wimbley, Damon); All You Can Eat (C/L: Blow, Kurtis; Morales, Mark; Robinson, Darren; Wimbley, Damon); Can You Rock It Like This (C/L: Smith, J.T.; Rubin, Rick; Smith, Larry); I Want You to Be My Girl (C/L: Levy, Morris; Barrett, Richard); Fat Boys (C/L: Blow, Kurtis; Waring, William; Miller, Ronald; Morales, Mark; Wimbley, Damon); Can't Stop the Street (C/L: Hartman, Dan; Midnight, Charlie); You

Notes   It is not known if any of these were written for the film.

L

3163 ✦ LA BAMBA
Columbia, 1987

Musical Score Santana, Carlos; Goodman, Miles

Producer(s) Hackford, Taylor; Borden, Bill
Director(s) Valdez, Luis
Screenwriter(s) Valdez, Luis

Cast Morales, Esai; De Soto, Rosana; Pena, Elizabeth; Phillips, Lou Diamond

Notes No cue sheet available. There are no original songs in this film.

3164 ✦ LABYRINTH
Tri-Star, 1986

Musical Score Bowie, David
Composer(s) Bowie, David
Lyricist(s) Bowie, David

Producer(s) Rattray, Eric
Director(s) Henson, Jim
Screenwriter(s) Jones, Terry

Cast Bowie, David; Connelly, Jennifer; Froud, Toby; Thompson, Shelley; Malcolm, Christopher; Henson, Brian

Song(s) Underground; Dance Magic; Chilly Down; As the World Falls Down; Within You

Notes No cue sheet available.

3165 ✦ LA CAGE AUX FOLLES
United Artists, 1978

Musical Score Morricone, Ennio; Travia, Maria

Producer(s) Danon, Marcello
Director(s) Molinaro, Edouard
Screenwriter(s) Veber, Francis; Molinaro, Edouard; Danon, Marcello; Poiret, Jean
Source(s) *La Cage Aux Folles* (play) Poiret, Jean

Cast Tognazzi, Ugo; Serrault, Michel; Galabru, Michel; Maurier, Claire; Laurent, Remi; Luke, Benny; Scarpitta, Carmen; Maneri, Luisa

Song(s) I Am Waiting (C: Morricone, Ennio; Travia, Maria; L: Boom, J.P.)

3166 ✦ LA CAGE AUX FOLLES II
United Artists, 1981

Musical Score Travia, Maria; Morricone, Ennio

Producer(s) Danon, Marcello
Director(s) Molinaro, Edouard
Screenwriter(s) Veber, Francis

Cast Tognazzi, Ugo; Serrault, Michel; Bozzuffi, Marcel; Borboni, Paola; Vettorazzo, Giovanni; Onorato, Glauco; Bisacco, Roberto; Luke, Benny; Galabru, Michel

Song(s) Darling (C: Travia, Maria; Morricone, Ennio; L: Smith, S. Duncan)

3167 ✦ LA CONGA NIGHTS
Universal, 1940

Musical Score Skinner, Frank
Composer(s) Skinner, Frank
Lyricist(s) Lerner, Sam

Producer(s) Goldsmith, Ken
Director(s) Landers, Lew
Screenwriter(s) Clork, Harry; Smith, Paul Gerard

Cast Herbert, Hugh; O'Keefe, Dennis; Moore, Constance; Quillan, Eddie

Song(s) Havana; Carmenita McCoy [2]; Chance of a Lifetime; Unfair to Love [1]

Notes [1] Used instrumentally only. [2] Also in TIGHT SHOES.

3168 ✦ LADIES' MAN (1947)
Paramount, 1947

Composer(s) Styne, Jule
Lyricist(s) Cahn, Sammy
Choreographer(s) Daniels, Billy

Producer(s) Dare, Danny [2]
Director(s) Russell, William D.
Screenwriter(s) Beloin, Edmund; Rose, Jack; Meltzer, Lewis

Cast Bracken, Eddie; Daley, Cass; Spike Jones and His Orchestra; Welles, Virginia

Song(s) What Am I Gonna Do About You?; Away Out West; I Gotta Gal I Love (In North and South Dakota) [1]; I'm As Ready As I'll Ever Be

Notes Spike Jones also performs "Dark Eyes;" "The Volga Boatman's Song;" "Holiday for Strings" and "Cocktails for Two." "Mama Yo Quero (I Want My Mama)" with special lyrics by Sol Meyer is used. [1] Written for unproduced movie musical THE UMPIRE'S DAUGHTER. [2] Billed as Daniel Dare.

3169 ✦ THE LADIES' MAN (1961)
Paramount, 1961

Musical Score Scharf, Walter
Composer(s) Warren, Harry
Lyricist(s) Brooks, Jack
Choreographer(s) Van, Bobby

Producer(s) Lewis, Jerry
Director(s) Lewis, Jerry
Screenwriter(s) Lewis, Jerry; Richmond, Bill

Cast Stanley, Pat; Lewis, Jerry; Benet, Vicki; Traubel, Helen; Freeman, Kathleen; Lester, Buddy; Raft, George; Harry James and His Band

Song(s) Don't Go to Paris; He Doesn't Know [1]; Birthday Song [2] (C: Brown, Louis Yule; L: Lewis, Jerry); Ladies' Man [2]; Finale and Death Scene [3] (C: Scharf, Walter; L: Traubel, Helen; Scharf, Walter)

Notes [1] Instrumentally presented only. [2] Not used. [3] Not used. From the opera THE FATAL LOVE. German libretto by Traubel, English lyrics by Scharf.

3170 ✦ LADIES MUST LIVE
Warner Brothers–First National, 1940

Musical Score Jackson, Howard
Composer(s) Chaplin, Saul
Lyricist(s) Cahn, Sammy

Producer(s) Jacobs, William
Director(s) Smith, Noel
Screenwriter(s) Kent, Robert E.
Source(s) *The Hometowners* (play) Cohan, George M.

Cast Morris, Wayne; Lane, Priscilla; Karns, Roscoe; Patrick, Lee; Reeves, George; Taylor, Ferris; Williams, Lottie; Saum, Cliff; Hopper, DeWolf

Song(s) Show You What Love Can Do; I Could Make You Care

3171 ✦ LADIES OF THE CHORUS
Columbia, 1948

Composer(s) Roberts, Allan; Lee, Lester
Lyricist(s) Roberts, Allan; Lee, Lester

Producer(s) Romm, Harry
Director(s) Karlson, Phil
Screenwriter(s) Sauber, Harry; Carole, Joseph

Cast Monroe, Marilyn; Brooks, Rand; Jergens, Adele

Song(s) Ladies of the Chorus; Anyone Can See; Every Baby Needs a Da-Da-Daddy [2]; Crazy for You; Ubangi Love Song (C/L: Ram, Buck); Where Am I Without You [1] (C: De Paul, Gene; L: Raye, Don); You're Never Too Old

Notes [1] Not written for picture. [2] Also in THE TRAVELING SALESWOMAN.

3172 ✦ LADY AND GENT
Paramount, 1932

Director(s) Roberts, Stephen
Screenwriter(s) Jones, Grover; McNutt, William Slavens

Cast Bancroft, George; Gibson, Wynne; Starrett, Charles; Gleason, James

Song(s) Everyone Knows It but You [2] (C: Johnston, Arthur; L: Coslow, Sam); My Own United States [1] (C: Traditional; L: Stange, Stanislaus)

Notes [1] Based on music of "When Johnny Comes Marching Home." [2] Also used in UNMARRIED.

3173 ✦ LADY AND THE TRAMP
Disney, 1954

Musical Score Wallace, Oliver
Composer(s) Lee, Peggy; Burke, Sonny
Lyricist(s) Lee, Peggy; Burke, Sonny

Producer(s) Penner, Erdman
Director(s) Luske, Hamilton; Geronimi, Clyde; Jackson, Wilfred
Screenwriter(s) Penner, Erdman; Rinaldi, Joe; Wright, Ralph; DaGradi, Don
Voices Lee, Peggy; Roberts, Larry; Baucom, Bill; Felton, Verna; Givot, George; Millar, Lee; Luddy, Barbara; Thompson, Bill; Freberg, Stan; Reed, Alan; McKennon, Dallas; The Mello Men

Directing Animator(s) Kahl, Milt; Thomas, Franklin; Johnston, Ollie; Lounsbery, John; Reitherman, Wolfgang; Larson, Eric; King, Hal; Clark, Les

Song(s) Bella Notte; Peace on Earth; Siamese Cat Song; He's a Tramp; What Is a Baby; La La Lu; Lady [1] (C: Wallace, Oliver; L: Fine, Sid; Penner, Erdman); Had I Known [1] (C: Wallace, Oliver; L: George, Gil); I'm Free as the Breeze [2] (C: Daniel, Eliot; L: Gilbert, Ray); Jim Dear [2]; Lady and the Tramp [2] (C: Wrubel, Allie; L: Gilbert, Ray); Old Trusty [2]; Summer Love [1] (C: Wallace, Oliver; L: George, Gil; Wallace, Oliver); That Fellow's a Friend of Mine [2]; Singing ('Cause He Wants to Sing) [2]

Notes Animated feature. There is also a "vocal" of "Home Sweet Home" by Bishop and Payne sung, or rather howled, by a group of dogs. [1] Used instrumentally only. [2] Not used.

3174 ◆ LADY BE CAREFUL
Paramount, 1936

Producer(s) Glazer, Benjamin
Director(s) Reed, Theodore
Screenwriter(s) Pasker, Dorothy; Campbell, Alan; Ruskin, Harry
Source(s) *Sailor Beware* (play) Nicholson, Kenyon; Robinson, Charles

Cast Ayres, Lew; Carlisle, Mary; Crabbe, Buster; Baker, Benny; Withers, Grant

Song(s) Printemps Ala Rumba (C: Revel, Harry; L: Gordon, Mack)

Notes "Love in Bloom" by Ralph Rainger and Leo Robin was also featured briefly.

3175 ◆ LADY BE GAY

See LAUGH IT OFF.

3176 ◆ LADY BE GOOD
Metro–Goldwyn–Mayer, 1941

Musical Score Edens, Roger
Choreographer(s) Berkeley, Busby

Producer(s) Freed, Arthur
Director(s) McLeod, Norman Z.
Screenwriter(s) McGowan, Jack; Van Riper, Kay; McLain, John

Cast Powell, Eleanor; Sothern, Ann; Young, Robert; Barrymore, Lionel; Carroll, John; Skelton, Red; O'Brien, Virginia; Conway, Tom; Dailey, Dan [3]; Owen, Reginald; Hobart, Rose; Silvers, Phil; The Berry Brothers [1]; Russell, Connie

Song(s) Oh Lady Be Good (C: Gershwin, George; L: Gershwin, Ira); You'll Never Know (C/L: Edens, Roger); Your Words and My Music (C: Edens, Roger; L: Freed, Arthur); The Last Time I Saw Paris (C: Kern, Jerome; L: Hammerstein II, Oscar); Fascinating Rhythm (C: Gershwin, George; L: Gershwin, Ira); I'd Rather Dance [2] (C: Brown, Nacio Herb; L: Freed, Ralph); All I Want to Do Is Love You [4] (C: Brown, Nacio Herb; L: Freed, Ralph)

Notes [1] James, Warren and Nyas. [2] Deleted from final print. [3] Billed as Dan Dailey Jr. [4] Not used.

3177 ◆ LADY CALLED LOU
Paramount, 1947 unproduced

Composer(s) Loesser, Frank
Lyricist(s) Loesser, Frank

Song(s) Goldie Goes with the Mine; Misty Eyed; What Kind of Fool

3178 ◆ THE LADY CONFESSES
PRC, 1946

Producer(s) Stern, Alfred
Director(s) Newfield, Sam
Screenwriter(s) Martin, Helen

Cast Beaumont, Hugh; Hughes, Mary Beth

Song(s) It's All Your Fault (C/L: Walker, Cindy); It's a Fine World (Don't Let Anyone Kid You) (C/L: Smith; Kuhstos; Blonder); Dance Close to Me Darling (C/L: Unger, Robert; Seaman, Al)

Notes Cue sheet doesn't differentiate between vocals and instrumentals.

3179 ◆ LADY FOR A NIGHT
Republic, 1941

Lyricist(s) Meyer, Sol
Choreographer(s) Gould, Dave

Producer(s) Cohen, Albert J.
Director(s) Jason, Leigh
Screenwriter(s) Dawn, Isabel; DeGaw, Boyce
Source(s) "Lady from New Orleans" (story) Brown, Beth

Cast Blondell, Joan; Wayne, John; Middleton, Ray; Merivale, Philip; Yurka, Blanche; Barrett, Edith; Kinskey, Leonid

Song(s) Conjur Man Melodies (C: Whipper, Leigh); Has Anybody Seen My Man (C: Styne, Jule)

3180 ◆ THE LADY FROM CHEYENNE
Universal, 1941

Producer(s) Lloyd, Frank
Director(s) Lloyd, Frank
Screenwriter(s) Scola, Kathryn; Duff, Warren

Cast Young, Loretta; Preston, Robert; Arnold, Edward; George, Gladys; Craven, Frank; Best, Willie; Ralph, Jessie; Charters, Spencer; Fields, Stanley

Song(s) Ladies from Paree (C: Previn, Charles; L: Lerner, Sam)

3181 ◆ LADY FROM LARIAT LOOP
Paramount, 1948 unproduced

Cast Hutton, Betty

Song(s) Pindy-Fendy [1] (C/L: Loesser, Frank); Batten Down Her Hatches (C/L: Loesser, Frank)

Notes [1] More an Indian chant than a song.

3182 ◆ LADY FROM LOUISIANA
Republic, 1941

Producer(s) Vorhaus, Bernard
Director(s) Vorhaus, Bernard

Screenwriter(s) Caspary, Vera; Hogan, Michael; Endore, Guy

Cast Wayne, John; Munson, Ona; Middleton, Ray; Stephenson, Henry; Westley, Helen; Pennick, Jack; Dandridge, Dorothy

Song(s) Tres Bien (C: Styne, Jule; L: Cherkose, Eddie)

3183 ◆ LADY FROM SHANGHAI
Columbia, 1948

Producer(s) Welles, Orson
Director(s) Welles, Orson
Screenwriter(s) Welles, Orson
Source(s) *Before I Die* (novel) King, Sherwood

Cast Hayworth, Rita [1]; Welles, Orson; Sloane, Everett; Anders, Glenn; De Corsia, Ted; Sanford, Erskine; Schilling, Gus

Song(s) Please Don't Kiss Me (C/L: Roberts, Allan; Fisher, Doris)

Notes [1] Dubbed by Anita Ellis.

3184 ◆ LADY IN A JAM
Universal, 1942

Producer(s) La Cava, Gregory
Director(s) La Cava, Gregory
Screenwriter(s) Thackerey, Eugene; Cockrell, Frank; Lovering, Otho

Cast Dunne, Irene; Knowles, Patric; Vassar, Queenie; Bellamy, Ralph; Pallette, Eugene; Hinds, Samuel S.; Garland, Jane; McWade, Edward; Homans, Robert

Song(s) My Darlin' Nellie's Grave (C/L: Dodd, Jimmy); I Come from a Line o' Cowhands (C/L: Bellamy, Ralph)

3185 ◆ LADY IN THE DARK
Paramount, 1944

Musical Score Dolan, Robert Emmett
Composer(s) Weill, Kurt
Choreographer(s) Pan, Hermes [5]

Producer(s) DeSylva, B.G.
Director(s) Leisen, Mitchell
Screenwriter(s) Goodrich, Frances; Hackett, Albert
Source(s) *Lady in the Dark* (musical) Weill, Kurt; Gershwin, Ira; Hart, Moss

Cast Rogers, Ginger; Baxter, Warner; Milland, Ray; Hall, Jon; Auer, Mischa; Sullivan, Barry; Russell, Gail

Song(s) My Ship [1]; Jenny [1] [2] (L: Gershwin, Ira; Burke, Johnny); Girl of the Moment [1]; Whereas and Secundus [1]; Suddenly It's Spring [6] (C: Van Heusen, James; L: Burke, Johnny); Tschaikowsky [1] [3]; Ladies and Gentlemen [1] [4]; Attorney for Prosecution [1] [4]; Milland's Best Years [1] [4]; Lawyer for Defendant [1] [4]; Jon Hall's Best Years [1] [4]; Ginger Rogers

Tra-La-La [1] [4]; Liza's to Be Married [1] [4]; Entry of the Gladiators [1] [4]

Notes The titles might not be exactly as known for the Broadway musical but they are what appeared on the Paramount cue sheets. The dance to "Suddenly It's Spring" with Rogers and Don Loper was arranged by Robert Russell Bennett. The dance with Rogers and Jon Hall ("Artist's Waltz") was arranged by Robert Emmett Dolan. (Another piece of Dolan's scoring was recorded on a 78 rpm record as "A Message for Liza.") There are snatches of many other songs from the original score but since they are only brief pieces I did not include them. [1] From original production. [2] Additional lyrics were written by Johnny Burke and Ira Gershwin. Gershwin was responsible for the lyrics about Jenny becoming an artist's model and how her chassis would be recognized from Troy to Tallahassee. Johnny Burke wrote how Jenny went to Labrador for a weekend where she was nicknamed Aurora Borealis and how she went on a Carribean voyage where her talent had no limit. He also wrote about Jenny at 38 where she learned about native customs and upset the tropics. [3] This was recorded by Mischa Auer but not used. [4] Based on a Gershwin and Weill song from the original. These titles are from the cue sheets. [5] Billy Daniels also assisted in the choreography. [6] Used instrumentally though recorded by Ginger Rogers.

3186 ◆ THE LADY IS WILLING
Columbia, 1942

Musical Score Grant, James Edward; McCleery, Albert
Choreographer(s) Dean, Douglas

Producer(s) Leisen, Mitchell
Director(s) Leisen, Mitchell

Cast Dietrich, Marlene [2]; MacMurray, Fred; Ford, Ruth; Clark, Roger; MacMahon, Aline; Ridges, Stanley; Judge, Arline; Keane, Robert Emmett

Song(s) I Find Love [1] (C/L: King, Jack; Clifford, Gordon)

Notes [1] Later published as "Strange Thing." [2] Dubbed by Virginia Rees.

3187 ◆ LADY JANE
Paramount, 1986

Musical Score Oliver, Stephen
Composer(s) Oliver, Stephen
Lyricist(s) Oliver, Stephen

Producer(s) Snell, Peter
Director(s) Nunn, Trevor
Screenwriter(s) Edgar, David

Cast Carter, Helen Bonham; Elwes, Cary; Wood, John; Hordern, Michael; Bennett, Jill; Lapotaire, Jane; Kestelman, Sara; Stewart, Patrick; Ackland, Joss

Song(s)   Never Had Man; Flowers of May; Love Theme from Lady Jane; The Coronation

3188 ◆ LADY L
Metro–Goldwyn–Mayer, 1966

Musical Score   Francaix, Jean

Producer(s)   Ponti, Carlo
Director(s)   Ustinov, Peter
Screenwriter(s)   Ustinov, Peter
Source(s)   *Lady L* (novel) Gary, Romain

Cast   Loren, Sophia; Newman, Paul; Niven, David; Dalio, Marcel; Parker, Cecil; Noiret, Philippe; Dauphin, Claude

Song(s)   Italian Song (C: Francaix, Jean; L: Ustinov, Peter)

3189 ◆ LADY, LET'S DANCE!
Monogram, 1944

Composer(s)   Grouya, Ted
Lyricist(s)   Oppenheim, Dave
Choreographer(s)   Gould, Dave [1]

Producer(s)   Dunlap, Scott R.
Director(s)   Woodruff, Frank
Screenwriter(s)   Panaleff, Michael; Milne, Peter

Cast   Bolita; Ellison, James; Frick and Frack; Catlett, Walter; Littlefield, Lucien; St. Clair, Maurice; Busse, Henry; Harvey, Harry; Henry Busse and His Orchestra; Eddie LeBaron and His Orchestra; Mitchell Ayres and His Orchestra; Lou Bring and His Orchestra

Song(s)   Lady, Let's Dance; Dream of Dreams; Rio; In the Days of Beau Brummel; Happy Hearts; Ten Million Men and a Girl; Silver Shadows and Golden Dreams (C: Pollack, Lew; L: Newman, Charles)

Notes   No cue sheet available. [1] Ballet choreographed by Michael Panaieff.

3190 ◆ THE LADY OBJECTS
Columbia, 1938

Composer(s)   Oakland, Ben
Lyricist(s)   Hammerstein II, Oscar

Producer(s)   Perlberg, William
Director(s)   Kenton, Erle C.
Screenwriter(s)   Lehman, Gladys; Kenyon, Charles

Cast   Ross, Lanny; Stuart, Gloria; Marsh, Joan; Benson, Roy; Watkin, Pierre; Paige, Robert; Loft, Arthur; Andrews, Stanley; Flowers, Bess; Doran, Ann

Song(s)   When You're in the Room; Victory Song (L: Drake, Milton); A Mist Is Over the Moon [1]; Sky High (L: Drake, Milton); Naughty Naughty (L: Drake, Milton); That Week in Paris; Home in Your Arms; Alma Mater [1] (L: Drake, Milton)

Notes   [1] Also in TALK ABOUT A LADY. [2] Listed in some sources but not cue sheet.

3191 ◆ LADY OF BURLESQUE
United Artists, 1943

Composer(s)   Akst, Harry
Lyricist(s)   Cahn, Sammy

Producer(s)   Stromberg, Hunt
Director(s)   Wellman, William A.
Screenwriter(s)   Gunn, James
Source(s)   *The G-String Murders* (novel) Lee, Gypsy Rose

Cast   Stanwyck, Barbara; Adrian, Iris; Dickson, Gloria; Martin, Marion; O'Shea, Michael; Bromberg, J. Edward; Fenton, Frank

Song(s)   So This Is You; Take It Off the E String (Put It on the G String)

Notes   No cue sheet available. Released as STRIPTEASE LADY overseas.

3192 ◆ A LADY OF CHANCE
Metro–Goldwyn–Mayer, 1928

Musical Score   Axt, William

Director(s)   Leonard, Robert Z.
Screenwriter(s)   Goulding, Edmund; Younger, A.P.
Source(s)   "Little Angel" (story) Scott, Leroy

Cast   Shearer, Norma; Sherman, Lowell; Lee, Gwen; Brown, Johnny Mack [1]; Besserer, Eugenie; Messinger, Buddie

Song(s)   (Just a Little Bit of) Driftwood (C/L: Lyman, Abe; Davis, Benny; Davis, Dohl); Crossroads [2] (C: Axt, William; L: Mendoza, David)

Notes   [1] Billed as John Mack Brown. [2] Also in SHOW PEOPLE.

3193 ◆ A LADY OF SCANDAL
Metro–Goldwyn–Mayer, 1930

Choreographer(s)   Lee, Sammy

Director(s)   Franklin, Sidney
Screenwriter(s)   West, Claudine; Mayer, Edwin Justus
Source(s)   *The High Road* (play) Lonsdale, Frederick

Cast   Chatterton, Ruth; Rathbone, Basil; Forbes, Ralph; O'Neil, Nance; Kerr, Frederick; Bunston, Herbert; Chadwick, Cyril; Ellsler, Effie; Bolder, Robert

Song(s)   Say It with a Smile (C: King, Jack; L: Janis, Elsie)

Notes   There is also a vocal of "Smiles" by J. Will Callahan and Lee G. Roberts.

3194 ✦ LADY OF THE LAKE
FitzPatrick Pictures, 1930

Producer(s) FitzPatrick, James A.
Director(s) FitzPatrick, James A.
Screenwriter(s) FitzPatrick, James A.
Source(s) "The Lady of the Lake" (poem) Scott, Sir Walter

Cast Marmont, Percy; Hume, Benita; Butt, Lawson; Carewe, James; Mason, Haddon; Bartlett, Hedda

Song(s) Eileen, Sweet Eileen (C: Shilkret, Nathaniel; L: Ryskind, Morrie)

Notes No cue sheet available.

3195 ✦ LADY OF THE PAVEMENTS
United Artists, 1929

Director(s) Griffith, D.W.
Screenwriter(s) Scarborough, George
Source(s) La Paiva Vollmoeller, Karl Gustav

Cast Velez, Lupe; Boyd, William; Goudal, Jetta; Conti, Albert; Fawcett, George; Armetta, Henry; Bakewell, William; Pangborn, Franklin

Song(s) Where Is the Song of Songs for Me? (C/L: Berlin, Irving)

Notes No cue sheet available.

3196 ✦ LADY OF THE TROPICS
Metro–Goldwyn–Mayer, 1939

Musical Score Waxman, Franz

Producer(s) Zimbalist, Sam
Director(s) Conway, Jack
Screenwriter(s) Hecht, Ben

Cast Taylor, Robert; Lamarr, Hedy; Franklin, Gloria; Tilbury, Zeffie; Cossart, Ernest; Schildkraut, Joseph; Moorhead, Natalie; Cunningham, Cecil; Porcasi, Paul

Song(s) Each Time You Say Goodby (I Die a Little) (C: Ohman, Phil; L: Carling, Foster)

Notes There is also a vocal of "Ai Tuoi Piedi Son" from MANON LESCAUT by Puccini.

3197 ✦ LADY POSSESSED
Republic, 1951

Musical Score Scott, Nathan

Producer(s) Mason, James
Director(s) Spier, William; Kellino, Roy
Screenwriter(s) Kellino, Pamela; Mason, James

Cast Mason, James; Havoc, June; Dunne, Stephen; Compton, Fay; Kellino, Pamela; Geray, Steven; Myrtil, Odette; Mosler, Enid

Song(s) My Heart Asks Why (C/L: May, Hans); It's You I Love (C/L: Wrubel, Allie); Calypso Number (C/L: Young, Marl); More Wonderful than These (C/L: Thompson, Kay; Spier, Bill)

3198 ✦ LADY SINGS THE BLUES
Paramount, 1972

Producer(s) Weston, Jay; White, James S.
Director(s) Furie, Sidney J.
Screenwriter(s) McCloy, Terence; Clark, Chris; de Passe, Suzanne

Cast Ross, Diana; Capers, Virginia; Williams, Billy Dee; Pryor, Richard; Melton, Sid; Callahan, James; Crothers, Benjamin "Scatman"

Song(s) Those Low-Down Shuffle Blues (C: Askey, Gil; L: Robinson, William)

Notes There are also renditions of "Tain't Nobody's Bizness If I Do" by Porter Grainger and Everett Robbins; "All of Me" by Seymour Simons and Gerald Marks; "The Man I Love" by George Gershwin and Ira Gershwin; "Them There Eyes" by Maceo Pinkard, William Tracey and Doris Tauber; "Gimme a Pigfoot and a Bottle of Beer" by Wesley Wilson; "I Cried for You" by Abe Lyman, Gus Arnheim and Arthur Freed; "What a Little Moonlight Can Do" by Harry Woods; "Fine and Mellow" by Billie Holiday; "Mean to Me" by Roy Turk and Fred E. Ahlert; "Strange Fruit" by Lewis Allen; "Good Morning Heartache" by Irene Higgenbotham, Ervin Drake and Dan Fisher; "Lover Man" by Jimmy Davis, Jimmy Sherman and Roger (Ram) Ramirez; "Lady Sings the Blues" by Billie Holiday and Herbie Nichols; "Don't Explain" by Billie Holiday and Arthur Herzog, Jr.; "Our Love Is Here to Stay" by George and Ira Gershwin; "You've Changed" by Bill Carey and Carl Fischer; "God Bless the Child" by Billie Holiday and Arthur Herzog, Jr.; "My Man" by Maurice Yvain, A. Willemetz, Jacques Charles and Channing Pollock; "Had You Been Around" by Ronald Miller, Avery Vandenberg, Bernard Yuffy and Richard Jacques; "Fancy Passes" by William O'Malley, Ronald Miller and Avery Vandenberg; "Hello Broadway" by Ronald Miller, and William O'Malley.

3199 ✦ A LADY'S MORALS
Metro–Goldwyn–Mayer, 1930

Composer(s) Straus, Oscar
Lyricist(s) Grey, Clifford
Choreographer(s) Lee, Sammy

Director(s) Franklin, Sidney
Screenwriter(s) Meehan, John; Richman, Arthur

Cast Moore, Grace; Howland, Jobyna; Martino, Giovanni; Reicher, Frank; Porcasi, Paul; Denny, Reginald; Beery, Wallace; Emery, Gilbert; Marion, George F.

Song(s) Is It Destiny?; Students' Song; Oh Why (C: Woods, Harry; Stothart, Herbert; L: Freed, Arthur); Swedish Pastorale (C: Stothart, Herbert; L: Johnson, Howard); I Hear Your Voice (L: Freed, Arthur; Grey, Clifford); I'll Remember You [1] (L: Freed, Arthur); A New Love Song [1] (C: Stothart, Herbert; Woods, Harry; L: Freed, Arthur); What Will Become of Me [1] (C: Stothart, Herbert; Woods, Harry; L: Freed, Arthur)

Notes Originally reviewed as THE SOUL KISS, then retitled. There are also vocals of "Chacun le Sait" and "Rataplan" from DAUGHTER OF THE REGIMENT by Donizetti; "Chorus" and "Casta Diva" from NORMA by Bellini and "Lovely Hour" by Carrie Jacobs Bond. [1] Not used.

3200 ✦ THE LADY TAKES A SAILOR
Warner Brothers–First National, 1949

Musical Score Steiner, Max

Producer(s) Kurnitz, Harry
Director(s) Curtiz, Michael
Screenwriter(s) Freeman, Everett
Source(s) "The Octopus and Miss Smith" (story) Gruskin, Jerry

Cast Wyman, Jane; Morgan, Dennis; Arden, Eve; Douglas, Robert; Joslyn, Allyn; Tully, Tom; Romay, Lina; Frawley, William; Clark, Fred; Meredith, Charles; Stevens, Craig; Prager, Stanley

Song(s) Porque Te Amei (C/L: Amaral, Nestor)

Notes It is not known if this was written for the picture.

3201 ✦ THE LADY VANISHES
Metro–Goldwyn–Mayer, 1938

Producer(s) Black, Edward
Director(s) Hitchcock, Alfred
Screenwriter(s) Gilliat, Sidney
Source(s) *The Wheel Spins* (novel) White, Ethel Lina

Cast Redgrave, Michael; Lockwood, Margaret; Whitty, Dame May; Lukas, Paul; Travers, Linden; Clare, Mary; Parker, Cecil; Radford, Basil; Wayne, Naunton

Song(s) The Code Song (C: Levy, Lou)

3202 ✦ THE LAIR OF THE WHITE WORM
Vestron, 1988

Musical Score Syrewicz, Stanislas

Producer(s) Russell, Ken
Director(s) Russell, Ken
Screenwriter(s) Russell, Ken
Source(s) *The Lair of the White Worm* (novel) Stoker, Bram

Cast Donohoe, Amanda; Grant, Hugh; Oxenberg, Catherine [1]; Capaldi, Peter; Davis, Sammi; Johns, Stratford; Brooke, Paul; Gable, Christopher

Song(s) The D'Ampton Worm (C/L: Machado, Emilio Perez; Powys, Stephen)

Notes No cue sheet available. [1] All dialogue dubbed.

3203 ✦ LAKE PLACID SERENADE
Republic, 1944

Director(s) Sekely, Steven
Screenwriter(s) Hyland, Dick Irving; Gilbert, Doris

Cast Ralston, Vera Hruba; Livingston, Robert; Catlett, Walter; Corrigan, Lloyd; Pallette, Eugene; Bachelor, Stephanie; Ray Noble and His Orchestra; Harry Owens and his Royal Hawaiians; Rogers, Roy; McGowan and Mak; Watts, Twinkle; The Merry Messiters

Notes No cue sheet available. It is not known if there are any original vocals in this film. Songs include "Deep Purple" by Mitchell Parish and Peter De Rose; "My Isle of Golden Dreams" by Walter Blaufuss and Gus Kahn; "National Emblem March" (inst.) by E.E. Bagley; "Intermezzo" by Robert Henning and Heinz Provost; "Waiting for the Robert E. Lee" by L. Wolfe Gilbert and Lewis F. Muir; "When Citrus is in Bloom" and "Drigo's Serenade" by Ricardo Drigo and "While Strooling Through the Park One Day" by Robert A. King.

3204 ✦ LA LUNA
Twentieth Century–Fox, 1979

Producer(s) Bertolucci, Giovanni
Director(s) Bertolucci, Bernardo
Screenwriter(s) Bertolucci, Giuseppe; Peploe, Clare; Bertolucci, Bernardo; Malko, George [1]

Cast Clayburgh, Jill; Barry, Matthew; Lazar, Veronica; Salvatori, Renato; Gwynne, Fred; Valli, Alida

Song(s) Kiss [2] (C: Newman, Lionel; L: Gillespie, Haven)

Notes [1] Malko did the English adaptation. [2] Also in NIAGARA.

3205 ✦ LAMBERT THE SHEEPISH LION
Disney, 1952

Musical Score Dubin, Joseph S.

Director(s) Hannah, Jack
Screenwriter(s) Peet, Bill; Wright, Ralph; Banta, Milt
Narrator(s) Holloway, Sterling

Song(s) Lambert the Sheepish Lion (C/L: Pola, Eddie; Wyle, George)

Notes Short subject.

3206 ✦ THE LAMBETH WALK
CAPAD, 1940

Musical Score Levy, Louis
Composer(s) Gay, Noel
Lyricist(s) Furber, Douglas

Producer(s) Havelock-Allan, Anthony
Director(s) De Courville, Albert
Screenwriter(s) Carstairs, John Paddy; Edmunds, Robert; Grey, Clifford
Source(s) *Me and My Girl* (musical) Gay, Noel; Rose, Louis Arthur; Furber, Douglas

Cast Lane, Lupino; Hicks, Seymour; Gray, Sally

Song(s) Lambeth Walk; Me and My Girl

Notes This is a British picture distributed by M-G-M.

3207 ✦ LA MELODIA PROHIBIDA
Fox, 1933

Composer(s) Akst, Harry
Lyricist(s) Gilbert, L. Wolfe

Song(s) The Islands Are Calling Me; Till the End of Time; Como Tu y Yo (C/L: Grever, Maria); Cuando Me Vaya (C/L: Grever, Maria); Derelict Song

Notes No other information available.

3208 ✦ LA MUJER QUE QUIERE A DOS
Twentieth Century–Fox, 1946

Composer(s) de la Vega, Jose
Lyricist(s) de la Vega, Jose

Song(s) La Bienvenida; En Que Quedamos por Fin (C/L: Baena; Federico); Ma Mujer Que Quiere a Dos (C/L: Monge, Chucho); Romanza; Asi Soy Yo; Ya Semos Dos (C/L: Monge, Chucho); Los Arbolitos (C/L: Gil, Chucho Martinez)

Notes No other information available.

3209 ✦ THE LAND BEFORE TIME
Universal, 1988

Musical Score Horner, James

Producer(s) Bluth, Don; Goldman, Gary; Pomeroy, John
Director(s) Bluth, Don
Screenwriter(s) Krieger, Stu
Voices Hingle, Pat; Shaver, Helen; Damon, Gabriel; Erwin, Bill; Hutson, Candy; Byrnes, Burke; Barsi, Judith; Ryan, Will

Song(s) If We Hold On Together (C: Horner, James; L: Jennings, Will)

Notes This is an animated feature.

3210 ✦ THE LAND BEYOND THE LAW
Warner Brothers, 1937

Musical Score Spencer, Tim; Jackson, Howard
Composer(s) Jerome, M.K.
Lyricist(s) Scholl, Jack

Producer(s) Foy, Bryan
Director(s) Eason, B. Reeves

Screenwriter(s) Ward, Luci; Watson, Joseph K.
Source(s) "The Last Bad Man" (story) Jackson, Marion

Cast Foran, Dick; Perry, Linda; Kendall, Cyrus W.; Strange, Glenn; Woods, Harry; Cobb, Edmund; Otho, Henry; Franklin, Irene

Song(s) The Prairie Is My Home [2]; The Circle Bar [1]; Whisper While You're Waltzing

Notes [1] Also in WEST OF THE ROCKIES. [2] Also in EMPTY HOLSTERS, PRAIRIE THUNDER and GUNS OF THE PECOS.

3211 ✦ THE LANDLORD
United Artists, 1970

Musical Score Kooper, Al
Composer(s) Kooper, Al
Lyricist(s) Kooper, Al

Producer(s) Jewison, Norman
Director(s) Ashby, Hal
Screenwriter(s) Gunn, William
Source(s) (novel) Hunter, Kristin

Cast Bridges, Beau; Grant, Lee; Sands, Diana; Bailey, Pearl; Bey, Marki; Gossett, Lou; Anspach, Susan

Song(s) Brand New Day; Car Commercial; Let Me Love You; A Man; Doin' Me Dirty; God Bless the Children (C/L: Holiday, Jimmy)

3212 ✦ LAND OF THE OPEN RANGE
RKO, 1941

Composer(s) Whitley, Ray; Rose, Fred
Lyricist(s) Whitley, Ray; Rose, Fred

Producer(s) Gilroy, Bert
Director(s) Killy, Edward
Screenwriter(s) Grant, Morton
Source(s) "Homesteads of Hate" (story) Bond, Lee

Cast Holt, Tim; Whitley, Ray; Waldo, Janet; White, Lee "Lasses"; Cavanaugh, Hobart

Song(s) Ki-O; Land of the Open Range

3213 ✦ LANDRUSH
Columbia, 1946

Composer(s) Burnette, Smiley
Lyricist(s) Burnette, Smiley

Producer(s) Clark, Colbert
Director(s) Keays, Vernon
Screenwriter(s) Simmons, Michael L.

Cast Ozie Waters and Colorado Rangers; Starrett, Charles; Burnette, Smiley; Houck, Doris; Lynn, Emmett; Chesebro, George

Notes No cue sheet available.

3214 ✦ LARAMIE TRAIL
Republic, 1944

Producer(s) Gray, Louis
Director(s) English, John
Screenwriter(s) Cheney, J. Benton

Cast Livingston, Bob; Burnette, Smiley; Brent, Linda; Garralaga, Martin

Song(s) Dish Rag Blues (C/L: Burnette, Smiley)

3215 ✦ LARCENY ON THE AIR
Republic, 1937

Producer(s) Siegel, Sol C.
Director(s) Pichel, Irving
Screenwriter(s) Bohem, Endre; English, Richard

Cast Livingston, Robert; Bradley, Grace; Robertson, Willard; Watkin, Pierre; Burnette, Smiley; Bates, Granville; Newell, William; Hopper, DeWolf

Song(s) Sitting on the Moon [1] (C: Stept, Sam H.; L: Mitchell, Sidney D.)

Notes [1] Also in SITTING ON THE MOON.

3216 ✦ LARCENY WITH MUSIC
Universal, 1943

Composer(s) de Paul, Gene
Lyricist(s) Raye, Don

Producer(s) Benedict, Howard
Director(s) Lilley, Edward
Screenwriter(s) Harari, Robert

Cast Carrillo, Leo; Jones, Allan; Carlisle, Kitty; The King Sisters

Song(s) Please Louise; Only in Dreams [1] (C: Strauss, Johann; L: Lerner, Sam); They Died with their Boots Laced; Do You Hear Music?; For the Want of You (C: Styne, Jule; L: Cherkose, Eddie); Keep Smilin' Keep Laughin' Be Happy! (C/L: Singer, Lou); Marching Along Together (C/L: Pola, Eddie; Steininger, Franz

Notes There is also a vocal rendition of "When You Wore a Tulip" by Jack Mahoney and Percy Wenrich. [1] Based on the "Emperor Waltz" as arranged by Charles Previn.

3217 ✦ LAS FRONTERAS DEL AMOR
Fox, 1934

Composer(s) Sanders, Troy
Lyricist(s) Mojica, Jose

Producer(s) Stone, John
Director(s) Strayer, Frank R.

Cast Mojica, Jose; Moreno, Rosita

Song(s) Oh Where Are You [3]; Andar [1] (C/L: Lecuona, Ernesto); Estoy Cantando [2] (L: DeLeon, Fray Luis); Te Quiero Dar Me Vida; Recuerdas

Notes There are also vocals of "La Donna e Mobile" by Verdi; "Cielito Lindo" and "The Minstrel" by Easthope Martin and "Las Mananitas." [1] Not written for this film. [2] Lyric from "Vida Retirada." [3] Also in ONE MAD KISS.

3218 ✦ A LASSIE FROM LANCASHIRE
Republic, 1938

Producer(s) Corfield, John
Director(s) Carstairs, John Paddy
Screenwriter(s) Montgomery, Doreen; Dudley, Ernest

Cast Browne, Marjorie; Thompson, Hal; Sandford, Marjorie; Daly, Mark; The Three Music Hall Boys; Rio & Santos; Caryll & Hilda; Mundy, Billy; Munro, Ronnie

Song(s) Lassie from Lancashire (C: Murphy, C.W.; Lipton, Dan; L: Neat); For the First Time in Life I'm in Love (C/L: Parr-Davies, Harry); Fair, Fat and Forty (C/L: Haines, Will E.); Beside the Seaside (C/L: Glover-Kind, C.W.); Rainy Day (C: Walker; L: Carstairs, John Paddy); Algebra (C: Munro, Ronnie; Campbell, Jimmy; L: Noble, William); Between You and Me and the Gatepost (C/L: Gay, Noel); Jolly Good Luck to the Girl Who Loves a Soldier (C/L: Leigh; Lyle); I'll Be Your Sweetheart (C/L: Dacre, Harry); Three Gay Blades (C/L: Van Kirk; Stirling); Mad About Music (C/L: Gay, Noel); Goodnight Little Sweetheart of My Dreams (C/L: Parr-Davies, Harry)

Notes A British National picture.

3219 ✦ LASSITER
Warner Brothers, 1983

Musical Score Thorne, Ken

Producer(s) Ruddy, Albert S.
Director(s) Young, Roger
Screenwriter(s) Taylor, David

Cast Selleck, Tom; Seymour, Jane; Hutton, Lauren; Hoskins, Bob; Lauter, Ed

Song(s) Beware of the Winners (C: Thorne, Ken; L: Parker, John David; Tanja; Lang, Werner; Ockerse, Taco)

3220 ✦ LAST AMERICAN HERO
Twentieth Century–Fox, 1973

Musical Score Fox, Charles

Producer(s) Roberts, William; Cutts, John
Director(s) Johnson, Lamont
Screenwriter(s) Roberts, William
Source(s) articles by Wolfe, Tom

Cast Bridges, Jeff; Perrine, Valerie; Fitzgerald, Geraldine; Beatty, Ned; Busey, Gary; Lund, Art; Lauter, Ed; Ligon, Tom; Orsatti, Ernie

Song(s) I Got a Name (C: Fox, Charles; L: Gimbel, Norman)

3221 ✦ THE LAST BANDIT
Republic, 1949

Producer(s) Kane, Joseph
Director(s) Kane, Joseph
Screenwriter(s) Williamson, Thames

Cast Elliott, William; Booth, Adrian; Tucker, Forrest; Devine, Andy; Holt, Jack; Gombell, Minna; Withers, Grant; Brissac, Virginia; Andrews, Stanley; Crehan, Joseph; Middleton, Charles

Song(s) Love Is Such a Funny Thing [1] (C: Traditional; L: Elliott, Jack)

Notes [1] Music is from the song "Careless Love."

3222 ✦ THE LAST BARRIER
Studio Unknown, 1940

Composer(s) Drake, Milton
Lyricist(s) Drake, Milton

Song(s) I Feel at Home in a Saddle; Dogie Lullaby; Let's Go on Like This Forever

Notes No other information available.

3223 ✦ THE LAST COMMAND
Republic, 1955

Musical Score Steiner, Max

Producer(s) Lloyd, Frank
Director(s) Lloyd, Frank
Screenwriter(s) Duff, Warren

Cast Hayden, Sterling; Alberghetti, Anna Maria; Carlson, Richard; Hunnicutt, Arthur; Borgnine, Ernest; Naish, J. Carrol; Cooper, Ben; Russell, John; Grey, Virginia; Kruger, Otto; Roberts, Roy; Pickens, Slim

Song(s) Jim Bowie (C: Steiner, Max; L: Clare, Sidney; MacRae, Sheila)

3224 ✦ THE LAST CROOKED MILE
Republic, 1946

Producer(s) Abel, Rudolph E.
Director(s) Ford, Philip
Screenwriter(s) Gruskin, Jerry; Sackheim, Jerry

Cast Barry, Donald; Savage, Ann; Mara, Adele

Song(s) The One I Love Belongs to Somebody Else [1] (C: Jones, Isham; L: Kahn, Gus)

Notes [1] Also in I'LL SEE YOU IN MY DREAMS (Warner).

3225 ✦ THE LAST DANCE
Audible Pictures, 1930

Producer(s) Young, Lon
Director(s) Pembroke, Scott
Screenwriter(s) Townley, Jack

Cast Reynolds, Vera; Robards, Jason; Chandler, George; Short, Gertrude; Leighton, Lillian; Todd, Harry

Song(s) Sally, I'm Lovin' You, Sally (C: Moret, Neil; L: Gillespie, Haven)

Notes No cue sheet available.

3226 ✦ THE LAST DRAGON
Tri-Star, 1985

Musical Score Segal, Misha

Producer(s) Hitzig, Rupert
Director(s) Schultz, Michael
Screenwriter(s) Venosta, Louis

Cast Taimak; Vanity; Murney, Christopher; Carry III, Julius J.; Prince, Faith; O'Brien, Leo; Star, Mike; Reyes Jr., Ernie; Marrow, Esther; Macy, W.H.

Song(s) The Last Dragon (C/L: Whitfield, Norman; Miller, Bruce); Star (C/L: Crockett, Gregg; Barnes, Sharon; Fugua, Gwen Gordy); Dirty Books (C/L: Thompson, Nonnie; Cleary, Bob; Rubin, Danny); Upset Stomach (C/L: Wonder, Stevie); Inside You (C/L: Hutch, Willie); Coke Is It (C/L: DeLuca, Dave); 7th Heaven (C/L: Wolfer, Bill; Vanity); Stand Your Ground (C/L: Whitfield, Norman); The Shuttle (C/L: Ashby, Kerry; West, John; Williams, Steve); Peeping Tom (C/L: Rockwell; Cole, Janet; Greene, Antoine); Rhythm of the Night (C/L: Warren, Diane); Fire (C/L: Oliver, Charlene; Wild, Brian; Wright, Nigel); First Time on a Ferris Wheel (C/L: Schock, Harriet; Segal, Misha); Glow (C/L: Hutch, Willie)

Notes No cue sheet available.

3227 ✦ THE LAST FLIGHT OF NOAH'S ARK
Disney, 1980

Musical Score Jarre, Maurice

Producer(s) Miller, Ron
Director(s) Jarrott, Charles
Screenwriter(s) Carabatsos, Steven W.; Glass, Sandy; Bloom, George Arthur

Cast Gould, Elliott; Bujold, Genevieve; Schroder, Ricky; Gardenia, Vincent; Lauren, Tammy; Fujioka, John; Shimoda, Yuki; Ryan, John P.; Elcar, Dana

Song(s) Half of Me (C: Jarre, Maurice; L: David, Hal)

3228 ✦ LAST FRONTIER
Columbia, 1955

Musical Score Harline, Leigh

Producer(s) Fadiman, William
Director(s) Mann, Anthony
Screenwriter(s) Yordan, Philip; Hughes, Russell S.
Source(s) *The Gilded Rooster* (novel) Roberts, R.E.

Cast Mature, Victor; Madison, Guy; Preston, Robert; Whitmore, James; Bancroft, Anne; Collins, Russell

Song(s) Last Frontier (C: Lee, Lester; L: Washington, Ned)

Notes No cue sheet available.

3229 ✦ LAST FRONTIER UPRISING
Republic, 1945

Composer(s) Willing, Foy
Lyricist(s) Robin, Sid

Producer(s) Gray, Louis
Director(s) Selander, Lesley
Screenwriter(s) Gates, Harvey

Cast Hale, Monte; Booth, Adrian; Taggart, James; Barcroft, Roy; London, Tom; Van Zandt, Philip; Cobb, Edmund; Foy Willing and the Riders of the Purple Sage

Song(s) Song of the Trail; That's Why I Love Texas; You're the Sweetest Rose in Texas (C/L: Wakely, Jimmy); So Long to the Red River Valley (C/L: Spencer, Glenn)

3230 ✦ THE LAST MARRIED COUPLE IN AMERICA
Universal, 1980

Musical Score Fox, Charles

Producer(s) Feldman, Edward S.; Shaner, John Herman
Director(s) Cates, Gilbert
Screenwriter(s) Shaner, John Herman

Cast Wood, Natalie; Segal, George; Harper, Valerie; Benjamin, Richard; Ryan, Charlene; Sokol, Marilyn; Golonka, Arlene; DeLuise, Dom; Dishy, Bob

Song(s) We Could Have It All (C: Fox, Charles; L: Gimbel, Norman)

3231 ✦ LAST MOVIE
Universal, 1971

Composer(s) Wilkin, John Buck
Lyricist(s) Wilkin, John Buck

Producer(s) Lewis, Paul
Director(s) Hopper, Dennis
Screenwriter(s) Stern, Stewart

Cast Hopper, Dennis; Carcia, Stella; Adams, Julie; Kristofferson, Kris; Gordon, Don; Cameron, Rod; Fuller, Samuel; Stockwell, Dean; Law, John Phillip; Mitchum, Jim; Darden, Severn

Song(s) Wonkle My Tonk (C/L: Darden, Severn); Good for Nothing Good Enough for Me (C/L: Kristofferson, Kris); Me and Bobby McGee (C/L: Kristofferson, Kris; Foster, Fred); Golden Idol; My God and I; La De Da; The Daydream; Only; Maria Suenos (C: Granda, Chabuca; Aparicio, Jaime Delgado); Sympathetic Scarecrow (C/L: Hilton, Zack)

Notes It is not known if all these were written for this film.

3232 ✦ THE LAST MUSKETEER
Republic, 1951

Musical Score Butts, Dale

Producer(s) White, Edward J.
Director(s) Witney, William
Screenwriter(s) Orloff, Arthur

Cast Allen, Rex; Kay, Mary Ellen; Pickens, Slim; Anderson, James; Morgan, Boyd "Red"; Jones, Stan

Song(s) I Still Love the West (C/L: Willing, Foy)

3233 ✦ LAST NIGHT AT THE ALAMO
Cinecom International, 1984

Musical Score Pinnell, Chuck; Bell, Wayne
Composer(s) Sargent, John
Lyricist(s) Sargent, John

Producer(s) Henkel, Kim; Pennell, Eagle
Director(s) Pennell, Eagle
Screenwriter(s) Henkel, Kim

Cast Davis, Sonny Carl; Perryman, Louis; Matilla, Steven; Hubbard, Tina-Bess

Song(s) Apocalypso; Tear It Down; Tall Dark Stranger; Long Road Out of Here; Little Bit Crazy (C/L: Cox, Paul); Temporary Feeling (C/L: Cox, Paul)

Notes No cue sheet available.

3234 ✦ THE LAST OF SHEILA
Warner Brothers, 1973

Musical Score Goldenberg, Billy

Producer(s) Ross, Herbert
Director(s) Ross, Herbert
Screenwriter(s) Sondheim, Stephen; Perkins, Anthony

Cast Coburn, James; Benjamin, Richard; Hackett, Joan; Welch, Raquel; McShane, Ian; Mason, James; Cannon, Dyan

Song(s) Friends [1] (C/L: Linhart, Buzzy; Klingman, Mark)

Notes [1] It is not known if this was written for the film.

3235 ✦ LAST OF THE BADMEN
Allied Artists, 1957

Musical Score Sawtell, Paul

Producer(s) Fennelly, Vincent M.
Director(s) Landres, Paul
Screenwriter(s) Ullman, Daniel B.; Chantler, David T.

Cast Montgomery, George; Best, James; Kennedy, Douglas; Richards, Addison

Song(s) West of Gallatin (C: Sawtell, Paul; L: Davis, Gwen)

3236 ✦ LAST OF THE DUANES
Fox, 1930

Producer(s) Butcher, Edward; Lipsitz, Harold B.
Director(s) Werker, Alfred
Screenwriter(s) Pascal, Ernest
Source(s) "The Last of the Duanes" (story) Grey, Zane

Cast O'Brien, George; Brown, Lucille; Loy, Myrna; McGrail, Walter; Bradbury Jr., James; Pendleton, Nat; Frederici, Blanche

Song(s) Cowboy Dan (C/L: Friend, Cliff); The Outlaw Song (C/L: Friend, Cliff)

Notes A remake of the 1924 original.

3237 ✦ LAST OF THE MOBILE HOT-SHOTS
Warner Brothers, 1970

Musical Score Jones, Quincy

Producer(s) Lumet, Sidney
Director(s) Lumet, Sidney
Screenwriter(s) Vidal, Gore
Source(s) *The Seven Descents of Myrtle* (play) Williams, Tennessee

Cast Coburn, James; Redgrave, Lynn; Hooks, Robert; Hayes, Perry; King, Reggie

Song(s) Jesus Is a Soul Man (C/L: Reynolds, Lawrence; Cardwell, Jack); Plant a Watermelon on My Grave and Let the Juice Soak Through (C/L: Dumont, Frank; Lilly, R.P.)

3238 ✦ LAST OF THE PAGANS
Metro–Goldwyn–Mayer, 1936

Musical Score Finston, Nat

Producer(s) Goldstone, Philip
Director(s) Thorpe, Richard
Screenwriter(s) Farrow, John Villiers

Cast Mala; Lotus

Song(s) In a Little Bamboo Bungalow (C/L: Bambridge, Bill; Luber, Mildred); Tahitian Melodies (C/L: Jurmann, Walter; Kaper, Bronislau); Shadows on the Starlit Waters [1] (C/L: Jurmann, Walter; Kaper, Bronislau)

Notes [1] Used instrumentally only.

3239 ✦ LAST OF THE PONY RIDERS
Columbia, 1953

Producer(s) Schaefer, Armand
Director(s) Archainbaud, George
Screenwriter(s) Woodman, Ruth

Cast Champion; Autry, Gene; Burnette, Smiley; Case, Kathleen; Down, Johnny; Jones, Dick

Song(s) Sing Me a Song of the Saddle [1] (C/L: Harford, Frank); Sugar Babe (C/L: Unknown)

Notes No cue sheet available. [1] Also in the Republic pictures SUNSET IN WYOMING and SINGING KID FROM PINE RIDGE. Autry was given credit as songwriter for this picture but not previous usages. Autry was known to put his name on songs he did not write (much as Al Jolson and others have done).

3240 ✦ LAST OF THE RED HOT LOVERS
Paramount, 1972

Musical Score Hefti, Neal

Producer(s) Koch, Howard W.
Director(s) Saks, Gene
Screenwriter(s) Simon, Neil
Source(s) *Last of the Red Hot Lovers* (play) Simon, Neil

Cast Arkin, Alan; Kellerman, Sally; Prentiss, Paula; Taylor, Renee

Song(s) I'm There [1] (C: Hefti, Neal; L: Bergman, Alan; Bergman, Marilyn); Last of the Red Hot Lovers [1] (C/L: David, Mack; Curb, Mike; Osmond, Alan)

Notes [1] Song written for exploitation only.

3241 ✦ THE LAST OF THE SECRET AGENTS?
Paramount, 1966

Producer(s) Abbott, Norman
Director(s) Abbott, Norman
Screenwriter(s) Tolkin, Mel

Cast Allen, Marty; Rossi, Steve; Williams, John; Sinatra, Nancy; Jacobi, Lou; Marcuse, Theo

Song(s) The Last of the Secret Agents? (C/L: Hazlewood, Lee); Don Jose Ole! (C: King, Pete; L: Tolkin, Mel; Abbott, Norman); You Are (C/L: Hefti, Neal)

3242 ✦ LAST OF THE SKI BUMS
U–M, 1969

Producer(s) Barrymore, Dick
Director(s) Barrymore, Dick

Cast Funk Ron; Zuettel, Mike; Ricks, Ed

Song(s) Ski Bum (C/L: Strunk, Jud)

Notes No cue sheet available.

3243 ✦ THE LAST OUTLAW
RKO, 1936

Musical Score Steiner, Max

Producer(s) Sisk, Robert
Director(s) Cabanne, Christy
Screenwriter(s) Twist, John; Townley, Jack

Cast Carey, Harry; Gibson, Hoot; Tyler, Tom; Walthall, Henry B.; Callahan, Margaret; Mayer, Ray; Jans, Harry; Thomas, Frank M.; Hopton, Russell; Jenks, Frank

Song(s) My Heart's on the Trail [1] (C: Shilkret, Nathaniel; L: Luther, Frank)

Notes [1] Also in WE WHO ARE ABOUT TO DIE.

3244 ◆ THE LAST REMAKE OF BEAU GESTE
Universal, 1977

Musical Score Morris, John
Composer(s) Morris, John
Lyricist(s) Feldman, Marty

Producer(s) Gilmore, William S.
Director(s) Feldman, Marty
Screenwriter(s) Feldman, Marty; Allen, Chris

Cast Feldman, Marty; York, Michael; Ann-Margaret; Ustinov, Peter; Howard, Trevor; Milligan, Spike; Gibson, Henry; Terry-Thomas; Kinnear, Roy; Schreiber, Avery; Griffith, Hugh

Song(s) For France; My Boy Beau; Arabic Commercial; We Sing As We March; A Man's Gotta Be

3245 ◆ THE LAST ROUNDUP
Columbia, 1947

Producer(s) Autry, Gene
Director(s) English, John
Screenwriter(s) Townley, Jack; Snell, Earle

Cast Autry, Gene; Champion; Morgan, Ralph; Vincent, Russ; The Texas Rangers

Song(s) The Last Round-Up [1] (C/L: Hill, Billy); You Can't See the Sun (C/L: Fisher, Doris; Roberts, Allan); One Hundred and Sixty Acres [1] (C/L: Kapp, David); An Apple for the Teacher [2] (C: Monaco, James V.; L: Burke, Johnny)

Notes [1] Also in ONE HOUR LATE (Paramount), STAND UP AND CHEER (Fox) and the Republic pictures SINGING HILL and DON'T FENCE ME IN. [2] Written for THE STAR MAKER.

3246 ◆ THE LAST SHOT YOU HEAR
Twentieth Century–Fox, 1969

Musical Score Pearson, Johnny; Shefter, Bert

Producer(s) Parsons, Jack
Director(s) Hessler, Gordon
Screenwriter(s) Shields, Tim
Source(s) (play) Fairchild, William

Cast Marlowe, Hugh; Walker, Zena; Haines, Patricia; Dysart, William

Song(s) Only Yesterday (C: Shefter, Bert; L: Stevens, Stella; Ackerman, Jack)

3247 ◆ THE LAST STARFIGHTER
Universal, 1985

Musical Score Safan, Craig
Composer(s) Safan, Craig
Lyricist(s) Mueller, Mark

Producer(s) Adelson, Gary; Denault, Edward O.
Director(s) Castle, Nick
Screenwriter(s) Betuel, Jonathan R.

Cast Guest, Lance; O'Herlihy, Dan; Stewart, Catherine Mary; Bosson, Barbara; Snow, Norman; Preston, Robert

Song(s) Redeye Rowdy; Satisfy the Night; Just One Star Beyond (L: Mueller, Mark; Manchester, Melissa); Incommunicado

3248 ◆ THE LAST SUNSET
Universal, 1961

Musical Score Gold, Ernest

Producer(s) Frenke, Eugene; Lewis, Edward
Director(s) Aldrich, Robert
Screenwriter(s) Trumbo, Dalton
Source(s) *Sundown at Crazy Horse* (novel) Rigsby, Howard

Cast Hudson, Rock; Douglas, Kirk; Malone, Dorothy; Cotten, Joseph; Lynley, Carol; Toomey, Regis

Song(s) Pretty Girl in the Yellow Dress (C: Tiomkin, Dimitri; L: Washington, Ned)

Notes There is also a vocal of "CuCuRuCuCu, Paloma" by Tomas Mendez.

3249 ◆ THE LAST TIME I SAW PARIS
Metro–Goldwyn–Mayer, 1954

Musical Score Salinger, Conrad

Producer(s) Cummings, Jack
Director(s) Brooks, Richard
Screenwriter(s) Epstein, Julius J.; Epstein, Philip G.; Brooks, Richard
Source(s) "Babylon Revisited" (story) Fitzgerald, F. Scott

Cast Taylor, Elizabeth; Johnson, Van; Pidgeon, Walter; Reed, Donna; Gabor, Eva; Kasznar, Kurt; Dolenz, George; Moore, Roger

Song(s) Mademoiselle de Paris (C/L: Durand, Paul; Contet, Henri); Long . . . Long . . . Long (C: McHugh, Jimmy; L: Roger, Jeannine; Mottier, Jean Pierre); Danse Avec Moi [1] (C/L: Harvey, Andre; Lopez, Francis); Passe (C/L: De Lange, Eddie; Unknown)

Notes There are many vocals of "The Last Time I Saw Paris" by Jerome Kern and Oscar Hammerstein II. The French lyrics are by Pierre La Mure. It is not known if any of the above were written for the film. [1] Harold

Rome credited with lyrics on sheet music. Hervey is credited as Hornez on sheet.

3250 ✦ THE LAST TRAIL
Fox, 1933

Director(s) Tinling, James
Screenwriter(s) Anthony, Stuart
Source(s) "The Last Trail" (story) Grey, Zane

Cast Trevor, Claire; Brendel, El; O'Brien, George; LaVerne, Lucille; McHugh, Matt; Naish, J. Carrol

Song(s) Moanish Lady (C: Reed; L: Unknown); She's Only One of the Weaker Sex (C/L: Brendel, El)

3251 ✦ THE LAST TYCOON
Paramount, 1976

Musical Score Jarre, Maurice

Producer(s) Spiegel, Sam
Director(s) Kazan, Elia
Screenwriter(s) Pinter, Harold
Source(s) *The Last Tycoon* (novel) Fitzgerald, F. Scott

Cast De Niro, Robert; Curtis, Tony; Mitchum, Robert; Moreau, Jeanne; Nicholson, Jack; Pleasence, Donald; Milland, Ray; Andrews, Dana; Boulting, Ingrid

Song(s) You Have the Choice (C: Jarre, Maurice; L: Pinter, Harold)

3252 ✦ THE LAST UNICORN
Jensen Farley, 1982

Musical Score Webb, Jimmy
Composer(s) Webb, Jimmy
Lyricist(s) Webb, Jimmy

Producer(s) Rankin Jr., Arthur; Bass, Jules
Director(s) Rankin Jr., Arthur; Bass, Jules
Screenwriter(s) Beagle, Peter S.

Song(s) The Last Unicorn; Man's Road; Where Do Unicorns Go; That's All I Got to Say

Notes No cue sheet available. An animated feature.

3253 ✦ THE LAST VOYAGE
Metro–Goldwyn–Mayer, 1960

Musical Score Stone, Andrew L.; Stone, Virginia

Producer(s) Stone, Andrew L.; Stone, Virginia
Director(s) Stone, Andrew L.
Screenwriter(s) Stone, Andrew L.

Cast Stack, Robert; Malone, Dorothy; Sanders, George; O'Brien, Edmond; Strode, Woody; Kruschen, Jack; Marston, Joel; Furness, George; Marihugh, Tammy

Song(s) Song of the Shell (C/L: Stone, Andrew L.; Stone, Virginia)

3254 ✦ LAS VEGAS NIGHTS
Paramount, 1941

Composer(s) Lane, Burton
Lyricist(s) Loesser, Frank

Producer(s) LeBaron, William
Director(s) Murphy, Ralph
Screenwriter(s) Pagano, Ernest; Clork, Harry

Cast Dale, Virginia; Sinatra, Frank; Dorsey, Tommy; The Pied Pipers; Regan, Phil; Cornell, Lillian; Wheeler, Bert; Moore, Constance; Dale, Virginia; Haines, Connie

Song(s) I Gotta Ride; Mary, Mary, Quite Contrary [7]; I'll Never Smile Again [3] (C/L: Lowe, Ruth); The Lamp on the Corner (Farolito) [6] (C: Lara, Augustin; L: Washington, Ned); Dolores [5] (C: Alter, Louis); That's Southern Hospitality [1] (C/L: Coslow, Sam); Moments Like This [8]; On Miami Shore [3] [4] (C: Jacobi, Victor; L: LeBaron, William; Loesser, Frank); Trombone Man [2] [3] (C: Mooney, Hal; L: Prince, Hughie; Dorsey, Tommy)

Notes [1] Only 55 seconds on screen. Also in TURN OFF THE MOON. [2] Dorsey wrote special lyrics. [3] Not written for production. [4] Loesser wrote the prologue lyrics. [5] Also in DR. BROADWAY and SAIGON. [6] Also in TROPIC HOLIDAY and CHAMPAGNE FOR TWO. [7] Not used in COLLEGE SWING or DANCING ON A DIME. [8] Also in COLLEGE SWING, MONEY FROM HOME and recorded but not used in TRUE TO LIFE.

3255 ✦ LAS VEGAS SHAKEDOWN
Allied Artists, 1955

Producer(s) Broidy, William F.
Director(s) Salkow, Sidney
Screenwriter(s) Fisher, Steve

Cast O'Keefe, Dennis; Gray, Coleen; Winninger, Charles; Gomez, Thomas; Patrick, Dorothy; Hughes, Mary Beth; Armstrong, Robert

Song(s) Miss You So (C/L: Malneck, Matty)

Notes No cue sheet available.

3256 ✦ THE LAS VEGAS STORY
RKO, 1951

Musical Score Harline, Leigh
Composer(s) Carmichael, Hoagy
Lyricist(s) Carmichael, Hoagy

Producer(s) Sparks, Robert
Director(s) Stevenson, Robert
Screenwriter(s) Felton, Earl; Essex, Harry

Cast Russell, Jane; Mature, Victor; Price, Vincent; Carmichael, Hoagy; Dexter, Brad; Oliver, Gordon; Flippen, Jay C.; Wright, Will

Song(s) I Get Along Without You Very Well; Monkey Song; My Resistance Is Low (L: Adamson, Harold)

3257 ✦ THE LATE GEORGE APLEY
Twentieth Century–Fox, 1947

Musical Score Mockridge, Cyril J.

Producer(s) Kohlmar, Fred
Director(s) Mankiewicz, Joseph L.
Source(s) *The Late George Apley* (play) Kaufman, George S.; Marquand, J.P.; *The Late George Apley* (novel) Marquand, J.P.

Cast Colman, Ronald; Cummins, Peggy; Brown, Vanessa; Haydn, Richard; Russell, Charles; Ney, Richard; Waram, Percy; Natwick, Mildred; Best, Edna; Westman, Nydia

Song(s) Sweet Little Marigold (C: Lampe, J. Bodewalt; L: Carleton, Howard)

Notes "Every Little Movement" from MADAME SHERRY by Karl Hoschna and Otto Harbach is also used vocally.

3258 ✦ THE LATE SHOW
Warner Brothers, 1977

Musical Score Wannberg, Ken

Producer(s) Altman, Robert
Director(s) Benton, Robert
Screenwriter(s) Benton, Robert

Cast Carney, Art; Duff, Howard; Tomlin, Lily; Macy, Bill; Nelson, Ruth; Cassidy, Joanna; Considine, John; Roche, Eugene

Song(s) What Was (C: Wannberg, Ken; L: Lehrner, Stephen)

3259 ✦ LATIN FOR A DAY (UNPRODUCED)
Disney

Song(s) Latin for a Day [1] (C: Wolcott, Charles; L: Gilbert, Ray)

Notes This was an unproduced short. [1] Not used in THE THREE CABALLEROS.

3260 ✦ LATIN LOVERS
Metro–Goldwyn–Mayer, 1953

Musical Score Stoll, George; Sendrey, Al
Composer(s) Brodszky, Nicholas
Lyricist(s) Robin, Leo
Choreographer(s) Veloz, Frank

Producer(s) Pasternak, Joe
Director(s) LeRoy, Mervyn
Screenwriter(s) Lennart, Isobel

Cast Turner, Lana; Montalban, Ricardo [1]; Lund, John; Calhern, Louis; Hagen, Jean; Franz, Eduard; Bondi, Beulah; Garay, Joaquin

Song(s) Carlotta, Ya Gotta Be Mine; Voce Promete e Nao Da (C: Almeida, Laurindo; L: Amaral, Nestor); A Little More of Your Amor; I Had to Kiss You; Pappa Loves Mambo (C/L: Hoffman, Al; Manning, Dick; Reichner, Bickley); Come to My Arms [3]; Latin Lovers [3]; Night and Amor [3]

Notes [1] Dubbed by Carlos Ramirez. [2] Sheet music only. [3] Not used.

3261 ✦ LAUGHING ANNE
Republic, 1954

Choreographer(s) Buchel, Betty; Buchel, Philip

Producer(s) Wilcox, Herbert
Director(s) Wilcox, Herbert
Screenwriter(s) Bower, Pamela

Cast Corey, Wendell; Lockwood, Margaret; Tucker, Forrest; Shiner, Ronald

Song(s) I've Fallen in Deep Water (C: Grouya, Ted; L: Parsons, Geoffrey)

Notes A British picture distributed by Republic. There are also vocals of "All the World Is Mine on Sunday" by Roche and Parsons and "All the Nice Girls Love a Sailor."

3262 ✦ LAUGHING BOY
Metro–Goldwyn–Mayer, 1934

Musical Score Stothart, Herbert

Producer(s) Stromberg, Hunt
Director(s) Van Dyke, W.S.
Screenwriter(s) Colton, John; Mahin, John Lee
Source(s) *Laughing Boy* (novel) La Farge, Oliver

Cast Novarro, Ramon; Velez, Lupe; Davidson, William B.; Thunderbird, Chief; Rambula, Catalina

Song(s) Call of Love (C: Stothart, Herbert; L: Kahn, Gus)

3263 ✦ LAUGHING IRISH EYES
Republic, 1936

Composer(s) Stept, Sam H.
Lyricist(s) Mitchell, Sidney D.

Producer(s) Clark, Colbert
Director(s) Santley, Joseph
Screenwriter(s) Cooper, Olive; Ryan, Ben; Rauh, Stanley

Cast Regan, Phil; Kelly, Walter C.; Knapp, Evalyn; Walker, Ray; Gordon, Mary; Hymer, Warren; Bing, Herman; Muse, Clarence; Hatton, Raymond; Compson, Betty

Song(s) Laughing Irish Eyes; Bless You Darling Mother (L: Stept, Sam H.); Londonderry Air (C: Traditional); All My Life

3264 ✦ THE LAUGHING LADY (1929)
Paramount, 1929

Director(s)   Schertzinger, Victor
Screenwriter(s)   Cormack, Bartlett; Richman, Arthur
Source(s)   *The Laughing Lady* (play) Sutro, Alfred

Cast   Chatterton, Ruth; Brook, Clive; Harrigan, Nedda; Walburn, Raymond; Pendleton, Nat; Healy, Dan

Song(s)   Another Kiss (C/L: Schertzinger, Victor)

Notes   No cue sheet available. It is not known if the song is actually in the picture. Song also previously used in MANHATTAN COCKTAIL.

3265 ✦ THE LAUGHING LADY (1945)
Twentieth Century–Fox, 1945

Musical Score   May, Hans
Composer(s)   May, Hans
Lyricist(s)   Stranks, Alan

Producer(s)   Jackson, Louis H.
Director(s)   Stein, Paul
Screenwriter(s)   Whittingham, Jack
Source(s)   (play) d'Abbes, Ingram

Cast   Ziegler, Anne; Booth, Webster; Graves, Peter; Aylmer, Felix; Dupuis, Paul

Song(s)   Love Is the Key; Laugh at Life; Magical Moonlight; I'll Change My Heart; Brother Rat; In an Old Chateau; Wonderful Wine

Notes   A British National Films production.

3266 ✦ LAUGHING SINNERS
Metro–Goldwyn–Mayer, 1931

Choreographer(s)   Mosconi

Director(s)   Beaumont, Harry
Screenwriter(s)   Meredyth, Bess; Fitzgerald, Edith
Source(s)   *Torch Song* (play) Nicholson, Kenyon

Cast   Crawford, Joan; Hamilton, Neil; Gable, Clark; Rambeau, Marjorie; Kibbee, Guy; Edwards, Cliff; Karns, Roscoe; Short, Gertrude; Marion, George F.

Song(s)   Original (C/L: Edwards, Cliff); (What Can I Do) I Love That Man (C: Broones, Martin; L: Freed, Arthur); Barnyard Romeo (C: Alter, Louis; L: Goodwin, Joe; Freed, Arthur)

Notes   Original title: COMPLETE SURRENDER. Also known as TORCH SONG.

3267 ✦ LAUGH IT OFF
Universal, 1939

Composer(s)   Oakland, Ben
Lyricist(s)   Lerner, Sam

Producer(s)   Rogell, Albert S.
Director(s)   Rogell, Albert S.
Screenwriter(s)   Clork, Harry; Loch, Lee

Cast   Cunningham, Cecil; Moore, Constance; Downs, Johnny; Beecher, Janet; Rambeau, Marjorie; Hopper, Hedda; Kennedy, Edgar; Demarest, William; McMahon, Horace; Stone, Paula

Song(s)   Doin' the 1940; My Dream and I; Who's Gonna Keep your Wigwam Warm; Laugh It Off

Notes   Titled LADY BE GAY in Great Britain.

3268 ✦ LAUGHTER
Paramount, 1930

Producer(s)
Director(s)   d'Arrast, Harry d'Abbadie
Screenwriter(s)   d'Arrast, Harry d'Abbadie; Doty, Douglas; Stewart, Donald Ogden

Cast   Carroll, Nancy; March, Fredric; Morgan, Frank; Anders, Glenn; Ellis, Diane

Song(s)   Little Did I Know (1) [1] (C: Fain, Sammy; L: Norman, Pierre); Laughter Opening (Inst.) (C: Duke, Vernon); Laughter Symphony (Inst.) (C: Duke, Vernon); Little Did I Know (2) [2] (C: Fain, Sammy; Duke, Vernon; L: Kahal, Irving)

Notes   There might only be one song with all four songwriters sharing credit. [1] Performed instrumentally only. Irving Kahal also credited by ASCAP. [2] Not used.

3269 ✦ LAUGHTER IN THE AIR

See MYRT AND MARGE.

3270 ✦ LAUGH YOUR BLUES AWAY
Columbia, 1942

Composer(s)   Cherkose, Eddie; Press, Jacques
Lyricist(s)   Cherkose, Eddie; Press, Jacques

Producer(s)   Fier, Jack
Director(s)   Barton, Charles
Screenwriter(s)   Sauber, Harry

Cast   Gordon, Bert; Falkenburg, Jinx; Drake, Douglas; Elsom, Isobel; Clark, Roger; Kennedy, Phyllis; Elliott, Dick

Song(s)   Gin Rhumba; Prairie Parade [2] (C/L: Markes, Larry; Charles, Dick); Home on the Russian Range; He's My Guy [1] (C: DePaul, Gene; L: Raye, Don)

Notes   [1] First used in WHO DONE IT. [2] Later with additional contributions by Eddie DeLange the song became "Along the Navajo Trail." That song was used in THE BLAZING SUN, ALONG THE NAVAJO TRAIL and DON'T FENCE ME IN.

3271 ✦ LAURA
Twentieth Century–Fox, 1944

Musical Score   Raksin, David

Producer(s)   Preminger, Otto
Director(s)   Preminger, Otto

Screenwriter(s)   Dratler, Jay; Hoffenstein, Samuel; Reinhardt, Betty
Source(s)   *Laura* (novel) Caspary, Vera

Cast   Tierney, Gene; Andrews, Dana; Webb, Clifton; Price, Vincent; Anderson, Judith; Adams, Dorothy; Flavin, James; Mitchell, Grant; Howard, Kathleen

Song(s)   Laura [1] (C: Raksin, David; L: Mercer, Johnny)

Notes   [1] Lyric added for exploitation only.

3272 ✦ LAW AND ORDER
Universal, 1940

Musical Score   Skinner, Frank; Freed, Ralph

Producer(s)   Cowan, Will
Director(s)   Taylor, Ray
Screenwriter(s)   Lowe, Sherman

Cast   Brown, Johnny Mack; Baker, Bob; Knight, Fuzzy; O'Day, Nell

Song(s)   Oklahoma's Oke with Me (C/L: Dodd, Jimmy); Ride 'Em Cowboy (C: Rosen, Milton; L: Carter, Everett); Those Happy Old Days [1] (C: Rosen, Milton; L: Carter, Everett)

Notes   [1] Sheet music only.

3273 ✦ THE LAWLESS BREED
Universal, 1946

Musical Score   Skinner, Frank
Composer(s)   Rosen, Milton

Producer(s)   Fox, Wallace W.
Director(s)   Fox, Wallace W.
Screenwriter(s)   Williams, Bob

Cast   Grant, Kirby; Knight, Fuzzy; Adams, Jane; Hackett, Karl; Drake, Claudia; Brown, Harry

Song(s)   I Never Say Oui, Oui! (L: Brooks, Jack); Do the Oo-la-la (L: Carter, Everett); Bananas Make Me Tough [1] (L: Carter, Everett); Sittin' on the Inside (L: Brooks, Jack)

Notes   The cue sheet is titled THE LAWLESS CLAN. The word "Breed" is crossed out. [1] Also in MAN FROM MONTANA.

3274 ✦ LAWLESS PLAINSMEN
Columbia, 1942

Producer(s)   Fier, Jack
Director(s)   Berke, William
Screenwriter(s)   Ward, Luci

Cast   Starrett, Charles; Hayden, Russell; Edwards, Cliff; Walters, Luana; LaRue, Frank

Song(s)   Lady Luck (C/L: Unknown); Ridin', Just Ridin' On (C/L: Unknown)

Notes   No cue sheet available.

3275 ✦ LAWLESS RANGE
Republic, 1935

Producer(s)   Malvern, Paul
Director(s)   Bradbury, R.N.
Screenwriter(s)   Friedman, Harry; Parsons, Lindsley

Cast   Wayne, John; Manners, Sheila; Dwire, Earl; McGlynn Jr., Frank; Canutt, Yakima; Curtis, Jack

Song(s)   Cowboy Wail (C/L: Bradbury, R.N.); On the Banks of the San Juan (C/L: Strange, Glenn); Dusty Road (C/L: Sargent, Charles H.)

3276 ✦ LAW OF THE PAMPAS
Paramount, 1939

Producer(s)   Sherman, Harry
Director(s)   Watt, Nate
Screenwriter(s)   Jacobs, Harrison

Cast   Boyd, William; Hayden, Russell; Duna, Steffi; Blackmer, Sidney

Song(s)   La Jornada (C/L: Rojo, Leo); Habanera [1] (C/L: Gianotti, Carlos A.); Rosita [1] (C/L: Gianotti, Carlos A.); Los Gauchos [1] (C/L: Rojo, Leo)

Notes   Picture first titled ARGENTINA. [1] Not Used.

3277 ✦ LAW OF THE RANGE
Universal, 1941

Composer(s)   Carter, Everett
Lyricist(s)   Rosen, Milton

Producer(s)   Cowan, Will
Director(s)   Taylor, Ray
Screenwriter(s)   Lowe, Sherman

Cast   Brown, Johnny Mack; Knight, Fuzzy; O'Day, Nell

Song(s)   Six Gun Dan (C/L: Crawford, Bob); I Plumb Forgot; Forget Your Boots and Saddle; Little Pony (C/L: Cool, Gomer); Pals of the Prairie (C/L: Crawford, Bob)

3278 ✦ THE LAW OF THE TROPICS
Warner Brothers, 1941

Producer(s)   Stoloff, Ben
Director(s)   Enright, Ray
Screenwriter(s)   Grayson, Charles
Source(s)   "Oil for the Lamps of China" (story) Hobart, Alice Tisdale

Cast   Bennett, Constance; Lynn, Jeffrey; Toomey, Regis; Maris, Mona; Bosworth, Hobart; Stevens, Craig; Judels, Charles

Song(s)   Beso Tropical (C/L: Martinez, Ray; Durant, Eddie); Mia Morena (C/L: Castillon, Jesus); Burrito (C/L: Rojo, Leo)

3279 ✦ LAW OF THE UNDERWORLD
RKO, 1938

Producer(s)   Sisk, Robert
Director(s)   Landers, Lew
Screenwriter(s)   Granet, Bert; Hartmann, Edmund L.

Cast   Morris, Chester; Shirley, Anne; Ciannelli, Eduardo; Abel, Walter

Song(s)   The First Time I Saw You [1] (C: Shilkret, Nathaniel; L: Wrubel, Allie)

Notes   [1] Also in THE FALCON TAKES OVER, OUT OF THE PAST and TOAST OF NEW YORK.

3280 ✦ THE LAWYER
Paramount, 1970

Producer(s)   Dexter, Brad
Director(s)   Furie, Sidney J.
Screenwriter(s)   Furie, Sidney J.; Buchman, Harold

Cast   Gould, Harold; Newman, Barry; Muldaur, Diana; Crowley, Kathleen; Colbert, Robert

Song(s)   The Winds of Change [1] (C: Dodds, Malcolm; L: Nissenson, Gloria)

Notes   [1] Song written for exploitation use only.

3281 ✦ LAY THAT RIFLE DOWN
Republic, 1955

Composer(s)   Elliott, Jack; Kahn, Donald
Lyricist(s)   Kahn, Donald; Elliott, Jack

Producer(s)   Picker, Sidney
Director(s)   Lamont, Charles
Screenwriter(s)   Shipman, Barry

Cast   Canova, Judy; Lowery, Robert; Jarmyn, Jil; de Wit, Jacqueline; Deacon, Richard; Burton, Robert; Canova, Tweeny

Song(s)   The Continental Correspondence Charm School; Sleepy Serenade; I'm Glad I Was Born on My Birthday [1]

Notes   [1] Not on cue sheet but listed in *Film Daily Annual*.

3282 ✦ LAZY RIVER
Metro–Goldwyn–Mayer, 1934

Musical Score   Axt, William
Composer(s)   Axt, William
Lyricist(s)   Mendoza, David

Producer(s)   Hubbard, Lucien
Director(s)   Seitz, George B.

Screenwriter(s)   Hubbard, Lucien
Source(s)   *Ruby* (play) Freeman, Lea David

Cast   Parker, Jean; Young, Robert; Healy, Ted; Pendleton, Nat; Gordon, C. Henry; Franklin, Irene; Cawthorn, Joseph; Eburne, Maude; Hatton, Raymond

Song(s)   Cajun Love Song; Fifi from Fontenoy

Notes   The Mendoza lyric credit is unconfirmed.

3283 ✦ LEADBELLY
Paramount, 1976

Musical Score   Karlin, Fred

Producer(s)   Merson, Marc
Director(s)   Parks, Gordon
Screenwriter(s)   Kinoy, Ernest

Cast   Mosley, Roger E.; Benjamin, Paul; Sinclair, Madge

Notes   Huddie Ledbetter's songs "Go Down, Ol' Hannah;" "Po' Howard;" "Fannin' Street (Mister Tom Hughes' Town);" "Good Mornin' Blues;" "Keep Your Hands Off Her"; "Cotton Fields (The Cotton Song);" "Rock Island Line;" "Silver City Bound;" "C.C. Rider;" "Bring Me Li'l Water Silvy;" "De Kalb Blues;" "Old Riley (In Dem Long Hot Summer Days);" "Governor Pat Neff;" "Goodnight Irene;" "That Midnight Special;" "Green Corn;" "Black Corn" with lyric by Pat Behan and music by Cecil Sharpe and "That My Grave Is Kept Clean" by Lemon Jefferson are used. There are no original songs written for this production.

3284 ✦ LEAN ON ME
Warner Brothers, 1989

Musical Score   Conti, Bill

Producer(s)   Twain, Norman
Director(s)   Avildsen, John G.
Screenwriter(s)   Schiffer, Michael

Cast   Todd, Beverly; Gillaume, Robert; North, Alan; Thigpen, Lynne; Bartlett, Robin; Beach, Michael; Phillips, Ethan; Reaves-Phillips, Sandra; Shelton, Sloane

Song(s)   Eastside High School Alma Mater (C/L: Miller, Catherine Peragallo); Check It Out (C/L: Schiffer, Michael; Jackson, Tyrone); You Are the One (C/L: Lowery, K.; Gaskins, D.); Skeezer (C/L: Shante, Roxanne); Rap Summary (Lean on Me) (C/L: Kane, Big Daddy); I Ain't Makin' It (C/L: Hamilton, Arnold; Coulter, Bob; Bolton, Glen); All the Way to Love (C/L: Ballard, Glen; Garrett, Siedah); Everybody Is Somebody (C/L: Bailey, Winston); Hooky Player (C/L: Gathers, Nancy); Lean on Me (C/L: Withers, Bill)

Notes   It is not known how many of these were written for the movie. Some of these are background vocal uses. As always, songs which seemed to be taken from existing recordings aren't listed.

3285 ✦ THE LEARNING TREE
Warner Brothers, 1969

Musical Score   Parks, Gordon
Composer(s)   Parks, Gordon
Lyricist(s)   Parks, Gordon

Producer(s)   Parks, Gordon
Director(s)   Parks, Gordon
Screenwriter(s)   Parks, Gordon

Cast   Johnson, Kyle; Clarke, Alex; Evans, Estelle; Elcar, Dana; Waters, Mira; Fluellen, Joel

Song(s)   The Learning Tree; Baby's Gone Blues

3286 ✦ THE LEATHERNECK
Pathe, 1930

Director(s)   Higgin, Howard
Screenwriter(s)   Krafft, John

Cast   Hale, Alan; Boyd, William; Armstrong, Robert; Kohler, Fred; Ellis, Diane

Song(s)   Only for You (C/L: Zuro, Josiah; Gromon, Francis; Weinberg, Charles)

Notes   No cue sheet available.

3287 ✦ LEATHERNECKING
RKO, 1930

Composer(s)   Akst, Harry [1]
Lyricist(s)   Davis, Benny [1]
Choreographer(s)   Eaton, Pearl [2]

Producer(s)   Sarecky, Louis
Director(s)   Cline, Edward F.
Screenwriter(s)   Murfin, Jane
Source(s)   *Present Arms* (musical) Fields, Herbert; Rodgers, Richard; Hart, Lorenz

Cast   Dunne, Irene; Murray, Ken; Fazenda, Louise; Sparks, Ned; Tashman, Lilyan; Foy Jr., Eddie; Rubin, Benny; Santley, Fred

Song(s)   All My Life; A Lot o' Nuts (C: Rodgers, Richard; L: Hart, Lorenz); Shake It Off and Smile (C: Levant, Oscar; L: Clare, Sidney); Evening Star; Sailor's Hornpipe; Finaletto; Mighty Nice and So Particular; A Kiss for Cinderella [3] (C: Rodgers, Richard; L: Hart, Lorenz); You Took Advantage of Me [3] [4] (C: Rodgers, Richard; L: Hart, Lorenz); Careless Kisses [5]

Notes   The cue sheet does not differentiate between vocals and instrumentals. [1] The cue sheet and script make no mention of Harry Akst or Benny Davis. Only Oscar Levant and Sydney Clare are credited. However other sources seem to agree that the composers and lyricists should be credited as above. [2] Stanley Green in the *Rodgers and Hammerstein Fact Book* credits Mary Read with the choreography. [3] From Broadway production. [4] Green lists this song but the cue sheet does not. However the cue sheet lists the song "A Lot O' Nuts" which Green does not. There is no mention of "A Lot O' Nuts" in *The Complete Lyrics of Lorenz Hart* by Robert Kimball and Dorothy Hart. But they don't mention "Leathernecking" either. [5] Sheet music only.

3288 ✦ THE LEATHERNECKS HAVE LANDED
Republic, 1936

Producer(s)   Goldsmith, Ken
Director(s)   Bretherton, Howard
Screenwriter(s)   Miller, Seton I.

Cast   Ayres, Lew; Jewell, Isabel; Ellison, James; Burke, James; Naish, J. Carrol; Clement, Clay; Holmes, Maynard; Eburne, Maude

Song(s)   Singapore Sal (C/L: Stept, Sam H.)

3289 ✦ LEAVE HER TO HEAVEN
Twentieth Century–Fox, 1945

Musical Score   Newman, Alfred

Producer(s)   Bacher, William A.
Director(s)   Stahl, John M.
Screenwriter(s)   Swerling, Jo
Source(s)   *Leave Her to Heaven* (novel) Williams, Ben Ames

Cast   Tierney, Gene; Wilde, Cornel; Crain, Jeanne; Price, Vincent; Philips, Mary; Collins, Ray; Lockhart, Gene; Hickman, Darryl; Wills, Chill; Mitchell, Grant

Song(s)   Beedle Deedle Dum Dum (C/L: Wills, Chill)

3290 ✦ LEAVE IT TO LESTER
Paramount, 1930

Choreographer(s)   Gambarelli, Maria

Director(s)   Cambria, Frank; Cozine, Ray

Cast   Allen, Lester; Hoey, Evelyn; Thompson, Hal

Song(s)   I'm Yours (C/L: Green, Johnny)

3291 ✦ THE LEFT HANDED GUN
Warner Brothers, 1958

Musical Score   Courage, Alexander

Producer(s)   Coe, Fred
Director(s)   Penn, Arthur
Screenwriter(s)   Stevens, Leslie
Source(s)   "Billy the Kid" (teleplay) Vidal, Gore

Cast   Newman, Paul; Milan, Lita; Dehner, John; Hatfield, Hurd; Congdon, James; Best, James; Keith-Johnston, Colin; Dierkes, John; Paiva, Nestor

Song(s)   The Left Handed Gun Ballad (C: Courage, Alexander; L: Goyen, William)

3292 ◆ THE LEFT HAND OF GOD
Twentieth Century–Fox, 1955

Musical Score   Young, Victor

Producer(s)   Adler, Buddy
Director(s)   Dmytryk, Edward
Screenwriter(s)   Hayes, Alfred
Source(s)   *The Left Hand of God* (novel) Barrett, William E.

Cast   Bogart, Humphrey; Tierney, Gene; Cobb, Lee J.; Moorehead, Agnes; Marshall, E.G.; Porter, Jean; Sen Yung, Victor; Ahn, Philip; Fong, Benson

Song(s)   A Loaf of Bread [1] (C/L: Darby, Ken)

Notes   [1] Based on songs "The Old Grey Goose" and "Go Tell Aunt Susie."

3293 ◆ THE LEGACY
Universal, 1979

Musical Score   Lewis, Michael J.

Producer(s)   Foster, David
Director(s)   Marquand, Richard
Screenwriter(s)   Sangster, Jimmy

Cast   Ross, Katharine; Elliott, Sam; Standing, John; Hogg, Ian; Tyzack, Margaret; Daltrey, Roger

Song(s)   Another Side of Me (C: Lewis, Michael J.; L: Osborne, G.)

3294 ◆ LEGAL EAGLES
Universal, 1986

Musical Score   Bernstein, Elmer

Producer(s)   Reitman, Ivan
Director(s)   Reitman, Ivan
Screenwriter(s)   Cash, Jim; Epps Jr., Jack

Cast   Redford, Robert; Winger, Debra; Hannah, Daryl; Dennehy, Brian; Stamp, Terence; Hill, Steven; Glennon, David; McMartin, John; Dundas, Jennie; Browne, Roscoe Lee; Baranski, Christine; Botsford, Sara; Colton, Chevi; Quinton, Everett; Jabara, Paul

Song(s)   Good Lovin' (C/L: Resnick, Arthur; Clark, Rudy); Magic Carpet Ride [1] (C/L: Moreve, Rushton; Kay, John); Put Out the Fire (C/L: Hannah, Daryl; Monteleone, Michael); Love Touch (C/L: Chapman, Mike; Knight, Holly; Black, Gene)

Notes   It is not known if all the above songs were written for this film. [1] Also in MASK.

3295 ◆ LEGEND
Universal, 1986

Musical Score   Tangerine Dream

Producer(s)   Milchan, Arnon
Director(s)   Scott, Ridley
Screenwriter(s)   Hjortsberg, William

Cast   Cruise, Tom; Sara, Mia; Curry, Tim; Bennent, David; Playten, Alice; Barty, Billy; Hubbert, Cork; O'Farrell, Peter

Song(s)   Loved by the Sun (C: Tangerine Dream; L: Anderson, Jon); Is Your Love Strong Enough (C/L: Ferry, Bryan)

3296 ◆ THE LEGEND OF BILLIE JEAN
Tri-Star, 1985

Musical Score   Safan, Craig

Producer(s)   Cohen, Rob
Director(s)   Robbins, Matthew
Screenwriter(s)   Rosenthal, Mark; Konner, Lawrence

Cast   Slater, Helen; Gordon, Keith; Slater, Christian; Bradford, Richard; Gehman, Martha; Smith, Yeardley; Tubb, Barry; Stockwell, Dean; Coyote, Peter

Song(s)   Invincible (C/L: Knight, Holly; Clumie, Simon); Closing In (C: Safan, Craig; L: Mueller, Mark)

Notes   No cue sheet available.

3297 ◆ THE LEGEND OF LOBO
Disney, 1962

Musical Score   Wallace, Oliver

Producer(s)   Algar, James
Screenwriter(s)   Hauser, Dwight; Algar, James
Source(s)   "Lobo and other stories" (story) Seton, Ernest Thompson

Cast   Allen, Rex; Sons of the Pioneers

Song(s)   The Legend of Lobo (C/L: Sherman, Robert B.; Sherman, Richard M.)

3298 ◆ THE LEGEND OF LYLAH CLARE
Metro–Goldwyn–Mayer, 1968

Musical Score   De Vol, Frank

Producer(s)   Aldrich, Robert
Director(s)   Aldrich, Robert
Screenwriter(s)   Butler, Hugo; Rouverol, Jean
Source(s)   (teleplay) Thom, Robert; DeBlasio, Edward

Cast   Novak, Kim; Finch, Peter; Borgnine, Ernest; Selzer, Milton; Browne, Coral; Cortese, Valentina; Tinti, Gabriele

Song(s)   Lylah #1 (C: De Vol, Frank; L: Siegfried, Sybille); Lylah #2 [1] (C: De Vol, Frank; L: David, Mack)

Notes   [1] Sheet music only.

3299 ◆ THE LEGEND OF NIGGER CHARLEY
Paramount, 1972

Musical Score   Bennings, John

Producer(s)   Spangler, Larry G.
Director(s)   Goldman, Martin
Screenwriter(s)   Goldman, Martin; Spangler, Larry G.

Cast   Williamson, Fred; Martin, D'Urville; Colley, Dom Pedro

Song(s)   In the Eyes of God (C/L: Bennings, John); The Legend of Nigger Charley (C/L: Bennings, John)

Notes   Sheet music credits Elenora Bennings with the songs.

3300 ✦ THE LEGEND OF SLEEPY HOLLOW
Disney, 1949

Composer(s)   de Paul, Gene
Lyricist(s)   Raye, Don

Producer(s)   Sharpsteen, Ben
Director(s)   Kinney, Jack; Geronimi, Clyde; Algar, James
Screenwriter(s)   Penner, Erdman; Hibler, Winston; Rinaldi, Joe; Sears, Ted; Brightman, Homer; Reeves, Harry
Source(s)   "The Legend of Sleepy Hollow" (story) Irving, Washington
Voices   Crosby, Bing; Rhythmaires, The

Directing Animator(s)   Thomas, Franklin; Johnston, Ollie; Reitherman, Wolfgang; Kahl, Milt; Lounsbery, John; Kimball, Ward

Song(s)   Ichabod; Katrina; The Headless Horseman; Sleepy Hollow [1]

Notes   This cartoon is part of THE ADVENTURES OF ICHABOD AND MR. TOAD along with THE WIND IN THE WILLOWS. See also THE WIND IN THE WILLOWS. [1] Not used.

3301 ✦ THE LEGEND OF THE LONE RANGER
Universal, 1982

Musical Score   Barry, John

Producer(s)   Coblenz, Walter
Director(s)   Fraker, William A.
Screenwriter(s)   Goff, Ivan; Roberts, Ben; Kane, Michael; Roberts, William
Source(s)   "The Lone Ranger" (radio show; TV show) Trendle, George W.; Striker, Fran

Cast   Spilsbury, Klinton [1]; Horse, Michael; Lloyd, Christopher; Clark, Matt; Clay, Juanin; Robards Jr., Jason; Perry, John Bennett; Farnsworth, Richard

Song(s)   Legend of the Lone Ranger (C: Barry, John; L: Pitchford, Dean)

Notes   [1] Speaking voice dubbed.

3302 ✦ LEMON DROP KID (1934)
Paramount, 1934

Producer(s)   LeBaron, William
Director(s)   Neilan, Marshall
Screenwriter(s)   Green, Howard J.; McEvoy, J.P.
Source(s)   "The Lemon Drop Kid" (story) Runyon, Damon

Cast   Tracy, Lee; Mack, Helen; Gombell, Minna; Frawley, William

Song(s)   Just One More Chance [1] (C: Johnston, Arthur; L: Coslow, Sam)

Notes   "Dinah" by Harry Akst, Sam Lewis and Joe Young was also used as was "Carolina in the Morning" by Walter Donaldson and Gus Kahn. [1] Also in COUNTRY MUSIC HOLIDAY, THE MAGNIFICENT LIE and THIS RECKLESS AGE.

3303 ✦ THE LEMON DROP KID (1951)
Paramount, 1951

Musical Score   Young, Victor
Composer(s)   Livingston, Jay; Evans, Ray
Lyricist(s)   Livingston, Jay; Evans, Ray

Producer(s)   Welch, Robert L.
Director(s)   Lanfield, Sidney
Screenwriter(s)   Hartmann, Edmund L.; O'Brien, Robert; Tashlin, Frank [1]; Elinson, Irving
Source(s)   "The Lemon Drop Kid" (story) Runyon, Damon

Cast   Hope, Bob; Maxwell, Marilyn; Nolan, Lloyd; Darwell, Jane; King, Andrea; Clark, Fred; Bellaver, Harry; Flippen, Jay C.; Frawley, William; Melton, Sid; Welden, Ben

Song(s)   It Doesn't Cost a Dime to Dream; They Obviously Want Me to Sing; Silver Bells

Notes   [1] Tashlin credited on official credit sheet, though not in books.

3304 ✦ LEO AND LOREE
United Artists, 1980

Composer(s)   Asher, Jay
Lyricist(s)   Wakefield, Kathy

Producer(s)   Begg, Jim
Director(s)   Paris, Jerry
Screenwriter(s)   Ritz, James

Cast   Most, Donny; Purl, Linda; Huffman, David; Paris, Jerry; Franon, Shannon

Song(s)   I Only Want What's Mine; Ooh La La La La (C/L: Costadinos, Alec R.); (L.A. Is) Only a Movie; If We Could Turn Back Time (L: Asher, Jay)

Notes   No cue sheet available.

3305 ✦ LEONARD PART 6
Columbia, 1987

Musical Score   Bernstein, Elmer

Producer(s)   Cosby, Bill
Director(s)   Weiland, Paul
Screenwriter(s)   Reynolds, Jonathan

Cast Cosby, Bill; Courtenay, Tom; Baker, Joe Don; Gunn, Moses; Colbert, Pat; Foster, Gloria; Zabriskie, Grace; Kirby, George

Song(s) Positive (C/L: Quigley, Peter; Campbell, Alaster); Without You (C/L: Dozier, Lamont)

Notes No cue sheet available.

3306 ✦ LEONARD SILLMAN'S NEW FACES

See NEW FACES.

3307 ✦ THE LEOPARD MAN
RKO, 1943

Musical Score Webb, Roy

Producer(s) Lewton, Val
Director(s) Tourneur, Jacques
Screenwriter(s) Dein, Edward; Wray, Ardel
Source(s) *Black Alibi* (novel) Woolrich, Cornell

Cast O'Keefe, Dennis; Margo; Brooks, Jean; Jewell, Isabel; Bell, James; Landry, Margaret; Biberman, Abner; Parma, Tula; Bard, Ben

Song(s) Palomita Mia (C/L: Gonzales, Aaron)

3308 ✦ LEO THE LAST
United Artists, 1970

Musical Score Myrow, Fred
Composer(s) Myrow, Fred
Lyricist(s) Myrow, Fred

Producer(s) Winkler, Irwin; Chartoff, Robert
Director(s) Boorman, John
Screenwriter(s) Stair, Bill; Boorman, John
Source(s) *The Prince* (play) Tabori, George

Cast Mastroianni, Marcello; Whitelaw, Billie; Lockhart, Calvin; Forster-Jones, Glenna

Song(s) Dinosaur Man; Ours Is a Nice House, Ours Is (C/L: Rulie; Holt); Where Do the Dreams Go

3309 ✦ LEPKE
Warner Brothers, 1975

Musical Score Wannberg, Ken

Producer(s) Golan, Menahem
Director(s) Golan, Menahem
Screenwriter(s) Lau, Wesley; Hoffs, Tamar Simon

Cast Curtis, Tony; Comer, Anjanette; Callan, Michael; Berlinger, Warren; Russo, Gianni; Tayback, Vic; Wilcox, Mary; Berle, Milton

Song(s) I Sure Love My Poopsie (C: Wannberg, Ken; Lehner, Stephen)

3310 ✦ LE ROI DE COEUR

See KING OF HEARTS.

3311 ✦ LES GIRLS
Metro–Goldwyn–Mayer, 1957

Musical Score Deutsch, Adolph
Composer(s) Porter, Cole
Lyricist(s) Porter, Cole
Choreographer(s) Cole, Jack

Producer(s) Siegel, Sol C.
Director(s) Cukor, George
Screenwriter(s) Caspary, Vera

Cast Kelly, Gene; Gaynor, Mitzi; Kendall, Kay [1]; Elg, Taina; Bergerac, Jacques; Phillips, Leslie; Daniell, Henry; MacNee, Patrick; Vercoe, Stepehen; Tonge, Philip

Song(s) Flower Song (C/L: Chaplin, Saul); Les Girls; Ca C'est L'Amour; Ladies in Waiting; You're Just Too, Too!; Why Am I So Gone (About that Gal)?; Drinking Song [2]; High-flyin' Wings on My Shoes [2]; I Could Kick Myself [2]; My Darling Never Is Late [2]; My Little Piece O' Pie [2]; What Fun [2]; You're the Prize Guy of Guys [2]

Notes [1] Dubbed by Betty Wand for all notes above C. [2] Not used.

3312 ✦ LE SILENCE EST D'OR

See MAN ABOUT TOWN.

3313 ✦ LES PARAPLUIES DE CHERBOURG

See UMBRELLAS OF CHERBOURG.

3314 ✦ LESS THAN ZERO
Twentieth Century–Fox, 1987

Musical Score Newman, Thomas

Producer(s) Avnet, Jon; Kerner, Jordan
Director(s) Kanievska, Marek
Screenwriter(s) Peyton, Harley
Source(s) *Less Than Zero* (novel) Ellis, Bret Easton

Cast McCarthy, Andrew; Gertz, Jami; Downey Jr., Robert; Spader, James; Bill, Tony; Pryor, Nicholas; Mitchell, Donna; Yurasek, John

Song(s) A Hazy Shade of Winter (C/L: Simon, Paul); Rock and Roll All Night (C/L: Stanley, Paul; Simmons, Gene); Are You My Woman (C/L: Record, Eugene); Lil' Devil (C/L: Astbury, Ian Robert; Duffy, William Henry); Abele Dancer (C/L: Dubango, Manu); Fire (C/L: Hendrix, Jimi); You and Me (C/L: Danzig, Glen; Rubin, Rick); She's Lost You (C/L: Gage, Peter); Rockin' Pneumonia and the Boogie Woogie Flu (C/L:

Smith, Huey P.); Goin' Back to Cali (C/L: L.L. Cool J); Want To Go Rave (C/L: Johnson, Linton Kwesi); Bump and Grind (C/L: Roth, David Lee; Vai, Steve); In-a-Gadda-Da-Vida (C/L: Ingle, Doug); Christmas in Hollis (C/L: Simmons, J.; McDaniels, E.; Mizell, J.); Fight Like a Brave (C/L: Flea; Kiedis, Anthony; Slovak, Hillel; Irons, Jack); How to Love Again (C/L: Bell, Vinnie; Gordon, Frederick); Moonlight Drive (C/L: Manzarek, Ray; Densmore, John; Krieger, Robby); Bring the Noise (C/L: Ridenhour, Carlton; Saddler, Eric); Psychotic Reaction (C/L: Ellena; Chaney; Atkinson; Byrne; Michalski); Life Fades Away (C/L: Orbison, Roy; Danzig, Glen)

Notes It is not known which, if any, of these were written for this picture.

3315 ♦ LET FREEDOM RING
Metro–Goldwyn–Mayer, 1939

Producer(s) Rapf, Harry
Director(s) Conway, Jack
Screenwriter(s) Hecht, Ben

Cast Eddy, Nelson; Bruce, Virginia; McLaglen, Victor; Barrymore, Lionel; Arnold, Edward; Kibbee, Guy; Warner, H.B.; Butterworth, Charles; Walburn, Raymond

Song(s) Love Serenade (C: Drigo, Ricardo; L: Wright, Bob; Forrest, Chet); Pat - Sez He (C: Ohman, Phil; L: Carling, Foster); Dusty Road (C/L: Rene, Leon; Rene, Otis); Where Else But Here (C: Romberg, Sigmund; L: Heyman, Edward)

Notes There are also some public domain songs sung.

3316 ♦ LETHAL WEAPON
Warner Brothers, 1987

Musical Score Kamen, Michael; Clapton, Eric

Producer(s) Donner, Richard; Silver, Joel
Director(s) Donner, Richard
Screenwriter(s) Black, Shane

Cast Gibson, Mel; Glover, Danny; Busey, Gary; Ryan, Mitchell; Atkins, Tom; Love, Darlene; Wolfe, Traci

Song(s) Lethal Weapon (C/L: Kamen, Michael)

Notes No cue sheet available.

3317 ♦ LET NO MAN WRITE MY EPITAPH
Columbia, 1960

Musical Score Duning, George

Producer(s) Kaplan, Boris D.
Director(s) Leacock, Philip
Screenwriter(s) Presnell Jr., Robert

Cast Ives, Burl; Winters, Shelley; Darren, James; Seberg, Jean; Montalban, Ricardo; Fitzgerald, Ella; Acosta, Rodolfo; Ober, Philip; Burke, Walter

Song(s) Reach for Tomorrow (C: McHugh, Jimmy; L: Washington, Ned)

Notes No cue sheet available.

3318 ♦ LET'S BE HAPPY
Allied Artists, 1957

Musical Score Brodszky, Nicholas
Composer(s) Brodszky, Nicholas
Lyricist(s) Webster, Paul Francis

Producer(s) Hellman, Marcel
Director(s) Levin, Henry
Screenwriter(s) Morgan, Diana
Source(s) *Jeannie* (play) Stuart, Aimee

Cast Vera-Ellen [1]; Martin, Tony; Flemyng, Robert; Marshall, Zena; Horton, Helen

Song(s) Let's Be Happy; I'm Going to Scotland; The Man from Idaho; Hold on to Love; The Golfer's Glide; Pajama Ballet (C/L: Brodszky, Nicholas); The Rose and the Heather; One Is a Lonely Number; The Piper's Wedding (L: Morgan, Diana)

Notes An Associated British-Pathe film. [1] Dubbed.

3319 ♦ LET'S DANCE
Paramount, 1950

Composer(s) Loesser, Frank
Lyricist(s) Loesser, Frank
Choreographer(s) Pan, Hermes

Producer(s) Fellows, Robert
Director(s) McLeod, Norman Z.
Screenwriter(s) Scott, Allan; Lussier, Dane
Source(s) "Little Boy Blue" (story) Zolotow, Maurice

Cast Hutton, Betty; Astaire, Fred; Young, Roland; Warrick, Ruth; Watson, Lucile; Moffett, Gregory; MacLane, Barton; Strudwick, Shepperd; Cooper, Melville

Song(s) Oh, Them Dudes; Can't Stop Talking; Why Fight the Feeling; Tunnel of Love [2]; Jack and the Beanstalk; The Hyacinth; The Ming-Toy Noodle Company [1]; It Was Great While It Lasted; Let's Do It Again

Notes [1] Not used. [2] Not used in VARIETY GIRL.

3320 ♦ LET'S DO IT AGAIN
Columbia, 1953

Composer(s) Lee, Lester
Lyricist(s) Washington, Ned
Choreographer(s) Bettis, Valerie; Scott, Lee

Producer(s) Saul, Oscar
Director(s) Hall, Alexander
Screenwriter(s) Loos, Mary; Sale, Richard

Cast Treen, Mary; Booth, Karin; Ames, Leon; Ameche, Don; Wyman, Jane; Milland, Ray

Song(s) Anyone But You; Call of the Wild; Give Me a Man Who Makes Music; These Are the Things I Remember; Takin' a Slow Burn; It Was Great While It Lasted; Let's Do It Again

Notes No cue sheet available. Dick Haymes' voice is heard via a recording singing "Anyone but You."

3321 ✦ LET'S FACE IT
Paramount, 1943

Composer(s) Porter, Cole
Lyricist(s) Porter, Cole

Producer(s) Kohlmar, Fred
Director(s) Lanfield, Sidney
Screenwriter(s) Tugend, Harry
Source(s) *Let's Face It* (musical) Porter, Cole; Fields, Herbert

Cast Kerr, Donald [5]; Hope, Bob; Hutton, Betty; Arden, Eve; Pitts, ZaSu; Drake, Dona; Weaver, Marjorie; Povah, Phyllis; Willock, Dave; Richards, Cully; Tombes, Andrew; De Carlo, Yvonne

Song(s) Who Did? I Did, Yes - I Did [2] (C: Styne, Jule; L: Cahn, Sammy; Seelen, Jerry; Lee, Lester); Let's Not Talk About Love [1] (L: Porter, Cole; Cahn, Sammy); Plain Jane Doe [3] [4] (C: Styne, Jule; L: Cahn, Sammy); All the Way [3] (C: Styne, Jule; L: Gannon, Kim)

Notes The following numbers from the Broadway score appeared instrumentally: "Ace in the Hole," "Baby Games," "Farming" (Recorded vocally), "Let's Not Talk About Love" and "Everything I Love." Sammy Cahn wrote additional lyrics for "Let's Face It," "Let's Not Talk About Love" and "Farming" although two of these never made it into the picture as songs. [1] From Broadway version. Cahn fixed the lyrics for this film. [2] Jerry Seelan and Lester Lee wrote special lyrics for a chorus of this song. The lyrics are about a guy who never thought of himself as square and to whom purple looks brown. [3] Not used. [4] Recorded. [5] Dubbed for singing.

3322 ✦ LET'S FALL IN LOVE
Columbia, 1933

Composer(s) Arlen, Harold
Lyricist(s) Koehler, Ted

Director(s) Burton, David
Screenwriter(s) Fields, Herbert

Cast Lowe, Edmund; Sothern, Ann; Jordan, Miriam; Ratoff, Gregory; Meyer, Greta; Birell, Tala; Jarrett, Arthur; Gateson, Marjorie; Furness, Betty

Song(s) Let's Fall in Love [2]; Love Is Love Anywhere; This Is Only the Beginning [1]; Breakfast Ball [3]; She's Not the Type [4]

Notes Remade as SLIGHTLY FRENCH in 1949. [1] Used instrumentally only. [2] Also in JUKE BOX RHYTHM, ON THE SUNNY SIDE OF THE STREET, SENIOR PROM and SLIGHTLY FRENCH. [3] Not used. Later put in COTTON CLUB PARADE nightclub review. [4] Not used.

3323 ✦ LET'S GO COLLEGIATE
Monogram, 1941

Producer(s) Parsons, Lindsley
Director(s) Yarbrough, Jean
Screenwriter(s) Kelso, Edmund

Cast Darro, Frankie; Moran, Jackie; Jones, Marcia Mae; Moreland, Mantan; Storm, Gale; Luke, Keye; Sully, Frank; Coffin, Tristram

Notes No cue sheet available. Released in Great Britain as FAREWELL TO FAME.

3324 ✦ LET'S GO NATIVE
Paramount, 1930

Composer(s) Whiting, Richard A.
Lyricist(s) Marion Jr., George
Choreographer(s) Bennett, David

Director(s) McCarey, Leo
Screenwriter(s) Marion Jr., George; Heath, Percy

Cast MacDonald, Jeanette; Oakie, Jack; Francis, Kay; Hall, James; Gallagher, Skeets; Pallette, Eugene

Song(s) My Mad Moment; Let's Go Native; It Seems to Be Spring; Joe Jazz; I've Got a Yen for You; Don't I Do? [1] [2]; My Mad Moment [1]; The Flicker Tail [1]; Pampas Rose [1] [2]

Notes Called DANCING EYES prior to production. [1] Not used. [2] Recorded.

3325 ✦ LET'S GO PLACES
Fox, 1930

Composer(s) Conrad, Con; Gottler, Archie
Lyricist(s) Conrad, Con; Mitchell, Sidney D.
Choreographer(s) Dare, Danny

Director(s) Strayer, Frank R.
Screenwriter(s) Wells, William K.

Cast Wagstaff, Joseph; Lane, Lola; Lynn, Sharon; Richardson, Frank; Catlett, Walter; Lee, Dixie; Chase, Ilka; Judels, Charles; Steers, Larry

Song(s) Reach Out for a Rainbow; Paris—Minuet (C/L: Krier, Georges); Hollywood Nights; Boop-Boop-A-Doopa-Doo Fox Trot (C: Burke, Johnny; L: Little, George A.); Parade of the Blues; Snow Ball Man (C: Hanley, James F.; L: Brockman, James); Fascinatin' Devil (C: Monaco, James V.; L: McCarthy, Joseph); I'm Climbing Up a Rainbow [1] (C: Nelson, Edward G.; L: Pease, Harry); Let's Go Places [2] (C:

Monaco, James V.; L: Friend, Cliff); Out in the Cold [2]; Um, Um in the Moonlight [2]; The Snowball Man [3] (C: Monaco, James V.; L: Brockman, James)

Notes Originally titled FAST WORKERS. Several of these songs were first registered for copyright as written for the film HOLLYWOOD NIGHTS. Perhaps this is another early title for this film or it might have been an abandoned production. [1] Not used. Put into THE BIG PARTY. [2] Listed in some sources but not on cue sheets. [3] Not used.

3326 ◆ LET'S GO STEADY
Columbia, 1945

Composer(s) Torme, Mel
Lyricist(s) Torme, Mel

Producer(s) Richmond, Ted
Director(s) Lord, Del
Screenwriter(s) Lazarus, Erna

Cast Parrish, Pat; Moran, Jackie; Preisser, June; Lloyd, Jimmy; Ennis, Skinnay; Torme, Mel

Song(s) Tantza Babele; Sioux Falls S.D.; Baby Boogie; I Don't Want To Love You (C/L: Prichard, Henry)

Notes No cue sheet available.

3327 ◆ LET'S LIVE TONIGHT
Columbia, 1935

Musical Score Schertzinger, Victor

Producer(s) North, Robert
Director(s) Schertzinger, Victor
Screenwriter(s) Markey, Gene

Cast Carminati, Tullio; Harvey, Lilian; Beecher, Janet; Williams, Hugh; Alberni, Luis; Birell, Tala; Treacher, Arthur

Song(s) Love Passes By (C: Schertzinger, Victor; L: Scholl, Jack); I'll Live in My Dreams [1] (C/L: Schertzinger, Victor)

Notes [1] Used instrumentally only.

3328 ◆ LET'S MAKE LOVE
Twentieth Century–Fox, 1960

Composer(s) Van Heusen, James
Lyricist(s) Cahn, Sammy
Choreographer(s) Cole, Jack

Producer(s) Wald, Jerry
Director(s) Cukor, George
Screenwriter(s) Krasna, Norman; Kanter, Hal

Cast Monroe, Marilyn; Montand, Yves; Randall, Tony; Vaughan, Frankie; Hyde-White, Wilfrid; Burns, David; Lynn, Mara; Besser, Joe; Kennedy, Madge; Berle, Milton [1]; Crosby, Bing [1]; Kelly, Gene [1]; King Jr., Dennis

Song(s) Let's Make Love; Hey You with the Crazy Eyes; Specialization; Incurably Romantic

Notes Originally titled THE BILLIONAIRE and Gregory Peck was to costar and Alan Jay Lerner and Frederick Loewe were to write the songs. "My Heart Belongs to Daddy" by Cole Porter (with revised lyrics by Charles Henderson) and "Give Me the Simple Life" by Rube Bloom and Harry Ruby are used vocally. [1] Special guest stars.

3329 ◆ LET'S MAKE MUSIC
RKO, 1940

Musical Score Webb, Roy

Producer(s) Benedict, Howard
Director(s) Goodwins, Leslie
Screenwriter(s) West, Nathanael; Phillips, Helen [1]; Dougall, Bernard [1]

Cast Bob Crosby and His Orchestra; Rubin, Benny; The Bobcats; Rogers, Jean; Risdon, Elizabeth; Buloff, Joseph; Compton, Joyce

Song(s) Fight on for Newton High (C: Webb, Roy; Dreyer, Dave; L: Ruby, Herman); You Forgot About Me [2] (C/L: Hanley, James F.; Robertson, Richard); The Big Noise from Winnetka (C/L: Crosby, Bob; Haggart, Bob; Rodin, Gil; Bauduc, Ray); Central Park (C: Malneck, Matty; L: Mercer, Johnny)

Notes [1] Special dialogue for Bob Crosby. [2] Sonny Mysels also credited on sheet music.

3330 ◆ LET'S ROCK!
Columbia, 1958

Composer(s) Gohman, Don
Lyricist(s) Hackady, Hal
Choreographer(s) Gennaro, Peter

Producer(s) Foster, Harry
Director(s) Foster, Harry
Screenwriter(s) Hackady, Hal

Cast La Rosa, Julius; Newman, Phyllis; Janis, Conrad; Harman, Joy; Martindale, Wink; Hackady, Jerry; Gary, Harold; Janis, Conrad; Harman, Joy; Anka, Paul; Danny and the Juniors; Roy Hamilton and the Cues; Reese, Della; The Royal Teens

Song(s) Blast Off! (C/L: Jones, Ollie); There Are Times; Casual; Two Perfect Strangers; Lonelyville (C: Marks, Walter); Here Comes Love (C/L: Stone, Jesse); The Secret Path to Love (C/L: Singleton, Charles; Wood, Johnny R.); All Love Broke Loose (C/L: Singleton, Charles; Cathy, Lee); Crazy Crazy Party (C/L: Calhoun, Charles; Winley, Paul); At the Hop (C/L: Singer, Arthur; Medora, J.; White, David); Short Shorts (C/L: Austin, T.; Gaudio, Bob); I'll Be Waiting There for You (C/L: Anka, Paul); Squeegie [1] (C/L: Blackwell, Otis)

Notes Some of these might not have been written for the film. [1] BMI list only.

3331 ◆ LET'S SCARE JESSICA TO DEATH
Paramount, 1971

Musical Score Stoeber, Orville

Producer(s) Moss Jr., Charles B.
Director(s) Hancock, John
Screenwriter(s) Jonas, Norman; Rose, Ralph

Cast Lampert, Zohra; Heyman, Barton; O'Connor, Kevin

Song(s) Stay Forever My Love (C/L: Stoeber, Orville)

3332 ◆ LET'S SING AGAIN
RKO, 1936

Producer(s) Lesser, Sol
Director(s) Neumann, Kurt
Screenwriter(s) Swift, Don; Jarrett, Sam

Cast Breen, Bobby; Armetta, Henry; Houston, George; Osborne, Vivienne; Withers, Grant; Courtney, Inez

Song(s) Let's Sing Again (C: McHugh, Jimmy; L: Kahn, Gus); Lullaby (C: Riesenfeld, Hugo; L: Hautzik, Selma); The Farmer in the Dell (C/L: Pokrass, Sam; Locke, Charles; Tyler, Richard E.)

Notes No cue sheet available.

3333 ◆ A LETTER TO THREE WIVES
Twentieth Century–Fox, 1948

Musical Score Newman, Alfred

Producer(s) Siegel, Sol C.
Director(s) Mankiewicz, Joseph L.
Screenwriter(s) Mankiewicz, Joseph L.
Source(s) *Letter to Five Wives* (novel) Klempner, John

Cast Crain, Jeanne; Darnell, Linda; Sothern, Ann; Douglas, Kirk; Douglas, Paul; Gilchrist, Connie; Bates, Florence; Cavanaugh, Hobart; Ritter, Thelma

Song(s) Crazy Eddie [1] (C: Henderson, Charles; L: Mankiewicz, Joseph L.)

Notes [1] This is a commercial. It lasts less than 30 seconds on screen.

3334 ◆ LET THE GOOD TIMES ROLL
Columbia, 1973

Producer(s) Isenberg, Gerald I.
Director(s) Levin, Sid; Abel, Robert

Cast Berry, Chuck; Little Richard; Domino, "Fats; Checker, Chubby; Diddley, Bo; The Shirelles; The Five Satins; The Coasters; Danny and the Juniors; The Bobby

Comstock Rock and Roll Band; Bill Haley and the Comets; Nader, Richard

Notes No original songs in this documentary. Vocals include "I'm a Man" and "Hey Bo-Diddley" by Ellas McDaniel; "Rip It Up" and "Good Golly Miss Molly" by R.A. Blackwell and John S. Marascalco; "Lucille" by Richard Penniman and Albert Collins; "Save the Last Dance for Me" by Doc Pomus and Mort Shuman; "Sincerely" by Harvey Fuqua and Alan Freed; "Earth Angel" by Jesse Belvin; "(I'll Remember) In the Still of the Night" by Fred Parris; "I'll Be Seeing You" by Irving Kahal and Sammy Fain; "Mabellene" by Chuck Berry, Russ Fratto and Alan Freed; "Reelin' and Rockin';" "Johnny B. Goode" and "Sweet Little Sixteen" by Chuck Berry; "My Blue Heaven" by Walter Donaldson and George Whiting; "Blueberry Hill" by Al Lewis, Larry Stock and Vincent Rose; "At the Hop" by John Madara, Arthur Singer and David White; "Everybody Loves a Lover" by Robert Allen and Richard Adler; "Soldier Boy" by Luther Dixon and Florence Greenberg; "Poison Ivy" and "Charlie Brown" by Jerry Leiber and Mike Stoller; "School Day (Ring! Ring! Goes the Bell)" by Chuck Berry; "Party Time" by Don Covay and John Berry; "Let's Twist Again" by Kal Mann and Dave Appell; "The Twist" by Hank Ballard; "Rock Around the Clock" by Jimmy DeKnight and Max C. Freedman; "Shake Rattle and Roll" by Charles Calhoun and "Let the Good Times Roll" by Leonard Lee.

3335 ◆ LICENSE TO DRIVE
Twentieth Century–Fox, 1988

Musical Score Ferguson, Jay

Producer(s) Mueller, Jeffrey A.; Light, Andrew
Director(s) Beeman, Greg
Screenwriter(s) Tolkin, Neil

Cast Haim, Corey; Feldman, Corey; Kane, Carol; Masur, Richard; Avery, James; Ensign, Michael; Hanft, Helen

Song(s) Drive My Car (C/L: Lennon, John; McCartney, Paul); Rush Hour (C/L: Wiedlin, Jane; Rafelson, Peter); Mercedes Boy (C/L: Pebbles); Jazzy's in the House (C/L: Townes, J.); Soul Man [1] (C/L: Porter, David; Hayes, Isaac); Trouble (C/L: Harvey, Steve); I Feel Free (C/L: Bruce, Jack; Brown, Peter); Make Some Noise (C/L: Raider, Slave; Nagel, D.); Crucial (C/L: Johnson, Gary "Jellybean"; Keith, Lisa); Waiting for the Big One (C/L: Neigher, Rick; Cole, David); Time Starts Now (C/L: Lorber, Sam; Labounty, Bill); That's Life (C/L: Kay, Dean; Gordon, Kelly); Get Out of My Dreams (C/L: Lange, Robert John; Ocean, Billy)

Notes It is not known which, if any, of these were written for the picture. All are background vocals. There are also a couple of standards thrown in. [1] Also in ONE TRICK PONY.

3336 ✦ LIES MY FATHER TOLD ME
Columbia, 1975

Musical Score   Kaplan, Sol

Producer(s)   Bedrich, Anthony; Guikin, Harry
Director(s)   Kadar, Jan
Screenwriter(s)   Allan, Ted

Cast   Yadin, Yossi; Birman, Len; Lightstone, Marilyn; Lynas, Jeffrey; Allan, Ted

Song(s)   Rags, Clothes, Bottles (C/L: Kaplan, Sol)

3337 ✦ THE LIEUTENANT WORE SKIRTS
Twentieth Century–Fox, 1955

Musical Score   Mockridge, Cyril J.

Producer(s)   Adler, Buddy
Director(s)   Tashlin, Frank
Screenwriter(s)   Belch, Albert; Tashlin, Frank

Cast   Ewell, Tom; North, Sheree; Moreno, Rita; Jason, Rick; Tremayne, Les; Platt, Edward

Song(s)   Rock Around the Island (C/L: Darby, Ken)

3338 ✦ THE LIFE AND TIMES OF JUDGE ROY BEAN
First Artists, 1972

Musical Score   Jarre, Maurice

Producer(s)   Foreman, John
Director(s)   Huston, John
Screenwriter(s)   Milius, John

Cast   Newman, Paul; Bisset, Jacqueline; Hunter, Tab; Huston, John; Keach, Stacy; McDowall, Roddy; Perkins, Anthony; Principal, Victoria; Zerbe, Anthony; Gardner, Ava

Song(s)   Marmalade, Molasses and Honey (C: Jarre, Maurice; L: Bergman, Alan; Bergman, Marilyn)

3339 ✦ LIFE BEGINS IN COLLEGE
Twentieth Century–Fox, 1937

Composer(s)   Pollack, Lew
Lyricist(s)   Mitchell, Sidney D.

Producer(s)   Wilson, Harold
Director(s)   Seiter, William A.
Screenwriter(s)   Tunberg, Karl; Ettlinger, Don
Source(s)   stories by Ware, Darrell

Cast   The Ritz Brothers; Davis, Joan; Martin, Tony; Stuart, Gloria; Stone, Fred; Pendleton, Nat; Baldwin, Dick; Marsh, Joan; Prouty, Jed; Weaver, Marjorie; Nugent, J.C.; Cook Jr., Elisha

Song(s)   Our Team Is on the Warpath; Why Talk About Love?; Rumba Goes Nuts (C/L: Pokrass, Sam; Golden, Ray; Kuller, Sid); Big Chief Swing It; Indian Nuts (C: Pokrass, Sam; L: Kuller, Sid; Golden, Ray); Sweet Varsity

Sue [2] (C/L: Tobias, Charles; Mencher, Murray; Lewis, Al); Fair Lombardy [1]; Spirit of 76 (C: Pokrass, Sam; L: Kuller, Sid; Golden, Ray); Rhumba Goes Collegiate [3]

Notes   [1] Used instrumentally except for four bars. [2] Not written for this picture. [3] Sheet music only.

3340 ✦ LIFE BEGINS WITH LOVE
Columbia, 1937

Director(s)   McCarey, Ray
Screenwriter(s)   Mitchell, Thomas; Holmes, Brown

Cast   Parker, Jean; Montgomery, Douglass; Fellows, Edith; Hare, Lumsden; Urecal, Minerva; Beckett, Scotty

Song(s)   What Makes You So Sweet [1] (C: Oakland, Ben; L: Russell, Bennee)

Notes   [1] Used instrumentally only.

3341 ✦ LIFEGUARD
Paramount, 1976

Producer(s)   Silverman, Ron
Director(s)   Petrie, Daniel
Screenwriter(s)   Koslow, Ron

Cast   Elliott, Sam; Hall, Mark; Lichtig, Scott; Stevenson, Parker; Archer, Anne; Quinlan, Kathleen

Song(s)   Time and Tide (C/L: Williams, Paul); Falling in Love with the Wind (C/L: Mentin, Dale); Country Love (C/L: Mentin, Dale)

3342 ✦ LIFE IN THE RAW
Fox, 1933

Musical Score   Lange, Arthur
Composer(s)   Brulier; Anthony
Lyricist(s)   Anthony

Director(s)   King, Louis
Screenwriter(s)   Anthony, Stuart
Source(s)   (story) Grey, Zane

Cast   O'Brien, George; Nissen, Greta; Trevor, Claire

Song(s)   Once I Had a Gal Named Susie (C: Anthony); Angel Band; Harp and Crown

3343 ✦ A LIFE OF HER OWN
Metro–Goldwyn–Mayer, 1950

Musical Score   Kaper, Bronislau

Producer(s)   Vetluguin, Voldemar
Director(s)   Cukor, George
Screenwriter(s)   Lennart, Isobel

Cast   Turner, Lana; Milland, Ray; Ewell, Tom; Calhern, Louis; Dvorak, Ann; Sullivan, Barry; Phillips, Margaret; Hagen, Jean; Kirk, Phyllis; Haden, Sara

Song(s)   A Life of Her Own [1] (C: Kaper, Bronislau; L: Webster, Paul Francis)

Notes There is a vocal of "Easy to Love" by Cole Porter. [1] Used instrumentally only.

3344 ✦ THE LIFE OF THE PARTY (1930)
Warner Brothers, 1930

Composer(s) Loewe, Frederick
Lyricist(s) Crooker, Earle

Director(s) Del Ruth, Roy
Screenwriter(s) Caesar, Arthur

Cast Lightner, Winnie; Delroy, Irene; Whiting, Jack; Butterworth, Charles; Judels, Charles; Davidson, John; Hoyt, Arthur; Irving, William

Song(s) Can It Be Possible (C: Gottler, Archie; Meyer, Joseph; L: Mitchell, Sidney D.); One Robin Doesn't Make a Spring; Somehow; Mystery of Clothes [1] (C: Burke, Joe; L: Dubin, Al); You Ought to See the Horse [1] (C: Burke, Joe; L: Dubin, Al); He Got a Poison Ivy Instead of a Clinging Vine [1] (C: Burke, Joe; L: Dubin, Al)

Notes No cue sheet available. Most of this film's numbers were cut when musicals went out of vogue. [1] Not used.

3345 ✦ THE LIFE OF THE PARTY (1937)
RKO, 1937

Composer(s) Magidson, Herb
Lyricist(s) Wrubel, Allie
Choreographer(s) Lee, Sammy

Producer(s) Kaufman, Edward
Director(s) Seiter, William A.
Screenwriter(s) Kalmar, Bert; Ruby, Harry; Shore, Viola Brothers

Cast Penner, Joe; Raymond, Gene; Parkyakarkus; Hilliard, Harriet; Moore, Victor; Broderick, Helen; Gilbert, Billy; Miller, Ann

Song(s) Chirp a Little Ditty; Roses in December (C: Oakland, Ben; L: Magidson, Herb; Jessel, George); So You Won't Sing; Life of the Party; Let's Have Another Cigarette; Yankee Doodle Band

3346 ✦ LIFE WITHOUT ZOE
Touchstone, 1989

Musical Score Coppola, Carmine
Composer(s) Darnell, August
Lyricist(s) Darnell, August

Producer(s) Roos, Fred; Fuchs, Fred
Director(s) Coppola, Francis Ford
Screenwriter(s) Coppola, Francis Ford; Coppola, Sofia

Cast Shire, Talia; Giannini, Giancarlo; McComb, Heather; Novello, Don; Nichols, Jenny; Keane, James

Song(s) Zoe; People Will Talk; Daiquiri Daiquira (Inst.); Don't Lead Me On; Takin' a Holiday.

Notes This is one of three films in NEW YORK STORIES.

3347 ✦ THE LIGHT FANTASTIC

See LOVE IS BETTER THAN EVER.

3348 ✦ THE LIGHT IN THE FOREST
Disney, 1958

Musical Score Smith, Paul J.
Composer(s) Smith, Paul J.

Director(s) Daugherty, Herschel
Screenwriter(s) Watkin, Lawrence Edward
Source(s) *The Light in the Forest* (novel) Richter, Conrad

Cast Parker, Fess; Corey, Wendell; Dru, Joanne; MacArthur, James; Tandy, Jessica; McIntire, John; Calleia, Joseph; Lynley, Carol; Campos, Rafael; Ferguson, Frank; Seldes, Marian

Song(s) Light in the Forest (L: George, Gil); I Asked My Love a Favor (L: Watkin, Lawrence Edward); Indian Lament (L: Traditional)

3349 ✦ LIGHT IN THE PIAZZA
Metro–Goldwyn–Mayer, 1962

Musical Score Nascimbene, Milton

Producer(s) Freed, Arthur
Director(s) Green, Guy
Screenwriter(s) Epstein, Julius J.

Cast de Havilland, Olivia; Sullivan, Barry; Mimieux, Yvette; Brazzi, Rossano; Nevinson, Nancy; Hamilton, George; Dean, Isabel

Song(s) Light in the Piazza [1] (C: Nascimbene, Milton; L: Freed, Arthur)

Notes [1] Used instrumentally only though recorded.

3350 ✦ LIGHTNING GUNS
Columbia, 1950

Composer(s) Burnette, Smiley
Lyricist(s) Burnette, Smiley

Producer(s) Clark, Colbert
Director(s) Sears, Fred F.
Screenwriter(s) Arthur, Victor

Cast Starrett, Charles; Henry, Gloria; Bailey, William Norton; Dearing, Edgar; Bond, Raymond; Mahoney, Jock [1]; Burnette, Smiley; Houchins, Ken

Song(s) The Bath Tub King; Rambling Blood in My Veins; Our Whole Family's Smart

Notes [1] Billed as Jock O'Mahoney.

3351 ✦ LIGHTNING STRIKES TWICE
RKO, 1934

Musical Score Steiner, Max

Producer(s) Marcus, Lee
Director(s) Holmes, Ben
Screenwriter(s) Grey, John; Fields, Joseph

Cast Lyon, Ben; Todd, Thelma; Crews, Laura Hope; Chandler, Chick; Hale, John; Davidson, John; Dearing, Edgar; Kelton, Pert; Gallagher, Skeets; Catlett, Walter

Song(s) Isn't This a Night for Love [1] (C/L: Burton, Val; Jason, Will)

Notes [1] Also in THE WITNESS CHAIR.

3352 ✦ LIGHT OF DAY
Tri-Star, 1987

Musical Score Newman, Thomas

Producer(s) Cohen, Rob; Barish, Keith
Director(s) Schrader, Paul
Screenwriter(s) Schrader, Paul

Cast Fox, Michael J.; Rowlands, Gena; Jett, Joan; McKeon Michael; Waites, Thomas G.; Jones, Cherry

Song(s) Light of Day (C/L: Springsteen, Bruce); Stay with Me Tonight (C/L: Edmunds, Dave; David, John); Rabbit's Got a Gun (C/L: Jett, Joan; Laguna, Kenny); You Got No Place to Go (C/L: Poul, Alan Mark; Fox, Michael J.); Twist It Off (C/L: Christina, Fran; Hubbard, Preston)

Notes No cue sheet available.

3353 ✦ LIGHTS AND SHADOWS

See THE WOMAN RACKET.

3354 ✦ LIGHTS OF OLD SANTA FE
Republic, 1944

Composer(s) Spencer, Tim
Lyricist(s) Spencer, Tim
Choreographer(s) Ceballos, Larry

Producer(s) Grey, Harry
Director(s) McDonald, Frank
Screenwriter(s) Kahn, Gordon; Williams, Bob

Cast Rogers, Roy; Trigger; Evans, Dale; Hayes, George "Gabby"; Powers, Richard; DuBrey, Claire; Corrigan, Lloyd; Littlefield, Lucien; Sons of the Pioneers

Song(s) Amor [1] (C: Ruiz, Gabriel; L: Skylar, Sunny; Mendez, Ricardo Lopez); The Cowpoke Polka; I'm a Happy Guy in My Levi Britches; Ride 'Em Cowboy (King of the Range) [3] (C/L: Spencer, Tim; Rogers, Roy); Lights of Old Santa Fe [2] (C/L: Elliott, Jack);

Trigger Hasn't Got a Purty Figger; The Nerve of Some People (C/L: Elliott, Jack); The Cowboy Jubilee (C/L: Carson, Ken)

Notes [1] English lyrics by Sunny Skylar. [2] Also in RAINBOW OVER TEXAS. [3] Also in KING OF THE COWBOYS but without Rogers credit.

3355 ✦ THE LIGHT THAT FAILED
Paramount, 1939

Composer(s) Sanders, Troy
Lyricist(s) Kipling, Rudyard

Producer(s) Wellman, William A.
Director(s) Wellman, William A.
Screenwriter(s) Carson, Robert
Source(s) "The Light That Failed" (story) Kipling, Rudyard

Cast Colman, Ronald; Lupino, Ida; Huston, Walter; Angelus, Muriel; Digges, Dudley

Song(s) When We Go Go Go; He Must Be a Man of Decent Height

3356 ✦ THE LIGHT TOUCH
Metro–Goldwyn–Mayer, 1951

Musical Score Rozsa, Miklos

Producer(s) Berman, Pandro S.
Director(s) Brooks, Richard
Screenwriter(s) Brooks, Richard

Cast Angeli, Pier; Granger, Stewart; Sanders, George; Kasznar, Kurt; Calleia, Joseph; Keating, Larry; Williams, Rhys; Lloyd, Norman; Mazurki, Mike

Song(s) Viso Perduto (C: Rozsa, Miklos; L: Gray, Hugh)

3357 ✦ LI'L ABNER (1940)
RKO, 1940

Musical Score Moraweck, Lucien

Producer(s) Schlom, Herman
Director(s) Rogell, Albert S.
Screenwriter(s) Kerr, Charles; Johnson, Tyler
Source(s) *Li'l Abner* (comic strip) Capp, Al

Cast Owen, Granville; O'Driscoll, Martha; Ray, Mona; Morris, Johnnie; Keaton, Buster; Seward, Billie; Sutton, Kay; Eburne, Maude; Kennedy, Edgar; Post, Charles A.; Jamison, Bud; Elliott, Dick; Daniels, Mickey; Weaver, Doodles

Song(s) Li'l Abner (C/L: Oakland, Ben; Drake, Milton; Berle, Milton)

Notes Released as TROUBLE CHASER internationally.

3358 ✦ LI'L ABNER (1959)
Paramount, 1959

Musical Score Riddle, Nelson; Lilley, Joseph J.
Composer(s) de Paul, Gene
Lyricist(s) Mercer, Johnny
Choreographer(s) Wood, Dee Dee [5]

Producer(s) Panama, Norman
Director(s) Frank, Melvin
Screenwriter(s) Panama, Norman; Frank, Melvin
Source(s) *Li'l Abner* (musical) de Paul, Gene; Mercer, Johnny; Frank, Melvin; Panama, Norman

Cast Palmer, Peter [1]; Parrish, Leslie; Kaye, Stubby [1]; St. John, Howard [1]; Newmar, Julie [1]; Stevens, Stella; Hayes, Billie [1]; Marks, Joe E. [1]; Hoffman, Bern; Alvarez, Carmen [1]; Simmonds, Stanley

Song(s) Put 'Em Back; The Matrimonial Stomp; Jubilation T. Cornpone; I'm Past My Prime; The Country's in the Very Best of Hands; There's Room Enough for Us; It's a Typical Day; If I Had My Druthers; I Wish It Could Be Otherwise [6]; Unnecessary Town [2] [3]; Namely You; Oh! Happy Day [2]; In Society (inst.); Rag Off'n the Bush; What's Good for General Bullmoose [4]

Notes Jerry Lewis has a brief cameo appearance. This film was a faithful adaptation of the Broadway original with many of the original cast members including many chorus members. All songs but [6] written for Broadway musical. [1] From original Broadway production. [2] Used instrumentally only. [3] Recorded vocally. [4] Very, very brief. [5] Based on Michael Kidd's original staging. [6] Written for film version.

3359 ✦ LILAC TIME
Warner Brothers–First National, 1928

Musical Score Shilkret, Nathaniel

Producer(s) McCormick, John
Director(s) Fitzmaurice, George
Screenwriter(s) Wilson, Carey; Marion Jr., George
Source(s) *Lilac Time* (play) Cowl, Jane; Murfin, Jane

Cast Moore, Colleen; Cooper, Gary; McIntosh, Burt; Cooper, George; Moore, Cleve; McGuire, Kathryn; Besserer, Eugenie

Song(s) Jeanine, I Dream of You in Lilac Time (C: Shilkret, Nathaniel; L: Gilbert, L. Wolfe)

Notes No cue sheet available.

3360 ✦ LILI
Metro–Goldwyn–Mayer, 1952

Musical Score Kaper, Bronislau
Choreographer(s) Walters, Charles

Producer(s) Knopf, Edwin H.
Director(s) Walters, Charles

Screenwriter(s) Deutsch, Helen
Source(s) (story) Gallico, Paul

Cast Caron, Leslie; Ferrer, Mel; Aumont, Jean-Pierre; Gabor, Zsa Zsa; Kasznar, Kurt

Song(s) Don Act (C/L: Kaper, Bronislau); Hi-Lili, Hi-Lo (C: Kaper, Bronislau; L: Deutsch, Helen)

3361 ✦ LILIES OF THE FIELD
Warner Brothers–First National, 1930

Composer(s) Cleary, Michael
Choreographer(s) Mack, Roy

Director(s) Korda, Alexander
Screenwriter(s) Goodrich, John
Source(s) *Lilies of the Field* (play) Hurlbut, William

Cast Griffith, Corinne; Forbes, Ralph; Boley, May; Loder, John; Wood, Freeman; Paige, Patsy; Southern, Eve

Song(s) I'd Like to Be a Gypsy (L: Washington, Ned); Speed (L: Magidson, Herb; Washington, Ned)

Notes No cue sheet available.

3362 ✦ LILIOM
Fox, 1930

Musical Score Fall, Richard
Composer(s) Fall, Richard
Lyricist(s) Gardner, Marcella S.

Director(s) Borzage, Frank
Screenwriter(s) Behrman, S.N.
Source(s) *Liliom* (play) Molnar, Ferenc

Cast Farrell, Charles; Hobart, Rose; Taylor, Estelle; Tracy, Lee; Williams, Guinn "Big Boy"; Roach, Bert; Warner, H.B.; O'Day, Dawn

Song(s) Dream of Romance; Thief Song

3363 ✦ LILLIAN ROTH IN STORY CONFERENCE

See STORY CONFERENCE.

3364 ✦ LILLIAN RUSSELL
Twentieth Century–Fox, 1940

Musical Score Newman, Alfred

Producer(s) Zanuck, Darryl F.
Director(s) Cummings, Irving
Screenwriter(s) McGuire, William Anthony

Cast Faye, Alice; Ameche, Don; Fonda, Henry; Arnold, Edward; William, Warren; Carrillo, Leo; Westley, Helen; Peterson, Dorothy; Truex, Ernest; Bari, Lynn; Bruce, Nigel; Allister, Claud; Weber, Joe; Fields, Lew;

O'Connor, Una; Foy Jr., Eddie; Cawthorn, Joseph; Davidson, William B.

Song(s) Adored One (C: Newman, Alfred; L: Gordon, Mack); Blue Lovebird (C: Kaper, Bronislau; L: Kahn, Gus); Waltz Is King (C: Henderson, Charles; L: Gordon, Mack); Artist's Life (C: Strauss, Johann; L: Henderson, Charles); Back in the Days of Old Broadway (C: Newman, Alfred; L: Henderson, Charles); Check Song (C/L: Henderson, Charles)

Notes There are also vocal renditions of "Under the Bamboo Tree" by Bob Cole and J. Rosamond Johnson; "Comin' Thro the Rye" and "Brighten the Corner Where You Are" by Charles H. Gabriel and Ina Duley Ogdon; "The Band Played On" by Charles B. Ward and John E. Palmer; "Come Down Ma Evenin' Star" by Robert B. Smith and John Stromberg; "My Blushin' Rosie" by John Stromberg and Edgar Smith; "After the Ball" by Charles K. Harris and "He Goes to Church on Sunday" by E. Ray Goetz and Vincent Bryan. "The Last Rose of Summer" by Thomas Moore, and Richard Alfred Milliken was recorded but not used.

3365 ✦ LILY IN LOVE
New Line, 1985

Musical Score Fenyes, Szablcs; Fisch, Irwin

Producer(s) Halmi, Robert
Director(s) Makk, Karoly
Screenwriter(s) Cucci, Frank

Cast Plummer, Christopher; Smith, Maggie; Sommer, Elke; Green, Adolph; Sando, Szabo; Goldsmith, Merwin

Song(s) This Will Never Change (C: Fenyes, Szablcs; L: Labous, Martee)

Notes No cue sheet available.

3366 ✦ LIMEHOUSE BLUES
Paramount, 1934

Producer(s) Hornblow Jr., Arthur
Director(s) Hall, Alexander
Screenwriter(s) Phillips, Arthur; Hume, Cyril; Jones, Grover

Cast Raft, George; Parker, Jean; Wong, Anna May; Taylor, Kent; Bevan, Billy

Song(s) Limehouse Blues [1] (C: Braham, Philip; L: Furber, Douglas); Limehouse Nights (C/L: Coslow, Sam); Limerick Song [2] (C: Traditional; L: Gordon, Mack; Riskin, Harry); Tea Cup (inst.) (C: Rainger, Ralph)

Notes [1] Not written for the film. Originally in ANDRE CHARLOT REVUE OF 1924. [2] Not used.

3367 ✦ LIMELIGHT
United Artists, 1952

Musical Score Chaplin, Charles; Rasch, Raymond; Russell, Larry

Producer(s) Chaplin, Charles
Director(s) Chaplin, Charles
Screenwriter(s) Chaplin, Charles

Cast Chaplin, Charles; Keaton, Buster; Bruce, Nigel; Bloom, Claire; Lloyd, Norman; Bennett, Marjorie; Dryden, Wheeler; Pollard, Snub; Kent, Stapleton; Mudie, Leonard

Song(s) Eternally [1] (C/L: Chaplin, Charles; Phillips, Jeffrey; Parsons, James John)

Notes No cue sheet available. This film wasn't shown in Los Angeles until 20 years later which made it eligible for the Oscars. It won for Best Original Dramatic Score. [1] Sheet music credits Chaplin and Geoffrey Parsons.

3368 ✦ LINDA
Willis Kent Productions, 1929

Producer(s) Kent, Willis
Director(s) Reid, Mrs. Wallace
Screenwriter(s) Noy, Wilfred; Todd, Ruth
Source(s) "Linda" (story) Montague, Margaret Prescott

Cast Baxter, Warner; Foster, Helen; Beery, Noah; Lewis, Mitchell; Flowers, Bess

Song(s) Linda (C: Sherman, Al; L: Tobias, Harry; Tobias, Charles)

Notes No cue sheet available.

3369 ✦ LINDA BE GOOD
PRC, 1947

Musical Score Mason, Jack
Choreographer(s) Ceballos, Larry

Producer(s) Kemp, Matty
Director(s) MacDonald, Frank
Screenwriter(s) Vale, Leslie; Halasz, George

Cast Sir Lancelot; Knox, Elyse; Wilson, Marie; Hubbard, John; Richards, Gordon

Song(s) Linda Be Good (C/L: Herbert, Charles; Mason, Jack); Old Woman with the Rolling Pin (C/L: Sir Lancelot); Young Girls of Today (C/L: Sir Lancelot); My Mother Says I Mustn't (C/L: Mason, Jack; Miller, Sy)

Notes No cue sheet available.

3370 ✦ THE LION AND THE HORSE
Warner Brothers, 1952

Musical Score Steiner, Max

Producer(s) Foy, Bryan
Director(s) King, Louis
Screenwriter(s) Wilbur, Crane

Cast Cochran, Steve; Wildfire the Wonder Horse; Teal, Ray; Steele, Bob; Antrim, Harry; O'Hanlon, George; Jackson, Sherry

Song(s) The Rustler from Kanab (C/L: O'Hanlon, George)

3371 ✦ THE LIQUIDATOR
Metro–Goldwyn–Mayer, 1966

Musical Score Schifrin, Lalo

Producer(s) Penington, Jon
Director(s) Cardiff, Jack
Screenwriter(s) Yeldham, Peter

Cast Taylor, Rod; Howard, Trevor; St. John, Jill; Tomlinson, David; Tamiroff, Akim; Sykes, Eric; Licudi, Gabriella; Le Mesurier, John; Nimmo, Derek

Song(s) The Liquidator (C: Schifrin, Lalo; L: Callander, Peter)

3372 ✦ LIQUID SKY
Cinevista, 1983

Musical Score Tsukerman, Slava; Hutchinson, Brenda I.; Smith, Clive

Producer(s) Tsukerman, Slava
Director(s) Tsukerman, Slava
Screenwriter(s) Tsukerman, Slava; Carlisle, Anne; Kerova, Nina V.

Cast Carlisle, Anne; Sheppard, Paula E.; Doukas, Susan; Von Wernherr, Otto; Brady, Bob

Song(s) Me and My Rhythm Box (C: Gerasimon, Anatole; Zvereva, Helena; L: Tsukerman, Slava)

Notes No cue sheet available.

3373 ✦ LISBON
Republic, 1956

Producer(s) Milland, Ray
Director(s) Milland, Ray
Screenwriter(s) Battle, John Tucker

Cast Milland, Ray; O'Hara, Maureen; Rains, Claude; Furneaux, Yvonne; Lederer, Francis; Novello, Jay

Song(s) Lisboa Antigua [1] (C: Portela, Raul; L: Dupree, Harry)

Notes [1] Portuguese words by J. Calhardo. A. Dovale also credited on sheet music.

3374 ✦ LISBON STORY
Republic, 1946

Musical Score May, Hans
Composer(s) Parr-Davies, Harry
Lyricist(s) Purcell, Harold

Producer(s) Jackson, Louis H.
Director(s) Stein, Paul
Screenwriter(s) Whittingham, Jack

Source(s) *Lisbon Story* (play) Purcell, Harold; Parr-Davies, Harry

Cast Burke, Patricia; Farrar, David; Rilla, Walter; Tauber, Richard; O'Madden, Lawrence; Grappelli, Stephane; Percy, Esme

Song(s) We Must Never Say Goodbye; Song of the Sunrise; Song of the Drum; Someday We Shall Meet Again; Paris in My Heart; Le Roi D'ys (C: Lalo; L: Traditional); Pedro the Fisherman; Happy Days

Notes A British National picture.

3375 ✦ LISTEN, DARLING
Metro–Goldwyn–Mayer, 1938

Musical Score Axt, William [1]

Producer(s) Cummings, Jack
Director(s) Marin, Edwin L.
Screenwriter(s) Ryan, Elaine; Chapin, Anne Morrison

Cast Garland, Judy; Bartholomew, Freddie; Astor, Mary; Pidgeon, Walter; Hale, Alan; Beckett, Scotty

Song(s) Zing! Went the Strings of My Heart (C/L: Hanley, James F.); On the Bumpy Road to Love (C/L: Lewis, Al; Hoffman, Al; Mencher, Murray); Ten Pins in the Sky (C/L: Ager, Milton; McCarthy, Joseph)

Notes [1] Billed as Dr. William Axt.

3376 ✦ THE LITTERBUG
Disney, 1961

Musical Score Baker, Buddy

Director(s) Luske, Hamilton
Screenwriter(s) Berg, Bill; Nolley, Lance

Song(s) Litterbug, Shame on You (C/L: Leven, Mel); County Fair [1] (C: Baker, Buddy; L: Jackman, Bob)

Notes Short subject. [1] Used instrumentally only.

3377 ✦ LITTLE ADVENTURESS
Columbia, 1938

Director(s) Lederman, D. Ross
Screenwriter(s) Simmons, Michael L.

Cast Fellows, Edith; Fiske, Richard; Wells, Jacqueline; Edwards, Cliff; Howell, Virginia; Bradley, Harry C.

Notes No cue sheet available. Cliff Edwards sings one song.

3378 ✦ LITTLE AMERICA
Paramount, 1935

Song(s) Mush You Haulers [1] (C: Whiting, Richard A.; L: Coslow, Sam)

Notes This is a documentary on Richard E. Byrd's second expedition into the Antarctic. The cameramen were John L. Hermann and Carl O. Peterson. Also used is the tune "Home Again" by M.S. Pike. There is also a vocal of "Sweet Sue" by Victor Young and W.I. Harris. [1] Based on song "Bear Down Pelham" by Whiting and George Marion, Jr., which is used instrumentally.

3379 ✦ LITTLE AUDREY CARTOONS
Paramount, 1948

Song(s)   Little Audrey Says (C: Sharples, Winston; L: Kaye, Buddy)

Notes   Animated shorts.

3380 ✦ LITTLE BEAU PEPE
Warner Brothers, 1952

Musical Score   Stalling, Carl

Director(s)   Jones, Chuck
Screenwriter(s)   Maltese, Michael

Cast   Le Pew, Pepe

Song(s)   Le Regimente (C/L: Maltese, Michael)

Notes   Animated cartoon.

3381 ✦ LITTLE BIG SHOT
Warner Brothers, 1935

Musical Score   Roemheld, Heinz
Composer(s)   Wrubel, Allie
Lyricist(s)   Dixon, Mort

Producer(s)   Bischoff, Sam
Director(s)   Curtiz, Michael; McDonald, Frank
Screenwriter(s)   Wald, Jerry; Epstein, Julius J.; Andrews, Robert

Cast   Jason, Sybil; Farrell, Glenda; Armstrong, Robert; Horton, Edward Everett; LaRue, Jack; Vinton, Arthur; Naish, J. Carrol; Kennedy, Edgar; Richards, Addison

Song(s)   I'm Rolling in Money (C/L: Gibbons, Carroll); I'm a Little Big Shot Now; My Kid's a Crooner [1]

Notes   [1] Not in cue sheets. Listed in Hirshhorn.

3382 ✦ A LITTLE BIT OF HEAVEN
Universal, 1940

Musical Score   Skinner, Frank

Producer(s)   Pasternak, Joe
Director(s)   Marton, Andrew
Screenwriter(s)   Taradash, Daniel; Purcell, Gertrude; Goldman, Harold

Cast   Jean, Gloria; Stack, Robert; Herbert, Hugh; Smith, C. Aubrey; Grey, Nan; Pallette, Eugene; Butch and Buddy; Beery, Noah; Arno, Sig; Blue, Monte

Song(s)   High School Cadets [1] (C: Sousa, John Philip; L: Freed, Ralph); What Did We Learn At School (C/L: Ellis, Vivian); (Heaven) After Every Rainstorm

(C: Skinner, Frank; L: Lerner, Sam); The Dawn of Love (C: Previn, Charles; L: Freed, Ralph)

Notes   There are also vocals of "A Little Bit of Heaven" by J. Keirn Brennan and Ernest R. Ball; "Short'nin' Bread" by Clement Wood and Jacques Wolfe. [1] Also in THE UNDER-PUP.

3383 ✦ LITTLE BOY LOST
Paramount, 1953

Musical Score   Young, Victor
Composer(s)   Van Heusen, James
Lyricist(s)   Burke, Johnny

Producer(s)   Perlberg, William
Director(s)   Seaton, George
Screenwriter(s)   Seaton, George
Source(s)   "Little Boy Lost" (story) Laski, Marghanita

Cast   Crosby, Bing; Dauphin, Claude; Fourcade, Christian

Song(s)   Apropos De Rien; If It's All the Same to You (Cela M'est Egal); The Magic Window; My English Into French Dictionary [1]

Notes   There were also vocal performances of the following songs not written for the picture: "Mon Coeur Est un Violon (My Heart Is Like a Violin)" by Miarka Laparcerie; Shelton Brooks' "The Darktown Strutters' Ball" and Stephen Foster's "Oh Susanna." [1] Not used.

3384 ✦ THE LITTLE COLONEL
Fox, 1935

Producer(s)   DeSylva, B.G.
Director(s)   Butler, David
Screenwriter(s)   Conselman, William
Source(s)   *The Little Colonel* (novel) Johnston, Anne Fellows

Cast   Temple, Shirley; Barrymore, Lionel; Venable, Evelyn; Lodge, John; Blackmer, Sidney; Chase, Alden; Robinson, Bill; McDaniel, Hattie

Song(s)   Sun Shines Brighter (C: De Francesco, Louis E.; L: Kernell, William); I Went to the Market (C/L: Robinson, Bill); Little Colonel [1] (C: Pollack, Lew; L: Webster, Paul Francis); Love's Young Dream [1] (C: Mockridge, Cyril J.; L: Moore, Thomas)

Notes   There are also renditions of many Stephen Foster songs and other older tunes. [1] Sheet music only.

3385 ✦ LITTLE DARLINGS
Paramount, 1980

Composer(s)   Fox, Charles
Lyricist(s)   Sager, Carole Bayer

Producer(s)   Friedman, Stephen
Director(s)   Maxwell, Ronald
Screenwriter(s)   Peck, Kimi; Young, Dalene

Cast Blye, Maggie; O'Neal, Tatum; Assante, Armand; McNichol, Kristy; Dillon, Matt

Song(s) You and Me and Summer [1]; Little Darlin' [1]

Notes [1] Not used.

3386 ✦ THE LITTLE DRUMMER GIRL
Warner Brothers, 1984

Musical Score Grusin, Dave

Producer(s) Crawford, Robert L.
Director(s) Hill, George Roy
Screenwriter(s) Mandel, Loring
Source(s) *The Little Drummer Girl* (novel) LeCarre, John

Cast Keaton, Diane; Voyagis, Yorgo; Kinski, Klaus; Frey, Sami; Cristofer, Michael; Suchet, David; Danker, Eli

Song(s) Always in Love (C/L: Grusin, Dave; Jones, Raymond; LeVay, Sylvester)

Notes Background vocal use only.

3387 ✦ LITTLE FAUSS AND BIG HALSY
Paramount, 1970

Composer(s) Perkins, Carl
Lyricist(s) Perkins, Carl

Producer(s) Ruddy, Albert S.
Director(s) Furie, Sidney J.
Screenwriter(s) Eastman, Charles

Cast Redford, Robert; Pollard, Michael J.; Hutton, Lauren; Beery Jr., Noah; Benson, Lucille

Song(s) Ballad of Little Fauss and Big Halsy; Movin'; Wanted Man [2] (C/L: Dylan, Bob); True Love Is Greater Than Friendship; Rollin' Free (C/L: Cash, Johnny); The Little Man [1] (C/L: Cash, Johnny)

Notes [1] Not used. [2] Not written for picture.

3388 ✦ THE LITTLE FOXES
RKO, 1941

Musical Score Willson, Meredith

Producer(s) Goldwyn, Samuel
Director(s) Wyler, William
Screenwriter(s) Hellman, Lillian; Kober, Arthur; Parker, Dorothy; Campbell, Alan
Source(s) *The Little Foxes* (play) Hellman, Lillian

Cast Marshall, Herbert; Wright, Teresa; Carlson, Richard; Duryea, Dan; Davis, Bette; Collinge, Patricia; Dingle, Charles; Reid, Carl Benton; Hicks, Russell; Brissac, Virginia

Song(s) Never Feel Too Weary to Pray (C/L: Willson, Meredith)

3389 ✦ LITTLE GIANT
Universal, 1946

Musical Score Fairchild, Edgar

Producer(s) Gershenson, Joe
Director(s) Seiter, William A.
Screenwriter(s) De Leon, Walter

Cast Abbott, Bud; Costello, Lou; Dumont, Margaret; Verdugo, Elena; Joyce, Brenda; de Wit, Jacqueline; Cleveland, George; Gordon, Mary

Song(s) Alma Mater Song (C/L: Fairchild, Edgar)

3390 ✦ THE LITTLE HUT
Metro–Goldwyn–Mayer, 1957

Musical Score Farnon, Robert

Producer(s) Robson, Mark; Herbert, F. Hugh
Director(s) Robson, Mark
Screenwriter(s) Herbert, F. Hugh
Source(s) *The Little Hut* (play) Roussin, Andre; Mitford, Nancy [1]

Cast Gardner, Ava; Granger, Stewart; Niven, David; Chiari, Walter; Currie, Finlay; Cadell, Jean

Song(s) The Little Hut (C: Cochrane, Peggy; L: Maschwitz, Eric; Stellman, Marcel)

Notes [1] English Stage adaptation by Mitford.

3391 ✦ LITTLE JOE, THE WRANGLER
Universal, 1942

Producer(s) Drake, Oliver
Director(s) Collins, Lewis D.
Screenwriter(s) Lowe, Sherman; Beecher, Elizabeth

Cast Brown, Johnny Mack; Ritter, Tex

Song(s) Little Joe, the Wrangler [1] (C: Hollander, Frederick; L: Loesser, Frank); I'll Saddle My Pony (C/L: Wakely, Jimmy)

Notes [1] Also in DESTRY RIDES AGAIN (1939), MAN FROM MONTANA and THE OLD TEXAS TRAIL.

3392 ✦ LITTLE JOHNNY JONES
Warner Brothers–First National, 1929

Composer(s) Cohan, George M.
Lyricist(s) Cohan, George M.

Director(s) LeRoy, Mervyn
Screenwriter(s) Heilbron, Adelaide
Source(s) *Little Johnny Jones* (musical) Cohan, George M.

Cast Buzzell, Edward; Day, Alice; Murphy, Edna; Edeson, Robert; Oakman, Wheeler; Turner, Raymond; Reed, Donald

Song(s) Yankee Doodle Boy [1]; Give My Regards to Broadway [1]; Straight, Place and Show (C: Jerome,

M.K.; L: Ruby, Herman); Go Find Somebody to Love (C: Cleary, Michael; L: Magidson, Herb); My Paradise [3] (C: Cavanaugh, James; L: Magidson, Herb); Painting the Clouds with Sunshine [1] (C: Burke, Joe; L: Dubin, Al); She Was Kicked in the Head By a Butterfly (C: Cleary, Michael; L: Washington, Ned; Magidson, Herb); (I'd Better Not Try It) I Might Like It [2] (C: Cleary, Michael; L: Magidson, Herb; Washington, Ned)

Notes   No cue sheet available. [1] Also in THE GOLD DIGGERS OF BROADWAY and PAINTING THE CLOUDS WITH SUNSHINE. [2] Not used. Used later in PARAMOUNT ON PARADE. [3] Ned Washington and Michael Cleary are also credited on sheet music.

3393 ◆ THE LITTLE LAND
Disney, 1956 unproduced

Song(s)   The Little Land (C: Bruns, George; L: Speirs, Jack; Peet, Bill)

Notes   Unproduced short.

3394 ◆ LITTLE LULU CARTOONS
Paramount

Song(s)   Little Lulu [1] (C/L: Lippman, Sidney; Wise, Fred)

Notes   Animated shorts. [1] Buddy Kaye is also credited on sheet music.

3395 ◆ THE LITTLE MERMAID
Disney, 1989

Musical Score   Menken, Alan
Composer(s)   Menken, Alan
Lyricist(s)   Ashman, Howard

Producer(s)   Ashman, Howard; Musker, John
Director(s)   Musker, John; Clements, Ron
Screenwriter(s)   Musker, John; Clements, Ron
Source(s)   "The Little Mermaid" (story) Andersen, Hans Christian
Voices   Auberjonois, Rene; Barnes, Christopher Daniel; Benson, Jodi; Carroll, Pat; Edwards, Paddi; Hackett, Buddy; Marin, Jason; Mars, Kenneth; McClurg, Edie; Wright, Ben; Ryan, Will; Wright, Samuel E.

Directing Animator(s)   Henn, Mark; Keane, Glen; Marjoribanks, Duncan; Aquino, Ruben; Deja, Andreas; O'Callaghan, Matthew

Song(s)   Under the Sea; Kiss the Girl; Part of Your World; Poor Souls; Les Poissons; Fathoms Below; Daughters of Triton

3396 ◆ LITTLE MISS BROADWAY (1938)
Twentieth Century–Fox, 1938

Composer(s)   Spina, Harold
Lyricist(s)   Bullock, Walter

Choreographer(s)   Sawyer, Geneva; Castle, Nick; Brier, Audrene

Producer(s)   Zanuck, Darryl F.
Director(s)   Cummings, Irving
Screenwriter(s)   Tugend, Harry; Yellen, Jack

Cast   Temple, Shirley; Murphy, George; Durante, Jimmy; Brooks, Phyllis; Oliver, Edna May; Barbier, George; Ellis, Edward; Darwell, Jane; Brendel, El; Meek, Donald; Gillingwater, Claude

Song(s)   Be Optimistic; How Can I Thank You; If All the World Were Paper; We Should Be Together; Swing Me an Old Fashioned Song [1]; Little Miss Broadway; I'll Build a Broadway for You

Notes   [1] This was arranged by Jule Styne, David Buttolph and Walter Scharf.

3397 ◆ LITTLE MISS BROADWAY (1947)
Columbia, 1947

Producer(s)   Katzman, Sam
Director(s)   Dreifuss, Arthur
Screenwriter(s)   Dreifuss, Arthur; McLeod, Victor; Wright, Betty

Cast   Porter, Jean; Nichols, Dick; Donnelly, Ruth; Gargan, Edward; Jordan, Charles; Barnett, Vince

Song(s)   That's Good Enough for Me [2] (C/L: Roberts, Allan; Fisher, Doris); A Man Is Brother to a Mule [1] (C/L: Roberts, Allan; Fisher, Doris); Judy and Dick (C: Karger, Fred; L: McLeod, Victor; Wright, Betty); Cheer for the Team (C/L: Samuels, Walter G.; Newman, Charles; Moore, McElbert)

Notes   No cue sheet available. [1] Also in SINGING SPURS and THRILL OF BRAZIL. [2] Also in MARY LOU.

3398 ◆ LITTLE MISS MARKER
Paramount, 1934

Composer(s)   Rainger, Ralph
Lyricist(s)   Robin, Leo

Producer(s)   Schulberg, B.P.
Director(s)   Hall, Alexander
Screenwriter(s)   Lipman, William R.; Hellman, Sam; Lehman, Gladys
Source(s)   "Little Miss Marker" (story) Runyon, Damon

Cast   Dell, Dorothy; Temple, Shirley; Menjou, Adolphe; Bickford, Charles; Overman, Lynne

Song(s)   I'm a Black Sheep Who's Blue; Low Down Lullaby; Laugh You Son of a Gun

Notes   The title was once HALF WAY DECENT. It was released in Great Britain as GIRL IN PAWN. Brief vocal renditions of "Sidewalks of New York" by Charles B. Lawlor and James W. Blake; "The Bowery" by Percy

Gaunt and Charles H. Hoyt and "Sweet Rosie O'Grady" by Maud Nugent are also used.

3399 ✦ LITTLE MISS NOBODY
Twentieth Century–Fox, 1936

Producer(s) Wurtzel, Sol M.
Director(s) Blystone, John
Screenwriter(s) Breslow, Lou; Burger, Paul; Eliscu, Edward
Source(s) (story) Brennan, Frederick Hazlitt

Cast Withers, Jane; Darwell, Jane; Morgan, Ralph; Haden, Sara; Casey, Harry; Hainey, Betty Jean; Jackson, Thomas; Prouty, Jed

Song(s) Then Came the Indians (C/L: Tobias, Henry; Stern, Jack; Tobias, Harry)

3400 ✦ LITTLE MISS ROUGHNECK
Columbia, 1938

Composer(s) Oakland, Ben
Lyricist(s) Drake, Milton; Jessel, George

Director(s) Scotto, Aubrey
Screenwriter(s) Niblo Jr., Fred; Neville, Grace; Simmons, Michael L.

Cast Fellows, Edith; Carrillo, Leo; Colton, Scott; Wells, Jacqueline; Irving, Margaret; Palange, Inez; Hall, Thurston

Song(s) As Long As I Love; Pickaninny Paradise [1]; When I Truck on Down [1]

Notes [1] Not used.

3401 ✦ LITTLE MR. JIM
Metro–Goldwyn–Mayer, 1946

Musical Score Bassman, George

Producer(s) Dull, Orville O.
Director(s) Zinnemann, Fred
Screenwriter(s) Bruce, George
Source(s) *Army Brat* (novel) Madelton, Tommy

Cast Jenkins, Jackie "Butch"; Craig, James; Gifford, Frances; Patten, Luana; Byington, Spring; Lee, Chingwah; La Plante, Laura; O'Neill, Henry; Ankrum, Morris

Song(s) Little Jim [1] (C: Fain, Sammy; L: Freed, Ralph)

Notes [1] Used instrumentally only.

3402 ✦ LITTLE NELLIE KELLY
Metro–Goldwyn–Mayer, 1940

Musical Score Edens, Roger
Composer(s) Edens, Roger
Lyricist(s) Edens, Roger
Choreographer(s) Larkin, Eddie

Producer(s) Freed, Arthur
Director(s) Taurog, Norman
Screenwriter(s) McGowan, Jack
Source(s) *Little Nellie Kelly* (musical) Cohan, George M.

Cast Garland, Judy; Murphy, George; Winninger, Charles; McPhail, Douglas

Song(s) Nellie Is a Darlin'; A Pretty Girl Milking Her Cow [1] (C/L: Traditional); It's a Great Day for the Irish; Intro to Singing in the Rain; Singin' in the Rain [3] (C: Brown, Nacio Herb; L: Freed, Arthur); Nellie Kelly I Love You (C/L: Cohan, George M.); Nellie Kelly Waltz; You Remind Me of My Mother [2]

Notes [1] Arranged and adapted by Roger Edens. [2] Deleted from final print. [3] Also in SINGIN' IN THE RAIN, HOLLYWOOD REVUE and A CLOCKWORK ORANGE.

3403 ✦ A LITTLE NIGHT MUSIC
New World, 1977

Composer(s) Sondheim, Stephen
Lyricist(s) Sondheim, Stephen
Choreographer(s) Birch, Patricia

Producer(s) Kastner, Elliott
Director(s) Prince, Harold
Screenwriter(s) Wheeler, Hugh
Source(s) *A Little Night Music* (musical) Sondheim, Stephen; Wheeler, Hugh

Cast Taylor, Elizabeth [1]; Rigg, Diana; Cariou, Len; Down, Lesley-Anne; Gingold, Hermione; Guittard, Laurence; Guard, Christopher; Tunick, Jonathan; Dunlop, Lesley; Franks, Chloe

Song(s) Night Waltz (Love Takes Time) [2]; The Glamourous Life [3]; Now/Soon/Later; You Must Meet My Wife; Every Day a Little Death; A Weekend in the Country; It Would Have Been Wonderful; Send in the Clowns

Notes No cue sheet available. All songs but [2] and [3] from Broadway original. [1] Dubbed. [2] Lyrics written for film. [3] Written for film.

3404 ✦ LITTLE NIKITA
Columbia, 1988

Musical Score Hamlisch, Marvin

Producer(s) Gittes, Harry
Director(s) Benjamin, Richard
Screenwriter(s) Hill, John; Goldman, Bo

Cast Poitier, Sidney; Phoenix, River; Jenkins, Richard; Kava, Caroline; Bradford, Richard; Lynch, Richard; Devine, Loretta; Deakins, Lucy

Song(s) Paradise [1] (C/L: Mitchell, Charles; Adams, Kaylee); Till the Next Time (C/L: Mitchell, Charles)

Notes [1] Also in WHITE WATER SUMMER.

3405 ✦ LITTLE OLD BOSKO AND THE PIRATES
Metro–Goldwyn–Mayer, 1937

Musical Score Bradley, Scott
Composer(s) Bradley, Scott
Lyricist(s) Bradley, Scott

Song(s) Cookie Song; Pirates Shouting

Notes Animated cartoon.

3406 ✦ LITTLE OLD NEW YORK
Twentieth Century–Fox, 1940

Musical Score Newman, Alfred

Producer(s) Zanuck, Darryl F.
Director(s) King, Henry
Screenwriter(s) Tugend, Harry

Cast Faye, Alice; MacMurray, Fred; Greene, Richard; Joyce, Brenda; Devine, Andy; Stephenson, Henry; Carter, Ben; Bond, Ward; Feld, Fritz; Brissac, Virginia

Song(s) Who Is the Beau of the Belle of New York (C/L: Gordon, Mack)

3407 ✦ THE LITTLE PRINCE
Paramount, 1974

Composer(s) Loewe, Frederick
Lyricist(s) Lerner, Alan Jay
Choreographer(s) Fosse, Bob

Producer(s) Donen, Stanley
Director(s) Donen, Stanley
Screenwriter(s) Lerner, Alan Jay
Source(s) "The Little Prince" (story) de Saint-Exupery, Antoine

Cast Kiley, Richard; Warner, Steven; Fosse, Bob; Wilder, Gene; Ackland, Joss; Revill, Clive; Spinetti, Victor; Crowden, Graham; McKechnie, Donna

Song(s) I Need Air; I'm on Your Side; Be Happy; You're a Child; I Never Met a Rose; Why Is the Desert?; Snake in the Grass; Closer and Closer and Closer; Little Prince; Matter of Consequence [1]

Notes [1] Not used.

3408 ✦ THE LITTLE PRINCESS
Twentieth Century–Fox, 1939

Choreographer(s) Belcher, Ernest; Castle, Nick; Sawyer, Geneva

Producer(s) Zanuck, Darryl F.
Director(s) Lang, Walter
Screenwriter(s) Hill, Ethel; Ferris, Walter
Source(s) *The Little Princess* (novel) Burnett, Frances Hodgson

Cast Temple, Shirley; Greene, Richard; Louise, Anita; Hunter, Ian; Romero, Cesar; Treacher, Arthur; Nash, Mary; Jason, Sybil; Mander, Miles; Mercer, Beryl; Clive, E.E.

Song(s) Dream Sequence (C: Pokrass, Sam; L: Bullock, Walter)

Notes There are also vocals of "Wot Cher (Knock'd 'Em in the Old Kent Road)" and "Auld Lang Syne."

3409 ✦ A LITTLE SEX
Universal, 1982

Musical Score Delerue, Georges

Producer(s) De Laurentiis, Robert; Paltrow, Bruce
Director(s) Paltrow, Bruce
Screenwriter(s) De Laurentiis, Robert

Cast Matheson, Tim; Capshaw, Kate; Herrmann, Edward; Glover, John; Copeland, Joan; Dalton, Susanna; Malick, Wendie; Shawn, Wallace

Song(s) Your Place or Mine (C/L: Manchester, Melissa; Willis, Allee; Bryant, David)

3410 ✦ THE LITTLE SHEPHERD OF KINGDOM COME
Twentieth Century–Fox, 1961

Musical Score Vars, Henry
Composer(s) Vars, Henry
Lyricist(s) Dunham, "By"

Producer(s) Dexter, Maury
Director(s) McLaglen, Andrew V.
Screenwriter(s) Lyndon, Barre
Source(s) *The Little Shepherd of Kingdom Come* (novel) Fox Jr., John

Cast Rodgers, Jimmie; Patten, Luana; Wills, Chill; Hutchings, Linda; Kennedy, George; Hamilton, Neil; Dix, Robert

Song(s) The Little Shepherd of Kingdom Come; When Love Is Young

3411 ✦ LITTLE SHOP OF HORRORS
Warner Brothers, 1986

Composer(s) Menken, Alan
Lyricist(s) Ashman, Howard

Producer(s) Geffen, David
Director(s) Oz, Frank
Screenwriter(s) Ashman, Howard
Source(s) *Little Shop of Horrors* (musical) Ashman, Howard; Menken, Alan

Cast Moranis, Rick; Greene, Ellen; Gardenia, Vincent; Martin, Steve; Arnold, Tichina; Campbell, Tisha; Weeks, Michelle; Belushi, James; Candy, John; Guest, Christopher; Murray, Bill; Stubbs, Levi

Song(s) Little Shop of Horrors; Downtown/Skidrow; Da-Doo [1]; Grow for Me; Somewhere That's Green; Some Fun Now [1]; Dentist; Git It/Feed Me; Suddenly

Seymour; Suppertime; The Meek Shall Inherit; Mean Green Mother [1]; Fee-Nix [1]

Notes [1] Written for film.

3412 ✦ THE LITTLEST DIPLOMAT
Warner Brothers, 1937

Musical Score Jackson, Howard

Song(s) The Colonel of the Regiment (C: Jerome, M.K.; L: Scholl, Jack)

Notes No other information available.

3413 ✦ THE LITTLEST HORSE THIEVES
Disney, 1976

Musical Score Goodwin, Ron

Producer(s) Miller, Ron
Director(s) Jarrott, Charles
Screenwriter(s) Sisson, Rosemary Anne

Cast Sim, Alastair; Barkworth, Peter; Colbourne, Maurice; Tebbs, Susan; Harrison, Andrew; Franks, Chloe; Bolgar, Benjie; Scales, Prunella; McEwan, Geraldine

Song(s) Flash's Theme (C/L: Goodwin, Ron)

3414 ✦ THE LITTLEST OUTLAW
Disney, 1954

Musical Score Lava, William
Composer(s) Lava, William
Lyricist(s) Chandler, Jeff

Producer(s) Lansburgh, Larry
Director(s) Gavaldon, Roberto
Screenwriter(s) Walsh, Bill

Cast Armendariz, Pedro; Calleia, Joseph; Acosta, Rodolfo; Velasquez, Andres

Song(s) The Littlest Outlaw [1] (A Boy); El Padre [1]; The Moon Won't Let You Tell a Lie [1]; La Fiesta [1] (L: Jackman, Bob); Doroteo (C/L: Santos, Edmundo); This Lovely Night [1]; Celita [1] (L: Jackman, Bob)

Notes [1] Used instrumentally only.

3415 ✦ LITTLE TOOT
Disney, 1948

Musical Score Daniel, Eliot; Darby, Ken

Song(s) Little Toot (C/L: Wrubel, Allie)

Notes No cue sheet available. This cartoon is a part of MELODY TIME.

3416 ✦ LITTLE WOMEN
Metro–Goldwyn–Mayer, 1948

Musical Score Deutsch, Adolph

Producer(s) LeRoy, Mervyn
Director(s) LeRoy, Mervyn

Screenwriter(s) Solt, Andrew; Mason, Sarah Y.; Heerman, Victor
Source(s) *Little Women* (novel) Alcott, Louisa May

Cast Allyson, June; Lawford, Peter; O'Brien, Margaret; Taylor, Elizabeth; Leigh, Janet; Brazzi, Rossano; Astor, Mary; Watson, Lucile; Smith, Sir C. Aubrey; Ames, Leon; Patterson, Elizabeth; Davenport, Harry; Gilchrist, Connie

Song(s) At Christmas Time (C/L: Colombo, Alberto)

3417 ✦ LIVE A LITTLE, LOVE A LITTLE
Metro–Goldwyn–Mayer, 1968

Musical Score Strange, Billy
Choreographer(s) Regas, Jack; Baker, Jack [1]

Producer(s) Lawrence, Douglas
Director(s) Taurog, Norman
Screenwriter(s) Hoey, Michael A.; Greenburg, Dan

Cast Presley, Elvis; Carey, Michele; Vallee, Rudy; Porter, Don; Sargent, Dick; Holloway, Sterling; Yarnall, Celeste

Song(s) Wonderful World (C/L: Fletcher, Guy; Flett, Douglas); The Edge of Reality (C/L: Giant, Bill; Baum, Bernie; Kaye, Florence); A Little Less Conversation (C: Strange, Billy; L: Davis, Scott); Almost in Love (C/L: Starr, Randy; Bonfa, Luiz)

Notes [1] Regas choreographed the "Dream Sequence" and Baker choreographed "A Little Less Conversation."

3418 ✦ LIVE AND LET DIE
United Artists, 1973

Musical Score Martin, George

Producer(s) Broccoli, Albert R.; Saltzman, Harry
Director(s) Hamilton, Guy
Screenwriter(s) Mankiewicz, Tom
Source(s) *Live and Let Die* (novel) Fleming, Ian

Cast Moore, Roger; Kotto, Yaphet; Seymour, Jane; James, Clifton; Harris, Julius W.; Lee, Bernard; Maxwell, Lois

Song(s) Live and Let Die (C/L: McCartney, Paul; McCartney, Linda)

3419 ✦ LIVE FOR LIFE
United Artists, 1967

Musical Score Lai, Francis

Producer(s) Mnouchkine, Alexandre; Danciger, Georges
Director(s) Lelouch, Claude
Screenwriter(s) Lelouch, Claude; Uytterhoeven, Pierre

Cast Montand, Yves; Bergen, Candice; Girardot, Annie; Tunc, Irene; Ferjac, Anouck

Song(s) All at Once It's Love (Aujord 'Hui C'est Toi) (C: Lai, Francis; L: Barouh, Pierre; Keller, Jerry); Live for Life [1] (C: Lai, Francis; L: Gimbel, Norman)

Notes Original French title VIVRE POUR VIVRE. [1] Lyric writen for exploitation only.

3420 ✦ LIVE IT UP

See SING AND SWING.

3421 ✦ THE LIVELY SET
Universal, 1964

Musical Score Darin, Bobby
Composer(s) Darin, Bobby
Lyricist(s) Darin, Bobby

Producer(s) Alland, William
Director(s) Arnold, Jack
Screenwriter(s) Goldberg, Mel; Wood, William

Cast Darren, James; Tiffin, Pamela; McClure, Doug; Maxwell, Marilyn; Sommers, Joanie; Drake, Charles; Thompson, Mickey; Nelson, James; Carter, Duane; Krause, Billy; Miller, Ron

Song(s) Look at Me (L: Newman, Randy); Boss Baracuda (L: Melcher, Terry); If You Love Him; Casey Wake Up; The Lively Set

Notes A remake of JOHNNY DARK (1954).

3422 ✦ THE LIVING DAYLIGHTS
United Artists, 1987

Musical Score Barry, John
Composer(s) Barry, John
Lyricist(s) Hynde, Chrissie

Producer(s) Broccoli, Albert R.; Wilson, Michael G.
Director(s) Glen, John
Screenwriter(s) Maibaum, Richard; Wilson, Michael G.

Cast Dalton, Timothy; d'Abo, Maryam; Krabbe, Jeroen; Baker, Joe Don; Rhys-Davies, John; Malik, Art; Wisniewski, Andreas; Llewelyn, Desmond; Brown, Robert; Bliss, Caroline

Song(s) The Living Daylights (L: Waaktaar, Pal); Where Has Everybody Gone?; If There Was a Man

3423 ✦ LIVING IN A BIG WAY
Metro–Goldwyn–Mayer, 1947

Musical Score Hayton, Lennie
Choreographer(s) Kelly, Gene; Donen, Stanley

Producer(s) Berman, Pandro S.
Director(s) La Cava, Gregory
Screenwriter(s) La Cava, Gregory; Ravetch, Irving

Cast Kelly, Gene; McDonald, Marie; Winninger, Charles; Thaxter, Phyllis; Byington, Spring; Adair, Jean;

Sundberg, Clinton; Warburton, John; Phillips, Wm. "Bill"; Hayes, Bernadene

Song(s) Fido and Me (C: Alter, Louis; L: Heyman, Edward)

Notes Formerly titled LIFE'S FOR THE LOVING and TO KISS AND TO KEEP. There is also a vocal of "It Had to Be You" by Isham Jones and Gus Kahn.

3424 ✦ LIVING IT UP
Paramount, 1954

Composer(s) Styne, Jule
Lyricist(s) Hilliard, Bob
Choreographer(s) Castle, Nick

Producer(s) Jones, Paul
Director(s) Taurog, Norman
Screenwriter(s) Rose, Jack; Shavelson, Melville
Source(s) *Hazel Flagg* (musical) Hecht, Ben; Styne, Jule; Hilliard, Bob; "Nothing Sacred" (story) Street, James

Cast North, Sheree [2]; Lewis, Jerry; Martin, Dean; Leigh, Janet; Arnold, Edward; Clark, Fred; White, Sammy; Rumann, Sig; Loo, Richard

Song(s) Ev'ry Street's a Boulevard In Old New York [1]; That's What I Like; You Are the Bravest [3]; How Do You Speak to an Angel? [1]; You're Gonna Dance with Me, Baby [1] [4]; Champagne and Wedding Cake; Money Burns a Hole in My Pocket [1]; Sister of Tokio Rose [5]; Hallelujah Train Routine [5] [6]; I'm Glad I'm Leaving [1] [5]; A Hundred Miles from Nowhere [5]; One More River to Cross [5]

Notes The movie was once to be titled ALIVE AND KICKING. Styne was originally planning on filming the stage play from the stage of the Mark Hellinger Theatre. Paramount decided to film the musical in Hollywood. It was not originally bought as a vehicle for Martin and Lewis. [1] From Broadway musical. [2] Dubbed by Gloria Wood. [3] Titled "Who Is the Bravest?" in Broadway production. [4] Titled "You're Gonna Dance with Me, Willie" in Broadway production. [5] Not used. [6] Consisted of the numbers "Everybody Wave Goodbye," "Hallelujah Train" and "Thanks for Bringing Me Lillies."

3425 ✦ LIVING ON VELVET
Warner Brothers–First National, 1935

Producer(s) Chodorov, Edward
Director(s) Borzage, Frank
Screenwriter(s) Wald, Jerry; Epstein, Julius J.

Cast Francis, Kay; William, Warren; O'Neill, Henry; Hicks, Russell; Kennedy, Edgar

Song(s) Living on Velvet [1] (C: Warren, Harry; L: Dubin, Al)

Notes [1] Used instrumentally only.

3426 ✦ LIZZIE
Metro–Goldwyn–Mayer, 1957

Musical Score   Stevens, Leith

Producer(s)   Bresler, Jerry
Director(s)   Haas, Hugo
Screenwriter(s)   Dinelli, Mel
Source(s)   *The Bird's Nest* (novel) Jackson, Shirley

Cast   Parker, Eleanor; Boone, Richard; Blondell, Joan; Haas, Hugo; Roman, Ric; Arnold, Dorothy; Reach, John; Ross, Marion; Mathis, Johnny

Song(s)   Warm and Tender (C: Bacharach, Burt; L: David, Hal); It's Not for Me to Say (C/L: Stillman, Al; Allen, Robert)

3427 ✦ THE LLANO KID
Paramount, 1939

Composer(s)   Sanders, Troy
Lyricist(s)   Loesser, Frank

Producer(s)   Sherman, Harry
Director(s)   Venturini, Edward
Screenwriter(s)   Tuchock, Wanda
Source(s)   "A Double-Dyed Deceiver" (story) Henry, O.

Cast   Guizar, Tito; Clayton, Jan; Sondergaard, Gale

Song(s)   Lullaby (L: Sanders, Troy); El Huapango; Posada (C: Sanders, Troy; Reina, James J.); Starry Eyes [1]

Notes   The film was originally called THE DOUBLE-DYED DECEIVER. [1] Used instrumentally only.

3428 ✦ LLOYDS OF LONDON
Twentieth Century–Fox, 1936

Producer(s)   Zanuck, Darryl F.
Director(s)   King, Henry
Screenwriter(s)   Pascal, Ernest; Ferris, Walter

Cast   Bartholomew, Freddie; Carroll, Madeleine; Standing, Sir Guy; Power, Tyrone; Smith, C. Aubrey; Field, Virginia; Harvey, Forrester; Sanders, George; Love, Montagu; Hare, Lumsden; O'Connor, Una; Mander, Miles; Huntley, Hugh; Bevan, Billy; Clive, E.E.

Song(s)   English Street Cry (C: Mockridge, Cyril J.; L: Owen-Smith, Warwick)

3429 ✦ LOADED PISTOLS
Columbia, 1949

Producer(s)   Schaefer, Armand
Director(s)   English, John
Screenwriter(s)   Cummings, Dwight; Yost, Dorothy

Cast   Autry, Gene; Henry, Gloria; Holt, Jack; Jones, Dick; Buttram, Pat; Davis, Rufe; Waller, Eddy; Mapes, Ted; Champion

Song(s)   When the Bloom Is on the Sage [1] (C/L: Vincent, Nat; Howard, Fred); Loaded Pistols (C/L:

Unknown); A Boy from Texas, A Girl from Tennessee (C/L: Unknown); Pretty Mary (C/L: Unknown)

Notes   No cue sheet available. [1] Also in ROUND-UP TIME IN TEXAS (RKO).

3430 ✦ THE LODGER
Twentieth Century–Fox, 1943

Musical Score   Friedhofer, Hugo
Choreographer(s)   Williams, Kenny

Producer(s)   Bassler, Robert
Director(s)   Brahm, John
Screenwriter(s)   Lyndon, Barre
Source(s)   *The Lodger* (novel) Belloc-Lowndes, Marie

Cast   Oberon, Merle; Sanders, George; Cregar, Laird; Hardwicke, Sir Cedric; Allgood, Sara; Mather, Aubrey; Leonard, Queenie; Hare, Lumsden

Song(s)   The Parisian Trot [1] (C: Newman, Lionel; L: Henderson, Charles)

Notes   There are also renditions of other English music hall tunes. [1] Also in DOLL FACE.

3431 ✦ LOLLY-MADONNA XXX
Metro–Goldwyn–Mayer, 1973

Musical Score   Myrow, Fred

Producer(s)   Carr-Smith, Rodney
Director(s)   Sarafian, Richard C.
Screenwriter(s)   Carr-Smith, Rodney; Grafton, Sue
Source(s)   *The Lolly-Madonna War* (novel) Grafton, Sue

Cast   Steiger, Rod; Ryan, Robert; Bridges, Jeff; Wilson, Scott; Busey, Gary; Hughes, Tresa; Hubley, Season

Song(s)   Peaceful Country (C/L: Carnes, Kim; Ellinson, David)

3432 ✦ LONDON BY NIGHT
Metro–Goldwyn–Mayer, 1937

Musical Score   Axt, William

Producer(s)   Zimbalist, Sam
Director(s)   Thiele, William
Screenwriter(s)   Oppenheimer, George
Source(s)   *The Umbrella* (play) Scott, Will

Cast   Murphy, George; Johnson, Rita; Field, Virginia; Carroll, Leo G.; Zucco, George; Love, Montagu; Quillan, Eddie

Song(s)   Hi, Bill (C: Axt, William; L: Wright, Bob; Forrest, Chet)

3433 ✦ LONE COWBOY
Paramount, 1934

Director(s)   Sloane, Paul
Screenwriter(s)   Leahy, Agnes Brand; Vernon, Bobby
Source(s)   *Lone Cowboy* (novel) James, Will

Cast   Cooper, Jackie; Lee, Lila; Wray, John; Richards, Addison

Song(s)   Rich Widow Says She Loves Me [2] (C/L: LeMaire, William); Lone Cowboy [1] (C: Rainger, Ralph; L: Robin, Leo)

Notes   The picture was originally titled HE'S MY PAL. [1] Not used. Also not used in ROSE OF THE RANCHO though recorded. [2] Based on an old Southern melody.

3434 ♦ THE LONELY GUY
Universal, 1984

Musical Score   Goldsmith, Jerry

Producer(s)   Hiller, Arthur
Director(s)   Hiller, Arthur
Screenwriter(s)   Weinberger, Ed; Daniels, Stan
Source(s)   *The Lonely Guy's Book of Life* (novel) Friedman, Bruce Jay

Cast   Martin, Steve; Grodin, Charles; Ivey, Judith; Lawrence, Steve; Douglass, Robyn; Griffin, Merv; Brothers, Dr. Joyce; Greer, Michael

Song(s)   Love Comes Without Warning (C: Goldsmith, Jerry; L: Bettis, John); Don't Call Me Lonely (C/L: McMahon, Gerard); Oughta Know Love By Now (C/L: McMahon, Gerard); The Lonely Guy (C: Frey, Glen; L: Tempchin, Jack)

Notes   There are also vocals of "I'm in the Mood for Love" by Jimmy McHugh and Dorothy Fields and "You Made Me Love You" by Joseph McCarthy and James V. Monaco.

3435 ♦ THE LONELY MAN
Paramount, 1957

Producer(s)   Duggan, Pat
Director(s)   Levin, Henry
Screenwriter(s)   Essex, Harry; Smith, Robert

Cast   Palance, Jack; Perkins, Anthony; Brand, Neville; Middleton, Robert; Cook Jr., Elisha; Van Cleef, Lee; Aiken, Elaine

Song(s)   The Lonely Man (C: Van Cleave, Nathan; L: Brooks, Jack)

3436 ♦ LONESOME TRAIL
A.G.A. Durlam, 1930

Director(s)   Mitchell, Bruce
Screenwriter(s)   Uncredited

Cast   Delaney, Charles; Aubrey, Jimmy; Faire, Virginia Brown; Canutt, Yakima; Mix, Art

Notes   No cue sheet available. Songs may not be original.

3437 ♦ LONE STAR
Metro–Goldwyn–Mayer, 1951

Musical Score   Buttolph, David

Producer(s)   Griffin, Z. Wayne
Director(s)   Sherman, Vincent
Screenwriter(s)   Chase, Borden

Cast   Gable, Clark; Gardner, Ava; Crawford, Broderick; Barrymore, Lionel; Bondi, Beulah; Begley, Ed; Farnum, William

Song(s)   Lovers Were Meant to Cry (C: Traditional L: Brent, Earl)

3438 ♦ THE LONE STAR TRAIL
Universal, 1943

Producer(s)   Drake, Oliver
Director(s)   Taylor, Ray
Screenwriter(s)   Drake, Oliver

Cast   Brown, Johnny Mack; Ritter, Tex; Knight, Fuzzy

Song(s)   Welcome Home [2] (C: Rosen, Milton; L: Carter, Everett); Adios, Vaqueros (C/L: Drake, Oliver); I Got to See Texas Once More (C/L: Wakely, Jimmy; Reinhart, Dick); Trail Dreamin' [1] (C: Rosen, Milton; L: Wakely, Jimmy; Drake, Oliver)

Notes   [1] Also in BOSS OF HANGTOWN MESA and TRIGGER TRAIL. [2] Also in FIGHTING BILL FARGO.

3439 ♦ THE LONG DAY'S DYING
Paramount, 1968

Producer(s)   Fine, Harry
Director(s)   Collinson, Peter
Screenwriter(s)   Wood, Charles
Source(s)   *The Long Day's Dying* (novel) White, Alan

Cast   Bell, Tom; Beckley, Tony; Hemmings, David; Dobie, Alan

Song(s)   Long Day [1] (C: Lockyer, Malcolm; L: Fishman, Jack)

Notes   [1] Used instrumentally only.

3440 ♦ THE LONG DUEL
Paramount, 1967

Producer(s)   Annakin, Ken
Director(s)   Annakin, Ken
Screenwriter(s)   Yeldham, Peter
Source(s)   (story) Singh, Ranveer

Cast   Brynner, Yul; Howard, Trevor; Andrews, Harry; Keir, Andrew; Rampling, Charlotte; North, Virginia

Song(s)   When the World Is Ready (C: Scott, Patrick John; L: Black, Don)

3441 ✦ THE LONGEST DAY
Twentieth Century–Fox, 1962

Musical Score   Jarre, Maurice

Producer(s)   Zanuck, Darryl F.
Director(s)   Annakin, Ken; Marton, Andrew; Wicki, Bernhard
Screenwriter(s)   Ryan, Cornelius
Source(s)   *The Longest Day* (novel) Ryan, Cornelius

Cast   Wayne, John; Mitchum, Robert; Fonda, Henry; Burton, Richard

Song(s)   The Longest Day (C/L: Anka, Paul)

Notes   Written for exploitation only.

3442 ✦ THE LONGEST NIGHT
Metro–Goldwyn–Mayer, 1936

Musical Score   Ward, Edward

Producer(s)   Hubbard, Lucien; Marx, Samuel
Director(s)   Taggart, Errol
Screenwriter(s)   Andrews, Robert
Source(s)   "The Whispering Window" (story) Fitzsimmons, Cortland

Cast   Young, Robert; Rice, Florence; Healy, Ted; Haydon, Julie; Doucet, Catherine

Song(s)   The Longest Night (C/L: Wright, Bob; Forrest, Chet)

3443 ✦ THE LONGEST YARD
Paramount, 1974

Producer(s)   Ruddy, Albert S.
Director(s)   Aldrich, Robert
Screenwriter(s)   Wynn, Tracy Keenan

Cast   Reynolds, Burt; Albert, Eddie; Peters, Bernadette

Song(s)   Saturday Night Special (C/L: Van Zandt, Ronnie; King, Ed; Walden, Alan); Love Knows the Way [1] (C: De Vol, Frank; L: Kusik, Larry); I'm So Tired [2] (C/L: Morgan, Thomas "Shotgun")

Notes   Released as THE MEAN MACHINE. [1] Lyric for exploitation use only. [2] Not used.

3444 ✦ THE LONG GOODBYE
United Artists, 1973

Musical Score   Williams, John

Producer(s)   Bick, Jerry
Director(s)   Altman, Robert
Screenwriter(s)   Brackett, Leigh
Source(s)   *The Long Goodbye* (novel) Chandler, Raymond

Cast   Gould, Elliott; Bouton, Jim; van Pallandt, Nina; Hayden, Sterling; Rydell, Mark; Brody, Jo Ann; Berlinger, Warren

Song(s)   The Long Goodbye (C: Williams, John; L: Mercer, Johnny)

3445 ✦ THE LONG HOT SUMMER
Twentieth Century–Fox, 1958

Musical Score   North, Alex

Producer(s)   Wald, Jerry
Director(s)   Ritt, Martin
Screenwriter(s)   Ravetch, Irving; Frank Jr., Harriet
Source(s)   "The Hamlet" (stories) Faulkner, William

Cast   Newman, Paul; Woodward, Joanne; Franciosa, Anthony; Welles, Orson; Remick, Lee; Lansbury, Angela; Anderson, Richard; Marshall, Sarah; Albertson, Mabel; O'Malley, J. Pat; Walker, William

Song(s)   The Long Hot Summer (C: North, Alex; L: Cahn, Sammy); Hey Eula [1] (C: North, Alex; L: Cahn, Sammy)

Notes   [1] Sheet music only.

3446 ✦ THE LONG, LONG TRAILER
Metro–Goldwyn–Mayer, 1954

Musical Score   Deutsch, Adolph
Composer(s)   Deutsch, Adolph; Alexander, Jeff; Minnelli, Vincente
Lyricist(s)   Deutsch, Adolph; Alexander, Jeff; Minnelli, Vincente

Producer(s)   Berman, Pandro S.
Director(s)   Minnelli, Vincente
Screenwriter(s)   Goodrich, Frances; Hackett, Albert
Source(s)   *The Long, Long Trailer* (novel) Twiss, Clinton

Cast   Ball, Lucille; Arnaz, Desi; Main, Marjorie; Wynn, Keenan; Hurlbut, Gladys; Olsen, Moroni; Freed, Bert

Song(s)   My Compliments; The Recipe; Martha; Mario

Notes   There is also a vocal of "Breezin' Along with the Breeze" by Haven Gillespie, Seymour Simons and Richard A. Whiting and "Cui Cui" by Xavier Cugat, Curbelo and Al Stillman. Some of the above songs are very brief.

3447 ✦ LONG LOST FATHER
RKO, 1933

Producer(s)   Macgowan, Kenneth
Director(s)   Schoedsack, Ernest B.
Screenwriter(s)   Taylor, Dwight
Source(s)   (novel) Stern, G.B.

Cast   Barrymore, John; Chandler, Helen; Cook, Donald; Mowbray, Alan; King, Claude; Sharland, Reginald

Song(s)   It Isn't So Much That I Wouldn't (C: Lane, Burton; L: Adamson, Harold)

3448 ✦ THE LONG WAIT
United Artists, 1954

Musical Score Castelonuovo-Tedesco, Mario

Producer(s) Samuels, Victor
Director(s) Saville, Victor
Screenwriter(s) Samuels, Lesser; Green, Alan
Source(s) *The Long Wait* (novel) Spillane, Mickey

Cast Castle, Peggie; Kay, Mary Ellen; Smith, Shawn; Donlon, Dolores; Quinn, Anthony; Evans, Gene; Coburn, Charles

Song(s) Once (C: Spina, Harold; L: Russell, Bob)

3449 ✦ LOOKER
Ladd Company–Warner Brothers, 1981

Musical Score De Vorzon, Barry
Composer(s) De Vorzon, Barry
Lyricist(s) Towers, Michael

Producer(s) Jeffrey, Howard
Director(s) Crichton, Michael
Screenwriter(s) Crichton, Michael

Cast Finney, Albert; Coburn, James; Dey, Susan; Taylor-Young, Leigh; Harewood, Dorian; Rossovich, Tim; Hickman, Darryl; Witt, Kathryn

Song(s) Looker; High Wire

Notes All background vocals.

3450 ✦ LOOK FOR THE SILVER LINING
Warner Brothers, 1949

Choreographer(s) Prinz, LeRoy

Producer(s) Jacobs, William
Director(s) Butler, David
Screenwriter(s) Ephron, Phoebe; Ephron, Henry; Spitzer, Marian
Source(s) "Life of Marilyn Miller" (story) Ruby, Harry; Kalmar, Bert

Cast Haver, June [1]; Bolger, Ray; MacRae, Gordon; Ruggles, Charles; De Camp, Rosemary; Wilde, Lee; Wilde, Lyn; Simmons, Dick; Sakall, S.Z.; Catlett, Walter; Tupine, Oleg

Song(s) 'Twas the Night Before Christmas (C: Heindorf, Ray; L: Moore, Clement)

Notes With the exception of Ray Heindorf's musical setting to "'Twas the Night Before Christmas" there was no original music written for this film. Vocals include "Shine on Harvest Moon" by Nora Bayes and Jack Norworth; "Back Back Back to Baltimore" by Egbert Van Alstyne and Harry Williams; "Can't You Hear Me Callin' Caroline" by Caro Roma and William H. Gardner; "Pirouette" by Herman Finck; "Yama Yama Man" by Karl Hoschna and George Collin Davis; "Time on My Hands" by Vincent Youmans, Harold Adamson and Mack Gordon; "A Kiss in the Dark" by Victor Herbert and B.G. DeSylva; "Look for the Silver Lining" by Jerome Kern and B.G. DeSylva; "Sunny" and "Who" by Jerome Kern, Otto Harbach and Oscar Hammerstein II and "Wild Rose" by Jerome Kern and Clifford Grey. [1] Dubbed by Bonnie Lou Williams.

3451 ✦ LOOK IN ANY WINDOW
Allied Artists, 1961

Musical Score Shores, Richard

Producer(s) Alland, William; Mascott, Laurence E.
Director(s) Alland, William
Screenwriter(s) Mascott, Laurence E.

Cast Anka, Paul; Roman, Ruth; Nicol, Alex; Perreau, Gigi; Mathews, Carole; Dolenz, George; Cassidy, Jack

Song(s) Look in Any Window (C/L: Anka, Paul)

Notes No cue sheet available.

3452 ✦ LOOKING FOR LOVE
Metro–Goldwyn–Mayer, 1964

Musical Score Stoll, George
Composer(s) Hunter, Hank; Vincent, Stan
Lyricist(s) Hunter, Hank; Vincent, Stan
Choreographer(s) Sidney, Robert

Producer(s) Pasternak, Joe
Director(s) Weis, Don
Screenwriter(s) Flippen, Ruth Brooks

Cast Francis, Connie; Hutton, Jim; Oliver, Susan; Baker, Joby; Nichols, Barbara; Carson, Johnny; Hamilton, George; Mimieux, Yvette; Prentiss, Paula; Thomas, Danny; Flippen, Jay C.; White, Jesse; Lane, Charles; Marshall, Joan

Song(s) Looking for Love; Let's Have a Party; When the Clock Strikes Midnight; This Is My Happiest Moment (C/L: Murry, Ted; Davis, Benny); Be My Love [1] (C: Brodszky, Nicholas; L: Cahn, Sammy); I Can't Believe that You're in Love with Me (C: McHugh, Jimmy; L: Gaskill, Clarence); Whoever You Are, I Love You (C/L: Geld, Gary; Udell, Peter)

Notes [1] Also in BECAUSE YOU'RE MINE and THE TOAST OF NEW ORLEANS.

3453 ✦ LOOKING FOR MR. GOODBAR
Paramount, 1977

Producer(s) Fields, Freddie
Director(s) Brooks, Richard
Screenwriter(s) Brooks, Richard
Source(s) *Looking for Mr. Goodbar* (novel) Rossner, Judith

Cast Weld, Tuesday; Keaton, Diane; Atherton, William; Kiley, Richard; Gere, Richard

Song(s) Don't Ask to Stay Until Tomorrow (C: Kane, Artie; L: Connors, Carol); Looking for Mr. Goodbar [1] (C: Kane, Artie; Connors, Carol)

Notes [1] Sheet music only.

3454 ✦ LOOKIN' TO GET OUT
Paramount, 1982

Musical Score Mandel, Johnny

Producer(s) Schaffel, Robert
Director(s) Ashby, Hal
Screenwriter(s) Voight, Jon; Schwartz, Al

Cast Voight, Jon; Ann-Margaret; Young, Burt; Remsen, Bert; Farese, Jude

Song(s) Lookin' to Get Out (C: Mandel, Johnny; L: Doering, George; Doering, Jo Ellen)

Notes No cue sheet available.

3455 ✦ LOOPING THE LOOP
Paramount, 1929

Cast Krause, Werner; Jugo, Jenny

Song(s) Poor Punchinello [1] (C: Pollack, Lew; L: Young, Joe; Lewis, Sam M.)

Notes No cue sheet available. A UFA German film distributed by Paramount. [1] This is a silent film and so the song was written for exploitation only.

3456 ✦ LOOSE ANKLES
Warner Brothers, 1930

Composer(s) Wendling, Pete
Lyricist(s) Meskill, Jack
Choreographer(s) Mack, Roy

Director(s) Wilde, Ted
Screenwriter(s) Towne, Gene
Source(s) *Loose Ankles* (play) Janney, Sam

Cast Fairbanks Jr., Douglas; Young, Loretta; Fazenda, Louise; Nugent, Eddie; Courtney, Inez; Pollard, Daphne; Harlan, Otis; Wales, Ethel; Keane, Raymond

Song(s) Loose Ankles; Whoopin' It Up

Notes No cue sheet available.

3457 ✦ LORD BYRON OF BROADWAY
Metro–Goldwyn–Mayer, 1930

Composer(s) Brown, Nacio Herb
Lyricist(s) Freed, Arthur
Choreographer(s) Lee, Sammy; Rasch, Albertina

Director(s) Nigh, William; Beaumont, Harry
Screenwriter(s) Wilbur, Crane; Mack, Willard
Source(s) *Lord Byron of Broadway* (novel) Martin, Nell

Cast Kaley, Charles; Terry, Ethelind; Shilling, Marion; Edwards, Cliff; Lee, Gwen; Rubin, Benny; Demerest, Drew; Byron, John; Craven, Hazel

Song(s) A Bundle of Old Love Letters; Blue Daughter of Heaven (C: Tiomkin, Dimitri; L: Egan, Raymond B.); Should I; Woman in the Shoe; Old Pal, Why Did You Leave Me?; Only Love Is Real; You're the Bride and I'm the Groom; When I Met You [1]; Love Ain't Nothing but the Blues [1] (C: Alter, Louis; L: Goodwin, Joe)

Notes [1] Not on cue sheets.

3458 ✦ LORD LOVE A DUCK
United Artists, 1966

Musical Score Hefti, Neal
Composer(s) Hefti, Neal
Lyricist(s) Sheldon, Ernie

Producer(s) Axelrod, George
Director(s) Axelrod, George
Screenwriter(s) Axelrod, George; Johnson, Larry H.
Source(s) *Lord Love a Duck* (novel) Hines, Al

Cast McDowall, Roddy; Weld, Tuesday; Carey, Lynn; West, Martin; Korman, Harvey; Gable, Martin; Gordon, Ruth; Albright, Lola

Song(s) Lord Love a Duck; Lovers Lane; First Day Back; Ring a Ding Ding; Murder Attempt; Murder

3459 ✦ LORD OF THE RINGS
United Artists, 1978

Musical Score Rosenman, Leonard

Producer(s) Zaentz, Saul
Director(s) Bakshi, Ralph
Screenwriter(s) Conkling, Charles; Beagle, Peter S.
Source(s) *Lord of the Rings* (novel) Tolkien, J.R.R.

Song(s) Mithrandir (C: Rosenman, Leonard; L: Fleischer, Mark)

Notes Animated cartoon feature. No cue sheet available.

3460 ✦ LORDS OF DISCIPLINE
Paramount, 1983

Producer(s) Jaffe, Herb; Katzka, Gabriel
Director(s) Roddam, Franc
Screenwriter(s) Pope, Thomas; Fonvielle, Lloyd
Source(s) *The Lords of Discipline* (novel) Conroy, Pat

Cast Keith, David; Prosky, Robert; Breland, Mark; Spradlin, G.D.; Biehn, Michael

Song(s) Carolina Keep Us Faithful (C: Blake, Howard; L: Fonvielle, Lloyd)

3461 ✦ LOS HIJOS MANDAN
Twentieth Century–Fox, 1939

Song(s) Tenia Que Suceder (C: Menendez, Nilo; L: Kemp, Ramiro Gomez)

Notes No other information available.

3462 ✦ THE LOST BOYS
Warner Brothers, 1987

Musical Score Newman, Thomas

Producer(s) Bernhard, Harvey
Director(s) Schumacher, Joel
Screenwriter(s) Fischer, Janice; Jeremias, James; Boan, Jeffrey

Cast Patric, Jason; Haim, Corey; Wiest, Dianne; Hughes, Barnard; Herrmann, Edward; Sutherland, Kiefer; Gertz, Jami; Feldman, Corey; Newlander, Jamison

Song(s) Cry Little Sister (C/L: Mainieri, Michael; McMahon, Gerard); Some Other Day (C/L: Gould, Danny); Lost in the Shadows (The Lost Boys) (C/L: Gramm, Lou); Drop into Fog (C/L: Newman, Thomas)

Notes It is not known how many of these were written for the picture. Songs that seemed to be previously recorded were not listed.

3463 ✦ THE LOST CONTINENT
Twentieth Century–Fox, 1968

Musical Score Schurmann, Gerard
Composer(s) Phillips, Roy
Lyricist(s) Phillips, Roy

Producer(s) Carreras, Michael
Director(s) Carreras, Michael
Screenwriter(s) Nash, Michael
Source(s) *Uncharted Seas* (novel) Wheatley, Dennis

Cast Porter, Eric; Knef, Hildegard; Leigh, Suzanna; Beckley, Tony; McCallum, Neil; Stock, Nigel

Song(s) Lost Continent Theme; Oo-Ee Baby; I'm a Boy in Love

3464 ✦ LOST HORIZON
Columbia, 1973

Composer(s) Bacharach, Burt
Lyricist(s) David, Hal
Choreographer(s) Pan, Hermes

Producer(s) Hunter, Ross
Director(s) Jarrott, Charles
Screenwriter(s) Kramer, Larry
Source(s) *Lost Horizon* (novel) Hilton, James

Cast Finch, Peter; Ullmann, Liv; Kellerman, Sally; Kennedy, George; York, Michael; Hussey, Olivia; Van, Bobby; Shigeta, James; Boyer, Charles; Gielgud, John

Song(s) Lost Horizon; Share the Joy; World Is a Circle; Living Together, Growing Together; I Might Frighten Her Away; The Things I Will Not Miss; If I Could Go Back; Where Knowledge Ends; Reflections; Question Me an Answer

3465 ✦ LOST IN A HAREM
Metro–Goldwyn–Mayer, 1944

Choreographer(s) Donohue, Jack

Producer(s) Haight, George
Director(s) Riesner, Charles F.
Screenwriter(s) Ruskin, Harry; Grant, John; Crane, Harry

Cast Abbott, Bud; Costello, Lou; Maxwell, Marilyn; Conte, John; Dumbrille, Douglass; Jimmy Dorsey and His Orchestra

Song(s) What Does It Take? (C: de Paul, Gene; L: Raye, Don); Sons of the Desert (C: Fain, Sammy; L: Freed, Ralph); John Silver (C/L: Dorsey, Jimmy; Krise, Ray); It Is Written [1] (C: de Paul, Gene; L: Raye, Don)

Notes [1] Listed in some sources but not on cue sheets.

3466 ✦ LOST IN ALASKA
Universal, 1952

Musical Score Mancini, Henry
Composer(s) Hughes, Arnold
Lyricist(s) Herbert, Frederick
Choreographer(s) Belfer, Harold

Producer(s) Christie, Howard
Director(s) Yarbrough, Jean
Screenwriter(s) Ragaway, Martin A.; Stern, Leonard

Cast Abbott, Bud; Costello, Lou; Ewell, Tom; Green, Mitzi; Cabot, Bruce; Cody, Iron Eyes; Urecal, Minerva

Song(s) A Country Gal; There'll Be a Hot Time in the Igloo Tonight

3467 ✦ LOST IN THE STARS
American Film Theater, 1974

Choreographer(s) Kelly, Paula

Producer(s) Landau, Ely
Director(s) Mann, Daniel
Screenwriter(s) Hayes, Alfred
Source(s) *Lost in the Stars* (musical) Weill, Kurt; Anderson, Maxwell

Cast Peters, Brock; Davis, Clifton; Moore, Melba; Rogers, Paul; St. Jacques, Raymond; Kelly, Paula; Barnum II, H.B.; Weeks, Alan

Song(s) Lost in the Stars; Cry the Beloved Country; Little Gray House; Trouble Man; Bird of Paradise; Big Mole; Train Go Now to Johannesburg

Notes No cue sheet available.

3468 ✦ LOST LAGOON
United Artists, 1957

Musical Score Brannon, Terry; Smith, Hubert
Composer(s) Smith, Hubert
Lyricist(s) Smith, Hubert

Producer(s) Rawlins, John
Director(s) Rawlins, John
Screenwriter(s) Subotsky, Milton

Cast Lynn, Jeffrey; Barry, Lelia; Donat, Peter

Song(s) To You (C/L: Venneri, Darwin); Charlie Walker Story; Charlie Walker Calypso; Married Life Calypso; Istiamba-Ambastia Calypso

3469 ✦ THE LOST MAN
Universal, 1969

Musical Score Jones, Quincy
Composer(s) Jones, Quincy; Cooper, Dick; Shelby, Ernie
Lyricist(s) Jones, Quincy; Cooper, Dick; Shelby, Ernie

Producer(s) Muhl, Edward; Tucker, Melville
Director(s) Aurthur, Robert Alan
Screenwriter(s) Aurthur, Robert Alan
Source(s) *Odd Man Out* (novel) Green, F.L.

Cast Poitier, Sidney; Shimkus, Joanna; Freeman Jr., Al; Tolan, Michael; Bibb, Leon; Dysart, Richard

Song(s) Last Night 'Na Night Before; Try, Try, Try; He Said He Loves Me (C/L: Jones, Quincy; Cooper, Dick; Shelby, Ernie; Hildebrand, Diane); Sweet Soul Sister; Rap, Run It on Down

3470 ✦ THE LOST WEEKEND
Paramount, 1945

Producer(s) Brackett, Charles
Director(s) Wilder, Billy
Screenwriter(s) Wilder, Billy; Brackett, Charles
Source(s) *The Lost Weekend* (novel) Jackson, Charles

Cast Milland, Ray; Faylen, Frank; Wyman, Jane; Terry, Phillip; Da Silva, Howard; Dowling, Doris

Song(s) Champagne in the Sun (C: Terr, Max; L: Raleigh, Ben; Wayne, Bernie); Bal Masque [1] (C: Young, Victor; L: Coslow, Sam)

Notes There are also selections from LA TRAVIATA sung as well as the popular songs "My Love and I" by Erich Wolfgang Korngold and Oscar Hammerstein II (also in GIVE US THIS NIGHT); "It Was So Beautiful" by Harry Barris and Arthur Freed and "Louise" by Richard A. Whiting and Leo Robin. "Louise" is also in INNOCENTS OF PARIS and YOU CAN'T RATION LOVE. [1] Also in FATAL LADY.

3471 ✦ THE LOTTERY BRIDE
United Artists, 1930

Composer(s) Friml, Rudolf
Lyricist(s) Brennan, J. Keirn

Producer(s) Hammerstein, Arthur
Director(s) Stein, Paul
Screenwriter(s) Jackson, Horace; Rogers, Howard Emmett
Source(s) "Bride 66" (story) Stothard, Henry

Cast MacDonald, Jeanette; Garrick, John; Chisholm, Robert; Brown, Joe E.; Gribbon, Harry; Nye, Carroll; Pitts, ZaSu

Song(s) You're an Angel; I'll Follow the Trail; My Northern Light; High and Low [1] (C: Schwartz, Arthur; L: Dietz, Howard); Yubla

Notes No cue sheet available. [1] From Broadway musical revue THE BAND WAGON.

3472 ✦ THE LOTTERY LOVER
Fox, 1935

Composer(s) Gorney, Jay
Lyricist(s) Hartman, Don

Producer(s) Rockett, Al
Director(s) Thiele, William
Screenwriter(s) Schulz, Franz; Wilder, Billy; Hellman, Sam

Cast Ayres, Lew; Paterson, Pat; Fears, Peggy; Holloway, Sterling; King, Walter Woolf; Denny, Reginald; Dinehart, Alan

Song(s) There's a Bit of Paree in You; Ting a Ling a Ling; Close Your Eyes and See; Gaby Can Can (Inst.); Twilight Caresses (Inst.); Tia Juana (Inst.); All for the Love of a Girl [1]

Notes [1] Not used.

3473 ✦ LOUISIANA HAYRIDE
Columbia, 1944

Composer(s) Kent, Walter
Lyricist(s) Gannon, Kim

Producer(s) Barton, Charles
Director(s) Barton, Charles
Screenwriter(s) Yawitz, Paul; Seff, Manuel

Cast Canova, Judy; Hunter, Ross; Lane, Richard; Bridges, Lloyd; Willis, Matt; McKay, George; Urecal, Minerva; Cavanaugh, Hobart; Hicks, Russell

Song(s) You Gotta Go Where the Train Goes; Rainbow Road; I'm a Woman of the World (C: Chaplin, Saul; L: Seelen, Jerry)

Notes "Put Your Arms Around Me Honey" by Albert Von Tilzer and Junie McCree and "Short'nin Bread" by Jacques Wolfe and Clement Wood are also sung.

3474 ✦ LOUISIANA PURCHASE
Paramount, 1941

Composer(s) Berlin, Irving
Lyricist(s) Berlin, Irving

Producer(s) Wilson, Harold
Director(s) Cummings, Irving
Screenwriter(s) Chodorov, Jerome; Fields, Joseph
Source(s) *Louisiana Purchase* (musical) Berlin, Irving; Ryskind, Morrie

Cast Moore, Victor; Zorina, Vera [6]; Bordoni, Irene; Hope, Bob

Song(s) Lawyer's Letter; Girl's Opening Chorus (It's New to Us); You're Lonely and I'm Lonely [1]; Louisiana Purchase [1]; It's a Lovely Day Tomorrow [1]; What Chance Have I with Love [1] [2] [4]; Old Man's Darling [1] [3]; You Can't Brush Me Off [1] [7]; Dance with Me Tonight at the Mardi Gras [1] [5]

Notes Many of the other tunes from the Broadway show are used as background instrumentals. These include "The Lord Done Fixed Up My Soul," "Fools Fall in Love" and "Sex Marches On." [1] From Broadway musical. [2] Not used but recorded. [3] Not used. [4] Later used in film version of CALL ME MADAM. [5] Used instrumentally only. [6] Dubbed by Dona Drake. [7] Used instrumentally only but recorded by Bob Hope.

3475 ◆ LOVE
Metro–Goldwyn–Mayer, 1927

Musical Score Luz, Ernst

Producer(s) Goulding, Edmund
Director(s) Goulding, Edmund
Screenwriter(s) Moon, Lorna; Marion, Frances
Source(s) *Anna Karenina* (novel) Tolstoy, Leo

Cast Garbo, Greta; Gilbert, John; Hurst, Brandon; de Lacy, Philippe; Fawcett, George; Fitzroy, Emily

Song(s) That Melody of Love [1] (C: Donaldson, Walter; L: Dietz, Howard)

Notes This film has two endings, one happy one sad. [1] This is a silent film. The song was written for exploitation only.

3476 ◆ LOVE AFFAIR
RKO, 1939

Musical Score Webb, Roy

Producer(s) McCarey, Leo
Director(s) McCarey, Leo
Screenwriter(s) Daves, Delmer; Stewart, Donald Ogden

Cast Dunne, Irene; Boyer, Charles; Ouspenskaya, Maria; Bowman, Lee; Allwyn, Astrid; Moscovich, Maurice

Song(s) Sing My Heart (C: Arlen, Harold; L: Koehler, Ted); Wishing (C/L: DeSylva, B.G.)

3477 ◆ LOVE AMONG THE MILLIONAIRES
Paramount, 1930

Composer(s) Baer, Abel
Lyricist(s) Gilbert, L. Wolfe

Director(s) Tuttle, Frank
Screenwriter(s) Mankiewicz, Herman J.

Cast Bow, Clara; Smith, Stanley; Erwin, Stuart; Green, Mitzi; Gallagher, Skeets

Song(s) Love Among the Millionaires; That's Worth Waiting For; Believe It or Not I Found My Man; Don't Be a Meanie; Rarin' to Go

Notes Originally titled PALM BEACH.

3478 ◆ LOVE AND HISSES
Twentieth Century–Fox, 1937

Composer(s) Revel, Harry
Lyricist(s) Gordon, Mack

Producer(s) Zanuck, Darryl F.
Director(s) Lanfield, Sidney
Screenwriter(s) Kenyon, Curtis; Arthur, Art

Cast Winchell, Walter; Bernie, Ben; Simon, Simone; Lahr, Bert; Davis, Joan; Baldwin, Dick; The Peters Sisters; Terry, Ruth; Chandler, Chick; Chilton and Thomas; Brewster Twins

Song(s) Sweet Someone; I Wanna Be in Winchell's Column; Oh What a Man (C: Pollack, Lew; L: Mitchell, Sidney D.); Darling, Je Vous Aime Beaucoup [1] (C/L: Sosenko, Anna); Be a Good Sport; Broadway's Gone Hawaii; A Little Love a Little Kiss [1] (C/L: Silesu, Leo)

Notes [1] Not written for this film.

3479 ◆ LOVE AND KISSES
Universal, 1965

Musical Score Loose, Bill
Composer(s) Curtis, Sonny
Lyricist(s) Curtis, Sonny

Producer(s) Nelson, Ozzie
Director(s) Nelson, Ozzie
Screenwriter(s) Nelson, Ozzie
Source(s) (play) Block, Anita Rowe

Cast Nelson, Ricky; Nelson, Kristin; Kelly, Jack; Hines, Madelyn; Kelton, Pert; Wells, Sheila; Van Dyke, Jerry

Song(s) Love and Kisses; Come Out Dancin' (C/L: Ballard, Clint; Riela, Angela); Say You Love Me

3480 ◆ LOVE AND LEARN
Warner Brothers, 1947

Musical Score Steiner, Max
Composer(s) Jerome, M.K.
Lyricist(s) Scholl, Jack

Producer(s) Jacobs, William
Director(s) de Cordova, Frederick
Screenwriter(s) Conrad, Eugene; Swann, Francis; Diamond, I.A.L.
Source(s) "Gentlemen Are Born" (story) Sauber, Harry

Cast Carson, Jack; Hutton, Robert; Vickers, Martha; Paige, Janis; Kruger, Otto; Brown, Barbara; D'Andrea, Tom; Bates, Florence; Stevens, Craig; McGuire, Don

Song(s) The Moon Is in Tears Tonight [1]; I'm in a Jam with Baby [2] (C: Jerome, M.K.; Heindorf, Ray; L: Koehler, Ted); Happy Me; If You Are Coming Back to Me; Would You Believe Me (C: Heindorf, Ray; Jerome, M.K.; L: Tobias, Charles)

Notes [1] Six seconds worth. Also in KID GALAHAD (1937). [2] Also in RACE STREET (RKO).

3481 ✦ LOVE AT FIRST BITE
American International, 1979

Musical Score Bernstein, Charles

Producer(s) Freeman, Joel D.
Director(s) Dragoti, Stan
Screenwriter(s) Kaufman, Robert

Cast Hamilton, George; Saint James, Susan; Benjamin, Richard; Shawn, Dick; Johnson, Arte; Hemsley, Sherman; Sanford, Isabel; Gordon, Barry; Schell, Ronnie

Song(s) Fly By Night (C/L: Bernstein, Charles; Long, Joe; Hines, Steve); Dancin' Through the Night (C/L: Adcock, Robbie; Bernstein, Charles; Long, Joe; Hines, Steve)

Notes No cue sheet available.

3482 ✦ LOVE AT FIRST SIGHT
Chesterfield, 1930

Composer(s) Lee, Lester; Levison, Charles
Lyricist(s) Lee, Lester; Levison, Charles
Choreographer(s) Hale, Chester

Director(s) Lewis, Edgar
Screenwriter(s) Lee, Lester; Levison, Charles

Cast Keener, Suzanne; Foster, Norman; Rankin, Doris; Cole, Lester; Raynolds, Abe; Atchley, Hooper L.; Mathews, Burt; Adams, Dorothee; The Chester Hale Girls; Paul Specht and his Band

Song(s) Jig-a-Boo Jig [1]; Sunshine; What Is Living with You?; Love at First Sight

Notes No cue sheet available. There are five songs in the picture. [1] Sometimes referred to as "Let's Jig the Jigaboo."

3483 ✦ THE LOVE BUG
Disney, 1968

Musical Score Bruns, George

Producer(s) Walsh, Bill
Director(s) Stevenson, Robert
Screenwriter(s) Walsh, Bill; DaGradi, Don

Cast Jones, Dean; Lee, Michele; Tomlinson, David; Hackett, Buddy; Flynn, Joe; Fong, Benson; Ross, Joe E.; Kelley, Barry; Adrian, Iris

Song(s) Herbie (C: Bruns, George; L: Brook, Don E. [1])

Notes [1] Pseudonym for Bill Walsh.

3484 ✦ LOVE CHILD
Ladd Company, 1982

Musical Score Fox, Charles

Producer(s) Maslansky, Paul
Director(s) Peerce, Larry
Screenwriter(s) Gerard, Anne; Specktor, Katherine
Source(s) article by Freeman, Jean Todd

Cast Madigan, Amy; Bridges, Beau; Phillips, Mackenzie; Salmi, Albert; Merlin, Joanna; Pearlman, Rhea

Song(s) Something More (C: Fox, Charles; L: Simon, Carly)

Notes No cue sheet available.

3485 ✦ LOVE COMES ALONG
RKO, 1930

Composer(s) Levant, Oscar
Lyricist(s) Clare, Sidney
Choreographer(s) Eaton, Pearl

Director(s) Julian, Rupert
Screenwriter(s) Smith, Wallace
Source(s) *Conchita* (play) Knoblock, Edward

Cast Daniels, Bebe; Hughes, Monica; Love, Montagu; Sparks, Ned; Tell, Alma; Belmore, Lionel; Selbie, Evelyn

Song(s) Until Love Comes Along; Night Winds; Gay Love [1]; For I'm a Simple Maid; Sailor Song

Notes Cue sheet doesn't differentiate between vocals and instrumentals. [1] Also in THE DELIGHTFUL ROGUE.

3486 ✦ THE LOVE DOCTOR
Paramount, 1929

Director(s) Brown, Melville
Screenwriter(s) Bolton, Guy
Source(s) "The Boomerang" (story) Mapes, Victor; Smith, W.

Cast Dix, Richard; Collyer, June; Segar, Miriam

Song(s) Wait Till You See My Cherie [1] (C: Whiting, Richard A.; L: Robin, Leo)

Notes [1] Also in INNOCENTS OF PARIS.

3487 ✦ LOVE FINDS ANDY HARDY
Metro–Goldwyn–Mayer, 1938

Musical Score Snell, Dave
Composer(s) Revel, Harry
Lyricist(s) Gordon, Mack

Director(s) Seitz, George B.
Screenwriter(s) Ludwig, William
Source(s) characters by Rouverol, Aurania

Cast Rooney, Mickey; Stone, Lewis; Holden, Fay; Parker, Cecilia; Garland, Judy; Rutherford, Ann; Turner, Lana

Song(s) In-Between (C/L: Edens, Roger); It Never Rains - But It Pours; Meet the Beat of My Heart; What Do You Know About Love [1]

Notes "Bei Mir Bist du Schoen" recorded but not used. [1] Sheet music only.

3488 ✦ THE LOVE GAMBLER
Fox, 1931

Composer(s) Kernell, William
Lyricist(s) Kernell, William

Cast Emillio; Mojica, Jose; Elvira; Marie, Mona; Valverde, Rafael

Song(s) Horses and Women (C: Sanders, Troy; L: Mojica, Jose); When You Smile; Dear One; My Serenata (C/L: Grever, Maria); Recuerda (C: Sanders, Troy; Mojica, Jose; Kernell, William; L: Sanders, Troy; Mojica, Jose); Tree Song [1] (C/L: Mojica, Jose; Sanders, Troy; Kernell, William)

Notes Mojica contributed Spanish lyrics to the Kernell songs also. Whether they were original or translations of Kernell's English lyrics (if any) is not known. The Spanish title of this film was CUANDO EL AMOR RIE, previously titled EL DOMADOR DE MUJERES. [1] Sheet music only unless this is an English version of "Recuerda."

3489 ✦ THE LOVE GOD?
Universal, 1969

Musical Score Mizzy, Vic

Producer(s) Montagne, Edward J.
Director(s) Hiken, Nat
Screenwriter(s) Hiken, Nat

Cast Knotts, Don; O'Brien, Edmond; Francis, Anne; Gregory, James; Arthur, Maureen

Song(s) Summer in the Meadow (C: Murray, Lyn; L: Hiken, Nat); Mr. Peacock (C/L: Slivinski, Walter)

Notes There is also a vocal of "Love's Old Sweet Song" by G.C. Bingham and J.L. Molloy.

3490 ✦ THE LOVE GODDESSES
Paramount, 1965

Producer(s) Turrell, Saul J.
Screenwriter(s) Turrell, Saul J.; Ferguson, Graeme
Narrator(s) King, Carl

Song(s) The Love Goddesses [1] (C: Faith, Percy; L: David, Mack)

Notes Documentary. [1] The lyrics were for exploitation only.

3491 ✦ LOVE HAPPY
United Artists, 1950

Musical Score Ronell, Ann

Producer(s) Cowan, Lester
Director(s) Miller, David
Screenwriter(s) Tashlin, Frank; Benoff, Mac

Cast Monroe, Marilyn; Marx, Groucho; Marx, Harpo; Marx, Chico; Massey, Ilona; Burr, Raymond; Cooper, Melville; Vera-Ellen; Valentine, Paul; Hutton, Marion; Blore, Eric; Belasco, Leon

Song(s) Who Stole the Jam? (C/L: Ronell, Ann; Spina, Harold; Bullock, Walter); Love Happy (C/L: Ronell, Ann)

3492 ✦ LOVE, HONOR AND BEHAVE
Warner Brothers, 1938

Musical Score Roemheld, Heinz

Producer(s) Wallis, Hal B.
Director(s) Logan, Stanley
Screenwriter(s) Ripley, Clements; Buckner, Robert; Jacoby, Michel
Source(s) "Everybody Was Very Nice" (story) Benet, Stephen Vincent

Cast Morris, Wayne; Lane, Priscilla; Litel, John; Mitchell, Thomas; Foran, Dick; O'Neil, Barbara; Barrie, Mona; Irving, Margaret; Gayle, Gregory; Moore, Dickie; Leonard, Audrey

Song(s) Bei Mir Bist Du Schoen (C: Secunda, Sholom; L: Cahn, Sammy; Chaplin, Saul; Jacobs, Jacob)

3493 ✦ LOVE, HONOR AND GOODBYE
Republic, 1952

Producer(s) Grey, Harry
Director(s) Rogell, Albert S.
Screenwriter(s) Phillips, Arthur; Loeb, Lee; Hyland, Dick Irving

Cast Bruce, Virginia; Ashley, Edward; McLaglen, Victor; Asther, Nils; Broderick, Helen; Borg, Veda Ann; Moore, Jacqueline

Song(s) Close Those Eyes (C: Scharf, Walter; L: Washington, Ned)

Notes There is also a vocal of "These Foolish Things" by Holt Marvell, Jack Strachey and Harry Link.

3494 ✦ LOVE, HONOR AND OH BABY!
Universal, 1940

Director(s) Lamont, Charles
Screenwriter(s) Young, Clarence Upson

Cast Woods, Donald; Adams, Kathryn

Song(s) Wasn't It You? [1] (C: Skinner, Frank; L: Henderson, Charles)

Notes [1] Also in SWING, SISTER, SWING.

3495 ✦ LOVE IN A GOLDFISH BOWL
Paramount, 1961

Producer(s) Jurow, Martin; Shepherd, Richard
Director(s) Sher, Jack
Screenwriter(s) Sher, Jack

Cast Fabian; Sands, Tommy; Michaels, Toby; Sterling, Jan; Andrews, Edward; McGiver, John

Song(s) Love in a Goldfish Bowl (C: Bacharach, Burt; L: David, Hal); You're Only Young Once (C/L: Faith, Russell; Marcucci, Robert; DeAngelis, Pete [1])

Notes [1] Not credited on sheet music.

3496 ✦ LOVE IN BLOOM
Paramount, 1935

Composer(s) Gordon, Mack [2]
Lyricist(s) Gordon, Mack

Producer(s) Glazer, Benjamin
Director(s) Nugent, Elliott
Screenwriter(s) McEvoy, J.P.; Thompson, Keene

Cast Burns, George; Allen, Gracie; Morrison, Joe; Lee, Dixie; Nugent, J.C.; Carle, Richard; Foy, Mary; Baker, Benny

Song(s) Here Comes Cookie [3]; Let Me Sing You to Sleep with a Love Song (C: Revel, Harry); Got Me Doin' Things; My Heart Is an Open Book [6]; Would There Be Love? [1] [7]; It's a Chance of a Lifetime [1] (C/L: Noble, Ray); To Say I Love You [1] (C/L: Noble, Ray); (Do You Know) Why Stars Come Out at Night [1] (C/L: Noble, Ray); Lean Upon My Shoulder [1] (C/L: Noble, Ray); Touch of Your Lips [1] (C/L: Noble, Ray); What Do We Care [1] (C/L: Noble, Ray); Change Your Mind [1] [5] (C/L: Noble, Ray); None but the Lonely Heart [4] (C: Tchaikovsky, Peter; L: Goethe; Westbrook, Arthur)

Notes Originally titled WIN OR LOSE. [1] Not used. [2] Contracts for this production signed by Gordon and Revel specifically do not give composer credit to Harry Revel for these songs. However they are erroneously referred to elsewhere as Revel and Gordon songs. I went with the two different contracts since they were signed by the songwriters. Also, ASCAP and published songs do not credit Revel. [3] Also in HERE COMES COOKIE. [4] According to the cue sheet this was performed instrumentally only. The published sheet music says Joe Morrison sang it in the picture. Westbrook did the English adaptation of the lyrics. In ROMANCE IN THE DARK. [5] In SHIP CAFE. [6] Not used in COLLEGE RHYTHM. [7] Also in STOLEN HARMONY.

3497 ✦ LOVE IN LAS VEGAS

See VIVA LAS VEGAS (1965).

3498 ✦ LOVE IN THE AFTERNOON
Allied Artists, 1957

Composer(s) Malneck, Matty
Lyricist(s) Malneck, Matty

Producer(s) Wilder, Billy
Director(s) Wilder, Billy
Screenwriter(s) Wilder, Billy

Cast Cooper, Gary; Hepburn, Audrey; Chevalier, Maurice; McGiver, John; Olga Valery and the Gypsies

Song(s) Fascination (C/L: De Feraudy, Maurice; Marchetti, F.D.); C'est Si Bon (C/L: Hornez, Andre); Love in the Afternoon; Arlane; Hot Paprika

Notes No cue sheet available.

3499 ✦ LOVE IN THE ROUGH
Metro–Goldwyn–Mayer, 1930

Composer(s) McHugh, Jimmy
Lyricist(s) Fields, Dorothy
Choreographer(s) Lee, Sammy

Director(s) Reisner, Charles
Screenwriter(s) Farnham, Joe; Hopkins, Robert E.
Source(s) *Spring Fever* (play) Lawrence, Vincent

Cast Montgomery, Robert; Rubin, Benny; Jordan, Dorothy; Nugent, J.C.; McNulty, Dorothy [1]

Song(s) Like Kelly Can; I'm Doin' that Thing; I'm Learning a Lot from You; Go Home and Tell Your Mother [2]; One More Waltz

Notes A remake of SPRING FEVER (1927). [1] Later changed name to Penny Singleton. [2] Also in STRANGERS MAY KISS.

3500 ✦ LOVE IS A BALL
United Artists, 1963

Musical Score Legrand, Michel
Composer(s) Legrand, Michel

Producer(s) Poll, Martin H.
Director(s) Swift, David
Screenwriter(s) Swift, David; Waldman, Tom; Waldman, Frank
Source(s) *The Grand Duke and Mr. Pimm* (novel) Hardy, Lindsay

Cast Ford, Glenn; Lange, Hope; Boyer, Charles; Montalban, Ricardo; Savalas, Telly; Jacobson, Ulla

Song(s) Ne Crois Pas (L: Lemarque, Francis); Song for Millie (L: Lemarque, Francis); Gather Your Dreams [1] (L: Howard, Bart); Love Is a Ball [1] (L: Adler, Richard)

Notes International title ALL THIS AND MONEY TOO. [1] Sheet music only.

3501 ✦ LOVE IS A MANY-SPLENDORED THING
Twentieth Century–Fox, 1955

Musical Score Newman, Alfred

Producer(s) Adler, Buddy
Director(s) King, Henry
Screenwriter(s) Patrick, John
Source(s) *A Many Splendored Thing* (novel) Suyin, Han

Cast Holden, William; Jones, Jennifer; Thatcher, Torin; Elsom, Isobel; Gregg, Virginia; Loo, Richard

Song(s) Love Is a Many-Splendored Thing (C: Fain, Sammy; L: Webster, Paul Francis)

3502 ✦ LOVE IS BETTER THAN EVER
Metro–Goldwyn–Mayer, 1951

Musical Score Hayton, Lennie
Composer(s) Brent, Earl
Lyricist(s) Brent, Earl

Producer(s) Wright, William H.
Director(s) Donen, Stanley
Screenwriter(s) Flippen, Ruth Brooks

Cast Parks, Larry; Taylor, Elizabeth; Hutchinson, Josephine; Tully, Tom

Song(s) Ittsie Bittsie Spider (C: Traditional); Copa Routine; Fruit Basket; Opening Number—Recital (C: Hayton, Lennie; L: Flippen, Ruth Brooks)

Notes Released internationally as THE LIGHT FANTASTIC.

3503 ✦ LOVE IS NEWS
Twentieth Century–Fox, 1937

Producer(s) Wilson, Harold; Carroll, Earl
Director(s) Garnett, Tay
Screenwriter(s) Tugend, Harry; Yellen, Jack

Cast Power, Tyrone; Young, Loretta; Ameche, Don; Summerville, Slim; Digges, Dudley; Catlett, Walter; Sanders, George; Darwell, Jane; Fetchit, Stepin; Cook Jr., Elisha; Tannen, Julius; Moore, Pauline

Song(s) Love Is News (C: Pollack, Lew; L: Mitchell, Sidney D.)

3504 ✦ LOVE LAUGHS AT ANDY HARDY
Metro–Goldwyn–Mayer, 1946

Musical Score Snell, Dave
Choreographer(s) Donohue, Jack

Producer(s) Sisk, Robert
Director(s) Goldbeck, Willis
Screenwriter(s) Ruskin, Harry; Ludwig, William
Source(s) characters by Rouverol, Aurania

Cast Rooney, Mickey; Stone, Lewis; Haden, Sara; Granville, Bonita; Romay, Lina; Holden, Fay

Song(s) Jesusita en Chihuahua (Cactus Polka) (C: Riestra; Cortazar, Ernesto M.; Brent, Earl); Hail to Wainright (C/L: Snell, Dave; Brent, Earl)

Notes Formerly titled UNCLE ANDY HARDY and ANDY HARDY GOES TO COLLEGE. There is also a vocal of "Ay, Ay, Ay, Ay, Ay" by Harry Warren and Mack Gordon.

3505 ✦ LOVE LETTERS
Paramount, 1945

Producer(s) Wallis, Hal B.
Director(s) Dieterle, William
Screenwriter(s) Rand, Ayn
Source(s) *Pity My Simplicity* (novel) Massie, Chris

Cast Jones, Jennifer; Cotten, Joseph; Louise, Anita; Richards, Ann; Cooper, Gladys

Song(s) Love Letters (C: Young, Victor; L: Heyman, Edward)

3506 ✦ LOVE, LIVE AND LAUGH
Fox, 1929

Composer(s) Baer, Abel
Lyricist(s) Gilbert, L. Wolfe

Director(s) Howard, William K.; Kolker, Henry
Screenwriter(s) Jessel, George; Burke, Edwin
Source(s) *The Hurdy Gurdy Man* (play) Clemens, Leroy; Hymer, John B.

Cast Jessel, George; Lee, Lila; Rollins, David; Kolker, Henry; MacKenna, Kenneth; Reinhart, John; Armetta, Henry

Song(s) A Song of Margharita; Two Little Baby Arms; If You Believe in Me [1]

Notes No cue sheet available. [1] May also be in SOUTH SEA ROSE.

3507 ✦ LOVELY TO LOOK AT
Metro–Goldwyn–Mayer, 1952

Composer(s) Kern, Jerome
Lyricist(s) Harbach, Otto
Choreographer(s) Pan, Hermes

Producer(s) Cummings, Jack
Director(s) LeRoy, Mervyn
Screenwriter(s) Ruby, Harry; Wells, George; Solt, Andrew
Source(s) *Roberta* (musical) Harbach, Otto; Kern, Jerome

Cast Grayson, Kathryn; Skelton, Red; Keel, Howard; Champion, Marge; Champion, Gower; Miller, Ann; Gabor, Zsa Zsa; Kasznar, Kurt; Dalio, Marcel

Song(s) Opening Night [1] (L: Fields, Dorothy); I'll Be Hard to Handle [2] (L: Dougall, Bernard; Fields, Dorothy); Lafayette [4] (L: Fields, Dorothy); Yesterdays;

I Won't Dance [5] (L: Hammerstein II, Oscar; Fields, Dorothy); You're Devastating [2] (L: Harbach, Otto; Fields, Dorothy); Lovely to Look At (L: Fields, Dorothy; McHugh, Jimmy); The Most Exciting Night [3] (L: Harbach, Otto; Fields, Dorothy); Go Tell Aunt Rhody (C: Traditional; L: Skelton, Richard "Red"); Smoke Gets in Your Eyes; The Touch of Your Hand

Notes   ROBERTA first filmed by RKO in 1934. [1] Based on the music of "Don't Ask Me Not to Sing" (lyrics by Otto Harbach). [2] Revised lyrics by Dorothy Fields. [3] Lyrics revised by Fields from the song "Armful of Trouble." [4] Based on "Clementina" from ROBERTA. [5] Otto Harbach and Jimmy McHugh are credited with the lyrics to this song but they did not contribute.

3508 ✦ A LOVELY WAY TO DIE
Universal, 1968

Musical Score   Hopkins, Kenyon

Producer(s)   Lewis, Richard
Director(s)   Rich, David Lowell
Screenwriter(s)   Russell, A.J.

Cast   Douglas, Kirk; Koscina, Sylva; Wallach, Eli; Haigh, Kenneth; Green, Martyn; Peters, Gordon

Song(s)   A Lovely Way to Die [1] (C: Hopkins, Kenyon; L: Spencer, Judy)

Notes   [1] During end titles this song was titled "A Lovely Way to Live."

3509 ✦ LOVE ME FOREVER
Columbia, 1935

Composer(s)   Schertzinger, Victor

Director(s)   Schertzinger, Victor
Screenwriter(s)   Swerling, Jo; Buchman, Sidney

Cast   Moore, Grace; Carrillo, Leo; Allen, Robert; Byington, Spring; Dumbrille, Douglass; Hall, Thurston; Alberni, Luis; Bartlett, Michael; Barris, Harry; Kaye, Harry

Song(s)   Love Me Forever (L: Kahn, Gus); Whoa (L: Schertzinger, Victor)

Notes   Released as ON WINGS OF SONG in Great Britain. There are also several classical numbers sung.

3510 ✦ LOVE ME OR LEAVE ME
Metro–Goldwyn–Mayer, 1955

Choreographer(s)   Romero, Alex

Producer(s)   Pasternak, Joe
Director(s)   Vidor, Charles
Screenwriter(s)   Lennart, Isobel; Fuchs, Daniel

Cast   Day, Doris; Cagney, James; Mitchell, Cameron; Keith, Robert; Tully, Tom; Bellaver, Harry; Gaines, Richard; Leeds, Peter

Song(s)   Eddie Fulton Jingle (C/L: Alexander, Jeff); I'll Never Stop Loving You (C: Brodszky, Nicholas; L: Cahn, Sammy); Never Look Back (C/L: Price, Chilton)

Notes   Loosely based on the life of singer Ruth Etting. There are also vocals of "It All Depends on You" and "I'm Sitting on Top of the World" by Ray Henderson, Sam Lewis and Joe Young; "You Made Me Love You" by James V. Monaco and Joseph McCarthy; "Everybody Loves My Baby" by Jack Palmer and Spencer Williams; "Mean to Me" by Roy Turk and Fred Ahlert; "Stay on the Right Side Sister" by Rube Bloom and Ted Koehler; "What Can I Say After I Say I'm Sorry" by Walter Donaldson and Abe Lyman; "Sam, the Old Accordion Man" and "At Sundown" by Walter Donaldson; "Shakin' the Blues Away" by Irving Berlin; "I Cried for You" by Gus Arnheim, Abe Lyman and Arthur Freed; "My Blue Heaven" by Walter Donaldson and Richard A. Whiting; "Ten Cents a Dance" by Rodgers and Hart and "Love Me or Leave Me" by Walter Donaldson and Gus Kahn.

3511 ✦ LOVE ME TENDER
Twentieth Century–Fox, 1956

Musical Score   Newman, Lionel
Composer(s)   Presley, Elvis; Matson, Vera
Lyricist(s)   Presley, Elvis; Matson, Vera

Producer(s)   Weisbart, David
Director(s)   Webb, Robert D.
Screenwriter(s)   Buckner, Robert

Cast   Egan, Richard; Paget, Debra; Presley, Elvis; Middleton, Robert; Brand, Neville; Dunnock, Mildred; Bennett, Bruce; Drury, James

Song(s)   Love Me Tender; We're Gonna Move [1]; Let Me; Poor Boy

Notes   Originally titled THE RENO BROTHERS. [1] Originally titled "There's a Leak in This Old Building."

3512 ✦ LOVE ME TONIGHT
Paramount, 1932

Composer(s)   Rodgers, Richard
Lyricist(s)   Hart, Lorenz

Producer(s)   Mamoulian, Rouben
Director(s)   Mamoulian, Rouben
Screenwriter(s)   Young, Waldemar; Hoffenstein, Samuel; Marion Jr., George
Source(s)   *Tailor in the Chateau* (play) Marchand, Leopold; Armont, Paul

Cast   Chevalier, Maurice; MacDonald, Jeanette; Ruggles, Charles; Butterworth, Charles; Loy, Myrna; Smith, C. Aubrey; Patterson, Elizabeth; Griffies, Ethel; Frederici, Blanche; Cawthorn, Joseph; Greig, Robert; Wales, Ethel; Doran, Mary; Roach, Bert; Hayes, George "Gabby"; Sedan, Rolfe; Mundin, Herbert

Song(s)   That's the Song of Paree (Song of Paree); Isn't It Romantic?; Deer Hunt Ballet (Inst.); Lover; Mimi [4]; A Woman Needs Something Like That; Love Me Tonight; The Son-Of-A-Gun Is Nothing But a Tailor; The Poor Apache; The Man for Me (The Letter Song) [1]; Cleaning Up the Floor with Lulu [2] [3]; Give Me Just a Moment [2]

Notes   Paramount had a rating sheet made on each number which rated each as to its supposed publication value. The choices were Excellent, Fair, Good and Poor. Here (with many surprises) is S.R. Hawkins' assessment of the publication value of each song. "Love Me Tonight" - Excellent; "Song of Paree" - Poor; "Isn't It Romantic" - Excellent; "A Woman Needs Something Like That" - Poor; "Mimi" - Fair; and "Lover" - Poor. [1] This number was cut before release but Paramount files indicate it was included in foreign prints. [2] Not used. [3] This was an early version of "The Poor Apache." [4] Later used in PEPE (Columbia).

3513 ◆ THE LOVE MOON
Paramount, 1930 unproduced

Composer(s)   Baer, Abel
Lyricist(s)   Gilbert, L. Wolfe

Song(s)   Crystal Waters; The Sound of the Gourd [1]; Malihini Love Call; Always the Same

Notes   [1] Also in the unproduced BUDDY ROGERS MUSICAL.

3514 ◆ LOVE NEST
Twentieth Century–Fox, 1951

Musical Score   Mockridge, Cyril J.

Producer(s)   Bassler, Robert
Director(s)   Sale, Richard
Screenwriter(s)   Diamond, I.A.L.
Source(s)   *The Reluctant Landlord* (novel) Corbett, Scott

Cast   Haver, June; Lundigan, William; Fay, Frank; Monroe, Marilyn; Paar, Jack; Joy, Leatrice; Blake, Marie

Song(s)   Champagne Shampoo Jingle (C/L: Daniel, Eliot)

Notes   There are also vocals of "The Love Nest" by Louis A. Hirsch and Otto Harbach and "Lovely Lady" by Jimmy McHugh and Ted Koehler.

3515 ◆ LOVE ON THE RUN (1936)
Metro–Goldwyn–Mayer, 1936

Musical Score   Waxman, Franz

Director(s)   Van Dyke, W.S.
Screenwriter(s)   Mahin, John Lee; Seff, Manuel; Hurlbut, Gladys

Cast   Gable, Clark; Crawford, Joan; Tone, Franchot; Owen, Reginald

Song(s)   Gone (C: Waxman, Franz; L: Kahn, Gus)

3516 ◆ LOVE ON THE RUN (1979)
New World, 1979

Musical Score   Delerue, Georges

Producer(s)   Belleggingen, Elsenor
Director(s)   Truffaut, Francois
Screenwriter(s)   Truffaut, Francois; Pisier, Marie-France

Cast   Leaud, Jean-Pierre; Pisier, Marie-France; Jade, Claude; Dorothee, Dani

Song(s)   Love on the Run (C: Voulzy, Laurent; L: Souchon, Alain)

Notes   No cue sheet available.

3517 ◆ LOVE ON TOAST
Paramount, 1938

Composer(s)   Coslow, Sam
Lyricist(s)   Coslow, Sam

Producer(s)   Cohen, Emanuel
Director(s)   Dupont, E.A.
Screenwriter(s)   Storm, Jane; Connell, Richard; Malloy, Doris

Cast   Payne, John; Adler, Stella; Baker, Benny

Song(s)   I'd Love to Play a Love Scene (Opposite You); I Want a New Romance (C: Lane, Burton); My Imaginary Love [1]

Notes   [1] Not used.

3518 ◆ LOVE ON WHEELS
Paramount, 1936 unproduced

Song(s)   Tea on the Terrace (C/L: Coslow, Sam)

3519 ◆ THE LOVE PARADE
Paramount, 1929

Composer(s)   Schertzinger, Victor
Lyricist(s)   Grey, Clifford

Director(s)   Lubitsch, Ernst
Screenwriter(s)   Vajda, Ernest; Bolton, Guy
Source(s)   *The Prince Consort* (play) Xanrof, Leon; Chancel, Jules

Cast   Chevalier, Maurice; MacDonald, Jeanette; Lane, Lupino; Roth, Lillian; Pallette, Eugene; Belmore, Lionel

Song(s)   Champagne; Paris—Stay the Same; Dream Lover; Anything to Please the Queen; My Love Parade; Sylvania's Queen; Let's Be Common; March of the Grenadiers; Nobody's Using It Now (L: Grey, Clifford; Schertzinger, Victor); Oh-La-La [1]; The Queen is Always Right (Gossip Quarrel Number)

Notes Originally titled THE PRINCE CONSORT. [1] Not on cue sheet.

3520 ✦ LOVER BOY
Twentieth Century–Fox, 1955

Musical Score Vlad, Roman

Producer(s) Graetz, Paul
Director(s) Clement, Rene
Screenwriter(s) Mills, Hugh; Clement, Rene
Source(s) *M. Ripois and His Nemesis* (novel) Hemon, Louis

Cast Philipe, Gerard; Parry, Natasha; Hobson, Valerie; Greenwood, Joan; Johnston, Margaret; Marmont, Percy

Song(s) Song of Margaret (C/L: MacOrlan, P.; Marceau, C.)

Notes Originally titled LOVERS, HAPPY LOVERS.

3521 ✦ LOVER COME BACK
Universal, 1961

Musical Score De Vol, Frank

Producer(s) Shapiro, Stanley; Melcher, Martin
Director(s) Mann, Delbert
Screenwriter(s) Shapiro, Stanley; Henning, Paul

Cast Day, Doris; Hudson, Rock; Randall, Tony; Oakie, Jack; Adams, Edie; Kruschen, Jack

Song(s) Lover Come Back (C: De Vol, Frank; L: Spilton, Alan); Should I Surrender (C/L: Landau, William; L: Ross, Adam)

3522 ✦ LOVERS AND LIARS

See A TRIP WITH ANITA.

3523 ✦ LOVERS COURAGOUS
Metro–Goldwyn–Mayer, 1932

Director(s) Leonard, Robert Z.
Screenwriter(s) Lonsdale, Frederick

Cast Montgomery, Robert; Evans, Madge; Young, Roland; Kerr, Frederick; Owen, Reginald; Hobbes, Halliwell; Searl, Jackie; Mowbray, Alan

Song(s) Is That You, O'Reilly? [1] (C: Macdonald, Ballard; L: Unknown)

Notes [1] This might be a traditional song arranged by Macdonald.

3524 ✦ THE LOVES AND TIMES OF SCARAMOUCHE
Avco Embassy, 1976

Producer(s) Aicardi, Federico
Director(s) Castellari, Enzo G.
Screenwriter(s) Carpi, Tito; Castellari, Enzo G.

Source(s) *The Life of Scaramouche* (novel) Constantini, Angelo

Cast Sarrazin, Michael; Andress, Ursula; Maccione, Aldo; Prete, Giancarlo; Forest, Michael

Song(s) Scaramouche (C/L: Dammico; Bixio; Frizzi; Tempera)

Notes No cue sheet available.

3525 ✦ LOVE SLAVES OF THE AMAZONS
Universal, 1957

Producer(s) Siodmak, Curt
Director(s) Siodmak, Curt
Screenwriter(s) Siodmak, Curt

Cast Taylor, Don; Ciannelli, Eduardo; Segale, Gianna; Chalk, Harvey

Song(s) Song of the Amazons (C/L: Gnattali, Radames)

3526 ✦ LOVES OF AN ACTRESS
Paramount, 1928

Director(s) Lee, Rowland V.
Screenwriter(s) Lee, Rowland V.

Cast Negri, Pola; Asther, Nils; McAllister, Mary; Tucker, Richard; Strange, Philip; Lukas, Paul

Song(s) Sunbeams Bring Dreams of You (C: Hajos, Karl; L: Brennan, J. Keirn)

Notes No cue sheet available.

3527 ✦ THE LOVES OF CARMEN
Columbia, 1948

Musical Score Castelonuovo-Tedesco, Mario
Choreographer(s) Cansino, Eduardo; Sidney, Robert

Producer(s) Vidor, Charles
Director(s) Vidor, Charles
Screenwriter(s) Deutsch, Helen
Source(s) *The Loves of Carmen* (novel) Merimee, Prosper

Cast Hayworth, Rita [1]; Ford, Glenn; Randell, Ron; Jory, Victor; Moss, Arnold; Buloff, Joseph; Adler, Luther; Cansino, Jose; Wycherly, Margaret; Cansino, Vernon

Song(s) Amor Di Gitano (C/L: Stoloff, Morris; Karger, Fred); Estrellita [2] (C: Ponce, Manuel; L: Davis, George)

Notes [1] Dubbed by Anita Ellis. [2] Sheet music only.

3528 ✦ LOVE SONGS
International Spectrafilm, 1986

Musical Score Legrand, Michel

Producer(s) Chouraqui, Elie; Baylis, Robert
Director(s) Chouraqui, Elie
Screenwriter(s) Chouraqui, Elie

Cast   Deneuve, Catherine; Lambert, Christopher; Anconina, Richard; Perrin, Jacques; Mancuso, Nick; Gainsbourg, Charlotte

Song(s)   Leave It to Me (C: Legrand, Michel; L: Legrand, Michel; McDaniels, Gene)

Notes   No cue sheet available.

3529 ◆ LOVE STORY
Paramount, 1970

Musical Score   Lai, Francis
Composer(s)   Lai, Francis
Lyricist(s)   Simon, Norman; Mark, Lowell

Producer(s)   Minsky, Howard G.
Director(s)   Hiller, Arthur
Screenwriter(s)   Segal, Erich
Source(s)   *Love Story* (novel) Segal, Erich

Cast   MacGraw, Ali; O'Neal, Ryan; Marley, John; Milland, Ray

Song(s)   Where Do I Begin? (L: Sigman, Carl); Look Around (You'll Find Me) [1]; For Me Alone [1]

Notes   [1] Lyric for exploitation use only.

3530 ◆ LOVE THY NEIGHBOR
Paramount, 1940

Composer(s)   Van Heusen, James
Lyricist(s)   Burke, Johnny

Producer(s)   Sandrich, Mark
Director(s)   Sandrich, Mark
Screenwriter(s)   Morrow, William; Beloin, Edmund; Pagano, Ernest; Myers, Zion

Cast   Anderson, Eddie "Rochester"; Benny, Jack; Allen, Fred; The Merry Macs; Harris, Theresa; Martin, Mary; Teasdale, Verree; Carson, Jack; Dale, Virginia; Denning, Richard

Song(s)   Dearest Darest I; Isn't That Just Like Love; My Heart Belongs to Daddy [1] (C/L: Porter, Cole); Do You Know Why [2] [5]; At the Psychological Moment [2] [4]; Escapade [2]

Notes   [1] Written for Broadway musical LEAVE IT TO ME. [2] Not used. [3] The Merry Macs were Judd McMichael, Ted McMichael, Joe McMichael and Helen Carroll. [4] Originally written for the RKO picture MYSTERY IN MUSIC. [5] Recorded and published.

3531 ◆ LOVE TIME
Fox, 1934

Composer(s)   Conselman, William
Lyricist(s)   Starling, Lynn

Producer(s)   Wurtzel, Sol M.
Director(s)   Tinling, James
Screenwriter(s)   Conselman, William; Johnson, Henry

Cast   Patterson, Pat; Asther, Nils; Mundin, Herbert

Song(s)   The Bitter Heart; The Drummer Boy; Happy Little Children (C: Kaylin, Samuel; L: Tresselt, Frank)

3532 ◆ LOVE UNDER FIRE
Twentieth Century–Fox, 1937

Producer(s)   Johnson, Nunnally
Director(s)   Marshall, George
Screenwriter(s)   Fowler, Gene; Rivkin, Allen; Pascal, Ernest

Cast   Young, Loretta; Ameche, Don; Borrah Minnevitch and His Gang; Drake, Frances; Catlett, Walter; Carradine, John; Rumann, Sig; de Mille, Katherine; Clive, E.E.; Alvarado, Don

Song(s)   The Language of Love (C: Pokrass, Sam; L: Lawrence, Jack)

3533 ◆ LOVE WITH THE PROPER STRANGER
Paramount, 1964

Producer(s)   Pakula, Alan J.
Director(s)   Mulligan, Robert
Screenwriter(s)   Schulman, Arnold

Cast   Adams, Edie; Bosley, Tom; Bernardi, Herschel; Wood, Natalie; McQueen, Steve

Song(s)   Love with the Proper Stranger (C: Bernstein, Elmer; L: Mercer, Johnny)

Notes   Film and song originally titled LOVE WITH THE SPECIAL STRANGER.

3534 ◆ LOVING COUPLES
Twentieth Century–Fox, 1980

Musical Score   Karlin, Fred
Composer(s)   Karlin, Fred
Lyricist(s)   Gimbel, Norman

Producer(s)   Valente, Renee
Director(s)   Smight, Jack
Screenwriter(s)   Donovan, Martin

Cast   MacLaine, Shirley; Coburn, James; Sarandon, Susan; Collins, Stephen; Kellerman, Sally; Martin, Nan

Song(s)   And So It Begins; I'll Make It with Your Love; Take Me Away (L: Pitchford, Dean); There's More Where That Came From (L: Pitchford, Dean); Turn Up the Music (L: Pitchford, Dean)

Notes   No cue sheet available.

3535 ◆ LOVING YOU
Paramount, 1957

Choreographer(s)   O'Curran, Charles

Producer(s)   Wallis, Hal B.
Director(s)   Kanter, Hal
Screenwriter(s)   Baker, Herbert; Kanter, Hal
Source(s)   (story) Thompson, Mary Agnes

Cast Presley, Elvis; Scott, Lizabeth; Corey, Wendell; Gleason, James; Hart, Dolores

Song(s) Loving You (C/L: Leiber, Jerry; Stoller, Mike); Got a Lot o' Livin' to Do (C: Weisman, Ben; L: Schroeder, Aaron); Dancing on a Dare (C: Thomas, Edward; L: Wise, Fred); (Let's Have A) Party (C/L: Robinson, Jessie Mae); (Let Me Be Your) Teddy Bear (C: Lowe, Bernie; L: Mann, Kal); Hot Dog (C/L: Leiber, Jerry; Stoller, Mike); Lonesome Cowboy [1] (C/L: Tepper, Sid; Bennett, Roy C.); Mean-Woman Blues (C/L: DeMetrius, Claude); I Beg of You [2] (C/L: Unknown); We're Gonna Live It Up [2] (C/L: Leiber, Jerry; Stoller, Mike); Candy Kisses [2] [3] (C/L: Morgan, George); Fireworks [2] (C: Weisman, Ben; L: Schroeder, Aaron); Detour (C/L: Westmoreland, Paul); Peter Cottontail [4] (C/L: Rollins, Jack; Nelson, Steve)

Notes Formerly titled STRANGER IN TOWN, RUNNIN' WILD and LONESOME COWBOY. [1] Additional lyrics by Charles O'Curran. [2] Not used. [3] Used in DOWN DAKOTA WAY (Republic). [4] BMI list only.

3536 ✦ LUCAS
Twentieth Century–Fox, 1986

Musical Score Grusin, Dave

Producer(s) Nicksay, David
Director(s) Seltzer, David
Screenwriter(s) Seltzer, David

Cast Haim, Corey; Green, Kerri; Sheen, Charlie; Thorne-Smith, Courtney; Ryder, Winona; Boyd, Guy

Song(s) Walk of Life (C/L: Knopfler, Mark); Follow Your Heart (C/L: Rafelson, Peter); King for a Day (C/L: Bailey, Tom; Currie, Alannah; Leeway, Joseph)

3537 ✦ LUCKY BOY
Tiffany–Stahl, 1929

Musical Score Riesenfeld, Hugo
Composer(s) Axt, William
Lyricist(s) Young, Lewis

Director(s) Taurog, Norman; Wilson, Charles C.; Flothow, Rudolph
Screenwriter(s) Jessel, George

Cast Jessel, George; Rosanova, Rosa; Strauss, William K.; Lee, Gwen; Tucker, Richard; Quimby, Margaret; Whitman, Gayne

Song(s) Lucky Boy (C: Baer, Abel; L: Gilbert, L. Wolfe); My Mother's Eyes (C: Baer, Abel; L: Gilbert, L. Wolfe); California Here I Come (C: Meyer, Joseph; L: DeSylva, B.G.; Jolson, Al); My Blackbirds Are Bluebirds Now (C: Friend, Cliff; L: Caesar, Irving); Old Man Sunshine; My Real Sweetheart; Bouquet of Memories

Notes No cue sheet available.

3538 ✦ LUCKY CISCO KID
Twentieth Century–Fox, 1940

Producer(s) Wurtzel, Sol M.
Director(s) Humberstone, H. Bruce
Screenwriter(s) Ellis, Robert; Logan, Helen
Source(s) character by Henry, O.

Cast Romero, Cesar; Hughes, Mary Beth; Andrews, Dana; Venable, Evelyn; Martin, Chris-Pin

Song(s) A Stray Lost Sheep (C: Holden, Cally; L: Ellis, Robert)

3539 ✦ LUCKY COWBOY
Paramount, 1944

Cast Gibson, Julie; Dew, Eddie

Song(s) Headin' Home (C/L: Lee, Lester; Seelen, Jerry)

Notes Short subject. There are also vocal renditions of "My Old Flame" by Sam Coslow and Arthur Johnston and "Lucky Cowboy" written by Leo Robin and Ralph Rainger for RIDING HIGH.

3540 ✦ LUCKY DAYS

See SING A JINGLE.

3541 ✦ LUCKY DEVILS
RKO, 1932

Musical Score Steiner, Max

Producer(s) Cooper, Merian C.
Director(s) Ince, Ralph
Screenwriter(s) Johnston, Agnes Christine; Markson, Ben

Cast Boyd, William [2]; Wilson, Dorothy; Gargan, William; Rose, Robert; Ates, Roscoe; Bakewell, William; Cabot, Bruce; Hudson, Rochelle; Chaney, Creighton [1]; Fraser, Phyllis; Furness, Betty; Haydon, Julie

Song(s) Stunt Men of Hollywood (C: Steiner, Max; L: Chaney, Creighton [1])

Notes [1] Lon Chaney Jr. [2] Billed as Bill Boyd.

3542 ✦ LUCKY IN LOVE
Pathe, 1929

Composer(s) Stept, Sam H.
Lyricist(s) Green, Bud

Producer(s) Kane, Robert T.
Director(s) Webb, Kenneth
Screenwriter(s) Markey, Gene

Cast Downey, Morton; Lawford, Betty; Keith-Johnston, Colin; Hobbes, Halliwell; Kerrigan, J.M.

Song(s) Love Is a Dreamer; For the Likes O' You and Me; When They Sing the Wearin' of the Green in Syncopated Time

Notes No cue sheet available.

3543 ◆ LUCKY LADY
Twentieth Century–Fox, 1975

Musical Score Burns, Ralph
Composer(s) Kander, John
Lyricist(s) Ebb, Fred

Producer(s) Gruskoff, Michael
Director(s) Donen, Stanley
Screenwriter(s) Huyck, Willard; Katz, Gloria

Cast Hackman, Gene; Minnelli, Liza; Reynolds, Burt; Lewis, Geoffrey; Hillerman, John; Benson, Robby; Hordern, Michael; Holland, Anthony

Song(s) Get While the Gettin's Good; Lucky Lady

Notes Vocals are also presented of "Young Woman's Blues" by Bessie Smith; "Ain't Misbehavin'" by Thomas "Fats" Waller, Andy Razaf and Harry Brooks; "Hot Time in the Old Town Tonight" by Theodore M. Metz and Joe Hayden; "If I Had a Talking Picture of You" by B.G. DeSylva, Lew Brown and Ray Henderson and "All I Do Is Dream of You" by Arthur Freed and Nacio Herb Brown.

3544 ◆ LUCKY ME
Warner Brothers, 1954

Composer(s) Fain, Sammy
Lyricist(s) Webster, Paul Francis
Choreographer(s) Donohue, Jack

Producer(s) Blanke, Henry
Director(s) Donohue, Jack
Screenwriter(s) O'Hanlon, James; O'Brien, Robert; Elinson, Irving

Cast Day, Doris; Cummings, Robert; Silvers, Phil; Foy Jr., Eddie; Walker, Nancy; Hyer, Martha; Goodwin, Bill; Rorke, Hayden

Song(s) Lucky Me; I Speak to the Stars; Superstition Song; Men; Parisian Pretties; High Hopes; Take a Memo to the Moon; Burbank Bounce; The Blue Bells of Broadway (Are Ringing Tonight); I Wanna Sing Like an Angel (Dance Like the Devil); Love You Dearly

3545 ◆ LUCKY STAR
Fox, 1929

Director(s) Borzage, Frank
Screenwriter(s) Booth, John Hunter

Cast Farrell, Charles; Gaynor, Janet; Reicher, Hedwiga

Song(s) Little Black Sheep (C: Baer, Abel; L: Gilbert, L. Wolfe)

3546 ◆ LUCKY STARLETS
Paramount, 1936

Producer(s) Moulton, Herbert

Cast Holt, Betty; Holt, David; Lee, Billy; Weidler, Virginia; Bartlett, Bennie; LeRoy, Baby

Song(s) Monsieur Baby [1] (C: Rainger, Ralph; L: Robin, Leo); Lucky Starlets (C/L: Coslow, Sam)

Notes Short subject. [1] Also in A BEDTIME STORY.

3547 ◆ LUCY GALLANT
Paramount, 1955

Producer(s) Pine, William; Thomas, William
Director(s) Parrish, Robert
Screenwriter(s) Miller, Winston; Mahin, John Lee
Source(s) *The Life of Lucy Gallant* (novel) Cousins, Margaret

Cast Wyman, Jane; Heston, Charlton; Trevor, Claire; Ritter, Thelma; Demarest, William

Song(s) How Can I Tell Her (C/L: Livingston, Jay; Evans, Ray)

3548 ◆ LULLABY OF BROADWAY
Warner Brothers, 1951

Musical Score Jackson, Howard
Choreographer(s) White, Al; Prinz, LeRoy

Producer(s) Jacobs, William
Director(s) Butler, David
Screenwriter(s) Baldwin, Earl
Source(s) "My Irish Molly O" (story) Baldwin, Earl

Cast Day, Doris; Nelson, Gene; Sakall, S.Z.; De Wolfe, Billy; George, Gladys; Bates, Florence; Triola, Anne; Stafford, Hanley; The Page Cavanaugh Trio

Song(s) In a Shanty in Old Shanty Town (C: Young, Joe; L: Little, Little Jack; Siras, John); You're Dependable (C: Miller, Sy; L: Seelen, Jerry); I Love the Way You Say Goodnight (C: Wyle, George; L: Pola, Eddie)

Notes It is not known which of these were written for the movie, if any. There are also vocals of "Lullaby of Broadway" by Harry Warren and Al Dubin; "Just One of Those Things" by Cole Porter; "Zing! Went the Strings of My Heart" by James Hanley; "You're Getting to Be a Habit with Me" by Harry Warren and Al Dubin; "Somebody Loves Me" by George Gershwin, B.G. DeSylva and Ballard Macdonald and "Please Don't Talk About Me When I'm Gone" by Sam Stept and Sidney Clare.

3549 ◆ LULU BELLE
Columbia, 1948

Musical Score Russell, Henry
Choreographer(s) Castle, Nick

Producer(s) Bogeaus, Benedict
Director(s) Fenton, Leslie
Screenwriter(s) Freeman, Everett
Source(s) *Lulu Belle* (play) MacArthur, Charles; Sheldon, Everett

Cast Lamour, Dorothy; Montgomery, George; Dekker, Albert; Kruger, Otto; Farrell, Glenda; McClure, Greg; Wynters, Charlotte

Song(s) Lulu Belle [1] (C/L: Russell, Henry; DeLange, Eddie); Sweetie Pie [1] (C/L: Russell, Henry; Lehman, Johnny)

Notes Songs also include "I Can't Tell Why I Love You" by Gus Edwards and Will D. Cobb and "The Ace in the Hole" by George Mitchell and James Dempsey. [1] Sheet music only.

3550 ✦ LUMBERJACK
Paramount, 1944 unproduced

Song(s) The Place Your Heart Calls Home (C/L: Waters, Vernon "Ozie"; Johnson, Forrest "Trees"); Fighting Forty [1] (C/L: Hamilton, Grace; Stern, Jack)

Notes Originally titled TIMBER. [1] Not used.

3551 ✦ LURE OF THE WILDERNESS
Twentieth Century–Fox, 1952

Musical Score Waxman, Franz

Producer(s) Jacks, Robert L.
Director(s) Negulesco, Jean
Screenwriter(s) Lantz, Louis

Cast Peters, Jean; Hunter, Jeffrey; Smith, Constance; Brennan, Walter; Tully, Tom; Shannon, Harry; Wright, Will

Song(s) Starry Hill (C/L: Darby, Ken)

3552 ✦ LUV
Columbia, 1967

Musical Score Mulligan, Gerry
Composer(s) Bacharach, Burt
Lyricist(s) Schisgal, Murray

Producer(s) Manulis, Martin
Director(s) Donner, Clive
Screenwriter(s) Baker, Elliott
Source(s) *Luv* (play) Schisgal, Murray

Cast Lemmon, Jack; Falk, Peter; May, Elaine; Wayne, Nina; Mayehoff, Eddie; Hartman, Paul; Darden, Severn

Song(s) Alma Mater; Love Casts Its Shadow

3553 ✦ LUXURY LINER
Metro–Goldwyn–Mayer, 1948

Producer(s) Pasternak, Joe
Director(s) Whorf, Richard
Screenwriter(s) Lehman, Gladys; Connell, Richard

Cast Brent, George; Powell, Jane; Melchior, Lauritz; Gifford, Frances; Koshetz, Marina; Xavier Cugat and His Orchestra; Breen, Thomas E.; Derr, Richard; Ridgely, John; The Pied Pipers

Song(s) Spring Came Back to Vienna (C/L: Torre, Janice; Spielman, Fred; Rotter, Fritz); Vamo a Rumbia (C/L: Cugat, Xavier; Angulo)

Notes There are also vocals of the Finale of Act III of AIDA by Verdi; "Alouette" and "Yes, We Have No Bananas" by Frank Silver and Irving Conn; "Bottoms Up" and "Siegmund's Liebeslied" from DIE WALKURE by Wagner; "Scene and Gavotte" by Massenet's MANON; "Con Maraccas" by Dimaulig and Cugat; "Peanut Vendor" by Marion Sunshine, L. Wolfe Gilbert and Moises Simons; "Zita the Vamp" and "I've Got You Under My Skin" by Cole Porter; "Torna a Surriento" by De Curtis; "Ya Viechor Mlada;" and LOHENGRIN'S "Abschied" by Wagner.